The Routledge Handbook of Male Sex Work, Culture, and Society

Panoramic and provocative in its scope, this handbook is the definitive guide to contemporary issues associated with male sex work and a must read for those who study masculinities, male sexuality, sexual health, and sexual cultures.

This groundbreaking volume will have a powerful impact on our understanding of this challenging, elusive subject. While the internet has brought the previously hidden worlds of male sex work more starkly into public view, academic research has often remained locked into descriptions of male sex workers and their clients as perverse. Drawing from a variety of regions, the chapters provide insights into the historical, popular cultural, social, and economic aspects of sex work, as well as demographic patterns, health outcomes, and policy issues. This approach shifts thought on male sex work from a hidden "social problem" to a publicly acknowledged "social phenomenon." The book challenges myths and reconceptualizes male sex work as a discrete field. Importantly, it provides a vehicle for the voices of male sex workers and new and established scholars. This richly detailed, humane, and innovative collection retrieves male sex work from silence and invisibility on the one hand and its association with scandal and stigma on the other. The findings within have profound implications for how governments approach public health and regulation of the sex industry and for how society can make sense of the complexities of human sexualities.

A compelling scholarly read and a major contribution to a commercial sector that is often neglected in policy debates on sex work, this handbook will be of great interest to scholars of criminology, sociology, gender studies, and cultural studies and all those interested in male sex work.

John Scott, PhD, is a professor and the head of the School of Justice at Queensland University of Technology, Australia. Trained as a sociologist, John has published widely on a range of themes, including sexual and gendered crime, and is passionate about the promotion of social research from the global south. He co-edits the *International Journal for Crime, Justice and Social Democracy*, and his recent work includes the co-authored *Southern Criminology* (Routledge, 2018).

Christian Grov, PhD, MPH, is a professor in the Department of Community Health and Social Sciences at the CUNY Graduate School of Public Health and Health Policy. He is the editor of *Sexuality Research and Social Policy*. Dr. Grov's research focuses on the sexual health and well-being of sexual and gender minority individuals, with a substantial body of research on sex work, including having co-authored the book *In the Company of Men: Inside the Lives of Male Prostitutes*.

Victor Minichiello, PhD, is an adjunct professor at the School of Social Justice at Queensland University of Technology and an emeritus professor at University of New England in Australia. He has published a number of pioneering books that shaped the field of HIV/AIDS, gerontology, and qualitative research in Australia. His research on ageism, sexual health, and sexualities is internationally recognized. He pioneered a number of landmark quantitative and qualitative studies on male sex work in the early 1990s, when the topic was considered highly controversial and a taboo among funding bodies and mainstream society.

The Routledge Handbook of Male Sex Work, Culture, and Society

Edited by John Scott, Christian Grov, and Victor Minichiello

LONDON AND NEW YORK

First published 2021
by Routledge
2 Park Square, Milton Park, Abingdon, Oxon OX14 4RN

and by Routledge
52 Vanderbilt Avenue, New York, NY 10017

Routledge is an imprint of the Taylor & Francis Group, an informa business

British Library Cataloguing-in-Publication Data
A catalogue record for this book is available from the British Library

Library of Congress Cataloging-in-Publication Data
A catalog record for this book has been requested

ISBN: 978-0-367-71603-5 (hbk)
ISBN: 978-0-367-71604-2 (pbk)
ISBN: 978-1-003-15283-5 (ebk)

Typeset in Bembo
by Apex CoVantage, LLC

https://www.routledge.com/9780367716035

We owe great gratitude and admiration to the pioneering LGBTIQA+ publisher Bill Cohen, the original publisher of the book Male Sex Work and Society, *who sadly died in 2019. Bill was inspirational and relentless in his support for our work and one of the kindest and most considerate publishers any author could wish for. This book could not have been written without him, and his DNA is all over it. We miss you and thank you for all of your support and determination.*

Contents

Contents

Figures

Tables

Notes on contributors

Max Nicolai Appenroth is a trans activist and PhD student at the Institute of Public Health, Charité Universitätsmedizin Berlin, Germany. Max holds a BA in social work and an MA in sociocultural studies. His work focuses on intersectional barriers that trans people face in accessing healthcare services and on lifespan inequalities and the later-life outcomes of trans people. A global trans activist, Max is also a lecturer at Alice Salomon University of Applied Sciences in Berlin, Germany, and a freelance educator on the topic of gender diversity. More information is available at www.max-appenroth.com.

Marco Bacio is a double PhD student of sociology at the University of Milan, Italy (where he teaches sociology to undergraduate students), and of gender studies at Lund University, Sweden (where he teaches quantitative methods to postgraduate students). His research interests include LGBT studies, gender studies, sexualities, sex work, and sociology of culture. Since 2011, he has been a research fellow at GENDERS, the Centre for Gender and Equality in Research and Science, at the University of Milan. Since 2019, he has been a member of Minerva – Laboratory on Diversity and Gender Inequality of Sapienza University in Rome. Since 2018, he has been a member of the scientific committee of the gender studies section of AIS (the Italian Sociological Association). Since 2020, he has been a member of the national executive board of AIS. His recent papers in English include "Social Suffering as Structural and Symbolic Violence: LGBT Experiences in the Face of AIDS Film Archive" (2018, with Cirus Rinaldi) and "The Queer Researcher: Challenging Homonormativity in Research and Educational Settings" (2019, with Cirus Rinaldi).

Michael Bar-Johnson is currently an assistant teaching professor at the University of Massachusetts, Lowell, where he teaches courses on human sexuality and sexual identity. Previously he served as chair of the psychology department from 2008 to 2014 at the University of New York in Prague, a partner of SUNY Empire State College international programs. He received his MSc in experimental psychology from the University of California, Santa Cruz, and his PhD at the Sexology Institute of the 1st Medical Faculty of Charles University in Prague in the area of medical psychology and psychopathology with a specialization in sexology. He has also attended advanced training in sexual medicine at the University of Oxford on scholarship from the European Society of Sexual Medicine. He completed his clinical training at the Sex Offender Unit of the Prague Psychiatric Center and also led group counseling sessions for pre-operation transsexuals in the Czech Republic. His past research provided the first quantitative investigation of male sex workers in the Czech Republic, published in the *Journal of Sex Research*. His current research focuses on sexual identity and sexual health.

Heather Berg is an assistant professor of women, gender, and sexuality studies at Washington University in St. Louis. Her writing, teaching, and activism focus on sexuality, labor, and class in late capitalism. Her book, *Porn Work,* explores precarity and resistance in the U.S. porn industry. It is forthcoming with UNC Press. Heather's work appears in *Signs, Feminist Studies, WSQ, Porn Studies,* and *Jacobin,* among others.

Katie B. Biello is an associate professor of behavioral and social sciences and epidemiology at the Brown School of Public Health, as well as investigator at the Fenway Institute at Fenway Health. Her primary research interests are identifying and understanding the underlying, multilevel risk factors for social inequities in HIV/sexually transmitted infections (STIs) and developing behavioral interventions to reduce risk among racial, sexual, and gender minorities and vulnerable populations, including male sex workers and people who use drugs. Her research spans the United States, Latin America, India, and Vietnam, and it has been primarily funded through extramural research grants from the U.S. National Institutes of Health and other foundations. These efforts have resulted in 100 peer-reviewed scientific journal publications to date.

Paul Bouanchaud is a senior researcher for a global health INGO. He gained his PhD in demography from the London School of Economics and Political Science in 2014 for his mixed-methods research into the HIV risk environments of male sex workers in China and has a background in social research methods and anthropology. Paul has worked on research projects in over 20 countries. His research interests focus on the social determinants of health, research with marginal communities, the use of mixed methods, and applied research and evaluations for international development contexts. He currently acts as a technical advisor to research teams in over 10 countries across sub-Saharan Africa, focusing on health areas including family planning and reproductive health, HIV, malaria, cervical cancer, water, sanitation and hygiene, and COVID-19.

Yifeng Troy Cai is a PhD candidate in the department of anthropology, an MPH candidate at the School of Public Health, an Andrew W. Mellon graduate fellow in the collaborative humanities program, and a graduate fellow in gender and sexuality studies at Brown University. His major research interests include exchange theory, intimacy, queer theory, digital anthropology, medical anthropology, and urban sociality. Currently, he is writing up his dissertation based on three years of fieldwork in Shanghai, China, on urban gay men's experiences of intimacy, kinship, and precarity in an increasingly digitalized China. He is simultaneously conducting a project on social change under the impact of COVID-19 in China. His research has been supported by the National Science Foundation, the Wenner-Gren Foundation, the American Council of Learned Societies, and the Luce Foundation, among others.

Hilary Caldwell (PhD, MASc, MHSc) is a sexologist with an interest in gendered sexualities and the sex industry. Her research focuses on women and men buying sex in Australia. She has 10 years of experience in researching the sex industry and has spent countless hours counseling sex workers and their clients, which motivates her to publicize the private with a view to improving social conditions and promoting sex-positive lives.

Denton Callander studies sex, sexualities, and sexual health. His work employs mixed methods to explore the sexual health and well-being of diverse populations, including sex workers and transgender and gender-diverse people. Denton also specializes in the study of digital cultures and their impact on contemporary sexualities.

Rosie Campbell, OBE, is a post-doctoral research fellow in the Department of Social Policy and Social Work at the University of York. She has been involved in research projects exploring sex work in a range of sectors and geographical areas of the United Kingdom. She has particular interest in sex worker safety and hate crimes against sex workers, the policing of sex work, and multiagency and community responses to sex work. She has moved between research and front-line sex work support services, delivering and developing sex work projects and contributing to multiagency responses to sex work, including in Merseyside and Leeds. As a founding member of the UK Network of Sex Work Projects and board member of National Ugly Mugs, she has worked with sex work projects throughout the United Kingdom and been involved in national policy development. A co-chair of the UK Sex Work Research Hub, she is an advocate for participatory action research and evidence-based policies and law that enhance the safety and rights of sex workers. She was awarded an OBE in 2013. Dr. Campbell was a researcher and netreach officer on *Beyond the Gaze* until 2018.

José Félix Colón-Burgos completed his undergraduate studies at the University of Puerto Rico, Cayey campus, where he earned a bachelor's degree in psychology and mental health, with a minor in sociology. He continued his graduate studies at the Graduate School of Public Health of the University of Puerto Rico, where he earned a master's in science on health systems research and evaluation and a doctorate in public health, specializing in the study of the social determinants of health. José Félix has worked as a research evaluator with various community, state, and international organizations aiming to tackle social and public health problems from a social justice perspective. His research interests include the study of the social determinants of health and the social determination of health; the effects of inequality and social structures on health, maternal health, and child health; substance abuse and sexual risk behaviors; deportation and health; tourism and health access to health services; men's health; immigrant health; and the political economy of health. José incorporates the use of social theory, critical medical anthropology, and critical public health with ethnographic, qualitative, and quantitative research techniques to explore the pathways of health risk in socially marginalized populations.

Writer, activist, and former sex worker **Dale Corvino** is based in New York. His writings have appeared in various journals and anthologies, including online at *The Rumpus* and *Salon*. He received the 2015 Christopher Hewitt Award for Fiction and won the 2018 Gertrude Press Fiction Chapbook contest. *Worker Names* was published in 2019. Recent publications include a reflection on his visit to Santiago, Chile, during the massive popular uprising for *The Gay & Lesbian Review*, a contributing essay on growing constraints of adult online content in *Matt Keegan: 1996*, from New York Consolidated/Inventory Press, and "Swarthy," a reflection on the colorism experienced by his Sicilian grandfather, in *Via: Voices in Italian Americana* from Bordighera Press.

Thomas Crofts is a professor in the School of Law and Department of Social and Behavioural Sciences at City University of Hong Kong and a professor (fractional) in the School of Law at Northumbria University. His research in criminal law, criminology, and criminal justice centers on criminalization and criminal responsibility, comparative criminal law, and criminal law reform.

Stewart Cunningham is a freelance researcher who has experience as a researcher in academic, NGO, and activist settings. His research interests coalesce around sex work legal frameworks and human rights–based campaigns for sex work law reform. His PhD study examined how the concept of human dignity is mobilized in legal and political debates on sex work. He worked on various elements of the data collection, analysis, and writing for *Beyond the Gaze*. He currently works as a part-time research associate in international human rights law at the Hertie School of Governance in Berlin.

Ryan DeVeau is a sex worker, activist, and researcher who studies sex work, sexual cultures, and sexuality. His qualitative approaches to research focus on the well-being of his peers, who include sex workers and the LGBTIQ+ community. He believes in the authenticity of shared stories and creating visibility, both of which drive his research.

Nicholas de Villiers is a professor of English and film at the University of North Florida. He is the author of *Opacity and the Closet: Queer Tactics in Foucault, Barthes, and Warhol* (University of Minnesota Press, 2012) and *Sexography: Sex Work in Documentary* (University of Minnesota Press, 2017).

John de Wit (PhD, MSc) is a professor of interdisciplinary social science: public health at Utrecht University, The Netherlands, and a professor of social research in health at UNSW Sydney, Australia. John has 30 years' experience in researching sexuality, health, and well-being, and he has published widely on a variety of topics. His current interests encompass social inequalities in health and well-being, particularly as they relate to sexual preferences and practices. His research focuses on strengthening theory-informed understandings of sexual health and well-being to inform best practice policy and programs.

Carlos Disogra, PhD, is an adjunct professor of psychology in the Faculty of Psychology at the National University of Córdoba in Argentina. His research on male sex work and the general population is focused on understanding condom use and HIV prevention. He has written several articles and a book on condom use in Argentina.

Basil Donovan is a sexual health physician and researcher. He established Australia's first sexual health training course, and for decades, he has conducted research on the sexual health and well-being of sex workers, gay men, Indigenous Australians, prisoners, and young people.

Itai Doron is a lens-based artist and fashion photographer. He is the director of the Fashion Media Programme at the London College of Fashion, University of the Arts London. He has participated in numerous group and solo exhibitions in the United States, Europe, Japan, and Israel. He has authored several photography books, including *End of Real* (2005), *Yassin* (2009), *Chokras' Mahal* (*Boys' Palace*, 2011), and *Fifteen Minutes With You* (2012), and he has written a number of book chapters and academic journal articles. Doron's research focuses on the construction of fashion imagery and the crafting of masculine archetypes within it. His fashion photography has been published in many fashion and culture magazines, including *Numéro Berlin, Numéro Homme Berlin, Replica MAN*, and *HEROINE*. He lives and works in London.

Tinashe Dune, PhD, teaches health sociology and public health at Western Sydney University in Australia and is a provisional psychologist. Her research and teaching focus on marginalized populations, including the experiences of culturally and linguistically diverse people, those living with disability, aging populations, LGBTIQ-identifying people, and Indigenous populations.

Maxime Durocher, born in 1974, has been a straight male sex worker since 2011 and an activist for sex workers' rights since 2014. His prior careers were programmer, project manager, and finally department director. He studied biochemistry, genetic engineering, and computer science. He loves ancient history, architecture, writing, and climbing.

Jennifer V. Evans is a professor at Carleton University, Canada. She specializes in twentieth-century social history, including Germany and East Central Europe; history of sexuality, comparative nationalisms, Cold War, and national identity and everyday life. Her publications reflect these same interests in thinking conceptually as well as historically. Her first book, *Life Among the Ruins: Cityscape and Sexuality in Cold War Berlin* (Palgrave Macmillan, 2011), is a cultural history of reconstruction and traces the rebirth of the city's various subcultures in the aftermath of World War II.

Taylor Grey (formerly Taylor Harrington) holds professional qualifications in ICT, blockchain technology, and international business and has conducted fieldwork studies on male online escorting. He is a research assistant in the School of Social Justice at Queensland University of Technology, Australia, and he collected the data for the online survey reported in the chapter for this book.

Andrew Grossman is the editor of the anthology *Queer Asian Cinema: Shadows in the Shade*, a regular contributor to and editor of *Bright Lights Film Journal*, and a columnist for *Popmatters.com*. He has contributed chapters to numerous anthologies, including *Chinese Connections* (Temple University Press), *Asexualities: Feminist and Queer Perspectives* (Routledge), *Transnational Chinese Cinema: Corporeality, Desire, and the Ethics of Failure* (Bridge 21), *Movies in the Age of Obama* (Rowman-Littlefield), and *Hong Kong Horror Cinema* (Edinburgh University Press). He also produced and directed a feature documentary, *Not That Kind of Christian!!*, which was featured at the 2007 Montreal World Film Festival.

Katie Hindmarch-Watson is an assistant professor of modern British history at Colorado State University. She received her PhD from Johns Hopkins University. Her scholarship explores the entangled histories of gender, labor, mobility, sexuality, and technology in nineteenth- and early-twentieth-century Britain and the British Empire.

Travis S. K. Kong is an associate professor in the department of sociology at the University of Hong Kong. His research interests are homosexuality, prostitution, and transnational Chinese sexualities. His articles have appeared in *Gender, Work, & Organization*; *Body & Society*; *Sexualities*; *Deviant Behavior*; *Critical Asian Studies*; *Culture, Health, and Sexuality*; the *British Journal of Criminology*; *The Sociological Review*; *Urban Studies*; *Qualitative Research*; *The Lancet*; and *AIDS Care*. He is the author of *Chinese Male Homosexualities: Memba, Tongzhi, and Golden Boy* (London: Routledge, 2011; Chinese edition in 2018) and *Oral Histories of Older Gay Men in Hong Kong: Unspoken but Unforgotten* (Hong Kong Univeristy Press, 2019; Chinese edition in 2014) and co-editor of the journal *Sexualities: Studies in Culture and Society* (2012–).

Rodrigo Mariño is a public health researcher who has conducted survey studies on male escorts in Australia and Argentina. He is a professor in the Faculty of Medicine, Dentistry, and Health Sciences at the University of Melbourne.

Giovane Mendieta-Izquierdo is an assistant professor of the doctorate in bioethics of the Universidad Militar Nueva Granada, Bogotá, Colombia, and the leader of the research line in medical bioethics and public health. He is also an associated researcher and evaluator recognized by Colciencias–Colombia. His areas of interest include gender relations, masculinity, bioethics, and health. He has studied male prostitution; body and masculinity; masculinity and tobacco; masculinity, family, and unemployment; and gender and suicide in the elderly. He has published in specialized journals and books, and some of his publications are the product of international collaborations.

Matthew J. Mimiaga is a tenured professor of behavioral and social health sciences and eidemiology (School of Public Health) and a professor of psychiatry and human behavior (Alpert Medical School) at Brown University. He is also the director of the Division of Epidemiology and Global Health Research at The Fenway Institute, Fenway Health. His research program focuses on interventions to decrease sexual risk in HIV primary and secondary prevention; biobehavioral interventions to enhance antiretroviral medication uptake and adherence for both HIV treatment and prevention; psychosocial treatment interventions for stimulant use disorder and concurrent HIV risk; infectious disease and psychiatric epidemiology; and global health research within 11 resource-constrained countries in Asia, Africa, Latin America, and Europe. His funded studies involve a variety of populations at risk for HIV infection, such as marginalized and disenfranchised groups with vulnerabilities to health disparities or stigmatized conditions, including sexual and gender minorities, racial/ethnic minorities, and other groups that experience social, political, economic, and/or environmental disadvantage. To date, he has authored over 300 publications (peer-reviewed, original scientific journal articles and book chapters, meta-analytic reviews and commentaries) and is/has been the principal investigator of numerous federally funded research grants in the area of HIV prevention and public health.

Gregory Mitchell is an associate professor of women's, gender, and sexuality studies at Williams College and an ACLS Burkhardt Fellow in gender and sexuality studies at Princeton University. He is the author of *Tourist Attractions: Performing Race and Masculinity in Brazil's Sexual Economy* (University of Chicago Press, 2016), an ethnographic study of male sex workers and their clients in Brazil. His work also appears in *GLQ, American Ethnologist, Brasiliana*, and the edited volumes *Men Who Sell Sex: Global Perspectives, Sex: Ethnographic Encounters, Policing Pleasure: Sex Work, Policy and the State in Global Perspective*, and *The Routledge International Handbook of Sex Industry Research*. He has received awards from the National Science Foundation, Ford Foundation, and the American Anthropological Association. His next book is tentatively titled *40,000 Missing Girls: Global Sporting Events, Moral Panics, and the Spectacle of Sex Trafficking*.

Alice Orchiston is a lecturer in the School of Law at the University of New South Wales, Australia. Her research focuses on the regulation of commercial sex, gender-based violence, and issues connected with labor and employment. Her doctoral research project, titled *Brothels as Workplaces: Exploring Labor Regulation and Compliance in Australia's Legal Sex Industry*, examined empirically the ways in which regulators treat legal sex work differently from other types of work.

Mark Padilla, a professor of anthropology at Florida International University, is a medical anthropologist with research and teaching interests in gender, sexuality, race, migration, political economy, commercial or transactional sex, theories of tourism, and critical HIV/AIDS and drug research. His applied research has been conducted primarily in the Hispanic Caribbean, particularly the Dominican Republic and Puerto Rico. His books include *Caribbean Pleasure Industry: Tourism, Sexuality, and AIDS in the Dominican Republic* (University of Chicago Press, 2007), which analyzes the lives of young men in the Dominican Republic who engage in sexual exchanges with foreign men and women, and *Love and Globalization: Transformations of Intimacy in the Contemporary World* (Vanderbilt University Press, 2007), which examines issues of gender and intimacy across the globe. More recently he has been working with transgender women in Puerto Rico, documenting their experiences, stories, and challenging engagements with healthcare. His work seeks to shift research, dialogue, and policy by amplifying the voices and experiences of the communities he studies in order to raise awareness of social inequalities and provide directions for policy change, community engagement, and social transformation.

Voon Chin Phua is a professor of sociology at Gettysburg College. His research focuses on the intersectionalities of sex, gender, and sexuality, as well as cultural tourism. His works have been published in numerous journals, including *Sex Roles, Sexualities, Archives of Sexual Behavior, Sexuality and Culture, Men and Masculinities*, and *Culture, Health, and Sexuality*.

Better known as a novelist, memoirist, and playwright, **Felice Picano** also taught literature at Antioch University Los Angeles for several years. Currently he teaches three writing workshops at The West Hollywood Public Library and lectures nationally on film, LGBT culture, and literature. His Hollywood *roman à clef, Justify My Sins*, was published in 2019, his *Songs & Poems* in 2020, and in 2021 two novels, *Pursuit: A Victorian Entertainment* and *The Betrothal at Usk*, the second book in his *City on a Star* trilogy.

Jane Pitcher has worked at Warwick, Loughborough, and Strathclyde universities in addition to public and third-sector organizations. She has more than 20 years' research and evaluation expertise, including research studies on sex work in street and indoor settings. The focus of her ESRC-funded PhD at Loughborough University was the working experiences of sex workers in diverse indoor settings in Great Britain, drawing on in-depth interviews with adult female, male, and transgender sex workers. Other publications include Pitcher, Campbell, Hubbard, O'Neill, and Scoular, *Living and Working in Areas of Street Sex Work: From Conflict to coexistence* (Policy Press, 2006) and Sanders, O'Neill, and Pitcher, *Prostitution: Sex Work, Policy, and Politics* (Sage, 2018). She was a key member of the *Beyond the Gaze* team, working across methods and analysis work.

Garrett Prestage is an Australian sociologist who works in both quantitative and qualitative social and behavioral research and is committed to community-based research. Garrett's research interests include HIV transmission and prevention among gay men, the roles of identity and community in understanding how individuals negotiate risk and pleasure in their lives, and survey design and questionnaire development. Garrett has been actively involved in the gay community for over 30 years and has worked in gay community–based research since 1983.

Juliet Richters has worked for over 30 years in sexual health research and education. Her work includes national and local surveys of sexual behavior and attitudes, in-depth interview studies, and theoretical work on the sociology of sexual practice. Among other topics, she has studied family planning, condom use, circumcision, and prevention of HIV and other sexually transmissible infections.

Robert Ridinger is a professor on the university libraries faculty at Northern Illinois University and a longtime researcher on the histories of the LGBT and leather/BDSM communities. He holds BA degrees in anthropology and German, an MLS from the University of Pittsburgh, and an MA in anthropology from Case Western Reserve University. He served as a Peace Corps Volunteer librarian in the Kingdom of Lesotho from 1976 to 1980 and is currently a member of the board of directors of the Leather Archives and Museum in Chicago and a reviewer for *CHOICE*. His publications include *The ADVOCATE Index, 1967–1982; Speaking for Our Lives: Historic Speeches and Rhetoric for Gay and Lesbian Rights (1892–2000)*; the article "Negotiating Limits: The Legal Status of S/M in the United States" in the *Journal of Homosexuality*; and the bibliographical column *OFF THE SHELF*.

Cirus Rinaldi, PhD, is an associate professor of sociology of deviance at the Department of Culture and Society, University of Palermo, where he lectures on genders, sexualities, violence and masculinities, and crime and criminal justice. His main research topics are masculinity and violence, homophobia, deviance theory, and the sociology of sexualities. He is one among the few Italian scholars who has widely researched sociological aspects of sexuality, the sociology of LGBT people, and masculinity in male sex work. He has been a member of the scientific committee of the gender studies section of AIS (the Italian Sociological Association). He is currently coordinating the activities of the Research group on bodies, rights, and conflict at Palermo University. Among his latest publications are the first Italian academic research on male sex work, *Uomini che si fanno pagare. Genere, identità e sessualità nel sex work maschile tra devianza e nuove forme di normalizzazione* (DeriveApprodi, Rome, 2020) and the chapter "Sex and Sexuality" (in W. Brekhus, ed., *The Oxford Handbook of Symbolic Interaction, forthcoming*).

Peter Salhaney is a project coordinator in the Center for Health Equity Research at the Brown University School of Public Health. In his time there, he has completed a master's of science in behavioral and social health science and worked on multiple research grants alongside Matthew J. Mimiaga and Katie B. Biello. His primary research interests are sexual health (HIV/sexually transmitted infection prevention and treatment) and drug use among underserved populations, including male sex workers, people who inject drugs, and individuals involved in the criminal justice system.

Teela Sanders is a professor of criminology at the University of Leicester. She is a leading international scholar in research on the intersections between gender, regulation, governance, and crime, specifically in the sex industry. Sanders has written eight books and edited eight books and has over 50 peer-reviewed journal articles, based on research projects funded from major research councils. The recently completed Economic and Social Research Council study on Internet sex work, *Beyond the Gaze*, has created some of the largest datasets in the world. Its outcomes have involved practitioners' good practice, safety resources for sex workers, and police and practitioner training. Sanders is currently working on a Home Office project regarding corrosive substance crime and a sex work project in Nairobi.

Christopher Santostefano is a registered nurse and research assistant in the Center for Health Equity Research at the Brown University School of Public Health. His background is in emergency and intensive inpatient care, but he has since pursued a career in research with a focus on healthcare delivery, health service policy, and population health. He has previously joined disaster relief and infectious disease control teams in Haiti and Brazil. He now works for Katie B. Biello and Matthew J. Mimiaga on multiple grant-funded sexual risk and substance use harm reduction projects that concentrate on marginalized sexual and gender minority individuals in the United States.

Jane Scoular is a professor in law at the University of Strathclyde. Her work is a primary reference in the field of the legal regulation of commercial sex, and her scholarship includes original theoretical expositions in books (recently *The Subject of Prostitution: Sex Work, Law, and Social Theory*, Routledge, 2016) and internationally peer-refereed journals, as well as international empirical studies. She has been a visiting scholar at the Universities of New York and Stockholm, where she researched the Swedish law relating to prostitution. She was a member of the Scottish Parliament's Expert Panel on Prostitution and continues to advise on policy in this area. She sat on the Management Committee and co-chaired the scientific program "Prostitution Policies and Politics" in the COST Action IS1209: Comparing European Prostitution Policies. Scoular was a key member of the *Beyond the Gaze* team, leading work on policing and legal framework analysis.

Russell Sheaffer is an experimental filmmaker and producer with a PhD from the Department of Communication and Culture at Indiana University, Bloomington. His writing has focused on historiographic approaches to thinking about "stag film" and on representations of male sex work in film. His films have screened at venues including the Tribeca Film Festival, Ann Arbor Film Festival, Berlinale, UCLA, the University of Wisconsin at Madison, Torino GLBT Film Festival, and the Museum of Modern Art.

Ankur Srivastav is a PhD candidate in the School of Social Work at the University of Southern California, Los Angeles. His research is invested in identifying and examining sociopsychological and cultural factors related to minority stress among LGBTQ youth and their associated impact on mental well-being. His dissertation research aims at understanding how fluidity in sexual identity among youth is associated with changes in behavioral health outcomes. Additionally, he is a part of INQUIRY, an international consortium of social scientists working on sexuality research in the United States, United Kingdom, Canada, and Mexico.

R. Vaishno Bharati is a freelance social science researcher based out of New Delhi, India, with more than a decade of experience in the field of gender and sexuality. She received her graduate degrees from the University of Chicago, University of Delhi, and Tata Institute of Social Sciences. Her research has explored issues of branding in drag performances, construction of queer identities, livelihood and gender performativity among Aravanis and Jogappas. She is trained in the classical dance form of Bharatanatyam, and she has worked on understanding the brahamanical reconstruction of the art form.

Kevin Walby is an associate professor of criminal justice at the University of Winnipeg, Canada. He has authored or co-authored 120 articles in the *British Journal of Criminology*, *Qualitative Research*, *Punishment & Society*, *Policing & Society*, *Australian & New Zealand Journal of Criminology*, *Criminology and Criminal Justice*, and more. He is author of *Touching Encounters: Sex, Work, and Male-for-Male Internet Escorting* (2012, University of Chicago Press). He is co-author with R. Lippert of *Municipal Corporate Security in International Context* (2015, Routledge). He is co-editor of *Access to Information and Social Justice* with J. Brownlee (2015, ARP Books) and *The Handbook of Prison Tourism* with J. Wilson, S. Hodgkinson, and J. Piche (2017, Palgrave). He is co-editor of *National Security, Surveillance, and Terror: Canada and Australia in Comparative Perspective* with R. Lippert, I. Warren, and D. Palmer (2017, Palgrave). He is co-editor of the *Journal of Prisoners on Prisons*.

Andrea Waling, PhD, is an ARC DECRA senior research fellow at the Australian Research Centre in Sex, Health & Society (ARCSHS) at La Trobe University, Melbourne. She is co-leading a program of research at ARCSHS focusing on the intersections of technology, bodies, masculinity, sexuality, and sexual intimacies, and works across a range of other projects including LGBTIQ+ health and well-being and young people and sexual health. She has published across numerous journals on the aforementioned topics. She is the reviews editor for *Journal of Bodies, Sexualities, and Masculinities*, on the editorial board for *The Journal of Men's Studies*, author of *White Masculinity in Contemporary Australia: The Good Ol' Aussie Bloke* (2019), and is currently writing *Exploring the Cultural Phenomenon of the Dick Pic* (2022).

Drew A. Westmoreland is a post-doctoral fellow at the CUNY Institute for Implementation Science in Population Health in New York City. A behavioral and STD epidemiologist, she has published articles related to sexual health, relationships, and methods in sexual research in various populations.

Albert C. H. Yau obtained his PhD in the department of sociology at the University of Hong Kong. His PhD thesis researches Chinese men who sell sex in Hong Kong and China. He is currently a project officer (research) at the Association Concerning Sexual Violence Against Women, an NGO that provides support to victims of sexual violence in Hong Kong.

Yuriy Zikratyy, PhD, is a lecturer in the interdisciplinary program in sexuality Studies at Concordia University (Montreal). His research focuses on queer archives and autobiographies from the early- and mid-twentieth century, sex work, cross-class sexual relations, and the history of sexual science. His work has appeared in *Out of the Closet, Into the Archives: Researching Sexual Histories* (2015) and *The Journal of History of Sexuality*.

Iván Zaro is a social worker. He began his professional career in 2004, specializing in male sex workers and people with HIV. He has long experience in fieldwork with prostitutes, where he has had the opportunity to meet and maintain direct contact with the population. In 2007, he directed the first sociological study on male prostitution in Madrid. He has written several articles on the subject, and he collaborates with mass media as an expert in male prostitution. In 2011, he co-founded Imagina MÁS, a non-governmental organization that has run the Madrid city council's Attention to Male Prostitution Program since 2013. *La Difícil Vida Fácil* (2016) is his first book.

Introduction

New Understandings of Male Sex Work: From Pathology and Criminality to Intersectionality and Cultural Diversity

John Scott, Christian Grov, and Victor Minichiello

Keywords: male sex work, regulation, SESTA, FOSTA, Swedish model, public health

In 1996 an escort in Dallas developed the first website devoted to sex work. The following year, the first nationwide online escort advertising service, Eros.com, appeared in the United States. As the millennium drew to a close, the spread of graphical browsers marked a turning point for commercial online sex that would change the organization of sex work. In 2000 the online magazine *Slate* featured a female escort who claimed to have earned a small fortune because of the advantages of online markets. Yet despite these developments, most advertisements for sex work still appeared in print media. During the first decade of the twenty-first century, however, the Internet started to eclipse print media in the global north as the primary site for marketing sex work, assisted by wide-scale growth in high-speed residential broadband (Cunningham & Kendall, 2011). Although most growth was linked to male demand, shifting cultural norms were also making it possible to consider the male body as a commodity, and men started a large number of online services, some catering to a female clientele. At the end of the twentieth century, gay male pornography represented a sizable segment of the U.S. pornography market, accounting for about one-third to one-half of the $2.5 billion adult entertainment industry (Thomas, 2000).

During the 1990s, research on male sex work began to document some of the structural and paradigmatic changes that were occurring in the sex industry. In 1996 one of the editors of this volume, Victor Minichiello, coauthored a paper on male sex work that provided an overview of the research up to that time (Browne & Minichiello, 1996). Minichiello and his coauthor argued that male sex work needed to be "understood within the social construction of masculinity and the secular origins of both whoredom and homosexuality" (p. 30). Male sex work had mostly been considered a crime or a health problem, as well as a product of individual pathology and economic necessity. The pervasiveness of these narratives supported a representation of sex workers as passive and disempowered victims, exploited and coerced into prostitution. The male sex worker was either a psychopathological social misfit, a victim of childhood sexual abuse, or a heterosexual who was driven to sex work because of social disadvantage (Browne & Minichiello, 1996). In popular culture, male sex work had gained public visibility through media reports of sex workers or their clients becoming victims of bizarre and violent crimes, such as homicides and serial killings. Although the violent incidents made for good news copy, these were rare events that created a skewed impression of the everyday life of the majority of sex workers (West & de Villiers, 1993). Think, for example, of the widespread media coverage of Andrew Cunanan's alleged past as a sex worker, following his murder of clothing designer Gianni Versace in 1997. While the landscape of male sex work seemed bleak, occasional reports presented male sex work as a rational choice. As the HIV/AIDS crisis was contained in the global north following the release of highly effective antiretroviral therapy in 1996, research on male sex work shifted from grim and often moralistic accounts of risk to more holistic accounts of male sex workers' lives. Increasingly, research (such as Minichiello and Browne's) became exploratory and qualitative', rewriting the dark scripts of male sex work by capturing the diverse voices of male sex workers. This volume, in its multidisciplinary and global focus, embraces that tradition.

Recent work, much of it presented in these pages, shows that the intrinsic nature of sex work is not always oppressive. There are different kinds of worker and client experiences and varying degrees of victimization, exploitation, agency, and choice (see Minichiello, Mariño, & Browne, 2001). In addition, Weitzer (2009) describes three distinct paradigms operating in sex worker research. He suggests that the "oppression" and "empowerment" paradigms offer two diametrically opposed, one-dimensional perspectives on sex work and suggests the need for a third, alternative perspective that moderates the oppression and empowerment paradigms by reflecting on sex work as containing "a constellation of occupational arrangements, power relations and worker experiences" (p. 215). He terms this the "polymorphous" paradigm. Research has revealed male sex workers *as workers* who are neither psychologically unstable, desperate, nor destitute and who have engaged in sex work as an occupational choice; their choice of work was, ultimately, a rational economic decision (Minichiello et al., 2001). Clients come from diverse backgrounds in terms of age, social class, ethnicity, and sexual identification (Minichiello et al., 1999). As we note later in this book (Chapter 16), it is unhelpful to speak of *the* sex industry and sex markets, because such terms limit male sex work to a monolithic narrative. Instead, we should consider sex work in terms of diverse *communities*. The Internet has certainly given visibility to these communities and encouraged their formation and growth.

One way the Internet has done this is by increasing escorts' visibility. Often ignored in the early research, escorts came to dominate the online environment. Escorts were typically men in their twenties who identified as gay or bisexual and reported deriving satisfaction from their work. Many escorts were well educated and skilled, and they saw escorting as their primary job and main source of income. Researchers thus came to recognize male sex workers as agents and sex work as an occupation. Male sex workers also reported that many of their clients identified as nongay. Telecommunications technology, including the mobile phone, facilitated interactions, increased the number of male sex workers, and created new spaces in which sex work encounters could take place, expanding the client base for male sex workers (Holt & Blevins, 2007). The rapid growth in the online male sex industry provided sex workers with alternatives to existing modes of operating. The ability to advertise for and select clients online provided privacy and anonymity, protecting both clients and providers from harassment, embarrassment, and the potential for police sanctions. Instead of facing the difficulties associated with cruising streets for clients, male sex workers were able to choose from a range of online venues for contacts, such as escort agencies, personal pages, and instant messaging services. The range of the Internet allowed sex workers operating online to reach a broader audience of potential clients, in terms of both sheer numbers and sociodemographic characteristics (Ashford, 2009; Lee-Gonyea, Castle, & Gonyea, 2009).

The Internet also changed the quality and experience of sexual services. Weitzer (2009) noted that clients of indoor sex workers (including online sex workers) demanded much more than just a sexual experience: they wanted sex workers who were friendly, affectionate, and attentive. He drew attention to the rise of the "girlfriend experience," in which female sex workers playacted the attentiveness expected of a girlfriend in real life. Male sex workers similarly offered a "boyfriend experience," a term frequently found in sex worker marketing to this day. The Internet displayed the diversity of male sex worker populations in terms of age, body type, background, and services offered. This book documents that diversity over time and cross-culturally, clearly indicating the myriad meanings given to male sex work. It is thus difficult to make generalizations about male sex workers, their clients, and the experience of male sex work, but studies have revealed some significant facts regarding male sex workers' experience. As these pages show, we know that certain structural conditions, especially those associated with the regulation of sex work, can create problems for sex work communities. For example, we know that when sex work is illegal, the risk of physical violence toward sex workers and their clients increases; so does the risk of poor health outcomes. The global sex industry has never been more visible than it is today, but the majority of sex workers still operate underground and under stigmatized conditions.

There were numerous advantages to moving sex work online. In addition to the increased safety, the Internet's limited regulation allowed sex workers to harness a wider range of advertising techniques to attract clients, including using explicit language and color photographs, and working online reduced their dependence on and payments to third parties, such as pimps or brothel owners (McLean, 2013). This not to say that the move towards online sex work did not have its challenges. McLean (2012) has pointed to a range of harms associated with selling sex through the Internet, notably continued stigma and a lack of support networks. Although we have identified the professionalization of the sex industry as a positive development for managing stigma, McLean notes that this might lead to a form of professional distancing among male sex workers that increases stigma and social isolation. The literature also abounds with references to the role the Internet has played in facilitating the growth of sexual subcultures specifically dedicated to sexual risks (Bimbi & Parsons, 2005).

But the greatest danger to male sex workers remains the regulatory environments that isolate sex workers and force them underground, away from the safe-sex messaging offered by online health-care providers and away from service providers and sex work communities. Legal systems worldwide continue to criminalize same-sex relations and paid sex. In a special issue of *The Lancet* that published articles focused exclusively on HIV and sex work, Shannon et al. (2014) showed that the decriminalization of sex work could reduce HIV infections by 33 to 46 percent, a significant public health outcome. Notable gains have been made with respect to decriminalizing homosexuality. In 2006, ninety-two countries (48 percent of UN member states) criminalized same-sex sexual acts between consenting adults, but this number dropped to 75 countries (39 percent of UN member states) by 2015 (Carroll & Itaborahy, 2015). The picture for sex work, however, is more challenging, and progress toward reform is very slow. Indeed, advocacy and adoption of the so-called Nordic model of regulation, which criminalizes the buying of sex as opposed to selling of sexual services, suggests that there is a global punitive shift (Minichiello, Scott, & Cox, 2017).

With respect to male sex work, evidence of a punitive shift can be found in the Rentboy.com saga (see Callander & Scott, 2015). Rentboy.com was the 'oldest and most popular website for male sex workers, who paid a monthly fee to advertise to and connect with potential clients on the site. It had been in operation since 1997—longer than Google. It was the world's first online male escorting site, and it received an estimated four million hits annually and hosted 40,000 profiles. In August 2015 the New York City Police Department, in partnership with the U.S. Department of Homeland Security, arrested seven people at the Rentboy.com offices in New York and seized all assets pertaining to the website. Although site purported to help men connect for companionship only and promoted a philosophy of safe sex, authorities alleged that it had been used to "facilitate the promotion, management, establishment, and carrying on of an unlawful activity, namely an enterprise involving prostitution." Sex work is illegal across all of the United States, except in a few counties in Nevada, where it is subject to heavy regulation. The raid on Rentboy.com raised important questions about sex work concerning its visibility, the consumer demand for such services, and the ongoing marginalization of those who buy and sell sexual services. More recently, passage in 2018 of the Stop Enabling Sex Traffickers Act (SESTA) and Allow States and Victims to Fight Online Sex Trafficking Act (FOSTA) by the U.S. Senate and House made it illegal in the United States to knowingly assist, facilitate, or support sex trafficking. Online sex workers argued that the legislation would affect their safety, as platforms that they and their clients used to discuss sexual services began to shut down. Craigslist, Backpage, and other sites fearful of liability ceased to offer their "personals" sections, in which such advertising had appeared, in U.S. domains.

And so it is that despite two decades of growth in online sex work that produced new sex work communities and promised improved safety and health conditions for sex workers, sex work today faces unprecedented regulatory challenges. In this climate, we present the diversity of the male sex work experience. Despite the aspirations of sex worker advocates worldwide who wish to define it as an occupation, male sex work remains a relatively mysterious phenomenon. For example, we have no idea of the actual numbers of male sex workers worldwide or in any given country; existing estimates vary wildly. This volume cannot provide all the answers to questions surrounding male sex work, but it can and does capture the polymorphous nature of male sex work research, which in the two decades since 1996 has become highly interdisciplinary, diverse in its methods, and sophisticated in its theorizing. In this volume—the sequel to *Male Sex Work and Society*, published by Harrington Park Press in 2014—we continue to examine the diverse experiences of male sex workers and their clients.

Compiling this volume has been different, and easier, in several ways. First, the topic is much easier to research and write about now, especially in jurisdictions where sex work is legal or has been decriminalized. Second, as sex work advocacy has become a more visible global force, more voices from the industry provide important narratives about the sex work landscape. Third, today's scholars are turning their attention to studying the intersections between gender, sexualities, human rights, and sex work, generating insights into how sexual work is woven into all aspects of human life, including cinema, art, fashion, politics, law, medicine, discrimination, and commerce. Fourth, as societies become more accepting of same-sex relationships and sex work, male sex work is becoming, at the very least, a "permissible" topic of public discussion and research—which explains the length of this volume.

Finally, a note on terminology. The handbook adopts what has been described as a polymorphic framework to understand sex work (Weitzer 2011). This is a critical approach, which takes as its focus the historical, political, economic and social conditions and contexts in which people enter and work in the sex industry. As the term suggests, this framework avoids making generalizations about sex work. Involvement in the sex industry occurs in the context of a shifting spectrum of choice, circumstance and coercion (Albright et al. 2017).

Following from this, the focus of the handbook is 'sex work', rather than 'prostitution' or trafficking. According to the World Health Organization [WHO] (2017), the commercial sex industry involves the exchange of money or goods for sexual services, while sex workers include men, women and transgendered people who 'receive money or goods in exchange for sexual services, and who consciously define these activities as income generating even if they do not consider sex work as their occupation'.

The WHO definition is quite descriptive and does not capture critical aspects of the sex work definition or account for the genesis of the term. Commercial sexual exchanges may be described in terms of 'prostitution' and 'sex work'. According to Pheterson (1990), the category 'prostitute' is a mystification or ideological representation that operates to stigmatise persons labeled as such. It is a highly gendered term and is rarely used to describe the male supply of sexual services. This noted, similarly culturally loaded terms have been used to describe male sex workers, including 'hustler', 'rent boy' and 'kept boy'. However, to address the historic baggage associated with the term 'prostitute' liberal sections of the feminist movement and sex industry advocates have sought to counter-construct the prostitute as 'sex worker', arguing that those involved in the sex industry are no different from other people or employees. This industrial or occupational focus has gained much currency since the 1970s, despite the categorical limitations of the term 'sex worker' which has become an umbrella concept for a varied range of behaviours, not all of which would have traditionally been designated 'prostitution'. While in this handbook we have favored the use of the term sex worker, prostitute/prostitution has been adopted when describing ideological representations of commercial sexual exchanges or when referring to historical examples. In this respect, we adopt a constructionist position with regard to the use of terminology that is attentive to historic and cultural shifts in meaning (see Stein, 1992).

As for the distinction between sex work and human trafficking, it is important not to conflate voluntary sex work with enforced forms of labor. The United Nations separates human trafficking into two categories, these being sex trafficking and labour trafficking. Sex trafficking occurs when a person engages in sexual activity under conditions of 'force, fraud or coercion'.

The editors of this book are scholars who research sex work and do not claim to have expertise on the subject of human trafficking, beyond recognizing it as distinct from sex work. A key issue of distinction is consent: trafficking and associated conditions, such as slavery or debt bondage, lack consent. Nonetheless, the association of prostitution/sex work and trafficking has a long history, beginning with the International Agreement for the Suppression of the White Slave Traffic (1904). In 1950 the United Nations adopted Convention for the Suppression of Traffic in Persons and of the Exploitation of the Prostitution of Others which defined prostitution as incompatible with the dignity of the person. However, since the 1970s, sex work advocates have argued that the criminalization of sex work makes sex workers vulnerable to exploitation. Since this time feminists have debated supporting sex workers right to choose to engage in work or whether to view prostitution as an inherently violent and degrading practice, which harms women.

Benoit et al. (2018) in reviewing the research literature on 'the prostitution problem' conclude that the strongest empirical support is for 'labor exploitation' over the 'sexual exploitation' perspective. Despite this, recent years have seen growing global support for the sexual exploitation perspective, resulting in the introduction of repressive policies to 'protect' women from exploitation, despite evidence indicating that repressive policies fundamentally threaten sex workers', female and male, health and rights (Vanwesenbeeck 2019).

In contrast, in 2016 Amnesty International called for complete decriminalization of sex work as the best for the protection for the safety and human rights of sex workers. It opposed criminalization of both sex workers and clients, which resulted in these groups being marginalized in a hidden economy, increasing risks associated with sex work. Decriminalization is also supported by UNAIDS, Global Alliance Against Traffic in Women, Human Rights watch, Lambda Legal, American Civil Liberties Union. It is also the policy position overwhelmingly favored by those involved in the sex industry who feel the impact of policies and is a policy supported by the editors of this volume.

International organizations such as Amnesty International and the Global Commission on HIV and the Law have opposed the conflation of sex work and trafficking, arguing the following: it is counter-productive towards efforts to eliminate trafficking by pushing sex workers underground and criminalizing sex worker initiatives to improve working conditions; it leads to suppression of sex work, as opposed to suppressing trafficking in the sex industry; it diverts resources and attention from other industries where trafficking occurs; it increases health and safety threats to sex workers through the disruption of advocacy and support networks for sex workers (GSWOP 2019).

While there is exploitation and abuse of women and men involved in sex work, this should not be framed as a 'whole of industry problem' (Vanwesenbeck 2019: 1965). Trafficking is not a problem intrinsically linked to sex work, but is a problem of labor exploitation and exploitative work conditions can exist in any sector of the workforce (Kempadoo et al. 2005). The causes of exploitation include wider socio-structural conditions, including legal structures which criminalize the sex industry and compound the stigma and marginalization of sex workers. Oppressive legal structures are often perpetuated by the conflation of sex work with exploitation and violence and the conflation of exploitative work conditions in the sex industry with trafficking (GNSWP 2019). Trafficking campaigns can encourage governments to ignore conventional techniques for protecting work, such as occupational health and safety regulation and trade unions. Any efforts to combat exploitation should involve sex workers, but the presentation of sex workers as helpless victims or part of the problem makes it difficult for sex workers to be part of the solution (Vanwesenbeeck 2019).

Outline

Part I, "Male Sex Work in Popular Culture," explores the representation of male sex workers in various texts, taking us from early international silent cinema to contemporary Internet porn productions. While films associated with male sex work have been analyzed in some detail, including in the previous volume, subjects such as fashion and documentary film were largely ignored in the literature until recently.

Chapter 1, "Reframing the Cleveland Street Scandal of England," by Katie Hindmarch-Watson, offers a new perspective on London's notorious Cleveland Street Scandal of 1889, which resulted from the discovery of a brothel that offered the sexual services of adolescent telegraph boys to wealthy clients. The scandal fueled a perception of sex between men as an aristocratic vice that corrupted working-class youths. Most previous accounts of the scandal have concentrated on either the illustrious clients or the procurers, but Hindmarch-Watson focuses on the telegraph boys. She debunks the contemporaneous depiction of the telegraph boys as innocent victims sacrificed to rich men's vices, presenting them instead as sex workers. She explores the bureaucratic mechanisms by which the Cleveland Street brothel was discovered, and the telegraph boys' contributions to the contours of the scandal and to Victorian homoerotic markets.

In **Chapter 2, "Youth Male Prostitution in Post-Nazi Germany,"** Jennifer Evans explores how homosexual prostitution was policed in Berlin in the years after World War II. She explains not only the complex laws governing homosexual acts, sex with minors, and male prostitution in a divided city and country but also the police procedures developed to enforce those laws. Although male hustlers had long congregated in and around Berlin's train stations, or *Bahnhofen*, after the war the problems of male prostitution became intensely politicized. Despite conflicting beliefs among criminologists about the dangerous effect of "unnatural desire" on heterosexual maturation, it was the call boys, more than their clients, who were seen as posing a challenge to the reconstruction of respectable German masculinity in both the East and the West. In the mind of the postwar German public, "*Bahnhof* boys" had become predators, not prey.

In **Chapter 3, "'Kept Men' in Silent Gay Cinema,"** Andrew Grossman points to an early cinematic tradition in which male sex workers are depicted very differently from their modern representations. This earlier tradition, exemplified by Mauritz Stiller's *Vingarne* (1916) and Carl Dreyer's *Michael* (1924), which both feature "kept men," draws on Platonic notions of erotic work, especially in the relationship between an older man and a comely youth whom he teaches and mentors until he arrives at the age of maturity.

In **Chapter 4, "Male Prostitution and Fashion,"** Itai Doron examines how male sex workers have used fashion to communicate with potential clients. Ranging from depictions of sex workers in films and photographs in the mid-twentieth century to contemporary Internet profiles and selfies, Doron documents how male prostitutes catering to different clients use fashion and styling to embody sexual fantasy. While heterosexual gigolos hoping to attract women often emphasize class, style, and taste, hustlers seeking to attract gay clients frequently champion a style of working-class adornment calculated to signal raw masculinity and potential violence and danger.

Exploring the representation of male strippers in almost twenty films, Andrea Waling, in **Chapter 5, "Male Strippers in Popular Film,"** demonstrates how male stripping for women is viewed differently from what is normally thought of as sex work. Men's stripping for women embodies a set of gendered norms, values, and expectations that distinguish it from women's stripping for men and enable it to avoid the stigma and shame that often accompany women's sex work. Indeed, men's strip shows have been reframed as harmless naughty fun.

In **Chapter 6, "Gigolos in Popular Cinema,"** Russell Sheaffer demonstrates how recent films, such as *Magic Mike* (2012) and its sequel *Magic Mike XXL* (2015), place the male body and sex work on display in ways that differ from the grittiness and stigma that characterized earlier films, such as *Midnight Cowboy* (1969) and *American Gigolo* (1980). The gigolos in the earlier works regard homosexual male prostitution as abject in a way that is radically different from heterosexual prostitution, and they engage in homosexual sex only when their circumstances become dire. In contrast, the recent films—marketed to heterosexual women—avoid homophobic narratives and have found a large audience that includes straight women, gay men, and a whole sexual spectrum between.

In **Chapter 7, "Male Sex Work in Documentary Films,"** Nicholas de Villiers surveys and critiques recent documentaries about various forms of sex work, ranging from working in adult films, male strip clubs, and massage parlors to hustling and escorting. He raises important questions about their objectivity, explaining how rhetorical framing, interview techniques, settings, and editing all contribute to shaping the messages conveyed by the films. As he points out, "While it is crucial to listen to the actual voices of male sex workers talking about their experiences, it is equally important to be mindful of the ways in which their stories have been framed and edited, and to question the techniques and motives of the filmmakers and curious audiences consuming media about male sex work."

Chapter 8, Heather Berg's **"Male Sex Work in the Porn Industry,"** offers a fascinating discussion of the gender dynamics and material aspects of sex work in the American porn industry. Berg challenges the popular view of porn work as a site of female sexual abuse and vulnerability. This sensational view, promulgated by antiporn critics, draws attention away from the workplace risks that porn workers of all genders face. She points out that when performers speak about being "exploited" or "taken advantage of," they are almost always referring to working conditions and pay, not sex.

Part II, "Male Sex Work in Literature," features five chapters. They include a breezy survey of male sex workers in world literature; an account of the creation of Phil Andros, maybe the most famous hustler in literary history; an overview of the representations of male sex workers in comics and graphic novels; and a bibliographic essay documenting how male sex workers have been viewed by various observers since the early nineteenth century.

In **Chapter 9, "Male Sex Workers in World Literature,"** novelist and memoirist Felice Picano cites numerous examples of texts in which male sex workers are depicted. His examples include the earliest known epic poem, *Gilgamesh*, as well as classical Greek and Roman poetry, seventeenth- and eighteenth-century Japanese and Chinese tales, and modern European, English, and American novels.

In **Chapter 10, "Male Sex Work Diaries,"** Yuriy Zikratyy brings to the fore the diaries of two singular clients of male sex workers. Thomas N. Painter and Samuel M. Steward produced remarkable testimonies of their renegade sex lives, which consisted of numerous money-based relations with hustlers and other working-class men. In their diaries they not only described their sexual encounters with sex workers but also tried to analyze and interpret them. They shared the view that sex with hustlers, however dangerous, expensive, frustrating, or unsatisfactory, was an indispensable part of a certain segment of queer life, and that it possessed its own social, emotional, intellectual, and physical pleasures. These diaries offer a rare insider's view of the world of male sex work. Zikratyy looks at the drama of intimacy and performance played out in client-hustler relationships and raises questions about class-based notions of masculinity, the power-pleasure dynamic of sexual purchase, and the changing understanding of intimacy between men in that period.

In **Chapter 11, "Male Sex Work in Comics and Graphic Novels,"** Dale Corvino provides an overview of queer content in popular graphic formats. He examines the narrative structure, voice, and drawing styles of eight significant works, dating from 1996 to the present, to illustrate how authors and artists in this emergent subgenre grapple with such issues as disclosure, identity and agency, exploitation and freedom, and longing and intimacy. The works Corvino appraises counter persistent stereotypes of male sex workers with detailed characterizations and complex narratives. They examine the perils and pleasures of a working life at the margins of personal autonomy and legality, and explore complicated themes with surprising nuance.

In **Chapter 12, "Male Sex Work in the Library Collection,"** Robert Ridinger offers a bibliographic review of studies of male sex work. He reveals how male sex workers have been placed within contexts as antithetical as criminality and entrepreneurship, and perceived through lenses of both moral reform and titillation. Prior to the 1990s, most research on male sex workers was done in Europe and the United States. More recently, however, studies of South American, Australian, North African, and Asian sex workers have emerged. Over time there has also been a marked shift in the kinds of authors who write about male sex workers, from professionals (lawyers, police and security officials, physicians, and psychologists) to academics trained as anthropologists, historians, criminologists, and sociologists. Male prostitutes have always been a part of the literature as informants, but more recently individual sex workers have also told their personal stories in book-length accounts.

Part III, "Male Sex Work Online," focuses on how male sex work has been affected by technological advances and regulation, touching on some of themes outlined at the outset of this introduction. Topics in these five chapters range from the difficulty of counting male sex workers and attempts to regulate Internet-based sex work to the different ways that female and male sex workers use technology to sell sexual services. In contrast to the preceding parts, which largely draw on traditions in the arts and humanities, this section is more focused on social science. The authors qualitative and quantitative methodologies to provide a picture of male sex work in the cyber age. We are reminded that while the structure and organization of male sex work have been transformed significantly in recent years, the regulatory frameworks surrounding sex work have been slow to acknowledge and respond to those changes, posing health and safety challenges for sex workers and their clients.

Chapter 13, "Quantification of Global Male Sex Work Communities in the Technology Era," confronts the difficulties involved in counting male sex workers in individual countries and globally. Victor Minichiello and his coauthors argue that counting male sex workers is difficult because of the stigma and secrecy associated with male sex work. Not only does the idea of objectifying the male body run counter to many cultural norms, but same-sex attraction is also highly stigmatized and even criminalized in most countries. However, recent laws decriminalizing sex work and same-sex relations have created more open environments. Consequently, many Western democracies have attempted to use various methods to count the number of sex workers in their population; the resulting government sources and other published sources offer at least a beginning point for estimating numbers of male sex workers. Online advertising by escorts has also made it possible for researchers to access, observe, and count those who use the Internet to solicit clients.

In **Chapter 14, "Male Sex Work and Digital Regulation,"** Denton Callander and Ryan DeVeau point out that sex work flourishes in diverse online spaces, including escort directories, multiservice adult entertainment platforms, dating and hook-up apps, classified websites, content delivery platforms, agency websites, individual sex worker websites, and social media. Savvy workers operate across multiple platforms, maintain different kinds of profiles for different audiences, and attempt to build a recognizable brand in order to generate both online and offline revenue. While the Internet has been a great boon to sex workers, attempts to control sex work through social and legal mechanisms have also affect online sex workers. Various layers of moderation and censorship are imposed through the very structure of the digital spaces in which male sex workers operate. Often such regulation remains invisible because it is exercised by platforms that host websites or by the companies that distribute nearly all mobile content. In addition, laws intended to prevent human trafficking have had a negative impact on sex workers who have nothing to do with trafficking.

In **Chapter 15, "Male Sex Work and the Law,"** Thomas Crofts and Alice Orchiston argue that, in the United Kingdom and Australia, criminal law has traditionally taken a gendered approach to sex work, with sex work laws drafted and applied mainly with female workers in mind. While some sex work laws have been applied to men at certain points in history, those laws were directed more at male homosexuality than at male sex work as a distinct concept. The increasing shift to online-facilitated sex work has both reduced the imperative to regulate sex work and also made regulation more difficult. However, recent moves to combat online sex trafficking have had an impact on male sex work as well. The question is, will that impact remain incidental or will male sex work be placed under the direct regulatory purview of sex work laws.

In **Chapter 16, "Internet-Based Male Sex Work,"** Kevin Walby reports on interviews with male escorts who solicit clients through the Internet. He explores how escorts from diverse backgrounds engage in their work and negotiate interactions with their clients. This chapter uses the stories told by escorts to challenge some aspects of sexual-script theory, which posits that human sexual behavior follows a sort of predetermined script or set of shared expectations about sexual interactions in particular situations. He shows that the negotiations of online male escorts with clients include a spectrum of experiences, ranging from instrumental interactions in which workers maintain a distance from clients and provide routine services based on scripts, to interactions that workers describe as intimate, friendly, and creative.

In **Chapter 17, "Male Independent Sex Workers in the Digital Age,"** Teela Sanders and her colleagues offer a careful analysis of data derived from the largest survey of online sex workers in the United Kingdom ever attempted. The Internet has significantly shaped the way independent male escorts conduct their business. While male and female sex workers use technology to sell sexual services in similar ways, there are some notable differences. For example, male sex workers are less likely to report crimes to the police and to use sex worker forums than are female sex workers. These differences may reflect the fact that independent male escorts pursue their profession in greater isolation than female sex workers. In addition, as a result of legislation recently enacted in the United States and proposed in the United Kingdom, male sex workers may be forced to advertise their services more discreetly and to use dating apps.

Part IV, "Male Sex Work in Public and Community Health," consists of chapters on two related studies: one on the global epidemiology of HIV and other sexually transmitted infections among male sex workers and the other on male sex workers and behavioral health. These chapters draw on traditions in the health sciences, especially the vast body of research conducted since the start of HIV/AIDS crisis in the 1980s. They remind us that the health of male sex workers has significance in terms of both public health and occupational health and safety. The bulk of research on male sex work continues to be financed by health-care funding, and advocate organizations recognize public health as a vital battleground in attempts to change regulatory frameworks associated with sex work.

In **Chapter 18, "Global Epidemiology of HIV and Other Sexually Transmitted Infections among Male Sex Workers,"** Peter Salhaney and his colleagues review scientific studies of the risk of HIV and other sexually transmitted infections among male sex workers. They report on sexual risk behavior as well as psychosocial and structural factors that contribute to the spread of HIV. They also discuss access to HIV prevention and treatment, along with biomedical and behavioral interventions intended to reduce HIV acquisition and transmission. In addition, this chapter addresses the human rights implications of the studies and highlights new areas in need of research and exploration.

Chapter 19, "Male Sex Work and Behavioral Health," focuses on how psychosocial issues affect the health of male sex workers. Salhaney and his colleagues summarize the existing research on depression and anxiety, trauma and violence, and substance use among male sex workers, as well as how workers are affected by structural conditions such as homelessness, lower socioeconomic status, and involvement with the criminal justice system. They also describe how 'syndemi'c theory, which posits that co-occurring epidemics of poor mental health, substance use, and disadvantageous social conditions interact to adversely affect health, provides an understanding of the lives of male sex workers, whose experiences of stigma and marginalization as members of a sexual minority may be at the root of their psychosocial problems. The authors discuss the treatment and structural interventions that have been devised and tested in efforts to improve the health outcomes of male sex workers.

Part V, "Male Sex Worker, Escort, and Client Voices: 'Nothing about Us without Us'" presents three chapters highlighting the perspectives of sex workers and their clients. One recounts the experience of a heterosexual male sex worker who caters to female clients; another explores the perspectives of female clients who employ male sex workers; and the third offers perspectives on trans men in sex work. An important approach in recent research has been for researchers to work collaboratively with sex workers and their advocates. The authors in this volume, as in the previous one, have either been a part of a sex work community themselves or have worked closely with such communities to capture sex workers' voices and everyday experiences.

In **Chapter 20, "Male Sex Work and the Female Client,"** Maxime Durocher offers a firsthand account of his experience as a heterosexual man who works with female clients. He explains the practical difficulties of earning a living as an escort, the challenges of working with couples, erection and performance issues, and the need for communication, respect, consent, and privacy between sex workers and their clients. He insists that, as a whole, sex workers are 'normal' people who are often more motivated by a quest for freedom and autonomy than by money. While acknowledging the advantages for him of his job, he also emphasizes the therapeutic benefits that clients derive from his work.

Chapter 21, "Female Clients of Male Sex Workers," presents new research by Heather Caldwell and John de Wit on the experience of women in Australia who pay for sex with men. Their research suggests that the particular stigmas felt by the clients of sex workers are different for men and women. Whereas men who buy sex are stigmatized as exploitative, women who buy sex are widely considered either victims or sluts. Female clients use a number of strategies to cope with the stigma they experience. Many tightly control the information they share about their activity, sometimes telling only a very few people that they buy sex. Others cope by associating only with people they perceive as broad-minded so that they will not be negatively judged. Still others reframe the act of buying sex in terms of something more socially acceptable, such as mental or physical therapy.

In **Chapter 22, "Trans Men in Sex Work,"** Max Nicolai Appenroth helps to redress the paucity of resources for or about male-identified trans sex workers through his analysis of the few existing studies and the results of a new online survey. Trans individuals in the sex work industry are most often drawn to sex work out of economic necessity, because they are frequently excluded from the formal economy. Some trans sex workers may find the self-determination offered by sex work empowering and may discover in the sex industry a supportive group of fellow trans sex workers. The criminalization of sex work poses particular dangers for trans people, who face an elevated risk of being prosecuted based on their gender identity. Moreover, trans people are often victims of violence and discrimination. Because street sex work is problematic for male-presenting trans persons, most participate in sex work online rather than in the street or in brothels.

Part VI, "Male Sex Work in the Americas," presents chapters on male sex work in the United States and Canada, the Dominican Republic, Brazil, Argentina, and Mexico. This section and the final two parts of this volume provide glimpses of the global diversity of male sex work. As these chapters make apparent, the various ways in which masculinity is constructed around the world are key to understanding responses to male sex work in international contexts.

The chapters capture some of the research that has emerged recently in the global south, mostly since the mid-1990s.

Chapter 23, "Male Sex Work in North America," by Christian Grov and Drew Westmoreland, analyzes important recent studies of male sex workers in the United States and Canada, especially those who attract clients via the Internet. The authors find that male escorts make conscious—often entrepreneurial—decisions to engage in sex work. In addition, they appear to take fewer sexual risks with their commercial partners than expected. This research contradicts the stigmatizing narrative that scapegoats sex workers as morally bankrupt vectors for disease transmission. However, two recent events are likely to have considerable negative impacts on sex work in the United States: the raid of Rentboy.com in 2015 that shut down what was then the largest male escorting website in the world, and the 2018 enactment of U.S. legislation intended to stop sex trafficking.

Chapter 24, "Male Transactional Sex in the Dominican Republic," by José Félix Colón-Burgos and Mark Padilla, draws attention to the difficulties faced by male sex workers in the Dominican Republic who had emigrated to the United States and then been deported back to the DR. Many of the men found they had no real roots in the Dominican Republic, and they were stigmatized by virtue of having been deported. Consequently, they feel that they were forced to participate in sex tourism and drug trafficking in order to survive.

Chapter 25, "Brazilian Male Sex Workers," by Voon Chin Phua, offers a longitudinal study of the lives of the male sex workers in Brazil's *termas*—bathhouses that often provide spaces for social interaction and sexual services—who have begun to see their trade as a viable career that they can exit and reenter at will. The *garotos*, as they are known, are similar to independent male escorts, and like them they are often entrepreneurial. The experiences of the *garotos* help rebut the assumption that sex work is necessarily oppressive and that all sex workers are victimized.

Chapter 26, "Street Hustling in Brazil," by Gregory Mitchell, reports on recently discovered records of interviews conducted in the early 1990s with street hustlers in Rio de Janeiro. These interviews offer a vivid picture of the culture of street hustling soon after the end of Brazil's military dictatorship. The economic conditions of the 1990s, a period of widespread hyperinflation, drove many young heterosexually identified men to sell sex, even as the HIV epidemic roared across the country. These *michês*, or hustlers, reluctantly entered a sexual marketplace that was steeped in paranoia, fear, and desperation. Although the interviews document a great deal of hopelessness and a bleak sexual landscape, they also record moments of ambiguity in regard to power, emotion, and pleasure at a time when AIDS was reconfiguring the lives of sex workers in Brazil.

In **Chapter 27, "Male Internet-Based Escorting in Argentina,"** Carlos Disogra and his colleagues document the status of male sex workers in Argentina, where a large percentage of male escorts offer their services to both men and women. Male sex workers have typically been ignored or represented negatively in Argentine popular culture, but recently they have gained some visibility and received a more sympathetic hearing. Although there remains some hostility toward gay men and lesbians, the increased acceptance of homosexuality that led to marriage equality in Argentina has also fostered greater tolerance of male escorts.

Chapter 28, "Male Sex Work in Mexico," by Giovane Mendieta-Izquierdo, describes a particular form of male prostitution in Mexico, the practice of "virile prostitution" carried out in the plazas and parks of Guadalajara, Jalisco. In virile prostitution, the male sex worker assumes the role of dominator to the extent that he is the active penetrator, while the client, a passive receiver, is dominated. To be a *mayate* is to be a macho man who sells his masculinity and virility to other men. The clients of the *mayates* are men of diverse orientations who seek to satisfy their sexual needs with men who appear very masculine.

Part VII, "Male Sex Work in Europe," focuses on the status of male sex workers in Italy, Spain, Sweden, and the Czech Republic.

In **Chapter 29, "Male Sex Work in Italy,"** Cirus Rinaldi places contemporary male sex work in southern Italy in the context of a long history of sex work and Italian attitudes toward homosexuality. In the paradigm of Mediterranean homosexuality, a man may have sex with other men without losing his manly reputation and normative sexual status, so long as he is "active" and has a virile appearance. In contrast, those who perform a "passive" role in anal intercourse are considered a separate species to be exploited. While this pattern for sexual activity between men has recently been challenged by a model based on homosexual identity, the earlier model remains central to contemporary sex work in southern Italy.

In **Chapter 30, "Male Prostitution in Spain,"** Iván Zaro profiles male sex workers and the difficulties they face in Spain's capital, Madrid. Especially vulnerable are those who face multiple stigmas—as migrants, as sex workers, as homosexuals, and as a group particularly vulnerable to drug use and sexually transmitted infections. For various reasons, sex work in Madrid has begun to retreat from public spaces into more private settings, such as apartments and saunas. While this development may provide greater safety for sex workers, it also increases their invisibility and perpetuates their vulnerability.

Chapter 31, "Male Sex Work in Sweden," by Marco Bacio, reports on Sweden's feminist-inspired legislation that targeted clients rather than sex workers in an attempt to reduce prostitution and sex trafficking. The law has drastically reduced street prostitution (but not online prostitution) and has changed Swedish public opinion about prostitution. Swedes now not only strongly support the legislation but also believe that sellers of sex as well as the buyers should be punished, even though the aim of the legislation was to protect the "victims" (i.e., the sellers). This so-called Swedish model has been adopted in other countries, including Norway, Iceland, France, and Ireland, though with somewhat different effects.

In **Chapter 32, "Male Sex Work in the Czech Republic,"** Michael Bar-Johnson writes about the Czech Republic, which has emerged as a sex tourism destination and the home to a thriving pornography industry that focuses on male performers who are typically eighteen or nineteen but often appear younger. Most male sex work now occurs in clubs and bars and through escorting via the Internet. Because Czech attitudes toward sex are liberal, sex work is not highly stigmatized. It is often seen as a realistic way to earn money quickly and easily.

Part VIII, "Male Sex Work in the Asia-Pacific Region," presents chapters on sex work in India, mainland China, Hong Kong, and Australia.

Chapter 33, "Male Sex Work in India," by Ankur Srivastava and R. Vaishno Bharati, illuminates the working conditions of male sex workers in Mumbai, a city with a large number of venues for hiring sex workers—including public spaces and pubs—but where male sex workers live in the shadows. Although male sex work is not recognized or prohibited in the laws of India, it is nevertheless highly stigmatized. Even organizations that attempt to advocate on behalf of sex workers often ignore the presence of male sex workers.

In **Chapter 34, "Male Sex Work in China,"** an ethnographic study of app-based male sex work in urban China, Yifeng Cai reports on how apps have transformed transactional sex, especially by increasing the independence and agency of male sex workers and blurring the lines between hooking up and selling sex. Thanks to the rapid development of geolocative dating apps in China, male sex workers no longer need to secure employment through specific commercial sex venues. Instead, any man who wants to participate in the sex trade can simply create a profile on a dating app and engage in transactional sex. The dating apps not only make it easy for gay men to meet each another but also provide a convenient platform for male sex work.

Chapter 35, "Male Sex Workers in China: Repercussions of Local Germ Theories on Safe Sex, Hygiene, and Fatalism," by Paul Bouanchaud, stresses the importance of including the voices of marginalized groups in discussions of HIV prevention in China. Male and transgender sex workers in southern China are at high risk for AIDS and other sexually transmitted infections, but they are largely invisible to public health services, and their understanding of "safe sex" is often shaped by local germ theories and their own internalized shame and fatalism, rather than by medically accurate information.

In Chapter 36, "Male Sex Work and Masculinities in Hong Kong and Mainland China," Albert C. H. Yau and Travis S. K. Kong contrast the construction of "occupational masculinity" by male sex workers in Hong Kong and mainland China. In Hong Kong, male sex workers, known as *go-go-zai*, adopt a "craftsmanship masculinity." They attempt to reclaim their male identity by associating themselves with the skilled labor practiced by many other working-class men in Hong Kong. In mainland China, male sex workers, known as "money boys," adapt a "guerrilla masculinity" that reconfigures masculinity in terms of entrepreneurial aspirations. They highlight the business acumen and physical freedom required in their work in portraying it as a masculine pursuit.

In Chapter 37, "Male Sex Work in Australia," Denton Callander and his colleagues provide important information about the history of sex work in Australia, where a legacy of legal and social activism has established one of the most sex-work-friendly places on the planet. The authors profile those who participate in the buying and selling of sex, and detail the support available for male sex workers. They also speculate on how innovative technologies may affect sex work in Australia in the future.

References

Albright, E., D'damo, K. (2017). Decreasing human trafficking through sex work decriminalization. *AMA Journal of Ethics, 19*, 122-126

Ashford, C. (2009). Queer theory: Cyber-ethnographies and researching online sex environments. *Information and Communications Technology Law, 18*, 297–314.

Benoit, C., Smith, M., Janson, M., Healey, P. and Magnuson, D. (2018). 'The prostitution problem': claims, evidence and policy outcomes. *Archives of sexual behaviour.* 1905-1923.

Bimbi, D. S., & Parsons, J. T. (2005). Barebacking among Internet-based male sex workers. *Journal of Gay & Lesbian Psychotherapy, 9*(3–4), 85–105.

Browne, J., & Minichiello, V. (1995). The social meanings behind male sex work: Implications for sexual interactions. *British Journal of Sociology, 46*(4), 598–622.

———. (1996). Research directions in male sex work. *Journal of Homosexuality, 31*(4), 29–56.

Callander, D., & Scott, J. (2015, Aug. 27). The rise and fall of Rentboy.com. *The Conversation.*

Carroll, A., & Itaborahy, L. P. (Eds.). (2015). *State- sponsored homophobia 2015: A world survey of laws: Criminalisation, protection, and recognition of same-sex love*. Geneva: International Lesbian, Gay, Bisexual, Trans and Intersex Association.

Cunningham, S., & Kendall, T. (2011). Prostitution 2.0: The changing face of sex work. *Journal of Urban Economics, 69*, 273–287.

Doezema, J. (2000). Loose women or lost women: the re-emergence of the myth of white slavery in contemporary discourses in trafficking in women. *Gender Issues, 18,* 23-50.

Global Network of Sex Workers Projects (GNSWP) (2019). Written submission for CEDAW on the General Recommendation on Trafficking in Women and Girls in the Context of Global Migration (General discussion at TWGCGM). https://www.nswp.org/resource/briefing-note-written-submission-cedaw-discussion-the-general-recommendation-trafficking

Holt, T., & Blevins, K. (2007). Examining sex work from the client's perspective: Assessing Johns using online data. *Deviant Behavior, 28*, 333–354.

Kempadoo, K., Sanghera, J., and B. Pattanaik. (2005). *Trafficking and prostitution reconsidered: New perspectives on migration, sex work and human rights.* Boulder: Paradigm.

Lee-Gonyea, J., Castle, T., & Gonyea, N. (2009). Laid to order: Male escorts advertising on the Internet. *Deviant Behavior, 30*, 321–348.

Logan, T. D., & Shah, M. (2009). Face value: Information and signaling in an illegal market Working Paper 14841. National Bureau of Economic Research, Cambridge, MA.

McLean, A. (2012). New realm, new problems? Stigma, dissociation and isolation in online male sex work. *Gay and Lesbian Issues and Psychology Review, 8*(2), 70–81.

———. (2013). "You can do it from your sofa": The increasing popularity of the Internet as a working site among male sex workers in Melbourne. *Journal of Sociology, 51*(4), 887–902.

Minichiello, V., Mariño, R., Browne, J., Jamieson, M., Peterson, K., Reuter, B., et al. (1999). A profile of the clients of male sex workers in three Australian cities. *Australian and New Zealand Journal of Public Health, 23*, 511–518.

Minichiello, V., Mariño, R., & Browne, J. (2001). Knowledge, risk perceptions, and condom usage in male sex workers from three Australian cities. *AIDS Care: Psychological and Socio-medical Aspects of AIDS/HIV, 13*(3), 387–402.

Minichiello, V., Scott, J., & Callander, D. (2013). New pleasures and old dangers: Reinventing male sex work. *Journal of Sex Research, 50*(3–4), 263–275.

Minichiello, V., Scott, J., & Cox, C. (2017). Commentary: Reversing the agenda of sex work stigmatization and criminalization: Signs of a progressive society. *Sexualities, 21*(5), 730–735.

Pheterson, G. (1990). The category 'prostitute' in scientific inquiry. *The Journal of Sex Research*, 27, 397-407.

Shannon, K., Strathdee, S., Goldenberg, S., Duff, P., Mwangi, P., Rusakova, M., et al. (2014). Global epidemiology of HIV among female sex workers: Influence of structural determinants. *Lancet, 385* (9962), 55–71.

Stein, E. (Ed.). (1992). Forms of desire: Sexual orientation and the constructionist controversy. New York: Routledge.

Thomas, J. (2000). Gay male video pornography: Past, present and future. In P. Appleton (Ed.), *Male bodies: Health, culture and identity.* Buckingham, UK: Open University Press.

Vanwesenbeeck, I. (2019). The making of 'the trafficking problem', *Archives of Sexual Behavior*, 48: 1961-1967.

Weitzer, R. (2007). The social construction of sex trafficking: ideology and the institutionalization of a moral crusade. *Politics and Society, 35, 447-475.*

Weitzer, R. O. (2009). Sociology of sex work. *Annual Review of Sociology, 35*, 213–234.

Weitzer, Ronald (Fall 2011). Sex trafficking and the sex industry: the need for evidence-based theory and legislation". *Journal of Criminal Law & Criminology.* Northwestern University School of Law. 101. 1337–1370.

Weitzer, R. (2015). Human trafficking and contemporary slavery. *Annual Review of Sociology*, 41, 223-242.

West, D., & de Villiers, B. (1993). *Male prostitution.* New York: Harrington Park Press.

Worthen, M. (2011). Sex trafficking or sex work? Conceptions of trafficking among anti-trafficking organizations in Nepal *Refuge Survey Quarterly*, 30.

Part I
Male sex work in popular culture

1

Reframing the Cleveland Street Scandal in England

Telegraph boys, the service economy, and compensated sex

Katie Hindmarch-Watson

In the summer of 1889, the Confidential Enquiry Branch of Britain's General Post Office (GPO) discovered that telegraph boys from London's Central Telegraph Office were selling sexual favors to elite men in a house of assignation at 19 Cleveland Street, a Victorian townhouse just off Tottenham Court Road. The brothel's owner, Charles Hammond, had obtained a supply of teenage boys through various contacts at the GPO to service those gentlemen who arrived at his house without having already procured an escort. Chief among Hammond's suppliers was Henry Newlove, a former telegraph boy who had recently been promoted to third-class clerk and "tracer" in the telegraph secretary's office. According to unpublished statements taken by GPO constables, at least four telegraph boys had admitted to sexual encounters with Newlove in the basement lavatories of the Central Telegraph Office. After a series of these clandestine hook-ups, Newlove suggested to each of them that they could make money "going to bed with gentlemen" at 19 Cleveland Street. They took up his offer. When this came to light in July, Newlove was arrested and went on to implicate some of his more illustrious clients, including Lord Arthur Somerset, the son of the Duke of Beaufort and equerry to the Prince of Wales. This revelation set off a chain of events that led to the public exposure of one of London's most secretive cross-class underworlds.

As details of the confidential investigation into telegraph-boy rent with aristocrats were leaked to the radical Liberal press in September, scandalized commentators reinterpreted these sexual acts as vestiges of ancien régime debauchery forced upon respectable civil servants (the telegraph-boy lavatory encounters went unmentioned in the press). The Cleveland Street or "West End" Scandal generated three trials and countless headlines throughout the fall and winter of 1889, finally winding down in the spring of 1890. The scandal resulted in the permanent exile of Somerset and jail time for one of his lawyers, along with Newlove, an additional Cleveland Street procurer, and the radical journalist Earnest Parke, who publicly accused the Earl of Euston of being another Cleveland Street client and lost the resulting libel trial. The telegraph boys were dismissed but weathered the storm relatively well, depicted as innocent victims sacrificed to rich men's vices.

The cast of characters that drove the Cleveland Street Scandal—aristocrats, radicals, MPs, and telegraph boys—were actors in a political showdown between the radical Liberal press and the Conservative government (Hyde, 1976; Simpson, Chester, & Leitch, 1976; Kaplan, 2005, chap 3; Weeks, 1981, chap 5; Aronson, 1996; Fisher, 1995; Cocks, 2003, pp. 144–153). Media accusations based on leaked police reports ultimately became the subject of parliamentary debate when the radical Liberal MP Henry Labouchere accused the Tory administration of orchestrating a cover-up on behalf of Somerset, Cleveland Street's most notorious aristocratic patron. Shortly after Labouchere's parliamentary accusations in early 1890, all official sources pertaining to the Cleveland Street affair that had been kept out of the papers were rounded up and sealed by the government. No more leaked information appeared in the public arena, and "gross indecency" committed by debauched aristocrats became news again only in 1895, when Oscar Wilde's own disastrous libel trial led to his incarceration. The 1889–1890 archives of police reports and evidence, government memos, trial transcripts, indictments, and correspondence remained closed to the public for 86 years, during which time commentators and historians who remembered the scandal or uncovered "Labby's" accusatory speech were left uncertain of the validity of these claims.

Modern research on the Cleveland Street brothel began with the Public Records Office releasing the files. When the records were opened in 1976, the scandal was quickly taken up by scholars intent on documenting the truth behind the accusations. What H. Montgomery Hyde's *The Cleveland Street Scandal* and Simpson, Chester, and Leitch's *The Cleveland Street Affair* revealed was a conspiracy of foot-dragging and buck-passing on the part of Treasury officials, the attorney general, the lord chancellor, Prime Minister Lord Salisbury, and the Department of Public Prosecutions (Hyde, 1976; Simpson et al., 1976). These studies were also published at a moment in historiography that outlined and heaped significance on an archaic Victorian sexual system, and Cleveland Street was proof positive of the era's sexual prudishness, repression, and hypocrisy.

The characterization of Victorian England as a specific sexual epoch coincided with a growing interest in gay and lesbian history. As historians noted, the Cleveland Street or "West End" Scandal was the first widely publicized case subject to Labouchere's contribution to the 1885 Criminal Law Amendment Act: he authored Section 11, which invented and criminalized a new, broad category of male homosexual behavior labeled "gross indecency." Numerous studies have illustrated its significance for late-Victorian and twentieth-century sexual cultures (Weeks, 1989; for a revised analysis, Upchurch, 2009). Cleveland Street has most commonly been evoked both as an example of late-Victorian male prostitution and as the backdrop for Oscar Wilde's fate six years later. More recently, historians of gay and queer sexualities have raked the sources of the Cleveland Street Scandal for further evidence of male homosexual subcultures and the processes of regulating sexual acts between men (Cook, 2003; Cocks, 2003; Brady, 2005; Kaplan, 2005).

The Cleveland Street Scandal has been analyzed as a government conspiracy, a case study in the efficacy of the Criminal Law Amendment Act, and a window into homoerotic London. However, two major aspects of the scandal remain underexplored: the bureaucratic mechanisms by which the Cleveland Street brothel was discovered and the telegraph boys' contributions both to the contours of the scandal and to Victorian homoerotic markets.

Addressing the first issue exposes a significant distinction: Post Office authorities, not the Metropolitan Police, discovered the house of assignation at 19 Cleveland Street. This fact tends to be obscured in the existing literature; the different police forces that tracked down the brothel's clients are conflated, thus representing a unified state response. By disambiguating the

GPO police from the Metropolitan Police and other security forces, we can appreciate that a sophisticated network of GPO administrators, constables, and agents exposed the brothel and its patrons to pubic censure. This surveillance department, the Confidential Enquiry Branch, was a recent innovation in postal securitization. The GPO had been steadily expanding its internal police force since 1877, when the discovery of widespread prostitution among telegraph boys, and attendant conflicts with the Metropolitan Police, had prompted substantial administrative attention and more rigorous monitoring of both postal employees and information transferred through postal networks (Hindmarch-Watson, 2012). This leads directly into the second set of concerns. Telegraph boys were central not only in the Cleveland Street Scandal itself but also in the development of the means by which sexual markets between elite men and youthful urban workers were unearthed.

Understanding the relationship between telegraph-boy prostitution and the growth of communications policing demands a different set of theoretical approaches than those often relied on in queer history. The telegraph boys involved in the Cleveland Street Scandal left police statements but little other evidence of their thoughts on the matter. Questions relating to sexual subjectivity cannot form the basis of a thorough analysis of the telegraph boys' contributions to the affair. We are left with the significance of the work telegraph boys did and what it represented to various administrative authorities and sexually intrigued men. These youthful telecommunications workers were the public face of Britain's bourgeoning telegraph system, touchstones of technological progress and urban celebration. They were also youthful members of a rapidly expanding state communications bureaucracy. As Morris Kaplan has noted of telegraph boys' contributions to Cleveland Street, "Much was made of the youths' employment as uniformed messengers in the postal service; the implication was that their corrupters posed a threat to the nation itself" (Kaplan, 2005, p. 205). The GPO had worked hard in recent years to cultivate this respectable telegraph boy, one whose sexual corruption could actually pose a threat to a specific configuration of the nation (Hindmarch-Watson, 2012). But the potency of telegraph boys' "corruption" at the hands of elites emanated from their particular labor regimes within modernizing information networks, and in many ways, the telegraph boys involved in Cleveland Street were "corrupting" agents in their own right, undermining assumptions about information transmission between consumer and worker.

Britain's telegraph system depended on the cheap labor of these adolescent males. As telegraph wires went underground in urban spaces and the complex work of transmitting coded electronic language went on within grand GPO edifices, telecommunications developed as a state service whose cost-effective telegraph boys made the largely intangible electronic technology manifest and understandable. Telegraph boys were a new kind of working-class public servant. They were meant to be ubiquitous urban messengers, expected to cross boundaries between all kinds of public and private spaces as a matter of course. The vast majority of telegram deliveries took place between this young, economically vulnerable workforce and wealthy men. This intersection of space, class, and gender meant that telegraph boys had to combine established forms of personalized deference with new demands for accessibility, standardization, and expertise. Sexual encounters between teenage working-class messengers and elite information consumers were a direct consequence of this balancing act.

In engaging in and, more importantly, confessing to sexual acts with elite men, telegraph boys disrupted orderly flows of information. They conflated different forms of service, informational and sexual, and in doing so, they broke down carefully maintained Victorian boundaries between free intercourse and private discretion. They undermined assumed relationships between elites and personal service providers, and the force of this betrayal ushered in an increasingly authoritarian approach to communications surveillance.

Why was the delivery of telegrams so symbolically resonant to the late Victorians? Telegraph boys were key laborers in what Patrick Joyce has termed the "self-regulating city" of Victorian liberal capitalism (Joyce, 2003; Hindmarch-Watson, 2012, p. 595). Joyce has developed this concept by fusing a version of actor network theory—the attribution of agency to things as well as to people in complex "sociotechnical" networks—with Foucault's "governmentality" to describe how nineteenth-century British state authorities conceived of, rationalized, and regulated their subject populations (Joyce, 2003, pp. 6–7; Law, 1994; Foucault, 1991). For Joyce and other British historians and political theorists receptive both to aspects of actor network theory and to governmentalities at work in physical as well as discursive realms, the material world has proven a fruitful lens for analyzing the indirect power and subsequent durability of Victorian liberalism, a system in which "rule [was] ceded to a self that must constantly monitor the very civil society and political power that are at once the guarantee of freedom and its threat" (Joyce, 2003, p. 4). This "liberal materialist" approach complements other recent scholarly enquiries into Victorian sociopolitics. Literary critic Elaine Hadley has explored some of the internalized features of liberalism, the "principles of cognition" or thought organization emanating out of practiced "disinterest, impersonality, and individuality" (Hadley, 2010, p. 19). These cultivated mindsets "sought to formalize" an increasingly heterogeneous public sphere (Hadley, 2010, p. 36). What emerges from Hadley's work and other studies is a compelling portrayal of a self-regulatory state of mind and an elaborately coded, exclusionary mode of knowledge accumulation, and thus a style and a way of being, that preserved elite political control while presenting a veneer of democratic access.

Many of the scientists, engineers, administrators, and politicians who created the infrastructural systems that emerged in Victorian Britain, including telecommunications, strove to enable such liberal subjectivities. The telegraph system in Britain was nationalized in 1870 at the behest of elite businessmen and MPs who, frustrated with the expensive, uneven patchwork of private networks, demanded seamless, reliable, and cost-effective channels of information in order to intensify domestic and imperial commerce (Perry, 1992, chap 4). As Edwin Chadwick put it in advocating for nationalization, "The saving of time; the stuff of which business as well as life is made [depends on] . . . the cheapness of communication and its completeness in pervading the whole country" (Chadwick, 1867, p. 222). Other commentators spoke of the "nervous system" of the Empire, and historian Rhys Morus Evans has elucidated how the Victorian telegraph was indicative of culturally embedded regulatory powers, expressed in metaphors of bodily circulation and flow (Morus, 2000). However, at a shilling a telegram until 1885, and even with the rate of six pence per ten-word telegram thereafter, the vast majority of Britons were priced out of telegraphy. The telegraphic public remained overwhelmingly elite, commercial, and administrative.

For both overseers and consumers, the telegraph network resounded with productive, unresolved tensions inherent to thresholds of public and private spaces, information, and mentalities. The division between the private realm of individual cultivation and the public world of productive, remunerative work and civic responsibility was a major organizational concept for Victorian liberal sensibilities. Rigidly separate public and private domains were necessary for the encouragement and practice of nineteenth-century British notions of freedom, meaning, to borrow Lauren Goodland's phrasing, an active commitment to "projects of liberating individuals from illegitimate authority while simultaneously ensuring their moral and spiritual growth" (Goodland, 2003, p. viii). The idea of individual privacy, a mental, intellectual, and usually physical space of self-directed personal exploration, was a touchstone of liberal subjectivity.

By properly channeling one's thoughts, personal interactions, consumption, and pleasures into character building, one developed the proper styles of presentation, cognition, and fortitude necessary to influence an orderly public sphere.

The circulation of ideas, either through free intercourse with fellow individuals or through unlimited access to an open press, was a key ingredient in this potent brew; the liberal subject needed to be informed. The sanctity of information dovetailed with Victorian obsessions with privacy, resulting in a widely shared commitment to noninterference in the circulation of the written, typed, transcribed, and spoken word. State administrators publicly expressed the same generalized popular sentiments about the necessity of privacy in public electronic communications, and they took seriously the role telecommunications staff played in policing the boundaries between private and public information. They cultivated the image of a passive yet efficient workforce, skilled in the telegraphic arts yet automatized and docile mediators, unlikely to imprint their own intentions on wired transmissions or to reveal private information.[1]

Of course, purely private and public realms were conceptual shorthands impossible to maintain in practice, especially in a political environment where personal character was expected to deliver public order. The individual of liberal fantasy, who could easily navigate these boundaries as interest or duty demanded, was elite, deeply gendered, and prone to lapses in character. A lot of work went into liberal self-fashioning, and not just on the part of those who could achieve some measure of Victorian social capital. Unruly workers, promiscuous telegraph boys among them, enable us to perceive the relational, interpersonal processes necessary in making liberal subjects.

Understanding the "self-regulating" subject, his variants, and his limits demands an exploration of the labor necessary for liberal spaces and subjectivities. This means prioritizing a sector of the British economy usually defined by its mostly intangible but nonetheless highly valuable products and which has proved remarkably durable and prolific: we need to reassess the meaning and centrality of service industries—professional, financial, bodily, and informational—to modernizing British life. What of the workers who produced the conditions of respectability, who enabled the self-cultivated, rationalized perspective and movements of other social actors? What kinds of labor went into producing the efficient mobility, privileged stances, and knowledgeability of certain modern subjects, urban and otherwise? Liberal subjects required plenty of servicing, and the labor that developed in response to meeting ever-expanding individual expectations of self-cultivation deserves to be taken much more seriously if we are interested in the origins of modern socioeconomic networks.

Telegraph boys help us address some of these questions by highlighting processes of stratification and precariousness in the personal interactions necessary for late-Victorian information service work. Service labor's relative value depended (and still depends) on the flow of social capital between provider and consumer. Most face-to-face personal service work produced intangible surplus aesthetic, intellectual, physiological, or emotional value for the consumer, leaving the service provider in a more tenuous position. "Professionalism" was a crucial designation for mitigating or reversing service work's socially marginalizing effects. Telegraph boys could not lay claim to professional status, and the very knowledge required to successfully perform their duties—how to channel private discourse through public networks, how to navigate unruly urban environments and cross boundaries, and how to provide pleasures while hiding evidence of excess—could be detrimental to the consumer's processes of respectable self-fashioning if it were publicly rendered (Clark, 2013).[2] In a social order based on "character" defined by individual agency and self-control, discretion was a virtue of service provision and one that could make service providers potentially volatile laborers. Indeed, often the more intimate the encounter that service providers had with consumers, the more unsettling such service work potentially became. Marginalizing such work and rendering certain workers socially invisible was one response to this pressure.

Telegraph boys' lack of status allowed them access to many private enclaves and privileged environments. As the telegraph system's most public servants, they engaged with telegraphy's overwhelmingly elite consumers on a regular basis. They navigated public and private urban landscapes, embodying the new technology on city streets and consumers' doorsteps. All of these encounters involved careful administrative supervision (from uniform design to clandestine monitoring by inspectors), technical manipulations, highly specialized knowledge, awareness of public expectations, and the management of public frustrations and fantasies.

Telegram message-delivery policy further magnified the state's commitment to discretion and discipline over telegraph boys. One messenger could not hand off a telegram to another; telegraph boys could not themselves transcribe any return messages; their telegrams had to be carried in their GPO-issued pouches, along with all money received and various paper forms for payment and return delivery; and they had to ensure that a telegram was placed in the correct person's hands, or, quite frequently, in the correct person's servant's hands. Telegraph boys were also instructed to use the "double knock" on front doors that postmen in England had adopted the nineteenth century. This communications ritual signaled the special importance placed on both postal and telegraph communications. It also relayed to those inside a house or office that the deliverer had a right to linger on private thresholds.[3]

Their uniform may have marked them for potential disciplinary infractions, but it also permitted them free rides on omnibuses and entry into venues normally prohibited to working-class boys, so long as they were on duty. Telegraph boys' unfettered ability to move about town was legally enforceable: cab drivers received fines from police courts if they refused to drive boys on urgent deliveries ("Law and Police", 1875). The boys' uniforms functioned like a "press pass" to venues of pleasure and power, as Gregory Downey describes the similar work privileges experienced by American telegraph boys (Downey, 2002, p. 63). To further enhance the importance, prestige, and efficiency of this system, GPO administrators designed telegraph dispatches to appear to be single-message deliveries: unlike postmen, who carried multiple letters and delivered the post according to laid-out routes, urban telegraph boys were sent out with a single telegram as soon as it came up. At least, this was the theory; in practice at busy London offices, telegraph boys would be sent out with up to three messages at a time.[4] Regardless, they were instructed to appear as if the one message in their hand was the single focus of their run across town. This personalized service combined old ideas of deference with new expectations for the efficiency of wired communication.

The GPO's gendered parameters dictated that the work of delivering information in urban environments was a strictly male endeavor, and this resulted in novel possibilities for clandestine sexual practices associated with masculine street cultures. Some telegraph boys exploited the possibilities of London's sexual subcultures while embodying state order, efficiency, and prescribed mobility. As a result of sociotechnical development, telegraph boys added a new, uniformed dimension to long-standing pederastic prostitution networks in the capital. Their ubiquity and accessibility fueled both the imaginations of men looking for "rough trade" on the London streets and the anxieties of communications administrators, who located telegraph boys as the primary laboring constituency on which to enact state authority. Ironically, increased GPO regulation seemed to enhance their vaunted image among London's queer subcultures. Thanks to an internal investigation into telegraph-boy prostitution in 1876 and 1877, telegraph boys became even more visible erotic symbols of disciplined, working-class masculinity (Hindmarch-Watson, 2012). In an effort to clamp down on same-sex encounters and prostitution, telegraph boys became increasingly subject to public military-style drilling and parades in the 1880s. As the fin-de-siècle Uranian John Gambril Nicholson reminds us, the uniform on public display was the primary marker of these youths' erotic appeal: he wrote admirably about "the lad that's lettered G.P.O" (quoted in D'Arch Smith, 1970, p. 29). This cycle of discipline, service, and desire put the GPO's youthful foot soldiers on a collision course with more sexual trouble.

The exposure of queer telegraph-boy networks in the 1870s fomented a significant shift in the state's vision of what constituted public and private realms and the extent to which the latter could be intruded upon in the name of the former. The momentous reaction to disruptive telegraph boys in the later Victorian period changed the meaning of communications security, with far-reaching consequences. The 1889 Cleveland Street Scandal is an example of this new communications policing and its consequences on the balance of power between competing authorities. The sexual transactions at 19 Cleveland Street came to light when one of the numerous Confidential Enquiry Branch constables, during a routine frisking of Central Telegraph Office telegraph boys in a search for missing funds from the receiver-general's department, found 18 shillings on a young indoor messenger (the amount was likely three times his weekly earnings). During the ensuing interrogation, the nervous 15-year-old, Charles Swinscow, described sexual encounters with Newlove in the basement lavatories and his subsequent experiences at Cleveland Street. This set into motion both an internal GPO investigation and collaboration with the Metropolitan Police and the Department of Public Prosecutions (DPP). When police and DPP efforts lagged, GPO officials devoted substantial manpower and funding to bring Cleveland Street's denizens to justice, including having the brothel's owner followed across Europe.

Histories of the Post Office tend to mark the 1880s as a "golden age," when telegram delivery costs decreased for the public, GPO services greatly expanded, and labor relations substantially improved, mostly thanks to the progressive leadership of Henry Fawcett, "the Blind Postmaster-General," a leading reformer of the Liberal Party (Campbell-Smith, 2011, pp. 183–192). Improved working conditions, including more openings for women, and public approval of GPO services were indeed hallmarks of London's Post Office innovations in the mid-1880s. But overlapping with these developments was the exponential growth of clandestine monitoring operations. From a staff of 20 in 1877, by 1889, the Confidential Enquiry Branch had more than 80 staff members, including 15 plainclothes policemen. The Post Office, that seemingly benign institution, had a crucial role to play in quietly renegotiating acceptable barriers between public interest and private transactions. For the authorities, its telegraph-boy troubles became increasingly aligned with other London insurgencies, namely militant Irish anti-imperialism. From 1886, the more authoritarian postmaster-general, Conservative M. Henry Cecil Raikes, used the Confidential Enquiry Branch to keep an eye on postal union activity. Surveillance forces that were enhanced to monitor troublesome telegraph boys ultimately expanded their reach. In doing so, the Post Office's policing amplified inherent tensions in liberal doctrines of freedom, discretion, and state-controlled communications.

The Cleveland Street Scandal is a window into an expanded, well-funded information-monitoring network attempting to grapple with a long-standing flaw in the telegraph system. In one sense, its outcome was a victory of the vigilant state working for the "public good" over elite privilege built out of privacy, silences, and discretion. In the middle of this shifting legal, social, and moral landscape, young communications workers continued to forge unintended networks. Sexual encounters and imaginative possibilities between themselves and information consumers were a consequence of class and gender conventions colliding with the personalized yet rote service demanded of them. Administrative attempts to monitor and properly channel workers' interactions with consumers emphasized the erotic potentialities of early electronic communication systems and explained why sexual misconduct was a major stimulator of information surveillance in this period. Cleveland Street's revelations also underscore telegraph boys' struggles to negotiate authority and their own sense of value over their daily interactions. Telegraph boys' most potent act of disruption was to disclose the secrets of their wealthy clients to Post Office authorities—it was naming the sexual acts to Confidential Enquiry Branch agents, much more so than discreetly committing them, that disrupted Victorian communications on a number of levels. For authorities, the telegraph-boy trouble aligned with other unruly London networks. Surveillance forces that monitored miscreant telegraph boys ultimately expanded their reach. By doing so, the Post Office's internal policing amplified tensions between liberal doctrines of freedom and state monitoring of communications. Clandestine information surveillance, initially targeted at proscribed sexualities, continued to expand along the wires.

The momentous reaction to telegraph boys from the 1870s onward changed the meaning of communications security, with far-reaching consequences. We can appreciate this relationship by balancing the ideological imperatives of the late-Victorian period with the potential volatilities of the labor of liberal cities and subjectivities. Telegraph boys were service providers in an information industry that valued their marginality. In finding opportunities in this, some telegraph boys asserted their agency in highly disruptive ways. The telegraph boys involved in male prostitution in London in the last quarter of the nineteenth century manifest some of the queer dynamics of a modernizing telecommunications service system, as well as the politics of containing such subversions. A service-labor approach to other historical actors, industries, and institutions may prove a fruitful lens for reprioritizing and invigorating the history of labor within other historical disciplines while avoiding the pitfalls of fatalistic or overly determinist renderings of the meanings of work in specific historical contexts. Perhaps service work and service workers have much more to tell us about historical subjectivities and economies, sexual and otherwise.

Notes

1 A similar attitude was expressed toward (mostly female) stenographers and typists in the same period (Price & Thurschwell, 2005).
2 I am indebted to Jess P. Clark's research and insights on the late-Victorian beauty industry for this point.
3 Instructions for Telegraph Messengers in London, POST 68/116, British Postal Museum and Archive, London.
4 Telegraphs: Instructions for Messengers in London, 1887, POST 68/778, British Postal Heritage Museum and Archive.

References

Aronson, T. (1996). *Prince Eddy and the homosexual underworld* (2nd ed.). London: John Murray.
Brady, S. (2005). *Masculinity and male homosexuality in Britain, 1861–1913*. Basingstoke, Hampshire: Palgrave MacMillan.
Campbell-Smith, D. (2011). *Masters of the post: The authorized history of royal mail*. London: Allan Lane.
Chadwick, E. (1867). On the economy of telegraphy as part of a public system of postal communication. *Journal of the Society of Arts, 15*, 222.
Clark, J. P. (2013). Pomeroy v. Pomeroy: Beauty, modernity, and the female entrepreneur in fin-de-siècle London. *Women's History Review, 22*(6), 877–903.
Cocks, H. G. (2003). *Nameless offences: Homosexual desire in the nineteenth century*. London: I. B. Taurus.
Cook, M. (2003). *London and the culture of homosexuality, 1885–1914*. Cambridge: Cambridge University Press.
D'Arch Smith, T. (1970). *Love in Ernest: Some notes on the lives and writings of English "Uranian" poets from 1889 to 1930*. London: Routledge and Kegan Paul.

Downey, G. J. (2002). *Telegraph messenger boys: Labor, technology, and geography, 1850–1950*. New York: Routledge.

Fisher, T. (1995). *Scandal: Sexual politics in late Victorian Britain*. Stroud, UK: Sutton.

Foucault, M. (1991). Governmentality. In G. Burchell, C. Gordon, & P. Miller (Eds.), *The Foucault effect: Studies in governmentality* (pp. 87–104). Chicago: University of Chicago Press.

Goodland, L. (2003). *Victorian literature and the Victorian state*. Baltimore: Johns Hopkins University Press.

Hadley, E. (2010). *Living liberalism: Practical citizenship in mid-Victorian Britain*. Chicago: University of Chicago Press.

Hindmarch-Watson, K. (2012). Male prostitution and the London GPO: Telegraph boys' 'immorality' from nationalization to the Cleveland street scandal. *Journal of British Studies, 51*, 594–617.

Hyde, H. M. (1976). *The Cleveland Street Scandal*. London: W. H. Allen.

Joyce, P. (2003). *The rule of freedom: Liberalism and the modern city*. New York: Verso.

Kaplan, M. B. (2005). *Sodom on the Thames: Sex, love, and scandal in Wilde times*. Ithaca: Cornell University Press.

Law, J. (1994). *Organizing modernity: Social ordering and social theory*. Oxford: Blackwell.

Law and Police. (1875, March 20). *Illustrated London news*, 267.

Morus, I. R. (2000). The nervous system of Britain: Space, time and the electric telegraph in the Victorian age. *British Journal for the History of Science, 33*(4), 455–475.

Perry, C. R. (1992). *The Victorian post office: The growth of a bureaucracy*. Woodbridge, Suffolk: Boydell Press.

Price, L., & Thurschwell, P. (2005). *Literary secretaries/secretarial culture*. Aldershot, Hampshire: Ashgate.

Simpson, C., Chester, L., & Leitch, D. (1976). *The Cleveland street affair*. Boston: Little, Brown.

Upchurch, C. (2009). *Before Wilde: Sex between men in Britain's age of reform*. Berkeley: University of California Press.

Weeks, J. (1981). *Sex, politics, and society: The regulation of sexuality since 1800*. London: Longman.

Weeks, J. (1989). Inverts, perverts and Mary-Annes: Male prostitution and the regulation of homosexuality in the nineteenth and early twentieth centuries. In M. Duberman, M. Vicinus, & G. Chauncey (Eds.), *Hidden from history: Reclaiming the gay and lesbian past* (pp. 195–211). New York: New American Library.

2

Youth male prostitution in post-Nazi Germany

Policing the *Bahnhof* boys

Jennifer V. Evans

Although Germany's unconditional surrender swept away much of the political rubble of the Third Reich, the shattered physical and social geography of Berlin hampered official efforts to rebuild the former capital. In 1945, Berlin was divided into four sectors, each one occupied and administered by a different allied power—France, Britain, the United States, and the Soviet Union. Though an integrated municipal council was established, parochial interests surfaced through the rhetoric of unity. While crossing from one sector to another might be relatively painless, complications could arise in securing ration cards, fuel, work, and shelter. For many Berliners, however, clearing the streets of pulverized debris was simple compared to the monumental task of restoring traditional mores. The public licentiousness that lingered on for months and even years after 1945 was a constant reminder to them of the debasement brought about by war and amplified by defeat.[1]

At this juncture of defeat, occupation, reconstruction, and renewal that witnessed the creation of not one but two postwar German states, the experiences of men such as Otto N., a 49-year-old cashier, are illuminating.[2] The tale of his escapades in Berlin unfolds in the 1951 file of a Department of Youth Services caseworker. One night Otto picked up a young man at the pissoir near the Friedrichstrasse train station (*Bahnhof*), east of the city center. Carefully negotiating terms, he made the necessary arrangements for sex, taking a moment to guarantee the boy's age of majority. Settling on a price of five East German marks, they struck a deal quickly and, we are told, fulfilled its terms. Later that same night, when their paths crossed again at a local movie house, the pair took advantage of the chance encounter to arrange another rendezvous. Leaving the eastern sector, they drove to the West Berlin district of Neukölln in search of an underground bar. Along the way they befriended another man, and all three made plans to reunite later that morning after Otto's wife left for work. Although he managed to avoid his spouse's suspicions initially, in time Otto fell into the dragnet of the West Berlin police force and had his case heard in front of the Tiergarten Amtsgericht (district court).[3]

With prior convictions from both the Nazi and postwar years, Otto found himself in the shadow of both the fallen Reich and the new republic.[4] In a gambit to secure a lighter sentence, he implored the court to understand he was under the impression that in the eastern sector, where the pickup occurred, mutual masturbation was no longer a crime. While true, what Otto did not realize at the time was that the rules of evidence were different in the West, where the pair was eventually arrested, and that the boy he cruised, although 18, was still legally a minor. For Otto, what began as an innocent pickup at the Friedrichstrasse train station resulted in a six-month prison sentence.

An aura of order surrounds this faded file, whose yellowed statements, collated and cataloged, are preserved in Berlin's city archive. But Otto's case was one of many that confounded the police, courts, and social service workers entrusted with interpreting and enforcing Paragraph 175 of the German penal code during the years after Hitler's demise. Indeed, this case bears many of the hallmarks of the confusion that plagued the policing of same-sex sexuality in postwar Berlin, when men and youths frequently crossed over the internal sector boundaries for evening liaisons, tempting fate and risking possible incarceration under the slow-to-be-reformed Nazi-era antisodomy legislation. Whether negotiated obliquely through knowing glances in the *Bahnhof* waiting room or over a few drinks and a bite to eat (*cine Stulle*) in one of the city's bars and cafes, intergenerational paid sex was a key feature of the Berlin gay scene, one that baffled police and welfare workers grappling with increasing numbers of "endangered" youths, contradictory legal interpretations, and an ever-worsening political situation that would divide municipal departments as early as 1948.

Yet, from numerous police surveillance records, court documents, and social service reports, the story of the male sex trade can be pieced together, allowing us to map the topography of transgressive sexuality in postwar Berlin and expose the contours of an urban subculture that survived Nazi assaults on homosexuals.[5] Indeed, despite the concerted efforts of the Gestapo and criminal police to destroy Berlin's reputation as an El Dorado for same-sex-desiring men and women, the city remained an important site of nonnormative sexual expression in the years after the war, a situation that prompted renewed efforts to regulate it.[6]

Otto's story also sheds light on another important issue that has yet to gain the attention of German historians, namely the early postwar perceptions of jurisprudence, sexual identity, and gender difference. In this chapter, I examine four categories of sources that provide information about homosexual prostitution in postwar Berlin: the laws governing homosexual acts, sex with minors, and male prostitution; the police procedures developed to enforce those laws; the criminological literature that guided citizens seeking to assess and amend those laws; and the judgments reached in police precincts and municipal appellate courts. I focus on those narratives of regulation and enforcement that reveal how the male sex trade in postwar Berlin was understood and handled. Although the presence of male hustlers in and around Berlin's metropolitan train stations was anything but new,[7] many came to regard it as a product of the general crime wave that had engulfed the city at the war's end.[8] While social workers, police, and church officials might agree on the magnitude of the problem, they were confused about how to understand it, and with the onset of the Cold War, their discussions of male prostitution in this increasingly divided city became intensely politicized. Thus, sexual identity, Weimar and Nazi legislation, criminology, and policing practices were all reconsidered and renegotiated in the effort to regulate this activity. If there is any single trend to be observed in the surviving records, it is that by the 1950s, the public perception of young male prostitutes had shifted: call boys had ceased to be endangered victims and had become capricious villains.[9]

This chapter discusses the challenges faced by officials responsible for identifying, policing, and prosecuting call boys and their clients, known as johns, and examines some of the twists and turns that characterized the process of regulating homosexual sex in postwar Berlin. A careful reading of newly available police and court documents demonstrates not simply the confusion that Berliners faced in defining societal values at the war's end but the contours of a defiant homosexual subculture, one that had not been completely destroyed by Hitler and that was being restored to public view by the disorder of daily life.

In the city that was once the hub of a racially defined empire and was then divided, occupied, and administered by foreign powers, the train station is an appropriate site for analyzing postwar shifting sexual boundaries. Once illustrative of Germany's famed order and murderous efficiency, during the Cold War, the *Bahnhof* became a gateway to freedom in the West and an access point for cheap goods and services from the East. It also exposed the raw and attenuated existence of those who were caught in the ebbs and flows of rapid modernization. While the beggars, vagrants, whores, and street youths congregating in a *Bahnhof* waiting room could be in a scene out of a Weimar-era Alfred Döblin novel, in the years following capitulation, this disorder was considered an index of the moral depravity brought about by defeat.[10] The sexually delinquent youths who gathered at the *Bahnhof* began to generate fears about national renewal. The police came to regard them as delinquent homosexuals in the making; reformers and betrayed clients as blackmailing turncoats; and criminologists as passive asocials.[11] The *Bahnhof* symbolizes Germany at a crossroads, still reeling from the recent Nazi past and torn between an emerging Soviet-style dictatorship and a consumerist Christian democracy; its denizens, the call boys, reveal some of the tensions associated with Berlin's homosexual subculture as it evolved, after years of Nazi persecution, in the fractious world of Cold War debates over policing, social welfare, and criminality.[12]

Regulating same-sex sexuality before and after the war

Like their predecessors in the Wilhelmian and Weimar periods, boy prostitutes after World War II led catacomb lives.[13] In the many bombed-out bunkers that dotted the city's landscape as well as in pay-by-the-hour hotels, rented rooms (*Absteigequartiere*), and pungent pissoirs, they turned tricks to help support their liminal existence. Their lives were less ordinary than most, marked by loss, poverty, violence, and crime in such extremes that the state appeared unable to understand, much less solve, their problems. Who were these youths who fell into the call boy system? Were they hardened criminals, moral misfits, or mere unfortunates who merited social welfare and state intervention? To the denazified social workers and newly recruited police officers walking the beat in capitulated Berlin, *Bahnhof* boys, whether operating alone or in cliques, were a paradox.[14] Often in contact with social services, whether escaping from a remand home or spending time in jail, they were viewed as both victims of and contributors to postwar instability.

Of course, concern about male prostitution was not solely a postwar phenomenon; it had an elaborate history that predated Hitler and the Nazis. The lineage of Paragraph 175 of the German penal code, which penalized consensual liaisons among adult men as well as purchased sex with adolescent youths, can be traced to Paragraph 143 of the Prussian penal code, which criminalized all forms of bestiality.[15] This paragraph of the Prussian code was applied to a newly united Germany in Bismarck's 1871 statute (*Reichstrafgesetzbuch*, or *RGSt*). Despite the efforts of famed sexologist Magnus Hirschfeld, who petitioned the imperial Reichstag to have the paragraph revoked, voices for sexual reform had little success until after World War I. It was only in the mid-1920s, with the emergence of an urban gay and lesbian subculture and progressive delegates willing to take up the cause, that significant reforms passed through the chamber.[16] The 1926 modification of the penal code required that prosecutions for transgressing the provisions of Paragraph 175 must be supported by material evidence that "intercourse-like actions" (*beischlafsähnliche Handlung*) had in fact occurred. While this amendment was scant reward for sexual reformers who had petitioned for total decriminalization, it nevertheless established that penetration—whether anal or oral—was the sole criterion of illegal "unnatural sex."[17] Although homosexual sex remained illegal, reformers agreed to the compromise, believing that the threshold of evidence was so high that few people would actually encounter interference from the state. For a time, local police forces turned a blind eye to most infractions, preferring instead to focus their attention on the endemic problem of sexual blackmail, which Hirschfeld, among others, characterized as the inevitable result of continued criminalization.[18]

Shortly after the National Socialists gained power in 1933, same-sex sexuality among adult men (*einfache Homosexualität*) attracted renewed official interest. Efforts to enforce Paragraph 175 intensified, especially after the events of June 30, 1934, known as the Röhm Putsch, or the "night of the long knives."[19] What apparently began as an assault against Ernst Röhm's authority within the Nazi Party and an indictment of his previously tolerated sexual proclivities signaled a decisive shift in attitude toward the issue of homosexuality.[20] In vitriolic campaigns against all "deviants" (*Abartige*), which at times linked Jews, Communists, and homosexuals together as one mutually reinforcing group, the Nazis sought to foster public support for their vision of "healthy social mores" (*gesundes Volksempfinden*).[21]

With the homosexual threat to the party officially excised through the purge of Röhm and his followers, the Nazis began the process of weaving the nation's moral fabric into a pattern more suitably aligned with the party's emerging racial policies. Since homosexuality represented a challenge to the racial health and regeneration of the nation, the state had to ensure that transgressors were suitably punished. Through the use of Article 6 of the Law for the Amendment of the Criminal Code (Gesetz zur Änderung des Strafgesetzbuchs), Paragraph 175 was altered to reflect this changing political ambience. In the federal court (*Reichsgericht*) decision of June 28, 1935, the law was officially rewritten to expand the notion of malfeasance to include any behavior that represented the "shameless" use of another man's body for the purpose of sexual excitement. Gone was the stipulation requiring material evidence of an "intercourse-like act"; the Nazi version allowed prosecutors to rely on rumor and innuendo and prohibited mutual masturbation, sexual touching, kissing, and even letter writing (Baumann, 1968, pp. 48–49).[22]

While widening the range of homosexual acts subject to prosecution, the new version of Paragraph 175 sharpened the focus on same-sex prostitution by splitting the original imperial-code paragraph in two. Paragraph 175 continued to govern sex between consenting adult men, while Paragraph 175a, subsections 1 through 4, criminalized forced intercourse, the use of one's position of authority as a teacher or youth services worker to solicit sex with someone in care, and sex with minors (boys under 21), as well as the buying and selling of sex (*Reichsgesetzblatt*, 1935). Although offering oneself for the purpose of sexual arousal was illegal under the old code, the penalties for transgressions under the Nazi paragraph were amplified considerably.

Reformulating Paragraph 175 naturally resulted in greater numbers of prosecutions, but contradictions in Nazi racial/biological ideology and the pragmatics of waging war provided a way out for some homosexuals "willing" to renounce certain forms of sexual activity (Himmler, 1937).[23] While many men were ensnared by the Gestapo's dragnet and ended their lives in one of the concentration camps, others were sentenced to prison or sent to the front to serve with the Wehrmacht in the final days of the war. Some, like Berlin prostitute Fritz K., were released from detention as the Soviets marched toward the soon-to-be-defeated Reich.[24] Even prior to 1945, the understanding and implementation of the laws against homosexual acts varied greatly, often depending on who was applying the statute, who was accused of the crime, and under what circumstances it had occurred.

Far from inheriting a unified disciplinary apparatus, postwar lawmakers, police, and judges were faced instead with a contradictory legal framework that would be further challenged by social and political conditions in the divided city of Berlin. Following the collapse of the Third Reich, the Allies began the daunting task of dismantling key Nazi institutions, including the police and judiciary. In 1945, to eliminate many of the laws deemed reflective of Nazi racial policy and authoritarianism, the Allied military government issued Army Order Number One.[25] Paragraph 175 was not among the scores of laws initially revoked, however (*Amstblatt der Militärregierung Deutschland*, 1945).[26] Despite numerous Allied Control Commission statements and the explicitness of article 3 of the military government's order outlawing the future application of laws smacking of National Socialist dogma, German courts, especially those in the western zones of occupation, continued to prosecute homosexuals according to the 1935 law.[27] Although a number of state courts in the Soviet-occupied eastern zone argued that the Nazi version of 175 and 175a should be annulled as tainted legislation, others, primarily in the West, opted to observe the unaltered Nazi-era code (See Brandstette, 1951, p. 273; Kramp and Martin, 2000, p. 125).

In many ways, postwar decisions about which version of the law should be upheld broke down along the East/West axis. In the Soviet Occupation Zone, which in 1949 became the German Democratic Republic (GDR), the Supreme Court of Berlin decided on February 21, 1950, that the 1935 variant of Paragraph 175, which expanded the definition of what constituted a homosexual transgression, was an "instrument of power for the Nazi state to prepare for war" (Kammerge richt Berlin, 1950, p. 129). Thus, in the emerging GDR, charges that consenting adult men had transgressed Paragraph 175 again required physical proof, which was not the case in the western zone. In West Berlin and the Federal Republic of Germany, the 1935 variant of Paragraph 175 was retained for several more years. However, in considering the second part of the code governing homosexuality, the section that criminalized bought sex and sex with minors (Paragraph 175a), the Supreme Court of Berlin upheld the Nazi variant, since it promoted "sexual integrity and thus the healthy development of the youth." As Günter Grau has argued elsewhere, when it came to safeguarding the sexual mores of young males, the East and West upheld similar images of respectability and moral endangerment (Grau, 1999, 1996). While the collapse of the Reich set in motion changes in the process of identifying homosexual transgressions, Nazi-era attitudes about the protection of youth continued to influence the regulation of male prostitution in both Germanys.

Gendering deviance

To contemporaries, the enforcement of the various laws governing homosexual sex was as confusing as the juridical debates. Immediately following capitulation, the Allied military command bestowed on Berlin's police the authority to reorganize its ranks (see Besarin in *Befehl des Militärkommandanten der Stadt*, 1945, p. 99). From its headquarters on Dircksenstrasse, in the central district of Mitte, and under the supervision of its new chief, Paul Markgraf, the police set about this process.[28] Markgraf preserved the traditional subdivisions of Schupo (protective) and Kripo (criminal) police and reassembled the vice squad to investigate crimes against morality (*Sittlichkeitsdelikte*) (Bessel, 1996, p. 225). Task force MII/4 of the criminal police, staffed with two detectives and a rotating number of lower-ranking officers as well as occasional police-women (Weibliche Kripo, or WKP), was charged with investigating cases involving seduction, rape, molestation, incest, and samesex prostitution. Other units handled theft, sabotage, youth crimes, and female prostitution, corresponding to the different juridical understanding of the nature of these crimes.[29] Thus male prostitution and female prostitution were treated as distinct crimes, requiring different responses, and were handled by different administrative units.

Although in diary accounts describing capitulation, the accompanying mayhem is characterized as general, curiously little information has surfaced regarding the plight of young men.[30] Indeed, the writers whose eyewitness accounts have helped define this chaotic time as the "hour of the woman" were conscious of a gender imbalance: those raped en masse following the Russians' entry into Berlin were women; the faces that Allied authorities saw waiting in line for rations were typically female; the survivors who worked to clear Berlin's debris-congested streets were the "rubble women" (*Trümmerfrauen*) (Heineman, 1996, 1999; see also Höhn, 1993; Goedde, 1999; Willoughby, 1998; Tröger, 1986). In Berlin during this postwar "hour," many women assumed sole responsibility for those under their care.

Prostitution offered one way for women to support themselves and their broken families. Some walked the streets, while others congregated near black-market booths, in parks, in public washrooms, and at the *Bahnhof*. As recent research has demonstrated, after the initial period of sexual assaults, the boundary between victim and collaborator became blurred. Some Germans believed that women's social and sexual mores had been loosened by the influx of foreign soldiers and that in the postwar era, women were more licentious. Civic officials in the southwest neighborhoods of Steglitz and Lichterfelde, which housed a high-profile American army base on Finckensteinallee, found that the problem of female prostitution warranted repeated arrests of girls suspected of spreading disease.[31] Of course, not all girls chatting on street corners were "on the make," as one Steglitz raid made all too clear when the police forced a virgin (*unbescholten*) and a survivor of Soviet aggression to undergo painful gynecological exams despite their repeated claims of innocence.[32] Yet as one police officer was quoted as saying, "It is impossible to differentiate between good and bad girls," since even those from good homes have "discovered their bodies as a means by which to live an easy life."[33]

Although a well-respected West Berlin police officer would one day claim the contrary, in the early months following the war, call boys frequently took their place beside the many *Bahnhof* girls.[34] While *Bahnhof* boys were also thought to be attracted to the "easy life," they presented unique challenges to the police. Did they choose this life out of necessity or from desire?[35] Did they merit society's protection or punishment? In developing a viable policy for the surveillance and arrest of those boys suspected of "polluting themselves," the Berlin police force navigated a path lined with contradictions.[36]

Since it was commonly accepted that venereal disease (VD) originated with women, call boys were spared the raids designed to ensnare female prostitutes and wayward girls. While the mere presence of women congregating in a public space was grounds for police intervention and forced VD testing, male hustlers typically had to be caught in flagrante delicto or, at the very least, acting "in a call boy–like way" (*nach Strichjungenart*). This differentiated treatment on the part of the Berlin police force was based on a variety of factors, chief among them the American command's objective of limiting amoral troop activity by cracking down on female prostitution.

A 1946 report of one spot check conducted at the bunker neighboring Schlesischer Bahnhof in Berlin's eastern sector illustrates the situation. In her log entry, Officer Behr of the WKP noted that the women's detachment found six youths blocking the entrance to the bunker. All were sent to the precinct for processing, but the brothers Georg and Gerhard B. and a friend described only as S. were set free after a short interview. Rolf R., not quite 15 years old, was transferred to the youth welfare station at Dircksenstrasse, since he was homeless, underage, and without either a ration card or identification. The two girls in the group, likewise without identification, were sent to police detachment MII/3, where they were documented and held on suspicion of prostitution. One of the pair was eventually forced to undergo a gynecological exam (Raid report, 1946).

Officer Behr's log entry outlines the process in place to deal with wayward youths. Those found without appropriate identification were automatically sent to youth services if they appeared underage and seemed "endangered." Girls would more than likely be forced to submit to VD testing, since in the eyes of police, they were already compromised. The boys could have been accused of amoral proclivities, since the culture of the *Bahnhof* was renowned for producing such behavior.[37] That they were not illustrates both the differential understanding of risk associated with the boys' situation and the existence of a gendered double standard. The incongruity of the enforcement strategies that emerges in police memos, in logbooks, and in the field as to who warranted what type of response was based on deeply entrenched societal notions of what was at stake in allowing "asocial" behavior to continue unchecked. Girls were forced to submit to pelvic exams in the name of protecting the public's health from the tainted exploits of an increasing number of fallen women. Boys, although equally imperiled, were simply sent to crisis centers to help them cope with the harshness of their social situation, which police believed had forced them to the streets in the first place.[38]

Although the police report never explicitly acknowledges the possibility, Rolf R.'s profile fits that of the many call boys who plied their trade either on the *Bahnhof*'s platforms or in its surrounding bunkers and ruins: he was underage, without a home, and without work. Had he not yet turned to prostitution, the police might make a preemptive strike to prevent an innocent youth from falling into the hands of "waiting homosexuals," who were believed to frequent the train stations in search of bought sex. What was particularly worrisome to the authorities about these young men was the fact that they spurned traditional employment and turned to life on the street despite the overwhelming need for able-bodied men to fill the depleted ranks in industry and agriculture.[39] Doubtless many of them fancied the company of peers over their depressing, often broken home lives, although the "freedom" offered by life on the street was hardly carefree. Many were unable to obtain residence permits or ration cards, especially if their origins lay elsewhere in the old Reich. Without the support of families, some found prostitution the only way to earn the semblance of a living. Word of where one could earn some extra money spread easily among the city's informal network of itinerant and homeless boys.[40]

Upon discovering an increasingly "asocial" element of boys taking more than temporary shelter, guards at the city's train stations appealed to the police to intervene. As they did with female prostitutes, the police played a definitive role in scrutinizing, categorizing, and eventually disciplining deviant behavior, seeking to safeguard a particular image of "normal" masculine identity that the existence of *Bahnhof* boys actively belied. Boy prostitutes were considered dangerous because they undermined "productive citizenship" by jeopardizing their own involvement as future contributors to the state. In the youth facilities, they would be given a trade, taught how to find work, and sent back into the world with a healthful respect for productive labor, able to contribute to Germany's rebuilding.

Policing street-level sex

Well into the 1950s, when Berlin was divided administratively and sandwiched between two separate countries, movement from one sector to the other continued with relative ease. Although not without difficulty, as late as 1958, Berliners could "flee" the East simply by taking the suburban train (the S-Bahn) to freedom.[41] The *Bahnhof* was thus a potent symbol of political transgression as well as the site of much of the city's clandestine sex trade.

To control the sex trade, police in the western sector of Berlin focused their attention primarily on Bahnhof Zoo, the station near the Berlin Zoo; police in the eastern sector patrolled three train stations where the trade flourished most visibly: Alexanderplatz, Friedrichstrasse, and occasionally Ostkreuz, in the east of the city center. In pairs, plainclothes officers would watch for signs of suspicious behavior and follow suspects into the neighboring parks or bombed-out apartment blocks where sexual acts typically took place. The officers would hide carefully and allow some time to pass before identifying themselves to the suspects. Using techniques of surveillance perfected during the Nazi period, they strained to gain the best perspective, making sure to note in their logs that they had turned "on [their] flashlight in order to get a better look."[42]

Because of the porous nature of the boundary between East and West Berlin, it was not unusual for police in the Soviet sector to ensnare West Berliners buying sex there or, conversely, for boys with eastern addresses to find their way into the western-sector court system, paying their dues to society in the Plötzensee Prison youth jail in West Berlin. Some degree of cooperation between the eastern and western police forces existed in the initial years after the war. One night in May 1948, for instance, a police task force conducting a raid at Bahnhof Zoo in the heart of the British sector asked Horst D., an 18-year-old resident of the western district of Neukölln, why he was frequenting this "known hangout for homosexuals and call boys." Since Horst had "neither identification nor money on him," he was sent to the local police station for questioning. There it was discovered that he was wanted on charges of assault and robbery at two eastern-sector precincts. Despite the worsening political situation, not to mention an ideologically divided police apparatus, Horst was sent eastward for processing. By 1950, however, the political situation had changed dramatically, so much so that two West Berlin witnesses in a case against Hans L. refused to cross into the GDR to attend the young man's hearing.[43]

While efforts to contain female prostitution and the spread of venereal disease involved joint efforts by the police and the state health office, with occasional help from the Allied power most affected, male prostitution remained in the domain of the local police, who received support from youth services. As the first contact that call boys and johns had with the legal system, the police possessed broad discretion in determining what situations warranted further investigation. Moreover, in recounting the unfolding of events, the police also played an active role in constructing what counted as criminal conduct.

For officers in the field, determining what constituted a criminal offense was a highly subjective act, made more so by the ambiguities of Paragraph 175a. Depending on the nature of the transgression, who was involved, and how much the officers had in fact witnessed, call boys and johns could expect anything from an on-the-spot interview to being arrested and taken to the station house for clarification and processing. In most scenarios, police officers would force youths to come to the precinct simply for exhibiting advanced signs of "call boy–like" behavior, but they would release the johns on their own recognizance, despite overwhelming evidence (in one case, the presence of semen and a disheveled appearance). Thus *Bahnhof* boys could expect to be treated differently from so-called established homosexuals, who were sometimes sympathetically viewed as "afflicted" by their sexual persuasion.

Despite its appearance of uniformity, the surveillance process was implemented quite flexibly. When Gerhard Z. entered a bombed-out building on Georgenstrasse with 17-year-old Karl-Heinz S. after a rendezvous at Bahnhof Friedrichstrasse, he was unaware that two officers on foot patrol had followed them. On that night in early June 1948, Gerhard and Karl-Heinz aroused suspicion because the complex they sought was, according to police, "often used by homosexuals and call boys for unnatural sex."[44] But Officers S. and W. missed catching the suspects in the act, having startled the two before they could begin mutually masturbating. After checking both men's papers, the police admitted in their report that they had little evidence to go on. Despite the lack of physical proof, Gerhard Z. opted to accompany the officers to the station "to explain his actions," since he was married and wanted to ensure that his case would be handled with the utmost discretion. It is doubtful Gerhard was ever sentenced, since the "intention" of having sex with a hustler was not technically a crime under Paragraph 175a, as it was interpreted in the East. However, the call boy might have been detained, because simply offering himself for the "purpose of abuse" was grounds for intervention.

In a similar case involving an encounter between an off-duty East Berlin homicide detective and a known prostitute, the evidence was sufficient to cast doubt on the officer's innocence but not adequate to sustain a charge. Having struck up a conversation with 14-year-old Fred V. in the street near Bahnhof Friedrichstrasse, Werner W. invited him to a nearby bar for schnapps, beer, and a bite to eat. By the time they had finished drinking, the trains had stopped running, causing both to search for a hotel room to sleep off the imbibed spirits. On the way, they ran into the back courtyard of a ruined building in order to urinate. It was at this time, Fred claimed, that Werner touched Fred's penis before placing it in his mouth. The boy pushed him aside, ran into the street, and yelled for the attention of two officers on foot patrol.

At the station house, the police interviewed both Werner W. and Fred V. in an attempt to sort out their stories. Since the boy's particulars were already in the card index, there was little doubt that he was a prostitute who had most likely offered himself in exchange for food and shelter. But how guilty was Werner W.? A seasoned officer who had been a member of the force since 1946, Werner W. underscored his "normal" orientation ("ich bin normal veranlagt") by repeatedly mentioning his pregnant fiancée. In search of physical evidence to support the boy's charges, the arresting officers returned to the scene with a chemist to conduct an examination for traces of semen, but rain the night before had washed away any evidence. Regardless of the fact that their encounter seemed to fit the pattern of most interactions between call boy and john, not to mention the boy's statement, without physical proof, Werner's guilt remained unproven.[45]

While Werner W. was released, Fred V. was sentenced to no less than two years in a youth home, with the possibility of being sent away for an indefinite amount of time if he remained hostile to "reeducation."[46] Paradoxically, a law originally envisioned as protecting an innocent youth from the advances of a corrupt adult targeted the youth for more extreme discipline. In Fred V.'s case, seduction was not a factor because he was a call boy.

Obviously, it was not the function of the police to judge which suspect should receive what sentence. But the police had to know who and what represented the greater threat to public and private order. Although their actions might vary according to the situation, they were generally swift to combat perceived transgressors. When Werner P. and Karl-Heinz H. entered a destroyed building along the River Spree so that Karl-Heinz could earn his bus fare home, police intervened and questioned both men, claiming that they had acted suspiciously near the Friedrichstrasse station. Sixteen-year-old Karl-Heinz answered every question asked of him, telling how he and Werner had searched for a quiet spot in order to masturbate uninterrupted. Werner P. was implicated by the youth's confession, and, as a result, his counterclaims were dismissed out of hand. Interestingly, it was the youth, Karl-Heinz, who was taken to the station for questioning; after making a note of his particulars, the police saw fit to release Werner on-site.[47]

As two of the previous cases illustrate, johns who purchased sexual favors were often treated differently from the call boys whose favors they had solicited. Did such discrimination connote a different estimation of guilt and transgression? Was the treatment of johns more lenient than that of call boys? In the police reports, this is not often clear. To be sure, it was a relief to a john not to have to proceed to the precinct to clarify his story on the night of the incident in question. But he could expect to have his address registered by police, which ensured that his story would be investigated further and that he might receive a summons to contest the charge in court at a later date.

In all these cases, we see the enhanced role police played in teasing out the "truth" in otherwise complicated investigations. They pursued suspects before any crime had been committed, created files on known call boys, and handled situations differently based on those files as well as the suspects' status.

Although both East and West Germany upheld the Nazi variant of Paragraph 175a in order to protect vulnerable young men from the perils of seduction, these cases suggest that by the late 1940s the vision of victimization embodied in the law rarely shaped the actions of the police. Instead, the police intervened in the city's semipublic spaces to control wayward youths, the call boys. Without visual or physical evidence of intercourse-like behavior, johns might be able to negotiate their temporary release, but call boys rarely had such an opportunity.

Manhood, medicalization, and mitigating circumstances

Although criminology in the period before 1945 has garnered recent scholarly interest, few studies document its reemergence after World War II—a dearth of scholarly research that is incongruent with the intense interest that criminology aroused in the 1950s.[48] Then jurists, sociologists, psychologists, and biologists devoted endless hours to investigating the malaise of the postwar generation and its propensity for crime. Some prominent criminologists who had made their careers during the Nazi interregnum reissued sanitized accounts of the sociological origins of criminal behavior. For those who considered the family the fundamental social and political unit, the male sex trade was a threat, undermining the marital bond as well as the conception of manhood.[49] Thus, sexual morality was hotly debated in professional journals, newspaper editorials, and conference proceedings.

In their efforts to understand homosexuality and purchased sex, postwar legal reformers in both Germanys drew on pre-Nazi discourses. In West Germany, where discussions of deviancy appeared in the public sphere, the central issues were biological and medical.[50] Social reformer Hans Giese, for example, employed a model of medicalization to distinguish between affliction (applicable to known homosexuals) and corruption (associated with prostitutes and blackmailing youths). In shifting blame from the john to the call boy, Giese lobbied to end the prohibition of same-sex sexuality but continue the regulation of male prostitution.[51] In East Germany, where debates about deviance were relegated to backroom committee meetings restricted to party functionaries, the police, and ministry officials, the factors stressed were sociological and environmental. Because the medical model smacked of biological determinism, a Nazi scourge, Communist Party officials selected other Weimar-era criminological approaches—corrective education and the redemptive role of work—to set delinquents on a new course. While this is a topic requiring additional research, the distinction must have been significant, having profound implications for the men and boys caught in the judicial system.

Most West German social scientists, jurists, and criminologists relied on prewar sociobiological "types" (*Typus*) to guide their analyses of postwar crime.[52] The 1950 reissue of Ernst Seelig's landmark textbook *Lehrbuch der Kriminologie* is an excellent example of this. His views of male prostitution upheld Cesare Lombroso's late-nineteenth-century notion that prostitutes were passive asocials who, in countries where homosexuality was still illegal, were lazy itinerants and career blackmailers (Seelig, 1950, p. 94).

Like many other criminologists, Seelig assumed that most call boys were heterosexually oriented and entered into prostitution simply to make money. Call boys, he said, were "not always homosexually inclined" (*homosexual veranlangt*); instead, they offered homosexual men only the physical part of their identity from which they could generate income (Seelig, 1950, p. 94; Lombroso & Ferrero, 1896).[53] F. Wiethold, director of the Institute for Forensic and Social Medicine at the University of Frankfurt, expressed a similar view in an essay published in the West German sexological journal *Beiträge zur Sozialforschung* (1952). Call boys, he reported, were only loosely associated with the homosexual subculture. But while these boys were not genuine sexopaths (*Sexopathen*), he argued, their social derailment merited direct intervention by the state, since the more contact they had with homosexual men, the more likely they would be to "succumb" to that lifestyle (Wiethold, 1952).

Not every legal and medical professional agreed that premature exposure to homosexual sex would increase the chances of abnormal sexual development. In a later article published in the *Beiträge zur Sexualforschung*, Reinhard Redhardt, also at the University of Frankfurt's Institute for Forensic and Social Medicine, argued against the mainstream interpretation that "seduction through adult homosexuals plays a determining role" (Reinhardt, 1954, p. 75).[54] Based on 45 case studies and interviews conducted between 1947 and 1950, he proposed that male prostitution must be understood as its own entity, distinct from delinquency, female prostitution, and homosexuality. As a self-contained social category or condition, male prostitution required scrutiny on its own.

While a long-standing argument over endogenous and exogenous factors continued in the postwar discussion of male sexual deviance, proponents on both sides often marked *Bahnhof* boys, typically members of the urban underclass, as criminogenically predisposed to asociality. Their deviant behavior posed risks to society: their criminality might be passed on to future generations if left unchecked, their actions jeopardized sexological arguments for decriminalizing Paragraph 175 by sullying the image of the homosexual, and their presence raised fears that exposure to same-sex desire threatened the development of a "healthful" orientation. Rarely was the call boys' involvement in the sex trade understood as a protean search for community or intimacy among same-sex-desiring men.[55]

One of the most scathing indictments of male prostitution came from Botho Laserstein, a controversial jurist whose life story was as extraordinary as his professional insight into the problem of blackmail was damning.[56] In his quasi-documentary account of a typical street boy in postwar Düsseldorf, Laserstein emphasized the immorality of male prostitution. Out of a pastiche of former clients' experiences, he (re)constructed a cultural milieu within which innocent homosexual men were taken advantage of by cheeky young boys on the make (*auf dem Strich*). In this sordid underworld, instead of confirmed homosexuals corrupting heretofore innocent youth, gangs of *Bahnhof* boys plotted blackmail. Interestingly, by representing the call boy Karl D.'s entry into the male sex trade as induced by an uncle's unwelcome advances, Laserstein reinforced the seduction motif, echoing fears voiced by conservative opponents to the decriminalization of homosexuality.[57] Regardless, he claimed it was greed, not sexual orientation, that induced the fall of Karl and other call boys, whose depravity made them the "worst kind of criminal there is." (Laserstein n.d.b in *Strichjunge Karl*, 37). So long as consensual sex among men was criminalized, Laserstein argued, new clients for the boys would be generated, thereby putting honest and otherwise law-abiding men in harm's way (Laserstein in *Strichjunge Karl*, 54).[58]

By pathologizing call boys in his quest to abolish Paragraph 175, Laserstein revealed their precarious and sometimes contradictory position within the West German legal reform movement. While themselves the product of the continued criminalization of an otherwise harmless activity, they in turn made criminals out of otherwise upstanding citizens, and for this behavior, they deserved little sympathy.[59] From both progressives advancing the protection of homosexuals and conservatives advocating the protection of society at large, call boys received little sympathy and much contempt. Talk of their victimization was minimal.

As they dealt with homosexual infractions in the 1950s, East and West Berlin officials seized on different parts of this multihued argument, drawing from diverging pre-1945 discourses to substantiate the state's regulation of intergenerational sex. In the steady procession of cases that passed through the district courts, defendants and prosecutors, judges and witnesses, party officials and welfare officers, armed with the most recent definitions of abnormality and deviance, picked up where the police had left off in redefining the contours of aberrant behavior.[60]

Most johns charged with violating the provisions of Paragraph 175a were given summary punishments at the police precinct. Those with social status and sufficient resources usually opted to pay a fine, but others faced jail terms, which in West Germany during the mid-1950s ranged from a week to multiple months, depending on the circumstances of the case.[61] Johns who wished to appeal the precinct's charges could do so before a municipal court judge. Trial records for those cases brought to West Berlin's Tiergarten municipal court reflect the negative impressions of the call boy that appear in postwar sociobiological accounts of criminality. They also reveal how mutable the concept of a homosexual could be.

Because a call boy's confession (*Gestandnis*) was central to the process of laying charges and establishing a john's guilt, it is understandable that in court, a john would elect to debate the veracity of his accuser's claim.[62] Given the growing popular and professional belief in the male prostitute's moral depravity, the criminal climate within which he circulated, and his relatively low social position, many johns defended themselves by attempting to discredit their accusers in open court and by arguing that mediating circumstances needed to be taken into account. In making their defense, they were using legal maneuvers already embedded in the system.[63]

The case against Horst K., a writer, who picked up a hustler at the *Bahnhof* at Savignyplatz, illustrates this system of negotiation. After they returned to Horst's apartment for sex, the call boy demanded a 50-mark payment, threatening to destroy his host's apartment, give him a good thrashing, and report him to the police if his demands were not met. When he received only a portion of the money he had demanded, the call boy went straight to the police and placed a charge against Horst K. At the precinct, despite his obvious victimization, Horst confessed to his "crime."[64] Nevertheless, seeking retribution, he decided to contest the charge and forced the process to proceed to court.

In December 1956, without counsel or evidence to support his story, Horst K. appeared in court to outline his situation. Surprisingly, the presiding judge took his plight into consideration. Horst's compliance with the police, confession of guilt, lack of a previous criminal record, and upstanding social position all contributed to the judge's sentence of 100 marks instead of the proposed ten-day prison sentence. The judge recognized that, although an illicit transaction had in fact occurred, the partner was obviously a call boy and the deed did not offend public sensibilities, since it took place in private.[65]

In their pleas for leniency, rarely did defendants claim outright innocence or recant earlier confessions; they sensed that admitting some responsibility was the most likely way to secure favor with the presiding judge. In (re)constructing their stories to present mitigating circumstances, defendants chose among several different options. Some bravely proclaimed that they were gay and had never had sex with a woman; others employed the "drunk defense" to account for their momentary straying from the straight and narrow; some relied on marital status as evidence that theirs was a one-time homosexual dalliance; others drew attention to their military experience to explain their actions.

On June 1, 1955, Karl-Heinz A., a 41-year-old bookkeeper, employed the service of counsel when he appeared before an appeals committee at the Tiergarten district courthouse, hoping to reduce the sentence he had received for picking up the underage Herbert S. near Bahnhof Steg-litz. Admitting that he had engaged the youth in conversation at the train station, he explained how they had walked together along Finckensteinallee toward Karl-Heinz's house. Along the way they engaged in erotic conversation, sharing their earlier sexual escapades. The bookkeeper was intrigued by the boy's stories of his initial seduction by an African American soldier in the occupation force. When they reached his home, KarlHeinz asked the youth if he was interested in meeting again for another walk. At their second meeting, after returning to the subject of the boy's sexual experiences, the defendant said he became noticeably aroused. Finding shelter in a nearby bush, the two mutually masturbated and made preparations for a third rendezvous.

Although the court records do not convey how Karl-Heinz stumbled into the system, they do provide some interesting information about his defense strategy. The crux of it rested on two main points: that the accused was engaged to be married and not inclined toward homo-sexual sex ("ich bin nicht in dieser Richtung veranlangt") and that sexual touching did not meet the legal standard of intercourse-like behavior.[66] The appeals committee agreed that since this transgression was a one-time dalliance, some lenience could be granted, but it rejected the defense claim that intercourse-like behavior had not transpired. Because the defendant's actions included touching the youth to arouse pleasure, Karl-Heinz's actions constituted a sexual offense under Paragraph 175a. He was ordered to pay 105 marks and received a moderate reduction in his sentence.[67]

If defendants could forge a link between their sexual transgression and their war experiences, the court was inclined to grant extenuating circumstances. Although sex reformers and jurists pointed to the homoeroticism present in all-male environments like the army, prisons, and youth-care facilities, defendants rarely acknowledged this aspect of their experience as fostering an interest in same-sex relationships. Instead, they professed that injuries and illnesses sustained in combat or imprisonment made them unable to forge "healthy" relationships with women.

When Gerhard P., a 48-year-old laborer, was accused of having sex 15 to 18 times with an underage neighbor, he offered his wartime experiences in mitigation. It was less the sexual perversions Gerhard "got used to" as a Soviet captive and more the chronic lung condition he developed on his release that made physical contact with women impossible. Gerhard was accorded some lenience by the court, owing in large part to the widely held belief that return-ing soldiers with extensive physical and psychological injuries were prone to homosexuality.[68]

When his case was heard in the criminal court (Strajkammer) in 1951, Paul W. offered a simi-lar defense. After engaging in erotic conversation with 16-year-old Gerd W., Paul was accused of initiating an extended session of mutual masturbation. Since the boy accepted money for the transaction (he was, after all, in social services and met the profile of a call boy), the court recognized that he too was an active participant and not simply a victim of seduction. To help understand the defendant's behavior, the court solicited a physician's assessment of Paul W.'s personality. The physician, Dr. Weimann, concluded that the laborer was an intelligent man, fully in control of his faculties. Despite an excessively close relationship with his mother, he had little contact with other women, largely owing to injuries sustained during the war. Disgusted by the ugliness of his war wounds, the defendant had developed a kind of "cripple neurosis" (Krüppelneurose), Weimann said, that no woman could manage to understand. Based largely on this diagnosis, Paul W. was given the relatively light fine of 50 marks or ten days in jail.[69]

In connecting their crimes to their wartime experiences, both Gerhard P. and Paul W. were able to draw sympathy to themselves by evoking images of citizenship, responsibility, and sacrifice and to deflect any thoughts of the boy's victimization. In these cases, the dangers of intergenerational homosexual sex were downplayed, and the defendants' homosexual behavior was medicalized. The courts accepted implicitly some of the same arguments advanced by prominent sexologists of the day, who advocated the repeal of Paragraph 175 by arguing that homosexuality should be treated by physicians and not the police.

As these West Berlin court cases demonstrate, the men accused of sex with minors could mitigate the consequences of their acts. However, the boys charged with "hustler-like behavior" rarely escaped some form of incarceration. In cases involving underage youth, social workers made field visits and reported back to the central youth services about the cleanliness of the home, the mother's employment status, the parents' relationship—an investigation that assumed delinquency was linked to conditions within the overburdened working-class household. These reports might have helped build a case for mitigating circumstances in the event that a youth came from a troubled home, but more often than not, they served to confirm commonly held beliefs concerning the true source of depravity. This is certainly what occurred in the case against Peter S., whose advanced endangerment earned him a six-month sentence in a youth facility.[70]

For the boys arrested and tried in East Berlin's court in the downtown district of Mitte, mitigating circumstances were even more of a rarity. Instead, the boys were the focus of a multi-level governmental investigation that employed a mixture of welfare and penal strategies geared toward the active promotion and sustainment of socially useful behavior. Male prostitutes, like other delinquent youths deemed reluctant to contribute to the economic restructuring of the fledgling GDR state, were monitored by various agencies within the purview of the Ministry of People's Education (Volksbildung), whose mandate included monitoring children's aid and youth services in addition to promoting socialist principles in cultural affairs. Adolescents charged with crimes in youth court served their sentences in a variety of facilities, but it was the juvenile workhouse that was considered to have the greatest potential to rehabilitate waywardness by promoting socialist morality and hard work.[71]

Claiming to encourage corrective education and communitarian values, these facilities combined social welfare and penal strategies to inculcate socialist values among the nation's youngest citizens. Not simply a throwback to Weimar-era rehabilitative policy, youth penal policy inherited significant Nazi-era measures as well. Male prostitutes charged with plying their wares at Bahnhof Friedrichstrasse, for example, were charged with transgressions under the general criminal code as well as under the 1943 Nazi-amended Young Offenders Act (Reichsjugendgesetz). East Berlin judges, interested in curbing aberrant sexual behavior among the city's youth, employed the Nazi act to sentence the hustlers they deemed most depraved to unlimited sentences (*unbestimmte Dauer*) in one of the regions' youth work facilities.[72] Fred V., mentioned earlier, who had "fallen into homosexual circles at Bahnhof Zoo" before being arrested after his liaison with a member of the homicide police in East Berlin, was given a sentence of "no less than nine months and no more than two years," which he served at the workhouse in Neustrelitz in the surrounding province of Brandenburg and at a remand home in Berlin. His case bears resemblance to a Nazi-era case against the hustler Alfred B., who in 1941 was likewise sentenced to an unlimited spate in a youth facility for call-boy activity around Alexanderplatz.[73] In both cases, the educative measures of the Young Offenders Act were lauded by the presiding judge as affording the youths the opportunity to avail themselves of rehabilitative measures while still fulfilling the state's mandate to punish the offenses committed. Considering both boys came from troubled families, the redemptive role of hard work in modifying sexual behavior assured state officials of the imperatives at hand.

While adopting Nazi-era penal measures and casting them in the language of prewar welfare reform, the East German regulators of male prostitutes trod softly around any attendant biological assumptions. Although they certainly inherited those traditions, early GDR policy makers and practitioners emphasized social environment, class struggle, and material inequality as factors contributing to moral debasement and criminality. Biological explanations of homosexuality, such as those advocated by East German sexologist Dr. Rudolf Klimmer, while circulating in the West, made little impact on legal definitions of deviance in the GDR. The East German emphasis on the redemptive role of hard work, especially in cases of sexual delinquency, was much more aggressive than similar ideas at play in West Berlin. So distrustful was the East Berlin court of biological explanatory models that only after multiple suicide attempts and the intervention of two physicians was one trial judge persuaded to release an afflicted youth from his unlimited sentence.[74] While both East and West Berlin youth services may be seen as inheriting a similar strand of pre-1945 criminology, especially Lombrosian-inspired analysis of prostitution as passive asociality, in resurrecting unlimited sentences under the guise of humanist social reform, jurists in East Germany ensured that the state would play a more authoritarian role in resocializing wayward youths.

Conclusion

By the early 1950s, West Germany had revised aspects of the Nazi-inspired version of Paragraph 175 but stopped short of the Weimar-era definition stipulating that intercourse-like actions determined criminal comportment.[75] In East Germany, men accused of Paragraph 175 crimes might be summoned to trial, but without suitable visual or physical evidence, they could be cleared of charges. Despite East Germany's attempts to reform the criminal code in the early 1950s, the workers' uprising of 1953 caused the government to abandon its commitment to legal reform. After 1953, the Socialist Unity Party initiated a series of pronatalist policies designed to spark early marriages and child rearing to help control the population decline and counteract the effect of the mass exodus of GDR citizens. Viewing homosexuality as a remnant of bourgeois society, the party opted to maintain the Nazi variant of Paragraph 175a, which criminalized same-sex sexuality in the name of the "healthful mores of the working people."

West Germany's jettisoning of the Nazi version of Paragraph 175 likewise had little effect on the status of Paragraph 175a. Public debate on male promiscuity remained extremely contentious throughout the 1950s, and a steady stream of infractions made their way through West Berlin's judicial system. Despite increased sensitivity among some progressive jurists about the plight of hustlers, a number of high-profile murders in Frankfurt and Berlin, where male prostitutes had actually killed their johns, ignited widespread condemnation of this criminal lifestyle.[76]

Whether a preemptive strike against the possible corruptibility of youth or a natural offshoot of problematic legislation, the juridical engagement with same-sex prostitution demonstrates a parallel discourse of state intervention in both Germanys that focused on molding, shaping, and protecting respectable masculine behavior from perceived dangers lurking on the fringes.[77] Despite conflicting beliefs about the impact of so-called unnatural desire (*widernatürliche Unzucht*) on otherwise "healthful" and heterosexual maturation, call boys, more so than their johns, posed a direct challenge to the reconstruction of a respectable German masculinity in the East as well as the West. While contemporary jurists might continue to employ the concept of guardianship to justify their treatment of them, in the mind of the postwar German public, *Bahnhof* boys had become predators, not prey.

Notes: I would like to extend special thanks to Jason Bennett, Dan Healey, Lisa Heineman, Dagmar Herzog, Wulf Kansteiner, Ingeborg Majer O'Sickey, Angus McLaren, and Jean Quataert for their careful reading of early versions of the original article. Research support was provided by the Berlin Program for Advanced German and European Studies, as well as both the Department of History and the University Research Foundation at the State University of New York at Binghamton.

Notes

1 On the subject of "debasement" and criminality, see Karl Bader, *Soziologie der deutschen Nachkrieg-skriminalitat* (Tübingen, 1949); Hilde Thurnwald, *Gegenwartsprobleme Berliner Familien: Eine soziologische Untersuchung an 498 Familien* (Berlin, 1948).

2 Access to post-1945 police, court, and welfare-services case files was granted on condition that the names of those affected be "anonymized" to protect their privacy. I wish to thank Herr Marx and Nanzka for access to Amtsgericht Tiergarten trial records not yet cataloged in the Landesarchiv Berlin.

3 Landesarchiv Berlin (hereafter referred to as LAB) B Rep 013 Senatverwaltung für Jugend und Familie, Acc. 1052, Nr. 39. Case number (507) Jug Kms 65/51 and 2 Ju Kms 8/51.

4 In a different case file account of transgressions against Paragraph 175 of the German penal code, Meinhard (2000) shows that the Berlin district court continued to recognize previous convictions under the Nazi criminal code as late as 1961. For an account of the post-1945 experiences of men convicted in Nazi-era Berlin, see Pretzel (2002). I thank Andreas Pretzel for sharing his interesting research with me at an earlier stage.

5 In recent years, many important studies have emerged that document transgressive sexuality in the urban milieu. Some key examples of the city's role in fostering discourses of belonging and the emergence of subcultural identification include Chauncey (1994); *Goodbye to Berlin? 100 Jahre Schwulenbewegung* (Berlin, 1996); Healey (2001); Maynard (1994): Mort (1999): Stein (2000).

6 On Berlin's vibrant history, see *Polizei. Vom Zwangsverhdltnis zur Zweckehe?* (Dobler, 1996); Dobler (1992).

7 In fact, in Berlin, liaisons with boy prostitutes continued as late as 1944. For a comparative perspective from the Nazi period, see the police files and court case records concerning male prostitution in LAB A Rep 358–02 Generalstaatsanwaltschaft beim Landgericht Berlin 1933–45

8 Bessel (1996) suggests that property crimes in Berlin rose 885 percent between 1937 and 1946. Equally alarming was the increase in violent crime. For statistics governing violent criminal infractions, see LAB C Rep 303/9 Polizeipräsident in Berlin 1945–48, Nr. 246 Statistiken der Kriminalpolizei 1945–48.

9 Although the term *rent boy* is more familiar to Anglo-American readers, I have elected to employ the term *call boy* to refer to boy prostitutes because of its contemporary idiomatic usage in German. To date, very little has been written on the postwar period, due to privacy laws and the difficulties in accessing case files. Schiefelbein (1992) provides an interesting overview of a series of trials in Frankfurt am Main in 1950–51. These centered on the admission of guilt by a known call boy whose testimony led to the arrest and persecution of more than 100 men in the city. Whisnant is currently examining the postwar gay scene in West Germany's major metropolitan centers. For a case history of Hamburg, consult Whisnant (2001).

10 Grossmann (1995) makes this point eloquently in her article on the rape of German women by Soviet soldiers.

11 See von Rönn (1998) for a larger discussion of youth corruptibility in the Nazi era. Special thanks to Dagmar Herzog for this reference.

12 Many people who have examined the problem of incarceration have confined their attention to either the Nazi or the postwar period. Some important contributions in the German literature include Dobler, 1996, 1999; Jellonnek (1990); von Rönn (1998); Schoppmann (1999); Sparing (1997); Stümke (1989). Recent examples from the postwar period include the essays in Pretzel and Rossbach (1999).

13 For an example from the Weimar period, see Mackay's famous account of a call boy's life in the 1920s in *Der Puppenjunge* (reprint, Berlin, 1999), in English as *The Hustler* (Boston, 1985).

14 See the police logbook entries for descriptions of the train stations most frequented by male prostitutes, in LAB C Rep 303/9 Polizeipräsident in Berlin, Nr. 248 Tätigkeitsbuch MII/I—Aussendienst—, May 8, 1948—April 23, 1949, 60.

15 This link between bestiality and homosexuality has been researched in the Swedish context by Rydstrom (2000). For early histories of the regulation of illicit sex and German masculinity, see Dinges (1998); Gleixner (1994); Hull (1996).

16 On the early homosexual rights movement and legal struggles to decriminalize homosexuality, see Steakley (1975); Eissler (1990).

17 In the nineteenth century, various regional appellate courts debated what constituted homosexual sex, often promoting conflicting interpretations of the legal statute. As an example, on October 24, 1877, the Prussian Upper Tribunal defined "intercourse-like" acts as those that "worked to satiate sexual desire in much the same way as in the natural manner between people of the opposite sex." In 1875,

however, the Royal Saxon Appellate Court had dismissed such a narrow definition. Penetration itself was not necessary so long as arousal occurred with another person or through that person's actions. Whereas the Prussian court disregarded mutual masturbation as constitutive of homosexual sex, the Saxon tribunal upheld it as a viable symbol of criminal activity (Baumann, 1968).

18 For a history of the legal definitions of pre-Nazi homosexual criminality, including some discussion of early legal reform, see Baumann (1968), Dworek (1990); Hutter (1990); Kroger (1957). McLaren (2002) documents the comparative history of blackmail in sexual scandals of the nineteenth and early twentieth centuries.

19 Tamagne (2000) and Hekma (1999) both argue that the 1930s witnessed a general increase in intolerance vis-à-vis homosexuals.

20 There is a broad range of opinions about the exact nature and origins of Nazi animosity toward homosexuality and homosexuals. In his landmark study of nationalism and respectability, Mosse (1985) contended that homosexuals represented the evils of modernity, posing a distinct challenge to a militarized but chaste vision of male bonding. Oosterhuis (1991, 1997) has suggested that initially Hitler tolerated homosociality as one aspect of the new militarized masculinity that Mosse (1985) referred to in the years after the Great War. In order to sustain power and legitimacy, homosociability had to be purged from this vision of the New Man. Moeller (1995) advances a more pragmatic solution to this issue in arguing that although the "night of the long knives" was motivated by the need to eliminate a possible rival within the ranks, a more general disdain for Röhm's public sexual identity may, in fact, have aided the Nazis in winning broad-based support for the action against the SA. Grau (1993) moves away from militarized masculinity to emphasize instead that the new population policy helped marginalize homosexuals, who had removed their reproductive power from the regeneration of the German people. See also Hancock (1998).

21 Interestingly, Heinrich Himmler's statements support the argument that the increased persecution of homosexuals after the Röhm Putsch was part of National Socialist policy and not simply a knee-jerk reaction to the SA's pronounced homosexual contingent. In a speech to the SS leadership on February 18, 1937, he reminded the audience that "in the first six weeks of our work in this field in 1934 we sent more cases to trial than the entire Berlin police force over the past 25 years. Nobody can tell me that it was all on account of Röhm" (Smith in Stümke & Finkler, 1981, p. 436).

22 This change in legislation was immediately felt in terms of the number of men prosecuted under the new variant of the paragraph. Baumann (in Moeller, 1995) gives figures that suggest that of the 41,116 Germans convicted of violating laws protecting morality (*Sittlichkeitsdelikte*) between 1931 and 1933, fully 2,319 were prosecuted against Paragraph 175. In the two years before World War II, the numbers increased dramatically to 24,447 Paragraph 175 infractions out of a total of 65,155 *Sittlichkeitsdelikte* (Baumann in Moeller, 1995).

23 Giles (1992) has illustrated this point in his earlier work on Nazi policy, suggesting that no unified strategy was at work in dealing with homosexual infractions. His latest work (Giles, 2002) provides further examples to support this point in an important examination of the logic employed by the SS and police in dealing with same-sex misbehavior.

24 See the case against Berlin prostitute Fritz K., found in Thüringisches Staatsarchiv Gotha Strafgefängnis Eisenach (1933–51), Nr. 237, in which he was released from his sentence due to the changing situation in the final months of the war. On the issue of prison sentences, see Hoffschildt (1999a; 1999b). Efforts are under way to catalog the exact number of men who perished in the camps as well as those who fell victim to Nazi jurisprudence. Hoffschildt is currently constructing a database of names, while Pretzel is assembling a book of the dead that seeks to enumerate the number of men who may be traced through the Berlin police and court records as having died due to Nazi persecution. This is an especially difficult task, given the fact that many men had repeat offences, and where access is granted, case files are often incomplete.

25 See also Soviet general Besarin's Order of the Military Commanders of the City of Berlin from May 25, 1945, which stipulated that "in the interest of reestablishing normal life for the citizens of Berlin, in the interest of fighting against criminal offences and disturbances of the peace[,] . . . the self-government of the city of Berlin has received authorization from the command of the Red Army to organize a civic police force, court, and an office of the public prosecutor. These organs have already been formed on the 20th of May and have started about their normal work" (Ministerium des Inneren, Hauptabteilung Kriminalpolizei, 1945).

26 For a discussion of the Allied position vis-à-vis Nazi jurisprudence, see Heuer (1995)

27 Perhaps these attitudes in the East help explain why from 1946 until 1949, only 129 judgments were passed down on Paragraph 175. Grau (1999, 1996) has made this point discussing the fractious debate

over the possible decriminalization of homosexuality in the GDR. Grau (1996) includes a transcript of the deliberations of the legal reform committee from the Bundesarchiv-Lichterfelde.

28 After the division of Berlin's municipal services in 1948, Markgraf commanded the eastern zone's police force. According to the American Occupation Government in Berlin, the city's police force was the first municipal administrative unit to split in two, well before the city government as a whole (NARA, 1950).

29 Female prostitution was located among the subsections of Paragraph 361 of the penal code generally associated with forms of asociality, including chronic drunkenness, lascivious behavior, peregrination, drug abuse, and begging, whereas Paragraphs 173 to 184b dealt with more severe forms of immorality, specifically, crimes against public decency. These *Sittlichkeitsdelikte* include molestation, incest, rape, homosexuality, male prostitution, seduction, *Lustmord*, and procurement. In a sense, the difference between these two sections was a question of behavior versus action, but generally criminals accused of committing the more serious infractions were believed to possess many of the asocial traits housed under the asociality paragraph. In this way, criminals charged with "crimes against the family and marriage" (the heading under which *Sittlichkeitsdelikte* were listed in the criminal code) were recognized as coming from among the ranks of the asocial, but rarely were those criminals accused of *Sittlichkeitsdelikte* charged simultaneously with infractions under Paragraph 361. The difference in the legal statutes governing moral infractions of a sexual nature speaks to that which was recognized as protected through the state's intervention: integrity of personhood and the family ideal, as in the case of *Sittlichkeitsdelikte*, and an esoteric sense of community mores, as in Paragraph 361.

30 Biess (1998) and Moeller (1998) have begun to shift the focus to a consideration of returning soldiers and their experiences in postwar Germany.

31 See the letter from Dr. Eugene E. Schwarz of the Public Health Office of the Office of Military Government Berlin Sector (OMGBS) to the *Bürgermeister* of Berlin dated July 9, 1947, in which he states that "the Military Authorities have brought to our attention the fact that in the immediate vicinity of the more important military installations of the US Army, prostitution is increasing in an alarming way and that nightly a great number of girls are soliciting and accosting soldiers. Places affected are the Titania Palast on Schlossstrasse, the Roosevelt Barracks on Finckensteinallee, the Telefunken Building and the Motor Barracks on Winifriedstrasse." Newspaper articles printed letters from women who were outraged at being sent forcibly for VD testing. A letter to the *Nachtexpress* from April 2, 1946, details the author's frustration over the 19-hour examination session she experienced after being rounded up at her place of work: "On the 13.3.46 I was present in the Regina Bar due to my work. Around 8 pm the police conducted a raid, during which all women were loaded in a truck."

32 On November 28, 1945, four 15- and 16-year-old girls were rounded up by Steglitz police while returning from a Christmas shopping trip at three o'clock in the afternoon. Since they had no ID on them (which was suspicious enough for police to think they were possible prostitutes), the girls were taken to the local precinct and strip searched. Afterward, they were sent for an examination at the hospital, where they had to undress in view of the American MPs who took part in the raid. Despite the pleas of one girl not to conduct the exam since she was a virgin, all four underwent the gynecological test for gonorrhea and syphilis. Forced to spend a night in a police-requisitioned "Bunkerhotel," despite testing negative, they returned home to their worried parents, who had not been informed of the raid. The girls and their parents initiated a letter-writing campaign to the Steglitz police with letters from the girls' teachers testifying to their collective outrage that this could be allowed to happen to such good girls. LAB C Rep 303/9 Ministerium des Inneren, Polizeipräsident in Berlin 1945–48, Nr. 249 Weibliche Kriminalpolizei, 6–12.

33 LAB C Rep 303/9 Polizeipräsident in Berlin 1945–48, Nr. 243 Abteilung V. Meldungen und Berichte. See also the "Survey of Juvenile Delinquency in Berlin" (OMGUS, 1946). This report outlines the material hardships endured by Berliners in the year following the war. The survey pays particular attention to the problem of fraternization among German "girls" and American soldiers and calls for the use of spot checks and raids (*Razzia*). In Zehlendorf, one of the districts in southwestern Berlin under American control, it states that "the young girls are kept in locked rooms through the night and many remain there throughout the next morning for their turn for examination."

34 Despite empirical evidence to the contrary, in 1959, Inspector Schramm of the Landeskriminalamt Berlin stated that in the immediate postwar period there were no call boys on the streets of Berlin. Only with the stabilization of the social and political situation, he argued, did hustlers reemerge onto the scene (Schramm, 1957, p. 90). For examples from a different context, in this case early 1950s Cologne, see Schön, 2000.

35 Boys picked up for suspected prostitution were forwarded to temporary youth facilities, where Youth Court Counseling Services case workers (*Jugendgerichtshilfe*) researched the background of each offender to document the charge's family history, even, if necessary, creating a psychological profile to help identify the cause and extent of moral endangerment. Social workers then submitted these reports to the particular judge presiding over the youth's case. A direct carryover from the Weimar period, this service attempted to make the court more sensitive to the plight of wayward youths by drawing attention to milieu and family life as indicators of the need for corrective education instead of outright punishment. With careful intervention instead of incarceration, a young charge might learn the error of his ways and embrace reform. Far from simply indicating a preexisting criminal predisposition, however, these profiles reinforced widely held notions of asociality, tracing its origins and causes to the broken and overburdened family. In the early postwar era, indicators such as dirty living quarters and a working mother, which frequently gained mention in these evaluations, were more often the rule rather than the exception. For examples of the treatment of young offenders, in this case young men charged with male prostitution, see the 1947 court case files from the Amtsgericht Tiergarten, which include examples of information gathered both by the Department of Youth Services and the Jugendgerichtshilfe before the division of municipal services in 1948. LAB B Rep 051 Amtsgericht Tiergarten.

36 LAB C Rep 303/9 Polizeipräsident in Berlin 1945–48, Nr. 259. Again, this language suggests the fact that many officials dealing with male prostitution viewed the boys as, in fact, heterosexual, forced into the trade by circumstance, not desire. Indeed, most (but not all) boys explicitly denied a homosexual orientation (literally, in German, *Veranlagung*), although this admission must be viewed with some skepticism. Police statements suggest that call boys (and johns, for that matter) framed their "disposition" in ways to minimize the harshness of the pending sentence. For male prostitutes, an admission of desire could eliminate the possibility of mitigating circumstances, which had a very tangible effect on the length and type of sentence.

37 In fact, both youth services and the Protestant Church believed the "streams of impoverished eastern youth" regularly fell "victim to homosexual circles" in postwar Berlin (West Berlin Youth Services, 1951).

38 For a more detailed discussion of this problem and how it evolved in East Germany, see Evans (2014) and Jorns (1995).

39 See the case against Günter S. in LAB C Rep 341 Stadtbezirksgericht Mitte, Nr. 5287, court case 99 DLs 6/50, January 28, 1950. Special thanks to Bianca Welzing of the Landesarchiv Berlin for making me aware of these files.

40 Some, like 14-year-old Fred V. from the East Berlin district of Köpenick, heard about the city's hot spots from boys he had met in the Struveshof facility in provincial Brandenburg. Interestingly, he had originally been picked up in 1949 for suspicious behavior around Bahnhof Zoo in the West. See LAB C Rep 341 Stadtbezirksgericht Mitte, Nr. 4433, case number 98 Ds 34/50, June 23, 1950.

41 Gumbert (forthcoming) notes that an East German crime drama from the late 1950s depicts a man's attempted escape from Bahnhof Potsdamer Platz, which had yet to be sealed off from the West. In more than 800 accounts submitted as part of a 1976 competition sponsored by the Senator for Work and Social Well-Being, many Berliners recall the porous nature of internal boundaries in the years after the war. See LAB B Rep. 240 Erlebnisberichte aus der Berliner Bevölkerung über die Zeit des 2. Weltkrieges und danach, Acc. 2651, Nrs. 1–6. For a filmic depiction of *Bahnhof* girls, see the 1947 DEFA film *Strassenbekanntschaft*.

42 LAB C Rep 303/9 Polizeipräsident in Berlin, Nr. 248 Tatigkeitsbuch MII/I—Aussendienst—, May 8, 1948—April 23, 1949.

43 Ibid., 10.

44 While it might seem as though this was an act of defiance, and perhaps it was, the fact that the key witness was responsible for initiating charges of theft suggests that this was not the situation at hand. See LAB C Rep 341 Stadtbezirksgericht Mitte, Nr. 4743, case against Hans. L. 18 Ju Js 585.50–99 Ds 100.50.

45 According to the police file, Werner was never charged but instead had to face an internal hearing to determine whether disciplinary charges would be placed for conduct unbecoming an officer. See the police statements taken from both suspects in LAB C Rep 341 Stadtbezirksgericht Mitte, Nr. 4433, case 98 Ds 34/50, June 23, 1950.

46 Fred was sent to no fewer than three different institutions before serving out his sentence in August 1952. See the letter from Child Protective Services dated January 1, 1952, in ibid.

47 LAB C Rep 303/9 Polizeipräsident in Berlin, Nr. 248 Tatigkeitsbuch MII/1—Aussendienst—, May 8, 1948—April 23, 1949, 60. In this case, it is important to stress that procedures dictated that Werner would likely receive notice in the mail regarding a fine for having contravened the law. If he wished to contest the terms of the charge, he had the opportunity to appear in court in a formal hearing. Transgressions of this sort frequently substituted a fine for time in jail, and according to Tiergarten district court records, if they were able, many johns opted to pay their fine.

48 On the emergence of criminology as a discipline in the nineteenth century, see Wetzell (2000). For the postwar period, see Gödecke (in progress) and Rode (1996).

49 Very little work has thus far been generated on the history of masculinity and social policy. For a beginning discussion of masculinity and national belonging, see Biess (1998). Merkel (1994) draws attention to idealized images of femininity at work in the GDR.

50 On this subject, it is useful to compare Grau's (1996, 1999) and Moeller's (1995) discussions of legal reform initiatives in East and West Germany.

51 Hans Giese, arguably the most significant contributor to post-1945 West German sexology, shied away from Hirschfeld's third sex model, arguing instead in favor of innate heterosexuality. As Moeller (1995) has pointed out, Giese believed that a homosexual man was very much still a man, insofar as desire was hardwired as heterosexual and procreative. Deviations from the norm, Giese argued, should be treated as a medical or psychological condition, since homosexuality required the intervention of capable physicians and not the police or courts (Moeller, 1995, p. 268). Interestingly, as early as 1949, East German sexologist Dr. Rudolf Klimmer suggested that there existed a basis in nature for homosexual desire. He argued that gay men should not be prosecuted for their actions, since there were anthropological and ethnological origins to the behavior (Klimmer, 1949). Unfortunately, Klimmer's ideas (not to mention writings) were suppressed in the East, never being allowed to guide policy or practice in the GDR. Indeed, the GDR remained quite fearful of biological explanatory models until the mid- to late 1960s, when "personality-based" criminological studies proposed to reveal the origins of juvenile delinquency, a problem that had plagued the nation since its founding in 1949. On the issue of personality and sexual crime, see Eghigian (2002).

52 An exception was Freiburg law professor Karl Bader, who directed attention toward the social and political undercurrents surrounding the fear of blackmail in the male sex trade following the war.

53 Criminologist Franz Exner (1949) sided with Lombroso in defining prostitution as a female-specific form of asociality. Male prostitutes are similarly regarded as an asocial scourge, predisposed to blackmail and dangerously corrupt.

54 Of course, opposition to the seduction theory was a focus of the gay movement well before the 1950s, from the writings of Karl Heinrich Ulrichs to Magnus Hirschfeld. Himmler himself, according to Oosterhuis (1999), perpetuated this idea that the majority of men gravitated toward homosexuality as a result of seduction at an early age.

55 Unfortunately, it is beyond the scope of this article to engage a discussion of motivation and community. My larger project attempts a more qualitative analysis of what was at stake in these liaisons.

56 Laserstein was a stridently outspoken critic of the Adenauer regime. He published widely in homosexual journals advocating the decriminalization of Paragraph 175, defended homosexuals in court cases, and empowered gay men accused under the article with his guidebook to defense strategies entitled *Angeklagte steh auf!*, published in the early 1950s. His flagrant disregard for the Adenauer state caused him to be placed under surveillance by the Department of Constitutional Protection (Verfassungschutz), which investigated threats to the integrity of West German democracy. He committed suicide in 1955, tarnished in a blackmail campaign and vilified in the conservative press (Hoven, 1991).

57 For a filmic version of the seduction motif, see Veit Harlan's remake of the 1919 film of a similar name, for which Magnus Hirschfeld originally contributed the screenplay. The 1957 version, *Anders als du und ich (§175),* filmed under consultation with Hans Giese, sparked a national discussion of the quest to decriminalize Paragraph 175 in West Germany. The film was inherently controversial, due to both the subject matter and the director's professional history as a filmmaker during the Nazi period; he was responsible for one of the worst anti-Semitic feature films, *Jüd Suß*. A spirited account of the film and the controversy that engulfed it may be found in Fehrenbach (1995).

58 Of course, the fear of solicitation and blackmail was intense during the Nazi period. In Hamburg, for example, members of the Hitler Youth served as decoys, pretending, as Micheler argues, "to offer sexual services in order to entrap men" (2002, p. 125).

59 For a full-length study of blackmail with an emphasis on the English and French contexts, see McLaren (2002).

60 Court records from this period are difficult to work with, offering but a foggy window into the past. I wish to extend warm thanks to Herren Marx and Nanzka of the Amtsgericht Tiergarten, Berlin, for arranging access to valuable case files not yet archived at the Landesarchiv Berlin. For a discussion of the role of courtroom dramas and the place of the law in crafting acceptable and aberrant identities during the Nazi period, see Szobar (2002). For a self-conscious study of the possibilities provided by court cases and their place in narrating gay history, see Maynard (1997).

61 By the time cases proceeded to the Tiergarten courthouse, the accused had most likely appeared at the precinct to "explain the situation" and had been informed of his right to challenge the charge in court. In the West Berlin system, uncomplicated cases involving consensual sex among men often led to summary punishments where the accused received by mail a notice of the charges, the prospective fine, and the amount of time he would have to spend in jail if he was unable to meet payment. In accepting the opportunity to contest the charges, the accused could elect to have his case heard in front of the judge. Accordingly, his file and paperwork would be transferred to the state prosecutor's office in order to arrange for a timely trial date. Probably because of the exorbitant cost, defendants generally refrained from enlisting the support of counsel, opting instead to represent themselves. Only in the case of prolonged appeals did defense attorneys play much of a role.

62 Jurist Botha Laserstein published a guidebook that served to acquaint the reader with the reconstructed legal process. His informal guide was rumored to be used by homosexuals wishing to adopt the best possible defense against charges incurred under Paragraph 175. See Laserstein (n.d.).

63 Despite the fact that these explanations fell on deaf ears, during the Nazi period, police statements continued to reflect the accused's attempt to craft a narrative appeal to mitigating circumstances, which in the Weimar period would have been entered into evidence in court and considered in sentencing. For examples from Berlin, see chapters in Pretzel and Rossbach (Meinhard, 2000).

64 Case against Horst K., 277 Cs 399/56, Amtsgericht Tiergarten, December 22, 1956.

65 Horst's monthly income was tabulated in 1956 at about 400–500 marks, and while this is onerous, as a comparison, a transport worker with the Berlin Transit Authority charged in another case in 1956 earned 280 marks per month and was forced to pay the same fine. See ibid. In some cases, the findings of the district court could be appealed by the state prosecutor if the sentence seemed too light. See the example of the case against Peter Z., 276 Cs 111/57, Amtsgericht Tiergarten, May 15, 1956, and (534) 66 ns 56.57 (196.57) *Landgericht Berlin kleine Strafkammer* dated March 7, 1958.

66 Case against Karl-Heinz A., 274 Ds 100/55, Amtsgericht Tiergarten, June 1, 1955.

67 Karl-Heinz was not the only accused to claim marital status as a defense; generally, the court recognized marriage as grounds for mitigating circumstances. In one case involving a divorced man who made contact with homosexuals through written notices on the walls of pissoirs, the judge granted mitigated circumstances, since the man's wife had returned. Despite numerous transgressions between 1952 and 1957, landscaper Franz S. had his sentence reduced from six weeks in jail to probation because the court believed he had learned from his mistakes and would not fall into the system again. See case against Franz S., 275 Ds 58/57, Amtsgericht Tiergarten, March 30, 1957.

68 Internist Dr. Kilian (1957) published the results of his research on the reintegration of returning soldiers into family life. He found that between 10 and 20 percent of the soldiers had homosexual encounters while in captivity. For a similar mention of homosexual "derailment" among POWs, see (Tschadek, 1957, pp. 76–79). More recently, Biess (1998, pp. 57–82) has uncovered this connection in his research on the reintegration of POWs into East and West German society.

69 The only circumstance in which lenience was rarely granted was in cases where the defendant had prior convictions during the Nazi period. Despite efforts to democratize the court system by removing National Socialist laws, case files suggest that previous convictions incurred during the Nazis' 12-year rule were viewed as damaging to one's defense (*Strafschärfend*), since they demonstrated a pattern of behavior. Even when years had transpired between convictions, those contesting the summary judgment found themselves in the position of accounting for transgressions that occurred under Nazi law (Meinhard, 2000, pp. 287–289).

70 See the statements entered by the municipal social services department of the West Berlin district of Berlin-Tempelhof at the juvenile court proceeding against 18-year-old Peter S., LAB B Rep. 051 Amtsgericht Tiergarten Acc. 1687 Nr. 10685.

71 (Evan, 2014).

72 See the decision by the Merseberg court from August 12, 1947, on the continued use of the Nazi-era Young Offenders Act, in *Neue Justiz* Jg. 2 Nr. 7/8 (July/August 1948). Many contemporaries believed

that a heavy hand was needed in dealing with the rise in crimes committed by the young in the wake of the war.

73 On Fred V., see LAB C Rep 341 Stadtbezirksgericht Mitte, Nr. 4433. On Alfred B., see LAB A Rep 358–02 Generalstaatsanwaltschaft beim Landgericht Berlin 1933–45, Nr. 104046 from 1941.

74 See LAB C Rep 341 Stadtbezirksgericht Mitte, Nr. 4779, in which the youth is examined on several occasions, once to determine if he had the maturity and mental capacity to stand trial and twice after he made multiple suicide attempts while serving his sentence.

75 See LAB Berlin C Rep. 341 Stadtbezirksgericht Mitte, case Nr. 5075 against Karl H. and Gustav W. For more information on the early legal reform movement in the GDR, see Grau (1999).

76 Detective Superintendent Schramm of the Landeskriminalamt Berlin outlined the case of the call boy known only as Esche, who had been charged with the murder of one of his johns in 1957. Esche surfaced in the police records examined for this project around the same period as the murder, when he was naming the many johns he had been with and cooperating with the police by taking them to the johns' apartments (Schramm, 1957, p. 90).

77 See von Rönn (1998) for a larger discussion of youth corruptibility in the Nazi era.

References

Ausstellung des Schwulen Museums in der Akademie der Künste. (1996). *Goodbye to Berlin? 100 Jahre Schwulenbewegung.* Berlin: R. Winkel.

Bader, K. (1949). *Soziologie der deutschen Nachkriegskriminalitat.* Tübingen: J.C.B Mohr.

Baumann, J. (1968). *Paragraph 175: Über die Möglichkeit einfache, die nichtjugendgefährdende und nicht öffentliche Homosexualtät unter Erwachsenen straffrei zu lassen* (pp. 42–43). Berlin: Luchterhand.

Bessel, R. (1996). Grenzen des Polizeistaates. Polizei und Gesellschaft in der SBZ und frühen DDR, 1945–1953. In R. Bessel & R. Jessen (Eds.), *Die Grenzen der Diktatur. Staat und Gesellschaft in der DDR.* Göttingen: Vandenhoeck und Ruprecht.

Biess, F. (1998). Survivors of totalitarianism: Returning POWs and the reconstruction of masculine citizenship in West Germany, 1945–55. In Hanna Schissler (Ed.), *The miracle years: A cultural history of West Germany, 1949–68* (pp. 57–82). Princeton, NJ: Princeton University Press.

Brandstette. (1951). *StPO mit Nebengesetzen.*

Chauncey, G. (1994). *Gay New York: Gender, urban culture, and the making of the gay male world.* New York: Basic Books.

Dinges, M. (1998). *Hausväter, Priester, Kastraten: Zur Konstruktion von Männlichkeit in Spätmittelalter und früher Neuzeit.* Göttingen: Vandenhoeck & Ruprecht.

Dobler, J. (1992). *Eldorado: Homosexuelle Frauen und Männer in Berlin 1850–1950. Geschichte, Alltag und Kultur.* Berlin: Verein der Freunde eines schwulen Museums Berlin.

Dobler, J. (1996). *Polizei. Vom Zwangsverhdltnis zur Zweckehe?* Berlin: Metropol Verlag.

Dworek, G. (1990). 'Für Freiheit und Recht': Justiz, Sexualwissenschaft und schwule Emanzipation 1871–1896. In *Die Geschichte des §175: Strafrechtgegen Homosexuelle* (pp. 42–61). (Freunde eines schwulen Museum in Berlin e.V in Zusammenarbeit mit Emanzipation e.V Frankfurt am Main).

Eghigian, G. (2002). The psychologization of the socialist self: East German forensic psychology and its deviants, 1945–1975. unpublished manuscript.

Eissler, W. U. (1990). *Arbeiterparteien und Homosexuellenfrage.* Berlin: Verlag Rosa Winkel.

Evans, J. V. (2014). Repressive rehabilitation: Crime morality and delinquency in Berlin-Brandenburg, 1945–58. In Richard Wetzell (Ed.), *Crime and criminal justice in modern Germany, 1870–1960.* New York: Berghahn.

Exner, F. (1949). *Kriminologie.* Berlin: Springer.

Fehrenbach, H. (1995). *Cinema in democratizing Germany: National identity after Hitler* (pp. 174–177). Chapel Hill, NC: Campus Verlag.

Giles, G. J. (1992, Spring). The most unkindliest cut of all. *Journal of Contemporary History, 27,* 41–61.

Giles, G. J. (2002, January–April). The denial of homosexuality: Same-sex incidents in Himmler's SS and police. *Journal of the History of Sexuality, 11*(1–2), 256–290.

Gleixner, U. (1994). *"Das Mensch" und "Der Kerl." Die Konstruktion von Geschlecht in Unzuchtsverfahren der frühen Neuzeit (1700–1760)*. New York: Fischer Taschenbuch Verlag.

Gödecke, P. (in progress). Strafrechtswissenschaft und Strafrechtsreform in der Bundesrepublik Deutschland 1945 bis 1969 (PhD dissertation). Universität Bielefeld, Bielefeld.

Goedde, P. (1999, Winter). From villains to victims: Fraternization and the feminization of Germany, 1945–47. *Diplomatic History, 23*, 17.

Grau, G. (1993). *Homosexualität in der NS-Zeit*. Frankfurt am Main: Fischer Taschenbuch Verlag.

Grau, G. (1996). Im Auftrag der Partei: Versuch einer Reform der strafrechtlichen Bestimmungen zur Homosexualität in der DDR 1952. *Zeitschrift für Sexualforschung, 9*, 109–129.

Grau, G. (1999). Return of the past: The policy of the SED and the laws against homosexuality in Eastern Germany between 1946 and 1968. *Journal of Homosexuality, 37*, 1–21.

Grossmann, A. (1995, Spring). A question of silence: The rape of German women by occupation soldiers. *October, 72*, 43–65.

Gumbert, H. (forthcoming). Murder and other cross-border capers: Televisual representation and ideological boundaries in East German crime thrillers. In Rüdiger Steinmetz (Ed.), *Changing identities in film and television of Eastern Europe*.

Hancock. (1998). 'Only the real, the true, the masculine held its value': Ernst Röhm, masculinity, and male homosexuality. *Journal of the History of Sexuality, 8*, 616–641.

Healey, D. (2001). *Homosexual desire in revolutionary Russia: The regulation of sexual and gender dissent*. Chicago: Univeristy of Chicago Press.

Heineman, E. D. (1996, April). The hour of the woman: Memories of Germany's 'crisis years' and West German national identity. *American Historical Review, 101*, 354–396.

Heineman, E. D. (1999). *What difference does a husband make? Women and marital status in Nazi and postwar Germany*. Berkeley: Univeristy of California Press.

Hekma, G. (1999). Same-sex relations among men in Europe, 1700–1990. In Franz Eder, Lesley Hall, & Gert Hekma (Eds.), *Sexual cultures in Europe, vol. 2: Themes in sexuality*. (pp. 79–103). Manchester: Manchester Univeristy Press.

Heuer, U.-J. (1995). *Die Rechtsprechung der DDR, Anspruch und Wirklichkeit*. Baden: Nomos Verlagsgesellschaft.

Himmler, H. (1974). The question of homosexuality (speech, February 18, 1937). In B. F. Smith (Ed.), *Geheimreden 1933–1945*. (pp. 433–442). Frankfurt: Propyluen Verlag.

Höhn, M. (1993, Winter). Frau im Haus, Girl im Spiegel: Discourse on women in the interregnum period of 1945–1949 and the question of German identity. *Central European History, 26*, 57–91.

Hoven, H. (1991). *Der unaufhaltsame Selbstmord des Botho Laserstein: Ein deutscher Lebenslauf*. Frankfurt am Main: Luchterhand Literaturverlag.

Hull, I. V. (1996). *Sexuality, state, and civil society in Germany, 1700–1815*. Ithaca, NY: Cornell Univeristy Press.

Hutter, J. (1990). §175 RStGB im zweiten deutschen Reich 1890–1919. In *Die Geschichte des §175: Strafrecht gegen Homosexuelle* (pp. 62–80) (Freunde eines schwulen Museum in Berlin e.V in Zusammenarbeit mit Emanzipation e.V Frankfurt am Main).

Jellonnek, B. (1990). *Homosexuelle unter dem Hakenkreuz. Die Verfolgung der Homosexuellen im dritten Reich*. Paderborn: Ferdinand Schöningh.

Jorns, G. (1995). *Der Jugend werkhof im Jugendhilfesystem der DDR*. Göttingen: Cuvillier.

Kammerge richt Berlin. (1950). Urteil v. 21.2.1950. *Neue Justiz, 4*, 129.

Kilian, H. (1957). Das Wiedereinleben des Heimkehrers in Familie, Ehe und Beruf. *Beiträge zur Sexualforschung, 11*, 32–34.

Klimmer, R. (1949, November). Uber das Wesen der Homosexualität in Psychiatrie, Neurologie und Medizinische Psychologie. *Zeitschrift für Forschung und Praxis, 11*, 341–348.

Kramp, M., & Sölle, M. (2000). §175—Restauration und Reform in der Bundesrepublik. In Kristof Balser, Mario Kramp, Jürgen Müller, & Joanna Gotzmann (Eds.), *"Himmel und Hölle": Das Leben der Kölner Homosexuellen 1945–69*. Cologne: Emons.

Kroger, P. (1957). *Entwicklungsstudien der Bestrafung der widernaturlichen Unzucht und kritische Studie zur Berechtigung der §§175, 175a, 175b de lege ferenda* (Doctor of law dissertation). Freie Universität Berlin, Berlin.

Laserstein, B. (n.d.a). *Angeklagte steh auf!*

Laserstein, B. (n.d.b). *Strichjunge Karl. Bin kriminalistischer Tatsachenbericht.*

Lombroso, C., & Ferrero, G. (1896). *La Femme criminelle et la prostituée.* Paris.

Mackay, J. H. (1985). *The Hustler.* Boston: Aluson Publications.

Mackay, J. H. (reprint, 1999). *Der Puppenjunge.* Berlin: Saggita.

Maynard, S. (1994). Through a hole in the lavatory wall: Homosexual subcultures, police surveillance, and the dialectics of discovery, Toronto, 1890–1930. *Journal of the History of Sexuality, 5,* 207–242.

Maynard, S. (1997). 'Horrible temptations': Sex, men, and working-class youth in urban Ontario, 1890–1935. *Canadian Historical Review, 6,* 99–124.

McLaren, A. (2002). *Sexual blackmail: A modern history.* Cambridge, MA: Harvard Univeristy Press.

Meinhard, U. (2000). 'Auch nach heutiger Rechtsauffassung keine Bedenken.' Der lange Weg durch die Instanzen, 1943–1961. In Andreas Pretzel & Gabriele Rossbach (Eds.), *"Wegen der zu erwartenden hohen Strafe . . .": Homosexuellenverfolgung in Berlin, 1933–1945* (pp. 287–289). Berlin: Selbstverlag.

Merkel, I. (1994). Leitbilder und Lebenswesen von Frauen in der DDR. In Hartmut Kaelble, Jürgen Kocka, & Hartmut Zwahr (Eds.), *Sozialgeschichte der DDR* (pp. 359–382). Stuttgart: Klett - Cotta.

Micheler, S. (2002, January–April). Homophobic propaganda and the denunciation of same-sex-desiring men under national socialism. *Journal of the History of Sexuality, 11*(1–2), 125.

Moeller, R. (1995). The homosexual man is a 'man,' the homosexual woman is a 'woman': Sex, society, and the law in postwar West Germany. In R. G. Moeller (Ed.), *West Germany under construction.* Ann Arbor, MI: Univeristy of Michigan Press.

Moeller, R. (1998). The last soldiers of the 'Great War' and tales of family reunions in the Federal Republic of Germany. *Signs: Journal of Women in Culture and Society, 24*(1), 129–145.

Mort, F. (1999, Spring). Mapping sexual London: The Wolfenden committee on homosexual offences and prostitution, 1954–57. *New Formations, 37,* 92–113.

Mosse, G. (1985). *Nationalism and sexuality.* New York: Howard Fertig.

Oosterhuis, H. (1991). Male bonding and homosexuality in Nazi Germany. *Journal of Homosexuality, 22*(1), 242–262.

Oosterhuis, H. (1997, Spring). Medicine, male bonding, and homosexuality in Nazi Germany. *Journal of Contemporary History,* 187–205.

Oosterhuis, H. (1999). Male bonding and homosexuality in Nazi Germany. *Journal of Homosexuality, 22,* 242–262.

Pretzel, A. (2002). *NS-Opfer unter Vorbehalt: Homosexuelle Männer in Berlin nach 1945.* Münster; Verlag Münster.

Reichsgesetzblatt (RGBl) (1935). pt. 1, 839–841.

Reinhardt, R. (1954). Zur gleichgeschlechtlichen männlichen Prostitution. In *Beiträge zur Sexualforschung.* Stuttgart: Ferdinand Enke.

Rode, C. (1996). *Kriminologie in der DDR. Kriminalitätsursachenforschung zwischen Empiric und Ideologie.* Freiburg im Breslau: Max-Planck-Institut für Ausländisches und Internationales Strafrecht.

Rydstrom, J. (2000). 'Sodomitical sins are threefold': Typologies of bestiality, masturbation, and homosexuality in Sweden, 1880–1950. *Journal of the History of Sexuality, 9,* 240–276.

Schiefelbein, D. (1992). Wiederbeginn der juristischen Verfolgung homosexueller Männer in der Bundesrepublik Deutschland. Die Homosexuellen-Prozesse in Frankfurt am Main 1950/51. *Zeitschrift für Sexualforschung, 5,* 59–73.

Schön, M. (2000). Einsatz für die Sittlichkeit: Kölner Polizei und Homosexuelle. In Kristof Balser, Mario Kramp, Jürgen Müller, & Joanna Gotzmann (Eds.), *"Himmel und Hölle": Das Leben der Kölner Homosexuellen 1945–69* (pp. 155–168). Cologne: *Himmel und Hölle.*

Schramm, E. (1957). Das Strichjungenunwesen. In *Sittlichkeitsdelikte* (p. 90). Wiesbaden: Arbeitstagung im Bundeskriminalamt.

Seelig, E. (1950). *Lehrbuch der Kriminologie: Muller Verlag.*

Sparing, F. (1997). *". . . wegen Vergehen nach §175 verhaftet." Die Verfolgung der Düsseldorfer Homosexuellen während des Nationalsozialismus.* Mahn- und Gedenkstätte Düsseldorf: Arno Press.

Steakley, J. D. (1995/1975). *The homosexual emancipation movement in Germany.* New York: VS Verlag.

Stein, M. (2000). *City of sisterly and brotherly loves: Gay and lesbian Philadelphia, 1945–72.* Chicago: Univeristy of Chicago Press.

Stümke, H.-G. (1989). *Homosexuelle in Deutschland: Eine politische Geschichte.* Munich: Back.

Stümke, H.-G., & Finkler, R. (1981). *Rosa Winkel, rosa listen.* Hamburg: Rowohlt.

Szobar, P. (2002, January–April). Telling sexual stories in the Nazi courts of law: Race defilement in Germany, 1933 to 1945. *Journal of the History of Sexuality, 11*(1–2), 131–163.

Tamagne, F. (2000). *Histoire de l'homosexualité en Europe.* Paris: Seuil.

Thurnwald, H. (1948). *Gegenwartsprobleme Berliner Familien: Eine soziologische Untersuchung an 498 Familien.* Berlin: Weidmann.

Tröger, A. (1986). Between rape and prostitution: Survival strategies and possibilities of liberation of Berlin women in 1945–1948. In Judith Friedlander, Alice Kessler-Harris, & Carrol Smith-Rosenberg (Eds.), *Women in culture and politics: A century of change.* Bloomington: Indiana University Press.

Tschadek, O. (1957). Die Aufgabe des Staates gegenüber dem Heimkehrer. *Beiträge zur Sexualforschung, 11,* 76–79.

von Rönn, P. (1998). Politische und psychiatrische HomosexualitätsKonstruktionen im NS-Staat. *Zeitschrift für Sexualforschung, 11,* 220–260.

Wetzell, R. (2000). *Inventing the criminal: A history of German criminology, 1880–1945.* Chapel Hill, NC: University of North Carolina Press.

Whisnant, C. (2001). *Hamburg's gay scene in the era of family politics, 1945–69* (PhD dissertation). University of Texas at Austin, Austin.

Wiethold, F. (1952). Kriminalbiologische Behandlung von Sittlichkeitsverbrechern. *Beiträge zur Sexualforschung* 2. Heft, Methoden der Behandlung sexueller Störungen. Vorträge gehalten auf dem 2. Kongress der deutschen Gesellschaft für Sexualforschung in Konigstein.

Willoughby, J. (1998, January). The sexual behavior of American GIs during the early years of the occupation of Germany. *Journal of Military History, 62,* 156.

Historical documents and court cases

Landesarchiv Berlin (hereafter referred to as LAB) B Rep 013 Senatverwaltung für Jugend und Familie, Acc. 1052, Nr. 39. Case number (507) Jug Kms 65/51 and 2 Ju Kms 8/51.

Merseberg court August 12, 1947, decision on Young Offenders Act. In *Neue Justiz* Jg. 2 Nr. 7/8 (July/August 1948)

Peter S., LAB B Rep. 051 Amtsgericht Tiergarten Acc. 1687 Nr. 10685.

Alfred B, LAB A Rep 358–02 Generalstaatsanwaltschaft beim Landgericht Berlin 1933–45, Nr. 104046 from 1941.

Fred V, LAB C Rep 341 Stadtbezirksgericht Mitte, Nr. 4433.

LAB Berlin C Rep. 341 Stadtbezirksgericht Mitte, case Nr. 5075 against Karl H. and Gustav W

LAB Berlin C Rep. 341 Stadtbezirksgericht Mitte, case Nr. 5075 against Karl H. and Gustav W.

LAB C Rep 341 Stadtbezirksgericht Mitte, Nr. 4779.

LAB B Rep. 240 Erlebnisberichte aus der Berliner Bevölkerung über die Zeit des 2. Weltkrieges und danach, Acc. 2651, Nrs. 1–6.

LAB C Rep 303/9 Polizeipräsident in Berlin, Nr. 248 Tatigkeitsbuch MII/I—Aussendienst—, May 8, 1948—April 23, 1949.

Hans. L., LAB C Rep 341 Stadtbezirksgericht Mitte, Nr. 4743, 18 Ju Js 585.50–99 Ds 100

LAB C Rep 341 Stadtbezirksgericht Mitte, Nr. 4433, case 98 Ds 34/50, June 23, 1950.

LAB C Rep 303/9 Polizeipräsident in Berlin, Nr. 248 Tatigkeitsbuch MII/1—Aussendienst—, May 8, 1948—April 23, 1949, 60.

Günter S. in LAB C Rep 341 Stadtbezirksgericht Mitte, Nr. 5287, court case 99 DLs 6/50, January 28, 1950.

See LAB C Rep 341 Stadtbezirksgericht Mitte, Nr. 4433, case number 98 Ds 34/50, June 23, 1950.

See LAB C Rep 341 Stadtbezirksgericht Mitte, Nr. 4433, case number 98 Ds 34/50, June 23, 1950.

Karl-Heinz A., 274 Ds 100/55, Amtsgericht Tiergarten, June 1, 1955.

Franz S., 275 Ds 58/57, Amtsgericht Tiergarten, March 30, 1957.

Horst K., 277 Cs 399/56, Amtsgericht Tiergarten, December 22, 1956.

Peter Z., 276 Cs 111/57, Amtsgericht Tiergarten, May 15, 1956, and (534) 66 ns 56.57 (196.57) *Landgericht Berlin kleine Strafkammer* dated March 7, 1958.

1947 court case LAB B Rep 051 Amtsgericht Tiergarten

LAB C Rep 303/9 Polizeipräsident in Berlin 1945–48, Nr. 259.

Raid report (1946). Bunker Schlesischer Bahnhof, November 2. LAB C Rep 303/9 Polizeipräsident in Berlin 1945–48, Nr. 259, 310.

Dr. Eugene E. Schwarz of the Public Health Office of the Office of Military Government Berlin Sector (OMGBS) to the *Bürgermeister* of Berlin dated July 9, 1947 LAB B Rep 210 Bezirksamt Zehlendorf, Amerikanische Militär, Tätigkeitberichte (Fluchtlinge), 1945–50, Acc. 840, Nr. 88.

LAB C Rep 303/9 Ministerium des Inneren, Polizeipräsident in Berlin 1945–48, Nr. 249 Weibliche Kriminalpolizei, 6–12.

LAB C Rep 303/9 Polizeipräsident in Berlin 1945–48, Nr. 243 Abteilung V. Meldungen und Berichte.

See also the "Survey of Juvenile Delinquency in Berlin" from the Office of the Military Government of the U.S. Sector (OMGUS), Berlin Sector, dated August—October 1946. United States National Archives and Records Administration (NARA), College Park, Maryland, RG 260 OMGUS Berlin Sector, Public Welfare Branch, box 192.

NARA, RG 466 U.S. High Commissioner for Germany (HICOG), Berlin Element, Public Safety Division, Classified Subject Files 1946–51, Survey Report of the Public Safety Branch USCOB, circa 1950.

Befehl des Militärkommandanten der Stadt Berlin, BArch DO 1 5.0 Ministerium des Inneren, Hauptabteilung Kriminalpolizei, Nr. 18, 99.

Amstblatt der Militärregierung Deutschland, 1945.

LAB C Rep 303/9 Polizeipräsident in Berlin, Nr. 248 Tatigkeitsbuch MII/I— Aussendienst—, May 8, 1948—April 23, 1949, 26.

LAB A Rep 358–02 Generalstaatsanwaltschaft beim Landgericht Berlin 1933–45.

LAB C Rep 303/9 Polizeipräsident in Berlin 1945–48, Nr. 246 Statistiken der Kriminalpolizei 1945–48.

LAB C Rep 303/9 Polizeipräsident in Berlin, Nr. 248 Tätigkeitsbuch MII/I—Aussendienst—, May 8, 1948—April 23, 1949, 60.

Thüringisches Staatsarchiv Gotha Strafgefängnis Eisenach (1933–51), Nr. 237.

West Berlin Youth Services (1951) Berlin-Schöneberg year-end report submitted to the Protestant mission. Archiv Diakonisches Werk (ADW), CentralAusschuß für die innere Mission der deutschen evangelischen Kirche, Geschäftsstelle Bethel, CA 551.

3

"Kept men" in silent gay cinema
Between romanticism and didacticism

Andrew Grossman

In reviewing the history of queer cinema—and especially gay-themed cinema—one is immediately struck by the disproportionate number of films focusing on sex work. The countless gay films that plumb the often gloomy plights of male prostitutes, hustlers, and call boys might betray a failure of imagination among queer filmmakers, who repeatedly position the marginalized sex worker as a romantic outlaw or disaffected antihero. This generalization is not meant to oversimplify the matter: by embracing a figure typically suffused with fatalism, queer filmmakers have responded to a history—cinematic and otherwise—that pathologized homosexuality and marked the drifter not only as deviant but also as an enemy of bourgeois stability. In films such as *Midnight Cowboy* (1969) or *Fortune and Men's Eyes* (1971), Hollywood identified queer hustling and sexual servitude with neurotic deviance and pathology. Subverting that history, while manifesting the nihilism of the AIDS crisis, films in the New Queer Cinema genre of the early 1990s tended to darkly romanticize an assortment of hustlers, drifters, and hirable street punks. No longer the pathological type propagated by mainstream cinema, the hustler was now a defiant outlaw suffused with an aura of desire; Gregg Araki's *The Living End* (1992) is an archetypal low-budget example. The hustler of post–New Queer Cinema films undermines the ideals of monogamy and stability that attend the coming-out narratives that have dominated commercial gay cinema for the past two decades or so. After their tribulations, the uncloseted youths of such middlebrow movies—*Love, Simon* (2018), for instance—will presumably graduate into monogamous relationships and respectable careers unknown to the sex worker.

Usually the younger partner in intergenerational relationships, the cinematic hustler character seems to invoke the ghost of an ancient theme. In the intergenerational eros associated with sex work, we might see a modern reflection (or allegory) of the Platonic ideals of pedagogy and ephebophilia (a sexual attraction to postpubescent adolescents). Yet this notion is only an appearance or pretense. Much as in the Hollywood coming-out narrative queer people are folded into the mainstream, the Platonic ephebe would eventually become a privileged—and married—Athenian citizen. But the modern prostitute, more or less an outlaw, finds himself excluded from legitimate social networks. A deviant doomed to sociological or psychological analysis, he signifies a failure of capitalist masculinity.

Philosophically, there is a certain irony in deeming the male prostitute a capitalist failure. Within the ideology of self-made entrepreneurialism, prostitutes (regardless of gender) could well be ideal models, for they grow an enterprise from their own selfhood. Beyond the obvious legal concerns, where prostitutes "fail" is not in the selling of their body per se—for we all rent our bodies for some type of labor—but in their inability to commodify the bodily enterprise into a larger corporation. The prostitute, unlike the "legitimate" entrepreneur, is not technologized or bureaucratized. The prostitute possesses only what biology has bequeathed him and is seen as lacking the aptitude or ambition to expand on or transcend that biology.[1]

Common terms like *hustler* or *trade* emphasize the male sex worker's perceived economic pettiness while adding a gloss of lingering homophobia. Such terms are intended as cool, desexualized euphemisms—a hustler might just as well be hustling drugs or black-market goods instead of his tabooed flesh. In this amoral (not immoral) formulation, the hustler sells himself arbitrarily or only when he is unable to trade other goods. The fact that *hustle* (whether a noun or verb) is more or less interchangeable with *swindle* suggests that the male prostitute would rather think of himself as a thief than a whore, though one must wonder what exactly he is supposed to be stealing. Whereas the gangster parodies venture capitalism with his ruthless violence, the hustler sullies it with his buyable passivity. Excluded from socioeconomic networks, the upwardly *immobile* hustler invokes the class analysis proposed by David Matza: If "ambition contains within itself the seed of institutional frustration . . . the latent feature of ambition that will yield a reversal and mock its virtue is the reality of class barriers and restrictions on social mobility" (Matza, 1969, p. 77). Of course, a few slickly produced films, such as Paul Schrader's *American Gigolo* (1980) or Hong Kong director Yonfan's *Bishonen* (1998), glamorize the lives of hustlers who harbor upwardly mobile ambitions, but these films are little more than wish-fulfillment fantasies.

Certain currents in humanistic psychology also share the blame for labeling hustlers as failures, particularly within the bounds of a capitalistic society. Insofar as mainstream (American) psychology has connected self-actualization with productivity and industry, the drifter's aimlessness and profligacy seem neurotic, if not nihilistic. Abraham Maslow's hierarchical (and indeed bourgeois) pyramid often has been criticized, but its devaluation of sexual activity lingers. Even many progressives who support legalizing prostitution might still see sex not as a creative activity to cultivate but as a basic animal or social need to fulfill.[2] Altruists and liberals seldom see prostituted pleasures as a mass social benefit or as a means to sensually enrich everyday lives. But in a repressed society, the mental and sexual health of many citizens surely could be enhanced by a skilled practitioner of the erotic arts. Though sexology is 150 years old and queer theory has now entered the mainstream, the realm of sexual *practice* remains a field for which there is no legitimate pedagogy, whether amateur or academic, public or private, paid or free.

If we extend the ideas of Herbert Marcuse, the delegitimization of prostitution is only one part of a total plan to subordinate individual sexual expression to state and corporate interests. The conservative mind sees the inwardly directed, time-consuming search for personal erotic gratification as a luxury at odds with the strict schedule of postindustrial commerce. Those who would legalize prostitution would not merely strike a blow for libertarianism but would also reclaim sexual transactions as personally directed quests rather than procreative enterprises sponsored by the state. But sanguine or "artistic" conceptions of sex work inevitably collide with the demands of the capitalist system in which prostitutes operate. Even an autonomous prostitute must compete with cohorts for select clientele. Regardless of the gratifications an expert prostitute might provide, he winds up reflecting capitalist conventions with his hourly rates, stratified fee schedules, and public offerings. The sense of failure built into sex work therefore has more to do with "work" than with "sex." Rather than rescuing clients from the reality principle or puritan banality, sex work becomes just another supply-and-demand transaction.

Burdened with this built-in sense of bankruptcy, the hustler is something of a negative myth in cinema, a romantic figure of unattainable youth and beauty, destined for melancholy. Precociously world-weary and street-smart, he doesn't require (or operates beyond) the adolescent enlightenment central to the bildungsroman, the narrative of youthful self-discovery and moral development. One might even say that the standard street-hustler narrative is a kind of anti-bildungsroman, as it eschews the coming-of-age or coming-out story and sets forth premature disillusionment as its primary value. Aesthetically, hustler movies tend to indulge in sanctimonious realism—consider Gus Van Sant's *My Own Private Idaho* (1991), Scott Silver's *Johns* (1996), Miguel Arteta's *Star Maps* (1997), or Michael Cuesta's *L.I.E.* (1997).[3] Often the realism is glossed with a sense of sadomasochistic exploitation, as the hustler's frail body is framed as a naked object of desire—consider Lino Brocka's *Macho Dancer* (1988), Jochen Hick's *Via Appia* (1989), Carsten Sønder's *Pretty Boy* (1993), and Wiktor Grodecki's *Not Angels but Angels* (1994), *Body Without Soul* (1996), and *Mandragora* (1997). All of these movies present adolescent sex workers as modern Narcissuses doomed as much by their beauty as by cruel urban economies.

Some documentaries, such as Fenton Bailey and Randy Barbato's *101 Rent Boys* (2000), also exemplify this trend. Requiring nudity of most of their participants, the filmmakers interview young hustlers—some of them uneducated runaways—in sleazy motel rooms, where they display their wares and regret their life choices. The film inspires both pity and desire, especially when one teenage runaway wishes (probably futilely) for an older man who would rescue him. Granted, other films take a less duplicitous view, such as Eloy de la Iglesias's *Colegas* (1982) or Nick Deocampo's documentary *Oliver* (1983), which more directly critique the entrenched economic inequalities that lead poor men into prostitution. Even these films, however, do not hesitate to objectify the economically wounded male body. Today, when queer film festivals demand sex and nudity in nearly every film, the truly radical sex-work film might shun naked skin altogether.

Picturizing hustlers as tragic figures forestalls attempts at satire or burlesque.[4] Generally, the hustler is trapped within the realist mode to which most contemporary filmmakers adhere. We should pause to distinguish this contemporary realism from the kind of underground realism that—before the rise of film schools and screenwriting courses—freely incorporated elements of camp and absurd humor. When Andy Warhol and Chuck Wein's *My Hustler* (1965) and Paul Morrissey's *Flesh* (1968), *Trash* (1970), and *Heat* (1972) objectified the male body, the joke was at the expense of capitalism itself, not the hustler. The beautiful hipster bodies of Warhol's Factory—especially that of Joe Dallesandro—were spectacular rather than strictly commercial. In Morrissey's *Flesh* trilogy, Dallesandro freely offers his oft-naked body as an object of contemplation for ambisexual men and women. Unambitious and unselfconscious, he is not a failed exponent of capitalism but rather a free (and admittedly vapid) spirit for whom money means little. Warhol and Morrissey's vagabonds embrace rather than struggle against their marginality, satirizing the upward mobility for which the ambitious hustler strives but rarely achieves. If Dallesandro worries about paying the rent in *Trash* (1970), it is a source of low comedy, not the stuff of melodrama. Though superficially beautiful, he is (in *Trash*) also riddled with drugs, pimples, and pubic lice—a travesty of the seductive gigolo.

This sort of hipster comedy, a perverse offshoot of neorealism, could flourish only when assimilation was not an option. The underground queer cinema of the 1960s and 1970s necessarily posited the rebel as its hero, as did the New Queer Cinema of the late 1980s and 1990s. But our changing political landscapes have transformed popular aesthetics. The "homonormative" tendencies of twenty-first-century LGBTQ cinema obviously take a more accommodating path, avoiding leftist rebellion and embracing the now-realistic possibilities of legal marriage, upward mobility, and overall legitimation. Certainly, auteurs outside the realist tradition can shun gritty hustler tragedies and stories of assimilation alike. In various satirical and parodic films by John Waters, Rosa von Praunheim, and Bruce LaBruce, one finds liberated, revolutionary hustlers who proudly embrace their deviance and antiestablishment credentials. For our discussion, however, we will put aside idiosyncratic satire and farce and focus on the dominant mode of realism.

This realism is usually tragic or romantic, not revolutionary or contentious. When it comes to male sex work, mainstream cinema offers few broadsides or polemics for social reform—with the notable exception of *Anders als die Andern* (1919), discussed later in the chapter. For female sex work, long informed by radical feminism, the case has been somewhat different. In Chantal Akerman's feminist landmark *Jeanne Dielman, 23, quai du Commerce, 1080 Bruxelles* (1975), a widow goes about her daily chores—peeling potatoes, emptying the trash, wrapping a package— while making time to entertain middle-aged male clients. Over three unhurried hours, the camera lingers objectively on her chores in real time, affording them the same banal detail as her prostitution, which provides only one brief orgasm (after which she inexplicably stabs her client to death). Though the film is notoriously pedantic and excruciating, Akerman nonetheless demystifies sex work while also blurring the distinctions between erotic and noncerotic forms of bodily labor.[5] Vicky Funari and Julia Query's *Live Nude Girls Unite!* (2000) offers a more polemical example. This autobiographical, partly satirical documentary follows a female sex worker and queer-theory graduate student who fight to unionize female strippers and lesbian sex workers. One is hard pressed to find similar legitimation of male sex work, which still carries the intersecting stigmas of AIDS, petty criminality, and masculine "failure."[6] Because the passivity associated with male sex work is deemed a betrayal of gendered agency, male prostitutes have few apologists, let alone crusaders.[7]

A primitive romanticism: Mauritz Stiller's *Vingarne*

In the general trends outlined so far, I have emphasized cinema's "entrepreneurially" tragic model of male sex work. In reality, there are certainly other, more deeply psychological models to pursue, but commercial cinema, preoccupied with surfaces, generally refuses its hustlers moments of introspection or revolutionary awakening. Bleak cinematic realism usually dooms the generic hustler to tragedy or, at best, meager attempts at continued survival. Even if the self-abnegating prostitute of *Midnight Cowboy* has been replaced by New Queer hipsters (as in the films of Gregg Araki or Larry Clark), the hustler's trade remains a bankrupt form of capitalism, a doomed attempt to move up a nonexistent economic ladder. But I have also mentioned an older theme, the Platonic or ephebic relationship. It is the Platonic model, in fact, that informs cinema's earliest gay films—and not coincidentally because silent filmmaking overlapped with Edwardian notions of pederastic homosexuality. Rooted in the ethos of ancient Greece, the pederastic relationship involves an older partner who teachers and mentors (rather than exploits) a single youth until he arrives at the age of maturity.[8] Putting aside the obvious cultural differences between ancient and contemporary constructs of homosexuality, such relationships may be *partly* analogous to the modern notion of a "kept man." If the public sex worker is a desperate capitalist lacking an economic ladder to climb, the kept man attaches himself to a single patron whose elite education, class status, and social network can be mined and cultivated.

While the kept man or trophy-boy relationship superficially harkens back to Greek models, the analogy has clear limitations. The ephebic or pederastic relationship, normative among elite Athenians, was not a case of social deviance but rather a preparatory stage for citizenship.

Contrarily, the modern kept man represents (in a capitalist society) a deviation from the economic independence expected of adult citizens. Biologically and intellectually, he will outgrow his "kept" or student role, yet he remains dependent economically and perhaps sexually. Stuck in a stage of arrested development, the kept man undergoes an identity crisis, realizing that he has outgrown his adolescence, but does not have the autonomous future expected of adults (a narrative referred to earlier as the anti-bildungsroman).

This identity crisis was a hallmark of even the earliest queer films. Cinema's first gay films, in fact, directly engage the paradoxes of the Platonic model, even if they wind up reiterating a tragic aesthetic comparable to that of contemporary hustler films. Mauritz Stiller's *Vingarne* (*Wings*, 1916) and Carl Theodor Dreyer's *Michael* (1924), both adapted from the 1902 novel *Mikhael* by Dutch novelist Herman Bang (1857–1912), recount the tragedy of a middle-aged artist infatuated with his prized male model (and adopted son). *Mikhael* is very much steeped in themes typical of German Romanticism: the cult of the artistic genius, an emphasis on emotionalism over reason, a Gothic atmosphere, and a predilection for angst-ridden love. Bang's "kept man" tragedy is analogous to the hustler tragedies but more historically nuanced. If the hustler represents a failure of democratic entrepreneurship, Bang's rather Edwardian narrative occurs within a rigid class structure (the exclusive world of "old money") that prevents outsiders and upstarts from moving up the ladder. In between the Bang adaptations appeared Richard Oswald and Magnus Hirschfeld's better-known *Anders als die Andern* (*Different from the Others*, 1919). A didactic, rather artless plea for the decriminalization of same-sex relationships, *Anders* details an intergenerational Platonic relationship that, though not characterized by erotic work per se, is framed as such by the film's plotline.

The kept men of these early-twentieth-century narratives are admittedly not sex workers in the common sense of the term. One would be right to point out numerous superficial differences. Kept men engage in extended rather than fleeting relationships, they usually (but not necessarily) forge deeper affections for the older patron, and they expect long-term economic support rather than discrete (and discreet) cash payments. There are also clear class differences that should not be trivialized. Although he is not economically self-sufficient, the kept man (as we usually imagine him) is educated and bourgeois, if also wayward and a black sheep of his family. Constituting a more amorphous category, sex workers might come from a variety of class positions, from transient men struggling to survive, to lower-class men who might turn to sex work during difficult economic times, to enlightened individuals who embrace sex work as part of a socially progressive or liberating profession. Given this broad understanding of sex work, the kept man hardly seems to belong on the liberatory end of the spectrum—indeed, the degrading term kept clearly implies long-term ownership. The street hustler may not be economically free, but neither is the kept man, who forms a more deeply parasitic relationship with a single host. But even parasites eventually succumb to atrophy and depreciation. Once the kept man ages out of his callow role, he may not differ from a workaday, world-weary prostitute.

Although *Vingarne* and *Michael* cannot be reduced to contemporary notions of quid-pro-quo sexual labor, their stories of kept men engage themes ever present in hustler films: strained intergenerational relationships, tragic conclusions, an older partner longing for idealized youth, and the paradoxical position of the younger partner, who is economically disenfranchised yet erotically empowered. As narratives focused on artists and their creations, *Vingarne* and *Michael* add an overtly aesthetic element to the mix, focusing on the ways in which representational art—specifically, life-size sculptures of the kept man—alternately embodies, intermediates, and transcends the erotic relationship. Though obsessed with queer aesthetics, the two films stop far short of claiming erotic work as an artistic, cultivatable pursuit in itself. On the contrary, both

Vingarne and *Michael* idealize the world of (representational) art and mourn the petty jealousy that informs a decidedly nonidealized Platonic relationship.

We would be naive to think that early twentieth-century audiences could ignore or overlook the queer implications of either Bang's source novel or its two adaptations. By the time *Mikhael* was first published in 1902, Bang's homosexuality was as well known in Denmark as that of Oscar Wilde in England. Bang paid a price for his rare openness, and he was frequently targeted by the Danish yellow press. One newspaper reviewer, appalled by *Mikhael*'s homoeroticism, scoffed that the novel's protagonist, Claude Zoret, was "an undisguised homosexualist [*sic*]" (Quoted in Tybjerg, 2018). In 1906, Bang and other cultural elites were connected to a rent-boy scandal, prompting one yellow journalist to publish a shamelessly reactionary (and clumsily phrased) diatribe: "An unclean puff like Herman Bang must be beaten down because he is the worst of them all. Everything which is typical of the depravities and crimes we now watch rising from the depths of the swamp—like poisonous gas bursting up into the air and daylight—can be found in Herman Bang" (Quoted in Tybjerg, 2018).

An early work by Swedish cinema pioneer Mauritz Stiller, *Vingarne*, the first of the two Bang adaptations, was cinema's first feature film with a gay theme. No complete prints are known to exist, which partly explains its absence from older histories of queer cinema. Released in 1916, the film sits within silent film's awkward "transitional" period: feature-length narratives had begun to supplant two-reel shorts, but filmmakers had yet to standardize close-ups, reverse angles, and the elements of montage later introduced by Lev Kuleshov, Erich von Stroheim, Abel Gance, and other auteurs. In analyzing the film's themes of erotic power and desire, the lack of close-ups is especially important. Standard notions of erotic power in cinema have derived disproportionately from film theorist Laura Mulvey's conception of the male gaze, which assumes a heteronormative subjectivity created by the film and imposed on the audience. Numerous theorists have qualified Mulvey's formulation of visual pleasure (1975) by introducing female, feminist, and queer gazes to destabilize the assumption of straightness. In whatever guise, gaze theory tends to focus on the close-ups and leering camera angles that take the gazer's perspective. Gazers are inherently active, and their objects are de facto passive. In the case of *Vingarne*, however, standard gaze theory does us no good. Made in 1916, the film predates the visual grammar that focuses unambiguously on one body or that cuts between tight shots of gazers and their objects.[9]

As a result, *Vingarne* adheres to the stage-bound presentation typical of early silent films, and, as in the theater, characters emote not through highlighted facial tics but with their whole body. Without close-ups to telegraph characters' objects or degrees of desire, *Vingarne* clarifies its erotic design from the outset through a curious framing device unfortunately missing in extant prints. *Vingarne* was considered lost until 1987, when a truncated print about 47 minutes in length was discovered in a Norwegian archive. Though the "torso" of the film was mostly intact, the print was missing the original self-reflexive "framing" story in which director Stiller, playing himself, happens on an idea for a new film after encountering Swedish sculptor Carl Milles's *Wings*, a 1911 stonework that depicts Zeus's abduction of a naked Ganymede. To needlessly complicate matters, a title card then informs viewers that the narrative of the film proper takes its inspiration from the myth of Icarus, not Ganymede. Nevertheless, the mixed mythological metaphor does not detract from *Vingarne*'s theme of narcissistic-cum-tragic youth.

In the lost framing story (which has been re-created in extant prints through production prints), an aspiring actor comes across a want ad: "Young, intelligent man with a prepossessing appearance is sought for a movie production." In the next sequence, we see director Stiller worry about casting the lead role of Michael, an artistic youth who becomes the kept boy of the famous sculptor, Zoret. "Heavens, how can I find a young man who can handle this role?" an intertitle reads—an evasive yet self-conscious admission that the role requires an actor who can handle taboo subject matter. A production still from the missing metannarrative shows Stiller entering an audition room filled with young hopefuls, all depicted as dandyish and stereotypically queer. He chooses an actor slightly more mature than the one seen earlier and instructs him to peruse Bang's source novel, which his screenplay will faithfully follow.

At this point, the preparatory metanarrative segues into the narrative proper. We first see the middle-aged Zoret, a master sculptor in the Rodin mold, dressed in a flowing black cape and flamboyant hat as he walks across a pastoral landscape. A caricatured aesthete, he ponders his planned sculpture of Icarus when he spots Michael, a handsome, kerchiefed youth attempting to woo female passersby. Approaching the young man, Zoret, arms outstretched, proclaims, "But that is my Icarus in flesh and blood." Admiring Michael's talent, the master invites him to visit his Paris home. Cut to four years later, and Zoret has adopted Michael as his son. Their relationship clearly transcends filial devotion, however. We see Zoret's new "son" serving as his model, naked save for a white drapery veiling his nether regions (Figure 3.1). After Zoret's new sculpture of Michael becomes the toast of local elites, a wealthy patroness, Princess Zamikow, asks Zoret to paint her portrait. Once in Zoret's home, the princess becomes entranced by a plaster cast of Michael's nude figure. Meanwhile, Michael becomes enamored of the princess, fondling the robes she has removed for her portrait—much to the consternation of the master's butler, who knows Zoret will see Michael's heterosexual excursions as a betrayal.

Figure 3.1 Vignarne: Michael poses for Zoret.

In a crucial moment emphasized more intently in Dreyer's version, Zoret reaches an impasse while attempting to paint the princess's eyes. When Zoret momentarily steps away from the canvas, Michael enters, takes up the brush, and instinctively touches up the portrait's eyes, improving on the master's work and betraying an affinity for heteronormative beauty. We have already said that *Vingarne* predates the era of the extreme close-up. Through medium-long shots, Stiller makes clear the relationship between Zoret and Michael, and that between Michael and the princess, without intent gazing. In this scene, however, a subtler gaze of sorts is displaced into the eyes of the painting. If later cinema's subsequent conventions of cross-cutting juxtaposed close-ups to signify looks of empowered desire, here a female gaze lies dormant, hiding within the painting and waiting for Michael—rather than a directorial close-up—to actualize and activate it. Eroticism is quite literally aestheticized: as Michael perfects a painted gaze, the work of art accrues a liveliness embodied in the princess's heightened desire to possess Michael. Just as the princess alternately assumes active and passive roles, so Michael represents a juncture of erotic allure and economic dependence. Ultimately, however, Michael is defined more by dependence than by sexual power. When we see Michael and the princess kiss in private, she stands dominantly while he remains seated, his back submissively arched (Figure 3.2). He is as much a kept man for her as he is for Zoret.

As Zoret sinks into depression, Michael and the princess go out on the town, at Zoret's expense. Zoret seeks solace in his journalist friend Switt, who realizes Michael, now a young man, is yearning to free himself from the role of Zoret's "adopted son." "Let the boy go," Switt says in an intertitle. "He won't bring you happiness." Rather obliquely, Zoret responds, "No,

Figure 3.2   Vignarne: Michael adopts a submissive posture.

I will not die without a child," as if attempting to desexualize (and legitimize) his relationship with Michael. Michael himself is still deeply conflicted. In an admittedly crude moment, Stiller visualizes Michael's wracked conscience by superimposing Zoret's visage over a scene in which Michael and the princess kiss. As Zoret's transcendental image surveils Michael's private transgression, the gaze again becomes displaced. Because Zoret's spectral gaze is a vestige of Michael's unconscious guilt, it carries an additional dualism, for here Michael is both active subject (as conjurer of the image) and object. Nevertheless, Michael's nagging guilt does not stop him from imploring Zoret for more money, which Zoret gives begrudgingly—and through a servant, as if to emphasize the transactional nature of Michael's kept status. The princess, meanwhile, has been profligate as well. To pay off her debts, Michael sells the bronze statue in his likeness that Zoret had given him, an act that is rife with irony. In a sense, Michael now sells himself, or at least the aestheticized part of himself that retains its integrity.

Realizing he has lost Michael to the princess, an inconsolable Zoret collapses, suffering a heart attack. Feverishly writing his will, he bequeaths all he owns to Michael, and then he thinks of the plaster copy of Michael's naked likeness that stands in the garden. With arms outstretched, he runs outside to the statue, fondles its stony buttocks, clutches his own chest, and fatally collapses. (The actor playing Zoret, Egil Eide, unfortunately stoops to hammy theatrics, rendering the scene fairly ludicrous.) Michael returns home too late and knows that the master died of a broken heart. In the final scene, Michael rebuffs the princess's attempts to console him, realizing that each of his relationships has sabotaged the other.

The tragedy is offset by a final return to the self-reflexive framing sequence, in which Lars Hanson, the actor who plays Michael, reads reviews of *Vingarne* in the daily paper. Audiences approve of the film, he learns, but are dismayed by the tragic conclusion and wish he had remained with the princess, especially as she is played by Lili Beck, at the time one of Denmark's most popular actresses. Though the modernistic framing device is clearly intended to distance audiences from the film's plotline, one cannot properly call the distancing effect Brechtian, as the framing device has an apologetic rather than a didactic function (and it also predates Brecht's earliest plays by several years).[10] By breaking the fourth wall, however, the film displaces the gaze in an experimental fashion. Rather than characters directing desirous gazes at one other—a phenomenon later normalized by parallel editing and close-ups—the *filmmakers themselves* direct a knowing (and disruptive) gaze toward the audience. Within the primitive film vocabulary of 1916, this was a fairly radical move on Stiller's part, even if the distance mainly provides a self-conscious buffer against then-controversial subject matter.

A didactic interlude: Oswald and Hirschfeld's *Anders als die Andern*

For its time, *Vingarne* was sui generis, and Bang's novel, hardly a masterwork, was notable mainly as a literary novelty. Though remarkable for both its narrative framework and its subject matter, *Vingarne* is obviously apolitical. As a retrograde melodrama bathed in the neo-Hellenistic ethos, its storyline demands fatalism, not social enlightenment. By the mid-1910s, the sexologies of Havelock Ellis and Magnus Hirschfeld had gained some traction in academic quarters, but a commercial movie dealing with the realities of gay sex work remained beyond the pale. Then dominated by the melodrama of Cecil B. DeMille and the naturalism of D. W. Griffith (and indeed Stiller), cinema was aesthetically ill equipped to attempt erotic psychodrama.[11]

In between the two adaptations of Bang's novel, the only example of openly queer desire in film is found in *Anders als die Andern*. This didactic melodrama was the brainchild of Magnus Hirschfeld, who, partnering with the prolific director Richard Oswald, produced a series of so-called enlightenment or social hygiene films (*Sozial-hygienisches Filmwerk*) designed to expunge puritan values from Weimar Germany.[12] Released in 1919, *Anders* can be seen as an extension of the progressive sexology that Hirschfeld advanced through his Institute for Sexual Science (Institut für Sexualwissenschaft), which he launched that same year.[13] After its Berlin premiere on May, 28, 1919, *Anders* met with early praise from more progressive Weimar critics. In a July 19 review published in the film magazine *Film Courier*, Dr. Jürgen Bartsch extolled the film's liberality: "This work towers above the flood of seamy pornography unleashed by the first enlightenment films in its praiseworthy intent, its scientific seriousness, and its altogether tasteful treatment of the awkward subject matter" (Quoted in Kardish, 2010, p. 72).[14] Nevertheless, German authorities deemed Hirschfeld's pro-gay proselytizing too radical and in 1920 banned the film from public exhibition, permitting screenings only for psychologists and medical professionals. When the Nazi youth brigades torched Hirschfeld's institute in 1933, they made a special effort to burn every print of the film. For four decades, *Anders* was assumed lost, until a shortened version—retitled *Gesetze der Liebe* (Laws of love) and prepared by Hirschfeld himself in 1927—was found in a Soviet archive in 1979 (Quoted in Kardish, 2010, p. 72). Extant versions based on this print, running about 50 minutes, use title cards and production stills to fill narrative gaps.

Though it does not directly broach the idea of male prostitution, *Anders* hints at the theme as much as a film could in 1919, and its final plea to legalize same-sex relationships highlights the problems of blackmail often attached to sex work. The film's intergenerational gay relationship (between a middle-aged man and his young pupil) also echoes the themes of subordination, dependence, and guilt that inform the Bang adaptations. As the story begins, violin virtuoso Paul (Conrad Veidt) reads stories of suicide in the daily paper, including those of a judge who mysteriously shot himself and a young man who took his life before his wedding day, "motive unknown." Paul, a closeted gay man, intuits the motive. Before his eyes appears a ghostly march of great men persecuted for their homosexuality, from Tchaikovsky and Wilde to Friedrich II and Ludwig II.[15] Paul is then visited by Kurt, a young, worshipful admirer and prospective student. Worried about his son's apparent queerness and his attraction to Paul, Kurt's businessman father tries to marry him off to a wealthy young widow, Else (in extant prints, Else's lost scenes have been replaced with explanatory titles). When Kurt rejects her, his parents send him to a sexologist (Hirschfeld, playing himself), who both confirms their suspicions and palliates their anxieties. "He is not at all to blame for his orientation," says Hirschfeld. "It is neither a vice nor a crime, indeed, not even an illness, but instead a variation, one of the borderline cases that occur frequently in nature." When the doctor explains to Kurt's parents that he suffers not from homosexuality but from societal prejudice, they reluctantly allow him to continue his "musical" relationship with Paul.

Soon the plot turns away from the Platonic older-younger relationship and centers on a criminal who blackmails Paul to keep his illicit relationship with Kurt a secret. (Germany's antigay Paragraph 175, enacted in 1871, was not amended until the late 1960s and not fully annulled until 1994.) Though Paul at first acquiesces, the blackmailer's ever-increasing demands eventually infuriate Paul, who violently ejects him from his home. On his way out the door, the blackmailer cynically says to Kurt, "He's paying you too" (Figure 3.3). Though we've never seen Paul explicitly pay Kurt money, the blackmailer assumes what society at large would assume— that the pair are (more or less) a sugar daddy and his kept man. Rattled by the altercation, Paul recalls his anxious student days, from his expulsion from boarding school for intimacy with a roommate to the time he consulted a hypnotist to "cure" his homosexuality. Returning to the present, he consults Hirschfeld, who reassures him that "love for one's own sex can be just as pure and noble as love for the opposite sex" and that, as a gay man, he can "still make valuable

Figure 3.3   *Anders als die Andern*: Paul attempts to comfort Kurt after the younger man learns of the blackmailer's scheme.

contributions to humanity." Later, at a lecture, Hirschfeld informs an audience that many anti-gay laws were repealed after European countries adopted the Napoleonic Code and that such laws were reinstated only in the mid- to late-nineteenth century. After the lecture, Else asks Hirschfeld if she can "cure" Kurt with her love. He responds, "Nature itself forbids it."

As the plot winds down, police arrest the blackmailer, who gleefully exposes Paul. While the blackmailer receives three years in jail, Paul receives only a week, after Hirschfeld testifies on his behalf, arguing that Paragraph 175 is needless and bigoted. Yet Paul's light sentence provides little comfort. Outed during the trial, Paul finds himself a social pariah, and his concert promoter cancels his contract. In an ending destined to become a sour cliché of gay cinema, a grief-stricken Paul commits suicide. At Paul's funeral (a scene now lost), Else condemns those present for having shunned him. Meanwhile, Hirschfeld restrains Kurt from also taking his own life, instead encouraging the young man to fight social injustice, just as "Zola struggled on behalf of one who innocently languished in prison."[16] In extant prints, a title card appears to describe the film's final image, which is now lost: "A large hand appears, holding a brush [that] strikes out once and for all Paragraph 175, that horrible law to which clings so much blood and tears."

In accordance with principles of enlightenment films, Hirschfeld's final defense of Paul appeals to logos (logic) as much as it appeals to pathos (emotion), arguing that the law only manufactures new criminals. "For each homosexual prosecuted under the law," he says, "another 100 were victimized by blackmailers."[17] Technically square and artistically uninspired, *Anders* is unapologetically a work of social propaganda. As such, it does what Stiller's *Vingarne*—and later Dreyer's *Michael*—do not: it eschews the aesthetics of tragedy and makes an open plea for sociolegal reform. For that matter, precious few fiction films in all of New Queer Cinema (and its aftermath) make any expressly *legal* arguments. Avant-gardists rely on provocation to rupture the social fabric, and culturalists assume humanistic storytelling will sway public opin-ion. Explicit activism and policy proposals, meanwhile, are shunted to documentary filmmak-ing or demoted to one-hour television dramas. Apart from preconceived, categorical notions of "entertainment," however, there is no need to artificially divide culture and activism along neatly bifurcated lines of fiction and nonfiction. Though culture certainly is a kind of activism, it also turns the wheels of progress slowly, sometimes imperceptibly. How might progress on queer issues have been different, we may ask, if mainstream filmmakers were unafraid to take a page from Hirschfeld?

A more sophisticated romanticism: Carl Dreyer's *Michael*

Though gay critics (such as Vito Russo) had long acknowledged the significance of Carl Drey-er's *Michael*, the second adaptation of Bang's novel, much mainstream scholarship—including the lionizing essays that followed Dreyer's death in 1968—tended to minimize both its cine-matic relevance and its queer content. The standard dismissive view was established by Siegfried Kracauer, who observed that German producers of the silent era were obsessed with filming salacious novels: "The need for adaptations was so urgent that even Herman Bang's esoteric novel *Mikhael* was made into a film, perhaps because of its tinge of homosexuality" (Kracauer, 1947, p. 78). Perceptions of the film changed dramatically when the Danish Film Institute completed a pristine restoration in 2006, rekindling the interest of film scholars and unearthing visual splendors obscured in damaged archival prints.[18] In light of the coyness of later critics, contemporary viewers might be surprised to learn that film distributors in the 1920s grossly sensationalized (rather than disguised) the film's queerness. Adding a then-fashionable gloss of Hirschfeldian scientism, the film's first U.S. release "ran for a short time at New York's Fifth Avenue Playhouse as *Chained: The Story of the Third Sex*, with a 'scientific lecture' tacked on and without credit to Dreyer as the director" (Russo, 1987, p. 22). (The "tacked on lecture" has been excised from extant prints.) Reviewing *Chained* for its 1926 Manhattan premiere, *New York Times* columnist Mordaunt Hall balked at homosexual themes that were obvious to view-ers at the time. Filmmakers "bent on delivering such a theme to the screen," Hall admonished, "should have instead "picturize[d] Oscar Wilde's story, 'The Picture of Dorian Gray,' or Robert Hichens's novel, 'The Green Carnation,' two works which, distasteful though they may be, at least possess real dramatic values."[19] Hall's deference to the legitimacy of Wilde betrays a homo-phobic moralism.[20] As Russo suggests, Hall was not really interested in something with more dramatic value but in "something with a strong sense of moral judgment," which "Dreyer's direct and uncritical approach" clearly lacks (Russo, 1987, p. 22).

Though Dreyer is widely regarded as the father of Danish national cinema, *Michael*'s pedi-gree is distinctly Germanic. It was made at UFA studios, under the auspices of producer Erich Pommer. It was scripted by Thea von Harbou (the writer of *Metropolis* and wife of Fritz Lang), and it was lensed by Karl Freund, the cinematographer responsible for so much of the look of German expressionism.[21] To a certain degree, the film also continues the tradition of the *kam-merspielfilm*, which cinematized the confined chamber dramas advanced by theater impresario Max Reinhardt. Yet the film, marked by the expressionistic sets and art direction of architect Hugo Häring, also evinces an atmosphere of decadence and fatalism far removed from the psy-chological realism typical of fin de siècle chamber dramas. As part of its expressionism, *Michael* employs a judicious use of the facial close-up, which by 1924 had become a standard emotive device. Dreyer never depends excessively on close-ups to tell this story, however. Mostly limit-ing himself to medium close-ups, he rarely uses the extreme, soul-searching close-ups he would revolutionize in his subsequent *The Passion of Joan of Arc* (1928) and to which audiences have since become accustomed.

Here, Zoret is played by Benjamin Christensen, the Danish cinema pioneer better known as the director of *Häxan: Witchcraft through the Ages* (1922). The understatement of Christensen's Zoret, worlds removed from Egil Eide's performance in *Vingarne*, is strikingly modern and bereft of melodramatic excess. The novel's homoeroticism, partly suppressed in the narrative, is here projected expressionistically through the décor designed by Häring, who festoons Zoret's drawing room with outsize busts, paintings, and assorted nudes that dwarf the humanity of the characters (Figure 3.4). The film begins with a portentous epigraph: "I can now die in peace, for I have seen true love." In the first scene, a dapper, tuxedoed Michael is already living in Zoret's manor. As Zoret prepares to host a dinner party, he remarks to his friend Switt that he's been offered as much as $30,000 for his sketches of Michael, who prizes money above senti-ment. "We do not want to sell our most beautiful memories," explains Zoret, pulling playfully on Michael's hair. Among Zoret's dinner guests is a duke who reminds young Michael of his special aura: "Only the paintings for which you modeled," the duke observes, "finally earned the Master his fame." As Zoret's guests assemble around the dinner table, the conversation takes a dark turn when Zoret, in an unsubtle bit of foreshadowing, reveals a morbid sketch of his new painting. "I want to paint Caesar just as he is murdered by his adopted son, Brutus," he announces. With a naïveté at once disarming and exasperating, Michael asks, "And how is Brutus supposed to look?" Michael's indifference to Zoret's devotion is equaled only by his obliviousness to the fated metaphor.

Figure 3.4 Dreyer's *Michael*: Art dwarfs humanity.

After the dinner party, a visiting countess (analogous to the princess in *Vingarne*) asks Zoret to paint her portrait, but he, devoted erotically and aesthetically to Michael, refuses. In a series of medium close-ups that explicate what *Vingarne* left implicit, Michael gazes at the countess, disclosing his bisexuality. In turn, she becomes enraptured by Zoret's *The Victor*, a shamelessly large painting that depicts Michael as a nude Siegfried engaged in a sylvan frolic. In the next scene, Zoret dines alone with the countess and finally relents to her request for a portrait. Michael, arriving late, becomes jealous in a rather adolescent manner: "You started dinner without me?" he asks. There is no indication, however, that Zoret too is bisexual or that Michael logically should feel threatened. Rather, the scene stresses Michael's vanity and childish insecurity. Notably, here it is the youth who becomes jealous of the master's falsely perceived foray into heterosexuality, adding a wrinkle absent from Stiller's version.

Repeating a crucial scene found in *Vingarne* and in Bang's novel, an erotically frustrated Zoret discovers he is unable to capture the essence of the countess's eyes. Dreyer's use of the extreme close-up, a technique undiscovered by Stiller in 1916, becomes crucial in this scene. When Michael takes up the brush, completing the eyes that elude Zoret, Dreyer personifies the painting by cutting suddenly to a close-up of the countess's eyes before dollying dramatically toward Michael's face (the only abrupt dolly in the film). The series of close-ups thus activates and "completes" the deficient gaze displaced into the princess's unfinished eyes. Conceding Michael's success at reflecting heterosexual beauty, a temperamental Zoret leaves the countess with Michael, who, as if belatedly progressing through Freudian stages of development, seems to exit his exclusively homosexual attachment to Zoret and enter a phase of heterosexual exploration and self-determination. Though quaint, such a reading is not terribly far fetched, as Freud's notions of psychosexual development had become well known by 1924.

Whispers of Michael's nightly escapades with the countess travel through the chattering classes, and, as in Stiller's version, Zoret's journalist friend Switt informs him that Michael has been cuckolding him. "You are still the only one in the dark!" Switt says, apparently jealous that Michael has become Zoret's favorite and now relishing the Master's humiliation.[22] To hammer his point home, Switt publishes a devastating review of Zoret's recent portrait of the countess, lambasting its artificiality and singling out Michael's phantom contribution: "Only the eyes are an exception; so unreal is the rest of it that one could swear these eyes were painted by another hand."

Agitated by Switt's betrayal, Zoret throws himself into what will become his final painting, a triptych entitled *The Vanquished*, a resigned and moribund work at odds with his expressionistic sculptures (Figure 3.5). Its side panels feature a nude man and woman exchanging desirous gazes, while the central panel houses a wizened man, dejected and floating among the clouds. The old man is tiny, dwarfed by the male and female lovers, much as all the characters in the film are dwarfed by art itself in the form of the great Hugo Häring busts and paintings that adorn Zoret's house. Rather than providing succor or an outlet for his ego, art now swallows up Zoret, who becomes a prisoner of his own creation. Nevertheless, the assembled upper crust toast him: "To the painter of suffering, the glory of the nation!" But Michael is absent from the reception. Eventually returning, he guiltily tries to comfort Zoret, massaging his feet and putting on his slippers. Here, in the film's greatest scene of affection, we finally see Michael adopt the submissive posture we assume typified their earlier, offscreen relationship. In a moment rich with irony, Switt later regales Zoret with the reviews. "They all say that you've never created anything more beautiful than the sky in *The Vanquished*."

Zoret's death is more elaborate in this film than in *Vingarne*—and tinged with the transcendent religious fervor Dreyer would articulate more clearly in *Ordet* (1955) and *Gertrud* (1964). Whereas the Zoret of *Vingarne*, in a final burst of energy, bolts from his deathbed to clutch at

Figure 3.5   Dreyer's *Michael*: Zoret in the midst of working on *The Vanquished*.

Michael's naked, stony form, here a resigned Zoret dies beneath a great crucifix that hangs on his bedroom wall (Figure 3.6). With his final breath, he asks Switt to bury him, anonymously, in a field of green grass and symbolically sprouting seeds. "Now I can die in peace, because I have seen true love," he says. As he undergoes a deathly frisson, his eyes roll back ecstatically. In *Vingarne*, Zoret's death is a private affair; here, Switt broadcasts the master's death in the streets. Michael, meanwhile, finds bittersweet succor in the countess's arms, rather than rejecting his female lover as he does in *Vingarne*. Nevertheless, as the countess nurses him, there is no indication that Michael has graduated into an autonomous adulthood. He still seems an overgrown, developmentally arrested boy.

Bang's effusive ending in the novel does little to dilute the story's economic underpinnings and implicit themes of erotic commerce. Throughout Dreyer's film, Michael's kept status is reflected in the commercial value of Zoret's artworks, which include likenesses of Michael himself. In the film's final act, Michael, desperate for cash, secretly sells paintings and the rare bronze statue (of himself) that Zoret had given him (Figure 3.7). If Michael's "exchange value" is signified by the price his likeness fetches on the open market, he here attempts symbolically to reclaim his identity and self-worth. But the act is futile. The bronze statue may be idealized, but the real Michael has neither beauty nor soul to sell, for Zoret has already captured and transposed the young man's essence. When Zoret discovers Michael's unauthorized sales, he instructs an art dealer to buy back one of the paintings, initiating a contest to possess—economically and figuratively—Michael's second self. Zoret learns, however, that as soon as the rare bronze came onto the open market, his other works became devalued, a phenomenon that quite literally

Figure 3.6 Dreyer's *Michael*: Zoret on his deathbed, flanked by an erotic statue (left) and religious symbolism (right).

Figure 3.7 Dreyer's *Michael*: The countess has purchased Michael's nude painting, which now sits in her parlor; Michael stands in silhouette in the foreground.

reveals Michael's fetish value. In a sense, Bang's story inverts Plato's critique of representational art. Instead of a degraded imitation of reality, Michael's precious bronze becomes more valuable than his own flesh. In Bang's narrative, art necessarily degrades reality—a thesis possible only when romanticism reigns and eros is doomed.

Conclusion: beyond Bang's *Liebestod*

Though *Vingarne* and *Michael* have immeasurable value as queer history, Bang's scenario cannot really hide the hoary melodrama in its heart, its ruminations about aesthetics and fleeting eros notwithstanding. As tragedy, it's all rather pat, as the characters lack the moral complexity from which great tragedy should arise. Michael's tragic flaw is not hubris or some godlike pretense but the insecurities typical of a vain adolescent caught between economic dependence and a desire for autonomy. Zoret's downfall stems from a desire to capture ephemeral beauty in both fleshly and sculpted forms. Neither theme is terribly novel, especially by the standards of early-twentieth-century romanticism. The scenario's foregone conclusion is further manufactured by a narrative gap. While Zoret praises Michael's budding talent in their first meeting, both film versions immediately jump ahead to Michael's bankrupt stage as a kept man, skipping over the crucial years in which (presumably) he had slowly transformed from hopeful artist into disillusioned object of desire. Michael acts as creator only in the brief, tense moment in which he "completes" the princess's or countess's painted gaze—an aesthetic act that becomes tantamount to a (hetero)sexual betrayal.

Perhaps in keeping with its German pedigree, Dreyer's film climaxes with a *Liebestod* (literally "love-death"), the paradoxical formulation that Wagner distilled from Schopenhauer and made famous in *Tristan and Isolde*.[23] With his orchestra, Wagner represents the climactic *Liebestod* as an upward struggle in which surging strings achieve tier after tier of ecstasy before reaching a dissonant anticlimax—a musical paradox that conveys the contradictory notion of "love-death." The climax of Stiller's film, in which Zoret absurdly clutches at Michael's sculpted form, contrasts mortal flesh with lasting art. Dreyer's more sophisticated version foregoes melodrama for transcendence, but Zoret's death is still a one-dimensional resignation, not a Wagnerian struggle. Because Zoret is not allowed to enjoy lasting gratification with Michael—neither by the plot nor by the standards of early-twentieth-century morality—he has little choice but to seek transcendence. We are left with Zoret's enigmatic final words: "Now I can die in peace, because I have seen true love." The line is ambiguous, and Dreyer makes no attempt to identify the "true love" Zoret visualizes on his deathbed. Michael's duplicitous actions throughout the film cannot represent this true love, his final moment of contrition (the slippers scene) notwithstanding. Perhaps in a nod to Schopenhauer, the image of love Zoret sees on the edge of mortality is not only unknowable but also unrepresentable, whether in flesh, bronze, or the material spaces of the film itself.

In contrasting art and flesh, both film versions of Bang's novel evoke Jean Paul's notion of *weltschmerz*, the melancholy caused by the distance between the limitations of the material world and a mind that longs for transcendence. In the case of image-centered cinema, communicating the impossibility of transcendence becomes especially problematic. Within the realm of pure images, filmmakers too often represent transcendence through reductive symbols, such as Michael's bronzed form or the crucifix above Zoret's bed. But our inability to communicate transcendental meaning does not mean that we cannot change the social norms that, in turn, shape the art we create. If the standard money-boy narrative reflects the impossibility of love in ether a rigidly stratified society (as in *Michael*) or in a crassly capitalist one (as in street-hustler films), we have the right to ask why such relationships "need" to be impossible. We have the right to reject tragic conclusions and the assumption that sexual desire and personal freedom always work against each other. Would elements of *Michael* remain tragic if we could alter the prearranged class assumptions and social conditions that underpin the narrative? Would there even be a tragedy if there were not a taboo against intergenerational love? Would Zoret not require unrepresentable transcendence if we, as a culture, did not unduly romanticize youth and fleeting beauty?

The ideas underlying such questions obviously go beyond the scope of this discussion, but if we recognize the elements of Bang's tragedy as culturally artificial, we see that there is hardly a tragedy at all, for the flaws lie not in individual characters but in the sociohistorical norms that have shaped them. To avert Bang's "necessary" tragedy, we likely would have to abandon the worship of youth and embrace bisexuality and polyamory as new societal norms, insofar as jealousy and possessiveness catalyze the downfall of Bang's male characters. We might have to jettison, too, the Eriksonian or Maslovian norms that relate our successes and failures to particular stages of life or peg notions of maturity to arbitrary chronological markers. A young man, whether Michael or a Manhattan hustler, need not be marked a failure because his life does not dovetail with the timetables of psychiatry or the romantic assumptions of the bildungsroman. Of course, we would have to do more than merely reject old ideologies. We also would have to advance a new aesthetic culture that recognizes sexual expression and *practice* as forms of expression that are as culturally valid as writing a symphony, or as forms of therapy as legitimate as psychiatry.

To some contemporary audiences, *Vingarne* and *Michael* will seem like dated artifacts, and the didacticism of *Anders* will come across as quaint and inartistic. Yet the same audiences might not question the clichés of so many "realistic" hustler stories that inculcate us with their own masochistic formulas. After sufficient exposure to such despairing formulas, we come to believe this is the way things have always been and always must be. I am not suggesting filmmakers should put forth "positive" images of sex workers, hustlers, and rent boys, because such images would only reform and reinforce a morally bankrupt system of sexual competition and exclusivity in which the wealthiest patrons excel. Rather, we need revolutionary images that deromanticize youthful beauty, minimize themes of jealousy and exclusivity, and reimagine the erotic vitality of middle and old age.[24] We also need to reinvigorate an expressly political queer cinema, one unafraid to fold progressive legal issues (e.g., decriminalizing sex work) into its themes. Though *Anders* may seem quaint, Hirschfeld propounded a reformist optimism rare in fiction films today. Obviously, we cannot return to blunt lecturing, which audiences will reject as patronizing and artless. But we can attempt to recapture Hirschfeld's sanguinity, his unyielding belief that we can change the cultural conditions we have historically created. Is it too unreasonable, then, to embark on new "enlightenment" films for the twenty-first century, films that need not sacrifice optimism on the pedestal of art?

Notes

1 In the abstract, one might say the same thing of an athlete, yet athletes today are also corporatized and bureaucratized. The most successful athletes are those with sponsorship deals; one hardly expects even the most successful male prostitute to become a paid endorser for Nike. Not coincidentally, the most sexualized sports—bodybuilding, for instance—are also the least profitable for the athlete.

2 I suspect most filmmakers today would take a similar point of view. Auteurs are unlikely to abandon their cameras and take up sex work because they perceive the latter to be the more creative, aesthetically expressive, and self-actualizing path. Todd Verow's semiautobiographical *Between Something & Nothing* (2008) is the rare film that links hustling to the creative activity of an artist, yet it is the film itself, not the hustling it documents, that is ultimately the legitimate work of art. It is difficult to

imagine inverting the formula, such that a filmmaking career is the cheap prostitution and hustling the paragon of auteurism.

3 The trend toward street realism is found in the first film to deal explicitly with male hustlers, Palle Kjærulff-Schmidt and Robert Saaskin's *Sin Alley* (*Bundfald*, 1957). A cautionary tale about wayward youths led into crime and prostitution, this Danish drama reflects homophobic and pseudoscientific attitudes typical of the 1950s.

4 Some exceptions can be found in Hong Kong cinema, which in the early 1990s churned out a series of exploitation films about gigolos that combined sex and violence with tasteless comedy (e.g., *Friday Gigolo* [1992], *Gigolo and Whore* [1992], *Super Gigolo* [1993], etc.). More interesting is Chow Hoi Kwong's 2015 film *12 Golden Ducks* ("duck" is Cantonese slang for male prostitute), an absurdist comedy that features butch actress Sandra Ng in a cross-dressed role as an aging gigolo.

5 Akerman offers no direct causal link between sex work and the heroine's final act of murder. The viewer is left to wonder if her aimless, empty lifestyle, rather than her sex work per se, drives her to the film's final act of annihilation.

6 While some postfeminists have argued that prostitution can be a proactive or empowering choice for women, there does not seem be a parallel "postmasculinist" position that argues likewise for men.

7 Notable exceptions to this rule are found in this volume and its predecessor, *Male Sex Work and Society* (2014).

8 The Greek word *paiderastia* literally means "the love of a male child." Though the Greek root *paid-* or *ped-* is commonly translated as "child," the upper-class pederast of ancient Greece would partner with an adolescent male, approximately 13 to 17 years old. Adolescents who had begun to grow a beard usually were considered too old to serve as ephebes, or younger partners.

9 The use of facial close-ups to convey erotic desire or power would not become a film convention until the late 1910s and early 1920s. Some of the earliest examples of the "modern" erotic gaze are found in Erich von Stroheim's *Blind Husbands* (1919), one of the first feature films to edit together various characters' gazes (or eyeline matches) within a single scene.

10 I use the term *distancing effect* (*Verfremdungseffekt*, coined by Bertolt Brecht) as it is commonly employed, to describe an artist's use of antirealistic devices that force an audience to be consciously aware and critical of dramatic artifice.

11 Though expressionism would soon bring psychology to the cinema, it was an expressionism that seldom addressed sex head on, the monstrous appetites of F. W. Murnau's *Nosferatu* notwithstanding.

12 Among Oswald and Hirschfeld's other enlightenment films was the heterosexually themed *Prostitution* (1919), which argues for the liberalization of antiprocurement laws. In his collaborations with Oswald, Hirschfeld mainly shaped the didactic approach and subject matter, while Oswald handled directorial and technical matters. For example, a German poster for *Prostitution* reads, "Directed by Richard Oswald, with the cooperation and advice of Dr. Magnus Hirschfeld."

13 The work of Hirschfeld, then the world's leading sexologist and queer activist, should need little introduction. The Institute for Sexual Science expanded on the work of Hirschfeld's Scientific-Humanitarian Committee (*Wissenschaftlich-humanitäres Komitee*), founded in 1897. Through these organizations and his axiom "justice through science," Hirschfeld opposed German law's antigay Paragraph 175 and sought to liberalize attitudes and laws regarding same-sex relations, transgenderism, sex work, abortion, and pornography.

14 The "seamy pornography" to which Bartsch alludes would seem tame today. For instance, Oswald and Hirschfeld's *Opium* (1919) features a scene of nude female bathing.

15 With regard to famous political figures, it is worth noting that Hirschfeld was called for expert testimony in a series of sensational trials (the so-called Harden-Eulenberg affair) that revealed the homosexuality of several ministers of Wilhelm II.

16 Hirschfeld refers to Zola's famous defense of Alfred Dreyfus. As a gay German Jew, Hirschfeld obviously would have seen parallels between the era's anti-Semitism and homophobia.

17 From notes to the German DVD released by *Filmmmuseum*. Retrieved from www.edition-filmmuseum.com/product_info.php/language/en/info/p4_Anders-als-die-andern.html.

18 The restored version is available on DVD and Blu-ray from the UK-based distributor Eureka.

19 Mordaunt Hall, "Another German Contribution," *New York Times*, December 15, 1926. In his review, Hall notes that *Michael* had also been circulating in a version renamed *The Invert*, a title that shows the influence of Hirschfeld.

20 Hichens's once-notorious novel *The Green Carnation*—which Hall prefers to Dreyer's film—was a thinly veiled roman à clef based on the relationship between Wilde and Lord Alfred Douglas (an

acquaintance of Hichens's). The novel was published anonymously in 1894; its immediate notoriety contributed to Wilde's subsequent prosecution and persecution.

21 Near the end of the film's production, cinematographer Rudolph Maté, who would go on to lens Dreyer's *The Passion of Joan of Arc* (1928), filled in for Freund when the latter left the set to film F. W. Murnau's *The Last Laugh* (1924).

22 The relationship between Zoret and Switt, who are about the same age, is ambiguous. In Dreyer's version, Switt becomes oddly irritated by the attention that Zoret lavishes on Michael, suggesting the two older men might have had a prior sexual relationship. Casper Tybjerg notes that Dreyer's film is actually gayer than Bang's novel, for the character of Switt, depicted in the novel as a womanizer, is in the film an asexual loner jealous of Zoret and Michael's relationship.

23 Before Wagner, one finds the word *Liebestod* used more simply in Arnim and Brentano's *Das Knaben Wunderhorn* (The youth's miraculous horn), the 1805 compilation of German lore most familiar to us through Mahler's grandiose setting. The verse reads: "My heart that is so red around you / for you I carry these roses / I broke them for you in *Liebestod* / when I shed my (own) blood."

24 Though not ideal, Bruce LaBruce's *Gerontophilia* (2014) is an example of a film that romanticizes age instead of youth.

References

Christensen, B. 1922. *Haxan: witchcraft through the ages.* Sweden: Svensk Filmindustri.

Hall, M. (1926, December 15). Another German contribution. *New York Times.* Retrieved from www. nytimes.com/1926/12/15/archives/another-german-contribution.html?module=ArrowsNav&contentCollection=Archives&action=keypress&region=FixedLeft&pgtype=article.

Kardish, L. (2010). *Weimar cinema, 1919–1933: Daydreams and nightmares.* New York: Museum of Modern Art.

Kracauer, S. (1947). *From Caligari to Hitler.* Princeton, NJ: Princeton University Press.

Matza, D. (1969). *Becoming deviant.* Englewood Cliffs, NJ: Prentice Hall.

Mulvey, L. (1975). Visual pleasure and narrative cinema. *Screen, 16*(3).

Russo, V. (1987). *The celluloid closet* (revised ed.). New York: Harper & Row.

Tybjerg, C. (2018). *Michael.* DVD audio commentary. Masters of Cinema Series. London: Eureka Entertainment.

Annotated List of Films Cited

American Gigolo (Paul Schrader, 1980). Richard Gere stars as a high-class male prostitute embroiled in a murder mystery. Schrader's glamorous, mainstream drama is a daylit neo-noir that makes limp attempts at psychologizing and social commentary.

Bishonen (Yonfan, 1998). Queer Hong Kong director Yonfan's slickly photographed tale of ambitious male prostitutes features plenty of boyish eye candy but little emotional substance.

Body Without Soul (Wiktor Grodecki, 1996). Grodecki's second documentary about Czech boy prostitutes (following 1994's *Not Angels but Angels*) enters the realm of absurdism when interviewing the boys' callous pimp, who works a day job as a mortician. As the camera focuses unblinkingly on the pimp as he performs an autopsy, we realize that he sees the boys as little more than disposable slabs of meat.

Colegas (Eloy de la Iglesia, 1982). Affecting, realistic story of teenage best friends (the title translates as "buddies") who turn to delinquency and hustling on the tough streets of Madrid. One of Spain's most notable gay filmmakers, Iglesia had previously directed *El Diputado* (1978), which deals with a leftist politician blackmailed for his dalliance with a male prostitute.

Different from the Others (Richard Oswald & Magnus Hirschfeld, 1919). One of several so-called enlightenment films by Oswald and Hirschfeld, this is cinema's first gay activist film. Its thin story of a blackmailed gay musician makes a didactic plea for the repeal of Germany's homophobic Paragraph 175. Subject to frequent censorship, the film exists today only in a fragmentary version.

Flesh (Paul Morrissey, 1968). The film that made Joe Dallesandro a star and gay icon, this ultra-low-budget, mostly improvised trifle directed by Andy Warhol acolyte Morrissey features various Warhol "superstars" indulging in sex and squalor in late-1960s Manhattan. The focus is squarely on the often naked body of Dallesandro, who plays an adolescent hustler criminally unaware of his beauty.

Fortune and Men's Eyes (Harvey Hart, 1971). A naive young straight man sent to prison encounters drag queens; rape; sexual servitude; and a corrupt, uncaring penal system. Considered frank and daring in its time, the film now comes across as dated, stereotyped, and filled with the gay self-loathing typical of Hollywood films of the early 1970s.

Heat (Paul Morrissey, 1972). A sometimes amusing, mostly dull riff on *Sunset Boulevard* (1950), *Heat* features a long-haired Joe Dallesandro sexually servicing middle-aged female neurotics. Mostly an exercise in camp, with less nudity than its predecessors *Flesh* and *Trash*.

Jeanne Dielman, 23, quai du Commerce, 1080 Bruxelles (Chantal Akerman, 1975). A landmark feminist tract by the Belgian lesbian filmmaker Chantal Akerman, *Jeanne Dielman* focuses on the empty, alienated existence of a housewife who sells her body when she is not performing menial household tasks. The film culminates in a final act of senseless violence that only deepens her sense of alienation.

Johns (Scott Silver, 1996). Another gritty tale of young hustlers, this time on LA's Santa Monica Boulevard. The film had considerable success on the festival circuit, but it fails to transcend the mix of realism and sentimentality that often characterizes the male hustler subgenre.

L.I.E. (Michael Cuesta, 1997) A nihilistic 15-year-old—whose mother has just died—pimps himself out to local middle-aged men in this self-consciously twisted coming-of-age tale. The film manages to be both provocative and reactionary; director Cuesta goes to some lengths to humanize the grimy pederast who befriends the young hero, but he winds up killing him off nonetheless. (Compare Gianni Da Campo's *The Flavor of Corn* [1986], which offers a more sanguine relationship between an adult and an adolescent boy.)

Live Nude Girls Unite! (Vicky Funari & Julia Query, 2000). A lesbian sex worker and queer-theory graduate student fight to unionize underpaid workers at the Lusty Lady, a San Francisco sex club. Funari and Query's feature documentary is sharp, insightful, and filled with moments of delicious irony.

The Living End (Gregg Araki, 1992). Two nihilistic, HIV-positive lovers embark on a road trip filled with sex, violence, and a "fuck you" attitude. Angry and crude, the film is emblematic of New Queer Cinema's defiant response to Americans' puritanism and indifference to the AIDS crisis.

Love, Simon (Greg Berlanti, 2018). A white, popular, good-looking teenage boy finds his way out of the closet. This highly commercial, heavily cross-promoted film represents Hollywood's facile notion of "progress."

Macho Dancer (Lino Brocka, 1988). Gay Filipino director Lino Brocka's most internationally famous film, *Macho Dancer* is set in the world of Manila's male strip clubs and underground gay sex trade. Part exploitation film, part crime thriller, part melodrama, it gave rise to similarly themed films, such as Mel Chionglo's *Midnight Dancers* (1994) and *Burlesk King* (1999).

Mandragora (Wiktor Grodecki, 1997). Two teenage runaways become male prostitutes on the dangerous streets of Prague. Moving and engrossing, if also dramatically unsurprising, the film is director Grodecki's fictional counterpart to his documentaries *Not Angels but Angels* (1994) and *Body Without Soul* (1996).

Michael (Carl Dreyer, 1924). Dreyer's elaborately produced, subtly acted, semiexpressionistic adaptation of Herman Bang's novel of the same name is among the earliest gay-themed feature films. Benjamin Christensen's understated turn as the gay artist Zoret is one of silent cinema's great unsung performances.

Midnight Cowboy (John Schlesinger, 1969). Winner of the Oscar for Best Picture, Schlesinger's melodramatic buddy film once startled audiences with Jon Voight's portrayal of a naive country boy turned Manhattan hustler. Schlesinger's modish direction cannot negate the bitter sense of self-hatred that spoils much of the film. Originally rated X for its subject matter.

My Hustler (Andy Warhol & Chuck Wein, 1965). Two male prostitutes (Paul America and Joseph Campbell) on Fire Island entertain a balding client (Ed Hood) who tries to corrupt them. Filmed in only a few days, this improvisatory feature has Warhol's usual stretches of tedium, but Harvard-educated Hood is witty as the effete, lettered client, and this is among the first queer American films to openly broach the topic of male prostitution.

My Own Private Idaho (Gus Van Sant, 1991). Keanu Reeves and River Phoenix play male hustlers in Van Sant's acclaimed, once-popular queer buddy movie. Not a great film but a historically important bridge between commercial Hollywood and the ethics of early 1990s New Queer Cinema.

Not Angels but Angels (Wiktor Grodecki, 1994). In this depressing examination of sexual exploitation, Czech filmmaker Grodecki interviews a series of adolescent boys who hustle in the train stations of Prague. The boys—almost all of them straight trade—are runaways and victims of abuse, lacking both education and a social safety net. The film's religious imagery and soundtrack of sacred choral music evince feelings of grace and compassion, but the boys need a sociological solution, not a spiritual one. Followed by Grodecki's *Body Without Soul*.

Oliver (Nick Deocampo, 1983). Filipino director and film historian Deocampo's documentary follows Oliver, an impoverished drag performer who puts food on the table by working in Manila's gay bars. This is the first film in a trilogy that also includes *Children of the Regime* (1985) and *Revolutions Happen Like Refrains in a Song* (1987); all three examine the politicoeconomic realities of sex work during the Marcos regime.

101 Rent Boys (Fenton Bailey & Randy Barbato, 2000). In this exploitative yet sentimental documentary, the titular boys are interviewed and exposed in sleazy motel rooms. The directors create sympathy for their interviewees while stripping them bare in both flesh and spirit.

Pretty Boy (Carsten Sønder, 1993). A 13-year-old boy runs away from home, prostitutes himself on the streets of Copenhagen, and hooks up with a Dickensian band of hustlers led by a cross-dressing teenage girl. Dramatically involving but morally vacant; the original Danish version reportedly features explicit scenes cut from the U.S. release.

Star Maps (Miguel Arteta, 1997). A young Latino man is pressured by his father into continuing an old family tradition—prostitution. A story of Hollywood disillusionment and exploitation, the film mixes gritty realism with moments of dark comedy.

Trash (Paul Morrissey, 1970). The second film in Morrissey's unofficial Flesh trilogy, *Trash* is another exercise in improvisatory camp, centered around hustlers in New York's counterculture. As in its predecessor, *Flesh*, Joe Dallesandro's frequent and pendulous nudity is the primary attraction.

Via Appia (Jochen Hick, 1989). An HIV-positive male flight attendant searches Rio's red-light district to reconnect with a hustler with whom he shared a passionate night. The film's commentary on the AIDS crisis takes a back seat to plentiful nudity. German director Hick went on to make several documentaries on gay themes, including *Menmaniacs: The Legacy of Leather* (1995) and *Talk Straight: The World of Rural Queers* (2003).

Vingarne (Mauritz Stiller, 1916). Silent film pioneer Stiller's adaptation of Herman Bang's gay novel *Mikhael* is at once primitive and surprisingly modern, placing its story of love between an artist and his male model within a self-reflexive framing device in which Stiller himself selects the actors to portray the scandalous storyline. Unfortunately, the framing sequence is now lost. Extant prints replace the missing scenes with production stills and title cards. Later remade in 1924 by Carl Theodor Dreyer as *Michael*.

4

Male prostitution and fashion

Dressed to thrill

Itai Doron

Expose and conceal (the Italian connection)

Andrew Cunanan is arguably the most famous, or infamous, gay male escort of all time.[1] Figure 4.1 shows a prep school yearbook photograph of a beaming Cunanan—the man who killed Italian fashion designer Gianni Versace in 1997—capturing how clothing can work with pose to denote sexual availability. In the 1987 photograph, Cunanan wears a pair of belted, pleated trousers and a white, button-down dress shirt—unbuttoned and untucked, revealing his nipples and nicely built torso. A wide striped tie, hanging like a loose noose around his neck, metaphorically slashes Cunanan's fully exposed upper body. The words "nice bod" are scribbled across Cunanan's naked chest, as if two words sum up his entire personality, portraying his status as a sexual commodity to the world (the words are not shown in the version of the photo reprinted here). Anyone who has ever seen an all-male strip show will instantly recognize the male stripper/sex worker look, the faux sophistication of an apparently respectable young man accustomed to taking off all his clothes in order to earn a living. Because this photograph showcases Cunanan's lewdness and self-indulgence, it became one of the more popular images used by the press in telling the Cunanan-Versace story. Most of the news articles described Cunanan as a "high-class male prostitute," an accolade previously bestowed on him by his mother (Bull, 1997, p. 40). A moderately successful gay male prostitute, Cunanan later cultivated a more refined look that is more closely linked to typical images of heterosexual male prostitutes.

Following Versace's death, the media revealed that Cunanan was a "boy toy"—a kept companion of "sugar daddies" (wealthy, older, and sometimes closeted gay men). Due to his role as a boy toy, it was necessary for Cunanan to maintain an elegant and sophisticated look, wearing clothes that in the gender-defined nineties did not fully reveal his sexual orientation. Ten years after the yearbook photograph was taken, and following his shooting of Versace, Andrew Cunanan was dead from a self-inflicted gunshot wound, after days of being on the run from the police. Carlos Noriega, the homicide cop who found his body in a houseboat, recalled: "I walked up to the second floor and saw Cunanan on his back. He was wearing boxer shorts, no shirt, no shoes" (Woodfield, 2015). It is ironic that in death as in life, clothes—or the lack of them—came to define Cunanan and his image in the public mind.

Figure 4.1 Prep school yearbook photo of Andrew Cunanan.

The Assassination of Gianni Versace: American Crime Story (2018), a TV dramatization of the events leading up to Versace's murder, emphasizes the clothes worn by the murderer and his victim, especially Cunanan's clothes on and off the job. In his role as a male prostitute, when he is in the company of clients or lovers, Cunanan wears smart-casual clothes, sporting effortlessly rolled-up shirt-sleeves and a single-breasted blazer swung over a shoulder. When he is on his own, he wears scruffy sportswear. A number of scenes show him assembling outfits from his wardrobe before meeting each of the five men who became his victims. These scenes are reminiscent of those of Richard Gere in writer-director Paul Schrader's film *American Gigolo* (1980), in which Gere plays a Los Angeles male escort named Julian Kaye. *American Gigolo* is arguably the first mainstream film to focus on male sex work while emphasizing how male prostitutes use fashion, appearance, social mannerisms, etiquette, and poise in their work.

In *Representations of Male Sex Work in Film* (2014), Russell Sheaffer highlights Julian's fictional history and his "rise" from hustler (a term used for male sex workers who work gay male bars or the streets) to gigolo—a supposedly higher-ranking male prostitute catering to women—implying a hierarchy of male sex workers. An iconic scene in which the shirtless Kaye lays out an assortment of fancy Giorgio Armani[2] outfits on his bed (while doing a line of coke), then carefully matches his shirts and ties before getting dressed, offered audiences a glimpse into the fictional life of a successful male escort (for wealthy women). The scene stood in stark contrast the portrayals of the less flashy existence of the street-walking male prostitutes or bar hustlers, catering to gay male clients, that became more visible, especially in North America in the early 1960s.[3] Julian Kaye's career in *American Gigolo* allows him to expose or conceal his well-maintained and virile body through a selection of ultra-masculine but also somewhat feminine wardrobe choices. Kaye seduces a female client in her room at the Beverly Hills Hotel by wearing a smart, expensive-looking suit and tie and projecting a professional, highly sophisticated, and cultured masculinity. In another scene, he fascinates a different female client by showing off in an unbuttoned white linen shirt and minuscule shorts as he is tanning by the pool of the less grandiose Westwood Apartment Hotel, projecting a sensual, flirtatious, almost slutty, and slightly cheap version of masculinity. Meanwhile, the other, less refined menswear/fashion statements that *American Gigolo* promoted, such as a baggy cotton shirt unbuttoned to the navel or extremely short denim cut-offs and running shorts, are now more associated with late 1970s and 1980s gay fashion trends, mainly influenced by the hedonism associated with gay club culture and disco music and a knowing but nonchalant attitude toward dressing up, sex, and sexuality.

Another scene in *American Gigolo* perfectly illustrates the role, function, and effective use of clothing to provoke, seduce, and engage in self-promotion. In this scene, Kaye is doing dumb-bells exercise at home as he is hanging from a pull-up bar, wearing ankle grips and a small, tight pair of anthracite gym shorts. Gere is otherwise naked, and even today the image shows that a style of dress (rather than simple nudity and the act of undressing) can provoke desire. Peter Lehman (2007) draws attention to the background sound of Gere/Kaye's heavy breathing alternating with the sound of a language-learning tape (Kaye is practicing his Swedish as he exercises), adding to the scene's autoerotic sexual overtone. Sound, the character's choice of clothing (for a supposedly heterosexual character), and Gere's fine-looking and almost fully naked body come together to create a vision of the male body as commodity and as a fetish, with a particular focus on the eroticism of the male body-sex/machine. We find traces of this scene in countless social media accounts of the male fitness and bodybuilding enthusiasts who post workout video clips that focus on particular body parts, such as abs, arms, chest, back, and butt. Many websites that promote male sex work feature similar clips that draw attention to the male prostitute's body, providing more detail than profile pictures (some go even further and show the escort in action) in order to grab their prospective clients' attention.[4]

Comparing the theme of *American Gigolo* ("the inability to express love") with the life of a gigolo, Schrader labels the male escort "a character of surfaces." Influenced by Italian taste and fashion, Schrader then placed his protagonist in a world of "high style" that acknowledges style as an integral part of everyday life and focuses on "showing oneself off to one's best advantage" (Nardini, 1999, p. 5). It refers to a preoccupation with looking good, appearance and reputation, social status, and the cultivation of a stylish self, with fashion being naturally an important element in that context. Bella figura is an acquired social convention that is ultimately attributed to "self presentation and identity, performance and display" (Nardini, 1999, p. 7). As we see in Figure 4.2, Julian Kaye's personal style signals the distinctive sexual and intellectual aesthetic experience that he offers to his clients. To borrow from literary theory, "A very common view of style is that it is a matter of the careful choice of exactly the right word or phrase, *le mot juste*" (Haynes, 2006, p. 2), and so Julian carefully chooses a shirt that he precisely matches with a pair of well-fitting trousers and a color-coordinated blazer to compose a fully coherent and distinctive and superficial, but nevertheless fully convincing, social reality for himself. He then sells this fabricated self-presentation to his clients.

Figure 4.2   American Gigolo: Julian Kaye's style.

In Schrader's portrayal of a male prostitute, we can recognize the use of fashion as a device that highlights the character's visual representation and metaphorical transformation. Julian Kaye communicates his (aspirational) social class status through fashion and style. At the same time, he conveys his availability as an object of desire for his clients. In addition, Schrader's evocation of the *Italianness* of Italian commodities (mainly through the use of Italian menswear clothing style) ensures Kaye's status as a Latin lover and a vehicle of rampant eroticism. In her discussion of the Latin lover image, Jacqueline Reich notes that "Italian men have never avoided fashioning themselves as objects of the gaze, by embracing male sexuality and eroticism in both their attitude and the clothes they wear" (2004, p. 46). Reich elaborates on the perception of the Latin lover as a byproduct of Italian masculinity and stereotypical, foreign perceptions of Italy, noting that the Latin lover has become "the 'imagined' embodiment of the primitive whose unrestrained and exotic passion contrasts sharply with the more civilized and restrained Northern European or American society." Reich suggests that clothing plays a key role in the

Latin lover's projection of a casual, elegant, and refined manner and in the process of turning this character into a commodified object of desire.

In Tennessee Williams' *The Roman Spring of Mrs. Stone* (2013), Paolo di Leo is a young and greedy Roman gigolo who is financially supported by Karen Stone, a former actress and a wealthy American widow who is 30 years his senior. Williams evokes the romantic allure of Rome and of Roman masculinity and emphasizes Paolo's narcissism and understanding of the relationship between clothing and sexual identity, capturing Paolo as he

> rushed toward the mirror as if it were water and his clothes were on fire. Without a glance in Mrs. Stone's direction, he gazed and preened in the glass, and finding it somewhat crowded by their two reflections, he murmured Excuse me and gave her a slight push to one side. Then he turned his back to the long mirror and, looking over his shoulder, he lifted the jacket over his hips so that they both, she and he, could admire the way that the flannel adhered to the classic callipygian shape of his firm young behind.
>
> *(2013, p. 88)*[5]

Paolo enhances the sense of his body through fashion confidence while engaging in the act of narcissistic adulation. He is at the same time a spectator and a spectacle. He sees and he is being seen, watching women watching him as he offers them the gift of his potential companionship, his body and lovemaking skills, while exuding elegance at every turn. He epitomizes an unapologetically peacocky masculinity, performed as an act of self-fashioning and paraded for public consumption. Like the English dandy, Paolo represents an Italian masculinity seen through the lens of the cultural custom of the *bella figura* ("beautiful figure"), conveying his manliness, his aspirations, and his outlook on life through his clothes, turning his performing male body into an object of spectacle in an urban environment. There is a fundamental narcissism in this form of masculinity that attempts to cover up insecurities "through the outward manifestation of grandiosity and excessive self worth" (Reich, 2004, p. 9).

Expose and conceal (take a walk on the wild side)

The Roman Spring of Mrs. Stone also presents us with an unnamed "young man" who stands at the other end of the men-as-sexual-objects spectrum. This character still has to climb the social ladder to reach Paolo's level of stylistic sophistication. At the beginning of the story and by the end of it, beauty is the young man's only visual asset:

> It was the sort of beauty that is celebrated by the heroic male sculptures in the fountains of Rome. Two things disguised it a little, the dreadful poverty of his clothes and his stealth of manner. The only decent garment he wore was a black overcoat which was too small for his body. Its collar exposed a triangle of bare ivory flesh; no evidence of a shirt. The trouser-cuffs were coming to pieces. Naked feet showed through enormous gaps in his shoe leather.
>
> *(2013, p. 4)*

The young man represents here the "cultural symbol of the Italian as other . . . the 'imagined' embodiment of the primitive, whose unrestrained and exotic passion directly affronts the more civilized and restrained Northern European or American society" (Reich, 2004, p. 26). Williams then describes an exchange of glances between the mysterious, poor-looking young man, who "had descended from the shell of a town among the hills south of Rome" and an affluent

American male tourist at the Piazza Trinita di Monte, illustrating the basic street hustler-client cruising decorum:

[H]e observed without looking at it the figure of an American tourist who had stopped a little space away from him. . . . But the young man knew that the hand in the pocket was about to produce a package of cigarettes and that he would offer him one. If accepted, that offer would have a sequence of others, dispelling hunger and every other discomfort for days to come. Still without returning the stranger's glances, his eyes assessed the value of the camera hung by a leather strap from his shoulder and the gold band at his wrist and even the approximate size of his shirt and shoes.

(2013, pp. 5–6)

The young man's "acquisition" and, even more so, his transformation into another, equally impeccable "Paolo" (the archetypal street hustler as social climber) happens beyond the last page of the story and only in the reader's (and Williams') imagination. But his presence adds another, darker dimension to the story. As he follows Mrs. Stone in the streets, we are introduced to an aspect of male sex work that Williams borrows directly from his life as a single gay man: the element of danger associated with cruising for "rough trade" male prostitutes. Williams' preference for "rough trade" sex is fully documented in his autobiography (*Memoirs*, 1975), as he and some of his contemporaries such as Samuel Steward used to frequent the intersection of Broadway, Seventh Avenue, and Forty-Second Street and Times Square in midtown Manhattan in the early 1940s, looking for sailors on shore leave—heterosexually identified "real men" who doubled up as hustlers. Steward, a major twentieth-century gay literary figure, tattoo artist, and academic and sexual renegade, had meticulously documented his encounters with "rough trade" hustlers in his infamous *Stud File*. He gave special mention to the sailor's uniform:

Most uniforms make the bodies beneath them more exciting . . . the sailor's uniform top[s] the list. . . . The uniform surrounds him with the shimmering glitter of an illusion, and we are frozen into our positions of adoration and desire. The uniform is the psychic link—the gazing-glass through which we look into another world.

(Spring, 2010, p. 82)

In this context, it is interesting to note American historian Anne Hollander's (1994) study of the modern men's suit as a masculine uniform, highlighting how it exudes sensuality by accentuating the legs, shoulders, and waist. She calls it "a costume of perfect nudity." As an item of clothing, it suggests a combination of power and pleasure, obscuring what needs to be kept private but simultaneously proposing that what's underneath is a well-proportioned, symmetrical body. It is designed to suggest that the wearer is a well-balanced and self-composed person, which can be considered very attractive or even sexually expressive. Both Steward and Hollander, though from different perspectives, highlight the notion of illusion and control as part of the erotic allure of uniforms and their appeal to both sexes. Throughout his life, Steward was a consumer of sexual services provided by homosexual and heterosexual male prostitutes. In the introduction to Steward's *Understanding the Male Hustler* (2012), John P. De Cecco defines the age group of hustlers as between 15 and 25, and he splits them into different types as they existed at the time of Steward's engagement with them:

The younger ones are the street hustlers; the older hustlers sometimes avoid the streets altogether and confine their hunting and affairs to the gay bars that are known and recognized as hustler bars. . . . Some of the particular handsome men are known as "call boys," often older and more experienced than the street hustlers; they present themselves through newspaper ads, gay strip shows, houses of prostitution, and modeling or escort services. . . . A few, the "kept boys," find rich "sugar daddies," older men who dazzle them with money, cars, clothes, swimming pools, travel, and more money.

(2012, Introduction, para. 7)

About half a decade earlier, Thomas Painter, a cultured and progressive gay man and an avid customer of "rough trade" prostitutes, conducted observational research of the Times Square and Forty-Second Street hustler scene between 1934 and 1943. Painter describe his ideal young, heterosexual white male hustler as someone who denoted insubordination and rebelliousness through his clothing and conduct:

> [S]lightly coarse, even slightly brutal. . . . A casual defiance of convention as to wearing of clothing is intensely exciting—i.e., wearing too few, too light, or too much en dishabille[6] clothing to suit the place or occasion is most erotic. A very "tough" youth in dress and manner.

(Minton, 2001, p. 129)

Painter's research elaborates on the presentation and display of the street hustler's body as object of desire in New York in the 1930s. According to Barry Reay (2010), Painter gave an account of the hustler's fashion style, dividing it into two types. The first was the style of his favored "roughly dressed" delinquents, laborers, sailors, and working-class drifters: "This was the masculine garb of dungarees, blue jeans, short-sleeved summer polo shirts, caps, studded belts, and boots." The second was the style of the "smooth": street hustlers who looked at sharply dressed gangsters and their rough and tough masculine identities for fashion inspiration. Painter noted that this second style could appear "cheap and flashy," an indication of the wearer's social and economic conditions.

Painter's pre-WWII observations and evaluations substantially contributed to our understanding of the street hustler's fashion choices decades later (2010, pp. 206–209). American documentary and street photographer William Gedney's 1969 short sequence of pictures provides a further visual record of the New York City male prostitution scene, showing how a personal fashion style has the ability to reflect particular choices associated with a sexual lifestyle. The sequence shows what appears to be a male hustler standing on a street corner.[7] As Figure 4.3 shows, Gedney's hustler is hanging out near a theater entrance, next to a poster for the *Curley McDimple* musical,[8] projecting nonchalant sexual availability: hands stuck in his back pockets, his open shirt revealing his torso, the outline of his penis against the light-colored fabric of his trousers. Gedney's May 2, 1969, notebook entry quotes Henry Miller: "I know exactly how one stands with hand in pocket and coat collar turned up—a sort of glorious feeling of disreputability."[9] The overtly masculine, assertive pose in Gedney's images, alongside the display of a fashion style associated with Stanley Kowalski-esque, blue-collar workers, provide good examples of the influence of masculine culture on gay male identities and the interplay between straight and gay fashion styles in the 1960s and 1970s.[10]

In noting the trade's uniform appeal to gay men, it is worth examining its key role in the link between client and prostitute. Fashion items associated with "rough trade" erotica were crucial in defining gay masculinity; they included Levi's trousers and denim jackets, tight white T-shirts and white wifebeater tank tops, plaid work shirts, work boots, and leather jackets—all items of "macho"-style clothing that were adopted by the gay community

Figure 4.3 William Gedney's *Hustler* (1969).

(alongside other hetero-signifiers such as facial hair and a muscled body) in the process of eroticizing masculinity. Gay men wore these items as a form of a self-conscious parody of the tough-guy look (gay clones), challenging the notion that gay men are "feminine." Rather than finding fashion inspiration in peacocky upper-class men, whom gay middle-class men considered too effeminate, clones tried to emulate the look of rough, white working-class men whose manliness seemed so apparent as to be unquestionable and who traditionally projected a hyper-masculine silhouette through their utilitarian work clothes or uniforms. Martin P. Levine lists nine major butch clone looks and their associated fashions: Western, Leather, Military, Laborer, Hood, Athlete, Woodsman, Sleaze, and Uniforms: "The men favored the hood, athlete, and woodsman looks for everyday leisure attire. They wore the Western, leather, military, laborer, and uniform looks for going out or partying. Lastly, they favored the sleaze look for cruising" (1998, p. 60). These tight-fitting garments were worn in a way that accentuated the body and specific body parts, such as the genital area, the chest area, and the buttocks and arms, and they came to define what gay men would consider "hot" and very attractive:

They often highlighted these features by not wearing underwear, wallets, or shirts. Some men even left the top or bottom button of their Levis undone, in part to signal sexual availability. . . . Clones wore waist-length down or leather jackets over Levis. The shortness of these jackets exposed the bulge of their genitals and buttocks.

(p. 65)

Although Levine's theory of fashion appropriation and articulation of a masculine style mainly relates to 1970s and 1980s gay subcultures, there has been a revival of butch gay clones in recent years, which I believe has shaped the way gay male prostitutes reimagine themselves through their clothing. Gary Lee Boas' picture *In Front of Badlands at the Corner of Christopher and West Street* (Figure 4.4), part of his collection of photographs that illuminate the adult entertainment scene of downtown Manhattan between 1979 and 1985, features the various fashions worn by the bar's gay clientele. The photograph looks like it was taken recently, showing a mix of casual classics styles, including Levi's jeans and Doc Martens, hoodies, windbreakers, and trainers (sneakers). Boas' *Hustler* (Figure 4.5), taken around the same period, shows a fit, preppy-looking young man hanging around a phone booth on a street corner, wearing a tight white T-shirt, white striped sports socks, white men's plimsolls, and very short shorts. This image shows how hot pants for men, traditionally considered an item of clothing associated with gay clones, project an image of sexual frivolity and sexual availability. The outfit seems to fall under Levine's Athlete category (*Butch Sign-Vehicles in Clone Fashion*, table 1998) with gym shorts, tank tops, sweatpants, jock straps, white crew socks, and running shoes considered must-haves to complete

Figure 4.4 In Front of Badlands at the Corner of Christopher and West Street, by Gary Lee Boas (undated, from the series *New York Sex,* 1979–85).

Figure 4.5 Hustler, by Gary Lee Boas (undated, from the series *New York Sex,* 1979–85).

the look. The guy depicted in Boas' *Hustler* is successfully "passing" as a virile, manly athlete by combining clothes and pose in the category of the sportsman as an erotic gay fantasy figure, in much the same way that "drag queen realness is an authenticity based on a collective gay male fantasy of a real woman" (Han, 2015, p. 147).

Hal Fischer's *Gay Semiotics: A Photographic Study of Visual Coding Among Homosexual Men* (1977, 2015) depicts similar features in a photo accompanied by the header "STREET FASH-ION JOCK." As we see in Figure 4.6, the image shows a bearded man wearing a sleeveless undershirt, Adidas trainers, white striped sports socks, and a pair of tight-fitting satin gym shorts (very much in the style of those worn by Gere/Kaye in *American Gigolo's* dumbbells exercise scene) that leave very little to the imagination. This photograph is part of a collection of images that Fischer captured in San Francisco's Castro and Haight-Ashbury districts in the late 1970s, a

Figure 4.6   *Street Fashion Jock*, by Hal Fischer, from the series *Gay Semiotics* (1977).
Source: Courtesy of the artist

significant pre-AIDS period in the city. The photographs focus on the codes of sexual orientation and identification within the gay community at the time, "ranging from such sexual signifiers as handkerchiefs and keys, to depictions of the gay fashion 'types' of that era—from 'basic gay' to 'hippie' and 'jock'" (Figure 4.7).[11]

In *Untitled (Go-Go Dancing Platform)* (1991), Cuban-born, American artist Felix Gonzalez-Torres placed a gay male go-go dancer on top of a square wooden platform encased in light bulbs and invited the diverse gallery audience, through a dance performance, to take a sneak peek into gay bars and club culture, where the sexual identity of male performers (go-go boys) is overtly on display (Watney, 2002, p. 161). According to UrbanDictionary.com, go-go boys are "dancers who are employed to entertain crowds at a club. Usually gay clubs." While the audience routinely tips them directly for their performance, go-go boys are technically or legally not considered prostitutes. As in *Untitled (Go-Go Dancing Platform)*, they are typically very scantily dressed in hot pants or briefs, calling to mind the young muscular toughs of physique or beefcake magazines, first launched in 1951 by American photographer Bob Mizer and titled *Physique Pictorial*.

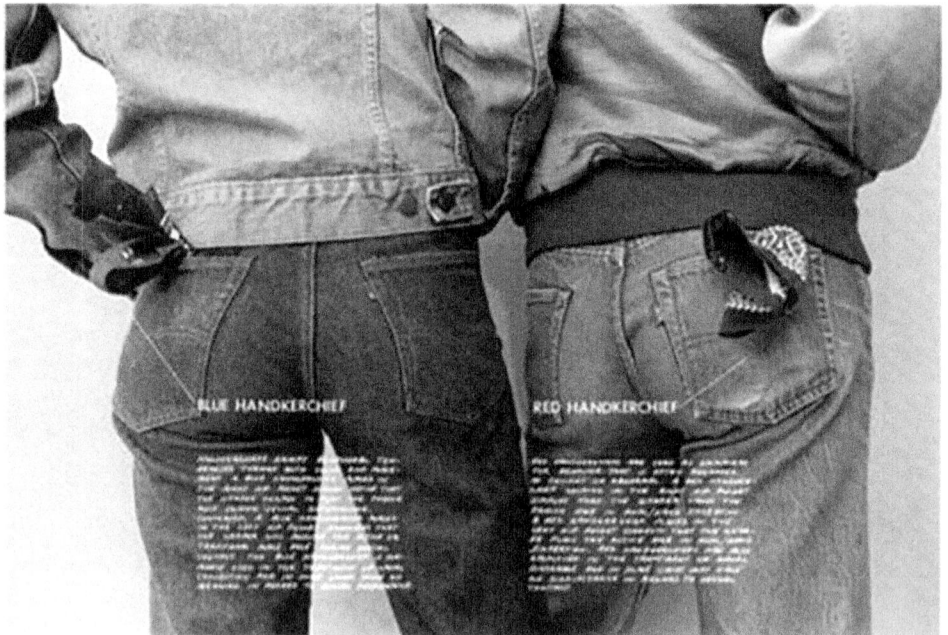

Figure 4.7   Handkerchiefs, by Hal Fischer, from the series *Gay Semiotics* (1977).

The alternative to more explicit gay erotica, which was forbidden at that time, physique magazines portrayed young male models wearing clothes that accentuated and revealed their bodies, emphasizing bulging muscles and naked skin. The magazines featured semi-nude and full-frontal nudity, along with stylized variations on gay male icons and fantasy figures such as the uniformed policeman, the army man, the cowboy and the sailor. Highly theatrical, and referencing heavily Hollywood westerns and sword-and-sandal aesthetics, beefcake photography placed an emphasis on clothing and props as means of extending the sexual models' appeal, mimicking the visual language of mid-twentieth-century fashion and advertising photography. Beefcake photographers used rear projection and studio props such as pillars, Greek columns, fishnets, and draperies to simulate hypermasculine, primarily heterosexual environments and stimulate the predominantly gay audience that beefcake magazines were aiming to reach. Some of the men depicted in physique magazines also prostituted themselves, with their magazine spreads discreetly functioning as advertisements for their services. For example, J. Brian Donahue's *Golden Boys* magazine, operating from 1963, showcased a selection of good-looking young California men who were also available for hire, operating from a boy brothel that was apparently frequented by Truman Capote and Tennessee Williams (Escoffier, 2009, p. 150). Mizer developed a system of symbols that he marked photos with, each symbol denoting the model/prostitute's sexual orientation, active/passive role, penis size, and so on:

> An "x" with prongs on all four ends marked the model as having a boastful and arrogant personality. A circle with a downward-pointing arrow denoted the model as having a dominant, forceful personality. An "x" with a black circle above it marked the model as physically dangerous, and so on.
>
> *(Bell, 2017)*

One of Mizer's most famous physique male models/hustlers was Joe Dallesandro, immortalized in Lou Reed's song "Walk on the Wild Side" (1973). In his physique images, and in the films he made in the early part of his career, Dallesandro appears unclothed, his naked body in full view for an audience of admirers. Dallesandro, probably drawing on his own experience as a hustler, starred in Andy Warhol's production of Paul Morrissey's 1968 film titled *Flesh*, playing a NYC street hustler in the first of a trilogy (the other films are *Trash*, 1970 and *Heat*, 1972). The cover of the videotape's 1996 release reinforces the cultural perception of male prostitutes as a street-savvy conmen. Dallesandro peers at the viewer, a red bandana tied around his greasy hair, looking very much like a Latino boy offender in a late fifties street gang (such as the Sharks, depicted in the 1961 film production of *West Side Story*). Reay describes one of the few instances in the film where Dallesandro is actually wearing clothes and how Morrissey's camera "cruises him on the street, scanning upwards: lingering briefly on his blue-jeaned crotch, belt, black T-shirt, open light blue shirt, and red bandana" (2010, p. 206).[12]

In the 1970s, Californian documentary photographer Anthony Friedkin featured black and Hispanic hustlers in his more racially and ethnically diverse visual investigation of male sex work and the urban scene in Los Angeles.[13] The photographs were part of *The Gay Essay* (1973) portfolio, a body of work that focuses on representations of the lesbian and gay communities in Los Angeles and San Francisco in the early 1970s. In the *Hollywood* (1971) section of the photographic essay, Friedkin looks at and focuses on the male prostitution scene that he encountered on Selma Avenue, just off Hollywood Boulevard. As Figure 4.8 illustrates, Friedkin's black-and-white images of hustlers show tough-looking young men who would not necessarily be described as attractive or good-looking, dressed in various garments straight out of the rough-trade hustler's closet: tight denim trousers, a denim or leather jacket, a wide belt and buckle, a

Figure 4.8 Anthony Friedkin's *Hustlers, Selma Avenue, Hollywood* from *The Gay Essay* (1973).

muscle-hugging shirt, or a wife-beater tank top. Friedkin captures the guys sitting or standing on street corners, looking around, waiting for a car to pull up. In an interview, Friedkin commented on the elements of physical and mental sexual violence that were integral to the scene he observed. It is clear that as a heterosexual male, Friedkin found the setting odd, dangerous, and to some extent worrisome, and it is interesting to note that the exact same setting will probably continue to trigger and elicit sexual arousal in some gay men, clients and artists alike. By the mid 1970s, it seems clear that the appeal of "rough trade" prostitution exclusively occupies the gay imagination and seems to be completely absent in images of heterosexual male prostitutes who sell sex to women.

"I know what you're thinking. You know what I'm thinking. We have our own methods of communication": Male Escort Fashion Online[14]

Streetwalking male sex workers do not necessarily always cater exclusively to a gay clientele. In *Portrait of an Ageing Hustler* (1979), writer and contributing editor to *New York* magazine Orde Coombs portrays the life and times of Bobby Vignolo, a 36-year-old male prostitute struggling to make ends meet in New York City in the late 1960s and 1970s. As a typical young heterosexual male, Vignolo identified his target customers as female. However, the article suggests that as he grew older and his looks faded, he expanded his business and began catering to gay men as well. His friend Kelly had no better luck. Kelly was an aging African American escort whom Vignolo has taken Coombs to meet in a Black hustlers' bar on 42nd Street. In their heyday, Bobby and Kelly exchanged sexual services for money or goods. When Kelly was the sexual companion of "the wife of one of the biggest white civil-rights lawyers in the country," she bought him clothes from Barneys and men's jewelry from Tiffany & Co. After she left him, he didn't manage to find another "good meal ticket, and now he's forced to hustle at the Ramrod—a late-night, all-male movie house on Broadway at 49th." Back to Vignolo, in his "tight-fitting denim suit which sits well on his five-foot-ten-inch frame," the article establishes and confirms a street hustler stereotype: "As he walks he puts his hands in his pockets and pulls down the red tank top he's wearing. He must, always, show the trimness of his body, the glistening pectoral muscles."

Coombs charts Vignolo's descent from a young, optimistic 21-year-old guy who just finished his army service, trying his luck in the big city, to the moment when he "stopped wearing the suits that he could no longer afford to clean" and convinced himself that "he looked sexier in jeans." Coombs describes a poignant moment when Vignolo first locked eyes with a wealthy German woman sitting by herself at the bar he'd been working in, cigarette dangling from the corner of his mouth, calling him "juvenile pap moving into congealed hustler shape." One can recognize a thread of narcissistic and at times nihilistic self-awareness evident in the way male hustlers such as Bobby Vignolo choose to represent themselves once they have acquired a sympathetic audience. This narcissism is often seen in today's male prostitutes mostly via the use of selfies and *plandids* (planned candid photographs) on websites and social media platforms.

Portrait of an Ageing Hustler emphasizes the difficulties that male sex workers like Vignolo and Kelly face in obtaining consistent work and a steady clientele as they rely mainly on chance or one-time encounters. But one can't help but imagine the impact of the Internet on Vignolo and Kelly's livelihood had they been in business today, given the various possibilities and numerous ways of promoting oneself online. By 2009, 30 years after Coombs documented Bobby Vignolo's struggles with reinvigorating his career, use of the Internet had become a key advertisement tool for prostitutes to attract customers (Lee-Gonyea, Castle, & Gonyea, 2009, p. 335). Almost a decade later, by 2018, the presentation of self and lifestyle through photographs via online platforms had become part of many individuals' daily reality, and an electronic presence features heavily as a prime and strategic marketing tool for escorts. For contemporary male prostitutes advertising online, the selfie is the most important and accessible self-marketing tool. Selfie self-portraits are "pleasure, attention, and validation all in one" (Eler, 2017, n.p.). Moreover, selfies "empower individuals to be active agents in defining their own beauty, gender, and sexuality" (Eler, 2017, n.p.). In addition, the plandid—a hybrid of "planned" and "candid" subjective shot—elaborates on the selfie by offering an opportunity to construct meticulously composed, nonchalant-appearing images that suggest a perfect, desirable moment in a wonderful, attractive lifestyle. By pointing a readily available smartphone or digital camera at themselves, men and women choose to either replicate or challenge contemporary notions of beauty and appearances. With the online representation of masculinity and the male body, men can now be called "narcissistic," "social climbers," or "fashion conscious", or they can be classified as "sexually available" or "objectified," labels that were previously attributed to, and primarily associated with, women.

Using their online profiles as a product package that customers judge and evaluate has become almost ubiquitous among male prostitutes. Roberto Dulce, also known as Sweet Roy, is probably Italy's most famous and popular gigolo, a regular on Italian TV talk shows. He collects between 500 and 2000 Euros (approximately $700 to $3000) for the services that he offers solely to single women. Dulce's personal Instagram account page (@roberto_roy_dolce, where he calls himself a "happiness consultant") features 50 selfie and plandid images of himself dressed in all sorts of expensive, fancy-looking clothes: two- and three-piece suits; formal shirts; a variety of ties and other accessories, including a chunky, expensive-looking watch; glasses; belts (with a very visible silver Hermes "H" buckle); and other male jewelry items. His thick dark hair, eyebrows, and beard are all well manicured. The profile contains few photographs in which Dulce is wearing casual clothes; only four photographs show him in underwear or focus on his half-naked body. Dulce's *bella figura* photographs seem to lack any sense of self-irony as he fully embraces the stereotype of the Italian Playboy and the Latin Lover—a Hollywood-influenced Italian Romeo, posing as a sophisticated, suave, sensual, sexy ladies' man. One plandid shows him in typical *American Gigolo* mode (and to a certain extent, *American Gigolo* attire) as he's walking down the street, nonchalantly carrying his suit jacket over his shoulder.

Dulce is an example of a growing number of contemporary male prostitutes using social media platforms and dedicated escort websites as direct promotion tools, showcasing the escorts' awareness of fashion as a marketing tool. Allan Tyler looks at various strategies that are employed by (mainly gay) male sex workers to promote their professional services in his essay "Advertising Male Sexual Services" (2014). Due to the decline of print media and the continuous rise of digital media, it is probably fair to say that the majority of male sex workers now advertise their services and communicate with their clients on dedicated business pages (Facebook, Twitter, Instagram) or via escort agency websites. In the section titled "A Picture Is Worth a Thousand Words," Tyler highlights the importance of photography to "reinforce identities that are based on physical or personal characteristics, or on particular services." In addition, over the past ten years or so, changes in the visual and photographic modes used in advertising male sex work also depict a cultural change in the perception of the sexual behavior of male homosexuals in general, and those involved in male prostitution in particular. Tyler compares a relatively tame image from the early 1990s of "an attractive, well-groomed young man in a white sleeveless T-shirt" with the more sexually explicit images that we see today. Rapid dissemination of such images has been made possible by social/sexual networking and e-commerce sites and environments such as Gaydar, Manhunt, and Grindr (2014, pp. 96–98). Grov and Smith (2014) add that in the digital age, once escorts have paid an initial fee, their profiles/advertisements can include

> long descriptions of their services as well as photographs and short videos, which was not possible in print. This allowed sex workers to present a more professional face and to reach potential customers in a more compelling and targeted manner.
>
> *(2014, p. 250)*

Having looked at a variety of European and international websites that are dedicated to promoting sex work[15] and that feature profiles of male sex workers, I noticed that there is a very clear difference between the perception and promotion of male sex work based on sexual orientation. Gay male prostitution seems to be primarily associated with the body, carnality, sex, promiscuity, and sordidness. Straight male prostitution is associated with high class, companionship, the finer things in life, and—if it comes to it—being positive about sex. Those connotations are reflected in the promotion strategy and visual language that escorts use on their profile pages. Straight male escorts focus on creating a sensual enigma (very much in the style of Christian Grey, the fictional character from the *Fifty Shades of Grey* trilogy; some straight escorts even use "Grey" as a fictional surname.) In contrast, gay male escorts focus on body parts in the personal information they provide and in the photos they display ("8" thick & cut," "big and ripped," "Brazilian monster cock," "chunky thighs and arse," "full of cum," "gold virgin ass," and so on).[16]

Dan G, a 27-year-old former paratrooper from York, United Kingdom, apparently chooses to offer men and women companionship and joyful sex because he is "a very understanding person who can relate to people lives and emotions and just like to give people a great time and make some wonderful memories," as he describes himself on his profile page on *The Male Escort Agency* website (2018). The photos on his page show him alternating personas. In some photos, he presents himself as a sophisticated, worldly gigolo standing by a piano dressed in a black tuxedo, a white shirt, and a black bow tie; in others as the life of the party, wearing a suit jacket with his jeans, holding a bottle of champagne and a flute glass; in others, projecting gay escort realness as he pulls down his white aussieBum briefs. The photos on Dan G's profile are typical in how they reinforce stereotypical views of male escorts. Rather than opting for standard and straightforward mirror selfies, the model performs for the camera his ideas about what his clients would like to see: the fantasy-turned-reality that he is, or who he might be, rather than who he really is. Quite a few escorts include the sentence "What you see is what you get" as a form of "guarantee" or reassurance. Some gay male escorts use more elaborate text specifically to enhance the fantasy element. Russian James advertises his unique selling proposition on www.sleepyboy.com, a UK site for male escorts and sex workers catering to gay men:

> In Western country, men talk about being alpha to hide insecurity of being little girl and puff tiny little chest to look like tough man. In mother Russia, we no need talk. We are real men, alphas, gods. Look at our president. If I make Putin look like pussy, what do I make you look like fag? I come from cold country but will make your life fiery hell. Do not pretend you do not secretly wish for this. Come worship young fitness muscle god from Siberia.
>
> *(2018)*

Accompanying this intentionally vulgar manifesto, which replaces real representation with cultural stereotypes and probably offers prospective clients a turn-on narrative, is a portfolio of photographs primarily showing Russian James posing bare-chested, or wearing nothing at all, making the most of his stereotypical pumped-up gym body. Because Russian James is a "man's man," the other images show him smoking a "manly" cigar or posing for selfies in front of a gym mirror. As his profile says, Russian James will also meet women, so some images show a softer side as he engages in cooking activities or present him as more respectable looking as he stands in a reflective pose, wearing a tight, white button-down shirt and black-rimmed eyeglasses. (Of course, it is very unlikely that women will look for a companion on www.sleepyboy.com, as Russian James's profile epitomizes classic gay escort style and lifestyle aspiration.)

Because the main service for sale is sex, gay male prostitutes' selfies focus on body image, presenting the male body as an object of desire, highlighting the goods on offer: cock, ass, muscles, feet. The few items of clothing worn do not serve the purpose of proposing a coherent outfit but rather function more to highlight various body parts. Fashion here fulfills a role similar to the role it played in physique photography: to draw the audience's eyes and minds to what lies underneath. It also fosters a user experience of seeing through clothes and imagining sexual scenarios rather than looking at clothing and appreciating them and the role they perform in the social construction of identity. While today's selfies of male escorts often contain the visible branding of favorite underwear brands such as Calvin Klein, aussieBum, Andrew Christian, C-IN2, 2(x)ist, and Charlie by Matthew Zink, other than that, we don't see much difference between them and 1950s physique pictures. As far as gay men's erotica is concerned, little clothing (men's underwear; posing pouches), or a complete lack of clothing, is one of the main factors that determines how sexually desirable an escort could turn out to be.

The Internet is awash with pages and services like those described in this chapter. Whether intended for heterosexuals or homosexuals, they all seem to communicate similar messages in similar ways. Clearly, many personal factors influence these advertisements, including economic and social class, cultural background and upbringing, diverse sexual orientations and preferences, and each escort's individual level of motivation and involvement in prostitution. But when it comes to the visual representation and the systems of signs used to represent, denote, signify, or evoke desire and seduction, it seems everyone is relying on relatively limited elements, as we see on sites such as The Men's Company (www.gigolo-escort.co.uk), RentMen.com, and Friendboy.pro, which cover multiple locations around the world.

Wanting to be wanted

In previous research, I explored the representation of the rough-trade prostitution scene, focusing on the intensities of the character of the white, hetero-flexible, working-class man as a gay fantasy figure since the late 1940s. In the aftermath of World War II, perhaps influenced by the hypermasculine image of the American GI and the Liberation experience,[17] French artists such as Jean Cocteau, Antonin Ivanovitch Soungouroff, Jean Boullet, Paul Smara, and Roland Caillaux featured in their erotic drawings characters of tough-looking sailors, soldiers, factory workers, and down-and-outs who could be identified as "gay-for-pay" male prostitutes. The 1960s and 1970s saw the continued prominence of the figure, from the nonchalant, streetwise swagger captured in the documentary pictures of Larry Clark and Danny Fields; to the passive postures of Joe Dallesandro and other male physique and bodybuilding models; and later to the representation of male prostitution in art in the work of Bill Rice, John S. Barrington, Kenny Burgess, Mark Morrisroe, Pedro Slim, George Dureau, Philip-Lorca DiCorcia, and Eve Fowler;

and in contemporary fashion photographs (in the work of Matthias Vriens-McGrath, Mert Alas & Marcus Piggott, and Willy Vanderperre, to name just a few).

One of the key goals of my study was to highlight the criminal element closely associated with male prostitution and to suggest that criminal fantasy plays a key role in the hustler-client relationship. Relying on the rich history of male prostitution as it is depicted in literature, visual arts, and film, I considered how artists were drawn to associate prostitution with rough, coarse, lower-class men who performed a fantasy of hypermasculinity mainly for white middle-class gay male clients. There was always a strong element of risk and danger associated with rough-trade hustling, due in part to the illegal status of homosexuality and prostitution and to the shame and stigma associated with both. Stigma and criminalization had forced male sex workers to operate at the fringes, in environments and places that are both private and dangerous. In the big cities, backstreets and dingy hotel rooms; old piers, docks, and waterfront areas; industrial ghost areas; parks and public toilets became the real-life and fictional backdrops for tales of sex and desire. The bleakness and roughness of the location completed the fantasy of the rough encounter: having sex with a Real Man, a manly heterosexual, as opposed to a supposedly effeminate homosexual. The vicious real-life murder of some high-profile gay clients (including silent film actor Ramon Novarro, film director Pier Paolo Pasolini, and fashion designers Gianni Versace and Rudolph Moshammer) by their rough-trade, gay-for-pay male hustler companions brought to light (and to public awareness) the particular circumstances of the gay hustler-client associations and the dangerous implications of their encounters, starkly highlighting the different socioeconomic status between male hustlers and their clients.

The starting point of my current research was this strong negative association, the promiscuity and the despair associated with homosexual prostitution, compared with the celebration of masculinity associated with a heterosexual gigolo who appears powerful, even triumphant. My goal was to identify the male sex worker's "uniform" by looking at the different ways in which male prostitutes use fashion and styling as an extension of their personae and the impact of specific fashion clothing styles on their clients' imagination. It became apparent that the visual systems employed by male sex workers are still almost exclusively derived from traditional ideas about heterosexual masculinity, with their personal style denoting the distinctive sexual, intellectual, and aesthetic experience that they offer to their clients. For male prostitutes serving female customers, being style conscious and impeccably dressed implements the conventional approach to what is considered sexually attractive in Western heterosexual culture. Within gay male prostitution, there is still a focus on clone fashion, tight-fitting clothing, and "straight-acting" demeanor,[18] showcasing a lack of appreciation for the complexities of the style of dress associated with alternative gay masculinities such as the feminized gay Twink, Club Kids, Gay Goths, and so on.[19]

In addition, there is evidence that the style of clothing and relatively limited "looks" worn by male prostitutes directly correspond to their clients' desire for more rounded psychosexual experiences. Other than sex, these experiences can include, for women, the extremely popular "boyfriend experience"; domestic/international travel; dinner dates; shopping, social events, and parties; days out and evenings in—which require paid male companions to dress in conservative, sartorial fashion. For gay men, these experiences can include sexual dominance, kinks, raw (condomless) sex, sex parties and orgies, massage, spanking, fist-fucking, role play, dirty talk, foot fetishism, muscle worship, and any other activity covering the gamut of sexual practices and sensibilities—and so the overall rent boy fashion style is more likely to be body revealing, accentuating parts of the male body that are sexually desirable. On careful examination of the scenarios that male clients and female clients of male prostitutes may seek to simulate, whether "normal couple activities" or anything *but* replicating romantic experiences, it appears that fashion plays a pivotal role in the shaping and facilitation of the indispensable fantasy element associated with the act of being sexually involved with another person.[20]

Notes

1 Research recognizes various types of male sex workers, including street hustlers (including the sub-category of trade hustlers), escorts, callboys, and masseurs (Caukins & Coombs, 1976; Pruitt, 2005). This chapter mainly focuses on street/trade hustlers and gay and straight Internet escorts.

2 Armani's *American Gigolo* wardrobe, with its fabric palette of grey, beige, greige, anthracite, taupe, and brown, not only catapulted the designer to international fashion stardom, but has also redefined menswear and become part of the vocabulary of menswear tailoring, referenced to this day in the menswear collections of contemporary brands such as *Bottega Veneta* and *Rag + Bone*.

3 See Parsons, J. T., et al. (2001). Sexual compulsivity among gay/bisexual male escorts who advertise on the internet. *Sexual Addiction and Compulsivity, 8*(2), 101–112.

4 For example, there is plenty of uncensored video blogging (vlogging) on gay and straight escort pages on Twitter.

5 *American Gigolo* is marked by a number of scenes that highlight (through Schrader's use of tracking shots set up from behind Richard Gere) the strategic importance of Gere/Kaye's well-shaped buttocks, encased in a variety of perfectly fitted trousers. The protagonist's status as a sexual object and the focus on his backside is present pretty much from the film's very first scene, and regardless of Kaye's occupation as prostitute, this focus on the male derrière alone can be perceived as highlighting a more feminine take on sexuality, as well as a homosexual gaze.

6 "The state of being dressed in a casual or careless style" (Merriam-Webster, n.d.).

7 Duke University's Digital Repository library staff notes: "In addition to strip club storefronts, there seem to be photographs of male prostitutes or hustlers."

8 A spoof on Shirley Temple's high-camp, Depression-era musicals.

9 In post-WWII Paris and, later, New York in the 1950s and 1960s, much attention was given to the streets and urban life by writers, artists, and documentary photographers. Street hustlers became by default the subject of documentary photography.

10 See pp. 5–6 in Doron, I. (2015). Queering foreign bodies: Discourse and identity in visual representations of straight migrant men. In Jillian E. Cox (Ed.), *Ways of queering, ways of seeing* (pp. 115–147). Oxford: Inter-Disciplinary Press.

11 "HAL FISCHER," Cherry and Martin, accessed August 18, 2018. A similar outfit of sneakers and gym shorts (minus the sleeveless t-shirt) was adopted and worn by the young, scantily clad busboys at legendary New York City nightclub *Studio 54* in the late 1970s, enhancing the club's mood of debauchery.

12 The red bandana is also an established fashion item associated with gay male cloning culture. Fischer notes it as a signifier for "top" or "bottom" gay sexual roles—depending on where it is placed in the back pocket (right pocket signifies "passive," while left pocket signifies "active"). Figure 4.8 shows the photo that accompanies the red and blue handkerchief entry in *Gay Semiotics* is reminiscent of the front and back cover of the Rolling Stones' *Sticky Fingers* (1971) album, featuring Dallesandro's life-size denim crotch (complete with a real zipper) and denim-encased tight buttocks.

13 For additional photographic representation of ethnically diverse street hustlers, see the work of George Dureau, Pedro Slim, and Larry Clark.

14 Julian Kaye's opening lines in the *American Gigolo* movie script by Paul Schrader.

15 *Gentlemen4Hire* (UK); *Dukes of Daisy* (UK-US); *The Men's Company* (Belgium); *The Men's Company* (UK); *Elite Male Models* (Spain); *London Privé* (UK); *Escorta* (Italy); *Societyservice* (Netherlands); *Redlights* (Netherlands); *Charisma Beauties* (Germany); *Callboy* (Germany); *Meine Begleitung* (Germany); *Gayescortclub* (Germany); *Topczechescort* (Czech Republic).

16 See Lee-Gonyea, J. A., et al. (2009). Laid to order: Male escorts advertising on the internet. *Deviant Behavior, 30*, 342–344.

17 See Roberts, M. L. (2013). *What soldiers do: Sex and the American GI in World War II France*. Chicago, IL: University of Chicago Press, for a discussion about representations of masculinity and the hard-hitting American GI in France at the time.

18 A term that refers to gay men whose behavior corresponds to, and seeks to simulate, stereotypical heterosexual masculinity. It is a frequent feature in user profiles on gay dating apps and used by gay male

prostitutes that define their masculinity as non-feminine. The term implies that the body language associated with gay men is significantly different from that of "normative" heterosexual men.

19 See Trevon D. Logan's discussion of hegemonic masculinity contextualized with clients' preferences in (2014). *Economic analysis of male sex work* (pp. 113–116). New York: Harrington Park Press.

20 Many of the observations in this section are based on my own research and understanding rather than on specific empirically based research that cites specific numbers.

Bibliography

Bancroft, A. (2012). *Fashion and psychoanalysis: Styling the self.* London: I. B. Tauris.

BBC Online. (2018). Backpage.com sex advert website owners face charges. *BBC.co.uk.* Retrieved from www.bbc.co.uk/news/technology-43699203

Bell, D. (2017). Character analysis revealed the core of Mizer's models. *Bob Mizer Foundation.* Retrieved from http://bobmizer.org/blog/2017/character-analysis-revealed-the-core-of-mizers-models

Boas, G. L. (2003). *New York sex, 1979–1985.* Paris: Edition Kamel Mennour.

Bull, C. (n.d.). Trophy boys. *The Advocate.* Retrieved from https://books.google.co.uk/books?id=GGMEAA AAMBAJ&pg=PA40&dq=cunannan+the+advocate+1997&hl=en&sa=X&ved=0ahUKEwie39u mu-3cAhXCDcAKHYjnBXwQ6AEIKTAA#v=onepage&q=cunannan%20the%20advocate%20 1997&f=false

Burston, P., & Richardson, C. (2005). *A queer romance: Lesbians, gay men and popular culture.* Abingdon: Routledge.

Caukins, S. E., & Coombs, N. R. (1976). The psychodynamics of male prostitution. *American Journal of Psychotherapy, 30*(3), 441–451.

Coombs, O. (1979, December 3). Portrait of an ageing hustler. *New York Magazine,* 46–54.

Doron, I. (2015). Queering foreign bodies: Discourse and identity in visual representations of straight migrant men. In J. E. Cox (Ed.), *Ways of queering, ways of seeing* (pp. 115–147). Oxford: Inter-Disciplinary Press.

Doron, I. (2016). Tinker, soldier, sailor, thief: The visual representations and appropriations of the male sexual outlaw as a gay fantasy figure in the arts and in fashion imagery. *Critical Studies in Men's Fashion, 3*(2), 79–93.

Eck, C., McAllister, J., & van de Vall, R. (1995). *The question of style in philosophy and the arts.* Cambridge: Cambridge University Press.

Eler, A. (2017). *The selfie generation: How our self-images are changing our notions of privacy, sex, consent, and culture.* New York: Skyhorse Publishing.

Eglinton, J. (2018). *A "new Puritanism"? Those who sneer at #MeToo could stand to learn from the Puritans.* Retrieved from www.abc.net.au/religion/articles/2018/03/02/4811225.htm

Escoffier, J. (2009). *Bigger than life: The history of gay porn cinema from beefcake to hardcore.* Philadelphia, PA: Running Press.

Fischer, H. (1977, 2015, 2019). *Gay semiotics: A photographic study of visual coding among homosexual men.* Los Angeles, CA: Cherrydelosreyes. Retrieved from www.cherryandmartin.com/publications/halfischer gaysemiotics

Gedney, W. (2000). *What was true: The photographs and notebooks of William Gedney.* New York: W. W. Norton & Co.

Gedney, W. (n.d.). *William Gedney contact sheet: 1588.* Duke University Libraries Digital Repository. Retrieved from https://repository.duke.edu/dc/gedney/gedst026006003

Gilmour, P. (2017). A male escort answers 21 questions about getting paid to sleep with successful women. *Cosmopolitan.* Retrieved from www.cosmopolitan.com/uk/love-sex/sex/a11658313/male-escort-questions-answered

Grov, C., & Smith, M. D. (2014). Gay subcultures. In V. Minichiello & J. Scott (Eds.), *Male sex work and society* (pp. 242–259). New York: Harrington Park Press.

Han, C. W. (2015). *Geisha of a different kind: Race and sexuality in Gaysian America.* New York, NY: NYU Press.

Haynes, J. (2006). *Style.* Abingdon: Routledge.

Hollander, A. (1994). Interview of Anne Hollander about her book *Sex and Suits*. Interview by Michael Kinsley, *Heads Up*, CNN. Retrieved from www.youtube.com/watch?v=EXro-3KQK1c

Hollander, A. (2016). *Sex and suits: The evolution of modern dress*. London: Bloomsbury Publishing.

Kouvaros, G. (2008). *Paul Schrader (contemporary film directors)*. Champaign, IL: University of Illinois Press.

Lee-Gonyea, J. A., Castle, T., & Gonyea, N. E. (2009). Laid to order: Male escorts advertising on the internet. *Deviant Behavior*, *30*(4), 321–348. https://doi.org/10.1080/01639620802168858

Lehman, P. (2007). *Running scared: Masculinity and the representation of the male body*. Detroit, MI: Wayne State University Press.

Levesley, D. (2016). How has the male escort industry changed since its biggest website was shut down? *Vice Media*. Retrieved from www.vice.com/en_uk/article/kwk7ez/how-has-the-male-escort-industry-changed-since-its-biggest-website-was-shut-down

Levine, M. P. (1998). *Gay macho: The life and death of the homosexual clone*. New York: NYU Press.

The Male Escort Agency. (2018). "Dan G." Retrieved from www.themaleescortagency.com/portfolio/dan-g/

McNamara, M. (2004, April 25). When gay lost its outré. *Los Angeles Times*. Retrieved from http://articles.latimes.com/2004/apr/25/entertainment/ca-mcnamara25/2

Merriam-Webster. (n.d.). *Definition of "dishabille."* Retrieved from www.merriam-webster.com/dictionary/dishabille

Minton, H. L. (2001). Thomas Painter and the study of male prostitution, 1935–43. In H. L. Minton (Ed.), *Departing from deviance: A history of homosexual rights and emancipatory science in America* (pp. 122–158). Chicago, IL: University of Chicago Press.

Murphy, R. (2018) *The Assassination of Gianni Versace: American Crime Story*. USA: FX.

Nardini, G. (1999). *Che bella figura!: The power of performance in an Italian ladies' club in Chicago*. Albany, NY: SUNY Press.

Parsons, J. T., Bimbi, D., & Halkitis, P. N. (2001). Sexual compulsivity among gay/bisexual male escorts who advertise on the Internet. *Sexual Addiction and Compulsivity*, *8*(2), 101–112.

Perry, K. (2012, March 29). The style of *American Gigolo*. *GQ magazine*. Retrieved from www.gq-magazine.co.uk/article/american-gigolo-paul-schrader-armani-suits

Pruitt, M. V. (2005). Online boys: Male-for-male Internet escorts. *Sociological Focus*, *38*(3), 189–203. https://doi.org/10.1080/00380237.2005.10571265

Reay, B. (2010). *New York hustlers: Masculinity and sex in modern America*. Manchester: Manchester University Press.

Reich, J. (2004). *Beyond the Latin lover: Marcello Mastroianni, masculinity, and Italian cinema*. Bloomington, IN: Indiana University Press.

Roberto Roy Dolce (@roberto_roy_dolce). (2018). *Instagram*. Retrieved from www.instagram.com/roberto_roy_dolce/?hl=en

Roberts, M. L. (2013). *What soldiers do: Sex and the American GI in World War II France*. Chicago, IL: University of Chicago Press.

Rodriguez, M. (2015). Here's how sex work changed after the government shut down rentboy.com. *Mic Daily*. Retrieved from https://mic.com/articles/129355/here-s-how-sex-work-changed-after-the-government-shut-this-male-escort-website-down#.Qzyn8ahKV

Schrader, P. (1980). *American Gigolo first draft*. Script City.

Sheaffer, R. (2014). Representations of male sex work in film. In V. Minichiello & J. Scott (Eds.), *Male sex work and society* (pp. 52–79). New York: Harrington Park Press.

Sleepyboy. (n.d.). "Russian James." Retrieved from www.sleepyboy.com/uk/london/escort/siberiangod

Spring, J. (2010). *Secret historian: The life and times of Samuel Steward, professor, tattoo artist, and sexual renegade*. New York: Farrar, Straus and Giroux.

Steward, S. (2012). *Understanding the male hustler*. New York: Routledge.

Tyler, A. (2014). Advertising male sexual services. In V. Minichiello & J. Scott (Eds.), *Male sex work and society* (pp. 84–106). New York: Harrington Park Press.

Urban Dictionary. (n.d.). Definition of "gogo boy." Retrieved from www.urbandictionary.com/define.php?term=gogo%20boy

Vanderbilt, A. (2014). *The best-kept boy in the world.* New York: Riverdale Avenue Books.

Watney, S. (2002). *Imagine hope.* Abingdon: Routledge.

Williams, T. (1975). *Memoirs.* New York: Doubleday.

Williams, T. (2013). *The Roman spring of Mrs. Stone.* New York: New Directions Publishing.

Woodfield, G. (2015, April 25). Cop who found Andrew Cunanan dead in houseboat reveals true story—and what haunts him about Versace killer's suicide. *Daily Mirror.* Retrieved from www.mirror.co.uk/news/world-news/andrew-cunanan-suicide-true-story-12120128

5

Male strippers in popular film

Representations disrobed

Andrea Waling

> "This man only wants to give you pleasure . . . the Rocket's got a supercharged love cannon for ya. . . . Fasten your seatbelts ladies; it's going to be a bumpy ride!"
>
> *A Night in Heaven* (1983)

Men's stripping, in particular for women, has in the last few years become much more visible and embedded in Western culture. Indeed, the male stripper or sexualized male has become a staple for many women's hen's nights. Some have suggested the increased popularity of male stripping is the result of women's increased sexual empowerment and represents positive gains in gay rights liberation movements (Rohlinger, 2002). However, it is important to note that a sexualized male body is not a new phenomenon. Sexually fluid men have been involved with the eroticized body for decades now. From Tom of Finland and Physique Pictorial to the Magic Mike films, the muscular male body has become sexualized and, in many ways, objectified.

In the last 40 years, however, the male body has been increasingly perceived as designed for a presumed heterosexual female gaze[1] (Bordo,1999; Cahill, 2012). With the rise of women's "liberated" sexuality and sexual empowerment in a postfeminist[2] climate (Gill, 2016), along with the increased visibility of women gazing at men's bodies for sexual desire and pleasure (Smith, 2002; Neville, 2015), men's stripping for women has become common in Western culture. Yet, unlike other forms of male sex work and unlike women's stripping, men's stripping for women seems to hold a different set of social norms. While perceptions of women's stripping sit on both sides of the spectrum—it has become normalized in terms of fitness activities relating to pole dancing, but it remains stigmatized because it is sex work—men's stripping in some (but not all) cases seems to avoid stigmatization. Men's strip shows, including the Chippendales (Las Vegas), Thunder from Downunder (Las Vegas), and Manpower (Australia), reframe men's stripping as erotic entertainment, and they have become what many regard as harmless, naughty fun for girls' nights and bachelorette parties. It is perhaps unsurprising, then, that men's stripping has become a feature in many popular films, and it seems to avoid the pathologization that female strippers often encounter (Bradley, 2007). When an activity is *pathologized*, it is treated as psychologically abnormal or unhealthy. Such pathologization includes the idea that female strippers are dirty and riddled with disease, have severe emotional issues and/or a history of abuse, are all victims in need of saving, have questionable morals, and lack self-respect.

This chapter looks at men's heterosexual stripping for women. I use the phrase *men's stripping*, but this term does not include men stripping for other men.[3] Nor does it include transmen who engage in stripping work. Rather, I focus here on the phenomenon of (assumed) heterosexual men's stripping for a female audience.[4] Instead of focusing on a single film, I seek to identify patterns of the representation of men's stripping across films (see Appendix A at the end of this chapter). I draw from a number of films[5] to exam how men's stripping is often seen as separate from, or exclusive, of sex work. I argue that men's stripping in film is represented as a legitimate enterprise, unlike women's stripping. Men's stripping is presented in a number of positive ways: as *humorous, ordinary*, and *average*; as *harmless, naughty*, and *communal;* as inherently *heterosexual, romantic*, and *affectionate*; as representative of *skill, technique*, and *mastery*; and as an activity that is *entrepreneurial, tactical*, and *promotional*. In short, men's heterosexual stripping for women holds a different set of gendered norms, values, and expectations that has enabled it to avoid the stigma, shame, and pathologization that often accompanies women's sex work.

Men's stripping: a review of the literature

Examination of men's stripping starts with the work of Dressel and Petersen (1982a, 1982b), Petersen and Dressel (1982), Prehn (1983), and Clark (1985). The works of Dressel and Petersen (1982a, 1982b) and Petersen and Dressel (1982) consider the question of role transcendence. They look at the extent to which men's and women's roles transfer across in the male strip setting (with men as object and women as subject). They note that women who watch male strippers tend to be more hypersexual and to behave more as men are expected to behave in terms of an aggressive heterosexuality (see Beasley, 2015). They also argue that homosociality among women allows this hypersexuality to emerge. However, even though some male strippers feel objectified and treated like "one-night-stands," male heterosexuality and instrumentality remain in place. That is, men are seen as sexually aggressive, and women remain passive objects rather than active subjects. Further, they contend that "while females initiate expressions of sexual interest within the club, subsequent tactile components of the act do not necessarily reflect gender role transcendence and may reinforce the notion of male instrumentality in sexual matters" (Dressel & Petersen, 1982a).

More recent work has explored male strip shows as homosocial bonding spaces for women (Montemurro, Bloom, & Madell, 2003); men's lived experiences of stripping (Tewksbury, 1993, 1994; Margolis & Arnold, 1993; Scull, 2013, 2015, 2017); the interactions between male strippers and female consumers (Wosick-Correa & Joseph, 2008; Liepe-Levinson, 2002; Smith, 2002); women's motivations for attending strip shows (Montemurro, 2001; Montemurro et al., 2003; Johnson, 2002; Tye & Powers, 1998); and gay, bisexual, and straight men's experiences of stripping for other men (Tewksbury, 1993; DeMarco, 2007). Montemurro et al. (2003) contend that the male strip show and/or club is a space that empowers women and enables them to engage in homosocial bonding, finding solidarity through the desiring of muscular men. Johnson (2002, p. 42) suggests that male strip shows for women allow women to develop a "female-defined heterosexuality without heterosexism." Smith (2002) notes that it is not the male stripper's body that is desirable but rather the eroticism of his movements. Recent ethnographic work by Scull (2017) maintains that male strippers are targets of "fag discourse" and "slut shaming" by women and that the profession is a threat to heterosexuality and masculinity. Scull also contends that male strippers who strip for women avoid such stigma by professionalizing their work, respecting women, avoiding male patrons, and resisting potential feminization by embracing traditional masculine characteristics, such as muscular bodies.

However, some scholars are critical of the male strip show and the claims regarding female empowerment, homosociality, and the ability to engage in female sexuality outside of a heterosexist framework. Wosick-Correa and Joseph (2008) note that, while it appears that women can "get away" with more in terms of touching and treatment of male bodies than men can in the reverse situation, the power dynamics are not the same because women are "not taken seriously as customers who might become carried away in the heat of the moment and violate personal (or even legal) boundaries with dancers" (p. 213). Liepe-Levinson (2002) argues that male strippers often make eye contact to create "connection" with their female audience, which requires women to either look back or look away. Liepe-Levinson also maintains that women do not have the opportunity to gaze at male bodies freely; rather, they are constrained within the dynamics of the space. Margolis and Arnold (1993) note that male strippers present themselves as sexual aggressors and interact only as performers. Their work is perceived as artistic and sexy, rather than sleazy, and they receive more compensation than female strippers do. In their work on amateur strippers, Calhoun, Cannon, and Fisher (1996) contend that men are more positively rewarded than women for sexually oriented behavior.

Pilcher (2009) argues that the female patrons of strip clubs are often directed by a male host or drag queen in how to behave, which includes encouraging women to scream, yell, act raunchy, and touch. Pilcher (2016) notes, "The host reproduces the assumption that women's sexuality needs to be excited, and supervised, or that women do not know how to express sexuality in a public, and non-romantic way" (p. 84). Pilcher (2013) also explores the interactions between male dancers and female audiences, noting that male strippers often perform imitations of sex acts on women. These simulated sex acts are often aggressive, and as Dressel and Petersen (1982a, 1982b) suggest, representative of active male sexuality. Pilcher (2013, 2016) suggests that such performances humiliate women rather than encouraging them to express their sexuality. Waling (2018) looks at the role of the female feminist researcher within the male strip-show space. She argues that male strip shows do not allow for female bonding and homosociality. Rather, they encourage competition among women to be objects in the male stripper's gaze. Thus, as Waling (2018) notes, "Homosociality within this space, in this understanding, is not through the collective act of objectifying men, but rather, the collective act of *being* objectified by these men" (p. 723).

Research exploring representations of men's stripping has been rather limited, focusing mostly on the films *The Full Monty* (1997) and the *Magic Mike* (2012, 2015) series. Scholars have described *The Full Monty* (1997) as a portrayal of the feminization of men and labor in the wake of economic austerity, which requires men to reclaim their masculinity through a feminized form of work (Hicks, 2000). Others debate the film's enactment of a "female gaze" representing the gaze of a female viewer. *Female gaze* is a feminist and theoretical term building on Mulvey's (1975) work on the male gaze. Here, female gaze refers to how men might be portrayed in film to suit women's preferences and sexual subjectivities. Goddard (2000) sees men's stripping in *The Full Monty* (1997) as a complete form of sex-role reversal (men as objects and women as subjects). Farrell (2003) and Cahill (2012) are critical of this interpretation, arguing that the female gaze is constructed in favor of supporting and encouraging men rather than denigrating them or reducing them to objects. Contemporary scholarship on the *Magic Mike* (2012, 2015) series is also divided. Some scholars argue that *Magic Mike* (2012) demonstrates a failed sexualization of men because Mike must leave his stripping career to find happiness (Perfetti-Oates, 2015). It also demonstrates the presence of an objectifying, heterosexual female gaze (Leona & Arimbi, 2016). Chow's (2017) analysis of the *Magic Mike* series offers a more nuanced perspective, exploring the role of austerity, neoliberalism, entrepreneurship, and the appropriation of erotic Black bodies.

It is within this context of this research that I examine the broad cultural representations of men's stripping in film. Ultimately, I show how such representations legitimize men's stripping as valid and justifiable in ways that are not true of women's stripping.

Humorous, ordinary, average

Numerous films feature men's stripping in a way that emphasizes the men's averageness or ordinariness. Often, the characters who strip for women are presented as normal, everyday men who might engage in stripping as a humorous activity for a loved one or as a part-time job. *The Full Monty* provides a quintessential example of ordinary men who are experiencing severe disenfranchisement in Northern England and turn to stripping as a way to make money.

The film takes a humorous and touching approach to the idea of "ordinary" men stripping. The film focuses on the main character, Gaz (Robert Carlyle), who is looking for a better way to pay his child-support payments after being laid off from working at the steel mill. Inspired by a local ladies' night where Chippendale dancers grace the premises, Gaz gathers his friends to engage in a similar venture to earn money. Their routine is less than masterful, with simple movements and a diverse range of older and young bodies. The characters are relatable, accessible, and, as Hicks (2000) argues, able to use a feminized form of labor to win back their "failed" masculinity.

In *Forces of Nature* (1999), the main leads, Ben Holmes (Ben Affleck) and Sarah (Sandra Bullock), find themselves in a gay men's strip bar needing to make a few dollars (Figure 5.1). Sarah convinces Ben to get on stage and strip, as the clients would be uninterested in her. Awkward and resistant, Ben refuses to engage at first, leaving Sarah, who has a background in exotic dancing, to manipulate his body for him. Using him as a pole, Sarah begins to strip his clothes off in a sexually teasing but humorous way. Soon, Ben pushes Sarah's hands away. He begins to strip and engage with the audience as his confidence builds, while Sarah collects money from the men. In this scene, Ben is able to avoid potential homosexualization and feminization through

Figure 5.1 Forces of Nature (1999).

the presence of Sarah on stage while benefiting financially. Because Ben does not rely on strip-ping as an ongoing profession, he is able to maintain his status of being an ordinary and average guy through the humorous representation of his strip-tease (see Cahill, 2012). Further, Sarah's presence functions as what Sedgwick (1985) calls a *token object* in negotiating relations between men. While Sedgwick (1985) refers to relationships between straight men, Sarah acts a media-tor for Ben's heterosexuality on stage with the gay men who view him. Such mediation enables Ben to remain an average, ordinary heterosexual guy, and it removes any vulnerability or sense of threat from his stripping activity in the presence of gay men (see Scull, 2017).

While it does not feature a traditional strip show setting, *Slapshot* (1977) contrasts men's stripping with the aggressive antics of ice hockey. The main character, Ned Braden (Michael Ontkean), is opposed to the rink violence encouraged by his coach, who believes that violence will excite fans. The striptease scene forms the climax of the film. While numerous players of the opposing teams engage in fist fighting, Ned begins to skate around the ice rink, stripping off each item of his hockey gear, accompanied by a live marching band playing the iconic "The Stripper."[6] Ned's striptease is lighthearted, warm, and affectionate, laughable in its absurdity as other hockey players engage in brutality on the ice. By portraying himself as a "lover, not a fighter," Ned manages to halt the violence happening at the other end of the rink and win back his wife's affection. Ned's striptease is noteworthy for its inherent lack of forceful sexuality or inherent sexiness. While Ned is an attractive and fit man, his stripping is intended to be humor-ous, and Ned is an ordinary, everyday guy.

In *13 Going on 30* (2004), Jenna (Jennifer Garner) unexpectedly receives a lap dance from her boyfriend Sam (Alex Carlson). As in other films, the striptease is humorous rather than sexy, with Sam engaging in dance moves that allow him to flex his muscles. The emphasis is on the narcissism of Sam, who is more interested in how his body looks than arousing his partner. Such emphasis is intended to be humorous, with Jenna responding with embarrassment and disgust rather than arousal. Older films like *Pennies from Heaven* (1981) feature a similar scene, with Tom (Christopher Walken) engaging in a theatrical striptease that is not erotic. Rather, the striptease exaggerates femininity, allowing Tom to appear absurd as he transgresses his gender role as male. The stripping is accompanied by skilled tap dancing to further highlight its theatrical and humorous, rather than erotic, nature.

In all of these examples, the use of humor combines with the men's ordinariness to downplay any sense of harm or vulnerability to these men who strip. Stripping is thus seen as fun and light rather than as indicative of a deeper pathology.

Harmless, naughty, communal

Unique to men's stripping is the fact that it is often done in the format of a show rather than as private one-on-one dances. In female strip clubs, women move about the space both as strip-pers on stage and as waitresses, functioning as dispensable decorative objects and background (Margolis & Arnold, 1993). Men's stripping is often presented as touchable only within a par-ticular set of circumstances that are controlled by the strippers themselves rather than the cli-entele. That setting allows the strippers to move about and control the space, while women are directed in how they can approach and touch the men (see Pilcher, 2009, 2013, 2016; Waling, 2018). Thus, men stripping for women is fundamentally different from men stripping for men or women stripping for men. The possibility that clients may harm a stripper is framed around the idea that only men can be sexually aggressive (Pilcher, 2013).

In *Magic Mike* (2012), the opening scene shows Dallas (Matthew McConaughey) on stage, identifying the "rules" regarding where the women in the crowd can touch the men's bodies.

Touching his nipples, crotch, and bum, he asks the women if they can "touch here" as they cheer him on. He shakes his finger and says "No no no no" in a teasing and flirtatious manner. Dallas then goes on to note that he sees "a lot of law breakers up in this house . . . and I don't see a goddamn cop in sight," insinuating that the women in the audience are free to break the rules he has laid out. In *Magic Mike XXL* (2015), the male stripper Andre (Donald Glover) wanders the convention hall in the film's climax, singing to women. He tells one woman, "It's okay, you can touch," when she attempts to reach out and then pulls back. It has been noted that women are more able to "freely" touch male strippers than men are permitted to touch women strippers, but as Wosick-Correa and Joseph (2008) contend, it is the unequal power dynamics in which women are not taken seriously as clients or customers in the male stripping space that allow this touching to occur. The films in the *Magic Mike* series are quintessential examples. The women are encouraged to touch the strippers, but such touching is permitted and controlled by the male performers in the strip show.

Communal love and adoration for the men is another lens through which men's stripping is represented as harmless. In *The Proposal* (2009), the Latin American Ramone (Oscar Nunez) works many jobs. He is the only male exotic dancer in Sitka, a small town in Alaska. Ramone does not embody the muscular physique associated with contemporary men's stripping, nor is his dancing masterful. Rather, he is clumsy, with a body more representative of a dad bod,[7] short, soft around the belly, and not overly muscular. When Margaret (Sandra Bullock) is forced to sit onstage as part of her surprise bachelorette party, she is uncomfortable as Ramone dances around her in a sexually explicit manner while the crowd cheers, echoing some women's observations about feeling uneasy in the space (Pilcher, 2009, 2013, 2016; Waling, 2018). Ramone is framed as ordinary here, but more importantly, he is non-threatening. He is well loved by the women in his small community. The men of *The Full Monty* (1997) are similar; as Cahill (2012, p. 78) notes, "The women in the audience know the men and relate to them as husbands, ex-husbands, and members of their own community." According to Cahill (2012, p. 78), when

> the women in the audience clap and cheer, they are not applauding the men for having met a set of expectations or standards developed by and for women. Rather, they are recognizing the men in and of themselves, saying that they are welcome and worthy as they are, affirming them in their personhood and their masculinity.

Both *The Full Monty* (1997) and *The Proposal* (2009) feature male stripping as connected to community, where the audience members are not strangers but rather women who love and care for these men. In both films, the men maintain their personhood, and they are regarded with pride and encouragement rather than seen as flawed, damaged, sex workers.

Even in the documentary *La Bare* (2014, Figure 5.2), the male strippers have female family members who are either supportive and encouraging or who are involved in running portions of the business of male stripping. Randy "The Master Blaster," the older male erotic dancer and owner of the club who trains and mentors the younger men, works alongside his 78-year-old mother. She helps run the financial aspects of his business, which includes not only dancing at La Bare but also related ventures, such as sending men out to strip at bachelorette parties. Other male strippers have family members, such as their mothers, sisters, and female cousins, attend their shows. Some women attend regularly to support the boys:

> I feel like they're my friends. Even though every time I give them, I get a hug I give them a dollar, I still feel like they're my friends . . . but you know several more of them are on my Facebook and you know it's, it really is its camaraderie you know I when I'm lonely

Figure 5.2 *La Bare* (2014) is produced and directed by Joe Manganiello, one of the stars of the *Magic Mike* series (2012, 2015). The documentary provides a behind-the-scenes look at the world of men's heterosexual stripping for women. It also touches on issues relating to gang violence.

or when I'm having a bad day I can come here and I can you know say hi to the guys and I smile, I'm happy and it cheers me up it makes me feel good.

Margaret, regular patron of La Bare

Margaret highlights the communal nature of the club, which is not an anonymous space but rather a place she can go to connect with the dancers and feel at home. Such encouragement is a stark contrast to attitudes toward women's stripping, where the conventional wisdom holds that girls who strip do so as a result of dysfunctional relationships with male members of their family, making it is unlikely that family members will come to the club and support their work. In the films discussed previously, the men do not necessarily have to hide their activities or forms of labor. Rather, they are known to work in erotic entertainment, and their work is encouraged rather than stigmatized.

Skill, technique, mastery

Women's stripping requires extensive skill and coordination, especially for those who engage in complex pole routines. It also requires emotional labor. However, these facts are generally not recognized. Men's stripping, in contrast, is built on the recognition of the skills required in terms of men's dancing and work on the body to gain an idealized muscular physique. Classics like *The Full Monty* and newer films, in particular the *Magic Mike* series, the *Chocolate City* (2015, 2017) series, and the documentary *La Bare* (2014), all emphasize the skill, mastery, and technique of dancing as part of the overall male stripper experience. This emphasis presents men's stripping as an art form, repositioning men's stripping as a valid career choice that requires discipline, athleticism, and hard work (Hicks, 2000; Chow, 2017).

In *The Full Monty* (1997), the men watch *Flashdance* (1983) as part of their training. They focus not on the early scenes of Alex's (the lead in *Flashdance*) stripping at her local strip club but rather on her audition and practice for getting into the ballet academy (Hicks, 2000). Further, *The Fully Monty* focuses on athletic pursuits, such as jogging, playing football (soccer), and other physical activities to support the men's training, as opposed to learning to move in erotic and sensual ways (Hicks, 2000). The men also engage Gerald (Tom Wilkinson), a trained ballroom dancer, to help them with their routine. Gerald emphasizes skill, technique, and discipline as key to their performance. Men's striptease is thus positioned as a form of skilled dance rather than as a form of sex work (Hicks, 2000).

The *Magic Mike* and *Chocolate City* series also emphasize skill and technique. Numerous scenes not only depict highly complicated and stylized dancing but also illustrate the behind-the-scenes activities of practicing choreography and training in the gym to achieve such physical feats. The climax performance of *Magic Mike XXL* (2015), where Mike (Channing Tatum) and Malik (Stephen "tWitch" Boss) engage in a dance duet, highlights such skill. A large frame on the stage acts as a mirror, where the two men mimic in time their dancing to two young women sitting back to back. The performance is difficult, with the men engaging in complex body movements that require them to be in time and in step with each other and that require them to synchronize how they interact with the two women on stage.

In the documentary *La Bare* (2014), the male strippers note that women's stripping requires less skill and discipline. Interviews with female strippers in the documentary support this view. The female strippers believe that male strippers work harder and have an overall mastery over the profession that female strippers lack:

> Girls don't do routines. The guys, all of them have to do an actual act and put on a show and stuff.
>
> *Female Stripper 1,*[8] La Bare

> I don't have to go on stage, I'm all about VIP upstairs more personal clients talking but in conversation, having dinner.
>
> *Female Stripper 2,* La Bare

> Actually no skill involved in being a female stripper just get some big titties and a little decent ass, whereas we actually put work into it.
>
> *"JD," male stripper,* La Bare

In other words, both men and women see men's stripping as fully dependent on physical fitness. In addition, the guys have to prepare and perform an act rather than just taking off their clothes in seductive manner. In the previous quotation, JD reduces female stripping to looking at the body, and he suggests that men's stripping requires extensive fitness regimens and practice. This comparison is not accurate. Rather, it relies on the paradox in which women are expected to work on their bodies to achieve an ideal look, but such work needs to be, or is regarded as, invisible (Bartky, 2002). In contrast, men's bodies are viewed as the result of hard work and discipline, and the work they do to achieve such bodies is visible and well regarded.

Also noteworthy is the dismissal of emotional labor as a form of work and skill. While male strippers do engage in emotional work when engaging with their audience members, it is brief and momentary. The emotional work done by female strippers, in particular what Female Stripper 2 highlights in terms of female strippers' having personal conversations with their clients and tending to their needs, is disregarded. The recognition of athleticism, skill, and discipline is vital to the legitimization and professionalization of men's stripping.

Heterosexual, romantic, affectionate

Cahill (2012, p. 78) argues that male strippers who strip to make a living, such as the Chippendales, are feminized, emasculated, and lessened due to the nature of their work. However, I argue that the opposite is true. Specifically, the circumstances of a male strip show allow male strippers access to power and permit them to reinstate gender norms concerning heterosexuality that circumvent potential feminization and emasculation. Films like *Just Can't Get Enough* (2002), *The Chippendales Murder* (2000), *For Ladies Only* (1981), *A Night in Heaven* (1983), *Mr. Mom* (1983), and *Summer School* (1987) all highlight male strippers' sexual eroticism and power. Each of these films contains male strip show scenes where women cheer and applaud the men, and it is the men who choose the women they engage with rather than women choosing them (see Waling, 2018).

In *A Night in Heaven* (1983), Faye (Lesley Ann Warren) is a college teacher who has flunked her student, Ricky (Christopher Atkins). Later, she finds herself at a male strip show, where Ricky is the main stripper known as Ricky the Rocket Man. He seduces her through his dancing, maintaining eye contact with her to make her uneasy and uncomfortable (see Wosick-Correa & Joseph, 2008), then thrusts his pelvis in her face, before kissing her and moving on to the next patron. She is left perplexed and confused, and later in the film, she sleeps with Ricky, only to be humiliated by him when she catches him with his girlfriend. In *Summer School* (1987), Freddy Shoop (Mark Harmon) is a high-school teacher who attends a male strip show and finds himself surprised when he recognizes his student Larry (Ken Olandt) as one of the main performers. Freddy watches, perplexed, while standing next to two older women who beg Larry to come their way. When he does, they kiss him[9] and give him money. When Freddy catches Larry, he attempts to convince him to come back to class to catch up on missed assessments. Larry responds, "Mr. Shoop, think about what you're saying. I mean if you could be 17 again, only you knew then, what you know now." Freddy raises his eyebrow and nods in agreement, and Larry responds, "Well, I know." The exchange is a reference to knowledge about women's pleasure and sexual activity, with Larry noting how his occupation has helped him be successful with women. In both films, men's heterosexual prowess is reaffirmed through women's admiration of them and through the ease with which they can use their jobs as male strippers to engage sexually with women outside of the striptease show.

Newer films like the *Magic Mike* series emphasize the strippers' emotional connection with their female audience. In *Magic Mike* (2012), Dallas (Matthew McConaughey) teaches the recruited Adam/"The Kid" (Alexander Richard Pettyfer) how to move on stage. Dallas begins by circling his own hips in front of the mirror, explaining how a stripper should move around the stage and move his body:

[Dallas circling his own hips in the gym mirror] You're the man, on the stage, thousands of women, eyes on you. You are their vision, so what do you do? You don't just fucking throw your clothes off, do you? You fucking make it count baby. You walk out. You look around, you tease, you seduce. You lock eyes but you don't lock in on any of 'em. They gotta believe you're already inside every single one of 'em. And when the time's right, and you'll know it, you stick it [Pelvic thrust]. And that right there, that's hitting the g-spot. Every. Single. Time.

Dallas then moves Adam's hips to circulate in front of the gym mirror, telling him:

You're not just stripping. You are fulfilling every woman's wildest fantasies. You are the husband they never had. You are that dreamboat guy that never came along. You are the one-night stand, that free, fling of a fuck that they get to have, tonight, with you on stage and still go home to their hubby and not get in trouble because you baby, you made it legal. You are the liberation.

Dallas emphasizes that stripping is not just about getting naked for women. Rather, it is fulfilling a fantasy in a way that is deemed harmless, fun, and enticing rather than crossing the boundary into illegal prostitution. Dallas reminds Adam that stripping and dancing are about connecting with women, albeit superficially, drawing from conventional beliefs that women desire emotional connection and romance over physical attraction and desire. Furthermore, Dallas highlights a fundamental difference between women's stripping and men's stripping: Women's stripping for men can include "private" dances that may include sexually explicit activities such as oral or vaginal sex, while men's stripping for women generally does not permit these activities.[10] Last, Dallas removes the vulnerability that Adam might feel in being an object of a female gaze (see Cahill, 2012) by reminding Adam that he is metaphorically "fucking" these women as the aggressor with his dancing and movements on stage. The film thus reinforces aggressive male heterosexuality throughout. Men's presumed roles as active, sexual aggressors, or those who "do" things to others, remain at the forefront of the male stripping space for women.

In *Magic Mike XXL* (2015), Mike and the gang arrive at Domina, a private, members-only establishment in a former plantation mansion in Savannah, Georgia, on their way to a male stripping convention in Myrtle Beach, South Carolina. Seeking some support after they crash their van into the swamp, they visit Rome (Jada Pinkett Smith), Mike's former lover and boss, who affectionately calls him "White Chocolate." Rome runs a male erotic entertainment-for-women business. Multiple rooms of her home are filled with African-American women who are being entertained by muscular and attractive African-American men.[11] Rome wanders the house as the Master of Ceremonies, checking on her "queens" (the women patrons) and instructing her dancers to take care of various chosen queens throughout the night. Rome emphasizes the need to care for her patrons and to remind them that they are beautiful, and she instructs her dancers to attend to their whims and desires, which are soft touching and romancing, rather than direct sexual gratification. While viewers are led to believe that the home is a privately run brothel, Rome's house does not allow women to pay for sexual pleasure beyond dancing and gentle touching. Thus, while Rome's establishment replicates private, alluring, and decadent sexual play parties, it continues to present female sexuality as interested in romance rather than sex (Tolman, 2000), and it does not cross the boundary into explicit sexual activity.

Entrepreneurial, tactical, promotional

While women's stripping can be, and is, an entrepreneurial endeavor, rarely is it seen as such. In contrast, men's stripping is often considered an entrepreneurial activity in which male strippers are not so much strippers as they are men who use their bodies either as a business venture in and of itself or as a stepping stone to secure funds for future ventures. Unlike women's stripping, often considered the last resort of desperate women or the result of a bad childhood that makes stripping inevitable rather than a life choice (Bradley, 2007), men's stripping is often considered an active, artistic, and decent pursuit.

In the *Magic Mike* series, the main character Mike uses stripping as a way to build monetary assets so he can start his own furniture business. The money that Mike earns stripping, while enabling a lavish lifestyle, has a more fundamental goal: to help him secure a loan. Chow (2017) argues that Mike's entrepreneurship is also established through the way Mike's body becomes both a tool and a product of his labor, whereby "autonomy, creativity, and freedom are manifested in everything from his chiseled muscles and carefully groomed hairlessness to his outstanding choreography" (Chow, 2017). In *Magic Mike XXL* (2015), Mike and his crew begin to experience personal crises regarding their performance routines, recognizing that they feel no connection with the roles they play on stage. Mike encourages the strippers to think outside of the box, to find something that speaks to them and will help create a more authentic performance. He asks the strippers what they are, and they respond they are "male entertainers." Later, when they arrive at the convention, they are greeted by Mike's old friend, Paris (Elizabeth Banks), who runs the convention each year. Paris calls the men "strippers," and they correct her by saying they are male entertainers. They use the same phrase to psych each other up when they prepare to go onstage. Thus, Chow (2017, para. 8) argues, the *Magic Mike* series reconfigures sex work, and in particular men's stripping, as "an opportunity for greater self-actualization and entrepreneurship." *Magic Mike* presents stripping, and stripping performances, as an art form and as entertainment rather than as sex (Chow, 2017).

The *Chocolate City* series (Figure 5.3) focuses on the plight of a young African-American man struggling to make ends meet while attending a local college. Focusing on issues including racism and poverty, the film is less humorous and much more interested in exploring male stripping in the context of austerity, precariousness, and complex social issues. Michael (Robert

Figure 5.3 *Chocolate City* (2015) was created as a response to the lack of African-American representation in the *Magic Mike* (2012) film. Director Jean-Claude La Marre felt it was vital to include people of color, with the film touching on black culture, class tensions, racism, and poverty.

Ri'chard) turns to stripping as a way of paying his college tuition. Like the *Magic Mike* series, the *Chocolate City* series frames men's bodies as a business. During one scene, Michael gets into an altercation with another dancer at the club, Adrian "Rude Boy" (Tyson Beckford), who calls him "Sucker Chocolate" instead of his stage name, "Sexy Chocolate." The looming fight is broken up by the owner and manager Princeton (Michael Jai White), who tells Adrian, "Don't you mess up my money." In other words, Michael and his body are a major money-maker for the club, and Michael's body is the product that is sold.

La Bare (2014) also notes the entrepreneurial nature of men's stripping. Dancers work to build themselves as a brand rather than engaging in erotic dancing solely for money. Presented as independent contractors, the male strippers are encouraged to build up their bodies and to see their bodies as a business:

> We have gotten such a big push now to really get in like fantasy man shape. We train like athletes you know, I'm getting ready for a photo shoot right now you know it's like 45 minutes a day cardio, on top of your workout which you better be wearing your sweat suit so you lose all your water weight. It's intense and there's no off season, you want to have an off season you're not gonna get paid.
>
> *"Chase,"* La Bare

Not only do the male strippers perform shows, they also engage in a series of promotional activities, including photo shoots and convention appearances. Although many female strippers engage in similar promotional work, the male strippers see these promotional activities as fundamentally different from those of female strippers:

> Their job is completely different from ours. Everything about it is different. Everything: how we handle the customers, how we get the money, how much money we make, like with them it really encompasses their entire life, I mean from beginning to end. I mean if they're not training they're eating because they're supposed to be training. You know they have to look a certain way all the time. They have to go to promotions all the time, they have to go do parties all the time, they have to do flyers, they have to model, they have to you know, constantly promote promote promote.
>
> *Female Stripper 1,* La Bare

As Female Stripper 1 notes, the men at La Bare build and structure their lives around their work and build themselves up as a brand.

Conclusion

In film, representations of men's stripping for women reveal a specific set of values, expectations, and belief systems. By portraying men's stripping as humorous and harmless, by emphasizing skill and entrepreneurship, and by replicating traditional scripts of aggressive male sexuality and masculinity, films portray men's stripping as a valid, fun, and financially rewarding occupation for men. The differences in cinematic portrayals of women's stripping and men's stripping do not suggest a gender role reversal regarding sexual objectification, as scholars such as Leona and Arimbi (2016) contend. Nor do they represent the emergence of an autonomous and liberated female gaze (see Perfetti-Oates, 2015). Rather, men's stripping as represented in film reflects what scholars have noted in actual strip venues: It maintains traditional gender hierarchies where men control the space, emphasizing conventional heterosexual romance narratives and assumptions regarding women's sexual desires as tied to romance rather than sex. It also values men's muscular bodies as the results of discipline and athleticism rather than as decorative or sexual objects. Further, in the films discussed in this chapter, promoting oneself as a male erotic dancer and building the body as a brand are essential for continued employment.

While Cahill (2012) maintains that men who strip to make a living wage are feminized, I have argued that many film representations of men's stripping demonstrate the opposite. Men who strip for money engage in entrepreneurship and build their bodies as a business in order to legitimize their occupation. Men's stripping can be understood as a way of "celebrating an ideology of entrepreneurship, which has been embraced in recent years by neoliberal ideologues (and sometimes counterhegemonic voices), as 'a means of insertion into increasingly competitive labor markets,' and a panacea to neoliberalism's collateral damages" (de Sa Mello da Costa & Saraiva, 2012, cited in Chow, 2017, para 2). This normalizing of men's stripping, and how it is presented as erotic entertainment rather than as sex work, allows men who strip for women to avoid the stigma and pathologization associated with women's stripping.

Notes

1 I say "presumed" here to not suggest that men's stripping has been designed for a heterosexual female gaze but rather that such a gaze, and the wants of women, are not necessarily representative of women's actual desires (Cahill, 2012).
2 Gill (2016) is skeptical of the notion that we are now in a postfeminist climate, instead maintaining that we are in what she calls a postfeminist sensibility, in which women are inundated with contradictory feminist and anti-feminist ideas under the guise of sexual empowerment and gender equality. Here, narratives such as women having a "free" sexuality that is not constrained within patriarchy are juxtaposed against what many feminist scholars argue is a heterosexist reconfiguration of women's sexuality as "empowered" but in actuality designed to please men.
3 This chapter does not attend to men's stripping for other men or transmen who might strip for men, though much can be said in terms of how heterosexual men's stripping for women is treated quite differently socially. My focus on men's stripping for women is premised on the invisibility of women's place and role as sex consumers where men are the sex workers. Men's stripping for women is widely recognized as a legitimate leisure activity for women, and yet it is not often considered a form of sex work.
4 By "assumed," I am referring to the belief that men who strip for women are heterosexual, when this is in fact not always the case.
5 I note that all of the films analyzed in this piece were produced in the United States. As such, this analysis is situated within a predominantly white and Western framework.
6 By late American composer David Rose, this jazz-influenced instrumental piece is iconic, using prominent trombone slides to evoke the feeling of music believed to accompany striptease artists.
7 A "dad bod" is a male physique associated with middle-aged men, commonly fathers, whose familial responsibilities have made it difficult for them to maintain strict fitness routines. This physique is a cross between soft muscularity and being overweight.
8 The names of the female strippers interviewed in *La Bare* are not provided, but female patrons and family members are named. Perhaps the women strippers did not want to reveal either a real or stage name; however, the film's unwillingness to name the strippers does in some way illustrate a lessening of personhood for these woman, whose identity is reduced to "stripper."
9 It is important to note that generally the men choose the women they'll provide a dance for, and this choice becomes a major focal point of the show. In contrast, in female strip clubs, the women wander around the space until chosen by a client. Men might be given money during their performance, but it is a token gesture as opposed to a full payment for an individual dance. In both the fictional films and in *La Bare*, male strippers will also give women a quick hug or kiss on the cheek after giving them a lap dance. Such action is understood as "respecting" women and meant to dissolve any potential notion of sexual harm toward women by engaging in signs of affection (Scull, 2017).
10 This is not to suggest that male strippers do not sleep with their clients. In the case of the *Magic Mike* Series, the men often sleep with female patrons but outside of their employment. In *La Bare*, "Don't

fuck your money" is a common phrase the men repeat to themselves and to each other. In other words, sleeping with clients means those clients will no longer attend the club because their fantasy has been "fulfilled."

11 While not the focus of this chapter, Chow's (2017) analysis of *Magic Mike XXL* looks at the portrayal of Black female desire, intimacy and enjoyment. Chow contends that the scene in Domina is "radical in its celebration of desirous [Black] bodies without shame" but is critical of the appropriation of Blackness and token gestures toward slavery within the film.

References

Bartky, L. (2002). *Sympathy solidarity and othwer essays*. London: Rowman & Littlefield.

Beasley, C. (2015). Libidinal heterodoxy: Heterosexuality, hetero-masculinity, and "transgression." *Men and Masculinities, 18*(2), 140–158.

Bordo, S. (1999). *The male body: A new look at men in public and in private*. New York: Farrar, Straus and Giroux.

Bradley, M. S. (2007). Girlfriends, wives, and strippers: Managing stigma in exotic dancer romantic relationships. *Deviant Behavior, 28*(4), 379–406.

Cahill, A. J. (2012). *Overcoming objectification: A carnal ethics*. London: Routledge.

Calhoun, T. C., Cannon, J. A., & Fisher, R. (1996). Amateur stripping: Sexualized entertainment and gendered fun. *Sociological Focus, 29*(2), 155–166.

Chow, B. (2017). Every little thing he does: Entrepreneurship and appropriation in the Magic Mike series. *Lateral: Journal of the Cultural Studies Association, 6*. https://doi.org/10.25158/L6.1.3.

Clark, R. (1985). Male strippers: Ladies' night at the meat market. *The Journal of Popular Culture, 19*(1), 51–56.

DeMarco, J. R. G. (2007). Power and control in gay strip clubs. *Journal of Homosexuality, 53*(1–2), 111–127.

de Sa Mello da Costa, A., & Saraiva, L. A. S. (2012). Hegemonic discourses on entrepreneurship as an ideological mechanism for the reproduction of capitalism. *Organization, 19*(5), 587–614.

Dressel, P. L., & Petersen, D. M. (1982a). Becoming a male stripper: Recruitment, socialisation, and ideological development. *Work and Occupations, 9*(3), 387–406.

Dressel, P. L., & Petersen, D. M. (1982b). Gender roles, sexuality, and the male strip show: The structuring of sexual opportunity. *Sociological Focus, 15*(2), 151–162.

Farrell, K. (2003). Naked nation: *The Full Monty*, working-class masculinity, and the British image. *Men and Masculinities, 6*(2), 119–135.

Gill, R. (2016). Post-postfeminism? New feminist visibilities in postfeminist times. *Feminist Media Studies, 16*(4), 610–630.

Goddard, K. (2000). Looks maketh the man: The female gaze and the construction of masculinity. *The Journal of Men's Studies, 9*(1), 23–39.

Hicks, H. J. (2000). Postindustrial striptease: *The Full Monty* and the feminization of work. *Colby Quarterly, 36*(1), 48–59.

Johnson, M. L. (2002). *Jane sexes it up: True confessions of feminist desire*. New York: Four Walls Eight Windows.

Leona, A., & Arimbi, D. A. (2016). Man's body on the line: Male objectification in *Magic Mike* (2012). *Allusion, 5*(2), 191–199.

Liepe-Levinson, K. (2002). *Strip show: Performances of gender and desire*. New York: Routledge.

Margolis, M. L., & Arnold, M. (1993). Turning the tables? Male strippers and hierarchy. In B. Miller (Ed.), *Sex and gender* (pp. 334–350). Cambridge, MA: Cambridge University Press.

Montemurro, B. (2001). Strippers and screamers: The emergence of social control in a noninstitutionalized setting. *Journal of Contemporary Ethnography, 30*(3), 275–304.

Montemurro, B., Bloom, C., & Madell, K. (2003). Ladies night out: A typology of women patrons of a male strip club. *Deviant Behavior, 24*(4), 333–352.

Mulvey, L. (1975). Visual pleasure and narrative cinema. *Screen, 16*(3), 6–18.

Neville, L. (2015). "Male gays in the female gaze": Women who watch M/M pornography. *Porn Studies, 2*(2–3), 192–207.

Perfetti-Oates, N. (2015). Chick flicks and the straight female gaze: Sexual objectification and sex negativity in *New Moon, Forgetting Sarah Marshall, Magic Mike*, and *Fool's Gold. Gender Forum: An Internet Journal for Gender Studies, 51*, 18–31.

Petersen, D. M., & Dressel, P. L. (1982). Equal time for women: Social notes on the male strip show. *Journal of Contemporary Ethnography, 11*(2), 185–208.

Pilcher, K. E. M. (2009). Empowering, degrading or a "mutually exploitative" exchange for women? Characterising the power relations of the strip club. *Journal of International Women's Studies, 10*(3), 73–83.

Pilcher, K. E. M. (2013). A "sexy space" for women? Heterosexual women's experiences of a male strip show venue. *Leisure Studies, 30*(2), 217–235.

Pilcher, K. E. M. (2016). *Erotic performance and spectatorship: New frontiers in erotic dance*. New York: Routledge.

Prehn, J. W. (1983). Invasion of the male strippers: Role alignment in a small-town strip club. *The Journal of Popular Culture, 17*(2), 182–186.

Rohlinger, D. A. (2002). Eroticising men: Cultural influences on advertising and male objectification. *Sex Roles, 46*(3–4), 61–74.

Scull, M. T. (2013). Reinforcing gender roles at the male strip show: A qualitative analysis of men who dance for women. *Deviant Behavior, 34*(7), 557–578.

Scull, M. T. (2015). The self-concept as a side bet: How stripping enhances the self-views of men who dance for women. *Deviant Behavior, 36*(11), 890–909.

Scull, M. T. (2017). Managing identity in a dirty occupation: Male strippers experiences with social stigmas. *Sociological Spectrum, 37*(6), 390–411.

Sedgwick, E. K. (1985). *Between men: English literature and male homosocial desire*. New York: Columbia University Press.

Smith, C. (2002). Shiny chests and heaving g-strings: A night out with the Chippendales. *Sexualities, 5*(1), 67–89.

Tewksbury, R. (1993). Male strippers: Men objectifying men. In C. L. Williams (Ed.), *Doing "women's work": Men in non-traditional occupations* (pp. 168–181). London: Sage Publications.

Tewksbury, R. (1994). A dramaturgical analysis of male strippers. *The Journal of Men's Studies, 2*(4), 325–342.

Tolman, D. (2000). Object lessons: Romance, violation, and female adolescent sexual desire. *Journal of Sex Education and Therapy, 25*(1), 70–79.

Tye, D., & Powers, A. M. (1998). Gender, resistance and play: Bachelorette parties in Atlantic Canada. *Women's Studies International Forum, 21*(5), 551–561.

Waling, A. (2018). I can't/can I touch him? Erotic subjectivity, sexual attraction, and research in the field. *Qualitative Inquiry, 24*(9), 720–727.

Wosick-Correa, K. R., & Joseph, L. J. (2008). Sexy ladies sexing ladies: Women as consumers in strip clubs. *The Journal of Sex Research, 45*(3), 201–216.

Appendix A
List of films discussed

Avildsen, J. G. (1983). *A Night in Heaven* [Motion Picture]. United States: 20th Century Fox.

An American romance film that tells the story of a college professor (Lesley Ann Warren) in an unhappy marriage who has a short, passionate affair with one of her male students (Christopher Atkins) after learning he is a stripper.

Bross, E. (2000). *The Chippendales Murder.* [Motion Picture]. United States: USA Network.

A dramatization of the true story of the rise of the Chippendales (male exotic dancers). This film focuses on the partnership between Steve Banerjee, Bruce Nahin, and Nick De Noia and their worldwide enterprise, which ultimately leads to the contracted death of De Noia by Banerjee.

Cattaneo, P. (1997). *The Full Monty* [Motion Picture]. United States: Fox Searchlight Films.

A British comedy film focusing on the lives of six unemployed steel workers struggling to make ends meet after their steel mill shuts down. The men turn to stripping for women as a way to make money and reclaim their masculinity.

Damski, M. (1981). *For Ladies Only* [Motion Picture]. United States: Artisan Entertainment.

An American drama film that focuses on a young male actor struggling to find work who turns to moonlighting as a stripper for women.

Dragoti, S. (1983). *Mr. Mom* [Motion Picture]. United States: 20th Century Fox.

An American comedy film that tells the story of a young couple reversing their gender roles as housewife and breadwinner after Jack Butler (Michael Keaton) loses his job as an engineer. Jack takes over the household responsibilities (which leads to much chaos and frustration), while Caroline returns to work in advertising. One scene in the film focuses on Jack's attendance at a male strip show with a group of women. The film focuses on the difficulties both partners face in these new roles, with Jack ultimately returning back to work and Caroline staying home to raise their children.

Fletcher, A. (2009). *The Proposal* [Motion Picture]. United States: Walt Disney Studios Motion Pictures.

An American romantic comedy starring Sandra Bullock and Ryan Reynolds, *The Proposal* tells the story of a hard and stoic executive editor-in-chief of a New York book publishing company who blackmails her assistant into marrying her so she does not lose her green card and right to work in the United States.

Hill, G. R. (1977). *Slapshot* [Motion Picture]. United States: University Pictures.

An American sports comedy film starring Paul Newman and Michael Ontkean. A local town is primarily supported by a mill that is about to lay off a high number of its workers. In addition, the local hockey team is at risk for disbandment. Dunlop (Paul Newman) uses extreme violence during play as a way to reinvigorate the team, which holds major consequences for its star player Ned Braden (Michael Ontkean).

Hughes, B. (1999). *Forces of Nature* [Motion Picture]. United States: DreamWorks Pictures.

An American romantic comedy film, *Forces of Nature* focuses on Ben Holmes (Ben Affleck) a writer who is trying to get to Savannah, Georgia for his wedding. En route, he meets Mary (Sandra Bullock), a free-spirited woman with whom he begins to develop a close bond, causing him to question whether he should get married.

Jacobs, G. (2015). *Magic Mike XXL* [Motion Picture]. United States: Warner Brother Pictures.

An American comedy-drama film starring Channing Tatum as Magic Mike, this film tells a story about a young man who strips in order to save money to start his own custom furniture business. Loosely based on Channing Tatum's actual experiences as a stripper when he was quite young, the film explores issues of drug culture, loyalty, and finding one's self.

La Marre, J. C. (2015). *Chocolate City* [Motion Picture]. United States: Paramount Home Media Distribution.

An American comedy-drama film starring Robert Ri'Chard, the film explores the life of a struggling African-American college student who strips as way to make money to pay his bills and finds a whole other world that he enjoys. The film is often touted as the black version of *Magic Mike*, and it was created as a response to the lack of people of color within *Magic Mike*.

La Marre, J. C. (2017). *Chocolate City: Vegas Strip* [Motion Picture]. United States: Open Road Films.

An American comedy-drama film that is the sequel to *Chocolate City*. In this story, the club at which Michael works is at risk of closing, and so he and his fellow strippers travel to Las Vegas to compete for $500,000 to prevent the club from closing. The film draws many parallels to *Magic Mike XXL*, in which the men engage in a similar adventure of competing in a national strip competition.

Manganiello, J. (2014). *La Bare* [Motion Picture]. United States: Filmbluff.

La Bare is a documentary film that explores the lives of men who strip at the La Bare club in Dallas, Texas. The film looks at their stripping routines, eating and workout practices, their reasons for stripping, how they feel about stripping, and their future goals and aspirations. It also focuses on what the men need to do to ensure success in the field of stripping for women, and it covers the loss of a close friend due to gang violence.

Payne, D. (2002). *Just Can't Get Enough* [Motion Picture]. United States: Regent Releasing.

An American drama, this film is similar to the *Chippendale's Murder* (2002); it is another dramatization of the lives of Steve Banerjee, Bruce Nahin, and Nick De Noia.

Reiner, C. (1987). *Summer School*. [Motion Picture]. United States: Paramount Pictures.

An American comedy, the film focuses on a failing high school gym teacher, Freddy Shoop (Mark Harmon), who is forced to teach a remedial English class during the summer. The film focuses on Freddy's interactions with his students, helping each one with specific life issues and becoming closer to them as a result.

Ross, H. (1981). *Pennies from Heaven* [Motion Picture]. United States: United Artists.

An American musical romantic drama film that tells the story of married Arthur Parker (Steve Martin) who has an affair with a young woman, Eileen (Bernadette Peters) and gets her pregnant. Arthur leaves Eileen to go back to his wife, leaving her to become a prostitute and take up with Tom (Christopher Walken), who doubles as her pimp. The film ends with Arthur returning to Eileen but being falsely accused of murder and ending up on death row.

Soderbergh, S. (2012). *Magic Mike* [Motion Picture]. United States: Warner Brother Pictures.

An American comedy-drama film starring Channing Tatum as Magic Mike, this film tells a story about a young man who strips in order to save money to start his own custom furniture business. Loosely based on Channing Tatum's actual experiences as a stripper when he was quite young, the film explores issues of drug culture, loyalty, and finding one's self.

Winick, G. (2004). *13 Going on 30* [Motion Picture]. United States: Columbia Pictures.

An American fantasy romantic comedy that tells the story of a young 13-year-old girl who is desperate to be in with the popular group of girls at school. After a horrendous 13th birthday crying in the closet and wishing she was older, she wakes up as a 30-year-old woman working for her favorite magazine and living what appears at first glance to be a charmed life, only to discover numerous problems, betrayals, and less-than-kind behavior on her part.

6

Gigolos in popular cinema

Magic Mike, American Gigolo, and the queerness of heterosexuality

Russell Sheaffer

Revisiting cinema's "hustler"

In film, male sex work has historically been portrayed as a "problem" that is fundamentally linked to the "problem" of homosexuality. *Midnight Cowboy* (1969) and *American Gigolo* (1980) presented some of the first widely accessible images of the male prostitute in American cinema. The gigolos in those films openly acknowledge and embrace the idea that homosexual male prostitution is abject in a way that is radically different from heterosexual prostitution, and they engage in homosexual sex only when their circumstances become dire.[1] It was not until the emergence of New Queer Cinema, a term coined by B. Ruby Rich in 1992 to describe LGBT films that were appearing at festivals in the United States, that things began to shift.[2] Informed by the AIDS crisis and the U.S. government's poor response to it in the late 1980s, New Queer Cinema (or NQC) pushed for new ways of seeing gay characters, including male sex workers.

In my chapter in *Male Sex Work and Society* (2014), I argued that

> post-NQC, the use of the character type of the male sex worker has flourished and become dramatically fractured. While major studio productions like *Deuce Bigalow: Male Gigolo* (1999) and *The Wedding Date* (2005) work to sanitize the gigolo, maintaining strict heterosexuality and presenting homosexual sex work as abject. . . [independent American and international films] have worked to push the male sex worker in a variety of other directions.
>
> *(Sheaffer, 2014, pp. 72–73)*

Since I wrote that chapter, depictions of the "hustler" character type have continued to flourish but in ways that I did not predict. In my earlier chapter, I had more or less written off contemporary Hollywood's representation of the male sex worker, noting a progression toward often homophobic (and generally sex-phobic) representations in Hollywood films throughout the 1990s and early 2000s. However, mainstream films and TV programs released over the course of the past decade demand a reexamination of that argument.

Far more complex representations have pushed the male sex worker into pleasure-embracing terrain in such films as *Magic Mike* (2012) and *Magic Mike XXL* (2015). Other films, including

The Extra Man (2010), *Ringo* (2011), *Fading Gigolo* (2013), *Rough Night* (2017), and *How to Be a Latin Lover* (2017), and HBO's television show *Hung* (2009–2011), all employ strippers, hustlers, gigolos, and escorts for comedic purposes. And films such as *Notre Paradis* (2011), *Aleksandr's Price* (2013), *Boulevard* (2014), *All Yours* (2014), *Cuatro Lunas* (2014), and *Sauvage* (2018) have included the male sex worker in dramatic, New Queer Cinema–inspired narratives.

While contemporary independent work often ruminates on the grittier elements of its characters' lives, Hollywood product has veered toward the comedic and (occasionally) celebratory. These mainstream films not only linger on the male bodies that they put on display; they have also helped usher in discussions of a "female gaze." This newly popular term is an inversion of Laura Mulvey's (2009) theory of the "male gaze," which understands the viewing politics inherent in Hollywood films to be that of a masculine gaze that objectifies the female body. While newer films (*Magic Mike* and its sequel, in particular) are often marketed to heterosexual women, queer readings of these films also provide evidence of a (sometimes acknowledged, sometimes implicit) viewing position for queer-identified men. As the stigma of same-sex desire continues to become less prevalent in the United States, mainstream films that feature male sex workers as characters have become less likely to villainize their characters' homosexual desire. Where Richard Gere's character in *American Gigolo* refuses to do any of "that fag stuff" and *Midnight Cowboy's* Joe Buck stoops to gay sex only when his career is at its worst, gay viewers are welcomed in *Magic Mike XXL*.

Although characters in these contemporary films may not explicitly engage in homosexual sex, the films do not actively stigmatize same-sex desire in the way that earlier Hollywood films did. Thus, *Magic Mike* takes us into important new territory. It is one of the first mainstream blockbusters that wholeheartedly embraces the pleasure and beauty of its male characters without working to undercut that pleasure through a moral critique of sex work.

In light of these changes, the goal for this chapter is to examine Hollywood's changing relationship with the character of the male sex worker.[3] I will focus on contemporary Hollywood films, considering them in two central ways. First, I look at representations of the male sex worker character type, examining how Hollywood films about male sex workers have shifted from queer-phobic (*American Gigolo*) to ambivalent (*Magic Mike*) and occasionally queer-embracing (*Magic Mike XXL*). Second, I examine Hollywood's morphing relationship to an LGBTQ+ demographic, using Alexander Doty's book *Flaming Classics: Queering the Film Canon* (2002) as a jumping-off point. Specifically, these films provide a lens that magnifies Hollywood's blossoming understanding of the LGBTQ+ community as cultural consumers worthy of attention. Looking at films from the past decade, I argue that, in a post-NQC landscape, specific Hollywood films have taken up the torch for progressive representation in ways that have diverged from U.S. and international independent films.

Representation: *Magic Mike*, the fallen woman, and economic critique

When Steven Soderbergh's *Magic Mike* was released in 2012, critics and viewers immediately noted its inversion of the protagonists' traditional gendered roles. In her *New York Times* review of the film, Manohla Dargis noted:

> What happens [in *Magic Mike*] will be familiar if you've ever seen one of those variations on the fallen-woman movie. An elastic genre popular in the 1920s and '30s, these flicks usually involve a working-class young miss who comically scrambles or crudely tramps her way into a mink, swank digs and finally either tragedy or redemption, depending on whether

she's doomed or saved. . . . In the past the movies were very much preoccupied with the moral regulation of women, but here the stress is on Mike's struggle.

(Dargis, 2012)

Magic Mike certainly draws from the structure that Dargis astutely notes, insofar as Mike (Channing Tatum) is caught in a "struggle to succeed as he juggles his part-time gigs (dancing, auto detailing and construction) with his desire to build custom furniture" (ibid.). For Mike, the end goal may be designing furniture, but unlike the moral tales that Dargis references, *Magic Mike* does not lean nearly as hard on a desire to push its protagonist toward moral retribution.

In *Magic Mike*, legality and morality are linked in malleable but important ways. Dallas (Matthew McConaughey), who owns the Xquisite Strip Club where Mike dances, constantly works to make the legality of stripping a crucial part of the conversation. The film opens with Dallas onstage (Figure 6.1), explaining to his patrons Florida's laws regarding touching strippers:

> Now, I want to go over a few rules with y'all tonight. . . . This is the "what can you touch and not touch" rules. Can you touch this? [Dallas rubs his chest.] No, no, no. . . . Can you touch this. . .? [Dallas grabs his rear.] No, no, no. And finally. . . [l]ast one, ladies. Can you touch this? [Dallas grabs his crotch.] Can you ever touch this? Well, that's who the law says you cannot touch. But I think I see a lot of lawbreakers up in this house tonight. And I don't see a cop in sight.

While Dallas encourages some rule breaking, here he is invested in rhetoric that posits his line of work as, first and foremost, legal. In addition to being the master of ceremonies for the "cock-rocking kings of Tampa," he acts as his business's accountant, he is concerned with the age of the club's hosts, and he emphasizes the importance of the legality of fantasy

Figure 6.1   Dallas (Matthew McConaughey) addresses the crowd at the Xquisite Strip Club in the opening scene of *Magic Mike* (2012).

fulfillment to Adam, a new hire at the club (played by Alex Pettyfer) in their first training session together. When Adam first enters the club early in the film, Dallas clearly states that his strip club "is not a fucking joke. All right? It's not a fucking hobby. This is a serious business I'm running."

For *Magic Mike*'s title character, too, stripping is a serious business that is far from immoral. Other characters, though, pressure Mike to think of his stripping in those terms. For example, Mike is frequently criticized by Brooke (Cody Horn), Adam's sister and Mike's love interest throughout the film, who has a hard time taking him seriously as an "entrepreneur-slash-stripper" (or is it "stripper-slash-entrepreneur?" she jokingly asks). While Mike never hits a point at which stripping becomes an area of moral concern in his life, throughout the film, he does articulate concerns about stripping and aging. Speaking to Brooke late in the film, Mike explains, "I don't want to fucking be some forty-year-old stripper. I want to *own* something." This desire for ownership is one of the crucial tensions in the film. It is not that Mike dislikes his work as a stripper or that he finds it immoral or distasteful in the way that fallen-woman films of the 1920s and 1930s would have clearly positioned sex work. Instead, a lack of stability and a lack business ownership are particularly troubling to Mike.

Rather than portraying stripping as an immoral act, *Magic Mike* positions the culture surrounding the Xquisite Strip Club where Mike dances—specifically, drug dealing and drug use—as the central issue in need of "moral regulation." Although *Magic Mike* is ostensibly about Mike, he does not embody the downward character arc that is so crucial to the fallen-woman genre that Dargis understands the film to be inverting. That downward spiral, though, is central to Adam's character arc. As Adam becomes a part of the clique at Xquisite, he begins selling ecstasy to young women, under the mentorship of Xquisite's resident disc jockey, Tobias (Gabriel Iglesias). When Adam leaves his backpack full of pills at a client's house after a brawl breaks out, Mike fronts him $10,000 in cash to keep Adam safe from his suppliers. Then, having sacrificed nearly his entire savings, Mike decides to leave stripping, hoping to start a "new [life] plan" with Brooke. Although *Magic Mike* does end with Mike ending his stripping career, it purposefully complicates any reading of the film that ties his exit to an understanding of stripping as "immoral." Mike continually refuses to think about his work as a stripper in those terms.

American Gigolo, a history of hustling, and cinematic homophobia

While engaged in very different types of sex work than *Magic Mike*'s title character, *American Gigolo*'s Julian (played by Richard Gere) and *Midnight Cowboy*'s Joe Buck (played by Jon Voight) are important characters in the cinematic lineage that leads to Mike. Unlike Mike, both Julian and Joe have penetrative sex for pay, and their narratives mark homosexual sex work as a particularly abysmal form of this labor. For *Midnight Cowboy*'s Joe, homosexual sex is a way to try to make ends meet when his career is at its worst, while *American Gigolo*'s Julian has graduated out of homosexual sex work entirely. *American Gigolo* depicts its protagonist as the heterosexual stallion that *Midnight Cowboy*'s Joe Buck so desperately wants to be. *Chicago Metro Times* reviewer Rocsan Richmond makes this connection perfectly clear in her review of *American Gigolo*, where she writes, "I'd looked forward to seeing 'American Gigolo' ever since I'd learned of its subject matter a year ago. . . . I was hoping [Richard Gere] might take over where Jon Voight left off in 'Midnight Cowboy'" (Richmond, 1980, p. 10).

Similarly, *Magic Mike* has allowed critics to draw a line back to *American Gigolo*. While Mike is not quite "taking over" where Julian left off in *American Gigolo*, *Gigolo* is understood as a necessary predecessor to the male objectification that is so central to *Magic Mike*.[4] Worth quoting at length, film critic Elena Lazic describes how *American Gigolo*'s objectification of Richard Gere's body (Figure 6.2) laid the foundation for *Magic Mike*:

> Decades before *Magic Mike*, *American Gigolo* was busy unashamedly objectifying its straight, male lead. But unlike almost every female character in mainstream cinema, Gere's Julian is a man who always actively participates in his own objectification.
>
> Julian spends a lot of time taking care of his appearance and enjoys the attention that preparation brings. Considering the depressing debates that Instagram selfies still spark today, it is incredibly refreshing to see a film made thirty-six years ago that does not condemn male narcissism. Instead, it unabashedly salutes its protagonist with flattering close-ups and extended takes. For much of the film's runtime there is simply nothing to do but watch Gere walk with the most obscenely sensuous gait, or sit with the coolest nonchalance.
>
> He is always the best dressed man in the room for obvious reasons. Under the pretense of [being a] "guide or translator" for rich, often much older women visiting Los Angeles, Julian sells much more than his company.
>
> *(Lazic, 2016)*

Lazic is not alone in drawing this line from *American Gigolo* to *Magic Mike*. Journalist Julie Hinds (2012) notes that "not since 1980's 'American Gigolo,' which featured a young Richard Gere as an expensive male escort, has a movie about beefcake been so exuberant." The celebration of male narcissism and exuberance in *American Gigolo* to which Lazic and Hinds point is certainly an element of the embrace of pleasure that is also central to *Magic Mike*. Mike and his fellow strippers are so deeply pleasurable to watch in part because they *know* they are gorgeous, and they are able to harness that excitement for their audience.

Figure 6.2 *American Gigolo* (1980) puts the body of Julian (Richard Gere) on display.

It is a crucial nuance in Lazic's argument, however, that the celebration of male narcissism in *American Gigolo* must be a heterosexual male narcissism. If we understand that Gere's performance is also consumable by or intended for gay-identified men, we simply cannot argue that the film "unabashedly salutes its protagonist" without also acknowledging the way in which that salute demonizes the queer individuals consuming the film. This is the crucial shift in representation between *American Gigolo* and *Magic Mike*: where Julian frequently reminds the audience that his body is available for heterosexual consumption, the films *Magic Mike* and *Magic Mike XXL* are strikingly unconcerned with the audience consuming their images.

While *Magic Mike* may not engage in a moral critique of sex work, the film is saturated with economic critique, which is a fundamental part of Mike's struggle and the film's structure. As Ben Sachs (2012) notes in the *Chicago Reader*,

> The primary characters here are a vain up-and-coming stripper (Alex Pettyfer) who sleeps on his sister's couch because he can't afford his own place, a burgeoning entrepreneur (Channing Tatum) who manages three separate businesses when he isn't stripping, and a seemingly dimwitted emcee (Matthew McConaughey, often hilarious) who turns out to be a shrewd accountant. The dance numbers, choreographed by Allison Faulk, are inventive and athletic, but not really erotic; Soderbergh never lets you forget that, for these men, dancing is above all a job.

Mike is constantly working to make ends meet as he juggles his different jobs. Scrambling to take on as much work as possible, he saves up his cash in the hope that he will be able to get a bank loan to open a custom furniture business. While Mike is not actively engaged in trading money for penetrative sex, his constant hunger for a dollar and his sometimes baffling amalgamation of work situate Mike as a prime example of American cinema's "male hustler."

To a certain extent, the male hustler was a character type in cinema decades before he became famous in 1969's *Midnight Cowboy* for trading cash for sex, but not in the way the term has come to be defined. In popular understandings of the term, *hustler* most often applies to men who "[engage] in homosexual behavior" for pay (Steward, 1991, p. xi). If we equate hustlers with individuals who have homosexual sex for pay, then the title character of *Magic Mike* does not qualify. However, if we understand the term *hustler* as film scholar Robert Lang (2002) does, as someone who hustles to make a living and is "looking for something, and who sooner or later finds himself pretending to be something he isn't, or thinks he isn't, or wishes he were, or doesn't realize he wishes he were" (p. 249), we raise the possibility that a hustler may be hustling for any number of things—clothes, a place to stay, or money, for example—and may exchange other services, such as time or companionship, without explicitly selling sex (Sheaffer, 2014, p. 53).

Mapping *Magic Mike*'s title character onto Lang's paradigm clearly frames him within the hustler narrative. Mike is absolutely looking for something: a relationship, a protégé, and a life that balances his love of stripping with his love of making furniture. His realization that he does not want to become an aging stripper (embodied in the film by Matthew McConaughey's Dallas) is one of the driving forces behind the film's narrative. Finally, Mike's ability to take time outside of the Xquisite Strip Club to woo women to come to the club is a central part of his business practice, essentially embracing the notion that time spent with potential show-goers outside the confines of the club can convert into dollars later thrown on the stage and put into his pocket.[5] In both *Magic Mike* and *Magic Mike XXL*, Mike is selling much more than just a dance; he's selling an idea of what it means to be with a charming, fun-loving male stripper.

For example, in one scene in *Magic Mike*, Mike and his protégé, Adam, approach two young women in a dance club. Calculating how to handle the encounter, Mike sends Adam to talk to the women at the bar. There to celebrate one of the women's 21st birthday, they complain to Alex that they cannot get the bartender's attention to order a drink. Like an alcohol-wielding guardian angel, Mike approaches with four shot glasses. "We can't find anybody to take these," Mike says to the women. "Do y'all want them? We can't drink them all ourselves." As they continue to talk, Mike riles the women up in charming fashion, chiding one for not having her friend "drunk already" on her 21st birthday. Playfully exchanging glances while handing the women a flyer for the Xquisite Strip Club, Mike says, "If you'd like to get a wee bit crazy, why don't you come down and see the show?" Playing along, one of the women responds, "Maybe we'll come if your little friend [Adam] comes, too." "That's an easy 'if,'" Mike responds, "because he will be there . . . you're going to come?" "Yeah," the woman responds, "I promise."

For a film marketed for its scenes of famous male actors stripping, these scenes may seem inconsequential; they are the interstitial moments between the film's striptease acts. It is in these scenes, however, that we see the *hustle* behind Mike's onstage work. As Dallas explicitly tells Adam during a pep talk,

> "You are fulfilling every woman's wildest fantasies. You are the husband that they never had. You are that dreamboat guy that never came along. You are that one-night stand, that free fling of a fuck that they get to have tonight with you on stage and still go home to their husbands."

In pursuit of satisfying his clients' fantasies (along with a cut of the money made at Xquisite's door), Mike frequently reveals a persona that allows him to hustle a potential paying customer into the club for his performances.

As Sachs (2012) rightly notes, and as these scenes demonstrate, the focus on the economic exchange of stripping (the way in which it is "above all a job") is central to the film's larger goals. While this kind of exchange explicitly transforms much of Mike's free time into labor (he is nearly always hustling in one form or another), *Magic Mike* clearly demonstrates Mike's love of his work as both a furniture maker and as a stripper. This focus on the economics of male sex work is also crucial to *Midnight Cowboy* and *American Gigolo*; both of those films take pleasure in their protagonists' hustle but ultimately place that pleasure in conflict with the economic position of the films' characters. It is *Magic Mike*'s ability to balance the focus on its strippers' work as *work* with its love and embrace of that work that makes *Magic Mike* so groundbreaking. *Magic Mike XXL*, the all-pleasure-all-the-time sequel helmed by *Magic Mike*'s producer and first assistant director, Gregory Jacobs, further emphasizes that embrace.

Pleasure, structure, and *Magic Mike XXL*

In *Magic Mike XXL*, visual pleasure is the paramount goal. While both *Magic Mike* and the sequel follow a group of men hustling to achieve their dreams, the two films are structured differently with regard to their stripping scenes. *Magic Mike* uses stripping routines in a highly theatrical way, allowing them to exist as (often singular) onstage numbers scattered throughout the film. In these scenes, the literal stage is the only location in which stripping occurs. While *XXL* occasionally offers dance scenes that occur in the everyday lives of its characters, outside of a strip club, it does not show its central characters' stripping until the film's end. Instead of featuring interstitial stripping scenes as in the first *Magic Mike* film, *XXL* builds to an epic 20-minute theatrical strip show that closes the film.

In *XXL*, the narrative tension relies completely on the ability of the "cock-rocking kings of Tampa" as they travel up to Myrtle Beach to perform one last show together. Throughout the film, the men discuss the perils of aging, their employment goals, their prospects outside of stripping, and their desire to embody—or to no longer embody—different masculine archetypes ("the fireman" or "the sailor," for example; see Figure 6.3), but there is never a question that they desperately *want* to be stripping together in Myrtle Beach.

XXL sets up this desire when Mike first hears that his old crew is planning a road trip to Myrtle Beach for a stripping convention. Early in the film, Mike is lured to a pool party by his old crew from the Xquisite Strip Club. There, Mike learns that Dallas and Adam (McConaughey and Pettyfer's characters in the *Magic Mike*) have run off together to start a new show in China, leaving the other members of the crew behind. To have one last hurrah before turning to more conventional jobs, the men are planning a trip to Myrtle Beach to "go down in a tsunami of dollar bills" at a stripping convention, rather than letting their last "memory of [stripping] be getting laid off." In these early moments, the film quickly reinforces the economic implications of stripping for these men. Stripping is still "above all a job."

With its characters more or less accepting the end of their stripping careers, *XXL* is far more interested than the first film in celebrating the pleasure that the job has given its characters. If viewers had understood the first *Magic Mike* as harboring any moral concerns about stripping, *Magic Mike XXL* works to rectify that by giving them a celebratory romp. In the scene following the pool-party encounter, for example, we see Mike back in his furniture workroom. After a quick exchange with an employee in which Mike explains that his business is not quite able to cover health insurance yet, we see Mike working a late night alone, putting in the labor required to make his furniture business successful. His passion for furniture making is just as strong as it was in the first *Magic Mike* film, but business ownership is not quite as glorious as he had expected. At the moment we see Mike begin welding—the first time in either film that the audience actually sees Mike crafting a piece of

Figure 6.3 Richie (Joe Manganiello) dons fireman attire during an onstage strip routine in
         Magic Mike (2012).

Figure 6.4 Mike (Channing Tatum) revives his popular "Pony" routine in *Magic Mike XXL* (2015).

furniture—Ginuwine's song "Pony" comes on the radio (Figure 6.4). Completely alone in his workshop, Mike revives one of his most popular dance routines from the first *Magic Mike*. As Mike grinds on his workbench, his workshop becomes his stage and his drills become his props. Panting while lying down after finishing his private solo routine, it is obvious that stripping is a personal pleasure that Mike misses. If we consider *Magic Mike* and *Magic Mike XXL* together, these moments of dancing *away* from the strip club are a crucial next act in *Magic Mike*'s narrative. Mike's obvious pleasure in dancing alone works as a corrective to readings of the first film that might have understood it as distancing Mike from stripping on moral grounds.

Audience and reception: the female gaze and the Hollywood marketing machine

While critics found the plot of *XXL* less enjoyable than the original, online message boards are populated with praise for the film. On Metacritic, for example, one viewer wrote in 2015: "More than anything, I felt recognized by Magic Mike XXL [*sic*]. It's sweet, feminist, funny, weird, erotic. For a movie about a bunch of straight fellas on a road trip, it's one of the most female-centric films I've ever seen." On the other hand, a slightly less positive filmgoer wrote the same year: "If you want to believe your wife and girlfriend are going to see this movie for the 'plot,' then be my guest. It's just a threadbare excuse to throw hunky guys onscreen in exchange for the ticket price."

These comments are very much in line with *New York Times* critic Manohla Dargis's notes about the first *Magic Mike* film:

> In 'Magic Mike,' men exist to be looked at, and women do the looking, a reverse of the old cinematic divide between the sexes that finds so-called passive women who are looked at by so-called active men. In one school of thought Hollywood movies are always organized

for the visual pleasure of the male spectator, which pretty much leaves the female spectator sidelined. There's no leaving her out any longer—or the gay or confident heterosexual
male spectator, either.

(Dargis, 2012)

Dargis is referring to Laura Mulvey's famous theory of the "male gaze," first described in her
1975 article "Visual Pleasure and Narrative Cinema," which understands the cinematic "pleasure in looking" as being "split between active/male and passive/female" (Mulvey, 2009, p. 19).
In the relationship between viewers and the moving images they consume, Mulvey understands
men as the lookers and women in a traditionally "exhibitionist role . . . with their appearance
coded for strong visual and erotic impact so that they can be said to connote *to-be-looked-at-
ness*" (p. 19, emphasis in original). This dynamic is one of the central inversions that *Magic Mike*
advances; in that film, as Dargis wrote, "men exist to be looked at, and women do the looking."
This is a key shift in the Hollywood production and marketing machine that *Magic Mike* and
Magic Mike XXL help make obvious: it *is* possible (and extremely profitable) for women to have
an active viewing position beyond simply inhabiting the "male gaze."[6]

This female gaze also provides a viewing position for queer-identified men. J. Bryan Lowder,
the editor of the queer blog Outward for *Slate* magazine, notes that his alternative viewing position as a gay man is a prominent part of the film's pleasure for its audiences:

The original *Magic Mike* was one of the most memorable moviegoing experiences of my
life. However, it's not the film itself . . . that sticks in my mind. It's the context of seeing the film I hold on to: A small group of gay friends and I picked the gayest theater we
could think of . . . got liquored up on girly drinks beforehand, and giggled with delight
when, as we stepped off the escalator on the mezzanine, we saw that the theater had hired
go-go boys to add festivity to the opening night. Throughout all this, there was a sense that
we were doing something slightly transgressive—turning a movie that was ostensibly for
straight women into one of the gayest events of the year.

(Lowder, 2015)

As a demographic, queer audiences have been actively creating viewing positions and counterreadings of straight culture for at least a century. Explaining his investment in queer readings
of mainstream texts, film scholar Alexander Doty (2000) writes that, for an LGBTQ audience,
"the coding of classic or otherwise 'mainstream' texts and personalities can often yield a wider
range of non-straight readings because certain sexual things could not be stated baldly—and still
cannot or will not in most mainstream products" (p. 1). As Doty explains, these counterreadings
are not "about co-opting and 'making' things queer" but more about "discussing how things
are, or might be understood as, queer." When you cannot speak directly about sex and sexuality,
nearly anything can be read in potentially unintended ways. In fact, for Doty, "any text is always
already potentially queer" (p. 2).

These contemporary female gaze–inspired films add another layer to Doty's analysis because
they usually discuss or show sex in far more explicit ways than the earlier, canonical films Doty
discusses in his book *Flaming Classics*.[7] In films like *Magic Mike* and *Magic Mike XXL*, queer
audiences are either implicitly invited to gaze on the male bodies on display, or they are more
explicitly welcome to create their own viewing positions because they are not actively shamed
for their gaze, as they were in films like *American Gigolo*. These alternative, queer viewing positions are made all the more pleasurable by access to far more explicit images of the male body
than Hollywood had previously allowed.

In discussing a drag scene in *Magic Mike XXL*, Lowder writes:

> When it first became clear that the boys (all of them straight) were going to a drag show, I tensed up: The temptation for the comedy to become lazily homophobic in such situations is strong. Luckily, *Magic Mike XXL* is smarter than that. . . .
>
> The trouble with this kind of direct appeal to gay folks is that it can often come off as Gaga "Born This Way" blunt and annoying. No one likes a hard sell, and gays have a long history of repurposing straight culture for our own uses—as my friends and I did with the first *Magic Mike*. When subtle subversion is your preferred approach, directness can feel somehow vulgar. The great thing about the draggy aspects of *Magic Mike XXL*, though, are that they make total sense in the world of the story, both logically and thematically. . . .
>
> And then, of course, there's the sense in which the entertaining Mike and the others are doing is really just drag of another gender. The roles and scenarios the guys use as their framing devices—both the old firemen/military routines and the new ones they debut in Myrtle Beach—are drag that eroticizes, exaggerates, and sends up traditional masculinity. Just as drag queens are playing with our ideas of the feminine rather than making fun of real women, male strippers similarly toy with the masculine. When you think about it, the two are really a perfect fit. . . . [I]n the film's attempt to welcome gay audiences more directly, it managed to add more depth than you might expect from similar summer romps.
>
> *(Lowder, 2015)*

This interest in attracting a gay male audience was also on the minds of the film's cast and crew. According to critic Julie Hinds, the actor Joe Manganiello "says *Magic Mike* should appeal to a wide audience that includes women, gay men, and even straight men, who he's convinced will find the comic elements hysterical" (Hinds, 2012). Helping *Magic Mike* cast a sweeping net for potential straight and gay audience members is a cast that appeals to a wide demographic. Channing Tatum and Joe Manganiello are straight celebrities who both have a gay following, and the film also heavily features Matt Bomer, an out gay actor who frequently oscillates between straight and gay roles. While the film's actors have embraced the idea that their performances are equally appealing to gay men and straight women, and with a cast that includes members and allies of the LGBTQ+ community, it is striking that the first *Magic Mike* film mostly avoids any conversations about queerness and features no queer characters.

Although the first *Magic Mike* does not explicitly acknowledge its gay consumers, neither it nor *XXL* incorporates the homophobic rhetoric that was central to past films featuring sexualized male bodies. *American Gigolo* is a prime example of the antiquated relationship between male objectification, sex work, and engrained homophobia that helps that film maintain its guise of straightness. In *American Gigolo*, homosexual sex work is considered one of the bottom rungs of the ladder that one must climb to become a successful gigolo—a rung to which that film's main character, Julian (Richard Gere), never wants to return. Positioned in direct opposition to Leon (Bill Duke), the film's antagonist who is a homosexual pimp, Julian repeats time and again that he absolutely will not do that "fag" or "kinky stuff." Julian has graduated from the world of the abject (gay/dirty/bad/kinky) into the world of the vanilla (heterosexual/clean/good/as close to heteronormative as possible).

By contrast, the characters in *Magic Mike* are already in the world of the vanilla: Heterosexuality is assumed and, as discussed earlier, the Dallas character understands the men's work as good, clean, *legal* fun. There is, however, one crucial scene in the first *Magic Mike* in which a character's sexuality is broached head-on. After returning home from her work as a medical assistant, Brooke (Adam's sister) finds a suitcase full of Adam's newly acquired stripping accoutrements. While Adam stands over the sink in the bathroom, shaving his legs, Brooke yells through the door, "Adam, I need to talk to you . . . about this box of boots and thongs and sailor hats and tube socks." "It's for work," Adam explains. "Don't lie to me!" Brooke responds. "I'm your sister, I love you, I don't judge you. . . . You know I don't care what your preferences are, man." Piecing together the assumed queerness in his sister's comments, Adam responds, "Whoa, hey! It is not what it looks like." In this fleeting moment between Adam and Brooke, the film establishes a couple of key things. First, through Brooke's assumption that her brother is gay, the film understands the appeal of its characters' performances to a gay demographic. These tube socks and sailor hats are a crucial element of what Lowder (2015) describes as "eroticiz[ing], exaggerat[ing], and send[ing] up traditional masculinity." Second, the film works to quickly and efficiently shut down any narrative implications that the men of Xquisite are, in fact, gay.

Given a history of films that have deeply stigmatized gay male sexuality, Brooke's comment to her brother that she loves him, will not judge him, and does not "care what [his] preferences are" is a crucial and striking adjustment. The more explicit and extended acknowledgment of a queer audience in XXL's drag scene functions as another attempted corrective, pushing even further for queer acceptance than the first Magic Mike film. Not only do the men of XXL go to a drag show, they are active participants in it. By having the whole crew vogue as a part of a competition for the "best amateur queen," XXL explicitly works to embrace and encourage its characters' objectification by a gay audience. In doing so, XXL acknowledges that gay men are a viable audience for both Magic Mike and Magic Mike XXL.

This shift is likely thanks in large part to the growing acceptance of LGBTQ+ people in the United States. With stigma around homosexuality and queerness diminishing, films have begun incorporating queer characters without making big, self-congratulatory advertising pushes that highlight their queer content. As film critic Lena Wilson notes in an article for Slate, the major Hollywood release Blockers (2018) provides a good example of this shift. Blockers features a lesbian coming-out story in the midst of a teen sex comedy. While the film

> was advertised . . . in the tradition of Porky's and American Pie . . . viewers were then pleasantly surprised to learn that the movie is not only hilarious but contains hidden depths. . . . Namely, a touching coming-out arc following one of the trio's members, Sam (Gideon Adlon), who begins the film as a closeted lesbian. This key plot point was not included in any of the film's promotional materials. . . . If anything, [the film's] promos paint Sam as an enthusiastically (if overeagerly) heterosexual nerd. . . . While Sam's lesbianism is crucial to the Blockers narrative, it's incidental to the film's off-screen perception—the movie is a teen movie before it is a gay movie. . . . Sam's narrative is also notable given that coming-out stories rarely venture out of gay cinema into mainstream genre films—much less into teen sex comedies. Lesbians in raunch-coms are typically objects of the male gaze (as in American Pie 2 or Dodgeball) or butt-of-the-joke gender deviants (as in Mike and Dave Need Wedding Dates or When We First Met). In big-budget blockbusters, meanwhile, gay characters hardly appear at all, except, recently, in a few blink-and-you'll-miss-it moments.
>
> *(2018)*

This desire to be a "teen movie before it is a gay movie" demonstrates a crucial shift in the way that queerness is highlighted in popular cinematic representation. If queerness is not inherently culturally stigmatized, it can simply be another character trait for Hollywood's movie-making machine. As LGBTQ+ characters find their way into more Hollywood films without fanfare, LGBTQ+ audiences are also more clearly embraced as the consumers of content (both "straight" and not).

LGBTQ+ cultural consumers have become a strikingly large market. While in prior decades it had been nearly career suicide for an actor to be gay and out, many mainstream celebrities—gay and straight—now specifically market themselves to queer audiences. The actor and singer Nick Jonas, for example, has been avidly marketed to the gay male community. As a part of his tour for his 2016 album *Last Year Was Complicated*, Jonas performed at numerous gay clubs, making headlines when he performed the song "Chains" at a London club while being literally chained onstage by drag queens (Stutz, 2015).[8] In interviews after these appearances, Jonas frequently noted the welcoming environment that the clubs and gay fans provided. When asked about what he "would . . . say to straight guys who might not feel as comfortable going to a gay club," Jonas responded that he thinks "insecurity drives a lot of really poor decision-making. I think as long as you can be confident and comfortable in your own skin and who you are then you don't really have to be worried about that" (Azzopardi, 2016). Jonas's advice to "be confident and comfortable in your own skin" could just as well be the tagline for *Magic Mike XXL* and the new mainstream system that welcomes the LGBTQ+ community as potential consumers of "straight" cultural products.

This is where *Magic Mike* and *American Gigolo* diverge in their understanding of the intersection of sex work and queerness. Where *Magic Mike* (partially through the corrective lens of *XXL*) embraces its queer audience, *American Gigolo* was produced at a moment when homosexuality was an obviously stigmatizing plot point for the film's characters. There is no doubt that queer audiences took pleasure in Richard Gere's body and performance in *American Gigolo*, perhaps in a way similar to that of Nick Jonas's gay fan base, but that film explicitly uses narrative threads that make such a relationship all the more taboo. *Magic Mike*, in contrast, works to avoid conversations regarding the sexuality of its characters and its audience. Instead, it basks in the consumability of the male body without concern for the audience's rationale or motivations for consuming those images. Where *American Gigolo* constantly works to remind its audience that Julian is available only to those who are women—and wealthy, white, and (usually) married—*Magic Mike* and *Magic Mike XXL* place no restrictions on their patrons.

Conclusions and future analysis

In the preceding volume of this work, *Male Sex Work and Society*, I argued that Hollywood's representation of male sex workers at that point in the twenty-first century (2014) paled in comparison with their representation in international and independently produced films. As *Magic Mike* and its sequel have demonstrated, however, it is not fair to simply dismiss mainstream Hollywood content as homophobic or sex-phobic. While perhaps sex-phobic, the Hollywood films that I criticized in *Male Sex Work and Society* (specifically, *Deuce Bigelow: Male Gigolo* and *The Wedding Date*) opened up the idea that men who sell sex (in many different forms) can be a profitable area of interest for mainstream cinematic product.[9]

Pulling from reviews as a way to understand the connections that viewers make between films, the progression in cinematic representation that links *Midnight Cowboy* to *American Gigolo*, *Magic Mike*, and *Magic Mike XXL* becomes apparent. Where *Magic Mike* works to move forward from *American Gigolo*, removing the homophobic rhetoric that is central to Richard Gere's performance in that film, it still maintains its distance from questions regarding its characters' sexuality. In multiple ways, *XXL* takes another step forward, addressing sexuality in playful ways that embrace an LGBTQ+ demographic while still insisting on its characters' heterosexuality.

The landscape of independent films produced in the past decade demonstrates a strikingly different momentum. While Hollywood films have found ways to weld the comedic and dramatic, allowing for space that celebrates the bodies it represents on screen, many independent films have continued on in the wake of the drama-saturated 1990s, occasionally rehashing older paradigms. While this chapter has focused on Hollywood content, it is worth briefly pointing out the ways in which independent and international films have sometimes stalled in their dramatic, stigma-battling representations of male sex work. The 2018 Cannes Semaine de la Critique (International Critic's Week) selection, *Sauvage*, is an example par excellence of this trend. *Sauvage* follows the struggles of Léo, the French film's 22-year-old protagonist, as he "recklessly roams the streets, nightclubs and backwoods of Strasbourg in search of more than just the physical contact he's freely selling" (Lodge, 2018).

Léo wholeheartedly embraces his work, much as Mike does in *Magic Mike*, but the two films provide very different endings for their two characters. As *Variety* reviewer Guy Lodge (2018) argues, "Léo is a little too personally invested in his prostitution for his own good: He's hurt when clients rebuff him, and gives a little too much of himself away in exchange not just for money, but for fleeting human connection with men who mostly treat him like a toy." While it is worth praising a contemporary representation that embraces male sex workers who love their job, *Sauvage* consistently uses Léo's line of work as a way to punish him. Léo is physically unhealthy, he is beaten time and again by his clients and his fellow sex workers, and the film toys with the idea of his running away from sex work to find a better life.

Sauvage would have been groundbreaking had it been made in the 1990s, with its sympathetic character being beaten down time and again by his surroundings and the work that he loves deeply. For films produced during the New Queer Cinema period of the 1990s, the HIV/AIDS crisis and the U.S. government's poor response to it often manifested in a gritty aggression and urgency that were visible in both subject matter and style. At this point in cinematic history, though, *Sauvage* lifts so thoroughly from Gregg Araki's *The Living End* (1992) and Gus Van Sant's *My Own Private Idaho* (1991) that its representation reads as a regression to the aggressive violence of the films of the 1990s, without the urgency that was central to their production and representation.[10] In fact, the parallels between *Sauvage* and *The Living End* are striking. Both *The Living End*'s Luke and *Sauvage*'s Léo are facing life-threatening illness, but where Luke is battling HIV, Léo struggles with asthma. What was so vital and political in the NQC films loses its urgency when rehashed in films like *Sauvage*. With films like *Magic Mike* actively embracing the pleasure that is a central concern of sex work, the hopelessness of films like *Sauvage* becomes all the more palpable.

Recent independent and international films' revisiting of familiar traumas is a crucial element in the representation of male sex workers in cinema, and therefore it is an area in need of further criticism and analysis. Because of the interconnections between Hollywood and independent or underground films, I am optimistic that we will see an uptick in independent films that do not feel it necessary to villainize their characters' work. Furthermore, as stigma surrounding non-normative sexualities continues to decrease, and as the critical reception of films like *Blockers* and *Magic Mike XXL* continues to be positive, I am hopeful that we will continue to see LGBTQ+ audiences more clearly embraced as consumers of content, both "straight" and not.

Notes

1 See Sheaffer (2014) for an in-depth analysis of this difference.

2 For more on New Queer Cinema, see B. Ruby Rich's article "New Queer Cinema" in *Sight & Sound* 2, no. 5 (Sept. 1992).

3 For an analysis of representations of male sex work in independent cinema (specifically with regard to New Queer Cinema of the 1990s), see Sheaffer (2014).

4 While critics made the connection between *Magic Mike* and *American Gigolo*, the two central characters of those films are engaged in very different forms of sex work. Specifically, throughout both *Magic Mike* and *Magic Mike XXL*, Mike never engages in penetrative sex for pay.

5 Mike receives a cut of the door sales at Xquisite in exchange for hustling for the club before the nightly shows. In the film, this is a marked difference between Mike and the other strippers: because his pay increases when the club is packed, Mike is particularly invested (both emotionally and financially) in the success of the club as a whole, not just in his own strip routines.

6 Both *Magic Mike* films have been box-office successes. The first *Magic Mike* had a budget of $7 million and brought in $167 million. *Magic Mike XXL* had a budget of $14.8 million and brought in $122 million.

7 In *Flaming Classics: Queering the Film Canon* (2000), Doty focuses on queer readings of *The Cabinet of Dr. Caligari* (Robert Wiene, 1921), *The Wizard of Oz* (Victor Fleming, 1939), *The Women* (George Cukor, 1939), *The Red Shoes* (Michael Powell and Emeric Pressburger, 1948), *Gentlemen Prefer Blondes* (Howard Hawks, 1953), and *Psycho* (Alfred Hitchcock, 1960).

8 While some fans embraced Jonas's appeal to an LGBTQ demographic, numerous articles accused him of queer baiting (using sexual ambiguity to target a specific, queer market). He addressed those accusations briefly in an interview for *Out* magazine (Moore, 2016).

9 With a budget of $17 million, *Deuce Bigalow: Male Gigolo* brought in more than $92 million. *The Wedding Date* had a budget of $15 million and brought in more than $47 million.

10 Although *Sauvage* does rehash a New Queer Cinema–inspired narrative in familiar aesthetic terms, it is absolutely unafraid of featuring full frontal male nudity, a definite progression from the more shielded bodies of the sex workers in New Queer Cinema.

References

Azzopardi, C. (2016). Nick Jonas on inspiring drag kings, his "very welcoming" gay club experience and how his man bod changed his life. *Pride Source*. Retrieved from https://pridesource.com/article/76311-2/

Dargis, M. (2012, June 28). The body politic. *New York Times*. Retrieved from www.nytimes.com/2012/06/29/movies/magic-mike-by-steven-soderbergh-with-channing-tatum.html

Doty, A. (2000). *Flaming classics: Queering the film canon.* New York: Routledge.

Hinds, J. (2012, June 28). Some moviegoers "nearly panting" for "Magic Mike." *Kentucky*. Retrieved from www.kentucky.com/entertainment/movies-news-reviews/article44366280.html

Lang, R. (2002). *Masculine interests: Homoerotics in Hollywood films.* New York: Columbia University Press.

Lazic, E. (2016, November 14). How *American Gigolo* flipped Hollywood objectification on its head. *Little White Lies*. Retrieved from https://lwlies.com/articles/american-gigolo-paul-schrader-objectification/

Lodge, G. (2018, August 17). Film review: "Sauvage." *Variety*. Retrieved from https://variety.com/2018/film/reviews/sauvage-review-1202808458/

Lowder, B. (2015). Magic Mike's XXL perfect sculpted gay pandering. *Slate Magazine*. Retrieved from https://slate.com/human-interest/2015/07/magic-mike-xxls-gay-appeal-is-surprisingly-deep.html

Moore, C. (2016, May 10). From teen heartthrob to gay icon, who is Nick Jonas? *Out Magazine*. Retrieved from www.out.com/entertainment/2016/5/10/teen-heartthrob-gay-icon-who-nick-jonas

Mulvey, L. (2009). Visual pleasure and narrative cinema. In *Visual and other pleasure* (2nd ed., pp. 14–27). Basingstoke, UK: Palgrave Macmillan. First published 1975.

Rich, B. R. (1992). New Queer Cinema. *Sight & Sound, 2*(5).

Richmond, R. (1980, February 9). Fragmented story dilutes "Gigolo." *Chicago Metro Times*, p. 10.

Sachs, B. (2012, June 29). Now playing: Magic Mike and a new generation of "bad news." *Chicago Reader*. Retrieved from www.chicagoreader.com/Bleader/archives/2012/06/29/now-playing-magic-mike-and-a-new-generation-of-bad-news

Sheaffer, R. (2014). Representations of male sex work in film. In V. Minichiello & J. Scott (Eds.), *Male sex work and society* (pp. 50–79). New York: Harrington Park Press.

Steward, S. M. (1991). *Understanding the Male Hustler.* Philadelphia: Haworth Press.

Stutz, C. (2015, July 21). Nick Jonas gets chained up by drag queens at London gay bar: Watch. *Billboard*. Retrieved from www.billboard.com/articles/columns/pop-shop/6640913/nick-jonas-chained-up-drag-queens-london-gay-bar-video

Wilson, L. (2018, April 17). *Blockers* didn't market its coming-out story: Here's why that matters. *Slate*. Retrieved from https://slate.com/culture/2018/04/blockers-unadvertised-gay-storyline-could-have-a-big-impact.html

Annotated List of Films and Television Shows

Aleksandr's Price (Pau Masó & David Damen, 2013). After losing his mother to suicide, a young Russian man turns to sex work as a way to survive. The film draws on a lineage of films that grapple with the seedy underbelly of the New York party scene.

All Yours (David Lambert, 2014). *All Yours* follows a young Argentinian hustler who moves to Belgium to become the apprentice of an older Belgian baker, only to fall for one of the baker's female employees.

American Gigolo (Paul Schrader, 1980). Like *Midnight Cowboy*, this Hollywood film is central to the history of male sex work in cinema. *American Gigolo* features Richard Gere as a male sex worker who has graduated from the abject realm of homosexual prostitution into the vanilla world of heterosexual male sex work. This film is a particularly important one in terms of content that lead to the *Magic Mike* films.

American Pie (Paul Weitz & Chris Weitz, 1999). A frequently cited teen sex comedy, *American Pie* follows a group of friends who make a pact to lose their virginity before they graduate from high school. Wildly successful, this film spawned multiple sequels and has proved to be an ongoing inspiration to teen sex comedy writers. The 2018 film *Blockers* was marketed as a work in the lineage of *American Pie*.

American Pie 2 (J. B. Rogers, 2001). This sequel to *American Pie* follows the characters from the first film as they prepare to throw a summer party. Critic Lena Wilson notes that lesbian characters in *American Pie 2* are objects of the "male gaze."

Blockers (Kay Cannon, 2018). This teen-sex comedy follows a group of friends who make a pact to lose their virginity on prom night. Following directly in the wake of the *American Pie* franchise, *Blockers* is particularly fascinating because it features a lesbian coming-out story without all of the marketing fanfare that would have accompanied that sort of inclusion in decades past. In so doing, Lena Wilson notes, the film functions as a "teen movie before it is a gay movie."

Boulevard (Ditto Montiel, 2014). One of Robin Williams's last films, *Boulevard* follows a married, bored, middle-aged man as he strikes up a mostly paternal relationship with a young hustler named Leo. The film is an interesting counter to some of the affective notes in Yaara Sumeruk's short film *Ringo* (2011).

The Cabinet of Dr. Caligari (Robert Wiene, 1921). Wiene's German expressionist masterpiece has long been a part of the canon of early cinema. It is also one of the texts Alexander Doty discusses in his book *Flaming Classics: Queering the Film Canon* (2000). Doty argues that the film's tagline "You must become Caligari" could also be read as a "call to queerness."

Cuatro Lunas (Sergio Tovar Velarde, 2014). This Mexican film follows four stories of gay love, one of which involves a retired, married man who solicits a hustler in a gay sauna.

Deuce Bigalow: Male Gigolo (Mike Mitchel, 1999). The film follows the exploits of a laughable male sex worker named Deuce (Rob Schneider), who also works as an aquarium cleaner. Although both sex-phobic and homophobic, *Deuce Bigalow* is a crucial work in the lineage of representations of male sex work in film. It is one of the movies of the late 1990s that demonstrated that films about male sex workers could be wildly successful.

Dodgeball: A True Underdog Story (Rawson Marshall Thurber, 2004). This Hollywood comedy features Ben Stiller and Vince Vaughn playing the captains of two opposing Las Vegas dodgeball teams. Critic Lena Wilson notes that lesbians in *Dodgeball* are objects of the "male gaze."

The Extra Man (Shari Springer Berman & Robert Pulcini, 2010). This film follows Henry Harrison (Kevin Kline), a failed playwright turned escort who takes a young writer (Paul Dano) under his wing. Seen alongside such films as *Fading Gigolo* and *How to Be a Latin Lover*, *The Extra Man* is part of a turn in representation that focuses on aging and male sex work.

Fading Gigolo (John Tuturro, 2013). Helmed by and featuring John Tuturro, *Fading Gigolo* follows an older man named Murray (Woody Allen) who tries to become a pimp in an effort to scrounge up extra cash. Along with *The Extra Man* and *How to Be a Latin Lover*, *Fading Gigolo* focuses on aging and male sex work.

Gentlemen Prefer Blondes (Howard Hawks, 1953). This musical features Marilyn Monroe and Jane Russell as showgirls who are actively looking for husbands. While the film focuses on the women's heterosexual relationships, it also heavily features their own relationship as a central element of the plot. Alexander Doty reads the film as an example of a bisexual text because of the film's interest in the women's relationship above their heterosexual exploits.

How to Be a Latin Lover (Ken Marino, 2017). The film's story follows Maximo (Eugenio Derbez), a once-hot-now-not gigolo who has wound up back on the market after he being thrown out by his 80-year-old wife. A cultural reimaging that lands somewhere between the sensibility of *Deuce Bigalow: Male Gigolo* and the sincerity of *American Gigolo*, this film relies on the assumed comedic nature of older men working as gigolos.

Hung (HBO, created by Collette Burson and Dmitry Lipkin, 2009–2011). This HBO television series follows the exploits of a high school teacher, Ray Drecker (Thomas Jane), who takes up male sex work as a way to pay his bills when he is short on cash. Although the series situates its protagonist as strictly heterosexual, its serialized format functions as a consistent, nuanced study of Drecker's character and motivations.

The Living End (Gregg Araki, 1992). *The Living End* follows Luke (a spontaneously violent hustler, played by Mike Dytri) and Jon (a film critic, played by Craig Gilmore) as they struggle with the implications of being HIV-positive. It is a foundational part of the New Queer Cinema movement that B. Ruby Rich saw emerging on the film-festival scene in the 1990s.

Magic Mike (Steven Soderbergh, 2012). Described by critic Manohla Dargis as inverting the "fallen woman" genre, this film's exploration of the economics of desire follows Mike, a stripper-entrepreneur who is saving up to start his own custom furniture business. Soderbergh's film has been a central part of conversations surrounding the "female gaze" (an inversion of Laura Mulvey's famous theorization of the "male gaze").

Magic Mike XXL (Gregory Jacobs, 2015). Helmed by *Magic Mike* producer Gregory Jacobs, the sequel picks back up with the crew from the former Xquisite Strip Club as they head to a stripping convention. This film wholeheartedly embraces the visual pleasure that was central to the marketing and reception of the first *Magic Mike* film.

Midnight Cowboy (John Schlesinger, 1969). This classic American film features Jon Voight and Dustin Hoffman as sex workers in New York City. One of the early, explicit examples of male sex work in cinema, the film is often referenced in later works ruminating on the same themes. Importantly, *Midnight Cowboy*'s hustlers understand homosexual male prostitution as abject while they idealize heterosexual male prostitution.

Mike and Dave Need Wedding Dates (Jake Szymanski, 2016). This film follows two party-loving brothers (played by Zac Efron and Adam Devine), who are forced to find "respectable" dates for their sister's wedding. Unlike in the film *Blockers*, critic Lena Wilson notes that, in *Mike and Dave Need Wedding Dates*, lesbians are "butt-of-the-joke gender deviants."

My Own Private Idaho (Gus Van Sant, 1991). This New Queer Cinema classic features River Phoenix and Keanu Reeves as young hustlers on a journey of self-discovery and connection. The film allows its characters to have deeply nuanced relationships with one another as well as within their roles as sex workers.

Notre Paradis (Gaël Morel, 2011). Inspired by the films of the New Queer Cinema movement, *Notre Paradis* follows an aging Parisian hustler who takes a young man under his wing.

Porky's (Bob Clark, 1981). Set in 1954, this film follows the exploits of a group of high school students in Florida. *Porky's* is a teen-sex comedy par excellence, becoming fodder and inspiration for generations of teen film writers.

Psycho (Alfred Hitchcock, 1960). Hitchcock's *Psycho* is frequently considered a masterpiece of horror cinema, but it is also central to Alexander Doty's queer reimagining of the Hollywood canon in his book *Flaming Classics: Queering the Film Canon* (2000). Doty is particularly interested in the way(s) that viewers may read Norman Bates's sexuality as straight, gay, bisexual, or completely nonsexual.

The Red Shoes (Michael Powell & Emeric Pressburger, 1948). *The Red Shoes* follows a ballerina who is torn between her new dance company and her love interest. Alexander Doty, in *Flaming Classics: Queering the Film Canon* (2000), describes *The Red Shoes* as emblematic of the queerness of the Hollywood art film of the 1940s and 1950s.

Ringo (Yaara Sumeruk, 2011). This short dark comedy follows an interaction between an older woman and a young hustler named Ringo. Although Ringo thinks he is there to have sex, it becomes obvious that the protagonist has hired Ringo to play out her maternal fantasies and traumas.

Rough Night (Lucia Aniello, 2017). This dark comedy finds Jess (Scarlett Johansson) panicked after a male stripper accidentally dies at her bachelorette party. Reinforcing the notion of male sex work as abject and taboo, this film regresses to a late-1990s, sex-phobic, comedic portrayal of the male sex worker that is akin to that in *Deuce Bigalow: Male Gigolo*.

Sauvage (Camille Vidal-Naquet, 2018). A selection of the Semaine de la Critique at the 2018 Cannes Film Festival, *Sauvage* follows Léo, a young hustler working the streets of Strasbourg in search of human connection. The film is deeply inspired by films produced during the New Queer Cinema movement, particularly Gregg Araki's *The Living End* (1992).

The Wedding Date (Claire Kilner, 2005). This Hollywood romantic comedy follows the story of Kat (Debra Messing) who hires a male escort to pose as her date at her sister's wedding. The film strictly maintains its male escort's heterosexuality, providing a stark, sanitized contrast to films like Gus Van Sant's *My Own Private Idaho* and Gregg Araki's *The Living End*.

When We First Met (Ari Sandel, 2018). This film features Adam Devine as a man who travels back in time to get out of the heterosexual friend zone with the girl of his dreams. Unlike in the film *Blockers*, Lena Wilson notes that, in *When We First Met* (as in *Mike and Dave Need Wedding Dates*), lesbians are "butt-of-the-joke gender deviants."

The Wizard of Oz (Victor Fleming, 1939). Victor Fleming's famous film is frequently referenced as a Hollywood classic, and it has also played a crucial role in the history of queer reading and community building. Alexander Doty cites Fleming's *The Wizard of Oz* as a central case study in his book *Flaming Classics: Queering the Film Canon* (2000), in which he reads the film as a lesbian fantasy.

The Women (George Cukor, 1939). This cult comedy with an all-female cast is one of the films highlighted by Alexander Doty in *Flaming Classics: Queering the Film Canon* (2000). Doty uses the film to discuss numerous queer-reading approaches for comedic works, including the interpretation of a queer, camp sensibility.

7

Male sex work in documentary films

Rhetorical and ethical frameworks

Nicholas de Villiers

Male sex workers are not usually given the same media treatment as female sex workers. Audiences are much less likely to hear about "trafficking" or men being tricked into sex work, but that does not mean the *agency* of male sex workers is completely unproblematic. Instead, the agency of male sex workers is frequently questioned in relation to maturity, drug use, and sexual identity (sexual orientation or preference versus sexual behavior). The figure of the male sex worker is often employed in documentary as a way to comment on capitalism, geopolitical/population shifts, or the HIV/AIDS crisis and the problems of reaching men who have sex with men (MSM) but do not identify as gay. In short, this media coverage often has a sociological or epidemiological focus (see, for example, the Current TV short documentary *Male Sex Workers in India*, 2006, about safe-sex outreach to MSM and male sex workers in Chennai, India).

This chapter surveys a range of primarily millennial documentaries from around the globe. It examines the various forms of male sex work in those documentaries with the goal of identifying common features of rhetorical framing, interview techniques, settings, and topics. While it is crucial to listen to the actual voices of male sex workers talking about their experiences, it is equally important to be mindful of the ways in which their stories have been framed and edited and to question the techniques and motives of the filmmakers and curious audiences consuming media about male sex work.

Many documentaries about male sex workers continue what Brian Winston has critiqued as the "tradition of the victim" in documentary (1988). Jay Ruby glosses Winston's critique in his essay "Speaking For, Speaking About, Speaking With, or Speaking Alongside—An Anthropological and Documentary Dilemma" (1991):

> At the same time as subjects are asserting their right to control their own image, there is the growing recognition on the part of the independent documentary community that it is difficult to justify making films about the private acts of the pathological, socially disadvantaged, politically disenfranchised, and the economically oppressed. . . . Until recently, most victims have passively allowed themselves to be transformed into aesthetic creations, news items, and objects of our pity and concern.
>
> *(Ruby, 1991, p. 52)*

Ruby also notes a crisis (or even death) of the notion of the objectivity of documentary:

> Ironically, the traditional form of the journalistic documentary not only denied a voice to subjects but to the filmmakers as well. 'Objective' documentaries have no authors, only reporters who present the 'who, what, where and whys' of the 'truth.' So the move toward a multivocal documentary form has also involved a renewed and increased role for the filmmaker—an overt acceptance of authorial responsibility.
>
> *(1991, p. 54).*

We should, therefore, be skeptical about the idea of objective "truth" in journalistic documentary. Nonetheless, this chapter addresses (with some irony) the traditional journalistic questions regarding the who, where, when, what or how, and why of documentaries purporting to convey the truth about male sex work. The chapter concludes by considering how male sex workers (1) negotiate stigma and (2) critique and resist the way their personal stories are solicited and framed.

Who? subjects and players

Male sex work takes many forms, from working in adult film, male strip clubs, host clubs, and massage parlors, to street-based hustling and "entrepreneurial" escorting. The last two are contrasted in the short BBC News documentary *Men for Sale: Life as a Male Sex Worker in Britain* (2017; Ruby, 1991). Documentary filmmakers typically select a number of individuals working within these specific milieux or venues to interview as informants. The filmmakers often conduct interviews in ways that resemble social-science approaches ranging from the sociological or criminological to the medical (assessing "risk groups"). The subjects are usually identified only by first names/stage names. In the case of the documentary *101 Rent Boys* (2000), they get assigned a number (as in sexology case studies). Sometimes the faces of male sex workers are blurred to conceal their identity.

In most cases, the filmmakers do not appear in front of the camera, but they can often be heard asking questions, even though documentary conventions frequently call for these questions to be edited out and reconstructed from the responses given. Clients also rarely appear in documentaries about sex work, for reasons of privacy and privilege, resulting in a lopsided "monologue" on what is in fact a transaction involving multiple parties (as noted by sex worker rights advocate Lola Davina [personal correspondence]). These parties include sex workers, clients, managers (sometimes called "pimps"), club owners, social service organizations (drop-in centers and clinics), and, in the case of these mediated representations, the camera and sound crew. Yet, typically, documentaries show only the male sex workers, often isolated in a semi-private setting, talking directly to the camera, and framed in close-up so that the viewer can pick up on subtle facial expressions, perhaps indicating shame or other emotions, as they talk about their interactions with clients, their backgrounds and families, and their feelings about selling sex. This close-up confessional framing is especially vivid in Wiktor Grodecki's documentaries about young male sex workers in Prague, *Not Angels But Angels* (1994) and *Body Without Soul* (1996), two films in a mode I have called "confession porn" (de Villiers, 2017; cf. de Villiers, 2018).

Where? spaces and venues

Sometimes filmmakers shoot on location at hustler strolls in major cities, but typically male sex work documentaries are shot inside hotel rooms, in drop-in centers, in gay bars, or in the backstage areas of male strip clubs. Typically the sex worker is isolated in these interviews for the sake of privacy and sincerity, which can downplay any sense of community or camaraderie. A rare exception appears in *Too Much, Too Young: Chickens* (1995), the controversial documentary about two young "rent boys" in Glasgow, Scotland. The film shows how friendship and camp humor help the boys cope with social stigma and exclusion (the controversy over the film is discussed toward the end of this chapter).

Space plays a significant role in documentaries about male sex work. The Canadian film *Men for Sale* (2008), which is shot in a drop-in center, follows a group of 11 young men over the course of one year as they talk about hustling, drug use, and clients/sugar daddies in Montréal (Figure 7.1). In many ways, the film mirrors the sympathetic but health-risk-assessment-focused approach to Montréal's male sex workers in Michel Dorais's book *Rent Boys: The World of Male Sex Workers* (2005). Both show how hustling is embedded in a complex societal network that includes friendships among male sex workers and features a variety of "types"

Figure 7.1   Men for Sale (Rodrigue Jean, 2008) film poster. ©2008 National Film Board of Canada. All rights reserved.

whom Dorais identifies as Outcasts (who might be homeless or drug-addicted), Insiders (those who are strongly embedded in the sex-worker community), Part-Timers (who separate their occasional sex work from their "straight" lives), and Liberationists (for whom sex work is part of exploring their sexuality). The workers have divergent life trajectories and attitudes toward their sex work, their clients, "sex entrepreneurs" (those making money off their sex work, including facilitators and drug dealers), and authorities, including police, health-service providers, and "moral entrepreneurs." Another attempt at a "longitudinal study" of hustling is German queer activist director Rosa von Praunheim's *Rent Boys* (2011). It examines the history of the hustler scene in Berlin centered on the Bahnhof Zoo train station since the 1960s, as told by current and former sex workers (many of whom are immigrants from Eastern Europe) looking back on their lives in sex work.

The U.S. film *101 Rent Boys* is primarily shot in motel rooms, with sex workers sitting on the bed or the floor, talking about their work as hustlers/escorts in the area of Santa Monica Boulevard in Los Angeles. The Ugandan film *Men of the Night* (2017) explains in rapid montage how relatively less visible male sex workers in Kampala work in "slums, hotels, bars, highways, and motels." In the Current TV documentary *Male Sex Workers in India*, reporter Adam Yamaguchi follows safe-sex outreach workers and commercial sex workers on a tour of the woodland cruising areas for MSM near a train station in Chennai, India. The Vocativ documentary short *The Beach Boys: Objects of Desire* (2013) focuses on the men who work the beaches of Mombasa, Kenya, typically Masai warriors in costume courting white female tourists looking to act out an exotic sexual and/or romantic fantasy.

The Japanese film *Boys for Sale* (2017) is shot in the Shinjuku 2-chome district of Tokyo and depicts the young, predominantly straight-identified men who work in *urisen* (rent boy) host bars. While it interviews some of the management side of the enterprise, it mostly features interviews with the male sex workers in tiny private rooms with beds where they can take their usually older male clients (Figure 7.2). The film also offers an important historical archive of

Figure 7.2 Boys for Sale (Itako, 2017), *urisen* bar signs in Tokyo Shinjuku 2-chome.
Photo credit: Adrian "Uchujin" Storey for *Boys for Sale*. Reproduced with permission from the filmmakers.

the queer history of the neighborhood. *Boys for Sale* makes for an interesting comparison to an earlier documentary, *The Great Happiness Space: Tale of an Osaka Love Thief* (2006), about professionally charming young men who work in a host bar in Osaka entertaining female clients (some of whom are themselves sex workers looking to be catered to during their off hours). Both films point to a long tradition of companionship for hire in Japan, including various forms of "bounded authenticity" and intimacy (Bernstein, 2007).

The U.S. film *All Male, All Nude* (2018) features a famous male strip club, Swinging Richard's in Atlanta, Georgia, and is quite exhaustive in its attention to every space and aspect of the strippers' working environment: the locker room, stage, VIP lounge and private rooms, and even the parking lot as the strippers arrive for work (Figure 7.3). The variety of spaces also means that the film features interviews with a wider range of people within the enterprise: the often straight-identified male strippers (who sometimes refer to their peers as "hustlers"), the club owner and managers, bartenders, and some customers, including female clients who enjoy visiting the nonetheless explicitly gay-male-oriented club. The Australian short documentary program *A Gigolo's Life: Male Sex Workers* (2014) also features a female client and a straight male sex worker with mostly female clients (and some couples), plus the two female managers of a male escort agency, shot in hotel rooms and a suburban home office in Melbourne.

Grodecki's Czech documentaries include interviews with young male hustlers and pimps in the Prague central train station, arcades, gay clubs, and rented rooms. They also feature some footage recorded on the set of an amateur porn film, as well as a morgue where the porn director also works cutting up a cadaver (echoing the title *Body Without Soul*, a phrase used by one of

Figure 7.3   All Male, All Nude (Gerald McCullouch, 2018) film poster.

Reproduced with permission from Gerald McCullouch.

the most ashamed of the straight-identified boys in an interview about how he feels "selling his body" to older homosexuals). Grodecki also inserts images of leering "dirty old men" (whom we assume represent clients) and statues of angels implying Catholic guilt. While these images attempt to capture a complex social fabric affected by a newly capitalist economy in a range of locations and involving multiple parties including tourist clients and exploitative porn producers, Grodecki's films often isolate his subjects in intimate confessional interviews that focus on individual feelings of shame.

When? history and context

Documentary films offer a snapshot of a particular historical moment in geopolitical and urban history, and they often attempt to comment on major economic and population shifts. This agenda is certainly apparent in Grodecki's films, which are arguably more about Grodecki's desire to critique capitalism and sex tourism than they are about the concerns of young male sex workers per se (Moss, 2006; de Villiers, 2017). Chinese filmmaker Cui Zi'en's quasi-documentary *Night Scene* (2005), featuring both actual sex workers and actors reading scripted dialogue, tells the stories of migrant workers within Beijing's gay nightlife during a profound shift toward marketization in China's economy. It focuses on a gay bar with drag and go-go boy entertainment known as the Fish Bar, where not all the workers sell sex (de Villiers, 2017). The documentary *Men of the Night* about male sex workers in Uganda includes voiceover explaining how Kampala's business district turns into a red-light district at night. It suggests that while people usually think of sex workers as female, the contribution of male sex workers to the "booming" industry is beyond measure. Each of these films is also framed in terms of HIV/ AIDS prevention and the problem of reaching men who do not identify as gay or even necessarily as male sex workers.

Some documentaries about male sex work are explicit critiques of sex tourism (cf. Ryan & Hall, 2001). *Beach Boys* features European women with exotic fantasies about Kenyan men, but these fantasies do not exclude the possibility of romance, even though such relationships are marked by colonial, racial, and economic inequality. Much more explicitly negative coverage is seen in the France 24 English news documentary short *Morocco: The Hellish World of Sex Tourism* (2011), which shows how Moroccan boys are being pimped or selling sex directly to "pedophile" European sex tourists out of dire economic need. The RT (formerly Russia Today) exposé *Sex, Drugs, and Refugees* (2018) focuses primarily on Syrian and Afghan refugees in Athens, Greece who resort to selling sex to Greek and other European men around Parliament Square. But we might have reasons to be skeptical these exposés' agendas: What are the vested interests or biases of French reporters telling these particular stories about former colonies, or Russian state news reporters intending to expose the corrupt side of Europe during the Syrian refugee crisis? Moreover, these exposés collapse many factors into one: Young men's sense of humiliation and anger at being homeless and lacking access to food and government services is conflated with the humiliation of being "gay for pay."

What?/how? questions and framing

We should thus be critical of the ways in which male sex workers—especially those who are young, and whose sense of control over their "fate" might be quite limited—are questioned in these documentaries. Filmmakers and audiences seem particularly preoccupied with the sexual identities and orientations of male sex workers—How it can be possible for them to have sex with men for money but not identify as gay?—echoing a long history of middle-class sexological research into male sex work and homosexuality more concerned with classifying sexual identity rather than behavior and less concerned with the social and material conditions and motives of male sex workers (Kaye, 2003).

The questions asked, and the terms used, often determine the answers given (Goffman, 1981). Male sex workers' responses to questions about how they started selling sex; what risks they take and why; and how they identify their sexual identity, orientation, preferences, and/or behavior involve complex negotiations of stigma. These responses are therefore constrained by (male) whore stigma, homophobia, and scripts of normative masculinity (machismo). Interviews with male sex workers on camera often demonstrate the problem identified by Erving Goffman's study *Stigma* in terms of "the management of spoiled identity" (1963). Criminological studies like Donald West's *Male Prostitution* (1993) have demonstrated some reflexive awareness of constraints in the answers given by young male sex workers (interviewed at a drop-in center in London), especially those identifying as straight. Sex-work researchers have also noted the potential "research fatigue" of sex workers interacting with those doing outreach repeatedly asking the same questions (Shah, 2014). And yet, documentary filmmakers often flatter themselves (and their audiences) that they are offering a rare sympathetic ear to a seemingly invisible or outcast population.

More accurately, male sex-work documentaries framed as exposés examine "open secrets" of gay urban subcultures, including cruising and hustling, drug use, pornography, and the issues of intergenerational and gay-for-pay sex. Some documentaries reveal how deeply the history of gay culture and the porn industry are intertwined. *Seed Money: The Chuck Holmes Story* (2016) tells the story of the San Francisco pornographer behind Falcon Studios, Chuck Holmes, whose work helped define post-Stonewall gay identity and ideals, and who in later life became a philanthropist for gay causes like the Human Rights Campaign. German filmmaker Jochen Hick's *Sex/Life in L.A. 2: Cycles of Porn* (2005) juxtaposes interviews with young gay actors hoping to make it in the relatively low-budget Los Angeles porn industry with the lives of three men now retired from making porn.

Other documentaries about the adult film industry examine the idealization of straight men in gay porn: *I'm a Porn Star: Gay 4 Pay* (2016) features interviews with several straight-identified but gay-for-pay performers (working for sites like Men.com, Sean Cody, and Bromo), as well as some gay men who have worked with them (porn performers and a director), along with *vox populi* (people on the street) interviews speculating about what it means to do gay porn but identify as straight. The U.S. reality television series *Broke Straight Boys TV* is a fascinating portrait of the gay-for-pay porn studio Broke Straight Boys, including both the producers and the performers, who can face rejection from family and friends when they "come out" as having sex with men on camera for money (de Villiers, 2018). Both *I'm a Porn Star: Gay 4 Pay* and *Broke Straight Boys TV* suggest that gay-for-pay performers understand homophobia more intimately after people learn they do gay porn.

The testimonials of male sex workers regarding their struggles with family rejection, homelessness, drug use, or financial desperation might be considered a kind of "affective labor," where the subject is aware of how to solicit sympathy from clients or filmmakers to make them feel that they are helping rather than exploiting the male sex worker. In his article "Sex and the Unspoken in Male Street Prostitution," Kerwin Kaye notes how male sex workers craft "sympathetic victim" personas in their interactions with social services (downplaying their individual agency or choice) that stand in contrast with the more "tough" image they project among their peers on the street for protection or respect (Kaye, 2010, p. 114).

But many male sex workers explain their emotional labor in terms of acting as therapists to their clients, fulfilling specific fantasies or offering release, comfort, exploration, or someone to confide in. In *All Male, All Nude*, one dancer jokes, "Some of the shit people say in your ear is hard to bear," while another dancer explains how "you find yourself reminding the customers quite often that, you know, there are still boundaries . . . this is still a place of work. It is a place of fantasy, but the fantasy does have guidelines." As these dancers point out, managing such "social intimacy" requires etiquette, intelligence, and tact in not just exposing oneself to the clients, but also in "exposing people to themselves." As many testimonials in these documentaries reveal, part of the emotional work of sex work involves dealing with burden of clients' shame or their projection of that shame onto the sex worker.

A major problem in many "confessional" documentary interviews with male sex workers is that the filmmakers often reinforce rather than alleviate stigma by focusing their questions on risk, disease, drug addiction, or feelings of shame and rejection. As Jo Weldon notes, research into sex work is often obsessively focused on questions about trauma (especially sexual abuse in childhood) but strangely uncurious about financial motivations for doing sex work, as if it is harder to talk about money than about sex, at least in American culture (Weldon, 2010, pp. 147–148). Editing also plays an important role in shaping the overall narrative effect of what are often diverse opinions regarding sex and money within one documentary. Sometimes interviews are edited to create a sense of "dialogue" among the sex workers interviewed, with contrasting takes on a particular topic, but often one tone will end up dominating the narrative (Grodecki's films are a good example).

Critical reflexivity is also required when considering the conditions in which interviews are recorded. In both *101 Rent Boys* and *Men for Sale*, female sound recordists attach microphones to the male sex workers, something remarked upon by the men, some of whom seem uncomfortable talking about sex frankly in the presence of a woman rather than in an all-male "homosocial" environment. Their hesitation foregrounds gender rather than race, class, or gay/ straight differentials between the interviewed subjects and the film crew, even though these differentials are also important to consider. It is also worth noting that female clients appear to be more likely to be interviewed in the documentaries discussed in this chapter, and they may experience a different form of stigma.

Filmmakers are often constrained in terms of how sexually explicit their documentary footage can be, a problem solved by the filmmakers of *Boys for Sale* by using Japanese *manga* (comics) style illustrations of the sexual activities between the male sex workers and their clients (Uchujin, 2017) (Figure 7.4). The porn documentaries mentioned previously are more sexually explicit, but they still work to differentiate themselves from pornography (even as before and after interview and making-of scenes are also staples of gay porn, and such documentaries can often feel like extended commercials for these studios). Music can also affect the tone of the interview or illustrative footage, whether it is the dance music favored by *All Male, All Nude* and *101 Rent Boys* or the mournful classical music (Mozart's Requiem) in Wiktor Grodecki's films.

Documentary tone also varies according to modes of distribution, suggesting different ways of reaching different audiences: special-interest documentary rental, pay-per-view, or subscription-based streaming (Netflix, Amazon, HereTV, YouTube); sensational exposés or sober online news journalism; films intended for international and LGBT film festivals; or documentaries made for educational outreach use by sex worker rights organizations (for example, *Men of the Night* was created by an organization also called Men of the Night, which advocates for the rights and visibility of male sex workers in Uganda and was promoted by the African Sex Workers Alliance).

Documentary has always had an ambivalent relationship with Hollywood filmmaking and Hollywood as an institution, especially when it comes to sexuality and representation. The sympathetic documentary *Scotty and the Secret History of Hollywood* (2017) interviews famous

Figure 7.4   *Boys for Sale* (Itako, 2017) film still of the *manga* style that is used for illustrating sexual activities between *urisen* and clients.

Illustration credit: N Tani Studios for *Boys for Sale*. Reproduced with permission from the filmmakers.

Hollywood call boy Scotty Bowers about his life and tell-all book recounting his work as a "call boy" and procurer of call boys for celebrity male and female clients in Hollywood, running his operation out of a gas station in Los Angeles. The film offers a critical take on the history of Hollywood's "closet." Juliana Piccillo's documentary *Whores on Film* (2019) also features interviews with male sex workers reflecting critically on the impact of Hollywood's images of hustlers and why audiences seem so fascinated by specific narrative tropes about male sex work.

Why? Motives and critiques

Finally, because this article has focused on how filmmakers and male sex workers frame questions of agency in their interviews, it is important to consider how male sex workers can resist the confessional framework of the interviews or even challenge the filmmakers' ethics. Several of the interviewees in *101 Rent Boys* call attention to what they see as the potentially exploitative nature of the enterprise: how little they are paid for participating ($50 USD, sometimes handed to them on camera at vulnerable moments), whether the interview is itself a form of prostitution or solicited performance, and *why* they should expose themselves (body *and* soul) for the camera and the voyeuristic spectator.

Fictionalization, or "faking," presents another ethical dilemma. For example, *Too Much, Too Young: Chickens* includes faked scenes of clients picking up the rent boys in cars (the clients were actually members of the crew), and the young men sued the filmmakers for misrepresenting them in the film, accusing them of scripting the interview responses. Additional controversy focused on the fact that the boys were paid for participating, and some blamed the filmmakers for putting the boys in harm's way by airing the documentary (McCann, 1999; Seenan, 1999; "Seduced by 15 Minutes of Fame", 1999).

However, obvious and deliberate fictionalization can be deployed effectively in a critical and reflexive fashion, as in the work of quasi-documentary filmmakers like Cui Zi'en (*Night Scene*) or Nicola Mai. For Mai's films about migrant sex workers in Europe, *Normal* (2012) and *Samira* (2014), Mai hired actors to perform and embody the stories of his ethnographic interview subjects (to protect their privacy but also to question some of the assumptions of authenticity in ethnographic documentaries). Cui and Mai also appear in their films as "characters," which is one way to accept authorial responsibility. Fictionalization here sensitizes us to irony, both the irony of soliciting the confessional performance of the sex worker subject and the smirking irony expressed by the sex workers in their interviews as a way of navigating various forms of stigma attached to selling sex.

Male sex workers often sharply criticize the hypocrisy of their clients or society at large for judging them even as the clients clearly enjoy their services and the release they provide. The best examples of multivocal and non-judgmental documentary investigation into the male sex industry—in all its various forms across the world—provide space for sex workers' critiques of the biases of non-sex workers who have demonstrated seemingly inexhaustible curiosity about the lives, habits, motives, fears, and dreams of male sex workers. An outstanding example is when, in *Boys for Sale*, the filmmakers acknowledge that they are renting the male sex workers' time for the interview, and they ask them at the end if being interviewed for the documentary is more difficult than having sex with a client, thereby inviting critique of the documentary enterprise itself.

References

Bernstein, E. (2007). *Temporarily yours: Intimacy, authenticity, and the commerce of Sex*. Chicago, IL: University of Chicago Press.

Cowan, M. (2017, December 13). Life as a male sex worker in Britain today. *BBC's Victoria Derbyshire Programme*. Retrieved from www.bbc.com/news/uk-42265838

de Villiers, N. (2017). *Sexography: Sex work in documentary*. Minneapolis, MN: University of Minnesota Press.

Dorais, M. (2005). *Rent boys: The world of male sex workers* (Peter Feldstein, Trans.). Kingston, Ontario: McGill-Queen's University Press.

Goffman, E. (1963). *Stigma: Notes on the management of spoiled identity*. New York: Simon and Schuster.

Goffman, E. (1981). *Forms of talk*. Philadelphia, PA: University of Pennsylvania Press.

Itako (2017) *Boys for sale* [documentary]. Ian Thomas Ash, Japan.

Kaye, K. (2003). Male prostitution in the twentieth century: Pseudohomosexuals, hoodlum homosexuals, and exploited teens. *Journal of Homosexuality*, *46*(1–2), 1–77.

Kaye, K. (2010). Sex and the unspoken in male street prostitution. In M. H. Ditmore, A. Levy, & A. Willman (Eds.), *Sex work matters: Exploring money, power and intimacy in the sex industry* (pp. 85–116). London: Zed Books.

McCann, P. (1999, February 5). C4 admits new fake and bars film's producer. *The Independent*. Retrieved from www.independent.co.uk/news/c4-admits-new-fake-and-bars-films-producer-1068771.html

Moss, K. (2016). Who's renting these boys? Wiktor Grodecki's Czech hustler documentaries. *Interalia*, 1. Retrieved from http://interalia.org.pl/pl/artykuly/2006_1/05_whos_renting_these_boys.htm#przy pisy_11

Ruby, J. (1991). Speaking for, speaking about, speaking with, or speaking alongside—An anthropological and documentary dilemma. *Visual Anthropology Review*, *7*(2), 50–67.

Ryan, C., & Hall, C. M. (2001). *Sex tourism: Marginal people and liminalities*. New York: Routledge.

Seduced by 15 Minutes of Fame. (1999). *Scottish Daily Record*. Retrieved from www.thefreelibrary.com/SEDUCED+BY+15+MINUTES+OF+FAME.-a060430053

Seenan, G. (1999, March 18). Youth in faked rent boy documentary to sue. *The Guardian*. Retrieved from www.theguardian.com/uk/1999/mar/19/gerardseenan

Sex, Drugs & Refugees: Syrian teenagers in Athens resort to prostitution to survive. (2018, February 28). *RT Documentary Channel*. Retrieved from https://rtd.rt.com/films/sex-drugs--refugees/

Shah, S. (2014). *Street corner secrets: Sex, work, and migration in the city of Mumbai*. Durham, NC: Duke University Press.

Uchujin (aka Adrian Storey). (2017, June 22). *Boys for Sale*—Gaining a community's trust to shoot a two-year documentary project in Japan. *Newsshooter*. Retrieved from www.newsshooter.com/2017/06/22/boys-for-sale-documentary-project-japan/

Weldon, J. (2010). Show me the money: A sex worker reflects on research into the sex industry. In M. H. Ditmore, A. Levy, & A. Willman (Eds.), *Sex work matters: Exploring money, power, and intimacy in the sex industry* (pp. 147–154). London: Zed Books.

Winston, B. (1988). The tradition of the victim in Griersonian documentary. In L. Gross, J. S. Katz, & J. Ruby (Eds.), *Image ethics: The moral rights of subjects in photography, film, and television* (pp. 34–57). New York: Oxford University Press.

Movie Titles, Directors, Year of Release (in alphabetical order)

101 Rent Boys (Fenton Bailey & Randy Barbato, 2000). Candid motel-room interviews with 101 hustlers/escorts working in the area of Santa Monica Boulevard in Los Angeles, with each paid $50 for the interview (often paid on camera).

All Male, All Nude (Gerald McCullouch, 2018). A behind-the-scenes documentary about the male dancers and management of the gay-male-oriented strip club Swinging Richard's in Atlanta, Georgia, with an emphasis on the social skills the job requires.

The Beach Boys: Objects of Desire (Vocativ, 2013). Documentary short on the men who work the beaches of Mombasa, Kenya, typically Masai warriors in costume courting white female tourists looking to act out an exotic fantasy.

Body Without Soul (Wiktor Grodecki, 1996). Polish director Wiktor Grodecki interviews migrant male teenagers who work in amateur pornography in Prague, and his probing, confessional interviews emphasize the young men's feelings of shame about "selling their bodies" and their fears about HIV/AIDS. Grodecki also interviews an exploitative porn producer and coroner in a morgue.

Boys for Sale (Itako, 2017). A smart and self-reflexive documentary featuring interviews with young, predominantly straight-identified men who work in *urisen* (rent boy) host bars in the Shinjuku 2-chome district of Tokyo, along with some managers and bartenders. The film makes innovative use of *manga*-style illustrations for the stories told by the sex workers about their mostly older male clients.

A Gigolo's Life: Male Sex Workers (SBS Two/The Feed, 2014). A short news documentary that interviews a straight male sex worker, a female client, and two female managers of a male escort agency in Melbourne, Australia, with an emphasis on de-stigmatizing women buying sexual services from men.

The Great Happiness Space: Tale of an Osaka Love Thief (Jake Clennell, 2006). Documentary about the young men who work in a host bar in Osaka entertaining female clients, some of whom are themselves sex workers.

I'm a Porn Star: Gay4Pay (Charlie David, 2016). U.S. documentary featuring behind-the-scenes interviews with several straight-identified but gay-for-pay performers as well as some gay men who have worked with them, along with *vox populi* (people on the street) interviews speculating about what it means to do gay porn but identify as straight.

Male Sex Workers in India (Grace Baek, 2006). Short Current TV documentary report on safe-sex outreach to MSM and male sex workers in Chennai, India.

Men for Sale (Rodrigue Jean, 2008). A sympathetic documentary following a group of 11 young men over the course of one year as they talk about hustling, drug use, and clients/sugar daddies in Montréal, Canada, shot in a drop-in center with an emphasis on health risks.

Men for Sale: Life as a Male Sex worker in Britain (Michael Cowan, 2017). Short BBC News documentary that juxtaposes street-based hustling with entrepreneurial male escorting.

Men of the Night (Men of the Night, 2017). NGO-produced documentary, advocates for the rights and visibility of male sex workers in Uganda.

Morocco: The Hellish World of Sex Tourism (Aziza Nait Sibaha & Karim Hakiki, 2011). France 24 exposé of sex tourism in Morocco—youths selling sex to foreign tourists.

Night Scene (Cui Zi'en, 2005). Chinese queer activist filmmaker Cui Zi'en's quasi-documentary features a deliberately ambiguous mix of actual sex workers and actors reading scripted dialogue telling the stories of migrant workers within Beijing's gay nightlife.

Normal (Nicola Mai, 2012). An artistic documentary by director and anthropologist Nicola Mai bringing the real life stories of male, female, and transgender migrants working in the sex industry in Albania, Italy, and the United Kingdom to the screen but using actors to embody real research interviews. This technique protects the anonymity and safety of the original interviewees, but it also questions notions of authenticity in ethnography.

Not Angels But Angels (Wiktor Grodecki, 1994). Polish director Wiktor Grodecki interviews teenage male hustlers in Prague's train station and clubs about their feelings, hopes, and fears faced with HIV/AIDS and the Czech Republic's newly capitalist economy. The film also interviews a "pimp" who helps them meet tourist clients. Images of angels and classical religious music underscore the Catholic tone of the film's confessional interviews.

Rent Boys (Rosa von Praunheim, 2011). Queer activist filmmaker Rosa von Praunheim's documentary interviews current and former male hustlers, many of whom are migrants from Eastern Europe, who work around the central Zoo train station in Berlin, along with some bar owners, clients, and social workers.

Samira (Nicola Mai, 2014). A two-screen "ethnofictional" installation presenting the life history of Karim, an Algerian migrant man selling sex as a transvestite at night in Marseille. Filmmaker and anthropologist Nicola Mai (who also appears in the film) uses actors to embody real people and real life histories in order to protect their privacy but also to question what counts as authentic reality or credibility in humanitarian and scientific work on migrant sex workers.

Scotty and the Secret History of Hollywood (Matt Tyrnauer, 2017). A charming documentary portrait of famous Hollywood call boy Scotty Bowers recounting his life and tell-all book on his work as a "call boy" and procurer of call boys for celebrity male and female clients in Hollywood.

Seed Money: The Chuck Holmes Story (Michael Stabile, 2015). A documentary portrait of the San Francisco pornographer behind Falcon Studios, Chuck Holmes, who became a philanthropist for gay causes.

Sex, Drugs, and Refugees (Alexander [Aleksandr] Avilov, 2018). Russian exposé about Syrian and Afghan refugees in Athens, Greece, who sell sex to Greek and other European men out of desperation.

Sex/Life in L.A. 2: Cycles of Porn (Jochen Hick, 2005). A documentary juxtaposing interviews with young gay actors hoping to make it in the relatively low-budget Los Angeles porn industry with the lives of three men now retired from making porn.

Too Much, Too Young: Chickens (Marie Devine, 1995). Controversial documentary about two young "rent boys" in Glasgow, Scotland. The filmmakers were accused of faking some of the scenes and exposing the young men to danger by airing the program on television.

Whores on Film (Juliana Piccillo, 2019). Embodying the ethos of "nothing about us without us," a diverse group of sex workers (male and female) speak back to historical representations of sex workers on screen (especially Hollywood film), and critique tropes of victimhood and rescue.

8

Male sex work in the porn industry*

Gendering risk and protection

Heather Berg

Dave Pounder, a porn performer/director/producer, laughed when I asked what he thought of straight porn's gender dynamics, especially the convention of paying men half the rates women command. I wanted to know if, having been a performer himself, Dave had tried to do things differently when he was writing the cheques. Dave explained that *the* question for him in deciding rates is "What is the lowest rate I can pay people where I'd still get people to shoot for me?":

> Most guys want to do porn. Most girls don't want to do porn. If you find someone who's willing, the only reason they want to do it is because they're getting paid. If you pay the guys half of what you pay the girls, they're still gonna want to do it. . . . I don't want to lowball guys. If I get a crappy guy who can't perform, I paid the location, I paid for the girl, if he climaxes in two minutes I have to shoot all over again.

(2014)

Dave's response points to the central—and contradictory—features of cisgender[1] men's work in the porn industry. Their work is both subject to intense pressure—a man's performance can make or break a scene—and systematically devalued. Thus, men performers are at once marked as disposable and in possession of hard-to-find skills.[2]

In this chapter, I explore how gender shapes working conditions in the U.S. porn industry, along with the public policy responses to those conditions. On the one hand, an employment law apparatus organized around a Fordist[3] workplace makes porn workers, like other feminized and contingent workers, precarious. On the other hand, anti-porn critics construct porn work as a site of sensationalized feminine sexual vulnerability. The result directs policy and popular attention away from the mundane workplace risks that porn workers of all genders face. In fact, when performers speak about feeling "exploited" or "taken advantage of," they are almost always referring to working conditions and pay, not to bad or violent sex. And, contrary to the dominant narrative, cisgender (or "cis") women are not uniquely vulnerable to workplace abuse.

I begin this chapter by describing porn work as feminized labor. As a kind of work associated with physical and emotional intimacy, porn work should be understood as feminized work even when the performers are not cis women workers. I then provide an overview of the conditions of porn work and the ill-fitting legal structures that attempt to regulate the work. The workplace strains that workers identify as most pressing emanate directly from an employment law system that excludes feminized jobs. Finally, I explore how gender norms shape men's experience of porn work on set. This chapter asks, "What can a Materialist[4] feminist lens reveal about men's porn work?"

The interviews I quote here come from my research on labor in the porn industry, which explores labor politics and work processes in porn's various genres. The research is grounded in 81 interviews I conducted between 2012 and 2015 with U.S. adult film industry performers, managers, and crew of diverse gendered, ethnic, age, sexual, and other identities. My fieldwork also included observations of porn sets, trade meetings, and conventions. This chapter's focus on cis men performers reveals the specific conditions they encounter. It also identifies the strains that many porn workers describe as they labor in jobs that are at once largely invisible as sites of economic struggle and hyper-visible as sites of gendered violence.

Porn as feminized labor

Porn work is feminized labor in two key ways. First, like other sexual labors, it is dominated by women workers, though not to the extent most scholars assume (see Smith, 2012). Second, porn work is feminized in the more expansive sense in which Materialist feminists deploy the term. Here, "feminization" signals not only workers' identities but also the work's gendered meanings. Feminized labor is work that, as Rosemary Hennessy describes it, carries "the marks of femininity," and workers of all genders can find their labor thus marked (2006b, p. 390). Femininity marks labor as unskilled, cheap, and replaceable. It also works as "the glue that binds corporate and state impunity," subjecting feminized workers to workplace risk (Hennessy, 2006b, p. 390). Similarly, Christina Morini describes the ways that feminization shapes the *"administration* of labour (precariousness, mobility, fragmentary nature, low salaries)" and its "contents . . . capacities for relationships, emotional aspects, linguistic aspects, propensity for care" (2007, p. 42).

Hennessy refers to the feminization of factory labor and Morini to labor in what she calls "cognitive capitalism," but their analyses help to explain power in porn too. Regardless of the genders of those performing in any given scene, porn and other sex work are marked as feminized and thus made precarious. Porn work is certainly subject to "corporate and state impunity"— as we see in the industry's propensity for flouting labor law and the state's concerted lack of interest in enforcing it.[5] We also see in porn work the marks of feminization that Morini describes. It is precarious and fragmented, with short career spans for most performers. It is also marked by hypermobility, with workers performing multiple roles and moving among sectors of the industry. Most performers make a middling income, and so the low-salary criterion does not quite fit here. Sex work is unique in this respect; it is one form of feminized work in which the "marks of femininity" do not translate into lower pay.

Porn carries the marks of femininity in terms of its "contents" too. With intense demands for emotional and bodily labor, it blurs the boundaries between life and work—another characteristic of feminized work (see Boris & Parreñas, 2010). "Work" here means "less and less a circumscribed part of life and more and more a *comprehensive action*" (Morini, 2007, p. 44). Indeed, porn workers encounter a boundless workday, populated by labors done off set and off the clock—self-marketing, readying the body for work, and resting from it.

Porn workers of all genders do this feminized labor, a reality that gets obscured in readings that reduce "feminized" to simply "done by women."[6] Nicola Smith warns of this tendency in sex work research especially, describing a

> conceptual leap in which the sex industry is not only explored as a feminized sphere of work—that is, as marginalized and denigrated because of its association with the private realm of erotic/affective life—but is also directly attached to female bodies—that is, as labor that is not just discursively constructed as "women's work" but that is, in reality, "women's work."
>
> *(2012, p. 590)*

In such constructions, sex work comes to be understood as an exclusively heterosexual phenomenon, with men buying and women selling. Here, even feminist analyses posit a "gender order in which sexual objectification is tied to female bodies and sexual subjectivity is tied to male ones" (Smith, 2012, p. 590). Such analyses reflect trans workers' self-identifications unevenly, sometimes constructing trans women as vulnerable *as women* and trans men as invisible *as men*, sometimes mis-gendering them, and sometimes ignoring their existence all together.

We see gendered stereotypes even where research engages sex workers who do not identify as cis women. In this text's previous volume, John Scott and Victor Minichiello describe the tendency to present female sex workers "as a passive 'supply' population, and male ones as 'more active'" (2014, p. xvi). My research suggests, instead, that when we understand sex work through the lens of political economy, such gendered assumptions do not hold. Instead, workers of all genders are active agents in navigating working conditions but within constraints over which they have limited control. This is not to say that power relations here are not gendered. On the contrary, gender forms a "second skin" (Hennessy, 2006a) that shapes workplace dynamics in countless ways. But fixed assumptions about female passivity and male subjectivity obscure more than they reveal, in the porn workplace and beyond.

Unlike other feminized jobs such as secretarial work or domestic labor, porn and other sex work are overwhelmingly understood through the lens of (typically white) cis women's vulnerability as sexual subjects rather than as workers.[7] Thus, sex work becomes what Brooke Beloso calls a "declassified" allegory for gender politics rather than a form of work in its own right (2012, p. 48). Shannon Bell describes prominent anti-porn feminist Catherine MacKinnon's move to perpetuate the idea of "the whore as woman's fundamental position in masculinist societies" (1994, p. 97). In this context, "exploitation" signals objectification and sexualized violence rather than the extraction of surplus value through waged labor (see Berg, 2014).

These framings of porn and sex work have two key effects. First, they erase the sexual labor of men and trans people (Logan, 2014, p. 111; Scott & Minichiello, 2014, p. xvi; Smith, 2012). "No one seems too worried about men being exploited by the porn industry," says Laura Kipnis, "which says something about just how beset with stereotypes these discussions are" (1999, p. xii).[8] Second, they cut off conversations about sex work and policymaking from materialist analysis. The result is performative concern for cis women's sexual vulnerability coupled with a silence around other forms of workplace risk. Anti-porn feminists focus on underage sex, double penetration, and BDSM (see MacKinnon, 1988, pp. 128, 138, 147) and not union busting, independent contractor status, and racist pay inequality. As I have argued elsewhere, because porn scholarship tends to frame itself in direct response to anti-porn feminist analysis, this field of vision sets the terms for the conversation (Berg, 2014).

There is a clear line tracing anti-porn discourse to the poorly designed policies it inspires. For example, the most regularly enforced porn industry regulation (and thus the regulation that porn managers most reliably enforce) is the set of federal "2257" recordkeeping statutes.[9] These require producers to maintain records of performers' legal names and copies of their photo identifications in order to demonstrate that performers are over 18. Workers say that the 2257 statutes present serious privacy concerns, leaving them vulnerable to stalking and public exposure. Such regulations also address a largely imaginary problem. According to my interviewees, producers aren't seeking out underage girls (other underage people are rarely the subject of these concerns) in hopes of duping them into porn performance. Even managers with the lowest ethical standards said they found the idea of trolling for underage workers distasteful. Managers note that with a seemingly limitless pool of willing (and legal) workers, there is no reason to take the effort and legal risks associated with cajoling unwilling workers. "A lot of people don't understand," explained producer/director Matt Frackas, "we do not need to seduce or convince or trick girls into this. There's always a supply" (2013). The specter of predatory producers tricking young women into appearing in porn distracts from the very real concerns faced by the workers in porn's always renewable labor force.

Gendering workplace policy

Focusing on porn as a source of women's *sexual* vulnerability obscures the reality that the vast majority of the workplace strains and abuses that porn workers describe are about work, not sex. These abuses are not explained by porn managers' special antipathy toward women, or, as many anti-porn feminists suggest, male consumers' desire to watch violence against women play out on screen. Porn workers are exploited at work because that is how the employer/employee relationship works, and workers described conditions similar to those described by other workers.

When I asked performer Richie Calhoun about the benefits available to performers, he responded, "We have nothing, we have no medical insurance, we have no union, we have no residuals or royalties" (2013). Like others treated as independent contractors, porn workers are overwhelmingly denied protections under wage and hour regulations such as overtime and minimum-wage requirements. Porn workers' liminal employment status and the lack of clarity around antidiscrimination policy also create the conditions for ubiquitous and unchecked racial inequality in work opportunities and pay. Mr. Marcus talked about the routine racism he encountered as a Black man in the industry. "When they shoot Black," he explained, "they automatically think they can pay less" (2013). Workers' de facto independent contractor status also makes them vulnerable to poverty upon retirement. "The thing with being an outlaw," 30-year industry veteran Carter Stevens told me, "is that the retirement package sucks" (2013). Finally, treating performers as independent contractors affects occupational health practices, shaping the level of risk that workers encounter on set and determining what happens when they sustain an infection or injury.

These conditions are made possible by an employment law system that was designed to fit a workplace that is less and less a reality for U.S. workers. Feminist legal scholars suggest that labor law modeled on male-dominated mass production manufacturing is especially ill equipped to address work in today's flexible, service-based, feminized economies (Stewart, 2013). It is also worth noting that such flexible labor arrangements aren't at all new for sex workers and others whose working arrangements fall outside the full-time, long-term, single-employer model of the twentieth century.[10]

Gendered dynamics at work

Male performers must navigate the combined force of these exclusions *and* their invisibility as sex workers who might be vulnerable to employer abuse. This status, as Pounder's earlier comment suggests, is heavily structured by normative ideas about gender and sexuality: Men are always ready for sex, but women need a bit more cajoling (see Beres, 2007). The idea of men's sexual readiness was compounded by the advent of Viagra, which opened porn work to men who were previously unable to perform under the conditions it requires. Viagra and injectable erectile dysfunction drugs de-skilled men's jobs by opening the field up beyond the select few who could maintain an erection for hours-long shoots, in strenuous positions, with crews watching, and with partners with whom they may or may not have had chemistry. With Viagra, "any guy could be a porn star," and pay "took a nose dive," explained Carter Stevens, a veteran of porn's "golden era" of the 1970s (2013).

The idea that men are always ready for sex emerged again and again in my interviews with both performers and managers. It is in some ways the inverse of a common refrain in other forms of feminized labor, one that suggests that low wages result from the supposed effortlessness of the work. But for men in porn, the popular perception is not so much that their work is easy. Workers and managers agree that even with chemical supports, maintaining an erection for hours at a time and ejaculating on command, in addition to men performers' various other job tasks, are skilled work. The threat of "failing a scene"—being unable to maintain an erection, ejaculating too early or not at all—always looms. It emerged again and again in my interviews with male performers as a major source of anxiety, and one that encouraged often risky overuse of erection-enhancing medications.

Although managers generally see men's porn work as skilled, they nonetheless see it as too desirable to command high pay. Access to no-strings-attached sex becomes a sort of supplementary payment. Mathieu Trachman found a similar dynamic in his study of French porn work. Here too, men confront a dynamic is which an erection is both an essential—and pressure-inducing—part of the job *and* visible evidence that one is not really working but instead experiencing pleasure (Trachman, 2015, p. 83). Men in my interviews described sex as a reward as a common management response when they demand better pay. "Everyone has this little thing they like to poke you with," Mr. Marcus explained, "like, 'I know guys who will do it for free, I know guys who will do it for cheaper.' Girls won't do it for free, but they might do it for less" (2013). Marcus insisted that managers pay the rate he set, not just because he wanted higher pay but also because he wanted to make a political point about the devaluation of Black men's labor. As one of few Black men cast to perform in higher-paying scenes with white women, he was in a better position than most to make such demands. Most men take what they can get, and Black men in particular find their work particularly devalued in a system that, as Mireille Miller-Young describes, sees Black workers as "hypersexual" and cheaply available (2014).

For most male performers, the idea that willing replacements would happily step in restricts negotiating power. When I asked if he felt he could negotiate work terms, white gay performer Christopher Daniels explained, "When I hear models negotiate, I'm just like, 'You're pretty brave.' If you don't want to do it, they'll find someone who will" (2014). This perceived labor surplus shapes efforts at collective bargaining too. Male performers were more likely to tell me they had tried to initiate unionizing efforts, partly because they tend to have longer careers in the industry and partly because they often have less power to negotiate on individual terms. But when they attempt to organize, they are again confronted with the idea that if they have complaints about the work, a string of replacements will be happy to step in. Of an unsuccessful organizing attempt, industry veteran Herschel Savage told me, "The producers and production companies have the power, the cash . . . you have no negotiating power" (2013). The same is true for all porn workers, not just men, but porn's gendered dynamics mean that men have not only reduced negotiating power but also the outward appearance of having less to organize around in the first place.

Men's comparatively reduced access to alternative income streams compounds these barriers to collective organizing. While women can ease out of performing with erotic dance tours, high-paying escort gigs, and branded merchandise, men's wages often dry up as soon as their porn gigs do. Men who do sexual labor aimed at male clients can access some of these opportunities, with escorting, personal appearances at events, and stripping and go-go dance gigs (Grov & Smith, 2014, p. 248), but on the whole, these pay less than similar work available to women sex workers. So, while women performers who make significant money in side gigs can afford to negotiate harder with managers because "a scene is just a marketing tool" and not a primary income source, the same is not true for most men performers (Berg, 2016).

Male performers can, however, take on behind-the-scenes work as (usually) low-budget directors and producers. In rare cases, performers can amass enough start-up capital to produce major scenes in their own right, but here, as for worker/producers of all genders, piracy and the explosion of user-generated content make production much less lucrative than it once was. And so the reality remains that when men performers work for others, they have very limited bargaining power.

Gendering consent

Most male performers accept the terms on offer not only in terms of rates but also in negotiating consent and the conditions of a scene. Women performers are expected to compile "yes" lists of men they are willing to work with, and they can generally refuse partners without fear of losing a casting. Meanwhile, men *might* be permitted a short "no" list of women they refuse to work with. Likewise, casting directors know beforehand what types of scenes and what specific sex acts women performers are willing to perform—whether they will film anal scenes, for instance. The general assumption, however, is that men are up for anything. Agency websites reveal this gap. Women performers' pages usually include a list of the types of scenes for which they are available, while men's "available for" lists are typically blank. For the few straight production companies that allow performers to decide whether to use condoms—most film only without condoms—the option is available in practice only to women performers. This policy is not explicit but rather is enforced by cultural norms that presume cis women's sexual vulnerability and men and trans women's lack thereof.

Directors proudly told me about the consent procedures they use with cis women performers, but they never mentioned their consent procedures (if any) for men and trans women. This was the case even where directors were otherwise respectful of trans women's gender identity. Here, still, they tended to view trans women's consent needs through the prism of men's sexual invulnerability. Trans woman performer Venus Lux described, for example, directors and crew treating her as one of the guys (2014). The focus on feminine sexual vulnerability, rather than workers' vulnerability as *workers*, means that no one seems vulnerable on a gay porn set. Gay performers suggest that the cursory check-ins directors do on straight sets are largely absent in their workplaces. "It still pisses me off to this day," Christopher Daniels explained, "sometimes [directors] don't even tell me who my scene partner is" (2014).

But on the whole, men complained about these conditions much less frequently than I expected them to. Instead, they tended to excuse such practices by referring to norms of feminine passivity and vulnerability. In response to another performer's suggestion that porn is "a woman's game," performer Richie Calhoun replied, "I think [that] makes perfect sense" (2013). I asked why. His response: "Because sex, still to a certain extent, no matter what you do to it . . . heterosexual sex is largely . . . someone doing something to someone else . . . I'm not saying that's a categorical thing, but in a lot of instances, *women are having things done to them . . .*

it only makes sense that that person should have more say" (2013). For men who perform in straight scenes who adopt such a perspective, managing their own identity as the person *doing* things to women requires intense emotion and identity management.

In her fieldwork with male sex workers in San Francisco, Nicola Smith found a similar faithfulness to gendered dichotomies. Interviewees were careful to position themselves as agents, rather than victims, and they did so in part through gendered and racialized tropes (2012, p. 597). In my interviews, too, men often located vulnerability "over there," even as they also described limited access to full consent, safe working conditions, and fair pay.

Gendering scene work

Reducing porn work to the sex performed also erases the intense creative and emotional labor that workers perform. Performers described—and in set observations I saw—the careful work of cultivating a connection with co-stars. On gay and straight sets, male performers (at least those who hope to get cast again) participate in this work alongside their co-stars. They calm their own nerves and those of partners, work to generate familiarity and chemistry, and do the emotional work of tuning into their partner's needs during a scene. In doing so, they confront broader cultural ideas that emotional connection in sex is unimportant for men and, in straight scenes, industry-specific conventions that often place women at the center and reduce men to a de-personalized penis. Industry veteran Herschel Savage talked about how proud he was to be known among women performers as a considerate partner, and how frustrating it was to be treated as "a piece of meat" by management (2013).

Men encountered a similar attitude toward their physical labor. Here, again, ideas about female vulnerability and male invulnerability erase common workplace strains. Dick Chibbles' account of his experience playing Chewbacca in a *Star Wars* porn parody provides just one example of the workplace health risks that go unreported:

> I was wearing thirty pounds of fur, it was about 135 degrees inside that outfit, they actually used a thermometer. The sex scene itself took five hours to shoot, every 5 minutes I had to cool down for 10. . . [I felt I was] going to faint.
>
> *(2014)*

Even in scenes without the extenuating circumstance of the Chewbacca costume, workers experience the various health risks associated with intense bodywork—muscle strain, dehydration, and nerve damage, for instance—in addition to the risk of STI transmission and side effects from overuse of erectile dysfunction medications, steroids, and other performance enhancers.

A common frustration among the workers I interviewed was outsiders' tendency to view porn's health risks only in terms of sexual danger. This myopia ignores the other risks that workers of all genders face and reinforces anti-sex and anti-sex-worker stigma. The state of California has, for example, engaged in a years-long campaign to enforce on-set condom use, an intervention that workers overwhelmingly oppose. Meanwhile, workers achieve little success in pursuing better enforcement of occupational health regulations that would protect them from mundane workplace risks such as staph infections. In the event of a sprained ankle, they find an opaque worker's compensation system that offers no relief. These are the costs of working in an industry that is both feminized and typically regarded only through the prism of women's sexual vulnerability.

Conclusion

This chapter pushed against the idea that only cisgender women porn workers are susceptible to poor working conditions while also arguing that such vulnerability is feminized. As such, I have focused on points of vulnerability rather than the ways that workers resist them. But in porn as in other forms of work, workers develop creative strategies, ranging from collective action to subtle workarounds, for making their work less precarious. For men, the costs of a system that views work in porn only through the lens of feminine sexual vulnerability are clear. But this framework fails workers of all genders. It forces workers to operate at the precarious intersection of the state's hyper-scrutiny surrounding imagined dangers and violent non-interference around real dangers. Legal scholar Deborah Dinner asks, "Who is left behind when appeals for safe workplaces rely on gendered ideas of which bodies need protection?" (2017). In the context of porn work, the answer is: all workers.

Notes

* (Daniels, 2014)
1 *Cisgender* refers to those whose gender identity matches the sex they were assigned at birth.
2 While Dave is speaking about men who work in straight porn, my research found that this dynamic largely applies to men who work in gay films also. Here, too, the idea that "most guys want to do porn" shapes the labor market.
3 *Fordism* refers to the male-dominated mass manufacturing typical of the early-mid twentieth century.
4 *Materialist feminism* refers to a tradition of feminist thought focused on the relationship of gendered subordination to capitalism.
5 Notable exceptions include intense but selective state enforcement of occupational health law, which is not designed to fit the porn work context and often places workers at greater risk (see Webber, 2015).
6 Some scholars suggest that this tendency is specific to the U.S. and western European contexts. In the Greek context, for example, a different history around feminist sexuality debates places porn in a different discursive context (Tsaliki & Chronaki 2016, p. 176). I focus on the United States, as my fieldwork was based in that country.
7 I specify *white* women here because constructions of sex worker vulnerability overwhelmingly frame white femininity as uniquely vulnerable, contrasting it with the "hypersexuality" of Blackness (Miller-Young, 2014).
8 A notable exception is Jeffrey Escoffier's work on gay male performers (2007).
9 *Record Keeping Requirements, 18 U.S. Code § 2257*, 2005.
10 Here we can look to the work of labor scholars such as Noah Zatz and Eileen Boris, who identify the processes by which contingent workers have been systematically denied access to basic benefits and coverage under labor law (2014, p. 96).

References

Bell, S. (1994). *Reading, writing, and rewriting the prostitute body*. Bloomington, IN: Indiana University Press.
Beloso, B. M. (2012). Sex, work, and the feminist erasure of class. *Signs, 38*(1), 47–70.
Beres, M. (2007). "Spontaneous" sexual consent: An analysis of sexual consent literature. *Feminism & Psychology, 17*(1), 93–108.
Berg, H. (2014). Labouring porn studies. *Porn Studies, 1*(1–2), 75–79.
Berg, H. (2016). "A scene is just a marketing tool": Alternative income streams in porn's gig economy. *Porn Studies, 3*(2), 160–174.
Boris, E., & Parreñas, R. S. (2010). Introduction. In E. Boris & R. S. Parreñas (Eds.), *Intimate labors: Cultures, technologies, and the politics of care* (pp. 1–12). Stanford, CA: Stanford Social Sciences.
Calhoun, R. (2013). Interview by author, Los Angeles, CA.
Chibbles, D. (2014). Interview by author. Granada Hills, CA.
Daniels, C. (2014). Interview by author. Los Angeles, CA.

Dinner, D. (2017, June 2). *Equal by what measure: Masculinity, antidiscrimination law, and labor protection, 1964–1991*. Presented at the Berkshire Conference on the History of Women, Genders, and Sexuality, Hempstead, NY.

Escoffier, J. (2007). Porn star/stripper/escort: Economic and sexual dynamics in a sex work career. *Journal of Homosexuality, 53*(1–2), 173–200.

Frackas, M. (2013). Interview by author, phone.

Grov, C., & Smith, M. (2014). Gay subcultures. In V. Minichiello & J. Scott (Eds.), *Male sex work and society* (pp. 240–259). New York: Harrington Park Press.

Hennessy, R. (2006a). The value of a second skin. In D. Richardson, J. McLaughlin, & M. Casey (Eds.), *Intersections in feminist and queer theory: Sexualities, cultures and identities* (pp. 125–150). Basingstoke, UK: Palgrave Macmillan.

Hennessy, R. (2006b). Returning to reproduction queerly: Sex, labor, need. *Rethinking Marxism, 18*(3), 387–395.

Kipnis, L. (1999). *Bound and gagged: Pornography and the politics of fantasy in America*. Durham, NC: Duke University Press.

Logan, T. (2014). Economic analysis of male sex work. In V. Minichiello & J. Scott (Eds.), *Male sex work and society* (pp. 106–147). New York: Harrington Park Press.

Lux, V. (2014). Interview by author, phone.

MacKinnon, C. (1988). *Feminism unmodified: Discourses on life and law*. Cambridge, MA: Harvard University Press.

Marcus, Mr. (2013). Interview by author. Balboa Park, San Diego, CA.

Miller-Young, M. (2014). *A taste for brown sugar: Black women in pornography*. Durham, NC: Duke University Press.

Morini, C. (2007). The feminization of labour in cognitive capitalism. *Feminist Review, 87*(1), 40–59.

Pounder, D. (2014). Interview by author, phone.

Record Keeping Requirements. (2005). *18 U.S. Code § 2257*.

Savage, H. (2013). Interview by author. Los Angeles, CA.

Scott, J., & Minichiello, V. (2014). Introduction: Reframing male sex work. In V. Minichiello & J. Scott (Eds.), *Male sex work and society* (pp. xii–xxvii). New York: Harrington Park Press.

Smith, N. (2012). Body issues: The political economy of male sex work. *Sexualities, 15*(5–6), 586–603.

Stevens, C. (2013). Interview by author. Skype.

Stewart, A. (2013). Legal constructions of body work. In C. Wolkowitz, R. L. Cohen, T. Sanders, & K. Hardy (Eds.), *Body/sex/work: Intimate, embodied, and sexualized labour* (pp. 61–76). Hampshire, UK: Palgrave Macmillan.

Trachman, M. (2015). The market for actresses: Gender, reputation, and intermediation in French pornography. In V. Roussel & D. Bielby (Eds.), *Brokerage and production in the American and French entertainment industries: Invisible hands in cultural markets*. London: Lexington Books.

Tsaliki, L., & Chronaki, D. (2016). Producing the porn self: An introspection of the mainstream Greek porn industry. *Porn Studies, 3*(2), 175–186.

Webber, V. (2015). Public health versus performer privates: Measure B's failure to fix subjects. *Porn Studies, 2*(4), 299–313.

Zatz, N., & Boris, E. (2014). Seeing work, envisioning citizenship. *Employee Rights and Employee Policy Journal, 95*, 95–109.

Part II
Male sex work in literature

9

Male sex workers in world literature

A sampling from historical times to the modern era

Felice Picano

Female sex workers enter into world literature fairly early: a case could made that they are there from the very beginning. Not so for male sex workers, partly because the earliest literatures that have come down to us beyond king lists and commercial inventory lists are Greek and later Greek-influenced Roman writings. Romantic love was understood to be primarily between two males, equal or unequally aged, with mixed-gender love the outlier. Females served as child bearers, housekeepers, and, later on, as commercial partners.

This seems to be true in early Asian and American empires too. But it began to slowly change in imperial Roman literature. By medieval times in the Western world, a major shift was evident in Europe which severely delimited not only who could be loved by whom but how and if it could be written about. As it was persecuted, sex and romance between same-gender people went underground, and homosexuality all but vanishes from our literature.

In the East, it remained potent, with writings by Saikaku in Japan, a tradition of Persian and Sufi poetry (with their adoration of "moon-faced boys"), and a tradition of "cut-sleeve" romances in China. It's only in eighteenth-century England and France—the cultural sophisticates of the age— that we once more see glimmers of same-sex encounters at all, and those are more widespread in graphic than in written form. We have evidence of male prostitution in the era that we can read.

It is not until late in the repressive Victorian era that male sex workers flourish again in public, brought to light via obscenity and libel trials. By the beginning of the twentieth century, however, not only male sex workers but also writing about them begins to proliferate. As with female prostitution, social and economic class, as well as stagnation versus mobility among the classes, become the defining agents and the crucial issues of male sex work. Especially in Britain, upper-class writers begin to reify the "common man" and, in so doing, elevate the sex-working male into an object of high regard and sometimes into a love object.

In France, Germany, and the rest of Europe, a more practical approach to male sex workers results in their being more integrated into the social and economic life and thus into the writings of the era by authors like Proust, Gide, Cocteau, Doeblin, and so on. When mid-century British authors—Isherwood, Auden, Spender, Waugh—visited, they too became engaged with male sex workers in less classist terms and wrote about it.

In Puritanical America, "sin" loomed large, and it was only when literary movements like realism, naturalism, and regionalism freed up subject matter that male sex workers entered New World literature, most evidently in Spanish and Portuguese literatures of Central and South America, while to the north, male sex workers featured in the literature haltingly and in writings that are either moralistic or "coded." It would require a generation of Americans living in Europe over a period of time (C. H. Ford, Tennessee Williams, Sam Steward, et al.) for American literature to begin to openly, if still ambiguously, treat the subject.

I propose to use those authors and others to illustrate this thesis.

The very first piece of recognized Western literature, Sin-leqi-unninni's *Epic of Gilgamesh*, (ca. 1700 BCE) has an unusual section in which the king orders a woman brought to the wild man Enkiddu. Her purpose is to "tame" Enkiddu, to physically wear him out, which she does only after seven days of intercourse. But also to "socialize" him as preteens and teenage boys are socialized by school, church, the Boy Scouts, school dances, and so on. Since Shammat has a purpose she must fulfill with a person deemed uncivilized and therefore undesirable, we may assume she was hired. Many texts from not much later in this part of the world mention sacred temple prostitutes of the Goddess Ishtar, or Venus. It isn't difficult to conclude that Shammat is the first sex worker in Western literature, right at its very inception, 1,000 years before Homer.

The next time such a person appears in Western literature, it is in the form of a hetaera in the ancient Greek city-states. These are professional women, often literate and even more cultured, and at times quite high up on the social scale. Greek males do not seem to ever have been sex workers, for the simple reason that, after all, Greek love was *primarily* between males, usually of different ages, and therefore they could get sex from other males without paying for it. Wives, while sometimes friends, were seldom the receivers of passion from Greek males. Even Socrates, whom contemporary writers agree was "froglike" in personal appearance, had male lovers, including Alcibiades, the handsomest young man of his day. The classic *Greek Anthology* is full of poetry about such young men and the boys who love them and leave them: Meleager (90–25 BCE) and Anacreon (570–500 BCE) are among the best and most prolific of the poets. Along with Ibycus and Pindar, they write both about the joys and the hardships of loving boys and young men: "Oh, boy with a girl's eyes/I look for you and follow you/but you ignore me, and do not recognize/my soul's charioteer." And "The love of a boy/is like a hungry wolf/hidden under your shirt." But it was the Hellenistic Syrian Meleager of Gadara who made the first collection of these shorter poems and fragments in his 60 BCE book, *The Garland*.

Roman times were similar, since they copied Greek culture closely. Marriage, as it has come down to us, is a Roman ritual and was primarily a commercial agreement between two families. (Meaning that all those who want to preserve the so-called sanctity of marriage are—unsurprisingly, given their capitalist bent—supporting the sanctity of *a business contract!*) In Petronius's prose work *Satyricon*, there are several boys and young men who, if they aren't called hustlers or prostitutes, definitely appear to today's reader to act like them. The young Eumolphus, for example, whom our two heroes, as well as everyone else, lust after throughout that book, breaks hearts left and right, and true to his work ethic eventually opts for the richest and most powerful lover and not the hotties. But it's not that fixed, because as the two scamps who are the protagonists show, one day the buyer can also become the seller.

Catullus, Gaius Valerius (87–54 BCE), often considered the best Republican poet, imitated Sappho as well as well as those classical and Hellenistic models. Of his over 200 poems, Western culture has chosen to honor those addressed to "Lesbia," an older woman who was unfaithful to him. But those represent only an eighth of his output. Most of his love poetry is addressed to Juventus, a high-born lad. (And also the name of a successful Roman soccer team, leading one to wonder. . .) The later, Augustan poets of love, Ovid, Horace, Vergil, Propertius, and Martial, all follow Catullus's lead: writing of boys who demanded gifts or were even outright prostitutes. Ovid's letters mention a young man with an "extremely large penis" suddenly appearing at his local bathhouse and causing a sensation among the regulars. Since there is graffiti in the ruins of resorts like Herculaneum and Pompeii showing such amplitudes in drawings, with names attached, it's not difficult to believe that certain men were for sale—and what? Operated by moving from one bathhouse to another? Possibly. Then there are all the Horatian odes addressed to athletes and other cuties. No wonder generations of British schoolboys indulged in mutual masturbation and more, given all the time they had to spend glossing and translating into English these paeans to male pulchritude.

Romans also began to love women with passion equal to their loves for youths. At least in literature, they did. Tellingly, literary and historical portraits of the Roman era about ambitious, powerful, and sexual women like the emperor Augustus's wife, Livia, and the emperor Claudius's wife, Messalina, are more cautionary tales than actual history. From Livy to Procopius, including even the generally objective Plutarch, Roman-era authors make sure strong women are denigrated and warned against.

The misogyny continued and deepened while almost all else changed with the widespread acceptance of Christianity, which succeeded only at the cost of repudiating the previous four millennia of culture. John Boswell's still necessary *Christianity, Social Tolerance and Homosexuality* covers the baffling varieties and many internal contradictions even in local areas regarding sexuality in this medieval period, which was by no means uniform across continental Europe. Gay love might be condemned in one town, while in the next one over, gay men were married in church. There is little *sensual* literature of the Middle Ages to look at. Unless, of course, we consider Rabelais, somewhat later on, who writes from a medieval mindset and whose characters certainly indulge mostly in the sin of gluttony. The Italian Renaissance, with its reawakening of classical culture, however, was more tolerant; one painter's nickname was La Sodoma. Michelangelo's and Shakespeare's sonnets address men and women equally.

But more to the point are Caravaggio and Benvenuto Cellini, great artists who are agreed to have consorted with various "low-lifes" of their time. The former's paintings of biblical subjects were controversial because he often used boyfriends, exes, and what we might call "Christopher Street trash" (i.e., dirty boys) as models for his saints and sinners alike. Other people easily recognized the boys. Meaning what? That they were male streetwalkers? Probably.

Perhaps Caravaggio would have been less conspicuous in Florence than in Rome. According to recent studies, during the brief but frantic "reform era" of Savonarola, a box was placed outside each church where you could anonymously place the names of "sodomites." The boxes were so quickly filled up they had to be emptied daily. The beautiful young Leonardo da Vinci (who counted the king of France among his more notable clients) as well as Michelangelo were denounced on a daily basis. Who knows what written works by them or by their compeers containing portraits or tales of male sex workers may exist hidden in vaults in the Vatican Library? So far they are safe from prying eyes. Once again, those town-by-town laws and punishments for breaking laws against homosexuality widely differed. In Venice, you could be burned at the stake for an offense that simultaneously would cost you a mere 25-florin fine in Florence.

Unfettered prurience returns to Western culture in late-seventeenth-century Europe with the courtly shenanigans of Charles II of England and especially those of Louis XIV, who had several publicly acknowledged mistresses going, along with his wife. But Louis's younger brother, known as "Monsieur," was a notable homosexual with his own subcourt and his own band of male lovers, mostly macho, upper-echelon officers in the armed forces. In his wonderfully complete and catty memoirs of the court at Versailles, Louis de Rouvroy, a.k.a. the Duke of Saint-Simon, several times retells (or retails) the general belief that Cardinal Richelieu, "the

Kingmaker", very early on in the two young royals' lives, decided to "satisfy and further stimulate" Louis's little brother's queer proclivities. Why? So that he would be too busy flirting and screwing around to ever threaten the Sun King's position. However, Louis loved his brother and protected him. Monsieur seems to have been an all-around nice guy whom even St. Simon couldn't find fault with. And the king married his little brother to a formidable woman who also adored him and protected him.

If Western literature of that time is reticent about male sex or male sex workers, classical Japanese literature is anything but. The greatest writer of the seventeenth century, Ihara Saikaku's first prose work was *Life of an Amorous Man*. That was successful enough that he next published *Five Women Who Lived for Love*. But all agree that his masterpiece is the encyclopedic *Great Mirror of Male Love*, issued in two volumes around 1687 that became massive best sellers. Most of the first volume and part of the second is concerned with samurais—that is, warriors—and their male lovers. Tales of sacrifice and of instances of such utter devotion between male lovers abound, with stories titled "A Sword His Only Memento" and "Boy Who Sacrificed His Love" common. In the second and by far larger volume, Saikaku's subject is Kabuki boy actors who portray women on stage. Saikaku is a great storyteller of the "Floating World" of Japan. In his tale "A Secret Vault," he writes, "Male actors of female roles in the old days . . . were not particularly concerned about looking like women. They simply placed towels on their heads and applied some rough makeup, and theater-goers used their imaginations to fill in the rest"—cattily adding, "The scenarios, too, were terrible, by today's standards."

All that has changed, however, by Saikaku's own time. In his tales, famous courtesans come to boy actors for makeup tips and young noblewomen for costuming choices to land a husband. More typical is this: "None matched Heihachi in beauty. With a single glance, wise men and fools, noblemen and commoners, all fell in love with him." But because they were both adored and poorly paid, the boys all prostituted themselves, although "their beauty only lasted five or six years." So, most of the remaining volume of *The Great Mirror* contains tales of boy actors selling themselves with sometimes sad, tragic, haunting, but also happy, wise, and hilarious results. This was the subject Saikaku enjoyed writing about most, and the tales form an entire subgenre of Japanese literature. In one story, "Bamboo Clappers," a long-in-the-tooth boy actor's real age is revealed by a psychic to be—astonishingly—38! In that same tale, a drunken bully of a samurai demands a boy actor from a merchant who has already paid for him. The boy gets him even more drunk and complains of his beard. He ends up shaving half of the samurai's whiskers off, leaving him drunk-asleep and looking like a fool when he awakens. This breadth of styles and genres in writing about male hustling will be unique until the mid-twentieth-century writers like John Rechy and Sam Steward.

By the middle of the eighteenth century, sexuality returns to Western literature, too. That's when we come upon John Cleland's novel, *Memoirs of a Woman of Pleasure* of 1749, also known as *Fanny Hill*. Cleland tells a story Defoe and others had told before, how an upright young woman is abandoned by her lover and finds herself in a house of prostitution. But as she is a good woman, eventually she finds love again. What's different with *Fanny Hill* is page after page of closely descriptive physical erotica told in a delightfully florid, eighteenth-century style. The book was a hit in its own time but censored. It was rereleased and was a sensation again. And it was again when it was reprinted in the 1960s.

While Cleland is completely open and detailed about the heterosexual goings-on in the book, there is a section in which Fanny is waiting in a room at an inn for a stagecoach and hears people making love in the next room. She climbs a chair and pokes a hole in a paper screen and witnesses a young man undressing a teenage boy, and then the two engaged in sex. Cleland does not describe what they are doing, as he does in such detail with male-on-female sex, but he states that Fanny is shocked and "disgusted" by what she sees. The age difference and her great ire suggests that the younger of the two is actually stealing clients away from ladies like herself. Before she can do anything about it, however, her chair falls and she is knocked out.

All this is odd enough for the book. But it is directly followed by a scene back at her "house" in which an intellectually challenged teen, "Simple Dick," who sells the ladies of the night posies, is seduced by Fanny in league with her colleague, Louisa. Abetted by Fanny, Louisa induces the lad into intercourse with her—which again is spelled out in detail. This is what today we would call child molestation, even rape.

What are those scenes doing in the book? In tandem, the two scenes point to the author's recognition of male-on-male sex between different classes and also confirm the idea that teenaged boys were viewed as desired and paid-for sexual objects. Use of the inn for sexual encounters is also fairly common. In *Queer City: Gay London from the Romans to the Present Day*, Peter Ackroyd writes that innkeepers in the city often hired out particular rooms for the express purpose of being used by rent boys and their clients.

Also in the eighteenth century, two classic Chinese novels, Li Po's *The Prayer Mat of Flesh* (1716) and Cao Xuen's multivolume *The Story of the Stone* (1760), found widespread distribution and readership due to progress in printing methods. In both books, scenes of male-on-male romance appear interpolated into heterosexual scenes. Especially in the first, more cynical book, where the hero is determined to have every kind of physical pleasure available, the boys are for pay.

These stories follow a long Chinese "cut-sleeve" tradition going back thousands of years: legends of kings who cut their sleeves rather than wake the sleeping boys they spent the night with. Many classic love and erotic poems of the Sung and T'ang periods may also be about boys and young men. We cannot tell, as there is no gender signifier in classic Chinese poetry. There is also a long history of uncredited sex stories in which boys and young men couple. By 1823, when a story collection titled *The Precious Mirror of Fragrant Flowers* was published anonymously, everyone knew its real title was *The Precious Mirror of Boy Actresses*, in a nod to Saikaku. They probably all knew who the author was too, although that is now lost.

Late in the nineteenth century, another anonymous author, this time British, wrote the spectacularly erotic *My Secret Life: Diary of a Victorian Gentleman*. Recent studies have identified "Anonymous" as Henry Spencer Ashbee, and the dates of the diaries as 1888 to 1894. The bulk of the diary is about heterosexual intercourse between "Walter," its narrator, and several female sex workers, especially one favorite, "Sarah." But he does eventually ask to have sex with a young man, and one is provided. This youth's pay will be a sovereign—worth about $112.00 today—and as the undernourished young man "of 20 or 21" makes clear, "I've not had meat for over two weeks." So, this is a completely fiduciary affair. At first it is all about looking, touching, and some masturbation; neither male reaches orgasm until Sarah is present. However, some weeks later Walter calls for the young man again, and this time both of them are comfortable enough together that they engage in mutual fellatio—sixty-nining—for which even more is paid.

The Cleveland Street Scandal of 1889 illuminated an entire subworld of British rent boys and their paying customers. Eight years before this, however, a text titled *Sins of the Cities of the Plain*, by another "Anonymous," was published. Its author was later confirmed as Jack Saul, one of the men arrested in the Cleveland Street Scandal. He testified in court not only that he and others were openly prostituting themselves to upper-class men but that they were pretty much ignored by the police while they did so. Saul also testified that a small portion of their customers wanted not virile young men but instead "Mary Anns," that is, men and boys whom today we'd

Felice Picano

call trans or, at the very least, cross-dressers. His *Sins of the Cities of the Plains* introduces these gender-nonconforming male sex workers to Western literature for the first time.

Meanwhile, across the channel, as Marcel Proust was nearing the end of his multivolume set of books, *À la recherche du temps perdu*, he placed a brilliant, ebon-black jewel of a scene in the final volume, titled *Le temps retrouvé*. One oddity is how utterly modern this volume seems compared with the earlier ones. It feels contemporary with Joyce, Woolf, Sinclair Lewis, and Theodore Dreiser. We'd been edging into the twentieth century, book by book, with Proust, but chiefly through objects: telephones, automobiles, airplanes—the first death in a car accident is in Proust, as is a scene where upper-class party-goers ascend to the Paris rooftops to watch French dirigibles fill the sky, and their headlights criss-cross searching for German Fokker planes. But now, suddenly, in the final volume, we are also psychologically in a modern arena too. Many of the upper-crust males we've met before are revealed to be closet cases. Robert de Saint-Loup, a character we've been meant to admire from volume two on, is suddenly witnessed making a sex date with the elevator boy in the resort hotel at Balbec. Obviously for pay. The reader naturally wonders how many decades he's been doing that sort of thing.

The section of *Le temps retrouvé* that is most modern, and that I think could actually have been one raison d'être for Proust in writing the entire 3,200 pages, comes when Marcel's car breaks down and his chauffeur decides to stop to fix it. When the rain worsens, the chauffeur places his unwell master out of the cold and rainy street while he gets help to repair it.

Where does he place the narrator? In the kitchen of a house of male prostitutes, where working-class guys moonlight. Little by little, as they come and go from the kitchen, we realize that several of them were hired specifically to flog men of the upper-crust until the peers reach orgasm. Well paid and laughing about their work, the proles spill out all the details of their encounters around the kitchen table to whomever might be around—including the quiet fellow huddled up in a coat and hat in the corner—Marcel. It is such a shocking scene, a century after it was written, that you just know Proust was aware that he would not be around to see it in print during his lifetime. For Proust, it epitomizes a collapse of everything that preceded it—not only the "family values" or the Catholicism of the earlier sections, but also the chivalric past, the myths and legends from medieval times. It does so by revealing an underside of Marcel's world that no doubt really existed. Those perfect surfaces that he so lovingly and so completely rendered throughout begin to tremble and then shiver before falling into pieces. Did Proust himself engage in such activities? We don't know. We do know that for years he kept a young, handsome, very macho bisexual servant, Agostino. He bought him a Hispano-Suiza limousine (advertised as "the Automobile of Kings") and even a biplane, in which Agostino eventually crashed and died.

How much this kind of high-low nightlife continued in London, despite the Cleveland Street Scandal and the Oscar Wilde trial not long after, can be gleaned from the life and work of openly gay author J.R. Ackerley. The founding editor and the voice of the BBC Radio network, and simultaneously editor of the prestigious magazine *The Listener* during the first four decades of the twentieth century, Ackerley enthusiastically promoted the work of his gay circle of friends, including E.M. Forster, Christopher Isherwood, Stephen Spender, and W.H. Auden.

Ackerley's delightful "travel book," *Hindoo Holiday* (1933), is unlike any other in existence. As a young man out of university, Ackerley went to work for a wealthy gay rajah in India. His job: to put together a traveling troupe and to redact Shakespeare's plays for the potentate's boy lover, an aspiring actor, as well as for a more demotic mixture of Indian audiences. In other books, like *My Dog Tulip*, Ackerley never hides his homosexuality. In his best-known title, *My Father and Myself*, the author discovers not only that his grand, handsome, and domineering father had a secret second family in London but also that among his parent's early forms of employment was as a Tower of London guardsman. E. M. Forster's policeman lover confides to Ackerley that pretty much each man in that unit—bred for stature and looks—which resided in the Albany Barracks at (often-cruisy) Regents Park, had "gentlemen sponsors." He concludes that Ackerley Senior was one of those soldiers for sale.

So, while it was not until late in the sexually repressive Victorian era of English-speaking countries that male prostitutes seemed to flourish again in people's consciousness, brought to light in a variety of obscenity and libel trials, their presence also started to filter down into literature then. By the twentieth century, however, male prostitutes and also writings about them begin to proliferate not only in France and England but also increasingly in the United States. As with female prostitution, social and economic class are crucial, as well as stagnation versus mobility among the classes. These become the defining agents and the crucial issues of male prostitution, especially in Britain, where upper-class writers who attended "Oxbridge" and were influenced by Ruskin begin to reify the "common man" and "common day laborer" and in so doing also elevate the sexual working male into an object of higher regard and sometimes into a love-object—as E. M. Forster does in his posthumously published *Maurice*.

In France, Germany, and the rest of Europe, a more practical approach to male sex workers resulted in their being more openly integrated into the social and economic life, especially during the Great Depression of the 1930s. When mid-century British authors visited those lands, they too became involved in relationships with male sex workers in less classist terms—namely, the letters of Isherwood, Auden, Spender, Waugh, Scott Moncrieff, and others. All of them engaged in it, and most of them wrote about it sooner or later. The correspondence by those authors back to the United Kingdom abounds in anecdotes, so we know that they generally supported not only their German boyfriends but sometimes their boyfriends' families too. It was pretty much how many German men in contact with foreigners got by in those economically lean years. The Count in Isherwood's *Mr. Norris Changes Trains* goes on at some length about the good old days before Hitler came to power, when working men for hire were cheap and plentiful.

Other writings of the era by forward-looking authors like Gide, Musil, Doeblin, and especially Jean Genet include male sex workers. Genet took on the subject with a passion few had previously displayed, mixing it with the criminal class and raising both to a higher and, for him, more mythic level. In his first novel, *Our Lady of the Flowers*, Genet describes the funeral of Divine, his titular hero/heroine: "And all of them, the girl-queens, the boy-queens, the aunties, fags and nellies who I am speaking of assembled at the foot of the stairway." Never before have we read of so many distinctions of homosexuals. He goes on: "The girl-queens are huddled together and chattering and cheeping around the boy-queens who are straight, motionless, and vertiginous, as motionless and silent as branches. All are dressed in black." This isn't just one or two hustlers, but an entire society composed of or containing many varieties of male sex workers.

Genet's other contribution, which no one had presented before, was the Pimp. "Their rattle stopped. There was in his supple bearing the weighty magnificence of a barbarian who tramples choice furs beneath his muddy boots. The torso on his hips was a king on a throne. Merely to have evoked him is enough for my left hand in my torn pocket to . . ." That is, the Pimp is what the gay set and even the author all masturbate to. The rest of the book is really just a peroration of these themes and memes, with nods to Genet's "gods": those men who murder and whose photos he keeps on the walls of his jail cell. While in his plays Genet would go on to explore other themes—especially power, corruption, and racism—the remaining novels all take their cues from the first one, and he continues his investigation with mythologizing of the world of the criminal French male hustler.

In puritanical America, however, "sin" still loomed large, and it was only when powerful literary movements—realism, naturalism, and regionalism—had achieved their varied break-throughs, freeing up subject matter, that male sex workers would begin to enter New World literature. They are hinted at or alluded to mightily in the works of Dreiser, Anderson, Hemingway, Langston Hughes, Erskine Caldwell, Mike Quin, and John O'Hara, but usually only as a way of establishing the "damned system" which the authors are trying to break through for their young heroes and heroines.

But slowly and eventually, it happens. So that Tennessee Williams could open his story "One Arm," in the volume of stories of that same name (1948), this way: "In New Orleans in the winter of '39 there were three male hustlers usually to be found hanging out on a certain corner of Canal Street and one of those streets that dove narrowly into the ancient part of the city." He means the French Quarter, or Vieux Carré. He goes on, "Two of them were just kids of about seventeen and worth only passing attention, but the oldest of the three was an unforget-table youth." Oliver Winemiller, or One Arm, is the ultramacho boxer who was left mutilated by an automobile accident. Still beautiful, he can earn his living with his body. When he gets involved with a porno filmmaker who wants to exploit his single-armedness not as a grace but as a bizarre fetish, Oliver loses it and kills him. That, then, not his working as a hustler, is Williams's real story.

The next time an American writer takes on the theme of male hustling, it will John Rechy's encyclopedic, bicoastal tome on the subject, *City of Night* of 1963. Like Williams, Rechy uses the theme and its many memes to evoke a larger host of significance, to explore its tragic-comic aspects. Along the way, he details the male hustling scenes of Manhattan and downtown Los Angeles with a specificity and denseness that is too real to be merely fictional. He presents characters of such individuality—the obese john in the chauffeured limo who nightly buys several "Angels"—that the book becomes larger than its subject. Of course, it didn't hurt that Rechy himself was a hustler, and his most-used photos show him shirtless, in tight jeans and engineer's boots, leaning against a wall and quite obviously waiting for a purchaser.

Meanwhile, Samuel M. Steward, friend and colleague of the moderns in Paris, especially Gertrude Stein and Alice B. Toklas (with whom he corresponded for decades), would pen his own book on the joys of male hustling—*Stud*—in 1966, as "a reaction" to Rechy's book. Writing as Phil Andros, his avowed purpose was to show how normal and ordinary homosexuality is and how easy it is for a good-looking youth to find himself being sold for sex no matter where he may be, working at a hotel, a ranch, and so on. Steward covers a wider swath of gay life of his day and places, and he's not afraid to include among "Phil's" clients oddities and fetishists who come to various sticky ends. Above all, swagger and a "butch attitude" seem to protect the sex workers. But Steward seldom looks into the more ambiguous world of modern "Mary Anns." These sex workers existed and still exist in every major city, and clubs devoted to them are known by name by nongay males looking to "walk on the wild side." Had he explored them, he might have seen a nexus of far closer connections between straight and gay males.

But few books can actually vie with the last text to be discussed. At the time of its publication by the Oliver Layton Press in 1963, and its republication a decade later, *The Asbestos Diary* was a fun/fabulous find. Many readers speculated who the author of this book of male/boy love could possibly be. Some even suggested it was post-*Lolita* Nabokov himself, having more extraliterary fun, probably because of the playful, erudite, at times delicious writing in the book. Brian Drexel, writing as "Duke,"—Casimir Dukahz, the narrator—goes through boy after clever, cute, mercenary boy, tale after tale. Pretty much all of the incidents are pickups, but it soon becomes clear that Duke is the one being picked up by the boys and that not only do the boys have an agenda for their time with Duke and what they can get out of him, he has been "marked" by an informal network of boys as a willing victim. At times the book is haunting: "And so the first of September," he writes sadly about a naive boy named August who ran away from him and into even worse luck, ". . . was the end of August."

What stands out in *The Asbestos Diary* is that all of them are playing the Game and, aside from poor August, they all know the rules of said Game. Man gets boy—for a short period of his boyhood glory—and pays through the nose for it. Boy goes off with an easily forgettable experience and some cold hard cash—or jewelry, or gold coins, or a convertible.

Clever and as amusing as the book usually is, it seems to have returned the idea of male sex work to what those original Greek and Roman lads of 25 centuries ago understood: without the various trimmings of aesthetics, philosophy, or even psychology our more modern authors have insisted upon. What it comes down to in the end is a deal: maybe some affection, some fun times together. But really just buy and sell, nothing but a deal.

Bibliography and works cited

Ackerley, J. R. (1933). *Hindoo Holiday*. London: Chatto and Windus.

Andros, P. (1966). *Stud* (Samuel Steward). Boston: Alyson Press.

Anonymous. (1823). *Precious mirror of fragrant flowers (a.k.a. Precious mirror of boy actresses)* (Keith McMahon, Trans., pp. 70–109).

Ashbee, H. S. (1966). *My secret life: Diary of a Victorian gentleman by Anonymous, 1889–1894*. New York: Grove Press.

Boswell, J. E. (1980). *Christianity, social tolerance and homosexuality*. Chicago: University of Chicago Press.

Boswell, J. E. (1994). *Marriage of lives: Same sex unions in premodern Europe*. New York: Villard Books.

Cameron, A. (Trans.). (1916). *The Greek anthology*. Book 5. Loeb Classical Library. Boston: Harvard University Press.

Cao Xueqin. (1977). *The story of the stone, vol. 4: The debt of tears* (David Hawkes, Trans.). London: Penguin Classics.

Chandler, G. (2016). *The sins of Jack Saul: The true story of Dublin Jack and the Cleveland Street Scandal* (2nd ed.). Tolworth, Surrey: Grosvenor House Publishing.

Cleland, J. (1966). *The memoirs of a woman of pleasure (a.k.a. Fanny Hill), 1749*. New York: Grove Press.

Dukahz, C. (1966). *The asbestos diary* (Brian Drexel). New York: Oliver Layton Press.

Genet, J. (1951). *Our lady of the flowers* (Bernard Frechtman, Trans.). Traveller's Companion Series. Paris: Olympia Press.

Granarolo, J. (1967). *L'oeuvre de Catulle: Aspects religieux, éthiques et stylistiques*. Paris: Les Belles Lettres.

Hajek, N. J. (2015). Still a rivalry: Contrasting Renaissance sodomy legislation in Florence and Venice. *Black & Gold, 1*. Retrieved from http://openworks.wooster.edu/blackandgold/vol1/iss1/2

Jou Pu Tuan: The Prayer Mat of Flesh, attributed to Li Yu. (1977). Translated by Richard Martin from the German version by Franz Kuhn. New York: Grove Press.

Mitchell, S. (Trans.). (2004). *Gilgamesh: A new English version*. New York: Free Press.

Norton, L. (Trans.). (1972). *Memoirs of the Duke de St. Simon a.k.a. Louis de Rouvroy 1739–1750* (Vol. 3). London: Hamish Hamilton.

Norton, R. (1997). *My dear boy: Gay love letters through the centuries*. San Francisco: Leyland Publications.

Proust, M. (1927). *Le temps retrouvé*. Paris: Gallimard. In English, *The Past Recaptured*. (1932). (F. A. Blossom, Trans., Modern Library ed.). New York: A. C. Boni-Liveright.

Raffel, B. (Trans.). (2004). *Pure pagan: Seven centuries of Greek poetry and fragments* (Modern Library ed.). New York: Modern Library.

Rechy, J. (1963). *City of night*. New York: Grove Press.

Rocke, M. (1996). *Forbidden friendships: Homosexuality and male culture in renaissance Florence*. New York: Oxford University Press.

Ruggiero, L. (2006). The forbidden fruit or the taste for sodomy in Renaissance Italy. *Quaderni d'italianistica, 27*(1), 31–52.

Saara Lilja. (1983). *Homosexuality in Republican and Augustan Rome.* Commentationes humananun litterarum 74. Helsinki: Societatis Scientiarum Fennicae.

Schalow, G. P. (Trans.). (1990). *The great mirror of male love, Ihara Saikaku, 1687.* Stanford, CA: Stanford University Press.

Sins of the cities of the plain: Or, the recollections of a Mary-Ann, with essays on sodomy and tribadism, attributed to Jack Saul, 1881. (2012). Richmond, VA: Valancourt Classics.

Stevenson, M., & Cuncun, W. (Trans. & Eds.). (2013). *Homoeroticism in imperial China: A sourcebook.* London: Routledge.

Verstraete, B. (2012, Winter). Reassessing Roman pederasty in relation to Roman slavery: The portrayal of *pueri delicati* in the love-poetry of Catullus, Tibullus, and Horace. *Uluslararası Sosyal Araştırmalar Dergisi/ The Journal of International Social Research, 5*(20), 157–167. Retrieved from William A. Percy.com/wiki/index/php.title

Williams, T. (1948). *One arm and other stories.* New York: New Directions.

10

Male sex work diaries

Archival discoveries from the journal entries of Thomas Painter and Sam Steward

Yuriy Zikratyy

The emergence and consolidation of gay male communities that took place in the modernized West roughly in the period of one century, between the 1870s and the 1960s, revealed the close connection between the worlds of homosexuality and prostitution. In large urban centers from San Francisco to Berlin, queer and nonbinary men shared spaces with female sex workers, emulating their styles and adopting their argot and survival strategies in the streets (Chauncey, 1994; Healey, 2001; Houlbrook, 2005; Peniston, 2004). Female prostitutes and other "tough girls" provided a cultural script for the queer underground subculture to develop. The scientific and popular discourses that reported on the two phenomena saw them as essentially the same: a symptom of society's moral degeneration, a metaphor of urban chaos brought about by immigration and industrialization, or a physical embodiment of the new sexological concept of perversion (Ben, 2018).

The connection of sex and money was also conspicuous within the queer community itself. A gender-based model of same-sex desire, in which one male partner in a couple is heterosexual and masculine ("normal") while the other is effeminate and queer, was by no means the only model of homosexuality at the time, but it was influential and helped shape the sexual lives of many. It inevitably positioned "normal" men as the only possible objects of queer desire, but they were at the same time inherently unavailable, as, according to this logic, they would always prefer a "real" woman to its male imitation. These normal men had to be purchased. In the words of French writer Marcel Proust, queer men (he called them "inverts") were

> lovers to whom the possibility of that love . . . is all but closed, simply because they are much taken with a man having nothing of the woman about him, with a man who is not invert and cannot, in consequence, love them; so that their desire would be forever unsatis-fiable were money not to deliver up real men to them, and imagination not finally to lead them to mistake the inverts to whom they prostituted themselves for real men.
>
> *(2004, p. 17)*

The quick and anonymous nature of commercial sex also befitted many queer men who were closeted or led risky double lives. In pre-1970s gay archives, both public and private, the theme of buying and selling sex is often present, and the whole cultural image of a male hustler emerges. He is longed for and at the same time pitied as a figure of fragile white masculinity. He is also idolized (and racialized) as a sex instructor of sorts, a guide into an exotic, more sexually open culture (Friedman, 2003; Kaye, 2004). The realities of male-to-male commercial sex and its representations in personal testimonies and subcultural press contributed to modern gay identity.

As the practice of recording one's sexual experiences in the form of diaries, memoirs, and private correspondence grew in popularity by the turn of the twentieth century, it became an important means of self-expression for sexual minorities, from unusually adventurous heterosexuals (*My Secret Life*, 1888) to nonbinary "third sexers" (*Autobiography of an Androgyne*, 1918). Sex workers rarely wrote these works, but they were their frequent subjects. In fact, numerous sexual records examined by historians as narratives of queer sexuality can be equally seen as the testimonies of sex workers' clients. In them, we see that hustlers often held some power over their clients, defining the terms and conditions of sexual exchange. These written records offer a rare insider's view into the world of male sex work. In this chapter, I examine the diaries of two singular men who hired male prostitutes. I focus mostly on Thomas N. Painter, but I also provide quotations from Samuel M. Steward, who published his work under the pseudonym Phil Andros.

Diaries from the twentieth century

Thomas N. Painter (1905–1978) and Samuel M. Steward (1909–1993) produced remarkable testimonies of their renegade sex lives, which consisted of numerous money-based relations with hustlers and other working-class men. They not only described their own sexual encounters with sex workers (hundreds of men in both cases) but also tried to analyze and interpret them for themselves and for the reader. They kept diaries, took photographs, and even wrote books about the world of paid sex—Painter's *Male Homosexuals and Their Prostitutes* (1942, unpublished) and Steward's *Understanding Male Hustler* (1991). Their shared point was that sex with hustlers, however dangerous, expensive, or unsatisfactory, was an indispensable part of a certain segment of queer life and possessed its own social, emotional, intellectual, and of course purely physical pleasures. At the same time, however, it must be observed that for both men, their sexual obsessiveness, which structured nearly every aspect of their lives, was hardly typical of most homosexuals of their time. Moreover, their fetishization of working-class straight men was by no means universally shared.

In the first half of the twentieth century, the eroticization of working-class and criminal masculinity was widespread in gay male communities (Chauncey, 1994; Gardiner, 1992; Herring, 2007). It was an omnipresent feature of queer cultural production in the period, from Jean Genet's novels to the paintings of Paul Cadmus. Steward and Painter shared the erotic image of "rough trade" as their ideal sexual partner, of which the Painter wrote:

> My type . . . were big, tall, heavily muscular virile extroverts, extremely masculine and with all the usual male characteristics of thought and action of the rough and tumble, devil-may-care type of adventurous, feckless, fiercely independent, strong minded young athlete. They were tough, and had none of the niceties and refinements such as careful dressing and appearance, gentility of speech, behavior or manner.
>
> *(LR,?/12/44)*

Steward enjoyed the risks involved in sex with these men—"feasting with panthers," in Oscar Wilde's famous words. "Once in a while," he wrote in the 1947, "the 'rough trade' (that means sailors, truck drivers, taxi drivers, and others who won't do anything with you, who are tough, and whom you take an awful chance with) get rough but I love it" (quoted in Spring, 2010, p. 100). Painter was permanently frustrated by the troubles—violence, robberies, blackmail, drugs, and so on—brought by contacts with rough trade. He preferred partners who, while visually resembling street toughs, were well-behaved and compliant in bed, their "roughness" being a carefully cultivated demeanor or merely a hustler's costume (jeans, sailor's cap, leather jacket). Painter and Steward repeatedly visualized this figure in numerous photographs and drawings that portrayed sailors, manual laborers, athletes, or gangsters in various homoerotic scenes, as illustrated in Figure 10.1 (Zikratyy, 2013). Steward even transformed his apartment into a brothel-like dungeon decorated with murals of rough trade in action (Spring, 2011a).

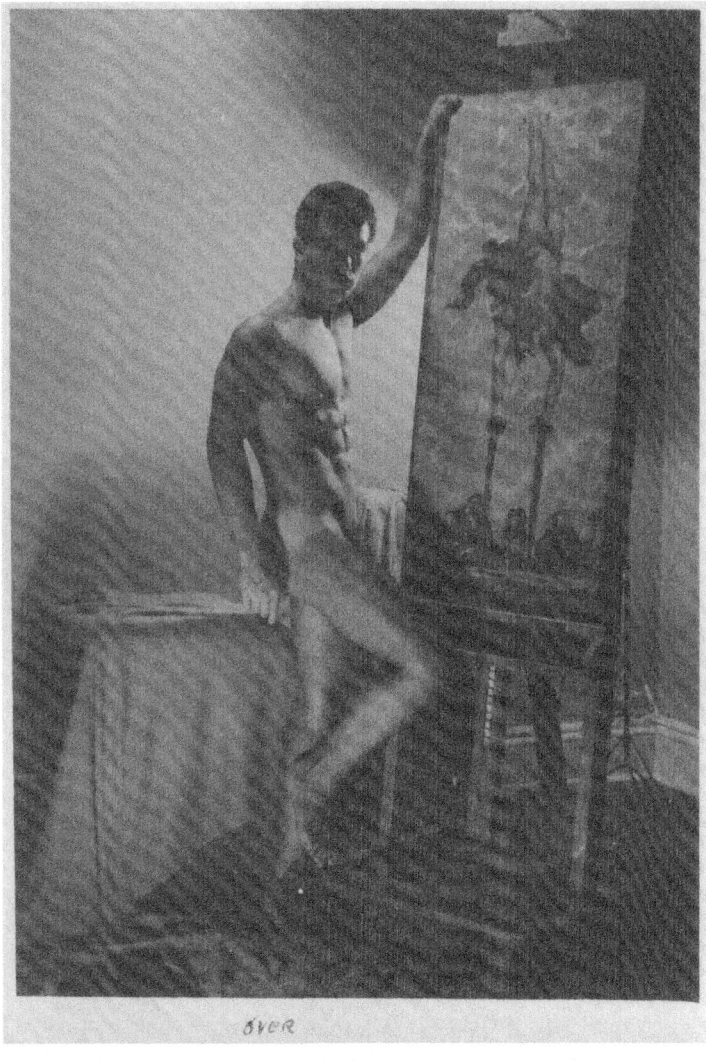

Figure 10.1 Thomas Painter, untitled photograph, 1950.

Image courtesy of the Kinsey Institute for Research in Sex, Gender, and Reproduction.

Sex with rough trade often but certainly not always involved money. Five dollars (a standard amount in the 1940 and 1950s) was a necessary ingredient in these encounters, as it ensured that the rough-trade partner was indeed heterosexual enough and was doing it "just for money." To Painter, for example, signs of a partner's pleasure in male-to-male sex revealed the man's possible homosexuality, a highly unappealing quality that ruled out Painter's desire to have sex with him again. "Unless I have visible evidence that he is the sort of boy who does not want to do it," Painter wrote, "I'm not interested in having it done. . . . I must be sure that he is properly all male" (LR,?/06/44). Similarly, Steward's "particular preference had always been for 'straight trade'" (Spring, 2010, p. 328). In his unpublished 1942 manuscript, Painter even included a "Blue Book of Homosexual Etiquette" in which he outlined his advice to fellow rough trade chasers: pay the man a minimum of three dollars, feed him and take care of his other immediate needs, keep your face below the partner's waist and do not try to kiss him, be suspicious of those who are too eager, never carry lots of cash or submit to blackmail, and avoid minors.

Money, especially if politely disguised as cab fare or a photo model's fee, to protect the man's self-image, functioned as a lubricant between buyer and seller. However, the exchange of sex for money between men did not always go smoothly. Muggings, robberies, and extortion were frequent. Painter writes:

> I have been robbed pretty regularly, and thoroughly at times, in the time I have been living here. (Some 2½ years.) You remember the loss of my typewriter by a boy named Angelo. He also took a wrist watch. Later a boy who was here only a week—whom Red introduced me to—while I was at work cleaned up the place suitcase full. An electric clock (a handsome $15 one), a lot of clothes (mostly old, as I never get around to buying new ones), the radio Roger has left here. Johnny R. needed a raincoat one cold, wet night. I lent him my brand new $25 one. He has never returned it. I also lent him $25. I have never seen any of that either. I '"lent" Red $25 to pay fine to avoid going to jail. One boy pretended to understand his price was $10 rather than $5, and I gave it to him—such things disgust me more than anger me. Another stole another wrist watch. . . . I have never been robbed before my face, or had money taken under threat or duress. But the total of the above probably is large (I have no intention of adding it up. I hate the whole subject. I regard the matter as necessary expenses involved in living the way I do. But I don't like it, anymore a man does his wife's bills for hats and dresses.)
>
> (LR, 21/8/48)

While anonymous cruising in bars, parks, train stations, and beaches was an important part of both Painter's and Steward's sex life and oftentimes led to exciting and fulfilling experiences, they met most of their partners through friends and acquaintances. Such arrangements protected queers from dealing with possibly dangerous strangers and ultimately created an underground network whose members shared not only practical tips or pornographic photographs but also contacts with willing and friendly hustlers. Painter writes about one such queer friend, Alan W., who shared his taste for Puerto Rican men and published a small samizdat physique magazine, *Chevere*, that specialized in erotic portraits:

> Visited this photographer friends of Indio's again. . . . And in trooped assorted Puerto Rican trade of his, sat around to visit. They were none of my exact type, but some were near enough to be very pleasant to talk to. He says he has 'demasiado mucho' of them

anyway and if and when I want some he will be delighted to get rid of some of them—especially in that it seems the ones I like best he likes least.

(LR, 25/2/58)

An entry from Steward's diary likewise illustrates how widespread paid sex with rough trade was among his circle and how casually these encounters were arranged with help of other queer men:

On January 16, Red arranged for me to go over to a hotel just south of Roosevelt Road to a truck driver named Bob Clark; he'd had him that morning. Christ, what a sordid dirty little experience. The man was fat, in bed naked in a hot dark room; he couldn't get a hard-on with my swinging, and finally I had to jack him off—all this for three bucks, which I left instead of five. That's the last time I take seconds on one of Red's tricks in the same day, at any rate.

(Spring, 2011b)

Red Jackson (a different person from the Red mentioned by Painter in the preceding quotation) was Steward's neighborhood friend who procured willing men to have sex with Steward. Another such friend was Chuck Renslow, a prominent physique photographer. Painter had his own friend circle of photographers-cum-procurers—for instance, Robert Gebhart ("Gebbe"), whose services Painter used to privately develop and print his own obscene pictures, and the famous "Lon of New York," who clandestinely sold illicit images (full nudes, including with erections). By the 1940s to the 1960s, many of the physique photography studios operated as prostitution networks, supplying their trusted customers with X-rated versions of their images and contacts with sexually agreeable bodybuilders, as may be represented in Figure 10.2. Some physique models were particularly open and businesslike about the additional services they offered and even ran their own brothel-like establishments. Painter writes about one such model named Arthur U.:

As was the vogue at the time (maybe it still is) the muscle boys were all whores, and so Arthur became one too. I don't say that like my Puerto Ricans they obliged sexually if approached nicely—they were aggressive and common whores to anyone to do anything. . . . Well Arthur didn't stop being a whore as almost all other boys do at a certain age (they get a good job, marry or just tire of it). . . . The sex business (and I mean business) is not a hobby; it is another job, moonlighting so to speak. His own apartment is the whore house all the time cluttered with hustlers and/or queers.

(IP)

Historians have noted not only the importance of physique imagery in the development of twentieth-century queer culture but also the crucial role that queer networks of physique photographers and bodybuilding enthusiasts played in the consolidation of the gay male community (Waugh, 1996).

Throughout their lives, Painter and Steward had sex with literally hundreds of men; dozens were regular lovers. These men were a motley crew of "floundering boys," to use Painter's expression (LR, 15/4/47). Even if one describes them in the most general fashion as young men of working and criminal classes (laborers between jobs, seamen, immigrant street youth, and so on), the life circumstances that led them into male prostitution varied greatly and so did their

Figure 10.2   Thomas Painter, untitled photograph, ca. late 1940s.
Image courtesy of the Kinsey Institute for Research in Sex, Gender, and Reproduction.

attitudes regarding homosexuality. Both Painter and Steward kept, in addition to a regular diary, detailed indexes of each and every one of their sex partners (Steward called his "Stud File"). These stories reveal a diverse world of rough trade. For example, Painter's paid partners ranged from those who were clearly repulsed by the male touch to oversexed complete bisexuals who aggressively pursued sex with both men and women. Painter describes one Howie S., of the latter kind:

> Despite him being essentially a stupid youth, a rather typical fourth class boxer, he seems to have caused considerable havoc in my life, though not with me. . . . [Our apartment] being what it was, there was one evening when I had Howie, he went into the next room and was fellated by Gerric and into the last room to be pedicated [anally penetrated] by Edward. Bill used to relate that in fellating Howie the first time he would come would be

just preliminary. And he loved all of it: wanted me to pedicate him, to fuck Gerric, and for all I know, fellate Edward. His heterosexual life was equally uninhibited and enthusiastic.

(IP)

Painter speaks of the havoc that occurred after Gerric K., Painter's roommate, married a woman who then quickly abandoned him and moved in with Howie instead. Many of Painter's partners were for all intents and purposes straight, but they enjoyed receiving oral sex, not "psychically, but animally, physically" (*LR*, 22/6/44). Others were "half-queers" who genuinely responded to male advances but were also embarrassed and distressed about them. There were always self-absorbed bodybuilders who got pleasure and pocket money from being worshipped for their muscular physique. Painter wrote about Lou D., a physique model who later went on to become a star of Italian sword-and-sandal movies:

> He proved to be the duplicate of the others ['muscle boys']. A mirror throws him into an egocentric trance. He wants to be told his pectorals are better than, say, Z.'s (which, I refer you to his pictures, is a great deal). He wants to be raved about and complemented continuously and shamelessly. If you don't he will prompt you, with direct questions. Incidentally his pectorals are better: they are fantastic.
>
> *(LR, 19/4/51)*

As many of Painter's lovers came from immigrant backgrounds, the sexual and gender categories of their native cultures (southern Italian, Puerto Rican) differed from those they encountered in the United States, complicating the two partners' understanding of what men can do sexually with each other and what makes a man queer. The hustlers' individual personality traits and temperaments were equally dissimilar; some of Painter's lovers were sexually compliant but bored and resentful, others "psychopathic" and violent but passionate in bed. The differences among Painter's rough trade companions could be illustrated by the opposite attitudes of two young men who associated with him in the 1930s and whose first-person testimonies were collected as case studies by psychiatrist George W. Henry. One, Salvatore N., a homosexual, was "disgusted" at the goings-on at Painter's place, which he described as a meeting place of "mercenary" male prostitutes. Another, hustler Leonard R., had sex with both women and men. He called Painter "a hell of a swell roommate" but explained that their relationship was "pure friendship" with no sex involved (Henry, 1948, pp. 179, 460).

Having rough trade for paid lovers could be exhausting, risky, and frustrating, but both Painter and Steward gradually became skilled at developing friendly relations with them. They were good listeners to the often troubled men, sympathetic in their reactions and willing to help at a moment's notice. Working as a parole officer and a tattoo master, respectively, Painter and Steward had everyday contact with working-class youths and came to value their company over that of prissy, well-off queers. Writing in 1954 after visiting a clandestine homosexual social club, Steward expounded:

> I hate bitch parties . . . I tolerated [tonight's] better than usual, however, for at the end of the evening I knew there lay waiting for me . . . Bob Berbich, the lanky truck-driver with his skull-like face, his body in which each muscle stands out, with the skin of the worker who never has the time to seek out the sun and who retains the winter whiteness all year round. . . . [He has been] faithful all these years, with his poor grammar, his limited view, his total and utter absence of "culture" in any form, his proletariat pleasures (a new car

every year, the old one traded in)—and [I imagine him] standing there, cock uplifted, his hands clasped behind his head (fearful that if he should touch me while I kneel before him, that some of my queerness will rub off on him), and leading me here and there around the room, my following him around the room almost on my knees—and then his final going to the bed, where . . . his head elevated on the pillow, his hands still behind his head . . . we set to work in earnest. . . . [A]t the moment of orgasm, there is only a slight, very slight contraction, a tiny spasm, and a little "oh!" escaping muffled from his mouth, or a small exhalation of air. When I go to spit, I know that by the time I get back he will be up and dressing, his shorts on—and then a final handshake, a promise to call me next week, an admonition to get some new "pitchers" to stimulate him, and off he goes.

(Spring, 2010, pp. 207–208)

In this account, the reader recognizes Steward's pride in associating with "real men" and being allowed to pleasure them. Bob Berbich was an ex-serviceman who held assorted blue-collar jobs over the 16 years he knew Steward: "a sailor, a motorcycle delivery boy, a taxi-driver, a night steelworker, a truck driver and a uniformed guard." Despite being married and ostensibly heterosexual, Bob had no scruples about being fellated by Steward and certainly enjoyed it; he was a "real man" whose confidence about his masculinity was so strong that sex with queers could not compromise it. Being accepted as a buddy by a working-class tough, if only to a limited degree, delighted and excited Steward, especially considering the stigma and opprobrium he faced among middle-class heterosexuals and even many other queers. One finds a similar sentiment in Painter's diary when he writes about spending an evening drinking and socializing with two Puerto Rican teenagers at a neighborhood bar: "It was sort of a make-believe evening . . . where I was what I would like to be—an accepted buddy and peer with two nice, beautiful, half-naked, friendly boys" (*LR*, 5/9/53).

The romantic (or even fetishistic) view of rough trade that one encounters in Painter and Steward had a distinct misogynistic and femmephobic strain to it; femininity in other queers and effete middle-class heterosexuals was a profound turnoff for both men. Benefiting, so to speak, from the working-class culture of aggressive phallic masculinity that permitted men to have an equally active role in sex with women and with queers, Painter and Steward came to inevitably share it to some degree. One may even describe Steward's masochistic submission to straight men as a tortured manifestation of his internalized homophobia. However, there is also an important cross-class dimension to Painter's and Steward's erotic vision of the lower classes. Being educated middle-class men (Painter studied to become a religious teacher, while Steward worked in academia for over ten years), they idealized and exoticized the "urban proletariat" as sexually liberated, devoid of the puritanical prejudices and inhibitions that Painter and Steward had grown up with and had to overcome. One can argue that Painter's and Steward's sexual diaries reveal intimate, affective histories of the two queer men's sexual emancipation, in which their pride in transgressing social boundaries and disregarding mainstream conventions combined with the pleasures of openly expressing and realizing their erotic desires, deemed immoral and pathological by others.

But how "not bound" by social norms and conventions were the interactions that this subset of queer men had with straight hustlers and rough trade? In the next part of this chapter, I look at Thomas N. Painter's sexual diary in more detail to examine the tensions and contradictions around the notions of masculinity, class, and money that defined such relations in the mid-twentieth-century America. I explore crucial questions about power, pleasure, and exploitation in male-to-male commercial sex in the period, reconstructing the affective microdynamics of Painter's relations with his paid working-class lovers.

Conflicts

Writing about *My Secret Life*, the voluminous sex journal of an anonymous Victorian gentleman who recounts in pornographic detail his sexual relations with innumerable prostitutes, domestic servants, and other working-class women, Steven Marcus addressed a profound question about the role of the objectification of others in the individual project of sexual emancipation. "Walter," the author of this famous memoir, was a fascinating if precocious representative of the modern liberal ideology of sexual freedom and diversity. He rejected the idea of a universal, God-given sexual norm and despised society's censorship of pornography. He was uninhibited about his desires, consciously fought his own prejudices about sex, and experimented with unconventional sexual practices. "Nothing can perhaps be justly called unnatural which nature prompts us to do," he argued, anticipating the progressive voices of sex reformers from the next century.

But Walter was a well-to-do upper-class man—most probably, the prominent civil engineer Colonel William Haywood—who was cynical and even brutal in using his power and money to obtain sex (Pattinson, 2002). He treated poor women as always available and ultimately powerless objects to be manipulated for his pleasure; he spoke of them as a man of his time and class would of horses or hunting dogs. Walter paid to deflower virgins, examined the genitals of his sex partners with a biologist's curiosity, raped several women who refused him, sexually harassed servants and other subordinate women on a daily basis, and forced prostitutes to enact his extravagant fantasies, however bizarre and dehumanizing. Marcus (1964) argues that this contradiction at the heart of *My Secret Life*—its author's impulse of sexual emancipation being thoroughly tied to a rigid, oppressive system of social inequalities, which he regularly exploits and never questions—is representative of the limitations, perhaps even the failure, of the Western sexual liberation project. As more recent discussion of race and sexuality has also shown (for instance, in the analysis of racism in gay male communities), most liberated forms of sexual behavior can comfortably coexist with most backward racial prejudice or dehumanizing fetishistic fantasies. "It may be useful to remind ourselves," emphasizes Marcus, "that the struggle for sexual freedom, at least in the lives of individual persons, requires considerable stepping over the bodies of others" (Marcus, 1964, p. 159).

One can identify obvious parallels between *My Secret Life* and the homosexual autobiographies of Thomas Painter and Samuel Steward: the view of members of the lower classes as sexually uninhibited and available, as well as the crucial role of money in facilitating sexual relations with them. There is an important difference, however: Painter's and Steward's partners were working-class men, not women, at a time when sex between men was socially proscribed, highly stigmatized, and downright illegal. In *My Secret Life*, the vector of power relations is brutally clear. It is directed from the aggressive phallic potency of Walter toward objectified and fragmented bodies of servant girls and prostitutes, whom he repeatedly abuses. The power dynamic of queer men's relations with straight hustlers was much more complex. Hustlers and rough trade, who usually were heterosexual working-class men, physically strong and streetwise, did not occupy the same subordinated and powerless position in paid sex as did the poor women of *My Secret Life*, especially vis-à-vis their queer clients, whom they considered weak and womanlike. Presenting Steward's understanding of his lifelong relationships with male hustlers, Justin Spring explains:

> The roles of hustler and customer were at that time defined in a way that was entirely to the physical, psychological, and monetary advantage of the hustler. In this well-established exchange, the hustler (who was understood to be primarily heterosexual) allowed the

homosexual customer to perform oral sex on him. That was all. There was no exchange of affection, no variety, and no reciprocation. As a result, the hustler retained his heterosexual identity, asserted physical and emotional dominance over the homosexual client, and at the same time profited financially from what was to him an inconsequential (and basically pleasurable) sensation.

(2010, p. 299)

The hustlers' advantage was certainly limited, as they were subject to the objectification and fetishization ubiquitous in sex work and did not always experience sexual advances from men as innocuous and inconsequential. The position of their queer clients was similarly twofold. Money allowed queers to obtain sex from underprivileged and marginalized young men, often from immigrant groups or racial minorities, but the stigma of homosexual "perversion" and the risk of legal persecution for sodomy or corrupting minors made them at the same time easy targets for extortion, blackmail, robbery, and assault. One can argue that queer–hustler relationships were an arena of conflict and negotiations between different vectors of privilege and oppression (economic, class- or gender-based, racial, generational) in which neither party could completely get the upper hand. The autobiographical testimonies of Thomas N. Painter reveal and articulate these conflicts.

The impossibility of reciprocity in homosexual relations is an overarching theme in Painter's diary and memoirs. In his view, queers wanted only straight men who were unable to genuinely respond to their desires, and money was an unfortunate but necessary way of resolving this deadlock. Among miscellaneous memorabilia included in Painter's archive at the Kinsey Institute, there is a short poem, "Broadway Love. Homosexual," which ends with the following lament:

> Hell was at its most fiendish moment
> When it devised a heart full of and hungry for love
> Then twisted the mind and body thus endowed so it must not find end to its yearning.
> And finally put in the same world glorious boys
> Who will imitate the Goal, willow-the-wisps,
> For a time, for money. Then are gone.
> And we see ourselves merely
> In a choking mire. Alone.

Written in 1935, it reflects Painter's frustration at his first experiences in New York's gay underworld and echoes homophobic cultural discourses of the time in which queers figured as "sad young men"—pallid sickly youths, driven to death or suicide by their "perverse" desires (Dyer, 2002, pp. 116–130). Gay life, as Painter saw it at the time, was a life of loneliness; one-sided infatuations with murky characters; and hasty, dangerous, and generally unsatisfying sex. Nearly 40 years later, organizing his writings for a future biographer, he wrote a short essay titled "Long Search" that highlighted his lifelong pursuit, often sidetracked and by and large disheartening, of reciprocated intimacy and companionship with men. The essay concludes with the section "1963–1968. Search Fulfilled." It is devoted to his last boyfriend, Gilbert, who was at last able to accept Painter as an equal partner and who fully enjoyed physical intimacy with him. "I became a 'companion,' I find myself completely needed and useful, I find reciprocated love, response, as never before," Painter declared. The pathos of this statement emphasizes the frustration and disillusionment he felt with many of his other partners, whom he found to be mercenary or physically cold. Poignant passages like the following from Painter's diary reveal the intimate, emotional side of sex with hustlers:

> Speaking of curious sensations. The last time Carmine was here, as we were about to leave and both were fully clothed, for the street, and he was standing there, I felt an impulse and went up to him and '"hugged" (embraced) him—rubbing my face and mouth against his neck and ear. This was an impulsive expression of affection, of the purest sort. And as I did so I felt the constriction of my throat which comes in deep emotion (related to weeping). And I felt the emotion too, instantaneously—for about five seconds, I guess. Then he responded by placing his arm around me—routinely, in the utter minimum of response suggested to my action. At this point I had the reaction: I could have wept, raged, or laughed, as I did, a sort of bitter, ironic half-laugh, as if to say "I should have known better than to give way to my affection to this paid boy who can't, and couldn't possibly, respond any other way than he did, but who did what he felt was required, in his own lazy, half-hearted, boy way."
>
> (LR, 7/5/53)

Painter could not escape the homophobic social climate of the time and ultimately regarded his homosexuality as a curse and a handicap. In his resigned view, the only relationship a queer could hope for was inauthentic and sordid love for pay. "And to those who cannot even buy / They may stand and dumbly want / Or they may haggle and cheat / Or they may weep, dry tears," Painter wrote in "Broadway Love: Homosexual."

In modern societies, money has been a widespread and effective means of asserting one's dominance. Giving money to others, especially those in dire circumstances, can also produce an immediate, and thoroughly false, sense of intimacy. It is therefore no surprise that, being at a disadvantage in their relations with hustlers and rough trade, queer men like Painter resorted to using money to smooth out the tensions inherent in their attraction to working-class straight men. Within the rigid system of asymmetrical sex roles adopted by many at the time, homosexual men were regarded exclusively as submissive partners obliged to sexually service others. They occupied a woman's (or more specifically, a prostitute's or an "easy" woman's) position in the working-class hierarchies of gender. Money and other attributes of higher social status allowed queers, otherwise treated as proxy women, to express masculine dominance in their interactions with working-class men and exercise some degree of control when buying sex from them.

In 1964, responding to the sex researcher John Gagnon, who asked Painter why he had always paid men for sex instead of finding a reciprocal and financially equal relationship, Painter provided a straightforward answer: "Non-paid I must please *him*. To do so I must fellate or be pedicated neither of which do I enjoy. . . . So I want to pay and command" (*LR*, 1/2/64). This statement is unusually blunt for Painter, who typically devised more elaborate and nuanced rationalizations for his actions, but it reveals his lifelong perception of money as an always-available resource with which one could obtain whatever one wanted from other people. Born into the upper-middle class, Painter described himself as growing up in "complete disregard of money," considering it "some sort of token stuff that you passed people when you wanted something" (*LR*, 20/11/62). As Painter quickly spent all of his family's fortune in the 1930s and in the following decades led a rather impoverished existence working as a parole officer and then as a bookstore clerk, this idea of money as a means of dominating others became to him less a fact of his everyday life than a powerful component of his erotic imagination. In fact, Painter singled out "forcing sex on an unwilling person . . . by giving (or withholding) money which he needs" as one of the predominant themes of his homoerotic artwork (*LR*, 8/5/66). Many of his pornographic drawings depict scenes of domination and sexual servitude in pseudo-historical, sword-and-sandal settings: for instance, a powerful ruler is offered captured enemy soldiers or newly purchased slaves, whom he orders to be stripped naked, tortured, and raped while he oversees the process (Zikratyy, 2013). Painter admitted he was excited by such sadistic fantasies of absolute control over another man's body and its unrestrained violation, but he never attempted to recreate those fantasies in real life (unlike Steward, he was not interested in sadomasochistic play).

In Painter's biography, the nexus of sexual domination and economic coercion took a softer, more indirect form of cross-class sexual patronage—a Horatio Alger–style scenario of a wealthy, educated man raising a slum boy to middle-class respectability in exchange for companionship and occasional sexual favors. Painter writes about his ideal relationship:

> My "daydreams," my erotic fancies however are all with me wholly dominant. Over strong, independent spirited, muscular, dominant youths. My dominance, in these situations, arises from vast wealth and power, which I exert to rescue and raise them from the most extremely low and desperate social situations—intense poverty, slavery, imprisonment, threat of death. Thus I can be dominant, in a way, while allowing them to be dominant personalities at the same time. They need me unequivocally, due to their situation . . . and I need them for their sexual attraction and to need someone to help, who needs me. Eventually, due to living with me (the rich and powerful person), they become educated, sophisticated, suave and able-to-take-care-of-themselves-very-well-thank-you—and I release them and find another who needs me.
>
> (LR, *9/2/66*)

This vision of mutually beneficial cross-class and cross-generational friendship with benefits was crucial to Painter's understanding of homosexual relations. It was a humane, even noble solution to what he saw as his sordid sexual predicament—his "unnatural" attraction to men who by definition could not reciprocate his feelings. Painter's professed goal was to befriend and mentor underprivileged young men involved in prostitution to queers, and other delinquent activities, and to help them reform and make an honest living. Putting aside Painter's genuine attempts to help his lovers, who often found themselves in trouble of one sort or another, one can clearly recognize in this "daydream" his desire to maintain dominant status in relationships by asserting middle-class masculinity and its values (responsibility, self-control, education, duty, service) over the rough, uncivilized, animal-like virility of the lower classes. In this philanthropic scenario, the submissive, humiliating position in which a queer partner was placed during the sexual contact itself—being forbidden caresses of any sort and allowed only to orally service the hustler, his own pleasure unimportant—was compensated by the economic power he could exercise in nonsexual spheres of life.

Painter enjoyed situations in which he felt respected, was treated as a trusted confidant, or was asked for help or advice. His Puerto Rican lovers showed particular regard for his status as an older, white, educated "Americano." His regular financial benefactions to them—some of them genuine gestures of help, others more pragmatic transactions—made him feel, for a time, like an affluent foreign guest toward whom everybody is uniformly friendly and compliant. The fact that as a queer man Painter remained vulnerable to public opprobrium, violence, and blackmail prevented him from becoming as ruthless and exploitative as the author of *My Secret Life*. In Painter's life, money was one of the few resources and privileges available to someone who was otherwise considered a sick and dangerous "pervert." It therefore served as the only available—but ultimately precarious—negotiation card in arranging sex with rough trade, who were nearly always worse off than Painter economically but arguably held more power as straight and physically strong young men.

What could money buy Painter? First of all, companionship. A long-term "kept lover" would join him during social outings or vacations; a horny straight soldier whom Painter had picked up on Coney Island would stay overnight, having no other place to go; a group of Puerto Ricans would join him for a picnic. It is important to stress how lonely life could be for a middle-aged homosexual man at the time and how rewarding even such simple social activities were to Painter. In these situations, money operated in a manner consistent with the long-standing working-class-leisure notion of "treating" as courtesy between men and a respectable way to gain and secure a woman's company. Since at least the mid-nineteenth century, working-men treated each other to rounds of beer in male bonding rituals and treated their girlfriends to dancehall outings and new dresses in exchange for sexual liberties (Peiss, 1986). To many of his lovers, Painter became something of an eccentric older hanger-on whose company was tolerated and maybe enjoyed so long he paid the expenses and supplied pocket money. At times, groups of cash-strapped young men formed around Painter and used his apartment as a place to spend a night and make a few dollars. About one such group, Painter wrote:

> The boys now have developed a special meaning of this in reference to me: one has or has not "joined the union" depending on whether or not he has been to bed with me. There was some comment in the car that Perez has joined the night before, and veiled speculation as to whether Indio would that night, as he now was the only non-union member of the group. This all in the spirit of good clean fun, in a kidding, humorous manner.
>
> *(LR, 15/7/55)*

Painter remarked that, unlike other queers who limited their interaction with rough trade to sexual transactions, he got genuine pleasure from socializing with his working-class sex partners. Part of the explanation lies in Painter's voyeuristic desire to observe them during everyday activities; Painter particularly enjoyed watching them when they were seminaked in the summer.

On the other hand, in nonsexual interactions, Painter could behave as an older friend and mentor and assume a dominant masculine role unavailable to him in sex with these men. This is how Painter described his relationship with his lover Efrain: "I hold the unique position of receiving the intimate confidences and the willing cooperation in answering my questions of a boy whom no other educated, upper-class person could even approach. (Not even as a queer, as he loathes them)" (*LR*, 7/10/60). He further explained:

> I am sure that part of my pleasure in Efrain is in his very dangerousness—and the fact that *I* can sit by him and stroke his hair and talk soothingly—and he will smile his nicest back at me. . . . Like having a pet panther who slashes anyone but purrs for me—I keep trusting.
>
> *(LR, 24/11/60)*

The pleasure and pride that Painter felt in this exceptional status, however illusory, were twofold. He asserted his middle-class superiority over the powerful but unbridled masculinity of working-class youth; he called himself a "wild animal trainer." And through his proximity to the lower classes and their authentic, natural virility, as Painter regarded it, he grew to see himself as more masculine as well. For Painter, this masculine rejuvenation in the slums—a long-standing practice among middle-class reformers and philanthropists (Koven, 2004;

Murphy, 2008)—counteracted the ubiquitous feminizing medical discourses that portrayed queers as quasi-women.

Another thing that money could buy Painter was of course sex itself, but the physical dimension of his relationships with hustlers and rough trade was also the most intricate. While many queers enjoyed the submissive position afforded to them in sex with straight men, Painter found it unsatisfying and repulsive; it undermined his masculine self-image. He avoided penetrative sex, in part because it presupposed a clear-cut hierarchy of roles, and instead enjoyed more neutral caresses, frottage, and mutual masturbation. Individual factors probably played a major role in how different men responded to Painter's sexual requirements. Some enjoyed an easy client who simply "worshipped" their body and did not expect them to do much; others were uncomfortable about any form of male touch outside of the strict protocol of unreciprocated anal and oral penetration; yet others were disappointed that Painter did not have "real sex" and did not give them the pleasure they expected. This is how Painter described the sexual mores of the young Puerto Ricans who became his frequent paid lovers in the 1950s and 1960s:

> The Puerto Rican boy is not only willing but eager for sex with a male . . . but he expects pedication [anal penetration], to be the pedicator. . . . Hence when they encounter my requirements they undergo several reactions: (1) they find they are not going to get detumescence [sexual release], which is [a] serious disappointment and frustration for them, as they are all in a terrific state of sexual starvation. (2) They find themselves called upon to allow me to make love to them, especially involving body and face, by my hands and mouth. This (as noted above) is, generally, foreign to their experience. Moreover it is psychologically repugnant: instead of being the dominant, aggressive, primitive pedicator, they become the passive object of my sexual attentions. Bad enough, but I want them, if they will, to make love to me—to embrace, intertwine, even kiss me. This is wholly foreign and seems homosexual to them, making love to a man, or even having him make love to them.
>
> (LR, 2/5/56)

Painter was something of a muscle fetishist fascinated by public displays of the seminaked male body (on the beach, during exercise, at labor). He was attracted to a well-developed physique in men, especially in their upper body. His sex partners often found themselves in an ambiguous position of being elevated to a demigod-like status while at the same time treated as cardboard mannequins whose only valued characteristics were their "splendid pectorals," "bulging biceps," and "fantastic latissimus dorsi." The rapid growth and visibility of the bodybuilding subculture in the postwar years introduced into American society—through beefcake magazines, sword-and-sandal movies, and Mr. Universe competitions—a new image of the young muscleman as an object of desire. But this newly sanctioned celebration of the male body remained a contested area, where more traditional ideas about what makes a man (dominance, action, a strong mind) clashed with his feminizing objectification. One sees this conflict clearly in the reactions of Painter's sex partners to his erotic worship of their muscular physique. There often appears to be a kind of narcissistic cockiness in the way they were ready to display their naked body for a queer's lustful gaze, combined with an unease, sometimes rather profound, about being essentially treated as a two-dimensional sex object, as seen in Figure 10.3.

The ultimate arena of conflict in Painter's sexual relations with hustlers and rough trade was ethical. Suspicions of moral corruption and sexual exploitation hung over such relationships—a middle-age man coaxing underprivileged youth into sex for money—in part owing to homophobic media representations of queers as child molesters and serial killers in the 1950s and

Figure 10.3 Thomas Painter, untitled photograph, 1950.
Image courtesy of the Kinsey Institute for Research in Sex, Gender, and Reproduction.

1960s, in part a result of their inherently problematic circumstances. The broken-home backgrounds and troubled behavior of some of Painter's lovers, who were often unemployed, homeless, or involved in petty crime and street gangs, both made them more willing to sell sex to queers and made this sexual-economic exchange ethically challenging, as it was essentially a form of survival sex. A romantic person with religious background, Painter tried to negotiate in his mind the conflict between his masculine pleasures at easily possessing these young poor men's bodies and his middle-class scruples about exploiting others' dire circumstances in so sordid a manner. In the summer of 1961, he wrote a short essay called "Moral Code" in which he described the ethical dimension of paid sex and articulated his own attitudes about it:

> Living a life of paying for sex with teenage underprivileged boys makes for thin ice skating on the "coercion for money" part of [the moral code]. I have always avoided it when

I sensed it, have only had boys who were perfectly willing and in no sense unhappy about it. . . . I have always verbalized my approach and taken no for an answer at once, without discussion (even if they didn't mean it, as it later developed). I have never used stimulants (erotic pictures) or drugs (alcohol) to "make" a boy. Frequently I have been so careful and hesitant and sensitive that the boys have been vaguely irritated. I have tried to minimize, in the sex act, my role down to necessity, never be greedy or boring or demanding. I stop at any slightest sign of disapproval of any detail. I try, as you know, to be friendly and interested in the person, fair in my dealings, respectful of their dignity as persons, sensitive to their feelings and attitudes.

(Painter, 1961)

This passage is clearly self-justificatory and not thoroughly truthful in its details (Painter did show his sex partners pornographic pictures on more than a few occasions, according to his own diary), but it reveals his genuine preoccupation with the ethics of paid sex. Interestingly enough, the essay was written during the time in Painter's life when he himself felt exploited and abused by rough trade. Just two months earlier, in May 1961, he had been raped by the aforementioned Efrain, who, according to Painter, showed no sexual desire for anal penetration at all and did it only to humiliate him. Seeing his life spiraling out of control as Efrain and his gang of "Dragons" took complete control of his finances through violence and blackmail, Painter suspected that he, in a way, had brought these troubles upon himself by coaxing poor, socially marginalized teenagers to be his paid lovers. In his diary entries from July 1961, Painter talks of still being shaken by his memories of *Suddenly Last Summer*, a Tennessee Williams movie he'd watched a year before, whose homosexual protagonist, Sebastian, dies at the hands of Spanish street boys whom he was blatantly buying for sex during his summer vacation. He could not help but wonder whether he was going to end up like Sebastian, who, despite being "obviously brilliant and talented, was at the end devoured by the half-wild boys he chose to devote himself to" (*LR*, 24/1/60).

In the "Moral Code" essay, Painter mournfully described his sexual biography as "forty years of paying underprivileged boys for sex." Painter's preoccupation with the impact of his actions on the lives of these men—was he helping or spoiling and corrupting them?—had been present in his autobiographical writing since the 1930s. In his archive, he preserved a brief one-page note written by one Charlie O., a typical street tough, a Jersey City gang member who was involved in many robberies and even a murder, went to prison for burglary, and was, at one point, addicted to heroin. On meeting Painter, who took a special fancy to him and encouraged him to make an honest living, Charlie resolved to go back to work as a merchant marine and returned to the sea in the spring of 1935. His note to Painter from June of that year reads:

Dear Tom
am doing very nice with my job, and just can't wait till the ship leaves, <u>I did not think that it was so easy to work for a living, but I have you to thank for that</u>. I have received my first pay yesterday, then went up town to pay Bill [Painter's queer friend] the money I owed him, we had a few drinks then had dinner, then we—.

By preserving this letter among his personal memorabilia as well as underlining the sentence, Painter wanted to communicate to future readers of his "Life Record" how he sought to positively influence his delinquent lovers and at times succeeded in reforming them; as late as 1967, he still described his friendship with Charlie as his "greatest success in helping someone" (*LR*, 14/8/67). This letter also served as a proof that, while true physical reciprocity was perhaps impossible in paid sex between queers and rough trade, their relations did not necessarily involve coercion and exploitation but could instead resemble regular, nonsexual friendship. Charlie is mentioned repeatedly throughout Painter's diary as an example of someone whom society viewed as immoral and criminal but, when approached with sympathy and understanding, turned out to be kind, loyal, and grateful. Even when Painter went broke in February 1935 and was quickly deserted by his other lovers, Charlie remained, living with him, and years later, after receiving a large insurance settlement for a work trauma, he gave some money to Painter in an attempt to compensate him for his previous help. The last incident especially reaffirmed Painter in his belief that queers could "love their boys, not just suck their semen" and that "the boys will, in their fashion, respond with friendliness and liking, some of them" (*LR*, 27/5/63).

"Some of them" is a key phrase here. Charlie was a rather exceptional figure in Painter's sexual biography, which was largely populated by either rough and sinister characters who ruthlessly exploited Painter's attraction to them, at times resorting to robbery and extortion, or "glorious youths" who, even if sexually available for money, showed little amiability and affection and naturally had no interest in establishing romantic relations or friendships with older queers. Furthermore, despite Painter's idealistic pronouncements about the positive role that he wanted to play in the lives of his working-class lovers, the effects of his paying them for sex were often demoralizing, and they often used the money they obtained from Painter to support a desultory semicriminal lifestyle of drinking, gambling, and drug use. Painter regularly pondered this issue, very much like the social reformers of the time who wondered whether dispensing money and material goods to the poor had any positive impact on their life situation or if it merely made them idle and dependent on charity.

The dangers of spoiling young lower-class men with his money, instead of reforming them, were obvious to Painter, for instance, in his relationship with Peter D., who was his "kept" boyfriend in 1939–1941. Peter was one of the "Depression boys," as Painter called them; he came to New York from the small industrial town of Palmerton, Pennsylvania, where his Ukrainian-immigrant parents worked in a zinc mill. Painter saw in Peter a "nice boy" who needed to be rescued from the underworld of male prostitution, where he'd ended up owing to economic hardship, not some inner depravity. Painter attempted to socially elevate the young man who, according to him, "acquired a hatred for books, school and reading in general, and for everything connected with learning," having been raised by poor and backward parents (*LR*,?/12/44). As Peter was unwilling to devote time to what Painter called "self-improvement" and, it seems, rather put off by Painter's overtly patronizing and possibly humiliating manner in insisting that he did so, hardly anything came out of Painter's "educational" efforts. A series of letters that Painter received from a friend of Peter's in 1941 suggests that the effect of Painter's relationship with Peter was harmful and turned the young man into a complete loafer without any serious goal in life. Peter's friend wrote:

> I am really concerned about [Peter's] attitude and mental outlook, on things in general. Having known Peter before you, I feel I am in a fairly good position to note the amazing change that has come over the kid. . . .
>
> *He has lost all sense of values*, both in money, and people. He doesn't seem to realize, *who his real friends are*, and if he did, not particularly impressed with the knowledge. . . . As I see it, Pete wasn't mentally equipped to keep up with the pace, that he has traveled this past year. His life for the past year, has been one beautiful vacation, after the other. He acts exactly like a movie star, who actually believes all the things that are said about them. In the house, on the street, he always seems to be conscious of himself.

[Peter] told me, that he really wanted to do something constructive for himself, and that pleased me very much. Ned [another friend] told him, before leaving, that he would assist in obtaining him a position. Ned has kept his word, he's even worried himself sick over it, but La Peter has shown a definite lack of interest. . . . It's apparent—that he doesn't want work. . . . So the kid—is just drifting along. Gets up in the afternoon, about one o'clock, usually spends couple of hours before the mirror, then takes a little stroll, has a lovely dinner, the price of which is of no consequence. Takes in a movie, the price, still of no consequence. Then he goes to bowl, in an alley, the location of which, I definitely don't like. It's on North Miami Ave. And long about, two or three in the morning, he comes strolling in, makes a careful toilet, and goes to bed. That has been going for days and days.

We both know—that it was partly your money, that brought about such a state of mind. . . . And I for one, would appreciate your taking him in hand, and try and mold him into something—*very different.*

The situation depicted in this letter was a far cry from Painter's ideal of helping an economically underprivileged lover to establish himself in life. Instead, it exposes the negative effects that "keeping" a straight young lover could entail. Peter's conflicted feelings about his relationship with Painter—Peter clearly enjoyed the financial opportunities it afforded him, demanded more and more money, and flaunted luxuries, but he remained averse to physical intimacy with Painter (and other men) and was ashamed about being his "kept boy"—further complicated the case and eventually led to their separation. Later in life, Painter regretted ever starting this affair and described it as "a horrible, complete waste of time, opportunity, money and everything else" (*LR*, 24/9/67).

In his diary, Painter expounds on his repeated romantic disappointments, like the breakdown of his relationship with Peter D. and other troubles caused by his association with hustlers and rough trade. On numerous occasions, he expresses his exasperation at being taken advantage of by the "mercenary" youngsters he pursued as sex partners.

Pete has no faintest conception of friendship or affection or appreciation: he uses me for his convenience, as a comfort station, a flop, a refuge, and a source of small contributions of cash in emergencies—but never has he come around without wanting something. Social and friendly intercourse are beyond his ken. . . . He has no friends—as none of these people do—merely companions who are temporary useful and convenient.

(LR, *14/9/52*)

This passage describing another Peter, a teenage "hustler and clip artist" who briefly lived with Painter in 1952, illustrates Painter's usual grievances about the paid lower-class lovers who turned out to be immature, unreliable, insensitive, ungrateful, opportunistic, unscrupulous in financial matters, or dangerously violent. Besides giving vent to romantic frustrations, these negative judgments reveal a profound conflict at the intersection of sex, class, and money that gave rise to the misunderstandings and fallings-out that beset Painter's sex life.

To fully understand this conflict, one needs to approach Painter as a modern middle-class subject who shared the new liberal notion of sex as consensual physical intimacy, whether romantic or purely recreational. Painter was, in a broad sense, a competent consumer able to safely navigate the underground sexual marketplace. Painter's attitude was egalitarian and transactional, and arguably thoroughly capitalist: two free individuals agree, via respectful negotiation, on a mutually beneficial exchange of sex for money. The modern capitalist logic of sexual contracts that enabled and shaped masochism as one of the paradigmatic modern "perversions" (Deleuze, 1991) equally served Painter the homosexual in resolving the deadlock of queer desire toward straight men. The cultural matrix of economic exchange made "impossible" relations (domination by a woman, sex between men) possible within the preestablished limits of articulated or implicit contract. All in all, Painter's preferred sex partners were safe and easy-to-deal-with "nice boys," a category he used to describe paid or kept lovers who were reliable, considerate, and uncomplicated in their sexual dealings. Many bodybuilding models belonged to this group:

> "Muscle boy" means the real weight-lifting, pictures-in-the-magazine set, mostly, it developed from the Brooklyn YMCA gym, where they all knew one another. . . . They were all, as opposed to the hustlers, boys living at home, going to school (and even college), honest, non-delinquent, otherwise decent and well-behaved boys. One had their telephone numbers and made appointments if they were not home—"to pose for me." They used the photographs as proof.
>
> *(IP)*

As active participants in the sexualized market of mail-order physique photography, these muscle boys were already familiar with the rules and workings of sexual-economic exchange. Their attitude was both courteous and businesslike: they appeared when called for, performed agreed-on sexual activities, collected their fee, and left.

However, what Painter encountered among more socially and economically marginalized young men was a view of sex not as mutual exchange but as an arena for asserting one's phallic dominance over the weaker and inferior partner, be it a woman or a queer man. Tensions inevitably arose as Painter found his middle-class masculinity devalued and undermined within such hierarchic relations. He aimed to remold these partners according to his middle-class ideal of philanthropic mentorship, but the subordinate role of dependent protégé was equally emasculating to these young working-class men, who would inevitably try to compensate for it, often through violence. Such young men often perceived male sexual pleasure not in modern terms of mutuality and consent but as organized around physical domination and the aggressive pursuit of genital relief. As such, it was fully reconcilable with violence and exploitation. As historian Matt Houlbrook argues:

> In sliding between intimate friendship and brutal assault, workingmen's encounters with the queer transcended contemporary understandings of "homosexuality" or "homophobia." Intimacy, sex, blackmail, theft, and assault constituted a continuum within the *same* cultural terrain, underpinned by dominant conceptions of masculinity as toughness and resourcefulness. . . . Men played roles that reproduced a *difference* from their sexual partners, articulating a toughness that asserted their physical and moral superiority.
>
> *(2005, pp. 178–179)*

Painter's relations with hustlers and rough trade were in a way a continuous power struggle around the changing, class-conflicted notions of masculine dominance. And like every power struggle, the struggle was open to erotic possibilities that energized and perpetuated it. The rough styles of masculine expression, culturally legitimized in the working-class and underworld milieus, were Painter's lifelong erotic fetish, but they also remained a source of danger, frustration, and disappointment, as they clashed with his own masculine self-image and his middle-class values and ideals.

Buying sex: then and now

Painter's affluent New England family shunned him; after graduating from the Union Seminary, he was denied every teaching job because of his "problem," and his upper-class friends refused any contact with him. Ultimately, buying sexual services from other men, especially those who were at the same time hypermasculine and economically vulnerable, allowed Painter to compensate for the powerless and abhorred position he found himself in as an openly queer man. Commercial sex allowed Painter to temporarily enjoy the fantasy world of sexual plenty (New York of the 1930s through 1960s had a bursting underground of male sex work) and sexual subservience (even the most tough-looking straight man could be transformed into docile sex object for an hour) and thus, in a way, repair his damaged sense of manhood.

What Painter desired as his ideal relationship with a young working-class straight partner is familiar to us today as "the boyfriend (or girlfriend) experience," a commercially based transaction that exceeds mere genital relief and offers some kind of emotional connection to the client, however limited or temporary. This type of relationship has recently attracted scholars' attention as a form of sexual-economic exchange that values genuine connections with otherness (as in the "authentic" experiences offered by tourist destinations and foreign cuisines) but also thoroughly commodifies and thus fully contains them (Earle & Sharpe, 2008; Sanders, 2008; Milrod & Monto, 2012). As studies show, the client's and the sex worker's experiences of these relations often differ strikingly: the client indulges in the fantasy of mutual intimacy and appreciates the seemingly genuine warmth and friendliness of the paid partner, while the sex worker carefully and consciously controls the emotional boundaries of the encounter (Peniston & Erber, 2007). The insightful theoretical notion of intimate or emotional labor (Boris & Parreñas, 2010) captures these new postindustrial economies of commercialized eroticism. But how new are they? I would argue that the relations that some queer men had with hustlers and rough trade were, in a way, a prototype of this new post–"sexual revolution" framework of intimacy and commerce. Queer men who actively participated in urban sexual underworlds, like Painter or Steward, explored new modes of relating to others outside of the socially sanctioned domains of work and domesticity. Their firsthand testimonies reveal their ingenious strategies of using money and the cultural capital of middle-class consumerism to bypass multiple conflicts around masculinity and same-sex desire and ultimately to lead plentiful and exciting (if frequently frustrating and dangerous) sex lives.

One way to look at the erotic universe captured in the voluminous sexual diary of Thomas N. Painter is to see an archaic system of gender identities and sexual roles in which straight men were "not quite straight" and could be cajoled into allowing another man to perform oral sex on them. This centuries-old world of flexible sexual orientation remains fascinating today, as the ideologies of gender are undergoing a dramatic transformation under the influence of trans and nonbinary movements. But an equally important revelation from Painter's "Life Record" is the complex admixture of intimacy and commerce enabled by urban capitalism that allowed new relations to emerge and develop between men. The tropes and formulas of consumer capitalism and the service economy provided a blueprint for a variety of informal semi-underground networks and connections that enabled commercial sex between men. Sites of mass public leisure (bars, pools, beaches, public playgrounds), the mail-order consumer industry, emerging public representation of male nudity, and new technologies of image-making and reproduction all became vital ingredients in shaping modern gay subcultures. In reading the diary of Thomas N. Painter, a self-identified queer man and a lifelong client of male sex workers, one encounters a rich firsthand illustration of a central thesis of the social theory of sexuality—the profound connection between capitalism and gay identity (D'Emilio, 1983).

References

Ben, P. (2018). Global modernity and sexual science: The case of male homosexuality and female prostitution, 1880–1950. In V. Fuechtner, D. E. Haynes, & R. M. Jones (Eds.), *A global history of sexual science, 1880–1960* (pp. 29–50). Oakland, CA: University of California Press.

Boris, E., & Parreñas, R. S. (Eds.). (2010). *Intimate labors: Cultures, technologies, and the politics of care*. Stanford, CA: Stanford University Press.

Chauncey, G. (1994). *Gay New York: Gender, urban culture, and the making of the gay male world, 1890–1940*. New York: Basic Books.

Deleuze, G. (1991). *Masochism: Coldness and cruelty*. New York: Zone Books.

D'Emilio, J. (1983). Capitalism and gay identity. In A. Snitnow, C. Stansell, & S. Thompson (Eds.), *Powers of desire: The politics of sexuality*. New York: Monthly Review Press.

Dyer, R. (2002). *The culture of queers*. London: Routledge.

Earle, S., & Sharpe, K. (2008). Intimacy, pleasure, and the men who pay for sex. In G. Letherby, et al. (Eds.), *Sex as crime?* (pp. 63–79). New York: Routledge.

Friedman, M. (2003). *Strapped for cash: A history of American hustler culture*. Los Angeles: Alyson.

Gardiner, J. (1992). *A class apart: The private pictures of Montague Glover*. London: Serpent's Tail.

Healey, D. (2001). Masculine purity and "gentlemen's mischief": Sexual exchange and prostitution between Russian men, 1861–1941. *Slavic Review, 60*(2), 233–265.

Henry, G. W. (1948). *Sex variants: A study of homosexual patterns*. New York: Paul L. Hoeber. First published 1941.

Hersoh, A. (1918) *Autobiography of an Androgyne*. New York: Medico-legal Journal.

Herring, S. (2007). *Queering the underworld: Slumming, literature, and the undoing of lesbian and gay history*. Chicago: University of Chicago Press.

Houlbrook, M. (2005). *Queer London: Perils and pleasures in the sexual metropolis, 1918–1957*. Chicago: University of Chicago Press.

Kaye, K. (2004). Male prostitution in the twentieth century: Pseudohomosexuals, hoodlum homosexuals, and exploited teens. *Journal of Homosexuality, 46*(1–2), 1–77.

Koven, S. (2004). *Slumming: Sexual and social politics in Victorian London*. Princeton, NJ: Princeton University Press.

Marcus, S. (1964). *The other Victorians: A study of sexuality and pornography in mid-nineteenth-century England*. New York: Basic Books.

Milrod, C., & Monto, M. A. (2012). The hobbyist and the girlfriend experience: Behaviors and preferences of male customers of Internet sexual service providers. *Deviant Behavior, 33*(10), 792–810.

Murphy, K. P. (2008). *Political manhood: Red bloods, mollycoddles, and the politics of progressive era reform*. New York: Columbia University Press.

Painter, T. (1942). Painter's *male homosexuals and their prostitutes*. Unpublished.

Painter, T. (1961). *Moral code*. Unpublished.

Pattinson, J. P. (2002). The man who was Walter. *Victorian Literature and Culture, 30*(1), 19–40.

Peiss, K. (1986). *Cheap amusements: Working women and leisure in turn-of-the-century New York*. Philadelphia: Temple University Press.

Peniston, W. A. (2004). *Pederasts and others: Urban culture and sexual identity in nineteenth-century Paris*. New York: Harrington Park Press.

Peniston, W. A., & Erber, N. (Eds.). (2007). *Queer lives: Men's autobiographies from nineteenth-century France*. Lincoln: University of Nebraska Press.

Proust, M. (2004). *The fugitive*. New York: Viking.

Sanders, T. (2008). Male sexual scripts: Intimacy, sexuality, and pleasure in the purchase of commercial sex. *Sociology, 42*(3), 400–417.

Spring, J. (2010.) *Secret historian: The life and times of Samuel Steward, professor, tattoo artist, and sexual renegade*. New York: Farrar, Straus and Giroux.

Spring, J. (2011a). *An obscene diary: The visual world of Sam Steward*. New York: Antinous Press.

Spring, J. (2011b). *Obscene diary: The secret archive of Samuel Steward, professor, tattoo artist, pornographer.* Exhibition curated by Justin Spring and Sarah Forbes. The Museum of Sex, New York. July 14, 2011—January 15, 2012.

Steward, S. (1991). *Understanding male hustler.* New York: Taylor & Francis.

Waugh, T. (1996). *Hard to imagine: Gay male eroticism in photography and film from their beginnings to Stonewall.* New York: Columbia University Press.

Zikratyy, Y. (2013). *Cross-class escape and the erotics of "proletarian" masculinity in Thomas Painter's sexual record and visual archive* (PhD dissertation). Concordia University, Montreal.

11

Male sex work in comics and graphic novels

Representations from an emerging genre

Dale Corvino

In both fine and popular art forms, there is a shift away from prevailing narratives centering on voices of privilege (by wealth, status, class, race, and/or gender) and toward a broader representation of and by marginalized people. Writers and artists from backgrounds long underrepresented in literature are gaining increasing acceptance and readership. They bring to the fore new voices, bring complexity to story lines and nuance to characters often reduced to stereotype. Nigerian-born novelist Chimamanda Adichie is known for her lyrical novels as well as her lecture "The Danger of the Single Story," in which she asserts, "The problem with stereotypes is not that they are untrue, but that they are incomplete." While stereotypes of many types of marginalized people persist, the problem is particularly acute with prevailing representations of male sex workers.

Michael Morgan, a prolific researcher of media effects, draws this conclusion from decades of research: "I think the moral argument is self-evident. Stories matter. Stories affect how we live our lives, how we see other people, how we think about ourselves." From the research on the effects of under- and misrepresentation, one may conclude that robust representation is merely a corrective to past deficiencies, but writer Gabrielle Bellot articulates an affirmative case for the project of queer representation: "Our literature has offered a vision to the world of the possibilities that may exist within each person, of our ability to resist and persist, of our ability to make and remake ourselves, even in the face of unspeakable pain." The shift toward broader representation expands our culture, and the inclusion of sex workers' narratives that present a more complicated picture than prevailing stereotypes is a part of this expansion. In the concise language of Twitter hashtags, representation matters.

Male sex workers may well face additional challenges when claiming space for their representation. The problem of disclosure is often primary to sex workers, compounding the risks that queer authors may face. In countries with oppressive laws against queer representation, merely speaking out or promoting certain content can subject individuals to prosecution or violence. In the United States, which has made progress toward attaining legislative as well as representational equality, many states still allow employment discrimination based on sexual orientation and/or gender identity; there are cases of schoolteachers being fired for expressing their identity, as well as cases of teachers being doxxed and subsequently fired for prior sex work.

The past two generations of writers have expanded the scope of male sex worker representation not only by countering stereotypes but also by representing the under-, mis-, and unrepresented in popular genres such as science fiction, young adult novels, and comics. The absence of particular characters and narratives in a given genre compounds the problem of persistent stereotypes. The existence of a body of sci-fi works without queer characters or story lines, for example, tacitly implies a queerless future; the picture is incomplete. In the works appraised in this chapter, writers and artists have engaged the popular comic genre to counter persistent stereotypes with immediate, explicit, and detailed characterizations and narratives.

Graphic novels and comic books: superhero hustlers

A comic book or graphic novel typically advances narratives with a combination of image and text: expositional blocks, dialogue bubbles, framed sequences of drawings, and insets. While a comic book is typically serialized, a graphic novel is a stand-alone volume. One of the strengths of the medium is the graphic depiction of bodies in motion, a strength that lends itself to the sexually graphic scenes of much adult content. Comic books are perhaps best known for the supernatural abilities of their superheroes, anthropomorphic content for both children and adults, and humor, whereas political and social commentary are typically the purview of serial comic strips and single-panel comics appearing in newspapers and magazines.

While comics in the West date back to the early nineteenth century and the advent of mass printing of newspapers and periodicals, the emergence of queer content in comics is far more recent. Comic artist Justin Hall surveyed the emergent queer comic subgenre, tracing its origin to the early 1950s and Tom of Finland's illustrations for *Physique Pictorial* and other titles. During the queer liberation movement of the 1970s, underground queer comic content flourished in San Francisco and other centers of queer life. Founded there in 1980 was the long-running anthology *Gay Comix*, which brought the emergent underground queer content to a wider audience. In the 1990s, mainstream comic publisher DC Marvel sought to capitalize on the popularity of underground content with the establishment of Vertigo Comics, an imprint for adult-themed graphic novels. Since Hall's 2013 survey of the landscape of queer comics, the subgenre has burgeoned, and some creators (for example, Alison Bechdel, creator of *Dykes to Watch Out For* and *Fun Home*; Germany's Ralf König) have gained wide mainstream audiences.

Representation of male sex workers in comics and graphic novels has come about far more recently than it has in literature; it is part of the burgeoning scope of the queer subgenre. For male sex workers, comics can be an accessible medium for telling stories based on true experiences without endangering individuals by disclosing their identities. The medium also allows for tighter creative control by the author or artist than is possible with highly collaborative and expensive endeavors such as film or television. The creative production of most of the comics considered in this chapter was in the hands of one or two individuals, many with professed experience in sex work. This aspect of artistic control may well insulate the creative process from commercial pressures, which tend to reinforce stereotypes.

A groundbreaking work representing male sex work in comic-book form is 1996's graphic novel *Seven Miles a Second*, developed by the artist and writer David Wojnarowicz with artist James Romberger and colorist Marguerite Van Cook, and first published by Vertigo Comics. The publication of *Seven Miles a Second* helped establish Vertigo as an adult, alternative-leaning imprint; the source material was decidedly outside the bounds of the industry's self-enforced standards, the Comic Code, and therefore unsuitable for a mainstream imprint. The story told is of teenage Wojnarowicz's destitution and despair in the face of his surroundings. It is told in first-person, confessional mode. In the first half, the narrator recounts, in the past tense, his start

as a teenage hustler. From the outset, desire and longing are entwined with violence and degradation; his first customer goads him into watching through a peephole as a female sex worker
services her customer, while the narrator himself is serviced by his customer. In a graphically
powerful frame, the female sex worker turns around to reveal extensive slash marks on her torso,
which the narrator describes as "fresh wounds" (Figure 11.1). The teen is thus introduced to sex
work alongside voyeurism and menacing violence.

Figure 11.1 Panel depicting the narrator's gruesome introduction to sex work, in *Seven Miles a
Second*, David Wojnarowicz, James Romberger, and Marguerite Von Cook, 1996.

In the second part of the book, the narrator switches to present tense to document the effect of prolonged, AIDS-related illness on his body and spirit and the impact of the epidemic on his circle of friends. He sinks into an apocalyptic rage against the cruelties of the universe, in particular, the government's indifference to gay men's suffering. The work exploits the potential of comic art to convey a story in frames while amplifying the emotional impact, in this case, of monstrous cruelty and suffering. For the illustrations, the artist Romberger summoned his experience in illustrating the horrors of oppressive urban poverty in his work for *World War 3*, a comics series that provided social and political commentary on the issues affecting New York's East Village during the Reagan era.

Wojnarowicz stoked controversy in the art world of his day by making overtly political statements denouncing the U.S. government's homophobia and lack of action in response to the AIDS epidemic. In the graphic novel treatment of *Seven Miles a Second*, Wojnarowicz and Romberger subverted the comic form by using its pulpy effects to convey Wojnarowicz's suffering. Comic books in the superhero genre typically depict a central character who, through some accident of fate, is heroically transformed and bestowed with special powers. Wojnarowicz achieves his special power during his teenage hustler years through the repeated degradations of his body and spirit. His suffering gives him the vision to see the world for what it is.

Wojnarowicz worked on *Seven Miles a Second* and other collaborative projects until he died of AIDS in 1992; the final section of the graphic novel was completed by his collaborators Romberger and Marguerite Van Cook. Wojnarowicz's demand that his suffering serve his art echoes a major theme in the work of French writer and hustler Jean Genet. In *Journal du voleur (The Thief's Journal)*, Genet outlines his aesthetic mission: "If I cannot have the most brilliant destiny, I want the most wretched, not for the purpose of a sterile solitude, but in order to achieve something new with such rare matter." As a representation of male sex workers, Wojnarowicz chronicles the abjection of his teenage self facing the disaffection and poverty that led him into sex work, and the transformation of his suffering into art.

The Japanese term *manga* broadly corresponds to the comics genre. While the history of manga dates back to twelfth-century scrolls that combine drawings and text, as with Western comics, there are categories of manga for many sorts of readers: children, teens, and adults. There is a huge body of erotica, much of which explores kinks, fetishes, and the taboo. A subgenre of manga erotica called *yaoi*, or boy's love (BL), is centered on male same-sex pairings and commonly features story lines about fetishes or taboo subjects. The *yaoi* genre is largely targeted toward women readers who are aroused by homoerotica.

The prolific *yaoi* creator Kano Miyamoto has explored male sex work in one of her series. *Say Please*, which is available in an English-language translation, features a male sex worker protagonist. While the text is translated into English, the graphic frames are printed as they are read in the original Japanese, from right to left. The character Ryoichi is a young sex worker operating out of a *urisen*, or male brothel. He is hired by Sakura, a closeted high school teacher, for the night, but the two wind up spending a week together after Ryoichi negotiates a rate with Sakura without involving the brothel (a practice described as "stiffing the house"). The two characters enter into an emotionally fraught and passionate entanglement that threatens the teacher's job and the male sex worker's sexual autonomy. In the *yaoi* context, the sex work aspect of the narrative serves as a device to throw a boyish young man together with a young professional, and it contributes to the forbidden aspect of their pairing.

The graphic style of *Say Please*, printed in black and white, includes sparely linear frames, closely observed details of intimacy, and an atmospheric use of shading to convey mood (Figure 11.2). Many of the pages include angular and overlapping frames, splicing together setting, action, and detail. The frames depicting sexual interactions between Sakura and Ryoichi

Figure 11.2 Panel depicting the offsite negotiation ("stiffing the house") between Ryoichi and Sakura, from *Say Please*, Kano Miyamoto, 2008.

explore the shifting power dynamics in their initially transactional pairing, as the emotional arc bends from cruelty and obsession toward dominance and revulsion. As is common in *yaoi*, rape is depicted in *Say Please* as a kink fantasy; after being forcibly penetrated by a sexually frenzied Sakura, Ryoichi agrees to return "tomorrow," that is, for another encounter. Also as is common in *yaoi*, the younger male, Ryoichi, is androgynous, permitting representations of sex acts to flutter between homosexual and heterosexual interpretations.

Presenting a contrast to the brooding, emotionally fraught style of the Japanese *yaoi Say Please* is the full-color, pornographic comic series *Satisfaction Guaranteed*, drawn and written by Canadian homoerotic artist Patrick Fillion. In this series, an evil pimp, Laburnum, controls the lives of a stable of male escorts through the machinations of his corporation, the SG Corp. The protagonist, Elias Shelby, is a young accountant unwittingly sold into servitude by his financially strained uncle. Each of the other escorts depicted has woeful backstory. They are different types, though all are idealized. Elias is rescued from his anguish over his downfall by Dane, another escort. These studs-in-distress are all locked into airtight contracts and have no choice but to service SG Corp.'s wealthy, sadistic clients in repeated acts of sexual debasement. By the end of the series, Elias plots to take the SG Corp. away from Laburnum and enslave him in revenge for his years of cruelty, and Dane has fallen in love with the bearish client who has secretly provided Elias with the financing for his hostile takeover.

The plot allows for repeat depictions of extreme sexual encounters, each involving a measure of coercion. Stylized depictions of common fetishes (bondage, restraint, BDSM) serve the series' central motif: wealth as the ultimate dominating force over the individual. The drawing style of the series is vivid, glossy, and explicit, and the escorts are drawn as hypermasculine ideals, showing influences of the work of Tom of Finland. Even supernatural characters (elves, devils, clowns) are idealized; all are impossibly well-endowed, muscular sexual athletes. As a depiction of sex workers' lives, the comic grapples with real-life themes of financial motivation, personal agency, and relationship dynamics, albeit in a highly exaggerated, fictionalized context.

Another full-color homoerotic comic series, *Payday*, was written and drawn by Sunny Victor, the pseudonym of a creator who has his own disclosure challenges because he resides in a country with oppressive laws and social prohibitions against homosexual depictions. *Payday* brings readers the story of Adrian, a self-actualized, upscale escort. In the course of the narrative, Adrian creates a myth around himself as the most exclusive and upscale escort—before he even meets one client. The hype proves to be irresistible for wealthy men who feel they deserve only the best.

In the first issue, Adrian is both narrator and protagonist. He recounts his origin story to a new client, a well-known author who wishes to write about Adrian's experiences. There are layers of representation, as Adrian is telling the story of telling his story, so that it can be told, in fictionalized form, to a wider audience. This frame-within-a-frame narrative device provides voyeuristic readers with an idealized story of an male sex worker who has access to wealth and luxury.

The style of the artwork in *Payday* is crisp, with sharp line drawings and realistic shading and color. The frames are episodic, of mostly static scenes, with breaks denoting action or dramatic emphasis; there are occasional insets for sexually graphic detail. Action is conveyed in sequential frames and from multiple points of view. Adrian's body is drawn as perfectly sculpted and with large genitals, though not to the exaggerated degree of the figures in *Satisfaction Guaranteed*. The story's jet-set global destinations are drafted with precision. In contrast to the other works' harrowing stories of economically stranded teen boys who have little agency in their sex work, Adrian is economically advantaged, college educated, and calculating; his first client offers to buy him a house after Adrian turns him down repeatedly. Despite Adrian's performance of mild sexual submission for his enthralled wealthy clients, *Payday* depicts an idealized fantasy of a sex worker who has ultimate agency—the power to create his own reality from his imagination.

Room for Love, a graphic novel, is a passion project of the British artist known as ILYA, who has created work for such major comics publishers as Marvel, DC, and Dark Horse, as well as manga for the Japanese market. Set in London, *Room for Love* opens on the separate lives of Cougar, a homeless Irish street hustler, and Pamela, a lonely, middle-aged romance novelist who has run out of romantic stories. The panels depicting Pamela's cozy yet sterile milieu are done in cool blue tones, while Cougar's life on the streets is represented in warm sepia shades. After Pamela's unwitting actions lead to Cougar's eviction from his sleeping place under a bridge, she invites him to live with her. Their unlikely romance is depicted in blended gray-colored panels. The spare drawing style and color coding drive the narrative's examinations of identity and intimacy.

Pamela's illusion of romance crashes when her gay male friend recognizes Cougar as a fellow queer, and Cougar reveals to Pamela that he is "not just a boy, a boy you can enjoy, a rent boy!" While Cougar sparks Pamela's creativity anew, Pamela offers Cougar an escape from his identification as someone for whom love is "professional, transactional." In *Room for Love*'s depiction of male sex workers, the realm of the hardened street hustler and the cozy comforts of a middle-class writer collide. From Cougar's perspective, their story is largely transactional—the titular room is provided to him in exchange for intimacy—whereas Pamela sees their pairing as her making room for love in her life, which is as drained of love as it is of romance story lines. Pamela meditates presumptuously on their relationship and how it has refueled her creative output.

Although the contours of the story bring nuance to the representation of male sex workers—Cougar identifies as gay, yet finds he is able to perform intimately with a woman (under the right inducements), while Pamela's unawareness of Cougar's sex work history blurs the boundaries between the transactional and the personal—at its core, *Room for Love* is the story of a young migrant street worker with limited options who, once Pamela learns of his sex work, reveals his history of sexual abuse. While perpetuating a stereotype of male sex workers as damaged, as incapable of and undeserving of love, the story illustrates how two parties in a relationship—whether transactional, personal, or somewhere in between—can operate under divergent understandings of the terms of that relationship.

The Lengths, another independently produced graphic novel rendered in black and white, was written and drawn by Howard Hardiman, a British graphic artist. Originally self-published in installments, the complete story was published in 2013 by Soaring Penguin, a UK-based publisher of graphic novels. This graphic novel centers on Eddie, an art-school dropout who is drawn to escorting by his encounters with Nelson, a successful, muscle-bound escort who takes on the role of Eddie's mentor. Hardiman, who has acknowledged his own experience with sex work during college, carried out extensive research to create *The Lengths*, interviewing male sex workers in London about their beginnings, work practices, highlights, and low points.

In nonsequential, alternating sequences, *The Lengths* examines Eddie's double life. He and his circle of friends and lovers index his relationship struggles and the circumstances that led him to drop out of school. Eddie is depicted as a well-meaning, somewhat adrift young man who bounces from one relationship to another. In his interactions with Nelson, the reader is introduced to "Ford," Eddie's escort persona, as Nelson brings him in on calls with his clients, helps him to set expectations, and advises him on how to market himself. In advising Eddie to get a second phone, Nelson seeks to impart the importance of keeping one's sex work and personal life in separate silos, but Eddie struggles with the strict separation. His newest romantic partner, Dave, finds out that he is escorting, and Dave accepts his partner's career. They use "weird hours" as a catch-all euphemism in discussing Eddie's sex work.

Much of the story in *The Lengths* is told in flashbacks, and there is no exposition other than the inclusion of the characters' profiles on "Trackr" (a dating app loosely based on Grindr) and occasional glimpses of text messages on a phone screen (Figure 11.3). In the online era, technology is a pervasive frame; the isolating nature of contemporary sex work, once relegated to the streets and now virtual, is a major theme. Absent a narrator, most of the scenes are drawn from the point of view of Eddie's interlocutors, with occasional switches to Eddie's view of the scene. This choice positions the reader somewhere in the frame as Eddie navigates his split existence. It has the effect of keeping the reader close to Eddie in his struggle to maintain his dual life and his search for intimacy and purpose. In the absence of expository blocks, all of the text is dialogue. Eschewing speech bubbles, most of the dialogue floats in the blank space of the frame, imparting a weightlessness to the exchanges.

A prevalent motif of the comic form is anthropomorphism, commonly the use of animal characters with human drives and motives. One highly regarded example of anthropomorphized characters deployed in the service of telling adult stories is *Maus*, a graphic novel by Art Spiegelman. In his treatment of his father's experience in Poland during the Holocaust, Spiegelman depicted Nazis as cats, Jews as mice, and the complicit Poles as rabbits. Another well-known example is R. Crumb's underground sensation *Fritz the Cat*, a comic strip featuring a horny, neurotic feline who lives in a city populated by other animals. In *The Lengths*, all the characters are drawn as dogs of varying breeds. Eddie resembles a bull terrier, Nelson is a mastiff with cropped ears, and Dan, Eddie's newest partner, is a shaggy-faced schnauzer. Though the characters have canine heads, they have mostly human bodies. Hardiman has stated that he based his characters on sex workers he's known, and that rendering the characters as dogs not only made for easier graphic identification but also dispelled potential problems of disclosure.

American comic-book author and tattoo artist Dave Davenport has tackled the topic of male sex work, notably in his homoerotic series *Hard to Swallow*, a compilation cocreated with Justin Hall and published by queer comics publisher Northwest Press. Of his interest in male sex workers, Davenport has stated, "I've known sex workers at all points of my life . . . and I may

Figure 11.3 Panel depicting "Trackr" profiles of the main characters in *The Lengths*, Howard Hardiman, 2013.

have had to hustle to make the rent. . . . It's a part of life, it always has been, and always will be. It needs to be a part of comics as well."

The *Hard to Swallow* series' pages are printed in black and white, with full-color covers. Set in Fogtown, a fictionalized locale that blends features of San Francisco and Santa Cruz, the series features a trio of characters with interwoven story lines. Doug is a compact young tough who works as a stripper at a gay club. He has a special bond with two supernatural characters: Grant, a preppie gay man who transforms into a sexually ravenous werewolf (Feral), and Mitch (the Ghost Skater), a skateboarding former lover of Doug's, who after his death was transformed into a horny ghost. With each story line, the characters' unashamed, raucous sexuality is an instrument of resolution. After rescuing Doug from danger, the supernatural characters engage in a three-way with him.

Doug's work as a stripper roots the comic's supernatural action in the gritty reality of sweaty sets, groping customers, and jockstraps stuffed with bills. The conceit that a gay male stripper is linked to the supernatural is an affirming depiction of a male sex worker, as it connects gay sexual agency and autonomy to the heroic. For this series Davenport employs a loose style of thick-lined cartoons with heavy shading. The pages are densely drawn, with runaway and overlapping frames. Sex is graphically depicted as rowdy and very much enjoyed, while danger takes the form of homophobic street punks. The overall effect of the energetic drawing style reinforces the sex and sex-work positivity of the series.

Davenport also collaborated with New York–based male sex worker Bryan Knight on the creation of *Velvet Collar*, which is planned as a series, although to date only the first issue has been published. Like many of the works discussed in this chapter, *Velvet Collar* was published independently; its full-color production was financed through crowdsourcing. In expository blocks, *Velvet Collar* provides background on the personal lives of five different male sex workers. The story was written by Knight; each main character is based on an actual male sex worker (escort, porn performer, dancer) who consented to participate in the project or is a composite based on two participating male sex workers. Where necessary, names have been changed to avoid disclosure, while individuals' likenesses are fairly closely rendered by Davenport from photos and videos.

Davenport's hand in drawing *Velvet Collar* is tighter than in *Hard to Swallow*, perhaps because there are more characters and interwoven stories to depict. The characters are faithfully rendered and colored, and the New York City settings are drafted with precision. The story is told sequentially, in the third-person present tense; the reader shifts from one main character's individual story to the next via a chain of phone calls made to gather the group to attend an event at the offices of Rentman, depicted as the world's largest online escort listing service. This narrative device centers on technology, reflecting the new reality of online sex work. As in *Hard to Swallow*, the sex—both personal and transactional—is depicted as explicit, raucous fun.

Part of the mission of *Velvet Collar* is to depict male sex workers as fully realized protagonists with complex emotional lives. The series follows the lives of five different workers who represent a diverse range of ethnicities, body types, and ages. The character Abel Rey is based on a Latino male sex worker active in New York. In his frames, he is seen arguing with a love interest who has "discovered" that he's a sex worker, despite his previous disclosure of this "on (their) second date." The sequence, charged with both emotion and sexual heat, resolves with Abel saying, "Other people pay cash, all you have do is pay attention." The sequence highlights the challenges male sex workers may face in navigating intimate, nontransactional relationships.

The character Billy is shown in the midst of a call with a submissive client who worships his hairy body and large belly. Billy is a "bear" type; his depiction runs counter to pervasive stereotypes of male sex workers as paragons of physical perfection, or as ephebic ideals (*ephebe* is the Greek term for a beautiful male youth on the cusp of manhood). The character named Rica Shay is a composite, partly inspired by a Los Angeles–based gay hip-hop performer and dancer. Frames depict him saying good-bye to a loving partner while pursuing his career as a performer, which is in turn financed by his sex work. In his interactions with a regular customer, it is made clear that the customer is well aware of Rica Shay's musical ambition and fully supports it. The character is depicted as successfully navigating a relationship, his creative aspirations, and his sex-work client's expectations.

The fourth male sex worker character, Storm, is based on the true experience of a "downlow" escort who requested that Knight withhold his name and likeness. He is African American, married with a wife and child; in the opening sequence, the separate silos of his life as male sex worker and as a father and husband come crashing down when his young daughter announces, "Dad, I know you're a prostitute," as he is getting ready to take her to school. Storm had been able to conceal his sex work from his family until he agreed to be photographed. This story grapples with deeper questions of disclosure in the lives of male sex workers. While his daughter is understanding, his wife raises potential serious consequences: "If child services finds out, they'll take her away from you."

The last of the quintet of male sex worker characters is Scott, a.k.a. Daddy. Daddy is actively working, both as a trapeze instructor and a sex worker, at the age of 62. This character is also a composite, drawing from the experience of an acquaintance of Knight's with 40 years of sex work experience, a "veteran" whose longevity defies the expectations and stereotypes of male sex workers. These five male sex workers convene at the launch party for an ad campaign in which they are featured at the offices of Rentman, on the occasion of the company's twentieth anniversary. The party is interrupted by a raid, depicting in thinly veiled fictional form the true events surrounding the federal prosecution of Rentboy.com in 2015. Federal agents in black crash the party and overrun the office with force (Figure 11.4). The five central characters, who are just coming around the corner, are astonished to see Rentman's handcuffed employees being perp-walked toward a police cruiser.

Of his motive for writing *Velvet Collar*, Knight has said,

> Right now gays are in the mainstream, we have marriage, and part of that strategy has been desexualizing everything we are[,] so this particular comic pushes us back into that realm where sex and identity are intertwined. . . . [T]he narratives of acceptance have been, "We're just like you!" but the truth is, we're not. . . . [A] lot of naked truths get exposed.

Figure 11.4 Cover illustration depicting the raid on the offices of Rentman. From *Velvet Collar*, Bryan Knight and Dave Davenport, 2017.

Beyond this mission, and that of expanding the representation of male sex workers to include men of different ages, races, ethnicities, and body types, there's a clear effort to document the new focus on criminalizing and prosecuting sex workers' online spaces. The illustration on the cover of *Velvet Collar* depicts the founder of Rentman bound up in yellow crime-scene tape. While the depiction is stylistic and graphically dynamic, it accurately conveys the circumstance of Jeffrey Hurant, the real-life founder of Rentboy, who, after being arrested and charged with promoting prostitution and conspiracy to commit money laundering, was convicted and sentenced to six months in federal prison. In a Department of Justice press release, the acting U.S. attorney who prosecuted the case described the business as an "Internet brothel."

Before it was shuttered, Rentboy was the single largest global advertising platform for male sex workers; its splash page around the time of the raid promised access to "over 10,500 men in 2,100+ cities worldwide." Prior to the 2015 arrests, it had operated without any significant scrutiny from federal authorities. The Rentboy raid was part of a coordinated law enforcement effort to shut down sex workers' online presence (Backpage, a major platform for female sex workers, was later also seized by federal authorities). In the aftermath of the seizures of Rentboy and Backpage, sex workers have attested to facing more dangerous situations and having less agency over their lives since the loss of those established, verifiable platforms.

Law enforcement officials commonly justify this new targeting of online content as necessary in order to prevent the sex trafficking of minors, a view that conflates adult, consensual sex work with coerced victims of child trafficking. This conflation is evident in a 2014 Issue Paper from the United Nations on the topic, in which the authors assert that "consent is always irrelevant to determining whether the crime of human trafficking has occurred." *Velvet Collar* chronicles a new era for sex work in which once-stable online platforms have left all sex workers scrambling for platforms free from scrutiny.

Conclusion

In a short span of time—just over two decades—representations of male sex work in this accessible, popular medium have done much to counter stereotypes. Authors and artists who are male sex workers have found varied solutions to problems of disclosure while grappling with major themes of identity and agency. This body of work offers detailed and often nuanced takes on how male sex workers negotiate complicated dualities of exploitation and freedom, longing and intimacy. The comics and graphic novels examine the perils and pleasures of a working life at the margins of personal autonomy and legality, and they have indexed a period of transition in male sex work from the mean streets to the open frontiers of the Internet, and on to the present reality of criminalized online spaces.

Bibliography and reference lists

Bellot, G. (2016, November 18). Queer writers in the age of Trump. *The Atlantic*. Retrieved from www.theatlantic.com/entertainment/archive/2016/11/queer-writers-in-the-age-of-trump/507854/

Boboltz, S., & Yam, K. (2017, February 24). Why on-screen representation actually matters [article quoting Michael Morgan]. *Huffington Post*. Retrieved from www.huffingtonpost.com/entry/why-on-screen-representation-matters_us_58aeae96e4b01406012fe49d

Carr, C. (2014). *Fire in the belly: The life and times of David Wojnarowicz*. New York: Bloomsbury Press.

Corvino, D. (2017, November 1). *Velvet collar*: The Rentboy raid inspired comic book. *Tits & Sass*. Retrieved from http://titsandsass.com/velvet-collar-the-rentboy-raid-inspired-comic-book/

Garcia, Ramon. (2003). Interview with John Rechy. *The Free Library*. Retrieved from www.thefreelibrary.com/Interview+with+John+Rechy.-a0104681248.

Genet, J. (1965). *The thief's journal.* London: Blond.

Hall, J. (2013). *No straight lines: Four decades of queer comics.* Seattle: Fantagraphics Books.

Istrati, P., & Sawyer-Lauçanno, C. (2010). *Kyra Kyralina.* Greenfield, MA: Talisman House.

Kordic, A., Pereira, L., & Martinique, E. (2016, September 24). A short history of Japanese manga. *Widewalls Editorial.* Retrieved from www.widewalls.ch/japanese-manga-comics-history/

Ngozi, C. (2009). The danger of the single story. *TEDGlobal.* Retrieved from www.ted.com/talks/chimamanda_adichie_the_danger_of_a_single_story/transcript

Rechy, J., et al. (1973). An interview with John Rechy. *Chicago Review, 25*(1). Retrieved from www.jstor.org/stable/25294804

Rudick, N. (2013, May 8). "This brighter path": An interview with James Romberger and Marguerite Van Cook. *Comics Journal.* Retrieved from www.tcj.com/an-interview-with-james-romberger-marguerite-van-cook/

Senate Committee on the Judiciary. (1955). *Comic books and juvenile delinquency, interim report.* Washington, DC: U.S. Government Printing Office. Retrieved from www.thecomicbooks.com/1955senateinterim.html

Sneddon, L. (2013, October 13). Comics interview: Howard Hardiman on "The Lengths." *New Statesman America.* Retrieved from www.newstatesman.com/cultural-capital/2013/10/comics-interview-howard-hardiman-lengths

United Nations Office on Drugs and Crime. (2014). *The role of "consent" in the trafficking of persons protocol* [issue paper]. Retrieved from www.unodc.org/documents/human-trafficking/2014/UNODC_2014_Issue_Paper_Consent.pdf

U.S. Department of Justice, U.S. Attorney's Office, Eastern District of New York. (2015, August 25). *Largest online male escort service raided.* [press release]. Retrieved from www.justice.gov/usao-edny/pr/largest-online-male-escort-service-raided.

A Chronology of Male Sex Workers in Fiction, Nonfiction, and Comics and Graphic Novels

Entries are listed in order of their discussion in the chapter. Asterisks indicate author(s) with stated experience in sex work.

Fiction

Kyra Kyralina, Panait Istrati, 1924. The earliest representation of a male sex worker in modern literature. A vagabond recounts his youth as the kept boy of a young and sensual Turkish bey during the waning days of the Ottoman Empire.

The Hustler, John Henry MacKay, 1926. Set in Weimar-era Berlin, this novel chronicles a young man's attraction to a homeless teenage hustler.

★*Notre Dame des fleurs* (*Our Lady of the Flowers*), Jean Genet, 1943. Written in prison, Genet's debut novel chronicles his experience in the Parisian homosexual underworld of hustlers, pimps, and drag queens. Its erotically charged, free-flowing prose sets forth Genet's transvaluation of betrayal as devotion and the eroticism of the abject.

★*Journal du voleur* (*The Thief's Journal*), Jean Genet, 1949. Genet's third novel, also autobiographical, recounts a series of romantic entanglements and his career as a hustler and a thief throughout 1930s Europe.

Last Exit to Brooklyn, Hubert Selby Jr., 1957. A collection of interrelated tales of working-class life in 1950s Sunset Park, Brooklyn, capturing a milieu of sexual violence, street gangs, drugs, and sex work. Features the character of Georgette, a female-presenting male sex worker.

★*City of Night*, John Rechy, 1963. Rechy's breakthrough autobiographical novel, drawn from his career as a hustler in New York and Hollywood, examines the longings of his "scores" and the systemic oppression of the gay underworld.

Midnight Cowboy, James Leo Herlihy, 1965. A meditation on loneliness, the novel presents the story of Joe Buck, a Texan stud with a sexual past rooted in trauma, who travels to New York to make it as a hustler. There he bonds with a disabled con man named Ratso, only to lose him to pneumonia on a bus ride to Florida.

★*$tud*, Phil Andros (Samuel Steward), 1966. A collection of erotic tales about Phil Andros, the titular stud for hire. In his travels to major American cities, he explores various kinks and fetishes, and larger topics, such as race. A chronicler of gay life in the 1960s, Andros unabashedly embraces his outlaw sexuality.

★*Numbers*, John Rechy, 1967. Johnny Rio is an aging hustler who returns to Los Angeles, his old proving ground, after years away, and goes on a mission to rack up numbers in a ten-day period.

★*My Brother, My Self*, Phil Andros (Samuel Steward), 1970. Andros's search for his long-lost twin brother, Dennis Andrews, leads him on a series of erotic adventures.

★*Shuttlecock*, Phil Andros (Samuel Steward), 1972. In Berkeley, California, Andros rescues a hippie from a bad drug trip and subsequently sends him off to the police academy, in order to fulfill his own fantasy of being dominated at the hands of a cop.

Enchanted Boy, Richie McMullen, 1989. An autobiographical novel about a boy growing up in postwar Liverpool who, after experiencing physical and sexual abuse, finds an escape and some agency as a "boy prostitute."

Enchanted Youth, Richie McMullen, 1990. The follow-up to *Enchanted Boy*, depicting the protagonist's teen years as a hustler and his transition to adulthood.

★*Neons*, Denis Belloc, 1991. The stark tale of Denis, whose childhood in rural France in the 1950s was marred by penury and abuse. Finding solace in anonymous sexual encounters in public toilets, he eventually makes his way to Paris and lives a hardened life of sex work and petty crime.

★*Hello, Darling, Are You Working?* Rupert Everett, 1992. A gay farce presenting the fate of ruined soap-opera star and former hustler Rhys Waveral.

Los novios búlgaros (*The Bulgarian Boyfriends*), Eduardo Mendicutti, 1993. A novel presenting the entanglement of a bourgeois gay Spaniard with Kyril, a sex worker, and his tribe of fellow Bulgarian exiles.

Martin and John, Dale Peck, 1994. The story of John, a New York hustler, who falls in love with Martin, a man dying of AIDS, is interwoven with the story with another pair of men with the same names.

Rent Boy, Gary Indiana, 1994. This epistolary novella tracks Danny, a college student and hustler, as he falls in with a black-market organ theft ring.

User, Bruce Benderson, 1994. Set in 1980s New York City, the novel centers on Apollo, a heroin-addicted hustler, as he races through his diminishing options after slashing the bouncer at a Times Square porn theater, disrupting the netherworld he inhabits.

Boy Culture, Matthew Rettenmund, 1996. A rickety love triangle between X, a hustler, and his two roommates, a sexually confused virgin he pursues and the precocious teenage party boy who pursues him.

After Nirvana, Lee Williams, 1997. Set in the Pacific Northwest in the1990s, the novel is narrated by Davey, a street hustler, as he moves between his tricks, his girlfriend, and his boyfriend.

Sarah: A Novel, JT LeRoy, 2000. Narrated by an unnamed boy whose mother, Sarah, is a "lot lizard," or truck-stop prostitute, in West Virginia. Longing for her love, he seeks to outdo her as Cherry Vanilla, his own lot lizard persona.

The Sluts, Dennis Cooper, 2005. Set largely on the pages of an online forum for escorts and their johns, this epistolary novel tracks one escort, Brad, as his review devolves into lurid metafiction.

Setting the Lawn on Fire, Mack Friedman, 2005. The coming-of-age story of Eye, whose journey of sexual discovery takes him to some far-flung places and states of longing, until he pursues his art while supporting himself as a hustler.

Murder Most Fab, Julian Clary, 2008. A comic novel tracking the rise and fall Johnny Debonair, a television star, rent boy, and serial killer.

★*Shuck*, Daniel Allen Cox, 2008. A novel based on the experiences of the author, its episodes center on Javeen, as he navigates his porn and sex work career, his meth addiction, his writing ambitions, and his bond with an obsessed artist.

What Belongs to You, Garth Greenwell, 2016. The story of a lone American in Sofia, Bulgaria, whose encounter with a hustler named Mitko in a public toilet initiates a quest for intimacy laced with abjection.

Nonfiction

★*Close to the Knives*, David Wojnarowicz, 1991. A collection of memoir essays by the artist, recounting his violent childhood, his life on the streets of New York, and his iconoclastic career as an artist.

★*Memories That Smell Like Gasoline*, David Wojnarowicz, 1992. A collection of four autobiographical short stories about the artist's life as a teenage hustler and his public battle against AIDS, with illustrations by Wojnarowicz.

Wonder Bread and Ecstasy: The Life and Death of Joey Stefano, 1996, Charles Isherwood. The tragic tale of Joey Stefano, from his meteoric rise in porn to his death by overdose at age 26.

★*Diary of a Hustler*, Joey (William Maltese) 1997. The story of an 18-year-old operating out of an elite call-boy agency in Las Vegas who finds himself drawn to the agency owner's assistant.

★*Assuming the Position*, Rick Whitaker, 1999. Armed with a degree in philosophy, Whitaker confronts his emotional detachment and drug addiction while hustling in New York in the 1980s.

★*Suburban Hustler: Stories of a Hi-Tech Callboy*, Aaron Lawrence, 1999. A collection of 24 stories chronicling Lawrence's experiences as an escort in suburban New Jersey during the early and open frontier of online interactions.

A Thousand and One Night Stands: The Life of Jon Vincent, H. A. Carson, 2001. Drawn from transcripts of interviews with the subject, this biography of the late bisexual bodybuilder and porn star chronicles his abusive childhood, his stint in professional baseball, his porn career, and his heroin addiction.

★*Chicken: Self-Portrait of a Young Man for Rent*, David Henry Sterry, 2002. Memoir recounting Sterry's vulnerability as a teenager newly arrived in Hollywood, suddenly homeless and preyed upon by sexual assailants, and his becoming a sex worker for women.

Blue Days, Black Nights, Ron Nyswaner, 2004. Nyswaner battles depression despite his success as a screenwriter. When he meets Johann, a leather-clad Hungarian hustler, he is drawn into a prolonged drug binge and romantic obsession.

The Romanian: Story of an Obsession, Bruce Benderson, 2006. Benderson's "erotic autobiography" chronicles his romantic obsession with Romulus, a street hustler he meets in Budapest. While laying bare the economic realities that drive Romulus, a poor migrant, to sex work, the memoir threads examinations of Romanian history and culture with intimate personal and familial narratives.

★*All I Could Bare*, Craig Seymour, 2008. Seymour's memoir of his life as a graduate student in Washington, DC, where he strips at one of the city's notorious gay clubs while navigating his studies, his relationship, and his family life.

★*Hos, Hookers, Call Girls, and Rent Boys: Professionals Writing on Life, Love, Money, and Sex*, edited by David Henry Sterry and R.J. Martin Jr., 2009. A collection of stories from sex workers of all stripes, organized thematically.

★*Full Service*, Scotty Bowers, 2012. Memoir of an ex-marine and gas station attendant who went on to become a sex worker and pimp to the stars of Hollywood.

★*Johns, Marks, Tricks, and Chickenhawks: Professionals and Their Clients Writing about Each Other*, edited by R.J. Martin Jr. and David Henry Sterry, 2013. A second collection of sex-worker stories that includes entries by sex workers' clients.

★*Money's on the Dresser*, Christopher Daniels, 2013. Memoir of a Las Vegas–based porn performer and escort.

★*Prose & Lore: Memoir Stories about Sex Work, Collected Issues 1–5*, edited by Audacia Ray, 2015. A compendium of literary journals from the writing program of the Red Umbrella Project, a now-defunct organization that advocated for the rights of sex workers.

Graphic Novels and Comics

★*Seven Miles a Second*, David Wojnarowicz (author), James Romberger, and Marguerite Van Cook (artists), 1996.

Say Please, Kano Miyamoto (author/artist), 2008.

Satisfaction Guaranteed, Patrick Fillion (author/artist), 2010.

★*The Lengths*, Howard Hardiman (author/artist), 2013.

Payday, Sunny Victor (author/artist), 2013.

Room for Love, ILYA (author/artist), 2015.

Hard to Swallow, Dave Davenport (author/artist), 2016.

★*Velvet Collar*, Bryan Knight (author) and Dave Davenport (artist), 2017.

12

Male sex work in the library collection

Discoveries in the stacks

Robert Ridinger

The idea of identifying a body of writings that reflect the existence and issues of male sex workers in world culture from the nineteenth century to date is complicated by several factors. The very nature of male sex has shifted according to changing social mores over the centuries. Discussions of these men have been rare and, when extant, filtered through the narrators' professional, personal, and philosophical backgrounds. Also, the literature has frequently lumped both male sex workers and female sex workers together under the label of prostitution, obliging those interested in male sex work to sift out relevant case studies and references from more broadly framed discussions. These discussions range from investigations conducted by individual physicians and psychologists as part of their professional writings (for example, Richard von Krafft-Ebing's *Psychopathia Sexualis* and Alfred Kinsey's survey published as *Sexual Behavior in the Human Male*) or by a group commissioned by a political or social organization, as in the case of the 1911 report *The Social Evil in Chicago*.

In addition, paperback pornographic novels published for gay men included many titles featuring stereotyped images of male sex workers, but these novels are frequently difficult to locate and seldom reprinted. We may use these novels' content to track the changing perceptions of male sex workers, both within and outside the gay male community. Literature of the twentieth century has spanned the full range of opinion on male sex work, from the sodomy laws and city, county, and state ordinances to the explosion of gay-affirming publications that arose following the Stonewall Riots of June 1969 and continued into the twenty-first century, some in purely electronic form and including the autobiographies of male sex workers. This chapter examines the growth of this body of writings by surveying representative works generated predominantly in the northern hemisphere from the beginning of the nineteenth century to contemporary times.

In the beginning: the nineteenth century

The Phoenix of Sodom, which appeared as a pamphlet in London in 1813, is one of the earliest monographs in English dealing with an establishment that functioned as a male brothel. In keeping with the literary forms of the time, it has a lengthy subtitle explicating the cryptic nature of the title (Figure 12.1): "The Vere Street coterie: Being an exhibition of the gambols

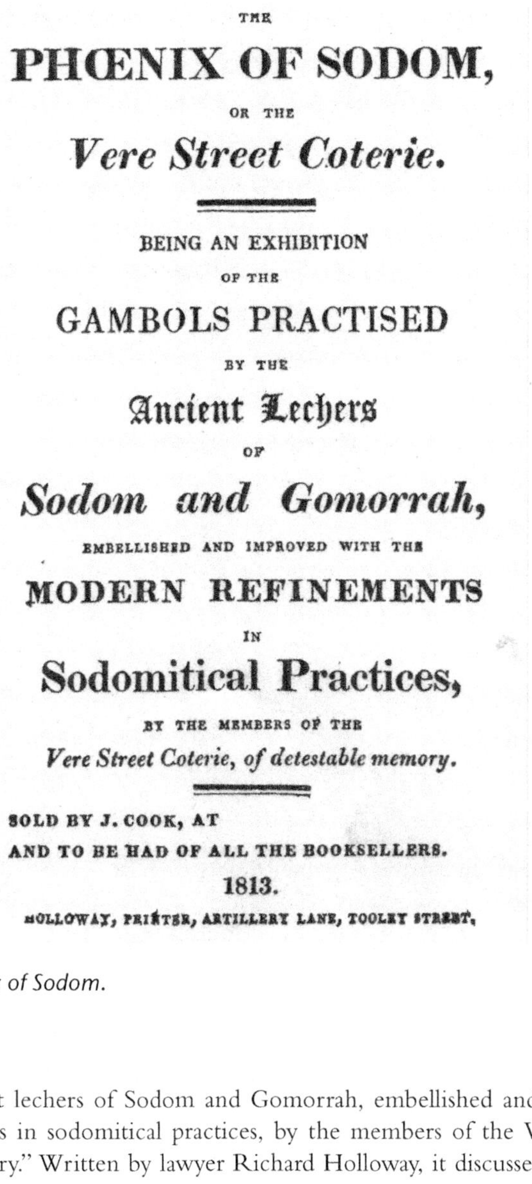

THE

PHŒNIX OF SODOM,

OR THE

Vere Street Coterie.

BEING AN EXHIBITION

OF THE

GAMBOLS PRACTISED

BY THE

𝔄𝔫𝔠𝔦𝔢𝔫𝔱 𝔏𝔢𝔠𝔥𝔢𝔯𝔰

OF

Sodom and Gomorrah,

EMBELLISHED AND IMPROVED WITH THE

MODERN REFINEMENTS

IN

Sodomitical Practices,

BY THE MEMBERS OF THE

Vere Street Coterie, of detestable memory.

SOLD BY J. COOK, AT

AND TO BE HAD OF ALL THE BOOKSELLERS.

1813.

HOLLOWAY, PRINTER, ARTILLERY LANE, TOOLEY STREET,

Figure 12.1   The Phoenix of Sodom.

practised by the ancient lechers of Sodom and Gomorrah, embellished and improved with the modern refinements in sodomitical practices, by the members of the Vere Street coterie, of detestable memory." Written by lawyer Richard Holloway, it discusses the incident in July 1810 in which London police raided the White Swan on Vere Street and arrested more than 20 individuals, including the landlord. Although most of the defendants were released due to lack of evidence, seven were sentenced to imprisonment and to stand in the pillory, where the mob pelted them with refuse and offal. The case received vivid coverage in the London press of the time.

Seven decades later saw the 1886 publication of *Psychopathia Sexualis* by Krafft-Ebing. It included an entry on male prostitution, reprinting a February 1884 article in a Berlin newspaper about "The Woman-Haters Ball." Krafft-Ebing commented:

> These facts deserve the careful attention of the police, who should be placed in a position to cope with male prostitution, as they now do with that of women.

Male prostitution is certainly much more dangerous to society than that of females; it is the darkest stain on the history of humanity.

From the statements of a high police official of Berlin I learn that the police are conversant with the male demimonde of the German capital and do all they can to suppress blackmail among pederasts—a practice which often does not stop short of murder.

(Psychopathia Sexualis, 1886, p. 593)

In 1887, François Carliers's *Les deux prostitutions, 1860–1870*, a section on "prostitution antiphysique" dealt with the question of homosexuals. In *Strangers: Homosexual Love in the Nineteenth Century* (2004), Graham Robb offers valuable context for Carlier's view of the subject:

François Carlier, who ran the Paris vice squad in the 1860s, thought that "pederasty" deprived the sufferer of courage, family feeling, and patriotism. "Normal" prostitutes, who were registered by municipal doctors, performed a useful function, in his view, by sating the lusts of potential rapists, whereas pederasts were inherently useless and should not be tolerated. . . . Mass round-ups were standard police procedure for dealing with prostitution (approximately 12,000 female prostitutes were arrested each year) and French policemen seem to have found it impossible to distinguish between male prostitutes and their customers.

(Robb, 2004, p. 28)

More specifically, these round-ups were carried out due to the perceived role of homosexuals as disruptors of the civic peace:

From the point of view of the police, homosexual acts, especially those committed in public, not only caused a scandal, which disrupted the ordinary life of the neighborhood, but also led to all kinds of petty crimes, such as thievery and blackmail, as well as violent crimes such as assault and murder. Most of these crimes were associated with male prostitution. According to François Carlier, the chief officer of the Parisian vice squad, which monitored prostitution in the city, it was a small step from petty thievery to grand larceny, with or without violence, for most of these men, especially for those who were too old to work profitably on the streets. Blackmail, one of the worst crimes associated with male prostitution, could involve false representation, forgeries of one kind or another, fraud and extortion, and in extreme cases, murder. Violence in one form or another was often perpetrated by or against male prostitutes. In Carlier's opinion, male prostitution clearly constituted a major criminal problem that needed to be more effectively controlled by the police. He advocated more stringent laws against male prostitution in particular and against male homosexual activity in general.

(Peniston, 1996, p. 130)

In 1899, Flammarion in Paris published a three-volume set of memoirs *L'amour à Paris*, authored by the former head of the French secret police, Marie-François Goron. Its third volume, titled *Les parias de l'amour*, drew on Goron's years of experience with the Parisian underworld and included a discussion of male prostitution in the city. The full text of this work is available online in the *Gallica* database.

The early twentieth century

From the end of the nineteenth century to the beginning of World War II, known book-length works dealing in whole or in part with male prostitution are limited, with the greatest concentration appearing during the 1920s and 1930s. The newly emerging field of sexology framed the discussion through the writings of Magnus Hirschfeld, Edward Carpenter, and Havelock Ellis, all of whom acknowledged the existence of male prostitution within their more general discussions of homosexuality. In 1904, Magnus Hirschfeld's study *Berlins Drittes Geschlecht* (*Berlin's Third Sex*) offered the reader a literary tour of the city's homosexual world and drew a distinction between "respectable" homosexuals who were victimized by the legal prohibitions against male same-sex activity and criminal male prostitutes who preyed on them. Between 1905 and 1907, the ten-part series *Das Berliner Dirnentum* (*Prostitution in Berlin*), written by German sociologist and cultural historian Hans Ostwald, was published in Leipzig. Its fifth section in 1906 was devoted *to Männliche Prostitution* (*Male Prostitution*) and issued in 1907 under the expanded title *Männliche Prostitution im kaiserlichen Berlin*. A more typical example of the journal articles appearing in the scientific literature of the time is a 1913 article by Hirschfeld on the causes and manifestations of male prostitution, published in Leipzig. In 1915, the third edition of Havelock Ellis' *Sexual Inversion* included references to male prostitution.

In his essay on the history of homosexuality in England, Jeffrey Weeks noted that "it is significant that writings on male prostitution began to emerge simultaneously with the notion of 'homosexuals' being an identifiable breed of persons with special needs, passions, and lusts" (1980, p. 113). A valuable and highly detailed overview of the evolution of attitudes toward male prostitution and the literature generated about it from the Victorian period into the mid-twentieth century is Kerwin Kaye's lengthy 2003 article in the *Journal of Homosexuality*, "Male Prostitution in the Twentieth Century: Pseudohomosexuals, Hoodlum Homosexuals, and Exploited Teens." Topics addressed include the role of social class in male prostitutes' views of themselves, the impact of sexological explanations for homosexuality on hustlers' self-images over time, and the political and psychological forces that male prostitutes were forced to cope with.

An excellent example of the typical attitudes of large U.S. cities toward any type of prostitution prior to the First World War is the 1911 report *The Social Evil in Chicago: A Study of Existing Conditions with Recommendations by The Vice Commission of Chicago*. The "social evil" of the title was public prostitution, and while the report focuses almost exclusively on women prostitutes and their life circumstances, men involved in the trade do receive a scant acknowledgment. Contained in the seventh chapter, "The Social Evil and Its Medical Aspects," is the following paragraph:

> Male Prostitutes. (Principally perverts.) They spread infection. They have a high mortality and morbidity rate. They increase the number of drug habitués.
>
> (Social Evil, *1911, p. 290*)

Male prostitution also made a brief appearance on the London stage during the period between the two world wars. The Independent Labour Party Arts Guild was engaged in promoting socialism through a series of productions, titled "Plays for the People," staged at various London theaters. One of them, *Bringing It Home: A Play in One Act*, by V. T. Murray, opened in the summer of 1926 at the Red Lion. The play used as its plot elements the issues of male prostitution and capital punishment.

The rise of the Nazis in Germany in 1933 signaled the end of the period of tolerance for writings on homosexuality. The Nazis destroyed the movement for homosexual rights and instituted punitive laws against gay men. One of the notable incidents in 1933 that contributed to the difficulty of assessing the extent of information available on male prostitutes was the sacking of Hirschfeld's Institute for Sexual Reform and the public burning of all the seized material.

The postwar era

Male prostitution surfaces again in the research literature of the post-World War II period in the massive research project on American male sex activity chaired by Dr. Alfred Kinsey and published in 1948 as *Sexual Behavior in the Human Male*. In the outline of information to be collected in individual sex histories, the eighth category, "Homosexual History," includes a section on homosexual prostitution, with questions addressing the subjects' experience either as active prostitutes or as clients purchasing their services. In Chapter 20, "Intercourse with Prostitutes," Kinsey makes the following observation:

> There is, however, a homosexual prostitution among males who provide sexual relations for other males; and such homosexual prostitutes are, in many large cities, not far inferior to the females who are engaged in heterosexual prostitution. Male homosexual prostitutes less often derive their main income from such activities, and less often engage in prostitution for any long period of years.
>
> *(Kinsey, Pomeroy, & Martin, 1948, p. 596)*

The next year, an autobiographical novel by the prominent homosexual French author Jean Genet appeared in Paris. In *Journal du voleur (The Thief's Journal)*, the reader accompanies the narrator on a journey across Europe in the 1930s during which he works as a male prostitute.

One of the first works on male sex workers to appear at mid-century was *Boy Prostitution*. It was published in Copenhagen in 1956 and written by the chief of the Danish morality police (a post similar to that held by François Carlier 80 years earlier). The work was briefly reviewed in 1957 by a faculty member at the University of Massachusetts, who noted that the study focused on urban Denmark and was based on statistical data, personal documents, and observation and found that male and female prostitutes existed in equal numbers, with the males "predominantly young . . . destitute migrants from the rural community" (Driver, 1957, p. 439). It should be noted that the 1950s also saw the publication of the first periodicals of what would come to be termed the "homophile" movement, *ONE* (1953–1964) and *The Mattachine Review* (1955–1966). While much of their reportage and discussion centered on the lack of civil rights for homosexuals, neither publication discussed male sex work directly as an area deserving of activism.

In 1957, a major investigative report was published in Great Britain by Her Majesty's Stationery Office. The title was the *Report of the Committee on Homosexual Offences and Prostitution*. Often called the "Wolfenden Report" after the peer who chaired it, it recommended specific reforms to English law and police procedures relating to both its target populations. The report briefly covered males who offered themselves to other men as a commercial transaction in its discussion of the practice of "importuning." The Commission recommended that the existing laws about living on the earnings of prostitution be expanded to include male prostitutes and that males charged with importuning for immoral purposes should be entitled to a trial by jury. Paragraph 116 of the Report notes that importuning "is an offense, punishable with six months' imprisonment on summary conviction or with two years' imprisonment on indictment, for a male person to persistently solicit or importune in a public place for immoral purposes" (Wolfenden Committee, 1957, p. 42). Parliament adopted the recommendations regarding prostitution into law in 1959. The Report also recommended legalizing homosexual acts committed in private, with consent, between persons at least 21 years of age and not members of the merchant navy or the armed forces, a piece of advice that Parliament noted but did not act on for another decade until the passage of the Sexual Offenses Act in 1967, which legalized homosexuality in England and Wales. In addition, further limitations on privacy were added, including the prohibition of same-sex acts in public accommodations such as hotels and in private homes with a third person present.

The early 1960s were marked by the publication in 1963 of two novels that dealt with male prostitution, one in the United States and the other in France. The latter is Jean Genet's *Our Lady of the Flowers* (originally written while the author was in prison in 1943 and presented to the U.S. reading public in this translation) and John Rechy's darkly autobiographical *City of Night*. The title character of Genet's work is a hustler who is eventually arrested and executed. Similarly, the narrator of *City of Night* works as a hustler, and the novel follows him in his journey across the margins of America.

In 1966, a collection of stories, *$tud*, written by tattoo artist and academic Samuel Steward under the pseudonym of Phil Andros (one of Steward's several documented pseudonyms) was published in the United States. Steward followed up this volume with a series of eight pornographic novels for the popular pulp market. All the novels featured the narrator Phil Andros, a working hustler. Steward is perhaps the most identifiable of the pool of authors who produced pornographic gay novels for the mass market during the 1960s, many of them published by Masquerade Books in New York. The decade closed with the publication in 1969 of *Boys for Sale: A Sociological Study of Boy Prostitution* by Dennis Drew and Jonathan Drake. Both of the authors wrote under pseudonyms and were in fact faculty members at Western Michigan University and Yale, Professor Dennison W. Nichols and Professor George Parker Rossman. In a 1977 interview, Nichols stated that Rossman provided the information for the book's contents. Much of the book is devoted to discussing and presenting documentation on the existence of boy prostitution worldwide, beginning with the classical civilizations of Greece and Rome and covering 20 countries and regions. The final chapter on the United States also includes case studies and a profile of how boys working in the trade earned their income and what its range was. A major defect of this book is that no bibliography or data sources are provided, making it difficult to assess the validity of its arguments and conclusions. The work was also never reviewed in the professional literature of the social sciences.

The 1970s

The literature on male prostitution continued into the 1970s. The year 1973 saw the publication of Mervyn Harris's *The Dilly Boys: Male Prostitution in Piccadilly*. Harris was a South African journalist then resident in London who spent 1969 researching the subject commencing. The book is based on a series of recorded conversations with a group of male homosexual prostitutes in their late teens and early twenties. Three years later, a U.S. counterpart to Harris's volume appeared, *For Money or Love: Boy Prostitution in America*, by investigative reporter Robin Lloyd. Written for a general audience, its treatment of the subject is based on an impressive range of interviews with police officials, politicians, social workers, gay rights activists, clergymen, hustlers, and clientele gathered from across the United States. Its chief value lies in the detailed picture it presents of the complex arguments being made about male prostitution in the United

States in the immediate aftermath of several nationally publicized cases regarding the abuse and murder of juveniles in 1973.

In 1976, two books were published about the same event in the history of male prostitution, the Cleveland Street Scandal. The incident in question occurred over a period of eight months in 1889–1890 and involved the discovery of a male brothel at 19 Cleveland Street in London and the subsequent (and complicated) legal actions taken to identify and prosecute its patrons, some of whom were prominent aristocrats. The first book was written by a trio of English journalists and authors, the second by barrister and former Member of Parliament H. Montgomery Hyde. In the prologue to *The Cleveland Street Affair*, by Colin Simpson, Lewis Chester, and David Leitch, the writers state that their work is "based primarily on the previously secret records of the Director of Public Prosecutions, which have now become available for the first time" (1976, p. 8). The authors provide extensive social background information on Victorian London and the principal characters involved, quoting from the government records. Hyde's book, *The Cleveland Street Scandal*, also draws on these original materials and discusses court proceedings and police actions in detail. Terming the event a "scandal "reflects both the Victorian attitude toward male prostitution and the events' potentially devastating impact on the monarchy.

The direct voice of the hustler last heard in the 1966 collection *$tud* resurfaced in 1977 with the publication of John Rechy's second book, *The Sexual Outlaw: A Documentary: A Non-Fiction Account, with Commentaries, of Three Days and Nights in the Sexual Underground*. Within the frank narration about the weekend experiences of a gay man in Los Angeles, Rechy considers the condition of being homosexual in America through documents illustrating various forms of oppression and offers insights gained from his own sexual and political identity. In addition, an American book paralleling the collection of life stories that formed the basis of *The Dilly Boys* also appeared in 1977. In *Bughouse Blues: An Intimate Portrait of Gay Hustling in Chicago* ("Bughouse Square" is a nickname for Chicago's Washington Square, the primary venue for the gay hustler trade), Richard Raff and his co-author "portray the milieu in which the gay hustler lives and operates" (1977, Preface, unpaged) and the variety of men who participated in the trade through dramatized stories of their lives. Given that *Bughouse Blues* was written in the first decade after the birth of the gay liberation movement at the Stonewall Riots in New York City, it is notable that the authors view the lives of gay men as tragic and marked by discrimination and police harassment, which were being successfully challenged. The book is similar to *Boys for Sale* in that it completely lacks any bibliographical references to either historical or sociological literature on Chicago, but it does offer a vivid illustration of male hustlers' social world in a major U.S. city in the later twentieth century.

The 1980s

Much of the literature produced in the 1980s reflected the impact of the AIDS pandemic on same-sex relationships, both private and commercial. From 1979 to 1981, a consulting firm in San Francisco conducted a study for the U.S. Department of Health and Human Services. Its goal was

> to develop an in-depth demographic and descriptive knowledge base on adolescents involved in prostitution and to examine the relationship of that phenomenon to involvement in pornography and other forms of sexual exploitation, child abuse and neglect, and runaway behavior. . . . The emphasis of that research was on adolescent male prostitution.
>
> *(Weisberg, 1985, p. xi)*

Data were collected in multiple forms, including a review of the literature on prostitution, ethnographic research in San Francisco and New York City, and a survey of existing social service programs that served adolescent prostitutes and runaway youth in seven large U.S. cities. A group of 79 male prostitutes was eventually identified, and a profile of each prostitute included such factors as family background, prostitution lifestyles, and involvement with the juvenile justice and social services systems. Law professor D. Kelly Weisberg presents and analyzes the results of this project in her 1985 book *Children of the Night: A Study of Adolescent Prostitution*. Of particular value is the chapter titled "Federal and State Legislation on Juvenile Prostitution," which presents a detailed picture of the U.S. legal responses beginning with the passage of the *Protection of Children against Sexual Exploitation Act* in 1977. The author observes that "legislative policy on juvenile prostitution has been formulated only in the past decade. Similarly, social science research on the phenomenon has been conducted only recently. This poses a dilemma in that legislation has been enacted largely without the benefit of empirical knowledge" (1985, p. 207).

Across the Pacific, 1985 also saw the publication in Sydney, Australia, of Roberta Perkins and Garry Bennett's *Being a Prostitute: Prostitute Women and Prostitute Men*, a comparative study focused on Sydney and based on sociological questionnaire data, in-depth interviews, and observations. The authors note in the preface that "absolutely nothing existed on male prostitution in Australia before the recent publication of. . . *Young and Gay*" (Perkins, 1985, p. xv), a reference to Garry Bennett's book locally published in 1983 by Twenty-Ten, a Sydney gay youth volunteer agency. The book's opening chapter defines seven categories of male homosexual prostitutes by clientele and/or skill and then provides lengthy transcriptions of interviews with ten men whose involvement in prostitution ranges from running an escort service to street hustling. The fifth appendix, "Profiles of Male Prostitutes," lists the questions asked of the hustlers in the sample and the range of their responses.

The 1990s

The last decade of the twentieth century opened with the sequential publication of two books by one of the more colorful characters in the world of male sex work, Samuel Steward, whose careers included teaching English literature, writing S/M pornography, becoming a prominent tattoo artist, and serving as one of the researchers for the Kinsey study. In *Bad Boys and Tough Tattoos: A Social History of the Tattoo with Gangs, Sailors, and Street-Corner Punks, 1950–1965*, published in 1990, Steward uses material he recorded in a diary he kept over several years (at Kinsey's request) to portray the lives of the clientele of his State Street tattoo shop in Chicago, many of whom were hustlers. A year later, his second work, *Understanding the Male Hustler*, appeared. The text is unusual in that it takes the form of a series of thoughtful extended conversations between Steward and his alter ego, the hustler Phil Andros. Their discussion explores the career arc of becoming a hustler, the history of the male prostitution and pornography scenes in the United States, and a wide variety of subjects ranging from the psychology of hustling to the types of clientele, AIDS, and aging. Steward's literary training is clear in the numerous references to writers and specific books. Readers will find it useful to compare Steward's depiction of hustling with later general works on the topic.

In 1992, British historian Rictor Norton returned to the world of eighteenth-century London and what it meant to be homosexual at that time with a work similar to the 1813 pamphlet *The Phoenix of Sodom*. Both recount police constabulary action against an establishment catering to men seeking sex with other men. Norton's book, *Mother Clap's Molly House: The Gay Subculture in England, 1700–1830* (Figure 12.2) introduces the reader to then-contemporary slang

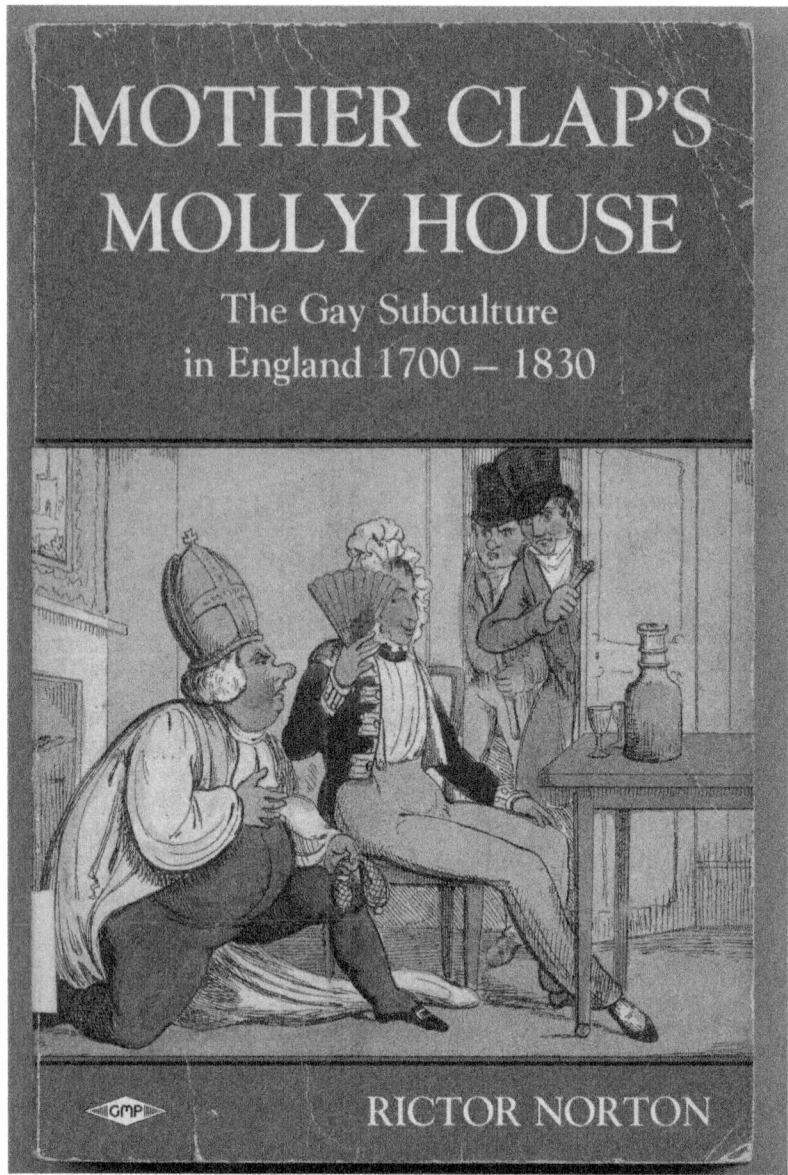

Figure 12.2   Mother Clap's Molly House.

for gay men ("mollies") and details the history of one of the houses they frequented, run by a woman named Margaret Clap. It was raided in February 1725. Forty men were arrested, some of whom received sentences as severe as being made to stand in the pillory and execution. Norton's extensive use of primary sources, such as court records, reveals the degree to which male prostitution was a part of what would now be termed the gay subculture of London 90 years before the writing of *The Phoenix of Sodom*.

London remained the focus of male prostitution research in 1993 with the publication of the lengthy study *Male Prostitution*, by Donald West and Buz de Villiers. Based on data gathered from interviews with 50 men in the late 1980s, the book's three main sections explore the world of street workers (the largest portion of the text), the male sex industry and its advertising, and social issues in commercial sex. Topics explored with the street workers include family backgrounds, their sexual orientation, childhood sexual abuse, homelessness, ways of entering the working life of prostitution, transactions with clients (both successful and less so), sexually transmitted diseases, drug use, and interactions with the law. The section on commercial sex presents data on the types of clients who engage male prostitutes, the involvement of children, legal control (both legislative and as exerted by the police), and foreign venues where male prostitution communities can be found. These last include Amsterdam, San Francisco, Morocco, and Thailand. A notable feature of the book is the inclusion of the complete questionnaire used for the survey interviews.

Three years later, another study of an urban group of male prostitutes was published, *Young Men in the Street: Help-Seeking Behavior of Young Male Prostitutes*. Its content is similar to that of the West book, but it centers on Washington, DC and takes a social-work perspective. The author, Cudore L. Snell, a faculty member in the Howard University School of Social Work, draws on interview data from 70 male prostitutes to evaluate their contact with helping agencies, these agencies' ability to build rapport with hustlers, hustlers' strategies for securing resources, and the quality of assistance rendered. The author concludes that "although individual members of the professions struggle to help, the helping professions themselves have not yet made a formal commitment to deal with issues related to prostitution in general and young male prostitutes in particular" (Snell, 1993, p. 93).

While ethnographic research on male prostitution in New York City was of the subject of the 1986 study *Children of the Night* by D. K. Weisberg, it was not until 1994 that the city was the main subject of its own book. Robert McNamara's *The Times Square Hustler: Male Prostitution in New York City* began as a sociological study carried out between January and December 1992. Originally an investigation into how members of high-risk populations dealt with AIDS, it expanded to consider how the hustlers formed a community and the dynamics of living in that community. The extensive use of excerpts from interviews with the network of hustlers who came to trust McNamara brings an immediacy to the text.

Immediacy of lived experience also characterizes the thoughtful 1996 memoir *Against My Better Judgment: An Intimate Memoir of an Eminent Gay Psychologist* by Roger Brown. In it, he describes the loss in his late 60s of his longtime partner and his coping efforts, which included turning to male prostitutes for company and affection. His interactions with and the lessons drawn from the three men he became involved with make this book an important contribution to the literatures of male sex work and gay male aging. Brown died in 1997 at age 71. His story has parallels in the other work on male sex workers published in 1996, which take a vividly different perspective. In *Honey, Honey, Miss Thang: Being Black, Gay, and on the Streets*, black gay criminologist Leon Pettiway presents the lives of five African American men who cross-dress and work as hustlers in their own direct and powerful words, gathered as part of a larger urban research project in the United States.

One of the most comprehensive explorations of prostitution (both male and female) is the lengthy anthology *Prostitution: On Whores, Hustlers, and Johns*, edited by James Elias, Vern L. Bullough, Veronica Elias, and Gwen Brewer (1998). Most of the material on male prostitution is in the fourth section, "Rent Boys, Hustlers, and She-Males." This section includes several important articles. Donald West followed up his 1993 book *Male Prostitution* with a paper, "Male Homosexual Prostitution in England." Also notable is Michael Knox's study, "Negotiations and Relationships Among Male Sex Workers and Clients in Liverpool, Merseyside, United Kingdom." "She-Male Prostitutes: Who Are They, What Do They Do, and Why Do They Do It?" is an important article by Dwight Dixon and Joan Dixon. "Out of CASH: The Rise and Demise of a Male Prostitutes' Rights Organization" by Jacqueline Boles and Kirk Elifson reports on the three-year life of the Coalition Advocating Safer Hustling, an outgrowth of an amFAR grant to study the prevention of HIV/AIDS among male sex workers. The seventh section of the anthology, "Research with Sex Workers," contains a personal account by Craig Seymour, "Studying Myself/Studying Others: One (Professional) Boy's Adventures Studying Sex Work," covering five years of ethnographic research in Washington, DC's male strip clubs.

In contrast to most of the published monographs on male prostitution, which usually focus on the hustler population in a specific city or national context, the 1999 collection *Men Who Sell Sex: International Perspectives on Male Prostitution and HIV/AIDS* provides a broader perspective. Issued as part of the *Social Aspects of AIDS* series published by the University of London, it reports on male sex workers in Sri Lanka, Thailand, the Philippines, Morocco, Peru, Bangladesh, India, Costa Rica, the Dominican Republic, Brazil, France, Canada, Mexico, the Netherlands, the United Kingdom, and the United States. Most of the authors bring direct experience of their work in HIV prevention to their writing, and they describe the ongoing attempts to accurately describe the roles played by gender, sexuality (and its social definitions), and politics.

Useful complements to *Men Who Sell Sex* are studies conducted by individual nations, such as *M Is for Mutual, A Is for Acts: Male Sex Work and AIDS in Canada* published by Health Canada in 1999. Its full text is available online at www.walnet.org/members/dan_allman/mutualacts/index.html. A similar work from 1999 is *Lady Boys, Tom Boys, Rent Boys: Male and Female Homosexualities in Contemporary Thailand* by Peter A. Jackson and Gerard Sullivan, which neatly complements the Thai data in *Men Who Sell Sex*. An unusually frank yet literary memoir from Rick Whitaker, who served as the executive assistant to the director of the New York City Opera, recounts his 20 months working for an escort service to gain income to support his cocaine habit. Whitaker's book, *Assuming the Position: A Memoir of Hustling*, would be reprinted in English in 2001 and translated into German in 2010.

The 2000s

The early years of the new millennium saw the appearance of Kerwin Kaye's 2003 article on the shifting history of male prostitution in the twentieth century and the first attempt to provide an historical grounding for the ethnographies of male sex work in the United States. This was Mack Friedman's *Strapped for Cash: A History of American Hustler Culture*, published by Alyson Publications and covering the period from 1607 to 2000. Its sources range from personal papers held by the Kinsey Institute library to 50 interviews that Friedman conducted with gay and trans hustlers to news stories on male prostitution from the popular press of the nineteenth century. *Strapped for Cash* is also notable for its extensive use of quotations from primary texts and illustrations, including prints; black-and-white photographs; line drawings; and street maps of the hustler districts in New York, San Francisco, and Los Angeles.

Published studies on male sex workers and their histories continued in 2004 with the publication of William Peniston's *Pederasts and Others: Urban Culture and Sexual Identity in Nineteenth-Century Paris* and Graham Robb's *Strangers: Homosexual Love in the Nineteenth Century*. The male sex work literature available on Southeast Asia also expanded in 2004 with the publication of Gerrie Lim's *Invisible Trade: High-Class Sex for Sale in Singapore*. It includes a chapter, "Boys in the Hood," containing interviews with several men in the trade. An English-language translation of social work professor Michel Dorais' 2003 book *Travailleurs du sexe* was published in 2005 by McGill-Queen's University Press as *Rent Boys: The World of Male Sex Trade Workers*. Based on interviews with 40 men in Montreal and Quebec City, the 2005 edition contains additional material on the role of organized crime, child prostitution, the legalization of prostitution, and then-current international literature to place the original study in a broader context.

In 2007, the *Journal of Homosexuality* published a themed issue, *Male Sex Work: A Business Doing Pleasure*, which also appeared as a separate monograph from Harrington Park Press (Figure 12.3). Its 12 articles are divided into three general topics: the Internet, strip clubs, and the opening section "On the Streets" on traditional male prostitution. The three papers in "On the Streets" are "Male Prostitution: Pathology, Paradigms, and Progress in Research," by David Bimbi; "Sex and the Unspoken in Male Street Prostitution," by Kerwin Kaye; and "Exploring the Interpersonal Relationships in Street-Based Male Sex Work: Results from An Australian Qualitative Study," by David Leary and Victor Minichiello. Bimbi's paper provides a valuable summary and analysis of the ways in which paradigms of male sex work in social science research have been based on specific samples of the hustlers, research designs, and assumptions made about the male sex worker (MSW) population prior to the actual studies being done. Paradigms reviewed are homosexuality, psychodynamics, gender roles, sex work as pathology,

Figure 12.3 Male Sex Work: A Business Doing Pleasure.

the existence of a range of types of male sex workers, MSWs as vectors for the transmission of disease (and thus a public health problem), and the idea of sex work as a job. Bimbi notes that

> the concurrent emergence of the sex as work paradigm and the introduction of the Internet have created a new venue. . . . However, the Internet as a venue for sex work has yet to be investigated fully. . . . The other aspect of male sex work that warrants investigation is the personal lives of MSWs.
>
> *(2007, p. 29)*

A second book by Gerrie Lim, *Invisible Trade II: Secret Lives and Sexual Intrigue in Singapore*, appeared in 2008, but it has only one chapter dealing with male escorts. (Editor's note: For studies that examine the role of the Internet in male sex work, see Part III of this book.)

The 2010s

The 2010s have seen the publication of new works in the established categories of male prostitution literature and the reissue of older works in electronic form. In 2010, Barry Reay's *New York Hustlers: Masculinity and Sex in Modern America* (see Chapter 10 of this book for a reprinted chapter from that work) continued the historic focus on New York City begun by George Chauncey in 1994 in *Gay New York*, which includes a short description of the types of male prostitutes active in the city over several decades and the transformation of Times Square into a center of the trade (Figure 12.4). Reay's *New York Hustlers* focuses on the 1940s through the 1960s, although it includes substantial information on the scene in the 1920s and 1930s as context. Reay notes the shift from the open effeminacy of these decades toward a more masculine presentation by the 1950s. He also makes extensive use of literary and artistic works and personal archives as sources for his detailed portrayal of the male prostitutes and their lives within the social worlds of New York City.

2011 saw the publication of two additional books on male sex work that moved beyond city studies such as *Bughouse Blues* and *New York Hustlers* into other dimensions of the hustlers' world. With *In the Company of Men: Inside the Lives of Male Prostitutes*, Michael D. Smith and Christian Grov report the results of their unique study of a group of men who work for an escort agency in the electronic age. Two appendixes offer demographic information on the escorts and the wider social network based in the agency. The other 2011 book, an anthology titled *Policing Pleasure: Sex Work, Policy, and the State in Global Perspective*, presents 14 ethnographic papers on sex workers in nine countries, including Mexico, Thailand, South Africa, China, Kenya, Brazil, India, and the United States (upstate New York). Only one paper, Gregory Mitchell's "Organizational Challenges Facing Male Sex Workers in Brazil's Tourist Zones," deals specifically with male prostitution. And in 2012, Kevin Walby's *Touching Encounters: Sex, Work, and Male-for-Male Internet Escorting* extended the research on male sex workers participating in the online landscape begun with *In The Company of Men* by presenting data based on interviews with 30 MSWs in Toronto, Montreal, Ottawa, Houston, and London. An online edition of William Peniston's 2004 work *Pederasts and Others: Urban Culture and Sexual Identity in Nineteenth-Century Paris* appeared in 2012 but contained no additional material.

A notable contribution to the body of books dealing with male prostitution is the massive collection of color photographs of 69 male sex workers taken by Philip-Lorca diCorcia on five trips to Los Angeles, California, in the late 1980s and early 1990s during the AIDS pandemic and published as the oversize volume *Hustlers* in 2013. The project was funded by the National Endowment for the Arts in 1989, with the proviso that whatever work produced would not be

Figure 12.4   New York Hustlers: Masculinity and Sex in Modern America.

obscene. That proviso was the result of pressure from conservatives reacting to a controversial exhibition of the work of Robert Mapplethorpe, who had also been supported by the NEA. The photos were taken on a set prepared by diCorcia in a hotel room, and each is accompanied by the individual's name, age, place of birth, and usual price for his services. A "Notes" section provides copies of the photographer's original notebook pages about some of the subjects. The collection was exhibited in 1993 at the Museum of Modern Art in New York City under the title *Strangers*.

In 2014, Peter Aggleton produced a second edited collection, *Men Who Sell Sex: Global Perspectives*, reusing the title of his 1999 volume. The new edition contains 17 chapters and expands the geographic scope of male sex work literature with research on southern and eastern Europe (Albania, Romania, and Macedonia), the Middle East (Turkey), Pakistan, South Africa, Australia, and China. 2014 also saw the publication by Harrington Park Press of *Male Sex Work and Society*, edited by Victor Minichiello and John Scott. It is divided into four sections, with the opening group of chapters examining the economic, historical, cultural, and social settings of male sex work. The second section looks at the marketing of MSWs through the media of advertising and the Internet, while the third examines the depiction of male sex work as a social problem and the reactions to this categorization has. The papers tackle topics as diverse as the clientele who hire men for sex, attempts at legal regulation of male prostitution and the actual regulations enforced, mental health and wellness issues, and how the changes in the definition of gay subcultures from the homophile era to the online age have been reflected in the venues and populations that male sex workers inhabit. The last chapters discuss the impact of sociocultural factors on male sex work in Hong Kong, eastern and southern Africa, Latin America, post-Soviet Russia, Germany, and Ireland (both the Irish Republic and Northern Ireland). Readers will find the concluding chapter by the editors, "Future Directions in Male Sex Work Research," especially valuable for its discussion of subjects related to male sex work that have received only partial attention, particularly race, age and ageism, clientele, geographic and sociopolitical contexts, public health/HIV, and online dialogues as sources of data.

Picking up on the chapter on Brazil in the 2011 anthology *Policing Pleasure*, Gregory Mitchell's 2015 volume *Tourist Attractions: Performing Race and Masculinity in Brazil's Sexual Economy* recognizes that

> there is a genuine and ethically grounded need for ethnographic studies that take seriously intersections of sexuality, race, and economics as experienced . . . in everyday life. Academics, students of sexual economies, and the general public know far less about sex workers as people than they do about sex workers as medical subjects or purported victims.
>
> *(2015, p. 3)*

Mitchell's detailed study provides a clear picture of the intricacies of Brazil's sex tourism industry and the men who inhabit it, based on ten field trips made between 2006 and 2015. Indonesia was added to the countries in which ethnographic research on male sex workers has been done with the 2016 publication of Matteo Alcano's *Masculine Identities and Male Sex Work between East Java and Bali: An Ethnography of Youth, Bodies, and Violence*.

Despite researchers' longstanding recognition that male sex work is basically an economic transaction, most published studies minimize attention to this aspect of male prostitution. Trevon Logan's 2017 *Economics, Sexuality, and Male Sex Work* is an exception, with a data set created by scanning the online paid advertisements posted by male escorts on a host website. This approach allowed the author to quantify the types of information related to male sex workers in the United States (for example, performing safe sex) not previously subjected to formal statistical analysis. Logan notes that

> the main contribution of this book is to treat male sex work as the market it is and use that market feature to its fullest advantage. . . . Until now, this information has not been exploited by social scientists looking for comprehensive information about this market.
>
> *(p. 4)*

The other major contribution to the international ethnography of male sex workers in 2017 came from Cenk Özbay, whose essay "'Straight' Rent Boys and Gays Who Sell Sex in Istanbul" appeared in *Men Who Sell Sex: Global Perspectives* in 2015. Study of these same two populations is continued and expanded in Cenk Özbay's *Queering Sexualities in Turkey: Gay Men, Male Prostitutes, and the City*, in which the author uses the concept of masculinity to explore the interactions of gender, class, urban spatial and social geographies, and sexual identity.

Thematic groupings

Within the diverse body of male sex work literature, certain thematic groupings can be discerned. Geographically, the majority of research and fiction works produced prior to the 1990s are situated in the northern hemisphere, chiefly in France, Germany, the United Kingdom, Denmark, and the United States. Within this region, a second pattern emerges: Urban areas are chosen as the sites for investigation and fieldwork, a natural consequence of the migration of many gay men to such places in search of opportunity, both economic and sexual, and the formation of homosexual communities that can support male prostitution. Cities represented in the literature include Berlin, Paris, London, Copenhagen, New York, Chicago, Los Angeles, and San Francisco. A third pattern evident in the literature over time is a shift in the type of authorship. Earlier works were written by professional men (lawyers, police and security officials, physicians, and psychologists) working outside academia. Later publications are often based on fieldwork done by social scientists trained as anthropologists, historians, criminologists, and sociologists. A fourth, less pervasive, theme is research done at the behest of task forces created by local and national governments to research specific social issues. Personal accounts by men who work as male prostitutes have always been a part of the literature, but a fifth theme is that of life stories told by individual sex workers in book-length accounts.

The paperback pornographic novel

A genre that has always been both relevant to and problematic for tracking the history of writing on male sex work is the paperback pornographic novel. The roots of popular fiction about male sex workers can be found in the late nineteenth century. These early novels drew on an interwoven body of work composed of scientific and philosophical monographs: articles and essays on the nature, origins, and character of the human sexual instinct and news reportage on incidents involving same-gender sexual activity, often heavily peppered with medical and psychological terminology. These three streams of writing provided channels through which the concept of men who sell sex to other men gradually diffused into the intellectual landscape of Western culture.

The popular novels intended for the general public were printed on low-quality paper and sold so cheaply that they earned the nickname "dime novels." They also served a less visible function, as noted in Shelley Streeby's 2011 essay, "Dime Novels and the Rise of Mass-Market Genres" in *The Cambridge History of the American Novel*:

> Although dime novels have frequently been derided and rarely read today, they helped to shape some of the most important genres of U.S. mass culture, including the romance, the detective story, the Western, science fiction, and stories of war and imperial adventure, as new media adapted and transformed their stories for the twentieth century.

(p. 587)

The classic dime novels and later, similar works such as *Stud* featuring hustlers as major and minor characters were written to be sensational through the depiction of subjects beyond generally accepted social experience (including, in the twentieth century, same-gender commercial sex).

The genre of popular fiction about male sex workers, such as Samuel Steward's 1970 novel *My Brother The Hustler* or Glenn Langdon's *The Last Retreat* (1962), poses a range of challenges to researchers due to several factors. One major issue is the physical construction of the books, which were printed on high-acid paper that does not age well and thus makes the books difficult to preserve. The result is condition problems for those libraries and archives that have chosen to include these books in their collections, as well as for the increasing number of online sources offering individual titles for sale. The fugitive nature of these books (due in part to limited publication runs now difficult to assess from primary business records) likewise makes their acquisition and assembly problematic. These problems are reflected in the WORLDCAT online database, whose holdings records for male sex worker fiction list only a small number of institutions with a collection of these books available for research.

A secondary problem in tracking the history of this genre is that most of its publishers in the United States are no longer in business, with some exceptions such as New York's Masquerade Books. Thus, ascertaining which titles sold the most copies has not as yet been possible. The complex question of author identification must also be acknowledged, as most of the paperback novels were written under pseudonyms or anonymously due to censorship concerns, although some writers such as John Rechy and Samuel Steward bravely published under their real names. Male sex workers as characters are also found within the genre of gay male fiction, making it difficult to trace the range of plots and themes that utilized them. The relevant and available works of fiction from North America should also reach beyond familiar writers such as Genet to an international assessment of the presence of male sex workers in world literature. Another potentially valuable avenue of research is the degree to which MSW literary works were censored and the grounds used to justify the censorship.

In 1966 (the year *Stud* was published), Steven Marcus's *The Other Victorians: A Study of Sexuality and Pornography in Mid-Nineteenth-Century England* appeared, noting that "there is almost no literature of a homosexual kind surviving from the period and that as far as can be determined very little was produced" (1966, p. 261). Four decades later, Julie Peakman reached a similar conclusion in her 2003 book, *Mighty Lewd Books: The Development of Pornography in Eighteenth-Century England*, which states that "unless other material is uncovered, as far as we can tell with currently available sources, fictionalized pornography directed at homosexual readers did not emerge until the nineteenth century" (p. 3). The emphatic enforcement of morally defined limitations regarding what was permitted to be published under the censorship regulations (with their varying definitions of obscenity) of the United Kingdom, Germany, France, and the United States from Victorian times until the post-World War II era made discussing male sex work openly a dangerous and challenging proposition for writers of all genres. And yet the stubborn literary thread of the lives of men who sell sex to other men was not extinguished. Instead, it has survived into contemporary times, exploring a variety of lived experiences and the passions, hungers, and sexual identities of male sex workers.

Bibliography

Aggleton, P. (Ed.). (1999). *Men who sell sex: International perspectives on male prostitution and HIV/AIDS.* Philadelphia, PA: Temple University Press.

Aggleton, P., & Parker, R. G. (Eds.) *Men who sell sex: Global perspectives* (2nd ed.). New York: Routledge.

Alcano, M. C. (2016). *Masculine identities and male sex work between East Java and Bali: An ethnography of youth, bodies, and violence*. New York: Palgrave Macmillan.

Allman, D. (1999). *M is for mutual, a is for acts: Male sex work and AIDS in Canada*. Ottawa, Ontario: Health Canada.

Andros, P. (1966). *$tud*. Washington, DC: Guild Press.

Barker, C., & Gale, M. B. (Eds.). (2000). *British theatre between the wars 1918–1939*. Cambridge: Cambridge University Press.

Bennett, G. (1983). *Young and gay*. Sydney: Twenty-Ten.

Bimbi, D. S. (2007). Male prostitution: Pathology, paradigms, and progress in research. In T. G. Morrison & B. W. Whitehead (Eds.), *Male sex work: A business doing pleasure* (pp. 1–35). Binghamton, NY: Harrington Park Press.

Boles, J., & Elifson, K. (1998). Out of CASH: The rise and demise of a male prostitutes' rights organization. In J. E. Elias, V. Bullough, V. Elias, & G. Brewer (Eds.), *Prostitution: On whores, hustlers and johns* (pp. 267–278). New York: Prometheus Books.

Brown, R. (1996). *Against my better judgment: An intimate memoir of an eminent gay psychologist*. New York: Harrington Park Press.

Cassuto, Leonard (2011). *The Cambridge history of the American novel*. New York: Cambridge University Press.

Carlier, F. (1887). *Les deux prostitutions, 1860–1870*. Paris: Dentu.

Dewey, S., & Kell, P. (Eds.). (2011). *Policing pleasure: Sex work, policy, and the state in global perspective*. New York: New York University Press.

diCorcia, P.-Lorca. (2013). *Hustlers*. Göttingen: SteidlDangin.

Dixon, D., & Dixon, J. K. (1998). She-male prostitutes: Who are they, what do they do, and why do they do it? In J. E. Elias, V. Bullough, V. Elias, & G. Brewer (Eds.), *Prostitution: On whores, hustlers, and johns* (pp. 260–266). New York: Prometheus Books.

Dorais, M. (2005). *Rent boys: The world of male sex trade workers*. Montreal: McGill-Queen's University Press.

Drew, D., & Drake, J. [pseud]. (1969). *Boys for sale: A sociological study of boy prostitution*. New York: Brown Book Co.

Driver, E. D. (1957). *Boy prostitution* by Jens Jersild. Copenhagen, Gad, 1956. Reviewed in *Journal of Criminal Law, Criminology, and Police Science, 48*(4), 438–439.

Elias, J. E., Bullough, V., Elias, V., & Brewer, G. (Eds.). (1998). *Prostitution: On whores, hustlers, and johns*. New York: Prometheus Books.

Ellis, H. (1915). *Sexual inversion*. Philadelphia, PA: F. A. Davis Company.

Friedman, M. (2003). *Strapped for cash: A history of American hustler culture*. Los Angeles, CA: Alyson Publications.

Genet, J. (1949). *Journal du voleur*. Paris: Gallimard.

Genet, J. (1963). *Our lady of the flowers*. New York: Grove Press.

Goron, M.-F. (1899). *L'amour a Paris*. Paris: Flammarion.

Harris, M. (1973). *The dilly boys: Male prostitution in Piccadilly*. London: Croom Helm.

Hirschfeld, M. (1904). *Berlins drittes geschlecht*. Berlin: Seemann.

Hirschfeld, M. (1913). *Einiges über die Ursachen und Erscheinungsformen der männlichen (nicht erpresserischen) Prostitution*. Leipzig: F. C. W. Vogel.

Holloway, R. (1813). *The phoenix of Sodom, or, The Vere Street coterie: Being an exhibition of the gambols practised by the ancient lechers of Sodom and Gomorrah, embellished and improved with the modern refinements in sodomitical practices, by the members of the Vere Street coterie, of detestable memory*. London: Sold by J. Cook, . . . and to be had of all the booksellers.

Hyde, H. M. (1976). *The Cleveland street scandal*. London: W. H. Allen.

Jackson, P. A., & Gerard Sullivan. (1999). *Lady boys, tom boys, rent boys: Male and female homosexualities in contemporary Thailand*. New York: Harrington Park Press.

Jersild, J. (1956). *Boy prostitution*. Copenhagen: Gad.

Kaye, K. (2003). Male prostitution in the twentieth century: Pseudohomosexuals, hoodlum homosexuals, and exploited teens. *Journal of Homosexuality*, *46*(1/2), 1–77.

Kaye, K. (2007). Sex and the unspoken in male street prostitution. In T. G. Morrison & B. W. Whitehead (Eds.), *Male sex work: A business doing pleasure* (pp. 37–73). Binghamton, NY: Harrington Park Press.

Kinsey, A. C., Pomeroy, W. B., & Martin, C. (1948). *Sexual behavior in the human male*. Philadelphia, PA: W. B. Saunders Co.

Knox, M. P. (1998). Negotiations and relationships among male sex workers and clients in Liverpool, Merseyside, United Kingdom. In J. E. Elias, V. Bullough, V. Elias, & G. Brewer (Eds.), *Prostitution: On whores, hustlers, and johns* (pp. 236–259). New York: Prometheus Books.

Krafft-Ebing, R. von. (1886). *Psychopathia sexualis*. Stuttgart: Enke.

Langdon, G. (1962). *The last retreat*. Fresno, CA: Fabian Press.

Leary, D., & Minichiello, V. (2007). Exploring the interpersonal relationships in street-based male sex work: Results from an Australian qualitative study. In T. G. Morrison & B. W. Whitehead (Eds.), *Male sex work: A business doing pleasure* (pp. 75–110). Binghamton and New York: Harrington Park Press.

Lim, G. (2004). *Invisible trade: High-class sex for sale in Singapore*. Singapore: Monsoon Books.

Lim, G. (2008). *Invisible trade II: Secret lives and sexual intrigue in Singapore*. Singapore: Monsoon Books.

Lloyd, R. (1976). *For money or love: Boy prostitution in America*. New York: Vanguard Press.

Logan, T. D. (2017). *Economics, sexuality, and male sex work*. Cambridge: Cambridge University Press.

Marcus, S. (1966). *The other Victorians: A study of sexuality and pornography in mid-nineteenth-century England*. New York: Basic Books.

McNamara, R. (1994). *The Times Square hustler: Male prostitution in New York City*. Westport, CT: Praeger.

Merkin, R. (2000). The religion of socialism or a pleasant Sunday afternoon? The ILP Arts Guild. In C. Barker & M. B. Gale (Eds.), *British theatre between the wars 1918–1939* (pp. 162–189). Cambridge: Cambridge University Press.

Merrick, J., & Ragan, B. T. (Eds.). (1996). *Homosexuality in modern France*. New York: Oxford University Press.

Minichiello, V., & Scott, J. (2014a). Future directions in male sex work research. In V. Minichiello & J. Scott (Eds.), *Male sex work and society* (pp. 462–469). New York: Harrington Park Press.

Minichiello, V., & Scott, J. (Eds.). (2014b). *Male sex work and society*. New York: Harrington Park Press.

Mitchell, G. (2015). *Tourist attractions: Performing race and masculinity in Brazil's sexual economy*. Chicago, IL: University of Chicago Press.

Morrison, T. G., & Whitehead, B. W. (Eds.). (2007). *Male sex work: A business doing pleasure*. Binghamton, NY: Harrington Park Press.

Murray, V. T. H. (1926). *Bringing it home: A Play in one act*. London: Labour Pub. Co.

Nicoll, A. (1973). *English drama 1900–1930: The beginning of the modern period*. Cambridge: Cambridge University Press.

Norton, R. (1992). *Mother Clap's molly house: The gay subculture in England, 1700–1830*. London: GMP.

Ostwald, H. (1905–1907). *Das Berliner dirnentum*. Leipzig: W. Fiedler.

Ostwald, H. (1906). *Männliche prostitution im kaiserlichen Berlin*. Berlin: Janssen.

Özbay, C. (2015). "Straight" rent boys and gays who sell sex in Istanbul. In P. Aggleton & R. Parker (Eds.), *Men who sell sex: Global perspectives*. Oxford: Routledge.

Özbay, C. (2017). *Queering sexualities in Turkey: Gay men, male prostitutes and the city*. London: I. B. Tauris.

Peakman, J. (2003). *Mighty lewd books: The development of pornography in eighteenth-century England*. New York: Palgrave Macmillan.

Peniston, W. A. (1996). Love and death in gay Paris: Homosexuality and criminality in the 1870s. In J. Merrick & B. T. Ragan (Eds.), *Homosexuality in modern France* (pp. 128–145). New York: Oxford University Press.

Peniston, W. A. (2004). *Pederasts and others: Urban culture and sexual identity in nineteenth-century Paris*. New York: Harrington Park Press.

Perkins, R., & Bennett, G. (1985). *Being a prostitute: Prostitute women and prostitute men*. Sydney: George Allen & Unwin.

Pettiway, L. (1996). *Honey, honey, Miss Thang: Being black, gay, and on the streets*. Philadelphia, PA: Temple University Press.

Protection of children against sexual exploitation act of 1977. Public Law No. 95–225 18 USC 2251.

Raff, R., & Nicosia, G. (1977). *Bughouse blues: An intimate portrait of gay hustling in Chicago*. New York: Vantage Press.

Reay, B. (2010). *New York hustlers: Masculinity and sex in modern America*. Manchester: Manchester University Press.

Rechy, J. (1963). *City of night*. New York: Grove Press.

Rechy, J. (1977). *The sexual outlaw: A documentary: A non-fiction account, with commentaries, of three days and nights in the sexual underground*. New York: Grove Press.

Report of the Committee on Homosexual Offences and Prostitution. (1957). Committee on Homosexual Offences and Prostitution, the Home Office, Great Britain. London: HMSO.

Robb, G. (2004). *Strangers: Homosexual love in the nineteenth century*. New York: W. W. Norton.

Seymour, C. (1998). Studying myself/studying others: One (professional) boy's adventures studying sex work. In J. E. Elias, V. Bullough, V. Elias, & G. Brewer (Eds.), *Prostitution: On whores, hustlers and johns* (pp. 361–367). New York: Prometheus Books.

Simpson, C., Chester, L., & Leitsch, D. (1976). *The Cleveland Street affair*. Boston, MA: Little, Brown.

Smith, M. D., & Grov, C. (2011). *In the company of men: Inside the lives of male prostitutes*. Santa Barbara, CA: Praeger.

Snell, C. L. (1993). *Young men in the street: Help-seeking behavior of young male prostitutes*. Westport, CT: Praeger.

The social evil in Chicago: A study of existing conditions with recommendations by the Vice Commission of Chicago. (1911). Chicago, IL: Gunthorp-Warren.

Steward, S. (1970). *My brother the hustler*. Gay Parisian Press.

Steward, S. (1990). *Bad boys and tough tattoos: A social history of the tattoo with gangs, sailors, and street-corner punks, 1950–1965*. New York: Haworth Press.

Steward, S. (1991). *Understanding the male hustler*. New York: Haworth Press.

Streeby, S. (2011). Dime novels and the rise of mass-market genres. In *The Cambridge history of the American novel* (pp. 586–599). New York: Cambridge University Press.

Walby, K. (2012). *Touching encounters: Sex, work, and male-for-male Internet escorting*. Chicago, IL: University of Chicago Press.

Weeks, J. (1980). Inverts, perverts and Mary-Annes: Male prostitution and the regulation of homosexuality in England in the nineteenth and early twentieth centuries. *Journal of Homosexuality, 6*(1/2), 113–134.

Weisberg, D. K. (1985). *Children of the night: A study of adolescent prostitution*. Lexington, MA: Lexington Books.

West, D. J. (1998). Male homosexual prostitution in England. In J. E. Elias, V. Bullough, V. Elias, & G. Brewer (Eds.), *Prostitution: On whores, hustlers and johns* (pp. 228–235). New York: Prometheus Books.

Whitaker, R. (1999). *Assuming the position: A memoir of hustling*. New York: Four Walls Eight Windows.

White, E. (2017). *Navigating force and choice: Experiences in the New York City sex trade and the criminal justice system's response*. Center for Court Innovation (U.S.); issuing body; National Institute of Justice. Retrieved from www.ncjrs.gov/pdffiles1/nij/grants/251504.pdf

Wolfenden Committee. (1957). *Report of the Committee on Homosexual Offences and Prostitution (Cmnd 9678)*. London: HMSO.

Part III
Male sex work online

13

Quantifying global male sex worker communities in the technology era

Revisions in definitions and statistics

Victor Minichiello, John Scott, Taylor Harrington,
Denton Callander, and Christian Grov

Emerging global sex work communities

Who "belongs" in sex workers' communities? We suggest a wide membership, and as sex workers themselves have long argued, the boundaries of such communities are highly porous and fluid. As we demonstrated in the first volume of *Male Sex Work and Society* (2014), outside of an occupational context, sex workers and their clients belong to multiple communities and have complex identities. Indeed, it is not always clear how we should define "sex workers." Do they have to be involved in the occupation for a minimum period of time? Do they have to be currently and actively engaged in sex work? Should sex work be their primary occupation, or do we include people who engage in sex work only part-time or occasionally? What services must they provide? These questions might seem straightforward, but using them to identify who is a sex worker is complicated.

Let us consider some of these complications. If we want research into sex work communities to be empirical and if we want to consider sex work as an occupation, it is seems logical to define who is a sex worker and to estimate the number of people engaged in this sort of work. However, it is difficult to find accurate information, given the stigma and secrecy associated with sex work. Male sex work often includes a double stigma because the idea of the male body being objectified or commercialized as a sexual object runs counter to many cultural norms. Same-sex attraction is also highly stigmatized and remains criminalized in many countries. Research has suggested that much male sex work occurs on a casual or part-time basis and that very few men become full-time sex workers or remain in the occupation for an extended period of time. Rather, much of the work is clandestine or opportunistic. Moreover, many people who engage in what might be considered male sex work may never view themselves as sex workers or adopt that term as a primary occupational or other identity. As in most occupations, there are full-time, part-time, and casual sex workers. Some view it as a career, some view it in a more limited context, and some fraudulently pose as sex workers for criminal or other reasons. In addition, there are aspirational or prospective sex workers who seek to earn income in the occupation but who are at an early stage of a career that involves learning skills, developing resources, and building a client base. Some aspiring sex workers may succeed, while others fail. Any of these people may or may not identify as a sex worker.

Understanding the male sex work counting space

Sociological concepts such as time and space are relevant when attempting to count male escorts (Giddens, 1985). Both of these elements influence how same-sex activity and male sex work are positioned in society, including their visibility and distribution. History clearly documents that male sex work is not a modern phenomenon, but its visibility has fluctuated across time and culture (Minichiello & Scott, 2014). Attempts to account for sex work will also be influenced by definitions of what constitutes sex work—for example, whether it is a full-time occupation or opportunistic (Callander & DeVeau, 2019). Such definitions are highly variable in the research literature, partly due to debates whether how sex work should be understood and studied as a problem or an occupation or whether the term *prostitution* or *sex work* should be used (Minichiello & Scott, 2014). Scholars have also identified a range of methodological issues associated with measuring the size and scope of sex work and the associated ethical issues in conducting such research (Sanders, Campbell, Cunningham, Pitcher, & Scoular, 2018).

Until recently, at least in Western democracies, laws criminalizing sex work and/or same-sex relations forced male prostitution to go underground, making it difficult to identify and count. Recent laws that decriminalize sex work and same-sex relations create environments that are more open to public visibility and the normalization of paid sexual relations between men (Minichiello, Scott, & Cox, 2018). Also, the opportunity for escorts to advertise online and researchers to easily access, observe, and count online male escorts was not available prior to the 1990s.

Today, sex workers organize the sale of their sexual services via a number of venues: the street, brothels/parlors, bars, and other public places where people go to dance and party, such as saunas, websites, and, more recently, apps. Often escorts use more than one of these venues, and the prominence of a particular venue depends on the local laws and customs. Hidden sex work, where the interaction between buyers and sellers takes place via chats, clubs, hotels, massage, and saunas is particularly difficult to quantify, partly because this information is often held by gatekeepers who do not release this information publicly or who must follow privacy laws. In contrast, counting the number of approved brothels is much easier because they are on the public record. In some parlors and brothels, the organization and structure of the business allow for some degree of formal or informal quantification regarding work shifts and profitability. However, much of male sex work is independent and not subject to management or formally structured into shifts. Rather, it occurs informally and often operates on an ad hoc basis according to highly variable market circumstances that impact levels of demand, but it is more visible via apps and websites. Each of these forums has its own set of specific methodological obstacles and barriers in terms of accurately identifying the number of escorts or clients in a time and place, let alone the nature and content of their interactions.

Research shows that, at least in Western countries, a large number of escorts increasingly use online advertising, which accounts for anywhere from 40 to 75% of their business (Prestage et al., 2015). A study commissioned by the municipality of The Hague, Netherlands, into the nature and extent of sexual services provided by males reported that for the years 2009–2012, the average number of male escorts advertising on the internet was 209, and that three-quarters of all male escorts in this region were active on the Internet (Van Gelder, 2014). One distinguishing feature between male sex work and female sex work is that many male sex workers enter the paid sex industry voluntarily and work on their own (Cheng et al., 2011). Male sex workers are, generally speaking, also more likely than female sex workers to initiate contact with clients electronically (for example, by phone and online) and work as private escorts rather than in a brothel-based environment (Donovan et al., 2010). In some countries, especially those where sex work is illegal and the Internet is regulated, as in Asia and the Middle East, where prostitution is illegal, massage parlors often host male employees (Lee & Gee-Hyun, 2015).

The most prominent male escort websites internationally are mostly run from countries where the provision of sexual services in return for payment is not criminalized. These e-commerce websites include marketing features that allows buyers to sort information on the website to find their preferences via search features relating mostly to the physical attributes of the "escort," such as height, weight, age and body features (Kumar, Minichiello, Scott, & Harrington, 2017). These sites are easily accessible and often require no user registration, and they often contain a consent agreement with the user such as those displayed in Figures 13.1 and 13.2.

Some researchers have noted that a reduction in street prostitution, at least in the male sex industry, may be partly due to the digital and technological developments taking place in the last decade or so (Callander & DeVeau, 2019). Studies commissioned by the Swedish National Board of Health and Welfare, with the most recent survey conducted in 2014, reveal an increase in the sale of sexual services via the Internet and social media, including men selling sex to other men (Mujaj & Netscher, 2015). One survey in the United Kingdom included 6,965 advertisements (as opposed to number of different individuals). In almost half of the profiles, sex workers reported their ages as 18–30, and the number of advertisements involving men selling sexual services to men doubled from 2010 to 2014 (House of Commons Home Affairs Committee, 2016).

It is always important to consider legal requirements. Where street prostitution in the form of red-light districts is legal, the purchase of sexual services on the streets is more widespread. Since the 1990s, street prostitution has significantly declined in many countries. For example, there has been a 50% decrease in street prostitution in Sweden since the 1990s (Eriksson & Gavanas,

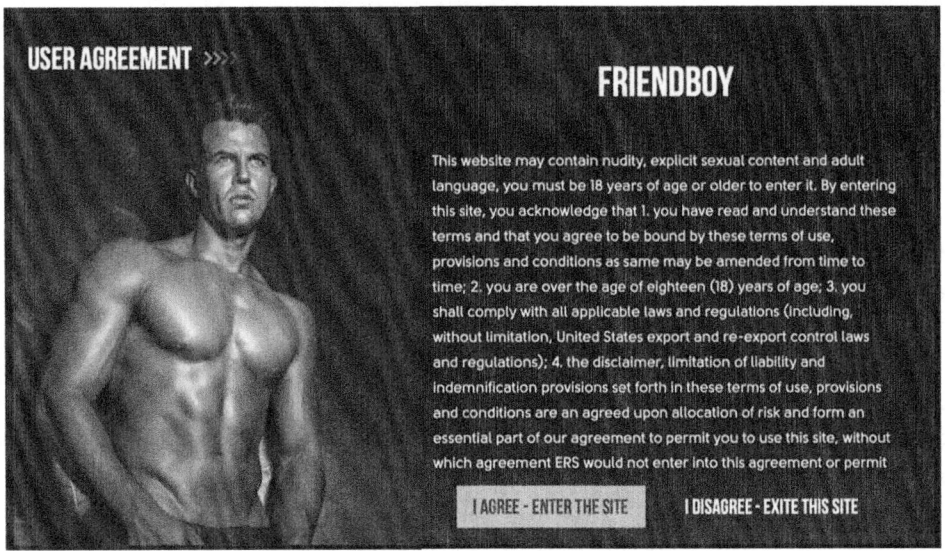

Figure 13.1   Consent agreement found on male escort website Friendboy.

Figure 13.2   Agreement statement found on male escort website Rent.Men.

2008). Street prostitution varies by geographic space (Garcia, Van Voss, & Melkerk, 2017). For example, evidence since the 1980s shows that in the larger U.S. cities of Los Angeles, San Francisco, and New York, street sex workers account for 10 to 20% of the sex worker population, but in some smaller regional cities with limited indoor venues, street prostitution can account for up to 50% of sex workers (Prostitutes Education Network, 1997). A more recent report funded by the U.S. National Institute of Justice shows that while street sex work, Internet-based sex work, brothels, and massage parlors existed in each of the eight U.S. cities included in the survey, there were regional differences that influenced their relative proportions (Dunk et al., 2014). In one of the few studies that has attempted to account for the geographical dimensions of male sex work, Logan (2010) found that the location of male sex workers (MSWs) closely follows the size of metropolitan statistical areas, rather than gay location patterns.

In Australia, according to the Sex Workers Outreach Project in New South Wales (SWOP NSW), the proportion working as street-based sex workers has been estimated to be 5 to 10%, respectively, of all sex workers in New South Wales (Donovan et al., 2012), and the trend is toward a decrease in the number of street sex workers. These proportions may not be observed in other Australian jurisdictions, due to the different laws regarding private and brothel work, and some Australian states report higher proportions of street workers. Street-based sex workers in the United Kingdom are just over a quarter of all sex workers, and these numbers are either remaining stable or declining (House of Commons Home Affairs Committee, 2016). Based on this evidence, a proposition can be put forward. In jurisdictions where sex work is illegal, prostitution is more likely to be found in the streets, massage parlors, and bars.

Brothels and escort agencies also vary considerably across countries depending on local law, policy, police culture, and custom (TAMPEP, 2009). One study of 25 European countries reported that the percentage of sex workers working outdoors ranged from 2 to 64%, with seven countries listed as having more than half of sex workers working in outdoor settings like streets, highways, and parks (TAMPEP, 2009). However, following a series of policy and legislative changes, Europe has seen a tremendous shift from outdoor to indoor sex work, although there are regional and perhaps gender differences. Unfortunately, the report does not provide an analysis of the gender of the sex workers.

The numbers of sex workers in the world

Using security services estimates, reporting by public health programs, and other monitoring data from global criminal justice programs, a Havocscope report (2018) estimates that there are close to 14 million prostitutes in the world, but it does not provide a male-female break-down. A report conducted by Foundation Scelles (2018) estimates that the figure is closer to 40–42 million, with 80% of world sex workers being female and about 8 to 8.42 million being men. Non-government organizations and sex workers' organizations are increasingly reporting male escorts in countries. For example, the NGO SWEAT (Sex Workers Education and Advocacy Taskforce) estimates that there are 153,000 sex workers in Africa, including 8,000 male escorts (Foundation Scelles, 2018). Countries with over 1,000,000 sex workers include China, India, and the United States. Countries with between 400,000 and less than 1 million sex workers include the Philippines, Mexico, and Germany (Havocscope, 2018). One thing is clear: While the number of sex workers increases with population size, a perfect correlation does not necessarily exist. For example, while Sweden has a larger population than the other Nordic countries, Sweden's prostitute population is approximately one-tenth of Denmark's and one-eighth of Norway's (End Prostitution Now, 2016). Although the three countries have similar economic and social profiles, it is reasonable to assume that the reduction or perhaps the lower visibility of prostitution in Sweden can be attributed to Swedish law and how laws influence the statistical count. (For more on prostitution in Sweden, see Chapter 31 of this book.)

Government reports on the actual number of sex workers, and male sex workers in particular, are not readily available, particularly from Asia and Africa. According to a report commissioned by the European Parliament, it is estimated that the Netherlands and Germany respectively have approximately 10,000–15,000 and 400,000–450,000 sex workers, of which 90% are female (TAMPEP, 2009). A report on prostitution published by the House of Commons Home Affairs Committee (2016) reported that there are 72,800 sex workers in the United Kingdom and about 32,000 in London; another report estimates 80,000 sex workers in the United Kingdom (TAMPEP, 2009). It is important to remember that when numbers are provided, even by government reports, disputes about accuracy abound. For example, Magnanti (2014) argues that the estimate of the United Kingdom's Office for National Statistics of 60,879 sex workers who contribute £5.314 billion to the economy is too high, citing a number of wage calculation assumptions and methodological flaws. Meanwhile, Fogg (2014) argues that these numbers are too low. Using an extractor to collect data from Adultwork (an advertisement platform for escorts launched in 2003, and known as "the eBay of sex"), which includes male escorts, Fogg estimates that there are 104,964 sex workers in the United Kingdom, contributing £8.7 billion pounds to the economy.

The number of sex workers in Asia is large, but government reports are not easily available. Four of the top ten countries with the most sex workers per 10,000 people are from Asia, according to *The Ultimate Guide* for the retiree, expat, investor, and entrepreneur (Foynes, 2013). A government report on prostitution in India states that there are at least 2 million female sex workers in India (Hays, 2015), although some commentators report that the figure is much higher (Havocscope, 2018). The number of male sex workers is not available or cited, which is not surprising given that male prostitution is not recognized in any law in India, and up until recently, consensual anal intercourse was illegal under section 377 of the Indian Penal Code (Patidar, 2018). However, a Google search reveals Indian agencies that house male companions for women and men, sex tourism sites mention boys for hire, and the subject of male escorts is now discussed on social media (Pagadala, 2014).

Male sex worker numbers: some estimates

In the research literature, it is reported that men generally account for an estimated 5–10% of sex workers in liberal democracies, although estimates tend to vary widely among countries (Minichiello & Scott, 2014). In Europe, for example, about 7% of sex workers are male, and this number ranged from 1% in Estonia to 15% in Poland, with ten European countries reporting that men made up 10% or more of the total sex worker population (TAMPEP, 2009). While acknowledging that there are discrepancies in the reported number of male sex workers, a government report from the United Kingdom estimated that males make up about 17% of total indoor sex workers (House of Commons Home Affairs Committee, 2016). Other commissioned research reports much lower numbers. A review of escorts' profiles in Ireland shows that males account for 3.5% of the total number of escort advertisements (Maginn & Ellison, 2013). A recent report commissioned by the Dutch Minister of Security and Justice on prostitution in the Netherlands noted that 5% of their captured sample were male (Daalder, 2015). Elsewhere in Europe, a survey conducted by the Danish National Centre for Social Research found that of the 3,200 sex workers in Denmark in 2010, 100 or about 3% were male (Haahr, 2011). In a critique of prostitution counting methodologies, a recent report that includes male prostitution and uses AdultWork software, estimates that the United Kingdom has 104,964 sex workers, of whom 44,085 or 42% are males (Fogg, 2014).

Most commentators in the policy, sex industry, and media field agree that, generally speaking, the reported percentage of male sex workers in many reports is probably too conservative. Callander, Harrington, Scott, DeVeau, and Minichiello (2019) suggest using behavioral survey data on men who have sex with men to extrapolate male escort numbers beyond profile numbers found on escorting websites. In Australia, 39% of male sex workers report advertising through sex work websites, and only 16% of male sex workers sell sex at least weekly (Prestage et al., 2015). Using these numbers, Callander and his colleagues comment that the 2017 Male Escort Global Survey (MEGS) data for Australia reporting 561 male escorts advertising on escort websites (Scott, Minichiello, Callander, & Harrington, 2017) captured around 6.5% of male sex workers operating in Australia with a 95% confidence interval of 3% to 13%. Callander and his associates estimate that 7,939 male sex workers were operating in Australia in 2017, within a likely range of 3,969 to 17,200. This wide range shows the discrepancies that can result from using only profiles samples versus also using survey data to improve estimates of sex workers' population size.

An alternative way to gain insights on the number of male sex workers is via police arrest statistics. For example, statistics from U.S. government agencies in the 1980s on prostitution arrests offered the following profile: 70% female prostitutes, 20% male prostitutes, and 10% customers (Prostitutes Education Network, 1997). Another report, using data extracted from the National Incident-based Reporting System developed by the FBI, reports that men made up 34.1% of the 4,055 arrests for prostitution in 2001 (Vandiver & Krienert, 2007). Of course, arrest data may tell us more about police practices than it does about sex work. This noted, we have to be careful not to extrapolate too much from official crime statistics, because such data will always include a "dark figure" of unreported, unrecorded, and unprosecuted criminal activity. Further, such data may also tell us more about policy and policing practices in specific jurisdictions than it does about frequency of sex work activity in a jurisdiction.

Male Escort Global Survey of online male escorts in the world: the number

The Male Escort Global Survey conducted in 2017 on male escorts by researchers at the Queensland University of Technology (see Figure 13.3; Scott et al., 2017) was repeated again in

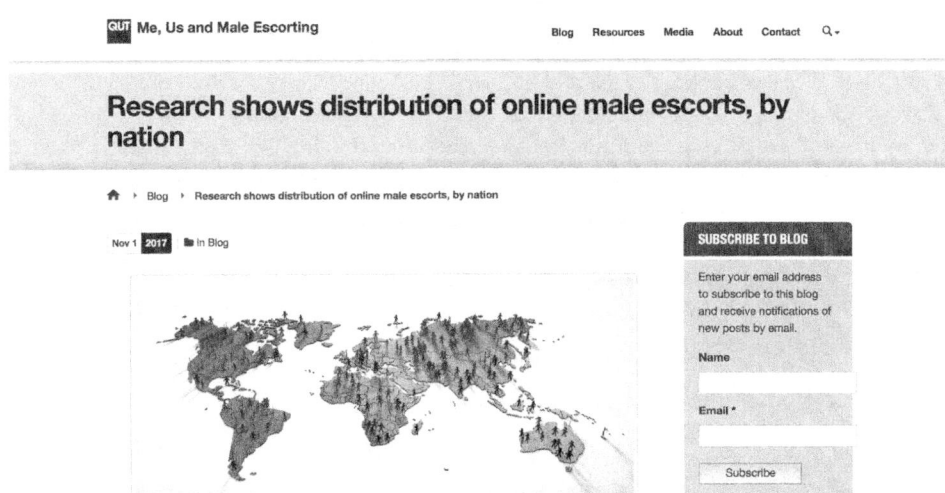

Figure 13.3   Blog that presents data on global survey of online male escorts found at research. qut.edu.au/aboutmaleescorting.

2018. Using a similar methodology developed by Kumar and colleagues (2017) to identify male escort websites, the researchers first verified the existing 2017 website list and then searched for new websites that went online after the earlier survey. The survey was conducted between March and May 2018. It relied on the data originally listed in the *Males* app (see Kumar et al., 2017), which offers a global listing of male sex work websites obtained through an online audit of sites first compiled in November 2016. Kumar and colleagues (2017) provide a detailed discussion on the methodology used to identity the online websites for male escorts.

We need to discuss some caveats before we present the results of the 2018 online male escorts survey and compare it with the previous year. First, the 2018 survey again measures the number of "available services" rather than actual demand or usage of those services. The best indicator of demand is a measure that records and counts paid clients or a client's specific request for a service via a booking, and across a number of different spaces where sex work operates. But such a measurement is difficult to operationalize in the field, due to obvious ethical issues, escorts' and clients' (un)willingness to share such information with researchers, and these two groups' general reticence to participate in such studies. Also, online escorting is only one venue and aspect of the sex industry (Scott et al., 2017) and therefore in itself does not offer an accurate or full picture of the sex work workforce. Others have also discussed some of the methodological and ethical issues and obstacles associated with counting the profiles of online escort profiles and advertisements (Sanders et al., 2018), and some have suggested protocols that can ensure greater accuracy when collecting such data (Callander et al., 2019).

Second, changes in the law regarding website requirements can have a profound impact on the traffic and viability of hosting such material. For example, two recent pieces of legislation, The Stop Enabling Sex Traffickers Act (SESTA) and Allow States and Victims to Fight Online Sex Trafficking (FOSTA), passed in the United States since our 2017 survey have exposed website owners to unclear criminal and legal risks, thus explaining the removal or shutdown of previously available sites that were hosted in the United States (Romano, 2018). For example, the following websites have been removed for legal reasons since the last survey: Men4RentNow, Boyscort, Cracker, Backpage. Other websites, including Connect2Men, have transferred their operation from the United States to other countries, where laws are more favorable to their business (Farokhmansh, 2018). Of the websites previously operating in the United States in the 2017 survey, 12 were no longer active, and a number of world escort websites no longer include the United States as a listed country, which may explain the lower numbers of escort profiles found in the United States in 2018. Not surprisingly, the survey found that a number of U.S. websites now include a message that mentions recent changes in the law and diverts the user to a company outside the United States (see, for example, companions4women.com).

Laws can also impact how sexual services are described. For example, the anti-prostitution laws in South Korea have created loopholes for male sex workers to work in the health and fitness sector as "male masseurs." Searching for "yeoseong massage" allows you to find men offering massage options to clients, including "Course C," which includes the use of adult sex toys (Lee & Gee-Hyun, 2015). In other parts of the world, such as the United Arab Emirates and African countries, the law influences how much information escorts provide about their sexual identity because homosexual activity is not legal and the law does not reference any protections against discrimination on the basis of sexuality (Equaldex, 2018). Sometimes terminology about sexual identity is influenced by cultural and sexual norms around masculinity (Minichiello, Dune, Disogra, & Mariño, 2014). For example, many of the websites in South America target both a male and female clientele rather than an exclusively gay market, with websites as a matter of routine providing information on whether the services are offered to "*attendemos homens, mulheres, e casais*" (we attend to men, women, and couples), "*ele, ela, & casais*" (him, her, and couples) or "*atención a hombres, mujeres, y parejas*" (attention to men, women, and couples).

Third, changes in the website's contract with users, which may require verification of identification or membership fees from escorts, can affect the volume of escort profiles and client usage of the site. For example, some websites, including Mx.mileroticos in Mexico and Vivalocal in Brazil, changed their verification and/or photo requirements, significantly reducing the overall number of profiles for those countries: from about 21,091 in 2017 to about 5,000 in 2018 for Brazil and from about 121,000 in 2017 to about 82,000 for Mexico in 2018.

Fourth, while it is true that some countries are being affected by new laws that are pushing escorting off social media platforms, other entrepreneurs and/or countries are either developing new products to respond to the legal challenges or seizing new or displaced market opportunities in promoting sex work via friendly social spaces. For example, two newer websites have used legal language to promote their services. Mintboys states that it follows the "Las Vegas model" where customers pay for time with an escort and adds the statement that "prostitution is illegal and we do not allow our escorts and clients to use this site for that purpose." As the site explains:

> It's a tumultuous time for the industry. Federal authorities have shut down Backpage. Craigslist has shuttered its personal sections. Men4RentNow, RentHotAngels, and other sites have shut down voluntarily, anticipating a government crackdown. Everyone wants to know what comes next in the aftermath of SESTA and FOSTA. MintBoys is "what comes next." It's the safe space where clients and escorts can return, and the result of years of careful planning. Despite the sudden passage of SESTA/FOSTA, and the uncertainty it's created, we believe MintBoys remains uniquely positioned to thrive in a rapidly evolving illegal environment.

FriendBoy, a new site operating from the Netherlands, states that "everything is very simple and easy on FriendBoy," implying that it is better or legally more secure than RentBoy (a website closed down by U.S. authorities) or RentMen.

Our 2018 survey also identified large sites like Escortbg in Bulgaria with over 20,000 profiles, which was either not available or not captured via our Google search in the 2017 survey, significantly increasing the number of escort profiles in that country. Other particularly large websites, such as Mileroticos, which previously focused on a few countries, have added new countries like Colombia and Italy, increasing the number of escort profiles in those countries. Finally, MEGS excluded countries where there were ten or fewer escorts. Excluded from the previous survey because of this criterion were Croatia, Jamaica, and Paraguay.

The Male Escort Global Survey 2018 survey results

A total of 65 countries are included in the 2018 survey. New in the 2018 survey are Azerbaijan, the Dominican Republic, Ecuador, Egypt, El Salvador, Lebanon, and Nigeria, with an average of 11 websites per country. Some countries had a much higher number of websites listing male escorts than others, with a range from 3 to 42. However, it is important to note that several international websites included escort profiles from countries around the world, such as Rentmen and Hourboy, and the host environments for these websites were often countries where prostitution was legal. The number of male escorts increased in 51 countries over the previous survey and decreased in only 7 countries. Using data from the 2017 MEGS survey, Callander and colleagues (2019) estimate that the rate of online sex work among men ranges from .04 per 100,000 (India) to 88 per 100,000 (Mexico), with a median value of 1.45 per 100,000. Globally, the overall rate was 4.9 online male sex workers per 100,000 adult men.

There were 294,067 male escort profiles online worldwide, and while this result is a decrease from the 325,852 profiles found in 2017, the total number of escorts when duplicate profiles are eliminated rose from 105,009 to 123,256. Overall, countries reported an increase from the previous survey in the number of male escorts for men and the number of male escorts for women and couples, as Table 13.1 shows.

Table 13.1 MEGS 2018: Estimates of Online Male Escort Numbers by Country

Country	No. of Websites	No. of Escort Profiles (EPs)	No. of Actual Escorts (AEs)	No. of Male Escorts for Men (MEMs)	No. of Male Escorts for Women/ Couples (MEWCs)	MEWC/ AE (%)
Argentina	11	433	262	80	182	69.46
Australia	30	782	668	525	143	21.40
Austria	16	213	192	166	26	13.54
Azerbaijan	6	22	20	13	7	35.00
Belgium	20	1,649	1,315	505	810	61.59
Bolivia	4	42	40	30	10	25.00
Brazil	35	5,610	4,240	2,924	1,316	31.03
Bulgaria	10	40,136	5,001	2,305	2,696	53.90
Canada	15	1,955	1,623	1,455	168	10.35
Chile	7	152	130	102	28	21.53

(Continued)

Table 13.1 (Continued)

Country	No. of Websites	No. of Escort Profiles (EPs)	No. of Actual Escorts (AEs)	No. of Male Escorts for Men (MEMs)	No. of Male Escorts for Women/ Couples (MEWCs)	MEWC/ AE (%)
China	30	1,867	1,750	1,728	22	1.25
Colombia	12	84,577	21,967	10,030	11,937	54.34
Costa Rica	3	53	49	46	3	6.12
Cyprus	4	64	64	24	40	62.50
Czech Republic	7	213	200	183	17	8.50
Denmark	11	54	42	38	4	9.50
Dominican Republic	3	131	106	95	11	10.37
Ecuador	6	223	187	169	18	9.62
Egypt	8	88	85	52	33	38.82
El Salvador	3	334	266	86	180	67.66
Estonia	4	63	44	27	17	38.63
Finland	7	322	111	109	2	1.80
France	18	1,400	1,044	680	364	34.86
Germany	19	1,252	1,006	708	298	29.62
Greece	13	427	282	122	160	56.73
Hong Kong	12	190	151	113	38	25.16
Hungary	10	213	199	108	91	45.70
India	10	731	704	443	261	37.07
Indonesia	11	302	286	194	92	32.16
Ireland	8	82	65	57	8	12.30
Israel	7	58	57	54	3	5.26
Italy	19	4,110	3,145	1,217	1,928	61.30
Japan	27	1,317	1,253	527	726	57.94
Kenya	4	59	59	9	50	84.70
Lebanon	4	131	125	107	18	14.40
Malaysia	8	140	119	94	25	21.00
Mexico	11	82,124	35,407	26,368	9,039	25.52
Netherlands	15	2,800	1,694	680	1,014	59.85
New Zealand	9	192	171	92	79	46.19
Nigeria	3	106	103	47	56	54.36
Norway	10	488	204	186	18	8.82
Panama	4	55	52	52	0	0
Peru	9	363	324	246	78	24.07
Philippines	10	510	501	367	134	26.74
Poland	6	60	53	50	3	5.66

Country	No. of Websites	No. of Escort Profiles (EPs)	No. of Actual Escorts (AEs)	No. of Male Escorts for Men (MEMs)	No. of Male Escorts for Women/ Couples (MEWCs)	MEWC/ AE (%)
Portugal	20	279	252	225	27	10.71
Romania	11	159	107	52	55	51.40
Russia	14	205	202	173	29	14.35
Singapore	18	439	324	281	43	13.27
South Africa	12	498	294	179	115	39.11
South Korea	6	74	72	56	16	22.22
Spain	29	10,088	6,559	4,301	2,258	34.42
Sri Lanka	4	666	621	23	598	96.29
Sweden	6	130	82	54	28	34.14
Switzerland	15	665	522	358	164	31.41
Taiwan	15	113	103	103	0	0
Thailand	15	202	126	88	38	30.15
Turkey	11	144	133	82	51	38.34
Uganda	3	35	35	4	31	88.57
Ukraine	8	45	45	28	17	37.77
United Arab Emirates	11	564	503	247	256	50.89
United Kingdom	42	13,364	7,828	4,106	3,722	47.54
Uruguay	5	61	60	14	46	76.66
United States	24	30,201	19,983	12,261	7,722	38.64
Venezuela	7	42	39	31	8	20.51
World Total	**M = 11.90 (median)**	**294,067**	**123,256**	**75,879**	**47,377**	**38.69**

Note: Countries with ten or fewer escorts are not included.

Key:

Indicates an increase since the 2017 survey

Indicates no change

Indicates a decrease.

No shading indicates a new country in the 2018 survey. Croatia, Jamaica, and Paraguay were excluded from the 2018 survey owing to low numbers.

Mexico, Colombia, the United States, the United Kingdom, and Spain were the countries with the highest number of escorts, 74% of the total male escorts. Some of the countries that reported the biggest increase since the previous survey included Bulgaria, Colombia, India, Italy, the Netherlands, the United Kingdom, and Sri Lanka. Countries with a modest increase include Canada, China, France, Japan, and the Philippines, while Brazil and the United States reported the largest decrease in number of male escorts.

Regionally, South and Central America account for the highest numbers of male sex workers (51%), followed by Europe (25%), North America (17%), Asia and the Middle East (5%), Oceania (Australia and New Zealand) (1%), and Africa (less than 1%). In contrast to the 2017 survey, South and Central America and Asia and the Middle East accounted for an increase in the total percentage of male escorts globally, while North America and Europe accounted for a decrease, and Oceania and Africa reported a similar result.

This distribution is perhaps not surprising when we look at the legality of same-sex intercourse and sex work. Anti-homosexuality laws that criminalize same-sex consensual activity are found in 72 countries, mostly located in nations of Africa, the Middle East, and Asia (Carroll & Itaborahy, 2015). When we look at the legal status of prostitution by country, most European and South American nations, Canada, Mexico, Australia, and New Zealand have laws that make prostitution legal in some form (ProCon.Org, 2018). Of the countries with the highest concentration of male sex work profiles on the Internet (see Table 13.1), same-sex relations and prostitution were legal in the following countries: Australia, Belgium, Brazil, Canada, Germany, Spain, and the United Kingdom. In China, Japan, Singapore, Taiwan, and the United States, one of these activities is illegal or restricted (see ProCon.Org, 2018; Erasing76Crimes, 2018).

Legislation associated with sex work, homosexuality, or same-sex relations influences the structure and organization of the sex industry and may restrict or increase opportunities to engage in sex work in various settings. For example, in jurisdictions where sex work and homosexuality are criminalized, using online platforms to market services may be problematic because the escort's identity is revealed via phone numbers, photographs, and information obtained when the escort registered on the site. Operating such sites may violate the law, as evidenced via the Rentboy.com case in New York State (Base, 2015). Law can also influence the terminology used to describe the types of service provided; for example, escorts may offer a "companion" service rather than an "escort" service. Moreover, sex workers can work separately in their own dwelling or as part of an agency in a company-registered facility that is operated by a third party. For example, in Asia, agencies are more often the norm than individual escort services because sex work is officially illegal but massage services are not (Kong, 2014; Lee & Gee-Hyun, 2015).

Clientele

Like the previous survey, the 2018 survey shows that male clientele is the primary market for male escorts. Table 13.1 shows that the majority of the escorts catered to gay men or men who have sex with men as customers. However, the overall figure has declined from 68% in 2017 to 61% in 2018.

The number of male escorts who advertised their services to women and couples rose from 32,948 to 47,975, as did the overall global percentage of male escorts catering to this group, which rose from 31% in 2017 to 39% in 2018. The top ten countries with the largest number of male escorts for women and couples were in order: Colombia (11,937), Mexico (9,039), the United States (7,722), the United Kingdom (3,722), Bulgaria (2,696), Spain (2,258), Italy (1,928), Brazil (1,316), the Netherlands (1,014), and Belgium (810). Seven of these countries also featured as the top countries for male escorts for women and couples in 2017. Again, Latin American and European countries feature prominently on the list, accounting for 48% and 29%, respectively, or, combined, more than two-thirds of all male escorts for women and couples globally. North America came next with 17%.

The results also reveal that 17 countries had more male escorts seeking female and couple clients than male escorts seeking male clients exclusively. The top ten countries with the highest percentage of escorts for women and couples were Sri Lanka (92.3%), Uganda (88.6%), Kenya (84.7%), Uruguay (76.7%), Argentina (69.5%), El Salvador (67.7%), Cyprus (62.5%), Belgium (61.6%), Italy (61.3%), and the Netherlands (59.9%).

Some methodological limitations of the online survey

Some limitations of the 2018 website survey are worth noting. Given the sheer number of MSW sites that exist, it is likely that this survey missed some sites. In jurisdictions where sex work or same-sex relations are heavily penalized, it is possible that escort sites are known only to participants within relatively closed social networks, such as subcultures of same-sex-attracted men. It may be that these sites are listed on the Tor network (a browser designed for anonymous Web surfing and protection against traffic analysis). No such sites were found in preliminary searches, but their existence is probable given the size of the Tor network (The Tor Project, Inc., 2015). Although we attempted to identify all possible slang terms for MSW in various languages, it is likely that we missed some terms and, consequently, some websites, especially given the cultural specificity of such terminology. It is also possible that some of the Google Translate terms are erroneous.

One thing is clear from the large number of websites on male escorting. It is increasingly important to acknowledge and recognize that male escorting is a business and social phenomenon. Research needs to develop a more comprehensive methodological approach to establishing a baseline dataset so that trends in the distribution of male sex workers across time and nations can be studied. Independent replication surveys that build on the method described in this chapter are highly desirable. Equally important is the development of a survey instrument that will facilitate the counting of male escorts working in outdoor settings (such as the streets) and indoor settings (such as brothels and third-party agencies); this survey should be developed in consultation with and administered by sex work organizations, NGOs, health agencies, and owners of brothels. Capturing all of the different sex work settings would offer a more comprehensive estimate of the number of male escorts globally. Studies can then draw on this dataset to frame their studies as they investigate the social, legal, and health content of male sex work in a cross-cultural context.

We must also acknowledge, as argued by Sanders and her colleagues (2018), that the mapping of the sex industry within countries and across the globe is fraught with methodological challenges that may never fully capture the size and changing dynamics of the sex work industry. The decriminalization and normalization agenda in the sex work industry, as called for by Amnesty International, calls for sex work to be treated like any other occupation (Murphy, 2015). It is our position that studies that attempt to count sex workers and describe the characteristics of sex work in a methodologically ethical and responsible manner, and conducted with sex workers' organizations as partners, may play an important role in supporting sex workers and their clients. Figure 13.4 reproduces a Facebook site calling for decriminalization and professionalization of male escorting.

Who is a male escort?

There is, of course, the larger question to be asked: Who can be classified as a male sex worker? Here, both gender and work come into play. First, let us consider gender. Is the sex worker a biologically born male with a penis or someone who self-identifies as male? Do male sex workers include females who transition to male? Most studies resolve the gender question by separating biologically born male escorts from transgender escorts. Escort websites also use these distinguishing categories, including the escort's sexual orientation, as a demarcation of their product.

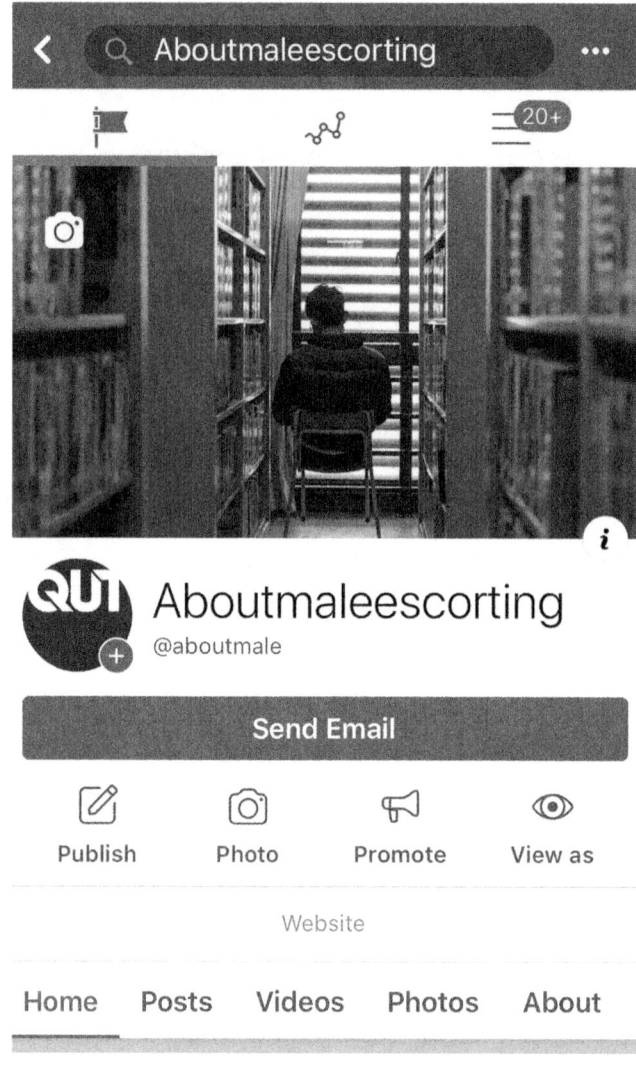

Figure 13.4 Facebook site calling for decriminalization and professionalization of male escorting.

Second, let us consider work. Is sex work performing sexual acts with another person for a fee? Most studies focus on the exchange of money for sexual favors. But reality is more complicated. In addition to money, people can exchange sexual services for drugs, housing, and other material goods, to list just a few items. If sex work were decriminalized, normalized, and professionalized like any other work, operationalizing this occupation would be much easier. For one thing, as Minichiello and Scott (2015) argue, there would exist accreditation, work standards, and training principles associated with the occupation of sex work, making it easier to agree on who can be counted as a sex worker. Unfortunately, a consensus regarding a set of benchmarks about sex work as an occupation does not currently exist.

As a result, there is a continued lack of clarity on who qualifies to be counted as a sex worker. Why is this lack of clarity an issue? As Morris (2017) argues, it is not uncommon for gay men (particularly young gay men) to use social platforms like Grindr, an online gay dating platform, to engage in incidental sex work. Morris sent the following message to 3,000 Grindr users in metropolitan areas: "Have you ever been offered money for sex online and said yes?" Of those who responded, 14.6% had been paid for sex on at least one occasion, and follow-up questions to this group revealed that only 2.3% had worked as professional escorts or porn actors, while 8.2% had engaged in incidental sex work or webcamming. This result is supported by a study conducted in the United States that recruited its sample of 7,217 men from a popular sexual networking website for men who have sex with men. Bond et al. (2019) gauged how often transactional sex occurred by asking the questions: "In the past 60 days, did you accept anything (money, drugs, etc.) in exchange for sex?" and "In the past 60 days, did you give anything (money, drugs, etc. in exchange for sex?" The researchers found that while 87% did not participate in any transactional sex activities, 13% did, and of these 5% were sellers of sex and 2% were both sellers and buyers of sex in exchange for money or drugs. Other studies reveal that the number of people who engage in incidental sex work outnumbers those involved in professional sex work (Sagar, Jones, Symons, & Bowring, 2015).

References

Base, T. (2015). CEO of largest online male service arrested on prostitution charges. *Time*. Retrieved from http://time.com/4010309/rentboy-ceo-arrested-prostitution/

Callander, D., & DeVeau, R. (2019). Technology and male sex work. In J. Scott, D. Bimbi, C. Grov, & V. Minichiello (Eds.), *Male sex work and society (Vol. 2): From contemporary perspectives to emerging trends.* New York: Harrington Park Press.

Callander, D., Harrington, T., Scott, J., DeVeau, R., & Minichiello, V. (2019). Male sex work online. In P. Maginn, E. Cooper, & M. Zebracki (Eds.), *Navigating sex work in the 21st century: Gender, justice, and policy.* London: Palgrave.

Carroll, A., & Itaborahy, L. (2015). *State sponsored homophobia 2015: A world survey of laws: Crimininalisation, protection, and recognition of same-sex love.* Geneva: International Lesbian, Gay Bisexual, Trans and Intersex Association (ILGA).

Cheng, L., de Die, L., & de Kroon, E. (2011). Just business? The unknown world of male prostitution in the Netherlands. *Humanity in Action* [Blog]. Retrieved from www.humanityinaction.org/knowledgebase/369-just-business-the-unknown-world-of-male-prostitution-in-the-netherlands

Daalder, A. L. (2015). *Prostitution in the Netherlands in 2014.* The Netherlands: Wetenschappeliijk Onderzork-en Documentatiecentrum. Retrieved from www.wodc.nl

Donovan, B., Harcourt, C., Egger, S., Schneider, K., O'Connor, J., Marshall, L., . . . Fairley, C. K. (2010). *The sex industry in Western Australia: A report to the Western Australian Government.* Sydney: National Centre in HIV Epidemiology and Clinical Research, University of New South Wales.

Donovan, B., Harcourt, C., Egger, S., Watchirs Smith, I., Schneider, K., Kaldor, J. M., . . . Tabrizi, S. (2012). *The sex industry in New South Wales: A report to the NSW Ministry of Health.* Sydney: Kirby Institute, University of New South Wales.

Dunk, M., Khan, B., Downey, P., Kotonias, C., Mayer, D., Owens, C., Pacifici, L., & Yu, L. (2014). *Estimating the size and structure of the underground commercial sex economy in eight major US cities.* Urban Institute Research Report. Retrieved from www.urban.org/research/publication/estimating-size-and-structure-underground-commercial-sex-economy-eight-major-us-cities

End Prostitution Now. (2016). *The challenge demand approach.* Retrieved from www.endprostitutionnow.org/challenging-demand.html

Equaldex. (2018). *LGBT rights in United Arab emirates.* Retrieved from www.equaldex.com/region/united-arab-emirates

Erasing 76 Crimes. (2018). *73 countries where homosexuality is illegal*. Retrieved from https://76crimes.com/news-by-country/

Eriksson, A., & Gavanas, A. (2008). *Prostitution in Sweden 2007*. Sweden: Socialstyrrlsen. Retrieved from www.socialstyrelsen.se/lists/artikelkatalog/attachments/8806/2008-126-65_200812665.pdf

Farokhmansh, M. (2018). Amid FOSTA crackdown, sex workers find refuge on Mastodon. *The Verge*. Retrieved from www.theverge.com/2018/4/11/17188772/trump-sesta-fosta-bill-switter-sex-workers-mastodon

Fogg, A. (2014). How much does prostitution contribute to the UK economy? [Blog.] *Import.io*. Retrieved from www.import.io/post/how-much-does-prostitution-contribute-to-the-uk-economy/

Foundation Scelles. (2018). *Prostitution by country*. Retrieved from www.fondationscelles.org/en/prostitution/prostitution-by-country

Foynes, D. (2013). *The countries with the most prostitutes*. Retrieved from www.liveandinvestoverseas.com/news/countries-with-most-prostitutes/

Garcia, M., Van Voss, L., & Melkerk, E. (2017). *Selling sex in the city: A global history of prostitution, 1600s-2000s*. Leiden, Netherlands: Brill.

Giddens, A. (1985). Time, space, and regionalization. In D. Gregory & J. Urry (Eds.), *Social relations and spatial structures* (pp. 265–295). London: Palgrave.

Haahr, U. (2011). *Mapping out prostitution in Denmark*. Retrieved from https://en.sfi.dk/news/news/mapping-out-prostitution-in-denmark/

Havocscope. (2018). *Prostitution statistics*. Retrieved from www.havocscope.com/prostitution-statistics/

Hays, J. (2015). *Prostitution in India*. Retrieved from http://factsanddetails.com/india/People_and_Life/sub7_3h/entry-4190.html

House of Commons Home Affairs Committee. (2016). *Prostitution, third report of session 2016–2017*. London: Home Affairs Committee. Retrieved from https://publications.parliament.uk/pa/cm201617/cmselect/cmhaff/26/26.pdf

Kong, T. (2014). Male sex work in China. In V. Minichiello & J. Scott (Eds.), *Male sex work and society*. New York: Harrington Park Press.

Kumar, N., Minichiello, V., Scott, J., & Harrington, T. (2017). A global overview of male escort websites. *Journal of Homosexuality, 64*(12), 1731–1744.

Lee, C., & Gee-Hyun, S. (2015). Exposing "invisible" male sex workers in South Korea. *The Korea Herald*. Retrieved from www.koreaherald.com/view.php?ud=20151108000311

Logan, T. D. (2010). Personal characteristics, sexual behaviors, and male sex work: A quantitative approach. *American Sociological Review, 75*, 679–704.

Maginn, P., & Ellison, G. (2013). The Scarlet Isle: The politics of male sex work in Ireland. *The Conversation*. Retrieved from https://theconversation.com/the-scarlet-isle-the-politics-of-male-sex-work-in-ireland-19404

Magnanti, B. (2014). Zombie statistics on sex work. *The Baffler*. Retrieved from https://thebaffler.com/latest/zombie-statistics-on-sex-work

Minichiello, V., Dune, T., Disogra, C., & Mariño, R. (2014). Male sex work from Latin American perspectives. In V. Minichiello & J. Scott (Eds.), *Male sex work and society*. New York: Harrington Park Press.

Minichiello, V., & Scott, J. (Eds.). (2014). *Male sex work and society*. New York: Harrington Park Press.

Minichiello, V., & Scott, J. (2015). *The professionalisation of male escorting*. Retrieved from https://research.qut.edu.au/aboutmaleescorting/2015/11/14/the-professionalisation-of-male-escorting/

Minichiello, V., Scott, J., & Cox, C. (2018). Commentary: Reversing the agenda of sex work stigmatization and criminalization: Signs of a progressive society. *Sexualities, 21*(5–6), 730–735.

Morris, M. (2017). *Introducing Internet-based "incidental sex work" and its implications*. Retrieved from https://research.qut.edu.au/aboutmaleescorting/2017/02/14/introducing-internet-based-incidental-sex-work-and-its-implications/

Mujaj, E., & Netscher, A. (2015). *Prostitution in Sweden 2014: The extent and development of prostitution in Sweden*. Stockholm: County Administrative Board of Stockholm.

Murphy, C. (2015). Sex workers' rights are human rights. Retrieved from www.amnesty.org/en/latest/news/2015/08/sex-workers-rights-are-human-rights/

Pagadala, T. (2014). Bodies for sale, by men too. *Indiatogether*. Retrieved from www.indiatogether.org/ realities-of-male-sex-workers-society

Patidar, V. (2018). What is section 377 of the Indian Penal Code. *Republic*. Retrieved from www.republic world.com/india-news/law-and-order/what-is-section-377-of-the-indian-penal-code-and-all-you-need-to-know-about-it

Prestage, G., Bradley, J., Hammond, M., Cox, C., Tattersak, K., & Kolstee, J. (2015). *Hook-up: A study of male sex work in NSW and Queensland, Report*. Sydney: Then Kirby Institute, University of New South Wales.

ProCon.Org. (2018). *100 countries and their prostitution policies*. Retrieved from https://prostitution.procon. org/view.resource.php?resourceID=000772

Prostitutes Education Network. (1997). *Prostitution in the United States—the statistics*. Retrieved from www. bayswan.org/stats.html

Romano, A. (2018). A new law intended to curb sex trafficking threatens the future of the Internet as we know it. *Vox*. Retrieved from www.vox.com/culture/2018/4/13/17172762/fosta-sesta-backpage-230-internet-freedom

Sagar, T., Jones, D., Symons, K., & Bowring, J. (2015). *The student sex work project*. Swansea: Swansea University, Centre for Criminal Justice and Criminology.

Sanders, T., Campbell, R., Cunningham, S., Pitcher, J., & Scoular, J. (2018). The point of counting: Mapping the Internet-based sex industry. *Social Sciences*, 7(5), 233–241.

Scott, J., Minichiello, V., Callander, D., & Harrington, T. (2017). *Research shows distribution of online male escorts, by nation*. Retrieved from https://research.qut.edu.au/aboutmaleescorting/2017/11/01/number-of-online-male-escorts-by-nation-2/

TAMPEP International Foundation. (2009). *Sex work in Europe: A mapping of the prostitution scene in 25 European countries*. RB Amsterdam, Netherlands: TAMPEP International Foundation. Retrieved from www.nswp.org/sites/nswp.org/files/TAMPEP%202009%20European%20Mapping%20Report.pdf

The Tor Project, Inc. (2015). *Tor project: Overview*. Retrieved from www.torproject. org/about/overview. html.en

Vandiver, D., & Krienert, J. (2007). An assessment of a cross-national sample of men and women arrested for prostitution. *The Southwest Journal of Criminal Justice*, 4(2), 89–105.

Van Gelder, P. (2014). *Boys online/boys offline: Update over seksuele dienstverlening door Internet escorts (M$M) in de Regio Den Haag*. Den Haag: Shop Den-Haag & Van Lier Research.

14

Male sex work and digital regulation

Control and censorship in online spaces

Denton Callander and Ryan DeVeau

The digitalization of male sex work is old news. Digital platforms for male sex work have proliferated for several decades, long enough to exhibit well-established norms and familiar structures. Male sex work flourishes in diverse online spaces, which means that savvy workers operate across multiple platforms, maintaining different kinds of profiles for different audiences and, in some cases, using content to build a recognizable brand, gain a following, and generate online and offline revenue. Brand management and cross-platform integration are "Internet 101" for small businesses of any kind, and for many men who sell sex, they have become part of the standard playbook for contemporary escorting.

While male sex workers may be spoiled for choice when it comes to advertising their services online, it is also important to consider the limitations that the digital world imposes on men who sell sex. In a practical sense, the time commitment of managing an online presence is substantial, and so are the fees that most services charge sex workers to advertise. And while on the surface it might seem that more platforms would benefit sex workers and clients by providing more ways to connect and engage, feelings of loneliness and isolation are not uncommon among men who use the Internet to sell sex (McLean, 2012; Koken & Bimbi, 2014). Thus, while digital environments bring new opportunities for male sex workers, they simultaneously give rise to new challenges.

Regulation has remained a persistent aspect of male sex work, even as that work has moved into online spaces. Society remains fixated on trying to control sex work through various social and legal mechanisms, so it is unsurprising that this commitment now finds focus on sex work's digital manifestations. In their highly comprehensive study of sex work online in the United Kingdom, Teela Sanders and her colleagues described several examples of the regulation of sex work online, including digital monitoring by police (2018). Their research, however, found that police were generally unwilling to police sex work online (at least in the United Kingdom), except in a small number of cases where they suspected human trafficking.

It is important to recognize that regulation online can take many forms, including those completely unrelated to conventional policing. In this chapter, we focus on expressions of regulation online that are far more surreptitious than the work of any police force, layers of moderation and censorship that are imposed on male sex work, sometimes through the very structure of the digital spaces in which it operates. As male sex work stretches further into the Internet's many nooks and crannies, it becomes a lens through which we can examine regulations that pervade every aspect of our online social world in ways that are often invisible and unchallenged. These regulations pose unique challenges to male sex workers, and they undermine the common myth that the Internet is "free."

A male sex worker's guide to building a media empire

In the past, sex work online was largely limited to posts on classified-driven websites, personal websites, and sex-work profiles. Over time, it has come to encompass a diverse offering of sex-work-specific and more general digital spaces. In their 2015 study, Sanders and her colleagues provided a useful overview of the different types of sex-work websites and mobile apps: escort directories, multiservice adult entertainment platforms, dating and hook-up platforms, classified websites, content delivery platforms, agency websites, individual sex worker websites, and social media (Sanders, Scoular, Campbell, Pitcher, & Cunningham, 2018). The diverse spaces in which sex work is advertised online can be further categorized into those designed for sex work and those that are not, a distinction that is highly relevant to the ways in which regulation takes place.

The many forms of advertising for male sex work online were also identified in an Australia-based study we conducted in 2018, which included an ethnographic investigation of male sex workers' online advertising. Men for whom sex work was a full- or part-time job (as opposed to those for whom it was mainly casual or contextual) clearly saw value in expanded digital reach, the ability to speak to different audiences in different tones, and to compartmentalize their self-expression online. One male sex worker we interviewed said:

> On my social media, it's very evident but it's more suggestive than actual. But that's, that's me in general, really. Well, it's, it's boring if you tell everyone everything in life, so . . . And that's, comes back to, you know, people being curious about you. They know it's intriguing. People wanna find out more in one way.
>
> *Zack, 25, Brisbane*

Zack (a pseudonym) discussed implicit and explicit signals that were typically sexual and focused on building interest in his sex work "brand." Like others with whom we spoke, these signals' explicitness was often context specific, reflecting a perceived need to adjust behavior among different digital spaces while highlighting the importance of working across many general and sex work-specific services. The extent of platform cross-pollination was revealed keenly in 2017 when we worked with colleagues to count all of the male sex work profiles that could be found online (Scott & Minichiello, 2017). Although we identified over 325,000 profiles for male sex workers in total, a third of these were duplicates, and this number does take into account how male sex workers use non-sex working spaces, like social media.

What is truly fascinating about the proliferation of sex work across digital platforms is not that it has occurred but rather the way in which it has mimicked more general trends of personal brand cultivation as a business strategy. Writing about women sex workers, journalist and sex work advocate Rae Story put it this way:

> Against the new cacophony of like-structured profiles, prostitutes had to start pushing themselves to "stand out from the crowd." We needed to post endless photographs of ourselves on our online profiles, write blogs, conduct webcam sessions, or phone chat to bloat out our "brand." Heck, some women even began to sell print photographs, calendars, and other merchandise. Because porn stars often worked as prostitutes, this also worked in

reverse: friends who had previously panicked if they were seen going into a brothel began posting short porn clips of themselves to earn extra cash and to encourage punters.

(2016)

Story describes how a sex worker's digital brand has become an important commodity. While her essay was generally critical of this development, the phenomenon is not surprising given the "microcelebrities" and social media "influencers" who rose to prominence in the second decade of the twenty-first century. Because those who engage in self-branding and image cultivation through online platforms can command sizeable incomes (Khamis, Ang, & Welling, 2017), it is common sense that male and female sex workers would adopt similar techniques of self-promotion. Interestingly, researchers have already started to explore strategies employed by male sex workers to generate personal brands online (Phua & Caras, 2008). However, the degree to which these digital techniques ultimately help or hinder sex workers is not yet clear.

Sex work and digital regulation

For better or for worse, the digital world has reshaped the sale of sex by men. We will not spend time discussing the pros and cons of sex work online. Instead, we focus on how sex work is regulated online. The term *regulation* refers to any method of social control, including those that are direct or indirect, formal or informal. Regulation is a part of everything we experience online, but it often remains invisible until challenged by "deviant" social practices, of which sex work is a prominent example. By operating in many different spaces, especially those not designed for sex work, male sex work tests different layers of digital regulation (Figure 14.1) and in doing so reveals their nature and occasionally their hypocrisy.

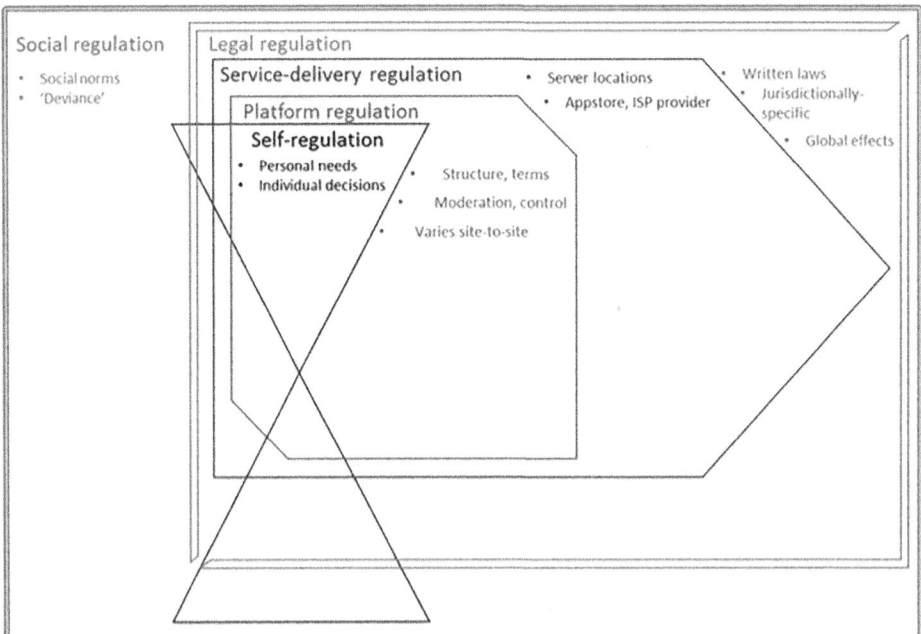

Figure 14.1 The layers of digital regulation.

Source: Ryan DeVeau.

1 Self-regulation

The first layer of online regulation is the self-regulation that each individual enacts online. When you decide whether to post an article or share a photo, this form of self-regulation is based on a complex milieu of context, short- and long-term need, and a range of factors that inform your online and offline decision-making on an ongoing basis. Self-regulation is never truly autonomous, and it can be argued that it is merely the enactment of the other layers of regulation detailed in Figure 14.1. Nevertheless, regulation of any kind ultimately starts and ends with the individuals who access a website or open a mobile app, sex worker or otherwise.

Although self-regulation online is not unique to sex workers, it seems to have a special place for male sex workers navigating different digital contexts. It is common, for example, for male sex workers to self-regulate their behavior in digital spaces where sex work or overt sexuality is not sanctioned. When we interviewed male sex workers in Australia, they told us that one of the most common strategies for self-regulation online is "signaling," which is the use of indirect but commonly understood tropes, symbols, or language to evoke secondary meanings. Gay men looking for sexual partners online also use signaling to disclose their HIV status. In short, signaling is a way for those "in the know" to communicate (Race, 2010). According to one of the sex workers we interviewed:

> Well, with Grindr, I don't know if you guys know, you can't put like . . . if you put cash signs, dollar bags, you know, your Grindr will get removed . . . So like I mean you can be subtle like . . . I wasn't going out of my saying, "Can you pay me?" but like guys would send me dollar bills and stuff and like question marks. So then obviously I would jump straight at that.
>
> *Rod, 23 years old, sex worker and porn performer, Sydney*

This quotation suggests that male sex workers and clients can use signaling, and it is a useful example of self-regulation in digital spaces not designed for sex work. But even in spaces where sex work is permitted, expressions of self-regulation can be found. When we reviewed the online profiles of male sex workers in the United States, for example, we found many examples of language that seemed to react to concerns about legal regulation. As the profile of one 28-year-old male sex worker in New York put it: "Any fees paid, or money exchanged is for my companionship or for modeling. Anything else that may or may not happen is a personal choice between two consenting adults of legal age." Here, the profile owner is responding to other layers of perceived regulation by modifying his profile even in a space that is obviously devoted to sex work.

2 Platform regulation

Self-regulation is always a response to other layers of regulation, which sit above and around the individual. In the previous quotation, Rod discussed how he self-regulated through language. His approach was not really an autonomous choice but instead an action dictated by the platform through which he found clients. He mentions Grindr, which is a useful example of the GPS-driven sex and dating platforms that are very popular with many different groups of people. Rod and other sex workers described their frustration at having their profiles deleted from these platforms, whose administrators alleged that they were using them to sell sex. When a profile is deleted, a second and more systemic layer of online control is revealed: platform regulation.

Many of us are familiar with long and largely unread "terms of access" that explain the rules of membership and participation in most commercial platforms, including websites and mobile apps. As part of our ethnography, we reviewed the terms of access for many different general and sex-work-specific websites and mobile apps. For general websites and apps, the terms are quite similar and very rarely mention sex work specifically. Grindr, for example, has terms that do not specifically exclude sex work but forbid the platform's use "for any commercial or non-private use, such as the sale or advertisement of goods or services" (Grindr LLC, 2018).

Because such language is common in platforms' terms of access, the question becomes: How do the individual platforms seek to enforce their particular terms of access as they relate to sex work? Men who sell sex through mobile apps frequently cited Grindr as an example of active and aggressive regulation of sex work. Most commonly, Grindr simply deletes the profiles of any men who appear to be involved with either buying or selling sex. Sometimes profiles just vanish, but in other cases male sex workers explained that they had been banned for using certain words but not others. Importantly, men described being unable to post certain words on their profiles; the Grindr app specifically forbade it without any human intervention (Figure 14.2). Through these experiences, it becomes clear that some aspects of platform regulation can actually involve manipulation of the software itself.

To explore how Grindr regulates language, we created a series of dummy user profiles and attempted to included various bits of language related to sex work among men. The software prevented us from entering the words "escort" and "hustler" into our profiles. When we entered these words, the software told us quite frankly, "That word is not allowed." While we were able to trick the app's software-driven censor—we were able to post mild alterations like "escorttt" and "hust-ler"—these victories were often short lived. Within an hour or two of posting, the dummy profiles were deleted without warning or explanation. However, profiles containing words like "generous" and "rent" remained uncensored. These words are not terribly surreptitious signals of sex work, and their permissibility highlights the potential fallibility of a platform's regulation.

In short, the platform itself restricts the language of male sex work, at least its most blatant forms. Our simple experiment revealed the nature and limits of this form of regulation, one that is not documented in the app's terms of access but is nevertheless part of how this platform regulates the behavior of its users. Interestingly, one male sex worker with whom we spoke thought that there might be variation in Grindr's underlying regulations in different parts of the world:

> In London itself, when someone advertises through Grindr, they don't get blocked. I remember this. The entirety of the two and a half weeks that I was remaining in London I had not lost my account once. I came back to Brisbane: instantly lost it.
>
> *Eden, 26 years old, sex worker, Brisbane*

It is unclear whether Grindr truly has different policies for regulating sex work in different parts of the world, but Grindr's policies are secondary to the fact that men perceive that differences exist. Many of the men with whom we spoke noted their perceptions of inconsistency both between and within individual platforms.

We see the inconsistent policing of sex work online by considering what other platforms do (or don't do). Specifically, we reviewed the terms of access for another sex and dating website not designed for sex work. Like Grindr, this website forbade its use "to distribute, promote or otherwise publish any material containing any solicitation for funds, advertising or solicitation for goods or service" (Wet-Media Inc., 2011). Despite this restriction, we observed explicit

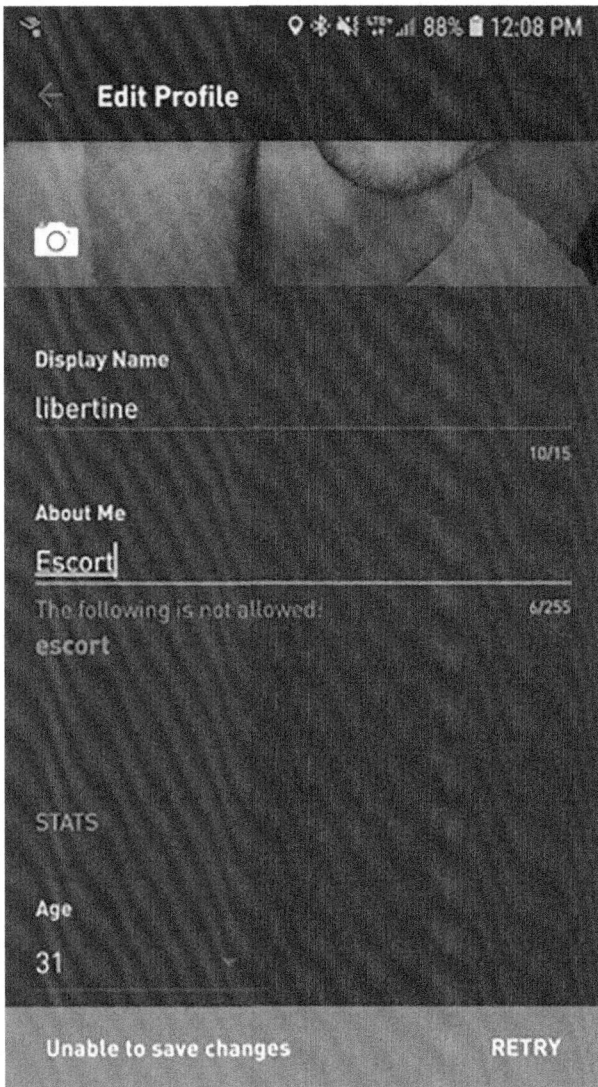

Figure 14.2 A popular mobile sex and dating app automatically rejects language perceived as relevant to sex work among men.

offers to buy and sell sex on several member profiles and in the website's forum section. When we contacted the website owners for clarification, they provided this written comment:

> Since we're a US-based company, we go by American regulations. Escorting is allowed, but as an escort, you're not allowed to advertise sexual suggestions or the trade of. Sex is for prostitutes and that is not allowed here. In terms of our policies, escorts are allowed on the site; however, even as an escort, escorts are not allowed to approach individuals and offer their services. All escorts are supposed to advertise in the profile heading that they are, in fact, escorts.

What makes this website different from Grindr? Why would such similar terms of access produce such remarkably different responses to materials advertising or soliciting sex work? The response from the website's managers references regulation in the United States (which we discuss later in this chapter), but is there some other layer of regulation that exists across many individual platforms?

3 Service-delivery regulation

On the surface, it might appear that platforms call all the shots when it comes to what is permitted online and what is not. As we have described, platform-driven regulation might be considered the primary form of digital regulation. A third, often overlooked, form of digital regulation can come from above, as it were, via the large corporations that control the Internet through market dominance, server ownership, or Internet access itself. In other words, the corporations that for all intents and purposes control the Internet have regulations of their own. They rarely impose these regulations on individuals, but the regulations often have powerful implications for the platforms that male sex workers use.

We have talked a lot about Grindr, not to single it out but because it is the original GPS-driven sex and dating app, the model upon which all others have been based. It is also notable because of its heavy-handed attempt to quash sex work. So fearful are its managers of any association with sex work that when we approached them in 2015 to discuss paid advertisements for an earlier study of sex work among men, their simple reply was: "For the sake of our users, we would never want to insinuate that there are a large number of sex workers on Grindr."

Why has Grindr typically reacted so forcefully when it comes to even the hint of sex work via its platform? As we have suggested, one possible explanation is another layer of regulation, one dictated by the companies the distribute nearly all mobile content: Apple and Google. Each of these behemoths owns and operates the marketplaces that distribute virtually all mobile software. This ownership allows them to dictate the terms of engagement for app developers, which must work with Apple's prohibition of "overtly sexual or pornographic material" (Apple Inc., 2018). While there is no clause specifically preventing the advertising or solicitation of sex work, Apple and Google are notoriously restrictive when it comes to sexual content and have purged apps that they perceived to be too sexual (Kincaid, 2010).

Being removed from distribution by either Apple or Google would, effectively, devastate a mobile app's business. Indeed, so potent is this possibility that it alone could explain why Grindr and its mobile compatriots have so vigorously policed sex-work-related content. This possibility might also explain why there are and have been almost no mobile apps devoted specifically to sex work—an odd gap when you consider the huge number of non-commercial sex apps, dating apps, and browser-based sex work websites. It seems entirely possible that service-delivery regulation in the mobile world has created a market of sex work content that is unbalanced between mobile and browser-based digital platforms.

Unlike mobile apps, websites are hosted and distributed by a huge number of services that have historically played little or no part in regulating content. Websites must adhere to regulations imposed by service deliverers like Web hosting services and Internet providers, but these organizations are very different from corporations like Apple or Google, and historically they have generally regulated content only when they receive a court order to do so. This difference may explain why websites have (at least historically) been far more comfortable with sex work content than mobile apps. However, as we discuss in the next section, regulation of sex work can affect browsers, and more directly than it affects mobile apps.

4 Legal regulation

The fourth layer of regulation that affects male sex workers online is the law. The Internet is not immune to laws, but often their implementation relies on the other layers of regulation we have described in this chapter, most notably through platforms and service delivery. Unlike laws, however, the Internet is not typically organized along geopolitical boundaries, so the enforcement and effects of laws can become tangled. In some locations, the laws concerning sex work tend to ignore its digital expressions, especially when it comes to sex work among men (Ashford, 2009).

The legal regulation of online male sex work is further complicated by the cornucopia of laws that regulate sex work globally. These laws differ widely between and even within countries. While it might seem strange for a male sex worker in Australia to be affected by a law introduced in the United States, physical servers that house Internet data have to exist somewhere and, as a result, they are always beholden to the laws of a particular land. This point is very important. It explains why local laws can affect male sex workers operating around the world, and it highlights the significant impact that legal regulation can have on digital spaces and practices.

The international impacts of local sex work laws were felt profoundly in 2015 when the United States Department of Homeland Security raided the offices of what was at the time the world's largest website for male sex work. RentBoy advertised profiles for male sex workers around the world but did so in violation of laws forbidding prostitution in New York State (Callander & Scott, 2015). Eventually, the website's owner pled guilty to charges of promoting prostitution, even though the judge agreed with the defense lawyer's argument that RentBoy had helped improve the lives and working conditions of male sex workers (Feuer, 2017). Rent-Boy operated from the United States but hosted members from countries around the world, including those where sex work is legal or decriminalized.

What can we learn from legal regulation in cyberspace? The RentBoy example forces us to confront an important truth: The internet is tangible. While the seemingly borderless nature of digital spaces can lull users into imagining a globalized utopia, the reality is not so fully realized as our digital experiences would have us believe. Further illustrating this reality is a series of laws introduced in the United States in 2018, legislation that quickly became infamous among sex workers: the *Stop Enabling Sex Traffickers Act* and the *Fight Online Sex Trafficking Act* or SESTA-FOSTA.

Designed to combat human trafficking, SESTA-FOSTA undermined previously enshrined ideals that platforms and service delivery institutions are not responsible for the content produced by their users (Romano, 2018). As we noted earlier, service delivery institutions (other than commercially driven app stores) have rarely been involved with regulating content. Indeed, this idea was enshrined in law prior to SESTA-FOSTA and was an important part of digital (non)regulation for decades. But the stiff penalties imposed by SESTA-FOSTA mean that many websites and hosting services meant find it not worth the risk to host sex-work-related content of any kind or to facilitate channels of communication for sex workers.

Within days of SESTA-FOSTA's passage, websites that were based in the United States but popular with male and female sex workers around the world started to disappear (Romano, 2018). As Aja Romano described in her piece for the website *Vox*, such are important from a safety standpoint because they allow sex workers to vet clients and, among other things, to share health information. Research echoes this conclusion (Young, 2018), including some of our own. In 2017, we conducted a linguistic analysis to explore the processes of sense-making around safer sex and biomedical prevention of HIV that took place via an online forum for male sex workers and clients (MagGibbon et al., in press). The men accessing that platform clearly found value in being able to share their ideas and experiences around sex work without judgment, and we observed the dissemination of helpful and accurate health information. SESTA-FOSTA threatens those spaces and has reshaped parts of the digital landscape for sex work.

As a tool for regulation, SESTA-FOSTA cut a wide swath across the layers of regulation that we have described in this chapter, another stark reminder that in the seemingly free space of the Internet, the law can still hold considerable sway. SESTA-FOSTA also reminds us how little policymakers seem to understand the Internet and how difficult it can be to predict the impact of laws on digital cultures and practices.

While SESTA-FOSTA had immediate effects, in the space of only a few days, new versions of the websites that had been taken down began to pop up in other countries around the world. One version of a popular website taken offline was launched in Australia, designed by and for sex workers (Cox, 2018). Similarly, after the fall of RentBoy, it was not long before a new website rose to claim market dominance. Its servers and offices are based in Germany, a country with some of the most progressive sex work laws in the world. From these outcomes, we might conclude that regulation is rarely unidirectional. Legal regulation that censors sex work may have powerful short-term (and short-lived) effects but unclear and unpredictable longer-term effects. It is important to remember, too, that while the digital impact of laws like SESTA-FOSTA is new, laws that seek to regulate sex work are certainly not, and they reflect a long social history of antipathy toward sex work. These laws, sold through a seemingly purposeful conflation with human trafficking, are the latest iteration of this antipathy, which brings us to the fifth and final layer of digital regulation.

5 Social regulation

All online regulation is underwritten by the high-level social systems that organize our social worlds. Laws are often the most tangled expressions of social regulation, but they do reflect the ways in which our societies think about and organize themselves, including the behaviors they deem "normal" or "deviant." Because sex work is something our societies (mainly) continue to view as deviant, it is subject to more intense social regulation than most other practices. Social regulation dictates the law, informs services, creates and shapes platforms, and dramatically guides individuals' decisions.

Social regulation permits and even encourages the many forms of sex work regulation we have explored thus far. Male sex work is subject to complex layers of regulation online all because of this "big picture" social regulation. This point is important. When seeking to understand the regulation of male sex work in online spaces, attending to broader social context is absolutely essential. A point that has been made a few times but which bears repeating: Societies around the world have long histories of seeking to control and regulate sex work offline (Scoular, 2010; Callander, 2017), and these efforts have now made their presence felt online. Male sex work is subject to complex layers of regulation online because of this "big-picture" social regulation. However, the proliferation of digital technologies around sex work has driven a need to rethink its regulation (Scott, 2017). The layers making up online regulation of male sex work intersect in reflexive ways, changing one another just as they are changed while contributing to new ways of doing and seeing sex work online as well as offline. Sherry Turkle, one of the earliest digital theorists, aptly described our online world as reflexively linked to our offline world (Turkle, 1995). These worlds were probably never truly divided, but any border has become less distinct and more porous as communication technologies continue to reshape our social experiences.

Mille foile: intersecting layers of digital regulation

There is no part of male sex work online that is not regulated. We have conceptualized this regulation in multiple layers, and each of our examples has hinted at the ways in which those layers overlap and intersect. Regulation in one layer easily bleeds easily into others as the bodies that constitute our societies—individuals, corporations, institutions, and governments—seek to contend with, produce, and control our online experiences. The multifaceted nature of this process is one of its most interesting aspects, but in focusing on the parts, we must not lose sight of the whole.

Another example perfectly encapsulates the overlapping layers of digital regulation. In the aftermath of the highly publicized RentBoy case, other websites involved with male sex work watched the legal landscape closely and were, understandably, somewhat nervous about what the future might hold. We interviewed the manager of a comparable website operating while the RentBoy drama unfurled. He said:

> I think once the spotlight was shone on RentBoy, it was like: well, could we be next or could we, you know, could there be a taskforce . . . looking at other sites that could fall foul of the law? And there were, there were lots of decisions to be made. Obviously, we considered moving the server . . . to a country that, you know, is more accepting.

In this case, legal regulation of one website for male sex work had an indirect effect on similar services. Driven by laws that were written for sex work in offline spaces, this layer of regulation bled through and influenced individual platforms. The manager also described the tangible steps his platform took to counter its risk, which included removing the ability to search specifically for men classified as "escorts" and working with members to alter profiles that referenced sex work. And as part of the functionality that allowed members to report problematic profiles (for example, "spam bots" and those that may have belonged to minors), they also added the option to report profile holders for suspected sex work.

We note that this website's owners and managers were ideologically opposed to the changes they implemented:

> And, you know, we could have continued as, as is but then, you know, there was various legal decisions to be taken . . . it was just seen as a too-risky item. I think for the board to say that it was too risky was really, was really sort of a heart-wrenching sort of decision. . . . And because of that, you know, the board took, you know, a long time to, to think about how we, how we deal with, you know, escorts on the site.

In this example, the regulation of male sex work operated in full force and on almost every layer. It started with a social context that in the state of New York facilitated the creation of laws prohibiting sex work (social regulation). Those laws were applied to one website (legal regulation), which served as a warning to similar services. The laws then led to at least one website altering its practices and structures to specifically exclude male sex workers (platform regulation). In doing so, it created the opportunity for members to report other members for perceived sex work practices (individual regulation).

Regulate me, babe

Regulation is not inherently bad. In fact, it is an essential component of our social world, the lubricant that keeps the whole machine chugging along. For sex workers, however, aggressive

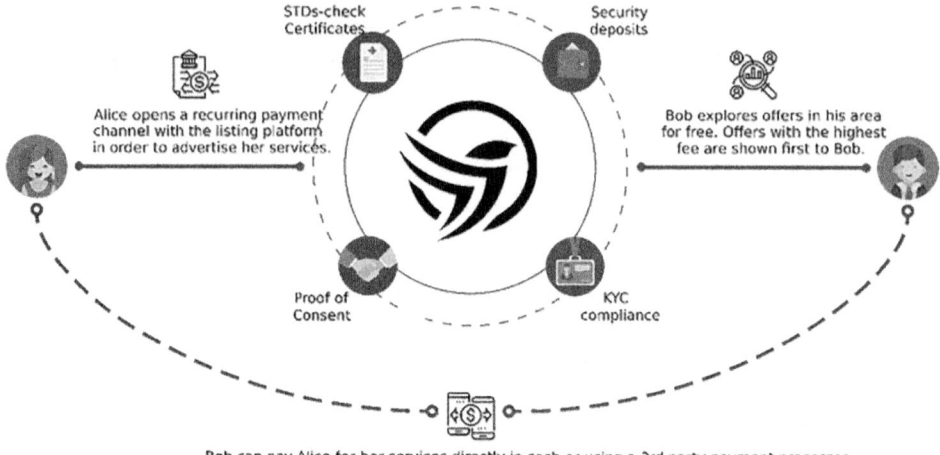

Figure 14.3 Schematic detailing the use of blockchain technology to facilitate payment while improving the health and safety of sex workers and clients.

Source: Peter Tuala.

regulation has often meant decreased autonomy and heightened risk. Offline, by any account, the most effective regulation of sex work thus far has been its decriminalization (Rekart, 2005; Harcourt et al., 2010). Extending the same approach into the digital world seems only reasonable. Sex work websites increasingly include information and resources to recognize, prevent, and report human trafficking, and by opening channels of communication, they may help sex workers and clients connect in ways that are safer than other contexts (Jones, 2015). Clumsy laws like SESTA-FOSTA and raids on digital organizations that the court sees as "[forces] for social good" (Feuer, 2017) are regressive. While their effects may be partly mitigated by the Internet's capacity to evolve, they continue to dictate a program of regulation that is paternalistic and outdated (Scott, 2017).

Digital spaces may be imbued with visible and invisible forms of regulation, but they can also help sex workers mitigate and address regulation online. In some parts of the world, payment for sexual services with cryptocurrency has become an alternative to banking institutions that discriminate against sex workers (McIntosh, 2018). Sex workers have set up social media groups to share information about collecting payment in cryptocurrency, and there is clearly an interest in its more advanced applications. For example, one website launched in 2017 is working toward a system whereby blockchain (the technology that is used to create cryptocurrency) can be used not just to pay for services but also to improve the health and safety of those involved in commercial sex by sharing proof of consent and details of sexual health testing (Ghosh, 2018). This model is outlined in Figure 14.3. In this model, regulation is recast as a tool for improving health and safety while weakening existing regulations that can harm sex workers and clients.

The bigger picture

This chapter has focused on the regulation of male sex work in digital spaces, but digital regulation and its effects are relevant to all sex workers. Women sex workers face many of the same challenges that men do when involved with sex work online, and research has found that both men and women who sell sex place considerable value on the Internet as a tool for minimizing risk and increasing safety (Kille, 2017). Notably, Sanders and her colleagues reported that three-quarters of their participants viewed the Internet as important to improving safety, and they detailed innovative digital safety strategies that included using telephone number checkers, discussing clients via online forums, and maintaining a database of problematic and dangerous clients (Sanders et al., 2018). As we have discussed, layers of regulation can endanger these techniques.

Regulation in and of digital spaces is also not unique to sex work. While sex work is likely subject to more overt and tangible regulation than many other social practices, everything we do online is regulated in some way. While it is simplistic to see regulation as inherently negative, an aspect of much digital regulation is its invisibility. Often, we do not realize the extent to which our online experiences and activities are manipulated through regulation or even that they are being regulated at all, which can lead to a false sense of freedom and perpetuate an uncritical approach to life online. Sex work among men illuminates the nature of digital regulation, but it is merely conceptually illustrative and not unique.

Even in its darkest corners, our digital world is regulated, if only by the structure it imposes on itself. Not only does regulation have practical considerations for male sex workers, but it has much broader theoretical and ideological implications for how our societies organize themselves online and offline. As more of our lives continue to move into and evolve within online spaces, we must continue to question and critique the nature and limitations of digital regulation.

References

Ashford, C. (2009). Male sex work and the Internet effect: Time to re-evaluate the criminal law? *The Journal of Criminal Law, 73*(3), 258–280.

Callander, D. (2017, December 1). *Our relationship with sex.* Presentation, UNSOMNIA 2.017, UNSW Sydney, Sydney, NSW, Australia.

Callander, D., & Scott, J. (2015, August 28). The rise and fall of Rentboy.com. *The Conversation.* Retrieved from http://theconversation.com/the-rise-and-fall-of-rentboy-com-46677

Cox, C. (2018, September 25). Opinion: Australian sex workers respond to FOSTA SESTA. *The Feed SBS.* Retrieved from www.sbs.com.au/news/the-feed/opinion-australian-sex-workers-respond-to-fosta-sesta

Feuer, A. (2017, August 2). Owner of Rentboy.com is sentenced to 6 months in prison. *New York Times.* Retrieved from www.nytimes.com/2017/08/02/nyregion/rentboy-jeffrey-hurant-sentence-sex-work.html

Ghosh, T. (2018). *Hussy ICO – How block chain will disrupt the sex workers industry?* Retrieved from LinkedIn https://www.linkedin.com/pulse/hussy-ico-how-block-chain-disrupt-sex-workers-industry-ghosh/

Grindr LLC. (2018). *Grindr terms and conditions of service.* West Hollywood, CA: Terms and Conditions of Service, Grindr LLC.

Harcourt, C., O'Connor, J., Egger, S., Fairley, C., Wand, H., Chen, M., . . . Donovan, B. (2010). The decriminalisation of prostitution is associated with better coverage of health promotion programs for sex workers. *Australian and New Zealand Journal of Public Health, 34*(5), 482–486.

Jones, A. (2015). Sex work in a digital era. *Sociology Compass, 9*(7), 558–570.

Khamis, S., Ang, L., & Welling, R. (2017). Self-branding, "micro-celebrity" and the rise of social media influencers. *Celebrity Studies, 8*(2), 191–208.

Kille, J., Bungay, V., Oliffe, J., & Atchison, C. (2017). A content analysis of health and safety communications among Internet-based sex work advertisements: Important information for public health. *Journal of Medical Internet Research, 19*(4), e111.

Kincaid, J. (2010, February 18). Did Apple just ban sexual content from the app store? *Tech Crunch.* Retrieved from https://techcrunch.com/2010/02/18/did-apple-just-ban-sexual-content-from-the-app-store/

Koken, J., & Bimbi, D. (2014). Mental health aspects of male sex work. In V. Minichiello & J. Scott (Eds.), *Male sex work and society* (pp. 223–240). New York: Harington Park Press.

MagGibbon, J., Donovan, B., Prestage, G., Bell, S., Cox, C., Minichiello, V., & Callander, D. (in press). From reluctance to advocacy: Sensemaking and collective negotiation of HIV pre-exposure prophylaxis among male sex workers and their clients. *Social Science and Medicine*.

McIntosh, R. (2018, June 7). Love, sex, bitcoins: The rise of blockchain in the adult industry. *Finance Magnates*. Retrieved from www.financemagnates.com/cryptocurrency/news/love-sex-bitcoins-rise-blockchain-adult-industry/

McLean, A. (2012). New realm, new problems? Issues and support networks in online male sex work. *Gay and Lesbian Issues and Psychology Review, 8*(2), 70.

Phua, V. C., & Caras, A. (2008). Personal brand in online advertisements: Comparing White and Brazilian male sex workers. *Sociological Focus, 41*(3), 238–255.

Race, K. (2010). Click here for HIV status: Shifting templates of sexual negotiation. *Emotion, Space and Society, 3*(1), 7–14.

Rekart, M. (2005). Sex-work harm reduction. *The Lancet, 366*(9503), 2123–2134.

Romano, A. (2018, April 18). A new law intended to curb sex trafficking threatens the future of the internet as we know it. *Vox*. Retrieved from www.vox.com/culture/2018/4/13/17172762/fosta-sesta-back page-230-internet-freedom

Sanders, T., Scoular, J., Campbell, R., Pitcher, J., & Cunningham, S. (2018). *Internet sex work: Beyond the gaze*. Basingstoke: Palgrave Macmillan.

Scott, J. (2017, August 7). Technology drives the need to rethink sex work industry regulations. *The Conversation*. Retrieved from https://theconversation.com/technology-drives-the-need-to-rethink-sex-work-industry-regulations-79656

Scott, J., & Minichiello, V. (2017). Research shows distribution of online male escorts, by nation. *Me, Us and Male Escorting*. Australia. Retrieved from www.webcitation.org/77fyPoR6c

Scoular, J. (2010). What's law got to do with it? How and why law matters in the regulation of sex work. *Journal of Law and Society, 37*(1), 12–39.

Story, R. (2016, February 22). Whoreburbia: The digital gentrification of "sex work." *Feminist Current*. Retrieved from www.feministcurrent.com/2016/02/22/whoreburbia-gentrification-sex-work/

Turkley, S. (1995). *Life on the screen: Identity in the age of the internet*. New York: Simon & Schuster.

Wet-Media Inc. (2011). *BBRT terms of service*. Burlington, NJ: Terms of Service, Wet-Media Inc.

Young, M. (2018, April 23). Sex workers in Australia say American law is creating devastating losses back home. *News.com.au*. Retrieved from www.news.com.au/lifestyle/relationships/sex/sex-workers-in-australia-say-american-law-is-creating-devastating-losses-back-home/news-story/09139a2f0d631cd72 84090d2336ca517

15

Male sex work and the law

Regulation of men selling sex within the context of female sex work

Thomas Crofts and Alice Orchiston

The legal regulation of male sex work has always been in the shadow of female sex work and male homosexuality. Legal, academic, and policy discussion and legal regulation reveal a fractured, gendered, and heterocentric approach to sex work. Laws criminalizing or regulating sex work have traditionally been drafted, interpreted, and applied only with female workers in mind, largely ignoring male sex workers.[1] Instead, male sex work has largely been dealt with separately and differently from female sex work, mainly through laws that criminalize male homosexuality without identifying whether sexual activity between men amounted to sex work. While some sex work-like laws have applied to males at certain points in history, they were directed more at male homosexuality in itself than at male sex work as a distinct concept.

This chapter explores this gendered, heterocentric approach to sex work, explaining why male sex work has remained in the regulatory shadow of female sex work and male homosexuality. The focus is on legal development and legal debate in the United Kingdom and Australia, particularly the State of New South Wales.[2] Despite this focus, many of the findings are applicable to other common-law countries with similar legal cultures. This chapter suggests three main explanatory factors. First, there has been a legal-conceptual linkage between male homosexuality and male sex work. Second, this linkage has made it largely unnecessary in practice to apply sex work laws to male sex workers. Third, there has been an inability or unwillingness to include male sex work within the dominant frameworks and conceptualizations of sex work, which focus on female workers and (more recently) their male clients. Finally, the chapter questions whether the effects of new technologies on sex work (both male and female) will challenge and end the gendered, heterocentric approach to sex work.

What has contributed to this gendered heterocentric approach?

Legal-conceptual indistinguishability of male homosexuality and male sex work in criminal law

One of the main factors explaining why male sex work has generally received little attention is that it has been fundamentally intertwined with the regulation and legal framing of male homosexuality.[3] Scott (2003a) notes that only recently has male sex work been rendered "socially problematic." This does not mean that male sex work has invariably been seen as unproblematic. Rather, "male prostitution has been problematized in a unique manner . . . understood as a moral problem, typically associated with gender deviation" (Scott, 2003a, p. 179a).[4] As Scott notes, in the nineteenth century the "close association of male prostitution with effeminate behavior led it to be increasingly associated with an emergent discourse on homosexuality that linked same-sex desire with gender transgression" (2003a, p. 180). This long-standing intertwining of male sex work with male homosexuality meant that the regulatory discourse surrounding male sex work was related to discourse surrounding the criminality of homosexuality itself. As Scott observes, "such behaviour was often not recognised as prostitution. No distinction emerged during this period [nineteenth century] to distinguish same-sex desire from commercial sexual activity involving males, both being conflated and assumed indistinguishable" (2003a, 181). As such, from early times, the main laws regulating male sex work and male homosexuality were laws directed at male homosexuality.

Sodomy and indecency laws

Laws criminalizing male homosexuality have historically been the primary vehicles for controlling male sex work. Initially, only anal sex attracted a criminal penalty in the United Kingdom through the *Buggery Act 1533* (UK), the *Criminal Law Amendment Act 1885* (UK), and the *Offences Against the Person Act 1861* (UK). Such laws were not passed to address a developed concept of the homosexual man but rather to regulate sodomy as a deviant sexual act (Weeks, 1991; Hough, 2004). It was only in the nineteenth century that the concept of the homosexual man started to take shape and with it the desire to control homosexuality through the criminal law (Weeks, 1991). The criminalization of non-penetrative sexual acts between men (the offense of indecency between males) through the *Criminal Law Amendment Act 1885* (UK) represented a growing understanding of homosexuality and a move to address concerns about the apparent increase in homosexual activity (Weeks, 1991). The offense created in 1885 carried a term of imprisonment for up to two years for "[a]ny male person who, in public or in private, commits, or is a party to the commission of, or procures or attempts to procure the commission by any male person of, any act of gross indecency with another male person."

Australian jurisdictions replicated these British offenses directed at homosexual conduct (Kirby, 2011, p. 25). The *Crimes Act 1900* (NSW), for instance, contained a division relating to "Unnatural Offences," including buggery and bestiality (section 79), attempts to commit buggery and bestiality (s 80), and indecent assault (s 81). Such prohibitions on homosexual conduct continued to exist in England and in the Australian jurisdictions in various forms until they were gradually repealed between 1967 and 1997 (see, for instance, Kirby, 2011, and for a broader jurisdictional discussion, see Hildebrandt, 2014).

Vagrancy laws

In the early nineteenth century, a set of laws was adopted through the *Vagrancy Acts* to criminalize sex workers. While the sex work provisions were directed at female work, certain provisions in these Acts also applied to male homosexuals and male sex workers. The *Vagrancy Act 1824* (UK),[5] section 3, made it an offense punishable by a fine of £5 or imprisonment for one month for "[e]very common prostitute wandering in the public streets or public highway, or in any place of public resort, and behaving in a riotous or indecent manner." The New South Wales equivalent provision in the *Vagrancy Act 1902* (NSW), section 4(1)(c), provides imprisonment with hard labor for a term not exceeding six months for a person who "being a common prostitute, wanders in any street or public highway, or is in any place of public resort, and in either case behaves in a riotous or indecent manner."

In the British case of *R v De Munck* (1918) 1 KB 635 at 637–638, it was found that the term "common prostitute" applied only to "a woman who offered her body commonly for lewdness for payment in return." This approach was also taken in New South Wales, where in the case of *Skinner v The King* (1913) 16 CLR 336 it was held that "common prostitute" referred to "the class of woman . . . who, whether in a street or in a house, carries on the trade or business of prostitution, and submits herself to men for the purpose of gain" (Barton ACJ at 340).

While these Acts did not prosecute male homosexuals and male sex workers as common prostitutes, these Acts also contained offenses for men soliciting or importuning for immoral purposes in public [*Vagrancy Act 1898* (UK), section 1 as amended by the *Criminal Law Amendment Act 1912* (UK), and *Vagrancy Act 1908* (NSW) as amended by the *Police Offences (Amendment) Act 1908* (NSW), section 4(2)(o)(ii)] and also knowingly living on the earnings of prostitution [*Vagrancy Act 1908* (NSW) section 4(2)(o)(i)]. These provisions were not designed to target male sex workers; rather, they were designed to apply to men who solicited for clients for female workers or lived off their earnings—for example, pimps. This approach was confirmed by the New South Wales case of *Ex parte Langley; Re Humphris* (1953) 53 SR (NSW) 324, where Owen CJ held that section 4(2)(o)(ii) of the *Vagrancy Act* (NSW) was intended to deal with "minor pests, not inaptly described as rogues and vagabonds"—that is, "men who live off the earnings of prostitutes, such as souteneurs and runners" (at 325).

There was a period where the soliciting and importuning provisions in the *Vagrancy Act* were applied to male sex workers and male homosexuals, but the offenses were applied whether men solicited for sex as sex work or not.[6] This application of the law suggests that no legal-conceptual distinction was made between male sex work and male homosexuality and, indeed, that the goal was to address male homosexuality itself. Several British cases reinforce this view. In *Horton v Mead* (1913) 1 KB 154, it was found that smiling "in the faces of gentlemen," pursing lips, and wiggling the body could amount to soliciting. In *Police v Cleary* (1948) 12 JCL 122, repeatedly visiting a men's public lavatory in a short space of time and appearing to talk to men was found to be an example of persistent importuning. In *R v Thompson* (1917) 2 KB 630, the accused was prosecuted for gross indecency because he was carrying two powder puffs, and when his room was searched, indecent photographs were found. Other cases highlight that men who behaved outside accepted norms of social behavior were targeted. Behaving effeminately or "inappropriately" (swinging the hips or arms, smiling at men in the face, visiting the public lavatory frequently), talking effeminately, dressing effeminately or looking effeminate (wearing feminine underclothes or make-up), or possessing effeminate objects (powder puffs) or objects associated with homosexual acts (Vaseline, photographs of nude men, letters expressing love for other men) were all considered evidence of the offenses (Hamilton, 1949). None of the cases discussed whether the motivation for the homosexual sexual behavior was for gain or payment.

These examples show that the prosecution of male sex work was based on either the vagrancy laws or other laws criminalizing sodomy or indecency. The fact that such offenses appear to have been applied interchangeably, at least in the United Kingdom, is confirmed by the commentary of Hamilton, a detective constable with Glasgow Police, who wrote an article in the *Police Journal* (1949) analyzing cases dealing with "male persons soliciting or importuning." In this article, Hamilton moves between detailing elements of cases of soliciting and cases of gross indecency without noting any difference between them. Furthermore, the cases he details show how broadly the concept of soliciting or importuning and indecency were understood and the lengths to which police officers would go to enforce these laws.

Hamilton's article points to the fact the laws were not primarily directed at male sex work but rather at male homosexuality more broadly.

The lack of a legal-conceptual distinction between male sex work and male homosexuality, with "both being conflated and assumed indistinguishable" (Scott, 2003a, p. 181), was not a simple, linear result of deliberate unwillingness or inability to make a distinction. To understand this conflation, it is important to consider the social context of homosexuality during this time, when forming and living a male homosexual lifestyle would have been extremely difficult. These difficulties meant that a subculture of homosexuality based on public interaction developed in the early 1900s (Smaal, 2007, p. 15):

> For most young men at the turn of the century, access to private space was a luxury and single men lived either with their family or in cheap, shared accommodation. Living conditions gave little privacy for sexually active men, and privacy was especially luxurious for homosexually inclined men. Single, wage-earning, working-class men pursued their relaxation in public places such as pubs, boarding houses and within city streets, rather than in the private sphere of the home.

This public homosexual subculture meant a fluidity between male sex work and male homosexuals, with both seeking sexual encounters in the same public cruising spaces. Furthermore, the legal approach to homosexuality and hostile social environment meant (see Weeks, 1991, p. 53) meant that

> homosexual activity was potentially very dangerous for both partners and carried with it not only public disgrace but the possibility of a prison sentence. This also fed into the market for prostitution and dictated much of the furtiveness, guilt, and anxiety that was a characteristic of the homosexual way of life.

The public nature of sexual encounters explains the vulnerability to prosecution of men soliciting for, and engaging in, sex in public spaces. Furthermore, class also played a role, with men from the middle and upper classes having "greater opportunity through money and mobility" to arrange sexual contact (Weeks, 1991, p. 55). As such, where there were such "great disparities of wealth and social position . . . the cash nexus inevitably dominated" (Weeks, 1991, p. 55). Thus, practically, there was a spatial, social, and economic intertwining of male sex work and male homosexuality that resulted from but also reinforced the legal and conceptual blurring of male homosexuality and male sex work.

The ending of vagrancy laws and harshening of the law

The approach of applying provisions in the *Vagrancy Act* to male homosexuals/male sex workers was ended, at least in New South Wales, in the mid-nineteenth century when it was determined that the soliciting provision in the *Vagrancy Act* was not designed to deal with such cases. In *Ex parte Langley; Re Humphris* (1953) 53 SR (NSW) 324, the appellant was convicted under the *Vagrancy Act* of being a male person soliciting for an immoral purpose after he invited another man to become an accomplice in the commission of "an unnatural sexual offence." Clancy J noted that this behavior could also have amounted to the offense of indecent or offensive behavior in a public place under s 8A of the *Vagrancy Act* or the offenses of inciting another to commit an "abominable crime of buggery" or indecent assault on a male person under ss 79 and 81 (respectively) of the *Crimes Act 1900* (NSW). This case confirms, once again, that the vagrancy provisions and provisions criminalizing sodomy or indecency were used interchangeably and without regard for whether the behavior amounted to sex work.

Taking the words of the provision alone, Clancy J held that there was no doubt that they could be interpreted to fit the appellant's behavior. His Honor noted that the soliciting provision in the *Vagrancy Act* and its equivalent in the United Kingdom had been applied to such behavior by men in New South Wales and in the United Kingdom (noting the similarity with the case of *Horton v Mead* (1931) 1 KB 154). However, His Honor noted that the question raised in this appeal, about whether the *Vagrancy Act* should apply, could not be dealt with merely by stating what had been assumed to be the correct approach in the past, nor could it be answered without regard to the words in their setting and in the whole Act. In contrasting the relevant offenses in *Crimes Act 1900* (NSW) with the offences in the *Vagrancy Act* (NSW), Clancy J found that the "crime of sexual relations between males" stood out "in sharp contrast in its nature and gravity" to the sorts of behaviors regarding prostitution addressed in the *Vagrancy Act* (NSW). Clancy J also noted that prior to the introduction of the offense of solicitation by male persons found in the *Vagrancy Act* (NSW), men engaging in behavior of the sort detailed in this case could be charged with incitement to commit an "abominable crime" in s 79 of the *Crimes Act 1900* (NSW), which carried a sentence of 14 years penal servitude.

Clancy J found that the significant difference in penalty between the offenses in the *Crimes Act 1900* (NSW) and the offense in the *Vagrancy Act* (NSW) (6 months) showed that the offense in the *Vagrancy Act* was not designed to displace the approach taken before the solicitation provision was included in the *Vagrancy Act*. If this were not the case, according to Clancy, the acts of the homosexual would receive the same penalty "as those who engage in practices such as fortune telling, playing or betting at an unlawful game" (at 327), which he clearly regarded as inadequate. In his view, the prohibition on soliciting by male persons in the *Vagrancy Act* (NSW) were

> more apt in describing the actions of a male who solicits another male to have intercourse with a female than where the result sought to be achieved by him is one which in the *Crimes Act* is grouped amongst "unnatural offences."

(at 327)

His Honor therefore concluded that the solicitation provision of the *Vagrancy Act* should not be used to charge men soliciting for sex with other men. Similarly, Owen CJ found that that s 4(2)(o)(ii) of the *Vagrancy Act* (NSW) was designed to deal with "minor pests, not inaptly described as rogues and vagabonds"—that is, "men who live off the earnings of prostitutes, such as souteneurs and runners" (at 325). It was not designed to deal with behavior such as that engaged in by the appellant. In confirming this view, Owen CJ referred to the fact that the equivalent provision in England was found in legal commentaries, such as Archbold, under the heading "Trading in Prostitution" and was found in the same place as offenses relating to women and girls (at 325).

Ex parte Langley; Re Humphris (1953) 53 SR (NSW) 324 made clear that the law viewed female sex work and men involved in female sex work differently than it viewed male sex work and men who have sex with other men. Research from the United Kingdom also finds that there was an increase in the prosecution of homosexual men in the years after the Second World War (and also the First World War) (Higgins, 1996). Higgins notes that this increased prosecution followed an increase in male homosexuality and male sex work that "greatly strengthened and expanded the homosexual subcultures" during this period (1996, p. 161). These changes can be explained partly by the fact that enlisting for service at wartime meant that young men were removed from families and females for long periods of time. Also, wartime "produced much greater sexual liberation generally" (Higgins, 1996, p. 161). Such liberation and increase in male homosexuality also produced a punitive moral reaction, with male homosexuality being seen as a threat to a nation's "health and economic and military efficiency" in the 1930s and 1950s (Minichiello, Scott, & Callander, 2013, p. 266).

In New South Wales, this harsher treatment during the middle of the twentieth century was further cemented by amendments made to the *Crimes Act 1900* (NSW) in 1955, which aimed to "eradicate" the "homosexual wave that unfortunately has struck this country—though not to the extent of continental countries" (Hansard 19/09/55 NSW Parliament [3230]). The *Crimes (Amendment) Act 1955* (NSW) introduced an offense punishable by two years' imprisonment for a male person committing, or being a party to the commission of, or procuring or attempting to procure an indecent act with another male in public or in private (s 81A). A male person soliciting, inciting, or attempting to solicit or incite a male to commit an indecent act, indecent assault, or buggery was subject to imprisonment for 12 months (s 81B).

Decriminalization of male homosexuality

Significant shifts occurred in the law's approach to male homosexuality and male sex work in the second half of the twentieth century following a period of increased punitiveness. As already noted, wartime saw a greater sexual liberation and an apparent expansion in male homosexual subcultures (Higgins, 1996, p. 161). However, increased visibility also meant increased moral concern and increased punitiveness. Such punitiveness also increased the public's awareness of male homosexuality, as the details of prosecutions of a number of high-profile homosexual men were salaciously represented in the media (see Higgins, 1996, pp. 65–72). Scientific research into sexuality and the understanding of homosexuality as a characteristic of a person increased with the rise in the visibility of male homosexual subculture. Against this background, the UK government established a committee chaired by Sir John Wolfenden to investigate the law relating to homosexuality and female sex work.

The terms of reference of the Wolfenden Committee specify that the Committee was to examine: "(a) the law and practice relating to homosexual offences . . . and (b) the law and practice relating to offences against the criminal law in connection with prostitution and solicitation for immoral purposes" (Home Office, 1957, para. 1). The Committee clearly understood (b) to refer only to female sex work (see Home Office, 1957, para. 13). The Committee looked at the purpose of criminalizing conduct and took the stance that "[i]t is not, in our view, the function of the law to intervene in the private lives of citizens, or to seek to enforce any particular pattern of behavior, further than is necessary to carry out the purposes we have outlined" (Home Office, 1957, para. 14). The purposes outlined were "to preserve public order and decency, to protect the citizen from what is offensive or injurious and to provide sufficient safeguards against exploitation and corruption of others" (Home Office, 1957, para. 13). In relation to homosexuality, the Committee recommended that private adult consensual acts should not be subject to criminalization. It was clear that the Committee had been influenced by the changing understanding of homosexuality, particularly Kinsey's research, which found that sexuality exists on a continuum. The Committee concluded that "homosexuals cannot reasonably be regarded as quite separate from the rest of mankind" (Home Office, 1957, para. 22). While recommending the partial decriminalization of male homosexuality, the Committee were in favor of retaining the offence of persistent importuning or soliciting for an immoral purpose by males, found in the *Sexual Offences Act 1957* (UK) and previously the *Vagrancy Act 1898* (UK),

(Home Office, 1957, para 116–124). It was felt that this offence had made the incidence of men importuning in the street negligible and therefore less of an "affront to public decency" than the street activities of female sex workers (Home Office, 1957, para 124). The reason to retain the offence was to ensure that the recommended partial decriminalization should "not be interpreted as an indication that the law can be indifferent to other forms of homosexual behavior, or as a general license to adult homosexuals to behave as they please" (Home Office, 1957, para 124). The discussion of this offence in the Report again confirms that it was seen as an offence relating to male homosexuality rather than male sex work.[7] Regarding female sex work, which was considered much more of a public nuisance, the Committee proposed an increase in the penalties for soliciting (Home Office, 1957, para 274–284).

The Wolfenden Committee's final report led to a vigorous discussion of homosexuality (Higgins, 1996) and debate about the role of criminal law in regulating matters of morality. It eventually led to the decriminalization of homosexuality in the United Kingdom, and in Australia, and it set the tone for prostitution policy in the following decades. Decriminalization of male homosexuality eventually weakened this inexorable legal-conceptual intertwining of male sex work and male homosexuality. After male sex work was set free from the legal connection to male homosexuality, it might have been expected that male sex work would come to fall under sex work regulation. However, that did not happen, because there was no practical need to use sex work laws to regulate male sex work because other criminal laws could be, were, and are used. A further explanation is the ongoing conceptualization of male sex work as a part of male sexuality (Vanwesenbeeck, 2001), and there was, and continues to be, an unwillingness or inability to conceptualize male sex work within the dominant narratives that frame female sex work and influence its regulation.

No practical need to expand sex work laws to male homosexuality

Laws initially enacted in the United Kingdom and Australian states and territories following the recommendations in the Wolfenden report generally did not fully decriminalize homosexuality. The age of consent tended to be higher, and certain specific offenses were retained for male homosexual sexual acts. The *Sexual Offences Act 1967* (UK) only decriminalized homosexual acts in private,[8] provided that both parties were aged 21 or over. Indecency between men remained a specific offense unless done in private (*Sexual Offences Act 1956* [UK], section 13). Full decriminalization was achieved only in 2000 when the age of consent was equalized through the *Sexual Offences (Amendment) Act 2000* (UK), section 1. Similarly, in Australia, similar steps to decriminalize homosexual sex acts were undertaken in most states and territories between 1972 and 1997 (see Bull, Pinto, & Wilson, 1991; Carbery, 2010; Kirby, 2011), although, as in the United Kingdom, the first step tended to be partial decriminalization with a higher age of consent and the retention of specific homosexual offenses. Full decriminalization occurred later in many states and territories. For instance, in New South Wales, partial decriminalization occurred in 1984 through the *Crimes Amendment Act 1984* (NSW) and full decriminalization in 2003 through the *Crimes Amendment (Sexual Offences) Act 2003* (NSW).

The initial partial decriminalization meant that residual offenses covering male homosexual sex acts could still be used to prosecute men who engaged in sex in public whether or not this public sex amounted to sex work. Even when these homosexual-specific criminal offenses were repealed to achieve equalization of the law, the criminal law still continued to be used to control sex acts between males in a way that sex acts between heterosexuals were not controlled (Johnson, 2012; Ashford, 2012). The longstanding views that standards of decency are "in diametric opposition to homosexuality" meant that police were still more likely to prosecute public sexual acts between homosexuals than they were to prosecute heterosexuals (Johnson, 2012, pp. 25–26).

A further set of criminal laws was adopted following the panic around the HIV/AIDS epidemic in the 1980s. Most jurisdictions either adapted existing grievous or actual bodily harm offenses to cover the transmission of a serious disease, or they created new offenses criminalizing the intentional or reckless transmission of HIV (or other serious disease). Some jurisdictions also adopted laws directed at sex workers, prohibiting people from working as sex workers when they know or could reasonably be expected to know that they are infected with a sexually transmitted disease, including HIV—for example, *Prostitution Act 1992* (ACT), s 25; *Sex Work Act 1994* (Vic), s 20. These provisions do not require that transmission occur, and in 2008, the Australian Capital Territory provision was used to prosecute an HIV-positive man for working as a sex worker (see Jenkins, 2008), even though there was no evidence that he had practiced unsafe sex or transmitted HIV. Coercive powers under health laws could also be used to control sex workers (Scott, 2003b). While these laws were not directed specifically at male sex workers, they did provide another avenue for regulation and control.

The range of laws that could be used to control male homosexuality following decriminalization and the effects of these laws has meant that there has practically been no need to use sex work laws to regulate male sex work. A further, and perhaps more fundamental, explanation for this heterocentric and gendered approach to sex work, which continues to focus on female sex work and bypass male sex work, is the traditional or ongoing inability or unwillingness to conceptualize male sex work within the dominant narratives that drive debate around the regulation of female sex work.

Inability or unwillingness to conceptualize male sex work within dominant frameworks and conceptualizations of sex work

Sex work laws to date have almost wholly framed sex work as something that female sex workers do for male clients. This conclusion is supported by the wording of sex work laws, the cases interpreting those laws, and the policy debates about those laws. Such laws, cases, and debates have rarely extended to male sex workers. The framing of sex work as something that women engage in might be due to male sex work being "understood within traditional perspectives of male sexuality, which may contrast sharply with ways in which female sex work contradicts traditional perspectives of femininity" (Vanwesenbeeck, 2001, p. 275; see also Browne & Minichiello, 1996). Regarding male sex work within the context of male sexuality has meant that male sex work has not fit neatly within any of the increasingly divergent ideological perspectives on female sex work.

On one end of the ideological spectrum lies a sex-positive, pro-sex work feminist frame of reference that emerged in the mid-1990s. This perspective regards sex work as legitimate work and "an empowering profession, because it provides an opportunity for women to subvert patriarchal domination and capitalise on their sexuality, and/or, because sex work fulfils an important social need" (Orchiston, 2017, pp. 54–55). Another frame regards sex work as context-specific embodied service work. In this view, sex work is neither intrinsically empowering nor exploitative. Instead, the degree of "power, control, and risk" experienced by sex workers is shaped by cultural and structural constraints, including regulation (Sanders, 2005; Weitzer, 2012; McDowell, 2009; Wolkowitz, 2006). Common to these approaches is an understanding that "the illegal status of sex work and its consequences do violate the civil and workers' rights and integrity of sex workers" (Vanwesenbeeck, 2001, p. 243). Furthermore, criminal laws directed at sex work are regarded as "discriminatory, criminogenic, and an overreach of the criminal law" (Egger & Harcourt, 1993, p. 116) and lead to poorer health and safety levels (Harcourt et al., 2010). In New South Wales, these arguments were influential in leading to the gradual repeal of criminal laws specific to sex work, while other Australian jurisdictions have either introduced regulation/licensing schemes (e.g., Queensland and Victoria) or continue to use a criminalization framework (e.g., South Australia and Western Australia) for addressing sex work (Harcourt, Egger, & Donovan, 2005; Crofts & Summerfield, 2007). Such a perspective on sex work does not encompass male sex work, because it sees no need for criminal law to be involved in the regulation of sex work.

At the other end of the ideological spectrum, many radical feminists frame sex work as a "gross violation of a woman's bodily integrity" and "both a manifestation and a cause of gender inequality" (Orchiston, 2017, p. 56). Dworkin has argued that sex work is not a matter of choice for women but rather a negation of choice and self-determination (Dworkin, 1987). Some have even described sex work as "an institution of male supremacy" akin to slavery (Cole cited in Overall, 1992, p. 707). Such a narrative, which has increasingly gained traction in recent years, posits female workers inexorably as victims and men as exploiters and users of women (Whowell & Gaffney, 2009; Ashford, 2009). Proponents of this model also tend to conflate sex work and trafficking of women (Orchiston, 2017; Sanders, Scoular, Campbell, Pitcher, & Cunningham, 2018). As Phoenix notes (2009, p. 10) in a policy context "sexual exploitation serves as a metonym for prostitution, with the result that human trafficking and prostitution become treated as though they are proxies for one another."

According to a radical feminist perspective, the decriminalization or legalization of sex work not only leads to direct harm to women involved in sex work but also breaks down "social and ethical barriers to treating women as sexual merchandise" (Raymond, 2004, p. 323). Recent models for regulating sex work (such as the Swedish model; see Chapter 31 of this book) adopt a radical feminist perspective aim to abolish sex work by criminalizing the client rather than the sex worker (Scoular, 2004). These models tend to be silent on male sex work, because

> [t]he great majority of it takes place between men within a world and a context that resist feminist analysis of patriarchal domination, the theoretical structure most often used to explain the imposition of sexuality, or even sexual slavery, upon women and children.
>
> *(Dorais, 2005, p. vii)*

Male sex work was largely absent in the debates surrounding the introduction of an abolitionist approach in Sweden (Gould, 2001, p. 239) and is generally overlooked within the trafficking discourse more generally (Levy & Jakobsson, 2014, p. 3), because many radical feminists are reluctant to conceptualize male sex work within what Weitzer calls the "oppression paradigm" (2011, p. 1338).

For instance, Jeffreys (1997, p. 92) argues that there are "crucial differences" between male and female sex workers: "Male gay sexual practice, which values quick, impersonal contacts in public places, does not differ greatly in procedure from what will take place for money. The act of being prostituted does not demean the man taking part" (1997, p. 107). Jeffreys asserts that male sex workers are able to gain sexual pleasure "from their work," whereas this is not the case for "prostituted women" (1997, p. 104). By taking a more nuanced view of male sex work than of female sex work, positioning the former as something that a (male) person can freely consent to notwithstanding a risk of being "damaged" by his involvement in it, Jeffreys conceptualizes male sex work as distinct from female sex work and effectively exempt from the abolitionist feminist narrative used to justify punitive sex industry laws.

In addition to the exclusion of male sex workers from dominant frameworks and conceptualizations of sex work, a final and related factor that contributes to the heterocentric and gendered approach to sex work is that male sex work has been, and is, carried out in ways that make it less visible and therefore less subject to regulation through sex work laws.

Visibility and the shift to online platforms

The forms and spaces in which male sex work takes place have always rendered it less visible to mainstream society and less likely to be seen as a "nuisance" that needs to be addressed through sex work laws. The historic criminalization of male homosexual activity pushed male sex work and male homosexuality into marginal spaces and clandestine communities (Weeks, 1981). As the Wolfenden Committee noted, the fact that the law could impose heavy penalties ensured that male importuning in the streets was negligible and did not nearly present the affront to public decency that the street activities of female sex workers did (Home Office, 1957, para 124). Male sex workers are more likely to work alone without the control of other individuals (Whowell & Gaffney, 2009) and are less likely to work from brothels or engage in street-based work (Minichiello et al., 2002; Dorais, 2005). Instead, they are more likely to seek clients through private advertisement (Minichiello et al., 2002).

Increasingly, both male and female sex work has shifted "into Internet-mediated private spaces" (Bernstein, 2007; Minichiello et al., 2013; MacPhail, Scott, & Minichiello, 2014; Sanders et al., 2018). Research conducted by McLean (2012) finds that male sex workers are turning to the Internet due to improvements in ease, convenience, accessibility, anonymity, autonomy, security, and profitability. The development of male sex work websites such as RentMen, Hunqz, Mintboys, and Jock2Go allow male sex workers to advertise without resorting to traditional methods or places to seek clients (e.g., street work, bars, beats, and so on).

The shift to Internet-mediated advertising has made it practically less imperative, and at the same time realistically more difficult, to apply criminal laws to male (and also to female) sex workers. The Internet is transforming what legislators may deem an unwanted public nuisance (i.e., public solicitation) into an "invisible" activity (Walker, Brock, & Stuart, 2006, p. 169) by hiding solicitation within websites that the vast majority of Internet users are unlikely to find. This has made it more difficult for law enforcement to trace sex workers' activities (Lee-Gonyea et al., 2009, p. 326). Policy relating to the policing of sex work (at least in the United Kingdom) has focused on street-based work (Sanders et al., 2018; Scoular & O'Neill, 2007), and law and policy have failed to acknowledge gender diversity or new forms of sexual exchange (Sanders et al., 2018; Ashford, 2006). It thus appears that at present there is only limited policing of Internet-based sex work (Sanders et al., 2018).

However, this situation may change because the

> increased focus on anti-trafficking, which is high on the policy agenda in the USA and many European countries, frequently conceptualized in terms of sexual exploitation and targeted mainly by criminal justice responses, means the Internet has become a new site for police surveillance of sex work.
>
> *(Sanders et al., 2018, p. 123, references omitted)*

Recent developments in the United States may signal growing regulatory interest in male sex workers online. The *Allow States and Victims to Fight Online Sex Trafficking Act 2017* (FOSTA) came into operation in April 2018, amending the *Communications Decency Act*, s 230, a provision that had protected online publishers from liability arising from user posts on their websites

(Goldman, 2018; Chamberlain, 2019). FOSTA conflates sex trafficking and sex work (Chamberlain, 2019, p. 2203) and, among other things, makes website owners, managers and operators criminally liable for advertisements posted on their websites for illegal sex work (Goldman, 2018). The reform was premised on a conception of trafficking that is expressly gendered and illustrative of an unwillingness to conceptualize males as trafficking victims. Consistent with a gendered and heterocentric approach, men and boys were absent in the Congressional debate that preceded the bill's enactment. Senator Rob Portman (OH-R), co-sponsor of the bill, described its goals in the following terms:

> The Communications Decency Act is a well-intentioned law, but it was never intended to help protect sex traffickers who prey on the most innocent and vulnerable among us. This bipartisan, narrowly crafted bill will help protect vulnerable women and young girls from these horrific crimes.
>
> *(Portman, 2017)*

Notwithstanding its gendered framing of trafficking, FOSTA has been applied to male sex work. The "real" (and unstated) reason for its enactment was ostensibly to outlaw sex worker advertising online, making it less visible, and the law has been enforced against both male and female sex work advertising sites. Shortly after FOSTA came into effect, Rentboy.com, the Internet's largest gay male escort site, was raided and permanently shut down and its operators charged with prostitution offenses. None of the charges related to human trafficking, nor was any evidence of trafficking asserted. Prior to its closure, the site generated A\$10 million in advertising fees from 2010 to 2015 (Indictment, 2016, p. 3). In addition, Backpage, a popular classified website that hosted sex worker ads, was shut down and its operators indicted (Chamberlain, 2019, p. 2089).[9] The closure of these websites sparked a wave of self-policing behavior on the part of other website operators, which also affected male sex workers' ability to advertise online. For example, the Web forum Reddit responded by banning its "male escorts" subreddit where male escorts advertised their services, along with "escorts," "hookers," and "sugardaddy" subreddits, which were used by sex workers of all genders. Craigslist closed its popular personals section, which had included sex worker ads, and escort site CityVibe shut down entirely (Romano, 2018). Tumblr banned all "explicit adult content and nudity" (D'Onofrio, 2018), forcing its sex worker users to remove explicit material or risk their blog being deleted.

FOSTA has had a significant impact outside of the United States, including in Australia and in the United Kingdom, because many of the websites used by sex workers internationally have U.S.-based servers and/or are operated by American businesses. For example, 30% of traffic to Rentboy.com was from users outside of the United States, equating to 150,000 unique hits per day (Indictment, 2016, p. 3). According to an Australian sex worker representative, FOSTA led to the loss of half of the sites used by male sex workers in Australia and, as a consequence, loss of income:

> There were a large range of sites that went down. I'd say we lost at least half the sites we use. . . . A lot of people are feeling the pinch very much. We all have rent to pay, some of us have family responsibilities—we're not all young, gay, and carefree, if you know what I mean.
>
> *(Young, 2018; see also Smiley & Lavoipierre, 2018)*

Lawless (2018) notes that the practical impact of website closures post-FOSTA may have been more severe for male sex workers than for female sex workers, because male sex workers generally work independently and have few, if any, other opportunities for off-street sex work, such as working from a brothel or an escort agency. Male brothels and escort agencies are concentrated in large metropolitan centers, and due to their scarcity, they tend to require workers to have a particular aesthetic. Older workers and workers who have alternative body types or attributes are less likely to have the option of working in a brothel or for an escort agency, even where they exist (Orchiston, 2017, p. 105). With reduced options for working indoors, it is possible that FOSTA has driven an increase in male sex workers engaging in street-based work, which leaves them more vulnerable to police scrutiny. Lending support to this proposition, there have been reports of growth in the number of street-based sex workers in the United States since the enactment of FOSTA (see, e.g., Andersen, Ravani, & Cassidy, 2018).

It is unclear whether this reform will lead to greater regulatory focus on male sex work at the domestic level. Because the trafficking framework on which FOSTA is based is highly gendered and heterocentric, it is likely that any domestic equivalent law would similarly position male sex work in the shadow of female sex work. At the same time, the U.S. experience shows that such a law could be used to target male sex workers.

Conclusion

This chapter has explored the reasons for the gendered, heterocentric approach to sex work that has seen male sex work pushed into the regulatory shadow of male homosexuality and sex work. Historically, male sex work and male homosexuality have legally and conceptually been treated as indistinguishable, or at least as so interconnected that there was no need to regulate male sex work distinctly. As such, laws criminalizing male homosexual sexual acts were primarily used to regulate male homosexuality and male sex work. For a period, provisions of the Vagrancy Acts in the United Kingdom and New South Wales prohibiting male solicitation were used interchangeably with laws criminalizing male homosexual sex acts. These laws have tended to be applied whether the behavior amounted to sex work or not, suggesting that the primary target was not male sex work specifically but rather male homosexuality in general. The middle of the nineteenth century saw an increasingly visible male homosexual subculture develop and increased scientific research interest in male homosexuality. It also witnessed an increasingly punitive approach toward male homosexuality and male sex work. When male homosexuality was decriminalized in the second part of the twentieth century, sex work laws were not expanded to cover male sex work, partly because residual criminal laws could still be used to regulate public male homosexual conduct and male sex work. In addition, we see the ongoing conceptualization of male sex work as part of male (homosexual) sexuality and the inability, or unwillingness, to conceptualize male sex work within dominant frameworks and conceptualizations of sex work. While these conceptualizations have shifted and co-existed at different times, they have in common a lack of reach to male sex workers, either by design or neglect. The increasing shift to online-facilitated sex work has reduced the imperative to legally regulate sex work and also made it practically more difficult. The question is whether the recent moves to combat online sex trafficking will also impact male sex work. While these laws generally conceptualize trafficking as a gendered issue and thus perpetuate the gendered, heterocentric approach to sex work, they have already had a practical impact on male sex work. The question remains whether this impact will remain incidental or whether male sex work will be brought out of the shadows and into the direct regulatory purview of sex work laws.

Notes

1 The focus of this chapter is on male sex workers providing sex work for men, because legal regulation of male sex workers has most visibly affected this subset of male sex workers. The contrasting of male sex work and female sex work in this chapter is not intended to suggest that a gender binary applies to sex work. Sex work is performed by trans, non-binary, and gender-diverse people, and clients may also be trans, non-binary, and gender diverse. While historically there has been little research on male sex work, even less attention has been paid to male sex workers providing services to women or to trans, non-binary, and gender-diverse workers and clients (Browne & Minichiello, 1996; Lee-Gonyea, Castle, & Gonyea, 2009; Smith, Laing, & Pilcher, 2014).

2 This chapter aims only to provide a snapshot of general developments and themes at different points in history in these jurisdictions. The legal sources for this exploration of "multiple marginalities" (Davies & Feldman, 1997) mean that the historical literature is patchy and legal approaches were not necessarily linear.

3 It should here be noted that while there has been a long history of the criminalization of sodomy, this was not linked to a concept of homosexuality, at least as a characteristic of a person. In law, little definitional distinction was made between sodomy with a male, female, or animal, but most prosecutions were for sodomy between men (Weeks, 1991; see also Hough, 2004). It was not until the nineteenth century that the concept of the homosexual developed and with it the drive to combat homosexuality through comprehensive criminal offenses (Weeks, 1991).

4 See Scott (2003a), Bimbi (2007), and Whowell and Gaffney (2009) for further discussion on the paradigm shifts in relation to male sex work. These shifts did not necessary take place in a linear progression; rather, some overlapped and existed at the same time. Bimbi argues that these discourses replaced one another based on the scientific community's conceptualization of homosexuality.

5 There were other laws and methods of controlling sex workers preceding the *Vagrancy Acts*, but these Acts had perhaps the most profound impact in controlling sex work. See, for instance, Laite (2008).

6 Weeks (1991, p. 52) suggests that this meant that "all homosexual males as a class were equated with female prostitutes." However, female workers were somewhat tolerated in a way that male homosexuals and male sex workers were not, suggesting that this is not a straightforward equation and that the primary drive was to combat male homosexuality.

7 It was noted that while in England, this offence was used mainly to prosecute men importuning other men for homosexual acts and occasionally for men importuning for clients for female workers, the equivalent provision in Scotland has been only applied to men importuning for clients for female workers and never to men importuning men for homosexual activities (Home Office, 1957, para. 117).

8 Section 2 of the Act made the meaning of private clear: "An act which would otherwise be treated for the purposes of this Act as being done in private shall not be so treated if done (a) when more than two persons take part or are present; or (b) in a lavatory to which the public have or are permitted to have access, whether on payment or otherwise."

9 The owners of Backpage.com were indicted under the Travel Act 18 USC§1952 (2012) for facilitating prostitution. FOSTA had not yet commenced at the time of indictment, but "[f]rom a policy standpoint the effects of the Backpage.com shutdown were not especially distinguishable from FOSTA's effects more generally" (Chamberlain, 2019, pp. 2089–2090).

References

Andersen, T., Ravani, S., & Cassidy, M. (2018, October 15). The Scanner: Sex workers returned to SF streets after Backpage.com shut down. *San Francisco Chronicle*. Retrieved from www.sfchronicle.com/crime/article/The-Scanner-Sex-workers-returned-to-SF-streets-13304257.php

Ashford, C. (2006). The only gay in the village: Sexuality and the net. *Information & Communications Technology Law, 15*(3), 275–289.

Ashford, C. (2009). Male sex work and the Internet effect: Time to re-evaluate the criminal law? *Journal of Criminal Law, 73,* 258–280.

Ashford, C. (2012). Heterosexuality, public places, and policing. In P. Johnson & D. Dalton (Eds.), *Policing sex* (pp. 41–53). New York: Routledge.

Bimbi, D. (2007). Male prostitution: Pathology, paradigms, and progress in research. *Journal of Homosexuality, 53*(1–2), 7–35.

Browne, J., & Minichiello, V. (1996). Research directions in male sex work. *Journal of Homosexuality*, *31*(4), 29–56.

Bull, M., Pinto, S., & Wilson, P. (1991). Homosexual law reform in Australia. In *Trends and issues in crime and criminal justice* (p. 29). Canberra: Australian Institute of Criminology.

Chamberlain, L. (2019). FOSTA: A hostile law with a human cost. *Fordham Law Review*, *87*(5), 2127–2211.

Crofts, T., & Summerfield, T. (2007). Licensing: Regulating prostitution or enforcing morality. *University of Western Australia Law Review*, *33*(2), 289–306.

Davies, P., & Feldman, R. (1997). Prostitute men now. In G. Scambler & A. Scambler (Eds.), *Rethinking prostitution: Purchasing sex in the 1990s*. New York: Routledge.

D'Onofrio, J. (2018). *A better more positive Tumblr*. Retrieved from https://staff.tumblr.com/post/180758987165/a-better-more-positive-tumblr

Dorais, M. (2005). *Rent boys: The world of male sex workers*. Montreal: McGill-Queen's University Press.

Dworkin, A. (1987). *Intercourse*. New York: Free Press.

Egger, S., & Harcourt, C. (1993). Prostitution in NSW: The impact of deregulation. In P. Easteal & S. McKillop (Eds.), *Women and the law: Proceedings of a conference held 24–26 September 1991*. Canberra: Australian Institute of Criminology.

Goldman, E. (2018). The complicated story of FOSTA and section 230. *First Amendment Law Review*, *17*, 279–293.

Gould, A. (2001). The criminalisation of buying sex: The politics of prostitution in Sweden. *Journal of Social Policy*, *30*(3), 437–456.

Hamilton, D. (1949). Male persons soliciting or importuning for immoral purposes. *The Police Journal*, *22*(2), 137–146.

Harcourt, C., Egger, S., & Donovan, B. (2005). Sex work and the law. *Sexual Health*, *2*, 121–128.

Harcourt, C., O'Connor, J., Egger, S., Fairley, C., Wand, H., Chen, M., . . . Donovan, B. (2010). The decriminalisation of prostitution is associated with better coverage of health promotion programs for sex workers. *Australian and New Zealand Journal of Public Health*, *34*, 482–486.

Higgins, P. (1996). *The heterosexual dictatorship: Male homosexuality in postwar Britain*. London: Fourth Estate.

Hildebrandt, A. (2014). Routes to decriminalization: A comparative analysis of the legalization of same-sex sexual acts. *Sexualities*, *17*(1/2), 230–253.

Home Office. (1957). *Report of the committee on homosexual offences and prostitution* (Cmnd 247). London: HMSO ("Wolfenden Report").

Hough, N. (2004). Sodomy and prostitution: Laws protecting the "fabric of society." *Pierce Law Review*, *3*, 101.

Jeffreys, S. (1997). *The idea of prostitution*. Melbourne: Spinifex.

Jenkins, M. (2008, January 18). Sex worker purposely spread STD. *The Australian*.

Johnson, P. (2012). The enforcers of morality? In P. Johnson & D. Dalton (Eds.), *Policing sex* (pp. 23–37). New York: Routledge.

Kirby, M. (2011). The sodomy offence: England's least lovely criminal export. *Journal of Commonwealth Criminal Law*, *1*, 22–43.

Laite, J. (2008). Taking Nellie Johnson's fingerprints: Prostitutes and legal identity in early twentieth-century London. *History Workshop Journal*, *65*(1), 96–116.

Lawless, T. (2018). *Since FOSTA*. Retrieved from https://meanjin.com.au/blog/since-fosta/

Lee-Gonyea, J., Castle, T., & Gonyea, N. (2009). Laid to order: Male escorts advertising on the Internet. *Deviant Behavior*, *30*(4), 321–348.

Levy, J., & Jakobsson, P. (2014). Sweden's abolitionist discourse and law: Effects on the dynamics of Swedish sex workers and on the lives of Sweden's sex workers. *Criminology and Criminal Justice*, *14*(5), 593–607.

MacPhail, C., Scott, J., & Minichiello, V. (2014). Technology, normalization and male sex work. *Culture, Health and Sexuality*, *13*, 137–155.

McDowell, L. (2009). *Working bodies: Interactive service employment and workplace identities*. Hoboken, NJ: Wiley-Blackwell.

McLean, A. (2012). New realm, new problems? Issues and support networks in online male sex work. *Gay and Lesbian Issues and Psychology Review*, *8*(2), 70.

Minichiello, V., Mariño, R., Browne, J., Jamieson, M., Peterson, K., Reuter, B., & Robinson, K. (2002). Male sex workers in three Australian cities. *Journal of Homosexuality, 42*(1), 29–51.

Minichiello, V., Scott, J., & Callander, D. (2013). New pleasures and old dangers: Reinventing male sex work. *Journal of Sex Research, 50*, 63.

Orchiston, A. (2017). *Brothels as workplaces: Exploring labour regulation and compliance in Australia's legal sex industry* (PhD thesis). University of Sydney, Sydney.

Overall, C. (1992, Summer). What's wrong with prostitution? Evaluating sex work. *Signs*, 705–725.

Phoenix, J. (2009). Frameworks of understanding. In J. Phoenix (Ed.), *Regulating sex for sale* (pp. 1–28). Bristol: Polity Press.

Portman, R. (2017). *Press release: Senators introduce bipartisan legislation to hold Backpage accountable, ensure justice for victims of sex trafficking (1 August 2017)*. Retrieved from www.portman.senate.gov/newsroom/press-releases/senators-introduce-bipartisan-legislation-hold-backpage-accountable-ensure

Raymond, J. (2004). Ten reasons for *not* legalizing prostitution and a legal response to the demand for prostitution. *Journal of Trauma Practice, 2*(3–4), 315–332.

Romano, A. (2018). *A new law intended to curb sex trafficking threatens the future of the Internet as we know it*. Retrieved from www.vox.com/culture/2018/4/13/17172762/fosta-sesta-backpage-230-internet-freedom

Sanders, T. (2005). *Sex work: A risky business*. Devon: Willan Publishing.

Sanders, T., Scoular, J., Campbell, R., Pitcher, J., & Cunningham, S. (2018). *Internet sex work: Beyond the gaze*. New York: Palgrave.

Scott, J. (2003a). A prostitute's progress: Male prostitution in scientific discourse. *Social Semiotics, 13*(2), 179–199.

Scott, J. (2003b). Prostitution and Public Health in New South Wales. *Culture, Health and Sexuality, 5*(3), 277–293.

Scoular, J. (2004). The 'subject' of prostitution: Interpreting the discursive, symbolic and material position of sex/work in feminist theory. *Feminist Theory, 5*(3): 343–355.

Scoular, J., & O'Neill, M. (2007). Regulating prostitution: Social inclusion, responsibilisation, and the politics of prostitution reform. *British Journal of Criminology, 47*(5), 764–778.

Smaal, Y. (2007). Coding desire: The emergence of a homosexual subculture in Queensland, 1890–1914. *Queensland Review, 14*, 13.

Smiley, S., & Lavoipierre, A. (2018, June 7). Australian sex workers struggling to survive after US bans online advertising. *ABC News*. Retrieved from www.abc.net.au/news/2018-06-07/fosta-the-us-law-punishing-australian-sex-workers/9842722

Smith, N., Laing, M., & Pilcher, K. (2014). Being, thinking and doing 'queer' in debates about commercial sex. In M. Laing, K. Pilcher, & N. Smith (Eds.), *Queering sex work* (pp. 1–9). Abingdon: Routledge.

Vanwesenbeeck, I. (2001). Another decade of social scientific work on sex work: A review of research 1990–2000. *Annual Review of Sex Research, 12*(1), 242–289.

Walker, D., Brock, D., & Stuart, T. (2006). Faceless-orientated policing: Traditional policing theories are not adequate in a cyber world. *Police Journal, 79*(2), 169–176.

Weeks, J. (1981). Inverts, perverts, and Mary-Annes: Male prostitution and the regulation of homosexuality in the nineteenth and early twentieth century. *Journal of Homosexuality, 6*(1–2), 113–134.

Weeks, J. (1991). *Against nature: Essays on history, sexuality and identity*. London: Rivers Oram Press.

Weitzer, R. (2011). Sex trafficking and the sex industry: The need for evidence-based theory and legislation. *Journal of Criminal Law and Criminology, 101*(4), 1337–1369.

Weitzer, R. (2012). *Legalizing prostitution: From illicit vice to lawful business*. New York: NYU Press.

Whowell, M., & Gaffney, J. (2009). Male sex work in the UK: Forms, practice and policy implications. In J. Phoenix (Ed.), *Regulating sex for sale* (pp. 99–119). Bristol: Polity Press.

Wolkowitz, C. (2006). *Bodies at work*. London: Sage.

Young, M. (2018, April 23). Sex workers in Australia say American law is creating devastating losses back home. *News.com.au*. Retrieved from www.news.com.au/lifestyle/relationships/sex/sex-workers-in-australia-say-american-law-is-creating-devastating-losses-back-home/news-story/09139a2f0d631cd7284090d2336ca517

Legislation

Allow States and Victims to Fight Online Sex Trafficking Act 2017 (US)
Buggery Act 1533 (UK)
Communications Decency Act
Crimes Act 1900 (NSW)
Crimes Amendment Act 1955 (NSW)
Criminal Law Amendment Act 1885 (UK)
Offences Against the Person Act 1861 (UK)
Police Officers Act
Policing and Crime Act 2009 (UK)
Public Health Act 1902 (NSW)
Public Health Act 2010 (NSW)
Public Health (Proclaimed Diseases) Amendment Act 1989 (NSW)
Prostitution Act 1992 (ACT)
Sex Work Act 1994 (Vic)
Sexual Offences Act 1967 (UK)
Sexual Offences (Amendment) Act 2000 (UK)
Travel Act (US)
Vagrancy Act 1824 (UK)
Vagrancy Act 1898 (UK)
Vagrancy Act 1902 (NSW)
Vagrancy Act 1908 (NSW)

Cases

Director of Public Prosecutions v Bull [1994] 158 JP 1005
Ex parte Langley; Re Humphris (1953) 53 SR (NSW) 324
Grivelis v Horsnell (1974) 8 SASR 43
Horton v Mead (1913) 1 KB 154
Police v Cleary (1948) 12 JCL 122
Skinner v The King (1913) 16 CLR 336
R v De Munck (1918) 1 KB 635
R v Thompson (1917) 2 KB 630

Other

United States v. Easy Rent Sys Inc., No. 1:16-cr-00045 (EDNY, 2016 January 28), ECF No. 68 (Indictment). Retrieved from https://tribwpix.files.wordpress.com/2015/08/rentboy-complaint-redacted.pdf

16

Internet-based male sex work

Varying roles of stories, scripts, and spontaneity

Kevin Walby

Introduction

This chapter examines how male Internet escorts from diverse backgrounds engage in their work and negotiate interactions with clients. By *male Internet escorts*, I mean men who use Internet communications to solicit clients for commercial sexual encounters. Focusing on male Internet escorts who sell sexual services to men, I consider how their negotiations with clients include a spectrum of experiences over time, ranging from interactions in which workers maintain distance from clients and provide mostly routine services based on scripts, to interactions that workers describe as intimate, friendly, and spontaneous.

To provide such an analysis, it is useful to draw from interactionist theories of sex and sexuality. The interactionist approach focuses on the complexities of communication, gesture, and meaning-making in small group situations. The notions of spontaneity and creativity have long interested interactionist scholars. Foremost among interactionist theories of sex and sexuality are two approaches that emerged in the mid-1970s: the work of Ken Plummer (1975, 1982, 1995) with respect to sexual stories and the work of John Gagnon and William Simon (1974) and their discussion of sexual scripts. This chapter draws out the differences between these approaches and shows the strengths and limits of both.

Jackson and Scott (2001, 2010) claim interactionist sociology is a way of grounding the claims made by queer theorists, but scripting theory does not fully explain the link between culture and discourse, scripts, and interaction. This chapter advances the idea that touching encounters are a way of reorienting interactionist theories of sex and sexuality. Sexual scripting does indeed happen, but there is a logic to sex work encounters between men that is often based on anonymous sociality. Sociologists must expand their theories of sexuality and sex work to explain spontaneous and anonymous encounters. Sexual scripting theory has not emphasized unanticipated meaning-making or bodily practices; it thus places too much weight on the script leading up to the encounter and neglects how the script breaks down or how touching alters the script.

First, I briefly explain interactionist theories of sex and sexuality and summarize the literature on male sex work for insights into how workers negotiate interactions with clients. Second, I offer a note on research design. Third, I analyze what male sex workers say about their sex work. Beyond extending and critiquing the sexual stories and sexual scripting perspectives, I also draw from Bernstein's (2007) notion of "bounded authenticity" to understand how male sex worker narratives signal different types of relations. Finally, I discuss the implications of my arguments for future empirical and conceptual approaches in the sociology of sex, sexuality, and sex work.

Stories, scripts, and encounters

Summarizing the sexual stories perspective, Plummer (1995, p. 34) argues, "No longer do people simply 'tell' their sexual stories to reveal the 'truth' of their sexual lives; instead, they turn themselves into socially organized biographical objects." The process of telling a sexual story in this sense is a process of constructing the self (Schrock & Reid, 2006), because the process of narration involves embellishing and revising past events and presenting them to an audience. The ways we narrate our sexual lives and the stories we tell about sex and ourselves are shaped and constrained by broader discourses. Plummer also suggests that people do not tend to tell sexual stories until there is a critical mass of people who are willing to articulate particular types of stories. For example, "coming out" stories or "sexual liberation" stories can be told only at certain points in history, based on the convergence of social, cultural, and political factors (also see Barker, 2005).

Summarizing the sexual scripting perspective, Gagnon and Simon suggest that the script acts as a metaphor for reproducing sexual meanings. Gagnon and Simon's *Sexual Conduct* (1974) was one of the first sustained considerations of sexuality to draw from interactionist sociology. The authors anticipated much of queer theory: scripting theory treats identity not as fixed but as something precarious that must be constantly achieved, and it focuses on the context in which sexual interaction takes place.

Sexual scripts, Gagnon and Simon suggest, operate on multiple levels. First, there are cultural scripts and contexts that provide instructions about how to have sex. Grand cultural scripts are interesting to study in comparative perspective (Farrer, Suo, Tsuchiya, & Sun, 2012). Second, there are interpersonal scripts that are patterned ways of interacting based on cultural scripts. An interpersonal scripts is the translation of a cultural script into an interaction between people. Third, there are intrapsychic scripts, which are the inner stories or dialogues of each participant, including their memories, plans, desires, and fantasies. If any attempt at scripting is rejected, an interaction may fail.

Matt Mutchler applied scripting theory in his study of how young men who have sex with men engage with one another sexually (Mutchler, 2000). Recent contributions have continued this work (see Carbonero & Gómez Garrido, 2018; Wiederman, 2015; Dworkin & O'Sullivan, 2007). Yet scripting theory presents challenges. The theory originally opposed biological determinism (the idea that all of our interests and capacities are determined in advance by biology), but it now involves a kind of cultural determinism. Some authors regard sexual scripts as "blueprints" for sexual behavior, detailing with whom one will have sex and how (Markle, 2008). Edward Laumann and John Gagnon (1995, p. 190) claim sexual scripts are cultural "instructions" for sexual conduct, including the "who, what, and when" of sexual conduct. Michael Wiederman (2005, p. 496) writes, "Social scripting theory rests on the assumption that people follow internalized scripts when constructing meaning out of behavior," such that "scripts provide meaning and direction for responding to sexual cues and for behaving sexually." These scholars suggest that people simply take on roles that are waiting for them.

The study of sexual scripts has also moved away from interactionist analysis toward a sexological concern for cataloguing behavior. As a result, meaning-making has been de-emphasized and the importance of bodies downplayed. Similarly, Gagnon and Simon's (1974) notion of scripting accounts only for recognizable types of sexuality based on well-known sex roles. For example, scholars claim that sex workers split the work self from the private self as a coping mechanism and that they feign intimacy, erecting a boundary between work sex and so-called real sex or home sex, by simply following scripts (e.g., Reiss, 1961). Yet key issues, such as the connection between sex and intimacy and the unanticipated or creative aspects of sex, remain unexplored because of this emphasis on surface acting.

Some scholars have tried to use the sexual stories and sexual scripting perspectives together (Sanders, 2008; Mutchler, 2000). I am more interested in how these perspectives diverge. The creator of the sexual stories approach, Ken Plummer (1982), argued that to emphasize scripts exclusively is to ignore open meaning-making tendencies in sexual encounters. Culture does not provide the sexual script in advance, I argue. Rather, this script must be produced by participants who learn what they can do together with their bodies. Scripts provide motifs and stereotypes, but touching, gestures, and interaction affect these scripts in ways that alter accepted meanings. In short, the idea of sexual scripts highlights the regularity of results rather than the more fluid outcomes and meaning shifts produced by the encounters themselves.

Instead of assuming that any script is determined in advance, I want to explore how touching during an encounter can produce sexual meanings. I emphasize the unanticipated elements of sexual encounters, how gestures and touch change scripts. However much scripting and roles may guide our interactions, there nevertheless remains an open tendency in encounters. With the act of touching, scripts can unravel and encounters can move in different directions. What is produced by the encounter is as important as the script going in. We can never fully anticipate the meanings that will be generated during an encounter, and we cannot assume there is a stable script in play throughout the encounter because meanings are modified through interaction (also see Bernstein [2007] on "bounded authenticity").

Scripting and male sex work

To supplement sexual scripting theory by focusing on the open tendency in encounters, I examine the work of male Internet escorts. Scholars and health policy makers have typically viewed sex workers as engaging in risky and deviant sexual behavior owing to an assumed poor upbringing. Such stereotypes are prominent in scholarly literature on female sex workers, but recent research on nonstreet female sex workers shows a wider spectrum of client negotiations (Bernstein, 2007; Murphy & Venkatesh, 2006; Sanders, 2005). Gaffney and Beverley (2001) argue that the diverse nature of male sex work, including on-street work, agency-based escorting, and Internet escorting, demands further research.

The new sociology of male sex work involves focusing more on off-street work than on-street sex work (see Grov, Wolff, Smith, Koken, & Parsons, 2014; Bimbi, 2007; Scott et al., 2005; Kaye, 2003; Browne & Minichiello, 1995) and on comparing samples of off-street and on-street workers. Wilcox and Christmann (2008), for instance, found that off-street workers view sex work like any job, tend to be better educated, and practice safe sex. Smith and Seal (2008), in their study of agency-based male escorts, noted that male escorts do not feel as much pressure or face the same vulnerability as street-based workers. Pruitt (2005) has explored how male Internet escorts differ by socioeconomic status, sexual identity, and gender identity. Castle and Lee (2008) have investigated how male Internet escorts set prices and attempt to communicate with clients. Ashford (2008) argues that the move to Internet-based solicitation has resulted in a "McDonaldization" of sex work services, involving predictable service delivery based on set scripts, although this position has been contested by research showing that male Internet escorts' encounters with clients are multifaceted (see Walby, 2012).

Wilcox and Christmann (2008) note that little is known about the negotiated encounters between male sex workers and their clients. Insights are needed on sexual scripting and sex work and on the so-called feigning of intimacy in male sex work. Debates about feigned intimacy practiced by male sex work began with Reiss (1961, p. 118), who wrote that male hustlers pursue "affective neutrality" and desexualize the sexual services they offer, rationalizing the exchange as purely economic. Feigned intimacy based on set sexual scripts represents an instrumental or purely rational approach to client relations. However, a focus on feigned intimacy reduces sex work to a predictable commercial transaction similar to routine provision of service, one that simply follows a set script. Such an approach glosses over issues such as affection, friendship, spontaneity, and intimacy.

The study

I conducted 30 narrative interviews with male Internet escorts between 2010 and 2012 (see Walby, 2012). Four of the Internet escorts lived in Ottawa, another 4 lived in Montreal, 13 lived in Toronto, 1 lived in Houston but traveled to Toronto and New York City regularly for work, 4 lived in New York City, and 4 lived in London. For inclusion in the sample, escorts had to work in one of these cities. I contacted escorts via the websites on which they advertised. These websites allow users to create a commercial profile that potential clients consult (Tyler, 2014). Profiles are searchable based on city location, escorts' features (e.g., age, ethnicity), services offered, and price (on such websites, see Burghart, 2018; Lee-Gonyea, Castle, & Gonyea, 2009).

For the study I contacted approximately 550 escorts on three different sites (Canadianmale.com, boys2rent.com, men4rentnow.com) and received 56 responses. Of those respondents, 26 potential participants chose not to participate because they deemed the 50-dollar honorarium approved by the ethics board inadequate. I conducted all of the interviews in person except for the interview with the participant in Houston, which took place by phone. Two of the escorts self-identified as Black, 4 as Latino, 1 as Lebanese, and the remaining 23 as white. Twenty-three participants reported being enrolled in or having completed college or university. The participants' actual average age was 34, and ages ranged from 20 to 64. The average length of time they had been working as an escort was six and a half years. One escort had been in the industry for less than a year, and four had been doing the work for a decade or more. Only two of the escorts began working in the sex industry via street-level prostitution. A few had worked for escort agencies but said they left because they felt that independent escorting provided more income and freed them from control by managers. One limit of this study is that I did not interview clients or other people involved in sex work (such as friends or families of sex workers).

Stories, scripts, and spontaneity in male-for-male sex work

The way that male escorts talk about their work suggests there is no set script used across the industry. Instead, sexual scripting occurs in certain contexts with specific clients. Sometimes there is not much of a plan, and the escort and the client "feel it out." Other times there is a very set approach that follows some kind of predetermined fantasy (as in, e.g., rough trade encounters, where there is some element of risk, physicality, or harm involved). Following a set script is what I call the *closed tendency* of the encounter, in which the participants fit their conduct into fixed categories of sexuality and set scripts for sex. As one escort said: "It's not about having the best body in the world. It's not about having the biggest dick. It's about being able to relate to people and to make people feel comfortable and to figure out what people want from you sexually. It stills shocks me to this day, even when people are paying for sex they have difficulty articulating exactly what they want." The closed tendency of the encounter requires finding out what script the client wants to follow and sticking to it. Clients thus play a part in moving the interaction one way or another. Scripts might be about kinds of sex, such as rough trade, safe sex, or a boyfriend experience (Tewksbury & Lapsey, 2017). For example, often escorts do not police their own body or their clients' bodies because clients are so afraid of disease that they ensure safe sex themselves: Most guys I find are really protective of themselves because they think you're a diseased whore. . . . [I]f you're fucking in the doggie style position, they're forward and you're behind they'll spend the whole time being fucked looking back to make sure you haven't slipped the condom off. . . . I had one guy he wouldn't even let me blow him without a condom because he had a fear of getting something. I talked him into it because I didn't want to blow him with a condom on but he wouldn't blow me. He needed condoms. He should have come over in a body bag frankly, with some holes cut out.

This example shows how escorts negotiate the prominent sexual script of "risky sex." They negotiate risk not in an abstract or calculating way but more often through the spontaneous touching that occurs during an encounter or by following the client's lead.

All the male Internet escorts I interviewed reported amicable relations with their clients, although some described encounters with clients as routine and predictable. For example:

I only push somebody's boundaries if they want them pushed. I'm not interested in trying to force or convince somebody to do something they don't want to do. I am interested in helping somebody explore something that they want to explore but have issues of discomfort around but I don't want to force anything on anybody. . . . Every once in a blue moon I'll get a client that wants something that I have sort of either never thought of before or haven't done, or is new to me[,] and most of the time when that happens it's kind of exciting because there is sort of a truism to the fact that men are all the same, like most clients are looking for exactly the same thing. So when you get somebody who wants something different it's kind of . . . finally I get to experiment or do something beyond the standard one-hour package.

This escort describes his encounters with clients as instrumental or purely rational, primarily because clients come looking for the "standard one-hour package," when in fact the escort appreciates more unique sexual situations with clients. But he also indicates there is more to the encounters than following scripts.

Although these examples indicate that some male sex workers feign intimacy with clients and take an instrumental approach to the work, other narratives show that sex workers' relationships with clients are often more complicated and fluid. Sometimes male sex workers experience such encounters as more creative. Escorts also have various understandings of intimacy, and sex is not always part of the picture. One escort discussed the pleasure he experiences with clients:

The guy I've known for 15 years, that's always fun. It's always different, he lets me be creative and he'll give me parameters to work with him and I take it from there. He likes to be surprised, so that's always thrilling for me. We always have a good time together.

Some escorts emphasize they are not faking or acting with clients:

> It comes out of trust and honesty. The thing I hear the most often is, "Wow, you resemble your picture, thanks, you didn't lie. You are what you say you are, you're not pretentious, you're not arrogant. You seem down to earth. You seem to honestly be having a good time with me. You're not just doing it and watching your watch." . . . Because a lot of them have been with enough guys to know when a guy or the person is just faking it. I am what I say I am, how I look, I'm genuinely interested and I have fun.

Not only does this escort describe clients as varied, but he also narrates his encounters as enjoyable for both himself and the client. In this case, the sex of male escorting cannot be fully explained by set scripts.

If all sexual encounters followed a set script, then nothing about sex would ever change and the meanings of sex would never vary. In other words, sexual scripting theory places too much emphasis on the predictability of sexual encounters, thus detaching it from the interactionist tradition in sociology. Scripts unravel, and the types of scripts can change drastically during an encounter, which raises the question: Is any set script truly prominent in an encounter? Some encounters begin as commercial affairs and then drift toward friendship and noncommercial interactions:

> There was a guy who I treated, he actually saw my ad on CanadianMale but he wanted only to have an erotic massage. So I went to a downtown hotel and met him. [W]e had chatted on the phone a couple of times and we had quite a few emails between us because when he had contacted me [he] said, "Oh I'm going to be coming down to Toronto in a couple of months," so he seemed like a really nice guy. And then finally when he arrived we had set a date and I went over and I treated him, really, really nice. And then he took me out to dinner. He really liked me as a person and said, "Oh do you want to go back to my hotel room, we could just hang out and watch TV and everything like that." And it was like kind of cool, so we did that and then I ended up spending the night. There was no, like, no sex involved whatsoever and we even kept in touch for a while after that. So it was great. Sometimes you meet some really nice people.

This escort suggests that this encounter, which started out as a commercial affair, engendered elements of friendship. It was a contingent friendship and it was not long term, but the escort's narrative hints at something more than a simple commercial transaction or a feigning of intimacy. The development of a relationship like this is similar to what Bernstein (2007) describes as "bounded authenticity," which captures the way that instrumentality and intimacy can be blurred in sex work encounters. For Bernstein, authenticity can be experienced, but it is constrained and shaped by the context and structural conditions, as well as the interaction itself.

An encounter can spontaneously fluctuate between a scripted and a nonscripted interaction sequence, or it can shift from script to script. Often intimacy occurs when the lines are blurred. Intimacy is like justice; both terms are almost impossible to define but also the subject of endless analysis. Bernstein (2007) has commented on how intimacy can become part of sex work, and this also serves to explain the fluctuating presence of scripts during encounters. It occurs when there has been a "shift from a relational to a recreational model of sexual intimacy," she argues (p. 141). In this sense, male sex work is not simply based on feigned intimacy; rather, it is influenced by the recreational model of sexual intimacy. Male Internet escorts I interviewed spoke about encounters they found exciting and more in line with their regular life, especially male Internet escorts who delivered sexual services to men: "There are times when I am tired. Bored, no. You have to love it to do it. It has to be fun. . . . I do not have a boyfriend so this is partly my sex life. . . . It is not boring but just [when I am] tired . . . then I enjoy it a little less." The ups and downs of escorts' lives affect their ability to provide fun and recreation for the client. This situation of bounded authenticity points to the possibility of intimacy, although it is contingent on the backgrounds of the worker and client and the circumstances of their encounter.

Some male Internet escorts' narratives reflected this sense of bounded authenticity:

> I have experienced it. Sometimes it is because the connection with the guy is really good, the sex is hot, he is doing things most do not do[,] like giving it to me, giving me a back rub when usually it is being requested from you; he is taking his time and you are actually turned on, and it is like wow. Those are moments that do happen[,] and I guess I form some kind of connection there.

The same respondent then shifted his narrative from noninstrumental relations that can be described as reflecting bounded authenticity to noting other issues that arise in the course of his work:

> As for genuine feelings[:] No. First of all, for long-term clients or repeat clients it is a bad idea. The rules have been defined from the start. You are the client, I am the escort, you pay me, no we are not going to have coffee some time.

During the same interview, again without prompting, the sex worker described how bounded authenticity, intimacy, and instrumental relations are all part of his work and relations with clients:

> If I did that, if my clients became my friends the line would be so blurred. I had that happen with one guy, he was a good customer and we always had a great time. He wanted to be my friend, come over and have pizza and watch a movie. Eventually we broke it off; he had to break it off with me because he was starting to have real feelings and that is not what I wanted to hear and I knew that was somehow happening. . . . I am all business when I do this. I will like you but I will not love. It takes years to form certain bonds.

Another male Internet escort noted that it is difficult to negotiate intimacy, and he talked about using feigned intimacy based on scripts as part of his encounters:

> I think that [in] sex trade work, like other professions like being a psychotherapist or a counselor, there's a creation of what some people would term false intimacy. . . . [I]n those situations, you're both working in the context of where you work in a one-hour block; frequently you're only working [for] an hour and you have to create an intimate environment with your client whether you're a psychotherapist or a counselor or a sex trade worker. . . . [T]hat was one of the things that I was actually a bit surprised about when I first started sex trade work, I thought it would be a lot more hot, horny, dirty, fucking all over the place and I would say not, certainly not all, but some, probably a slight majority of clients, somewhere over 50 percent, that's really what they're craving in terms of sex trade work. . . . [T]hey're looking for someone who will kind of provide an emotional physical intimacy with them. . . . [I]n the situation that I'm in now where I'm only seeing a couple of clients a week . . . one of the kind of regular clients that I have in Montreal is like a hardcore S&M top, so within the context of the work that I'm doing here, I'm finding I'm

craving more emotional intimacy from the other primary partner that I have right now just because I'm not getting it through my sex trade work.

This escort indicates that emotional intimacy emerges from work encounters when he or his clients are specifically seeking intimacy, even though it is not permanent. The escort is not only negotiating intimacy issues during work but also as an element of his personal and sex life. This overlap between private and working sex lives may be one significant difference between what male sex workers who work with male clients find compared with male sex workers who work with female clients. As Davies and Feldman (1999) suggest, male sex workers sometimes share affection and form friendships with regular male clients.

One reason male Internet escorts' encounters with clients can involve intimacy is that the escorts engage in the sexual activities that they would with a regular partner:

> I do everything I would do with a boyfriend almost. . . . I'm very limited sexually, but intimate-wise I have no problem, kissing, because for them you can get a blowjob any-where, like I can get a blowjob in 90 seconds right now, but getting someone to snuggle for an hour is not the same thing, and just to talk, watching TV with somebody naked on the bed, for some people that's a bigger thrill than anything else. And there are busy, suc-cessful, not necessarily lonely, I think mostly busy, people [who] are too busy to get out and meet people, and for me it actually, it works for me too because I don't have a boyfriend.

As in their personal sexual life, some of the escorts' sexual activities are scripted, while other activities are less so or not scripted much at all. What the workers describe as intimacy may be scripted or not. But the mention of intimacy shows that scripts can shift during interactions, and scripts can also be discarded in the fluidity and spontaneity of the encounter.

This integration of work and private or personal sex lives inverts how the sex of sex work is often theorized in sex work research, which has relied on the notion of feigned intimacy to explain how sex workers can participate in sex work. However, the way that sex workers narrate their encounters depends on the client and on the escort's physical and sexual preferences. Scripts can be sought out and worked up depending on the desires of the client on any given evening. One male Internet escort commented on the diverse meanings of intimacy in commercial encounters and also the barriers to intimacy and how his work life compares with his relationships outside sex work:

> It is a different kind of intimacy than you have with a partner or someone [when] you are not getting paid for it. With a one-night stand you can have a kind of intimacy where afterwards you are completely spent, there is nothing else you need to do, a nice moment, there is that kind of intimacy, but it has got all these barriers that need to be vocalized, but you do not need to be worried. There are a few who want boyfriends, and maybe this is being callous but if you are getting paid for it you do not have to worry about that . . . you know you can be very full on, and that is fine, because you do not have to hold back, because it has a natural end.

The respondent found that sex work has barriers to ongoing intimacy, which again suggests bounded authenticity (Bernstein, 2007). Another male Internet escort suggested that there is the possibility for intimacy at work, but that it should be limited and not spill over into personal life:

> I do not think the two things are incompatible. The fact that you are playing a role, the line is sometimes blurred—a couple clients I am close with, they know my real name and not

just my escort name—you get to know them on a personal level as well, and they find it sometimes odd, that dividing line, when I am just being me and when I am just being the escort. But even then there is always a little bit of the escort in me. If they get too close, I will say do not make the mistake of falling in love with an escort, I do not like to exploit the clients. I think it is a very honest profession, there is a contract, a deal made, they pay for the time I give them, I do not exploit them beyond that, I do not try to get extra money out of it, I feel happier that the job is done well and there is no other contract outside of it.

This escort called sex work an "honest profession" and pointed to the balance between intimate and instrumental relations that male sex workers strike. Yet sometimes the interaction spontaneously spirals out of control in ways the two parties do not anticipate, moving from one script to another or going off script completely.

Discussion and conclusion

Male sex work is neither purely instrumental nor purely intimate. It varies with the clientele, the scripting involved, and how those scripts are resisted or rejected. To the extent an interaction is instrumental, cultural scripts reign. To the extent that some unanticipated, spontaneous, and creative touching and negotiations occur, encounters also have an open tendency. Otherwise there would be no new meaning to be made from the way we touch one another.

As I have shown with these interviews, some male Internet escorts work in a context that supports intimacy and friendship with male clients as well as unanticipated sexual relations (also see Pitcher, 2019). There is an overlap between personal and work sex life for some of male Internet escorts that emerges primarily with repeat clients. Male Internet escorts also report using the Internet to screen and select clients in a way that is not feasible for other sex workers, such as on-street sex workers (also see Minichiello, Scott, & Callander, 2013). The ability to screen clients is an important factor that creates a context for what I call touching encounters.

Conceptually, it is important not to conflate the sexual-stories and sexual-scripting perspectives. There are differences, and both have limits. The way that people touch pulls the encounter away from a set sexual script. Meanings of sex change according to cultural trends, but they also shift in the corporeal present. We must supplement sexual scripting theory to emphasize the unanticipated aspects of encounters, and the examples of male commercial sexual encounters in these interviews help to explore this idea. By focusing on touching encounters, I have tried to show how sex relations are based on scripts of sex and sexuality while also acknowledging that pervasive cultural scripts can be broken down and recomposed (see Bernstein [2007] on "bounded authenticity"). The two tendencies of the encounter, the closed tendency toward following sexual scripts and the open tendency toward creativity, spontaneity, and unanticipated outcomes, each lead to sequences of interactions, produced by and modified through the ongoing conversation of gestures and confessions that make up sexual interactions and the stories we share about them.

References

Ashford, C. (2008). Sex work in cyberspace: Who pays the price? *Information and Communications Technology Law*, *17*(1), 37–49.

Barker, M. (2005). This is my partner, and this is my . . . partner's partner: Constructing a polyamorous identity in a monogamous world. *Journal of Constructivist Psychology*, *18*, 75–88.

Bernstein, E. (2007). *Temporarily yours: Intimacy, authenticity, and the commerce of sex*. Chicago: University of Chicago Press.

Bimbi, D. (2007). Male prostitution: Pathology, paradigms, and progress in research. In T. Morrison & B. Whitehead (Eds.), *Male sex work: A pleasure doing business* (pp. 7–35). New York: Haworth Press.

Browne, J., & Minichiello, V. (1995). The social meanings behind male sex work: Implications for sexual interaction. *British Journal of Sociology, 46*(4), 598–622.

Burghart, K. O. (2018). What's on sale? A discourse analysis of four distinctive online escort advertisement websites. *Sexuality & Culture, 22*(1), 316–335.

Carbonero, M. A., & Gómez Garrido, M. (2018). Being like your girlfriend: Authenticity and the shifting borders of intimacy in sex work. *Sociology, 52*(2), 384–399.

Castle, T., & Lee, J. (2008). Ordering sex in cyberspace: A content analysis of escort websites. *International Journal of Cultural Studies, 11*(1), 107–121.

Davies, P., & Feldman, R. (1999). Selling sex in Cardiff and London. In P. Aggleton (Ed.), *Men who sell sex: International perspectives on male prostitution and HIV/AIDS* (pp. 1–22). Philadelphia: Temple University Press.

Dworkin, S. L., & O'Sullivan, L. F. (2007). It's less work for us and it shows us she has good taste: Masculinity, sexual initiation, and contemporary sexual scripts. In M. Kimmel (Ed.), *The sexual self: The construction of sexual scripts* (pp. 105–121). Nashville, TN: Vanderbilt University Press.

Farrer, J., Suo, G., Tsuchiya, H., & Sun, Z. (2012). Re-embedding sexual meanings: A qualitative comparison of the premarital sexual scripts of Chinese and Japanese young adults. *Sexuality & Culture, 16*(3), 263–286.

Gaffney, J., & Beverley, K. (2001). Contextualizing the construction and social organization of the male sex industry in London at the beginning of the twenty-first century. *Feminist Review, 67*(1), 133–141.

Gagnon, J., & Simon, W. (1974). *Sexual conduct: The social sources of human sexuality*. Chicago: Aldine.

Grov, C., Wolff, M., Smith, M., Koken, J., & Parsons, J. (2014). Male clients of male escorts: Satisfaction, sexual behavior, and demographic characteristics. *Journal of Sex Research, 51*(7), 827–837.

Jackson, S., & Scott, S. (2001). Embodying orgasm. *Women & Therapy, 24*(1–2), 99–110.

Jackson, S., & Scott, S. (2010). Rehabilitating interactionism for a feminist sociology of sexuality. *Sociology, 44*(5), 811–826. https://doi.org/10.1177/0038038510375732

Kaye, K. (2003). Male prostitution in the twentieth century: Pseudohomosexuals, hoodlum homosexuals, and exploited teens. *Journal of Homosexuality, 46*(1/2), 1–77.

Laumann, E., & Gagnon, J. (1995). A sociological perspective on sexual action. In G. Parker & J. Gagnon (Eds.), *Conceiving sexuality: Approaches to sex research in a postmodern world* (pp. 183–213). New York: Routledge.

Lee-Gonyea, J. A., Castle, T., & Gonyea, N. E. (2009). Laid to order: Male escorts advertising on the internet. *Deviant Behavior, 30*(4), 321–348. doi:10.1080/01639620802168858

Markle, G. (2008). "Can women have sex like a man?" Sexual scripts and *Sex in the city. Sexuality & Culture, 12*(1), 45–57.

Minichiello, V., Scott, J., & Callander, D. (2013). New pleasures and old dangers: Reinventing male sex work. *Journal of Sex Research, 50*(3–4), 263–275.

Murphy, A., & Venkatesh, S. (2006). Vice careers: The changing contours of sex work in New York City. *Qualitative Sociology, 29*(2), 129–154.

Mutchler, M. (2000). Young gay men's stories in the States: Scripts, sex, and safety in the time of AIDS. *Sexualities, 3*(1), 31–54.

Pitcher, J. (2019). Intimate labour and the state: Contrasting policy discourses with the working experiences of indoor sex workers. *Sexuality Research and Social Policy, 16*(2), 138–150.

Plummer, K. (1975). *Sexual stigma: An interactionist account*. London: Routledge.

Plummer, K. (1982). Symbolic interactionism and sexual conduct: An emergent perspective. In M. Brake (Ed.), *Human sexual relations*. New York: Pantheon Books.

Plummer, K. (1995). *Telling sexual stories: Power, change, and social worlds*. London: Routledge.

Pruitt, M. (2005). On-line boys: Male-for-male Internet escorts. *Sociological Focus, 38*(3), 189–203.

Reiss, I. L. (1961). Standards of sexual behavior. In A. Ellis & A. Abarbanel (Eds.), *Encyclopedia of sexual behavior* (pp. 996–1004). New York: Hawthorn Books.

Sanders, T. (2005). It's just acting: Sex workers' strategies for capitalizing on sexuality. *Gender, Work, and Organization, 12*(4), 319–342.

Sanders, T. (2008). Male sexual scripts: Intimacy, sexuality, and pleasure in the purchase of commercial sex. *Sociology, 42*(3), 400–417.

Schrock, D., & Reid, L. (2006). Transsexuals' sexual stories. *Archives of Sexual Behavior, 35*(1), 75–86.

Scott, J., Minichiello, V., Mariño, R., Harvey, G., Jamieson, M., & Browne, J. (2005). Understanding the new context of the male sex work industry. *Journal of Interpersonal Violence, 20*(3), 320–342.

Smith, M., & Seal, D. (2008). Motivational influences on the safer sex behavior of agency-based male sex workers. *Archives of Sexual Behavior, 37*(5), 845–853.

Tewksbury, R., & Lapsey, D. (2017). Male escorts' construction of the boyfriend experience: How escorts please their clients. *International Journal of Sexual Health, 29*(4), 292–302.

Tyler, A. (2014). Advertising male sexual services. In V. Minichiello & J. Scott (Eds.), *Male sex work and society* (pp. 82–105). New York: Harrington Park Press.

Walby, K. (2012). *Touching encounters: Sex, work, and male-for-male Internet escorting.* Chicago: University of Chicago Press.

Wiederman, M. (2005). The gendered nature of sexual scripts. *The Family Journal, 13*(4), 496–502.

Wiederman, M. (2015). Sexual script theory: Past, present, and future. In J. DeLamater (Ed.), *Handbook of the sociology of sexualities* (pp. 7–22). London: Springer.

Wilcox, A., & Christmann, K. (2008). Getting paid for sex is my kick: A qualitative study of male sex workers. In G. Letherby, K. Williams, P. Birch, & M. Cain (Eds.), *Sex as crime?* (pp. 118–136). Cullompton, UK: Willan.

17

Male independent sex workers in the digital age

Online male escorting in the United Kingdom

*Teela Sanders, Jane Pitcher, Jane Scoular, Rosie Campbell,
and Stewart Cunningham*

We can look at the development of Internet-enabled sex work through the lens of technological and structural transformations in the global economy. Free markets and the value placed on individual enterprise in many Western states, beginning in the late twentieth century, have been accompanied by a growth in consumer culture. The new consumer culture has changed what it means to be a worker, blurring work-based and consumption-based identities (du Gay, 1996). At the same time, technology and particularly digital communication have profoundly affected how we organize our lives, conduct our relationships, and take part in commercial and retail transactions (van Dijk, 2012). These technological developments have had a significant impact on social organization and the spatial distribution of human activities. Indeed, Castells (2000) has coined the term *network society* to describe the new social structures. These changes have also affected the organization of sex work, with evidence suggesting that Internet-enabled sex work is a growing and developing sector of the economy (Cunningham & Kendall, 2011; Sanders, Scoular, Campbell, Pitcher, & Cunningham, 2018).

Although there are fewer studies of male and transgender sex workers than female sex workers, several recent studies explore the experiences of male Internet-based sex workers (e.g., Koken, Bimbi, Parsons, & Halkitis, 2004; Uy, Parsons, Bimbi, Koken, & Halkitis, 2004; Bimbi & Parsons, 2005; Lee-Gonyea, Castle, & Gonyea, 2009; McLean, 2012; Walby, 2012; MacPhail, Scott, & Minichiello, 2015; Minichiello, Scott, & Callander, 2013). Male sex workers advertising via the Internet often identify as gay or bisexual (Koken et al., 2004; Bimbi, 2007). Men advertising sexual services for men tend to use specialist sites for commercial sexual services, as well as social networking sites such as Gaydar. Ryan (2019) explores the lives of Brazilian and Venezuelan migrant men selling sex in Dublin, noting the strong role of social media sites and specialist apps such as Grindr that allow individuals to build instant and transient sex worker profiles and to develop their own brand and digital identity in the male sex work scene. Other recent studies demonstrate that online technology is pivotal to male sex workers' relationships with clients; it also allows them to develop their own professional business and "occupational strategies" (Kuhar & Pajnik,

2019). However, as Tyler (2015) notes, these sites may impose a specific structure on individual advertisements that may restrict their content.

It has been suggested that the Internet may lead to positive changes in working practices. For example, Parsons and colleagues (2004) noted that independent male sex workers advertising on the Internet commented on the difference in the type of customers they attracted, their ability to engage in safer sex practices, and the fact that they had fewer concerns about law enforcement compared with workers in other sectors. However, the legal situation in the United Kingdom becomes more complex when male sex workers wish to work in collectives (Pitcher & Wijers, 2014).

The Beyond the Gaze (BtG) study is the largest study of the online UK sex work market to date, and it has produced some major data sets from which new and important knowledge has emerged. The study's methodological tools consisted of a survey of sex workers ($n = 641$); a survey of customers ($n = 1,323$); interviews with sex workers ($n = 62$); and 54 interviews with other individuals, including police officers (across 16 forces in England, Wales, Scotland, and Northern Ireland), website platform owners, website moderators, and IT specialists. The recruitment drive for participants was initiated through the goodwill and "buy-in" from credible online websites that specialized in male sex work. We were fortunate to have research support that allowed us to run both constant online banners and '"pop ups" during the three months the survey was open. In addition, we received regular re-tweets and re-posts on social media platforms, important online spaces where sex workers gather.

We also conducted a qualitative mapping of online sex work advertising spaces and a longitudinal survey project with sex work support services to assess the types of online services they provide. Additional details about the project can be found in the book *Internet Sex Work: Beyond the Gaze* (Sanders, Scoular et al., 2018); in an open-access journal article about the spaces of online sex work, "Behind the Screen: Commercial Sex, Digital Spaces, and Working Online" (Cunningham et al., 2018); and in two articles specifically addressing crime and safety (Campbell, Sanders, Scoular, Pitcher, & Cunningham, 2018) and mapping (Sanders, O'Neill, & Pitcher, 2018).

In this chapter, we examine information we gathered about male sex workers who operate online. In the BtG survey, male sex workers formed 19.4 percent ($n = 124$) of the total respondents. For the qualitative element of the study, we conducted sixteen interviews with male sex workers.

Profile of Beyond the Gaze male sex worker respondents

Among the 124 men who completed the survey, the dominant form of sex work was independent escorting. However, many worked in more than one sex market, an interesting finding that reflects the fluidity and cross-fertilization in the industry (Table 17.1).

While 39.5 percent of the respondents ($n = 49$) worked in only one sector, 24.2 percent ($n = 30$) worked in two sectors, 14.5 percent ($n = 18$) worked in three sectors, and the remainder worked in more than three sectors. Some interview participants had moved between sectors—transitioning, for example, from street-based work to escorting—whereas others told us they went directly into Internet sex work. As the interviews confirmed, many of the men held other mainstream jobs in addition to their sex work job. Eight participants noted they worked concurrently in other jobs, including counseling, accountancy, information technology, office work, care work, modeling, and employment at a sex worker rights organization.

Male survey respondents were slightly younger overall than their female counterparts. For example, while 30.1 percent ($n = 37$) of men were ages 18 to 24, only 16.8 percent ($n = 79$) of

Table 17.1 Cross-Market Work Among 124 Male Sex Workers

Type of sex work	No. participating (%)
Independent escorting	110 (88.7%)
Sexual massage	41 (33.1%)
BDSM	31 (25.0%)
Webcam sex	30 (24.2%)
Phone sex	20 (16.1%)
Adult films	19 (15.3%)

women were in that age category at the time of the survey. This age difference corresponds with other studies that suggest that many men may engage in the exchange of sexual services for money while comparatively young (see Sanders, O'Neill et al., 2018). Nonetheless, more than a third of the men (37.4 percent, $n = 46$) and women (36.9 percent, $n = 173$) were ages 25 to 34. While 21.1 percent ($n = 26$) of men were 35 to 44, compared with 29 percent ($n = 136$) of women, 11.4 percent of men ($n = 14$) were 45 and older, compared with 17.1 percent ($n = 80$) of women.

Most survey respondents overall had entered the sex industry between the ages of 18 and 24 or in their 30s. Although proportionately more men than women had started doing sex work when under 18 (14.9 percent, $n = 17$, compared with 3.4 percent, $n = 15$), and slightly more women than men were 35 to 44 when they first engaged in sex work (14 percent, $n = 61$, compared with 8.8 percent, $n = 10$), there were otherwise no substantial gender differences relating to age of entry. The qualitative interviews revealed that the circumstances of men entering into sex work were not dissimilar from what we know concerning women's entry into the business. For example, participants mentioned being introduced to the industry by friends and being presented with the opportunity to sell sexual services through other forms of work, such as massage or modeling. Men's reasons for doing sex work were also similar to those presented by women, including funding their education, general financial reasons, enjoyment of the work, and the flexibility and relative freedom of independent sex work, as also noted in Pitcher (2019). When asked about their own sexuality, there were some interesting gender differences among respondents. The majority of men described themselves as gay (63.7 percent, $n = 79$), but the number of female sex workers who did so was very small. Yet the rate of bisexuality was much higher in the female sample compared with the male sample.

Minichiello et al. (2013) also note that large proportions of male escorts identify as gay or bisexual. Bimbi (2007) suggests that stigma directed at sex workers may be less pronounced in gay communities, partly because escorting is now often seen as a profession and Internet advertising takes place in online gay spaces as well as on websites specifically for escorts. However, as Koken and colleagues (2004) found, male sex workers still encounter sex work–related stigma in some circumstances.

Customers of male sex workers are predominantly male (Minichiello et al., 2013). While nearly all male interviewees in the BtG study provided services to male clients, some also worked with women and couples. As Redman's (2017) work on male and female escorts notes, the demand from female customers for male sex workers is small but evident, and there is also a market for couples who are willing to pay for sexual services from escorts.

As with the female respondents, the large majority of the male participants were white (82.3 percent, $n = 102$). As a proxy measure for migrant workers, 21.2 percent ($n = 24$) of the men were of non-British nationality, compared with 13.8 percent ($n = 62$) of women. A London-based study of migrant workers in the sex industry (Mai, 2009) found that female interviewees tended to work across different indoor settings, whereas male and transgender participants were more likely to work independently than to participate in other forms of sex work. However, there has been no comprehensive research on the distribution of migrant sex workers in the United Kingdom, and thus it is not possible to confirm whether the proportions noted here are representative of the wider online migrant sex worker population.

Nearly a third of male respondents (31.9 percent, $n = 38$) lived in Greater London: a higher proportion than the survey average (20 percent; 126 of all respondents lived in Greater London). This finding might partly relate to the relatively younger ages of men compared with women responding to this question. Overall, survey respondents age 44 and younger were more likely to live in London than those in the older age groups. This finding corresponds with the younger age structure of cities such as London compared with rural areas (ONS, 2018).

The majority of male respondents, 58.1 percent ($n = 72$), classed themselves as single, compared with 45.1 percent ($n = 210$) of women. These data may relate partly to the younger age of male sex workers in the survey. Only 11.4 percent ($n = 14$) of male respondents had financial dependents, compared with 33.8 percent ($n = 158$) of women. Census data for the United Kingdom show that women are more likely to be unpaid caregivers than men, particularly in the younger age groups (Dahlberg, Demack, & Bambra, 2007).

The highest level of education among men was not significantly different from the survey average. Men were slightly more likely to be educated to the degree level or higher (41.8 percent, $n = 51$) compared with respondents overall (37.6 percent, $n = 239$). Other studies of male and female Internet sex workers (e.g., Bernstein, 2007; Walby, 2012) have also found that they are relatively highly educated compared with sex workers in other sectors, or they are studying at the same time that they are doing online sex work.

Marketing services online

As the literature shows (e.g., Tyler, 2015; Sanders, Scoular et al., 2018), men advertising sexual services for other men tend to use different online platforms from their female counterparts, including specialist escort sites and men-to-men dating sites. The main online advertising site used, by 95 male survey participants in the BtG study (76.6 percent of the sample), was a major UK-based platform specifically for male escorts and erotic masseurs. Survey respondents also used a number of other smaller UK and international sites aimed at male sex workers who provide escorting, webcam, and phone chat services. Additionally, survey respondents also advertised on dating sites aimed more generally at male-to-male sexual encounters; one such site was used by 27.4 percent ($n = 34$) of respondents. Other sources included websites advertising services offered by female as well as male sexual providers. For example, one-third of the male respondents ($n = 41$) advertised via the major international platform used by the majority of the female survey respondents. More than one-fifth of respondents also used general commercial listings.

Respondents used social media as well, for advertising sexual services and networking with other sex workers. For example, 14.5 percent of male respondents ($n = 18$) used Twitter. While some interview participants did not want to mix their personal and business online activities because of concerns about anonymity, others said they had integrated their profiles on different marketing sites with their social media presence. Spartan (25, works in a number of sectors, including escorting, webcam sex, and massage), told us:

> And I've not been on Twitter for too long but I've been pushing quite hard recently and I've been finding quite a bit of success, certainly gaining followers. And I've integrated

that into my website now as well. I've also integrated it through my AdultWork profile. So whenever I interact with AdultWork, whenever I integrate with the webcam software that AdultWork owns, that now pops up new Twitter messages. And that also then pings straight onto my website and goes onto all the different pages as well.

Escorts use social media and blogging to provide further information about their lifestyle and preferences and to provide feedback on interactions with clients. These marketing practices may extend their range of clients and encourage repeat visits:

> It's about the real me and what I get up to. So it's . . . just full of normal stuff. It's like if I pop to the supermarket, I might take a picture at the supermarket. Or if I'm cooking something, I'll mention what I'm having for lunch. And I'll mention things that's gone on. I discuss clients. Not in, not in a personal like identifying way, but I'll say, "Had a wonderful gentleman in a couple of hours ago." I don't say like, "He's just gone two minutes ago, so look out for him." . . . There's a Twitter feed built into my website, so people can see my tweets through the website as well without going onto Twitter, and it bigs clients up. . . . Because they do read it and they'll read something about themselves, that I enjoyed the appointment and enjoyed seeing them.
>
> *(Ben, 43, independent escort/masseur)*

Attwood (2013, p. 205) has observed that men as well as women may be the objects of "erotic gazing" in cyberspace. Moreover, some online sex workers may present different aspects of their personality as an integral part of their working identity.

Women survey respondents were more likely to have their own website than men (31.7 percent, *n* = 147, compared with 16.9 percent, *n* = 21). Male interview participants who had developed their sex work business and expressed a wish to stand out from the competition or to establish a particular brand appeared more likely to have developed their own website. Having their own site enabled them to provide more information than they could in online directories, to provide a more professional profile, and to facilitate marketing to particular types of clients.

> Well, the key for me is my personal website. That accounts for about 70 percent of my business, although I have probably over thirty profiles on various sites. The fact that I can put a link to the site, so they might initially find my details on another site[,] but invariably the feedback is, it's the web, my website is the clincher. And quite a few find it via Google, via search engines.
>
> *(Michael, 57, independent escort)*

> I decided that the website was to appeal to chief executives, senior manager types, and academics, because, if you read my website, it's all grammatically correct, no spelling mistake in it anywhere, and it's geared towards an executive clientele. Whereas opposed to the Backpage and Craigslist adverts, which are just, they're just like Mr. White Van Man, if you understand. I use different . . . mediums to attract different types of clients. White Van Man isn't gonna look at my website; he's gonna look on a contact site. But an executive who's coming up to [this city] from London for three or four days, he will look at my website and plan that he wants to see me for four hours. And the website is geared towards the four hours, executive overnight appointments. I travel all over the world. I was in Germany six times last year. So, you know, it's geared to those types of clients.
>
> *(Ben, 43, independent escort/masseur)*

As noted in Cunningham et al. (2018), customer reviews on advertising platforms or other forums can be useful for marketing, but they may also run the risk of breaching sex workers' anonymity or become a source of harassment, as discussed later in this chapter.

Work organization and time spent in sex work

More men had been doing their current sex work job for less than a year, compared with women (26.6 percent of men, $n = 33$, compared with 12.4 percent of women, $n = 58$). While there was not a substantial difference between the proportions of men and women who had been in their sex work job for one to ten years (65.3 percent, $n = 81$, and 71.1 percent, $n = 333$, respectively), women were more likely than men to have been in their current sex work job for more than ten years (16.6 percent, $n = 78$, compared with 8.1 percent, $n = 10$). Proportionately more women than men had been providing sexual services online for three years or more (59.8 percent, $n = 279$, compared with 48.4 percent, $n = 60$). These numbers largely correspond with the length of time they had been in sex work.

A higher proportion of men than women worked ten or fewer hours per week providing services to clients (around two-thirds of men, $n = 80$, compared with just over half of women, $n = 233$). Sanders, Scoular and colleagues (2018) note that the differential between the earnings of male and female sex workers may relate partly to the number of hours worked, with men earning slightly less (and working slightly less) on average than women. In addition to contact time with clients, sex work also involves largely unpaid time spent maintaining a sex work business. Nearly two-thirds of men also spent up to ten hours per week on other tasks associated with their sex work. As with women's earnings in the sex industry, men's earnings could fluctuate significantly, and thus many interviewees held other jobs alongside their sex work. For example, Marcus (42), an independent sex worker/masseur who also worked in various other mainstream jobs, observed that his weekly sex work earnings could be "anything from zero to £1,000. . . . I can go three months and see four clients. It's awful. That's partly why I do other stuff as well."

Women were more likely than men to use the professional services of third parties. For example, 35.2 percent ($n = 146$) of women said they used an accountant at least sometimes, but only 13.6 percent of men ($n = 15$) used a similar service. Although 38.2 percent ($n = 153$) of women used a photographer, only 29 percent ($n = 31$) of men used that service at least sometimes. Interview participants were the most likely to refer to IT professionals when discussing their use of third parties to help them with their business.

Most survey respondents (72.1 percent) did not share premises with other sex workers. Of those who did, just over 28 percent ($n = 35$) of men and just under 27 percent ($n = 125$) of women shared premises with others at least some of the time. Some participants were aware that the current UK law presented difficulties for sex workers based in the same premises. This legislation may particularly affect women, whose online activities are more likely to be monitored by authorities (see Sanders, Scoular et al., 2018), but it also has implications for men working together. Spartan (25, working across various sectors) commented on the law and how two people operating as sex workers from the same premises may be interpreted in law as a brothel: "I think that's a really, really stupid law. It's—it's blatantly dangerous and serves no purpose to the benefit of an adult worker."

Working practices: centrality of the Internet

Both male and female respondents were very positive about the advantages the Internet gave them in their work. For example, 94.3 percent of men ($n = 116$) and 97.4 percent of women

($n = 457$) tended to agree or strongly agree that having access to the Internet helped them to organize their work:

> The great thing about the Internet is you can put an ad on in five minutes. If you put a print ad on, it can, you can wait a month for it to get published. So with the Internet it's instant. And when I very first started doing the sexual massage after my break, I didn't have a website because I'd let that go, didn't have time to put a print press ad, so I, all I did was put one advert on Gumtree, which was very cryptic because you're not allowed to put sexual adverts on there. I, I remember very clearly I put it on on the Monday and by the Thursday I'd seen ten clients.
>
> *(Marcus, 42, independent sex worker/masseur)*

Although in slightly lower proportions than women, a high percentage of men tended to agree or strongly agree that the Internet had improved the quality of their working life (74.4 percent, $n = 90$ men, and 82.3 percent, $n = 376$ women). This response partly related to length of time in the sex industry: men who had worked in the industry for more than three years were more likely to agree with the statement than those who had been sex workers for a shorter time, suggesting that the Internet was all the latter group had known.

The centrality of the Internet to sex work was noted by many survey respondents: 64.2 percent of men ($n = 79$) and 66.5 percent of women ($n = 307$) tended to agree or strongly agree that they would not do sex work without the Internet. Some independent interview participants had started in sex work before the Internet became a central part of their working practice. When participants had not been working in the sex industry as long, however, the Internet was all they had known. Dylan (18, independent sex worker/escort) noted that his working life "wouldn't exist if it wasn't for the Internet." Those with more experience noted that if the Internet were not available, "Sex workers [would] always find a way" (Ruzgar, 27, independent escort). Working without the Internet is not an option for webcam workers, however, and others, such as Rab (38, independent escort/masseur), who observed that working practices would have to change significantly without access to the Internet.

Respondents also saw the Internet as important for safety. For example, 86.2 percent of men ($n = 106$) and 87.3 percent of women ($n = 400$) tended to agree or strongly agreed that the Internet enabled them to monitor enquiries. Interview participants noted that access to the Internet gave them the ability to get more information about clients by undertaking background checks, including by networking with other sex workers and receiving safety alerts from websites such as National Ugly Mugs, which enabled them to learn about potential risks or problem clients. Although still a high proportion of respondents, a slightly lower percentage of men compared with women felt that the Internet enabled them to find out about their rights (79.5 percent, $n = 97$, compared with 84 percent, $n = 389$).

There were also concerns about using the Internet, however. For example, 54.1 percent of men ($n = 66$) and 61.6 percent of women ($n = 284$) tended to agree or strongly agree that they were worried that friends or family might find out about their work through the Internet. Interview participants also commented on the disadvantages as well as advantages of Internet-based sex work. For example, the easy access to advertising sources that has been described was also seen as increasing competition, as long-standing sex workers found themselves advertising alongside less experienced newcomers to the profession. As Boyd (32, works in various sectors, including escorting, webcamming, BDSM, and massage) noted about the Internet and working online,

I think it's made it easier and made things quicker and more efficient. But in other ways I think it's probably made it more competitive. So there's a lot of people coming in who are unprofessional and unskilled, so you have to weed through them to get to the guys that are actually doing the job properly.

The increased competition may also result in a reduction in rates and create the need to engage in marketing or to focus on niche markets: "There's a lot of pressure on me to market myself and to stand out against all the competition" (Marcus, 42, independent sex worker/masseur).

Many respondents also tended to agree or agreed that the Internet had increased the amount of time they spent managing their work (62.3 percent of men, $n = 76$, and 67.7 percent of women, $n = 312$). The Internet has also potentially increased the amount of time sex workers waste online. As Michael (57, independent escort) noted:

The problem with all this technology, it's a Pandora's box for timewasters. You know it's just that, but that's, you know, it goes with the territory. You have to be very, very thick skinned in this business, very thick skinned. But this can also relate to how you market your services, which clients you aim at and which sites you use.

Despite the disadvantages, very high proportions of men and women said they were satisfied with working conditions in their sex work job: 84.6 percent of men ($n = 104$) were satisfied or very satisfied with their working conditions, as were 83 percent of women ($n = 386$). Similarly, nearly all men and women felt they were good at their job some, most, or all of the time.

In relation to factors contributing to or detracting from job satisfaction, men were more likely to agree that they were always enthusiastic about their job (31.7 percent of men, $n = 39$, compared with 16.6 percent of women, $n = 77$). However, a higher proportion of women than men agreed that they were enthusiastic some or most of the time (75.3 percent of women, $n = 350$, compared with 62.6 percent of men, $n = 77$). Men were also more likely than women to feel their job was socially useful: 84.3 percent of men ($n = 102$) and 70.9 percent of women ($n = 327$) felt their job was socially useful some, most, or all of the time. And men were less likely than women to feel isolated in their work: 47.5 percent of men ($n = 58$), compared with 59.5 percent of women ($n = 276$), felt isolated at least sometimes. However, men were less likely than women to agree that they were well paid for their work (76.4 percent, $n = 94$, compared with 85.6 percent, $n = 398$). This difference may partly relate to the comparatively lower earnings for male sex workers discussed earlier.

Relatively low proportions of men and women felt they got emotionally involved in their work: 49.2 percent of men ($n = 60$) and 44.6 percent of women ($n = 206$) felt they were emotionally involved at least some of the time. Men were less likely than women to feel exhausted at the end of the working day: 59 percent of men ($n = 72$) felt exhausted at least sometimes, compared with 70.3 percent of women ($n = 326$). Similarly, a lower proportion of men than women experienced stress in their work: 55.7 percent of men ($n = 68$) and 64.8 percent of women ($n = 300$) said they experienced stress at least sometimes. Men were somewhat less likely than women to worry about their neighbors finding out about their work; 45.5 percent ($n = 56$), compared with 53.9 percent of women ($n = 248$), tended to agree or strongly agree with that statement. Nonetheless, the fact that more than two-fifths of men were concerned about their neighbors also suggests, as noted earlier, that male sex workers may be susceptible to social stigma in certain circumstances.

Although proportions were high for both gender groups, men were slightly less likely than women to agree that they made decisions on how to organize their work; 93.5 percent of men ($n = 115$), compared with 96.8 percent of women ($n = 450$), tended to agree or strongly agree with that statement. There were also slightly lower proportions of men tending to agree or strongly agreeing that they could decide themselves when to work (89.4 percent, $n = 110$, compared with 96.3 percent, $n = 448$) and where to work (85.2 percent, $n = 104$, compared with 91.3 percent, $n = 421$). Slightly lower proportions of men than women tended to agree or strongly agree that they could refuse clients according to their own judgment (91.9 percent, $n = 113$, compared with 97.4 percent, $n = 453$). Minichiello et al. (2013) have also noted that Internet-based independent sex work gives workers greater control over their working conditions than many other forms of sex work, although, as we will discuss, there are also safety concerns that accompany online work.

Crimes and privacy online

Sex workers of all genders in the study said they had been the victims of certain crimes in the past five years, and some crimes were more common than others. Nonpayment or attempting to underpay was a key issue for more than half of the men and women surveyed (54 percent of men, $n = 67$, and 52.9 percent of women, $n = 248$). Their experiences had led some interview participants to charge clients at the start of a transaction. One sex worker observed that when he used to ask for payment at the end of a transaction, he sometimes felt coerced into meeting certain demands in order to be paid for his services:

> There was a time when I used to charge—I used to ask for the money—when the service was—at the end of the massage. And there were certainly people who turned up who came across as the nicest, most respectful, loveliest person you could ever imagine. And you gave them the massage and then do all the hard work and give them a really great massage, and then it—come to the climax of the session, they became very pushy and demanding and powerful in their requests. And I suppose I felt, unless I go along with what they want now, then I'm not going to be paid for the service that I just provided. . . . Now is that a crime? Was I raped? I don't know. I certainly felt abused and manipulated.
>
> *(Liam, 38, masseur)*

Online harassment occurred more frequently than in-person harassment or stalking, a finding that appears to be consistent with national trends (see later discussion). Slightly higher proportions of women than men said they had experienced threatening or harassing text messages, calls, or emails in the past five years (58.4 percent of women, $n = 274$, and 46.8 percent of men, $n = 58$). Receiving persistent or repeated unwanted contacts through email or social media was an issue for many women and men; it was reported by 66.1 percent ($n = 310$) of women and 55.6 percent ($n = 69$) of men.

Although there is limited research regarding online crimes overall, it appears that sex workers may be somewhat more likely than the general population to experience online abuse. For example, an online survey commissioned by Amnesty International (2017) of 504 women in the United Kingdom, ages 18 to 55, found that 21 percent had experienced abuse or harassment online. A national survey in the United States (Duggan, 2017) found that 41 percent of U.S. adults had encountered some form of online harassment. While men were somewhat more likely to have experienced online harassment, women were more likely than men to report being sexually harassed. A UK-based study of 353 participants accessed through the website of Network for Surviving Stalking (Maple, Short, & Brown, 2011) suggests that cyberstalking is becoming more common than face-to-face harassment. Nearly 30 percent of the 324 survey respondents in this study who said they had experienced some form of harassment through electronic communication were men.

Slightly higher proportions of men than women in the BtG survey had also experienced repeated unwanted contacts, attempts to contact, or persistent following in person (33.1 percent of men, $n = 41$, and 27.5 percent of women, $n = 129$). Verbal abuse had also been a problem for both women and men, having been experienced by 50.3 percent of women ($n = 236$) and 44.4 percent of men ($n = 55$).

Proportionately, men were slightly more likely to have encountered threats of violence (27.4 percent; $n = 34$, compared with 24.3 percent; $n = 114$ of women). While numbers are relatively low, they were also more likely to have experienced theft or robbery (19.4 percent, $n = 24$, for men, compared with 12.4 percent, $n = 58$, for women). Comparatively low proportions of all survey respondents had experienced physical or sexual assault in the past five years: 12.9 percent ($n = 83$) of respondents overall reported experiencing physical assault, and 19.5 percent ($n = 125$), sexual assault. Among men alone, the numbers were lower for both crimes: 8.1 percent ($n = 10$) and 12.9 percent ($n = 16$), respectively.

In summary, there was relatively little gender difference regarding sex workers' experience of crimes overall, but men were slightly more likely than women to have experienced nonpayment, in-person unwanted contact, threats of violence, and theft or robbery. For other types of crimes, the proportions for men were slightly below those for women, and somewhat lower when it came to online threats or persistent online contact or harassment.

Men were less likely to report incidents to the police. Only 16.5 percent of men ($n = 15$), had ever reported an incident in which they had been victimized, compared with 25.4 percent of women ($n = 93$). Similarly, a lower proportion of men than women said they were quite likely or very likely to report incidents in the future (28.1 percent of men, $n = 34$, compared with 37.1 percent of women, $n = 172$). Similarly to women who do sex work (see, e.g., Pitcher & Wijers, 2014; Sanders, Scoular et al., 2018), one reason men gave for not reporting was a previous experience of reporting a crime when they had not been taken seriously or the violence was dismissed as a feature of their profession. For example, Mac (25, independent escort and BDSM services) said that he had reported a physical assault to the police

> but the police were more or less, more bothered in how come I was meeting this client. So rather than [saying], hang on a minute it's—still classed as an offense to do whatsit, they were more interested in how come I was down there meeting a guy.

Ruzgar (27, independent escort) described how he and a fellow student had reported to the police a nonpayment incident that culminated in violence against them. He felt that because they told the police that they were escorts, their attitude was "'You deserved it,' basically." Moreover, he was a migrant, and sex workers who are migrants are particularly vulnerable because of their uncertain residency status and fear of deportation, as also noted by Mai (2009). Said Ruzgar,

> I don't think I would call the police in any of the, you know, even if I'm beaten up like very badly. It's never happened but, er, I don't think I would call the police at all. Mostly because I am a sex worker but, even more than that, because I am a migrant, I think.

Other participants described a more positive experience in reporting crimes to the police, however, and Liam (38, masseur) noted the importance of setting an example so that the police would take future crimes seriously:

> I realize that there might be certain consequences as a result of [reporting to the police], you know, attracting the police to—to me. But I think I just have to live with the consequences. And I'd rather live with the consequences than the consequence of letting a criminal know that I'm easy game and that this is a venue that you can return to any time you've run out of cash.

The reasons for reporting and not reporting are complex for sex workers (Klambauer, 2017). The examples described demonstrate the deliberations that are required when a crime has taken place in the sex work context and how sex workers have to assess the consequences of contacting the police (Campbell et al., 2018).

Some BtG interviewees did not have views on whether changes to the laws were needed in order to make their working practices safer. With respect to online advertising for sexual services, most felt there was sufficient regulation related to age verification. Regarding regulation of sex work more generally, the majority of participants felt that if it was to be regulated at all, it should be treated like to other professions, and that policing priorities should focus on protecting sex workers who report crimes.

Safety

Male survey respondents used a number of mechanisms to enhance their safety (Figure 17.1). The main methods were avoiding drugs and alcohol at work (60.5 percent), seeing only or mostly regular clients (36.3 percent), and screening potential clients (32.3 percent).

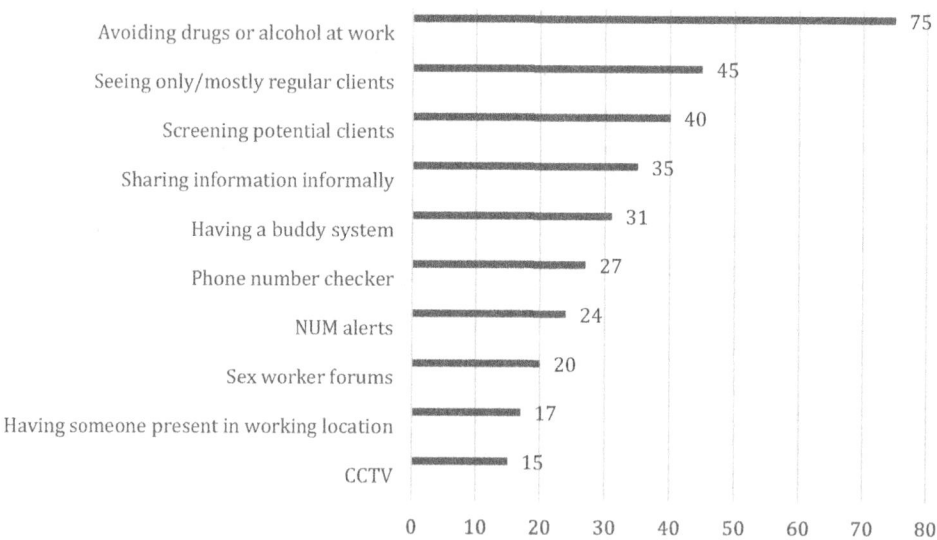

Figure 17.1 The main methods used by male respondents to enhance their safety at work (*N* = 124). ("NUM alerts" refers to alerts on the website for National Ugly Mugs, a national organization in the UK designed to warn sex workers about dangerous individuals.)

There were no substantial gender differences, except that women were more likely than men to use sex worker forums (33.5 percent, $n = 157$, compared with 16.1 percent, $n = 20$) and NUM alerts (30.7 percent, $n = 144$, compared with 19.4 percent, $n = 24$), to share information informally (37.1 percent, $n = 174$, compared with 28.2 percent, $n = 35$), and to have someone else present in their working location (21.5 percent, $n = 101$, compared with 13.7 percent, $n = 17$).

Men were substantially less likely than women to be concerned about their privacy online: 34.4 percent of men ($n = 42$), compared with 51.7 percent of women ($n = 242$), answered in the affirmative to this question. Men were also less likely than women to state that information they had put online had been used without their consent (28.2 percent, $n = 35$, compared with 39.6 percent, $n = 184$).

Most respondents ($n = 620$) took steps to protect their identity online, including using a pseudonym (91.5 percent, $n = 567$), not linking work and personal profiles (87.6 percent, $n = 543$), not giving out personal details (76.5 percent, $n = 474$), and obscuring their face (48.9 percent, $n = 303$). Only 19 respondents overall (3 percent) said they did not take any of the steps mentioned to protect their identity. Women were slightly more likely than men to be cautious about revealing their identity. Among male respondents, 79.8 percent ($n = 99$) used a pseudonym, 71.8 percent ($n = 89$) did not link their personal profiles, 54 percent ($n = 67$) did not give out personal details, and 36.3 percent ($n = 45$) obscured their face—in all cases, lower rates than those for all survey respondents.

While some interview participants described taking steps to protect their privacy, such as keeping a separate phone for their sex work business or maintaining separate online identities, others accepted that there was a risk of being outed because of their online presence. Said Dylan (18, independent escort):

> I wouldn't do this work if, like, I came into—because my partner [had] done it for a number of years. Like when I was first doing it, he told me from the very start that unless you're prepared fully for the possibility for people in your personal life—or even a disgruntled client [to see] details in the local area that you're living in about what you do, then you shouldn't get into this industry, because I can guarantee at some point somebody's gonna find out or somebody's gonna try something. So I've known that from the beginning.

Sources of support and networking

Men were substantially less likely than women to agree strongly that the Internet gave them access to networks and peer support (47.2 percent, $n = 58$, compared with 65.8 percent, $n = 302$). However, when we combined respondents who either tended to agree or strongly agree with this statement, the differences were not substantial (78 percent of men, $n = 96$, compared with 82.8 percent of women, $n = 380$).

The main website used by male respondents for advice or support was a forum specifically for male escorts (used by 19.4 percent of men, $n = 24$). Men were less likely than women to use National Ugly Mugs for support: 26.4 percent of women ($n = 124$) reported using it, compared with 17.7 percent of men ($n = 22$). National Ugly Mugs (NUM) is a third-party reporting system in the UK designed to protect sex workers; sex workers (and organizations) can report crimes and incidents to NUM, which then sends them out as legally sanitized alerts to its more than 6,000 members. There were also some gender differences in the use of social media: 26 percent ($n = 122$) of women compared with 12.9 percent ($n = 16$) of men used Twitter for support, although similar proportions of men and women used Facebook for that purpose (10.5 percent, $n = 13$, and 10.2 percent, $n = 48$, respectively).

Some interview participants felt there were relatively few sources of external support for male sex workers, although this response depended in part on their location, as workers in some large cities had greater access to dedicated sex work support projects. For some male sex workers, their main sources of support were the safety networks they had access to and providers of sexual health services, where they could decide whether it was appropriate to disclose their working status. The importance of nonjudgmental support was noted, although one respondent from England's Midlands region, Aaron (30, independent escort also providing other sexual services), felt that there was less stigma and more of a focus on "It's work, and let's make sure they're safe and stuff like that." Rab (38, independent escort/masseur) used a London-based sex work project for sexual health advice and testing and found the specialized knowledge helpful:

> I've had like [an] STD test with somebody who wasn't familiar with the business side of it, and I think I definitely felt their lack of knowledge or lack of what this meant for me in terms of it's a business; if I had a diagnosis like that at the [specialist project for male sex workers], everything is truly done on an equal level, like my sexual health, public health and the fact that it's a business, like, and there's an understanding of that.

Concluding comments

Male sex work has been organized through digital technologies for the past 20 years, and the Beyond the Gaze project has demonstrated that while sex workers who use online technology to sell sexual services do so in similar ways, there are some nuanced differences with male sex workers (who usually sell services to other men). The most notable differences were that male sex workers were less likely to report crimes to the police and were less likely to be engaged in sex worker forums or online networking. These results suggest that the isolated nature of sex work may be more of a feature for male sex workers than for female sex workers.

The passage in 2018 of the Stop Enabling Sex Traffickers Act (SESTA) and Fight Online Sex Trafficking Act (FOSTA) in the United States has already had major ramifications for the ways in which sex work is sold. Those laws, whose stated intention is to stop trafficking, make it a crime to operate "an interactive computer service" with "intent to promote or facilitate the prostitution of another person." On April 6, 2018, the FBI seized the major online advertising site Backpage.com. The effect has rippled out to the businesses of thousands of sex workers across the world who advertise in the adult services sector. Sex workers in the United Kingdom have begun pulling their own advertisements, and adult website platforms have begun self-regulating to avoid becoming embroiled with such charges. Discussions in the UK House of Commons in July 2018 show that the moral panic and misinformation about the relationship between adult services websites and trafficking and exploitation have spread into political circles (Hansard, 2018).

SESTA and FOSTA have major implications for the livelihoods of sex workers and the safety of their working practices; sex workers are changing their original safer practices and attempting to operate more secretively. Male sex workers, of course, are not immune from the effects of increased and significant surveillance of adult platforms, and while much of this activity is centered in the United States, the ramifications are affecting sex workers throughout the Western world, where digital technologies are central to sex businesses.

It is possible that male sex work advertising will retreat further to spaces that less overtly advertise commercial sex. Instead, sex work advertising online may merge with geographic applications (phone apps that base information on geographical location), thus identifying and linking people available for dating in a specific location, as well as dating sites and apps. In some senses, this outcome would return male sex workers to the subtle ways in which they advertised and negotiated 20 years ago, prompting new and alternative ways of connecting seller and buyer. It is only over the next decade that we will see the full effects of today's moral panic and politics on the nature and organization of the sex industry. We will then be able to trace how different groups of sex workers have navigated these surveillance and eradication tactics. In ways yet to be seen, the sex industry will likely move into different spaces, create new networks, and harness innovative ways to advertise and provide its services.

References

Amnesty International. (2017). *Amnesty reveals alarming impact of online abuse against women.* Retrieved from www.amnesty.org/en/latest/news/2017/11/amnesty-reveals-alarming-impact-of-online-abuse-against-women/

Attwood, F. (2013). Through the looking glass? Sexual agency and subjectification online. In R. Gill & C. Scharff (Eds.), *New femininities: Postfeminism, neoliberalism, and subjectivity.* Basingstoke, UK: Palgrave Macmillan.

Bernstein, E. (2007). Sex work for the middle classes. *Sexualities, 10*(4), 473–488.

Bimbi, D. S. (2007). Male prostitution: Pathology, paradigms, and progress in research. *Journal of Homosexuality, 53*(1), 7–35.

Bimbi, D. S., & Parsons, J. T. (2005). Barebacking among internet-based male sex workers. *Journal of Gay and Lesbian Psychotherapy, 9*(3–4), 85–105. doi:10.1300/J236v09n03_06

Campbell, R., Sanders, T., Scoular, J., Pitcher, J., & Cunningham, S. (2018). Risking safety and rights: Online sex work, crimes, and "blended safety repertoires." *British Journal of Sociology.* doi:10.1111/1468-4446.12493

Castells, M. (2000). *The rise of the network society: Information age: Economy, society, and culture.* London: Wiley Blackwell.

Cunningham, S., & Kendall, T. D. (2011). Prostitution 2.0: The changing face of sex work. *Journal of Urban Economics, 69*(3), 273–287.

Cunningham, S., Sanders, T., Scoular, J., Campbell, R., Pitcher, J., Hill, K., et al. (2018). Behind the screen: Commercial sex, digital spaces, and working online. *Technology in Society, 53*, 47–54.

Dahlberg, L., Demack, S., & Bambra, C. (2007). Age of gender and information careers: A population-based study in the UK. *Health and Social Care in the Community, 15*(5), 439–445.

Du Gay, P. (1996). *Consumption and identity at work.* London: Sage.

Duggan, M. (2017). *Online harassment 2017.* Washington, DC: Pew Research Center. Retrieved from www.pewresearch.org/internet/2017/07/11/online-harassment-2017/

Hansard. (2018, July 4). *Commercial sexual exploitation* (Vol. 644). UK Parliament, House of Commons Hansard. Retrieved from https://hansard.parliament.uk/Commons/2018-07-04/debates/50911795-3525-4F4A-B047-EF87047B5176/CommercialSexualExploitation

Klambauer, E. (2017). Policing roulette: Sex workers' perception of encounters with police officers in the indoor and outdoor sector in England. *Criminology and Criminal Justice, 18*(3), 255–272.

Koken, J. A., Bimbi, D. S., Parsons, J. T., & Halkitis, P. N. (2004). The experience of stigma in the lives of male Internet escorts. *Journal of Psychology and Human Sexuality, 16*(1), 13–32.

Kuhar, R., & Pajnik, M. (2019). Negotiating professional identities: Male sex workers in Slovenia and the impact of online technologies. *Sexuality Research and Social Policy, 16*(2), 227–238.

Lee-Gonyea, J. A., Castle, T., & Gonyea, N. E. (2009). Laid to order: Male escorts advertising on the Internet. *Deviant Behavior, 30*, 321–348.

MacPhail, C., Scott, J., & Minichiello, V. (2015). Technology, normalisation, and male sex work. *Culture, Health, and Sexuality, 17*(4), 483–495.

Mai, N. (2009). *Migrant workers in the UK sex industry: Final policy-relevant report*. ESRC Final Project Report. London: Metropolitan University.

Maple, C., Short, E., & Brown, A. (2011). *Cyberstalking in the United Kingdom: An analysis of the ECHO pilot survey*. Luton, UK: University of Bedfordshire, National Centre for Cyberstalking Research.

McLean, A. (2012). New realm, new problems? Issues and support networks in online male sex work. *Gay and Lesbian Issues and Psychology Review, 8*(2), 70–81.

Minichiello, V., Scott, J., & Callander, D. (2013). New pleasures and old dangers: Reinventing male sex work. *Journal of Sex Research, 50*(304), 263–275.

Office for National Statistics (ONS). (2018). *Population estimates for England and Wales, Scotland, and Northern Ireland: Mid-2017*. London: ONS.

Parsons, T. J., Koken, J. S., & Bimbi, D. S. (2004). The use of the Internet by gay and bisexual male escorts: Sex workers as sex educators. *AIDS Care, 16*(8), 1021–1035.

Pitcher, J. (2019). Intimate labour and the state: Contrasting policy discourses with the working experiences of indoor sex workers. *Sexuality Research and Social Policy, 16*(2), 138–150. doi:10.1007/s13178-018-0323-3

Pitcher, J., & Wijers, M. (2014). The impact of different regulatory models on the labour conditions, safety, and welfare of indoor-based sex workers. *Criminology and Criminal Justice, 14*(5), 549–564. doi:10.1177/1748895814531967

Redman, S. (2017). *Female and male escorts in the UK: A comparative analysis of working practices, stigma, and relationships* (PhD thesis). University of Leeds, Leeds.

Ryan, P. (2019). *Male sex work in the digital age: Curated lives*. New York: Palgrave Macmillan.

Sanders, T., O'Neill, M., & Pitcher, J. (2018). *Prostitution: Sex work, policy, and politics* (2nd ed.). London: Sage.

Sanders, T., Scoular, J., Campbell, R., Pitcher, J., & Cunningham, S. (2018). *Internet sex work: Beyond the gaze*. Cham, Switzerland: Palgrave Macmillan.

Tyler, A. (2015). M$M@Gaydar: Queering the social network. In M. Laing, K. Pilcher, & N. Smith (Eds.), *Queer sex work*. London: Routledge.

Uy, J. M., Parsons, J. T., Bimbi, D. S., Koken, J. A., & Halkitis, P. N. (2004). Gay and bisexual male escorts who advertise on the Internet: Understanding reasons for and effects of involvement in commercial sex. *International Journal of Men's Health, 3*(1), 11–26.

Van Dijk, J. (2012). *The network society* (3rd ed.). London: Sage.

Walby, K. (2012). *Sex, work, and male-for-male Internet escorting*. Chicago: University of Chicago Press.

Part IV
Male sex work in public and community health

18

Global epidemiology of HIV and other sexually transmitted infections among male sex workers

Emerging approaches in prevention and treatment

Peter Salhaney, Katie B. Biello, and Matthew J. Mimiaga

This chapter provides an overview of the global epidemiology of HIV and other sexually transmitted infections (STIs) among male sex workers, with an emphasis on sexual risk behavior, as well as psychosocial and structural factors that increase the likelihood of HIV's spread. It discusses access to HIV prevention and treatment along with effective biomedical and behavioral interventions to reduce HIV acquisition and transmission among this group. Finally, it highlights new areas for exploration and knowledge to be gained. It is important to keep in mind that there are various types of male sex workers, including Internet escorts, street workers, masseurs, and dancers, and each type may have considerable differences in sexual risk behaviors, which may influence epidemiological data across different contexts and world regions. For example, male sex workers who solicit clients on the Internet may have a different risk profile from those whose work is predominantly street-based. Similarly, individuals who self-identify as male sex workers and for whom sex work is their primary source of income may differ significantly from men who do not identify as sex workers and who exchange sex only intermittently or informally. We use the term male sex worker (MSW) throughout this chapter to refer broadly to men who engage in transactional sex with other men for money, goods, drugs, or other items of value.

Global epidemiology of HIV and other sexually transmitted infections among male sex workers

According to the United Nations AIDS (UNAIDS) approximately 38 million people are living with HIV/AIDS infection globally, of whom 1.7 million were newly infected in 2019 (UNAIDS, 2020). Amid these cases, male sex workers (MSWs) represent a largely understudied population at particularly elevated risk for HIV and other sexually transmitted infections.

Owing to the lack of routine epidemiological data collected on MSWs worldwide, there is considerable variation in regional estimates of HIV and STI incidence and prevalence within this group.

Studies using convenience sampling consistently show a high burden of HIV among MSWs, with prevalence rates exceeding that of female sex workers (FSWs) and men in the general population (Friedman, Guadamuz, & Marshal, 2011). We performed a literature review of seven electronic databases, national surveillance reports, and conference abstracts for reports of MSWs published between 2004 and 2013. Drawing from 66 selected studies, representing 31,924 MSWs in 28 countries, pooled biological assay-confirmed HIV prevalence was 10.5 percent (95 percent confidence interval [CI] = 9.4 to 11.5 percent). The highest pooled HIV prevalence was in sub-Saharan Africa (31.5 percent, 95 percent CI = 21.6 to 41.5 percent), followed by Latin America (19.3 percent, 95 percent CI = 15.5 to 23.1 percent), North America (16.6 percent, 95 percent CI = 3.7 to 29.5 percent), and Europe (12.2 percent, 95 percent CI = 6.0 to 17.2 percent) (see Figure 18.1). Men who engaged in transactional sex had an elevated burden of HIV compared with the overall male population (probability [PR] = 20.7, 95 percent CI = 16.8 to 25.5) (Oldenburg, Perez-Brumer et al., 2014).

In a similar meta-analysis examining the prevalence of HIV among MSWs in 2015, the rate ranged from 5 to 31 percent, much higher than in the general population (Baral et al., 2015). A study in Côte d'Ivoire, one of the West African countries most severely affected by HIV/AIDS, found that among 96 MSWs, 50 percent were living with HIV, 12.8 percent with gonorrhea, and 3.2 percent with chlamydia infections (Vuylsteke et al., 2012). Cross-sectional national surveillance data of MSWs attending STI clinics in the Netherlands from 2006 to 2012 found that 18.1 percent of STI clinic encounters included a diagnosis of at least one bacterial STI (Fournet et al., 2015). Similarly elevated rates of HIV and other STI diagnoses have been demonstrated by studies conducted in Canada (Weber et al., 2001), Thailand (Toledo et al., 2010), Brazil (Cortez, Boer, & Baltieri, 2011), Vietnam (Nguyen, Nguyen, Le, & Detels, 2008), and Nigeria (Vu et al., 2013), as well as Europe (Belza, 2005; Sethi et al., 2006), Australia (Callander et al., 2015), and Latin America (Segura et al., 2010).

Reports of higher HIV prevalence among men who have sex with men (MSM) and who engage in sex work versus MSM who do not engage in sex work have not been entirely

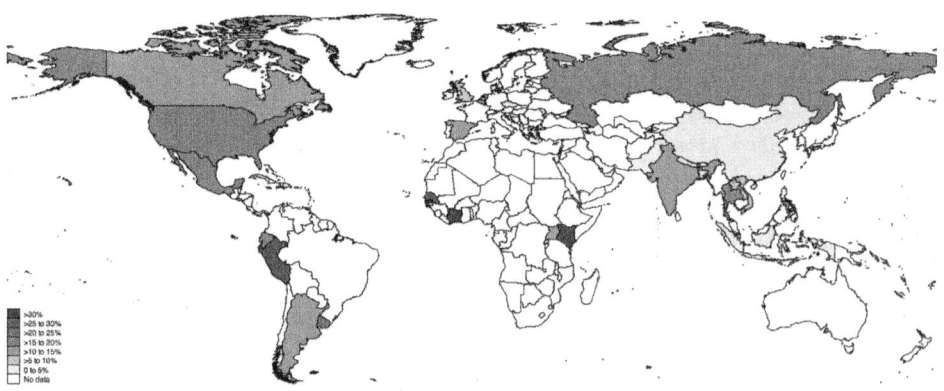

Figure 18.1   Pooled HIV prevalence by country from 66 studies reporting biologically confirmed HIV prevalence with a sample size of ≥50.

Source: Oldenburg, Perez-Brumer et al., 2014.

consistent across studies, likely as a result of different sampling methods. Similarly, in different world regions, the magnitude of this relationship varies with local cultural, political, economic, and structural factors, particularly those that enable or restrict the practice of sex work or same-sex practices. For example, Callander (2017) outlined how HIV and STI rates among MSWs are influenced by the local rates of infection overall: if infection rates are elevated in a country overall, rates are also likely to be high among MSWs in that population.

Notwithstanding this variation, a recent systematic review and meta-analysis of 33 studies in 17 countries, comparing MSM who engaged in transactional sex with those who did not incorporating(n = 78,112 MSM) showed that, overall, transactional sex was associated with a statistically significant elevation in HIV prevalence (odds ratio [OR] = 1.34, 95 percent CI = 1.11 to 1.62). This increase was most pronounced in Latin America (OR = 2.28, 95 percent CI = 1.87 to 2.78) and sub-Saharan Africa (OR = 1.72, 95 percent CI = 1.02–2.91) (Oldenburg, Perez-Brumer, Reisner, & Mimiaga, 2015). In Sydney, Australia, investigators found an HIV prevalence of 6.5 percent among MSWs, which was greater than the prevalence among FSWs (0.4 percent) but less than the prevalence among MSM who did not report engaging in sex work (23.9 percent) (Estcourt et al., 2000). These comparisons, however, should be interpreted with caution, as these were not probability samples, and the three groups ranged in size from 94 (MSWs) to 3,541 (MSM). In the same study, the prevalence of genital warts, the most commonly reported STI, was higher among MSWs than MSM who were not sex workers (12.2 percent) and FSWs (4.6 percent) (Estcourt et al., 2000). A separate analysis conducted in China also found that "money boys"—a term analogous to MSW—had a lower HIV prevalence (4.5 percent) than MSM not reporting sex work (7.0 percent) but a higher prevalence than the general population (0.04 percent) (Liu et al., 2012; UNAIDS, 2015a). As in the study by Estcourt et al. (2000), readers should take into consideration the fact that these analyses did not use probability sampling. Together, these findings suggest that MSWs consistently remain at elevated risk for HIV and other STIs compared to the general population, FSWs, and most MSM who do not engage in sex work. There are, however, regional differences in HIV incidence and prevalence, related to unique context-specific factors, that are essential to informing HIV treatment and prevention interventions for MSWs worldwide.

Sexual behavior, sex partners, and negotiating safer (or riskier) sex with clients

Biological, psychosocial, and structural factors play a meaningful role in HIV and STI-related risk-taking behaviors among MSWs. The biological risks associated with HIV transmission through condomless anal intercourse overlap for both MSWs and other MSM (Baggaley, White, & Boily, 2010). Having another STI can also increase the risk of acquiring HIV if exposed; thus, it is common for HIV to be diagnosed with a co-occurring STI (Rodríguez et al., 2002). According to the Centers for Disease Control and Prevention, individuals infected with an STI are two to five times more likely to acquire HIV after unprotected sexual exposure than people who are not infected with an STI (CDC, 2018), because ulcerations on the genitals and other parts of the body, often produced by syphilis and herpes simplex virus, become vulnerable entry points for HIV infection. Similarly, chlamydia and gonorrhea cause inflammation, which amplifies the concentration of cells in genital secretions to which HIV can successfully bind (Ward & Rönn, 2010).

Behavioral risks for HIV taken by MSWs typically include having multiple concurrent sexual partners (Beyrer et al., 2012) and greater numbers of condomless anal or vaginal sex acts with both male and female clients (Baral et al., 2015; Nerlander et al., 2017; Rietmeijer, Wolitski, Fishbein, Corby, & Cohn, 1998). Commonly reported factors related to condom negotiation include physical or emotional attraction to the client, the type of sex (oral versus anal), and the length or steadiness of the client–sex worker relationship (Ballester-Arnal, Gil-Llario, Salmeron-Sánchez, & Giménez-García, 2014; Shinde, Setia, Row-Kavi, Anand, & Jerajani, 2009). For example, a study in Spain found that nearly all MSWs (99.6 percent) reported using a condom during anal intercourse, but only 76.8 percent used a condom during oral sex (Ballester-Arnal et al., 2014). These behaviors extend the risk for HIV and STI transmission to others; specifically, MSWs are more likely than their non–sex worker MSM counterparts to engage in condomless sex with their primary male and female partners (Elwood, Williams, Bell, & Richard, 1997; Estcourt et al., 2000; Rietmeijer et al., 1998). Further findings from Bacon and colleagues (2006) estimated that 42 percent of seropositive MSWs in San Francisco were unaware of their HIV infection, suggesting that many MSWs may unknowingly be transmitting HIV to both clients and nonpaying partners, making them a particularly important "bridge" population on whom interventions should be focused (Elwood et al., 1997; Estcourt et al., 2000; Rietmeijer et al., 1998).

Across much of the literature, inconsistent condom use by MSWs appears to be motivated by socioeconomic need, as MSWs are often offered more money if they agree not to use a condom with a paying client (Mimiaga, Reisner, Tinsley, Mayer, & Safren, 2009). One study conducted in India found that more than two-thirds of MSW participants reported being offered more money if they would not use a condom with a client, and 74.2 percent of those MSWs had accepted the proposition; the investigators also found that 86.0 percent of MSWs had not used a condom during their most recent paid sexual encounter (Biello, Thomas et al., 2017).

The degree of risk for acquiring HIV and other STIs from sex work encounters varies widely depending on the context. For example, in 2009, a research team found that while most MSWs in the United States were offered more money by clients for condomless sex, street-based MSWs were far less likely to refuse such offers compared with Internet-based escorts (Mimiaga et al., 2009). Additionally, the street-based MSWs were more likely to engage in riskier sexual behaviors for more money out of financial desperation, and they more commonly exchanged sex for drugs, as well, reporting a higher frequency than Internet escorts of crack and cocaine use in the past 12 months. Such differences in risk-taking behavior between street-based and Internet-based MSWs are consistent across the literature (Minichiello et al., 2000; Morse, Simon, Baus, Balson, & Osofsky, 1992; Parsons, Koken, & Bimbi, 2004; Rietmeijer et al., 1998). However, Smith and Seal (2008) found that Internet escorts had a higher probability of participating in risk-taking behaviors with their casual sex partners or clients, owing to the fact that most Internet-based escorts in their sample primarily used sex work on a "part time" basis to supplement other sources of revenue (Smith & Seal, 2008). These subgroup distinctions should be factored heavily into the effective design and implementation of public health interventions that will meet the unique needs of MSW subgroups.

Factors potentiating HIV and sexually transmitted infection risk among MSWs

Over the past decade, research on sexual and gender minorities has suggested that psychosocial problems may represent intertwined "syndemics" (Mimiaga et al., 2015; Mustanski, Garofalo, Herrick, & Donenberg, 2007; Reisner et al., 2009; Stall et al., 2003). The term *syndemic* was first developed to describe the co-occurring and mutually reinforcing epidemics of substance use, violence, and AIDS in poor urban communities, and it emphasizes how disadvantageous social conditions interact to adversely affect health outcomes within marginalized communities. There is a substantive body of literature revealing that MSWs disproportionately face psychosocial problems such as depression, substance abuse, childhood sexual abuse, and intimate partner violence

(Burnette et al., 2008; Panchanadeswaran et al., 2008). A study from the northeastern United States found that 41 percent of MSWs had experienced childhood sexual abuse, a rate that is considerably higher than in the general male U.S. population (Mimiaga et al., 2009). Furthermore, several studies in the United States and Australia have highlighted the elevated frequency of illicit drug use among MSM who engage in transactional sex compared to those who do not (Biello, Oldenburg et al., 2017; Underhill et al., 2014; Weber et al., 2001). In an analysis of twenty metropolitan U.S. cities, Nerlander and colleagues (2017) found that 22.6 percent of men who reported engaging in transactional sex had injected drugs at some time, compared with only 5.4 percent of men who had not. Similar trends were identified related to the use of noninjection drugs, including crack cocaine (26.7 percent versus 3.2 percent) and methamphetamine use (24.2 percent versus 5.3 percent), in the past 12 months (Nerlander et al., 2017).

In addition to these psychosocial burdens, MSWs also experience structural and socioeconomic marginalization (Marshall et al., 2010), lower educational attainment (Weber et al., 2001), and incarceration (Nerlander, Shannon, Kerr, Zhang, & Wood, 2017), as well as stigma, poverty, and discrimination (Underhill et al., 2015). The literature that is only beginning to emerge on the lived experiences of MSWs beyond their risk for acquiring HIV reveals that MSWs often perceive or experience high rates of discrimination when receiving health care (Brookfield, Dean, Forrest, Jones, & Fitzgerald, 2019; Crowell et al., 2017; Jones, Dean, Brookfield, Forrest, & Fitzgerald, 2018; Lazarus et al., 2012; Oldenburg, Biello, Colby, Closson, Mai et al., 2014; Scorgie et al., 2013). Male sex workers may face discrimination related to their sexual identity, sex work, HIV status, or other associated factors (e.g., homelessness, low literacy, mental health, and substance use). A recent meta-analysis of 22 qualitative papers addressing barriers to accessing sexual health services for MSWs found that stigma was the predominant obstacle identified in all but one of the studies (Brookfield et al., 2019). The spectrum of reported stigma in health care settings ranged from, in the United States, an unwarranted focus on a person's sex work–related history (Xavier et al., 2013), to disregard for patient confidentiality, ridicule (Scorgie et al., 2013), and even, in sub-Saharan Africa, the refusal of care (Okanlawon, Adebowale, & Titilayo, 2013).

For MSWs, feeling stigmatized and criminalized, and fearing disclosure of their identity, can create overwhelming barriers to accessing health care. Because of the personal nature of discussing one's sexual activity, health care–related stigma can lead individuals to avoid such undesirable experiences, distrust their medical providers, and choose not to disclose certain sex work–related behaviors (Underhill et al., 2015). Notably, these negative coping strategies may mean MSWs receive improper health guidance, incomplete risk assessments and risk reduction counseling, only partial disease screening, and prescriptions for medications that are not specific to their health needs. It is well documented that stigmatization makes individuals less likely to seek care, thereby delaying opportunities for testing, diagnosis, and treatment and increasing the likelihood of poor health outcomes overall (Boynton & Cusick, 2006; King, Maman, Bowling, Moracco, & Dudina, 2013; Krüsi et al., 2014; Lazarus et al., 2012; Restar et al., 2017; Scambler & Paoli, 2008; Scorgie et al., 2013; Callander, 2017). Male sex workers in Lebanon reported avoiding HIV testing because they knew that they would lose their employment at a brothel if they were found to be infected (Aunon et al., 2015). Because of such consequences, when faced with barriers to care or experiences of stigma, many MSWs rely on health services provided in nonconventional settings. One report in the United States found that the primary sources of HIV testing for MSWs were research studies, drug rehabilitation centers, needle exchange programs, street-based outreach, and correctional institutions. That same study found that, compared with their non–sex worker MSM counterparts, MSWs reported lower rates of non-HIV STI testing, less access to insurance coverage, and higher rates of unmet health care needs (Underhill et al., 2014).

Stigma as a barrier to health care access is often multilayered and interwoven with other structural, cultural, and legal influences. Interviews with MSWs from Lebanon and Kenya have highlighted the pervasive impact of deeply rooted cultural conservatism on perpetuating damaging social norms regarding sexuality, gender diversity, and sex work, which has ultimately impeded the coverage of targeted, evidenced-based HIV prevention strategies for this group (Aunon et al., 2015; Okal et al., 2009). As a consequence of these gaps, MSWs in Lebanon and Kenya reported limited knowledge of HIV-related risks and particularly low participation in HIV testing; instead, they relied heavily on other MSWs for social support and access to sexual health–related resources. Both studies concluded that truly effective outreach strategies seeking to facilitate access to HIV/STI information and services must be spearheaded by peer educators (i.e., men who have previously or are currently engaged in sex work) (Aunon et al., 2015; Okal et al., 2009). Research in Malaysia involving qualitative interviews with key stakeholders who worked with MSWs—health ministry officials, religious leaders, and people living with HIV—support these findings, underscoring how cultural and structural norms can affect sexual health promotion efforts among individuals who engage in transactional sex (Barmania & Aljunid, 2016).

The criminalization of sex work also has direct implications for how vulnerable MSWs are to HIV and other STIs. Globally, there is a lack of legislation and formal policy to protect sex workers from violence at the hands of law enforcement, primary partners, and sex work clients (UNAIDS, 2010). Shannon and Csete (2010) have reasoned that restricting legal protections reinforces sex workers' disempowerment and fear of violence, creates barriers to negotiating safe sex practices and seeking out health services, and thereby increases the risk of poor sexual health outcomes. Emerging data have also revealed that legalizing or decriminalizing sex work is imperative to addressing the HIV epidemic among people who engage in transactional sex because it would improve access to regular sexual health services (HIV and STI screening and treatment, preexposure prophylaxis [PrEP], postexposure prophylaxis [PEP], and antiretrovirals [ARVs] for HIV treatment), provide protection for sex workers when they are attempting to negotiate condom use with clients, and prevent further violence or abuse (Abel, Fitzgerald, & Brunton, 2009; Kerrigan et al., 2006; Krüsi et al., 2014; Shannon & Montaner, 2012; Shannon et al., 2015; UNAIDS, 2016). By mitigating individual fears of incarceration or legal hassles, eliminating legal constraints on sex workers would allow HIV prevention programs to be implemented more widely and effectively (Baral, Logie, Grosso, Wirtz, & Beyrer, 2013). In fact, a 2017 ecological analysis of data from 27 European countries found that HIV prevalence was much lower among sex workers in countries where sex work was fully or partially legal, compared with countries where sex work remained criminalized (Reeves et al., 2017). Overall, a 2015 report estimated that sex work decriminalization and comprehensive legal protections could prevent 33 percent to 46 percent of new HIV infections among sex workers and their clients over the next decade (Beyrer et al., 2015). By lifting social, cultural, and legal barriers, public health officials would also be able to better promote proper health care utilization, work toward improving the overall health of sex workers, and further prevent acquisition and transmission of HIV and other STIs between sex workers and their partners and clients (Steen, Chersich, & de Vlas, 2012).

Access to HIV prevention and treatment and to antiretroviral therapy

Expanded access to antiretroviral therapy among the general population through governmental and programmatic services, community organizations, and research entities has led to significant improvements in the overall health and well-being of people living with HIV. The benefit of consistent adherence to ART treatment is twofold: it protects one's immune system from the spread of the virus, and it reduces the individual's viral load and thus the likelihood of transmission through sexual activity and injection drug use (Lundgren et al., 2015; Schaecher, 2013). The advantages offered by ART are contingent on linkage to care shortly after HIV diagnosis, prompt initiation of antiretroviral medications, optimal adherence to the prescribed regimen, and ongoing retention in HIV care (Gardner, McLees, Steiner, del Rio, & Burman, 2011; Mugavero, Amico, Horn, & Thompson, 2013). The HIV care continuum has been developed to visualize and quantify the spectrum of engagement in HIV-related health care: testing and diagnosis, linkage to care, retention in care, delivery of ART, and achievement of viral suppression. While HIV care-continuum data are available for the general population and certain high-risk groups, including MSM overall, there is a dearth of statistical evidence related to MSWs. Given this, we have drawn on data from FSWs to highlight where potential risks may exist for their male counterparts.

A 2015 report from the Joint United Nations Programme on HIV/AIDS (UNAIDS) found that the proportion of FSWs who reported receiving an HIV test, with a result, in the past 12 months ranged widely by country, from 1.1 to 5.9 percent in Egypt, Vanuatu, and Afghanistan, to as high as 100 percent in Djibouti, Ireland, São Tomé and Príncipe, and Singapore (UNAIDS, 2015b). Another review of 52 low- and middle-income countries found that, in 2010, the median percentage of FSWs who had both been tested for HIV in the past 12 months and also knew their results was 49 percent (Bekker et al., 2018). In an attempt to measure global linkage to ART, a meta-analysis of 39 studies of FSWs living with HIV in Asia, Africa, North America, and South America found that a reported history of ever having taken ART was higher among FSWs in high-income countries (80 percent) than those in low- and middle-income countries (36 percent) (Mountain et al., 2014). This inequity in ART access exists within nations as well. According to UNAIDS (2019b), in Zimbabwe, 84.0 percent of all people living with HIV reported receiving ART, compared with 78 percent of FSWs living with HIV. In Pakistan, the rate of access to HIV care is even lower, with antiretroviral treatment reportedly received by 12 percent of those among the general population living with HIV and just 5 percent of FSWs with HIV (UNAIDS, 2019a).

As previously discussed, the lack of access to HIV treatment and deficient uptake of ART are results of the overlapping challenges facing sex workers who are living with HIV, including societal stigma, little to no legal protection for sex work, and fear of serostatus disclosure without consent. Although there are virtually no data specific to MSWs, it could be speculated that rates of HIV-care access and follow-through are even lower among MSWs compared with FSWs, given that men are less likely than women to attend health care visits and given the added stigma faced by MSWs for engaging in same-sex behaviors (Baker et al., 2014; Bertakis, Azari, Helms, Callahan, & Robbins, 2000; Wang, Hunt, Nazareth, Freemantle, & Petersen, 2013). To our knowledge, the only examination of the HIV care continuum among MSWs was conducted in Peru in 2017 by Bayer and colleagues, with a group of 209 MSWs. Their study found that, among the 34 MSWs in the study who tested positive for HIV (16.3 percent of the sample), 76 percent had attended at least one HIV-related appointment, only 59 percent were currently in care, 50 percent were actively taking ART, and only 32 percent had been on ART for six months or more. The primary reason reported for nonmaintenance in HIV care was the difficulty of managing multiple clinical visits over an extended period of time (Bayer et al., 2017).

Interventions focused on sexual risk reduction

Despite the fact that MSWs are disproportionately burdened by HIV and other STIs owing to their high-risk sexual activity, few behavioral interventions have been adapted to directly address the unique challenges MSWs face. This scarcity may be overshadowed by the extensive research focused on MSM who do not engage in transactional sex and on FSWs. The complex nature of the environment in which MSWs operate (transient, stigmatized, hidden) makes it nearly impossible to effectively tap into this population via traditional avenues of outreach. The most effective designs for behavioral intervention have incorporated interpersonal, biomedical, community, and structural approaches.

Formative research with MSWs in various global contexts has offered insight into which components are best included when tailoring interventions for MSWs. Recent findings from qualitative interviews with 32 MSWs in Boston suggested that key project elements to effectively promote behavioral change should integrate trauma-informed care for mental health, substance abuse treatment, accessible HIV/STI testing, readily available condoms and informational materials, support groups for those experiencing social isolation, and skills building for risk reduction with sexual partners (Mimiaga et al., 2009; Reisner et al., 2008). These recommendations highlight the need for broad, multifaceted interventions to meaningfully address the unique contextual barriers to care for MSWs (Ballester-Arnal et al., 2014; Baral et al., 2015; Vuylsteke, Das, Dallabetta, & Laga, 2009).

Behavioral interventions to reduce risk for HIV

As mentioned, there are few sexual risk reduction programs for MSWs and even fewer evaluations of the projects' utility. One intervention model makes use of peer-led outreach and education, in which a program-trained MSW or former MSW disseminates HIV- and STI-related information, promotes safer sexual behaviors, and facilitates links to care through referrals to sexual and social services. The effectiveness of this particular peer-led model for MSWs has varied by study. In New York City, for example, the paradigm demonstrated a significant reduction in the number of condomless anal sex (CAS) acts between MSWs and their clients (Miller, Klotz, & Eckholdt, 1998). Similarly, for 425 MSWs in Mombasa, Kenya, peer-based outreach considerably improved HIV knowledge and STI-prevention behaviors, including increased condom use with both paying and nonpaying male partners (Geibel, King'ola, Temmerman, & Luchters, 2012). A seven-module version of this intervention, called Harm Reduction and Sexual Health Promotion, was evaluated among 919 young MSWs in Vietnam. Results of the pre-post assessment found significant improvements in HIV- and STI-related knowledge, as well as intentions to attend a doctor's visit and to disclose same-sex behaviors to medical providers (Clatts, Goldsamt, Yu, & Colby, 2016). While the peer-led model has shown some success, there is concern that the initial efficacy eventually dwindles and the educational focus diffuses. To counteract these possibilities, peer outreach should be supplemented with behavioral interventions that are brief and that directly target individual actions, activities, and skills (McCamish, Storer, & Carl, 2000).

One group of researchers recently aimed to develop a behavioral intervention specifically for MSWs in Chennai, India (Thomas et al., 2017). First, the researchers collected in-depth qualitative feedback from 40 interviews with MSWs, and four focus groups with 35 key informants who had expert knowledge of the local MSW community, to inform the design of an HIV-prevention program. Participants discussed the need for content beyond basic HIV educational and psychological support, emphasizing a focus on psychological distress, alcohol-related risk, and sexual communication skills (Thomas et al., 2017). Respondents also raised concerns about confidentiality, privacy, and scheduling on implementation of the program. As in other parts of the world, MSWs in India increasingly rely on the use of mobile phones for sex work solicitation, and they endorsed a combination of in-person and mobile phone–delivered sessions as well as mobile phone messaging. Integrating mobile phone technology helped to mitigate some of the challenges associated with face-to-face counseling, such as execution, confidentiality, and resource consumption (i.e., time and money), while also proving to be both feasible and useful for MSWs (Thomas et al., 2017).

These findings served as the basis for a theoretically driven, manualized intervention program incorporating mobile phones for MSWs in the U.S. northeast (Mimiaga et al., 2019). This intervention was recently tested in a randomized, controlled pilot trial to examine participant acceptability, procedural feasibility, and preliminary efficacy in reducing sexual risk for HIV. Male sex workers ($n = 100$) were equally randomized into (1) a behavioral HIV prevention program integrating in-person and mobile phone—delivered HIV risk reduction counseling, plus daily personalized text messages used as motivating "cognitive restructuring" cues for reducing CAS acts, or (2) a standard of care (SOC) comparison condition (Mimiaga et al., 2019). The intervention was both feasible (98 percent retention at six months) and acceptable (>96 percent of all intervention sessions attended); all intervention participants rated the project as "acceptable" or "very acceptable." A reduction in the reported number of CAS acts by MSWs with paying male clients in the preceding month was seen in both study groups, but MSWs who received the intervention reported a faster rate of decline from the baseline (B) to both the three-month (B = −1.20; 95 percent CI = −1.68, −0.73; $p < 0.0001$) and six-month assessment visits (B = −−.44; 95 percent CI = −3.35, −1.53; $p < 0.00001$), compared with men in the SOC group. Specifically, at three months, participants in the intervention condition reported 1.43 CAS acts (standard deviation [SD] = 0.29) with paying male clients in the previous month, compared with 4.85 (SD = 0.87) in the SOC control group (p = 0.0003). Furthermore, at six months, the intervention-condition participants reported 0.24 (SD = 0.09) CAS acts with male clients in the previous month, compared with 2.79 (SD = 0.79) in the SOC control group (p < 0.0001) (Mimiaga et al., 2019). These preliminary findings are encouraging, and they suggest that similar behavioral HIV-prevention interventions for MSWs could be adapted and implemented more globally.

Another promising approach tested in the Philippines was a brief community mobilization program that included HIV and STI education, interactive training on proper condom use, instructions on seeking out community resources, and both individual and group goal-setting exercises (Urada et al., 2016). This project was uniquely grounded in a human rights framework, with a focus on mediating risks relevant to sex workers (i.e., rape, violence) and raising sex workers' awareness and understanding of the laws protecting them against abuse and discrimination. Among 87 sex workers (27 men and 60 women), pre-post test scores revealed significant increases in scores across all domains assessed (each rated out of 10): HIV knowledge (pre-test score 3, post-test score 7), STI knowledge (2 pre, 5 post), human rights knowledge (3 pre, 6 post), intentions to use condoms consistently with causal partners (4 pre, 10 post), and intentions to get tested for HIV (6 pre, 8 post) (Urada et al., 2016).

Contingency management, another behavioral-change model, provides monetary incentives for achieving a targeted health behavior and has been shown to be an acceptable and feasible means of supporting HIV-risk reduction among MSWs (Galárraga et al., 2014; Landovitz et al., 2015; Mitchell et al., 2018). For example, MSWs in Mexico City were given economic incentives for having negative (uninfected) test results for HIV and other STIs at periodic clinical visits. This study demonstrated lower rates of HIV and STI diagnoses among MSWs assigned to the intervention group compared with those in the control group, suggesting that financial compensation may be effective in promoting harm-reduction behaviors among MSWs (Galárraga, Fletcher, Shoptaw, & Reback, 2014).

Recent research has revealed that MSWs also engage in adaptive behavioral strategies to decrease their vulnerability to HIV. For example, an analysis of 23 MSWs in Vietnam found that the men experienced both felt and enacted social stigma related to sex work, which increased their susceptibility to HIV and other STIs by way of riskier sexual behaviors, as the literature has indicated. In response to such shame and discrimination, the MSWs employed stigma-management techniques aimed at concealing their involvement in sex work, such as controlling communication with nonpaying sexual partners and seeking increased social support from family and friends (Closson et al., 2015). Other risk-reduction strategies used by MSWs in this sample included engaging in oral or manual sex instead of anal sex, selecting male clients whom they perceived to be lower-risk clients, and reducing their overall number of partners by choosing to work with repeat transactional sex clients (Mimiaga et al., 2013).

Treatment as prevention

Biomedical approaches that use antiretroviral drugs to treat HIV have been groundbreaking in addressing the HIV epidemic. The PARTNER study, which examined HIV-positive partners taking ART in couples where the other partner is HIV negative, has concluded. Final results subsequently confirmed that individuals living with HIV who are on effective ART, adhere to their medication regimen, and have an undetectable level of HIV in their blood are unable to transmit the virus to others (Rodger, Cambiano, Bruun, Vernazza, Collins, Degen et al., 2019; Rodger, Cambiano, Bruun, Vernazza, Collins, Van Lunzen et al., 2016). This method, known as treatment as prevention (TasP), serves as both primary and secondary prevention for HIV-acquired individuals and their sexual partners (Hollingdrake et al., 2019; Rodger et al., 2016; Saag et al., 2018; WHO, 2012). As previously established, access and adherence to ART are vital to the success of TasP, yet they remain suboptimal among disenfranchised populations, including MSWs.

To facilitate linkage to care and treatment uptake, certain initiatives have been promoted, including "test and treat," in which individuals who test positive for HIV immediately receive ART, regardless of their CD4 cell count or viral load. Early treatment, on a biological level, promotes viral suppression while simultaneously improving retention in HIV-related care at a structural level (Mugavero et al., 2012). In 2009, investigators in South Africa used mathematical modeling and estimated that combining test-and-treat strategies with other prevention methods would reduce the worldwide prevalence of HIV to 1 percent by 2059 (Granich et al., 2009). Though the test and treat model may ultimately reduce HIV transmission and improve HIV-related outcomes, it does not address the roots of stigma, discrimination, and other structural barriers that prevent MSWs from seeking out health care services in the first place, which is why it must be supplemented with concurrent behavioral and structural interventions to meet the needs of MSWs and other marginalized populations.

PrEP/PEP

In addition to biobehavioral approaches employing antiretroviral drugs for treatment, preexposure prophylaxis (PrEP) and postexposure prophylaxis (PEP) have also proven to be effective in stemming HIV transmission among high-risk groups (Fonner et al., 2016; Grant et al., 2010). Since the approval of PrEP by the FDA in 2012, narrowly focused health communications and marketing strategies have primarily targeted gay and bisexual cisgender men, leading to deficient awareness of PrEP among MSM who do not identify as gay or bisexual (i.e., many MSWs) and other at-risk groups, including transgender women. Thus, despite the fact that both medication regimens are highly efficacious (>90 percent reduction in risk), knowledge and uptake of PrEP and PEP remain low. Findings from a study across 20 major U.S. cities found that out of 585 MSM who reported exchanging sex for money or drugs, only 20.5 percent had ever heard of PrEP (Nerlander et al., 2017). Furthermore, this statistic has been globally consistent: 21.7 percent of MSWs sampled in Kenya were familiar with PrEP, and none had ever taken it (Restar et al., 2017). Similarly, among 31 MSWs in Providence, Rhode Island, only 19.4 percent had ever heard of PrEP (Underhill et al., 2015).

Despite minimal awareness of PrEP among MSWs, research reveals that, upon learning of its efficacy, these men are generally interested in and willing to use PrEP for HIV prevention. For example, during individual interviews, Underhill and colleagues found that among 31 MSWs in Providence, 20 (64.5 percent) were interested in taking PrEP, compared with 12 (48 percent) of 25 MSM who did not engage in sex work (Underhill et al., 2015). In a study in Vietnam, nearly all (95.4 percent) of the 281 MSW participants indicated they would be willing to take PrEP, although the percentage dropped substantially when participants were asked whether they would take PrEP given potential side effects (Oldenburg, Biello, Colby, Closson, Nguyen et al., 2014). Out of 12 MSWs in Puerto Rico in 2016 who had heard of PrEP, 9 expressed high levels of interest in taking the medication (Giguere et al., 2016). The year prior, among 40 people in Canada who inject drugs and engaged in transactional sex, 70 percent also reported that they would consider taking PrEP in the future (Escudero et al., 2015). The most common reasons stated by MSWs for a lower interest in and nonuptake of PrEP are concerns about side effects, a lower perceived risk for HIV, lower socioeconomic status (income, education, employment), less engagement with health services, lack of health insurance, and not identifying as gay or bisexual (Biello, Oldenburg et al., 2017; Giguere et al., 2016; Oldenburg, Biello, Colby, Closson, Nguyen et al., 2014; Underhill, Guthrie et al., 2018; Underhill, Morrow et al., 2015). However, among 300 MSWs in Vietnam, those who had previous contact with a peer educator were approximately twice as likely to be interested in taking PrEP than those who did not have contact with a peer educator (OR = 2.01, 95 percent CI =1.22 to 3.31). These results suggest that peer education may play a key role in informing MSWs about PrEP and promoting other risk-reduction practices (Oldenburg, Biello, Colby, Closson, Nguyen et al., 2014).

In modeling the potential impact of PrEP, a team in Peru estimated that by providing PrEP to 20 percent of MSWs in the capital city of Lima, approximately 3.4 percent of HIV infections within that population could be avoided over the course of ten years (Gomez et al., 2012). Given the low use of condoms and elevated number of sex partners among MSWs, increasing the acceptability of PrEP and PEP among this population would be a transformative addition to current risk-reduction practices. To the best of our knowledge, only one behavioral intervention has been developed and tested specifically to increase PrEP uptake among MSWs, in Providence, Rhode Island, where approximately 80 MSWs were randomized to receive either (1) a strength-based case management intervention implemented by nonclinical staff (including motivational interviewing, appointment and transportation assistance, and problem solving), or (2) SOC referrals to the local PrEP clinic. Participants randomized to the case-management arm were 2.6 times as likely to initiate PrEP within two months of baseline compared to those in the SOC arm (57 percent versus 22 percent, p = .002; relative risk = 2.64, 95 percent CI = 1.34 to 5.20) (Biello et al., 2019). Overall satisfaction with the intervention was also very high. Thus, promotion and facilitation of PrEP among MSWs remains an important element of future HIV risk-reduction studies.

HIV self-testing

Recognizing the lack of access to and engagement in HIV testing and counseling, public health officials have strived to establish innovative strategies that promote the availability and accessibility of preventative sexual health resources. One method that has been adopted in many countries is HIV self-testing (HIVST), wherein individuals collect their own biological specimen (oral fluid or blood) and perform a rapid HIV test on the sample themselves (Napierala Mavedzenge, Baggaley, & Corbett, 2013). This high-impact, low-cost option may allow MSWs to overcome substantial barriers to HIV testing, such as concerns about confidentiality and stigma. A growing number of studies conducted with MSM and FSWs have found that HIVST is highly acceptable, but there are concerns about user error, lack of professional counseling, and poor test accuracy (Lippman et al., 2018; Marley et al., 2014; Ortblad et al., 2018; Witzel, Rodger, Burns, Rhodes, & Weatherburn, 2016). Additionally, very few projects have explored the opinions and feasibility of HIVST among MSWs. In a small sample of cisgender male and transgender female sex workers in Puerto Rico, 91.6 percent said they would "likely" or "definitely" use rapid HIVST (Giguere et al., 2016). Some participants believed that HIVST offered an opportunity for sex workers to self-test with their clients; however, others feared such discussions would complicate exchanges with clients or even trigger violence toward sex workers (Giguere et al., 2016). Still, HIVST has the potential to reach MSWs who are reluctant to be tested for HIV and who would otherwise not seek out or have access to HIV testing services. Because empirical evidence is still limited, effective HIV self-testing programs for MSWs must continue to comprehensively monitor for quality assurance (i.e., adequate training and proper use), laboratory confirmation of test results, and rapid linkage to the counseling and care that are necessary for individuals testing, both positive (HIV-acquired) and negative (HIV-uninfected) (Napierala Mavedzenge et al., 2013).

Community-based programs

In response to structural challenges when seeking or navigating health care services where sex work is criminalized, many MSWs have collaborated with local stakeholders on peer-driven, community-based efforts to address health disparities. For example, the Sex Workers' Rights Advocacy Network (SWAN) is a group in Central and Eastern Europe and Central Asia that advocates for the human rights of male, female, and transgender sex workers and is led by sex workers who sit on the network's steering committee and advisory board (www.swan net.org). In Myanmar, the Targeted Outreach Project (TOP) began in 2004 and has been implemented in 18 cities across the country, reaching more than 62,000 sex workers annually (Ditmore, 2012). TOP establishes drop-in centers where sex workers can go for peer support and access to free health care, without the stigma they often experience. Local sex workers in each city (known as "community educators") lead their respective sites by offering empowerment, advocacy, and emotional support for their communities (Ditmore, 2012). Project Weber/ RENEW is a peer-led nonprofit organization for male, female, and transgender sex workers in Rhode Island. Weber/RENEW provides sexual health resources (HIV and STI testing, safer sex materials), harm reduction (clean needle exchange, overdose prevention programs), and substance-abuse recovery support for its members (www.weberrenew.org). A recent review of 22 global "community empowerment–based" programs led by sex workers in India, Brazil, and the Dominican Republic were found to be significantly associated with national reductions in HIV and STI diagnoses as well as increases in consistent condom use with clients. Of significant importance to these findings is that the effectiveness of many of the programs was moderated by structural barriers, including funding constraints, criminalization of sex work, and pervasive stigma, discrimination, and violence toward sex workers (Kerrigan et al., 2015). Thus, high levels of social, financial, and political support are needed to implement such community-based programs in a comprehensive way.

Cost considerations and access to prevention and treatment

With the emergence of improved treatment options, HIV/AIDS is now viewed as a manageable chronic condition in most developed countries. Yet the condition requires long-term and costly medical management, support services, and prescription drugs. Data from the United States reveal that the lifetime medical cost for an individual living with HIV in 2017 was, on average, $379,668 (CDC, 2017). Conversely, an analysis by Schackman et al. (2015) found that the average lifetime cost for high-risk individuals who remain uninfected was approximately $96,700 per person, corresponding to a savings of approximately $280,000 per person for each infection averted. Preventative biomedical drugs such as PrEP cost more than $2,000 per month out of pocket in the United States (Adamson, Carlson, Kublin, & Garrison, 2017). Without health care coverage, many MSWs may not be able to afford these drugs. The costs of other medications, food, and housing must also be considered. Taken as a whole, these high costs represent substantial financial barriers to accessing services for both HIV-infected and uninfected MSWs.

Financial limitations vary by country, state, and type of health care system. For example, in Norway, which has a government-funded national health care system, costs for HIV care and prevention services are covered, leaving citizens with little to no out-of-pocket costs (PEI, 2017). In Canada, there is a great deal of interjurisdictional heterogeneity of drug costs, which are primarily dependent on one's geographical location (Gogolishvili, 2019; Yoong, Bayoumi, Robinson, Rachlis, & Antoniou, 2018). For example, while the governments of Alberta, British Columbia, Northwest Territories, Nunavut, and Prince Edward Island offer universal coverage of ART for all residents living with HIV, other provinces, such as Quebec, collect a yearly income-based premium for the same medications (Yoong et al., 2018). In Australia, there are similar inconsistencies across both inter- and intrajurisdictions. For example, the Northern Territory and Western Australia provide free HIV and sexual health services, such as ART (Wilkinson et al., 2015). Within jurisdictions, one study found that copays for ART were free of charge at a major sexual health clinic in Victoria but cost money in more rural parts of Victoria (Wilkinson et al., 2015). In the United States, access to treatment and prevention varies by state and type of insurance. For example, low-income MSWs who lack private health insurance and meet certain eligibility criteria may qualify for Medicaid, the federal- and state-funded health insurance program. Compared with the rest of the country, U.S. states in the South have been more restrictive in their coverage of services and their eligibility criteria, requiring that people with HIV must also meet a disability requirement to qualify for such programs (Adimora, Ramirez, Schoenbach, & Cohen, 2014). Even for those who do qualify, benefits and coverage in southern states are generally substandard compared with other parts of the country (Kates, 2011). Limited insurance policies and coverage of sexual health services are directly linked to elevated rates of HIV and STIs; in the United States, the South accounts for more than half (52 percent) of new diagnoses nationwide, and the region has the highest rates of chlamydia, gonorrhea, and syphilis (CDC, 2018; Workowski & Berman, 2011). And regardless of the state or the insurance plan, insurance deductibles and copays in the United States remain significant barriers to accessing prevention options and treatment compliance (Eaddy, Cook, O'Day, Burch, & Cantrell, 2012; Underhill et al., 2014; Wohl et al., 2017; Yehia et al., 2015).

Gaps in the literature and future directions

As we have made clear, MSWs remain largely overlooked by public health efforts in the context of the global response to HIV/AIDS and STIs. Most of the emerging data from systematic surveillance of HIV/AIDS and STIs is limited to nonprobability samples, but these studies overall reveal that MSWs continue to experience unique biological, behavioral, and structural challenges that increase their risk for poor sexual health outcomes. Given the inherent heterogeneity of this population, health and governmental officials must seek to generate and implement innovative HIV and STI treatment and prevention approaches for MSWs. As highlighted throughout this chapter, a multilevel methodology is necessary to optimize the effectiveness of such programs. Future studies should aim to develop and test novel behavioral interventions tailored to the specific needs of MSWs. Moreover, such interventions should be integrated with biomedical approaches that address the complex psychosocial factors and risk-taking behaviors of MSWs. To comprehensively address the sexual health disparities among MSWs, it is essential to concentrate on key structural factors, including the decriminalization of sex work, the reduction of sex work–related stigma and discrimination, and increasing access to services such as mental health, sexual health, and substance abuse treatment. Local and federal agencies would benefit from including MSWs in strategic planning and developmental efforts aimed at improving access to and participation in HIV treatment and prevention. Ultimately, committed advocacy, funding, surveillance, programmatic efforts, and research are central not only to public health but also as a foundation for social justice and human rights.

References

Abel, G. M., Fitzgerald, L. J., & Brunton, C. (2009). The impact of decriminalisation on the number of sex workers in New Zealand. *Journal of Social Policy, 38*(3), 515–531.

Adamson, B., Carlson, J., Kublin, J., & Garrison, L. (2017). The potential cost-effectiveness of pre-exposure prophylaxis combined with HIV vaccines in the United States. *Vaccines, 5*(2), 13.

Adimora, A. A., Ramirez, C., Schoenbach, V. J., & Cohen, M. S. (2014). Policies and politics that promote HIV infection in the Southern United States. *AIDS (London, England), 28*(10), 1393.

Aunon, F. M., Wagner, G. J., Maher, R., Khouri, D., Kaplan, R. L., & Mokhbat, J. (2015). An exploratory study of HIV risk behaviors and testing among male sex workers in Beirut, Lebanon. *Social Work in Public Health, 30*(4), 373–384.

Bacon, O., Lum, P., Hahn, J., Evans, J., Davidson, P., et al. (2006). Commercial sex work and risk of HIV infection among young drug-injecting men who have sex with men in San Francisco. *Sexually Transmitted Diseases, 33*, 228–234. doi:10.1097/01.olq.0000204914.91923

Baggaley, R. F., White, R. G., & Boily, M.-C. (2010). HIV transmission risk through anal intercourse: Systematic review, meta-analysis and implications for HIV prevention. *International Journal of Epidemiology, 39*(4), 1048–1063.

Baker, P., Dworkin, S. L., Tong, S., Banks, I., Shand, T., & Yamey, G. (2014). The men's health gap: Men must be included in the global health equity agenda. *Bulletin of the World Health Organization, 92*(8), 618.

Ballester-Arnal, R., Gil-Llario, M. D., Salmeron-Sánchez, P., & Giménez-García, C. (2014). HIV prevention interventions for young male commercial sex workers. *Current HIV/AIDS Reports, 11*(1), 72–80.

Baral, S. D., Friedman, M. R., Geibel, S., Rebe, K., Bozhinov, B., Diouf, D., et al. (2015). Male sex workers: Practices, contexts, and vulnerabilities for HIV acquisition and transmission. *The Lancet, 385*(9964), 260–273.

Baral, S. D., Logie, C. H., Grosso, A., Wirtz, A. L., & Beyrer, C. (2013). Modified social ecological model: A tool to guide the assessment of the risks and risk contexts of HIV epidemics. *BMC Public Health, 13*(1), 482.

Barmania, S., & Aljunid, S. M. (2016). Navigating HIV prevention policy and Islam in Malaysia: Contention, compatibility or reconciliation? Findings from in-depth interviews among key stakeholders. *BMC Public Health*, *16*(1), 524.

Bayer, A. M., Díaz, C. M., Chiappe, M., Baker, A. N., Egoavil, M. S., Pérez-Lu, J. E., et al. (2017). The odyssey of linking to and staying in HIV care among male sex workers in Peru. *Journal of HIV and AIDS*, *3*(1).

Bekker, L.-G., Alleyne, G., Baral, S., Cepeda, J., Daskalakis, D., Dowdy, D., et al. (2018). Advancing global health and strengthening the HIV response in the era of the sustainable development goals: The international AIDS society—Lancet commission. *The Lancet*, *392*(10144), 312–358.

Belza, M. J. (2005). Risk of HIV infection among male sex workers in Spain. *Sexually Transmitted Infections*, *81*(1), 85–88.

Bertakis, K. D., Azari, R., Helms, L. J., Callahan, E. J., & Robbins, J. A. (2000). Gender differences in the utilization of health care services. *Journal of Family Practice*, *49*(2), 147–152.

Beyrer, C., Baral, S. D., Van Griensven, F., Goodreau, S. M., Chariyalertsak, S., Wirtz, A. L., et al. (2012). Global epidemiology of HIV infection in men who have sex with men. *The Lancet*, *380*(9839), 367–377.

Beyrer, C., Crago, A.-L., Bekker, L.-G., Butler, J., Shannon, K., Kerrigan, D., et al. (2015). An action agenda for HIV and sex workers. *The Lancet*, *385*(9964), 287–301.

Biello, K. B., Chan, P., Olson, J., Maynard, M., Holcomb, R., Salhaney, P., et al. (2019). *PrEPare for work: An intervention to increase PrEP uptake among male sex workers*. Paper presented at the International AIDS Conference, Amsterdam.

Biello, K. B., Oldenburg, C. E., Mitty, J. A., Closson, E. F., Mayer, K. H., Safren, S. A., et al. (2017). The "safe sex" conundrum: Anticipated stigma from sexual partners as a barrier to PrEP use among substance-using MSM engaging in transactional sex. *AIDS and Behavior*, *21*(1), 300–306.

Biello, K. B., Thomas, B. E., Johnson, B. E., Closson, E. F., Navakodi, P., Dhanalakshmi, A., et al. (2017). Transactional sex and the challenges to safer sexual behaviors: A study among male sex workers in Chennai, India. *AIDS Care*, *29*(2), 231–238.

Boynton, P., & Cusick, L. (2006). Sex workers to pay the price. *BMJ*, *332*(7535), 190.

Brookfield, S., Dean, J., Forrest, C., Jones, J., & Fitzgerald, L. (2019). Barriers to accessing sexual health services for transgender and male sex workers: A systematic qualitative meta-summary. *AIDS and Behavior*. doi:10.1007/s10461-019-02453-4

Burnette, M. L., Lucas, E., Ilgen, M., Frayne, S. M., Mayo, J., & Weitlauf, J. C. (2008). Prevalence and health correlates of prostitution among patients entering treatment for substance use disorders. *Archives of General Psychiatry*, *65*(3), 337–344.

Callander, D. (2017). Sexually transmissible infections and male sex work (blog). Me, Us and Male Escorting, Queensland University of Technology (QUT). Retrieved from https://research.qut.edu.au/aboutmaleescorting/2017/09/15/sexually-transmissible-infections-and-male-sex-work/

Callander, D., Read, P., Minichiello, V., Hamilton, R., Chow, E., Ali, H., et al. (2015). P14.25 HIV and STIs among male sex workers attending Australian sexual health clinics. *Sexually Transmitted Infections*, *91*(Suppl. 2), A207–A208. doi:10.1136/sextrans-2015-052270.537

CDC (Centers for Disease Control and Prevention). (2017). *HIV cost-effectiveness*. Retrieved from www.cdc.gov/hiv/programresources/guidance/costeffectiveness/index.html

CDC (Centers for Disease Control and Prevention). (2018). *HIV in the United States by region*. Retrieved from www.cdc.gov/hiv/statistics/overview/geographicdistribution.html

Clatts, M. C., Goldsamt, L. A., Yu, G., & Colby, D. (2016). Sexually transmissible infection and HIV prevention and treatment for young male sex workers in Vietnam: Findings from the SHEATH intervention. *Sexual Health*, *13*(6), 575–581.

Closson, E. F., Colby, D. J., Nguyen, T., Cohen, S. S., Biello, K., & Mimiaga, M. J. (2015). The balancing act: Exploring stigma, economic need and disclosure among male sex workers in Ho Chi Minh City, Vietnam. *Global Public Health*, *10*(4), 520–531.

Cortez, F. C. P., Boer, D. P., & Baltieri, D. A. (2011). A psychosocial study of male-to-female transgendered and male hustler sex workers in São Paulo, Brazil. *Archives of Sexual Behavior*, *40*(6), 1223–1231.

Crowell, T. A., Keshinro, B., Baral, S. D., Schwartz, S. R., Stahlman, S., Nowak, R. G., et al. (2017). Stigma, access to healthcare, and HIV risks among men who sell sex to men in Nigeria. *Journal of the International AIDS Society, 20*(1), 21489.

Ditmore, M. (2012). *Targeted Outreach Project (TOP): Scaling up HIV programming in Burma by mobilizing sex workers.* Case Study Series. AIDSTAR-One (USAID's AIDS Support and Technical Assistance Resources, Task Order One). Retrieved from https://aidsfree.usaid.gov/sites/default/files/tops_sw_burma.pdf

Eaddy, M. T., Cook, C. L., O'Day, K., Burch, S. P., & Cantrell, C. R. (2012). How patient cost-sharing trends affect adherence and outcomes: A literature review. *Pharmacy and Therapeutics, 37*(1), 45.

Elwood, W., Williams, M., Bell, D., & Richard, A. (1997). Powerlessness and HIV prevention among people who trade sex for drugs ("strawberries"). *AIDS Care, 9*(3), 273–284.

Escudero, D. J., Kerr, T., Wood, E., Nguyen, P., Lurie, M. N., Sued, O., et al. (2015). Acceptability of HIV pre-exposure prophylaxis (PrEP) among people who inject drugs (PWID) in a Canadian setting. *AIDS and Behavior, 19*(5), 752–757.

Estcourt, C. S., Marks, C., Rohrsheim, R., Johnson, A. M., Donovan, B., & Mindel, A. (2000). HIV, sexually transmitted infections, and risk behaviours in male commercial sex workers in Sydney. *Sexually Transmitted Infections, 76*(4), 294–298.

Fonner, V. A., Dalglish, S. L., Kennedy, C. E., Baggaley, R., O'Reilly, K. R., Koechlin, F. M., et al. (2016). Effectiveness and safety of oral HIV preexposure prophylaxis for all populations. *AIDS (London, England), 30*(12), 1973.

Fournet, N., Koedijk, F., van Leeuwen, A., van Rooijen, M., van der Sande, M., & van Veen, M. (2015). Young male sex workers are at high risk for sexually transmitted infections: A cross-sectional study from Dutch STI clinics, the Netherlands, 2006–2012. *BMC Infectious Diseases, 16*(1), 63.

Friedman, M., Guadamuz, T., & Marshal, M. (2011, August 14–17). *Male youth engaged in sex work: Health disparities and outcomes in early adulthood.* Paper presented at the National HIV Prevention Conference, Atlanta.

Galárraga, O., Sosa-Rubí, S. G., González, A., Badial-Hernández, F., Conde-Glez, C. J., Juárez-Figueroa, L., et al. (2014). The disproportionate burden of HIV and STIs among male sex workers in Mexico City and the rationale for economic incentives to reduce risks. *Journal of the International AIDS Society, 17*(1), 19218.

Gardner, E. M., McLees, M. P., Steiner, J. F., del Rio, C., & Burman, W. J. (2011). The spectrum of engagement in HIV care and its relevance to test-and-treat strategies for prevention of HIV infection. *Clinical Infectious Diseases, 52*(6), 793–800.

Geibel, S., King'ola, N., Temmerman, M., & Luchters, S. (2012). The impact of peer outreach on HIV knowledge and prevention behaviours of male sex workers in Mombasa, Kenya. *Sexually Transmitted Infections, 88*(5), 357–362.

Giguere, R., Frasca, T., Dolezal, C., Febo, I., Cranston, R. D., Mayer, K., et al. (2016). Acceptability of three novel HIV prevention methods among young male and transgender female sex workers in Puerto Rico. *AIDS and Behavior, 20*(10), 2192–2202.

Gogolishvili, D. (2019). Out-of-pocket costs associated with HIV in publicly funded high-income health care settings. Rapid Response Service no. 137, Ontario HIV Treatment Network, Toronto. Retrieved from www.ohtn.on.ca/wp-content/uploads/2019/05/RR137_out-of-pocket-costs-associated-with-HIV.pdf

Gomez, G. B., Borquez, A., Caceres, C. F., Segura, E. R., Grant, R. M., Garnett, G. P., et al. (2012). The potential impact of pre-exposure prophylaxis for HIV prevention among men who have sex with men and transwomen in Lima, Peru: A mathematical modelling study. *PLoS Medicine, 9*(10), e1001323.

Granich, R. M., Gilks, C. F., Dye, C., De Cock, K. M., & Williams, B. G. (2009). Universal voluntary HIV testing with immediate antiretroviral therapy as a strategy for elimination of HIV transmission: A mathematical model. *The Lancet, 373*(9657), 48–57.

Grant, R. M., Lama, J. R., Anderson, P. L., McMahan, V., Liu, A. Y., Vargas, L., et al. (2010). Preexposure chemoprophylaxis for HIV prevention in men who have sex with men. *New England Journal of Medicine, 363*(27), 2587–2599.

Hollingdrake, O., Lui, C.-W., Mutch, A., Dean, J., Howard, C., & Fitzgerald, L. (2019). Factors affecting the decision to initiate antiretroviral therapy in the era of treatment-as-prevention: Synthesis of evidence from qualitative research in high-income settings. *AIDS Care, 31*(4), 397–402.

Jones, J., Dean, J., Brookfield, S., Forrest, C., & Fitzgerald, L. (2018). *TaMS: Factors influencing transgender and male sex worker access to sexual health care, HIV testing and support study (TaMS) report*. Respect Inc., Brisbane, Queensland, Australia. Retrieved from https://respectqld.org.au/tams-report-2018/

Kates, J. (2011). *Medicaid and HIV: A national analysis*. Menlo Park, CA: Kaiser Family Foundation.

Kerrigan, D., Kennedy, C. E., Morgan-Thomas, R., Reza-Paul, S., Mwangi, P., Win, K. T., et al. (2015). A community empowerment approach to the HIV response among sex workers: Effectiveness, challenges, and considerations for implementation and scale-up. *The Lancet, 385*(9963), 172–185.

Kerrigan, D., Moreno, L., Rosario, S., Gomez, B., Jerez, H., Barrington, C., et al. (2006). Environmental-structural interventions to reduce HIV/STI risk among female sex workers in the Dominican Republic. *American Journal of Public Health, 96*(1), 120–125.

King, E. J., Maman, S., Bowling, J. M., Moracco, K. E., & Dudina, V. (2013). The influence of stigma and discrimination on female sex workers' access to HIV services in St. Petersburg, Russia. *AIDS and Behavior, 17*(8), 2597–2603.

Krüsi, A., Pacey, K., Bird, L., Taylor, C., Chettiar, J., Allan, S., et al. (2014). Criminalisation of clients: Reproducing vulnerabilities for violence and poor health among street-based sex workers in Canada— A qualitative study. *BMJ Open, 4*(6), e005191.

Landovitz, R. J., Fletcher, J. B., Shoptaw, S., & Reback, C. J. (2015). Contingency management facilitates the use of postexposure prophylaxis among stimulant-using men who have sex with men. *Open Forum Infectious Diseases, 2*(1), ofu114. doi:10.1093/ofid/ofu114

Lazarus, L., Deering, K. N., Nabess, R., Gibson, K., Tyndall, M. W., & Shannon, K. (2012). Occupational stigma as a primary barrier to health care for street-based sex workers in Canada. *Culture, Health & Sexuality, 14*(2), 139–150.

Lippman, S. A., Lane, T., Rabede, O., Gilmore, H., Chen, Y.-H., Mlotshwa, N., et al. (2018). High acceptability and increased HIV-testing frequency after introduction of HIV self-testing and network distribution among South African MSM. *Journal of Acquired Immune Deficiency Syndromes (1999), 77*(3), 279–287.

Liu, S., Zhao, J., Rou, K., Chen, L., Cai, W., Li, L., et al. (2012). A survey of condom use behaviors and HIV/STI prevalence among venue-based money boys in Shenzhen, China. *AIDS and Behavior, 16*(4), 835–846.

Lundgren, J. D., Babiker, A. G., Gordin, F., Emery, S., Grund, B., Sharma, S., et al. (2015). Initiation of antiretroviral therapy in early asymptomatic HIV infection. *New England Journal of Medicine, 373*(9), 795–807.

Marley, G., Kang, D., Wilson, E. C., Huang, T., Qian, Y., Li, X., et al. (2014). Introducing rapid oral-fluid HIV testing among high risk populations in Shandong, China: Feasibility and challenges. *BMC Public Health, 14*(1), 422.

Marshall, B. D., Shannon, K., Kerr, T., Zhang, R., & Wood, E. (2010). Survival sex work and increased HIV risk among sexual minority street-involved youth. *Journal of Acquired Immune Deficiency Syndromes (1999), 53*(5), 661.

McCamish, M., Storer, G., & Carl, G. (2000). Refocusing HIV/AIDS interventions in Thailand: The case for male sex workers and other homosexually active men. *Culture, Health & Sexuality, 2*(2), 167–182.

Miller, R. L., Klotz, D., & Eckholdt, H. M. (1998). HIV prevention with male prostitutes and patrons of hustler bars: Replication of an HIV preventive intervention. *American Journal of Community Psychology, 26*(1), 97–131.

Mimiaga, M. J., Bogart, L. M., Thurston, I. B., Santostefano, C. M., Closson, E. F., Skeer, M. R., . . . Safren, S. A. (2019a). Positive strategies to enhance problem-solving skills (STEPS): A pilot randomized, controlled trial of a multicomponent, technology-enhanced, customizable antiretroviral adherence intervention for HIV-infected adolescents and young adults. *AIDS Patient Care and STDS, 33*, 21–24. https://doi.org/10.1089/apc.2018.0138

Mimiaga, M. J., O'Cleirigh, C., Biello, K. B., Robertson, A. M., Safren, S. A., Coates, T. J., et al. (2015). The effect of psychosocial syndemic production on 4-year HIV incidence and risk behavior in a large cohort of sexually active men who have sex with men. *Journal of Acquired Immune Deficiency Syndromes (1999), 68*(3), 329.

Mimiaga, M. J., Reisner, S. L., Closson, E. F., Perry, N., Perkovich, B., Nguyen, T., et al. (2013). Self-perceived HIV risk and the use of risk reduction strategies among men who engage in transactional sex with other men in Ho Chi Minh City, Vietnam. *AIDS Care, 25*(8), 1039–1044.

Mimiaga, M. J., Reisner, S. L., Tinsley, J., Mayer, K., & Safren, S. (2009). Street workers and Internet escorts: Contextual and psychosocial factors surrounding HIV risk behavior among men who engage in sex work with other men. *Journal of Urban Health, 86*(1), 54–66.

Minichiello, V., Marino, R., Browne, J., Jamieson, M., Peterson, K., Reuter, B., et al. (2000). Commercial sex between men: A prospective diary-based study. *Journal of Sex Research, 37*(2), 151–160.

Mitchell, J. T., LeGrand, S., Hightow-Weidman, L. B., McKellar, M. S., Kashuba, A. D., Cottrell, M., et al. (2018). Smartphone-based contingency management intervention to improve pre-exposure prophylaxis adherence: Pilot trial. *JMIR mHealth and uHealth, 6*(9). doi:10.2196/10456

Morse, E. V., Simon, P. M., Baus, S. A., Balson, P. M., & Osofsky, H. J. (1992). Cofactors of substance use among male street prostitutes. *Journal of Drug Issues, 22*(4), 977–994.

Mountain, E., Mishra, S., Vickerman, P., Pickles, M., Gilks, C., & Boily, M.-C. (2014). Antiretroviral therapy uptake, attrition, adherence and outcomes among HIV-infected female sex workers: A systematic review and meta-analysis. *PLoS ONE, 9*(9), e105645.

Mugavero, M. J., Amico, K. R., Horn, T., & Thompson, M. A. (2013). The state of engagement in HIV care in the United States: From cascade to continuum to control. *Clinical Infectious Diseases, 57*(8), 1164–1171.

Mugavero, M. J., Amico, K. R., Westfall, A. O., Crane, H. M., Zinski, A., Willig, J. H., et al. (2012). Early retention in HIV care and viral load suppression: Implications for a test and treat approach to HIV prevention. *Journal of Acquired Immune Deficiency Syndromes (1999), 59*(1), 86.

Mustanski, B., Garofalo, R., Herrick, A., & Donenberg, G. (2007). Psychosocial health problems increase risk for HIV among urban young men who have sex with men: Preliminary evidence of a syndemic in need of attention. *Annals of Behavioral Medicine, 34*(1), 37–45.

Napierala Mavedzenge, S., Baggaley, R., & Corbett, E. L. (2013). A review of self-testing for HIV: Research and policy priorities in a new era of HIV prevention. *Clinical Infectious Diseases, 57*(1), 126–138.

Nerlander, L. M., Hess, K. L., Rose, C. E., Sionean, C., Thorson, A., Broz, D., et al. (2017). Exchange sex and HIV infection among women who inject drugs: 20 US cities, 2009. *Journal of Acquired Immune Deficiency Syndromes (1999), 75*(Suppl. 3), S333.

Nguyen, T. A., Nguyen, H. T., Le, G. T., & Detels, R. (2008). Prevalence and risk factors associated with HIV infection among men having sex with men in Ho Chi Minh City, Vietnam. *AIDS and Behavior, 12*(3), 476–482.

Okal, J., Luchters, S., Geibel, S., Chersich, M. F., Lango, D., & Temmerman, M. (2009). Social context, sexual risk perceptions and stigma: HIV vulnerability among male sex workers in Mombasa, Kenya. *Culture, Health & Sexuality, 11*(8), 811–826.

Okanlawon, K., Adebowale, A. S., & Titilayo, A. (2013). Sexual hazards, life experiences and social circumstances among male sex workers in Nigeria. *Culture, Health & Sexuality, 15*, 22–33.

Oldenburg, C. E., Biello, K. B., Colby, D., Closson, E. F., Mai, T., Nguyen, T., et al. (2014). Stigma related to sex work among men who engage in transactional sex with men in Ho Chi Minh City, Vietnam. *International Journal of Public Health, 59*(5), 833–840.

Oldenburg, C. E., Biello, K. B., Colby, D., Closson, E. F., Nguyen, T., Trang, N. N., et al. (2014). Engagement with peer health educators is associated with willingness to use pre-exposure prophylaxis among male sex workers in Ho Chi Minh City, Vietnam. *AIDS Patient Care and STDs, 28*(3), 109–112.

Oldenburg, C. E., Perez-Brumer, A. G., Reisner, S. L., Mattie, J., Bärnighausen, T., Mayer, K. M., et al. (2014). Global burden of HIV among men who engage in transactional sex: A systematic review and meta-analysis. *PLoS ONE, 9*(7), e103549. doi:10.1371/journal.pone.0103549

Oldenburg, C. E., Perez-Brumer, A. G., Reisner, S. L., & Mimiaga, M. J. (2015). Transactional sex and the HIV epidemic among men who have sex with men (MSM): Results from a systematic review and meta-analysis. *AIDS and Behaviour* (12), 2177–2183. PMID: 25652233.

Ortblad, K. F., Chanda, M. M., Musoke, D. K., Ngabirano, T., Mwale, M., Nakitende, A., et al. (2018). Acceptability of HIV self-testing to support pre-exposure prophylaxis among female sex workers in Uganda and Zambia: Results from two randomized controlled trials. *BMC Infectious Diseases, 18*(1), 503.

Panchanadeswaran, S., Johnson, S. C., Sivaram, S., Srikrishnan, A. K., Latkin, C., Bentley, M. E., et al. (2008). Intimate partner violence is as important as client violence in increasing street-based female sex workers' vulnerability to HIV in India. *International Journal of Drug Policy, 19*(2), 106–112.

Parsons, J. T., Koken, J. A., & Bimbi, D. S. (2004). The use of the Internet by gay and bisexual male escorts: Sex workers as sex educators. *AIDS Care, 16*(8), 1021–1035.

Reeves, A., Steele, S., Stuckler, D., McKee, M., Amato-Gauci, A., & Semenza, J. C. (2017). National sex work policy and HIV prevalence among sex workers: An ecological regression analysis of 27 European countries. *The Lancet HIV, 4*(3), e134–e140.

PEI (PrEP in Europe Initiative). (2017). *PrEP Access in Europe.* Retrieved from www.avac.org/sites/default/files/u3/PEI_Report_May2017.pdf

Reisner, S. L., Mimiaga, M. J., Mayer, K. H., Tinsley, J. P., & Safren, S. A. (2008). Tricks of the trade: Sexual health behaviors, the context of HIV risk, and potential prevention intervention strategies for male sex workers. *Journal of LGBT Health Research, 4*(4), 195–209.

Reisner, S. L., Mimiaga, M. J., Skeer, M., Bright, D., Cranston, K., Isenberg, D., et al. (2009). Clinically significant depressive symptoms as a risk factor for HIV infection among black MSM in Massachusetts. *AIDS and Behavior, 13*(4), 798–810.

Restar, A. J., Tocco, J. U., Mantell, J. E., Lafort, Y., Gichangi, P., Masvawure, T. B., et al. (2017). Perspectives on HIV pre- and post-exposure prophylaxes (PrEP and PEP) among female and male sex workers in Mombasa, Kenya: Implications for integrating biomedical prevention into sexual health services. *AIDS Education and Prevention, 29*(2), 141–153.

Rietmeijer, C. A., Wolitski, R. J., Fishbein, M., Corby, N. H., & Cohn, D. L. (1998). Sex hustling, injection drug use, and non-gay identification by men who have sex with men: Associations with high-risk sexual behaviors and condom use. *Sexually Transmitted Diseases, 25*(7), 353–360.

Rodger, A. J., Cambiano, V., Bruun, T., Vernazza, P., Collins, S., Degen, O., et al. (2019). Risk of HIV transmission through condomless sex in serodifferent gay couples with the HIV-positive partner taking suppressive antiretroviral therapy (PARTNER): Final results of a multicentre, prospective, observational study. *Lancet (London, England), 393*(10189), 2428–2438. doi:10.1016/S0140-6736(19)30418-0

Rodger, A. J., Cambiano, V., Bruun, T., Vernazza, P., Collins, S., Van Lunzen, J., et al. (2016). Sexual activity without condoms and risk of HIV transmission in serodifferent couples when the HIV-positive partner is using suppressive antiretroviral therapy. *JAMA, 316*(2), 171–181.

Rodríguez, M. D. M. P., Obasi, A., Mosha, F., Todd, J., Brown, D., Changalucha, J., et al. (2002). Herpes simplex virus type 2 infection increases HIV incidence: A prospective study in rural Tanzania. *AIDS, 16*(3), 451–462.

Saag, M. S., Benson, C. A., Gandhi, R. T., Hoy, J. F., Landovitz, R. J., Mugavero, M. J., et al. (2018). Antiretroviral drugs for treatment and prevention of HIV infection in adults: 2018 recommendations of the international antiviral society—USA Panel. *JAMA, 320*(4), 379–396.

Scambler, G., & Paoli, F. (2008). Health work, female sex workers, and HIV/AIDS: Global and local dimensions of stigma and deviance as barriers to effective interventions. *Social Science & Medicine, 66*(8), 1848–1862.

Schackman, B. R., Fleishman, J. A., Su, A. E., Berkowitz, B. K., Moore, R. D., Walensky, R. P., et al. (2015). The lifetime medical cost savings from preventing HIV in the United States. *Medical Care, 53*(4), 293.

Schaecher, K. L. (2013). The importance of treatment adherence in HIV. *American Journal of Managed Care, 19*(Suppl. 12), s231–s237.

Scorgie, F., Nakato, D., Harper, E., Richter, M., Maseko, S., Nare, P., et al. (2013). "We are despised in the hospitals": Sex workers' experiences of accessing health care in four African countries. *Culture, Health & Sexuality, 15*(4), 450–465.

Segura, M., Bautista, C. T., Marone, R., Sosa Estani, S., Rey, J., Montano, S. M., et al. (2010). HIV/STI co-infections, syphilis incidence, and hepatitis B vaccination: The Buenos Aires cohort of men who have sex with men. *AIDS Care, 22*(12), 1459–1465.

Sethi, G., Holden, B. M., Gaffney, J., Greene, L., Ghani, A., & Ward, H. (2006). HIV, sexually transmitted infections, and risk behaviours in male sex workers in London over a 10-year period. *Sexually Transmitted Infections, 82*(5), 359–363.

Shannon, K., & Csete, J. (2010). Violence, condom negotiation, and HIV/STI risk among sex workers. *JAMA, 304*(5), 573–574.

Shannon, K., & Montaner, J. S. (2012). The politics and policies of HIV prevention in sex work. *The Lancet Infectious Diseases, 12*(7), 500–502.

Shannon, K., Strathdee, S. A., Goldenberg, S. M., Duff, P., Mwangi, P., Rusakova, M., et al. (2015). Global epidemiology of HIV among female sex workers: Influence of structural determinants. *The Lancet, 385*(9962), 55–71.

Shinde, S., Setia, M. S., Row-Kavi, A., Anand, V., & Jerajani, H. (2009). Male sex workers: Are we ignoring a risk group in Mumbai, India? *Indian Journal of Dermatology, Venereology, and Leprology, 75*(1), 41.

Smith, M. D., & Seal, D. W. (2008). Motivational influences on the safer sex behavior of agency-based male sex workers. *Archives of Sexual Behavior, 37*(5), 845–853.

Stall, R., Mills, T. C., Williamson, J., Hart, T., Greenwood, G., Paul, J., et al. (2003). Association of co-occurring psychosocial health problems and increased vulnerability to HIV/AIDS among urban men who have sex with men. *American Journal of Public Health, 93*(6), 939–942.

Steen, R., Chersich, M., & de Vlas, S. J. (2012). Periodic presumptive treatment of curable sexually transmitted infections among sex workers: Recent experience with implementation. *Current Opinion in Infectious Diseases, 25*(1), 100–106.

Thomas, B., Closson, E. F., Biello, K., Menon, S., Navakodi, P., Dhanalakshmi, A., et al. (2017). Development and open pilot trial of an HIV-prevention intervention integrating mobile-phone technology for male sex workers in Chennai, India. *Archives of Sexual Behavior, 46*(4), 1035–1046.

Toledo, C. A., Varangrat, A., Wimolsate, W., Chemnasiri, T., Phanuphak, P., Kalayil, E. J., et al. (2010). Examining HIV infection among male sex workers in Bangkok, Thailand: A comparison of participants recruited at entertainment and street venues. *AIDS Education and Prevention, 22*(4), 299–311.

UNAIDS. (2010). *Global report: UNAIDS report on the global AIDS epidemic 2010.* Retrieved from www.unaids.org/globalreport/Global_report.htm

UNAIDS. (2015a). *2015 China AIDS response progress report.* National Health and Family Planning Commission of the People's Republic of China. Retrieved from www.unaids.org/sites/default/files/country/documents/CHN_narrative_report_2015.pdf

UNAIDS. (2015b). *Global AIDS response progress reporting 2015.* Retrieved from www.unaids.org/sites/default/files/media_asset/JC2702_GARPR2015guidelines_en.pdf

UNAIDS. (2016). *Prevention gap report.* Retrieved from www.unaids.org/sites/default/files/media_asset/2016-prevention-gap-report_en.pdf

UNAIDS. (2019a). *Country factsheet—Pakistan.* HIV and AIDS Estimates. Retrieved from www.unaids.org/en/regionscountries/countries/pakistan

UNAIDS. (2019b). *Country factsheet—Zimbabwe.* HIV and AIDS Estimates. Retrieved from www.unaids.org/en/regionscountries/countries/zimbabwe

UNAIDS. (2020). *Global HIV & AIDS statistics—2020 fact sheet.* Retrieved from www.unaids.org/en/resources/fact-sheet

Underhill, K., Guthrie, K. M., Colleran, C., Calabrese, S. K., Operario, D., & Mayer, K. H. (2018). Temporal fluctuations in behavior, perceived HIV risk, and willingness to use pre-exposure prophylaxis (PrEP). *Archives of Sexual Behavior, 47*(7), 2109–2121.

Underhill, K., Morrow, K. M., Colleran, C., Holcomb, R., Calabrese, S. K., Operario, D., et al. (2015). A qualitative study of medical mistrust, perceived discrimination, and risk behavior disclosure to clinicians by US male sex workers and other men who have sex with men: Implications for biomedical HIV prevention. *Journal of Urban Health*, *92*(4), 667–686.

Underhill, K., Morrow, K. M., Colleran, C. M., Holcomb, R., Operario, D., Calabrese, S. K., et al. (2014). Access to healthcare, HIV/STI testing, and preferred pre-exposure prophylaxis providers among men who have sex with men and men who engage in street-based sex work in the US. *PLoS ONE*, *9*(11), e112425.

Urada, L. A., Simmons, J., Wong, B., Tsuyuki, K., Condino-Enrera, G., Hernandez, L. I., et al. (2016). A human rights-focused HIV intervention for sex workers in Metro Manila, Philippines: Evaluation of effects in a quantitative pilot study. *International Journal of Public Health*, *61*(8), 945–957.

Vu, L., Adebajo, S., Tun, W., Sheehy, M., Karlyn, A., Njab, J., et al. (2013). High HIV prevalence among men who have sex with men in Nigeria: Implications for combination prevention. *Journal of Acquired Immune Deficiency Syndromes*, *63*(2), 221–227.

Vuylsteke, B., Das, A., Dallabetta, G., & Laga, M. (2009). Preventing HIV among sex workers. In M. K (Ed.), *HIV prevention: A comprehensive approach* (pp. 376–406). San Diego, CA: Elsevier.

Vuylsteke, B., Semde, G., Sika, L., Crucitti, T., Traore, V. E., Buve, A., et al. (2012). High prevalence of HIV and sexually transmitted infections among male sex workers in Abidjan, Cote d'Ivoire: Need for services tailored to their needs. *Sexually Transmitted Infections*, *88*(4), 288–293.

Wang, Y., Hunt, K., Nazareth, I., Freemantle, N., & Petersen, I. (2013). Do men consult less than women? An analysis of routinely collected UK general practice data. *BMJ Open*, *3*(8), e003320.

Ward, H., & Rönn, M. (2010). The contribution of STIs to the sexual transmission of HIV. *Current Opinion in HIV and AIDS*, *5*(4), 305.

Weber, A. E., Craib, K. J., Chan, K., Martindale, S., Miller, M. L., Schechter, M. T., et al. (2001). Sex trade involvement and rates of human immunodeficiency virus positivity among young gay and bisexual men. *International Journal of Epidemiology*, *30*(6), 1449–1454.

WHO (World Health Organization). (2012). *Antiretroviral treatment as prevention (TasP) of HIV and TB*. Retrieved from www.who.int/hiv/pub/mtct/programmatic_update_tasp/en/

Wilkinson, A., McMahon, J., Cheah, Y., Bradshaw, C., El-Hayek, C., & Stoové, M. (2015). Paying the price in an era of HIV treatment as prevention: A retrospective study of the cost burden of HIV treatment for people living with HIV in Victoria, Australia. *Sexual Health*, *12*(1), 34–38.

Witzel, T. C., Rodger, A. J., Burns, F. M., Rhodes, T., & Weatherburn, P. (2016). HIV self-testing among men who have sex with men (MSM) in the UK: A qualitative study of barriers and facilitators, intervention preferences, and perceived impacts. *PLoS ONE*, *11*(9), e0162713.

Wohl, D., Kuwahara, R., Javadi, K., Kirby, C., Rosen, D., Napravnik, S., et al. (2017). Financial barriers and lapses in treatment and care of HIV-infected adults in a southern state in the United States. *AIDS Patient Care and STDs*, *31*(11), 463.

Workowski, K. A., & Berman, S. M. (2011). Centers for disease control and prevention sexually transmitted disease treatment guidelines. *Clinical Infectious Diseases*, *53*(Suppl. 3), S59–S63.

Xavier, J., Bradford, J., Hendricks, M., Safford, L., McKee, R., Martin, E., et al. (2013). Transgender health care access in Virginia: A qualitative study. *International Journal of Transgenderism*, *14*(1), 3–17.

Yehia, B. R., Stewart, L., Momplaisir, F., Mody, A., Holtzman, C. W., Jacobs, L. M., et al. (2015). Barriers and facilitators to patient retention in HIV care. *BMC Infectious Diseases*, *15*(1), 246.

Yoong, D., Bayoumi, A. M., Robinson, L., Rachlis, B., & Antoniou, T. (2018). Public prescription drug plan coverage for antiretrovirals and the potential cost to people living with HIV in Canada: A descriptive study. *CMAJ open*, *6*(4), E551.

19

Male sex work and behavioral health

Structural risks, stigma, and psychosocial considerations

Peter Salhaney, Matthew J. Mimiaga,
Christopher Santostefano, and Katie B. Biello

Male sex workers (MSWs) may be doubly stigmatized, by virtue of having sex with other men and being classified as sex workers; however, while substantial research has examined the mental health, substance use history, and structural conditions of female sex workers (FSWs), the literature on these psychosocial factors among MSWs is much more limited. Importantly, the conceptual framing of poor psychosocial health among MSWs is generally presented from two distinct angles: (1) poor psychosocial conditions are consequences of engaging in sex work, or (2) negative psychosocial conditions are antecedents to sex work. Unfortunately, the lack of historical or longitudinal studies limits drawing causal conclusions or determining directionality of the associations reported in the literature. In this chapter, we summarize the existing research on mental health, substance use, and structural conditions for MSWs; describe how syndemic theory provides an understanding of these conditions and their impact on health; and discuss behavioral and psychosocial treatments and structural interventions that have been developed and tested among MSWs to improve health-related outcomes.

Psychosocial aspects of health

Depression and anxiety

The literature suggests that MSWs disproportionately experience problems stemming from negative mental health, including depression, alcohol dependence, illicit drug use, and violence victimization, regardless of the study setting (e.g., domestic versus global, community versus clinic). Risk factors for mental health complications are complex and multifactorial, as are the health consequences of these conditions.

Depression and anxiety are two of the most commonly assessed and frequently occurring mental health problems among MSWs. Studies conducted in North America show rates of depression and psychiatric distress in this population ranging from 33 to 50 percent (Mimiaga,

Reisner, Tinsley, Mayer, & Safren, 2009; Smith & Seal, 2008). Studies in Asia indicate the prevalence there is comparable or even higher. One such analysis of more than 300 MSWs in Ho Chi Minh City, Vietnam, revealed rates of depression approaching 60 percent (Biello, Colby, Closson, & Mimiaga, 2014). Another study, conducted among a sample of "money boys" (a term analogous to MSW) in Shanghai, China, found that more than 60 percent of participants expressed high levels of depressive symptomatology (Wong et al., 2010). While rates of anxiety among MSWs tend to be lower, they remain elevated compared with the general population: among 710 Vietnamese MSWs, one-fifth reported moderate levels of anxiety on the Beck Anxiety Inventory (Goldsamt, Clatts, Giang, & Yu, 2015). It is also hypothesized that these rates of mental health problems may be underestimated in regions where mental health conditions are highly stigmatized, causing some MSWs to underreport negative psychological symptoms (Wong et al., 2010).

Depression and anxiety are also more common among MSWs compared with men who have sex with men (MSM) who do not identify as sex workers. An intervention program for individuals entering substance abuse treatment in the United States observed that men who reported ever engaging in transactional sex (n = 157) had higher levels of anxiety (28.5 percent) and depression (66.8 percent) than their male counterparts (n = 498) who had never engaged in transactional sex (20.5 percent and 50.9 percent, respectively) (Burnette et al., 2008). In Shanghai, investigators examined the prevalence of depressive symptoms among 200 MSWs and 200 MSM who did not engage in sex work; the MSW group had nearly twice the rate of depression (70 percent versus 46 percent) (Huamei et al., 2014). In this same study, social support, which was associated with lower rates of depression (odds ratio [OR] = 0.92, 95 percent confidence interval [CI] = 0.89–0.96), was also lower for MSWs versus MSM who did not engage in transactional sex. These results provide support for the "stress-buffering" hypothesis, which highlights the effect of social support in lessening the burden of negative mental health conditions (Gellert et al., 2018).

Rates of depression and anxiety among MSWs vary depending on their sexual orientation and gender identity. Research from Eastern Europe suggests that depression most often occurs in straight-identifying MSWs (47 percent), followed by bisexual MSWs (42 percent) and those who identify as gay (Bar-Johnson & Weiss, 2014). The authors also found that while no gay-identifying MSWs reported anxiety, 17 percent of MSWs identifying as straight and 28 percent of those identifying as bisexual displayed anxious symptoms. Similarly, a team in Vietnam discovered that non–gay-identifying and non–male-identifying MSWs had the highest rates of anxiety (Goldsamt et al., 2015). Together, these findings suggest that internal conflict regarding sexual identity and gender expression appear to be correlated with poorer mental health outcomes.

Trauma and violence

Research also reveals that MSWs endure high rates of trauma and violence, including childhood sexual and physical abuse, intimate partner violence, and violence victimization. Among a sample of 30 indoor-based MSWs in the United States, two-thirds (66.7 percent) reported a history of childhood sexual abuse (30 percent) and/or physical abuse (85 percent) (Smith & Seal, 2008). A similar study including 32 MSWs in the United States indicated that the cohort's frequency of childhood sexual abuse was 41 percent (Mimiaga, Reisner et al., 2009). In Vietnam, nearly one-fifth of the 300 MSW respondents were victims of childhood sexual abuse (Biello et al., 2014)

Intimate partner violence (IPV)—physical, sexual, or emotional harm perpetrated on an individual by a sexual partner—is also inordinately common among MSWs. In fact, MSWs face elevated rates of violence from both paying clients and nonpaying intimate partners. Of 100 MSWs recently surveyed in the United States, 24 percent reported that they had experienced violence (emotional, physical, or sexual) committed by a nonpaying partner in the preceding six months (Brown, Mimiaga, Safren, Mayer, & Biello, 2018). More than half (57 percent) of money boys surveyed in Shanghai said they were abused by a primary male sexual partner at least once in the past five years, compared with only 45 percent of MSM who did not engage in transactional sex (Dunkle et al., 2013). Money boys also tended to report multiple types of abuse more often than their non–sex worker MSM counterparts (32 percent versus 24 percent); the most prevalent manifestations included "overall abuse, threats, and financial abuse" (Dunkle et al., 2013). An earlier study in Vietnam had demonstrated that MSWs were significantly more likely than MSM who did not identify as sex workers to have ever been forced to have sex against their will (11.2 percent versus 2 percent, respectively) (Clatts, Giang, Goldsamt, & Yi, 2007). A regional analysis across 17 Latin America countries supports these findings: 53.9 percent of MSWs, compared to only 33.8 percent of general MSM, were victims of IPV (Oldenburg, Perez-Brumer et al., 2015). Similarly, investigators in Uganda found that male students who had ever engaged in transactional sex were 12 times as likely as male students who had not participated in sex work to have faced physical violence in the previous 12 months (OR = 12.4, 95 percent CI = 6.5–23.9) (Choudhry, Östergren, Ambresin, Kyagaba, & Agardh, 2014).

Violent acts committed by clients are widespread in the sex work community. Twenty percent of Vietnamese MSWs ($n = 300$) reported having experienced sexual violence as an adult (Biello et al., 2014). Among 100 MSWs in Chennai, India, 44 percent said they had been verbally abused in the context of sex work, 29 percent were victims of physical abuse, 43 percent were forced to not use a condom, 13 percent were forced to have anal sex, and 24 percent were forced to drink alcohol (Bello et al., 2017). In this study, reports of verbal abuse and forced anal sex were significantly more common among MSWs whose only source of income was sex work, suggesting a perceived powerlessness owing to their economic dependence on the work (Bello et al., 2017). In Kenya, 36 MSWs participated in qualitative interviews in which they described instances of abuse inflicted by clients, such as not being paid after sex or being abandoned in a remote and dangerous location (Okal et al., 2009). MSWs in this same sample also revealed that abuse and harassment were not inflicted solely by clients; in fact, receiving verbal or physical abuse from the general public was reportedly so ordinary that MSWs in Kenya considered acts of violence as "normal" or "part of the job" (Okal et al., 2009). These findings were consistent with findings in the United States, where 15 of 100 MSWs surveyed reported they had experienced an act of violence—including verbal abuse (22 percent), physical abuse (10 percent), rape (8 percent), and forced condomless anal sex (9 percent)—perpetrated by a client in the preceding six months (Brown et al., 2018). In an earlier qualitative analysis, 32 MSWs in the United States explicitly described some of these abusive or traumatic encounters, including being raped, having a gun or knife pulled on them, being spat on and hit, and even getting into a car accident while giving oral sex to a client (Reisner, Mimiaga, Mayer, Tinsley, & Safren, 2008).

The literature suggests that MSWs also suffer violence and unjust treatment at the hands of law enforcement. Kenyan MSWs interviewed by Okal and colleagues in 2009 recounted instances of police harassment, arbitrary arrests for loitering, and extortion for money or sexual services by police officers. Such reports demonstrate a dual problem, wherein MSWs are confronted by violence from primary partners, clients, and even the general public but cannot report this violence to the police owing to their fear of violent treatment by the police.

Given that trauma and violent victimization in both childhood and adulthood have been shown in other populations to be associated with negative mental health outcomes, the frequency of these lived events among MSWs may contribute to their disproportionate rates of mental health sequelae, including mental health hospitalization, psychoactive substance abuse, depression, and suicidal thoughts or actions (Khoury, Tang, Bradley, Cubells, & Ressler, 2010; Kilpatrick et al., 2000; Negele, Kaufhold, Kallenbach, & Leuzinger-Bohleber, 2015; Turner, Finkelhor, & Ormrod, 2006; Xie et al., 2018). Despite the evidence linking high rates of abuse or violence with negative health consequences, we still lack research and evidence-based interventions addressing trauma among MSWs. A systematic review of the global prevalence and correlates of violent acts against sex workers identified no studies that specifically examined MSWs (Deering et al., 2014).

Stigma

Experiences of stigma, which can broadly be characterized as negative attitudes, relative powerlessness, and loss of status related to a particular characteristic (King, Maman, Bowling, Moracco, & Dudina, 2013), are common among MSWs owing to their status as both sex workers and MSM. Oldenburg et al. (2014) found that more than one-third of 300 MSWs surveyed in Vietnam said they had been "made fun of" for engaging in sex work, nearly 15 percent had been assaulted for engaging in sex work, and 75 percent felt that they would be disliked if people knew that they engaged in sex work. In a study of 500 Kenyan MSM, MSWs were significantly more likely than other MSM to report experiencing stigma or discrimination in the previous 12 months (59 percent versus 29 percent; $p < 0.001$) (Onyango-Ouma, Birungi, & Geibel, 2005).

The illegality of sex work perpetuates stigmatizing incidents by making MSWs' lives more unstable and less safe, as well as by creating barriers to physical and mental health care (Decker et al., 2015). Sex work criminalization enables the development of a culture of discrimination and exploitation by both police and clients, thereby increasing the vulnerability of MSWs to violence and infectious diseases, such as HIV and other sexually transmitted infections (STIs) (Krüsi et al., 2014). Moreover, constant police surveillance and social isolation have damaging impacts on MSWs' emotional and mental health, leading to anxiety, post-traumatic stress disorder, depression, and even suicide (NSWP, 2017). In fact, research consistently demonstrates that experiences of stigma and discrimination are correlated with social isolation, depression, drug or alcohol abuse in the context of sexual encounters, and other high-risk sexual behaviors (Diaz, Ayala, Bein, Henne, & Marin, 2001; Fitzgerald-Husek et al., 2017; Oldenburg et al., 2014; Thomas et al., 2012).

Data collected on MSWs suggest that many of these men use stigma-management techniques to help them maintain relationships with family, friends, and sexual partners, and most importantly, to maintain their sense of identity in the face of societal disapproval (Koken, Bimbi, Parsons, & Halkitis, 2004). For example, in the Dominican Republic, 72 MSWs described specific strategies they employed to minimize the impact of stigmatization, such as inventing or obtaining jobs to explain sex work income, creating alibis for prolonged absences, and using sexual relationships with women to express heterosexuality to their peers (Padilla et al., 2008). Emphasizing heteronormative traits and reaffirming masculinity were primary stigma-management techniques described during qualitative interviews with MSWs in Hong Kong (Kong, 2009). Those men said they intentionally hid the "deviant" and "feminine" attributes that they perceived to be typically associated with other MSWs; they disassociated themselves from the concept of sex work by identifying themselves with more neutral terms (e.g., "male masseur," "public relations person"); and they reframed their occupation to make it appear more service-oriented, emphasizing the provision of "quality" services to satisfy clients' emotional, physical, and sexual needs (Kong, 2009).

Substance use and health

Substance use and sex work tend to reinforce each other in a cyclical fashion (Friedman et al., 2014). Given the large body of evidence showing that substance use is correlated with poorer health outcomes, including HIV infection (Chesney, Barrett, & Stall, 1998; Stall et al., 2003; Zenilman, Shepherd, Smith, Rompalo, & Celentano, 1994), hepatitis C infection (Osher et al., 2003), and negative mental health (Grant et al., 2004; Regier et al., 1990), understanding substance use patterns among MSWs is crucial to improving their overall quality of life.

Alcohol

Research shows high rates of alcohol use among MSWs globally. In one study in the United States, 55 out of 100 MSWs displayed symptoms of alcohol dependence (Brown et al., 2018). Another recent study, with migrant and nonmigrant MSWs in Thailand, revealed that nearly half (47.6 percent) were heavy alcohol users (Guadamuz, Clatts, & Goldsamt, 2018). Further sexual-risk data from the sample in Thailand suggest that MSWs who engaged in heavy alcohol use were nearly three times as likely to use stimulants during sex (adjusted odds ratio [aOR] = 2.67, 95 percent CI = 1.16–6.15) and more than twice as likely to have had more than 15 male paying clients in the preceding 30 days (aOR = 2.16, 95 percent CI = 1.02–4.58), highlighting how intertwined alcohol use is with increased sexual risk. Moreover, almost all (99 percent) of 654 MSWs surveyed in Vietnam in 2015 reported having used alcohol at some point, with 84 percent having used it in the past 30 days (Clatts, Goldsamt, & Yu, 2015).

There is also substantial evidence demonstrating that sex work is associated with higher rates of alcohol use among men. For example, a team in South Africa found that men with heavy episodic drinking were nearly three times as likely to have engaged in transactional sex compared with nondrinkers (OR = 2.6, 95 percent CI = 1.7–4.1) (Bello et al., 2017). Similarly, a separate study of Kenyan MSM revealed that those who engaged in transactional sex had a 30 percent higher prevalence of hazardous alcohol use, compared with MSM who were not sex workers (adjusted probability ratio [aPR] = 1.34, 95 percent CI = 1.12–1.60) (Korhonen et al., 2018). In many instances, alcohol consumption becomes a normalized component of sex work encounters, as men often drink alcohol before or during sex with their clients (Niccolai, King, Eritsyan, Safiullina, & Rusakova, 2013; Yang, Guadamuz, Lim, Koe, & Wei, 2016; Yu, Goldsamt, & Clatts, 2016).

Drug use

Data collected on MSWs also indicates above-average rates of both injection and noninjection illicit drug use. A U.S. study by Brown and colleagues found that 90 out of 100 MSWs sampled in 2018 had used illicit drugs in the previous six months (Brown et al., 2018). Moreover, in the northeastern United States, Underhill and colleagues (2014) measured higher rates of both injection drug use (52 percent) and noninjection drug use (68 percent) in MSWs than in MSM who did not participate in sex work (4 percent and 28 percent, respectively). Substance use was elevated but less common among MSWs in Vietnam versus those in the United Stats: of 700 Vietnamese MSWs surveyed, more than a quarter (28 percent) had ever used cannabis, and 10 percent were currently using it; nearly one-third had ever used and 17 percent were currently using methamphetamines; and almost half (46 percent) had used one or more types of opiates and/or stimulants in their lifetime, including 8 percent who reported having injected heroin (Yu, Clatts, Goldsamt, & Giang, 2015).

A high prevalence of substance use is also seen among men who may not identify as sex workers but may engage in more informal or infrequent transactional sex. For example, in a recent analysis by Nerlander and colleagues, out of 8,411 men in 20 major U.S. cities, 23 percent of those who had engaged in transactional sex in the preceding year had ever injected drugs, compared with only 5 percent of those who had not exchanged in transactional sex in the past year (Nerlander, Hess, Sionean et al., 2017). A separate analysis from California found that crack use (OR = 3.7, 95 percent CI = 2.24–6.18) and injection drug use (OR = 2.3, 95 percent CI = 1.19–4.37) were both associated with a substantial increase in the odds of engaging in transactional sex (Newman, Rhodes, & Weiss, 2004). Likewise in Brazil, a history of STIs and current crack use by men corresponded to a 15 percent increase and a 10 percent increase, respectively, in the prevalence of transactional sex (aPR = 1.15, 95 percent CI = 1.01–1.21; aPR = 1.10, 95 percent CI = 1.02–1.18) (Guimarães et al., 2016).

Polydrug use

Evidence is building that the simultaneous use of multiple substances is correlated with and highly common among MSWs. Findings from 433 MSM in India revealed that those who reported polysubstance use were 1.15 times as likely to have engaged in transactional sex (p = .057), compared with MSM who did not engage in polysubstance use (Wilkerson et al., 2018). A similar relationship was found among 343 black South African people who use drugs, wherein testing positive for two drugs (adjusted odds ratio [aOR] = 2.7, 95 percent CI = .96–7.58) or three drugs (aOR = 4.2, 95 percent CI = 1.37–12.62) was associated with higher odds of transactional sex (Floyd et al., 2010). In Australia, a study by Minichiello and colleagues (2002) revealed that more than 50 percent of 185 MSWs surveyed in three different cities had used multiple substances simultaneously on at least one occasion.

The impact of polysubstance use may vary depending on the specific substances mixed, yet each drug carries its own risks. For example, combining multiple stimulants (such as cocaine and ecstasy/MDMA) may exacerbate symptoms of psychosis, anxiety, or panic attacks, and it may result in impaired thermal regulation and cardiac functioning (SAHealth, 2012). Mixing stimulants and depressants (alcohol, opioids, marijuana) can lead to heart problems or respiratory infections; it can also cause a person's breathing and heart rate to decrease dangerously. In fact, when cocaine is mixed with alcohol, the combination may be more toxic to the heart and liver than either substance alone, and combining heroin and cocaine often leads to overdose because the cocaine causes the body to use more oxygen, while the heroin reduces the respiratory rate (SAHealth, 2012). A study of 153 drug users in the United Kingdom who had experienced a nonfatal drug overdose found that in 111 of the cases (73 percent) more than one drug had been consumed (Neale, 2001).

Substance use in the context of sex work

As stated, the relationship between sex work and substance use is likely bidirectional: substances may be used as a coping response to stressors caused by sex work, and engagement in sex work may also be motivated by a need to pay for drugs. Studies have shown that MSWs tend to abuse substances during or before sexual work encounters for a number of reasons, including to ease the "shame" felt (Yu et al., 2015), to enhance sexual performance (Clatts et al., 2007; Lasco, 2018; Minichiello, Mariño, Khan, & Browne, 2003; Vu et al., 2012), and because they are forced to do so by clients (Brown et al., 2018). In a sample of 32 MSWs in the United States, 75 percent indicated they had used marijuana in the context of sex in the previous 12 months,

53 percent had used cocaine, 31 percent had used crack, 22 percent had used crystal meth, and 3 percent had used heroin; nearly all (91 percent) reported having had sex while drunk (Mimiaga, Reisner et al., 2009). Notably, other analyses have suggested that MSWs may be more likely to use substances in the context of sex with primary sexual partners than with clients, citing concerns about safety with clients if they were to become too intoxicated (Yu et al., 2015).

Engagement in sex work as a result of substance use (i.e., to pay for drugs) is particularly common when transactional encounters with clients are based on the exchange of sex for drugs, rather than for money or other incentives (DeBeck, Shannon, Wood, Li, Montaner, & Kerr, 2007; Deering, Shoveller, Tyndall, Montaner, & Shannon, 2011). A review of MSM in Long Beach, California, found that a large majority (74 percent) of transactional events with clients involved an exchange of drugs (primarily methamphetamine: 60 percent of cases), with the remaining exchanges being for money or shelter (Newman, Rhodes, & Weiss, 2004). A qualitative study done in the United States by Mimiaga and colleagues (2009) further described this relationship, quoting one MSW participant: "I think if I quit coke, I probably wouldn't be doing it [sex work]. Really, because that's why I do it, to get high. . . . [T]hat money, that's my drug money."

Substance use and associated health risks

Substance use has a substantially demonstrated link with sexual disinhibition and an increased risk for STI and HIV acquisition. In 1994, Graaf, Vanwesenbeeck, Zessen, Straver, and Visser observed that MSWs who struggled most with drug addiction were also less discriminating in their choice of clients and were more likely to engage in high-risk behaviors, such as condomless sex or receptive anal intercourse, for more money. Similarly, among more than 300 MSWs in Vietnam, substance use was associated both with depression (OR = 2.9, 95 percent CI = 2.2–3.9) and high-risk sexual behaviors (Biello et al., 2014). Moreover, specific substances may put MSWs at an even greater risk of contracting HIV: data from 2010 showed that stimulant use (cocaine/crack and methamphetamine) more than doubled the odds of the user's engaging in unprotected anal sex with casual male partners (aOR = 2.61, 95 percent CI = 1.05–6.42) and increased threefold the odds of problematic alcohol use (aOR = 3.31, 95 percent CI = 1.312–8.38) and clinical depression (aOR = 3.11, 95 percent CI = 1.45–6.66). Other findings have confirmed that stimulant use is correlated with low rates of condom use and increased numbers of sexual partners (Benotsch, Lance, Nettles, & Koester, 2012; Halkitis, Parsons, & Stirratt, 2001), which also increase the likelihood of HIV infection (Koblin et al., 2006; Oldenburg, Jain, Mayer, & Mimiaga, 2015). Additionally, excessive alcohol consumption has proven to be an underlying cause or contributing factor for more than 30 adverse health conditions, including infectious disease, cancer, diabetes, neuropsychiatric disease, cardiovascular disease, liver and pancreatic disease, and both unintentional and intentional injury (Rehm, 2011). As such, higher rates of substance use among MSWs are likely to increase their risk for further physical and mental health complications.

Structural factors and health

MSWs are disproportionately affected by structural burdens like homelessness (Marshall, Shannon, Kerr, Zhang, & Wood, 2010), lower socioeconomic status (e.g., lower levels of income, employment, and education), and involvement with the criminal justice system (Nerlander, Hess, Sionean et al., 2017). These burdens act as barriers to health care access, increase the risk of poor health outcomes, and result in lower quality of life (Adler & Newman, 2002; Arpey,

Gaglioti, & Rosenbaum, 2017; Binswanger, Redmond, Steiner, & Hicks, 2012; Freed, Hansberry, & Arrieta, 2013; Goldenberg, Krüsi, Zhang, Chettiar, & Shannon, 2017).

Data have indicated that the employment and education levels of MSWs may be lower than in the general MSM population. For example, one U.S. sample of 52 MSWs and 42 MSM who did not identify as sex workers revealed that 28.8 percent ($n = 15$) of MSWs had not completed high school, versus 13 percent ($n = 6$) of the MSM comparison group (Underhill et al., 2014). This same study found that 62 percent of the MSWs were unemployed, compared with only 20 percent of MSM who reported not engaging in sex work (Underhill et al., 2014). This distinction mirrored earlier results from a project in Vancouver, where MSWs were more likely than their MSM counterparts to have less than a high school education (40 percent and 12 percent, respectively) (Weber et al., 2001). Additionally, more than twice as many MSWs as non-sex worker MSM reported making less than $10,000 annually (58 percent vs. 26 percent) (Weber et al., 2001). Another team found that among 185 Australian MSWs across three sites, nearly one-third (31 percent) of participants had not completed a secondary education, though this number varied by the men's method of sex work; specifically, 55 percent of street-based sex workers had not finished their secondary education, whereas 41 percent of online-based male escorts reported attending tertiary studies beyond their secondary education (Minichiello et al., 2002). This disparity in educational attainment was also noted in the northeastern United States, where 68 percent of street-based MSWs surveyed reported having a high school diploma or less education, compared with 8 percent of online male escorts (Mimiaga, Reisner et al., 2009). Investigators also observed that street-based MSWs were more likely than Internet escorts to be unemployed (89 percent and 23 percent, respectively) (Mimiaga, Reisner et al., 2009). Findings from China were similar: 342 of 394 MSWs sampled (87 percent) had only a high school degree equivalent or less education (Cai et al., 2010).

Studies across varied geographic settings have demonstrated that engagement in transactional sex is strongly associated with homelessness. In fact, homelessness is known to be a primary risk factor leading youth to enter into sex work (Deisher, Robinson, & Boyer, 1982; Luckenbill, 1985). In 2011, about 31 percent of a sample of 41 heterosexual-identifying men in New York City who engaged in transactional sex with other men were homeless (Jenness et al., 2011). More recently, in an analysis of 100 MSWs in the northeastern United States, nearly half (43 percent) were found to be unstably housed (Brown et al., 2018). In a Rhode Island study, rates of homelessness among MSWs were elevated: 58 percent were currently homeless, and 62 percent had been homeless in the previous month (Landers et al., 2014). Landers and colleagues also found that homelessness in this sample was highly correlated with injection drug use (aOR = 5.5, 95 percent CI = 1.0–29.4) (Landers et al., 2014). Another study had similarly reported several years earlier that men who were homeless in the U.S. South were three times as likely (OR = 2.9, 95 percent CI = 2.2–3.9) to engage in transactional sex than those who were not homeless (Bobashev, Zule, Osilla, Kline, & Wechsberg, 2009). In fact, across 20 different cities in the United States, transactional sex was more commonly reported among MSM who had experienced homelessness in the preceding 12 months (31 percent) than among those who had not (5 percent) (Nerlander, Hess, Sionean et al., 2017).

In the United States, sex work is also closely related to involvement with the criminal justice system. In fact, MSM who had been incarcerated were more than five times as likely (OR = 5.2, 95 percent CI = 2.0–13.6) as MSM without a history of incarceration to have engaged in transactional sex, according to evidence from the 2011 U.S. National HIV Behavioral Surveillance System (Philbin et al., 2018). Likewise, Nerlander and colleagues observed in 2017 that sex work was more common among MSM who had been incarcerated (19 percent) than among MSM who had never been incarcerated (3 percent) (Nerlander, Hess, Sionean et al., 2017). Additionally, in a UK study of 145 MSWs in England, Wales, and Northern Ireland who injected drugs, three-quarters said they had been to prison; those MSWs also tended to have entered the prison system at a younger age, and a higher proportion of them continued to inject while in prison compared with their MSM counterparts who did not engage in transactional sex (27 percent versus 17 percent) (Croxford et al., 2015).

Syndemic theory as a framework for understanding health outcomes

Syndemic theory has previously been used to describe the often-overlapping psychosocial and structural risks faced by distinct populations, with substantial focus on MSM. Syndemic theory posits that co-occurring epidemics of poor mental health, substance use, and disadvantageous structural conditions interact to adversely affect health (Biello et al., 2014; Oldenburg, Perez-Brumer, & Reisner, 2014; Singer & Clair, 2003). Thus, a syndemics perspective highlights how synergistic interactions among psychosocial and biological conditions underlie patterns of health within social, political, and economic, and structural contexts (Bazzi et al., 2019). Moreover, according to Stall's theory of syndemic production, experiences of social stigma and marginalization as a sexual minority are at the root of these psychosocial problems (See Figure 19.1) (Stall, Friedman, & Catania, 2008; Wolitski, Stall, & Valdiserri, 2008).

A large body of research has demonstrated that greater numbers of coexisting psychosocial health problems are associated with high-risk sexual behaviors and a higher prevalence of HIV infection among MSM overall. Compounding the stigma surrounding same-sex behavior, MSWs also experience high rates of social marginalization owing to their sex worker status. Thus, a syndemic framework may be useful for understanding the role these factors play in risk-taking and poor health outcomes among MSWs, particularly in the context of HIV, hepatitis C, and other STIs.

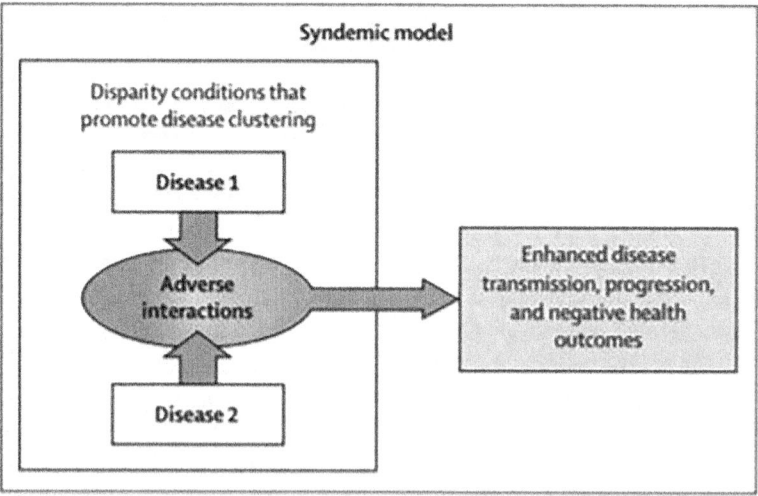

Figure 19.1 Model of a syndemic interaction.

Source: Singer, Bulled, Ostrach, & Mendenhall, 2017.

As we have detailed, MSWs face inordinate challenges posed by comorbid mental health, substance use, and structural health risks. Moreover, as described in Chapter 18, these psychosocial and environmental dynamics correlate with increased HIV risk among MSWs across the globe. However, no published research that we are aware of has examined the longitudinal relationship among co-occurring syndemic mental health, substance use, and structural-risk factors on HIV sexual risk among MSWs. Our research team of Mimiaga, Hughto, and Biello (2012) has just analyzed data from a longitudinal cohort study of 100 MSWs and found that the odds of participating in condomless anal sex (CAS) were highest for MSWs who reported more psychosocial problems over the study follow-up. Specifically, compared with those who had no psychosocial problems (7 percent of the sample), MSWs with four or more psychosocial problems (15 percent) had more than five times the odds of engaging in CAS with a male client, and those with two or three psychosocial problems had more than three times the odds of having CAS with a male client over the follow-up period. Similarly, in a sample of 300 Vietnamese MSM surveyed by Biello et al. (2014), experiencing four or more psychosocial health problems—such as depression, alcohol dependence, illicit drug use, sexual violence victimization, and childhood sexual abuse victimization—was significantly associated with having CAS with a client (OR = 4.7; 95 percent CI = 1.5, 14.9), and every unit increase in the number of psychosocial health problems reported was related to a 25 to 30 percent increase in the likelihood of engaging in CAS with clients and non–sex work partners. A recent qualitative study among sex workers in Kenya (Bazzi et al., 2019) similarly demonstrated that substance use, the criminalization of sex work, and violence inflicted on sex workers directly informed sex workers' vulnerability to HIV and their attitude toward PrEP as an HIV-prevention strategy.

Future projects should consider applying the syndemic framework to better understand and describe the impact of multilevel, concurrent mental health, substance use, and structural risks on the health of MSWs, which in turn will foster the development of interventions and programs tailored specifically to the unique and complex needs of this population.

Programmatic and community-based response

Despite the high burden of psychosocial and environmental challenges faced by MSWs, to date there are to our knowledge no published, effective, evidence-based interventions that simultaneously address mental health, substance use, and structural risk factors for MSWs. A few programs have been created through grassroots efforts by community organizations that provide services specifically to MSWs. For example, Project Weber/RENEW in Providence, Rhode Island, is a peer-based harm-reduction and recovery-services operation for high-risk male, female, and transgender sex workers (Figure 19.2). The organization offers recovery counseling and case management and links sex workers to drug treatment programs, detox services, and mental health care. It also hosts support groups for sex workers who continue to struggle with adverse mental health or substance abuse. In line with the peer-centered model of this institution, all staff members have direct experience with sex work, substance abuse, or mental health problems and, as such, they are well versed in culturally competent services that concentrate on the unique challenges endured by sex workers (see www.weberrenew.org). RÉZO, in Montreal, is a nonprofit organization for MSM, with a specialized focus on MSWs. In addition to facilitating access to medical services (HIV/STI testing, vaccinations, dental care) through its drop-in center, RÉZO also engages in outreach to street-based MSWs by providing "information, listening, referral, and support," with the goal of promoting the development of real-world skills necessary to help them increase their independence, improve self-efficacy, and find stability

Figure 19.2   Project Weber/RENEW staff members at their drop-in center in Providence.
Photo credit: Alberto Edeza.

(www.rezosante.org). In the Czech Republic, Project Sance (Project Chance) provides support for children and young adults who are victims of childhood sexual abuse or human trafficking. The group focuses on helping these individuals reintegrate into society by finding housing, employment, and health care for them, and by helping them to avoid interactions with the criminal justice system. One of the primary reasons that programs such as Weber/RENEW, RÉZO, and Sance have been successful in connecting with MSWs is that they address issues specific to people who do sex work (stigma and confidentiality, homelessness, mental health, trauma and abuse, and substance use) in spaces that are welcoming, nonjudgmental, and supported by peers.

In light of the multilevel, systemic obstacles that MSWs must overcome, interventions that address intertwined syndemic factors may be most effective at reducing negative mental health symptoms and substance abuse. Evidence-based projects developed for and shown to be efficacious among FSWs could be a starting point for testing and implementing interventions that may also be culturally appropriate for MSWs (Beattie et al., 2010; Surratt & Inciardi, 2010; Hong & Li, 2007; Wechsberg, Luseno, Lam, Parry, & Morojole, 2006). Similarly, studies that seek to reduce negative mental-health risks (Safren et al., 2016; Alvy et al., 2011) and substance-use risks (Mimiaga et al., 2012; Shoptaw & Frosch, 2000) among the general MSM population may be adapted for MSWs. However, it is imperative that future programs take into account the lived realities of MSWs in the setting where the research is being done. For example, future interventions should consider the diversity of MSW subpopulations, including their self-identified sexual orientation (Bar-Johnson & Weiss, 2014) and whether they are street-based workers or they primarily solicit clients online (Mimiaga, Reisner et al., 2009). Accounting for the variation among these subgroups will help to ensure that ongoing research endeavors for regarding MSWs are culturally appropriate and responsive to their needs.

References

Adler, N. E., & Newman, K. (2002). Socioeconomic disparities in health: Pathways and policies. *Health Affairs*, *21*(2), 60–76.

Alvy, L. M., McKirnan, D. J., Mansergh, G., Koblin, B., Colfax, G. N., Flores, S. A., et al. (2011). Depression is associated with sexual risk among men who have sex with men, but is mediated by cognitive escape and self-efficacy. *AIDS and Behavior*, *15*(6), 1171–1179.

Arpey, N. C., Gaglioti, A. H., & Rosenbaum, M. E. (2017). How socioeconomic status affects patient perceptions of health care: A qualitative study. *Journal of Primary Care & Community Health*, *8*(3), 169–175.

Bar-Johnson, M., & Weiss, P. (2014). Mental health and sexual identity in a sample of male sex workers in the Czech Republic. *Medical Science Monitor: International Medical Journal of Experimental and Clinical Research*, *20*, 1682.

Bazzi, A. R., Yotebieng, K., Otticha, S., Rota, G., Agot, K., Ohaga, S., et al. (2019). PrEP and the syndemic of substance use, violence, and HIV among female and male sex workers: A qualitative study in Kisumu, Kenya. *Journal of the International AIDS Society*, *22*(4), e25266. doi:10.1002/jia2.25266

Beattie, T. S., Bhattacharjee, P., Ramesh, B. M., Gurnani, V., Anthony, J., Isac, S., et al. (2010). Violence against female sex workers in Karnataka state, South India: Impact on health, and reductions in violence following an intervention program. *BMC Public Health*, *10*(476).

Bello, B., Moultrie, H., Somji, A., Chersich, M. F., Watts, C., & Delany-Moretlwe, S. (2017). Alcohol use and sexual risk behaviour among men and women in inner-city Johannesburg, South Africa. *BMC Public Health*, *17*(3), 548.

Benotsch, E. G., Lance, S. P., Nettles, C. D., & Koester, S. (2012). Attitudes toward methamphetamine use and HIV risk behavior in men who have sex with men. *American Journal on Addictions*, *21*, S35–S42.

Biello, K. B., Colby, D., Closson, E., & Mimiaga, M. J. (2014). The syndemic condition of psychosocial problems and HIV risk among male sex workers in Ho Chi Minh City, Vietnam. *AIDS and Behavior*, *18*(7), 1264–1271.

Binswanger, I. A., Redmond, N., Steiner, J. F., & Hicks, L. S. (2012). Health disparities and the criminal justice system: An agenda for further research and action. *Journal of Urban Health*, *89*(1), 98–107.

Bobashev, G. V., Zule, W. A., Osilla, K. C., Kline, T. L., & Wechsberg, W. M. (2009). Transactional sex among men and women in the South at high risk for HIV and other STIs. *Journal of Urban Health*, *86*(1), 32–47.

Brown, E., Mimiaga, M., Safren, S., Mayer, K., & Biello, K. (2018). *Violence victimization among male sex workers in the U.S. Northeast.* Paper presented at the 22nd International AIDS Conference, Amsterdam, Netherlands.

Burnette, M. L., Lucas, E., Ilgen, M., Frayne, S. M., Mayo, J., & Weitlauf, J. C. (2008). Prevalence and health correlates of prostitution among patients entering treatment for substance use disorders. *Archives of General Psychiatry*, *65*(3), 337–344.

Cai, W.-D., Zhao, J., Zhao, J.-K., Raymond, H. F., Feng, Y.-J., Liu, J., et al. (2010). HIV prevalence and related risk factors among male sex workers in Shenzhen, China: Results from a time-location sampling survey. *Sexually Transmitted Infections*, *86*(1), 15–20.

Chesney, M. A., Barrett, D. C., & Stall, R. (1998). Histories of substance use and risk behavior: Precursors to HIV seroconversion in homosexual men. *American Journal of Public Health*, *88*(1), 113–116.

Choudhry, V., Östergren, P.-O., Ambresin, A.-E., Kyagaba, E., & Agardh, A. (2014). Giving or receiving something for sex: A cross-sectional study of transactional sex among Ugandan university students. *PLoS ONE*, *9*(11), e112431.

Clatts, M. C., Giang, L. M., Goldsamt, L. A., & Yi, H. (2007). Male sex work and HIV risk among young heroin users in Hanoi, Vietnam. *Sexual Health*, 4(4), 261–267.

Clatts, M. C., Goldsamt, L. A., & Yu, G. (2015). Sexual practices, partner concurrency and high rates of sexually transmissible infections among male sex workers in three cities in Vietnam. *Sexual Health (Online)*, 12(1), 39.

Croxford, S., Platt, L., Hope, V. D., Cullen, K. J., Parry, J. V., & Ncube, F. (2015). Sex work amongst people who inject drugs in England, Wales and Northern Ireland: Findings from a National Survey of Health Harms and Behaviours. *International Journal of Drug Policy*, 26(4), 429–433.

DeBeck, K., Shannon, K., Wood, E., Li, K., Montaner, J., & Kerr, T. (2007). Income generating activities of people who inject drugs. *Drug and Alcohol Dependence*, 91(1), 50–56.

Decker, M. R., Crago, A.-L., Chu, S. K., Sherman, S. G., Seshu, M. S., Buthelezi, K., et al. (2015). Human rights violations against sex workers: Burden and effect on HIV. *The Lancet*, 385(9963), 186–199.

Deering, K. N., Amin, A., Shoveller, J., Nesbitt, A., Garcia-Moreno, C., Duff, P., et al. (2014). A systematic review of the correlates of violence against sex workers. *American Journal of Public Health*, 104(5), e42–e54.

Deering, K. N., Shoveller, J., Tyndall, M., Montaner, J., & Shannon, K. (2011). The street cost of drugs and drug use patterns: Relationships with sex work income in an urban Canadian setting. *Drug and Alcohol Dependence*, 118(2–3), 430–436.

Deisher, R., Robinson, G., & Boyer, D. (1982). The adolescent female and male prostitute. *Pediatric Annals*, 11(10), 819–825.

Diaz, R. M., Ayala, G., Bein, E., Henne, J., & Marin, B. V. (2001). The impact of homophobia, poverty, and racism on the mental health of gay and bisexual Latino men: Findings from 3 US cities. *American Journal of Public Health*, 91(6), 927.

Dunkle, K., Wong, F., Nehl, E., Lin, L., He, N., Huang, J., et al. (2013). Male-on-male intimate partner violence and sexual risk behaviors among money boys and other men who have sex with men in Shanghai, China. *Sexually Transmitted Diseases*, 40(5), 362.

Fitzgerald-Husek, A., Van Wert, M. J., Ewing, W. F., Grosso, A. L., Holland, C. E., Katterl, R., et al. (2017). Measuring stigma affecting sex workers (SW) and men who have sex with men (MSM): A systematic review. *PLoS ONE*, 12(11), e0188393.

Floyd, L. J., Hedden, S., Lawson, A., Salama, C., Moleko, A. G., & Latimer, W. (2010). The association between poly-substance use, coping, and sex trade among black South African substance users. *Substance Use & Misuse*, 45(12), 1971–1987.

Freed, C. R., Hansberry, S. T., & Arrieta, M. I. (2013). Structural and hidden barriers to a local primary health care infrastructure: Autonomy, decisions about primary health care, and the centrality and significance of power. In J. J. Kronenfeld (Ed.), *Social determinants, health disparities, and linkages to health and health care* (pp. 57–81). Bingley, UK: Emerald Group Publishing.

Friedman, M. R., Kurtz, S. P., Buttram, M. E., Wei, C., Silvestre, A. J., & Stall, R. (2014). HIV risk among substance-using men who have sex with men and women (MSMW): Findings from South Florida. *AIDS and Behavior*, 18(1), 111–119.

Gellert, P., Häusler, A., Suhr, R., Gholami, M., Rapp, M., Kuhlmey, A., et al. (2018). Testing the stress-buffering hypothesis of social support in couples coping with early-stage dementia. *PLoS ONE*, 13(1), e0189849.

Goldenberg, S. M., Krüsi, A., Zhang, E., Chettiar, J., & Shannon, K. (2017). Structural determinants of health among im/migrants in the indoor sex industry: Experiences of workers and managers/owners in Metropolitan Vancouver. *PLoS ONE*, 12(1), e0170642.

Goldsamt, L. A., Clatts, M. C., Giang, L. M., & Yu, G. (2015). Prevalence and behavioral correlates of depression and anxiety among male sex workers in Vietnam. *International Journal of Sexual Health*, 27(2), 145–155.

Graaf, R. D., Vanwesenbeeck, I., Zessen, G. V., Straver, C., & Visser, J. (1994). Male prostitutes and safe sex: Different settings, different risks. *AIDS Care*, 6(3), 277–288.

Grant, B. F., Stinson, F. S., Dawson, D. A., Chou, S. P., Dufour, M. C., Compton, W., et al. (2004). Prevalence and co-occurrence of substance use disorders and independent mood and anxiety disorders:

Results from the national epidemiologic survey on alcohol and related conditions. *Archives of General Psychiatry, 61*(8), 807–816.

Guadamuz, T. E., Clatts, M. C., & Goldsamt, L. A. (2018). Heavy alcohol use among migrant and non-migrant male sex workers in Thailand: A neglected HIV/STI vulnerability. *Substance Use & Misuse, 53*(11), 1907–1914.

Guimarães, R. A., Rodovalho, A. G., Fernandes, I. L., Silva, G. C., Felipe, R. L. D., Vera, I., et al. (2016). Transactional sex among noninjecting illicit drug users: Implications for HIV transmission. *Scientific World Journal, 2016*, article ID 4690628, 7 pp., https://doi.org/10.1155/2016/4690628

Halkitis, P. N., Parsons, J. T., & Stirratt, M. J. (2001). A double epidemic: Crystal methamphetamine drug use in relation to HIV transmission. *Journal of Homosexuality, 41*(2), 17–35.

Hong, Y., & Li, X. (2007). Behavioral studies of female sex workers in China: A literature review and recommendation for future research. *AIDS and Behavior, 12*(4), 623–636.

Huamei, Y., Wong Frank, Y., Zhen, N., Yingying, D., Nehl Eric, J., Lavinia, L., et al. (2014). Social support and depressive symptoms among "money" boys and general men who have sex with men in Shanghai, China. *Sexual Health, 11*, 285–287.

Jenness, S. M., Kobrak, P., Wendel, T., Neaigus, A., Murrill, C. S., & Hagan, H. (2011). Patterns of exchange sex and HIV infection in high-risk heterosexual men and women. *Journal of Urban Health, 88*(2), 329–341.

Khoury, L., Tang, Y. L., Bradley, B., Cubells, J. F., & Ressler, K. J. (2010). Substance use, childhood traumatic experience, and posttraumatic stress disorder in an urban civilian population. *Depression and Anxiety, 27*(12), 1077–1086.

Kilpatrick, D. G., Acierno, R., Saunders, B., Resnick, H. S., Best, C. L., & Schnurr, P. P. (2000). Risk factors for adolescent substance abuse and dependence: Data from a national sample. *Journal of Consulting and Clinical Psychology, 68*(1), 19.

King, E. J., Maman, S., Bowling, J. M., Moracco, K. E., & Dudina, V. (2013). The influence of stigma and discrimination on female sex workers' access to HIV services in St. Petersburg, Russia. *AIDS and Behavior, 17*(8), 2597–2603.

Koblin, B. A., Husnik, M. J., Colfax, G., Huang, Y., Madison, M., Mayer, K., et al. (2006). Risk factors for HIV infection among men who have sex with men. *AIDS, 20*(5), 731–739.

Koken, J. A., Bimbi, D. S., Parsons, J. T., & Halkitis, P. N. (2004). The experience of stigma in the lives of male internet escorts. *Journal of Psychology & Human Sexuality, 16*(1), 13–32.

Kong, T. S. (2009). More than a sex machine: Accomplishing masculinity among Chinese male sex workers in the Hong Kong sex industry. *Deviant Behavior, 30*(8), 715–745.

Korhonen, C., Kimani, M., Wahome, E., Otieno, F., Okall, D., Bailey, R. C., et al. (2018). Depressive symptoms and problematic alcohol and other substance use in 1476 gay, bisexual, and other MSM at three research sites in Kenya. *AIDS (London, England), 32*(11), 1507.

Krüsi, A., Pacey, K., Bird, L., Taylor, C., Chettiar, J., Allan, S., et al. (2014). Criminalisation of clients: Reproducing vulnerabilities for violence and poor health among street-based sex workers in Canada—A qualitative study. *BMJ Open, 4*(6), e005191.

Landers, S., Closson, E. F., Oldenburg, C. E., Holcomb, R., Spurlock, S., & Mimiaga, M. J. (2014). HIV prevention needs among street-based male sex workers in Providence, Rhode Island. *American Journal of Public Health, 104*(11), e100–e102.

Lasco, G. (2018). Call boys: Drug use and sex work among marginalized young men in a Philippine port community. *Contemporary Drug Problems, 45*(1), 33–46.

Luckenbill, D. F. (1985). Entering male prostitution. *Urban Life, 14*(2), 131–153.

Marshall, B. D., Shannon, K., Kerr, T., Zhang, R., & Wood, E. (2010). Survival sex work and increased HIV risk among sexual minority street-involved youth. *Journal of Acquired Immune Deficiency Syndromes (1999), 53*(5), 661.

Mimiaga, M. J., Hughto, J. W., & Biello, K. B. (2012). *Longitudinal analysis of syndemic psychosocial problems predicting HIV risk behavior among male sex workers in Massachusetts and Rhode Island.* Manuscript submitted for publication.

Mimiaga, M. J., Noonan, E., Donnell, D., Safren, S. A., Koenen, K. C., Gortmaker, S., et al. (2009). Childhood sexual abuse is highly associated with HIV risk-taking behavior and infection among MSM in the EXPLORE study. *Journal of Acquired Immune Deficiency Syndromes (1999)*, *51*(3), 340.

Mimiaga, M. J., Reisner, S. L., Pantalone, D. W., O'Cleirigh, C., Mayer, K. H., & Safren, S. A. (2012). A pilot trial of integrated behavioral activation and sexual risk reduction counseling for HIV-uninfected men who have sex with men abusing crystal methamphetamine. *AIDS Patient Care and STDs*, *26*(11), 681–693.

Mimiaga, M. J., Reisner, S., Tinsley, J., Mayer, K., & Safren, S. (2009). Street workers and internet escorts: Contextual and psychosocial factors surrounding HIV risk behavior among men who engage in sex work with other men. *Journal of Urban Health*, *86*(1), 54–66.

Minichiello, V., Marino, R., Browne, J., Jamieson, M., Peterson, K., Reuter, B., et al. (2002). Male sex workers in three Australian cities: Socio-demographic and sex work characteristics. *Journal of Homosexuality*, *42*(1), 29–51.

Minichiello, V., Mariño, R., Khan, M. A., & Browne, J. (2003). Alcohol and drug use in Australian male sex workers: Its relationship to the safety outcome of the sex encounter. *AIDS Care*, *15*(4), 549–561.

Neale, J. (2001). Don't overdo it—overdose extent and prevention: The extent of illicit drug overdose and strategies for prevention. *Druglink*, *16*(4), 18–22.

Negele, A., Kaufhold, J., Kallenbach, L., & Leuzinger-Bohleber, M. (2015). Childhood trauma and its relation to chronic depression in adulthood. *Depression Research and Treatment*, *2015*. 650804. doi:10.1155/2015/650804

Nerlander, L. M., Hess, K. L., Rose, C. E., Sionean, C., Thorson, A., Broz, D., et al. (2017). Exchange sex and HIV infection among women who inject drugs: 20 US cities, 2009. *Journal of Acquired Immune Deficiency Syndromes (1999)*, *75*(Suppl. 3), S333.

Nerlander, L. M., Hess, K. L., Sionean, C., Rose, C. E., Thorson, A., Broz, D., & Paz-Bailey, G. (2017). Exchange sex and HIV infection among men who have sex with men: 20 US cities, 2011. *AIDS and Behavior*, *21*(8), 2283–2294.

Newman, P. A., Rhodes, F., & Weiss, R. E. (2004). Correlates of sex trading among drug-using men who have sex with men. *American Journal of Public Health*, *94*(11), 1998–2003.

Niccolai, L. M., King, E. J., Eritsyan, K. U., Safiullina, L., & Rusakova, M. M. (2013). "In different situations, in different ways": Male sex work in St. Petersburg, Russia. *Culture, Health & Sexuality*, *15*(4), 480–493.

NSWP (Global Network of Sex Work Projects). (2017). *The impact of criminalisation on sex workers' vulnerability to HIV and violence*. Retrieved from www.nswp.org/sites/nswp.org/files/impact_of_criminalisation_pb_prf01.pdf

Okal, J., Luchters, S., Geibel, S., Chersich, M. F., Lango, D., & Temmerman, M. (2009). Social context, sexual risk perceptions and stigma: HIV vulnerability among male sex workers in Mombasa, Kenya. *Culture, Health & Sexuality*, *11*(8), 811–826.

Oldenburg, C. E., Biello, K. B., Colby, D., Closson, E. F., Mai, T., Nguyen, T., et al. (2014). Stigma related to sex work among men who engage in transactional sex with men in Ho Chi Minh City, Vietnam. *International Journal of Public Health*, *59*(5), 833–840.

Oldenburg, C. E., Jain, S., Mayer, K. H., & Mimiaga, M. J. (2015). Post-exposure prophylaxis use and recurrent exposure to HIV among men who have sex with men who use crystal methamphetamine. *Drug and Alcohol Dependence*, *146*, 75–80.

Oldenburg, C. E., Perez-Brumer, A. G., Biello, K. B., Landers, S. J., Rosenberger, J. G., Novak, D. S., et al. (2015). Transactional sex among men who have sex with men in Latin America: Economic, socio-demographic, and psychosocial factors. *American Journal of Public Health*, *105*(5), e95–e102.

Oldenburg, C. E., Perez-Brumer, A. G., & Reisner, S. L. (2014). Poverty matters: Contextualizing the syndemic condition of psychological factors and newly diagnosed HIV infection in the United States. *AIDS (London, England)*, *28*(18), 2763.

Onyango-Ouma, W., Birungi, H., & Geibel, S. (2005). *Understanding the HIV/STI risks and prevention needs of men who have sex with men in Nairobi, Kenya. Horizons final report*. Washington, DC: Population Council.

Osher, F. C., Goldberg, R. W., McNary, S. W., Swartz, M. S., Essock, S. M., Butterfield, M. I., et al. (2003). Blood-borne infections and persons with mental illness: Substance abuse and the transmission of hepatitis C among persons with severe mental illness. *Psychiatric Services*, *54*(6), 842–847.

Padilla, M., Castellanos, D., Guilamo-Ramos, V., Reyes, A. M., Marte, L. E. S., & Soriano, M. A. (2008). Stigma, social inequality, and HIV risk disclosure among Dominican male sex workers. *Social Science & Medicine*, *67*(3), 380–388.

Philbin, M. M., Kinnard, E. N., Tanner, A. E., Ware, S., Chambers, B. D., Ma, A., et al. (2018). The association between incarceration and transactional sex among HIV-infected young men who have sex with men in the United States. *Journal of Urban Health*, *95*(4), 576–583.

Regier, D. A., Farmer, M. E., Rae, D. S., Locke, B. Z., Keith, S. J., Judd, L. L., et al. (1990). Comorbidity of mental disorders with alcohol and other drug abuse: Results from the Epidemiologic Catchment Area (ECA) study. *JAMA*, *264*(19), 2511–2518.

Rehm, J. (2011). The risks associated with alcohol use and alcoholism. *Alcohol Research & Health*, *34*(2), 135.

Reisner, S. L., Mimiaga, M. J., Mayer, K. H., Tinsley, J. P., & Safren, S. A. (2008). Tricks of the trade: Sexual health behaviors, the context of HIV risk, and potential prevention intervention strategies for male sex workers. *Journal of LGBT Health Research*, *4*(4), 195–209.

Safren, S. A., Bedoya, C. A., O'Cleirigh, C., Biello, K. B., Pinkston, M. M., Stein, M. D., et al. (2016). Cognitive behavioural therapy for adherence and depression in patients with HIV: A three-arm randomised controlled trial. *The Lancet*, *3*(11), PE529–E538.

SAHealth (South Australia Health). (2012). *The dangers of mixing drugs*. Retrieved from www.sahealth. sa.gov.au/

Shoptaw, S., & Frosch, D. (2000). Substance abuse treatment as HIV prevention for men who have sex with men. *AIDS and Behavior*, *4*(2), 193–203.

Singer, M., Bulled, N., Ostrach, B., & Mendenhall, E. (2017). Syndemics and the biosocial conception of health. *The Lancet*, *389*(10072), 941–950.

Singer, M., & Clair, S. (2003). Syndemics and public health: Reconceptualizing disease in bio-social context. *Medical Anthropology Quarterly*, *17*(4), 423–441.

Smith, M. D., & Seal, D. (2008). Sexual behavior, mental health, substance use, and HIV risk among agency-based male escorts in a small US city. *International Journal of Sexual Health*, *19*(4), 27–39.

Stall, R., Friedman, M., & Catania, J. A. (2008). Interacting epidemics and gay men's health: A theory of syndemic production among urban gay men. In R. J. Wolitski, R. Stall, & R. O. Valdiserri (Eds.), *Unequal opportunity: Health disparities affecting gay and bisexual men in the United States* (pp. 251–274). New York: Oxford University Press.

Stall, R., Mills, T. C., Williamson, J., Hart, T., Greenwood, G., Paul, J., et al. (2003). Association of co-occurring psychosocial health problems and increased vulnerability to HIV/AIDS among urban men who have sex with men. *American Journal of Public Health*, *93*(6), 939–942.

Surratt, H. L., & Inciardi, J. A. (2010). An effective HIV risk-reduction protocol for drug-using female sex workers. *Journal of Prevention & Intervention in the Community*, *38*(2), 118–131.

Thomas, B., Mimiaga, M. J., Mayer, K. H., Perry, N. S., Swaminathan, S., & Safren, S. A. (2012). The influence of stigma on HIV risk behavior among men who have sex with men in Chennai, India. *AIDS Care*, *24*(11), 1401–1406.

Turner, H. A., Finkelhor, D., & Ormrod, R. (2006). The effect of lifetime victimization on the mental health of children and adolescents. *Social Science & Medicine*, *62*(1), 13–27.

Underhill, K., Morrow, K. M., Colleran, C. M., Holcomb, R., Operario, D., Calabrese, S. K., et al. (2014). Access to healthcare, HIV/STI testing, and preferred pre-exposure prophylaxis providers among men who have sex with men and men who engage in street-based sex work in the US. *PLoS ONE*, *9*(11), e112425.

Vu, B. N., Mulvey, K. P., Baldwin, S., & Nguyen, S. T. (2012). HIV risk among drug-using men who have sex with men, men selling sex, and transgender individuals in Vietnam. *Culture, Health & Sexuality*, *14*(2), 167–180.

Weber, A. E., Craib, K. J., Chan, K., Martindale, S., Miller, M. L., Schechter, M. T., et al. (2001). Sex trade involvement and rates of human immunodeficiency virus positivity among young gay and bisexual men. *International Journal of Epidemiology, 30*(6), 1449–1454.

Wechsberg, W. M., Luseno, W. K., Lam, W. K., Parry, C. D., & Morojole, N. K. (2006). Substance use, sexual risk, and violence: HIV prevention intervention with sex workers in Pretoria. *AIDS and Behavior, 10*(131).

Wilkerson, J. M., Di Paola, A., Rawat, S., Patankar, P., Rosser, B. S., & Ekstrand, M. L. (2018). Substance use, mental health, HIV testing, and sexual risk behavior among men who have sex with men in the state of Maharashtra, India. *AIDS Education and Prevention, 30*(2), 96–107.

Wolitski, R. J., Stall, R., & Valdiserri, R. O. (2008). *Unequal opportunity: Health disparities affecting gay and bisexual men in the United States.* New York: Oxford University Press.

Wong, F. Y., He, N., Huang, Z., Young, D., O'Conor, C., Ding, Y., et al. (2010). Migration and illicit drug use among two types of male migrants in Shanghai, China. *Journal of Psychoactive Drugs, 42*(1), 1–9.

Xie, P., Wu, K., Zheng, Y., Guo, Y., Yang, Y., He, J., et al. (2018). Prevalence of childhood trauma and correlations between childhood trauma, suicidal ideation, and social support in patients with depression, bipolar disorder, and schizophrenia in southern China. *Journal of Affective Disorders, 228*, 41–48.

Yang, C., Guadamuz, T. E., Lim, S. H., Koe, S., & Wei, C. (2016). Factors associated with alcohol use before or during sex among men who have sex with men in a large Internet sample from Asia. *LGBT Health, 3*(2), 168–174.

Yu, G., Clatts, M. C., Goldsamt, L. A., & Giang, L. M. (2015). Substance use among male sex workers in Vietnam: Prevalence, onset, and interactions with sexual risk. *International Journal of Drug Policy, 26*(5), 516–521.

Yu, G., Goldsamt, L. A., & Clatts, M. C. (2016). Sexual initiation and complex recent polydrug use patterns among male sex workers in Vietnam: A preliminary epidemiological trajectory. *Archives of Sexual Behavior, 45*(4), 975–981.

Zenilman, J. M., Shepherd, M., Smith, P., Rompalo, A., & Celentano, D. (1994). Alcohol and other substance use in STD clinic patients: Relationships with STDs and prevalent HIV infection. *Sexually Transmitted Diseases, 21*(4), 220–225.

Part V

Male sex worker, escort, and client voices

"Nothing about us without us"

20

Male sex work and the female client

Accounts from a straight male escort

Maxime Durocher

First contact with an alien race

When I say I'm an escort for women, I get four different types of standard reactions.

Disgust

The first reaction is disgust, either in words or attitude, and it is the most common response. This reaction is what makes our job difficult, sometimes unbearable. Our clients are humans; they're not the problem. Stigma is. It is stigma that leaves a mark. It is what everyday people think of us that brings violence to us. Stigma makes people turn a blind eye toward that violence; stigma makes people think that we chose that violence, that, in a way, we deserve it. But we are humans, too. We can choose our own line of work, and we should be free of violence or judgment while engaging in our work. However, when the general population thinks less of us, then violent offenders see us as the perfect victims, as proven by the scores of unreported and uninvestigated sex worker deaths.

The only way to remove this mark is to have the law on our side. Decriminalization is not only good for our health and our security, it is also a good way to tell the population at large that we deserve respect, that we are not criminals but rather people doing their job.

Decriminalization would mean that I could tell my clients they have nothing to fear, that they would not be committing a crime (in Canada, buying sex is a crime but not selling it). Nobody wants to break the law. Just as importantly, it would mean that my fellow sex workers, those most marginalized, could more easily get the help and services that would make their lives so much easier.

Glamorization

The second reaction is glamorization. People think I'm living the dream, having sex with all the women I want—as if, as a man, that is all I want out of life. As if enjoying myself is my job. No, that's not my job. My job is to give pleasure, not to take it. I push back my own needs, what I want, to concentrate on giving my client what she wants, if it's something I can give her.

At the same time, I (and most other sex workers) follow a moral code. We require protection for sex. We do not take on clients we do not feel safe with. We don't sell out our clients. We stay very discreet. We count the money twice, but we want our clients to be satisfied—at least those we like and want to come back.

Curiosity

There third type of response I get is curiosity. Those who are even a little bit curious by nature and who encounter a profession they know little about, let alone one shrouded in mystery as sex work is, will invariably have questions popping up in their head like dried corn kernels on a hot plate. However, the questions are almost always the same: How do I keep it up? How ugly are my clients?

This curiosity has led me to avoid saying what I do for work. I don't avoid offending those who are likely to be disgusted, but unless I know a person well, I won't get into this discussion. It can get bizarre quickly and it can be very uncomfortable, with strangers delving into personal areas without realizing just how insensitive their questions are.

For the record: I tend to see things that please me in every client. That's what's keeping it up. Yes, I have encountered difficult situations where I haven't performed to my standard, but I have a mouth, I have hands, I have a body, and most important, I have a brain. A failing erection will not keep me from giving pleasure. In fact, the problem concerning my erection is not my clients'. Rather, it's my self-imposed pressure to perform, to give all I can to the women who are buying my time. That's a much bigger issue.

Also: My clients aren't ugly. How dare anyone judge them? The ugly ones are those who dare voice such opinions. There's beauty in everyone, and those who have truly turned me off were those I disagreed with on some fundamental level. It is the people with negative personalities with whom I have the most trouble.

Trouble comes in many different forms for a straight male sex worker, but most of the difficulties are psychological or behavioral. A client who drinks too much and gets difficult to deal with. A demanding or clinging patron who doesn't understand the concept of limits and who tries to wring everything out of you with no tool other than an earnest yearning. A panic attack in the middle of a session. Prejudice against sex workers. Being seen as a victim. Having to avoid work-related talks with the people you casually meet.

Indifference

The rarest of responses is indifference, and it is the one that I love. Being seen as just another worker is a blessing. I can just go on talking about whatever I was talking about, and that is sweet. Why? Because I love causing silent waves of change. I love it when people know what I do, because I'm proud of what I do. I see it as a badge of honor to give women what they want or crave.

How do I want people to react to the revelation that I am a sex worker? I want their eyes to widen, their jaws to drop a fraction, their heart skip a beat or two. I want them to wonder quietly: Why? He's normal. Does he really do that? Yes, I do, and I'm no different from you. I don't come from an alien race, a special prostitution nursery, a broken family, or a convention for drug addicts. Those are all convenient fabrications that are designed to isolate us.

In fact, we, sex workers as a whole, are normal people. We are students, single parents, debtors, or people just tired of doing 9 to 5. More than money, we are looking for freedom. We want to have time to study, time to take care of our children, to be free from financial worries or corporate machinery. I wanted to have time to climb, write, and create. I wanted to be my own boss. Sex work gives you that freedom, and it's a beautiful gift.

For many of those I talked with, it's also that freedom they were looking for. Some feel the need for freedom as powerfully as I do. I know that my nightmares are filled with going back to a 9-to-5 routine or going back to school. I wake up with my heart beating fast, feeling an urgent need to ground myself, to get away from it all, desperately clawing to get out of that terrible trap and to convince myself I'm still a whore. When I do, a wave of relief washes over me, and I slump back down in my bed under those soft and embracing comforters.

The perils of entrepreneurship

Like many other sex workers, I run a small business. There's only one source of anxiety in my current job: finding my next appointment. Like all independent workers, I strive to achieve a steady stream of income. Like any entrepreneur, I defined my product and keep refining it as I go, I created my image, I built my online presence, I publicized my business with interviews and meetings, and I set my prices according to value and demand.

However, my business, unlike those of my friends who cater to men, is different. My target audience is not only unaware that I exist but also unaware that the type of services I offer even exist. It's like trying to sell cola when everybody drinks water and nobody knows that soft drinks exist. The market's lack of awareness is the biggest challenge that I, and all straight male escorts, face.

It took me six months to get my first date. I still remember it. The clients were a couple. Very nice, polite, eager, middle-aged professionals. It went very well, and for an hour I got $160. I remember walking back home in the crisp fall air, telling myself how easy it had been.

The challenges of couples

Despite my initial positive experience, I've found that couples are not all that easy. For a while I refused to see couples anymore, owing to a particularly unpleasant encounter. In my naïveté, I had talked only to the husband, and then realized in the middle of the action that the wife might have felt as though she was being raped. Being unaware of the couple's dynamic, I couldn't tell if consent was really part of the equation. She wasn't resisting or saying no, and she seemed really compliant, but something was not completely right. Had I talked to her beforehand, maybe I would have realized that everything was fine, or maybe I would have decided that she did not really want to live that experience.

Being the second man in a threesome is a different challenge than being the second woman. Both have specific rules to play by. In the context of a threesome, being heterosexual is also different from being bisexual or homosexual. In any case, it's a balancing act. Mine is to give the woman as much pleasure as possible while giving the man all the room he needs. I need to concentrate on her while monitoring his reactions without looking at him. I need to keep them both happy at all times.

Still, I can fail. One woman told me a few days later that after the encounter her partner had reproached her for complimenting my hands more than she had ever complimented his. Another woman told me just after I arrived that she was doing it for her husband, that she was really interested only in women. Another woman made unloving comments about her husband before he joined us. Messy situations are a part of life. If you can't accept that, you're in trouble.

Now, with couples, I simply ask to speak with the lady. In our chat, I make sure that she's part of the process, that she really wants to do this. I also try to connect with her, glean her desires. I make sure that both partners understand the need to talk about this experience, fix limits if necessary, establish rules, and plan for possible events. A good threesome is all about good communication.

Unsatisfied customers

Although I've had great success in my career, there are a few ladies who weren't satisfied with my services. One felt that I didn't give her what she wanted. One felt that she should have left a bigger impression on me. One was angry because I couldn't perform a second time in the day. I know perfectly well that a service provider cannot possibly satisfy every possible client, but it's always a disappointment when I face such cases. It hurts to be held responsible for simple human failings. Some clients fail to see that behind every service provider, sexual or otherwise, there's a human being and that we have feelings just as they do, that we deserve respect as much as they do.

Erection and performance problems

A man's erection is psychological, and as a society we're so hung up on performance that it can lead to trouble. As a professional, I put too much pressure on myself, but some women take it personally when an erection fails. I've had clients cry because they couldn't make me come. That's how much pressure society puts on us to perform. We define ourselves by our successes and failures instead of simply enjoying what fun we can.

Putting more pressure on ourselves only makes matters worse. It's a vicious circle. As sex workers, we're trying our best. The erection may not be here today, but we still have the rest of our body. Personally, I prefer oral sex to penetration. So much fun. And very personal, more intimate, even. But that's just my opinion.

Political and social differences

I am always myself, and it's difficult for me not to argue or defend things I believe in when I'm with a client. The few clients who never booked me a second time were women with whom I didn't see eye to eye on social or political issues. Do you take the risk of antagonizing your client by disagreeing with her? That's a decision that every sex worker has to make.

Communication, respect, consent, and privacy

I put a lot of stock in communication, as you can see on the home page of my website (Figure 20.1). Two individuals should communicate their desires, expectations, fear, and anxieties, and they should be able to adjust to each other's needs. Communication is central to a good experience.

However, when I talk about the importance of communication, I'm not saying that both parties need to reveal everything all the time. That's a huge mistake. We need a secret garden or else we lose our individuality.

Equally important are respect and consent. Without respect, you cannot have true consent, and consent is key. Respect brings harmony. Consent brings safety. Communication brings pleasure.

An important part of respect is privacy. Paramount in my mind is respect for my clients' privacy. When I began this work, I used to ask my clients about their motivations and a bit of

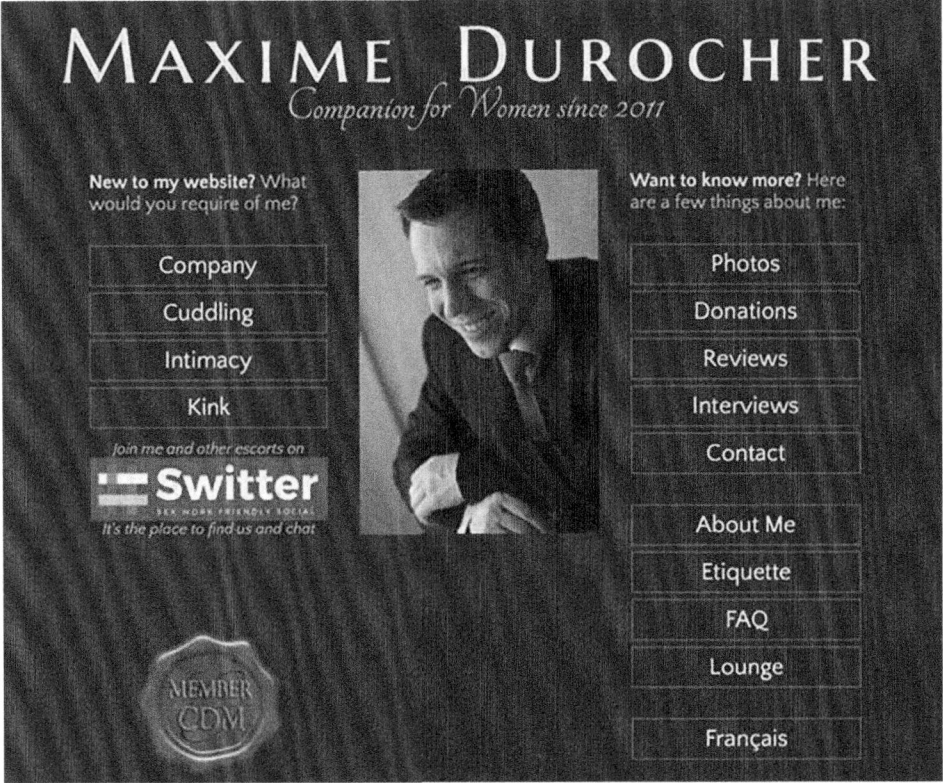

Figure 20.1 The home page of the author's website, MaximeDurocher.com.

their background. Doing so helped me establish the right mood and know what kind of attitude I should have during the date. However, I stopped asking for that information because I found it a bit intrusive. Now I let the lady give me the information she wishes me to have. It's more natural, and most of the time I get the information I need without asking intrusive questions.

The only thing I ask is that my client tell me what kind of encounter she's looking for and if she has any special requests. I'm not a mind reader, and if there's something a lady absolutely wants to have or to avoid, it should be clear from the outset.

The benefits to clients

What my clients want is much more than simply sex. Even if the encounter is short, they have personal contact with another human being. If that weren't part of the equation, they'd be masturbating. My clients love to talk, share their lives, and feel me close to them, the warmth of my body and soul. I offer them an irreplaceable experience in exchange for a livelihood.

The beauty of calling on a professional is that the experience is clean and clear. If a lady calls me for my services, she doesn't have to play a game. She doesn't have to seduce. She doesn't have to go along with prescribed societal norms. She can be whatever she wants to be. She can be herself and nothing else. She can also be coy, secretive, mysterious. She doesn't have to care, so long as respect and consent are part of the equation.

The rules and etiquette also give me a lot of freedom, because I know that she's interested in me. So, I can be as charming as I want. I can be frank. I can let my guard down and not be afraid of being rejected. I don't have to pretend or play a game. The seduction is pure and unadulterated. Its effect is strong and heady for my clients. It carries me to a wonderful place where joy and pleasure are the only rulers.

Without the tentacular social expectations, we don't have to call each other again, and there won't be any awkward moments when she gets back in touch with me a year or two later. What we do is simple and joyful. In fact, I know that some women see me for the therapeutic effect our meetings have on them.

Many of my clients start preparing for our date well in advance. They bring back all the self-care they may have abandoned a while back. They think about what they're going to wear. They get massages, they go to see their favorite esthetician, they might buy this or that. Step by step, they're rebuilding their confidence, their self-worth.

To others, I give strength. They might be in a difficult marriage they're unwilling to break, often in consideration of their children. They might call on me after an ugly divorce, or years after an assault.

To some, I give what's missing in their current relationship: an attentive ear, affection, oral caresses, or even just plain sex, feeling desired. Such deficiencies can leave gaping holes in their lives if ignored, but they do not always provide enough motivation to leave a partner.

Sex workers tend to save marriages and make them happier. Those outside our community do not see that we help maintain society's fabric. We're not evil; we're not trying to ensnare your spouse. We don't want them as you want them. We're just there to help them. We're professionals offering a service. In the end, they go back to you, and that's fine with us.

A great connection with a client can last years. I help her through difficult moments, share her intimate thoughts, and know her aspirations, tribulations, joys, and ups and downs. Even if the connection isn't spectacular, it still can be a great experience. I love to meet all the many different women who have been short-changed by circumstances or societal paradigms. Society wanted them to believe in a Prince Charming who would be their perfect life partner, the soul mate who would make them complete. The reality is very different, of course. I can help my clients make up for Prince Charming's shortcomings.

That said, I love it when a client contacts me for a follow-up. It shows that she appreciated me and wants more of me. It makes me feel all warm and fuzzy. It makes me feel desired. It makes me feel attractive. It's a heady drug. Just as powerful is the look in her eyes when she tells me: "You're so hot!" That sends a shiver of pleasure down my spine. I love it when they grab my cock through my pants with longing.

Defining love, sex, and relationships

As a society, we define sex through orgasm when we aren't defining it through penetration. Both of these definitions are wrong. Sex is just an experience we share with one or more people. It's a great, fun way to share intimacy and feelings.

So when I work, my goal is to make sure my client feels comfortable and has a good time. The goal isn't penetration or orgasm. It's what we can weave between us. It's much closer to a moment of escape. A second reality, where we start with a clean slate and build a fantasy castle we can revisit again and again.

When I talk about fantasy, I don't mean something false, which most people assume and most clients dread. No; the relationship I have with my clients is real. I give part of myself, and together we build a relationship.

Different relationships are based on different things. Some relationships are based on friendship, some on work, others on love. In sex work, the relationship is based on service. But that doesn't mean the relationship is fake. It's just different. The relationships I build are more intimate than friendship, more sexual, but they don't have the depth that usually comes with love. So long as the client does not think she is getting love out of the relationship, then she will be fine.

The only hiccup is that our society wants to equate sex with love, and we're very much conditioned to equate them. So the elation a client can feel as she is interacting with a sex worker is often confused with love. That's normal, but as a sex worker, I can't let my client be blinded by that. What she can feel coming from me is not love; it's just me opening up to her.

I can anticipate your next question. No, I have never seen a relationship successfully transition from a base of service to one of love. Never. You see, when you meet a service provider, you get only a part of him. We don't argue, we don't ask for anything, we don't go against your wishes. We block a part of ourselves from your view. That means you get only the best of us. Once you get the whole picture, inevitably the relationship will change.

My life in a nutshell

My work is almost 24/7. I'm always checking my emails or trying to find new ways to connect with potential clients, but I do have free time, lots of it. What do I do with it? I nourish my imagination. I watch movies, play games, read, write, and create. That's my passion. That and climbing, but I know I will never make money climbing.

As a sex worker, I also get to appreciate ballet. I get to try many new restaurants. I see a lot of museum exhibitions. I love taking the train or a plane, seeing new countries. I meet many different women, get exposed to many different points of view, and learn intimate details, which I'm always curious about. I just love to talk to women. They fascinate me.

You may be surprised to learn that outside work, I don't have that much sex, and I don't think about it very often. I prefer a good movie to lousy sex. Quality before quantity, always. Same with my relationships. I see few people, but good people. People who bring me joy. Women who are affectionate and often kinky.

What's more, monogamy is long behind me. I think it's an inadequate form of relationship that few can really be happy with without worry or jealousy. I prefer to live without those sentiments. I think it's saner and more respectful.

Of course, the media have always been curious about me, my work, and my life. Some are very respectful. A few are insightful, and most try to be juicy. After an interview I can feel dirty or elated, depending on the type of interview. I hold my own, point out fallacies, misconceptions, and bias, hoping to help people understand why we, sex workers, fight for our rights. But in the end, the journalists do what they want with the interview.

On the other end of the spectrum, researchers are much more respectful. Circumscribed by ethics and protocols, more often than not they are our allies, because data and science are on the side of human rights, every time. Their strength is their downside, however. Being impartial, most of them have never hired a sex worker or been one, so they lack true emotional knowledge of our work, sometimes even disbelieving what we tell them, going as far as saying we are wrong.

I'm always happy to talk with both: journalists, to spread the word to as many people as I can; researchers, to build scientific knowledge about our work. Both are important, and both need to be better at what they do.

QUT Me, Us and Male Escorting

The Benefits of Prostitution to Society

A Male Escort's Perspective

Guest Blogger: Maxime Durocher, a male sex worker in Montreal, Canada

First, let me clear the air. Yes, not all is rosy in my domain, but the dark side is not intrinsic to prostitution, just as there is nothing wrong with homosexuality, only how people treat homosexuals. It's a question of moral views. I can't convince those who believe that prostitution is immoral to change their opinion, no more than I can convert a monogamist to open up her relationships to multiple partners.

Figure 20.2 The author's guest blog post, "The Benefits of Prostitution to Society: A Male Escort's Perspective," on *Me, Us and Male Escorting,* https://research.qut.edu.au/aboutmaleescorting/2016/05/31/the-benefits-of-prostitution-to-society/.

I have written a blog for an academic forum on male escorting. In it I explain my views and perspectives on the benefits of sex work for society (Figure 20.2).

Changing the discourse

As a male sex worker, I stand outside most social paradigms, even more so because my clients are women. They haven't been taught that they can hire the services of a prostitute if they want to. Even worse, the current societal context tells them that they are failures as women if they can't find a mate. The thought of hiring a professional might affect their self-esteem even more negatively.

However, hiring a professional is smart. For a woman, picking up somebody in a bar just because she wants some company, affection, or sex is disappointing at best, risky at worst. What

Figure 20.3   Calling for respect and understanding (Kermond, 2016).

I would say to women is this: Why not contact me or one my colleagues, make an appointment, have a good time, and then use your time to find someone worth sharing your life with?

The chance of finding that great partner in a club, on a dating website, or on some matching app is slim. The best connections are made under natural circumstances. Those take time. In the meantime, a professional can be there for you.

What's stopping you? Social conventions and stigma. You were taught all your life that prostitution is bad, that those poor women are being exploited. What's exploitative about a professional choosing to offer a service for money? Because part of it is sex? That's moralistic at best. Think about the reason you're considering emailing me or one of my colleagues. That's what's important, because it's about you. We assure you: We're not being exploited. We are just offering a service.

We need to create new discourses about sex workers and the sex work arena. The discourse surrounding respect and understanding, as explained in an article published in the *Sydney Morning Herald*, in which I was interviewed, is important to changing attitudes (see Figure 20.3).

When we march for our rights, we ask for the right to work in peace, so that we can be safe and healthy. We don't ask anybody to change their views on sex. Rather, we ask that they respect our views on sex. Sex happens between two consenting adults, and it should never be regulated by laws. Laws don't exist to impose morals; they exist to defend the basic rights of individuals.

I started being an activist barely a year after I started sex work. Why, when I hadn't participated in any other social movement? Because for the first time, after studying for most of my life and having a ten-year career in technology with a meteoric rise through the ranks, I feel like I truly belong. That's how much I believe in the value and importance of sex work as real work.

References

Durocher, M. (2016). The benefits of prostitution to society: A male escort's perspective. *Me, Us and Male Escorting.* Retrieved from https://research.qut.edu.au/aboutmaleescorting/2016/05/31/the-benefits-of-prostitution-to-society/

Kermond, C. (2016, June 17). Male sex workers call for respect, understanding. *Sydney Morning Herald.* Retrieved from www.smh.com.au/national/male-sex-workers-call-for-respect-understanding-20160609-gpf5qy.html

21

Female clients of male sex workers
Managing stigma

Hilary Caldwell and John de Wit

Buying sex is both stigmatized and stigmatizing. Although engaging in sex, commercial or otherwise, is not inherently harmful, stigmatization has harmful consequences (Weitzer, 2017a; Vanwesenbeeck, 2001). Stigma arising from participation in a deeply discrediting or discreditable activity (Goffman, 1963) manifests in labeling, stereotyping, separating, status loss, discrimination, and negative representations in public opinion, the media, and political discourse (Weitzer, 2017a; Phillips, Benoit, Hallgrimsdottir, & Vallance, 2012). Stigma also seeps into broader sociocultural structures, including social welfare policies and other determinants of health advantage and disadvantage (Phillips et al., 2012; Cama et al., 2018). Experiences of stigmatization include negative impacts on self-concept and identity formation, leading individuals to conceal their activities and to lead double lives, which may prevent them from engaging in normal social interaction (Phillips et al., 2012; Weitzer, 2017b). Nonetheless, stigma reflects societal norms, which constantly change. This chapter clarifies some social norms and the stigma associated with buying sex.

Prior to the 1950s, buying sex was an expected male pastime that has been systematically demonized by campaigners who consider female sex workers degraded, damaged goods, and exploited victims of men. According to Scott and Minichiello (2014), these exploitation narratives explain why buying sex is more stigmatizing than selling it. Though the ideas that sex work is inherently harmful and that male clients are fundamentally violent are highly contested (Abel, 2014; Minichiello, Scott, & Cox, 2017; Phipps, 2017; Sanders, 2008; Scott & Minichiello, 2014; Sullivan, 2007; Vanwesenbeeck, 2013; Weitzer, 2010), the idea that sex work equals exploitation continues to dominate the discourse.

While some research has pointed to high levels of psychological distress in sex workers as confirmation of the harms perpetrated by male clients, Vanwesenbeeck (2001) suggests that social stigma regarding the sex industry drives the negative outcomes. This chapter investigates the effects of stigmatization on the lived experiences of female clients of sex workers, exposing weaknesses in exploitation arguments and revealing additional stigmas that may affect only women.

Female clients of sex workers have only recently come to the attention of academic researchers. The previous lack of awareness and research may have reflected a perceived low number of women buying sex based on surveys in which few women reported buying sex. In recent years, however, women buyers of sex have come to the attention of popular media, increasing their visibility and raising questions about gendered understandings of the sex industry, consumerism, female sexual agency, and what it means to be a woman in a postfeminist era (West Morris, 2012).

This chapter draws on a study in which we investigated the Australian social discourse about women who buy sex. We also interviewed sex workers with female clients and women who bought sex (Caldwell, 2018). We begin by considering the positioning of women who buy sex in popular exploitation discourse about the sex industry and within narratives regarding female sexual agency and how these discourses affect women who buy sex.

Contemporary Australian discourse on women buying sex

Ideas about women buying sex in contemporary Australia come from media representations that include messages about female sexuality and the sex industry (Caldwell & de Wit, 2015). Discourse in media is considered powerful in terms of developing the public understanding of any social setting (Rose, 2001; Wadham, Pease, Atherton, & Lorentzen, 2012). The media actively produce gender and reinforce gender norms (Butler, 1999; Gill, 2007).

We used textual analysis to identify and analyze Australian discourse about women who buy sex (McKee, 2003). Specifically, we analyzed a televised commercial advertisement depicting sexual tension between a woman holidaying in Bali and a local waiter (Figure 21.1).

The highly popular advertisement prompted a good deal of social and commercial media commentary, including online audience engagement. Initially, less than 20 percent of audience members who responded online to the television commercial interpreted it as possibly portraying female sex tourism or commercial sex. Only after journalistic commentary suggested this interpretation did two-thirds of the audience participating in the online debate agree that the advertisement portrayed commercial sex. The initial lack of audience awareness to the possibility of women buying sex illustrates the general idea that society does not foreground women's sexual agency.

Two distinct and polarized discourses regarding sex work were evident in audience comments: (1) sex work is work, and women who buy it are empowered, and (2) sex work is inherently exploitative, the women who buy it are as bad as men. These discourses directly reflect the analysis of Weitzer (2009), who examined the body of sociological study with regard to sex work and who identified the two main theoretical perspectives underpinning study design.

Figure 21.1   Australian television advertisement promoting Balinese holidays.

These theoretical perspectives either desire to oppress the sex industry due to its presumed intrinsic violence against women, or they consider the industry empowering for its workers and clients. Both of these paradigms rely on assumptions of male customers and female sex workers. Our study revealed that client stigma is gendered: Men who buy sex are seen as abusive, and women who buy sex are either victims or sluts.

The near-equal representation of commercial sex as either work or exploitation found in Australian discourse may represent a cultural shift away from exploitation narratives, which dominate in societies that have criminalized the buying and selling of sex. Australian sex industry regulation varies in each state and territory and is mostly progressive, with commercial sex either legalized or decriminalized.

Sex worker's perceptions of female-client stigma

We used thematic analysis of interview data from 17 sex workers who had been engaged by female clients. Ten of these sex workers identified as female, six as male, and one as gender non-conforming. None of the female workers described her orientation as straight, including one who described herself as gay for pay. Of the male sex workers, three said they were straight, one said he was straight for pay, one said he was gay, and one did not describe his orientation. Sex workers spoke about stigma directed toward all involved in the sex industry. Some of the female-identifying sex workers felt society treats their female clients "like us, dirty sluts," and other sex workers thought that women who buy sex are not considered to be like other women. They thought female clients are considered odd or unacceptable anomalies, with society believing something is wrong with them. Sex workers thought these perceptions might build on skewed interpretations of male clients that assume that all clients of sex workers are "creepy and ugly and horrible" rather than regular people. Some sex workers stressed that buying sex is not necessarily an indulgence and that "women's mental and physical health is well served by being able to access sex workers." One sex worker went on to describe the stigma and discrimination that women living with disabilities face when attempting to buy sexual services.

Sex workers were generally keen to participate in the study because they recognized the voices of female clients being silenced through stigmatization. Some sex workers noted that society wishes to silence women who buy sex through a compulsion to control female sexuality and desire and also to maintain the status quo regarding dominant narratives of (male) clients as violent. None of the interviewed sex workers felt exploited by their work or by male customers in general, noting that the Swedish model (which aims to criminalize clients) rests on unrealistic gender moralizations. A sex worker from Victoria noted the enactment of the licensing system and legislation surrounding the sex industry in that state treats all sex workers as women and all clients as men, suggesting that the voices of female clients might disrupt this state of affairs.

Women's experiences of stigma when buying sex

We interviewed 21 women who had paid for sex. Through an interpretative phenomenological analysis, we explored their motivations and experiences. Potential interviewees contacted the researcher after responding to online advertisements placed in social media often used by sex workers and in online spaces where sex workers advertise. Some women were motivated to become involved in the study due to the aggressive campaigning in the media for the Swedish model of regulation and the subsequent Parliamentary Inquiry in New South Wales at the time of recruitment.

Our interviewees were diverse, and they bought various types of sexual services. The women we interviewed were all female-identifying people, including one trans-identifying woman. Their ages ranged from 18 to 69, with 12 women under 45 the first time they bought sex and nine women over 45. Most Australian states are represented in the sample. Three interviewees had secondary schooling, 4 were university graduates, 11 had post-graduate qualifications, and 3 did not say their education level. Several interviewees had been buying sex for several years while in and out of various personal relationships. At the time of interview, 12 described themselves as single and 9 as partnered, some in open relationships. All 21 interviewees were Caucasian. Income levels were high for seven interviewees, medium for seven, medium to low for four, and low for three. Most of the interviewees would not have participated had they not been assured anonymity. One created a generic email address for the occasion, and another conducted the interview in her car, which she called "the only private place in her life."

In most interviews, experiences of stigmatization were expressed explicitly and spontaneously. In addition, specific questions asked whether women told other people about their experiences and if they would recommend buying sex to a friend. During data analysis, a relationship emerged between stigma and most other themes, demonstrating that stigma often subverts other concerns.

Two of the women who bought sex denied feeling stigmatized and described situations in which they actively avoided feeling stigmatized by using strategies such as secret keeping. The two interviewees who denied feeling stigmatized appeared to confuse stigma with shame, and most interviewees said they felt no shame for buying sex. One interviewee spoke at length about stigma directed toward sex workers and needed specific prompting to address the stigmatization of buying sex. Weitzer (2017b) points out that individuals internalize ideas about their identity and behavior in diverse ways.

Most interviewees understood the concept of stigma and how it affected them. For example: "Well it is certainly not something that I would be comfortable being widely known, so yeah, I guess I have to acknowledge that there is a massive stigma associated to it" (Interviewee 11, woman who bought sex [WBS]). WBS Interviewee 20 said, "There is so much stigma attached to things like this and it just isn't like that. It is a really wonderful thing." Our interviewees considered the possible reactions if other people found out they had bought sex. For example one WBS said, "Coming forward and saying that I am a woman and I have been with a sex worker, that is a massive, that is like an A bomb has just been dropped" (WBS Interviewee 12). Another said, "I look like, I guess your, quintessential female, and I think my colleagues would be most surprised to find out about my double life . . . and probably horrified" (WBS Interviewee 8), while another said, "My family would think what they already think of me . . . that I'm a sexual deviant. They already think some fucked up shit about me because I am a lesbian" (WBS Interviewee 21). Sanders (2017) explains that an abundance of stigma affects all actors directly connected to commercial sex, exposing a "bleak analysis of how much of society views and treats sex workers" (p. 1).

The women interviewed who bought sex were aware of social narratives regarding the victimization of female sex workers and the demonization of clients, who are generally labeled as perpetrators of violence. WBS Interviewee 11 said that she "suspects women buying sex suffer less stigma than men" due to exploitative narratives. WBS Interviewee 8 said these narratives "make sex buyers into uncaring people," and WBS Interviewee 11 "found the current positioning of sex work as assault to be deeply offensive to everyone engaged in it and particularly to women cast as victims." While some interviewees rejected exploitation narratives as not directed toward them, others were aware of the stigmatizing effects for all clients, and some were sympathetic to male clients, to whom they can now hypothetically relate. In short, the stigma experienced by players in the sex industry contain complex intersections between activity and gender.

Activity-based stigma

Women who bought sex described feeling stigmatized and shamed for their sexual orientations or practice when buying any sexual service other than regular heterosexual services. WBS Interviewee 2 said,

> people [male friends] would get terribly offended that you are more into it [the female dancers at the strip club] than them. Because, obviously it's fine that you are gay but you are not supposed to be demonstratively gay in public. . . [and] you would get the phenomenon where sometimes the dancers would refuse to come near you. Because obviously, they didn't want to catch the gay.

Regarding paying for same-sexual services, WBS Interviewee 2 said, "You are hiding away those things, then you are pretending that the sex you have purchased is heterosexual sex."

WBS Interviewee 3 felt her interest in BDSM was stigmatizing. WBS Interviewee 3 would like to work as a sex worker if not for the stigma, and she coined the phrase "Stigma steals power." WBS Interviewee 4 said she experienced such excessive stigma around being a person who is transgender that buying sex seemed insignificant. WBS Interviewee 4 said, "There was a lot of stigma against non-operative transwomen . . . and I like to say jokingly that I like country and western music. God, I've faced enough prejudice as it is."

Several women felt the stigma was more about exchanging sex for money rather than having free sex (WBS Interviewees 7, 8, 9, and 12). WBS Interviewee 9 said, "I think that's actually the core of the stigma is that you are exchanging money." While the cost of paying for sex may be a barrier for some women, Interviewee 8 made an important point in saying that many women "believe in their entitlement to free sex," effectively preventing their purchase of it. Women who bought sex felt additional concerns about paying for sex; those concerns may not affect men who buy sex, including heteronormative notions of women owning sex that men have to earn. de Beauvoir (1997) explains, "From primitive times to our own, intercourse has always been considered a 'service' for which the male thanks the woman by giving her presents or assuring her maintenance . . . a woman gives herself, man pays her and takes her" (pp. 395–6). When women pay for sex, they challenge ideas that they own sex and that they must give it. Women buying sex spoke about their choices not to *pick up* in a bar or club, and some said they felt pressure from society to have free sex and not pay for it.

In an academic opinion piece, feminist writer Sheila Jeffreys (2003) implied that if women buy sex, they do so chiefly to satisfy the voyeuristic desire of men. One interviewee bought sex to satisfy her partner's desire. WBS Interviewee 6 considered stigma to be more about how sex was purchased rather than the sex itself. She said,

> I don't think it's about paying for sex, I think that it was about him instigating it and not me. Had it been me, chatting around saying, 'Right, I've got an itch, no one is scratching it, I am just going to call an agency,' and that would have been fine. Submitting to the wishes of a partner who wanted it is more, it's more humiliating, demeaning, I don't know. It puts it in a different box.

The individual circumstances that motivated someone to buy sex appear to be important in terms of meeting social expectations that buying sex is empowering for women, as portrayed in some media.

Gendered stigma

Experiences of stigma are gendered. Sex workers noted that all commercial sex involvement induces stigma, that women suffer less stigma than men due to exploitation narratives, and that women who buy sex suffer more stigma than men who buy sex due to slut shaming. Attwood (2007) describes societal double standards of sexual behavior where damage to a woman's reputation occurs through derogatory labels such as "slut," which are used to police female submission to men. Most interviewees revealed that women who bought sex were aware of, and affected by, stigmatizing notions of sluttiness and sex shaming that do not generally apply to men. Interviewees felt that slut shaming is grounded in ideas that "female pleasure is not regarded as important" (WBS Interviewee 5) and is "unauthentic and dirty" (WBS Interviewee 20). They also said that female sexuality "makes people deeply uncomfortable" (WBS Interviewee 17), because the "stigma is about women having sexual desire full stop" (WBS Interviewee 19).

Interviewees also believe that there is more stigma for women with sexual dysfunction than men with sexual dysfunction (WBS Interviewee 12), and that men are perceived to have high sexual desire while women are considered to desire love (WBS Interviewee 9). For example, WBS Interviewee 7 said,

> Um, so yeah, I mean it is very complex and I think there is a lot of judgment against women. Like you know, if you are seeking services then you must be a raging nympho or something or you must be broken or completely insecure. But, with men it is like just another Friday night or, whatever. So like, there is judgment and it sucks.

The mainstream media influence social constructions of expected female sexual behavior. For example, feminist writer Tankard Reist wrote a newspaper article about the rising media attention about women buying sex, noting that there is "no social construction of men as sluts who enjoy their own degradation" (Tankard Reist, 2010). However, there is some evidence, found in the analysis of Australian contemporary discourse, that some social commentators consider slut-shaming shameful. Paradoxically, the analysis also revealed a small number of commentators who simultaneously described male clients as perpetrators of violence and female clients as empowered. This gendered double standard reveals that although men and women who buy sex are subject to stigmatization, the source of discomfort for those commenting lies in mixed messages about female sexual agency and the conflation of sex work with male violence against women.

Stigma management

Given the disempowering nature of receiving stigma, it is useful to examine the strategies that the stigmatized use to manage stigma. Women who bought sex described the various methods they use to reduce the impact of stigma on them. The most common themes were controlling the flow of information by either not telling people or by associating only with broad-minded people. A strong and perhaps less conscious method of controlling information was to deflect or reframe the act of buying sex into something more socially acceptable.

Goffman (1963) describes information control as a means of "passing" without stigma. Most women interviewed had kept their buying of sex a secret in an effort to avoid stigmatization. WBS Interviewee 9, who initially denied feeling stigmatized told, "*everyone* [emphasis added] except for like, my parents and relatives, yeah. Like, about 10 people, I have told." WBS Interviewee 10 denied being affected by stigma but said that she kept her buying of sex a secret from most of her friends. The remaining interviewees described feeling stigmatized, and all but two others told few people about it.

The chosen confidants were different for different interviewees. For example, WBS Interviewee 8 wanted the people she cared most about to know:

> I suppose I don't find it really hard to live a double life in my work, because what I do in my personal life is my business. I would find it very hard if my friends didn't know. And, I wouldn't be able to maintain that type of double life. It would be too tricky.

However, WBS Interviewee 16 said she told all manner of strangers and health professionals about buying sex but not a single friend or family member.

In contrast, Interviewees 13 and 15 told most people important to them, including extended family and work colleagues. In practice, however, most interviewees told very few people, reflecting their awareness that buying sex is, at this time, a stigmatized activity. WBS However, Interviewee 8 saw stigma as changing with current social norms:

> I was like, really unsure whether I should tell any of my friends, you know because I didn't know how they would all react. Because I think society has raised us all to have a bit of a taboo about it. And I think, as the new generation comes in and probably I think as society changes anyway, um, you know, it is becoming more acceptable.

In addition to secret keeping, another strategy for managing stigma is associating with only sex industry allies. WBS Interviewee 2, who is a current sex worker, said,

> I made a decision that I would not involve, I was not going to have anyone in my life that didn't know that I was both queer and a sex worker and they, if they had a problem with any of those things then they were to fuck off. So, that made life a lot simpler.

Deflecting and reframing

Another strategy to deflect stigma identified by Goffman (1963) is to combine the stigmatized activity with another attribute, one that has significantly less stigma attached to it, effectively reframing the activity. For example, WBS Interviewee 4, as mentioned previously, felt that the stigma associated with being a transwoman weighed heavier than stigma associated with buying sex. For most interviewees, buying sex was their most stigmatizing attribute, and they used deflection and reframing effectively. For example, WBS Interviewee 3 said, "I was being mentored as a dominant. I think it would have been very, very different for all of the boys in my family, if I had been mentored as a submissive." This strategy of managing stigma deflects the stigma to a group perceived to be more marginalized.

About half of the women interviewed cited "therapy" as their main motivation for buying sex, and very few cited sexual tension or desire as a major motivation. WBS Interviewee 12 said, "And I really looked at it as physio. You go to a physio if you have a sore back, he is going to touch your sore back to see how bad it is." Considering a sex worker a health professional was also a strategy used by WBS Interviewee 3: "I see it as no different if I was to see a psychologist." WBS Interviewee 5 said, "So, I think of him more of, like a secular mentor. And therapist." WBS Interviewee 13 used a health professional to endorse her activity: "I always use my psychologist as something that makes it sound less dodgy. I said my psychologist supports me seeing an escort."

Some interviewees had bought sexual services for therapeutic reasons and entertainment at different times and were able to recognize the relationship of stigma to those different motivations. For example, WBS Interviewee 4 said,

> Actually, I just remembered something. What helped me begin to shift that was that I did work with a somatic body worker about 5 years ago. Yeah, I totally forgot that. [laughing] And that helped just to begin to shift some of my internalized stigma I suppose.

In addition, WBS Interviewee 5 recalled, "I've talked more about the therapy than I have about the male escort. So obviously I feel some stigma about that, cause I really would only talk to my closest friends about that."

WBS Interviewee 17 had preconceived ideas about buying sex as being only physical when she said she has

> like an aversion to the phrase 'buying sex.' Because for me it is like something so much bigger than that. It is actually a much broader experience than the sexual act. Because I thought there is so much around the experience of being with a male sex worker that isn't just about . . . I don't know, buying sex for me is where you go and you have sex and then that is it. You know?

In sum: All the interviewees used controlling information, deflecting, reframing, and renaming sexual services to reduce their feelings of being negatively judged by others. But what happened when these same women wanted to share information about buying sex?

Promotion of sexual services

All women who bought sex were asked if they would recommend buying sex to a friend and how many people they told about it. By asking these questions, we sought to examine the less-conscious effects of being stigmatized and the relationship between promotion of sexual services and secret keeping. Twelve women who had bought sex said they would unconditionally recommend it to friends, and the others said the answer might depend on the friend's circumstances and values. Desires to recommend buying sex confirmed their sense of positive outcomes and of having had made the right decision to buy sex. WBS Interviewee 12 said,

> Why is it OK for us to go to the hairdresser and have our hair cut because we don't want to do it at home, we are not skilled enough to do it at home, but we frown upon the situations when a woman or a man goes out and buys sex? . . . Yeah, it is a problem with the perceptions of sex that we have as a society rather than the actual act of buying isn't it.

SW Interviewee 2 thought it would be good to normalize women buying sex so more women might have access to sexual services. The women interviewed were stuck between a desire to promote buying sex and to protect their reputations because of the negative effects of being stigmatized. WBS Interviewee 7 said, "And it would make them feel more empowered and it would open their minds up, but I couldn't suggest it to them because it would sink like a lead balloon. Like, they just would not cope with it."

WBS Interviewee 18 said, "If I met [a good sex worker] I would give his business cards to all my friends." Interviewee 1 "highly recommends it" and went on to say, "Some [people] get offended and it is like . . . yeah, go home and make your own coffee then and don't buy one in a shop either." Other, conditional recommendations to friends were "It would depend on the circumstances. But I would not, not recommend it" (Interviewee 6), "If I think someone was not coping then yes" (Interviewee 10), and "If I had that sort of relationship with a friend" (Interviewee 11).

WBS Interviewee 9 said:

> I was so excited when I saw the ad about this, about your survey. I thought, Yes, this is totally about time that we women start like actually start challenging this and publishing the findings and like. I just wish that every woman who ever gets themselves in a situation where they feel like they didn't do something for their own sexual satisfaction, I just wish all of them would have the confidence to do it. And something that I am realizing from having lots of just general casual sex at the moment is look, it's all in our heads. We create all of these self-doubt sort of things ourselves. And you can take charge of it. Once you take charge of it it is, then you will feel so liberated. Whether it is paying for it or just having casual sex, when you actually take charge and you know what you want, it is amazing.

In sum: The interviewees had clear desires to promote sexual services while wanting to preserve their status by secret keeping, demonstrating cognitive dissonance as a consequence of stigma.

Implications of stigma

For our interviewees, the negative implications of stigmatization were clear. For example, Interviewee 17 said, "The risk of being publicly shamed is like, really scary." Goffman (1963) explains that keeping secrets about stigmatized activities results in anxiety and insecurity because a person cannot know for sure who "knows" and who does not know. WBS Interviewee 2 described "existing in a permanent state of tension." WBS Interviewee 3 felt that other people knowing about her buying sex could affect her possible career choices, and WBS Interviewee 19 worried that her former partner might attempt to discredit her in family court if he found out, threatening her custody of their children. WBS Interviewee 20 said, "I guess my main worry would be, would be like the school community like, where your kids go to school. I don't really want to be, you know, I don't want to be someone's gossip."

Stigmatization is an effective means of social control and may well be the reason why buying sex is not a common pastime. WBS Interviewee 5 said, "It is stigma that prevents women buying sex and missing the therapeutic benefits." It might well be that some people who are otherwise motivated to buy sex do not do so because they fear the response from others. WBS Interviewee 5 also said,

> If the stigma of sex work were to alleviate a bit, I think you find quite a large emerging market in sex services that were therapeutic for women. And yeah, when I see people that are coming into tantra communities, yeah, there is a lot of women that we are talking about, seeking that.

WBS Interviewee 7 also considered the social taboo against buying sex a major deterrent.

While stigmatization may limit people's access to buying sex, it may also influence their ability to access other services. The CRSH Stigma Indicators project (Cama et al., 2018) found that capacity to access to other health services due to stigma is associated with mental health issues and social isolation and can prevent people from using health care.

Individual motivation to control personal information seems paramount to feeling safe, but it has a negative effect in terms of silencing sex workers' clients who wish to advocate for a broader understanding of the sex industry. WBS Interviewee 17 said,

> And, that, you know, that is only pushing me and my story deeper underground. Like a, because I feel really frightened, that you know, I see myself as a really strong feminist and there are other women out there who are going to shame me around this. And that is too frightening for me then, and it becomes a harder thing for me to talk about.

WBS Interviewee 15 tried to tell her story on Twitter; she felt her experience was dismissed because it did not fit the prevailing narrative of an exploitative male client and a female sex worker:

> And that is what I wanted to bring up because they were talking about criminalization and abolition. And, that is why I brought it up because my experiences do count if you are talking about criminalizing it. I get very frustrated that they conflate sexual abuse and certainly childhood sexual abuse with sex work because there is no relation and I have been in both situations. I mean, I am obviously not a worker myself, but I found it quite disturbing that people can't see the difference between somebody wanting to do sex work and between someone who has been trafficked or abused when it is not their choice. . . . When I had written on twitter, one person claimed that I was being exploited. That female sex workers and female clients are being exploited . . . they just want to try to make all women into victims. . . . And it is frustrating that people, you know, these people won't acknowledge that "Yes, that did happen to me but I cannot make the choice to see a sex worker," you know, now I can make the choice to go out to a bar and pick someone up, which is certainly less safe.

A further problem with silencing is the inaccurate generalizations that are made in influential spaces. WBS Interviewee 17 complained that clients of sex workers are talked about with "no authority" and neglected during public inquiries. The interviewees in this study were adversely affected by exploitation narratives, and their experiences caused them to question the truthfulness of negative sex industry narratives. However, their inability to be heard as bona fide clients permits a one-sided political debate that seeks to criminalize them. Some women who bought sex were concerned about being considered criminals should Swedish models of regulation be adopted in Australia.

Stories of stigma inform

Details of these women's stories, generously and anonymously given, inform us about female sexual behavior and sex industry involvement in ways that are usually unmentionable. The motivations for most of the women to participate in our study about buying sex was to collectively have a voice in sex industry debate with a view to reducing stigma. Stigma placed on the commercialization of sexual acts is challenged by women's stories of achieving therapeutic outcomes when buying sex. In addition, stigma that is based on male entitlement to women's bodies is challenged when women buy sexual services from all genders. Slut shaming is another type of stigma experienced by women who buy sex. Ultimately, stigma about buying sex results in negative outcomes for individuals leading double lives and silences their ability to lead efforts toward positive changes for broader society.

Future directions and stigma reduction

The stigmatization of sex industry clients results in limited access to services, threats to relationships and mental well-being, and inappropriate representation with serious political and legal ramifications. The project of stigma reduction through the normalization of the sex industry, as described by Sanders (2017), is an enormous task in which legal reform is essential. The decriminalization of sex work is a first and crucial harm-reduction technique. Unfortunately, decriminalization does not erase stigma (Weitzer, 2017b; Abel, 2014), but it may reduce some fear about accessing sexual services and increase acceptability and citizens' rights.

An important stigma reduction measure would consider buying sex an option for all genders. Women's sexual desire and capacity to buy sex are not only overlooked in contemporary Australian discourse but also denied, indeed sanitized, in academic discourse, as exemplified by papers positioning female sex tourism as *romance tourism*, a phenomenon separate from male sex tourism (Pruitt & LaFont, 1995; Taylor, 2006; Tornqvist, 2012). Men and women buy sex for similar reasons and in similar fashions, and they experience similar outcomes (Sanders, 2008; Vanwesenbeeck, 2001; Caldwell, 2012; Caldwell & de Wit, 2016). While female clients of sex workers may escape some stigma experienced by male clients, female clients also suffer from being considered inconsequential. Particular stigma experienced by men buying sex from men may be different again. By encouraging broader thinking about the sex industry, thinking about men and women as buyers of sex disrupts ideas of *all* clients as being engaged in exploitation narratives and *all* women as either victims or sluts.

Brents and Sanders (2010) note that representations of the sex industry have moved toward a subtle shift in the perceived respectability of middle-class consumers and workers. Brents and Sanders also point to the adult industry's marketing to women as evidence of mainstreaming or normalizing the sex industry. The media's power to mainstream the sex industry was demonstrated when more than half of the women interviewed in our study said they bought sex after reading a positive media article about other women buying sex.

More research is needed regarding women who buy sex. We need to enable and encourage women to disclose to researchers when they buy sex, we need to assist women to identify as sex buyers without denial and deflection, and we need to reject political attempts to make them invisible.

Currently, sex workers who assert the benefits of their services are often discounted as unrepresentative or as aggressive marketers. Meanwhile, women who buy sex risk slut shaming, stigma and being reduced to anomalies. Female client voices are vital in challenging gendered narrative about female sexuality and increasing understanding of the sex industry. Sex industry stigma steals power.

References

Abel, G. (2014). A decade of decriminalization: Sex work "down under" but not underground. *Criminology and Criminal Justice*, *14*(5), 580–592. doi:10.1177/1748895814523024

Attwood, F. (2007). Sluts and riot grrls: Female identity and sexual agency. *Journal of Gender Studies*, *16*(3), 233–247. doi:10.1080/09589230701562921

Beauvoir, Simone (1997), ""Introduction" to The Second Sex", in Nicholson, Linda (ed.), The second wave: a reader in feminist theory, New York: Routledge, pp. 11–18.

Brents, B., & Sanders, T. (2010). Mainstreaming the sex industry: Economic inclusion and social ambivalence. Journal of Law and Society, 37(1), 40–60.

Butler, J. (1999). Gender trouble (10th ed.). New York, NY: Taylor & Francis.

Caldwell, H. (2012). Long-term clients who access commercial sexual services in Australia (Dissertation). University of Sydney.

Caldwell, H. (2018). Women who buy sex in Australia: From social representations to lived experiences (Dissertation). University of New South Wales.

Caldwell, H., & de Wit, J. (2015). Australian attitudes about heterosexual power relations when women participate in sex tourism. In 22nd Congress of the world association for sexual health. Singapore: Journal of Sexual Medicine.

Caldwell, H., & de Wit, J. (2016). Sex workers describe the market of female clients in Australia. In HHARD conference, CRSH margins and belonging. Sydney.

Cama, E., Broady, T., Brener, L., Hopwood, M., de Wit, J., & Treloar, C. (2018). Stigma indicators monitoring project: Summary report. Sydney: Centre for Social Research in Health, UNSW.

Gill, R. (2007). Gender and the media. Cambridge: Polity Press.

Goffman, E. (1963). Stigma: Notes on the management of spoiled identity. London: Penguin.

Jeffreys, S. (2003). Sex tourism: Do women do it too? Leisure Studies, 22(3), 223–238. doi:10.1080/0261 43603200075452

McKee, A. (2003). Textual analysis: A beginner's guide. London: Sage.

Minichiello, V., Scott, J., & Cox, C. (2017). Commentary: Reversing the agenda of sex work stigmatization and criminalization: Signs of a progressive society. Sexualities, 0(0), 1–6. doi:10.1177/1363460716684510

Phillips, R., Benoit, C., Hallgrimsdottir, H., & Vallance, K. (2012). Courtesy stigma: A hidden health concern among front-line service providers to sex workers. Sociology of Health & Illness, 34(5), 681–696. doi:10.1111/j.1467-9566.2011.01410.x

Phipps, A. (2017). Sex wars revisited: A rhetorical economy of sex industry opposition. Journal of International Women's Studies, 18(4), 306–320. Retrieved from http://vc.bridgew.edu/jiws/vol18/iss4/22

Pruitt, D., & LaFont, S. (1995). For love and money. Romance tourism in Jamaica. Annals of Tourism Research, 22, 422–440. doi:0160-7383(94)00084-0

Rose, G. (2001). Visual methodologies: An introduction to the interpretation of visual materials (3rd ed.). London: Sage.

Sanders, T. (2008). Male sexual scrips: Intimacy, sexuality and pleasure in the purchase of commercial sex. Sociology, 42, 400. doi:10.1177/0038038508088833

Sanders, T. (2017). Unpacking the process of destigmatization of sex work/ers: Response to Weitzer "Resistance to sex work stigma". Sexualities, 0(0), 1–4. doi:10.1177/1363460716677731

Scott, J., & Minichiello, V. (2014). Clients of male sex workers. In J. Scott, D. Callander, & V. Minichiello (Eds.). Male sex work and society. E-book: Harrington Park Press.

Sullivan, B. (2007). Rape, prostitution and consent. The Australian and New Zealand Journal of Criminology, 40(2), 127–142.

Tankard Reist, M. (2010, April 22). Women buying men for sex is not equality. The Sydney Morning Herald. Retrieved from www.smh.com.au/opinion/society-and-culture/women-buying-men-for-sex-is-not-equality-20100422-tf2q.html

Taylor, J. S. (2006). Female sex tourism: A contradiction in terms? Feminist Review, 83, 42–59. Retrieved from www.jstor.org/stable/3874382

Tornqvist, M. (2012). Troubling romance tourism: Sex, gender and class inside the Argentinean tango clubs. Feminist Review, 102, 21–40. Retrieved from https://doi.org/10.1057/fr.2012.12

Vanwesenbeeck, I. (2001). Another decade of social scientific work on sex work: A review of the research 1990–2000. Annual Review of Sex Research, 12, 242.

Vanwesenbeeck, I. (2013). Prostitution push and pull: Male and female perspectives. The Journal of Sex Research, 50(1), 11–16. doi:10.1080/00224499.2012.696285

Wadham, B., Pease, B., Atherton, C., & Lorentzen, P. (2012). The sex factor: Media representations of men and women in Australia. In J. Little, B. Wadham, B. Pease, C. Atherton, & P. Lorentzen (2012). Centre for Citizenship and Globalisation research paper series: The sex factor: Media representations of men and women in Australia, *3*(3). Special Issue. Deakin University. Retrieved from www.deakin.edu.au/arts-ed/ccg/

Weitzer, R. (2009). The sociology of sex work. *Annual Review of Sociology, 35*, 213–234. doi: 10.1146/annurev-soc-070308-120025

Weitzer, R. (2010). The mythology of prostitution: Advocacy research and public policy. *Sexuality Research and Social Policy, 7*, 15–29. doi:10.1007/s13178-010-0002-5.

Weitzer, R. (2017a). Additional reflections on sex work stigma. *Sexualities, 0*(0), 1–4. doi:10.1177/1363460716684513

Weitzer, R. (2017b). Resistance to sex work stigma. *Sexualities, 0*(0), 1–13. doi:10.1177/1363460716684509

West Morris, D. (2012). The sex wars continue: Hung's postfeminist debate. *The Communication Review, 15*(3), 204–217. doi:10.1080/107144212.2012.702007

22

Trans men in sex work

Prevalent but overlooked

Max Nicolai Appenroth

Introduction to language

In this chapter, the term *trans* is used as an umbrella term to describe a diverse community. *Trans* refers to people who do not identify with their gender assigned at birth. This term is inclusive of many possible identities, including trans men, trans women, gender diverse and non-binary people, transsexuals, and transgender. The term *transsexual*, first used in the early twentieth century, is often rejected by the trans community as a term created to divide "sick" from "healthy" people (Stryker, 2017). To counter its pathologizing effect and to encompass a range of identities beyond the binary options of "male" and "female," the community has come up with the word *trans*. *Trans* also differs from the term *transvestite*. Transvestism, which refers to as cross-dressing, addresses a person's desire to change their outer appearance to match the stereotypical appearance of the "opposite" sex. Cross-dressing does not (always) affect a person's gender identity or the wish to transition permanently.

The terms *cis* and *cisgender* refer to people who identify with their gender assigned at birth. In this chapter, I focus on people who were assigned female at birth and who identify as trans masculine.

In many Indigenous cultures, the concept of diverse gender expressions has been deeply rooted for centuries. These concepts of gender diversity do not necessarily align with more recent ideas in the global north of what *trans* means, and they have suffered from oppression by colonizers. Nevertheless, it is important to mention their existence. Gender diversity has been and is being expressed by, for example, Two-Spirit people in the Northern Americas, Muxes in Mexico, Hijras in India and Pakistan, and Fa'afine in Samoa, among others.

Like *trans, sex work* is a multifaceted term. It may include, but it is not exclusive to, street sex work, (full) escort services, acting in porn, stripping or erotic dancing, professional dominance or submission, phone sex, and online webcam performances. I use *sex work* to describe an exchange of sex or sexual activity for money, housing, food, drugs, or other goods and services. Many trans sex workers trade sex for hormones and other needed medical expenses. I use the term *survival sex* to describe "the trading of sex for survival needs" such as housing, food, and clothing (Fitzgerald, Patterson, & Hickey, 2015, p. 8). The concept of survival sex needs specific attention when talking about trans sex workers.

Information about trans masculine sex workers is very scarce. Based on existing literature and resources, this chapter provides some (legal) context about the United Stated, Germany, and few other European countries.

Whom are we talking about?

When we think about trans sex workers, we commonly think about female-presenting trans identities. The dominance of women selling sex to men is also present in this context. The focus on trans female embodiments in the sex work industry reinforces gendered stereotypes, "in which sexual objectification is tied to female bodies and sexual subjectivity is tied to male ones" (Smith, 2012, p. 590). Sexual objectification and stereotypical images of trans women in society often lead to the assumption that all trans female identities *must* be sex workers. In addition, prostitution laws "deeply affect many non-sex worker trans people who are perceived, through hypersexualized prejudices, as sex workers" (Fedorko & Berredo, 2017, p. 10). Meanwhile, society's belief that all sex workers are female-presenting individuals leads to the invisibility of sex workers who do not present as female. In other words, the assumption exists trans men cannot be sex workers.

If not for some fierce trans female sex workers of Color who played an important role in the Stonewall Riots of June 1969, we would not have had the so-called Gay Liberation (Stryker, 2017). The underrepresentation of trans people in historical storytelling is a common issue. And, unfortunately, in research and academic discussions, trans individuals have often been grouped among sexually diverse persons and subsumed under the acronym LGBT. The common mistake of mixing gender identity and sexual preferences makes the trans community even more vulnerable, rendering their specific needs and struggles invisible. Another common mistake in research is to include trans women in the MSM (men who have sex with men) category. The focus of data collection appears to be strictly on genitalia and sexual behavior rather than on identity. By ignoring the diversity of trans bodies, researchers can misrepresent this cohort.

With respect to trans identities in the sex work industry, researchers have long focused on trans female sex workers, and several articles can be found regarding this cohort. See, for example, Nuttbrock's *Transgender Sex Work and Society* (2018). However, there are only a handful of resources for and/or about trans male sex workers. Through a thorough analysis of (the little) existing literature, the outcomes of an online survey (specifically conducted as research for this chapter), and an interview with a trans masculine–identified sex worker in Germany, I provide an introduction to and overview of this particular group of sex workers.

What do we know about trans communities?

According to a survey conducted by the Williams Institute at the University of California Los Angeles, approximately 0.6% of adults living in the United States are trans (Flores, Herman, Gates, & Brown, 2016). The number of gender questioning people is most likely higher. Recent studies of the Flanders region in Belgium have revealed that an estimated 2.5% of the general population have an ambivalent feeling about their gender identity; an incongruent gender identity is reported by 1.1% of the general population (Van Caenegem et al., 2015). Similar rates were found in a study of high school students in New Zealand, where 1.2% of the respondents indicated a trans identity and an additional 2.5% said that they were unsure about their gender identity (Clark et al., 2014). These outcomes indicate that the number of trans-identified people in society is much higher than often believed. However, the diversity of this community, as well as the many different ways of describing one's personal identity, makes it difficult to offer an all-inclusive statement. Additionally, the oppression faced by trans people does not allow everyone to openly live their desired identity. Thus, many trans people hide their true selves or don't live them at all, and they refrain from taking part in research and surveys that could put them at risk.

Similarly, criminalization and stigma faced by sex workers often force them to live and/or work hidden. To start a public discussion and to call attention to sex workers' rights, St. James Infirmary ran a media campaign in 2010–2011 with the slogan "Someone You Know Is a Sex Worker" (St. James Infirmary, s.a.). This slogan may be very accurate for not only cisgender people but also for trans people.

The most comprehensive study about trans identities to date was conducted in the United States in 2015. The U.S. Transgender Survey (USTS) included the responses of 27,715 trans adults (18 and older) in the United States. Of the respondents, 33% identified as trans women, 29% identified as trans men, and 35% identified as non-binary. Eighty percent of the non-binary participants were female assigned at birth (James et al., 2016).

Trans individuals in the sex work industry face more risks and obstacles than their cisgender peers do. The motivation for engaging in sex work may differ between these two groups, as the incidence of trans people living below the average income in many countries is much higher than it is for the cisgender mainstream society. To live in poverty as a single individual in the United States, for example, means having an income of $12,486 or less per year (U.S. Census Bureau, 2018). The numbers from the USTS report indicate that almost one in five participants (18%) earned no money at all or had a yearly income of less than $10,000. In comparison, 5% of the general U.S. population faces a similar financial situation. Of all USTS participants, almost one-third (29%) were living in poverty, which is more than double the rate (14%) of the general U.S. population. Poverty was more prevalent among people living with HIV (51%), people living with a disability (45%), and people of color (38%)—an example of intersecting oppressive categories (James et al., 2016).

An overrepresentation of people who face multiple forms of oppression can be found among sex workers in general. Structural discrimination influences an individual's decision to become a sex worker, and it also influences the encounters while doing sex work (Amnesty International, 2016). The USTS report showed that nearly one in five participants (19%) had exchanged sexual activity for money, food, housing, or other goods and services. Out of these 19% of the overall sample, 19% identified as trans men and 23% as non-binary and female assigned at birth (James et al., 2016). Trans individuals of color, undocumented residents, participants who experienced homelessness, and "those who have lost a job because of their gender identity or expression" were more likely to have engaged in sex work (James et al., p. 159).

Similar dynamics can be found throughout Europe, where trans migrants face hostility, exclusion, and few options for legal employment. Furthermore, "many [trans people] are systematically excluded from the formal economy, as their identification documents do not reflect their gender, gender identity, and/or gender expression, and they face hostile transphobic environments at workplaces" (Fedorko & Berredo, 2017, p. 7). In addition, sex work can also be seen as a withdrawal from transphobic and discriminatory work settings. By entering a self-determined work environment, many trans sex workers find themselves in a supportive group of other trans sex workers, and the community and the activism that emerge from these alliances are seen as tools for empowerment that often cannot be found in other work environments:

> For many transgender people, the sex trade can offer greater autonomy and financial stability compared to more traditional workplaces, with few barriers to entry. However,

economic insecurity and material deprivation can increase one's vulnerability to harm and decrease the ability to make self-determined choices.

(Fitzgerald et al., 2015, p. 7)

The criminalization of sex work comes with additional risks for trans people. In addition to facing potential arrest for engaging in illegalized[1] sex trade, trans people face an elevated risk for being prosecuted based on their gender identity. In Greece and Turkey, for example, laws have been introduced that allow only unmarried, cisgender women to work legally in the sex industry (Fedorko & Berredo, 2017). These laws specifically exclude trans people, and they force trans masculine people to perform sex work in their gender assigned at birth—that is, as women: "As trans people are often associated with and read as the sex/gender they were assigned at birth, they are impacted by arrest, prosecution, imprisonment, and even death penalty in the same way as cis lesbian, gay, and bisexual individuals" (Fedorko & Berredo, p. 11).

Risks of trans masculine sex workers

Work environment and legal frameworks

Multiple facets affect a sex worker's environment, particularly with regard to escort services and trade of sex for money or other goods. In many countries, sex work is illegalized, which forces many sex workers to work in the underground. Trans identities add another obstacle. Many countries do not have a legal gender recognition (LGR), and even if they do, trans people are very often victims of violence and discrimination. The result is a situation in which trans sex workers cannot access legal support when they experience violence or harm at work.

When legislation allows sex work, the laws may not recognize a trans person's preferred and lived gender identity, due to the lack of LGR. In cases where sex work is lawful and LGR exists, trans people still may choose to live and work outside of the juridical measures. Many countries where sex work is not illegalized ask workers to register and undergo regular health and STI screenings, but medical environments are prone to discrimination against trans people. The US Transgender Survey showed that one out of three participants who sought treatment or advice from a healthcare provider had negative experiences because of being trans. These participants reported being verbally harassed, being refused the treatment that they needed, or being pushed into a role of a "trans healthcare expert" who had to teach their provider about trans-specific care (James et al., 2016). Furthermore, trans sex workers may experience discrimination when registering with the authorities.

Samuel,[2] a trans male escort form Germany, said during a 2018 interview:

I would never register as a sex worker in Germany. First of all, I don't want it to be written down anywhere that I do this kind of work. I don't know how times and policies will change and it could be used against me one day. I also want to protect my "real" life outside of sex work. The thing with the "whore pass" also puts me at risk that clients find out my real identity. I never carry any personal documents, when I go and see my clients. . . . STI checkups are done by the public health department and I would never consider going there. They are not aware of trans bodies, they don't know what to do with us. And I'm afraid of discrimination. I go and get checked regularly at my GP [general practitioner], but she doesn't know I'm a sex worker. I can't tell her, because I'm afraid she then would see me with different eyes.

The purpose of Germany's new prostitution law is to reduce human trafficking. The law was implemented in 2017 and requires a formal registration for sex workers, mandatory health counseling, and the obligatory use of condoms. Registered sex workers receive a registration certificate (which Samuel called the *whore pass*) that they must carry at all times when working. There is the option of stating an alias name for the certificate; nevertheless, a person's legal name and personal information are stored by the authorities (GSSG, 2017). The registration requires a notify address in Germany, which many sex workers, especially undocumented/illegalized migrants, refugees, and homeless people, cannot provide. That requirement has opened up a new market for *selling* addresses to register, which makes already vulnerable identities dependent on others. Although this law appears to be well intended, some sex workers consider it to be a control mechanism that allows the state to monitor the industry. This bureaucratic surveillance by the state also forces sex workers to pay income tax from their work.

Legal frameworks also determine where sex workers can advertise their services or find clients. Depending on a trans sex worker's body representation, the worker is limited to specific environments and settings in which they can work and approach potential clients. For example, street sex work can be problematic for a male-presenting trans person, as the possible clients may not be aware of what a trans man is. Although it is common for trans men to undergo double-mastectomy (colloquially called "top surgery"), very few trans men undergo what is colloquially known as "bottom surgery"[3] (metoidioplasty or phalloplasty). Clients' normative expectations for a male gender expression could put trans masculine sex workers at risk for violence.

A general lack of knowledge and stereotypical images around trans bodies in mainstream society likely affects almost every trans sex worker, opening up possibilities for new types of discrimination. As Samuel mentioned:

> You wouldn't believe what type of messages I receive and all the stupid things people say to me, because they have no idea what's going on. Although I clearly state in my online ads that I'm a masculine person with a vagina, I still receive many emails asking if I'd wear lingerie or other women's clothes for a date or if I could send them a picture "dressed up" [in women's clothes]. I was asked many times how big my dick is. . . . No matter if it's straight- or gay-identifying clients, some of them don't see my identity and think because of my genitals, I'm less of a man or even like a woman. I've had clients telling me, it was their first time having sex with a woman. Feels pretty weird, regarding my appearance, which is clearly masculine.

There are not many options for trans masculine sex workers outside of online advertising or online sex work in general. There are no known trans-masculine-inclusive brothels.[4] This lack of options adds another layer of risk, as many trans male sex workers have to operate without safety measures provided in brothels or within a community of street sex workers.

In the United States, the Stop Enabling Sex Traffickers Act (SESTA) and Allow States and Victims to Fight Online Sex Trafficking Act (FOSTA) were implemented in 2018 to fight human trafficking. SESTA-FOSTA "exposes Internet service providers to criminal charges if they are suspected of 'assisting, facilitating, or supporting sex trafficking.' This legislation impacts the ability of sex workers to use the Internet to advertise and provide services, share information, and protect themselves" (NSWP, n.d.). The Global Network of Sex Work Project (NSWP) has noted that it is a terrible mistake to link human trafficking with sex work and vice versa. Doing so negatively affects sex workers' ability to work in safe settings and achieve economic stability. It also makes them vulnerable to mistreatment, and it does not solve the problems of human trafficking. The implementation of this legislation particularly affects trans masculine sex workers, who cannot advertise online anymore.

Mental health

Research has shown that trans women who engage in sex work have a high prevalence of depression and other mental-health-related issues (Nemoto, Bödeker, & Imamoto, 2011). No research about mental health and sex work has been inclusive of trans masculine participants so far, but similar outcomes could be expected. The analysis of the National Transgender Discrimination Survey (USA; $n = 6,450$) showed a massive increase in suicide attempts among trans men who had engaged in the sex trade (75.5% vs. 44.3% of non-sex workers) (Fitzgerald et al., 2015). A major issue around trans people's mental health is a general lack of resources and counseling. Specifically, for trans masculine sex workers, there are no known inclusive services particularly targeting their needs. This cohort may be included in general trans services and community centers, but due to the dearth of information and literature about this group, efficient support is uncommon.

HIV and AIDS

Since 2014, the World Health Organization (WHO) has noted the need to care for trans people who have HIV/AIDS and who are at risk of contracting HIV. As mentioned previously, there is a persistent omission and exclusion of trans masculine and non-binary identities in the research. A comparison of global research projects on HIV/AIDS showed 32 published studies about trans female identities between 2012 and 2015, whereas only five looked into the HIV prevalence among trans men during the same period (Poteat, Scheim, Xavier, Reisner, & Baral, 2016). The U.S. Transgender Survey showed that respondents with sex work experience were nearly 16 times as likely to be living with HIV (7.9%), as compared to those who have never done sex work (0.5%) (James et al., 2016).

Based on the insufficient research and data collection, the prevalence for HIV in trans men can only be estimated. It is believed that trans masculine individuals have a higher risk of HIV transmission due to hormone intake through injections. Additionally, trans people are more likely to be illicit drug users (James et al., 2016). Hormone treatment may result in vaginal atrophy in trans men, leading to a greater exposure to HIV through vaginal intercourse (Poteat, 2016). The misconception that trans masculine identities predominantly engage in heterosexual intercourse with (cis)women leads may be another reason the experiences of trans men are not reported in HIV/AIDS research. Studies have shown that trans men who have sex with cis-men are more likely to engage in risky sexual behavior. A potential risk factor could be low negotiation skills, based on "unequal power dynamics, low self-esteem, and need for gender identity affirmation" (Sevelius, 2009, p. 398). The aforementioned findings, along with drug use and mental health problems, may affect a person's ability to negotiate safer sex practices with sexual partners or clients.

Furthermore, trans men are less likely to get tested for HIV, and they have less access to free or affordable testing, condoms, and lubricants (Scheim et al., 2016). In addition, there is a lack of research determining the effectiveness of the HIV pre-exposure prophylaxis (PrEP) in trans MSM. Trans men have broadly been excluded from PrEP trials, despite a similar or even elevated risk of HIV transmission compared to cisgender men. Medical professionals recommend an initial intake of PrEP for at least 20 consecutive days for trans men (Radix, n.d.). Based on research outcomes, however, it is believed that the effectiveness of PrEP in vaginal tissue highly differs from anal tissue. Specifically, vaginal tissue takes longer to build a protective shield against potential HIV infections than anal tissue does (Louissaint et al., 2013; Patterson et al., 2011). Due to a lack of research, we have no data about the effectiveness of PrEP in combination with hormone replacement therapy (HRT) in trans men. It is believed that trans men who undergo HRT are at elevated risk for HIV exposure based on a change in vaginal tissue as a side effect of testosterone (Poteat, Malik, Scheim, & Elliott, 2017).

Results of online survey

For purposes of this chapter, I conducted an online survey. The survey included 18 questions. Seven questions were multiple choice, and 11 were write-in. All questions included the option "prefer not to answer." The survey was active from February to August 2018, was conducted in English, and spread mostly through social media (Facebook, Twitter) and personal contacts to known sex workers and trans support organizations. Given the anonymous nature of the online study, it was exempt from an IRB approval. A total of 56 participants took part, of whom 37 answered all the questions. The results of these 37 participants are presented here. Inclusion criteria were that participants must identify somewhere on the trans male or trans male–presenting spectrum (including non-binary identities who were passing as masculine) and must have engaged in sex work in the past or present. Those criteria are based on self-determination, and no legal gender recognition and/or medical-related transition steps were required.

Demographics of participants

In total, 65% ($n = 24$) identified somewhere on the male spectrum, 27% ($n = 10$) were non-binary (27%), two were gender fluid, and one identified as "agender." In answering the question about how they are perceived by others, most (70% of $n = 37$) said that they were passing as male, about 19% were seen as the gender they were assigned at birth (female), and three respondents had mixed or unclear gender representation. Half (51%) were currently doing sex work, and 49% had done sex work in the past. The mean income of respondents who answered the question (valid $n = 25$) was $19,334/year. Of those who were currently engaging in some form of sex work, 14 stated that up to 50% of their monthly income was earned through sex work, and 5 respondents said that income from sex work accounted for 50 to 100% of their current income.

Work environment

Participants who answered the question about their current residence (valid $n = 34$) were based in Australia (14), the United States (10), Canada (4), Germany (4), the United Kingdom (2), and New Zealand (1). Most of their sex work experience took place in their country of residence. The legality of sex work varied not only from country to country but also from national region to national region. Nineteen (51.4%) respondents said they were not registered or registration was not required, seven (18.9%) stated that they could not register, 10 (27%) responded that sex work was illegalized in the country where they lived at the time of the survey, and only one (2.7%) person (from Germany) said that they were officially registered as a sex worker.

Participants indicated the genders of their clients. Nearly all (92%) said their clients were exclusively cis-men, and three participants said that their clients were exclusively cis-female.

Almost 90% found their clients exclusively online. Only one participant said he found his clients via street-based sex work or via brothels, but he added that he did so prior to transitioning. The write-in answers for the question asking about what services the participants offered included full (escort) service, taking part in porn, offering massage or BDSM sessions, phone or online cam sex work, and stripping or exotic dancing. For some participants, a medical transition changed how they experienced their work. For some it opened up a new market, while for others it determined how they approached sex work. One respondent wrote, "I did sex work as a cis-presenting woman and a trans male, and these experiences were radically different. . . . I also lost all business once I accessed genital surgery as I no longer have a vaginal canal" (Participant A). As previously mentioned, bottom surgery among trans men is rare compared to bottom surgery among trans women.

Reasons for engaging in sex work

The results of the survey also reflected the economically disadvantaged positions of trans people. The majority of participants (70%) said that they did sex work out of a need for money. However, some participants said that even though they engaged in sex work to survive, it also led to a feeling of self-empowerment and being able to explore a different sexual identity. One response about motivation for engaging in sex work was, "Initially, inability to find other work. Then I found empowerment in working with my diverse body" (Participant B). As mentioned earlier, sexual interactions with a cisgender person who does not know one is trans can be problematic and frustrating. When asked what motivated him to do sex work, another participant wrote, "Having sexual interactions that feel like education sessions or services that's not being paid for. So, I started charging for cis men to treat me like an attraction" (Participant C).

Although some respondents indicated empowerment through male embodiment, others experienced higher levels of dysphoria when performing sex work perceived as their gender assigned at birth. The need for money pressures individuals into roles and experiences that can cause serious trauma. One person stated, "I am trans masculine, but do sex work as a woman, because it pays better. . . . I was only motivated by my need for money. I respect others, who are sex positive and enjoy the work, but I sure as fuck do not" (Participant D).

Risks for trans sex workers

When asked what risks they see for themselves when performing any type of sex work, respondents provided diverse answers. Most respondents were afraid of physical violence, sexual assault, rape, and murder. The fear of potentially bad clients and experiencing hate crime was prevalent in most answers. Due to an illegalized status as a sex worker in some countries, many participants were afraid of being arrested and not being able to turn to the police when violent incidents occurred. An additional complication was the fear of being outed as a sex worker in other work or social and family settings.

When asked how the situation of trans masculine sex workers could be improved, many respondents noted that sex work must be decriminalized. Several participants requested trans-male-inclusive brothels and safe workspaces, which would increase their sense of security while being at work. Others expressed the need to reduce stigma and discrimination against sex workers and to make social and healthcare services more accessible. The need for networking among trans men was expressed alongside the wish for more options of gender expression in the industry.

Conclusion: where to next?

The diversity of the trans male community also reflects the variety of motivations for taking part in the sex trade. Previous studies show that trans people are more prone to be dependent on sex work due to socioeconomic disadvantages, based on structural and interpersonal discrimination and prejudice:

> The large representation of trans people in sex work around the world is undeniably a result of widespread structural, institutional, and interpersonal violence experienced by trans people from their early lives with regards to receiving support from their families and their immediate environments and accessing education and alternative employment.
>
> *(Fedorko & Berredo, 2017, p. 7)*

In addition to trans people's adverse and discriminatory experiences throughout the life course,

> trans sex workers face intersectional stigma and discrimination because of their trans and sex worker status, with other influencing factors including racism, misogyny, ableism, classism, and xenophobia. Many of them are impacted by housing discrimination, over-policing, and lack of access to justice, health services, and social benefits, as sex work is not recognized as work in their respective countries.
>
> *(Fedorko & Berredo, 2017, p. 9)*

Juridical systems fail to serve trans sex workers on many levels. First, the online survey showed that trans masculine sex workers fear being arrested for exchanging sex for money or other goods:

> The stigmatized and criminalized nature of sex work routinely forces sex workers to operate at the margins of society in clandestine and dangerous environments with little recourse to safety or state protection. As a result, sex workers face an increased risk of violence and abuse, and such crimes against them often go unreported, under-investigated and/or unpunished, offering perpetrators impunity.
>
> *(Amnesty International, 2016)*

Second, many gender-variant sex workers, especially trans people of color, encountered discrimination or apathy from police and state officials while seeking help from them (James et al., 2016).

Identifying the needs and particular risks of this highly underserved community should pave the way for a better understanding of trans men in the sex trade. Legalizing and decriminalizing the exchange of sex for money and other goods will also lead to opportunities for trans masculine sex workers to connect, build networks, establish organizations, find empowerment from within the community, and operate in safe working environments. Furthermore, society needs to diminish stigma against sex workers and trans people, which will help trans masculine sex workers advocate for their rights without the fear of being prosecuted and ostracized. Cis allies can become more active in the fight for equality and equity of trans people by calling for legal gender recognition, decriminalizing sex work, and calling out discrimination against trans people.

Notes

1 I use the term "illegalized" to highlight the active agency of juridical and governmental systems to declare something as illegal.
2 Name has been altered to protect the participant's identity. Samuel's statements have been translated from German to English by the author.
3 The U.S. Transgender Survey showed that only 3% of all trans masculine participants underwent phalloplasty (the construction of a penis) and 10% of all trans female respondents have had a vagino- and/or labiaplasty (the construction of a vagina and/or labia).
4 This statement is based on an extensive research over a period of more than one year. Up to submission of this chapter (April 2019), no information about trans-masculine-inclusive brothels could be found.

References

Amnesty International. (2016). *Amnesty International policy on state obligations to respect, protect and fulfil the human rights of sex workers*. Retrieved from www.amnesty.org/download/Documents/POL3040622016ENGLISH.PDF

Clark, T., Lucassen, M., Bullen, P., Denny, S., Fleming, T., Robinson, E., & Rossen, F. (2014). The health and well-being of transgender high school students: Results from the New Zealand Adolescent Health Survey (Youth'12). *Journal of Adolescent Health, 55*, 93–99.

Fedorko, B., & Berredo, L. (2017). *The vicious circle of violence: Trans and gender-diverse people, migration, and sex work*. TvT Publication Series, Vol. 16.

Fitzgerald, E., Patterson, S., & Hickey, D. (2015). *Meaningful work: Transgender experiences in the sex trade* (with new analysis from the National Trandgender Discrimination Survey). Retrieved from https://www.transequality.org/sites/default/files/Meaningful%20Work-Full%20Report_FINAL_3.pdf

Flores, A., Herman, J., Gates, G., & Brown, T. (2016). *How many adults identify as transgender in the United States?* Retrieved from https://williamsinstitute.law.ucla.edu/wp-content/uploads/How-Many-Adults-Identify-as-Transgender-in-the-United-States.pdf

Gemeinnützige Stiftung Sexualität und Gesundheit. (2017). *Info ProstSchG*. Retrieved from www.prostituiertenschutzgesetz.info/kontakt-fragen-prostschg/

Global Network of Sex Work Project (NSWP). (n.d.). *Briefing note: U.S.A FOSTA legislation*. Retrieved from www.nswp.org/sites/nswp.org/files/fosta_briefing_note_ 2018.pdf

James, S., Herman, J., Rankin, S., Keisling, M., Mottet, L., & Anafi, M. (2016). *The report of the 2015 U.S. transgender survey*. Washington, DC: National Center for Transgender Equality. Retrieved from https://transequality.org/sites/default/files/docs/usts/USTS-Full-Report-Dec17.pdf

Louissaint, N., Cao, Y., Skipper, P., Liberman, R., Tannenbaum, S., Nimmagadda, S., . . . Hendrix, C. (2013). Single dose pharmacokinetics of oral Tenofovir in plasma, peripheral blood mononuclear cells, colonic tissue, and vaginal tissue. *Journal of AIDS Research and Human Retroviruses, 29*(11), 1443–1450. Retrieved from www.ncbi.nlm.nih.gov/pmc/articles/PMC3809387/

Nemoto, T., Bödeker, B., & Imamoto, M. (2011). Social support, exposure to violence and transphobia, and correlates of depression among male-to-female transgender women with a history of sex work. *American Journal of Public Health, 101*(10), 1980–1988. Retrieved from www.ncbi.nlm.nih.gov/pubmed/21493940

Nuttbrock, L. (Ed.). (2018). *Transgender sex work and society*. New York, NY: Harrington Park Press.

Patterson, K., Prince, H., Kraft, E., Jenkins, A. Shaheen, N., Rooney, J., . . . Kashuba, A. (2011). Penetration of Tenofovir and Emtricitabine in mucosal tissues: Implications for prevention of HIV-1 transmission. *Science Translational Medicine, 3*(112). Retrieved from www.ncbi.nlm.nih.gov/pmc/articles/PMC3483088/

Poteat, T., Malik, M., Scheim, A., & Elliott, A. (2017). HIV prevention among transgender populations: Knowledge gaps and evidence for action. *Journal of Current HIV/AIDS Reports, 14*(4), 141–152. Retrieved from www.ncbi.nlm.nih.gov/pmc/articles/PMC5896563/

Poteat, T., Scheim, A., Xavier, J., Reisner, S., & Baral, S. (2016). Global epidemiology of HIV infection and related syndemics affecting transgender people. *Journal of Acquired Immune Deficiency Syndrome, 72,* 210–219. Retrieved from www.ncbi.nlm.nih.gov/pubmed/27429185

Radix, A. (n.d.). *PrEP and transgender people: Limited data point to similar efficacy; more scale-up is needed.* Retrieved from www.positivelyaware.com/articles/prep-and-transgender-people

Scheim, A., Santos, G., Arreola, S., Makofane, K., Do, T., Herbert, P., . . . Ayala, G. (2016). Inequities in access to HIV prevention services for transgender men: Results of a global survey of men who have sex with men. *Journal of the International AIDS Society, 19*(3/2). Retrieved from www.ncbi.nlm.nih.gov/pubmed/27431466

Sevelius, J. (2009). There's no pamphlet for the kind of sex I have": HIV-related risk factors and protective behaviors among transgender men who have sex with nontransgender men. *Journal of the Association of Nurses in AIDS Care, 20*(5), 398–410. Retrieved from www.ncbi.nlm.nih.gov/pmc/articles/PMC2785444/

Smith, N. (2012). Body issues: The political economy of male sex work. *Journal of Sexualities, 15*(5/6), 586–603. Retrieved from https://journals.sagepub.com/doi/abs/10.1177/1363460712445983

St. James Infirmary. (s.a.). *Media campaign.* Retrieved from https://stjamesinfirmary.org/wordpress/?page_id=1673

Stryker, S. (2017). *Transgender history.* New York, NY: Seal Press.

United States Census Bureau. (2018). *Poverty thresholds.* Retrieved from www.census.gov/data/tables/time-series/demo/income-poverty/historical-poverty-thresholds.html

Van Caenegem, E., Wierckx, K., Elaut, E., Buysse, A., Dewaele, A., Van Nieuwerburgh, F., . . . T'Sjoen, G. (2015). Prevalence of gender nonconformity in Flanders, Belgium. *Archives of Sexual Behavior, 44*(5), 1281–1287.

World Health Organization. (2014). *Consolidated guidelines on HIV prevention, diagnosis, treatment and care for key populations.* Retrieved from www.who.int/hiv/pub/guidelines/keypopulations/en/

Part VI

Male sex work in the Americas

23

Male sex work in North America

Frontiers of change in the United States and Canada

Christian Grov and Drew A. Westmoreland

Introduction

As in most of the world, sex work remains criminalized in most of the United States and Canada. However, with the majority of male sex work transactions today beginning online (as opposed to on street corners or in gay bars, bathhouses, or brothels)—and the increasing social acceptance of LGBT people more generally—there has been reduced interest in the enforcement of anti-prostitution laws, at least for male sex workers. One prominent exception was the 2015 raid and subsequent shutdown of rentboy.com in New York City, which has affected male sex work communities around the globe.

This chapter takes stock of prominent studies of male sex workers in the United States and Canada over the last two decades. Its goal is not to provide a laundry list of every research article that has mentioned male sex workers but rather to describe the major work done to advance our knowledge of male sex workers in these regions. Thus, it focuses on research conducted with male sex workers that has resulted in multiple publications or monographs, providing a comprehensive account of the results of each project.

The *Classified Project*

Prior to the Internet boom, most research on male sex workers focused on street or bar hustlers (Allen, 1980), call boys (Allen, 1980), rent boys (West, 2012; Bloor, McKeganey, & Barnard, 1990), and agency-based or hard-copy-advertised escorts (Hickson, Weatherburn, Hows, & Davis, 1994; Lumby, 1978; Salamon, 1989). In the late 1990s and early 2000s, researchers hypothesized that the Internet not only changed how male escorts advertised sex but also changed *who* was escorting and the logistics of *how* they performed their jobs. To better understand how Internet-based male escorts differed from more traditionally researched male sex workers, Parsons and colleagues conducted a study describing online male sex workers in New York City. The publications emerging from this study touched on three broad areas: *who* these men are, *why* they escort, and *what* the occupational considerations and risks associated with escorting are.

From August through October of 2000, the researchers identified 535 male escorts operating in New York by scanning American Online (AOL.com) member profiles for language that suggested someone might be advertising as an escort (e.g., either overt language such as "escort" or coded language such as "seeking generou$"). An email with information about the study was sent and successfully delivered to 370 of the 535 potential participants. From these, 60 called the researchers to screen for eligibility, and 57 met the study's criteria. Fifty (of the 57 scheduled) showed up for their study visit and completed the qualitative interview and self-administered quantitative survey (Parsons, Bimbi, & Halkitis, 2001). The qualitative interview focused on experiences working in the sex industry, while the quantitative survey covered topics such as sociodemographic characteristics, childhood sexual abuse, sex behaviors, sexual sensation seeking and compulsivity scales, and substance use (Uy, Parsons, Bimbi, Koken, & Halkitis, 2004).

Most participants were White (67%), identified as gay (83%), and had at least some college education (95.6%). Mean age was 31.8. Eighty-three percent were HIV-negative, and 4% ($n = 2$) reported that they had never been tested for HIV. Forty-six percent reported having been diagnosed with an STI other than HIV in their lifetimes. Over one-third (37%) reported having a primary sex partner, and only three participants reported that their partners did not know they engaged in sex work. Participants reported an average of 45 paying sexual partners and 25 non-paying sexual partners in the past three months. Over half reported having anal sex with a condom consistently with clients, and 39% reported at least some condomless anal sex. Significantly more participants (44% vs. 39%) reported having condomless anal sex with casual sex partners than with paying clients (Parsons, Koken, & Bimbi, 2007).

The average time spent escorting was 2.7 years (range 3 weeks to 25 years). Most reported charging approximately $200 per hour, ranging from $75 for bodywork (e.g., erotic massage) up to $250 for full service (oral/anal sex, "boyfriend experience"). The median annual income earned from sex work was $20,000 to $29,999 (Parsons et al., 2007). These factors all helped the researchers develop to a descriptive portrait of the characteristics of the male sex workers in the study.

One common theme in research about sex workers is the investigation of psychological traits and influences of past experiences, or trauma, on their current occupation. Parsons et al. (2001) contributed to this body of research by examining sexual compulsivity among participating male sex workers. The mean score on the Sexual Compulsivity Scale for the total sample was 19.2 (SD = 6.9), and these scores did not differ meaningfully by HIV status, by ethnicity, or by childhood sexual abuse status. However, sexual compulsivity was related to the number of casual sexual partners ($R^2 = 0.16$, p-value = 0.004) and frequency of condomless sexual acts with paying and non-paying sex partners: receptive condomless anal sex to ejaculation with non-paying sex partners ($R^2 = 0.12$, p-value = 0.01), receptive condomless anal sex to ejaculation with paying sex partners ($R^2 = 0.19$, p-value = 0.001), and insertive condomless anal sex to ejaculation with paying sex partners ($R^2 = 0.13$, p-value = 0.009). The results from this study were unable to confirm an association between sexual compulsivity and childhood sexual abuse previously found in the literature; however, sexual compulsivity was associated with sexual risk behaviors among both clients and casual sex partners (Parsons et al., 2001).

Parsons, Bimbi, Koken, and Halkitis (2005) further explored psychological states and experiences of gay and bisexual male Internet sex workers by investigating the prevalence and resulting effects of childhood sexual abuse. Childhood sexual abuse was defined as having been pressured, forced, or intimidated into doing something sexually before age 16. An affirmative answer to this question triggered a series of follow-up questions that assessed who the abuser was, how frequently the sex worker experienced abuse, and the emotional repercussions of these incidents. Twenty-eight (60.9%) participants reported some form of childhood sexual abuse, with most (61.5%) reporting abuse by a family member. The mean age when the abuse occurred was 11 (SD = 3.2), and participants who reported childhood sexual abuse had an earlier age of sexual debut (average age of 11 vs. 15.6). Men of color were eight times more likely to report childhood sexual abuse (vs. White participants), and participants identifying as bisexual were six times more likely (vs. participants identifying as gay) to report childhood sexual abuse. Finally, escorts who reported childhood sexual abuse were more likely to report having condomless anal sex, indicating a propensity to engage in riskier sexual behaviors (Parsons et al., 2005).

Why did these men escort? Many participants (39.1%) reported that they escorted because they liked sex, but, unsurprisingly, money was the main reason participants reported doing sex work (Uy et al., 2004). Once they started escorting, other benefits began to emerge. Twelve participants reported that they felt good about their work (Koken, Bimbi, Parsons, & Halkitis, 2004). Other benefits mentioned included traveling to new places, staying at new hotels, and meeting people from different social circles. Some noted their improved sense of self—28.3% reported an ego boost, while 26% reported increased self-confidence, outgoingness, or improved body image. In addition to an improved sense of self, participants also reported benefits to their sex life, such as an expanded sexual repertoire (Uy et al., 2004).

Despite these reported benefits of escorting, some participants also noted negative effects on their emotional well-being. They reported feeling used, guilty, detached, or empty, and most reported experiencing stigma related to being an escort (Uy et al., 2004; Koken et al., 2004). Some also found it difficult to "lead a double life" and were uncomfortable with the work's illegality (Koken et al., 2004). Nearly a quarter reported not telling anyone about their escorting, which negatively affected budding romantic partnerships (Koken et al., 2004).

Participants reported that escorting affected their sexual lives. They were less likely to cruise for sex or had less casual sex to save their libido for work (19.6%). Indeed, some escorts (6.5%) felt that it was hard to separate work sex from non-work sex, and some (15.2%) felt that their time spent as escorts had caused a loss of sexual satisfaction in non-work, personal encounters (Uy et al., 2004). Despite the reports of negative effects on their personal emotional well-being, some (35%) found comfort in thinking that they were helping clients who were lonely or elderly or who had body issues (Koken et al., 2004). This dichotomy of perceived positive benefits and negative effects from escorting probably contributes to the relatively short duration of working as a sex worker. Some men noted that escorting was not their full-time occupation or that they considered sex work a temporary financial solution (Uy et al., 2004).

In addition to examining *why* men chose to work as escorts, Parsons et al. (2007) examined how these men got started in sex work, as well as tools and resources they wished they had to better do their jobs. A common piece of advice that escorts (24%) gave for anyone thinking about starting in the business was to do one's research. Indeed, some participants reported talking to or scheduling a session with an escort prior to having their first client (Parsons et al., 2007). Other male sex workers were repeatedly mentioned as valued social support due to less worry about being stigmatized (Koken et al., 2004). Some participants even had partners who themselves were current (*n* = 5) or former (*n* = 1) sex workers, and all but two of the participants' primary partners knew about their sex work (Koken et al., 2004).

Once in the business, escorts stressed the importance of having a good personality, possessing special traits or characteristics (41%), being comfortable with one's own sexual identity, and engaging in self-care—that is, having social support inside and outside of the business and drawing personal/professional boundaries (24%). However, participants wished they had more information on certain topics in order to perform their jobs better and to remain healthier and safer. These topics included basic business practices and finances (22%), general safety information (20%) (e.g., knowing the warning signs of drugged-up and/or dangerous clients), safe sex information (48%), how to access affordable drug and alcohol counseling (20%), and avoiding undercover police (35%) (Parsons et al., 2007). The responses reported in various publications from the *Classified Project* make it evident that many participants do approach their sex work from an online business perspective (Parsons et al., 2007; Koken et al., 2004).

One of the foci of the *Classified Project* was to compare escorting through agencies and hard-copy publications to escorting on the Internet. In 2004, Parsons, Koken, and Bimbi described Internet-based escorting from the perspective of Internet-based escorts. Some participants reported advertising both on the Internet and in traditional hard-copy gay publications. Compared to previous methods of soliciting clients, Internet-solicited clients were generally thought to be classier, more intelligent, and more well-to-do. By soliciting clients on the Internet, participants reported that they worried less about law enforcement and more carefully screened for potentially dangerous clients. Generally, the Internet was seen as a more favorable venue to solicit clients because of its flexibility and better hours; it also offered participants more control than, say, working for an escorting agency. For example, escorts reported having more control over the types of services that they offered, including HIV risk behaviors such as unprotected sex. A majority (80%) of the escorts reported that they received requests for condomless anal sex ("barebacking") from clients. Many of these requests were made up front when scheduling an appointment; however, some requests were made during the appointment (Parsons, Koken, & Bimbi, 2004). Most participants reported refusing condomless anal sex requests—65.2% reported that barebacking was completely off limits (Parsons et al., 2004; Bimbi & Parsons, 2005). Those escorts who did refuse condomless sex experienced immediate financial repercussions, but they felt that the risks related to condomless sex were greater than lost revenue (Parsons et al., 2004). Many escorts took the opportunity to educate clients requesting condomless anal sex about the risks involved, the reasons they would not perform certain condomless sex acts, and safe sex practices. Only nine participants (19.6%) reported engaging in condomless anal intercourse with clients; more often, escorts reported engaging in condomless sex with casual sex partners (44%) (Parsons et al., 2004).

Sex work in the *Sex and Love* Study

In addition to their work on the *Classified Project*, Koken, Parsons, Severino, and Bimbi (2005) collaborated again to look at commercial sex encounters in New York City in an iteration of the *Sex and Love* Study. This study was a broader look at sexual risk behavior among gay and bisexual men that also included inquires about performing or soliciting sex work. In 2003, 1,072 men attending two large LGBT community events in New York City completed a brief paper-and-pencil survey; however, only men reporting sex outside of a monogamous relationship in the past three months were included in analyses ($n = 660$) (Koken et al., 2005).

The analyzed sample was mostly White (65% vs. 9% African American, 9% Asian/Pacific Islander, and 12% Latino), gay-identified (92% vs. 7% bisexual), and HIV-negative (63% vs. 9% HIV-positive, 7% unknown status). Many (42.7%) participants reported having had a commercial sex encounter, and, of these men, 36.5% reported paying for sex, 36.9% reported being paid for sex, and 26.6% reported both being paid and having paid for sex (Koken et al., 2005).

Three groups were compared in this study: (1) men with any commercial sex encounters (sub-categorized as having been paid, having paid, or both), (2) men with recent (past year) commercial sex encounters, and (3) men with no commercial sex encounters. First, men who had ever been paid for sex were, on average, younger than men who had paid for sex (33 years old vs. 40.5) and were more likely to report condomless receptive and insertive anal sex with casual, non-commercial sex partners compared to those with no experience as sex workers.

Participants who had ever been paid for sex were also more likely to report being HIV-positive. Substance use was more likely to be reported by men who were paid for sex and by men who both paid and were paid for sex compared to men who only paid for sex or men who had no experience with commercial sex (Koken et al., 2005).

Although nearly half of the participants reported commercial sexual encounters, only about a quarter (26.6%) reported a recent (within the last year) history of any commercial sex. Slightly more than half (54.7%) reported that they were paid for sex during these encounters, 25.3% reported having recently paid for sex, and 20% reported both paying for sex and being paid for sex in the past year. Men who reported any commercial sex encounters in the past year were more likely to report higher-risk behaviors such as unprotected receptive and insertive anal sex, (ever) having a non-HIV sexually transmitted infection (STI), and significantly more sex partners than men with no commercial sex encounters in the past year (Koken et al., 2005).

Overall, the findings from the *Sex and Love* study indicated that sexual risk behaviors were higher among men who have *any* experience with commercial sex, whether buying, selling, or both. Interestingly, there was quite a bit of overlap (26.6%) between men who both paid and were paid for sex. These men also fell between paid sex workers and paying clients on the continuum of sexual risk behaviors, with paid sex workers having the highest frequency of at-risk behaviors (i.e., unprotected anal sex, higher number of sex partners, and substance use). This study also illuminated the slight stigma surrounding commercial sex encounters among gay and bisexual men. Interestingly, gay and bisexual men acknowledged the commonality of commercial sex, but they did not seem to think that people in their immediate social circles were engaging in it (Koken et al., 2005).

The *RentBoy* study

From the 1990s until the U.S. federal government shut it down in 2015 (Friedersdorf, 2015; Clifford, 2015; Osborne, 2015), Rentboy.com was one of the leading websites on which male escorts (and some transgender escorts) advertised their services to male clients. Escorts advertised via profiles that included their photos, measurements (height, weight, and genitals), a description of their interests (both personal and/or sexual), hours of availability, and rates. RentBoy's market was predominately in the United States; however, it also included profiles from escorts from across the world. RentBoy was free for users (i.e., clients) to browse; it charged monthly subscription fees to escorts to maintain their profile/ad. RentBoy's headquarters were in New York City, and its managers were strong advocates for the LGBT community—they sponsored a float in the annual NYC Pride March, for example—and for escorts themselves. They also supported research with sex workers.

In 2013, Christian Grov, in collaboration with RentBoy and Hook-Online.com (a not-for-profit escort advocacy group, which also shuttered its doors because of the RentBoy raid), launched a cross-sectional online study of male escorts. The research opportunity was advertised on both websites and generated responses from 418 escorts. (Nearly all responses came via RentBoy.) As reported in Grov et al. (2014), the mean age of the sample was 34, and the majority were White (70.8%), gay-identified (74.3%), and U.S. residents (76.8%). The second and third most common nations were the United Kingdom ($n = 24$, 5.7%) and Canada ($n = 21$, 5.0%).

In total, 18.7% were HIV-positive and 8.6% did not know their status. More than half the participants had completed at least a college degree, and 44.4% earned over $60,000 (USD) in the past year. Nearly two-thirds (64.1%) maintained some kind of employment outside of escorting, and 28.2% were either currently married (or had a commitment ceremony or domestic partner) or in a relationship. For those in a relationship, married, divorced, or widowed, 84.8% indicated their partner is/was male. See Table 23.1.

Modal time spent escorting was between one and five years (43.7%), and a quarter of the respondents (25.9%) had been escorting for less than one year. Most (76.1%) had been hired exclusively by male clients, and the median number of hires in the last 30 days was 10 (IQR 4–18). More than two-thirds (69.7%) had not disclosed their escorting to any of their family

Table 23.1 Demographic Characteristics of Male Escorts From Rentboy.com, 2013

	M	SD
Age in years, valid *n* = 412*	34	10.7
	n	%
Race or Ethnicity, valid *n* = 414		
White	293	70.8
Black, Afric. Amer.	23	5.6
Latino	47	11.4
Asian/Pacific Islander	15	3.6
Multiracial or "other"	36	8.7
Resides in the USA, valid *n* = 409	314	76.8
HIV status, valid *n* = 418		
Negative	304	72.7
Positive	78	18.7
Don't know/unsure	36	8.6
Sexual identity, valid *n* = 416		
Straight, heterosexual	9	2.2
Bi, bisexual	87	20.9
Gay	309	74.3
Other	11	2.6
Total income in last year ($US), valid *n* = 388		
Up to $29,999	112	28.9
$30,000 to $59,999	104	26.7
$60,000 to $99,999	101	26.1
$100,000+	71	18.3
Education, valid *n* = 413		
Up to a high school degree	64	15.5
Some college	122	29.5
College degree	93	22.5
Graduate school	134	32.4
Employment status in addition to escorting, valid *n* = 415		
Not applicable, I only escort	149	35.9
Part-time (less than 35 hours/week)	135	32.5
Full-time (greater than 35 hours/week)	131	31.6
Relationship Status, valid *n* = 416		
Single	283	68.0
In a relationship	88	21.2
Married, had a commitment ceremony, domestic partner	29	7.0
Divorced	9	2.2
Widowed	7	1.7

* *n* = 6 did not answer this question but previously indicated they were over the age of 18

Source: Adapted from Grov et al. (2014). *Sexuality Research and Social Policy*, *11*(2), 176–185.

members. In contrast, more than three-quarters had disclosed their escorting to some of their friends. In total, 29.4% of escorts indicated they had engaged in condomless anal sex with the most recent male client who had hired them. Substance use was common: poppers (46.2%), marijuana (40.2%), cocaine (24.6%), prescription drug use without a prescription or not as prescribed (23.4%), methamphetamine (23.2%), GHB (19.6%), steroids (10.8%), ketamine (10.5%), crack or freebase (3.6%), heroin (1.9%), and methadone (1.2%). See Table 23.2.

Table 23.2 Behavioral Characteristics and Disclosure of Escorting to Others, Rentboy.com, 2013

	n	%
Length of time working as an escort, valid *n* = 412		
Less than a month	17	4.1
1 to 6 months	45	10.9
6 to 12 months	45	10.9
1 to 5 years	180	43.7
5 to 10 years	73	17.7
Greater than 10 years	52	12.6
Sex of people who have hired you . . . valid *n* = 418		
Exclusively male (100%)	316	76.1
Mostly male	79	19
Equally split between male and female	15	3.6
Mostly female	4	1.0
Other	1	0.2
Family knows about involvement in escorting, valid *n* = 413		
Not at all	288	69.7
Some	51	12.3
About half	7	1.7
Most	25	6.1
All	27	6.5
Not applicable (I don't have any family to tell)	15	3.6
Friends know about involvement in escorting, valid *n* = 412		
Not at all	102	24.8
Some	159	38.6
About half	43	10.4
Most	57	13.8
All	51	12.4
Condomless anal sex w/most recent male client		
Yes	123	29.4
Substance use in the last 12 months		
Poppers (nitrate inhalants)	193	46.2
Marijuana	168	40.2
Cocaine	103	24.6
Rx drugs (w/o a prescription or not as prescribed)	98	23.4
Methamphetamine	97	23.2
Ecstasy (MDMA)	92	22.0
GHB	82	19.6
Steroids	45	10.8
Ketamine	44	10.5

(Continued)

Table 23.2 (Continued)

	n	%
Crack or freebase	15	3.6
Heroin	8	1.9
Methadone	5	1.2
	Md	IQR
Number of times hired in last 30 days, valid *n* = 406	10	4 to 18
Md = Median, IQR = Interquartile Range		

Source: Adapted from Grov et al. (2014) *Sexuality Research and Social Policy*, *11*(2), 176–185.

Table 23.3 Workshops That Rentboy Escorts Thought Would Benefit Them, 2013

	Overall rank	
	n	%
Attracting the "right" clients and keeping them	253	65.0
Escorting and legal matters	249	64.0
How best to market yourself as an escort online	244	62.7
Financial planning and planning for the future (how to manage your money from escorting)	205	52.7
Affordable healthcare for escorts	184	47.3
Self-defense and protecting yourself with a client	168	43.2
Dating (relationships) and escorting	160	41.1
Ending an escorting career and transitioning to a new one	158	40.6
Balancing my career as an escort with another job	150	38.6
How to avoid burnout	148	38.0
Setting boundaries with clients	141	36.2
Talking to your healthcare provider about being an escort	132	33.9
How to negotiate safer sex with clients	119	30.6
Coming out to friends/family about being an escort	64	16.5

Source: Adapted from Grov et al. (2014) *Sexuality Research and Social Policy*, *11*(2), 176–185.

In a series of publications stemming from this dataset, Grov and colleagues (2014) examined the types of workshops escorts would prefer to attend, from a list of 14 topics ranging from "Attracting the 'right' clients and keeping them" to "How to negotiate safer sex with clients." Notably, more than half of participants expressed interest in topics that would improve their business as an escort. These included "Attracting the right clients and keeping them" (65.0%), "Escorting and legal matters" (64.0%), "How best to market yourself as an escort online" (62.7%), and "Financial planning and planning for the future (managing income from escorting)" (52.7%). Meanwhile, few were interested in workshops in coming out about escorting to friends/family (16.5%), strategies for negotiating safe sex with clients (30.6%), or talking with healthcare providers about being an escort (33.9%). The study concluded that escorts might feel that they have already mastered these skills or that these skills were unnecessary. Interestingly, the theme that escorts are looking for ways to become "better escorts" was shared by the RentBoy participants and those who participated in the *Classified Project* previously discussed. See Table 23.3.

Grov, Rodríguez-Díaz, Jovet-Toledo, and Parsons (2015) also compared how escorts' sexual behavior varied between their most recent client and their most recent non-commercial partner. Apart from research suggesting that male escorts were less likely to have condomless anal sex with their male clients compared with male non-clients (as highlighted in the *Classified Project* and *Sex and Love Study*), little is known about how male escorts' behavior differs between their clients and non-clients. The study found that encounters with non-commercial partners were more likely to involve a greater range of sexual behaviors, including giving oral sex to the partner, kissing, anal receptive sex, and sex without condoms. These findings suggested that escorts may display a greater sexual repertoire with non-commercial partners than with their clients. Encounters with non-commercial partners were also rated as more satisfying than encounters with clients. Prior researchers have noted that clients may wish to engage in intimate but not necessarily sexual behaviors, a conclusion that was supported by the *RentBoy* dataset. Escorts were significantly more likely to engage in erotic talk (78.0% vs. 64.2%), erotic massage (51.3% vs. 37.8%), and role play (35.7% vs. 28.0%) with their last client than they were with their last non-commercial partner.

In a third publication stemming from the dataset, Grov, Moody, and Kinkaid (2015) divided escorts into three mutually exclusive groups based on how "out" they were about being an escort. The three groups were escorts who were out to friends only (48.9%), escorts who were out to friends and family (26.6%), and escorts who were out to neither friends nor family (23.5%). The researchers hypothesized that men out to neither friends nor family would perform more poorly than the other two groups across indicators of health and well-being due to the lack of social support from friends and family. Although the not-out group reported lower satisfaction and pay from their last male client, the researchers' hypothesis was unsupported. Outness patterns were largely unassociated with social and sexual behaviors with the last male client, and the majority eschewed condomless anal sex with their last male client, suggesting that escorts—regardless of how out they are to friends and family—could navigate safer sex behaviors with their clients.

Men out to friends and family were significantly more likely than men in the other two groups to have been escorting for more than five years or to work at escorting full-time. This finding suggested that escorts who have been engaged in escorting for a long period and/or escorting full-time might be out to friends and family both out of necessity and inevitability: inevitable because it becomes increasingly difficult to conceal from friends and family sporadic work hours and sources of income, and necessary because friends and family have the potential to serve as powerful mechanisms of support in helping escorts navigate the emotional costs and stigma associated with sex work.

In a more recently published study, Grov, Koken, Smith, and Parsons (2017) compared the participants from the RentBoy study to a 2014–2015 sample of men who advertised as sex workers on the New York City men-seeking-men section of Craigslist.org ($n = 95$). To identify participants for the Craigslist sample, the research team reviewed ads in the men-seeking-men section to identify those who might be looking for paid sexual encounters (the ads often used terms like "seeking generous$") and then responded with an invitation to participate in an online survey. In multivariable modeling, compared to the RentBoy participants, Craigslist participants had significantly higher odds of being non-White (AOR = 5.32), gay-identified (AOR = 2.32), making less than $20,000 a year (AOR = 3.77), and having used marijuana in the past 12 months (AOR = 3.41).

Furthermore, compared to the RentBoy participants, Craigslist participants had significantly lower odds of escorting full-time (AOR = .24), kissing (AOR = .23), and having anal insertive sex with their last male client (AOR = .36). In additions, the odds were significantly lower that their last paid encounter lasted longer than one hour (AOR = .49) and that they'd been paid over $200 for that encounter (AOR = .19). They also had fewer clients in the past 30 days (AOR = .95). Craigslist participants were at greater economic disadvantage than the men from RentBoy; however, they were less likely to engage in HIV risk behaviors (anal sex and condomless anal sex). The study concluded that those advertising on Craigslist might be characteristically different from those advertising on RentBoy. In contrast to RentBoy, where escorts have to purchase advertising space for a minimum of one month, ads on Craigslist were free and could be removed immediately upon finding a suitable client. Many of the ads to which the researchers responded intimated that the advertiser (sex worker) was looking for a short-term financial solution (e.g., having enough money to pay the rent at the end of the month).

The *Escort Agency* study

As we have illustrated, much of what is known about male sex work has been derived from online samples or samples of escorts who advertise online. Considerably less is known about men who escort via an agency; there are fewer agency-based escorts than independent escorts on escorting websites. Starting in 2004, Dr. Michael Smith led a mixed-method study of $n = 30$ male sex workers based out of an escort agency within a small mid-Atlantic city (population of about 49,000) (Smith & Seal, 2008; Smith & Grov, 2011). The agency had been operating for about five years at the time of the study, and 94% of the men escorting for the agency took part in Smith's research project. Smith's work involved conducting qualitative interviews with escorts at the agency as well as the manager, doing ethnographic observation of the day-to-day activities at the agency, and collecting survey data from escorts and the agency manager.

Escorts from the agency served approximately 180–200 clients per month with about 95% of calls taking place at a client's residence or hotel room. The remainder occurred at the agency. Participants ranged in age from 18 to 35 years old (median = 22.4 years). The sample was predominantly Caucasian (70%), and the majority self-identified as gay (63.3%). Most (86.7%) had completed high school, and most had full-time jobs in addition to escorting. Just over half said they were in a steady relationship. Of these men, 88% said their partner was aware of their escort work.

In the series of publications stemming from the dataset, Smith and his colleagues noted that escorts were less likely to engage in HIV risk behavior with clients than with their non-commercial partners (Smith & Seal, 2008)—a finding that has been replicated in essentially every study we have discussed in this chapter thus far. Escorts themselves described playing active cognitive roles in mitigating their risk in the profession. They also noted that many of their clients were not seeking to engage in sexual behavior (particularly anal sex). Rather, many clients requested intimate behavior in one-hour sessions, with the majority of that time spent talking with a client or engaging in light touching/fondling/massage (Smith & Grov, 2011). A parallel phenomenon in the female sex work literature, termed a "girlfriend experience," has been likened to clients' desire for this "boyfriend experience" (Smith & Grov, 2011).

Smith's study included ethnographic components. Smith spent considerable time at the agency, which was based in a single-family home owned by the agency manager. Some escorts lived at the agency, often temporarily, while many others "hung out" at the agency regularly (e.g., played video games) and even brought friends over to hang out with them. In their ethnographic analysis of how the agency functioned, Smith, Grov, and Seal (2009) noted that the escorts established both physical boundaries (defined areas where clients were not invited) and psychological boundaries (limitations of relationship with clients, other escorts, and the agency manager) to construct personal and professional space regarding their sex work. The study further noted that physical and psychological boundaries often were blended (e.g., bringing friends/family to the agency, utilizing the agency as a "drop-in community center"). The agency further mitigated negative aspects of sex work by providing job training, social support, stigma management, and dual-use space (e.g., personal and professional).

In a third study stemming from these data, Smith, Grov, Seal, and McCall (2013) utilized a social-cognitive theoretical perspective to assess the interactions of behavioral, cognitive, and situational factors that influenced escorts' entry into the sex trade industry. The authors noted that—as predicted by a social-cognitive perspective—there were reciprocal influences of behavior and environment, environment and cognition, and behavior and cognition. Escorts developed more self-efficacy around engaging in sex work (i.e., behavior) and more positive outcome expectations with greater escorting experience. In contrast, moral conflict (i.e., believing that engaging in sex work was wrong) and lack of physical/sexual attraction to clients limited escorts' sense of self-efficacy. The study concluded that social-cognitive theory could serve as a model for understanding how individuals become sex workers and how they physically and psychologically cope with the work they do (Smith et al., 2013).

Finally, in the most recent study stemming from this dataset, Smith, Grov, Seal, Bernhardt, and McCall (2014) examined social situations and emotional correlates associated with male sex work in this sample. ("Emotional correlates" are commonly known as "emotional labor" in the female sex work literature.) They found that participants identified a range of social and emotional factors regarding their sex work and employed a variety of strategies to provide good customer service and adapt to negative experiences. For most, social support was inhibited due to fear of stigmatization that might result if participants disclosed sex work to significant others *outside* the agency. Instead, interactions *within* the agency provided core work-related social support for most of the escorts. The study concluded that socially connected agency-based sex workers were more satisfied with their work and that the social/emotional aspects of sex work were significant but unexpected aspects of their jobs.

Canadian sex work studies, *Touching Encounters*

With few notable exceptions (Corriveau & Greco, 2014; Jiao & Bungay, 2018), there is little published on male sex work in Canada; however, one notable study is *Touching Encounters* (2012) by Kevin Walby. The purpose of the book was to examine male sex work in the context of sex, sexuality, and labor theories. A review of the book and theoretical concepts was published in *Sexuality Research and Social Policy* in 2013. In this section, we highlight aspects of Walby's interviews with male escorts not addressed in previous sections of this chapter, and we recommend the full book and brief Grov review for anyone further interested in theoretical discussions of sex work (Grov, 2013; Walby, 2012).

For his research, Walby recruited male-for-male escorts with commercial profiles on escorting websites (Canadianmale.com, boys2-rent.com, and men4rentnow.com). He emailed information about the study to 550 escorts identified across the three websites, received 56 responses from those initial emails, and conducted 30 interviews from those 56 interested. Walby conducted all but one of the qualitative interviews in person. Most of the escorts lived in Toronto (*n* = 13), four lived in Montreal, four lived in Ottawa, four lived in New York City, four lived in London, and one lived in Houston, Texas. The interviews lasted from 37 to 80 minutes and were held in different venues according to the participants' preferences (e.g., coffee shops, bus stops, park benches, the escorts' homes).

The average age of the escorts was 34 (range 20–64), but the average age on their online profiles was 29. Mean time spent escorting was 6.5 years, but the range varied from less than one year to more than ten years. Most were White (n = 23), but two identified as Black, four identified as Latino, and one identified as Lebanese. A few of the escorts mentioned prior escorting experiences as street hustlers and working for escort agencies or massage parlors, and two worked in the porn industry. Most (n = 20) men worked other jobs in addition to escorting, and most (n = 23) were enrolled in or had completed college. From these escorts' interviews, Walby focused on describing the labor process of escorting, the escorts' worker identity, and the escorts' work-life balance (Walby, 2012).

One key aspect highlighted in *Touching Encounters* was the entrepreneurial nature of sex work (e.g., advertising, startup costs) and its relation to other types of work as described by participants. In Walby's view, escorts are entrepreneurs because they are, in fact, self-employed business owners. Self-employment afforded them autonomy and control over the clients they saw and the hours they kept, and the Internet helped them run their businesses efficiently. In comparison, the escorts with previous experience at escorting agencies reported feeling less control over their clients and schedules while at the agency, but some escorts reported other benefits from the agencies, such as safety and security. Escorting was inconsistent work, and escorts mentioned surges and lapses in demand. Walby drew comparisons to the rise of other forms of unsteady work that are more normative, such as freelance writing or consulting, and made more efficient by technology.

Technology, particularly the Internet, was an extremely important means of communication and a way for the escorts to market themselves to potential clients. Many escorts discussed the care they took in advertising themselves through their online profiles, including having photographers take professional headshots of them and managing the style of the images. For example, one escort discussed his marketing strategy of using a general photo for his main profile image and including leather-dressed photos of himself in less prominent positions on the page. He reasoned that a more general photograph was welcoming to a broader client base, and the leather photos indicate his ability to serve a niche market. In addition to the visual advertising through enticing photos, escorts' ads also included the sexual services they provided (often in code) and written descriptions of their physical traits (e.g., penis size, body hair), personality traits (e.g., charm, conversational skills), and sexual traits (e.g., performance ratings, identity, and preferences). Even sexual orientation was strategically advertised to increase escorts' appeal (e.g., a more fluid sexual orientation appeals to a broader client base). Technology benefited escorts by allowing them to efficiently advertise their services, but it also benefited clients through the reviews of escorts also posted on the sites.

Touching Encounters also made several unique contributions to the literature by analyzing the work itself. One important consideration is the operating expenses incurred as an escort. These operating expenses include fees for additional advertising (i.e., print ads) as well as purchasing sex toys and condoms. Operating expenses also include other forms of "body work," such as body maintenance (e.g., grooming, working out, douching) and occupational health concerns. Walby did not spend much time addressing escorts' unique occupational health concerns, such as safe sex and lowering the risk of STDs, including HIV. Instead, Walby focused on another occupational challenge: aging. Some escorts delay the inevitable "best by" date by lying about their age on their profiles. Most clients are looking for new experiences and younger escorts, but there is a niche market for older escorts, and some participants described being successful in it. According to these escorts, clients view older escorts as more mature and responsible. However, being an older escort brought additional physical challenges and operating expenses. Physical challenges arose from the natural limitations of their body and libido. Older escorts worked harder to stay in shape and be physically attractive. Additionally, older escorts were not able to see as many clients per day due to sexual performance limitations; however, the could overcome this limitation with erectile dysfunction medication, adding additional operating costs. Notably, however, younger escorts also reported investing in male enhancement supplements to ensure that they were able to perform sexually and meet their clients' expectations (Walby, 2012).

Touching Encounters also touched on escorts' work persona and work-life balance. Specifically, Walby focused on how and whether male escorts separate their personal lives and their professional sex lives. Some of the escorts reported that they did some surface-level acting when meeting clients, but others reported that successfully "faking it" was difficult, especially with repeat clients. Interviewees frequently brought up repeat clients, who helped them illustrate the complexities of separating personal and professional encounters. Sex was not equivalent to intimacy, the escorts emphasized. Intimacy did, however, play a role in how escorts described their actions with clients. Cuddling, kissing, and sleeping over were generally reported as intimate acts occurring between client and escort. Descriptions of these more intimate acts as "everything I would do with a boyfriend" support Walby's hypothesis that personal and professional sexual encounters were inextricably linked for male escorts. Indeed, many interviews highlighted how relationships developed between escorts and their clients and how these relationships and activities with clients could satisfy some of the escorts' intimacy and sexual needs. From a relationship perspective, male escorts' work-life balance seemed less like a balancing act and more like a Venn diagram with heavily overlapped circles. One distinguishing aspect between personal and professional was disclosure. Many participants were not open about their work and selective about the people with whom they shared this information.

Touching Encounters has done much to situate sex work within labor theory discourse. Walby took a worker-centric approach in his descriptions and discussions of the escorts he interviewed, tying together many different sexual and labor theories while also providing a matter-of-fact view of the daily operations of a self-employed escort.

Sex work in the *Together 5,000* cohort study

With the exception of the *Sex and Love* study, the previously discussed research on male sex workers was based on samples entirely made up of sex workers. These studies enable us to understand the lived experiences of sex workers, but they make it difficult to understand how those who engage in sex work compare with non-sex workers. Christian Grov and his colleagues are presently conducting the *Together 5,000* cohort study of 8,777 individuals who are at risk for HIV (Lopez-Rios et al., 2018; Grov et al., in press; Nash et al., in press). Nearly all (97.5%, *n* = 8,554) are cisgender male, 0.7% (*n* = 63) are transgender women, and 0.6% (*n* = 53) are transgender men who have sex with men. There are also *n* = 107 (1.2%) individuals who self-identify outside of the gender binary—all reported being assigned male at birth and reported having sex with men. In total, 50.9% are persons of color, and 25.3% are young individuals aged 16 to 24 years. To be eligible, participants had to indicate they are not taking HIV pre-exposure prophylaxis (PrEP), not known to be HIV-positive, and otherwise demonstrated moderate risk for contracting HIV (e.g., recent condomless anal sex with a man).

Participants reside in all 50 United States, Puerto Rico, and Guam. They were enrolled between October 2017 and June 2018 via men-for-men geo-social-sexual networking apps. The study itself was marketed to potential participants as an opportunity for free at-home HIV testing. Participants in the cohort complete annual online surveys as well as at-home self-administered HIV testing (sample mailed to a lab). At the time of this chapter's preparation, only baseline data on the cohort were available. Although *Together 5,000* is not designed as a study of sex workers, the cohort includes 1,339 (15.3%) individuals who self-reported having engaged in some form of sex work (receiving money, drugs, or housing) in the three months prior to enrollment (Grov et al., 2018). Notably, *Together 5,000* did not assess how participants met their clients (i.e., where they advertised or whether their sex work was street based, agency based, or Internet based).

Figure 23.1 displays a map of the distribution of those who engaged in sex work. Much like non-sex workers, these individuals reside in all 50 states and Puerto Rico. However, compared to non-sex workers, those who had engaged in sex work recently differed significantly from non-sex-workers in multiple ways. They were significantly younger, less likely to be White, and less likely to be employed full-time; they made significantly less annual income; and they were less likely to identify as gay and less likely to be cisgender male. They were significantly more likely to have experienced recent housing instability and significantly less likely to have been tested for HIV in the last year. With regard to sexual behavior, sex workers were significantly more likely to report sex with women, transwomen, and transmen in the last three months than non-sex workers. They also reported a significantly greater number of male partners and receptive condomless anal sex acts with their male partners in the last three months. Sex workers did not significantly differ from others with regard to whether they were in a relationship with a main partner—approximately one-quarter overall. All values are shown in Table 23.4.

Although the *Together 5,000* cohort study is not representative of all gay and bisexual men, sex work was common in the sample—approximately one in every seven participants reported having engaged in sex work in the prior three months—a phenomenon also observed in the *Sex and Love Study*. These participants also characteristically differed from others in the cohort in ways that are known to be associated with engaging in sex work (e.g., lower income, underemployment, housing instability), but sex workers in the sample also evinced greater needs with regard to HIV prevention. Specifically, those engaged in sex work would benefit from increased access to HIV testing, condoms, and PrEP. Given factors such as lower income, underemployment, and housing instability that were identified among sex workers, successful retention in PrEP care may require additional patient navigation and institutional support.

Figure 23.1   Geographic locations of sex workers in the *Together 5,000* cohort study, *n* = 1,339.

Table 23.4 Characteristics of Sex Workers in the Together 5,000 Cohort Study

	Non-sex workers		Sex workers			
	n	%	n	%	Chi-Sq	p
Race						
White	3732	50.2	577	43.1	39.3	< .001
Black	949	12.8	207	15.5		
Latino	1845	24.8	382	28.5		
Asian/Pacific Islander	282	3.8	29	2.2		
Other, multiracial	630	8.5	144	10.8		
Employment status						
Full-time	4827	64.9	568	42.4	280.2	< .001
Part-time	1486	20	377	28.2		
Unemployed	642	8.6	250	18.7		
Unemployed, student	483	6.5	144	10.8		
Sexual identity						
Gay	6264	84.2	1050	78.4	30.0	< .001
Bisexual	1086	14.6	260	19.4		
Other	88	1.2	29	2.2		
Gender identity						
Cis male	7287	98.0	1267	94.6	54.4	< .001
Transgender female	39	0.5	24	1.8		
Transgender male	39	0.5	14	1.0		
Something else (gender non-binary)	73	1.0	34	2.5		
Income						
≤$9,999	1247	16.8	446	33.6	335.3	< .001
$10K–$19,999	1094	14.7	280	20.9		
$20K–$29,999	1218	16.4	216	16.1		
$30K–$49,999	1865	25.1	260	19.4		
$50K+	2014	27.1	137	10.2		
Housing instability						
Never	5497	73.9	569	42.5	684.3	< .001
Within the last 5 years	1261	17.0	651	48.6		
Greater than 5 years ago	680	9.1	119	8.9		
Currently in a relationship	1980	26.6	335	25	1.5	0.22
Last HIV test						
Within the last year	4601	61.9	761	56.7	19.3	< .001
More than one year ago	1829	25.9	363	27.2		
Never tested	908	12.1	205	16.1		
Has never heard of PrEP	354	4.8	122	9.1	30.6	< .001
Sex with transmen, last 3 months	308	4.1	172	12.8	166.3	< .001
Sex with transwomen, last 3 months	182	2.4	109	8.1	114.7	< .001
Sex with females, last 3 months	688	9.2	253	18.9	110.3	< .001
	M	SD	M	SD	t	p
Age (M, SD)	30.8	7.9	28.3	7.4	10.7	< .001
# Male partners, last 3 months	5.4	6.7	9.6	15.3	16.8	< .001
# Female partners, last 3 months	0.5	2.4	1.4	5.3	10.5	< .001
# Condomless receptive anal sex acts w/males, last 3 months	3.63	8.5	7.01	18.0	10.9	< .001

Conclusion: the changing landscape for the online sex worker

In this chapter, we focused on a handful of studies of male sex workers in the United States and Canada. These studies are by no means exhaustive of every scholarly publication that has included or otherwise mentioned sex workers. And, notably absent from this chapter is research focused on street-based sex workers (Mimiaga, Reisner, Tinsley, Mayer, & Safren, 2009). However, this absence is emblematic of the fact that much of male sex work today is initiated in online environments. Even the *Escort Agency* study discussed in this chapter identified most of its clients via its webpage and digital advertisements (as opposed to a listing in a telephone book or print advertising in gay magazines). Escorts' use of the Internet highlights a common themes across the studies discussed in this chapter: Male escorts may possess more agency than we give them credit for. They make conscious decisions to enter sex work, and as sex workers, they are not looking for information about how to stop being sex workers or how to protect themselves against HIV and other STIs. Rather, they are seeking to be better escorts and to maximize their social support as sex workers. Furthermore, they appear to manage sexual risks with their commercial partners, a practice that directly contradicts the stigmatizing narrative that has scapegoated sex workers as vectors of disease transmission, morally bankrupt, and otherwise in need of being saved from their own bad decisions. But the landscape for sex work, particularly the digital landscape, is changing.

Aside from the *Together 5,000* cohort study, the research described in this chapter preceded two notable historical events that are likely to have considerable impact on sex work: the Rent-Boy raid and the passage of FOSTA/SESTA. As mentioned earlier, Rentboy.com—which at the time was one of the most-used male-for-male escorting websites in the world—was shut down by the U.S. federal government in 2015. The immediate reaction from sex workers, sex work advocates, and the larger LGBT community was condemnation. Many perceived the raid on RentBoy not only as a hostile act toward sex workers but also as an affront to the LGBT community (Friedersdorf, 2015; Clifford, 2015; Osborne, 2015).

Although other escorting websites have remained active since the RentBoy raid, the actions of the U.S. federal government have sent clear signals that any such site is subject to similar treatment. Its owners can be arrested, and the escorts advertising on the site can be prosecuted. We know that escorting (for both men and women) has largely transitioned to be online and independent (as opposed to working for an agency), and many facets of the online environment (such as having a digital communication trail with clients) enhance the safety of escorting, particularly over street-based sex work. We lack data on how the RentBoy raid has impacted sex workers both in terms of their mental health (e.g., fear of engaging in sex work) and their safety (e.g., will I be arrested?). We also lack data on how many individuals have entered or left online advertising for sex work and what happened to those who left.

More far-reaching than the RentBoy raid was the 2018 U.S. House of Representative's passage of the Fight Online Sex Trafficking Act (FOSTA) H.R 1865 and the U.S. Senate's Stop Enabling Sex Traffickers Act (SESTA) (Consumer Watchdog, 2018). The law was intended to stop sex trafficking (particularly child sex trafficking) by allowing prosecution of websites that might host sex traffickers (even if that is not the website's explicit purpose). Because websites are now liable for what their users may do, Craigslist (for example) proactively shut down its personals section in March 2018 (Kennedy, 2018), and the federal government shut down Backpage.com in April 2018 (Hugo, 2018), with a 93-count federal indictment (Department of Justice, 2018). Now, visitors to Backpage.com are greeted by the image shown in Figure 23.2.

Reaction to Backpage's shutdown has been mixed. Although some applaud the measure as a win against child trafficking and sex trafficking, it also impacts the community of consenting

Figure 23.2   Seizure of Backpage.com on April 6, 2018.
Source: Backpage.com.

sex workers, who are now further marginalized. It is too soon to determine the long-term impacts of Backpage's shutdown on the health and safety of sex workers. As a greater number of Internet-based activities are switching from computer websites to smartphone and app-based activities, it will be important to monitor not only how sex work shifts to accommodate these new platforms but also how these new apps are regulated both within and outside of the United States.

References

Allen, D. M. (1980). Young male prostitutes: A psychosocial study. *Archives of Sexual Behavior*, *9*(5), 399–426.

Bimbi, D. S., & Parsons, J. T. (2005). Barebacking among Internet based male sex workers. *Journal of Gay & Lesbian Psychotherapy*, *9*(3–4), 85–105.

Bloor, M., McKeganey, N., & Barnard, M. (1990). An ethnographic study of HIV-related risk practices among Glasgow rent boys and their clients: Report of a pilot study. *AIDS Care*, *2*(1), 17–24.

Clifford, S. (2015). *Raid of RentBoy, an escort website, angers gay activists*. Retrieved from www.nytimes.com/2015/08/27/nyregion/raid-of-rentboy-an-escort-website-angers-gay-activists.html?_r=0

Consumer Watchdog. (2018). *Consumer Watchdog welcomes law that holds websites like Backpage accountable for sex trafficking*. Retrieved from www.consumerwatchdog.org/index.php/privacy-technology/consumer-watchdog-welcomes-law-holds-websites-backpage-accountable-sex

Corriveau, P., & Greco, C. (2014). Misunderstanding (mis)understandings: Male sex workers and the Canadian criminal code. *Sexuality & Culture, 18*(2), 346–360.

Department of Justice. (2018). *Justice Department leads effort to seize backpage.com, the Internet's leading forum for prostitution ads, and obtains 93-count federal indictment.* Retrieved from www.justice.gov/opa/pr/justice-department-leads-effort-seize-backpagecom-internet-s-leading-forum-prostitution-ads

Friedersdorf, C. (2015). *A website for gay escorts gets busted by Homeland Security: Why was Rentboy.com a federal crime-fighting priority?* Retrieved from www.theatlantic.com/politics/archive/2015/08/a-web-site-for-gay-escorts-gets-busted-by-homeland-security/402343/

Grov, C. (2013). Applying a sociological lens to male-for-male Internet escorting. *Sexuality Research and Social Policy, 10*(2), 159–160.

Grov, C., Koken, J., Smith, M., & Parsons, J. T. (2017). How do male sex workers on Craigslist differ from those on RentBoy? A comparison of two samples. *Culture, Health & Sexuality, 19*(4), 405–421.

Grov, C., Moody, R. L., & Kinkaid, H. (2015). Differences in substance use, sexual behavior, and demographic factors by levels of "outness" to friends and family about being a male-for-male escort. *International Journal of Sexual Health, 27*(4), 369–382.

Grov, C., Rodríguez-Díaz, C. E., Ditmore, M. H., Restar, A., & Parsons, J. T. (2014). What kinds of workshops do Internet-based male escorts want? Implications for prevention and health promotion. *Sexuality Research and Social Policy, 11*(2), 176–185.

Grov, C., Rodríguez-Díaz, C. E., Jovet-Toledo, G. G., & Parsons, J. T. (2015). Comparing male escorts' sexual behaviour with their last male client versus non-commercial male partner. *Culture, Health & Sexuality, 17*(2), 194–207.

Grov, C., Stief, M., MacCrate, C., D'Angelo, A. B., Lopez-Rios, J., Hirshfield, S., & Nash, D. (2018, November 8–11). *Sex work and associated risks in a U.S. national cohort study of cismen-, transwomen-, and transmen who have sex with men.* Society for the Scientific Study of Sexuality, Montreal, Quebec.

Grov, C., Westmoreland, D. A., Carneiro, P., Stief, M., MacCrate, C., Mirzayi, C., & Nash, D. (In press). Recruiting vulnerable populations to participate in HIV prevention research: Findings from the *Together 5,000* cohort study. *Annals of Epidemiology*.

Hickson, F., Weatherburn, P., Hows, J., & Davis, P. (1994). Selling safer sex: Male masseurs and escorts in the UK. In P. Aggleton, P. Davies, & G. Hart (Eds.), *AIDS: Foundations for the future* (pp. 197–209). London: Taylor & Francis.

Hugo, K. (2018). *"People are going to die": Sex workers devastated after Backpage shutdown.* Retrieved from www.newsweek.com/people-are-going-die-sex-workers-devastated-after-backpage-shutdown-876486

Jiao, S., & Bungay, V. (2018). Intersections of stigma, mental health, and sex work: How Canadian men engaged in sex work navigate and resist stigma to protect their mental health. *The Journal of Sex Research*, 1–9. Retrieved from https://doi.org/10.1080/00224499.2018.1459446

Kennedy, M. I. (2018). *Craigslist shuts down personals section after Congress passes bill on trafficking.* Retrieved from www.npr.org/sections/thetwo-way/2018/03/23/596460672/craigslist-shuts-down-personals-section-after-congress-passes-bill-on-traffickin

Koken, J. A., Bimbi, D. S., Parsons, J. T., & Halkitis, P. N. (2004). The experience of stigma in the lives of male internet escorts. *Journal of Psychology & Human Sexuality, 16*(1), 13–32.

Koken, J. A., Parsons, J. T., Severino, J., & Bimbi, D. S. (2005). Exploring commercial sex encounters in an urban community sample of gay and bisexual men: A preliminary report. *Journal of Psychology & Human Sexuality, 17*(1–2), 197–213.

Lopez-Rios, J., D'Angelo, A. B., Stief, M., MacCrate, C., Mirzayi, C., Nash, D., & Grov, C. (2018, November 8–11). *Factors associated with polyamory in a U.S. national cohort study of cismen-, transwomen-, and transmen who have sex with men.* The Society for the Scientific Study of Sexuality, Montreal, Quebec.

Lumby, M. E. (1978). Men who advertise for sex. *Journal of Homosexuality, 4*(1), 63–72. doi:10.1300/J082v04n01_05.

Mimiaga, M. J., Reisner, S. L., Tinsley, J. P., Mayer, K. H., & Safren, S. A. (2009). Street workers and Internet escorts: Contextual and psychosocial factors surrounding HIV risk behavior among men who engage in sex work with other men. *Journal of Urban Health, 86*(1), 54–66. doi:10.1007/s11524-008-9316-5.

Nash, D., Stief, M., MacCrate, C., Mirzayi, C., Patel, V. V., Hoover, D., . . . Grov, C. (In press). Together 5,000 (T5K): An online, PrEP-era cohort of vulnerable, HIV-negative gay and bisexual men and trans-men and trans women who have sex with men in the United States and Puerto Rico. *Journal of Medical Internet Research.*

Osborne, D. (2015). *Why the rentboy.com raid hit such a nerve.* Retrieved from http://gaycitynews.nyc/rentboy-com-raid-hit-nerve/

Parsons, J. T., Bimbi, D. S., & Halkitis, P. N. (2001). Sexual compulsivity among gay/bisexual male escorts who advertise on the Internet. *Sexual Addiction & Compulsivity: The Journal of Treatment & Prevention,* 8(2), 101–112. doi:10.1080/10720160127562

Parsons, J. T., Bimbi, D. S., Koken, J. A., & Halkitis, P. N. (2005). Factors related to childhood sexual abuse among gay/bisexual male Internet escorts. *Journal of Child Sexual Abuse, 14*(2), 1–23.

Parsons, J. T., Koken, J. A., & Bimbi, D. S. (2004). The use of the Internet by gay and bisexual male escorts: Sex workers as sex educators. *AIDS Care, 16*(8), 1021–1035.

Parsons, J. T., Koken, J. A., & Bimbi, D. S. (2007). Looking beyond HIV: Eliciting individual and com-munity needs of male Internet escorts. *Journal of Homosexuality, 53*(1–2), 219–240. doi:10.1300/J082v53n01_10

Salamon, E. D. (1989). The homosexual escort agency: Deviance disavowal. *British Journal of Sociology, 40*(1), 1–21.

Smith, M. D., & Grov, C. (2011). *In the company of men: Inside the lives of male prostitutes.* Santa Barbara, CA: Praeger.

Smith, M. D., Grov, C., & Seal, D. W. (2009). Agency-based male sex work: A descriptive focus on physi-cal, personal, and social space. *The Journal of Men's Studies, 16*(2), 193–210.

Smith, M. D., Grov, C., Seal, D. W., Bernhardt, N., & McCall, P. (2014). Social-emotional aspects of male escorting: Experiences of men working for an agency. *Archives of Sexual Behavior, 44*(4), 1047–1058. doi:10.1007/s10508-014-0344-9.

Smith, M. D., Grov, C., Seal, D. W., & McCall, P. (2013). A social-cognitive analysis of how young men become involved in male escorting. *Journal of Sex Research, 50,* 1–10.

Smith, M. D., & Seal, D. W. (2008). Motivational influences on the safer sex behavior of agency-based male sex workers. *Archives of Sexual Behavior, 37*(5), 845–53. doi:10.1007/s10508-008-9341-1.

Uy, J. M., Parsons, J. T., Bimbi, D. S., Koken, J. A., & Halkitis, P. N. (2004). Gay and bisexual male escorts who advertise on the Internet: Understanding reasons for and effects of involvement in commercial sex. *International Journal of Men's Health, 3*(1), 11–26.

Walby, K. (2012). *Touching encounters: Sex, work, and male-for-male Internet escorting.* Chicago, IL: University of Chicago Press.

West, D. (2012). *Male prostitution.* New York: Routledge.

24

Male transactional sex in the Dominican Republic

The politics of labor exclusion

José Félix Colón-Burgos and Mark Padilla

There is extensive anthropological and sociological research on Caribbean sex tourism, much of which has focused on the colonial histories and contemporary global conditions that contribute to the availability of Caribbean bodies for "consumption" in tourism markets. For example, Kamala Kempadoo describes the colonial economies' use of enslaved populations to fulfill the erotic fantasies of foreigners, such that reproductive and sexual labor was tied since the beginning of the European colonization to the basic social and economic configuration of Caribbean societies (Kempadoo, 1999b). Her work draws on this historical legacy to place contemporary female sexual labor in the context of tourism. Contemporary ethnographers, such as Denise Brennan and Amalia Cabezas, have examined female sexual labor in the Dominican Republic (DR) and Cuba from the perspective of present-day transactions that routinely occur between tourists and locals throughout the region (Brennan, 2004; Cabezas, 2009).

Male sexual labor has been less extensively studied in the Caribbean. In particular, a persistent limitation in the literature has been the tendency to view male and female sexual labor through different analytic lenses. Discussions of women in the sex industry have tended to focus on women's disempowered gender position, which can lead to depictions of women's hyper-exploitation and vulnerability within the industry, while men are less often examined within a vulnerability framework. Indeed, depictions of men's involvement in sexual labor can overstate their capacity to control the conditions of their labor or its effects on their minds and bodies. For example, analyses of sex work among Caribbean men have occasionally described their labor as promoting masculine status, because sex work with female tourists can lead to an increase in masculine prowess. According to Pruitt and LaFont, for example, the Jamaican "rent-a-dread" or "rent-a-Rasta"—racialized terms used to refer to local men who seek foreign female tourists for transactional sex—are cultural categories that draw on traditional notions of male dominance to initiate relationships with foreign women (Pruitt & LaFont, 1995). Similarly, an early analysis of "beach boys" in Barbados argues that men's exchanges with female tourists are a form of resistance among young males against neocolonialism, as well as a means to gain masculine esteem among their peers (Press, 1978).

As Padilla (2007) has argued elsewhere, while heterosexually behaving Dominican male sex workers may gain certain kinds of masculine status through their participation in sex work, the unqualified notion that their participation in sex work does not pose any serious challenges to their status as men neglects entirely the commonality of discreet sexual exchanges with other men, the shame and homophobia that are often associated with these exchanges, and the ways that such exchanges are meticulously "covered" in intimate and familial relationships.

(p. 138)

Due to the stigma associated with male-male sex, such exchanges within the Caribbean tourism industry are infrequently examined, though they may constitute a rather large portion of the exchanges within the tourism economy. Indeed, Padilla's first study with Dominican male sex workers found that discreet contacts between Dominican men and gay male tourists were more common among the men interviewed than exchanges with women, despite these men's outward emphasis on their heterosexual conquests (Padilla, 2007).

While Padilla's earlier work sought to examine the notion of men's presumed masculine prowess as a consequence of their involvement in sex work, in this chapter, we take a slightly different tack on this line of argument. Specifically, we draw on our more recent study of Dominican men employed in tourism to describe how the combination of various factors constrains the options available to these men, leading ultimately to intense labor exclusion. Most importantly for our currently argument, we examine the role of deportation of Dominican men from the United States (US) as a phenomenon that results in continued labor exclusion when these men arrive in the DR. At first glance, deportation and involvement in the sex tourism industry might seem to be disconnected phenomena, and indeed they are rarely discussed together in the social science literature on migration and tourism. While tourism scholars have documented the commonality of migration among persons employed in tourism (Padilla, 2010; Kempadoo, 1999a; Burns, 1999), few analyses explain how global deportation regimes are linked to tourism economies and labor practices. As we have argued elsewhere (Padilla, Colón-Burgos, Varas-Díaz, Matiz-Reyes, & Parker, 2018), the Caribbean—a region witnessing an historic increase in repatriations, primarily from the United States—is a prime site for research on this topic.

Drawing on ethnographic engagement with deported Dominican men working in the tourism economies of the DR, we argue that patterns of deportation and labor exploitation within the tourism economy are intimately interrelated, an argument we illustrate with case studies of Dominican male sex workers. Drawing on semi-structured interview with 16 Dominican deportees, here we present a close case study analysis of three of these participants as a means of tracing the labor exclusions that are of interest in this chapter. We argue that the growing U.S. deportation regime—which sends approximately 1,989 Dominicans, of whom the majority are men, back to the DR annually (U.S. Immigration and Customs Enforcement, 2017)—leads to labor exclusion among the deported men. The patterns of labor exclusion experienced by these deportees are linked to larger patterns of absorption of marginalized and criminalized migrants into informal labor markets of sex and drugs. We therefore aim to explain the various factors, identified in our ethnographic research, that constrain labor options among male deportees and contribute to their exploitation within the sex tourism industry.

Social exclusion and the devaluation of the labor force

Scholars of migration have long discussed the complex tensions between "push" and "pull" factors that ultimately contribute to migratory decisions (Massey et al., 1993). Dominican migration has been similarly analyzed, identifying various migratory "push" factors from the DR to the US. These push factors include the "transnational" character of Dominican families; opportunities for work, education, and identity development; and economic and political policies or regimes (Grasmuck & Pessar, 1991). These migratory push factors are connected to larger global neoliberal conditions that have rearranged economic relations, placing structural constraints on nations, regions, or specific populations (Golash-Boza, 2015). Neoliberal principles, such as the free flow of capital across national boundaries, are applicable primarily to financial transactions, but the flow of human beings is subject to strategies of social exclusion via deportation regimes (De Genova & Peutz, 2012). As Linda Green has suggested, these strategies of exclusion are enforced culturally and structurally, and they draw on constructions of those who are deemed "human beings" and those who are "nobodies" (Green, 2011). In the case of the US, the Dominican community has been policed by what Kanstroom (2007) called the U.S. Modern Deportation System. This deportation system manifests in two ways: (1) through extensive border control and (2) through post-entry social control (Kanstroom & Brinton Lykes, 2015). Both have largely disrupted the Dominican community in the US. In this chapter, we focus on individuals who have been extensively impacted by the latter, because the majority of our sample had legal residence in the US before being deported. This research focus is unique, because it serves to debunk the common stereotype that deportees are hiding "illegally" for lengthy periods prior to their deportation.

Scholars have noted that deportation process is backed by social and legal policies[1] that help to institutionalize the xenophobic and racist rhetoric of the class in power. The combination of policies, discriminatory discourses, and immigration and criminal law ("crimmigration") (Beckett & Evans, 2015; García- Hernández, 2015; Stumpf, 2006), creates an easily deportable Other (Brotherton & Barrios, 2013; Brotherton, 2014). The case of Dominican deportees provides an example of how the U.S. deportation regime adapts, assimilates, and integrates immigrant cultures in a segmented manner. At the same time that large immigrant communities grow in places such as Washington Heights in New York City, the social and political climate systematically dehumanizes and removes certain members of the same immigrant communities when their labor is no longer needed (Brotherton & Barrios, 2011). The Dominican men whom we interviewed have been victims of these processes of social exclusion since their first migration to the US. According to Brotherton and Barrios (2009), Dominican deportees are socially displaced and removed three times in the course of their life: first, when they migrate to the US; second, when they are imprisoned in the US; and the third, when they are repatriated back to the DR.

To examine how regimes of migration and deportation are intertwined in the labor decisions and patterns that develop over time, we conducted qualitative in-depth interviews with 37 Dominican men *(16 of whom reported being deported from the US)* who had engaged in a wide range of tourism work. We recruited these men through ethnographic observations and interactions in tourist areas, including parks, streets, beaches, bars/clubs, hotels, restaurants, and sex establishments (e.g., brothels, saunas, or clubs known for sex work) in and around tourism enclaves in the DR. All participants were male-identified adults and were employed in tourism work in Santo Domingo or Boca Chica, located in the DR's south coast capital province. Ethnographic notes were taken during and after observations. The in-depth interviews were recorded and transcribed for later coding and analysis. In this paper, we draw on *three* such interviews, using pseudonyms to refer to individuals, to examine their individual life stories of deportation and labor exclusion.

From the moment they left for the US until they were forced to return to the DR, our participants' lives were shaped by a neoliberal economic ideology and global capitalist system. While in the US, they were victims of three processes of social exclusion: (1) criminalization, (2) institutionalization, and (3) deportation. This last social exclusion process (deportation) may be seen as a political response to sustained global capitalist relations, which operate largely by maintaining the *condition of deportability* (Robinson, 2008), a status in which an individual's immediate social environment is shaped largely by the policing of "illegals" who are always subject to expulsion. The social condition of deportability, in turn, intersects with the labor system, functioning to lower wages, to constrain work options in the North (Robinson, 2008) and to redistribute "disposable labor" from the global north to the periphery (Golash-Boza, 2015; Rodkey, 2016). As Robinson (2008) posits, "This condition assures the ability to super-exploit with impunity and dispose without consequence" (p. 313).

The experiences of the Dominican deportees described in this chapter provide useful examples of immigrants who have been victims of this condition of deportability in the United States. Furthermore, the incorporation of Dominican deportees into the Caribbean-based tourism industry post-deportation (Padilla et al., 2018) demonstrates how some Dominican men are re-made—through the deportation regime—into exploitable workers in the periphery. Through the words and life stories of the interviewed male deportees, we demonstrate how the processes of social exclusion devalue their labor. One outcome of this social exclusion is that some individuals are forced to engage in transactional sex with male and/or female tourists as a means of "making do."

Post-deportation: entering the Caribbean transnational market of transactional sex

During our ethnographic fieldwork, we met with several community leaders and members of non-governmental organizations (NGOs) who work with HIV/STD and drug abuse prevention in the southern province of Santo Domingo. One of these leaders was "Tyson," a community activist who was involved in several *luchas* (struggles) for the human rights and political recognition of the LGBTQ and other persons who use drugs in the DR. As part of our recruitment phase, the first author reached out to Tyson to see if he could help us recruit participants who met the sampling requirements for our study. While he was writing down our participant selection criteria[2] (which did not include deportation), he remembered a man who worked as a taxi driver in the area. Tyson started to narrate the story of Frank. According to Tyson, Frank was deported from the US. Like many deportees, Frank was forcibly sent to the DR, where he did not know anyone. Given Frank's fluency in English, he began to work in the tourism sector as a taxi driver. The problem was that Frank was a recovering addict in the United States. In the DR, in order to survive, he had to expose himself again to the world of drugs, because many of the tourists that he served with his taxi asked him for sex or drugs, exposing him to a world that he hoped to leave behind.

A week after meeting with Tyson, I (first author) had the opportunity to meet with Frank in person in one of the Colonial Zone's most historical parks, El Parque Colón. Frank, with his "Dominican York" accent, narrated to me a bit of his odyssey crossing the Mona passage to Puerto Rico (his first point of entrance to the US) and his subsequent life in New York City; later, we talked about his work in the Dominican tourist sector. We met in September, at the end of the low tourism season, in the middle of a renovation construction project in the Colonial Zone that was converting vehicular streets into pedestrian walkways. Both the season and the construction project were affecting Frank's business to the point that he had recently had to sell his taxi in order to get by.

Frank told me that he was known as the *transporta* and that his job consisted of getting everything the tourists want. Frank described aspects of informal tourism work as "an atrocity," which is significant given that he had been doing this type of work for many years of his life. Frank described obtaining sex workers and drugs for tourists as part of his work, and he told me about the myriad tasks he carries out in tourism performs in the Colonial Zone, emphasizing his role as caretaker and protector of tourists. He had virtual contact with his foreign clients through his email, which he reviews periodically at an Internet café on El Conde, a long pedestrian mall that bisects the Colonial Zone in Santo Domingo and typically attracts many tourists.[3]

Frank coordinated airport pick-ups and hotel transfers for clients. For those tourists who ask for "services" (implying female sex workers), he made it clear that did not look for minors and that he was going to let them know if the *"tipas son malas"* (if the women are bad). I asked him if he had taken a tourist guide course with the Dominican Ministry of Tourism, to which he quickly replied, "I have nothing to do with the State," expressing dissatisfaction with the Dominican government. He also added that given his immigration status as a deportee, he was unable to work or seek work in the country. Frustrated, began to tell me about his life in the DR after deportation, explaining how he returned to using crack and marijuana, among other drugs.

Frank told me a story related to a request from a tourist who seemed to be a regular client. The tourist asked him to have sex with a female sex worker and with him for US $100. The client offered him extra money if he joined the scene. Frank told me that he took care of getting the woman, paying her, explaining what she was going to do and taking them to *la cabaña* (motel). He explained to the woman that she was going to carry out what he called a *golo-golo* (oral sex with attention to the testicles). While taking part in the sexual act, Frank felt *"sucio"* (dirty) and didn't want to be there. He let the sex worker perform oral sex on him while the tourist penetrated her. While telling me the story, Frank spoke with a look tone of embarrassment and annoyance about the situation. He also talked about how disgusting Dominican tourism was:

Frank: *"Aquí lo que vienen son enfermos, el 90% viene algarete y el 10% viene tradicional. No te tires una mujer en el Conde ni con condón!"* [Here, what comes are sick people, 90% are crazy and 10% come to do traditional tourism. Don't have sex with a woman in El Conde even if you are going to use condoms!]

Frank wanted to show me his apartment, so we walked from el Parque Colón to a barrio at the north of the Colonial Zone called San Carlos. While we were walking, he told me a story about an Italian tourist who had lived in El Conde for several months and who asked sex workers to put bottles in his anus. Frank laughed and again emphasized that those who visit the Zone and El Conde were sick. When we arrived at his home, I gradually realized it was a ruined building and was very difficult to access. First we had to climb up what looked like a two-story house. From that house, we had to go to the roof of another building and through some improvised wooden stairs, where we reached the rooftop of another building that contained small rooms (like storage closets) converted into tiny apartments. In front of his apartment there was an improvised door tied with a chain and a padlock. Frank opened the door to his little room, and there he had a simple bed with a small desk, a TV set, and a DVD player. In the wall of his unit, he had a hole in the wall that simulated a window. Also, on the walls, there were drawings of landscapes and messages that alluded to freedom. One of the drawing showed an orca, or killer whale.

Narratives like Frank's were common among our interviewees who were informal tourist workers. Many deportees who return to the DR lack social networks or social capital to help them integrate into a society about which they are entirely unfamiliar. Pablo, a formal tourist worker in the Colonial Zone of Santo Domingo, explained how this lack of social networks and social capital affects deportees when they return:

I am already old and . . . I lost my youth there [US], all my friendships of youth are there. And then when I came here, when they deported me here in 2013, I did not have anyone. I came here, and I was in a strange country. I did not know anyone; dad and mom had died. All the neighborhoods where I lived, here in Los Mina . . . I did not know . . . the pharmacy that dad had in Los Mina, in Catanga, I did not recognize it. I didn't have any sibling or anything like that. I did not have anyone. And I still live here like if I was a tourist . . .

not a tourist, but as a foreigner, because I do not know anyone. I came here and I began to know these people now and to make friends. My family, siblings, all are in the United States.

Pablo, 9/25/2014

As anthropologist Rodkey (2016) documented in his study of the post-deportee experience in the DR, many deportees have to resign themselves to living in a place that is not their home, although it was their birthplace. Pablo's case shows us the reality of many of the deportees arriving in the DR. Starting over in this new "home" is extremely challenging, given that the men are equipped with few tools to survive. Importantly, deportees have to face Dominican society, the Dominican government, and the repressive institutions of the Dominican state, all of which consider them criminals and stigmatize them due to their deportee status. In Figure 24.1, we

El Nacional (https://elnacional.com.do)

Repatriados EU agravan inseguridad

Arzobispado llama poner atención a los deportados.

3 agosto, 2018
Por:
RICARDO RODRIGUEZ ROSA ricardo.rodriguezrosa@gmail.com
e-mail:
redaccion[@]elnacional.com.do

SANTIAGO. El Arzobispado de esta ciudad dijo hoy que la cantidad de dominicanos que han sido repatriados está agravando el problema de la inseguridad ciudadana del país, ya que muchos de estos son bombas de tiempo que generan violencia ante cualquier situación que se podría resolver con el diálogo. Expresa que resulta alarmante la cantidad de dominicanos que han sido enviados desde los Estados Unidos a República Dominicana en los últimos tiempos. Destaca que en el primer semestre de este año llegaron a suelo dominicano 807 ciudadanos luego de haber cumplido condenas en distintas cárceles estadounidenses. Sostiene que esos dominicanos participaron en delitos como secuestros, falsificación de documentos, asesinatos, venta y tráfico de drogas y otros hechos, que a su juicio empaña la imagen de la comunidad que reside en distintas ciudades de Estados Unidos.

Recordó que como allí el delito no queda sin castigo y las malas acciones tienen consecuencias, cada día seguiremos viendo más compatriotas deportados porque algunos se marcharon de aquí con la creencia de que allá podían actuar como chivos sin ley. "Ahora los tenemos aquí, agravando el problema de la inseguridad ciudadana que sufrimos. Muchos son bombas de tiempo que generan violencia ante cualquier situación que podría resolverse con el diálogo", ratifica. A través de su periódico digital Camino, el Arzobispado, llama a las autoridades competentes a que vigilen los pasos de estos ciudadanos, por considerar que perdieron el rumbo de la vida buscando en la riqueza fácil su felicidad. "Ojalá que estos hermanos nuestros logren reencontrarse con los valores que han perdido, y no les sigan causando más sufrimientos a sus padres, a quienes les duele profundamente la mala conducta de sus hijos", concluye el Arzobispado.

Figure 24.1 Local Dominican news article with stigmatizing rhetoric against Dominican deportees.

include an excerpt from a local newspaper in the Dominican Republic that verbalizes this stigmatizing rhetoric from a member of the clerical leadership (archbishop) of one of the main cities on the island country: "A number of Dominicans who have been repatriated are aggravating the problem of citizen insecurity in the country, since many of these are time bombs that generate violence in any situation that could be solved with dialogue." To this argument the archbishop added that the Dominican deportees were *chivos sin ley* (lawless goats) and a threat to the society (Rodriguez-Rosa, 2018, p. 1).

This discriminatory rhetoric permeates Dominican society, providing grounds for labor exclusion and stigma against the deportees. As Brotherton and Barrios (2011) note, "Deportees return to the DR with their identity spoiled on numerous levels and face being diminished and shunned because of both their moral and physical stigma" (p. 201). Due to the combination of stigmas, social displacement, and exclusion (Brotherton & Barrios, 2009; Golash-Boza, 2015), the deportees are excluded from most formal employment in the DR, forcing them into tourism work. Within this industry, they demonstrate their resilience by using some of their "portable" skills: their knowledge of and fluency with the English language and their familiarity with U.S. culture. Consider José, who described in an interview his experiences in the Dominican tourism industry:

J.C: But what do you work on?

José: I work in tourism as a guide. Tour guide. I tell the tourists where the dating houses are, as they say, where to find the girls, where to go for example to dinner, the best restaurants. I can tell you where the best and cheapest hotels are from where they are currently staying. I translate, and countless other things.

J.C: Do you do something else for the money, José?

E: Yes

JC: What other things you do?

E: Sometimes I look for substances for tourists.

JC: OK.

E: Sometimes I sell my body.

JC: Ok. I imagine that. . .

E: Do you want me to be honest?

JC: Yes . . . yes . . . one hundred percent.

E: Ok.

JC: Yes, that is what we are looking for. And do you do that here in Santo Domingo, or in Boca Chica?

E: Yes . . . yes. In different places. Sometimes they want you to go with them, spend the day up and down with them. To Boca Chica or any other site.

The first author met José while conducting participant observation in a corner café called Grands, but historically called Paco's,[4] in the corner entrance of El Conde, Ciudad Colonial. José was a 38-year-old light-skinned, green-eyed Dominican with *pelo bueno* (good hair, meaning straight hair), as it is often called in the country. José was born in La Vega, a rural town in the middle of the country. With his earnings as an informal tourist guide and sex worker, he tries to maintain a good appearance with a formal haircut and a cool beach vibe, with short pants, T-shirts and flip-flops. If you see him from afar, you might think he is a tourist from the US. He speaks perfect English, with a New York City (NYC) accent, and he speaks Spanish with a "Dominican York" accent. When he was five years old, he moved with his family to the capital province of Santo Domingo and then migrated to NYC five years later. He recalled when he migrated to the US for the first time:

JC: After Santo Domingo, at what age did you move to New York?
José: At 10 years old.
JC: 10 years.
José: Yes.
JC: And with whom did you go there?
José: I arrived alone. With the flight attendant.
JC: Ah. Okay. And who sent for you?
José: Mi papá me mando a buscar (My dad sent for me).

Like most Dominican migrants in the 1980 and 1990s, José migrated to Washington Heights, Manhattan, NYC (Grasmuck & Pessar, 1991; Hernández, 2002). He spent his adolescent years between NYC and Puerto Rico until he moved to Florida, where he was imprisoned and later deported nine years before our interview. When I asked José how this immigration process has affected his life, he responded:

José: Oh . . . one hundred percent. 360, it did a tremendous spin in my life.
JC: Yes?
José: Yes. It has changed everything . . . everything. It has even changed my personality, brother.
JC: Okay.
José: That "vaina" [situation] has hurt me a lot. Too much.
JC: Tell me, how do you feel it has. . .?
José: It has sunk me more into drugs. I have done things that I never would have done in my life, after I am here.
JC: Okay.
José: Because of the situation that I am deported. I cried tears of blood. I have blamed myself a lot. I have lost many loved ones. I lost many of my friends. I even lost my family. Because those people do not even remember me anymore. They do not write to me anymore, they do not call me anymore, or anything.

Deportation status had severed most of José's social ties, leaving him disconnected and vulnerable, ultimately resulting in his decision to engage in sex work to make ends meet. During the interview, José was clear that the clients upon whom he relied most were foreign gay men:

JC: And what type of clients do you normally work with?
José: Normal clients, but more gays. Almost always the majority.
JC: Okay. And what nationality are they?
José: Afroamericanos, blancos, boricuas . . . de todas las nacionalidades . . . dominicanos, Afro-Americans, whites, Puerto Ricans . . . Of all nationalities . . . Dominicans. . .
JC: Yes?
José: Yes.
JC: Dominicans who come from the United States to here?
José: And from here too [i.e., Dominicans also].
JC: From here too.

José: Yes, you know there are Dominicans with money and they are always touring and stuff.

JC: Yes. And from Europe?

José: Yes . . . yes, from Europe too. . .

José did not consider himself a *bugarrón*, which he declared was a "word that I hate." *Bugarrón* is a Dominican sexual identity category for a man who engages in insertive penetration only, has a masculine demeanor, and often receives payment or benefits from "passive" gay men in exchange for sex. José explained that despite the mythology about their masculine performance in bed, interactions with tourists often involved supposed *bugarrones* being penetrated:

José: They want to be *bugarrones* in the street, but in reality, they let themselves be penetrated. They let the tourists penetrate them. And they're gays, but they're hidden. They themselves don't know they're gays. But, they love that stuff!

Despite being critical of his peers in the tourism industry who "loved that stuff," José admitted in his interview that he was successful in getting the attention of gay male tourists:

Many of them get sweet on me because I speak English, because I can talk to them with— about things with New York and stuff. About the United States that I know. And they like that. They gain trust with me.

José was aware that the trust that he was able to obtain with these foreign men was a source of potential financial support, a lifeline to resources that had been restricted due to his deportee status and his exclusion from the formal labor market.

Conclusion

The deportation of immigrants has consequences for individual lives that exceed the mere act of deportation (Brotherton & Barrios, 2011). The social exclusion that deportees face when they are returned "home" are intense, based in large part on the negative attributions that accompany deportee status in places such as the DR. Brotherton and Barrios (2011) have eloquently described the stigmatization and criminalization of Dominican deportees once they return to the DR, leading many of them to resort to self-medication or trade in illegal substances, which often lands them in jail again. According to De Genova and Peutz (2012), non-citizen "deportables" are perversely subject to a number of social degradations globally, including high social and health vulnerability.

Our ethnographic research attempts to trace the influence of these social processes on individual lives, to understand how multiple factors intertwine to place individuals in vulnerable positions. One significant effect of these intertwining conditions is that individuals experience extreme constraints on productive capacity, due to their inability to find consistent wage or skilled labor. Social stigma and labor discrimination play an important role in this process, resulting in constrained options for deportees. Natural affinities with the tourism industry, such as English-language capacity and cultural knowledge that enables the development of trusting relationships with tourists, simultaneously push deportees toward informal tourism work. Finally, the saturation of the Caribbean tourism economy with commercial sex work and the drug economy—particularly "party" drugs like cocaine and ecstasy—mean that deportees are likely to depend on the income they receive from the trade in illegal substances that put many of them on the road to deportation in the first place.

Ultimately, we consider these processes to be little-understood expressions of global neoliberal relations, which seamlessly link the criminal (in)justice system in the United States, the politics of othering and forced removal that characterize the global deportation regime, and the absorption of criminalized informal labor into the Caribbean trade in sex and drugs serving U.S. tourists. Viewed systemically, neoliberal relations restructure global systems of labor through the criminalization of particular classes of migrants, who then are forced to provide personalized sexual services and drugs for those whose mobility is not similarly constrained. We believe that the life stories of these Dominican men illustrate the convergence of these complex dynamics, highlighting their implications for these men's labor. Future research should aim to identify the specific ways in which the health and well-being of deportees—numbering in the millions in the Caribbean—are affected by deportation, along with the means by which countries can support the health and human rights of this neglected population. This study provides evidence to support the creation of a program that help deportees live a healthy and productive life post-deportation while also providing de-stigmatization campaigns to debunk the notion that deportees are inherently criminal. As far as we are aware, no such programs currently exist in the Caribbean region, leaving men like Frank, Pablo, and José to fend for themselves in the treacherous economic and social environments of their purported "home."

Acknowledgments

This study was supported by a grant from the National Institute of Drug Abuse (NIDA) (Grant # 1 R01 DA031581–01A1;PI:Mark Padilla) a Supplement to Support Diversity in Health-Related Research for José Colón Burgos (3R01DA031581–03S1) and Award #S21MD010683 from the National Institute on Minority Health and Health Disparities (NIMHD) of the National Institutes of Health (NIH). The content is solely the responsibility of the authors and does not necessarily represent the official views of NIDA, NIMHD or the National Institutes of Health.

Notes

1 Policies such as the "Immigration and Nationality Act" (INA) and the "Illegal Immigration Reform and Responsibility Act" (IIR-IRA, 1996) exist to legally justify the othering process.
2 Our study required that the participants must: (1) be men, (2) report Dominican nationality (regardless of ethnic heritage), (3) be 18 years of age or older, (4) report a history of internal migration within the DR or external migration to the US and/or Puerto Rico in the last five years, and (5) be currently employed in the tourism sector in one of the research sites.
3 For a more detailed explanation of El Conde and its importance in the Colonial Zone transactional sex market, see Chapter 3 of Padilla's book, *Caribbean Pleasure Industry: Tourism, Sexuality, and AIDS in the Dominican Republic,* (2007), Chicago: University of Chicago Press, pages 76–105.
4 Paco's, as it is commonly known by the locals, is open for food and alcohol 24 hours a day, 365 days a year, and it (unintentionally) serves as a meeting place between sex workers (male and female) and tourists.

References

Beckett, K., & Evans, H. (2015). Crimmigration at the local level: Criminal justice processes in the shadow of deportation. *Law and Society Review.* doi:10.1111/lasr.12120.

Brennan, D. (2004). *What's love got to do with it? Transnational desires and sex tourism in the Dominican Republic.* Durham, NC and London: Duke University Press.

Brotherton, D. C. (2014). Jock Young and the criminological imagination as a life force. *Crime Media Culture, 10*(3), 227–237. doi:10.1177/1741659014558758.

Brotherton, D. C., & Barrios, L. (2009). Displacement and stigma: The social-psychological crisis of the deportee. *Crime Media Culture, 5*(1), 29–55. doi:10.1177/1741659008102061.

Brotherton, D. C., & Barrios, L. (2011). *Banished to the homeland: Dominican deportees and their stories of exile.* New York, NY: Columbia University Press.

Brotherton, D. C., & Barrios, L. (2013). The social bulimia of forced repatriation: A case study of Dominican deportees. In K. Franko-Aas & M. Bosworth (Eds.), *The borders of punishment: Migration, citizenship, and social exclusion.* Oxford, UK: Oxford University Press, pp. 1–307.

Burns, P. M. (1999). *An introduction to tourism and anthropology.* New York, NY: Routledge.

Cabezas, A. (2009). *Economies of desire: Sex and tourism in Cuba and the Dominican Republic.* Philadelphia, PA: Temple University Press.

De Genova, N., & Peutz, N. (Eds.). (2012). *The deportation regime: Sovereignty, space and the freedom of movement.* Durham, NC: Duke University Press.

Golash-Boza, T. (2015). *Deported: Immigrant policing, disposable labor, and global capitalism.* New York and London: New York University Press.

Grasmuck, S., & Pessar, P. R. (1991). *Between two islands: Dominican international migration.* Berkeley and Los Angeles, CA: University of California Press.

Green, L. (2011). The nobodies: Neoliberalism, violence, and migration. *Medical Anthropology, 30*(4), 366–385. doi:10.1080/01459740.2011.576726.

Hernández, C. C. G. (2015). *Detained and deported: Crimmigation-law.* Chicago, IL: ABA Book Publishing.

Hernández, R. (2002). *The mobility of workers under advanced capitalism.* New York, NY: Columbia University Press.

Kanstroom, D. (2007). *Deportation nation: Outsiders in American history.* London: Harvard University Press.

Kanstroom, D., & Brinton Lykes, M. (Eds.). (2015). *The new deportation delirium: Interdisciplinary responses.* New York and London: New York University Press.

Kempadoo, K. (1999a). Continuities and change: Five centuries of prostitution in the Caribbean. In *In sun, sex, and gold: Tourism and sex work in the Caribbean.* New York, NY: Rowman & Littlefield, pp. 3–33.

Kempadoo, K. (1999b). *Sun, sex and gold: Tourism and sex work in the Caribbean.* New York, NY: Rowman & Littlefield.

Massey, D. S., Arango, J., Hugo, G., Kouaouci, A., Pellegrino, A., & Taylor, E. (1993). Theories of international migration: A review and appraisal. *Population and Development Review, 19*(3), 431–466.

Padilla, M. B. (2007). *Caribbean pleasure industry: Tourism, sexuality, and AIDS in the Dominican Republic, worlds of desire.* Chicago, IL: University of Chicago Press. Retrieved from www.loc.gov/catdir/toc/ecip076/2006039087.html.

Padilla, M. B. (2010). *Getting there from here: The erotics and perversity of global mobility in Dominican tourism zones.* Translocations Conference: Travel, Migration, and Sexuality, Northwestern University, Chicago, IL.

Padilla, M. B., Colón-Burgos, J. F., Varas-Díaz, N., Matiz-Reyes, A., & Parker, C. M. (2018). Tourism labor, embodied suffering, and the deportation regime in the Dominican Republic. *Medical Anthropology Quarterly.* doi:10.1111/maq.12447.

Press, C. M. (1978). Reputation and respectability reconsidered: Hustling in a tourist setting. *Caribbean Issues, 4*(1), 109–119.

Pruitt, D., & LaFont, S. (1995). For love and money: Romance tourism in Jamaica. *Annals of Tourism Research, 22*(2), 422–444.

Robinson, W. I. (2008). *Latin America and global capitalism: A critical globalization perspective.* Baltimore, MD: The Johns Hopkins Univeristy Press.

Rodkey, E. (2016). Disposable labor, repurposed: Outsourcing deportees in the call center industry. *Anthropology of Work Review, 37*(1), 1–25.

Rodriguez-Rosa, R. (2018, August 3). Repatriados EU agravan inseguridad. *El Nacional.* Retrieved from https://elnacional.com.do/repatriados-eu-agravan-inseguridad/

Stumpf, J. (2006). The crimmigration crisis: Immigrants, crime, and sovereign power. *American University Law Review, 56*(2), 367–418.

U.S. Immigration and Customs Enforcement. (2017). *Fiscal year 2017 ICE enforcement and removal operation report, department of homeland security.* Retrieved from www.ice.gov/removal-statistics/2017.

25

Brazilian male sex workers

In and out of *termas*

Voon Chin Phua

Research on male sex work, specifically on men who sell sex for money (e.g., Smith, Grov, & Seal, 2008), has increased over the years. The range of topics studied is wide and diverse. Historically, research has focused on the more negative aspects of male sex work, such as HIV/AIDS, drug and alcohol use, history of childhood abuse, and violence. Many of these studies have focused on exploitation and victimization, examining children and youth in the sex trade, as well as sex trafficking. Reviewing research on sex work from 1990 to 2000, Vanwesenbeeck (2001) finds that most of the studies are STI/HIV related. Examining the occupational aspects of sex work is less common. However, in recent years, a growing number of studies have begun to examine other aspects of male sex work, such as marketing strategies, with a focus on sex workers' agency and work aspects of the trade. Still the examination of male sex work as *work* remains sparse. A notable exception is Benoit, Ouellet, Jansson, Magnus, and Smith's (2017) article that uses an occupational choice framework to examine entry into sex work in Canada.

The debate over whether male sex work is work in the sense of a legitimate occupation is complicated. The continued framing of sex work as exploitative and oppressive, the stigma surrounding homosexuality, the idea of sex as a commodity to be sold for money, and the legality of sex work all combine to discourage the examination of sex work as a viable career. Nevertheless, Kuhar and Pajnik (2018) report that recent studies on male sex work have increasingly framed male sex workers as having control over their work and have concluded that their involvement can be a rational career choice. For example, Weitzer (2007) and Benoit et al. (2017) have explicitly argued for framing sex work as work in which workers are willing participants.

Indeed, for some male sex workers, sex work is an occupational choice, and the decision to enter the trade is a rational one (e.g., Weitzer, 2005; Uy, Parsons, Bimbi, Koken, & Halkitis, 2004; Browne & Minichiello, 1996). Few studies, if any, have examined the career trajectory of sex work, because such studies require longitudinal data to track male sex workers' career movements. Hoping to bridge this gap, I examine sex workers' entry into and exit from the sex trade over ten years (2004–2015, 2018), based on data from participant observation and interviews with Brazilian male sex workers.

Sex work's career path

Entry

According to Benoit et al., "No studies could be found that situate reasons for initial entry in sex work within frameworks of occupational choice, nor sex work studies that directly focus on the interplay between agentic and structural factors" (2017, p. 4). They find that motivations to enter sex work include critical life events, personal appeal of the work, and the need for money. In her review, Vanwesenbeeck (2001) reports that "a host of conditions appear to be associated with entry into prostitution, including physical and sexual abuse, dysfunctional families, parental substance abuse, and sexual precocity" (p. 260). However, she also notes that these conditions are generally limited to the sample on whom the researchers focused, including but not limited to homeless youth and those working on the streets.

In recent years, an increasing number of researchers have argued that sex workers and their clients have varying experiences, with different levels of agency and choices (see, e.g., Phua & Caras, 2008; Scott et al., 2005; Browne & Minichiello, 1996). Male sex work includes a diverse group of actors, each navigating different circumstances and sociopolitical systems. Thus, the reasons and modes of entry into sex work greatly vary. Weitzer (2007) distinguishes between pathways to street-based and indoor sex work, with the former centering on survival and the latter on attaining financial independence. Uy et al. (2004) report that male sex workers achieved higher self-esteem and felt empowered by being paid for the sexual services they provide.

In addition, male sex workers are not necessarily location bound, as some solicit business at different sites. With improvements in transportation and communication technologies, many male sex workers are now advertising their services in a global market via the Internet: "Escorts now have websites, which include photos and descriptions of their services, and potential clients are able to e-mail these escorts or find them in popular Internet chat rooms" (Parsons, Bimbi, & Halkitis, 2001, p. 102). The popularity of and global access to the Internet provide male sex workers with a cost-effective way to advertise their services. Websites on which male sex workers advertise range from catering to only one specific city to covering a worldwide market. Even when male sex workers advertise on a website specific to a city or region, they are often mobile and offer delivery of their services across state and national borders (see, e.g., Pruitt, 2005).

Staying in the industry

Once male sex workers enter the trade, whether they remain in it or exit depends on many factors, including, but not limited to, how much control they have in their participation in the trade, the involvement of a third party (e.g., pimps or managers), how they view the work, the viability of other work options, and how well they manage the challenges of the work. Studies have examined the different strategies that sex workers employ to survive and remain in the profession. Vanwesenbeeck (2001) argues that the work-related issues on which researchers have focused fall into two broad categories: (1) male sex workers' "working routines, stresses, and risk" and (2) male sex workers' "management of work, risk, and identity" (2001, p. 265).

Current studies either directly or indirectly examine how male sex workers manage challenges that affect their well-being and attempt to increase their market share. These studies cover a range of topics, including but not limited to the management of clients (e.g., Phua, 2009, on the relationships between sex workers and their clients in Brazil), health (e.g., Kong, 2008, on condom use among sex workers in China), identity (e.g., Allen, 2007, on the idea of play labor to understand how male sex workers in Cuba manage work and identity), and specific marketing strategies (e.g., Phua & Caras, 2008, who examine how male sex workers market their services online).

Much research has focused on the relationship between health (specifically on STI/HIV) and sex work. These studies are mostly related to STI/HIV transmission (Bimbi & Koken, 2014), which can be included in the category of occupational health hazards. First, male sex workers have varying concerns about contracting STIs (e.g., Phua, Hopper, & Vazquez, 2002). Maintaining good health is important in sex work because it helps attract clients. Phua, Ciambrone, and Vazquez (2009) report that online male sex workers do not always share their health status, at least not in the early communications with possible clients.

Similarly, much research has examined identities in the context of male sex work. Most of these studies examine the complexities of gender identities, sexual identities, and sexual roles and activities. One study has argued that sex workers' presented identities can be viewed as tags that are not necessarily reflections of the true self but rather as marketable assets to increase business (Phua, 2010).

Several studies have examined the strategies that male sex workers use to increase their business. Clients might try to "buy time with an individual who is, or comes close, to the living version of an imagined fantasy" (Phua & Caras, 2008, p. 251). Studies indicate that male sex workers actively strategize and position themselves in the market to fulfill clients' desires. In part, doing so requires them to understand what clients are looking for. Logan's (2010) study is a unique quantitative approach examining the factors influencing prices in sex work. Phua and Caras (2008) report that self-marketing strategies include selling a package deal; commodifying specific body parts, race, and ethnicity; and offering non-sexual services such as chauffeur and tour services. Tyler (2014) examines the media in which male sex workers advertise and their promotional strategies. Tyler notes that over the years 1991–2011, more sex workers were willing to include photographs in their ads, particularly of their face. This willingness points to not only the importance of visual advertising (use of photographs) in sex work but also the increasing openness of this trade.

Exiting sex work

In their study of sex workers of different genders in Canada, Benoit and Millar (2001) report that their respondents attempted to exit on average 5.8 times before making a permanent break. Their respondents reported three key reasons for wanting to quit the trade: being burnt out and tired of the work, external pressure to quit, and a desire to end drug and alcohol dependencies. Benoit and Millar (2001) also report the challenges associated with leaving the lifestyle and the constant lures that pull them back. Scoular and O'Neill (2007) argue that the idea of helping (female) sex workers exit the trade, while important, generally assumes that the workers are trapped in the trade and sometimes understates the workers' different trajectories and lived experiences. In their study of 92 participants involved with sex work and drug use, Cusick, Brooks-Gordon, Campbell, and Edgar (2011) identify three types of exiters, in part differentiated by where they work (street versus indoor): (1) opportunistic exiters whose lifestyles had not changed but whose circumstances led to changes in their drug use and involvement in sex work, (2) gradual exiters for whom a cumulative chain of events distanced them from drug use and sex work, and (3) strategic exiters who developed a plan to eventually exit sex work. Cusick et al. also note that "some sex workers may not be willing to 'exit'" and conclude that "exit support is a vital part of holistic provisions, yet to only emphasize exit at a strategic level can erode other vital aspects of support" (2011, p. 154).

Clearly, sex workers are diverse, with different motivations to enter the trade. They solicit clients at different venues, and they have different work strategies, experiences, and trajectories. These differences are not only based on race, class, age, and other individual characteristics but also affected by structural factors such as familial relationships and local socioeconomic systems. In addition, some scholars note variations by country, including the country's attitudes toward sex and sex work and wealth and income disparities in the country (e.g., Vanwesenbeeck, 2001).

Methods

In this study, I examine male sex workers' work trajectories as they enter and exit the trade. I focus on male sex workers who solicit business in *termas* in Brazil, which are akin to Western bathhouses but are specifically known for sex work (e.g., Phua, 2010). These male sex workers are generally called "boys" or *garotos de programa*, but, for consistency's sake, I use the term *garotos*.

I used data from a larger study on Brazilian sexualities conducted between 2004 and 2015, with a follow-up in 2018. This broader study focused on the social constructions of Brazilian sexualities from a life-course perspective (Phua, 2016). I collected an oral history of each participant and documented these life stories chronologically. Of great importance in the larger study were the intersectionalities of race, class, gender, and sexualities and their effects on participants' experiences and identities. The sample was collected using a snowball approach. To minimize selection bias and to achieve a more diverse group of participants, I solicited participants at different locations (e.g., *termas*, bookstores, streets, bars, and universities) and from friends' recommendations. For the purpose of this study, I used interview data only if participants had been or were currently *garotos*.

Most of the interviews were conducted at a public location chosen by participants. Most of the interviews were tape-recorded and transcribed, with some hand-recorded. Most of the interviews were conducted in English and/or Portuguese. A Brazilian translator was employed where appropriate. I also recorded informal conversations where participants were aware of my research but chose not to sign consent forms. In some cases, they were either amused by or wary about the formality of consent forms.

I used a grounded theory approach to analyze the data. This approach allows themes and issues that participants deemed important to emerge. The goal is to develop a more in-depth understanding of the empirical world as experienced and presented by my participants. I first coded broad themes and later performed focused coding using those identified themes. To provide my interviewees with confidentiality, I used pseudonyms for all participants and did not include other demographic information.

First, I provide an overview of Brazilian *termas* and *garotos*. Next, I describe the work trajectories of the *garotos* who work in *termas*, from their entry to their presumed exit.

Studying male sex work in Brazilian *termas*

Stereotyped as one of the more sexually permissive countries in South America, Brazil is sometimes considered a destination for sex tourism (e.g., da Silva & Blanchette, 2009). While this reputation is not necessarily deserved, "the predominant, popular, international image of Brazilian sexuality carries connotations of the exuberance and display of carnival, scenes of Rio de Janeiro, and a sense of freewheeling sensuality and hedonism" (Ford, Vieira, & Villela, 2003, p. 53). Permissiveness and sexual fluidity are stereotypical images of Brazilian sexuality, especially during Carnival (Green, 1999). Many *garotos* congregate at Carnival for both pleasure and business, as the number of tourists soars during this festival (e.g., Kulick, 1998). This view of Brazil "often translates itself to Brazilians being perceived as sexually adventurous and as passionate lovers. The stereotypical image of Brazilian men being mulatto, muscular, and well-hung further enhances their desirability as sexual partners" (Phua & Caras, 2008, p. 242). In addition, the differentials in exchange rates between countries potentially make Brazil an attractive destination (Phua & Caras, 2008). Parker (1999) has mentioned sex work as a possible income source for Brazilian migrants into bigger Brazilian cities. Kulick (1998) specifically writes about *travesti* (a local version of transgender women) sex workers in Salvador.

In Brazil, *termas* are like western bathhouses with various amenities. Some of them are patronized by both *garotos* and potential male clients. These *termas* provide spaces for social interactions and sex work. Most of the *termas* also offer other forms of entertainment, including restaurants, workout stations, swimming pools, and go-go dancer and drag performances. *Termas* provide relatively safer environments because *garotos* are screened upon entering and, in some cases, need to have someone vouch for them. These *garotos* are better groomed when compared to street sex workers, and some of them also advertise their services online. These *garotos* provide interesting case studies because they are likely to be entrepreneurs and to view their work as an occupation.

Initiation into sex work

Friends and family members were one main route of entry into sex work among *garotos* in my study. This finding is consistent with earlier studies (e.g., De Graaf, Vanwesenbeeck, Van Zessen, Straver, & Visser, 1994; Kidd & Liborio, 2011). Through knowledge of friends and family members' involvement in the trade, these *garotos* became aware of the possibility. In a few cases, friends and family members initiated the conversation when they learned about the *garotos'* financial difficulties. For example, Pedro arrived in the city knowing only his brother, who was working as a *garoto* in the *termas*. After Pablo had searched for a job unsuccessfully for several weeks, his brother decided to reveal to him what he had been doing for money and brought him to the *termas*, initiating Pedro's introduction to the trade.

In other cases, potential *garotos* asked for more information, usually in jest but often with a sincere desire for more information. Introduction is paramount because it allows workers to have a mentor who can help them learn the rules of the trade, such as how to attract clients, negotiate prices, and learn the most productive days and times to work. Some *garotos* started in the business when clients made them an offer that introduced them to the trade (see, e.g., Kuhar & Pajnik, 2018). For example, Tiago was working as a waiter at a restaurant, and a customer he was serving suggested that he could make extra cash if he was interested. Workers in gay-friendly restaurants and hotels are more likely to receive such propositions.

A less common route is for potential *garotos* to explore on their own to test the waters. Some showed up at *termas* to check things out but never returned depending on their experiences—for example, whether clients expressed interest in them or whether they were disgusted by the sexual activities. Fabio, a medical student, was sitting alone when we began conversing. He explained to me that he came with a friend and was just checking the place out but decided that he could not do it even though he self-identified as gay. He said, "It is interesting to see what is happening but it is not for me. I don't think I will be back again." As the popularity of Internet increases, potential *garotos* can first explore the possibility in private. Junior had heard about the *termas* from friends but didn't start going there until he spent a few months testing the waters using the app *Hornet*.

Garotos in this study offered six reasons for their participation in the trade. First, some *garotos* complained that they have limited work options. An array of factors limited their opportunities, including unfamiliarity with a new city, lack of relevant work experience, lack of education, and low work aptitude. Second, they could not find a desirable job with acceptable perks (e.g., wages and work schedule). Third, they needed fast money, such as for an emergency like the hospitalization of a loved one. Fourth, they needed money for a desired purchase, such a motorcycle. Fifth, some *garotos* participated as a form of transgression. Some saw sex work as an affirmation of their power, self-esteem, and manhood. Sixth, sex work offered some form of enjoyment, socially and/or sexually.

Framing sex work: temporary work or potential career

Most *garotos* started their careers as sex workers in their late teens or early 20s when they were young—one of the most valuable assets in the trade. Flexible time, higher pay per hour, social and sexual activities, and access to an otherwise inaccessible or less accessible lifestyle are attractive to disadvantaged youth. Some of these *garotos* saw this work as temporary, an experimental phrase in their life. A few of them worked with specific goals in mind, such as paying for school or buying a motorcycle. Joao said,

> I am 19 and I have a job but I won't be able to buy the motorbike I want. My friend told me about this and I don't mind the sex. People are nice . . . I have friends and we talk about who is good or bad. I will work for another 3 months when I have enough money for my motorbike then I think I will quit.

Other *garotos* view sex work as transitional as they await opportunities for other jobs. None of the *garotos* in my study had planned to be in this trade for a long time when they began working at the *termas*. In part, the stigma of sex work coupled with the stigma of homosexuality continued to affect the perception of this form of work as legitimate. When the *garotos* frame their work as a temporary, experimental transgression, they are able to neutralize the stigma of the work and retain their prized masculinity and, for some, their heterosexuality.

However, a few *garotos* changed their minds as they immersed themselves deeper in the trade. Some *garotos* decided to stay in the trade because they became used to the lifestyle that the work affords, along with the peculiarities of the work and how to manage it. It can be difficult to walk away from the higher pay per hour. These *garotos* did not enjoy every aspect of the work; rather, they saw it as a means to an end. Also, they noted that it is challenging or inconvenient to explain their previous work to potential employers.

Over the course of my study, I have found that more *garotos* see the trade as a viable career option and stay in it longer. Some *garotos* also get involved in sex-work-related industries, such as pornography (e.g., Weitzer, 2009), which allows them to expand their market beyond Brazil if they become popular. A few *garotos* treated sex work as seasonal and worked only during the high tourist seasons in major cities. Upon closer examination, I realized that some of them simply moved among various cities working as *garotos* and, in doing so, appeared to potential clients as less professional, a trait that some clients prefer. In addition, *garotos* might lose some of their novelty if they frequent a *terma*, giving clients the impression that they depend on the trade for a steady income. While some clients might be more sympathetic to the *garotos'* financial situation, other clients might see it as an opportunity to negotiate their fees. Other *garotos*, who are more entrepreneurial and independent, treat sex work as a career choice (see, e.g., Marino, Minichiello, & Disogra, 2003). For example, Marcelo describes his experience:

> I started when I was 19 because I needed money and cannot find good work. I didn't think I was going to work for so long. It's like 12 years now. I cannot find a job that pays as well and gives me so much freedom. I don't mind the sex and you meet some good people. Some clients are crazy but I know how to avoid them and I can choose not to work with them. The longer I stay the more I learn how to handle so it becomes easier. Nowadays you can see some who have worked longer than me and still quite successful. I also need to change a little over time to stay in the work because I am not young anymore so I make sure I keep my body good. Lucky I am big and I am good at what I do so I have regular clients and can get new ones too. It's good for both of us.

Koken et al. report that some Internet escorts even reframe "sex work away from the stereotypical social problem model to sex work as a legitimate form of work which can be a constructive and positive force in the lives of those in the commercial sex industry as well as those who seek their services" (2004, p. 29). Similarly, a few *garotos* justify their involvement in the trade as a mutually beneficial engagement. Lukas had a 70-year-old client who showed up occasionally. The older man could barely walk. Lukas would go to his place and accompany him to the *termas*. It was striking how attentive Lukas was toward this client and how they seemed to enjoy each other's company. Lukas explained to me that this client has been good to him for many years and treats him like family. The client no longer expected many sexual favors from Lukas, and while he does give Lukas some money at the end of the day, Lukas claims that the money is not important as he could earn it from other clients. Rather, he offers his companionship as a way of repaying this older gentleman for his kindness and help over the years.

As noted earlier, Brazilian *termas* provide a space not only for sexual acts but also for social activities. Through interactions with coworkers and the possibility of a longer-term involvement, some *garotos* come to see sex work as a possible career path. The normalization of sex work over time can happen when *garotos* are more involved with sex work and stay in the business for a longer time. In addition, as more *garotos* remain in the profession, more "role models" are available to suggest its viability. Smith et al. (2008) report that working for an agency allowed sex workers to share information and support, which helped them learn how to manage the negative aspects of sex work. Interested *garotos* also can learn from the "long-timers" how to remain marketable as they age in the trade.

Notably, youth and beauty are two highly valued traits in sex work that fade with time. As *garotos* age, their marketability may decline, particularly if youth is one of their main assets. It is not just that they age but also that younger competitors will enter the market. To remain in the business, *garotos* have to reinvent themselves, and they can learn reinvention strategies from the more experienced workers. One common strategy is to sell themselves as a *man* rather than a *boy*, making a smoother transition in sync with aging while retaining the emphasis on masculinity. Studying online Brazilian rent boys, Phua and Caras (2008) find that providing additional services beyond sex is not uncommon. Expanding or specializing in certain sexual activities and roles is another strategy. One example of expanding the sexual repertoire includes being an exclusive top to being versatile; for some male sex workers, bottoming has become more acceptable over time, partly as a strategy to increase business. Having a large penis, a sculpted body, and a vivacious personality are also important assets that *garotos* can possess regardless of age.

What seems important to surviving and doing well in the trade is the information exchange among *garotos*. *Garotos* who have family members and friends in the trade learn from one another. This information exchange not only teaches them how to manage work challenges and how to do well in the trade; it also enables them to stay in the trade longer if they choose to do so. Luciano says, "If I don't have my brother and friends, I would not have started working here and stay so long. They help me with how to deal with clients and other boys, and my family."

Exiting sex work

Over the course of the study period, some *garotos* left the business. In most cases, those who remain and are still working provided updates about their friends and acquaintances who no longer do sex work. Some *garotos* have achieved their goals and no longer participate in the trade. Leaving the city or neighborhood where they used to work and returning to their home cities or neighborhood marks an exit route that is both literal and symbolic. Former *garotos* being in prison, having married, working in a different location, having new jobs, moving out of the city, finding sugar daddies or mommies, or dying are common reasons for no longer working in the trade.

Some self-declared former *garotos* continue to visit the *termas* periodically. While this finding is similar to Cusick et al.'s (2011) finding that exit from sex work may not be a one-time final departure, there is still a major distinction here due to the venue. *Termas* provide a place for entertainment, socializing with old and new friends, and a transgression from their routine lives. *Termas* allow some *garotos* to relive their past through familiar interactions and discourses. Being approached by clients also re-affirms their attractiveness and boosts their egos and self-esteem. The possibilities of earning extra cash and engaging in sexual and social activities are incentives. Thus, while they are not entering the *termas* as *garotos*, they may accept opportunities when they arise. In short, the door for re-entry into sex work is always open for them. Some former *garotos* comment on their visits to the *termas*:

> "I just stopped by before my security night shift to meet friends and have a beer. Sometimes some clients will pay for the beer and I might even work a little."
>
> "I don't work anymore. I come here to work out. It is cheaper than paying for a gym. If things happen, I am fine with it too. No one will complain about having more money."
>
> "I don't work as a boy anymore. I have a good job now but I come to see what happens."
>
> "I think I am too old to get work now. I come when I am bored and want something different. But it is fun to hang out with people and usually we get free drinks and even go out with old clients in a group. It is good fun."
>
> "I haven't work for three years now and come here sometimes. I cannot believe I still get offers. I am still good."

These quotations suggest that a final exit from sex work may be accomplished only by death. Having worked as a *garoto* offers workers an alternative. While this opportunity does not necessarily mean that former *garotos* will return to the trade in the future, sex work will always remain an option, however unlikely it might be for some. To successfully disengage from the scene depends on the *garotos*' ability and willingness. Their ability not to fall back on the trade is in part based on the social network and life they built having no or little connection to the trade. Also, their willingness to leave the trade for good depends on the extent to which they can resist the perceived advantages the trade provides. One interesting example is the case of Vitor:

> Vitor entered the trade in his late 20s, a little older than other *garotos* in terms of age of first entry. He was very popular because he was very attractive and friendly. He identified as heterosexual and was married to a very beautiful woman. His wife did not know about his work and his goal was to earn enough to start a restaurant with his wife. He only worked as a top as he claimed no interest in men, though he didn't mind the sex with clients. After working for a few years, he left the trade and the city and started a business with his wife. After being absent from the *termas* for several years, he returned to work. As a handsome older man now, he still has clients, but he is not as popular as before. He offers both top and bottom services now. He shared that his business did not work out, and he was divorced now. So he decided to return to the city and to start a new life. He was familiar with this work, and it offered him quick cash. After a year or so, I lost track of him, but according to others, he left the city again.

Conclusion

In this study, I have examined the work trajectories of Brazilian *garotos* who work in *termas*. In general, these *garotos* are similar to independent male escorts in other studies. Like *clients*, *the* garotos need to pay a fee (albeit lower) for entry, and they need to abide by certain safety rules set by the establishment (e.g., no weapons or drugs). In the *termas*, *garotos* establish friendships and social networks with one another and with clients. These networks facilitate information exchange and potentially provide role models that suggest the viability of sex work as a long-term career choice. However, *garotos'* motivations for entering sex work, their management of work-related challenges, and the ways they choose to distance themselves from sex work when they exit the trade are diverse.

The *termas* differ from brothels or agencies where, in most cases, a portion of sex workers' earnings is surrendered to the owners as payment for services or facilities provided. In contrast, *termas* provide a meeting space for a nominal fee regardless of whether the *garotos* make any money that day. It is important to note that not all Brazilian *garotos* work in *termas*, and for those who do, the *termas* might be one of several venues in which they solicit business. In addition, *termas* are also social spaces that sometimes merge a work space with a leisure space, creating a grey area that allows *garotos* some flexibility in terms of negotiating their roles. It is precisely this advantage that allows for the examination of work trajectories.

Sex workers' work trajectories are a challenge to study because the work has not been institutionalized, making it a part of the informal or underground economy. Legalizing and legitimizing the work might provide workers with more legal protection, more structured benefits (e.g., pensions), and perhaps greater acceptance and less stigma. However, it remains unclear how legalization/decriminalization might affect sex workers, particularly those in developing countries where work in the informal economy offers a certain flexibility. More research should be conducted that considers the pros and cons of redefining sex work as a legitimate career option with benefits similar to those provided by other valid employment (see Crofts, 2014, on regulating sex work).

While I have examined *garotos'* work trajectories and their potential for treating sex work as a career, I do not suggest that *garotos* do not face the challenges of engaging in sex work. Although Scott et al. posit that "the intrinsic nature of sex work is not all oppressive, and that there are different kinds of worker and client experiences and varying degrees of victimization, exploitation, agency, and choice" (2005, p. 321), sex workers face many challenges. Stigma associated with same-sex sexual activities and sex work, risks of STI/HIV infection, abuse of drugs and alcohol, lack of alternative work options, and potential discrimination and violence continue to haunt them. Perhaps further research will examine how these Brazilian sex workers manage these issues compared those who work in other venues.

References

Allen, J. S. (2007). Means of desire's production: Male sex labor in Cuba. *Identities: Global Studies in Culture and Power, 14*(1–2), 183–202.

Benoit, C., & Millar, A. (2001). *Dispelling myths and understanding realities: Working conditions, health status, and exiting experiences of sex workers.* Retrieved from http://web.uvic.ca/~cbenoit/papers/DispMyths.pdf

Benoit, C., Ouellet, N., Jansson, M., Magnus, S., & Smith, M. (2017). Would you think about doing sex for money? Structure and agency in deciding to sell sex in Canada. *Work, Employment, and Society, 31*(5), 731–747.

Bimbi, D. S., & Koken, J. A. (2014). Public health policy and practice with male sex workers. In V. Minichiello & J. Scott (Eds.), *Male sex work and society* (pp. 199–222). New York, NY: Harrington Park Press.

Browne, J., & Minichiello, V. (1996). Research directions in male sex work. *Journal of Homosexuality, 31,* 29–55.

Crofts, T. (2014). Regulation of the male sex industry. In V. Minichiello & J. Scott (Eds.), *Male sex work and society* (pp. 179–198). New York, NY: Harrington Park Press.

Cusick, L., Brooks-Gordon, B., Campbell, R., & Edgar, F. (2011). "Exiting" drug use and sex work: Career paths, interventions and government strategy targets. *Drugs: Education, Prevention & Policy, 18*(2), 145–156.

da Silva, A. P., & Blanchette, T. G. (2009). Sexual tourism and social panics: Research and intervention in Rio de Janeiro. *Souls: A Critical Journal of Black Politics, Culture, and Society, 11*(2), 203–212.

De Graaf, R., Vanwesenbeeck, I., Van Zessen, G., Straver, C. J., & Visser, J. H. (1994). Male prostitutes and safe sex: Different settings, different risks. *AIDS Care, 6,* 277–288.

Ford, N. J., Vieira, E. M., & Villela, W. V. (2003). Beyond stereotypes of Brazilian male sexuality: Qualitative and quantitative findings from Sao Paulo, Brazil. *Culture, Health, and Sexuality, 5,* 53–69.

Green, J. N. (1999). *Beyond Carnival: Male homosexuality in twentieth-century Brazil.* Chicago, IL: University of Chicago Press.

Kidd, S. A., & Liborio, R. M. C. (2011). Sex trade involvement in São Paulo, Brazil and Toronto, Canada: Narratives of social exclusion and fragmented identities. *Youth & Society, 43,* 982–1009.

Koken, J. A., Bimbi, D. S., Parsons, J. T., & Halkitis, P. N. (2004). The experience of stigma in the lives of male Internet escorts. *Journal of Psychology & Human Sexuality, 16,* 13–32.

Kong, T. S. K. (2008). Risk factors affecting condom use among male sex workers who serve men in China: A qualitative study. *Sexually Transmitted Infections, 84*(6), 444–448.

Kuhar, R., & Pajnik, M. (2018). Negotiating professional identities: Male sex workers in Slovenia and the impact of online technologies. *Sexuality Research and Social Policy.* Retrieved from https://doi.org/10.1007/s13178-018-0330-4

Kulick, D. (1998). *Travesti: Sex, gender, and culture among Brazilian transgendered prostitutes.* Chicago, IL: The University of Chicago Press.

Logan, T. D. (2010). Personal characteristics, sexual behaviors, and male sex work: A quantitative approach. *American Sociological Review, 75*(5), 679–704.

Marino, R., Minichiello, V., & Disogra, C. (2003). Male sex workers in Córdoba, Argentina: Sociodemographic characteristics and sex work experiences. *Pan American Journal of Public Health, 13,* 311–319.

Parker, R. (1999). *Beneath the equator: Cultures of desire, male homosexuality, and emerging gay communities in Brazil.* New York: Routledge.

Parsons, J. T., Bimbi, D., & Halkitis, P. N. (2001). Sexual compulsivity among gay/bisexual male escorts who advertise on the Internet. *Sexual Addiction and Compulsivity, 8*(2), 101–112.

Phua, V. C. (2009). The love that binds: Transnational relationships in sex work. *Sexuality and Culture, 13*, 91–110.

Phua, V. C. (2010). Negotiating sex and sexualities: The use of sexual tags in the Brazilian sex trade workplace. *Archives of Sexual Behavior, 39*, 831–841.

Phua, V. C. (2016). The prized connection: Portugueseness in Brazilians. *InterDISCIPLINARY Journal of Portuguese Diaspora Studies, 5*, 25–37.

Phua, V. C., & Caras, A. (2008). Personal brand in online advertisements: Comparing White American and Brazilian rent boys. *Sociological Focus, 41*, 238–255.

Phua, V. C., Ciambrone, D., & Vazquez, O. (2009). Advertising health status in male sex workers' online ads. *The Journal of Men's Studies, 17*, 251–258.

Phua, V. C., Hopper, J., & Vazquez, O. (2002). Men's concerns with sex and health in personal advertisements. *Culture, Health, and Sexuality, 4*, 355–363.

Pruitt, M. V. (2005). Online boys: Male-for-male Internet escorts. *Sociological Focus, 38*(3), 189–203.

Scott, J., Minichiello, V., Mariño, R., Harvey, G. P., Jamieson, M., & Browne, J. (2005). Understanding the new context of the male sex work industry. *Journal of Interpersonal Violence, 20*, 320–342.

Scoular, J., & O'Neill, M. (2007). Regulating prostitution: Social inclusion, responsibilization, and the politics of prostitution reform. *The British Journal of Criminology, 47*(5), 764–778.

Smith, M. D., Grov, C., & Seal, D. W. (2008). Agency-based male sex work: A descriptive focus on physical, personal, and social space. *The Journal of Men's Studies, 16*(2), 193–210.

Tyler, A. (2014). Advertising male sexual services. In V. Minichiello & J. Scott (Eds.), *Male sex work and society* (pp. 83–106). New York, NY: Harrington Park Press.

Uy, J. M., Parsons, J. T., Bimbi, D. S., Koken, J. A., & Halkitis, P. (2004). Gay and bisexual male escorts who advertise on the Internet: Understanding reasons for and effects of involvement in commercial sex. *International Journal of Men's Health, 3*(1), 11–26.

Vanwesenbeeck, I. (2001). Another decade of social scientific work on sex work: A review of research 1990–2000. *Annual Review of Sex Research, 12*, 242–289.

Weitzer, R. (2005). New directions in research on prostitution. *Crime, Law and Social Change, 43*, 211–235.

Weitzer, R. (2007). Prostitution as a form of work. *Sociology Compass, 1*(1), 143–155.

Weitzer, R. (2009). Sociology of sex work. *Annual Review of Sociology, 35*, 213–234.

26
Street hustling in Brazil
Historical glimpses of Rio de Janeiro

Gregory Mitchell

The cruising project

Sexual economies are always influenced by broader political economic circumstances, and Brazil is no exception to this rule. That is, the political and economic shifts that affect inflation, pricing, tourism rates, and levels of disposable income in the broader social landscape also affect the sex industry, including the number of men selling sex at a given moment, how much they charge, and the sex acts in which they are willing to engage. The macroeconomy plays out in the sexual microeconomy of individual lived experiences. Brazil makes an especially good case study for examining such connections because of its remarkable economic volatility over the last half century.

This chapter examines previously unanalyzed records of approximately 30 interviews that outreach workers conducted with street-based male hustlers (many of them heterosexual) selling sex to other men in Rio de Janeiro in the early 1990s,[1] just after the end of Brazil's military dictatorship (1964–1985). This post-dictatorship period was a time of widespread hyperinflation and great economic struggle as the country attempted to right itself, but it had not yet attained the economic gains of the 2000s, when soaring commodity prices and the discovery of new light sweet crude oil brought about a booming economy and the growth of a consumer class previously unknown in Brazil. With that explosion came thousands of men willing to sell sex in order to participate in conspicuous consumption and enjoy class mobility (Mitchell, 2010). Later, in the 2010s, Brazil would suffer the deepest economic crisis in decades when the prices charged by male sex workers came crashing down alongside major financial mismanagement and government corruption, further disrupting the sexual economy. But the economic peril of the early 1990s deserves special analysis because it drove many young heterosexually identified men to selling sex even as the HIV epidemic roared across the country, meaning these hustlers reluctantly entered a sexual marketplace that was steeped in paranoia, fear, desperation, and often self-loathing.

I began studying male sex workers (*garotos de programa*, or "*garotos*" for short) in Brazil in 2006 as a masters' student in cultural anthropology at the University of Chicago and continued my studies through my years as a PhD student at Northwestern University in performance studies and then as a professor of women's, gender, and sexuality studies at

Williams College. The project began as a thesis about the growth of gay consumerism and the tourist industry in Brazil, but—as I walked the beaches and saw handsome young Brazilian men on the arms of older "*gringo*" (foreign) tourists and bathhouses filled with men for hire—I hypothesized that the growth in tourism was not due to some rise in gay-friendly marketing or advertisements in travel magazines but rather the result of the availability of cheap, legal, high-end commercial sex services. My work was eventually published in *Tourist Attractions: Performing Race and Masculinity in Brazil's Sexual Economy* (2016), which was the first book-length monograph published in English to focus on *garotos* (rent boys) in Brazil and their clients.

In those days, a 40-minute *programa* (session with a client) cost about 80 US dollars. Now that the value of the Brazilian *real* has fallen from 1.5 *reais* per dollar to 4 *reais* per dollar, *programas* can now be purchased for around 25 US dollars. However, the introduction of geosocial sexual networking apps like Grindr, Scruff, and Hornet have disrupted the industry, allowing *garotos* to work more flexible hours, to be more selective, and to work from virtually anywhere. It also means that young men who were uncomfortable working in formal bathhouse or brothel venues or who were afraid to hustle on the street can now work online from the convenience of their phone. The result has been a large increase in supply.

I wanted to know what the market was like before my arrival on the scene in 2006, though. And so I tried to trace the history of male prostitution in Brazil, and in Rio de Janeiro specifically. (Brazil's prostitutes' rights movement has resisted widespread adoption of the term "sex worker," so in this article I use "prostitute" and "prostitution," but not pejoratively.) Although some other scholars had written about male prostitution as a minor theme (see Parker, 1999; Green, 1999; Trevisan, 1986), until *Tourist Attractions*, the only other book close to the subject was *O negócio do michê* (*The Business of the Hustler*), an ethnographic account of male prostitutes in São Paulo written in 1986 by Nestor Perlongher, an Argentine expat and anthropologist who had sex with as many as 11 hustlers a day. Perlongher was a surrealist poet who fled Argentina's dictatorship. He was obsessed with the macho straight men whom he paid to fuck him, especially the Black ones, whose dark bodies, as his contemporary João Trevisan explained, "filled him with fear—but also delight" (Trevisan, 1986, p. 38). He was a devotee of Antonin Artaud and The Theater of Cruelty, which saw divinity in suffering and degradation. Perlongher also moved to the Amazon jungle for a period to join a cult built around the powerful hallucinogen *ayahuasca*. He viewed condoms as an apparatus of the state that disciplined desire and subjugated the body. He was uncomfortable with the idea of "gay identity," which he saw as limiting possibilities and forcing labels that constrained and chafed. He died of AIDS-related causes in 1991 (see Bollig, 2006).

To read *O negócio do michê* is to get a glimpse into the dark and somewhat depressing underworld of São Paulo hustlers at that time. The book reads like the work of a poet, and Perlongher draws on the ever-ambling post-structuralist philosopher Gilles Deleuze, whose dense metaphysical prose Perlongher admired, as he drifts with readers "around the streets—and [moved] down—in terms of income, class, legal position, and physically onto the street, down into nightclub basements or public toilets—into the city" (26). As Ben Bollig points out, Perlongher's *michês* ("hustlers," now a somewhat pejorative term in Portuguese) are nomads, circulating along customary paths from point to point, client to client, always reaching a point in order to leave it behind rather than to dwell. It is in the state of cruising—when betwixt and between points—that Perlongher feels the *michê* is best understood. This instability allows the *michê* to remain a mercurial and romantic figure for Perlongher, and so it is difficult to say how the famed poet-anthropologist would have theorized the great migration of *michês* indoors, where they have become increasingly static and non-nomadic.

The archives

Shortly after Perlongher published his work on *michês* in São Paulo, another, more practical project emerged. In the late 1980s and 1990s, as Brazil succumbed to astronomical inflation rates that crippled the country, Projeto Pegação (The Cruising Project), a small group of five men led by a young social worker named Paulo Longo, began doing outreach work with street *michês* in Rio de Janeiro (Longo, 1998a, 1998b). Longo reports that his group was almost solely responsible for introducing and normalizing condom use among *michês*, who quickly adapted to them. Projeto Pegação worked exclusively with men on the street, although in the late 1990s, gay tourism in Rio became increasingly focused on indoor *sauna* (bathhouse) prostitution, which was far safer for all parties, more convenient, and generally free from police harassment. Whereas Perlongher conceived of *michês* as continually remaking their own meaning, Longo knew that AIDS was drastically reconfiguring all aspects of the *michês'* lives and worlds.

In Longo's time, *michês* worked in several main areas of male prostitution (see Figures 26.1 and 26.2; for a more visual cartography, see Angelo, 2002): Galeria Alaska (an indoor corridor of shops in Copacabana), the Rainbow Kiosk (a small nearby stand on the beach known as a gay hangout), Quinta da Boa Vista (a large public park), Central do Brasil (the train station), Bar Maxim's (a beachfront bar), Cinelândia (near the downtown business district), and nearby Via Ápia. Areas known for gay cruising, such as the bohemian neighborhood of Lapa and the Aterro do Flamengo (a public park and recreation area), also included some commercial sexual encounters mixed in with non-commercial gay sex. These spaces have changed considerably since Longo's team did their work. See, for example, Figure 26.3, which shows the Aterro do Flamengo park today, which has been developed and is filled with picnicking families, runners, cyclists, and tourists taking in the view of Sugar Loaf Mountain. Projeto Pegação suffered funding difficulties and internal management issues and disbanded before Longo's sudden death at the age of 42 from heart failure (see Larvie, 1999).

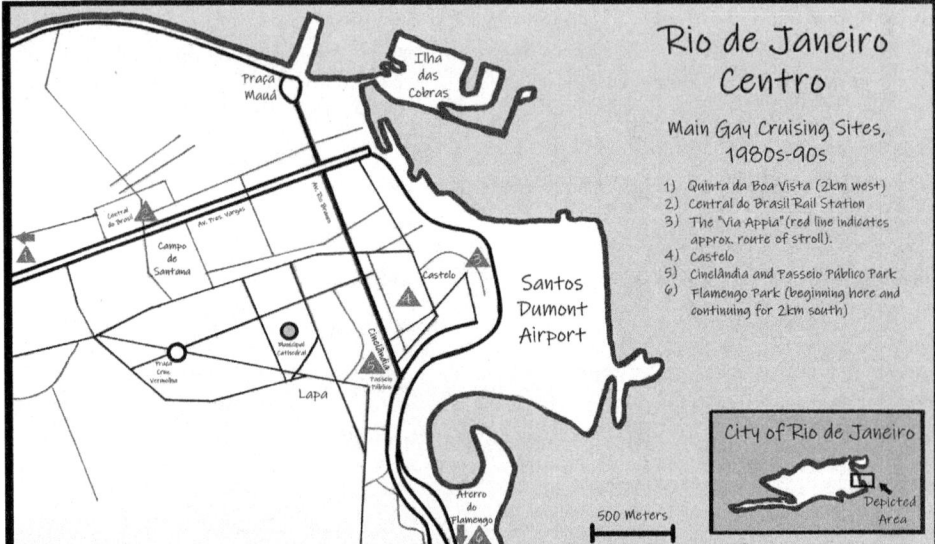

Figure 26.1 Main locations of commercial gay cruising in Rio de Janeiro's downtown.
Credit: Thaddeus Blanchette.

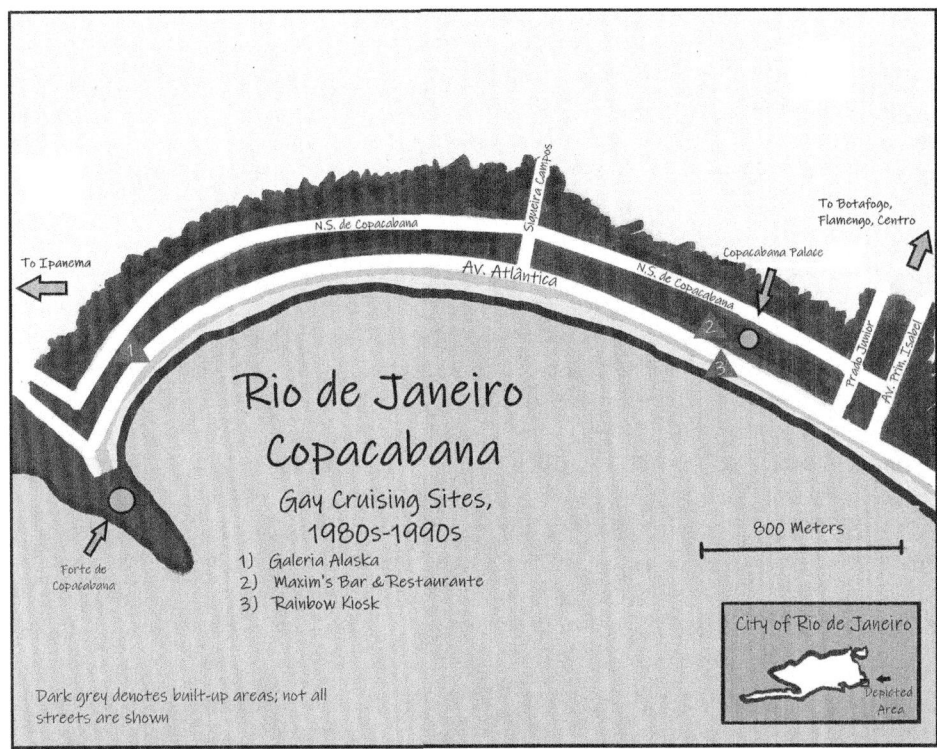

Figure 26.2 Main locations of commercial gay cruising in Rio de Janeiro's Copacabana neighborhood.

Credit: Thaddeus Blanchette.

Figure 26.3 Aterro do Flamengo in 2019.

Photo credit: Thaddeus Blanchette.

Some of the gay commercial sex spaces have taken a more ironic turn in terms of occupants. Galeria Alaska, the indoor corridor of shops in Copacabana, used to have not only hustlers but also a robust gay nightlife scene. A drag queen known as Eloína dos Leopardos was inspired by U.S. male striptease shows and created *Os Leopardos* (*The Leopards*), an erotic performance troupe whose show, *A Noite dos Leopardos* (*The Night of the Leopards*), featured cabaret numbers that used naked male dancers with erect penises, who sometimes even danced in showers onstage. Some of the performers worked in gay pornography and did sex work. Galeria Alaska also was the site of *Cabaret Prevenção* (*Prevention Cabaret*), a show put on by an NGO to raise awareness about HIV/AIDS awareness. Eventually, heterosexual tourists came to gawk at *Os Leopardos* as an example of exotic and erotic Brazilianness. Today, all of this has vanished, and Galeria Alaska is home to mundane businesses and even an evangelical Church (see Figure 26.4.)

The Rainbow Kiosk (Figure 26.5) still retains its name, but it has gotten a makeover. No longer a small hut serving drinks in a casual space, it has been remade as an upscale sit-down restaurant on a busy stretch of Copacabana Beach. A highly visible scene for heterosexual prostitution still abounds in this area at night, and plenty of gay men still frequent this part of the beach, but the *michês* are long gone.

Around 2007, I was visiting Davida, the sex worker rights organization, to interview its founder, Gabriela Leite, an aging communist and self-avowed *puta* (whore) who was the undisputed leader and charismatic figurehead of the prostitutes' rights movement in Brazil. Davida had an office in the bohemian neighborhood of Lapa (near Cinelândia) with a room

Figure 26.4   Galeria Alaska in 2019, now home to an evangelical church rather than a site for gay entertainment and male prostitution.

Photo credit: Thaddeus Blanchette.

Figure 26.5   The Rainbow Kiosk in 2019.

Photo credit: Thaddeus Blanchette.

upstairs that had been turned into a library. I spent many days sifting through their archive, looking at books, magazines, and reports. One afternoon, I found the original handwritten records from Projeto Pegação's interviews with *michês* in 1990. I also found a program evaluation done by the World Health Organization (WHO) under the direction of Richard Parker, a prominent anthropologist who had written several books on gay culture in Brazil (which included a few interviews with *garotos*). I photographed some of the pages from Projeto Pegação's files, as well as the evaluation by Parker and the WHO, but Davida had to surrender its office space during a budgetary crisis brought on by the George W. Bush administration's ban on foreign aid to organizations that supported decriminalization or legalization of sex work (Rohter, 2005).[2]

The archives were scattered, mostly housed in the attics and closets of Davida's members or their friends, family, and colleagues. Eventually, some of the material ended up at the Arquivo Público do Estado do Rio de Janeiro, a public archive. One day in 2016, while I was engaged in a project with some Davida members on heterosexual sex tourism during the World Cup and the Olympics, I met a student named Guilherme Alef, who was working for the research collective we had founded, *O Observatório da Prostituição* (The Prostitution Policy Watch). Guilherme had been in the library archives and had stumbled on some of the missing Projeto Pegação materials. Eventually, Guilherme scanned what was there, which included about 30 surviving interview records of the original 90.[3]

What follows are some glimpses of the lives of these young men, whose fates are unknown. Perhaps they died of AIDS. Perhaps they left *a vida* (the life) and settled down somewhere with wives and children. Perhaps they succumbed to drugs or were taken by the streets. Painting a partial ethnographic portrait of them here is my homage to Longo, whose haunting presence hung over the archive, which as I found it at Davida's office still included birthday cards from friends, notes from his long-time lover, and other ephemera. It is also an homage to Perlongher, who so often described hustlers in the poetic and elliptical language of mysticism. The two men, whom I never met before their early deaths, were the only other people I knew to have conducted research akin to my own and therefore the closest thing I had to academic interlocutors, even though they happened to be dead. These traces of the hustlers' lives—preserved by a handful of passionate gay activists, tossed from trunk to trunk for decades all over Rio de Janeiro, only to drift back up almost 30 years later and be scanned and shot across the world by a technological invention unthinkable at the moment of initial contact—reflect the circuitous and partial mode of emergence that Perlongher felt best captured the essence of the *michê*, always moving, always mercurial, always haunting the edges of queer desire.

The form

By today's standards, the three-page form deployed by Longo and his team seems quaint at best, or offensively misguided at worst. In addition to recording the street name, the geographic point of contact, and the male prostitute's number of clients, STD history, condom usage, and sexual practices, researchers also added their own observations on characteristics like "intellectual/cultural condition" (*condição intelectual/cultural*) and posture or manner (*postura*). In the commentary on intellectual/cultural condition, researchers make comments such as "poor vocabulary," "good verbal fluency," "lives with mother; estranged from father," or simply "good." For posture, they write evaluative words like: "masculine," "not extremely masculine," "nice," "presentable," "elegant," "chill and educated," (*tranquilo e educado*), "reasonable," or "humble." Based on scratched out answers and contradictory comments, the hustlers seemed confused by some technical questions about sexual activity, such as whether they are "active or passive in oral sex."

As a quantitative data set, the study doesn't seem all that reliable. But the details provided and quotations pulled and inserted into the section for notes and comments yield subtle but rich information. Here I discuss only eight of the interviewed men, because most of the other records lacked detail about the content of the interviews. The researchers made almost no notes about some of the interviewees and, for other interviewees, only illegible, brief notes about limited things such as location. Because these are public records, I've left the names that the men gave interviewers intact, though in my own ethnographic work I've observed that it is the norm for hustlers in Brazil to use *nomes de guerra* (street names, literally "names of war.") Working from these records, I attempt in the following to conjure the hustlers back into a more vivid ethnographic form, to enliven them and to offer a deeper sense of the hustlers' complex personhood behind and within these forms.

Ghosts from the past

Ricardo

Nineteen-year-old Ricardo was working in the historic downtown neighborhood of Cinêlandia (Figure 26.6) on a crisp winter evening when the researcher approached him. Ricardo was immaculately dressed, sporting a Benetton jacket and slicked-back hair. He loved clothes and dressing well. He had been doing *programas* (turning tricks) since he was 16. During that time, he had done a lot of *programas*, and one time he even fist-fucked a guy. That *maricona* (faggot)

Figure 26.6 A boulevard in Cinelândia, the area that Ricardo and other *michês* were working when approached by Longo's team.

Photo credit: Thaddeus Blanchette.

had given him surgical gloves to wear to do the deed, and while the client had not shit, he had bled (*não saiu feijão, mas sangrou.*)[4]

Ricardo was a total top (exclusively acts as the anal insertive partner), but in his non-hustling life he liked to have sex only with *travestis* (loosely translated as transgender women.) In fact, it had been many months since he had fucked a cisgender woman. His speech was peppered with slang he had picked up from the various *travestis* he had wooed, and he gotten into *candomble* (an Afro-Brazilian possession-based faith related to Vodou and Santeria that *travestis* often participated in or used for casting magic spells).

He used to work in Galeria Alaska, but he had to move over to Cinelândia because he had stolen a hair dryer from a *travesti* (presumably an ex-lover) when he needed some money, so he was avoiding her neighborhood now. For a while, a big dyke worked as his pimp for him, but she wasn't around to protect him anymore. While Ricardo was talking, a little gay guy walked past (*um gayzinho*). "He doesn't even know how to dress," Ricardo said. The interviewer asked Ricardo who had taught him so dress well. "I learned by myself," he replied.

Flavio

Flavio, aged 18, was living in a *favela* (shantytown) five years earlier, but he fled after running into some trouble with some guys who lived there. He went to live in Resende, an industrial city some distance from Rio. Later, he ended up in a boarding school on Paquetá, a small island near Rio de Janeiro. But in 1988, a couple years before the interview took place, he had gone to Recreio, a wealthy beachfront area west of the city to steal. He was in the process of stealing the radio and cassette player out of a car there when the vehicle's owner caught him. Rather than be angry or call the police, this old gay man befriended him, and eventually Flavio moved in. There was never sex between them, Flavio asserted; they were just friends. Later, Flavio had a fight with him, though. (What the fight was about remains a mystery in this record.)

And so Flavio moved out and started renting a room in a hostel in Cinelândia, where he turned his first trick. He remained friends with the older gentleman mentioned previously, though, and while he said that he still never had sex with him, he did sometimes round up some other guys from Madureira (a bustling lower-middle-class neighborhood in the city's north zone) all the way to Recreio to have paid sex with that older guy whom he used to live with. In addition to selling sex to other men on the streets and working as a procurer of hustlers for the wealthier older man, Flavio was trying to learn to drive. He wanted to become a professional driver and to get out of prostitution. He really wanted to return to his original home in the favela, but he was still afraid of the "bandits" there whom he had pissed off years earlier.

Jorge

Twenty-year-old Jorge estimated that he'd been in prostitution for only six months, but not consecutively. He was looking for work, and so he came into and went out of the industry, turning tricks in Galeria Alaska, a shopping area in Rio. He told Paulo, the leader of the project, that he had emigrated from Paraná, a state in the south of the country wedged between Argentina and the city of São Paulo. He was very masculine, though, and now that he was selling sex again, he was doing steady business—around 20 clients per month, making reasonably good money as a *michê*. He was looking for other work. Throughout the conversation, Jorge had difficulty making conversation. His vocabulary was poor. He seemed to have a very low level of education. He didn't know very much about AIDS, at one point asking Paulo "Are you sure you can't catch it from kissing?" He showed a bit of nervousness about some of the questions about the activities of a *michê* at first, but he was open and willing to discuss other subjects (like being in love with a woman). As the night wore on, he got more comfortable. He told funny stories about his more extravagant sexual experiences, like the client who wanted him to hide behind a curtain so that only his penis poked out (which the client would then masturbate.) He laughed about this and other funny stories. But he had a darkly cynical side, too. At some point in the night, a young man with a bruised face came by. When Paulo asked the guy what had happened, the guy claimed that he'd been injured in a motorbike accident. Jorge retorted that "every queer (*bicha*) who gets punched says they fell off their motorbike."

Martin

Martin, in his early to mid-20s, worked in Galeria Alaska, but he had just started selling sex three months prior. He was a well-spoken immigrant from Rio Grande do Sul in the south of Brazil. Unlike most of the hustlers, Martin seems to have been bisexual; he reported that he would have non-commercial sex with about five other partners a month—"with women or with men, depending on the attraction." So it wasn't the gay sex that bothered him about prostitution, but he nonetheless felt disgusted by it ("*mostrou-se revoltado*"). He had about 20 clients a month, which meant that at the time of the interview he had probably turned around 60 tricks to date. He said that he would never bottom for clients, though he did for other guys. He always used condoms with clients, but the only time he was rigorous in his condom use with other partners was when he would bottom. One thing he did not like was sucking dick, saying "I only suck women" ("*Só chupo mulher* [sic]"). The first time Paulo found him, he was ostensibly not trying to sell sex. At least that wasn't his first plan of action. Instead, a visibly drunk Martin had been trying to sell a pair of Reebok tennis shoes to make enough money to pay the rent. The next time Paulo encountered him, Martin said he was doing a *programa* to get some money. Throughout both of their encounters, Martin would interrupt the conversation to attempt to get some cocaine off of people.

Isac

Isac was 15 years old and working at Bar Maxim's, a beachfront bar in Copacabana where gays hung out. Isac had dropped out of school after the fifth grade. He'd been selling sex for six months, he said, and he usually got about ten clients every month. Sometimes he used the money for cocaine. He was solely a top, asserting that he had never bottomed or given a blow-job. The boy had gotten gonorrhea from a client once and was terrified of AIDS. He had done a blood exam not long before and had tested negative for HIV. However, he wanted to "submit to a seropositivity exam" (presumably the researcher's terminology, but it's unclear if these tests are different). The boy bemoaned that he would not know how to react if he discovered he was "contaminated" (*contaminado*). One of the clients, a guy named Kenedy whom Isac knew from working in Galeria Alaska, had recently told him that he was HIV-positive but was not yet showing symptoms. Isac wanted to use condoms because he knew they could prevent HIV, but a client had refused and called off the *programa* (session) because of it. As a result, Isac had lost 600 *cruzeiros*, a small but much-needed sum of money.

Ding-Don

Ding-Don (ding dong, like a doorbell) felt old at 34. (There's no explanation of how he got this nickname.) The interviewer described him as "masculine/virile" (*masculine-viril*). He had left school after seventh grade and worked various jobs. He had been in prostitution for only two years, but he was tired of it. He had only four or five clients a month, and even then he only let the men suck his dick. He spent all the money he made as a hustler on sex with female prostitutes, and he noted that the women sometimes stole all his money from him during a *programa*. He remarked that "money made from prostitution comes easily and goes just as easily." He refused to use condoms, even with the female prostitutes and even though he had gotten gonorrhea once, insisting that there was no risk of HIV from heterosexual sex, only anal sex with men, which he didn't have. He hoped to return to São Paulo soon and get a job as a taxi driver. But the money just went so quickly.

Name unknown

An unnamed hustler living in Duque de Caxias, a city just north of Rio, was working in Cinelândia. He said he was the oldest of eight brothers and that he would return every night, however late, to sleep at home. He hated to spend the night on the street, because it was not good sleep. It did not make up for the actual functions of real sleep. He was tired a lot. And when you are tired enough for enough of the time, he said, you will eventually go get a real job. He looked down on the other hustlers. He had a critical view of the *michês passivos*, the ones who bottom, which in his opinion was probably the majority of them (whatever they may have claimed). It is their fault that business is so poor right now, he said. He would top you for 200 or 300 *cruzeiros*, and he'd even accept a check, but only if he knew where you live.

Luiz

Luiz was 36 years old, practically ancient in Cinelândia. But he had been selling sex for two thirds of his life already, having done his first *programa* when he was just 13. Luiz was sexually versatile and he "works assiduously" in the area, but he complained that the place had been heavy with constant assaults and police pressure. He had been watching the outreach workers making contacts in the area. He was eager to talk to them because he planned to "change his life" soon. Just a short while ago, he became interested in learning more about AIDS. He began to use condoms 100% of the time just recently because he suspected that he had been "contaminated by HIV" because had spent so many years without using any protection. Moreover, he had been in prostitution for 23 years, and he had become jaded and showed bitterness toward the business of hustling. He said he was "feeling the weight of his years" in prostitution (though Roberto, the interviewer, made a note that Luiz doesn't appear to show his age). He complained that he disliked the "insincerity (*falsidade*) of the gay world." He didn't like the gay nightclubs, but he'd been to almost all of them. As a somewhat curious ending to his interview, he noted that he sells sex to men but he also hustles *gringas*, or foreign women, too.

Conclusion

It's impossible to know what became of these men—or the hundreds of others working in Rio de Janeiro at that time. Although the archive is painfully incomplete, a few themes emerged. AIDS haunts the edges of their lives, and there is general paranoia and a lack of information. There was a lot of hopelessness in the interviews. There are so many forces outside the control of the boys and men working the streets. The hopelessness was so pervasive that the government officially recommended de-emphasizing the lethality of AIDS in outreach work. Ana Filgueiras, Director of the Brazilian Center for the Defense of the Rights of Children and Adolescents, explained:

> Equating AIDS and death can blunt a campaign's effectiveness. If you say 'AIDS kills,' [they say] it's just another thing to kill us. The police kill us, too.' Killing is not serious to them. But if you tell them AIDS makes you very thin and weak, that's something they are afraid of.

The sexual landscape at that moment was bleak, yet there were moments of ambiguity regarding power, emotion, and pleasure. What to make of the man who caught Flavio stealing from him only to take him into his home (into an apparently non-sexual relationship)? Is this inspirational tale undercut by the fact that years later the man apparently was using Flavio to procure other young men for sex? Or was Flavio a clever entrepreneur who hooked up his buddies with an opportunity to make some cash off this "older gentleman"? What to make of Ricardo's tempestuous relationships with the *travestis* whom he alternately seems to be in love with and also prone to betraying as he runs off to hock their hair dryers and other belongings? How to understand Ricardo, a fancily dressed and ostensibly straight man hiring a "big dyke" to be his "pimp?" How does the complexity of the genderplay in his scenario reveal the intricacies of agency within this underground world of *travestis*, queer women, and hustlers? This ambiguity is tantalizing. Even as the country reeled from economic disaster and dictatorship, it was home to a rich queer sexual world whose inhabitants were influenced by major currents—AIDS, recessions, the violence meted out by the Brazilian military police—even as they struggled to live their lives day to day.

Today, male prostitution is largely indoors. Throughout the 2000s, *saunas* (bath houses) featuring brothel-style male prostitution became the preferred venue for many clients, including an increasing number of foreign gay tourists. These venues offered safety and luxury for both clients and prostitutes. Gradually, the city began to clean up blighted outdoor areas. When I worked in Copacabana, interviewing *garotos* from a nearby *sauna*, we would often hang out at a little bar overlooking a park. The guys who could not afford to pay the five-dollar door fee to get inside to work would still hustle in the park. A few years later, the city installed floodlights in the park, killing off the business. By the time I wrapped up my fieldwork in 2012, Grindr had arrived. Now young men who didn't want to commit to sex work as a profession (with a workplace, schedule, and so on) could hop into and out of the sexual economy, accepting a quick blowjob or fuck whenever they wanted some cash. Moreover, gay men who messaged any guy and found him nonresponsive could now offer a bit of cash to get his attention. Increasingly, I hear from Brazilian acquaintances, friends, and students that times are tough and they've accepted these offers (especially from foreigners), though they are offended if I suggest that this arrangement is prostitution.

The sexual economy of male prostitution in Brazil has become unruly, ill defined, less stable, more temporary, and quite flexible. These changes are responses to the economic crisis facing Brazil and the broader political economy wrought by the advent of the Internet. The features of male prostitution today, though, echo elements of the past. Apps have become a new kind of cruising, complete with signals (woofs, taps, and so on) and their own etiquette. HIV remains poorly understood and a source of stigma. And today, as before, there are complex relationships, feelings, attachments, and desires that exist between the *garotos* and their clients. Studying the history of male prostitution in Brazil is critical, allowing us to better see the pains and pleasures of queer community that were unfolding in the 1990s—phenomena that would cascade across the ensuing decades, riding the economic highs and lows, until that world of prostitution slowly transformed into the one that Brazilians and *gringos* alike can find in Rio de Janeiro today.

Notes

1 Because the interview records are partial, with some including only one page of the file, it is unclear precisely how many interview records are extant.
2 The statement condemning prostitution is contained in the United States Leadership Against HIV/AIDS, Tuberculosis and Malaria Act of 2003 and House Resolution 1298/Public Law 108–025.
3 In addition to thanking Guilherme Alef for help with this chapter, I also owe a deep debt to João Sodré for helping me to decipher some of the written records. I also wish to thank Thaddeus Blanchette for taking photos for this chapter and for helping to track down information on more precise locations.
4 Now archaic, *maricona* was a term meaning "faggot" that was more commonly used at that time.

References

Angelo, M. (2002). *Território e prostituição na metropole carioca*. São João de Meriti, Rio de Janeiro: Ecomuseu Fluminense.

Bollig, B. (2006). Exiles and nomads: Perlongher in Brazil. *Hispanic Research Journal*, 7(4), 337–351.

Green, J. (1999). *Beyond Carnival: Male homosexuality in twentieth-century Brazil*. Chicago, IL: University of Chicago Press.

Larvie, P. (1999). Natural born targets: Male hustlers and AIDS prevention in urban Brazil. In P. Aggleton (Ed.), *Men who sell sex: International perspectives on male prostitution and HIV/AIDS* (pp. 159–78). Philadelphia, PA: Temple University Press.

Longo, P. (1998a). *Michê*. Rio de Janeiro: Planeta Gay Books.

Longo, P. (1998b). The Pegação Program: Information, prevention, and empowerment of young male sex Workers in Rio de Janeiro. In K. Kempadoo & J. Doezema (Eds.), *Global sex workers: Rights, resistance, and redefinition* (pp. 231–239). New York, NY: Routledge.

Mitchell, G. (2010, Spring). Fare tales and fairy tails: How gay sex tourism is shaping the Brazilian dream. *Wagadu: A Journal of Transnational Women's and Gender Studies*, 9, 93–114.

Mitchell, G. (2016). *Tourist attractions: Performing race and masculinity in Brazil's sexual economy*. Chicago, IL: University of Chicago Press.

Parker, R. (1999). *Beneath the equator: Cultures of desire: Male homosexuality and emerging gay communities in Brazil*. New York: Routledge.

Rohter, L. (2005, July 24). Prostitution puts U.S. and Brazil at odds on AIDS policy. *New York Times*.

Trevisan, J. (1986). *Perverts in paradise*. New York: Alyson Publications.

27

Male Internet-based escorting in Argentina

Changing attitudes and laws

Carlos Disogra, Victor Minichiello, Rodrigo Mariño, John Scott, Taylor Harrington, and Tinashe Dune

Introduction

Popular culture and media portrayals of male sex workers (MSWs) are often simplistic and reductionist, and they have a tremendous effect in forming perceptions and stereotypes (frequently negative) about the MSW population. These effects are apparent in Argentina, where research on male escorts has been limited. To date, most studies have focused on counting the number of male escorts, describing their use of health services and their contact with police, and creating a sociodemographic profile of them (Disogra, Marino, & Minichiello, 2005; Marino, Minichiello, & Disogra, 2003), with an emphasis on how the sexual encounter is negotiated within Latin American culture (Minichiello et al., 2014) and identifying the sexual health risks of male escorts (dos Ramos Farías et al., 2011). As one would expect, within the Argentine sex work organizations, male escorts are less visible than female escorts. Perhaps this relative invisibility has contributed to misrepresentations of them, although recent attempts by the media to report their presence and give them a voice have started a dialogue that sometimes challenges old stereotypical views.

As we discussed in the first volume of *Male Sex Work and Society* (Minichiello et al., 2014), male sexuality and sexual behavior in Argentina and other Latin American countries tend to be fluid. The Western dichotomy of male sexual orientation—straight or gay—does not speak to how men actually experience their sexuality (Caceres, 2002; Padilla, 2008). Unlike the male escort online profiles found in North America, Europe, and Australia, where most escorts exclusively target male clients, male escorts in Argentina and other Latin American countries are more likely to offer services to both men and women (Minichiello et al., 2014; Scott et al. 2017). In addition, within the context of fluctuating economies and unemployment rates, sex work offers an opportunity to get ahead and to secure a consumer lifestyle that would be unattainable in other types of work (Rivers-Moore, 2007). Hence the services in which male escorts are willing to engage within their social and economic environment may have more to do with financial benefits than with the clients' or the sex workers' sexual identity (Padilla & Castellanos, 2008).

One of the more prominent studies conducted in Argentina with government research funding is a study on sexually transmitted infections (STIs) among male-to-female transvestites, transsexuals and transgender people, and male sex workers in Argentina (dos Ramos Farías et al., 2011). In a sample of 114 MSWs from seven Argentinean cities, the researchers found an HIV prevalence of 11.4%, Hepatitis B virus of 22.0%, Hepatitis C virus of 6.1%, and *Treponema pallidum* of 20.4%. A recent government report indicates that the prevalence of HIV in the total Argentine population is 0.3%. The last Argentine epidemiological report of AIDS of 2017 notes "the slight decrease in diagnoses in young women and the increase in diagnoses in older women" while reporting "the increase in diagnoses in men who have sex with others men, who represent 40% of the total number of new cases" (Dirección de Sida y ETS, Ministerio de Salud de la Nación Argentina, 2018, p. 4). While the 2017 report does not specify the prevalence of HIV in men who have sex with men (MSM), the last reported value dates to 2014: "The prevalence of HIV infection in MSM was 11.5%," which resulted from a measurement in a sample of 1,015 MSM (Dirección de Sida y ETS, Ministerio de Salud de la Nación Argentina, 2014, p. 55).

The figures for MSWs are consistent with those of men who have sex with men. They are also consistent with an UNAIDS report (2018) that reveals that gay men and other men who have sex with men in Argentina have an HIV prevalence of 11.4%. The government has been concerned that new HIV infections have increased by 16% since 2010 and has made it a national priority to reduce the rates, particularly among MSM. Since 2015, it has adopted a test-and-treat approach, and 64% of people living with HIV were receiving treatment and prophylaxis to prevent further transmission of HIV. Within Latin American countries, Argentina has the largest number of people accessing antiretroviral therapy (UNAIDS, 2018). Some commentators have argued that these rates can be lowered even further, given advances in preventive HIV and STD interventions in the MSW population in Argentina and elsewhere. These advances include greater condom usage and the new medications that reduce the likelihood of passing HIV to another person by at least 95% (Disogra, 2012; dos Ramos Farías et al., 2011).

Actively challenging misconceptions and erroneous representations of male escorting can play a role in ensuring a more tolerant legal status for sex work and creating responsible social and health-promotions programs. Within this context, this chapter offers an overview of the current male escorting situation in Argentina. The chapter is organized into three parts. It starts by reviewing how male escorts and escorting are presented in popular culture in Argentina. It also describes current legislation and attitudes toward sex work and same-sex relationships. The second part presents a landscape of online male escorting by analyzing secondary data provided by male escorting websites operating in Argentina. The final part of the chapter examines clients' concerns about male escorts in Argentina, including issues related to sexual health.

Sex work represented in popular Argentine culture

This section describes recent portraits of male sex workers reported in Argentinean popular culture. In our chapter in the first volume of *Male Sex Work and Society* (Minichiello et al., 2014), the media and film we described tended to focus on male escorts who worked on the street. We reported on negative aspects of this work, such as murderer, drugs, and young men's struggles with this work. Have conditions improved over the past five years given some significant reforms in sex work and gay rights in Argentina? While we did find a few media reports associated with the murders of male escorts, including a 60-year-old expat found murdered by a male escort in the city of Córdoba, the play and media reports we describe in the following were generally positive; they focused on presenting the escorts' attitudes and views of their work. However, we do need to acknowledge that the cinema has a tendency to focus on some negative aspects of male sex work and seldom captures the realistic experience of selling sex.

The play *Kill the Taxi Boy* (Aguilar, 2017; see Figure 27.1) is about a group of four older adult men planning to kill a male escort to retaliate for extortion. The themes of murder and violence are clearly found here. However, their plan leads them to a series of reflections on their lives: their homosexuality, family, secrets, old age, loneliness, illness, and happiness. In one production, the young actor Rodrigo Díaz played the MSW. The press described Díaz as an escort in real life, due to his previous relationship with the late Ricardo Fort, a famous and wealthy gay actor who was older than Díaz. Díaz denied having been a MSW and maintained that his relationship with Fort was romantic (Farandula Show, 2017).

Two prominent news stories on male escorts presented a more positive view of the lives and insights of people who work in this profession. *Infobae*, a national newspaper, printed an interview with Bruno, a 23-year old escort and activist (also known as Brune, which is the new way of creating a gender-neutral name in Spanish; Brune identifies as both male and female) (Luna, 2018). The story reflects on the escort's path into sex work and his political views. Brune says that she started her career almost by chance. At the beginning, she did not consider her activity a job until she realized that she earned the equivalent of a minimum salary. Identifying herself as a MSW was difficult for her, though. She declares that her adolescence was apolitical until she discovered feminism, Queer theory, and militancy, at which point "I politicized my identity, I politicized my work." Her family is aware of her profession, although she had to challenge her family's prejudices through the first-person account of her "compañeras" (female fellows).

Brune works at an NGO for people living with HIV/AIDS, where she is in charge of HIV prevention for MSW. Brune generally enjoys sex with some of her clients, and in a difficult economy, she makes good money. Brune sets limits with sexual situations that make her feel uncomfortable with clients. She notes that she feels more vulnerable with romantic partners and

Figure 27.1   Promotion leaflet for movie, *Matar Al Taxi Boy*.

has been abused by ex-boyfriends but not by clients. She talks about being discriminated against by a manager for whom she worked. Asked about the public's opinion on MSW, she says,

> I think that people in general are in favor, except for minority groups such as religious, the political right, and abolitionist feminism. In general, the people are in favor of the regulation of sex work, but from a public health perspective, it is called regulation.

She further explains:

> We are against that model of State, we do not want a health book or be seen as objects of care for other people's sexualities. The core of our conquest must be oriented to our human rights, our labor rights, to be able to have a benevolent organization, to contribute to our retirement, to have civil rights, right to free circulation in public spaces. We are in 2018 and still in 19 provinces you might be imprisoned or fined for standing in a corner, because there are valid regulations approved during the military dictatorship and it is the police that enforce them.
>
> *[Authors' translation]*

She believes that heterosexuality is still alive but meaningless, given that many of her clients have girlfriends and/or female partners. MSWs have a WhatsApp group where they warn about unpleasant or dangerous clients.

In a filmed interview with Juan, a MSW, published on YouTube (Staunsager, 2016), Juan defines himself as a professional sex worker and identifies as a man. Juan uses several work names, and he advertises on Facebook and sites with a classified advertisement. His view is that people do not respect sex work; rather, "they take it as a joke." As a result, he is selective with the customers he accepts. He felt guilty at first but with more work experience, he is "getting better at it." Juan has another casual job, but he is not happy with the pay, and it is physically hard and dangerous work. In contrast, Juan describes better working conditions in sex work and his sex work as self managed. He has had some bad experiences doing sex work, though, and after those episodes, he turned to friends and other sex worker support groups via Facebook and sex work community groups. In terms of the services that he provides, he does not have any specific requirements, as he is experimenting with them. Additionally, he is also considering a venture into porn.

The majority of his clients are married heterosexual men. One of the services that he provides is sex, and another is company, affection, and conversation. His family did not know about his profession until the video interview went public. Juan shares a house with four other people (who are not sex workers) and two cats. He says that when they ask him what he does for a living, they do not believe him.

Juan states that in the city of La Plata (where he lives and works), the red zone is changing because people do not like transvestite sex workers (TSWs), whose presence on the streets and in neighborhoods has attracted police, who arrest the TSWs. TSWs often get raped, beaten, imprisoned, injured, and exposed to cold winter conditions, he said. Juan also expressed the view that he feels judged by "normal people" all the time for being a MSW. He opposes the campaign "Without customers there is no trafficking" because being an MSW is a personal choice. He notes that people who print leaflets advertising sex work get fined. Although trafficking exists, Juan defends the existence of independent, self-employed sex workers. Juan asserts that he does not sell his body and that he is not being violated. Rather, he provides a service by doing sex work. Sex work is part of his sex life with some of his clients. He also has a sex life separate from sex work.

Sex work and homosexuality in Argentina: context

Historical summary and future directions of the Argentine laws on prostitution and sex work

Meir (2017) shows how Argentinean legislation on prostitution affects sex workers' workspaces. Using Buenos Aires as a case study, Meir illustrates that while independent sex work is legal at the federal level, at the local level in the City of Buenos Aires the law criminalizes the offer and demand of sex "in an ostentatious manner in non-authorized public spaces." An historical view of prostitution laws allows us to understand how sex workers face limitations "on the spaces they can use, both by explicit legislation (at the local level) and by law enforcement's interpretation of legislation" (p. 25). Cangas Arreola (2006) argues that during the Spanish colonial period in Latin America, prostitution was a sin because it did not comply with the commandment that forbids adultery, but it was tolerated as a necessary evil that prevented other evils. Ots Capdequí (1920) provides examples that range from tolerance to rigorous punishment of prostitutes. The latter practice in many ways still prevails today.

The first Argentine legal document about prostitution dates from 1875 (Benarós, 1975). "The houses of prostitution will be tolerated in the municipality, as long as they are subject to the prescriptions of this Regulation," reads Article 2. A municipal registration of the brothel was required. The brothel could be inhabited only by prostitutes, who could not live in any other house. These houses had to be at least two blocks away from temples, theaters, and schools. Clandestine prostitution that did not conform to the regulation was punished with 8 days' imprisonment for the first offense, 15 days for the second, and a month for the third and subsequent offenses.

A significant amendment occurred with Law 12.331 (1936) for the prevention of STDs, established in Article 15: "It is prohibited in all the Republic the establishment of houses or places where prostitution is practiced, or incited." It is often argued that this law was intended to control syphilis, whose transmission was attributed in part to prostitution (Miranda, 2012). In 1955, the situation changed, when the wife of the then president of the nation, the famous Eva Perón (also known as Evita), wanted to decriminalize prostitution and give prostitutes better working conditions. So the presidential Decree 4633 (1955), which referred to the so-called regulation of the "houses of tolerance," is attributed to her. The Decree established a long list of requirements. Sex workers were required to register with the Ministry of Public Health, and brothels had to conform to architectural and sanitary requirements to be officially authorized. The age of both prostitutes and clients was raised to a minimum of 18 years, and some provision were made that indicated a lot of concern for the welfare of prostitutes.

A summary of the current of federal law, Law N° 11,179, called the Penal Code of the Nation and Its Modifications, Act 25.087 (1999), and Crimes Against Sexual Integrity, Modification to the Penal Code, are the key pieces of federal law regulating sex work in Argentina. In addition, the 23 federated provincial states and the Autonomous City of Buenos Aires have their own laws, and in turn, the municipalities have distinct ordinances.

Regarding the legal future of sex workers in Argentina, López (2013) presented a reformist and progressive bill to regulate independent sex work, which did not pass. The bill was intended to create within the Ministry of Labor, Employment, and Social Security (Ministry), the Oficina

Nacional de la Protección al Trabajo Sexual (ONPTS) (National Office for the Protection of Sexual Work). The ONPTS would have comprised the Ministry staff and representatives of sex workers' organizations. ONPTS would have been self regulating. It would have monitored the law; studied and proposed updating the laws on sex work; promoted access to educational, medical, and legal information to sex workers; encouraged the coordination and harmonization of federal, provincial, and municipal regulations in the matter of sex work; granted a credential that authorizes the practice of the sex work; considered proposals for the improvement of living conditions of sex workers; and worked to incorporate sex workers into Argentina's pension systems, health and social assistance systems, and insurance systems. To practice sex work, sex workers would have needed to meet the following requirements: (1) be of legal age, (2) have no legal impediment to working in the country, and (3) attend a free qualifying course that would have been taught by ONPTS staff: "The qualification course should ensure, as a minimum requirement, content related to basic notions about: human rights, constitutional law, labor and criminal law; prevention of addictions; sexual health; and sexually transmitted infections" (p. 3).

Although the bill did not pass, Argentina, through its Ministry of Justice and Human Rights, has focused on human trafficking (for the purpose of sexual exploitation or other ends). It administers a program called "Programa Nacional de Rescate y Acompañamiento a las Personas Damnificadas por el Delito de Trata" (National Program for the Rescue and Support of Victims of Trafficking), providing a telephone number for complaints 24 hours a day, 365 days a year and using the slogan "Without customers there is no trafficking." The publication of sex work advertisement notices are forbidden by Decree 936 (2011) (Ministry of Justice and Human Rights, 2018).

A double standard exists in Argentina. On the one hand, sex work is not a crime, and there is even a law regulating it. At the same time, different acts connected with sex work are criminalized—for example, commercial sex advertisements and offering sexual services in public spaces. In its attempts to prevent human trafficking, the government has proceeded in such a way that some adult sex workers who practice in an independent and rational manner have been the victims of violence, raids, and thefts by security forces and by the State itself. In short, private commercial sex work between two consenting adults is de facto criminalized (Amnesty International, 2016).

This de facto criminalization of sex work has many negative effects. It makes it difficult for sex workers to access health and social services, particularly transgender sex workers, leaving them without State protection when they are victims of crimes. Amnesty International recommends ending this de facto criminalization by making a clear distinction between sex work involving consenting adults and trafficking of people; by changing any law that criminalizes any activity related to commercial sex work; and allowing sex workers to register as tradespersons, allowing them to access social, health, and retirement services and pay taxes (Amnesty International, 2016). Amnesty International's (AI) report on sex work in Argentina (2016) shows how the Argentine government's political ideology toward taking an abolitionist view, grounded in feminist theory regarding prostitution, is influencing the enforcement of the Federal Anti-trafficking Law adopted in 2008, and how sex work is regulated at the ground level. In essence, the legislation uses vague language that does not see sex work as a legitimate form of work, does not distinguish between forced and voluntary sex work, and perpetuates stigma and presumptions of sex workers' criminality. Equally interesting is the fact that the AI report did not discuss male sex work or interview any male escorts as part of its study sample.

It is also important to note that we tried to obtain official government arrest statistics for prostitution in Argentina. We could not find any reports or statistics on the incidence of sex work arrests over time. Some municipalities keep official statistics regarding sex work in the

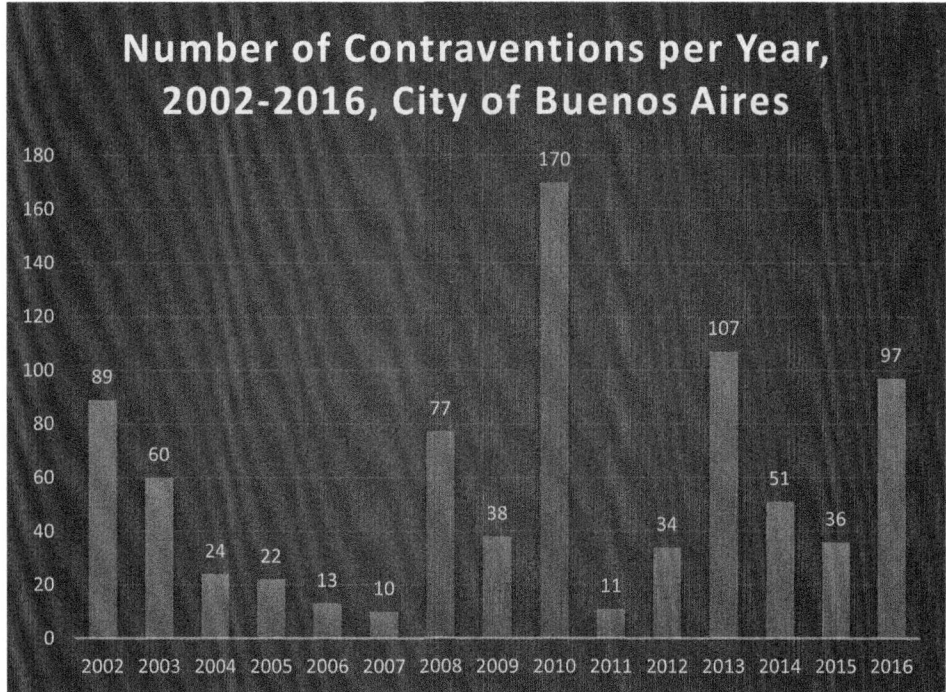

Figure 27.2 Number of Contraventions per Year, 2002–2016, City of Buenos Aires.
Adapted from Durand, 2016, p. 11.

streets. However, it is difficult to find information on the incidence of MSWs over time for a number of reasons. First, because prostitution is not a crime in Argentina, it is not possible to be arrested and charged for prostitution (male or female). However, a person offering sex services in the streets might be detained and charged with a contravention. *Contraventions* are minor infractions more closely related to social life than to crimes or offenses regulated in the Criminal Code. (Other contraventions include drinking alcohol in the streets.) Thus, if person offering sex services in the streets is charged with a contravention, the detainee will be registered in the category "contravenciones." The official number of contraventions per year (2002–2016) follows in Figure 27.2 (Durand, 2016, p. 11), but only for the city of Buenos Aires. The figures under-represent the victimization experienced by sex workers as reported by local sex work organizations (Webb, 2016).

Sex work and homosexuality in Argentina

Despite its machismo and Catholic culture, in 2010 Argentina became the first country in Latin America to recognize same-sex marriage. At the time, it was only the tenth nation worldwide to do so (Encarnación, 2011). How did this happen? The answer lies partly with changing social attitudes over time toward homosexuality and support from national governments. The Pew Research Centre Global Divide on Homosexuality survey (2013) reveals that Argentina has, in comparison to other countries, progressive social attitudes toward same-sex sexuality. Of all Latin American countries, it has the highest number of respondents (74%) stating that "homosexuality should be accepted by society," higher than the United States (60%) and slightly lower than Australia (79%) and Britain (76%). The majority of Argentines (67%) do not believe that being LGBTI should be a crime.

Gay rights in Argentina has a long history. Bazán (2004) writes a detailed history of homosexuality in Argentina, beginning with the edict of the Spanish king to kill those who practice sodomy at the stake in colonial times, and ending with the fight to legalize marriage between people of the same sex. Jorge (2012) attributes the equal marriage law in Argentina to the decrease in discriminatory attitudes toward homosexuals in Argentina. Jorge provides data showing that in 1991, 39% of Argentines did not want to have a homosexual as a neighbor. Since then, there has been a steady decrease in that number. For example, by 2010, it had dropped to 9% (Jorge, 2012).

Encarnación (2011) believes that changes in attitudes toward homosexuality in Latin America in general and particularly in Argentina result from a number of factors: first, gay Argentine social organizations' strategy to present gay rights as human rights; second, the growing public support for gay pride marches; and third, businesses recognizing the economic spending power of gay people. For example, the Argentina crisis of 2001 and the sharp devaluation of the Argentine currency made Buenos Aires a very popular tourist destination for Western gay travelers, bringing large financial benefits to the city. Additionally, Argentine gay activist groups sought support from all political parties, regardless of their position in the left-right spectrum. Last, but not least, there is a positive correlation between educational level and tolerance toward gays (access to higher education in Argentina is free to all).

In addition to changing public attitudes, other significant factors were at play. For example, Schulenberg (2012) explains that same-sex legislation was facilitated by the fact that there is no mention of marriage in the Argentine Constitution that requires the state to pass amendments to it in order to recognize lesbian and gay couples. Schulenberg also describes how gay rights activists in Argentina worked with the political elites as strong allies, eventually allowing this reform to be presented to Congress for a vote. Although the human rights strategy adopted by gay activists in Argentina has been successful, Encarnación (2011) argues that same-sex and other gay rights won in Latin America represent "more of a political victory than a social transformation" and are therefore vulnerable to backlashes or reversal from extreme right-wing politically organized forces. In other words, there remains hostility and intolerance toward gay men and lesbians by a significant number of citizens in Latin American countries. Citing the findings of the 2008 Americas Barometer survey of the Latin American Public Opinion Project, Encarnación observed that Argentina was only one of two countries in Latin America with an above 50% "high tolerance" toward homosexuality. The other country was Uruguay.

Online sex work in Argentina

There are no published government reports on the size of the sex industry in Argentina, let alone on the number of male escorts. However, we can make estimates based on some recent global data about online male escorts. In 2017, Scott and his colleagues found that Argentina had a total of 139 online male escorts, with 59.71% of the escorts indicating that they provide services to women and couples (Scott, Minichiello, & Callander, 2017). Argentina was one of only three countries around the world that reported having more male escorts seeking female and couples clients than male escorts seeking male clients (Scott et al., 2017). The researchers replicated the survey in 2018, and they found that the number of online male escorts had increased to 262. Again, Argentina reported a high percentage of male escorts (69%) who targeted women and couples in their advertisements (Minichiello, Scott, Callander, & Harrington, 2019).

Other research has examined Argentina's male websites. Minichiello and his colleagues (2014) undertook a survey of 145 online male escorts from the websites Soytuyo and Revista-ratones; their results were reported in Volume 1 of *Male Sex Work and Society*. They found that the majority of the escorts indicated that they provide services to males, females, and couples, and they identified their sexual position as "top." More than half indicated that they were aged between 20 and 24. Disogra (2012) also conducted a study with a sample of 145 MSW from two large Argentine cities (Buenos Aires and Córdoba) that included street escorts. He found that the average age was 25.2 years. The majority were Argentinean nationals (92.4%) and had completed secondary education (54.2%) or university studies (19.7%). As for the place where they offer their sexual services, 54.2% of MSW responded "private apartment," 21.1% "street," 18.4% "other," and 6.3% "agency." MSW reported an average of 4.57 commercial sexual encounters with male clients per week, ranging from zero to 25 encounters.

Our current website survey included five sites owned and operated in Argentina—Soytuyo, Revistaratones, Leonos, Onyce, and Sierrescalientes—and the largest international male escort website, Rentmen, operated from the Netherlands. Three of the Argentine sites (Soytuyo, Revistaratones, and Leonos) are well established and have been operating for at least a decade. For example, Soytuyo was established 17 years ago (Figure 27.3) and is a popular website in Argentina, with 4,437 daily views and 525,000 visits over the last 6 months.

Over 78% of the traffic to this website is from Argentina. Often these websites include some limited sociodemographic statistics, including about 50 words written by the escorts about their services, along with pictures and videos of the escorts (Figure 27.3).

Our survey of online male escorting in Argentina took place on March 19–23, 2018. One coder collected the following information from all six websites: the escort's city location; whether the escort's profile was duplicated across the sites; information about the escort, such as age, penis size, sexual role, and the gender of the clients to whom he offered sexual services;

Figure 27.3   Image from the website Soytuyo.

Source: https://www.soytuyo.com.

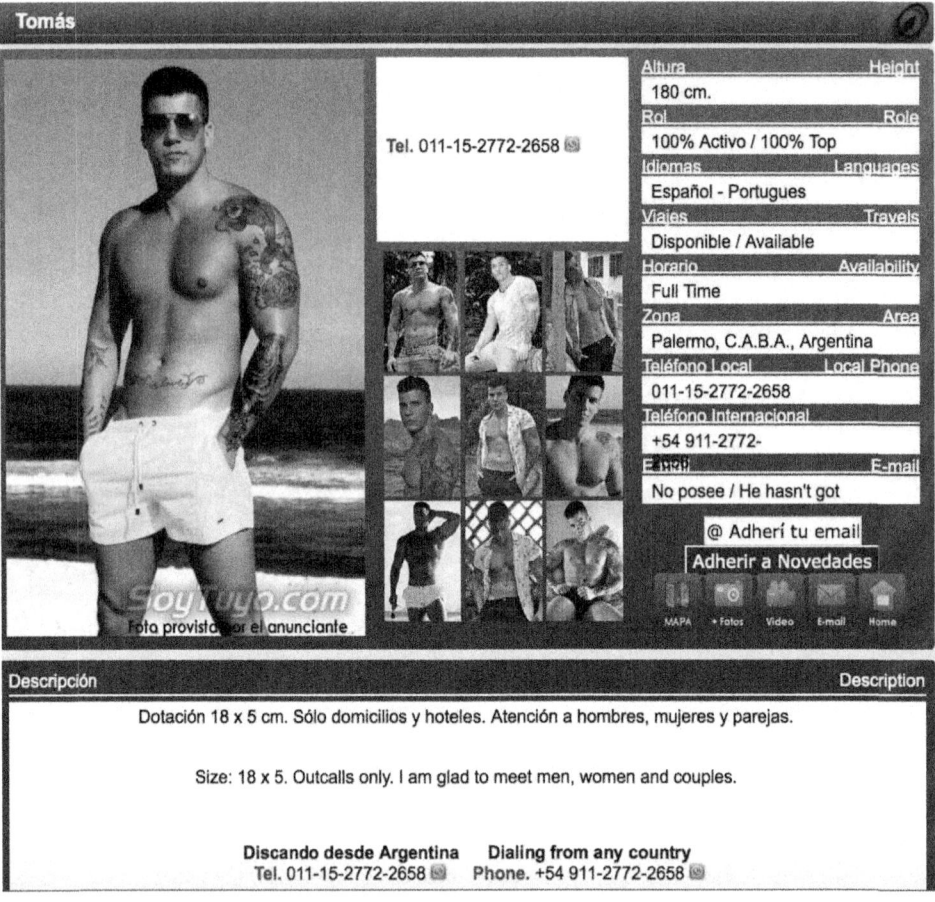

Figure 27.4   An example of profile information about escorts found on the website, Soytuyo. com.

Source: https://www.soytuyo.com.

whether the escort's descriptive profile used the words "morbose" (which, in Spanish, generally means a willingness to have raw or natural sex), "fulfill all fantasies," or "condoms"; and whether a video of the escort was included. A second coder randomly checked every 40th case to ensure reliability. The data were stored on Numbers, the Apple software spreadsheet program.

The data included 381 online escort profiles (see Table 27.1). Of these, 148 or 39% were duplicates, which meant there were 233 individual escorts, an increase from the previously published study in 2016. The current figures are likely to be higher, because our survey did not include all the websites mentioned in the world online study. The majority of escorts were located in Buenos Aires (87%), with Córdoba (6%) and Rosario (4%) being the next two cities with the largest numbers of online male escorts. The two largest escort websites were Soytuyo (39%) and Leonos (34%), followed by Rentmen (11%), Revistaratones (9%), Sierrascalientes (4%), and Onyce (3%). More than half of the profiles on the international Rentmen site were found on the local websites. The three largest websites have been in operation for at least a

Table 27.1 Profile of Online Male Escorts in Argentina, *n* = 381

Variables	N	%
Client Type		
Men, Women, Couples	176	46%
Men and Couples	31	8%
Men and Gay Couples	105	28%
Exclusively Men	69	18%
Mentions Penis Size		
Yes	228	60%
No	153	40%
Mentions word "morbose"		
Yes	67	18%
No	314	82%
Fulfils 'all Fantasies		
Yes	140	37%
No [SR1]	241	63%

decade, are national sites with most escorts from Buenos Aires, and offer similar profile information about the escorts. The other two local websites have recently been established, with one of them catering to escorts in Córdoba and the other including both female and male escorts. Rentmen is now the largest international male escort website, with over 7,000 escorts from most cities around world. The mean average age of the escorts in our survey was 24, consistent with the results of other studies (Logan, 2014). See Table 27.1.

As with previous studies conducted in Argentina, more than half (54%) of the male escorts reported offering their sexual services to men, women, and couples or to men and couples. The percentage of escorts offering their sexual services exclusively to men was 18%, and a further 28% offered services to men and gay couples. Less than half of the escorts offered services only to men or male couples. The majority of escorts reported a masculine sexual role, defined as a "top" (the person who penetrates the other in anal sex and is sexually dominant). A little less than one-third (29%) of the escorts reported that they were "100% top," and 18% indicated generally taking an active top role. About half (48%) reported being versatile, and only a minority (5%) reported being passive.

The profiles sometimes included a brief description of the escort, although what was allowed in the description varied by website. When we look at whether clues about intentions with respect to safe or risky behavior could be read into the statements, some interesting findings emerge. In the Spanish sexual culture, the word "morbose" can imply natural or raw sex, and in the online male sex work culture, the statement "fulfilling all fantasies" usually indicates a willingness to consider unsafe sexual practices. Interestingly, only a minority of the escorts (18%) mention the word "morbose," but a significant number, more than one-third (37%), mention "all fantasies." While this phrase can suggest unsafe sexual practices, mentioning condom sex or showing condoms being used in videos can imply the message that the escort engages only in safe-sex practices.

Studies have found that there is an association between sexual intentions and safe/unsafe sexual behavior (Sheeran, Abraham, & Orbell, 1999). In our survey we investigated whether the escort mentioned the word "condom" in his description statement or included a video with a condom on the penis. Only 5% did so, with the vast majority remaining silent on this issue. Consistent with other studies about the sexual intention of online male escorts, and as a result of the effectiveness of antiviral medication and the use of PrEP (Denton et al., 2017), condoms are increasingly less likely to be mentioned in escort profiles.

Clients' discourses

Foroescortsxp.com is an Argentine forum on the topic of female, transvestite, and male sex workers (SWs). Although it is mostly a forum for clients, it also includes the participation and voices of sex workers. The participation of MSWs, however, is infrequent (112 out of 365,517 posts or less than 1% of the total posts) and is practically limited to initial presentations or responding to comments made by clients about the escort.

The forum is divided into three main sections titled by the sex worker's gender: women, transvestites, and men. Each section has sub-forums with different themes: masseurs, provinces of Argentina and the city of Buenos Aires, rest of the world, porn, and a sub-forum for the participation of sex workers (a recent addition, as originally the participation of sex workers was not allowed).

The men's section has a gay sub-forum and a sub-forum for male sex workers for women. The forum requires registration, either free or with charge. The forum has 144,925 members, but only 8,738 are considered active. The proportion of posts on each of the three sections can be estimated as: women 75%, transvestites 15%, and men 10%. The total number of messages in the men's section, at the writing of this piece, was 365,517. Members must observe "terms and rules" and a "code of conduct" in their posts. There is always advertising of sex workers' pages and free HIV testing.

We will discuss the men's section of the forum only. The forum participants frequently describe their experiences with MSWs and ask questions. Reports of experiences are highly sought after by forum participants. Not only is the sexual experience reported, but a review of the MSW is conducted. An evaluation is reported with specific items rated from 0 to 10: venue, cleanliness, face, body, and penis, and qualified as "Yes" or "No" whether the MSW kisses, ejaculates, and allows himself to be penetrated. Finally, the reviewer lists the MSW's fees and renders a final verdict on whether to repeat the experience. Sometimes, the experience is described as "bad" and may act as a caution to the other parties. The "bad experiences" often have complaints about the hygiene of the venue or the lack of a MSW's erection.

There is little discussion of health issues in the forum. The use of condoms is not often discussed. Some participants have recently commented that they no longer wear condoms because they take the pre-exposure prophylaxis pill (PrEP). However, these comments were challenged by MSWs, who argued that the effectiveness of PrEP is not 100% but rather 90%. In addition, the local monthly cost of treatment is $12,051.25 pesos (about US $590), which is the average monthly income in Argentina, making it unviable for the vast majority of the local population and why the condom is still the preferred form of HIV prevention in Argentina. Because this is an online forum, several parties reported a nostalgia for the times before the Internet and the cell phone, when the meetings between the MSW and a client began face to face on the street.

Conclusion

Our research suggests that the numbers of male escorts in Argentina are increasing, and they are moving away from the streets to the online environment, a process that began around the turn of the last century. This increase had occurred despite social attitudes and regulations that clearly discourage sex work in general and raise additional concerns for the health and safety of male sex workers. Data from this and other studies indicate that the demand for unsafe sex in Argentina is increasing, as is the incidence of STIs and HIV. It may be that a combination of factors, including cultural articulations of masculinity, stigma, and a relative lack of resources all contribute to poorer health outcomes for MSWs. The ambiguous legal status of sex work in

Argentina must also be a factor in such outcomes. Furthermore, although Argentina has several organizations concerned with preventing STI transmission, including a female sex workers' union in Buenos Aires (Asociación de Mujeres Meretrices Argentinas), Argentina does not have any national sex workers' organization. Nor does it have community groups that are funded by the state with a mandate to offer services to sex workers or to run specific health promotion or peer education programs. Health promotion and education programs are by and large run by volunteers at a local level. These include human rights groups and sporadic and short-lived gay organizations. These observations and conclusions point to a need for improvement in the provision of services and public health support.

References

Aguilar, H. (2017). *Matar al taxi boy*. Retrieved from https://culturadelserproducciones.jimdo. com/2018/01/27/matar-al-taxi-boy

Amnesty International. (2016). *"What I'm doing is not a crime": The human cost criminalizing sex work in the City of Buenos Aires, Argentina*. Retrieved from https://www.amnestyusa.org/reports/what-im-doing-is-not-a-crime-the-human-cost-of-criminalizing-sex-work-in-the-city-of-buenos-aires-argentina/

Bazán, O. (2004). *Historia de la Homosexualidad en la Argentina. De la Conquista de América al siglo XXI*. Buenos Aires: Marea.

Benarós, L. (1975). Casas de prostitución en Buenos Aires, en 1875. *Todo es Historia, VIII*, 10–22.

Caceres, C. F. (2002). HIV among gay and other men who have sex with men in Latin America and the Caribbean: A hidden epidemic? *AIDS, 16*, S23–S33.

Cangas Arreola, O. D. (2006). El amor se volvió mujer. Las mujeres y el amor en el México colonial. *Avances, 132*, 1–24.

Decreto 4633. (1955). *Reglamenta el funcionamiento de las casas de tolerancia*. Poder Ejecutivo Nacional.

Decreto 936. (2011). *Proteccion Integral a las Mujeres. Promuévese la erradicación de la difusión de mensajes e imágenes que estimulen o fomenten la explotación sexual*. Poder Ejecutivo Nacional. Retrieved from http://servicios.infoleg.gob.ar/infolegInternet/anexos/180000-184999/184133/norma.htm

Dirección de Sida y ETS, Ministerio de Salud de la Nación Argentina. (2014). *Boletín sobre VIH, sida e ITS en la Argentina*. Año XVII, Número 31. Retrieved from www.msal.gob.ar/images/stories/bes/graficos/0000000601cnt-2015-01-29_boletin-epidemiologico-vih-2014.pdf

Dirección de Sida y ETS, Ministerio de Salud de la Nación Argentina. (2018). *Boletín sobre VIH, sida e ITS en la Argentina*. Año XX, Número 34. Retrieved from www.msal.gob.ar/images/stories/bes/graficos/0000001070cnt-2018-03_boletin-epidemio-vih-sida.pdf

Disogra, C. (2012). *Predictores de encuentros sexuales comerciales seguros entre hombres. Tesis doctoral no publicada*. Universidad Nacional de Córdoba, Argentina.

Disogra, C., Marino, R., & Minichiello, V. (2005). Self-reported use of health services, contact with police and views about sex work organisations among male sex workers in Cordoba, Argentina. *Journal of Psychology of Human Sexuality, 17*(1–2), 181–195.

dos Ramos Farías, M. S., García, M. N., Reynaga, E., Romero, M., Vaulet, M. L., Fermepin, M. R., . . . Avila, M. M. (2011). First report on sexually transmitted infections among trans (male to female transvestites, transsexuals, or transgender) and male sex workers in Argentina: High HIV, HPV, HBV, and syphilis prevalence. *International Journal of Infectious Disease, 15*, e635–e640.

Durand, V. (2016). *Una aproximación a los perfiles sociodemográficos y a la vida en situación de cárcel, de los privados de libertad en establecimientos de ejecución penal de Argentina*. Retrieved from www.jus.gob.ar/media/3268823/SNEEP%2015%20años%20-%20Perfil%20sociodemografico%20detenidos.pdf

Encarnación, O. G. (2011). Latin America's gay rights revolution. *Journal of Democracy, 22*, 2–16.

Farandula Show. (2017). Retrieved from www.youtube.com/watch?v=DjmNTPAwagU

Jorge, J. E. (2012). Same-sex marriage in Argentina tolerance and discrimination in political culture. *Journal of Research in Peace, Gender, and Development, 2*, 60–71.

Ley 12.331. (1936). *Organizando la profilaxis de las enfermedades venéreas en todo el territorio de la Nación.* Congreso de la Nación, Argentina.

Ley 25.087. (1999). *Delitos contra la integridad sexual.* Modificación al Código Penal. Congreso de la Nación, Argentina.

Logan, T. (2014). Economic analyses of male sex work. In V. Minichiello & J. Scott (Eds.), *Male sex work and Society* (pp. 107–147). New York, NY: Harrington Park Press.

López, O. (2013). *Proyecto de Ley Nacional para regular el Trabajo Sexual Autónomo.* Retrieved from www.ammar.org.ar/IMG/article_PDF/Proyecto-de-Ley-para-regular-el_a319.pdf

Luna, M. (2018). *La vida de un taxi boy: "No siempre disfruto el sexo, pero me voy feliz porque tengo los bolsillos llenos".* Retrieved from www.infobae.com/sociedad/2018/01/30/la-vida-de-un-taxi-boy-no-siempre-disfruto-el-sexo-pero-me-voy-feliz-porque-tengo-los-bolsillos-llenos/

Marino, R., Minichiello, V., & Disogra, C. (2003). Male sex workers in Cordoba, Argentina sociodemographic characteristics and sex work experiences. *Revista Panaamericana de Salud Publica, 13,* 311–319.

Meir, J. (2017). Sex work and the politics of space: Case studies of sex workers in Argentina and Ecuador. *Social Sciences, 6*(2), 42. doi.org/10.3390/socsci6020042

Minichiello, V., Dune, T., Disogra, C., & Marino, R. (2014). Male sex work from Latin American perspectives. In V. Minichiello & J. Scott (Eds.), *Male sex work and society* (pp. 363–395). New York, NY: Harrington Park Press.

Minichiello, V., Scott, J., Callander, D., & Harrington, T. (2019). *Result of 2018 survey of number of online male escorts by nation.* Brisbane: QUT. Retrieved from https://research.qut.edu.au/aboutmaleescorting

Ministerio de Justicia y Derechos Humanos. (2018). *Oficina de Monitoreo de Publicación de Avisos de Oferta de Comercio Sexual.* Retrieved from www.jus.gob.ar/areas-tematicas/trata-de-personas/oficina-de-monitoreo-de-publicacion-de-avisos-de-oferta-de-comercio-sexual.aspx

Miranda, M. (2012). Buenos Aires, entre Eros y Tánatos. La prostitución como amenaza disgénica (1930–1955). *Dynamis, 32,* 93–113.

Ots Capdequí, J. M. (1920). *Bosquejo histórico de los derechos de la mujer en la legislación de Indias.* Madrid: Reus.

Pew Research Centre Global Attitudes & Trends. (2013). *The global divide on homosexuality.* Retrieved from www.pewglobal.org/2013/06/04/the-global-divide-on-homosexuality/

Padilla, M. B. (2008). The embodiment of tourism among bisexually-behaving Dominican global imaginary. *Archives of Sexual Behavior, 37,* 783–793.

Padilla, M. B., & Castellanos, D. (2008). Discourses of homosexual invasión in the Dominican global imaginary. *Sexuality Research and Social Policy, 5*(4), 31–44.

Rivers-Moore, M. 2007. Affective sex: Beauty, race and nation in the sex industry. *Feminist Theory, 14*(2), 153–169.

Schulenberg, S. (2012). The construction and enactment of same-sex marriage in Argentina. *Journal of Human Rights, 11*(1), 106–125.

Scott, J., Minichiello, V., & Callander, D. (2017). *Number of online male escorts by nation.* Brisbane: QUT. Retrieved from https://research.qut.edu.au/aboutmaleescorting/2017/11/01/number-of-online-male-escorts-by-nation-2

Sheeran, P., Abraham, C., & Orbell, S. (1999). Psychosocial correlates of heterosexual condom use: A meta-analysis. *Psychological Bulletin, 125*(1), 90–132.

Staunsager, M. (2016). *Trabajo Sexual en Primera Persona—Juan Ejemplo.* Retrieved from www.youtube.com/watch?v=jSfPkr-t0gI

UNAIDS. (2018). *Country, Argentina.* Retrieved from www.unaids.org/en/regionscountries/countries/argentina/

Webb, H. (2016). *Sex work in Argentina: "We would invoice, if our work were recognised".* Retrieved from www.thebubble.com/sex-work-in-argentina-we-would-invoice-if-our-work-was-recognized

28

Male sex work in Mexico

Virile prostitution at the Plaza Tapatía of Guadalajara

Giovane Mendieta-Izquierdo

Introduction

This chapter is based on in–depth interviews with 13 men who engage in prostitution in *Plaza Tapatía*, and it is part of a larger research project published in the book *Prostitución viril: Un estudio fenomenológico del cuerpo* [*Virile Prostitution: A Phenomenological Study of the Body*] (Mendieta-Izquierdo, 2015). It uses the term *virile prostitution*[1] as practiced in the plazas or parks of Guadalajara, Mexico. In virile prostitution, the male sex worker assumes the role of dominator to the extent that he is the active penetrator, while the client, as the passive receiver, is dominated. The active male is understood to be dominant, reflecting the domination of the masculine over the feminine.

Prostitution is not illegal in Mexico; however, both the Penal Code and the police penalize and restrict this activity (Lamas, 1996). In addition, Mexican federal labor law excludes sex work, failing to accept it as a form of work in the country. The first study of prostitution in Mexico was conducted by Mexican sociologists Gomezjara, Barrera, and Pérez (1978), who wrote about several aspects of male homosexuality in their study of male and female prostitution in Mexico. Later studies have examined social and labor contexts, attitudes, and risk or prevention practices concerning AIDS among groups of transvestites and masseurs in Mexican public steam rooms. Men who work in the steam rooms come from low socioeconomic strata, and there are differences between the two groups regarding working conditions, exposure to risk, sexual practices, and preventative measures in terms of risk. Masseurs maintain an unquestioned heterosexual male identity despite having sex with other men so long as they maintain the role of penetrators in oral and anal sex, practice preventive behaviors, use condoms, and follow the rules of the establishment. In contrast, transvestites lead marginalized lives of constant daily confrontation. Although they are not exploited by others, they are nevertheless exposed to greater dangers and violence, and they are at increased risk. Transvestites are more open about their sexual practices and enjoyment, but their infrequent use of condoms is alarming (Liguori & Aggleton, 1998).

Researchers have also studied the body and its uses among male sex workers, particularly strippers, *mayates*,[2] and transvestites. A study of sex workers in the city of Xalapa in the state of Veracruz emphasizes that strippers exhibiting their body as spectacle, emphasizing beauty, a very masculine appearance, and youth. *Mayates* are active penetrators who maintain a masculine appearance. Among transvestites, the body is a fiction, with male bodies having the appearance of women (Córdova Plaza, 2005).

Male prostitution in public places—plazas or parks

In Mexico, the name used for men who engage in male prostitution is based on the place in which it is conducted, and the geographic spaces in which it occurs largely coincide with those of the gay scene, most notably closed spaces such as bars, discotheques, saunas and pornographic theaters. Notable in these spaces are strippers, masseurs, and sex workers who operate through spas, newspaper advertisements, shops, saunas, private apartments, bars, or clubs (Córdova-Plaza, 2005; Jackson, 2007; Demarco, 2007; Boden, 2007). Male prostitutes also work in public places such as streets, plazas, parks, corners, and bathrooms; this article discusses this second group of sex workers (Manzelli, & Pecheny, 2002, p. 119; Atkins, 2012; Schrimshaw, Downing, & Siegel, 2013).

In the spaces where male sex work and public sex occur, there are patterns of walking and waiting. Walking offers a means of understanding the potential opportunities that are available in the environment. The continual repetition of looking, walking, and standing around in a place allows the men involved in the sex trade (clients and sex workers) and men who have non-commercial sexual encounters to recognize one another (Carrier, 2003; Atkins & Laing, 2012).

Studies of street prostitution highlight social factors such as poverty (Kaye, 2007), youth, and dysfunctional family relationships (MCouns & Minichiello, 2007). Older men frequently act as support networks, and young people take advantage of their youth and project an image of aggressiveness, which is an aspect of survival that sometimes leads to violence in the streets (Kaye, 2007). The men who make use of these spaces have been identified as a group with specific needs for housing, sexual health, and the management of illegal substances and situations (Atkins, 2012).

Notable actors in these space include streetwalkers, within which we find the sub-categories of *mayates* and transvestites (Córdova-Plaza, 2005). Other recognized actor classifications found in this context include *chichifos*[3] and *chacales*,[4] although the latter two are not necessarily prostitutes and are not the subjects of this study.

What does it mean to be a *mayate* in Mexico?

The common features of male prostitution as performed by *mayates* in the *Plaza Tapatía*[5] are presented in the following based on individual case studies and on an analysis that seeks to identify the common characteristics of *mayates* with regard to virile prostitution. These features revolve around the body and corporeality, clients' desires, the characteristics of *mayates*, and ways of establishing contact. Figure 28.1 shows the panoramic view of Paseo Degollado, Plaza Tapatía, Guadalajara, Jalisco, México.

For this study, 20 in-depth interviews were conducted with 13 male prostitutes, in the Plaza Tapatía in Guadalajara, Mexico, from September 2010 to June 2013. Figure 28.2 shows the geographic location of ZMG Zona Metropolitana de Guadalajara, Jalisco, México. The researcher interacted directly with the men in the Plaza, making use of observation and participant observation (Mendieta-Izquierdo, 2015). Open coding was carried out for all the interviews, with groupings by themes and sub-themes, thus allowing the research to reveal the essence of the *mayate*.

Figure 28.1 Panoramic view: Paseo Degollado, Plaza Tapatía, Guadalajara, Jalisco, México.
Source: Toño Ceja. (Mendieta-Izquierdo, 2015).

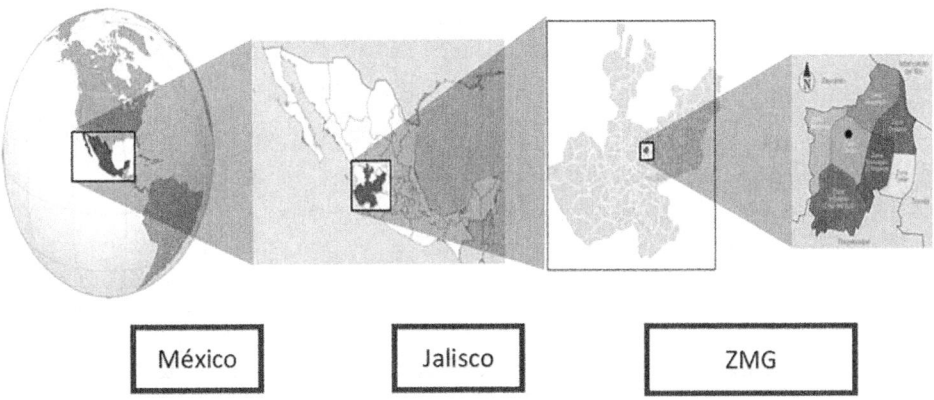

Figure 28.2 Geographic location: ZMG Zona Metropolitana de Guadalajara, Jalisco, México.
Source: (Mendieta-Izquierdo, 2015).

As noted earlier, the *mayate* is a man who engages in virile prostitution. The object of sale and desire is his virility as manifested through his body and masculine appearance. This is an appearance that clients seek and to which they assign value. The *mayate* is the macho man who is generally the active penetrator who exchanges sex for money, who sells his masculinity and virility to other men. He is also associated with drugs and alcohol. The *mayate*'s body allows for the realization and materialization of all the aspects that make up what it means to be a *mayate*, as the following interviewees make clear:

> A *mayate* spends his time giving sex to gays. He goes around fucking the *jotitos*.[6] That is what the *mayates* call them here in Mexico. They put that thing into shit, right? [Smiling] That is what *mayates* are for. You know what a *mayate* is? They are the ones that come out of the cow shit. So, based on that, that's what one is like. . .
>
> *Superman, 28 years old*

> The *mayate* always does this, day and night, just this, you understand me? The *mayate* is a guy who uses drugs, gets drunk, uses money for other things. . . . A *mayate* is a guy, a guy that, that explores and doesn't give a crap if the guy is taken or not, you understand me? He goes with gays or non-gays or bisexuals, right? A *mayate* is a *mayate*, he does just this, one hundred percent, for him, it's a business, for him, it's a job.
>
> *Batman, 25 years old*

> Well, here in Mexico, the little animal, the ones who go around in the shit. Well, since we go around in shit, supposedly we are getting it out. That's it! Get out shit.
>
> *Centella, 34 years old*

In short, the *mayate* is a man who sells sexual services to his clients, using the masculinity represented through his body. He is generally the active male penetrator, but not always. The *mayate* can also be penetrated:

> The *mayate* no longer wants to penetrate *jotos*, now the *joto* has to penetrate the *mayate*, here. That's the issue here now. Well, I have a friend who was telling me that. Because. . . [eats] because he likes gays, he is attracted to them, or he likes gay penises.
>
> *Batman, 28 years old*

The *mayate* can present as heterosexual or bisexual (a category that can come up short in explaining sexual complexity among this group of men). Because his sexual practices can be diverse, he experiences a type of *sexual existence*[7] without borders.

Characteristics of the mayate

This section presents some of the elements that are considered specific to a *mayate* who works in the plaza: identifying what one wants to be; being handsome; having charisma, patience, prudence, and vision; being intelligent, being honest with oneself and one's clients, and being a good person; having a large penis; wearing simple but clean clothes; not being afraid to have sex with another man; being responsible for one's health; and taking medical precautions.

1 Identifying oneself

Usually, the *mayate* is the active male penetrator, the *macho* who does the penetrating. As we've seen, some *mayates* engage in *inter*, which means both penetrating and being penetrated. Sexual practices and the role that the *mayates* assumes in them do not condition their identity and sexual orientation:

> Yeah, so, identifying yourself, what you want to be, active, passive, inter. Because there are all kinds with all kinds. [Smiling] Those who get 50 pesos are those who do everything or will have everything done to them. Yeah, whatever you want, it depends on each person's preference.
>
> *Centella, 34 years old*

2   Handsomeness

The term *guapetón* or handsome refers to certain characteristics that appeal to and attract clients. Attractive physical traits include being dark and thin, having short hair, not being effeminate, and being a subjectively good-looking young man:

> Here, a handsome boy is, well, yeah, yeah, you have to be handsome, right? To get the *jotitos*. [Laughter] Yeah, handsome!
>
> *Superman, 28 years old*

3   Charisma

Charisma is essential for establishing initial contact and sustaining a conversation that allows the client to trust the *mayate*, who through cheerfulness and flirting projects a rough, exaggerated, non-effeminate masculinity. This appearance is essential in the buying and selling of sexual services among virile prostitutes:

> Charisma, being cheerful with them, being cool, behaving well with them and getting them to trust you primarily because, first you chat with them, then they trust you and see if you're cool, they trust you and they go with you, otherwise they don't talk to you anymore and turn around and look at someone else, do you understand me?
>
> *Batman, 25 years old*

> Being kind of flirty, that's what a lot of people like, like *cholos*, you could almost say that 50% or 40% of the men like rough *cholos* that look really tough, really masculine because they don't want them to be very effeminate, they want them look like, wow! Like with a voice like this, and they're like that, like, they're like that, it's like that's what excites them and you have to have all the things and if you have them, you end up convincing someone.
>
> *Captain America, 26 years old*

4   Patience

Prostitution in public places such as plazas or parks requires a level of patience among those who engage in it. In the particular case of *Plaza Tapatía*, patience usually involves sitting and waiting on benches, window frames, or stairs until a potential client approaches or, instead, going and

Figure 28.3 Mayates awaiting their customers.
Source: Toño Ceja. (Mendieta-Izquierdo, 2015).

sitting on each bench and/or walking around the plaza in search of clients. Figure 28.3 shows *mayates* awaiting their customers. Waiting and searching require a great deal of patience:

Yes! It's not easy! Because you have to wait, you have to be very patient, it is like when a fisherman goes out to fish, he goes fishing for fish, so he gets into the water of the lagoon, takes out his rod and casts the lure, right? And he's there for hours and hours, sitting, waiting for the hours to pass and not a single fish bites, he's just there, he daydreams or reads a magazine or listens to the radio and then suddenly he feels a tug on the lure, right? [Coughs] And I was telling you that when you feel the tug, there's a fish biting and now it depends whether the fish is a big one and you go with that one, you don't need to cast again, but if it's a small fish, you have to wait for another. It's the same here. If a fish or a person comes along that has a way to help you out. Let them help you out! They may have dough. So you do it with that one and that's it. Now, if one wants to follow someone, that's up to them. And if you get a person with not a lot of money, who is poorer, well, I don't have to seek them out anymore! So that's how it is. The big fish! That would be like 500, 600, more or less. Those are very rare. [Smiling] For fishermen, too, big fish are very rare, but they do come!

Captain America, 26 years old

5   Prudence and Vision

Engaging in prostitution in a public place requires a certain level of prudence and vision, a different way of looking at the world, to identify and recognize men who are seeking sexual services and to avoid making mistakes. This skill is acquired over time in the plaza by relating with peers or simply meeting and sustaining the gazes of potential clients. In this context, eye contact an important initial step in approaching a client:

A lot of vision, seeing people, whether they are really there for that because you can also be wrong and get into trouble because it is also a public place, it's public, lots of families go and there are many men that are not part of the scene but are walking around, so sometimes you watch them wondering if they're gays, they might reply, "What are you looking at?" and there's a quarrel, yes, what are you looking at me for, or "Do I owe you something, or what?" So you have to be very careful and with a lot of vision, to see who is here for that. So, what one has to do is sit and watch the people who are walking around and then you detect who.

Captain America, 26 years old

Yes! To be accessible to people, more or less to figure out who is gay, who is a *mayate* and, well, over time, you start to figure out who is who.

Centella, 34 years old

6   Planning

Planning refers to things that must be considered and done before arriving at a hotel once the transaction is established. *Mayates* must plan and consider each and every one of the activities that they will perform with the client, the sexual activities that will take place, and the boundaries that will be established:

More than anything, intelligence, knowing what you are going to do before arriving at the hotel, so that you already know what you're going to do before you get there, you have to already be thinking, what am I going to do. When you are entering the hotel, you already know what you are going to do, you arrive and take off your clothes, you bathe, you lie down, you act like a statue and let them do whatever they want to you. Of course, always respecting how far it goes and that's it. Uh, uh, what you agreed on before, before kissing. In my case, it's: I arrive, I take off my clothes, I bathe, I lie down on the bed, I rest, without touching them, they touch me, uh, well, uh, I move my mouth to one side [turns face to one side] because sometimes they even try to steal kisses from you, stolen, sometimes it feels like that and they get you right to the right point and, and [smiling] damn! [laughter] and then that's it until they finish, and, and. . . [coughing].

Captain America, 26 years old

7   Being an honest, good person

Mayates generally do not commit acts of delinquency such as robbing or hitting clients, behavior that would generate mistrust among clients. However, some *mayates* do engage in such behavior, generating a contrast between the stereotyped image of the *mayate* and what may occur in reality:

> Being honest with yourself and with people; um, noble, I think, very much regardless of whether you use drugs or drink or not. Um, well, being good to others, it doesn't matter if you use drugs or drink, but don't meddle in the lives of others.
>
> . . .
>
> Yes, yes, yes! Be a good person. Well, I recommend, not doing stupid things, robbing or beating people. Because that way you get more. Yes, look at me, I don't do it! Sometimes I'm dying of hunger . . . because people don't want to go with you, because of those jerks.
>
> *Centella, 34 years old*

8   Large penis

Mayate is synonymous with virility and masculinity, which is also projected in penis size. The penis is synonymous with manliness, strength, and power. It is a part of the geography of the body that is commercialized and takes on singular importance in the *mayate's* sexual relations for money:

> Being good, and you especially have to have a good penis. Because if you come out with a dick like this, like 10 centimeters, no way! Well, it has to be 20 centimeters and up. Because these guys want only large penises, they only want large penises. . . . All of them. And tell me, what's yours like? Because if you say it's like this and then you come out with one like this? [gesturing with hands] Show it to me? I mark it for them like this on my pants, and, Oh man, let's go, let's go! [laughter] Because I also have a big one, mine I swear measures like 22 centimeters, hey. And just like that, they come running.
>
> *Superman, 28 years old*

9   Wearing simple but clean clothes

The way in which the bodily image is projected is important for achieving success with clients. Looking *cholón*[8] can have an effect, and dressing *pepón* [sexy] is related to bodily cleanliness, a situation that can affect whether clients approach a *mayate*. For this reason, *mayates* wear simple yet clean clothes; which makes clients more likely to approach them. However, clients do look for a diversity of appearances:

> Normal, tight, looking like a normal guy, easygoing, because if you look *cholón* to them, no, nobody likes you. Yeah, like this, with this cleft chin, and they tell me, don't look like a *malandrín* [scoundrel]! I'm just like this, like one of those lousy *malandrinotes* [scoundrels]! And not me, I just like to go around like this, but I am very easygoing, that's true, I am very easygoing.
>
> *Superman, 28 years old*

> Oh, well, well-dressed, well-perfumed, no, no, no! Seize the heat of the moment quicker, yes! Well-dressed means like dressing for a wedding or like for a part or something,

well-dressed, well-perfumed! Because you've already grabbed their attention, and if they don't see you clean, well perfumed, they may approach you and then just stare at you, right?

Aquaman, 28 years old

10   Not being afraid to have sex with another man

From a bodily perspective, when carrying out sexual practices with clients, the *mayate* should not be concerned, although this situation generates tension and concern among some for not adhering to heteronormative practices, a situation that is resolved through the use of the imagination and help from heterosexual pornographic films. Homoerotic contact is established within an economic framework because the discourse of the *mayates'* sexual identity does not affect their own identity, sexual orientation, and masculinity. For them, it is clear that the work is performed for money and is part of their sexual existence:

Well they love it! They like men's asses, that's it, in fact, they're not even gay, they do it for money. So, like for me, saying I do it for fun, because I love putting my penis in, not true! That's what it is to be a *mayate*.

Superman, 28 years old

Well, to not be afraid of fucking another dude because, what else—[smiling] What else?

Centella, 34 years old

11   Responsibility for health; taking medical precautions

The perception of a body that is susceptible to illness and exposed to constant risks, particularly sexually transmitted diseases, suggests the need to take medical precautions and specific HIV tests. *Mayates* express a concern for their health and the perception that they maintain a healthy body:

Well, what I would recommend is getting your blood test, I mean, it's not a requirement, but so that you are controlled. I do it. . . [takes from his pocket proof of two medical tests]. I like to be well.

Centella, 34 years old

I went alone, I didn't tell anyone, anyone. That is, they told me, do the test here, at this place, like this, like this, like this, and yeah.

Spiderman, 26 years old

G: They tell me that in Juarez they give out condoms and the test for free. What motivated you to take the test?

D: Curiosity, more than anything. Curiosity. I can calmly say that I don't have anything. . .

Hulk, 19 years old

F: I get myself tested every 3 months, I have always done it. Over in Vallarta! I go to [Social] Security!

Flash, 24 years old

What are clients seeking? The vast majority of those who solicit sexual services from *mayates* are men with diverse identities and sexual orientations who are seeking sexual release and the satisfaction of their sexual needs with men with a very masculine appearance:

> What do they look for in a *mayate*? Well, as I said: maybe [some are seeking] a release, but not others, for others it's their vice, assuming it's a vice, the penis! It's like, Oh! I want penis! I tell you, because I have friends that give it for free and do like it, these are guys who are really addicted to cock, that can't live without it. They pay and they pay some more, but why? Because, stay a little longer! Because they are people who aren't seeking a release, but rather, for them it's like a vice, they want cock all the time. That's a vice, more than anything! Those who come around looking for pleasure, don't talk to me about your past, don't ask me what they're after! There are others who do that, clients that are like, "How tall are you?" "Where are you from?" "What do you do?" "Why do you charge so much?" "Is this really worth it?" To all those questions, you're like, "Hey man, are you here to fuck, or what are you here for?" [smiling]
>
> *Aquaman, 28 years old*

> What they like, no? The [lowering voice] dick, that's what they like. Cock! No?
>
> *Robin, 19 years old*

> For me to do it to them [mimicking by making hands into fists and moving them towards abdomen].
>
> *Centella, 34 years old*

> Well, what they like, for one to have relations with them, for them to have anal sex and oral sex because they like it and it is something they inherited, since they were children they were abused and believed that this was their path and that is why they chose this path, and they see a man and they like a man, so they want it, no matter how yours is. . . . You understand me? That is, however long it is, your dick. Many people look for big ones, many people look for medium ones or for you to have, for you to know how to have sex or know how to impassion them, or know how to humiliate them, make them feel like women. . .
>
> *Batman, 28 years old*

Note that clients are perceived under a bicategorical, exclusive, and complementary heterosexual gender system that implies a perception of orientation, desires, and practices (Córdova Plaza, 2005). For this reason, they are denominated as deviant or abnormal and associated with gender reversal and passivity. Note that the *mayates* quoted here mention that many people want the *mayate* to "know how to have sex," "humiliate them," and "make them feel like women."

Interaction with the client

The way in which the *mayate* relates to his client are particular to prostitution in the plaza and can differ from other practices of street prostitution. In this context, *cotorreo* is the word that men use when they are seeking sex with other men:

> *Cotorreo*: having relations with men. That is the word here.
>
> *Batman, 25 years old*

1   The gaze

As described by Carrier (2003), body language and the gaze or eye contact is the mechanism by which initial contact is established. The gaze and eye contact are the first steps toward the paid sexual encounter:

> With the gaze, and if someone approaches me, well, great; if not, fine. Right? At the same time, I don't go around doing this, and well, if something comes up, then I do it. Just like you saw me sitting here and approached me and that's it.
>
> *Flash, 24 years old*

> Come, boy, come! Like, they send you signals with their eyes or stare here at your penis. That is a green light, that is a signal for you to come closer to them.
>
> *Superman, 28 years old*

> Raising your eyebrow, winking, making a gesture that's not too rude, that says, "should we or shouldn't we?" That says, "ooh, why are you winking at me?" "you sly guy, what time!" Assuming that they are gay, right? Because there are many that aren't; they go by and look at you and that's it, and it's like, what, are you gay or not? And when they say that to you, usually, "no, man, I'm not gay, I saw you go by!" "And why did you wink at me?"
>
> *Aquaman, 28 years old*

> They stare at you for a long time and because, uh, they stare at another guy and the other guy is also involved in this, so, like, was he staring at this guy? Like if they're going around looking for something, so you walk right by him and if he is attracted to you, he stares at you, and you stare at him from afar and you make a gesture with your head from afar, like, what's up, like that [moving head] and if he responds with the same answer, yeah! That's it! It means yes, so yeah, it depends on how you can, you can reach them and begin a conversation.
>
> *Captain America, 26 years old*

2   Initial conversation

After the gaze, the initial conversation is the next step. Either the client or the *mayate* must take the first step to initiate a conversation. There is no rule. It is a practice that is learned through experience, through surreptitious experiences in the plaza, and it is a situation that can lead to misunderstandings. It is a process of consecutive approaches, a sort of gallantry. There is also a differentiation between new clients and those who are already known. Once verbal contact is established, the questions differ from the final objective. The weather, the time, any situation is the pretext to continue with the encounter; they form a part of the process to continue the *cotorreo*. Otherness and how others see one are important during this phase of contact:

> Um, chit-chat, usually it is the same, the same, if the client does not come closer to you, you go to him. I come over, I say hello, I ask him the time, how is he doing, what is he doing—oh, well, *cotorreando*! He starts to say, "Where do you work?" "What do you do?" I'm here *cotorreando*, that is the word for it here, *cotorreando*! Either they approach, you go their way, or you take the initiative, um, you go, you go directly to the hotel, you go

directly to chit-chat about how big it is, if you do it well, I like it to be done like this, like this or like that.

Batman, 25 years old

You go up to them, if there's a guy, a *jotito* sitting there, you sit next to them and, "hey, what time is it?" Knowing you have a watch! Sorry, what's up! Right? Oh, thanks, what a nice afternoon. Right? And look [looking up] it's going to rain! Right? You're trying to get talking, and among the chit-chat, [determine] are you part of the scene or not? Are you *cotorreando* or not? And then they bowl you over; "I'm not looking for *cotorreo*!" There are some that aren't; they just come to mess around. New people!

Aquaman, 28 years old

Cotorreando, a *cotorreo*, starting [so that I can] go for breakfast or go eat. . . . No, well, you arrive and sit on a bench and since you're something new, it doesn't take long for a guy who is not from here to come up to you, "hey, you're not from here, right?" "What's up?" And, "do you suck, bite or chew?" "So, do you fuck or what?" I mean, it's a saying. "Do you fuck?" "Yeah, how much?" Since you're new to them. They see that you're new. "So what's up?" "What's yours like?" "No, it's 19." "Is it thick or thin?" "Normal," you say, more or less.

Centella, 34 years old

You usually start by saying, do you have a cigarette? Could you tell me the time? Or, I think I know you! If the other person wants something, they play along. Oh, yes, I think I recognize you too. And what's up and what do you do, and blah, blah, blah! Until the moment arrives. Because both play dumb. They play dumb! They are not dumb, they know, they are like, let's see who wins the game, it's like a game, let's see who wins. And if someone, uh, that is paying wants to go with you and if you're cautious and smart, you're going to convince them, otherwise they might say, no, you know what? Maybe another time! But if one is talkative and very intelligent, you keep them guessing, you keep them guessing and you keep them involved in your game until they say, all right, let's go!

Captain America, 26 years old

3   The "hook"

What drives virile prostitution is the marketing of virility. Masculinity is embodied and reduced to a corporeal level in the penis. It is the hook, the lure with which to attract and maintain clients, the motive and reason for male prostitution in *Plaza Tapatía*:

Well, you know, I have seen a lot of things here, I have seen that many people grab their thing" [Making reference to genitals, touching genitals].

Flash, 24 years old

Yes! What's up, man! Yeah, that's it! And they look at your penis. Later on, you say! This dude wants dick! Come on! And then you come up to them with more certainty, what up, son, what? Yeah, fresh today! [laughing] Yeah, fresh today! And then they say to you, well how big are you? And it's like that. No, well, I'm this big. And they don't believe you, man. They don't believe me that I measure 20, 22 centimeters. No, no way, so skinny and so short, how could you be packing such a hog? And I tell them, primo, it's true! I show them through my fucking pants, oh, yeah, man! Right?

. . .

Sometimes yes, and other times flaccid. They even say to you, even flaccid, show it to me, it's enough for a real connoisseur [laughing] for a real connoisseur, even if it's flaccid, you can tell if it's big. And it's true there are guys who have it like this even flaccid [gesturing with hands], and mine is like this flaccid [gesturing with hands again] And they say, oh, man, we'll see later. I tell them, didn't you see it well, that it's flaccid? No, later you'll see that it's big, let's go, like that, man! I tell you, that's how they've gone with me to fuck.

Superman, 28 years old

Well, almost the majority do it, I can stand it up, this one walks by and I grab it. That's it, like, that's a *mayate*!

Aquaman, 28 years old

You get hard there in the moment so that they can see it through your pants. I do it regularly, and it's like, oh! [making an expression of surprise]. The hook, that's the hook. Yes! Yes! I, I arouse myself so that it gets erect and I show how long it is so that you can see its size, and how thick it is, and they walk by, damn!

Centella, 34 years old

4   The agreement: the rate and sexual practices

The *mayate*'s body is assigned an economic value depending on the sexual practices that are to be performed, on the use or lack of use of a condom, and on the use or nonuse of drugs. In prostitution in public places, each individual establishes his rate:

No, sir! I'll do whatever you want! But how much are you going to charge me? No, I'll charge you three hundred pesos! Then, if he accepts, he says, no, less, two fifty! Well, all right, he takes you to the hotel and you begin to have relations with him.

. .

The client asks and whatever the client asks you, you have to answer. Why? So that you can reach an agreement with him, regarding money as well as the sexual relations.

. . .

Whatever the client asks for. Yes, up to a certain point. With the active ones, there's a certain limit, with the passive ones it's anything, including kissing and caressing, sucking each other but here no, here he sucks your member and you penetrate and so on. You caress him, you grab his chest, his butt, and so on. Yes?

Batman, 25 years old

Um, How long do you last? Um, do you kiss? Do you caress? Do you humiliate? How much do you charge? No, this much! Can it be cheaper? If he wants to and the money is worked out, then it's set.

G: And how much?

Two hundred. Caressing, humiliation, penetration, oral sex, kissing if you want. Well, kissing, I'll tell you, that depends on the person, too, not everyone is very nice to kiss.

Centella, 34 years old

445

How old am I, and, what's my name? and, um. . . . Where do I live, and . . . what do I like to do? Uh, I like to caress, kiss and all that, um, I like to get oral sex [lowering voice]. I like to get oral sex and all that, and that's it, well, if they want penetration, then penetration also, that's also what motivates them.

Robin, 19 years old

In summary: Sending signals with one's gaze, the initial conversation, the hook, and the agreement are the aspects that constitute the process of what is known in Mexico as *cotorreo*. The way in which the encounter occurs is a two-way street, and the client and the offeror (*mayate*) can use different strategies. It is a game with different tactics in which the ultimate goal is sexual contact. The client and the *mayate* are in a constant search to establish *cotorreo*, the difference between them being their ultimate interest; the former seeks a man to satisfy his sexual needs, and the latter seems only to seek money, without thinking about his broader sexual existence, which can provide him with diverse sensations, including enjoyment, pleasure, satisfaction, disgust, and rejection, situations that validate the work of the *mayate* and construct his masculinity.

Notes

1 The term *virile prostitution* was coined by Néstor Perlonger (1993, p. 6) to establish the difference in the sexual services carried out by *miché*, who are male sex workers who present themselves to clients with an exaggerated masculinity, making it possible to safeguard precisely that aspect of masculinity. It is different from sexual services provided by other types of homosexual prostitutes—for example, transvestites, who charge for their exaggerated representation of femininity (Perlonger, 1993). In Mexico, the term *miché* is not used; the term *mayate* is used instead. Assuming a dominant model of sexuality, it allows for the understanding of bisexuality as a result of a powerful and irrepressible male sexual impulse (Crawford, Kippax, & Prestage, 1996).

2 The *mayate*: Etymologically, the word *mayate* comes from the *Náhuatl* (*mayatl*) language. The Royal Academy of the Spanish Language defines *mayate* as "a beetle of different colors and regular flight." In Honduras and Mexico, it is also recognized colloquially as meaning a homosexual man (*Diccionario de la lengua Española*, 20th ed., 2014). In gay subculture, *mayate* means a low-income man who is an active penetrator and who provides homoerotic encounters for money. According to Carrier (2003), the word means "a young, macho, heterosexual man who has occasional sexual contact that is anal insertive in nature with anal-receptive and effeminate men of any age" (p. 12).

3 *Chichifos* are "young people who receive money in a systematic way for having sex with other men." Also, they "may have the connotation of being unsavory" (Carrier, 2003, p. 12). These men frequently establish relations with other men, receive financial or material gifts in exchange for sexual exclusivity, and are companions.

4 *Chacales* is a term popularly used to refer to a man who has very masculine characteristics and looks indigenous, although not reaching a level of excessive masculinity (Monsiváis, 1998).

5 *Plaza Tapatía*, in Guadalajara, Jalisco, Mexico, is located in a central area of the city and hosts multiple street vendors and a huge number of people and tourists. People are generally seen sitting on benches, and whole families go there for entertainment. The plaza and the surrounding shops are frequented by the general population. The plaza is ideal for wandering, as it is removed from city traffic and surrounded by several pedestrian walkways. It has a diversity of shops and informal commerce, and it is a place where countless street vendors and urban recreation activities converge. This study focuses on the areas of the *Plaza Tapatía* in which *mayates* are found, particularly Paseo Degollado, located in the center of Guadalajara behind the Degollado Theater, between Avenida Hidalgo and Paseo Morelos.

6 *Joto* is a colloquial term in Mexico used to refer to a homosexual man.

7 An individual's *sexual existence* is understood as "a dimension of their existence that involves anatomical/physiological aspects, psychic processes, and behaviors. It is a bio/psychic/social dimension of the individual, involved in the experience of pleasure and erotic desire" (Núñez-Noriega, 1999, p. 35). The notion of a sexual existence is preferred in this work to that of sexual identity because a sexual existence conceives of the subject's sex life as a dynamic state that is permanently being defined and transformed, distancing it from the hegemonic model of static, bicategorical sexuality. The term is described by

Núñez-Noriega (1999) in his book, *Sexo entre varones: Poder y resistencia en el campo sexual* [*Sex Between Men: Power and Resistance in the Sexual Arena*].

8 Colloquial term for a man careless in his appearance and dress.

Bibliography

Atkins, M., & Laing, M. (2012). Walking the beat and doing business: Exploring spaces of male sex work and public sex. *Sexualities, 15*(5–6), 622–643.

Boden, D. M. (2007). Alienation of sexuality in male erotic dancing. *Journal of Homosexuality, 53*(1–2), 129–152.

Carrier, J. (2003). *De los otros: Intimidad y homosexualidad entre los hombres del occidente y el noroeste de México.* México: Pandora.

Córdova-Plaza, R. (2005). Vida en los márgenes: la experiencia corporal como anclaje identitario entre sexoservidores de la ciudad de Xalapa, Veracruz. *Cuicuilco, 12*(34), 217–238.

Crawford, J., Kippax, S., & Prestage, G. (1996). Not gay, not bisexual, but polymorphously sexually active: Male bisexuality and AIDS in Australia. In P. Aggleton (Compiler), *Bisexualities and AIDS: International perspectives* (pp. 44–60). London: Taylor and Francis.

DeMarco, J. (2007). Power and control in gay strip clubs. *Journal of Homosexuality, 53*(1–2), 111–127.

Diccionario de la lengua Española (20th ed.). (2014). Retrieved from https://www.rae.es/obras-academicas/diccionarios/diccionario-de-la-lengua-espanola

Gomezjara, F., Barrera, E., & Pérez, N. (1978). *Sociología de la prostitución.* México: Ediciones Nueva Sociología.

Jackson, J. D. (2007). The closing of Atlantis. *Journal of Homosexuality, 53*(1–2), 153–172.

Kaye, K. (2007). Sex and the unspoken in male street prostitution. *Journal of Homosexuality, 53*(1–2), 37–73.

Lamas, M. (1996). *Violencia simbólica, mujeres y prostitución.* México: Plaza y Valdés.

Liguori, A. L., & Aggleton, P. (1998). Aspectos del comercio sexual masculino en la ciudad de México. *Debate Feminista, 9*(18), 152–185.

Manzelli, H., & Pecheny, M. (2002). Prevención del VIH/SIDA en hombres que tienen sexo con hombres. In C. Cáceres, M. Pecheny, & V. Terto (Compliers), *SIDA y sexo entre hombres en América Latina: Vulnerabilidades, fortalezas, y propuestas para la acción—Perspectivas y reflexiones desde la salud pública, las ciencias sociales y el activismo* (pp. 103–138). Lima: UPCH/ONUSIDA.

MCouns, D. L., & Minichiello, V. (2007). Exploring the interpersonal relationships in street-based male sex work: Results from an Australian qualitative study. *Journal of Homosexuality, 53*(1–2), 75–110.

Mendieta-Izquierdo, G. (2015). *Prostitución viril: un estudio fenomenológico del cuerpo.* Bogotá: Fundación Universitaria del Área Andina.

Monsiváis, C. (1998). La noche popular: Paseos, riesgos, júbilos, necesidades orgánicas, tensiones, especies antiguas y recientes, descargas anímicas en forma de coreografías. *Debate Feminista, 9*(18), 55–73.

Núñez-Noriega, G. (1999). *Sexo entre varones. Poder y resistencia en el campo sexual.* Ciudad de México: UNAM, El Colegio de Sonora.

Perlonger, N. (1993). *La prostitución masculina.* Buenos Aires: La Urraca.

Schrimshaw, E., Downing, M., & Siegel, K. (2013). Sexual venue selection and strategies for concealment of same-sex behavior among non-disclosing men who have sex with men and women. *Journal of Homosexuality, 60*(1), 120–145.

Part VII
Male sex work in Europe

29

Male sex work in Italy

Male hierarchies, honor, and sexual status in the South

Cirus Rinaldi

A short history of male sex work and homosexuality in southern Italy from ancient times to present day

Little study has been done on male sex workers in Italy (Barnao, 2004; Ferraris, 2004). Much of the published research broaches the topic only in passing, often blurring its boundaries with an investigation of sexual abuse, exploitation, and trafficking of minors or with the study of impersonal sexual relations between men in public places (where monetary exchange does not usually occur.) Several factors greatly hinder the study of male sex work in Italy, including a delay in the sociological analysis of sexuality; an emphasis on bio-psycho-medical approaches, rather than sociological approaches, to the study of sexuality; and the stigmatization of researchers who deal with sexuality-related topics, which are usually studied in the context of deviant behavior. In fact, some scholars' interest in male sex work is very recent (Oliviero, Russo, & Zaami, 2010; Rinaldi, 2012, 2013a, 2013b, 2014, 2017, 2018).

To consider the specific gender regimes that have developed in Southern Italy, we must briefly discuss the main historical developments and the relationships among homosexuality, masculinity, and male sex work today. Male prostitution in Southern Italy has an ancient history dating back to the classical age. In that period, as Michel Foucault has pointed out, the voluntary renunciation of the prestige associated with the male role was considered repugnant (Dover, 1978; Foucault, 1990). Traditional ideals about masculinity dominated thought and behavior, with a dichotomy between culturally constructed "feminine," passive roles and "masculine," active roles. Active agents clearly included adult and free men. Passive actors were the objects of pleasure, including women, boys, and slaves, who did not belong in the group of free men. The Romans maintained a strict and sharp dichotomy based on insertive and receptive sexual roles, leading men to assume a dominant sexual role with regard to women and other men (especially non-Roman individuals: slaves who could also be "used" sexually), in private as well as in public. The *impudicus*, who played the "passive" role during the sexual intercourse, was much despised. Freeborn men did not include sex workers, who were usually recruited from lower classes, foreigners, and slaves (Boswell, 2005). This situation mirrored economic disparity and created conditions for sex workers that are consistent with modern times (Friedman, 2014).

By the late nineteenth and early twentieth century, many commentators described Southern Italy as an erotic paradise for homosexual-identified persons. In a pamphlet entitled *Capri und die Homosexuellen* (Berlin, 1902), Dr. A. Sper argued that the islanders' heightened sexuality was deeply related to climate and geography. (In similar terms, Richard Burton, in the appendix to his translation of the *Arabian Nights* [1886], hypothesized the existence of the Sotadic Zone, a geographic area that encompassed parts of Southern Europe, North Africa, Asia, and South America in which "pederasty" was prevalent among the indigenous people.) According to Sper, environmental conditions made Italians sexually mature by the age of 12 (whereas Germans became mature between the age of 15 and 17). Foreigners visiting Southern Italy eroticized and exoticized Italian boys and men, who were thought to start playing sexual games and to become involved in juvenile (homo)sexuality rather earlier than their European peers (Aldrich, 1993).

The Grand Tour also offered many opportunities to enjoy classical beauty and museums as well as busboys, beggars, and fishers. This exotic fascination was also associated with "othering," social typing, and scientific observation. In Oscar Wilde's letters about his sexual encounters in Naples and Palermo, in Baron von Gloeden's pictures of young native models taken in Taormina, and in many other accounts, visitors to Southern Italy itemized Italian men's traits and features (handsome faces, muscled and firm bodies, dark skin and eyes) and developed fantasies about Italian males as complaisant sexual partners with specific physical and personality traits. These men were usually younger and poorer than their foreign admirers.

With the introduction of the Napoleonic Code in Italy between 1804 and 1809, "unnatural" acts were decriminalized, with the law enforced only against those who had sex with minors or offended the public morality. However, the rise of fascism brought a new view of homosexuality, which came to be considered an anomaly and a threat to morality and the gender order. Homosexuality was also associated with delinquency and criminal activity, including prostitution. After the unification of Italy, the fascists refused to make homosexuality illegal. The new penal code, the Codice Rocco, included no specific law forbidding homosexual relations, because this very provision would have implicitly recognized the existence of such a "nefarious vice," which was inconsistent with assumptions about fascist virility. Nonetheless, many homosexuals were convicted for indecent exposure and enticement; individuals were put on trial not so much for committing a crime or breaking the law but rather because their very nature threatened standards of masculine virility and predominant heterosexual norms (Benadusi, 2005).

Partly due to the influence of Cesare Lombroso (1835–1909) and his classification of criminal types, Italian police often arrested homosexual prostitutes, who were often minors. As a result, the public came to equate homosexuality with crime and immorality. The *pederasti passivi* (that is, homosexuals playing a "passive" role) were more harshly prosecuted than the *pederasti attivi* (that is, homosexuals playing an "active" role). While the latter played the traditional masculine role, the former abdicated that role, and in the eyes of their contemporaries, they appeared more similar to women than to men. In fact, many positivist scientists who were following the criminal theories of Cesare Lombroso used to consider passive pederasts natural prostitutes, associating them with female individuals and addressing them with female adjectives: *le prostitute masculine* (Dalla Volta, 1929; Di Tullio, 1927).

Lombrosian positivism "scientifically" sanctioned the connection between homosexuality and innate criminality (Lombroso, 1906). The main scientific discourses of the early twentieth century saw homosexuals as "perversely" criminal subjects because they predominantly "enticed boys." Thus homosexuality became a vexing issue for society and children; a risk in prisons, hospitals, and colleges; and a threat in everyday life. At the same time, homosexuals were viewed as natural victims because their moral disposition and pathologies favored the onset of other "diseases" (Messina, 1953; see also Dennis, 2017). Within this political and scientific climate, legitimized by the criminological and medical discourse, arose one of the most pressing concerns regarding homosexuality: male prostitution, stereotypically linked to homosexuality up to the present day (Rinaldi, 2012).

In the early twentieth century, following the teachings of Salvatore Ottolenghi, the founder of the School of Scientific Police in Rome and a pupil of Lombroso, police officers were trained in the physical and psychological identification of the "perverts" and the "sexually inverted" according to their tattoos and their way of speaking, walking, and dressing. The passive homosexual (the *cinaedus*, a synonym for *impudicus*) selling his sexual services is regarded as someone who relinquishes masculinity, mainly because he behaves in a way that is considered *naturally* feminine. In particular, perverts and the sexually inverted—the "active homosexuals" and the "passive homosexuals" (*cinaedi*), respectively—were classified as "habitual offenders of the libidinous type" alongside prostitutes, or "habitual sexual offenders of professional type" (Ottolenghi, 1907, p. 117).

In the transition from fascism to a democracy in Italy, dominated by the Christian Democratic Party, we can detect no discontinuity in repressive policies. An active vice squad and zealous judges united their efforts in order to curb practically any public expression of homosexuality (Pini, 2017). The repression of homosexuality became particularly strict in the late 1950s, when the control of public morality intersected with specific moments in the development of international relations. As a result of specific Interpol-issued police regulations, Italy initiated a process of (official) repression of homosexuality, following what had already happened as other countries attempted to purge homosexuals from state institutions: The police patrolled and raided public gardens, adult movie theatres, and public restrooms, eventually identifying nearly 23,000 homosexuals between 1947 and 1972 (Petrosino, 2017).

All the medical-legal and criminological literature of the time expresses concern with regard to minors and young people in general, accompanied by a focus on male homosexuality because, as reported in a popular, influential handbook of that time, "feminine [homosexuality] (tribadism, sapphism, lesbianism) generally occurs more discreetly." The same literature also strengthens the idea of "homosexual-as-enticer-and-crime-instigator." Although homosexuality was not in itself a crime, "it may give occasion to indecency, lewd behavior, sexual assault, and sexual offenses in general: more in particular, it paves the way to blackmail and crimes leading to bodily harm and murder" (Franchini & Introna, 1961, p. 544). We find the same types of concerns in the sociological research of the period. There, homosexuality is framed within delinquent activity, because homosexual practices are associated with the prostitution performed by young "racialized" men—that is, immigrants coming to a large extent from Southern Italy. Because of their own marginality, these young men were forced to work as prostitutes, thereby engaging in antisocial conduct and committing a crime that is not exactly traditional (that is, not "typically" masculine) (Bertolini, 1964).

Similarly, some writers feared the risk of "morbid epidemic" and "psychic contamination" with regard to the presence of homosexuals in detention facilities (Ferracuti & Palmieri, 1988, p. 236; Bolino & De Deo, 1970, p. 42). These writers portrayed homosexuals as people who, in order to satisfy their urges, are corruptors par excellence of respectable or defenseless subjects. Consequently, they considered homosexuality as a *crime factor* that is connected to "a considerable *social danger* as it is typical of criminal facts" (Messina, 1953, pp. 673–674, emphasis in original). In short, homosexuality creates crime (Ferracuti & Palmieri, 1988).

That said, the post-war years in Italy, especially the 1950s and 1960s, were in fact the "golden age" of homosexual sexual relations, during which young boys often offered sexual favors in exchange for money (Pini, 2003). Such was the life of the Roman *marchettari* (hustlers) described by Pier Paolo Pasolini (1922–1975) in his novel *Ragazzi di vita* (1955). The *marchettari* have been sentimentally defined as spontaneous prostitutes who had sex with men to make some quick money or who wanted to experiment with their own sexuality given the lack of available girls. (In compliance with the customs of the time, girls were seldom out on their own.) As homosexual liberation movements grew in Italy in the 1970s, homosexual male prostitution, along with other indirectly connected activities (pornography, modeling, and so on) flourished, and street prostitutes or call boys were free to advertise in publications targeted for the homosexual market. The period of sexual liberation and feminism coincided with the demise of spontaneous prostitution, and the young spontaneous *marchettari* gave way to marginalized young men, drug addicts, and immigrants coming from the South. Later, the sex work market in Italy opened up to non-EU citizens, primarily from North Africa, and then to young men from Eastern Europe.

Focusing on the most relevant scientific literature on the topic, we can list, following Aldrich (1993), the most significant social regulations concerning sex between men in the Mediterranean area and Southern Italy:

1   Society "allowed" homosexual relations between adult men and adolescents/young men as a normal part of the latter's sexual development
2   In exchange for sex, youth were usually given something in return (money, food, housing), and such "payments" were instrumental in removing guilt or neutralizing stigma
3   With regard to social status, relations were asymmetric (compared to their wealthier clients, Italian hustlers mostly came from working-class families; the same applies today to non-European sex workers)
4   Southern men (not unlike their counterparts coming from the Global South) were thought to have specific "racial" and behavioral characteristics that allegedly made them more prone to passion, exaggeration, sexual expression, crime, and deviance
5   Sexual intercourse is considered to be a naturalization process during which the virile individual enacts his traditional masculine natural role (performing anal penetration on the other man who, in return, is naturalized as a female or a "faggot")
6   A man must maintain his manly reputation and normative sexual status; if he is "active" and has a virile appearance, he can have sex with other men (adults or foreigners) without losing his virility
7   Those who perform a "passive" role in anal intercourse are considered a separate species and pigeonholed in a specific essentialist and racial category. They are seen as "faggots," "sick people," and "sinners" to be exploited, and their role is likened to that of an "available" female or a "social" female

Although active and passive roles in sex acts between men and boys have been replaced by a discrete homosexual identity grounded in a homosexual subculture, sexual conduct in male sex work mirrors some of those ancient and modern gender regimes and sexual stratifications.

Male sex work scenes and masculine reputation

Much of my research attempts to explain how male sex workers begin and continue their careers.[1] Figures 29.1 through 29.3 reproduce photos that I took during my field work. Here I show how young males involved in sex work neutralize stigmatizing labels (Goffman, 1963; Weitzer, 2018) and build and exchange sexual capital by creating hierarchies of bodies, practices, and desire.

The commercialization of the male body and the sale of homosexual sex have specific features compared to other types of sex work (such as escorting) (see Minichiello, Scott, &

Figure 29.1   Photo taken during fieldwork by Cirus Rinaldi.

Callander, 2013; Gagnon & Simon, 1974; Plummer, 1982). Because sex between men occurs within cognitive, interpretive, and cultural frames that define it as something "unnatural," sex between sex workers and clients can be explained by a series of motivations (Scott, Callander, & Minichiello, 2014) and sexual scripts. These scripts do not necessarily depend on the "nature" of the sex workers involved. Instead, they tend to identify clients as *predatory*, *insatiable*, and *depraved*. In short, the scripts prevent male sex workers from identifying with the cultural enemy (namely, "the faggot" client), allowing them perform dramatizations of masculinity and sexuality that help them maintain their masculine identity.

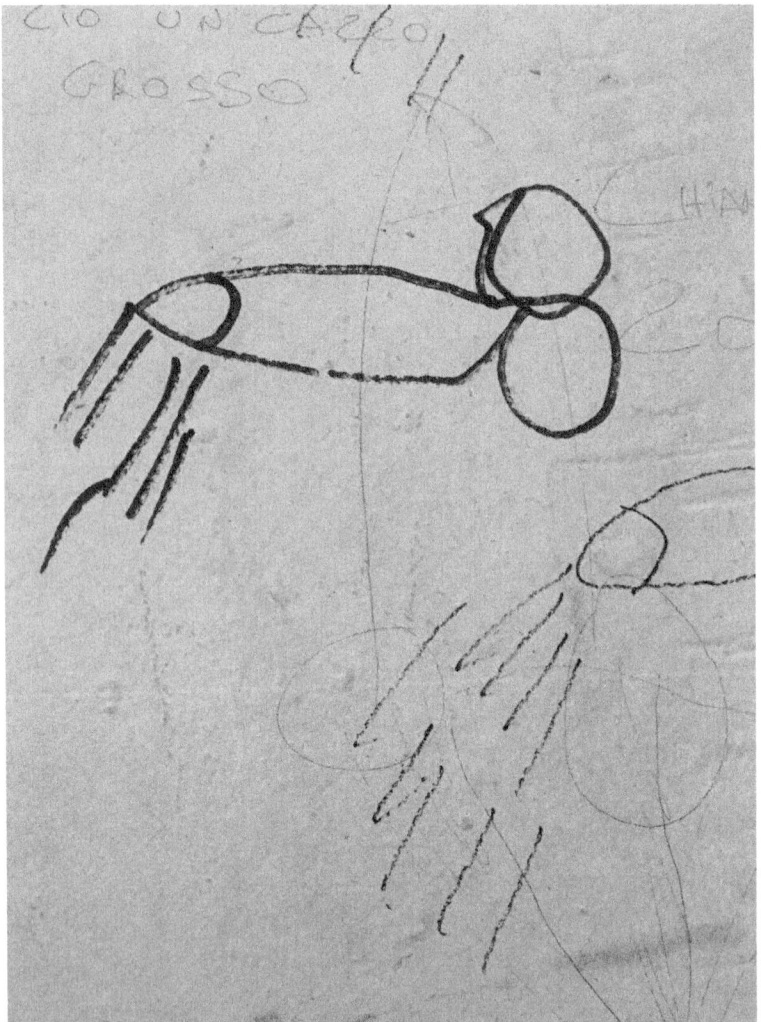

Figure 29.2   Photo taken during fieldwork by Cirus Rinaldi.

For Italian male sex workers, being a public sex worker, receiving pay for sexual services, or receiving little monetary compensation (and, therefore, being depreciated) often means being attacked in their male respectability and being treated as females. Italian male sex workers often interpret professionalization as a form of dependence on the client, on another male. This dependence reveals their deficiency as a male, which makes them appear less masculine, a man with a deficit. For these reasons, the sexual-economic exchange must appear as a *concession* that the sex worker himself grants to the client, a willing choice. Sex workers do not want to view the sexual exchange as something the client would grant to the sex worker. The following attitude is typical if Italian male sex workers: "I can come with you, but you have to pay me, if you didn't have money you'd make me sick, and still, with all the money you have, you

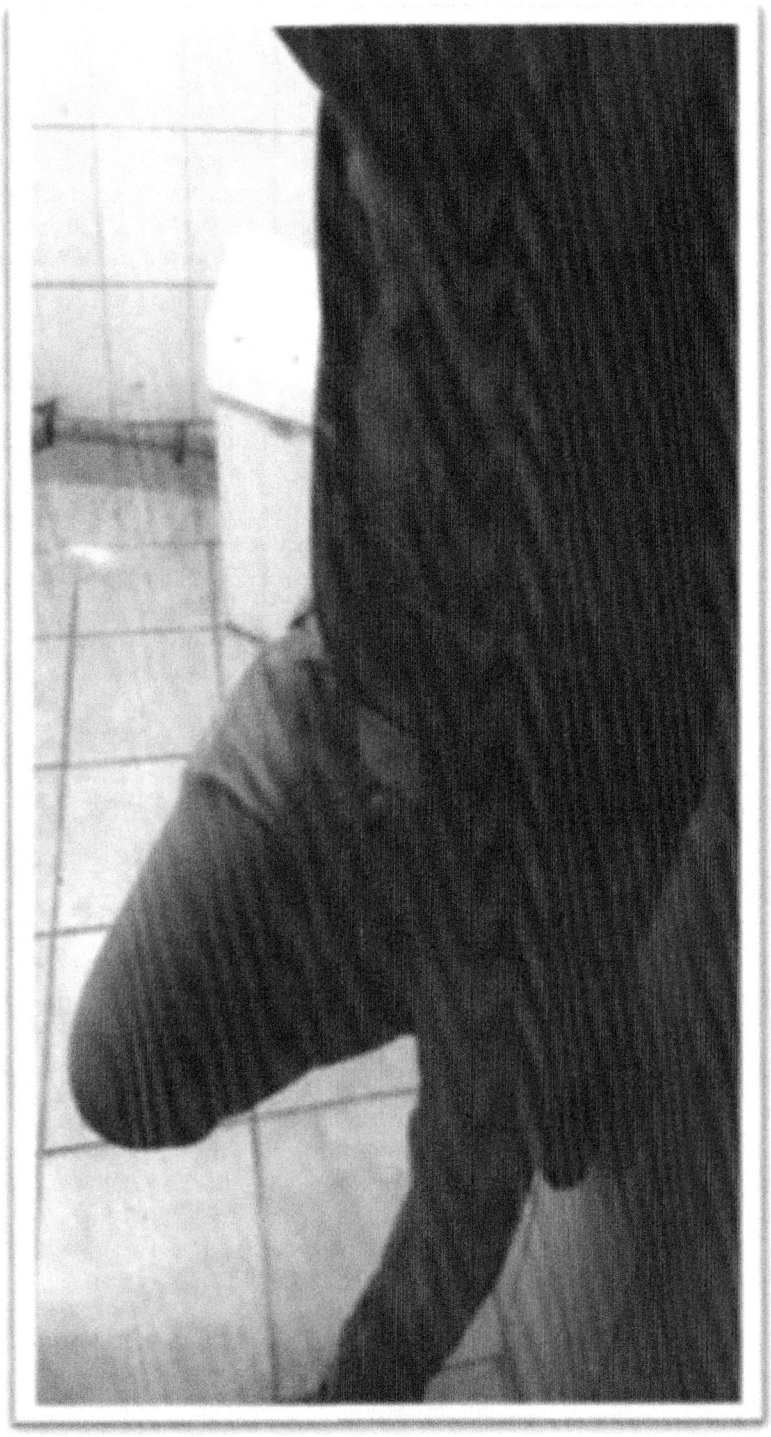

Figure 29.3   Photo taken during fieldwork by Cirus Rinaldi.

make me sick anyway" (*Anonymous, cinema, bathrooms*). The following interview extract may help clarify what I am discussing here:

> I do never solicit them [i.e., my clients]. That's embarrassing for me. It's them who must come to me, not the other way round. If they waste time . . . coming back and forth, that pisses me off big time. So I stop them and say: "Bro, what do you want?" [He brushes the tip of his forefinger with that of his thumb, indicating money.] "You must pay to come with me." See, I don't ask them, it's them who must come to me. They must knee down. [He says this in Sicilian dialect, alluding to oral sex.] I can't look like the needy type, like I'm a girl. Otherwise, I'd look like a fucking whore.
>
> *Hammouda, 22, Tunisian*

If you feel "depreciated" or "devalued," then you must preserve your respectability and "save your face" (Goffman, 1967). According to an expression used in the field, male sex workers usually achieve this goal by "making a scene," lest they are seen and identified as a *scafazzato*—that is, a "bum," a person "devoid of self-respect," "with no dignity" because they "charge little" and perform "indecent" sexual activities (such as passive anal intercourse, active fellatio, or masturbation). Therefore, they must always preserve their reputation as a man: It is an advantage from a privileged situation, an "incorporated capital" (Bourdieu, 1997). Both the sex workers and the clients constantly monitor and add value to masculinity, which is under a permanent threat. Sex workers fashion themselves so to appear as individuals exerting a direct control of their context and interactions, playing the "active part" and functioning as the decision-making center of the exchange. This active and spasmodic control of the sexual interaction makes us understand how sex work poses a constant threat to the sex worker's sexual and gendered self.

Justifying and negotiating masculinities

Entering the sex work scene often coincides with embarking on a "career" as a sex worker. As the worker takes up this role, he has to negotiate it constantly, because he risks losing his virile reputation (Connell & Messerschmidt, 2005). At the outset of their career, non-professional sex workers (that is, not street prostitutes)—who are mostly people of lower social status, working-class individuals, and racialized migrants—often construct legitimizing accounts of their conduct. These narratives are an attempt to neutralize the effects or repair the breach of social expectations (including the system of genders) caused by the sex workers' participation in behaviors that they and others label as "deviant." Sex workers feel the need to justify to themselves and to others *why they do what they do* and *why they intend to do what they intend to do*. Individuals engage in a discourse on motives when they consider what is happening as *questionable, inconsistent, problematic, inappropriate, unsolicited*, and/or *awkward*. Accordingly, we can say that sex workers, as potentially stigmatized individuals, engage in "identity work" (Snow & Anderson, 1987) to create and sustain social acceptance among the other males involved in the "trade" by rationalizing any allegedly unacceptable masculine behavior. By doing so, sex workers can regain their status as legitimate, masculine men.

The most common justifications that sex workers give to legitimize their behavior revolve around neutralizing the stigma that derives from having sex with other men. Their accounts show that sex workers subscribe to dominant social values and sexual norms, including the moral and social sanctions against homosexual conduct. Consequently, in attempting to neutralize their actions, they try to show their commitment to those dominant social values and to convince the "conventional others" that male sex workers should not be classified as deviants or "queers."

This process suggests that sex workers, while enacting the scripts of a specific sexual subculture, work within a broader regulatory system of values. Therefore, the world of sex work and the "conventional" world (that is, the setting in which men despise the other men with whom they have sex) intersect at many points. Sex workers come to learn when they can violate sexual norms and use that knowledge in a twofold way: after selling sex, to mitigate shame and sense of guilt, and before selling sex, to anticipate the transgressive action in order to facilitate it.

Sex workers use four main "motives" to explain and justify why they become a sex worker and continue pursuing this career:

1   "To make money"
2   "I'd rather do this than get into even worse trouble with the police"
3   "It's an easy job/easy money"
4   "It's the only thing I can do"

The first motive, "to make money," is associated with an impersonal activity whose moral sanctions are neutralized by a monetary exchange. The respondents justify their involvement by neutralizing any emotional or physical urge for offering their services:

> I started when I realized I could make some money . . . I'd never done it before, I started doing it when I saw the money.
>
> *Antonio, 19, Italian*

> I don't like sex with men, but I need the money. I live with my mum, my father is dead. I am responsible for my family.
>
> *Abdul, 21, Moroccan*

> I don't like it . . . you know . . . it's the easiest way to make money.
>
> *Roberto, 22, Italian*

The second motive, "I'd rather do this than get into even worse trouble with the police," is the most popular among illegal immigrants and young "offenders" involved in other illegal activities. They are usually forced to limit their visibility in public and semi-public areas so to reduce as much as possible their contact with the local authorities:

> So, as a boy, I went down a wrong path . . . you know, petty crime. Then, I realized that it was not the right path. So in order to make some money, I began, as they say, my career as a hustler.
>
> *Roberto, 22, Italian*

The third motive, "It's an easy job/easy money," is the most popular among Italian sex workers, who consider selling their body a second job. This motive is common among individuals from disadvantaged backgrounds and lower social classes, who go in search of extra money over the weekends. Others choose prostitution according to a basic cost-benefit analysis: Doing *it* is not just another way to make money; you can make a *lot of* money doing it, in a *very short* time, and in a *very simple* way:

> You don't even know how easy it is. You don't even have to move. They just come to you, as if you were all covered in honey. You don't even have the time to cum, that others line

up. You don't even realize that. What do you do, then? You *babbii* with them [Sicilian dia-lect for "joking"] until you have them blow you. Money . . . I'd leave with a lot of money.

Totò, 24, Italian

Sex workers use the fourth motive, "It's the only thing I can do," in order to solicit solidarity and sympathy from what George H. Mead called the "generalized other" (1934). This motive focuses on social inequalities and a lack of opportunities:

I came here to change my life, to find a job, to make a lot of money. I wanted to change my family's life in Tunisia. Moving to Italy could have been an opportunity to do so . . . I went around, looking for a job but didn't find one.

Rachid, 20, Tunisian

I don't have a visa, this is the only thing I can do. I can't go elsewhere or look for a job. I can only stay here and wait for a client.

Abdul, 20, Moroccan.

We stay here, on the street. . . . A real job could change our lives . . . this [sex work] is use-less. . . . What are my dreams? I have some dreams . . . to have a home, a girlfriend, a fam-ily . . . if I find a good job, once I've found it . . . I'll never look back and forget everything.

Arian, 22, Albanian

The stories that are based on "lack of opportunities" also draw on of victimization-based rhetoric strategies, which aim to elicit sympathy. The third and fourth motives can be included within a specific class of justifications called "sad tales" (Scott & Lyman, 1968). "Sad tales" are based on a reconstructed past described as terrible, painful, or sad. The goals of such accounts are to make heterosexuality appear essential, natural, and normal and to reinforce traditional ideas about masculinity (Simon, 1996). Thus, the practice of homosexuality becomes either a temporary, necessary activity replacing the heterosexual relationship, or its training phase. Homosexuality is tolerated to the extent that it does not preclude heterosexual relationships and marriage and to the extent it does not turn into a loving relationship that replaces marriage or leads to embracing a new identity.

Avoiding stigma

The study of male sex work entails a detailed analysis of the presentation of the masculine self and the negotiations that the actors undertake to define "what is happening" and to avoid stigma. In sex work settings, we can identify several important types of negotiation, including *definitions of the situations* in which the sexual activity takes place, *means of access* to the sexual experience, and *instructions* about social roles and statuses (race, gender, class) and group roles. Individuals who identify as heterosexual and who want to "be part of the trade" have to bypass the assumption that only "queers" take part in the sex work business. Therefore, they need to authorize themselves to participate in the sexual acts and experiences required by this work. In most cases, the explanation is chiefly economic, although other factors may play a part, includ-ing curiosity, latent homosexual fantasies, or "pleasure for its own sake." Sex workers become "scriptwriters" or "adapters." At the same time, they draw categories and materials from exist-ing cultural norms in order to turn their actions into scripts for specific behaviors (Gagnon &

Simon, 1986). The sex worker, then, participates in a dramaturgical production of the sexual act that demands an exhibition of unfeigned sexual signs (erection and orgasm), which require them to learn specific techniques (learning to feel pleasure, perceiving the positive effects):

> After some time it [my penis] started to work, I was going crazy. . . . But, in the end, I pulled it off.
>
> *Abdul, 25 Moroccan*

Sex workers behave in ways that question the representation of human sexuality as a mere reaction to stimulation. In fact, they prove how we attach meaning to what we feel on the inside (as well as what we perceive from outside) and how we are involved in a *symbolic translation* process that translates feelings into names, labels, and other linguistic categories. Male sex workers are almost always able to exercise some degree of voluntary control over their inner symbolic processes and to speed up, slow down, or completely inhibit their sexual responses and reactions. They have to learn how to achieve a symptomatic condition (an erection), interpret it, and assign to it a precise meaning so that they can "feel something," manage to "do something" (get an orgasm), or "work" without being identified as "faggots." To achieve these goals, they can adopt various learning techniques, including the dissembling or simulation of the sexual act:

Q: "Can you explain to me how you do it?"
I: "You trick them, have them on . . . without them realizing!"
Q: "So what do you do exactly?"
I: "Well in short . . . you need to . . . do lots of different things . . . or the fake cum shot."
Q: "And how do you do that?"
I: "So, for the fake cum shot, you can just fake it and cum on their ass, you spit on their ass and then rub your hand over it, you rub your dick, so that he can't tell, but you get some people that do get it and don't tell you, and others that normally . . . it's not like they don't get it, but they're so much into dick that they just don't realize it."

> *Luigi, 19, Italian*

The sexual hierarchy within the field

This last excerpt of conversation highlights how the *result* of the sex workers' *self-positioning* as "heterosexual" enables them to assert their traditional masculinity, showing contempt for the client or—as in the example—trying to swindle him. The convergence of traditional male gender roles, ethnic-sexual moral rhetorics ("We are the real [Italian] men"), and heteronormativity ("I do it, but only as a top. I'm a man. I'm not like them, they're faggots" or "I'm a man") allows sex workers to distance themselves from the *abject other*, as we see in the following excerpts:

> There are lots of queers, they fall in love with you and help you. Some of my friends manage to get loads of money from them, they have a car, a house a job . . . everything . . . they got lucky, you know? They're like women, they treat you like women do, they take care of you, they fall in love with you.
>
> *Roberto, 20, Romanian*

> I'm a top, I'm a real man . . . they're faggots.
>
> *Aziz, 24, Tunisian*

I'm a total top, they're sick, they like to be abused [be receptive in the sexual act].

Antonio, 19, Italian

I've made mistakes in my life, I always get into trouble . . . I've been also in jail but I could never be a faggot.

Richard, 22, Albanian

No, I've never bottomed. Never. Once, one wanted to pay me 500 Euros [sic] just to give him head but . . . as soon as . . . I just . . . I'd just put a condom on his dick and I was already going to kneel down when . . . I can't help . . . My body doesn't accept to bottom. [D: Not even if they offered you a shitload of money?] No, I can't . . . I can't even pretend. I just can't do it. Maybe putting . . . or licking him, . . . like . . . my dick against his, well that's something I usually do. [D: And what about masturbating him?]. Yes, I did that, sometimes. Every day, when my clients come, I happen to do it. While I fuck them from behind, I grab his dick and jerk him off, until he cums. [D: Are there boys that bottom? Like S., the guy you spoke to me about before. Is it easy to speak about it with the other boys?] Uhm . . . as far as I am concerned, it's not that easy.

Roberto, 22, Italian

The sex work field is highly specialized field. Its actors are unequally equipped with sexual capital (which depends on physical traits, self-presentation, and other characteristics that acquire monetary and symbolic value within the sex field) and therefore occupy different spaces in the hierarchy of sexual work, the "levels and layers of desirability" (Green, 2014). Effeminate gay men are considered "lower class" sexual actors, as opposed to racialized men or those who possess characteristics that are culturally associated with manliness. Based on the data collected, we can make the following generalizations about "erotic capital":

1   Male sex workers are sharply differentiated according to the sexual practices offered (bottom vs. top). By overtly despising effeminate individuals, male sex workers take a virile and contemptuous attitude, which clients especially value within the sexual exchange
2   The most attractive (profitable) sex workers have the ability to perform anal insertive intercourse; a virile body; specific racialized characteristics (skin color, the fact of being exotic or "Mediterranean"); traits associated with a lower-class status (a certain accent, defiant attitude, gait, coarseness of manners); and specific bodily features (large penis size; height; a fit, lean, young body)
3   Local (Italian) sex workers consider themselves more trustworthy than foreign sex workers, whom they stereotype as unclean or as thieves:

'Cos today the client comes and says I am the best at this. Tomorrow he meets a Tunisian boy that for 5 Euros does the same things I do. Still, with the Italian boys, including me, things are different: If you give me 20 Euros you will find a clean and honest person . . . I mean, you don't risk to catch some disease, while if you go with the Tunisian boy you get the same pleasure but can get some disease, because he's not a clean person aesthetically and physically.

Antonio, 19, Italian

They come here and steal away our clients.

Aldo, 22, Italian

They're all dirty.

Anonymous Italian male sex worker

Never trust them: They might be even sick.

Sergio, 25, Italian

However, foreign sex workers sometimes successfully differentiate themselves on the basis of their offers and physical traits:

Italians are all bottoms.

Momo, Moroccan, 20

I don't use condoms. Don't need them. I'm not a queer. . . . They [the local sex workers] can get sick, not me.

Lilian, Tunisian, 21

Italians have small dicks.

Rico, Tunisian, 21

4   Other factors associated with the sexual hierarchy include the qualities and "styles" of the sex offer. The sex workers highest in the hierarchy work to maintain privacy for their clients and for themselves; take a subtle approach to hooking up (not flashy or exaggerated), and offer sex in a comfortable or quasi-private location (never outdoors, never in the train station public toilets because women and children may catch you in the act)

Conclusions

Males endowed with a specific "physical" and "attractive" capital characterized by certain mannerisms, education, lifestyles, and cultural habits, are *naturalized, classed, sexualized*, and/or *racialized* according to the same features that lead to the marginalization of less desirable male sexual partners or sex workers. Within homosexual communities and societies at large, a "class" of treacherous, disgusting, and threatening individuals is constructed, whose dangerous and virile features cause attraction and repulsion. Sex work can threaten their respectability as males and their masculinity, leading sex workers to cultivate a hypermasculinity that compensates for their sacrificed masculinity. Male sex workers convey this hypermasculinity through aggressive manners and virile physicality. The study of male sex work in Italy allows us to understand what it means to perform a subordinate masculinity in between the old and the new, between the need for a real man to provide for a woman (and for himself) and the inability to acting like a "traditional man" as a result of limited opportunities and career choices. Because, as Luigi (22, Italian) says, "As soon as I make enough money, I need to buy new clothes, get some weed, and look for *fimmini* ["girls" in Sicilian dialect] . . . I wanna bring a girl to the disco, and if you don't have money enough, what would you give her?"

Note

1   I began studying male sex work in 2011. Since then, I have collected nearly 80 hours of ethnographic observation conducted in public sex environments (public parks, railway/bus stations, adult movie theaters, and other cruising sites) in two main cities in Southern Italy: Naples and Palermo.

I conducted 40 in depth-interviews with a number of foreigners and immigrants (ten from Tunisia, ten from Morocco, seven from Romania, and three from Albania) and ten Italian male sex workers. The topics covered included the beginning and continuation of their careers as sex workers, the activities performed, and their emotional involvement. The average age of the respondents was 22.5 years. All of interviewees, except for two who defined themselves as bisexual, identified as heterosexuals. Two of the patrons I met in an adult movie theater, whom we could define as "clients," have become regular informers. I was able to access the research field thanks to my personal knowledge of gay subculture and sexual exchange sites. However, at least in the earlier stage of my research, the method I used to infiltrate the observed groups (especially in semi-public sites such as movie theaters) was that of "passive" observation: I mingled with the various participants without taking on a specific role, such as that of sex worker or client but simply as an onlooker. Later, my behavior and level of involvement changed as I revealed myself as a researcher, especially to the sex workers with whom I came in contact.

References

Aldrich, R. (1993). *The seduction of the Mediterranean: Writing, art, and homosexual fantasy*. New York: Routledge.

Barnao, C. (2004). Uno "sguardo" sulla domanda: i clienti dei night club e i clienti della prostituzione maschile in luoghi pubblici. *Quaderni di strada (Provincia di Pisa)*, *2*, 131–137.

Benadusi, L. (2005). *Il nemico dell'uomo nuovo. l'omosessualità nell'esperimento totalitario fascista*. Milan: Feltrinelli.

Bertolini, P. (Ed.). (1964). *Delinquenza e disadattamento minorile: Esperienze educative*. Bari: Laterza.

Bolino, G., & De Deo, A. (1970). *Il sesso nelle carceri italiane: Inchiesta e documenti*. Milano: Feltrinelli.

Boswell, J. (2005). *Christianity, homosexuality, and social tolerance*. Chicago, IL: University of Chicago Press.

Bourdieu, P. (1997). The form of capital. In A. H. Halsey, H. Lauder, P. Brown, & A. Stuart Wells (Eds.), *Education: Culture, economy, society* (pp. 46–58). Oxford: Oxford University Press.

Burton, R. F. (1886). *A plain and literal translation of the Arabian nights' entertainments, now entitled the book of the thousand nights and a night with introduction explanatory notes on the manners and customs of Moslem men and a terminal essay upon the history of the nights*. London: Burton Club.

Connell, R., & Messerschmidt, J. W. (2005). Hegemonic masculinity: Rethinking the concept. *Gender & Society*, *19*(6), 829–859.

Dalla Volta, A. (1929). Una associazione a delinquere nel reato di violenza carnale contro natura. *Zacchia: Rassegna di studi medico legali*, *VIII*, 1–12.

Dennis, J. P. (2017). *The myth of the queer criminal*. New York: Routledge.

Di Tullio, B. (1927). Nella delinquenza minorile: reati sessuali e prostituziona maschile. *Bollettino Dell'amministrazione Carceraria*, *4*.

Dover, K. (1978). *Greek homosexuality*. Cambridge, MA: Harvard University Press.

Ferracuti, F., & Palmieri, V. M. (1988). Omosessualità e criminalità. In F. Ferracuti (Ed.), *Trattato di criminologia, medicina criminologica e psichiatria forense: Tomo VII Criminologia e psichiatria forense delle condotte sessuali normali, abnormi e criminali* (pp. 219–245). Milano: Giuffré.

Ferraris, V. (2004). Risultati di uno studio qualitativo e delle interviste con testimoni privilegiati in alcune aree metropolitane italiane. In *Ricerca sulla prostituzione maschile dei giovani stranieri* (pp. 2–66). Torino: IRES-CGIL.

Foucault, M. (1990). *The use of pleasure: Volume 2 of the history of sexuality*. New York: Vintage Books.

Franchini, A., & Introna, F. (1961). *Delinquenza minorile: Problemi medico-legali, psicologici e giuridico-sociali*. Padova: Cedam.

Friedman, M. (2014). Male sex work from ancient times to the near present. In V. Minichiello & J. Scott (Eds.), *Male sex work and society* (pp. 2–33). New York: Harrington Park Press.

Gagnon, J. H., & Simon, W. (1974). *Sexual conduct: The social sources of human sexuality*. Chicago, IL: Aldine.

Gagnon, J. H., & Simon, W. (1986). Sexual scripts: Permanence and change. *Archives of Sexual Behavior*, *15*(2), 97–120.

Goffman, E. (1963). *Stigma: Notes on the management of spoiled identity*. Englewood Cliffs, NJ: Prentice-Hall.

Goffman, E. (1967). *Interaction ritual: Essays in face-to-face behavior*. Chicago, IL: Aldine.

Green, A. I. (2014). The sexual fields framework. In A. Green (Ed.), *Sexual fields: Toward a sociology of collective sexual life* (pp. 25–56). Chicago, IL: University of Chicago Press.

Lombroso, C. (1906). Du Parallélisme entre l'homosexualité et la criminalité innée. *Archivio di psichiatria*, *XXVII*, 378–381.

Mead, G. H. (1934). *Mind, self, and society: From the standpoint of a social behaviorist*. Chicago, IL: University of Chicago Press.

Messina, S. (1953). L'omosessualità nel diritto penale. *Ulisse*, *3*(18), 670–676.

Minichiello, V., Scott, J., & Callander, D. (2013). New pleasures and old dangers: Reinventing male sex work. *Journal of Sex Research*, *50*(3–4), 263–275.

Oliviero, L., Russo, C., & Zaami, A. F. (2010). Vite ai margini: Sex workers al maschile. In A. Morniroli (Ed.), *Vite cladestine: Frammenti, racconti e altro sulla prostituzione e la tratta di esseri umani in provincia di Napoli*. Naples: Gesco.

Ottolenghi, S. (1907). *Poliziascientifica. Identificazione fisica e psichica, investigazioni giudiziarie: Quadri sinottici delle Lezioni tenute nella Scuola di Polizia*. Rome: Società Poligrafica Editrice.

Pasolini, P. (1955). *Ragazzi di vita*. Milano: Garzanti.

Petrosino, D. (2017). Il senso comune del pudore: La repressione dell'omosessualità nell'Italia republicana (1947–1981). In U. Grassi, V. Lagioia, & G. P. Romagnani (Eds.), *Tribadi, sodomiti, invertite e invertiti, pederasti, femminelle, ermafroditi . . . Per una storia dell'omosessualità, della bisessualità e delle trasgressioni di genere in Italia* (pp. 219–238). Pisa: RTS.

Pini, A. (2003). La prostituzione maschile in Italia. In Associazione on the Road (Ed.), *Porneia: Voci e sguardi sulle prostituzioni*. Padova: Il Poligrafo.

Pini, A. (2017). L'Italia contemporanea. In In U. Grassi, V. Lagioia, & G. P. Romagnani (Eds.), *Tribadi, sodomiti, invertite, invertiti, pederasti, femminelle, ermafroditi . . . per una storia dell'omosessualità, della bisessualità e delle trasgressioni di genere in Italia* (pp. 211–217). Pisa: ETS.

Plummer, K. (1982). Symbolic interactionism and sexual conduct: An emergent perspective. In M. Brake (Ed.), *Human sexual relations*. New York: Pantheon Books.

Rinaldi, C. (2012). Il sex work maschile (omosessuale): Rappresentazioni, mondi sociali e analisi. In C. Cipolla & E. Ruspini (Eds.), *Prostituzioni visibili e invisibili* (pp. 189–222). Milan: Franco Angeli.

Rinaldi, C. (2013a). Il sociologo come cruiser: Riflessioni intorno ai mondi sociali dei clienti e dei marchettari. In A. Morniroli & L. Oliviero (Eds.), *I clienti del sesso: I maschi e la prostituzione* (pp. 95–110). Naples: Intra Moenia.

Rinaldi, C. (2013b). Razza, genere e sessualità nelle arene del sew working maschile: Implicazioni autoetnografiche. In M. Grasso (Ed.), *Razzismi, discriminazioni e confinamenti* (pp. 175–188). Rome: Ediesse.

Rinaldi, C. (2014). Male prostitution. In C. J. Forsyth & H. Copes (Eds.), *Encyclopedia of social deviance* (Vol. II, pp. 406–409). Thousand Oaks, CA: Sage.

Rinaldi, C. (2017). Dalla messa-in-scena alla costruzione delle gerarchie: Riflessioni su copioni sesuali, maschilità e neutralizzazione dello stigma nel sex work maschile. In C. Rinaldi (Ed.), *I copioni sessuali: Storia, analisi e applicazioni* (pp. 324–355). Milan: Mondadori.

Rinaldi, C. (2018). A sociology of queer implications? Methodological inquietudes and ethical involvements in the study of non-normative sexualities. *BAGOAS—Estudos Gays: gênero e sexualidades*, *18*, 40–69.

Scott, J., Callander, D., & Minichiello, V. (2014). Clients of male sex workers. In V. Minichiello & J. Scott (Eds.), *Male sex work and society* (pp. 82–105). New York: Harrington Park Press.

Scott, M. B., & Lyman, S. M. (1968). Accounts. *American Sociological Review*, *33*(1), 46–62.

Simon, W. (1996). *Postmodern sexualities*. London: Routledge.

Snow, D., & Anderson, L. (1987). Identity work among the homeless: The verbal construction and avowal of personal identities. *American Journal of Sociology*, *92*, 1336–1371.

Sper, A. (1902). *Capri und die Homosexuellen: Eine psychologische Studie*. Berlin: Orania-Verlag.

Weitzer, R. (2018). Resistance to sex work stigma. *Sexualities*, *21*(5–6), 717–729.

30

Male prostitution in Spain

Vulnerability of the invisible

Iván Zaro

The sociological analysis of sex work in Spain has usually centered on cisgender female prostitutes hired by men, subordinating the male role to that of the sexual services client (Zaro, 2008). (A *cisgender* woman is a woman whose personal identity corresponds to the female sex she was assigned at birth.) This trend has fueled ignorance about and the invisibility of sex workers, offering a skewed and incomplete view of prostitution in Spain. This approach makes it difficult to analyze the vulnerability of male prostitutes (Schiffer & Giebers, 2003).

In some forms of prostitution, the relationship between the sex worker and client does not entail domination of one gender over another, as is the case with male prostitution (Latapie, 2009). The absence of scientific literature in Spanish and the lack of support for research add to our ignorance on the topic. This lack of social and scientific interest is perhaps explained by the double stigma suffered by male sex workers: Prejudice against prostitution itself (the set of prejudices, attitudes, and discrimination collectively called "slut shaming" in common parlance) combines with the stigma of being homosexual or being a man who has sex with other men (MSM), because most male prostitutes' clients are other men (Bimbi, 2007). This fact does not mean that women do not demand sexual services but rather that there is a shortage of studies on women clients (Scott, Callander, & Minichiello, 2014).

A male sex worker is a man who offers sexual services to other people in exchange for money (Zaro, Navazo, Vázquez, García, & Ibarguchi, 2016). Both parties agree on the sexual relationship and the price, as well as other points of negotiation such as drug use. Prostitution in Spain is not regulated and thus is understood socially to be outside of the law, even though it is not a crime. Nonetheless, the National Institute of Statistics counts prostitution, among other illegal activities, when calculating Spain's gross domestic product.

However, newer policies have aggravated the vulnerability and invisibility of Spanish prostitutes. These policies attempt to cleanse the streets of prostitution in the interests of tranquility and neighborhood quality. Therefore, prostitutes may occasionally leave the streets and other public spaces and move to closed spaces, such as clubs or apartments. In other words, the conditions in which prostitutes gather become hidden, a phenomenon aided by the digital revolution and the increased use of dating apps and other online resources.

Such policies are enacted at the local and national levels. For example, Barcelona has municipal ordinances that prosecute any form of misuse of public places, including the offer and acceptance of sexual services. The national Organic Law of 4/2015 (March 30) attempts to protect citizens' safety. Article 37.5 of this law contains two provisions that directly affect sex workers on the street. First, they can be fined up to 600 Euros if they perform obscene acts in public. Second, they can be fined up to 30,000 Euros if, after being notified by the authorities not to offer their services in public places, they continue to do so. By mid-2017, sex workers had been fined a total of 329 times throughout the country.

The law also fines the client through Article 36.11, which makes illegal

> the request or acceptance by the petitioner of paid sexual services in areas of public transit in the vicinity of places intended for use by minors . . . or when these conducts, by location in which they are carried out, can generate a traffic safety risk.

Madrid leads of the country in fines against those who solicit prostitutes, with a total of 665 fines between 2015 and 2017 according to the Ministry of the Interior.

Simultaneously, Madrid offers protections to the LGTBTI community through two laws: (1) Law 2/2016 (March 29), Identity and Expression of Gender and Social Equality and Non-Discrimination of the Community of Madrid, and (2) Law 3/2016 (July 22), Integral Protection Against LGTBIphobia and Discrimination for Reason of Orientation and Sexual Identity in the Community of Madrid. Both laws provide a normative framework that guarantees the right of all people not to be discriminated against because of their sexual orientation or gender identity. They also guarantee that the Administration of the Autonomous Community of Madrid will protect people who are victims of discrimination and hate crimes or who suffer discriminatory, humiliating, or degrading treatment based on their sexual orientation or gender identity.

The invisibility of male prostitution in Madrid can have positive consequences for male sex workers, such as not being subject to fines for selling sexual services or soliciting in the streets of Madrid. However, it has other repercussions that make the workers more vulnerable and excluded, as I discuss later in this chapter.

Characteristics of male prostitution in Madrid

Madrid is home to the largest number of sex workers in Spain (Zaro, 2016). In this section, I detail the main characteristics of male prostitution in Madrid, observed through 14 years of fieldwork in the city of Madrid, starting in 2006. These characteristics combine to oppress sex workers and hinder their access to basic rights.

Immigration and legal situation

Male prostitution in Spain is largely practiced by migrant men who have arrived from three large geographical areas (Menoyo et al., 2005). The first is Latin America. For years, the primary country of origin was Brazil, but in recent years, more and more male sex workers come from Venezuela, which shares a language and many cultural traits with Spain. Venezuela has faced serious shortages of antiretroviral treatments to control HIV infection. This humanitarian crisis has forced many Venezuelan men to migrate to Spain to try to survive. To generate income that they can send to their families back home, they request asylum for political or humanitarian issues, because people with HIV are not receiving adequate medical monitoring or treatment in Venezuela. Men who had never worked as prostitutes until they arrived in Madrid have found that sex work offers them a way to generate income to sustain themselves and their family members in the country of origin. In these cases, emigration is a matter of survival. Except on the street, Latin American men are found in practically in all the places in Madrid where male prostitutes congregate.

The second group consists of men from Eastern Europe, specifically Romania and Bulgaria. The venues that these men use to solicit clients are saunas and the street, specifically in the city center, Puerta del Sol. These populations are marked by strong levels of homophobia and cultural machismo, especially in men from Romania. This machismo often translates into violence—both verbal and physical—as a way for the men to establish relationships with one another and with potential clients, especially among street prostitutes in Madrid. Street sex workers are mostly Romanians who have little education, strong language barriers, and little to no professional experience in the normalized labor market. They often lack stable housing, and sometimes they have been incarcerated either in their home country or in Spain. The primary area for male prostitution on the streets is near Montera Street, a street that is also frequented by cisgender women prostitutes, many of whom also come from Romania.

The third group consists of men from Muslim countries such as Morocco, Cameroon, and Algeria. These men tend to be found in all areas of male prostitution from saunas to the Internet. In recent years, more men from sub-Saharan Africa have emigrated to Europe because their sexual orientation is a crime in their countries of origin. For example, gay men may emigrate from Senegal based on their desire to live a homosexual life with guaranteed human rights, although homophobia among their compatriots may cause them hide the true motivation for their emigration.

Illegal immigrants face particularly difficult challenges. They cannot access social services and the healthcare system, and they dare not report abuse by clients to the police. Their dual status as an illegal immigrant and a male prostitute increases their risk of social exclusion and increases their vulnerability.

Mobility

Mobility refers to the migratory flow of people motivated by economic concerns. In the context of sex workers, mobility refers to the trips that men make through Spanish and European territory to engage in sex work in destination places for a set period of time.

Mobility is a strategy to avoid the burnt-face effect (Zaro et al., 2016). To be a "burnt face" means to be known as a sex worker in a certain city or setting, thus making it difficult to compete in the same conditions with new sex workers who have recently arrived on the scene. Mobility allows sex workers to search for new spaces and cities in which to offer their services, which offers novelty to their clients. Therefore, mobility is a strategy for obtaining more clients and income.

Mobility occurs through different circuits, in private apartments managed by pimps and via the Internet through mobile applications and contact portals for sex workers. Because Madrid is a city with no coast, during the summer months most male prostitutes move to coastal areas with a greater influx of tourists.

Mobility can exacerbate sex workers' vulnerability. Being in constant transit makes it difficult for them to be aware of the available health resources in case of an emergency. It also makes it impossible to establish personal relationships and a familiar place of reference. Indeed, male sex workers often speak about suffering from their solitude.

Homophobia and identity

Although there is a tendency to associate male prostitution with homosexuality, there is great diversity among male sex workers. In Madrid, 46% of male sex workers define themselves as homosexual, 30% as heterosexual, and 22% as bisexual (Zaro et al., 2016). In Barcelona, 54% define themselves as bisexual, 33% as heterosexual, and 21% as homosexual (Benjumea, 2006). Sexual orientation therefore loses some of its relevance in a sector where workers and clients are men whose clients can be cisgender women. Often the sex workers who define themselves as heterosexual project a stigma onto their gay clients (Perlongher, 1993).

Despite the diversity of male sex workers and their clients, the model of hegemonic masculinity (the set of social attitudes that describe the male gender role as violent, non-emotional, and sexually aggressive and physically associated with tall, well-built, and hairy body types) is alive and well in male prostitution in Spain, especially in contact portals and mobile applications. Male sex workers advertise and sell their muscular bodies, which they've made muscular by using hormones and anabolic steroids (Zaro et al., 2007). A muscular physique commands higher rates and provides a higher income level for the sex worker (Logan, 2010), because a large majority of clients desire that physique, along with classically male behaviors (Logan, 2014).

However, there is a group of sex workers for whom sexual identity and gender are fluid and negotiable realities. These men's gender roles defy those required by hegemonic masculinity. Among these subversive identities we find men who exclusively play the receptive role in their sexual practices, including men who use female hormones and assume a feminine image. Because they are transgender, they can also claim a masculine identity in their sex work (Da Silva & Evangelista, 2004).

Homophobia and stigma

Stigma is "a profoundly discrediting attribute" (Goffman, 1963) that affects and influences how stigmatized individuals relate to their environment and to society in general. Stigma includes not only stigmatizing behaviors—such as rejection and discrimination—but also the responses and strategies used to reduce the negative consequences of stigma. Male sex workers face a double stigma, first for being men who have sex with other men (homophobia) and second for exchanging sex for money ("slut shaming"). Male sex workers often try to transfer the stigma they suffer onto their clients. By doing so, they maintain the masculine role of penetrator, essentially defining the homosexual as the receiver of the penetration (Mai, 2015). Homophobia among sex workers can generate violence among the sex workers themselves and toward their clients. Such violence can include bullying, verbal and physical aggressions, sexual abuse, and rape (Scott et al., 2005).

Spanish society in the Franco era culturally associated homosexuality with secrecy and crime. Cruising areas and male prostitution were inaccurately linked with spaces of crime. This view maintains homosexuality within the universe of deviant behavior—that is, outside of the norm and outside of socially accepted behavior. Currently in Spain, male prostitution is usually associated with the LGTBI community, even though, as we have seen, its borders are much broader. Thus, male sex work is often excluded from any debate about prostitution, because male prostitution is viewed as an autonomous and foreign world compared to that of female cisgender prostitution. This view permits most of society to remain ignorant about male prostitution while increasing male sex workers' invisibility and vulnerability. The more stigma that exists, the more difficult it is for members of this group to empower themselves and to use their own voices to push against inaccurate perceptions and negative stereotypes. Finally, the picture of prostitution will always be incomplete if society does not accept men as providers of sexual services, as opposed to only clients or consumers of sexual services.

Sexual health and serophobia

Currently, sex workers are one of the groups most vulnerable to HIV infection in Spain. According to data collected by Madrid's Sandoval Health Center, which specializes in the diagnosis and treatment of sexually transmitted infections, between 2013 and 2017 a total of 17,897 people were tested for HIV at first consultation, of which 1,290 were prostitutes. Of these, 997 were female sex workers (77.28%), 215 were male sex workers (16.66%) and 78 were transgender sex workers (6.04%). As Table 30.1 shows, test results showed that the group with the highest HIV prevalence is transgender women (30.8%), followed by men (20.4%) and women (0.4%). Thus, women, despite composing the majority of sex workers, have the lowest prevalence of HIV. These findings work to dismiss the false and macho belief in Spain that points to prostitutes as a transmission mechanism for STIs, and especially HIV. Meanwhile, transgender sex workers have an alarming prevalence of HIV, which can be a consequence of multiple factors. Transgender sex workers' HIV status generates inequality among sex workers. It also hinders the negotiation of safe sex with clients, reinforces homophobia and transphobia, and increases the stigma against prostitution.

The new diagnoses at the Sandoval Center reflect a masculinization of the infection. In 2017 alone, among 236 HIV diagnoses, 93% were men who have sex with men, of which 6% were sex workers. Regarding the region of origin, 45% were from Spain and 42% were from Latin America (42%). In addition, throughout 2017, 45 seroconversions occurred among MSM who had been coming to the Sandoval Center with previous negative serologies; 11% of these seroconversions occurred in sex workers. Here we find one of the worst consequences in the delay of the approval and regulation of pre-exposure prophylaxis, or PrEP, by the Spanish government. (PrEP is a pill that helps people who do not have HIV, but who are at substantial risk of contracting it, to prevent HIV infection.) The longer PrEP is not implemented with vulnerable populations such as sex workers, the longer they are exposed to a higher risk of HIV transmission. The profile of a seroconverter in Sandoval Center in 2016 was a man between 20 and 39 years old, with several previous negative HIV tests, repeated episodes of STIs, numerous sexual partners, and unprotected sex under the effect of recreational drugs.

This reality reflects the vulnerability of male prostitutes in Spain with regard to sexual health. A detailed investigation of sex workers examined the use of condoms. The study determined that condoms had a symbolic value as a physical barrier that distanced sex workers from their customers. However, sex workers often did not use condoms when they had sexual encounters with other sex workers or emotional partners, with playful and casual sex

Table 30.1 HIV Prevalence in Madrid's Sandoval Health Center, 2013–2017

	Female sex workers	Male sex workers	Transgender sex workers
HIV tests performed	997	215	78
HIV prevalence	0.4%	20.4%	30.8%

Source: Sandoval Health Center Madrid

partners, or even with regular clients with whom they had a relationship of trust (Zaro et al., 2007). However, Spanish health authorities still failed to approve PrEP as an HIV-prevention tool. Currently, without PrEP, sex workers' use of condoms is contingent on their ability to negotiate with their clients, which is often affected by urgent economic needs, tipping power relations in the clients' favor.

Male sex workers use *serophobia* (manifestation of fear and aversion toward people living with HIV) as a competitive tool. They also use it to exclude and marginalize those who are diagnosed with HIV. For this reason, those who have HIV often keep their serostatus secret for fear that their colleagues may use this information against them, disclosing their serological status in order to prevent potential clients from demanding their services. They also suffer exclusion and rejection by their peers in prostitution spaces such as saunas, apartments, and the street.

Drugs

Clients often view prostitution as something playful that includes the use of recreational drugs. Therefore, in sex work, it is common to find substance use, often demanded by the clients themselves. Several studies have linked substance use with a higher risk of unprotected sexual practices (Kumar, 2016). Analyzing the data of Imagina MÁS (discussed in detail subsequently) in relation to substance use among male prostitutes ($N = 82$) between the years 2012 and 2017, it is worth mentioning that the drugs most consumed with clients are alcohol (53.6%), cocaine (45.1%), Viagra (39.0%), and poppers (17.0%). The patterns of consumption in sex workers' private lives are somewhat different. Alcohol is the most widely consumed drug (59.7%), followed by cocaine (34.1%), cannabis (24.3%), and ecstasy (9.7%). In other words, the use of Viagra and similar drugs for erectile dysfunction (ED) are used as a professional tool, often without a prescription or medical follow-up. Combining ED drugs with cocaine and poppers puts sex workers' health, and even their lives, at risk. In addition, drug use directly affects the perception of risk (the more drug use, the lower the perception of risk), and it decreases sex workers' ability to negotiate condom use.

Unlike the recent phenomenon called Chemsex in Europe or "party and play" in the United States, in which MSM use recreational drugs to facilitate high-risk sexual activity (McCall, Adams, Mason, & Willis, 2015), in male prostitution, the use of drugs as a prelude to or during sex has been present for a long time. In Spain, male sex workers speak of selling services to "*clientes de colocón*," or high customers. These types of services tend to be longer and better paid than meetings where there is no substance use. Sex workers often refer to the emotional and physical wear and tear created by this type of service, which can last more than 15 hours.

Despite the incursion of new drugs into the LGTBI community, in male prostitution they are still relatively rare. For example, only 6.1% of male sex workers report using GHB (gamma-Hydroxybutryic acid, a naturally occurring neurotransmitter and a psychoactive drug) with their clients. They also report using mephedrone (3.6%) and methamphetamine (2.4%). However, these drugs can have serious consequences, including health damage and psychotic outbreaks. The consumption of GHB in Madrid seems to be increasing and caused several deaths among young gay men in 2018.

With regard to injected drugs, earlier research estimated that at least 16% of sex workers in Madrid had used injected drugs at some time in their lives (Belza et al., 2001). HIV prevalence among those who had injected drugs on at least one occasion (60%) was higher than among those who did had not used an injectable drug (11%). Currently in Madrid, we detect an increase in the use of injectable drugs, especially mephedrone and methamphetamine. Injecting drugs, sometimes known as *slamming*, tends to be associated with sexual encounters and eroticizes intravenous drug use (Zaro et al., 2016). The rise in slamming shows a rupture with the stereotype of the marginalized heroin consumer that existed in Spain during the 1980s.

Imagina: one solution

In 2011, in the midst of an economic crisis, the Imagina MÁS association was founded. It is a non-governmental organization (NGO) composed of a team of professionals from social work, social integration, psychology, education, medicine, and other disciplines. Its main purpose is to work in health, education, training, and STI prevention. It seeks to reduce stigma and discrimination, decrease social and labor exclusion, and promote equality and diversity, mainly in the most vulnerable groups: people with HIV and other STIs or at risk of acquiring STIs, women, immigrants, LGBTI people, people who practice prostitution (PEP), young people, and the elderly.

Imagina MÁS also seeks to facilitate people's access to the public health care system, to promote beneficial healthy habits for individuals and their personal development, to inspire and create new alternatives for social well-being, and to celebrate diversity through the recognition of human beings' dignity and equal rights.

The organization has managed since 2013 the Attention to Male, Transgender, and Genderfluid Prostitution Program of the Madrid city council. Madrid is the first, and to date only, city in Spain to launch a program that addresses the complex reality of male prostitution. The implementation of this program originated during a serious economic recession as a response to the group's multiple needs.

The Imagina MÁS program makes direct contact with male, transgender, and genderfluid sex workers in Madrid, establishes a bridge between the target population and the city's public health and social system, and provides training and education on the reduction of risky practices for the transmission of STIs and the reduction of harm in people who use drugs. Also, since 2014, the entity has managed, with the support of the Ministry of Health, the first residential resource for male, transgender, and genderfluid sex workers who are at risk of social exclusion. Half-stay apartments welcome people at risk of exclusion, offering them accommodation, food, transportation assistance, and a professional counseling staff. These apartments usually have six residents as well as one emergency room.[1]

The Program seeks to accomplish its mission through four main services:

1 Mobile unit

The mobile unit is composed of professionals from social work, social integration, and voluntary personnel. This team intervenes in the spaces where male prostitutes gather: the Puerta del Sol (zone of street prostitution), apartments managed by third parties, two saunas, and a nightclub. All of these spaces are located in the vicinity of Chueca, the city's main LGTBI neighborhood. Virtual interventions are also carried out via www.telechapero.com, the main contact website for sex workers in Spain. Professionals and volunteers in this unit maintain direct contact with sex workers and deliver free preventive material and basic information on sexual health.

2 Care center

The care center is located in the city center. The intake of all new cases, as well as individual interventions and group trainings, take place at the care center. The Social Work unit is responsible for the assessments, interviews, and social histories. The team designs a plan of action by working with (and maintaining contact with) the users of the service. The care center also provides psychological support service, legal advice, and rapid HIV testing, all confidential and without cost. The care center also provides translation services for clients who do not speak, or who have limited facility with, Spanish.

The care center also provides residential resources for some clients. For people who have entered the residence, the team has guards on weekends to attend to any emergency situation that may occur.

3 Group training

This Program offers training aimed at educating the target population on the important topics of sexual health, empowerment skills, negotiation of condom use, harm reduction in drug users, sexual diversity, and LGTBI rights. Occasionally the workshops are taught by professional experts outside the association. These experts include endocrinologists, who discuss the use of hormones and anabolics, and medical experts in drugs, who discuss the reduction of drug use and the interactions between drugs and antiretroviral treatment.

Since 2018, the Program has expanded its workshops to professionals in the social and health field with the aim of raising awareness about male and transgender prostitution. The Program also seeks to raise awareness about sexual diversity to improve the relationship between sex professionals and the LGTBI community.

4 Peer education

The team has trained sex workers in sexual health and basic tools of social intervention. The organization firmly believes that the community itself must take control in the process of empowerment, and therefore the mobile unit team includes sex workers. They play a key role in sending the message of self-care to the community of sex workers.

Sociodemographic summary

From its beginning in 2013 to 2017, the Program has made 6,177 interventions, of which 1,242 were first intervention (20.10%), compared to 4,935 that were follow-up (79.89%). The community of male prostitutes in Madrid is composed mostly of men who have pursued sex work in response to a chronic economic emergency. Before the economic crisis, the average time spent as a prostitute was around 19 months (Zaro et al., 2007).

Regarding the origin of sex workers served by the mobile unit (Figure 30.1), the majority were of foreign origin (78.8%) rather than Spanish (21.2%). Among foreigners, the main geographical area of origin was Latin America, which included almost half of the men served (45.5%). The countries of origin were Brazil (14.7%), Venezuela (11.8%), Argentina (1.3%), Chile (0.8%), Colombia (7.0%), Costa Rica (0.2%), Cuba (1.8%), Ecuador (1.4%), Honduras (0.3%), Mexico (0.6%), Paraguay (1.8%), Peru (1.4%), Puerto Rico (2.0%), Dominican Republic (0.2%), and Uruguay (0.2%).

The second geographical area of origin is Spain (21.1%), and the third is Eastern Europe (21.0%), specifically Romania (17.8%) and Bulgaria (3.2%). This fourth group was composed of men from Africa (7.1%); their countries of origin were Morocco (4.2%), Senegal (2.7%), and Algeria (0.2%). Finally, we found a small group of men whose country of origin was unknown (5.3%).

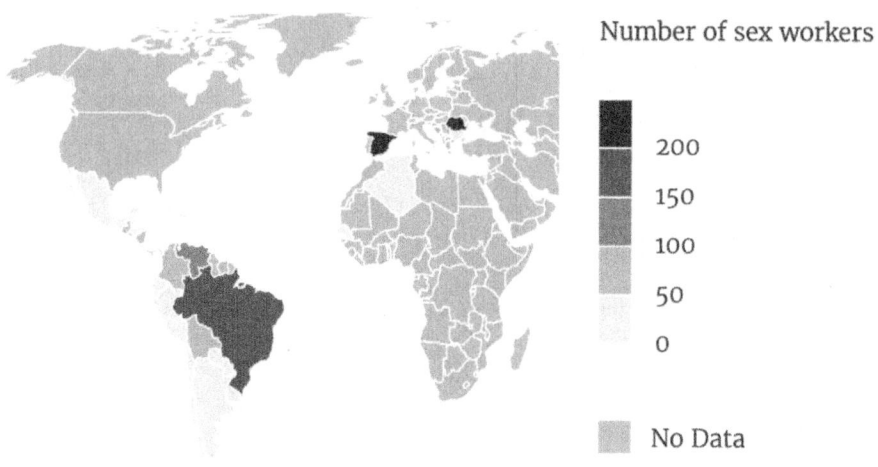

Figure 30.1 Volumes and country of origin of the male sex workers attended by the Male, Transgender, and Genderfluid Prostitution Program of the Madrid City Council, 2013–2017.

Source: Attention to Male, Transgender, and Genderfluid Prostitution Program of Imagina Más.

According to the data collected by the Program, the administrative situation of foreign male prostitutes in Madrid who have used the Program's services is mostly legal (58.5%), while 30.8% are undocumented and a minority (10.7%) have an unknown status. Undocumented men are especially vulnerable because lack of a residence permit entails a series of obstacles that make it difficult, and often impossible, to access the healthcare system and social services, to request any type of financial benefit, and to report hate crimes against LGTBI people.

As Figure 30.2 shows, the age of the male sex workers is mostly 26–35 years (52.3%), followed by those 18–25 years (43.8%) and 36–45 years (3.8%). Thus we see how the recent economic crisis has influenced long-term male prostitution. Younger male sex workers are concentrated in apartments managed by third parties; those apartments may be a starting space for sex work by young people, where they acquire knowledge of codes and rules while they gain experience in prostitution.

Where does male sex work occur in Madrid? Figures from program interventions (Figure 30.3) show the most popular locale is local saunas (27.5%), where clients can rent individual cabins where the sex workers perform their sexual services. The saunas in the city have often been spaces that permitted anonymous sexual contact between men without any economic transaction. In these places, prostitution is not allowed; men who are identified as sex workers are expelled. However, Madrid does have two exclusive saunas for male prostitution, where it is allowed and visible. In them, we find great heterogeneity in the origins of the sex workers, who report feeling more protected and less exposed. Because the saunas provide exclusive private premises for sexual encounters, misunderstandings such as those that occur in areas of street prostitution or bars can be avoided.

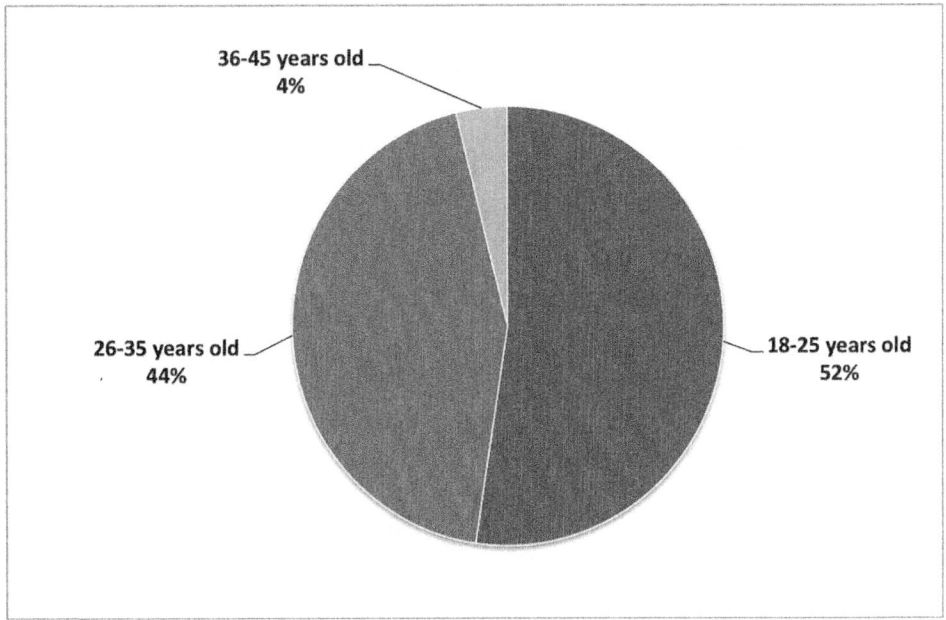

Figure 30.2 Distribution by age of the male sex workers attended by the Male, Transgender, and Genderfluid Prostitution Program of the Madrid City Council, 2013–2017.

Source: Attention to Male, Transgender, and Genderfluid Prostitution Program of Imagina Más.

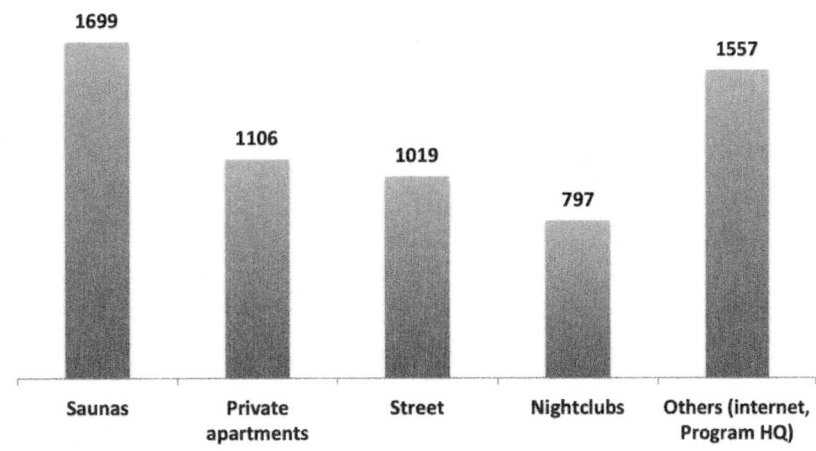

Figure 30.3 Places and volumes of intervention of the Male, Transgender, and Genderfluid Prostitution Program of the Madrid City Council, 2013–2017.

Source: Attention to Male, Transgender, and Genderfluid Prostitution Program of Imagina Más.

The second-largest area in terms of the volume of men served is private apartments managed by third parties (17.9%). In Spain, procuring is classified as a crime related to prostitution, sexual exploitation, and corruption of minors:

> The penalty of imprisonment of two to four years and a fine of twelve to twenty-four months will be imposed on anyone who profits by exploiting the prostitution of another person, even with the consent of the same. In any case, it will be understood that there is exploitation when any of the following circumstances occur: a) That the victim is in a situation of personal or economic vulnerability. b) That heavy, disproportionate or abusive conditions are imposed for its exercise.

In 2010, Spain dismantled, for the first time, a men's trafficking network for sexual exploitation that sponsored apartments in Madrid, Palma de Mallorca, Barcelona, and Alicante. It is estimated that 80 people were exploited, of whom 80% were cisgender men, 10% were transgender women, and 10% were cisgender women. As a result of this police operation, the number of apartments managed by pimps in Madrid decreased. Currently, there are only three apartments in the city, and the operation is similar to that of female prostitutes. Sex workers stay in the apartment for 21 days before moving to another apartment in a different city.

Male prostitution in the street (16.5%) is concentrated in the Puerta del Sol area, where we find the lowest level of prostitution among the men who are socially excluded. These sex workers face multiple problems, including homelessness, hunger, poverty, addiction, untreated mental illness, and threats from ex-convicts. On the street, we found men coming mostly from Eastern Europe, specifically Romania, and to a lesser extent Morocco. Homophobia, as well as a desire to avoid the stigma of prostitution, often leads these sex workers to relate to one another and to clients through physical and verbal violence. They often state that they are "fucking fags" out of necessity, never for pleasure. In this space, sex-worker aggressions toward clients are frequent (there was a murder case in 2008). Clients in this scenario are mostly elderly Spaniards who have lived their sexuality through adulthood using male prostitution and hiding. Nowadays, they avoid day centers and similar resources for the elderly, saying they feel more free in the Puerta del Sol.

Finally, the mobile unit has also intervened in the local nightlife (12.9%) at a bar located in the Chueca neighborhood aimed at the general public. There, male prostitution tends to go unnoticed. The typical profile of a male sex worker at the bar is often foreign, of Latin American origin, who has chosen this location because he can contact clients without feeling identified as a sex worker. This bar was sold in 2017, and the new management prohibited male prostitution inside its walls.

Sex workers have also been treated at the Program headquarters (25.4%). There, a team member facilitates access to public resources by physically accompanying the sex worker to help him overcome linguistic barriers or reduce the obstacles posed by the stigma associated with prostitution. The program team physically accompanied sex workers to health centers for the early diagnosis and emergency treatment of sexually transmitted infections (45.7%); to hospitals for access to antiretroviral treatment and medical follow-up (21.7%); to get specialized legal advice for asylum applications and residence permits (18.5%); to use social services to apply for financial aid, maintenance benefits, and/or housing (13.6%); and to mental health centers to coordinate cases with referred psychiatrists (0.5%).

Other resources used at the headquarters were group training sessions on health, legal rights, and social resources (44.4%); the individual counseling service (28.9%); anonymous and confidential rapid HIV testing (16.4%); psychological support (7.3%); peer volunteering (1.9%); and support groups for newly diagnosed people (0.9%).

Conclusions

The economic crisis has had an impact on all spheres of Spanish society, including male prostitution. The crisis has not meant an increase in the volume of men engaged in sex work but rather the persistence of sex work. The unemployment rate and the precariousness of employment in Spain have contributed to these men finding in prostitution a way of obtaining sufficient economic resources to survive. Spain's ongoing economic recovery had not yet been felt in most of the population of male sex workers, who continue to engage in male prostitution.

Immigration also plays a fundamental role in male prostitution in Spain. For example, men from Venezuela have emigrated from their home country for humanitarian reasons and begin to engage in prostitution once they arrive in Spain. For many of these men, prostitution has become a method of obtaining the economic resources they need so urgently. Prostitution over a limited period of time has become a drawn-out, chronic activity.

The vulnerabilities within male sex work are multiple and diverse. A lack of legal residency sometimes makes it impossible to access the health system and social benefits, perpetuating the exclusion of an invisible group in society. Within male prostitution in Spain, homophobia is a reality that affects the individual's identity and the ways in which male sex workers relate to others. Homophobia is the root cause of different types of violence—verbal, physical, and mental— that harms individuals physically and emotionally.

The high mobility of prostitution, based on the need to offer clients an ever-changing mix of new faces and bodies, hinders the establishment of stable social relations and the feeling of a permanent community. Combined with the strong stigma associated with prostitution, mobility thus hinders collective consciousness, empowerment, and activism by male sex workers. Male sex work therefore continues to be linked to clandestine activities and even crime, reinforcing xenophobic and homophobic beliefs that establish a direct relationship among homosexuality, prostitution, immigration, and crime. The absence of scientific literature describing male sex workers in Spain serves to heighten the group's exclusion from socio-health resources and prevent the implementation of policies that will mitigate their vulnerability. Although many (but certainly not all) male sex workers engage in sex work willingly, this willingness does not mean that sex workers do not experience multiple vulnerabilities and inequalities.

Male sex workers are currently the group most vulnerable to HIV and other STIs in Spain (24% of sex male workers in Madrid are HIV positive); their vulnerability is well above that of cisgender women prostitutes (1%). Despite these alarming data, the Spanish government has still not approved and provided access to pre-exposure prophylaxis (PrEP), which other countries have adopted to prevent the spread of HIV, especially among vulnerable groups such as prostitutes. PrEP could facilitate the empowerment of the community to care for their own health, diminishing clients' power and the social and economic inequalities that frequently pressure sex workers to engage in risky sexual practices.

The use of drugs is another challenge faced by male prostitutes. Drug use often increases inequality in relationships with clients, leads to addiction, has multiple adverse physical and mental effects, increases risky practices that lead to STIs, and leads to the exchange of sex for drugs. In addition, the current pattern of drug use among men who have sex with men in Spain includes especially dangerous and lethal substances, including GHB.

Finally, we see that male prostitution in Spain has begun to concentrate on private settings, such as apartments managed by third parties and saunas. Also, the use of mobile applications for contact between MSM and other specific online outlets for male prostitution is increasingly widespread. As a result, sex workers have begun to disappear from public spaces in Madrid.

In short, sex workers' silence and invisibility in Spain grows and perpetuates their vulnerability.

Note

1 A half-stay apartment is a kind of halfway house. It works as a shared apartment where people in need of help (those without a home or resources) can live for a short period until they can live on their own. They usually receive financial, psychological, and behavioral support while they live in the apartment.

References

Belza, M. J., Llácer, A., Mora, R., Morales, M., Castilla, J., & de la Fuente, L. (2001). Sociodemographic characteristics and HIV risk behaviour patterns of male sex workers in Madrid, Spain. *AIDS Care*, *13*, 677–682.

Benjumea, F. (2006). *Prostitución masculina actual en Barcelona: Usos y significados de las masculinidades en las relaciones sexuales remuneradas entre varones* [*Male prostitution in Barcelona: Analysis on masculinities in paid sexual relationships between men*]. Barcelona: Universidad de Barcelona.

Bimbi, D. S. (2007). Male prostitution: Pathology, paradigms, and progress in research. *Journal of Homosexuality*, *53*(1–2), 7–35.

Da Silva, L., & Evangelista, L. (2004). *La consomation de drogues dans le milieu de la prostitution masculine* [*Consumption of drugs in the field of male prostitution*]. Paris: Observatorie Français des Drogues et Toxicomanies.

Goffman, E. (1963). *Stigma: Notes on the management of spoiled identity*. Englewood Cliffs, NJ: Prentice Hall.

Kumar, N. (2016). *Negotiating masculinity in male independent escorting*. Queensland, Australia: University of Technology.

Latapie, H. (2009). *Doubles vies: Enquête sur la prostitution masculine homosexuelle* [*Double lives: Investigation into gay male prostitution*]. Paris: Le Gueuloir.

Logan, T. D. (2010). Personal characteristics, sexual behavior, and male sex work: A quantitative approach. *American Sociological Review*. doi:10.1177/0003122410379581

Logan, T. D. (2014). Economic analyses of male sex work. In V. Minichiello & J. Scott (Eds.), *Male sex work and society* (pp. 106–147). New York: Harrington Park Press.

Mai, N. (2015). Surfing liquid modernity: Albanian and Romanian sex workers in Europe. In P. Aggleton & R. Parker (Eds.), *Men who sell sex: Global perspectives*. Abingdon: Routledge.

McCall, H., Adams, N., Mason, D., & Willis, J. (2015). *What is chemsex and why does it matter?* London: BMJ Publishing Group Ltd.

Menoyo, C. et al. (2005). *Prevención del VIH/SIDA y otras ITS en hombres que ejercen la prostitución* [*Prevention of HIV/AIDS and other STIs in sex male workers*]. Madrid: Ministerio de Sanidad y Consumo, Plan Nacional sobre el SIDA.

Perlongher, N. O. (1993). *La prostitución masculina* [*Male prostitution*]. Buenos Aires: La Urraca.

Schiffer, K., & Giebers, M. (Eds.). (2003). *Final report*. Amsterdam: European Network Male Prostitution, ENMP.

Scott, J., Callander, D., & Minichiello, V. (2014). Clients of male sex workers. In V. Minichiello & J. Scott (Eds.), *Male sex work and society* (pp. 150–177). New York: Harrington Park Press.

Scott, J., Minichiello, V., Mariño, R. P., Harvey, G., Jamieson, M., & Browne, J. (2005). Understanding the new context of the male sex industry. *Journal of Interpersonal Violence*, *20*(3), 320–342.

Zaro, I. (2008). *Evitando conductas de riesgo en hombres que ejercen la prostitución* [*Avoiding risk behavior in male sex workers*]. Presentation at the 10th National AIDS Convention (Congreso Nacional sobre el SIDA). SEISIDA, San Sebastián.

Zaro, I. (2016). *La difícil vida fácil: Doce testimonios sobre prostitución masculina* [*Easy hard life: Twelve testimonials on male prostitution*]. Madrid: Punto de vista editores.

Zaro, I., Navazo, T., Vázquez, J., García, A., & Ibarguchi, L. (2016). *Aproximación al chemsex en España 2016*. Research paper by Imagina Más and Apoyo Positivo, Ministerio de Sanidad, Servicios Sociales e Igualdad, Gobierno de España. Retrieved from www.infochemsex.com

Zaro, I., Peláez, M., & Chacón, A. (2007). *Trabajadores masculinos del sexo: Aproximación a la prostitución masculina en Madrid 2006* [*Male sex workers: An approach to male prostitution in Madrid in 2006*]. Madrid. Retrieved from www.sidastudi.org

31

Male sex work in Sweden
Criminalization of the client

Marco Bacio

Sweden, located in northern Europe, is home to ten million people, making it the most populous country in Scandinavia (Denmark, Norway, and Sweden) and in the European Nordic Region (Scandinavia plus Finland and Iceland). Beginning in the late 1990s, Sweden became the worldwide leader in the fight against prostitution, making the country prominent in the literature and debate about sex work. However, the so-called "Swedish model" deliberately excludes male sex workers, and even today their presence is barely considered.

In this chapter, I explain how the Swedish model has diffused throughout the world. I explain the law (which is now 20 years old) and the feminist thought that supported the original legislation. I then summarize the three years of fieldwork that I carried out in Sweden. I interviewed 12 key informants (social workers, activists, a counselor, and a sexologist) in two of the three major Swedish cities (Stockholm and Malmö), and in Oslo (Norway) and Helsinki (Finland) to compare different countries and systems. To understand the effects of the Swedish legislation on the lives and on the work of male sex workers, I interviewed 25 male sex workers who work in Sweden. The conclusion summarizes the main results of my research.

It is important to understand the environment in Sweden with respect to research on prostitution/sex work. This issue is so sensitive that it seems impossible for the average person to have a neutral approach to it. Everyone must stand in favor of or against the legislation. And the words used to frame the discussions matter a great deal. The Swedish law uses the terms *prostitution* and *prostitute*, not *sex work* and *sex worker*. The government and those who support the legislation use the word *prostitution*, while those who wish to overturn the legislation use the term *sex worker*. For example, Swedish government institutions, such as local authorities and health services providers, use the word *prostitution*, but the two Swedish associations that fight for the rights of the country's sex workers (Fuckförbundet and Rose Alliance; see Figures 31.1 and 31.2) use the term *sex work*. I learned from my fieldwork that using the correct words with the people who live and work in Sweden is important. Indeed, some social workers or activists refused to talk with me because I used the "wrong" word with them; because the legislation is so controversial, few people believe that you are a neutral researcher who wants to study prostitution or sex work from an academic point of view. Attempting to

Figure 31.1 People with red umbrellas (a symbol of the sex workers' rights movement) on the Fuckförbundet floats during the EuroPride Parade in Stockholm on August 4, 2018.

be as neutral as possible, some researchers and social workers have used the term *sex for compensation*. Unfortunately, the phrase just sounds awkward to those who hear it and who want to know your position on the issue.

To maintain a neutral position, in this chapter I use both terms, in alphabetical order with a slash in between: *prostitution/sex work* or *prostitute/sex worker*. Before exploring the details of the Swedish legislation, it is important to understand the feminists thought that has framed the prostitution/sex work debate.

Figure 31.2   The Fuckförbundet floats from a street-level view during the EuroPride Parade in Stockholm on August 4, 2018. Sex workers and allies on the floats display their support for sex workers' rights in Sweden.

Feminist thought on prostitution/sex work

Due to space limitations, I offer two key elements of the debate: the different ideas regarding prostitution/sex work (as presented by Zelizer, 2005) and feminist thought on this topic (Scoular, 2004). The aim of Zelizer's book, *The Purchase of Intimacy*, is to analyze "the relationship between everyday practices and legal disputes when it comes to intimate economic interactions" (p. 1). As Zelizer notes, taboos exist against sex for hire. It is commonly believed that "intimacy corrupts economy and the economy corrupts intimacy. Yet . . . people often mingle economic activity with intimacy. The two often sustain each other" (p. 1).

Debates about money transactions and intimacy often focus on three competing ideas: separate spheres, "nothing-but," and connected lives. The hostile-worlds view "places rigid moral boundaries between market and intimate domains. It condemns any intersection of money and intimacy as dangerously corrupting" (Zelizer, 2005, p. 22). In contrast, the "nothing-but" view holds that "some simpler principle—economic, cultural, or political—actually explains what is going on" (Zelizer, 2005, p. 29). According to the hostile-world view, there is no possibility of contamination between economy and intimacy, but the "nothing-but" view holds that contamination can occur but only under negative circumstances, such as coercion: Prostitution is

> the result of coercive, and more specifically patriarchal, power structures. . . . Commercialized sex, as in prostitution, from this perspective is no different from unpaid sex in rape, dating, or marriage. The problem here is not commodification but men's coercion of women.
> *(Zelizer, 2005, p. 31)*

According to the third theory, connected lives,

> People create connected lives by differentiating their multiple social ties from each other, making boundaries between those different ties by means of everyday practices, sustaining those ties through joint activities (including economic activities), but constantly negotiating the exact content of important social ties.
>
> *(Zelizer, 2005, p. 32)*

Most discussions about intimacy, sex, and money (or economic transactions in general) in Sweden focus on tension between the separate-spheres and nothing-but viewpoints.

According to Scoular (2004), the main problem with discussions about the sexual market is the limitations involved in viewing prostitution as "straightforwardly paradigmatic, given the contingencies and diversity of the structures under which its materializes" (p. 343). Scoular divides the feminist perspectives on prostitution into three theories: domination theory, sex radicals, and postmodern subjects.

Domination theory is related to what Zelizer called the hostile world; it understands prostitution as violence against women, as "sexual slavery" (Barry, 1979), or as "male sexual behavior characterized by three elements variously combined: barter, promiscuity, and emotional indifference" toward another human being (Jeffries, 1997, p. 4). For domination theorists, there is no distinction between forced and voluntary prostitution, because men use prostitution to possess women: Womanhood is "confirmed in sexual activity, and when a prostitute contracts out the use of her body she is thus selling *herself* in a very real way" (Pateman, 1988, p. 207, emphasis in original). Thus "radical feminist theories reduce women's identity to a single trait, regardless of the structuring roles of money, culture, or race" (Scoular, 2004, p. 345). In contrast, sex radicals see prostitution/sex work as a complex, diverse, social practice. They are skeptical of equating commercial sex with erotic diversity, because they believe that prostitution/sex work reinforces the dominant norms of heterosexuality and femininity (Scoular, 2004). Feminists who see prostitutes/sex workers as postmodern-subjects focus on research, and they use the phrase *sex work* instead of *prostitution*. For example, O'Connell Davidson (1998) considers the variety of forms that sex work can take and sex workers' different degrees of control and power. O'Neill (2001) utilizes "a sophisticated combination of post-modern insight and ethnography to highlight the socioeconomic processes and structures that lead women into prostitution yet avoids viewing prostitution as either inherently oppressive or as an expression of sexual freedom" (Scoular, 2004, p. 349).

In other words, feminists have different opinions about prostitution/sex work. Feminists who subscribe to domination theory generally advocate for laws that stop and outlaw the sexual market. Sex radicals often prefer laws that would regulate the market, while the majority of feminists who regard sex workers as postmodern subjects aim to decriminalize sex work. It is now time to discuss the Swedish approach to prostitution/sex work. How does the law operate? Why has Sweden approved this legislation? Does it work?

The Swedish legislation and the criminalization of (men) clients

In general, countries have different ideas about how to regulate the market for sex work. As Garofalo Geymonat points out, "Often the fact that a country says 'no' or 'yes' to prostitution has no real impact on the decrease or increase of sexual market; it is more correlated with the local and world economic dynamics" (2014, p. 75, my translation). Along the same lines, Holmström and Skilbrei noted: "The prostitution market is both highly flexible and international and this means that its development is influenced by many different factors. In such a market, the law has limited scope to produce predictable outcomes" (2017, p. 91).

Nonetheless, many governments and politicians want to control sex work. In some cases, they want to end the sex trade in their country, and to do so they enact laws that ban sex work and criminalize the workers and/or the clients. But the only effect that they can truly control is related to the visibility of the sex trade, a phenomenon that has been called *spatial switching* (Hubbard, Matthews, & Scoular, 2008). In fact, sex work is more an international than a national phenomenon, and for that reason, local authorities find it difficult, perhaps even impossible, to manage it.

Nonetheless, politicians continue to pass laws aimed at eliminating sex work. As Östergen (2017) points out, we can divide the laws/policies into two categories: abolitionism and prohibitionism. The goal of abolitionism is to abolish the purchase of sexual services, while prohibitionism seeks to make all aspects of sex work illegal.

A second categorization scheme distinguishes among criminalization, legalization (or regulation), and decriminalization. The first category can be divided into "criminalization of the client" and "criminalization of the seller" (Östergen, 2017). A third typology, with four categories, comes from Garofalo Geymonat (2014): criminalization (or prohibition), regulation (or legalization), abolitionism, and decriminalization. With *criminalization*, a state completely outlaws the exchange of sex for money. These countries directly prosecute prostitutes/sex workers, who commit a criminal offense. Criminalization may apply to workers or to clients, as in Sweden. With *regulation*, the state recognizes prostitution/sex work (only among adults and without any restrictions) and regulates the sexual activities. With *abolitionism*, prostitution/sex work is not illegal per se, but certain activities are declared illegal and banned, such as trafficking and third-party gain (as in brothels and pimping). *Decriminalization*, the newest category, has been occurring only since 2003, when New Zealand became the first country to adopt this policy. In New Zealand there is no specific law on sex work, and selling sex and sexual services is equal to any other economic activity. Danna (2014) has suggested two additional categories: neo-prohibitionism (the criminalization of the client) and neo-regulationism (non-punitive toward sellers).

The Swedish Sex Purchase Act was first presented as part of the Women's Peace Bill. Its purpose was "to combat prostitution, which was seen as harmful, both for those directly involved and for society at large" (Holmström & Skilbrei, 2017, p. 83). This 1999 law had two major goals: reducing prostitution (in the short term by policing it and in the long term by changing public attitudes toward it) and reducing human trafficking for sexual purposes (Holmström & Skilbrei, 2017). To accomplish these goals, the law criminalized the clients of prostitutes (as we know, the law does not use the term *sex workers*). These clients, who commit a criminal offence, are punished with a fine and in theory even with prison (in 2011, the prison sentence increased from 6 months to 12 months), but only 200 cases are reported each year, and of these only 10% end in a fine or imprisonment (Garofalo Geymonat, 2014). Nonetheless, many other countries, including Norway, Iceland, France, and Ireland, have adopted the "Swedish model."

Twenty years later, we can ask: Did the Swedish Sex Purchase Act achieve its goals? According to Holmström and Skilbrei (2017), it is very difficult to determine the effects, if any, of the Swedish law in Sweden. First, let's examine the law's first goal: the reduction of prostitution. According to Kotsadam and Jakobsson (2014), prostitution is more prominent where it is legal (as in Denmark) and less prominent where it is illegal (as in Sweden). However, "visibility" usually refers to street prostitution. Since 1999, the number of women (and men) who sell sex on the street in Sweden has decreased significantly, but it is almost impossible to say the same about online prostitution. The law's second goal was to change society's perspectives on prostitution.

According to Jonsson and Jakobsson (2017), there is a higher rate of social acceptance for prostitution/sex work in countries where prostitution/sex work is legal and/or regulated than in countries where it is illegal or criminalized. Therefore, we can conclude that "the Sex Purchase Act has led to increased support in the [Swedish] population for banning not only buying sex but also selling sexual services" (Svedin, Jonsson, Kjellgren, Priebe, & Åkerman, 2012, p. 33). In other words, it appears that the Swedish population not only strongly favors its legislation but also believes that the law should also criminalize the sellers. But this belief works against the main intentions of the legislation, which aims to protect the victims (the sellers) and to criminalize the clients (Holmström & Skilbrei, 2017).

Another goal of the Swedish Sex Purchase Act was to end the trafficking of human beings for purposes of prostitution. The data produced by the Swedish National Police Board tend to confirm a decrease in trafficking, but the real problems are how to define trafficking and what to consider trafficking: "These problems make it very difficult to state that the Sex Purchase Act has decreased trafficking in Sweden" (Holmström & Skilbrei, 2017, p. 93).

It is important to remember that the Swedish legislation is gender neutral. So, the clients of men sex workers are criminals, as are the clients of women sex workers. But as this section has made clear, the legislation targets only the men who buy sex from women prostitutes/sex workers. Not only are men sex workers not acknowledged; they are deliberately excluded from the law. How can a man be harassed by a woman? Or how can a man be sexually harassed by another man? Paradoxically, one of the most advanced countries in terms of gender equality has built a law on stereotypes about women and men.

What are the effects of this law? Based on interviews with 12 key informants in three countries, the next section reveals the effects of the Swedish model on how researchers study it, how social workers provide assistance to both sellers and buyers, and how activists fight for sex workers' rights.

The effects of criminalization: daily life in Sweden

I interviewed nine key informants in Sweden, two in Norway, and one in Finland. The three interviewees outside Sweden were activists with the local national association that fights for the rights of sex workers: PION (*Sexarbeidernes Interesseorganisasjon*) in Oslo and *Pro-Tukipiste* in Helsinki. The interviewees in Sweden (four in Stockholm and two in Malmö) were three activists with RFSL (Swedish Federation for Lesbian, Gay, Bisexual, and Transgender Rights), one activist and two social workers with RFSL Ungdom (for people between 15 and 25 years old), one sexologist with RFSU (Swedish Association for Sexuality Education), one social worker at *Mikamottagningen* (now called KST—*Kompeten-scentrum Sexuella Tjänster* or Center for Sexual Services), and one counselor at a Stockholm center for sexual transmitted diseases that provides services to LGBT people. All the names in the following are real.

All the interviewees but one prefer to use the term *sex work*, even if it is open to attack from the outside:

> What I like about the term "sex worker" is that it clearly defines that it has to do with people older than 18. You can rely on a definition by UNAIDS: with people over 18 it is consensual and it is not trafficking. While "sex for compensation" could be basically anything—it could be kids, could be trafficking, yeah basically anything. . . [If you use the term *sex work*], you know that you are going to be attacked in the Swedish context.
>
> *Nicklas, RFSL activist*

According to all the experts I interviewed, the Swedish law is extremely ideological, and for this reason it is very difficult to study and to understand how the system works from a neutral perspective:

> It was very hard to be somewhere in-between if you talk about the legislation. Either you are supposed to be very much pro-legislation in Sweden or against it. So being in the middle, having a complex analysis that there are different experiences of sex work and selling sex, it was hard. There is a lot of ideology. . . . You are a victim, you have been exposed to sexual assault and this [sex work] is a consequence.
>
> *Jonas, RFSL activist*

The activists and service providers whom I interviewed are aware of the fact that the law and society as a whole do not consider men who sell sex. Indeed, in the Nordic countries, prostitution/sex work is widely considered a women's issue. Some of the men who sell sex to other men or to women want to take advantage of this situation:

> Then, men sex workers said that this is one thing which is good to be ignored because the law does not affect them because they do not exist officially. Everyone is interested in women in prostitution.
>
> *Jaana, Pro-Tukipiste activist*

Recall that the main goal of the Swedish legislation is to eliminate prostitution, because sex work is a form of a trauma for women who sell sexual services. This goal creates a contradiction for these services providers, who receive funds from the government. The most problematic part of the legislation, they say, is the third-party provision, which prevents a third party from interfering between sellers and buyers. The problem is that this third-party section of the law is also applied to service providers. They became the target of the law and, for this reason, criminals themselves:

> Well the purchase act is not the biggest problem, it is the third party legislation that is the biggest, biggest, problem, because you are not able . . . because it makes it hard for people like sex workers working together, helping each other. . . . It is quite challenging working with harm reduction—talking about safer sex, giving information about condom use—because that can be interpreted about making it easier to sell or buy sex.
>
> *Jonas, RFSL activist*

The accusation of facilitating the buying and/or selling of sex was widespread among all the interviewees. For example, social workers of the RFSL Ungdom project "Pegasus," which aims to help people between 15 and 25 years old who had or have experiences of selling sex, told me that they must be very careful in what they say to these young people:

> According to this model we do not give advice . . . so we do not really give advice on what they should or should not do. But I think it is more like asking questions and giving different perspectives.
>
> *Virag, RFSL Ungdom social worker*

Note that such information may not be very useful to young people who, instead of finding simple answers to their questions, receive more questions about feelings and "different perspectives." The boundaries of the Swedish law are very clear, and service providers do not want to be attacked by feminists or by the public, which is very supportive of the legislation. At the most basic level, the problem occurs because people who take part in the debate often mix human trafficking with simple organization or coordination among sex workers. As a social worker at *Mikamottagningen* explains:

> Often people in the debate mix up that if something is organized, then, it is human trafficking. Just because the prostitution is organized, it does not mean it is human trafficking. Human trafficking is a crime that is written in the law, how it is formulated—it is a very severe crime, but it is also very clear what it is. It does not have to be a crime because something is organized. It does not have to be a severe crime—it definitely does not have to be human trafficking. To be organized it could be that I feel safer if I sell sex if I do it through friends rather than if I do it alone, so we organize as a group to take care of each other—but it does not mean it is human trafficking. But people mix that up all the time.
>
> *Ylva, Mika Malmö social worker*

One of the paradoxes of the law is that social workers, nurses, counselors, and other professionals who participate in harm-reduction activities cannot give condoms and/or lube to sex workers and their clients because this activity is clearly interpreted as facilitation of an illegal activity. The Mika clinic solves this problem by placing bowls filled with condoms and small packages of lube in every room of the center; thus, the problem remains serious for people who work in outreach projects, harm reduction, and HIV prevention. They are the most affected by third-party legislation:

> I am staying away from politics as good as I can when I am working with the community, because that is the most important thing for me. If the Swedish model created the situation where the sex workers were healthy and non-stigmatized and free from HIV infection etc. etc., I would be pro-Swedish legislation. But the Swedish legislation does not work that way.
>
> *Nicklas, RFSL activist*

The Mika clinics in Sweden warrant additional discussion. There are three units in the country, one in each major city (Stockholm, Göteborg, and Malmö), they are publicly funded, and the local city authority pays the Malmö team. These clinics' official purpose is to reach prostitutes and to convince them to stop selling sex. But the reality is quite different. Indeed, sex workers who drop into the clinic know that nobody will ask them to stop selling sex. Instead, they find a welcoming environment where they can get tested for STDs, talk about their living situation, and sort out multiple questions, including questions about access to social services. The Mika clinics are not seeking to rescue people from prostitution. Rather, they seek to help the people working in this industry by helping them have a better quality of life, feel safer while engaging in transactional sex, and minimize the risk of contracting HIV and other STDs.

Finally, it is noteworthy that Sweden is trying to export its legislation abroad. Because the Swedish government sees the law as a way to end the sex trade, it is investing money to convince other countries to follow the same path:

> Sweden has used a lot of money to promote this. I think this is the biggest political export.
>
> *Jaana, Pro-Tukipiste activist*

> What if we spent less money on promoting the Swedish model abroad—not going to fancy meetings, not giving money to organizations to promote the Swedish legislation—instead, using that money to give a welfare net for vulnerable people that may be selling sex instead?
>
> *Nicklas, RFSL activist*

Even though the Swedish law has been successfully exported to other countries, including Norway, Iceland, France, and Ireland, each country has passed the laws under a different set of circumstances and with different effects. Consider the case of Norway. The decision to enforce the legislation was not led by feminists. Rather, it resulted from the increased presence of migrants (both legal and illegal) during the economic crisis of 2007. Indeed, the law passed two years later, in 2009.

> If radical feminists try to use traditional way of intimidation, they get criticized more here than in Sweden. I think that compared to Sweden it is a different world.
>
> *Andrés, PION activist*

In Norway, clients are criminalized as they are in Sweden, but this does not mean that the Norwegian population perceives them as criminals (in contrast to the Swedish population, which does perceive clients as criminals). Moreover, the third-party legislation is not a problem in Norway. Social workers can do outreach work and distribute condoms and lube without the fear of being attacked or being accused of facilitating commercial sex.

How do Swedish sex workers work? Are they affected by the Swedish legislation when selling sex in Sweden? The next section deals with the experiences of male sex workers in the country.

The invisibility of men who sell sex in Sweden

The sample is formed by 25 interviews with men who sell sex to other men in Sweden and who advertise online. The average age of the interviewees was 28. The youngest was 20 and the oldest 52. In terms of race and ethnicity, 18 were white, 5 were Asian, and 2 were Latino. In terms of their educational credentials: 8 have a master's degree, 7 an undergraduate degree (of which 3 were master's students at the time of the interview), 7 graduated high school, 2 did not go beyond middle school, and 1 did not declare his educational status.

I contacted all the sex workers exclusively online. As a first contact, I sent the same message. Moreover, I created a website for my research where the sex workers were able to check my identity and the goals of the project. I also paid for advertisements on different websites. In these ads, I put three pictures of me, a link to my personal website, and a link to my university webpage. I sent no more than 100 messages in Sweden, so my response rate was extremely high. The number of sex workers who advertise in Sweden is very low, so I sent a message, and sometimes even two or three messages, to every male sex worker who uses the Internet to find clients in Sweden. I gave them 500 Swedish Crowns (or 48 EUR, 42 GBP, 55 USD) to thank them for their time; each interview lasted between one hour and 30 minutes and two hours. Finally, to guarantee their privacy, I asked them to give me a fake name; Sweden is a small country, after all. The names that follow are not the names they gave me because I changed them to Swedish common names.

I can divide the 25 men I interviewed in Sweden into two sub-groups. The first is composed of people, both Swedish and non-Swedish citizens, who live permanently in Sweden. The second is composed of people, all non-Swedish citizens, who do not live in Sweden and were just traveling in the country at the time of the interview.

Before talking directly with the interviewees about the Swedish legislation, it was necessary to determine if the men who sell sex in Sweden are aware of the legislation in force in the country. The majority of them did not know about the legislation or had a very vague idea about it, even though it is not difficult to find information about the law. When I asked a sex worker where he had found information about the Swedish law, he replied, "It is not hard to find, it is just a Google away" (Gustav, 24 yo). However, the majority of the men I interviewed were not interested in conducting a simple Google search to understand the law of the country in which they live. Similarly, sex workers who travel across the world, and in different countries, typically did not know the local legislation, and they were not interested in the law of their country of origin either:

M: Do you know the legislations about sex work in the countries you visit?
C: Vaguely.
M: Also, in the US?
C: I just know that it is not technically legal, but I do not know any specifics besides that.
M: You said vaguely, what does it mean?
C: As I am aware because it takes no effort to know but I am also disinterested because it does not matter to me. Unless there are some countries out there where the penalty is death or something like that, then maybe I would be interested in knowing but it is not an important piece of information to me.
M: So, you did not check in advance before you came in Sweden?
C: No.
M: And also, in the US is a vague idea.
C: I think it is illegal in all states besides Nevada, I know that much.

Carl, 28 yo

This sex worker is aware that information is easily accessible, but he is not interested in spending time to find the answers. The key point here is that the sex workers in my sample did not think that they were committing a crime. Why were they so sure that they were not risking anything? Was it because they are men? Was it because they are not obligated to sell sex and that they had no bad experiences? Or was it because they never heard anything negative about men selling sex to men? Indeed, because the discourse in Sweden (and in some other countries) is much related to women who sell sex to men, the legislation comes last in these escorts' list of things to worry about; likewise, it does not appear to be a concern for the men who buy sexual services, who are technically committing a crime. Moreover, spatial shifting of sex works from the streets to the Internet (Hubbard et al., 2008) hides prostitution, making it more difficult for the police and the public authorities find and prosecute (Holmström & Skilbrei, 2017).

Because men sell sex to men online, I can affirm, this activity is just ignored. It is ignored because these sex workers are men (not women), Swedish or with a Western passport, or migrants who are not planning to stay in Sweden for more than a week. Indeed, when I asked if they ever had any problem with the police, only one sex worker answered yes. Interestingly, the man who answered "yes" was a student from Eastern Asia, living in Copenhagen and working on both sides of the Öresund Bridge (which connects Denmark and Sweden). When he started working in the sex industry, he received a visit from the Danish police, who wanted to check where he was living and if any coercion was involved in doing this work. This inquiry was perfectly fine with him because it is part of the Danish legislation. Male sex workers in Sweden are so outside of the debate, the focus of the legislation, and police activity that they do not to care about the law or its effects. Indeed, they often tell their clients that because they buy sex from men instead of women, they do not need to worry that they are committing a crime in Sweden.

To conclude: There may be no legal impact on sex workers' life or the work in Sweden. Other things scared them more, such as being recognized as sex workers by family or friends and going out with clients to dinner or public places in their own city.

Conclusions

In Sweden, in 1999, legislation was passed with the goal of ending prostitution and the violence that men perpetrate against women. The law deliberately excluded men who sell sex because men are not considered victims, either as buyers or as sellers. Some of these men are aware that they are not the target of the police or the other public authorities, which gives them some degree of freedom compared to women who sell sex to men. Meanwhile, the goal of eliminating the sale of sex is so widespread in Swedish society that outreach work, such as giving condoms and lube to sex workers, is viewed as a facilitation of the illegal encounter between seller and buyer. At the same time, HIV and STDs prevention programs, as well as giving advice to sex workers, are considered inappropriate. Nonetheless, some private organizations (such as RFSL, RFSL Ungdom, and RFSU) and public organizations (like Mika Clinic Malmö) do not attempt to convince women and men who sell sex to quit. Rather, they provide the services that sex workers need to remain safe and healthy.

I interviewed 25 men who sell sex to men in Sweden. None of these 25 men experienced any problem or issue with the police or any other public authorities. Nor did their clients, to the best of the interviewees' knowledge. Also, these male sex workers are barely aware of the Swedish legislation or any other legislation about prostitution/sex work. They know that because they are men, they do not risk facing any criminal charges for selling sex to other men (or women). The result is gender discrimination. Women are affected because they are women, and men are not affected because they are men.

We know that sex work is not a straightforward issue. As in many other matters, there are debates and different opinions. However, I argue that the Swedish government and key actors should try to understand the needs of the sex workers that work in the country instead of assuming that they are all victims of their past traumas who need to be rescued.

References

Barry, K. (1979). *Female sexual slavery*. Englewood Cliffs, NJ: Prentice-Hall.

Danna, D. (2014). *Report on prostitution laws in the European Union*. Milan: The University of Milan.

Garofalo Geymonat, G. (2014). *Vendere e comprare sesso: Tra piacere, lavoro e prevaricazione*. Bologna: Il Mulino.

Holmström, C., & Skilbrei, M. L. (2017). The Swedish sex purchase act: Where does it stand? *Oslo Law Review, 4*(2), 82–104.

Hubbard, P., Matthews, R., & Scoular, J. (2008). Regulating sex work in the EU: Prostitute women and the new spaces of exclusion. *Gender, Place and Culture, 15*(2), 137–152.

Jeffries, S. (1997). *The idea of prostitution*. Melbourne: Spinifex Press.

Jonsson, S., & Jakobsson, N. (2017). Is buying sex morally wrong? Comparing attitudes toward prostitution using individual-level data across eight Western European countries. *Women's Studies International Forum, 61*, 58–69.

Kotsadam, A., & Jakobsson, N. (2014). Shame on you, John! Laws, stigmatization, and the demand for sex. *European Journal of Law and Economics, 37*(3), 393–404.

O'Connell Davidson, J. (1998). *Prostitution, power, and freedom*. London: Polity Press.

O'Neill, M. (2001). *Prostitution and feminism*. London: Polity Press.

Östergen, P. (2017). *From zero-tolerance to full integration: Rethinking prostitution policies* (DemandAT Working Paper No. 10). Retrieved from http://www.demandat.eu/publications/zero-tolerance-full-integration-rethinking-prostitution-policies

Pateman, C. (1988). *The sexual contract*. Cambridge: Polity Press.

Scoular, J. (2004). The "subject" of prostitution: Interpreting the discursive, symbolic and material position of sex/work in feminist theory. *Feminist Theory, 5*(3), 343–355.

Svedin, C. G., Jonsson, L., Kjellgren, C., Priebe, G., & Åkerman, I. (2012). *Report on prostitution in Sweden*. Linköping: Linköping University Press.

Zelizer, V. A. (2005). *The purchase of intimacy*. Princeton, NJ and Oxford: Princeton University Press.

32

Male sex work in the Czech Republic

The intersection of cultural norms, sexual orientation, and economic disparities

Michael Bar-Johnson

The Czech Republic, since the fall of communism in 1989, has become a sex tourism destination (Bunzl, 2000; Golgo, 2003). It is also home to a thriving gay pornography industry that focuses on films with actors who are typically 18 or 19 but often appear much younger (Marritz, 2007). The country attracts many sex tourists seeking sex with very young men (Bar-Johnson & Weiss, 2015). Sex work is decriminalized in the Czech Republic, so it is not a crime for individuals to offer sexual services if they are over the age of 18 (see Havelková, 2018, for a complete review of Czech policy regarding sex work in general). However, the low age of consent, set at 15 years old, makes age restrictions difficult to enforce if the sex worker refuses to press charges (ECPAT International, 2014). Male sex work in the Czech Republic takes place mainly in clubs and bars dedicated primarily to sex workers, as well as via Internet escorting (Bar-Johnson & Weiss, 2015). Those still working the streets tend to be ethnic minority Roma, but police efforts have curtailed this aspect of sex work (Graham & Weitzer, 2017).

Sexuality and Czech culture

The Czech Republic is far more liberal than other post-Soviet countries in terms of its attitudes toward sex. While Russia moved toward further stigmatizing homosexuality, eventually leading to the passage of its anti-gay-propaganda laws, the Czech Republic moved toward the more liberal position of its Western European neighbors and eventually legalized gay registered partnerships (Sikes, 2010). In a radio interview, Dr. Petr Weiss, Director of the Sexology Institute at Charles University in Prague, speculated on the reason for the country's liberal attitude toward sex:

> The tolerance of Czechs in sexual questions is really very high. It's really high compared to attitudes in even the US or England and France. Czechs' attitudes on pre-marital sex, extramarital sex, contraception, abortion, homosexuality—really very liberal. We think that this is connected to the number of atheists in our society. I think this is the reason why we are so liberal when it comes to sex.
>
> *Weiss, in radio interview with Velinger, 2009*

The lack of a strong religious prohibition on sex, combined with the high value of personal privacy enshrined in the Czech constitution, has created an atmosphere where sexuality and sex work has become a part of the everyday landscape of many cities (Graham & Weitzer, 2017). In the Czech Republic, brothels, both gay and straight, are a feature of many quiet residential areas, and they exist without significant backlash from their communities or interference from police, despite operating in a grey area under the law. Thus, the commercial sex industry in general and the gay sex industry in particular have flourished in the absence of any real stigma or social opposition (Sikes, 2010).

Sex work in the Czech Republic

Hall (2007a) was the first to provide a scientific analysis of male sex workers in Prague in his ethnographic study on young Czech men's exchange of sex for money. Little has changed since his report; however, for the most part, police have driven sex workers from the street and train stations. Currently they offer their services mainly in bars and clubs that cater specifically to sex workers and their clients (Bar-Johnson & Weiss, 2015; Graham & Weitzer, 2017), or they offer their services via Internet portals for male escorts (Bar-Johnson & Weiss, 2015). Police control of the bars has also limited the number of underage sex workers, but it has not eliminated underage male sex work. Underage prostitution is more problematic among Internet escorts, who do not need to verify their age to create an online advertisement, whereas club owners typically try to enforce the age requirement of 18 for entry.

Government health officials have estimated that 5% all sex workers in the Czech Republic are male (Mann & Tarantola, 1996). Male sex workers in the Czech Republic have already been the topic of qualitative research (Hall, 2007b) and film documentaries by the Polish director Wiktor Grodecki, including *Not Angels but Angels* (1994), *Body Without Soul* (1996), and the fictionalized account *Mandragora* (1997), which may have helped to precipitate the police crackdown on child prostitution in the early 2000s (ECPAT International, 2014). A leading Czech journalist has assembled other interesting case studies of young male sex workers into the book *Your Son the Prostitute* (author's translation of Vlašík, 2009). Early quantitative research had mostly been devoted to the study of female sex workers (Zikmundová & Weiss, 2003, 2004).

Studies of male street prostitutes typically find that these sex workers have had dysfunctional childhoods and little or no family support (Leichtentritt & Arad, 2005) and are more likely the victims of abuse (Valera, Sawyer, & Schiraldi, 2001). They are often undereducated, lack other job skills, and need fast cash to survive (Flowers, 2001). They also frequently enter prostitution to support a drug habit (McCabe et al., 2011). However, research regarding male Internet escorts has typically found fewer social problems, with these sex workers being primarily motivated by money and the easy nature of the work (Uy, Parsons, Bimbi, Koken, & Halkitis, 2004).

Findings regarding sex workers in public bars and clubs in the Czech Republic (Figure 32.1) have shown similar results to those found in earlier studies of male street workers (Bar-Johnson & Weiss, 2015; Graham & Weitzer, 2017). These Czech sex workers typically began their sex life much earlier than the average Czech, although the extent of their childhood problems seems to be much less severe in Prague than among sex workers in other countries, such as Ireland (McCabe et al., 2011), the United States (Mimiaga, Reisner, Tinsley, Mayer, & Safren, 2007), or Russia (Minichiello & Scott, 2014). They are, however, somewhat more likely to be homeless, to have problems with drugs and alcohol, and to engage in risky sex (Bar-Johnson & Weiss, 2014). It seems that many have slipped through the relatively robust social safety net provided by the Czech government, so they have found in sex work what they perceive to be the only reasonable solution to their difficult financial situations. Few have any real plan to find other

Figure 32.1   Escorts often work for the club officially as strippers (Escape Club, Prague, now closed).

work; they have little education and few skills, as well as a poor work ethic. In the movie *Mandragora* (1997, Figure 32.2), a sex worker advises a new recruit that the secret to success is to "do as little work as possible for as much money as you can get" (author's translation). However, for sex workers who manage to find regular legal work, many will face stiff penalties from the government, which garnishes their legal wages for years in order to pay off the large debts they accrued for their unpaid health insurance during the time they worked on the black market as sex workers. Unfortunately, many sex workers do not know that they need to be registered as either a student or unemployed for the government to pay for their insurance (personal communication, MSW in clubs working to inform other sex workers, from Bar-Johnson, 2015).

It is worth commenting on the situation in the bars and clubs, which, according to the escorts, have improved in recent years. In the past, these bars were known as rather dangerous places to visit. The sex workers were often beaten or threatened by the club owners, and the clubs were subject to frequent police raids in the late 1990s, mainly to search for underage boys. Now, most clubs are under new ownership, and the owners take greater care to ensure that boys under 18 do not enter. The clubs also prohibit the open use of drugs (Graham & Weitzer, 2017). Barmen in two research studies (Bar-Johnson & Weiss, 2015; Graham & Weitzer, 2017) reported being instructed by the management not to admit any sex workers who appear visibly under the influence of drugs, in particular the locally popular methamphetamine, Pervitin. These changes have improved working conditions for many male sex workers, who no longer seek clients in the dangerous train station and now have a safer environment in which to look for clients. However, their work conditions rely in great part on the whims of a few, mostly

Figure 32.2   Movie poster from *Mandragora* (Grodecki, 1997).

foreign, club owners. Overall, the decriminalization of prostitution, combined with enforcement of laws against child prostitution and pimping, has had a generally positive effect on the conditions for male sex workers in the Czech Republic.

Previous research (Smith & Seal, 2008) suggested that supportive, healthy workplace environments also play an important role in promoting safer sex, which, however, was not observed in any of the research on these establishments; no condoms or any information about HIV were

Figure 32.3   Planet Romeo's specialized web portal for male escort advertisements (www. hunqz.com).

reported as available in any of the clubs. Future interventions should target clubs as a potential venue for decreasing risky sexual behavior.

Also surprising is the much larger group of Internet escorts in the Czech Republic (typically a few hundred are offering their services at any given time on the popular website, www.hunqz. com; Figure 32.3), precisely because they do not fit the typical profile of a sex worker (Bar-Johnson & Weiss, 2015). These escorts are for the most part fairly well educated, happy, and otherwise typical young men. Due to the ease of finding clients over the Internet and the lure of easy money, and the lack of explicit social stigma, their numbers seem to remain steady, with new escort profiles appearing on the Web almost daily as others disappear. These sex workers seem for the most part naïve to the inherent dangers of sex work, which is in fact greater for them due to the anonymity of the Internet. Many of these Internet escorts admitted to being the victim of a violent crime, a fact most of the young men who create Internet profiles at present are almost certainly unaware of, as there is no objective information available to these young sex workers about the inherent risks of the escort business.

Sexual identity and Czech male sex workers

The study of sexual orientation is difficult, with controversy surrounding even the definition of the term, so I will use the wider term *sexual identity*. In particular, scientists interested in human sexuality have engaged in a great deal of debate in defining bisexuality in males. Modern estimates of its prevalence in men are around 10% (Bancroft, 2009).

National representative surveys conducted in the Czech Republic reveal that 98% of males indicate their orientation as heterosexual, with less than 1% identifying as homosexual and approximately 2% reporting they are unsure of their orientation (Weiss & Zvěřina, 2001). For females in the general population, the findings are similar, with 97% reporting heterosexuality, 2% unsure, and less than 1% identifying as homosexual.

Regarding sexual identity among male sex workers, researchers in the United States typically have found a high percentage of bisexuals in their samples, ranging from 20% (Smith, Grov, & Seal, 2008) to nearly 40% (Boles & Elifson, 1994; Ross, Timpson, Williams, Amos, & Bowen, 2007). Studies of female prostitutes in the Czech Republic also found a much higher incidence of bisexuality among female sex workers (Zikmundová & Weiss, 2004) than in the general population (Weiss & Zvěřina, 2001). Half of all female sex workers reported same-sex sexual experience, 6% considered themselves lesbian, and 13% considered themselves bisexual (Zikmundová & Weiss, 2004).

In one of the few quantitative studies of Czech male sex workers (Bar-Johnson & Weiss, 2015), the majority of male sex workers investigated were in fact not homosexual. Rather, approximately one-third were heterosexual, and another third reported their orientation as bisexual. Although the study took great care to ensure that any man engaged in sex work at the time had a chance to be selected for the study and response rates were high, it is impossible to obtain a true representative sample of this population. Therefore, we should not draw any firm conclusions about the exact percentages of gay-for-pay sex workers in the Czech Republic, although the percentages mentioned previously are similar enough to those suggested by previous research on male sex workers in the United States (Boles & Elifson, 1994; Ross et al., 2007) that they are probably indicative of the population of Czech male sex workers in general.

Gay-for-pay pornography and male sex work in the Czech Republic

One might expect that the stigma associated with gay-for-pay behavior may be mitigated by the Czechs' liberal views regarding sexuality in general (Weiss & Zvěřina, 2001), as well as their pragmatic views regarding earning money. A comment indicative of this pragmatism occurred in one of our preliminary interviews with sex workers during the design phase of our study. In the research of Bar-Johnson (2015), one heterosexual escort (who also performed in gay porn) from a poor industrial region in the northeastern part of the country was asked if it was difficult for him as a heterosexual to perform sex acts with other men. He replied, "It's better than working in the (coal) mines" (author's translation).

It seems that Czechs' pragmatic view of sex work is that if foreigners are willing to pay good money, then it is completely up to the individual to decide if he is willing to work in this industry in the hopes of earning quick financial rewards (Sikes, 2010). This tolerance toward gay-for-pay sex work was evident in a 2005 case in which a popular Czech television station, TV Nova, first aired its version of the American *Big Brother* series. The producers threatened one of the housemates, Filip Trojovsky (Figures 32.4, 32.5), with expulsion when it was revealed that he had not disclosed making gay pornography in the past. Public outcries of unfairness got him reinstated on the show; however, he did lose a lucrative endorsement contract in neighboring Germany over the scandal. In a country where the sex business is everywhere and salaries are generally low, it seems that Czech society does not have a problem accepting that heterosexuals can perform homosexual acts for money without affecting their perceived sexual orientation or their popularity with the public.

Another important area to consider is the booming gay pornography industry in the Czech Republic, due to its close connection with the sex work industry. The reputation of the Czech Republic as a culture where young men are eager to exchange sex for money regardless of their sexual orientation is consistently reinforced by the large amount of gay porn produced there (Sikes, 2010):

> The past decade has witnessed a tremendous explosion in the production of all-male pornography in the Czech Republic; these pornographic performances, accessed either through recorded visual media or live via streaming video over the Internet, have flooded the international marketplace. In fact, a recent story in the popular press ranked the Czech nation just behind the United States in all-male pornographic production—a fact all the

Figure 32.4   Filip Trojovsky (left) in Bel Ami promotional photo.

Figure 32.5   Filip Trojovsky from the Czech version of *Big Brother*.

more remarkable considering that the Czech Republic has less than one-twentieth the population of the United States. Clearly, pornography attracts a large number of young Czech men into the business, especially given the relative size of the national job pool.

(p. 373)

In his review of Czech male pornography, Brennan (2017) points out a consistent theme of exploitation, with young heterosexual Czech men depicted as easily convinced to have sex with other men in exchange for money. Popular websites such as *Czech Hunter, Debt Dandy*, and *Dirty Scout* perpetuate this reputation and contribute to the perception that young Czech men are eager to engage in sexual activity for money, very likely contributing to the influx of

Figure 32.6   All Boys: Documentary film about small American-owned Czech gay production company.

sex tourists in search of young male sex workers (Brennan, 2017). This image of hypersexualized young Czech men began with the now famous gay pornography production company, Bel Ami, which has been promoting videos of exclusively teen men from the Czech and Slovak Republics since 1993 (www.belamionline.com). Its business model of recruiting young gay and gay-for-pay actors into a world of modeling which includes not only porn but mainstream promotion of swimwear and underwear has proven very successful, for example, their more recent cooperation with the popular gay brand ADDICTED (VOCLA.com, 2015). However, they also have a darker history of controversy, which includes being among the first to shoot mainstream gay incest pornography with the twin brothers Elijah and Milo Peters (Rogers, 2010). Regardless, their success became a model for many other less scrupulous foreign producers to set up shop in the Czech Republic, with serious consequences for young men in the industry as illustrated in the documentary film *All Boys* (Heikkinen, 2010; Figure 32.6). The documentary shows how the young men are provided accommodation and living expenses in lieu of higher wages for their sex work. As a result, they are left susceptible to sexual coercion and abuse with little chance to deny their employers' demands, and the film graphically depicts how some of the men eventually descend into depression, addiction, and homelessness.

Research on male sex workers suggest that Prague's internet sex workers were more likely to have first appeared in gay porn. Then, when their on-screen desirability waned, they turned to sex work, where their status as a porn star could be advantageous (Bar-Johnson & Weiss, 2014). However, sex workers in bars and clubs were more likely to be recruited at their place of work by smaller porn producers, often for risky, low-paying bareback (without condom) pornography.

Mental and sexual health and sexual identity

The relationship between sex work and poor mental health among female sex workers has long been established, with studies having found as many as two-thirds of these women suffering symptoms of PTSD (White, 1998) in addition to increased symptoms of depression (Roxburgh, Degenhardt, & Copeland, 2006). For many young men in the Czech Republic, this type of work is a means of survival and a way to earn easy money, so it is attractive not only to homosexuals but also to any young man who finds himself in financial difficulty, whether gay, straight, or bisexual (Bar-Johnson & Weiss, 2015). Yet despite the relatively open Czech culture, it still seems that for sex workers with a bisexual identity, sex work is associated with a higher degree of psychological distress. Many bisexual male sex workers reported levels of symptoms that would qualify them for a clinical diagnosis of major depression or an anxiety disorder, whereas for homosexuals and heterosexuals engaging in sex work in the Czech Republic, problems with psychological health were not as prevalent (Bar-Johnson & Weiss, 2015). Unfortunately, little other research has focused on the mental health issues of male sex workers, with the focus usually on HIV transmission (see Aggleton, 1999, for a historical review).

Sexual health of sex workers

HIV has not hit the Czech Republic as hard as it has hit many other post-communist countries, with 0.3% of the Czech population infected according to official government statistics, as opposed to Russia, which at 1% has triple the number of cases per capita (Gokengin et al., 2018). However, medical professionals caution that the actual rates of people living with HIV may be triple these reported figures (NeLP, 2014). Men who have sex with men (MSM) are the largest risk group for contracting HIV in the Czech Republic, although 70% of those with HIV are undergoing treatment, and close to 90% have achieved viral suppression, according to Brown et al. (2018). Although the Czech Republic fares much better than the vast majority of former Soviet countries, Gokengin et al. (2018) still found 30% of all cases presenting for the first time with late-stage HIV infection and 10% with advanced stage infection and male sex workers in the Czech Republic were found to have an infection rate of close to 1% (Bruckova et al., 2006).

Recent studies that considered sexual orientation as a variable have confirmed that the higher level of sexual compulsivity in both gay and bisexual men can lead to increased risk of HIV transmission (Parsons et al., 2008; Kelly, Bimbi, Nanin, Izienicki, & Parsons, 2009). Research regarding substance abuse found that among adolescents, bisexuals have a greater risk of substance abuse than gays (Kerr, Ding, & Chaya, 2014). Bar-Johnson and Weiss (2014) found that only those sex workers reporting a bisexual identity also reported regular or daily use of methamphetamines. Regardless, the risk of exposure to HIV either through sexual contact or sharing needles for the injection of methamphetamines remains serious for male sex workers in the Czech Republic in general and those with a bisexual identity in particular. This finding emphasizes the need for a more proactive testing and prevention programs for at-risk groups (NeLP, 2014), especially bisexual male sex workers. Bar-Johnson and Weiss (2015) were able to convince local drug harm reduction outreach programs to add the brothels to the list of sites they visit for education and needle exchanges, but otherwise there are no targeted interventions to reduce HIV transmission in this population.

Life after sex work

One thing that is missing in nearly all of the research is data on the long-term effects of sex work, so I will provide what insights I can from qualitative observations and informal interviews. Although participants were asked not to give their names in order to maintain their anonymity in the research of Bar-Johnson and Weiss (2014), many of the Internet escorts stayed to talk with the researcher following the completion of the survey, sometimes for as long as two hours. The issue of their sexual partners was the most common topic in these conversations. Some respondents made a point of emphasizing that they are not gay and that they have a girlfriend and that they are doing this job only for the money. One of the first respondents asked to meet in a coffee shop in the lobby of a luxury apartment complex where he lived to complete the survey. He said that he was able to afford such as exclusive address only because he and his girlfriend made a lot of money in the sex industry, both of them working as escorts.

Several other participants also raised the issue of partners, usually by first asking if the researcher had a girlfriend, to which the researcher responded that he was gay and had a male partner. In one case, one of the younger Internet escorts said that "maybe [he, the escort] should find a boyfriend too, as [he] has too many problems with his girlfriend," and although he obviously intended it as a joke, it is possible he was genuinely conflicted about his orientation.

Among those respondents who reported that they were gay, all used the opportunity to justify their engagement in sex work. One young man reported that he did so only to support himself until he finished school, and that he was already in the process of interviewing for jobs abroad as a paramedic. Another was raising money to finance a website with gay-oriented news and entertainment, while a third was raising money for costumes for his cabaret show. In each case, these young gay men made it very clear that they saw sex work only as a temporary stepping stone to finance some future career goal, which was not the case with any of the respondents who mentioned girlfriends. In contrast, the presumably heterosexual respondents (no bisexual respondents reported a partner in this research) usually mentioned that sex work allowed them to live a better life than any other type of work, but their focus was always on the present, and they did not mention future plans. On the contrary, two of the older respondents (mid-20s) expressed remorse that they had not planned for the future, as they were currently having trouble finding enough clients to survive. One respondent even broke down in tears, as he related his fall from his early days as an escort in an exclusive club where he earned a monthly wage over 10 times the national average salary that had allowed him to rent an expensive flat and live an extravagant lifestyle. When he got older and clients expressed less interest, he eventually became homeless and was currently desperately seeking an older, financially secure benefactor to take him in. He hoped to find someone abroad, but he was despondent that he might not be able to, and he clearly appeared to be suffering significant depression about his current situation. Although he claimed to be writing a book about his experiences and expressed dreams of becoming an author, he seemed to have no concrete idea what to do to survive other than to continue selling sex as his livelihood. His goal is consistent with the research of Hall (2007a), who found that becoming a "kept boy" is one of the goals of many young sex workers, because being kept involves a more stable life situation and continued access to the lifestyle to which they have become accustomed.

Case study

Because there is little longitudinal research about the career of a male sex worker, I include a case study here that was part of a dissertation (Bar-Johnson, 2015). In the tradition of grounded ethnological research, I had the opportunity to conduct a series of semi-structured follow-up interviews with one of the escorts from the study. He provided some insight into his own experiences in sex work, his emotional reactions to them, and a possible exit strategy for those leaving the business. The participant agreed to meet on several occasions in 2013 to answer questions regarding his experiences as a sex worker and his motivations and feelings associated with his trajectory into and out of the business. The interviews were conducted at a public café on four occasions over a six-month period during 2013. In the interest of protecting his anonymity, his responses are presented in more general language. The questions and his answers, as translated from field notes (the interview was conducted in Czech), follow.

When did you come to Prague and what was your motivation?

The participant was a Czech resident in his mid-20s and had come to Prague in the mid-2000s at the age of 18. He came from a small village in the east of the country with few job prospects. After completing technical high school, he chose to move to the capital, Prague, where he hoped to find more lucrative career opportunities, as well as to escape a difficult family situation. He came to Prague by bus with all his savings, the equivalent of 200 euro.

How did you first become involved in the sex industry?

He was young, tall, athletic, and attractive and therefore an obvious target for the booming pornography industry in Prague. Within one hour of arriving at the bus station, while getting something to eat there, he was approached by a pornography producer and asked if he would like to make a (straight) porno. He agreed. The producer arranged for accommodation, and he shot several scenes (compensated at about 150 Euro per scene). Within the next few weeks, he had made enough money to rent a small room in a shared apartment on a weekly basis. He continued his work in pornography only until he was able to secure another position, as a receptionist in a fitness center. He stated that aside from the financial rewards, he had little interest in working in the sex industry and did not enjoy his work in heterosexual pornography.

How did you then become involved in sex with men?

It was not long after gaining employment in the fitness center when a much older male client training there offered him a large amount of money (approximately 300 Euro) to do private stripping and posing for him at his home. He accepted this offer, which led to monthly visits with the client that eventually included providing oral sex, resulting in even greater monetary rewards. At this point, his sex work was mainly to supplement his income. He reported that he found giving oral sex to this much older man "disgusting at first," but later he came to appreciate that the man was nice to him and very generous, and he said that "he got used to it." This was his only homosexual experience up to this point in his life.

Do you have a girlfriend and does she know about your sex work?

During this period, he met his girlfriend through connections in the pornography industry, where she also worked at first as an actress and then later as an escort for men. At the time they began dating, she was spending about two weeks per month working in a legal brothel in another European country, and spending two weeks in Prague. He knew about her work and seemed unconcerned, as she made excellent money and she invited him to move into her luxury apartment as their relationship became more serious. She was aware of his appearances in heterosexual porn, but he did not tell her about his previous work with male clients, and he stopped meeting with his regular sponsor after he began living with his girlfriend. Although he expressed some concerns for her safety, he didn't feel that her sex work was an issue in their relationship, and he described them as being a happy couple for some time. However, as the relationship became more serious, problems began to arise, mainly over fights that she was making most of the money and he was not contributing enough to the relationship, which became his motivation to return to sex work.

How did you become more involved in sex work with men?

He reported that he first contacted some of Prague's many pornography producers. Within one day, he was offered a role in an erotic massage video in which he would be touched and masturbated by other men, but would perform no other sex acts. He did such scenes a few times, but the pay was rather low for this type of scene (100 Euro), and he did not want to engage in any other sex acts on film to protect his identity. Therefore, he decided that escorting would be the best solution. Like many young men in Prague, his first step was to launch an escort profile on www.gayromeo.com with a few headless pics of his torso. Because he was in very good shape, he had a client organized within one day of launching the profile. Within the first month, he had seen several clients and was making approximately 1000 Euro per month (the median Czech full-time salary) for working only a few hours per week. Several clients asked to meet him again, and he quickly developed a set of regulars. The types of encounters varied greatly, from muscle worship, posing, and masturbation, to sadomasochistic role-play, to both active and passive anal sex. He had several offers from clients abroad (mainly in New York) who offered him much larger sums of money (1000 USD or more per visit). However, he did not have a passport and was hesitant to travel.

How did you feel about having sex with men as an escort?

Although not excited or enthusiastic about the sex, he stressed that his clients were all nice to him, paid the fee (typically 200 Euro), and often gave him an additional tip or present. He also mentioned that they were younger and better looking than the man with whom he had his first experience, so he didn't find the experience disgusting anymore. This continued for approximately six months until after a fight with his girlfriend, one of his regular clients (married to a woman) offered him the chance to move into his house and be a full-time companion at a salary of 2000 Euro per month. As he had nowhere to live and found the client to be a generally nice guy, he accepted the offer and moved into his own room in the large house.

He was required to spend a few nights a week sleeping in bed with the client and engaging in active and passive anal sex; the rest of the time he was free to do as he liked. For the first few months, he found this situation very stressful, as every aspect of his life was de facto under his client's control, and this was the only time he reported feeling any anxiety. He discontinued his work with other clients and began to take on more roles as a personal assistant to the client, running errands, driving him, and in general doing what needed to be done.

After several months, however, the client tired of him sexually and decided to hire him officially as a personal assistant, and they agreed there would be no more sex work. During this time, he reconciled with his girlfriend, and he now spends some nights per week with her and some staying at his employer's house. The employer, meanwhile, has found another younger escort for a sexual relationship, apparently a pattern that has occurred several times, as at least two other "ex-boyfriends" are still employees of his company.

How would you describe your sexual identity?

When asked this question, he immediately answered that he is a bisexual. I asked how he knows that, and he said because although he is only genuinely excited about sex with women, he also feels a "loving bond" with his employer and after many sexual encounters together, he found aspects of sex with men pleasurable. When I asked if he would have sex with other men outside of a business relationship, he was less sure, stating that maybe it could happen but at the moment he is committed to his girlfriend and they are talking about getting married.

Do you foresee yourself getting involved in sex work again in the future?

His response to this question was a definitely "no," which he then qualified with "unless absolutely necessary." However, he did add that he had no regrets about his experiences as a male sex worker. Instead, he is building on his experience as a driver and opening his own small limousine business. He hopes to be successful enough that his girlfriend can stop working as an escort and they can start a family.

His story of forming a close bond with his regular client is reminiscent of the types of stories related by Walby (2012) in his interviews with high-end career Internet escorts in Toronto, London, and New York. The only difference is that he chose not to make international escorting a career but rather continued to view escorting as a short-term solution to his financial and housing problems with the goal of eventually leaving the business as soon as doing so was viable. This difference is most likely due to the fact that the escorts interviewed by Walby were gay, whereas this case involves the case of a predominantly heterosexual man with bisexual feelings. The concept of "mostly heterosexual" introduced by sex researchers might be the best way to characterize his orientation (Vranglova & Savin-Williams, 2012). Although this story appears to have a happy ending, it is simply one case study and in no way should be considered typical of Prague escorts. However, it does demonstrate how a young man with no previous homosexual experiences can easily become involved in the gay porn and escort industry in Prague, along with one possible outcome. I emphasize, however, this case is probably the best-case scenario. It does not necessarily reflect the experiences of the majority of the sex workers in Prague, whose fates remain unknown (Graham & Weitzer, 2017).

Hall (2007a) also reported on some formerly straight boys who found themselves involved in long-term relationships, originally based on money but later also on emotional attachment, which could lead to a reorganization of their own sexual identity to that of bisexual. This arrangement seems reminiscent of a form of pederasty, which was common in previous centuries (Naphy, 2006; Kaye in Minichiello & Scott, 2014). Some young working-class boys were mentored by older affluent men seeking sexual encounters but also providing valuable life skills that eventually allowed the boys to create a better life for themselves than would have been possible without such assistance. Homosexuality and bisexuality were not labeled at that time in the same way unless the males were very feminine in their behavior, so there was probably less pressure from society to form a bisexual identity than today. Now, with LGBTQ rights on the rise, increased social acceptance has brought an increased pressure to amend one's sexual identity to reflect one's sexual behaviors.

General conclusions

The trend in research on male sex workers has progressed through stages over the years (for a complete review, see Minichiello & Scott, 2014). Early research on male sex workers focused on the pathological characteristics of the sex workers as deviants; later, during the AIDS crisis, male sex workers as a vector for disease into the mainstream population; and later male sex work as a cause of psychological problems. The latest trend has been toward legitimizing sex work and attempting to reduce the stigma of this career option. However, I argue that this new trend focuses too heavily on the modern economies of the United States, Western Europe, and Asia, and it does not take into account the issues of income disparity across developing regions. Male sex workers in Prague have economic experiences more similar to those in other former Soviet countries and in modern Russia but with fewer government and social prejudices against them. Yet, for the majority of sex workers in Prague, sex work is not a viable career in the long term. Once they begin to engage in sex work, they find the lifestyle too attractive to leave until their age or appearance forces them to, because they have become accustomed to making good money for little effort and few have a viable exit strategy in place.

Recommendations

Research has highlighted the need for informational campaigns targeting escorts and sex workers in clubs, to advise young men of the risks and dangers inherent in sex work, such as physical and sexual violence and exposure to HIV (Bar-Johnson, 2015; Graham & Weitzer, 2017). In addition, although there currently exist extensive services for female sex workers (www.roz kosbezrizika.cz), as well as limited services directed at homeless young men, some of whom are sex workers (www.sance.info), there are currently no social services specifically targeting the complex needs of the majority of male sex workers in the Czech Republic (Graham & Weitzer, 2017). These workers often may require comprehensive services to start a new life after they exit sex work, including temporary housing, drug rehabilitation, psychological counseling, job training, and legal counseling, for example, in working with health insurers to negotiate repayment of debts. Other research has indicated the importance of community-based interventions beyond simple drug or alcohol rehabilitation and HIV information (Parsons, Koken & Bimbi, 2007); however, that research focused on older, more upscale, and more career-type sex workers than are found in the Czech Republic. Unfortunately, although it has long been established that job rehabilitation for young sex workers creates an atmosphere for stable social adjustment (Allen, 1980) and that failure to create alternative opportunities often results in an inevitable decline into social ostracism, drug abuse, and mental problems (Caukins & Coombs, 1976), little has been done to offer alternatives to these Czech sex workers. Informational campaigns and the creation of outreach intervention programs will be crucial to reducing the risk and harm for male sex workers in Prague. Reaching those who suffer from mental instability and those who are currently economically successful has proven difficult for such interventions in the past (Gandy & Deisher, 1970), and this difficulty likely continues today. However, the Czech Republic has been, and will likely continue to be, a destination for sex tourism, and therefore more needs to be done to ensure the health and safety of the Czech and Slovak male sex workers there.

In the last decade, research in the area of male sex work has exploded. Vast cultural differences and the wide variety of types of sex work make drawing generalizations difficult or impossible. Smith et al. (2008) provide a good example of how a small "family-run" brothel can be a positive experience, an outcome also noted by Bar-Johnson and Weiss (2015) and Graham and Weitzer (2017), but this outcome relies purely on the benevolence of the brothel owner. Although it has made great economic strides in the last 30 years, the Czech Republic remains a poor country relative to its rich neighbor, Germany. As a result, the influx of sexual tourists and the dominance of foreign-owned commercial sex enterprises in the Czech Republic are unlikely to decline, and male sex workers in Prague continue to play on a rather uneven playing field.

References

Aggleton, P. (Ed.). (1999). *Men who sell sex: International perspectives on male prostitution and HIV/AIDS.* London: UCL Press.

Allen, D. M. (1980). Young male prostitutes: A psychosocial study. *Archives of Sexual Behavior, 9*(5), 399–426.

Bancroft, J. (2009). *Human sexuality and its problems.* London: Churchill Livingstone Elsevier.

Bar-Johnson, M. D. (2015). *Sexual and psychological aspects of the lives of male sex workers in Prague* (Unpublished doctoral dissertation). Charles University, First Medical Faculty, Czech Republic, Prague.

Bar-Johnson, M. D., & Weiss, P. (2014). Mental health and sexual identity in a sample of male sex workers in the Czech republic. *Medical Science Monitor, 20,* 1682–1686.

Bar-Johnson, M. D., & Weiss, P. (2015). A comparison of male sex workers in Prague: Internet escorts versus men who work in specialized bars and clubs. *Journal of Sex Research, 52.*

Boles, J., & Elifson, K. W. (1994). Sexual identity and HIV: The male prostitute. *Journal of Sex Research, 31*(1), 39–46.

Brennan, J. (2017). Exploitation in all-male pornography set in the Czech republic. *European Journal of Cultural Studies.* doi:10.1177/1367549417719012

Brown, A., Attawell, K., Hales, D., Rice, B., Pharris, A., Supervie, V., . . . Noori, T. (2018). Monitoring the HIV continuum of care in key populations across Europe and Central Asia. *HIV Medicine, 19,* 431–439.

Bruckova, M., Bautista, C., Graham, R., Maly, M., Vandasova, J., Presel, J. . . . Earhart, K. (2006). HIV infection among commercial sex workers and injecting drug users in the Czech republic. *The American Journal of Tropical Medicine and Hygiene, 75*(5), 1017–1020.

Bunzl, M. (2000). The Prague experience: Gay male sex tourism and the neocolonial invention of an embodied border. In D. Berdahl, M. Bunzl, & M. Lampland (Eds.), *Altering states: Ethnographies of transition in Eastern Europe and the former Soviet Union* (pp. 70–95). Ann Arbor, MI: University of Michigan Press.

Caukins, S. E., & Coombs, N. R. (1976). The psychodynamics of male prostitution. *American Journal of Psychotherapy, 30*(3), 441–451.

ECPAT International. (2014). *Global monitoring: Status of action against commercial sexual exploitation of children: Czech Republic* (2nd ed.). Bangkok, Thailand: Author.

Flowers, R. B. (2001). *Runaway kids and teenage prostitution.* London: Greenwood.

Gandy, P., & Deisher, R. (1970). Young male prostitutes: The physician's role in social rehabilitation. *Journal of the American Medical Association, 212*(10), 1661–1666.

Gokengin, D., Oprea, C., Begovac, J., Horban, A., Zeka, A. N., Sedlacek, D., . . . Yurin, O. (2018). HIV care in Central and Eastern Europe: How close are we to the target? *International Journal of Infectious Diseases, 70,* 121–130.

Golgo, F. (2003). Všechno pořad při starém: Loňské policejní razie neskončovaly s mužskou prostitucí v ČR. In J. Čulík, F. Golgo, Š. Kotrba, R. Mokrý, K. Murphy, J. Paul, & J. Žytek (Eds.), *Jak Češi bojují: Výbor z Britských listů* (pp. 77–81). Praha: Britské listy.

Graham, E., & Weitzer, R. (2017). Young men doing business: Male bar prostitution in Berlin and Prague. *Sexualities, 21*(8), 1–20.

Grodecki, W. (1994). *Not angels but angels.* Czech Republic: Hillivres Multimedia.

Grodecki, W. (1996). *Body without soul.* Czech Republic: Hillivres Multimedia.

Grodecki, W. (1997). *Mandragora.* Czech Republic: Hillivres Multimedia.

Hall, T. M. (2007a). Rent-boys, barflies, and kept men: Men involved in sex with men for compensation in Prague. *Sexualities, 10*(4), 457–472.

Hall, T. M. (2007b). Forms of transactional sex in Prague among young men who have sex with men (1999–2004). *Czech Sociological Review, 43*(1), 89–109.

Havelková, B. (2018). Prostitution law and policy in the Czech Republic. In S. Jahnsen & H. Wagenaar (Eds.), *Assessing prostitution policies in Europe.* London: Routledge.

Heikkinen, M. (Dir. & Producer). (2010). *All boys.* Finland, Czech Republic. Retrieved from https://variety.com/2010/film/reviews/all-boys-1117943073/

Kelly, B., Bimbi, D., Nanin, J., Izienicki, H., & Parsons, J. (2009). Sexual compulsivity and sexual behaviors among gay and bisexual men and lesbian and bisexual women. *Journal of Sex Research, 46*(4), 301–308.

Kerr, D. L., Ding, K., & Chaya, J. (2014). Substance use of lesbian, gay, bisexual, and heterosexual college students. *American Journal of Health Behavior, 38*(6), 951–962.

Leichtentritt, R. D., & Arad, B. D. (2005). Young male street workers: Life histories and current experiences, *British Journal of Social Work, 35,* 483–509.

Mann, J., & Tarantola, D. J. M. (1996). *AIDS in the world II.* Oxford: Oxford University Press.

Marritz, I. (2007, April). 9.5. *Out,* 57–63.

McCabe, I., Acree, M., O'Mahony, F., McCabe, J., Kenny, J., Twyford, J., . . . McGlanaghy, E. (2011). Male street prostitution in Dublin: A psychological analysis. *Journal of Homosexuality, 58*(8), 998–1021.

Mimiaga, M. J., Reisner, S. L., Tinsley, J. P., Mayer, K. H., & Safren, S. S. (2007). Street workers and Internet escorts: Contextual and psychosocial factors surrounding HIV risk behavior in men who engage in sex work with other men. *Journal of Urban Health: Bulletin of the New York Academy of Medicine, 86*(1), 54–66.

Minichiello, V., & Scott, J. (2014). *Male sex work and society.* New York: Harrington Park Press.

Naphy, W. (2006). *Born to be gay: A history of homosexuality.* Gloucestershire: Tempus Publishing Limited.

NeLP—Network of HIV Low Prevalence Countries in Central and South East Europe. (2014). *Overcoming obstacles to testing.* Conference Proceedings. Retrieved from https://www.avert.org/professionals/hiv-programming/prevention/overview

Parsons, J. T., Koken, J. A., & Bimbi, D. S. (2007). Looking beyond HIV: Eliciting individual and community needs of male escorts. *Journal of Homosexuality, 53*(1–2), 219–240.

Parsons, J. T., Kelly, B., Bimbi, D., DiMaria, L., Wainberg, M., & Morgenstern, J. (2008). Explanations for the origins of sexual compulsivity among gay and bisexual men. *Archives of Sexual Behavior, 37*(5), 817–826.

Rogers, T. (2010, May 25). Gay porn's most shocking taboo. *Salon.* Retrieved from www.salon.com/2010/05/21/twincest/

Ross, M. W., Timpson, S. C., Williams, M. L., Amos, C., & Bowen, A. (2007). Stigma consciousness concerns related to drug use and sexuality in a sample of street-based male sex workers. *International Journal of Sexual Health, 19*(2), 57–67.

Roxburgh, A., Degenhardt, L., & Copeland, J. (2006). Posttraumatic stress disorder among female street-based sex workers in the greater Sydney area, Australia. *BMC Psychiatry, 624,* 12.

Sikes, A. W. (2010). Politics and pornography: Czech performance in the international arena. *Theatre Journal, 62*(3), 373–387.

Smith, M. D., Grov, C., & Seal, D. W. (2008). Agency based male sex work: A descriptive focus on physical, personal, and social space. *The Journal of Men's Studies, 16*(2), 193–210.

Uy, J. M., Parsons, J. T., Bimbi, D. S., Koken, J. A., & Halkitis, P. N. (2004). Gay and bisexual male escorts who advertise on the Internet: Understanding reasons for and effects of involvement in commercial sex. *International Journal of Men's Health, 3*(1), 11–26.

Valera, R. J., Sawyer, R. G., & Schiraldi, G. R. (2001). Perceived health needs of inner-city street prostitutes: A preliminary study. *American Journal of Health Behavior, 25*(1), 50–59.

Velinger, J. (Host). (2009). *Czechs and sex: A comprehensive survey* (Interview with author, P. Weiss). Radio Praha. Prague: Czech Republic.

Vlašík, C. (2009). *Váš kluk prostitut?* [*Your son the prostitute*]. Prague: Mladá Fronta.

VOLCA.com. (2015, April 8). *Addicted swimwear: Soaked and loaded with Bel Ami.* Retrieved from www.youtube.com/watch?v=qMkF-yKepI0

Vranglova, Z., & Savin-Williams, R. C. (2012). Mostly heterosexual and mostly gay/lesbian: Evidence for new sexual orientation identities. *Archives of Sexual Behavior, 41*(1), 85–101.

Walby, K. (2012). *Touching encounters: Sex, work, and male-for-male Internet escorts.* Chicago, IL: University of Chicago Press.

Weiss, P., & Zvěřina, J. (2001). *Sexuální chovaní v ČR—situatce a trendy* [*Sexual behavior in the Czech republic, the situation and trends*]. Prague, Portal: Charles University.

White, K. (1998). Posttraumatic stress disorder found to be common among prostitutes. *Journal of Women's Health, 7*(8), 943.

Zikmundová, M., & Weiss, P. (2003). Sexuální aktivity prostitute při výkonu profese. *Praktické Lékař, 83,* 714–716.

Zikmundová, M., & Weiss, P. (2004). Soukromý sexuální život prostitute. *Česká a Slovenská Psychiatrie, 100,* 66–72.

Part VIII

Male sex work in the Asia-Pacific region

33

Male sex work in India

Gendered sexualities and the market of Mumbai

Ankur Srivastav and R. Vaishno Bharati

The term *sex work* is gendered, primarily regarded as a job in which cisgender (a person whose gender corresponds with their sex assigned at birth) and trans women engage. It is one of those rare sources of livelihood that is entirely feminized and has attracted strong morality critics. In India, even organizations working to prevent sex work or "prostitution" and those working for and with sex workers for labor and heath rights often ignore the presence of male sex workers.

Though sex work with respect to women in India is not criminalized in and of itself, activities surrounding sex work, such as solicitation and brothel keeping, are illegal under the Immoral Traffic (Prevention) Act (1986). Women sex workers are prosecuted within a framework of crime, morality, and coercion, but this system does not acknowledge male sex workers. The colonial-era law, Section 377 of the Indian Penal Code (1864), which criminalizes sexual acts against order of nature, and the Shore Nuisance (Bombay and Kolaba) Law of 1983, which criminalizes soliciting in public places, were the two laws that have been used to prosecute male sex workers. While the Shore Nuisance Law can still be used against male sex workers in public spaces, Section 377 of the IPC was decriminalized in September 2018.

It needs to be noted that neither of these laws deals with transactional sex between men, and they have rarely been used to prosecute male sex workers. Instead, they have served as tools for extortion by the local police. However, the arrival of the HIV/AIDS epidemic brought to light the presence of men who sell sex (Khire, 2008). Most recent research has explored sex work, or "transactional sex," in terms of risk, safe sexual behavior, substance use, and health interventions (Biello et al., 2017; Baral et al., 2015; Dandona et al., 2006). However, ideas of the male body as a commodity and the methods that male sex workers use to navigate different masculinities have not received as much attention. In short, not much is known about the processes and experiences that underpin male sex work (Khan, 1999).

The chapter explores various meanings and expressions attached to masculinity by the men we interviewed. It also explores how men use their bodies and engage in body projects in order to negotiate desirability within the often-ignored market space of male sex work. Further, this chapter makes an effort to map the subtleties underlying transactions with bodies and the creation of vulnerabilities that require scrutiny and engagement.

Male sex work in India: an overview

The complex nature of social stratifiers such as caste, class, region, linguistics, and religion plays a very important role in defining self (Khire, 2008; Network of Indian Male Sex Workers, 2006). In India, not many men would actually label themselves as "male sex workers" because they are selling sex. The stigma attached to sex work also prevents men from identifying as male sex workers: "As individuals, many MSW suffer from a sense of low self-esteem [and] poor confidence fueled by stigma when identified as sex worker" (Network of Indian Male Sex Workers, 2006).

Shivananda Khan (1999) is against the label "sex work." He believes that for most men and women in sex work, selling their bodies in exchange for money, food, or shelter is their only option; thus, they do not have the power to negotiate or improve their working conditions. Khan has also demanded the use of a colloquial and culturally relative vocabulary to discuss sexuality and identity. These terms include *kothi* (a feminine homosexual person), *panthi* (a masculine homosexual person), and *double-decker* (a person who plays both active and passive roles in sex with men). In contrast, Khire (2008) believes that there is no political identity that is associated with selling sex and hence prefers to use scientific categories such as "male sex workers" while doing away with the cultural context and vocabulary entirely.

Shinde, Setia, Kavi, Anand, and Jerajani (2009) conducted a study in Mumbai with male sex workers (including men who have sex with men [MSM] and transgender persons) that primarily examined their risk behavior and vulnerabilities. The findings indicated that MSM are a high-risk group due to inconsistent condom usage and high STI/HIV infections. Shinde suggested that qualitative research would be essential in examining the social aspects of sex work and the negotiation of condom use.

In 2006, the Network of Indian Male Sex Workers Kolkata (NIMSW) conducted a study on male sex workers in three cities: Kolkata, Ahmedabad, and Vijayawada. The report mentions the difficulty of reaching out to the male sex worker (MSW) population for health intervention because members of the group are hidden and hard to identify. Economic need was listed as one of the key reasons that men engage in sex work. Unlike their female counterparts, in the absence of any laws that address male sex work, male sex workers are not organized as a collective. They are often subsumed under the LGBTQI movements in India, further sidelining their efforts to improve their physical and mental health.

Studies focusing on tourism and migration have explored issues faced by male sex workers along with issues of livelihood, race, and sexuality (Herold, Garcia, & DeMoya, 2001; Padilla, 2008). Factors such as migration, large-scale economic shifts, and even prominent political ideologies influence views of sex work (Shah, 2014; Stout, 2014). While migration from rural to urban spaces is common across India, the case of Mumbai is somewhat special. In addition to being a harbor city and therefore an economic hub for centuries, it is a major center of the Indian film and fashion industries, thus receiving a huge pool of diverse migrants both in terms of aspirations and skill sets. Many unskilled and illiterate people migrate from rural areas to Mumbai to generate income and sustain their families in villages. Similarly, a considerable number of skilled and educated people migrate to the city in search of better employment opportunities and high-paying jobs. Usually, this migration is a single-unit migration in which the migrant does not migrate with his or her family. These migrants slowly create and claim their own recreational spaces and facilities in the city (Bhagat & Jones, 2013; Tumbe, 2012). Mumbai has a night-life culture where alcohol, food, music, and sex are available until late in the night, and this availability cuts across social classes. On the one hand, the city has lounges, pubs, and discos that cater to the middle- and upper-class population, and on the other hand, the city also has liquor outlets (government permit shops) that sell cheap alcohol. The city also offers spaces where one can find men and women available for sex in exchange of money. The migrant population buys sex, and a small though significant segment of this population (including both men and women) sells sex.

However, there is insufficient literature or knowledge available regarding a market in which male bodies are desired and commodified (Liguori & Aggleton, 1999; Scott et al., 2005; Smith, 2012). However, with men entering previously female-gendered occupations such as secretaries, receptionists, and flight attendants, and women being regarded as consumers, the Indian media has been depicting the commodification of male bodies for over two decades now. The demand of male bodies has been seen in many spaces, evident in the many men's underwear advertisements and the numerous up-and-coming male catwalk models. This cultural shift has contributed to many men wanting to take up these professions.

Masculinity and desirability

Throughout history, bodies have undergone changes due to cultural forces and the power manifested in them. Chinese foot-binding, western corsets, tattooing, and piercing have for centuries involved the use of tools and materials to alter the shape and size of the body. In recent times, body projects have undergone a radical change with change in the technologies. For example, there have been more than two million breast implant and enhancement operations in United States since the 1960s (Lipworth & McLaughlin, 2012; Sarwer, Nordmann, & Herbert, 2000). Increasing numbers of men are also having chest implants to achieve a muscular appearance. These various body projects suggest what is acceptable and desirable in a particular culture (Benson, 1997).

The "gym culture," especially among men, is a direct effect of such an understanding of body and masculinity as demanded by various social and cultural forces. As Benson (1997) notes, the theatrical display of masculine bodies through photography contributed to ideal body images. The goal is to enhance body mass, often with the use of steroids. Muscularity is important to masculinity; the idea behind bodybuilding is to produce a body that is desirable in terms of size, muscularity, shape, and tone (Benson, 1997).

The so-called "clone" look during the 1970s (hairy chests and moustaches) epitomized social ideas of masculine men. But with changes in technologies, globalization, and modernization, ideas about what is appealing and desirable are changing. Waxed chests and clean-shaven faces have replaced hairy bodies as the new ideal (Kneas, 2017). A gym-toned body, six-pack abdominals, and big biceps now define the new metrosexual man (an image-conscious urban man who spends considerable resources on appearance and lifestyle) (Ervin, 2011; Sinclair, 2011). The male bodies on television appeal to a new market that considers both its women viewers and its gay viewership. This new market for the consumption of male bodies has raised concerns over the display of masculinity (Beggan & Allison, 2009; Parry & Light, 2016; Ramsay, 2017); shirtless men and men in underwear on television are shaping a new sense of sensuality, sexuality, and desirability (Rohlinger, 2002).

In one sense, the nude and semi-nude male bodies on display in the media set standards for men with regards to desirability (Blond, 2008; Hobza, Walker, Yakushko, & Peugh, 2007). However, with the increasing sensuality attached to men's bodies, a sense of homophobia is also created, with sensual and commodified bodies seen as a threat to masculinity (Alcalde, 2014; Anderson, 2013; Pompper, 2010). Men who are not comfortable with the notion of same-sex sexualities are made even more uncomfortable with the media's celebrated depictions of non-normative sexualities. Hence masculinity and public bodily displays cannot be understood in isolation; their linkage with sexuality becomes important. Jay Clarkson (2005), in his study of

U.S. television series and websites, has found that the media depict gay men in stereotypical ways, portraying gay men as feminine and engaging in non-traditional professions. Clarkson explains that gay men presented in the media are situated squarely between an emerging masculinity that targets female consumers and a traditional masculinity that is based in homophobia and misogyny, which targets male consumers. Still, the media seem to be moving masculinity away from its traditional presentation and recreating it in a way that represents a flamboyant sexuality.

Media and masculinity

The Hindi film industry (popularly known as Bollywood) has strongly influenced ideas about men and masculinity; we have seen Indian actors and their bodies displaying the new masculinities since the 1990s, thereby setting social trends and contributing to popular culture. The ideal male body has shifted and changed over time due to changing aesthetics, international influences, and sociocultural changes (Ciecko, 2001; Gehlawat, 2012). Two decades ago, the Hindi film industry celebrated the hairy bodies of Sunny Deol, Akshay Kumar, and Sunil Shetty, thus glamorizing the hyper-masculine (Om, Aag, Haseeno, & Replayy, 2016; Shandilya, 2014). This idealized male body also infiltrated Indian living rooms through advertisements and other sources. In the last decade or so, queer identities, bodies, and desires have also begun to occupy Indian homes. Depictions of non-normative genders and sexualities, both considerate and inconsiderate, have come from the mainstream media. It is difficult to speculate whether a movie like *Dostana* (Mansukhani, 2008), which portrays same-sex love between two mainstream male actors as a source of humor, was targeting the female market or the gay market (Gopinath, 2000; Srinivasan, 2011). Hindi cinema has also created movies such as *Oops* (Tijori, 2003) and *Desi Boyz* (Lulla, 2011), which showcase men in strip-tease and escort businesses serving women clients; however, both movies (Figure 33.1) fail to capture the seriousness and sensitivity of the issues regarding male sex work (Chanda, 2016; Talukdar, 2018).

Figure 33.1 Film posters from *Oops* (2003) and *Desi Boyz* (2011).

Figure 33.1 (Continued)

Sex work has always been stigmatized given the strict value systems that are laid by social, cultural, religious and political institutions in India (Cornish, 2006). The presence of strong stigma around same-sex behavior and the "shameful, immoral" act of selling sex, makes the men who sell sex to men prone to more stigma, harassment, and discrimination (Chakrapani, Newman, Shunmugam, McLuckie, & Melwin, 2007; Shinde et al., 2009).

The study

Our study aimed to explore the profiles of male sex workers, their sexual networks (pimps and clients), and the kind of body projects they used to increase their desirability. It also sought to explain how masculinity and sexuality get negotiated and redefined in the sex work market. Given the exploratory nature of our questions, we relied on a case study approach (Flick, 2008; Travers, 2001). Our methods helped us examine our participants' subjective lived experiences and their sociopolitical environment; they also allowed us to document individual participant experiences while exploring common elements (Hall, 2007). All study protocols were approved by the ethics and research committee of Tata Institute of Social Sciences (Mumbai), and data were collected in 2011 and 2012.

Participants and recruitment

Purposive snowball sampling was used to locate 10 participants using inclusion and exclusion criteria. Candidates could participate if they (1) identified as male, (2) were aged 18 years or older, (3) stated that transactional sex was their primary or secondary source of income, and (4) gave written consent to participate in the study. Because the population under study is hard to reach and some of the participants might be married and not open about their work, it was difficult to approach them directly. Therefore, we asked two social services organizations that work with this population in Mumbai to help identify potential study participants. Both these service organizations have targeted interventions under the Indian National AIDS Control Programme for HIV prevention among men who have sex with men and men who engage in transactional sex. One of the service organizations has worked with gender and sexual minorities for over two decades, and we asked for that organization's help in making initial contacts with the participants and also to gain insights on male transactional sex. After completing the interview, we asked participants to refer other individuals who might be willing to participate in the study and would meet inclusion criteria. Participants who met the eligibility criteria and gave written informed consent were interviewed in an enclosed room at the social services agency. Participants received 300 INR (~$4.50) as compensation for their travel and participation.

Data collection

A structured interview guide was used during data collection. Questions were framed in line with the objectives of the study and allowed in-depth assessment of each participant. The interview guide was intended to capture life history, significant details regarding entry into and maintenance of transactional sex, and various other dimensions. The interview guide had seven domains: (1) language, labels, and identities in male transactional sex; (2) sexual history before entering transactional sex; (3) transactional sexual narratives (experience, process, pimp or middlemen, clients); (4) non-transactional sexual narratives (sex for pleasure, intimate partners); (5) body and labor (body image, desirability, emotions, money, and work); (6) masculinity and transactional sex; and (7) social and sexual networks. We also collected some demographic information, but we discarded any identifying information in the coding process.

We collected the data in audio form, and we conducted most of the interviews in Hindi, a more familiar and comfortable language for the participants. The audio files were later translated and transcribed in English. The researchers ensured that the transcription was of good quality and that no culture-specific information was lost in the process of translation. Some of the words and concepts were transcribed in Hindi when the researchers felt that translation might harm the cultural relevance or meaning. Aliases have been given to all the participants.

Data analysis

Thematic analysis of the interviews was conducted following a process outlined by Boyatzis (1998). The process consisted of generating, revising, and determining the reliability of codes and themes by identifying positive and negative qualifications. The translated transcripts were uploaded to NVivo 7. An a priori codebook based on the identified domains was created, and the transcripts were independently coded by two researchers. New codes identified during the coding process were discussed between the two coders and after agreement were added to the coding trees in NVivo 7; text segments were ordered in each domain. The text segments were further evaluated by both frequency and theoretical salience. Effort was also made to revisit and clarify any questions arising in the coding process due to translation work to ensure cultural specificity and relevance. Common themes arising from coding and categorizing were compared to one another for conceptual fit with the theoretical framework. In addition, memos were kept to help identify theoretical topics and issues that need to be resolved in subsequent analyses. The researchers also used information received from talking to the members of the community and by spending time at the site, and these observations were also helpful in analyzing the data.

Study findings

Sociodemographic characteristics

The average age of the ten participants was 23.8 years (range = 20–27). More than half (*n* = 6, 60%) of the participants were originally from Mumbai, whereas the rest reported migrating from other states. More than two-thirds (*n* = 8, 80%) of the participants reported staying with their families in Mumbai. Half (*n* = 5, 50%) of the participants identified as bisexual, whereas others identified as straight, gay, or MSM. One of the participants reported not identifying with any sexual label. In terms of their client system, all participants reported that their clientele largely consisted of men, although a few reported having women as clients (see Table 33.1).

Table 33.1 Demographic Characteristics of Participants

		Age	Birthplace	Living Arrangement	Sexual Identity	Clients
1	Amit	22	Mumbai	Family	Straight	Men, women
2	James	25	Bhopal	Alone	Bisexual (more attracted to men)	Mostly men, couples
3	Nikhil	22	Rajasthan	Family	Bisexual	Men, women
4	Raj	25	Mumbai	Family	MSM, bisexual (mostly attracted to men)	Men
5	Abdul	24	Mumbai	Family	Bisexual	Men, couples
6	Rohan	20	Mumbai	Family	Gay	Only men
7	Sanjay	24	Mumbai	Family	Gay	Only men
8	Chetan	29	Goa	Family	None	Only men
9	Bunty	27	Delhi	Friends	Gay	Mostly men, couples
10	Dinesh	20	Mumbai	Family	Bisexual	Men, women

Note. MSM = men who have sex with men.

517

Identities, labels, and behaviors

The participants listed a varied range of sexual identities based on their perceptions of self and sexuality. Most based their understanding of their sexual identity on sexual attraction and sexual behavior. Those who identified as gay men based their identity on attraction to and sexual behavior with other men. Those who identified as bisexual based their identity on attraction or behavior or both. A few participants reported that they were primarily attracted to and preferred to have sex with women, but they also considered their ability to perform sexually with men in the process of labeling themselves as a bisexual person. One of the participants reported enjoying sex with both men and women and identified as a straight person. Similarly, one participant who is attracted to and has sex with both men and women did not apply any labels to himself. The straight-identified participants had very stereotypical perception of gay men as being effeminate, which creates a barrier in terms of accepting or associating with any same-sex-based identities.

> I am a bisexual; I can have sex with both men and women. Gay means those who are only interested in men, and they walk in a way that you can make out that he is kothi. You can also make out bisexual but mostly they look straight.
>
> *Dinesh, 20 years old, bisexual-identified participant*

> I say I am gay. Gay means gay, one who likes boys, has sex with boys, talks and shares with boys and more. . .
>
> *Rohan, 20 years old, gay-identified participant*

> I look straight, others look gay. Their way of talking, walking is different and by looking at their face one can make out that they are gay. When I walk and talk I don't look gay. Even though I have sex with men and get attracted to them, people think I am a normal person.
>
> *Abdul, 24 years old, bisexual-identified participant*

In terms of defining sex work, most of the participants understand it as sex in exchange for money and/or gifts. The participants described sex work based on their current situation, opportunities, client system, and the roles they play. For some participants, sex work offers them a way out of their current financial difficulties or the opportunity to save money for their future; for others, it is a fast and easy way to make money to support their lifestyle and to make up for their unstable careers. Though most of them reported entering into sex work due to financial need, some expressed their desire to continue with it as an additional mode of income generation. A few participants also described sex work as a comparatively easier and better way to earn money compared to other skill-based jobs with lesser income opportunities. Participants also reported working in escort and massage services, in addition to sex work:

> I don't know much, but I think it is an easy way to earn money, very easy way. You just need to go and sleep with someone for an hour and you will get 10,000 or 15,000 (INR) per session. So, I think it is an easy way to earn money.
>
> *James, 25 years old, bisexual-identified participant*

> Sex work is with clients. In sex sometimes we do oral sex, sometimes it is just spending time. There is an exchange of money, and sometimes we are given gifts like laptop, mobile, etc.
>
> *Rohan, 20 years old, gay-identified participant*

In terms of their sexual behavior, the straight-identified, non-identified, and few bisexual-identified participants reported being repulsed by the idea of being the passive partners (receptive in sexual acts), while the gay-identified were seemingly more accepting of passive roles. The terms of the market as widely accepted by the participants are laid down by the paying party and the market that produces the objectified body. Hence, sex workers sometimes participate in work that they dislike, in terms of the sexual acts or the people with whom they have to engage in said acts. Although negotiation in terms of sex acts and prices happens largely over the phone, at the site of sexual transaction, condom usage, sex roles, and the amount to be paid sometimes get re-negotiated. Clients sometimes prefer role-playing which may at times include cross-dressing, where the gender performance is considered part of the sex act:

> Sometime what happens is I need to also play passive role. So, in passive part, they like someone who is slim or average types. So, if I get gym build, then there are some who don't like that, so I think it's better to look normal.
>
> *James, 25 years old, bisexual-identified participant*

Soliciting and clients

Soliciting clients largely occurs in two ways: individual soliciting and through pimps (also referred as agents). Individual soliciting takes place on the streets and in public bathrooms, public transport, parties, pubs, and discotheques. The participants who do not identify with any sexual identity/labels prefer working only through a pimp, as they do not want to solicit on their own and they want to remain anonymous. Working through a pimp is considered a safer option, because the pimp's role is to find clients, negotiate fees, and provide support in any crisis situation. There is a very important market for the pimps, who function largely through newspaper ads and websites advertising about their services (Figure 33.2). They provide a strong link between the sex workers and the clients and make money through commissions:

> I go through pimp only. Yes, sometimes I need to mail my photo to the client, but pimps also have my photo. Pimps have portfolios of all sex workers working for them and they send a few pics to the client; and whoever the client picks, the pimp sent that one to the client. Pimps usually find clients through ads in newspapers and there are also Internet services. To be very frank I have also done it in loos. I will tell you about loos, I go to the loos with the excuse to pee. I stand there, there are usually a lot of people standing outside in the night. I keep looking at people, and those I think are ok, I mean they can give something. So, I go to them and tell, "Sir I charge." . . . So, we go either to their place, or his car or some other place.
>
> *James, 25 years old, bisexual-identified participant*

Clients are very diverse group, though most of them are men, with a smaller number of female clients and couple clients. Regardless of their sex, clients are usually above 30 years of age and come from an upper socioeconomic background. The male sex workers who identify as straight or bisexual provide services to both male and female clients. Those who provide services to couples are usually the bisexual-identified male sex workers, while the gay-identified, MSM, and non-identified male sex workers provide services only to male clients. In case of couple clients, the men usually play the role of passive participants and do not engage in the act directly. Rather, they give directions to the sex worker on how to perform the sexual act

Figure 33.2 Copy of newspaper advertising for male sex workers. Newspaper advertising is managed by pimps.

with the woman. The power hierarchy is evident here; the act is being performed for the male client's pleasure:

> Usually I get clients above 30 years of age. Some are older also. If you are young you will get anyone on the street men or women, but these are the old men who do not get anyone.
>
> *Raj, 25 years old, bisexual-identified participant*

> I get female clients through disco only. Sometime also near the walls in Colaba. For example, me and my friend were standing. We were standing at distance, one here and over there. So, they move in cars, they will look at us standing. They will keep looking at us from the car only. Then I know that they are the clients, so when they come out we make contact.
>
> *Amit, 22 years old, straight-identified participant*

Body, desirability, and market

A few participants reported on the emphasis on bodies and their desirability in sex work. We had participants who were regular gym goers; they emphasized that working out and maintaining a fit body was essential for their business. Several participants indicated that they regularly go to parlors to get facials, bleaching, eyebrow work, and waxing to make their body look desirable and attractive. Some participants who are frequent consumers of beauty services also have a desire to join the gym. These different body engagements suggest a market for a wide range of body types, although the boundary between gym goers and parlor goers is not a strict one. We found a relationship between a sex worker's sexual identity and desired perception in the trade with the kind of body he would like to have to present that image. For example, one of our participants recognizes self as a bisexual person and wants to have a girlfriend; therefore, he chose to have a gym-toned, fit, and in-shape body. Another participant who identifies as gay reported using parlor services to make himself look desirable.

> I get a shave done, apply powder and perfume . . . wear shoes, jeans, and goggles. I get a facial done once in a month. Also get bleach, eyebrows made and waxing.
>
> *Sanjay, 24 years old, gay-identified participant*

> I go to the gym, get massage at times, and follow a diet to maintain my look. Once, I got a facial. I take out my body hair myself with a blade. I wear formal clothes to attract clients. I follow my routine of workout. I don't have any pimples. I use and continue only one face wash. When I was working, I used to do body building also, so I thought I should make use of my body.
>
> *Abdul, 24 years old, bisexual-identified participant*

It is very likely that most of these body projects are undertaken to achieve a greater acceptance and admiration of self. Interestingly, one of the participants used media and popular celebrities to describe clients' desires. Salman Khan, a Bollywood actor and an icon many Indian youth, seems to be one of the most-sought-after male ideals within the sex work market. He has developed a prototype of the male body, consistently showcasing his six-packed, gym-toned body and encouraging a lot of his young fans to desire the same. Similarly, in sex work, many clients seem to demand such bodies. The sex worker's desire to have a gym-toned body is therefore linked to making himself look more appealing and desirable to others and also to attract more clients:

> I need to take care of my body like my life. Every week I get facial and bleach done, I also get full body waxing. I don't go to gym, but I need to start soon. Now people want gym bodies, after that Salman Khan movie, everyone wants a good body. . . . If I walk in feminine ways, then people will notice me, they don't notice straight-looking men. I roll my eyes, stare, and make eye contacts, give smile to attract men. I wear nice clothes, simple clothes, so that people look at me.
>
> *Raj, 25 years old, bisexual-identified participant*

Masculinity, sexuality, and sex work

Men in sex work often grapple with their sexuality and gender expression because sexual behavior sometimes does not correspond with their identity/perception of self. There may also be a resistance to identifying with certain groups or identities based on the stereotypes and stigma attached with them. In our study, participants who identified as straight or bisexual held a stereotypical image of gay men. They talked about gay men as a homogenous group who by their appearance are more likely to be recognized as "gay" persons in a public space. Appearance here goes beyond the way they dress and perform their gender; it also includes their mannerisms, such as staring at other men, which are deemed to be feminine. One of the participants also stated his aversion to the idea of men holding hands. The description they provided of a gay man in a public arena is a stereotype of a feminine gay man; such descriptions leave less room for varied gender expressions exhibited by men who have sex with other men. This stereotype also raises the issue of discomfort with femininity, which is experienced more than same-sex phobia:

> I look straight, others look gay. Their way of talking, walking is different and by looking at their face one can make out that they are gay. When I walk and talk I don't look gay. Even though I have sex with men and get attracted to them people think I am a normal person.
> . . . Straight means I look like normal men; others have a different way of walking and talking. I want to look normal and I don't want people to know. I don't want my friends to know. I want to have an affair with a girl. I don't like at all when men hold hands and walk.
> *Abdul, 24 years old, bisexual-identified participant*

In comparison to earlier narratives of gym-toned bodies, one of the participants cited the market value of a non-gym-toned body. This participant provided parlor services and was not a gym-goer. He pointed out that in sex work, one needs to look and maintain the body in a way that the client wants. Because there is no one client prototype, different clients make different demands. According to this participant, a non-gym-toned body is the most marketable. He mentioned that clients who are looking for passive partners might not like to have one with a gym-toned body; hence, an average body helps to cater to the desires of the active partner. In addition, a few participants talked about waxing to make their bodies desirable to their clients, noting that many clients do not like hairy men. Another participant talked about cross-dressing to attract more clients:

> I don't go to parlor, and I don't go to gym. I think the kind of body I have now is good. Sometime what happens is I need to also play passive role, so in passive part, they like someone who is slim or average types. If I get gym-built, then there are some who won't like that, so I think it's better to look normal. I don't like passive part, but for money I have to do it.
> *James, 25 years old bisexual-identified participant*

Participants also talked about how choice in terms of their sex partners and their role in sex is not available in commercial sex. Rather, the buyer (client) dictates the terms of the sexual act. Sex workers have to compromise with their choice of partner with respect to the client's age, looks, role in sex, and so on. Moreover, they need to engage in sexual activity with whoever is ready to pay for it. Sexual attraction then automatically becomes secondary, and money becomes the primary factor. One of the participants also points out that the sex is for the satisfaction of the client and not for the sex worker:

> I like kissing and body sex (non-penetrative sex). Mostly I have done top-sex, meaning fucking other people. And very few times I have been fucked. It all depends on the client, if his mood is that someone should fuck him then we fuck him. If he wants someone to suck him or to fuck someone, then we need to do that. Sometimes when we reach home, after watching us they change their mind and say I want to fuck you. Then we also change our rate. Clients get satisfied, but I don't.
> *Nikhil, 22 years old, straight-identified participant*

It is also important to look at the linkages between sexual behavior, sexual identity, and masculinity. One of the participants who identifies as straight drew a correlation between getting penetrated and being gay or homosexual. Similarly, a bisexual-identified participant who is attracted to and has sex with both sexes does not get penetrated. He further indicated that for a bisexual person, the sex of the other person doesn't matter, and the bisexual person would penetrate anyone, man or woman. A gay-identified participant reported that there is no sex possible between two gay men; hence, to be in a sexual relationship one man needs to be a *kothi* (a feminine homosexual man) and the other needs to be a *panthi* (a masculine man who often identifies as a straight person). From the narratives, there are strict definitions of bisexual men and gay men and who penetrates whom, and sex workers operate in accordance with these definitions. In addition, one of the bisexual-identified participants perceived being penetrated as a threat to his masculinity, because such an act is considered a "gay" or feminine thing to do. He also believed that engaging in such sexual practices would eventually result in him developing a liking for the same and would transform him into a gay-identified man. As a bisexual man, he engages in penetrative sex with a man or woman. Because he is the penetrator, his masculinity doesn't get questioned. However, he will allow himself to be penetrated only by bisexual person, as he believes that all gay men are receptive partners:

> I have got penetrated only once. I was having sex with a guy, and I penetrated him and then he wanted to do it to me, he was bisexual, so I let him. It felt weird, that I was doing him and now he is doing me. I was feeling a little odd. Gay people get anal sex and bisexual don't. With bisexual they just want to do sex so doesn't matter who is the person. . .
>
> I feel if I do it once, I will do it always. And then I might also get those feelings that I want to get penetrated. . . . First time it felt odd, but then I liked it; but then I won't ever do it again. If I do it often then I will also become like them (gay) and I will also behave and think of only men. And I don't know if I would want to have sex with women. If I start enjoying getting penetrated, then why will I go to women.
>
> *Dinesh, 20 years old, bisexual-identified participant*

Our study identified multiple gendered sexualities being performed by the participants. Non-gay-identified participants describe a "gay" man in a public arena as that of a stereotypically feminine gay man. These descriptions hint at the discomfort with femininity among male sex workers, irrespective of their sexual identities. In a public space, conforming to masculine norms permits a lot of men who are engaged in homosexual sex to go unnoticed. The non-gay-identified individuals also seem more uncomfortable with being associated with a gay identity or group. Only the gay-identified participants cross-dressed and got their bodies waxed. There are certain roles in sex that are considered non-masculine, and hence the non-gay-identified participants are reluctant to practice them. The straight-identified participant also displayed fear of becoming gay if he "gives in" and plays a passive role in sex. Similarly, the idea of being in a relationship with another man is resisted by the participants who do not associate with any same-sex-based identity.

Conclusion

This chapter has explored the negotiations involved in the construction of desirable male bodies as purchasable commodities in the market and the presence of a client system that desires these bodies. It has identified linkages among sex workers' identities, desirability, performativity, and the economics governing sexual transactions. The case studies described here helped us understand how male sex workers view and interrogate their sexuality, gender expressions, identity, and self-perception.

The city of Mumbai, by virtue of being the fashion and financial capital of India, provides all the necessary tools for production of male bodies in sex work, the sex market, and networks of agents and clients. In addition, the city has a large number of venues for hiring sex workers, including public spaces, pimps, privately run pubs, and parties. Consistent with other research, we found men in sex work to be a non-homogenous group (Logan, 2010); the men we interviewed differed in their sexual identities, gender performance, role in sex, soliciting practices, body projects, and client system.

Participants reported using various body projects to make their bodies look desirable (Frederick & Essayli, 2016). Literature on male body image further elaborates that men who are seeking to attract other men experience heightened social pressure to be attractive (Minichiello, Scott, & Callander, 2013), which in turn leads to experiencing a high level of sexual objectification (Engeln-Maddox, Miller, & Doyle, 2011) and self-objectification (Kozak, Frankenhauser, & Roberts, 2009; Rolnik, Engeln-Maddox, & Miller, 2010). In our study, participants reported using fitness (gym/body-building), beauty services, or both to appear more attractive and desirable to their clients. The choice of body projects was associated with their sexual identification and gender expression. Beauty services, which are regarded as feminine, are associated with gay men. A study of Dominican male sex workers presented similar findings; desirability and embodiments were associated with self-perception of masculinity and sexual identification. Non-homosexual-identified participants chose embodiments conforming to traditional masculinities (Padilla, 2008).

There is also a relationship between sexual roles, identities, and gender expression. Those identifying with non-homosexual identities reported being repulsed by passive roles in sex acts; in the literature, this attitude has been described as a means of reasserting one's masculinity (Padilla, 2008). However, because sex work is dependent on monetary exchange, personal choice in terms of partner or sex roles is limited (Khire, 2008; Ramakrishnan, 2006; Shinde et al., 2009). In addition, if a client is looking for a passive partner, the client might reject a man with a gym-toned body. Therefore, some men engaged in sex work try to have a body type that can fulfill both active and passive roles (Benson, 1997; Shinde et al., 2009). Sexual identity and preference for body projects in terms of physical appearance are thus negotiated by the norms of the market (Davidson, 2002).

Examining the relationship among male sex workers, pimps, and clients has presented points of negotiation, opportunities, and limitations that define the politics of the sex work market. In effect, it has also emphasized the need for body projects as essential to creating desirability in relation to one's sexual identification and gender expression. Finally, we note that given the current political milieu and recent decriminalizing of same-sex behavior in India, there is a need to conduct more social and behavioral research to document male sex workers' concerns in affirming their identities and rights and to advocate for sex workers' rights.

References

Alcalde, M. C. (2014). What it means to be a man? Violence and homophobia in Latino masculinities on and off screen. *The Journal of Popular Culture, 47*(3), 537–553.

Anderson, E. (2013). Adolescent masculinity in an age of decreased homohysteria. *Boyhood Studies, 7*(1), 79–93.

Baral, S. D., Friedman, M. R., Geibel, S., Rebe, K., Bozhinov, B., Diouf, D., . . . Cáceres, C. F. (2015). Male sex workers: Practices, contexts, and vulnerabilities for HIV acquisition and transmission. *Lancet, 385*, 260–273. doi:10.1016/S0140-6736(14)60801-1

Beggan, J. K., & Allison, S. T. (2009). Viva viva? Women's meanings associated with male nudity in a 1970s "for women" magazine. *Journal of Sex Research*, *46*(5), 446–459.

Benson, S. (1997). The body, health and eating disorders. In K. Woodward (Ed.), *Identity and difference: Culture, media and identities* (pp. 121–181). London: Sage.

Bhagat, R. B., & Jones, G. W. (2013). *Population change and migration in Mumbai metropolitan region: Implications for planning and governance*. Singapore: Asia Research Institute, National University of Singapore.

Biello, K. B., Thomas, B. E., Johnson, B. E., Closson, E. F., Navakodi, P., Dhanalakshmi, A., . . . Mimiaga, M. J. (2017). Transactional sex and the challenges to safer sexual behaviors: A study among male sex workers in Chennai, India. *AIDS Care*, *29*(2), 231–238.

Blond, A. (2008). Impacts of exposure to images of ideal bodies on male body dissatisfaction: A review. *Body Image*, *5*(3), 244–250.

Boyatzis, R. E. (1998). *Transforming qualitative information: Thematic analysis and code development*. Thousand Oaks, CA: Sage Publications, Inc.

Chakrapani, V., Newman, P. A., Shunmugam, M., McLuckie, A., & Melwin, F. (2007). Structural violence against kothi-identified men who have sex with men in Chennai, India: A qualitative investigation. *AIDS Education & Prevention*, *19*(4), 346–364.

Chanda, R. (2016). On-screen male sexuality and women spectators: Semiotic analysis of Hindi contemporary cinema. *Jankriti International Magazine*. ISSN:2454-2725.

Ciecko, A. (2001). Superhit hunk heroes for sale: Globalization and Bollywood's gender politics. *Asian Journal of Communication*, *11*(2), 121–143.

Cornish, F. (2006). Challenging the stigma of sex work in India: Material context and symbolic change. *Journal of Community & Applied Social Psychology*, *16*(6), 462–471.

Clarkson, J. (2005). Contesting masculinity's makeover: "Queer Eye", consumer masculinity, and "straight-acting" gays. *Journal of Communication Inquiry*, *29*(3), 235–255.

Dandona, L., Dandona, R., Kumar, G. A., Gutierrez, J. P., McPherson, S., Bertozzi, S. M., . . . the ASCI FPP Study Team. (2006). How much attention is needed towards men who sell sex to men for HIV prevention in India? *BMC Public Health*, *6*(1), 31–31. doi:10.1186/1471-2458-6-31

Davidson, J. O. (2002). The rights and wrongs of prostitution. *Hypatia*, *17*(2), 84–98.

Engeln-Maddox, R., Miller, S. A., & Doyle, D. M. (2011). Tests of objectification theory in gay, lesbian, and heterosexual community samples: Mixed evidence for proposed pathways. *Sex Roles*, *65*(7–8), 518–532.

Ervin, M. (2011). The might of the metrosexual: How a mere marketing tool challenges hegemonic masculinity. In E. Watson & M. E. Shaw (Eds.), *Performing American masculinities: The 21st century man in popular culture* (pp. 58–75). Bloomington, IN: Indiana University Press.

Flick, U. A. (2008). *Designing qualitative research* (1st ed.). London and Thousand Oaks, CA: Sage Publications.

Frederick, D. A., & Essayli, J. H. (2016). Male body image: The roles of sexual orientation and body mass index across five national US Studies. *Psychology of Men & Masculinity*, *17*(4), 336.

Gehlawat, A. (2012). "Aadat se Majboor"/"helpless by habit": Metrosexual masculinity in contemporary Bollywood. *Studies in South Asian Film & Media*, *4*(1), 61–79.

Gopinath, G. (2000). Queering Bollywood: Alternative sexualities in popular Indian cinema. *Journal of Homosexuality*, *39*(3–4), 283–297.

Hall, T. (2007). Rent-boys, barflies, and kept men: Men involved in sex with men for compensation in Prague. *Sexualities*, *10*(4), 457–472.

Herold, E., Garcia, R., & DeMoya, T. (2001). Female tourists and beach boys: Romance or sex tourism? *Annals of Tourism Research*, *28*(4), 978–997.

Hobza, C. L., Walker, K. E., Yakushko, O., & Peugh, J. L. (2007). What about men? Social comparison and the effects of media images on body and self-esteem. *Psychology of Men and Masculinity*, *8*(3), 161.

Khan, S. (1999). Through a window darkly: Men who sell sex to men in India and Bangladesh. In P. Aggleton (Ed.), *Men who sell sex: International perspectives on male prostitution and AIDS* (pp. 195–213). London: UCL Press Limited.

Khire, B. V. (2008). Male sex work (MSW). In R. Sahni, V. K. Shankar, & H. Apte (Eds.), *Prostitution and beyond: An analysis of sex work in India* (pp. 126–144). New Delhi: Sage Publications.

Kneas, D. (2017). Chest hair and climate change: Harrison Ford and the making of "lost there, felt here". *Environmental History, 22*(3), 516–526.

Kozak, M., Frankenhauser, H., & Roberts, T. A. (2009). Objects of desire: Objectification as a function of male sexual orientation. *Psychology of Men and Masculinity, 10*(3), 225.

Liguori, A. L., & Aggleton, P. (1999). Aspects of male sex work in Mexico City. In P. Aggleton (Ed.), *Men who sell sex: International perspectives on male prostitution and HIV/AIDS* (pp. 103–126). London: UCL Press Limited.

Lipworth, L., & McLaughlin, J. K. (2012). The safety of breast implants: Epidemiologic studies. In P. J. Walter (Ed.), *Biomaterials in plastic surgery* (pp. 121–153). Oxford: Woodhead Publications.

Logan, T. D. (2010). Personal characteristics, sexual behaviors, and male sex work: A quantitative approach. *American Sociological Review, 75*(5), 679–704.

Lulla, K. (2011). *Desi boyz*. Eros International.

Mansukhani, T. (2008). *Dostana*. Dharma Productions.

Minichiello, V., Scott, J., & Callander, D. (2013). New pleasures and old dangers: Reinventing male sex work. *Journal of Sex Research, 50*(3–4), 263–275.

Network of Indian Male Sex Workers. (2006). *Pilot study on male sex workers in three cities in India*. Kolkata: NIMSW.

Om, S., Aag, R. G. V. K., Haseeno, B. A., & Replayy, A. (2016). The retro noughties: 1970s Hindi films in 2000s Bollywood cinema. In P. Joshi & R. Dudrah (Eds.), *The 1970s and its legacies in India's cinemas* (pp. 101–105). New York: Routledge.

Padilla, M. B. (2008). The embodiment of tourism among bisexually-behaving Dominican male sex workers. *Archives of Sexual Behavior, 37*(5), 783–793.

Parry, D. C., & Light, T. P. (2016). Sexual desire in the digital leisure sphere: Women's consumption of sexually explicit material. In S. Carnicelli, D. McGillivray, & G. McPherson (Eds.), *Digital leisure cultures: Critical perspectives* (pp. 207–220). London: Routledge.

Pompper, D. (2010). Masculinities, the metrosexual, and media images: Across dimensions of age and ethnicity. *Sex Roles, 63*(9–10), 682–696.

Ramakrishnan, L. (2006). Putting the "B" back in LGBT: Bisexuality, queer politics, and HIV/AIDS discourse. In B. Bose & S. B. (Eds.), *The phobic and the erotic: The politics of sexualities in contemporary India* (pp. 291–300). London: Seagull, Berg Publishers.

Ramsay, G. (2017). Straight women seeing gay porn: "He's too good looking!" *Porn Studies, 4*(2), 157–175.

Rohlinger, D. A. (2002). Eroticizing men: Cultural influences on advertising and male objectification. *Sex Roles, 46*(3–4), 61–74.

Rolnik, A. M., Engeln-Maddox, R., & Miller, S. A. (2010). Here's looking at you: Self-objectification, body image disturbance, and sorority rush. *Sex Roles, 63*(1–2), 6–17.

Sarwer, D. B., Nordmann, J. E., & Herbert, J. D. (2000). Cosmetic breast augmentation surgery: A critical overview. *Journal of Women's Health and Gender-Based Medicine, 9*(8), 843–856.

Scott, J., Minichiello, V., Marino, R., Harvey, G. P., Jamieson, M., & Browne, J. (2005). Understanding the new context of the male sex work industry. *Journal of Interpersonal Violence, 20*(3), 320–342.

Shah, S. P. (2014). *Street corner secrets: Sex, work, and migration in the city of Mumbai*. Durham, NC: Duke University Press.

Shandilya, K. (2014). Of enraged shirts, gyrating gangsters, and farting bullets: Salman Khan and the new Bollywood action film. *South Asian Popular Culture, 12*(2), 111–121.

Shinde, S., Setia, M. S., Kavi, A. R., Anand, V., & Jerajani, H. (2009). Male sex workers: Are we ignoring a risk group in Mumbai, India? *Indian Journal of Dermatology, Venereology and Leprology, 75*(1), 41–46.

Sinclair, D. (2011). "Metro" men boost spa growth: Skin care (aroma & spa). *South African Pharmaceutical and Cosmetic Review, 38*(11), 18–20.

Smith, N. J. (2012). Body issues: The political economy of male sex work. *Sexualities, 15*(5–6), 586–603.

Srinivasan, R. (2011). "Gaylords" of Bollywood: Politics of desire in Hindi cinema. *Economic and Political Weekly*, 73–78.

Stout, N. M. (2014). *After love: Queer intimacy and erotic economies in post-Soviet Cuba*. Durham, NC and London: Duke University Press.

Talukdar, H. (2018). Masculinities and media culture in Indian Bollywood films. *International Journal of Smart Education and Urban Society (IJSEUS)*, *9*(2), 12–24.

Tijori, D. (2003). *oops!* Tijori Films.

Travers, M. (2001). *Qualitative research through case studies* (1st ed.). London and Thousand Oaks, CA: Sage Publications.

Tumbe, C. (2012). Migration persistence across twentieth century India. *Migration and Development*, *1*(1), 87–112.

34

Male sex work in China

Digital technology and its emerging role

Yifeng Troy Cai

Globally, geosocial dating apps such as Tinder and Grindr increasingly shape how people form intimate relations such as sex, dates, or marriage (Chan, 2018; Garcia, Reiber, Massey, & Merriwether, 2012; McGuire, 2016; Race, 2015). However, to date, little research has examined how dating apps shape the male sex industry. This chapter discusses the transformations that geosocial dating apps brought to the male-male sex industry by detailing the results of an ethnographic study in contemporary People's Republic of China (PRC). I argue that the rapidly developing app-infrastructure in China has given rise to a booming app-based male-male sex industry. As a result, male sex work is becoming increasingly individualized and independent of commercial sex venues in contemporary urban China. Additionally, in some cases, the digital infrastructure in China blurs the boundaries among sex, work, fun, and pleasure for male sex workers (MSWs). App-based male sex work allows researchers to critically reflect on our theoretical paradigms and research methodologies so as to improve future research and intervention with male sex workers in China and elsewhere.

I first briefly explain the ethnographic methods and field site used in this study. Then I situate app-based male sex work in China's legal, technological, and cultural contexts, and I provide an overview of the male sex industry. Next, I discuss in more detail the structural transformations of male sex work in China and provide ethnographic vignettes that portrays male sex workers' lived experiences of selling sex via geosocial dating apps. In the conclusion, I provide theoretical and methodological reflections on studying app-based male sex work.

Methodology

Overall, the design of this study is ethnographic. I conducted field study in Shanghai in the summers of 2017 and 2018, for a total of six months. Main research methods included online participant observation (Boellstorff, Nardi, Pearce, & Taylor, 2012), open-ended interviews, and informal conversations. During the fieldwork, I interacted with informants both on apps and in offline settings. As typical of ethnographic research (Hammersley & Atkinson, 2007), I gained permission from informants to spend time with them in informal everyday settings. For example, I went to movies, meals, coffee, and bars/clubs with my informants. In this way, I established trust with my informants and gained a more holistic understanding about the lived realities of MSWs in contemporary China. I also drew methodological insights from communication studies (Light, Burgess, & Duguay, 2018) in order to study male sex workers' app-based activities.

During my fieldwork, I created accounts on the four different apps most popular among Chinese gay men: Blued, Grindr, Jack'd, and Aloha. I stated clearly on my profiles my identity as a researcher and my academic affiliation, and I included a brief introduction to my project. Following the examples of other studies on apps (Light et al., 2018; Race, 2015; Wang, 2018), I used these apps daily during my fieldwork, on average approximately three hours per day. Because geolocative dating apps show profiles by proximity to the users, I traveled to different districts of Shanghai to use these apps in order to reach a more diverse set of research participants. Whenever I encountered a profile offering paid sexual services, I initiated a conversation, introducing myself and my research project, and asked if the users would be willing to talk more. Every now and then, other users would initiate conversations with me via dating apps, including MSWs, their clients, and gay men interested in sexual transactions among the gay community.

All together, I conducted 20 semi-structured, open-ended, in-person interviews with male sex workers in Shanghai. All of the interviews were conducted in mandarin Chinese. They were recorded with the informants' permission and later transcribed into Chinese and translated into English by me. Each interview lasted for about two hours. In these interviews, I asked broad questions as prompts, including *What do you think about male sex work in today's China? Why do you sell sex? What roles do you think dating apps play in male-male transactional sex? Do you have any memorable stories from selling sex that you are willing to share with me?* During the interviews, I encouraged interviewees to talk about anything they found relevant to the prompts. I also worked to ensure that the interview stayed focused on the theme of male sex work. I deliberately incorporated open-ended interviews into the research design to allow informants to articulate whatever they found important and significant about their experiences and subjective feelings about engaging in app-based male sex work in contemporary China.

Contextualizing app-based male sex work in contemporary China

As most archaeological discoveries in the rest of the world suggest, same-sex desires and practices can be found in many regions in pre-modern times (Blackmore, 2011). Historians of China have documented different forms of same-sex relations from China's ancient dynasties to modern times (Hinsch, 1990; Kang, 2010). I will not repeat their findings here. Interested readers should consult Travis S. K. Kong's (2014) chapter in the first volume of *Male Sex Work and Society* for a succinct summary of the history of male homosexuality and prostitution in China. In this section, I contextualize male homosexuality and male-male sex work in contemporary urban China from three angles: legal status, contemporary gay male hook-up culture, and forms of male sex work.

Legal status

The legal status of homosexuality and same-sex sex work in contemporary China is complicated. Although many scholars have rightly observed that same-sex desires/practices and same-sex prostitution have led to arrest and/or imprisonment (Kong, 2014; see also Zheng, 2015), it would be inaccurate to claim that homosexuality and male-male sex work are illegal or criminalized in China. In fact, the opposite seems to be true. Chinese legal scholar Guo Xiaofei (郭晓飞) points out that there is in fact no law that explicitly criminalizes homosexuality or same-sex sex work per se (Guo, 2007, p. 110). Guo also points out, however, that the ambiguity of the legal status of homosexuality and male-male prostitution in written law and regulations does not mean homosexuality and same-sex prostitution are not policed in mainland China. In reality, gay men and MSWs are constantly arrested and sentenced (Kong, 2014). In fact, Guo argues, the police still arrest gay men and male sex workers for "indecency" or "prostitution" even though specific laws may not exist (Guo, 2007, p. 119). Guo observes that, because the arrestees worry about their sexual orientation or activities being made public, most of the time these men accept fines or custody. Indeed, according to many of my informants, the police pretend to be clients on gay dating apps to approach MSWs and arrest them.

Gay hook-up culture

There are various ways Chinese gay men seek out other gay men for erotic and/or romantic relationships in contemporary urban China. For example, physical venues such as bars and clubs are important venues where Chinese gay men meet one another. Well-known gay clubs such as Destination in Beijing or Lucca 390 in Shanghai routinely host theme parties that attract gay men from around China as well as East and Southeast Asian countries. However, these physical venues are often closed, temporarily or permanently, due to police crackdowns. Sometimes these venues will reopen after a short period of time or relocate to a different area to restart their business.

Unlike some western countries such as the United States where gay bathhouses have been declining in the past several decades (Dean, 2009; Delany, 1999), bathhouses in East and Southeast Asia still appear to be booming, and they serve as important venues for gay men to meet one another for sex. During my NGO outreach work for HIV testing in Shanghai, the bathhouses were always packed, especially on Saturday and Sunday afternoons. These bathhouses were mostly segregated by age group, and, to a lesser degree, nationality. While some bathhouses were frequented by the older generation or by younger men seeking older men for sexual/romantic partners,[1] some attracted predominantly younger gay men in their 20s or were known to have more Western visitors. Even more so than clubs and bars, bathhouses are subject to police crackdowns. Between 2016 and 2017, two well-known bathhouses were shut down permanently in Shanghai.

Dating apps, in contrast, have become the most common, popular, and stable way for younger gay men to look for sex in urban China. China has a prosperous gay dating app market, with new apps being continuously developed or purchased from foreign companies. Grindr, the world's most-used gay dating app, for example, was purchased by the Chinese company Kunlun (昆仑) in 2016 (Cao, 2018). Some of the most popular gay dating apps in China are Blued, Grindr, Jack'd, and Aloha. According to one quantitative survey study, up to February 2018, Blued had over 40 million users worldwide and over 30 million users in mainland China ("Xtecher Statistical Analysis," 2017). When we consider the number of users of other dating apps, the number of dating app users in China may well exceed 30 million. According to the same study, over 60% of Blued users are between 20 and 29 years old, about 20% are between 30 and 34, about 10% are between 15 and 19, and 5% are between 35 and 39. These statistics suggest that gay men older than 40 years old are not the major users of dating apps. However, these numbers may be affected the prevalent ageism among the gay population in China, which could lead to users misreporting their age on dating apps. It is also possible that there are gay dating apps geared toward older gay men. However, I was unable to find such apps at the time of my fieldwork. Further studies are needed to address whether and to what extent the digitalization of gay men's social life affects older gay men's lived experiences.

The popularity of these apps can be partly attributed to their privacy features (Albury & Byron, 2016; Wu & Ward, 2018; and see McGuire, 2016, for a study of how privacy features can be breached and thus threaten the discreetness of dating app use). Rather than visiting gay bars, clubs, or cruising parks, men who are attracted to men, whether they are openly gay, closeted, or curious, and regardless of their relationship or marital status, can easily and discreetly register for one or multiple accounts and meet other men for sex and/or dates. In a social environment that is still not entirely comfortable with homosexuality (Engebresten, 2014; Zheng, 2015), the emergence and development of geosocial dating apps allows those who are closeted and/or married to a woman, as well as those who prefer more private modes of same-sex intimacy, to fulfill their desires without making their same-sex desires public. I encountered many profiles on gay dating apps with pictures showing only the torsos or even pictures of landscapes. While some will send pictures with their faces after talking on the apps for a while, some will resort to describing their appearances in words to their potential hook-up partners to protect their confidentiality. Apps' impact on urban gay life in China is revealed by yet another important phenomenon: Dating apps are literally *infiltrating* homoerotic encounters. Based on my ethnographic observation in clubs, bars, bathhouses, and at dance parties, app-based interactions frequently accompanied, and sometimes even replaced, in-person interactions. For instance, even on dance floors in gay clubs, some Chinese gay men still used dating apps to message people who might very well be standing right next to them. I observed the same behavior in bathhouses, where lines of gay men stood next to each other and browsed their gay dating apps. In this sense, dating apps do not just *facilitate* hook-ups among gay men; they *mediate* those hook-ups to the extent that they have become ingrained in the very fabric of homoerotic encounters, at least for the younger generation of gay men in urban China.

Forms of male sex work

Forms of male sex work appear to align with gay hook-up cultures. Although this chapter emphasizes app-based male sex work, it is worth noting that male sex work is organized and structured in diverse ways across urban China. App-based male sex work is by no means entirely replacing other forms of sex work in China. Partly due to China's regional differences in terms of political and economic conditions, history, local culture, and ethnic make-up, male sex work takes varying forms in different locations. In his landmark studies on female sex work in China, the leading Chinese scholar of sex work, Pan Suiming (潘绥铭, 1999, 2000) meticulously documented the drastically different structures of the sex industry in terms of clientele, pimp-sex worker relationships, pricing, and services in different towns and cities.

These differences also exist in the male sex industry across China. In *An Inquiry to Commercial Sex in MSM Community in China* (《中国男男性交易状态调查》, Ge, 2007), thus far the only book-length study providing a comprehensive overview of male-male sex work across China,[2] published by the well-known NGO Beijing Gender Health Education Institute (北京纪安德咨询中心), some of the most common forms of male sex work are street- or cruising park-based sex work; commercial sex venue-based sex work in bathhouses, karaoke bars, clubs, and massage parlors; and online male sex work. It is worth pointing out that these typologies are meant to provide broad strokes of the general forms of male sex work in China, and each category can be further divided into sub-categories. For example, while some street-based male sex workers sell sex to male clients as gay men, others dress up as women to sell sex (Lin, 2018).

Although both types of sex work are street or cruising park based, they are different in terms of clientele, sex workers' lived experiences, and their implications for gender and sexuality in general.

However, to the best of my knowledge, there is no mention of app-based male sex work in China in published studies, probably due to the fact that gay dating apps did not gain wide popularity in China until the early 2010s. Based on the ethnographic data from my observation and interviews, apps have become an increasingly important venue for male sex work in urban China. The remainder of this chapter discusses important transformations in the male sex industry brought about by gay dating apps.

Geosocial apps and the transformation of male sex work in China

In this section, I discuss the two (kinds of) apps that are most pertinent to male sex work in urban China: (1) a multifunctional app called WeChat and (2) gay dating/hook-up apps. The rapid development of apps has led to two major changes. First, male-male sex work is increasingly done through dating apps. Second, more and more MSWs enter the sex industry directly through apps or break free from commercial sex venues such as bathhouses or massage parlors and start selling sex independently, which leads to what I call the "individualization of the Chinese male sex industry."

Few visitors to China these days will fail to notice how important smartphone applications such as WeChat have become in Chinese people's everyday life. First developed as a messaging app, WeChat now has many functions, including audio/video chat, online banking, bill payment, investment, restaurant reservations, online games, and social networking. Among these, digital payment has had a palpable impact on transactional sex among men. WeChat allows business owners to charge clients discreetly and conveniently. Furthermore, clients can tip the male sex workers working in physical sex venues through WeChat, which makes the app-mediated payment even more desirable for all parties involved.

However, the many functions of WeChat pose challenges to the owners of commercial sex venues. Because the owners of these establishments make a large portion of their income through commissions, they prohibit their employees from seeing clients in their off-time. However, with WeChat, MSWs can easily connect with their clients without the constraints of physical locations or the prohibitions of MSWs' employers. Theoretically, WeChat gives male sex workers more agency in choosing to work independently instead of under an employer. However, relying on WeChat alone limits a MSW's clientele, because they can virtually connect only with clients they have already met. To reach a larger group of potential clients, male sex workers need to use geosocial dating apps.

Geosocial apps use a grid system, displaying users' profile pictures based on their distance from the user. One simply logs onto the app anywhere and sees other gay men near him, then clicks on the profile pictures to initiate a conversation. The features of hook-up apps differ, but most of them allow users to display at least one picture, physical statistics (height, weight, age, sexual position), and space to write whatever the users want to write (self-introduction, reasons for using the app, and so on). These dating apps not only make it easier for gay men to meet one another; they also provide a convenient platform for male sex work. Compensating for WeChat's inability to reach a wide clientele, hook-up apps allow MSWs to advertise their sexual services. In urban China today, it is easy to log onto a hook-up app and see profiles explicitly advertising their sexual services (Figure 34.1), whether in a business area or in a residential gated community. In sum, smartphone apps, particularly WeChat and gay hook-up apps, provide a digital infrastructure that enables a more individualized and flexible mode of transactional sex.

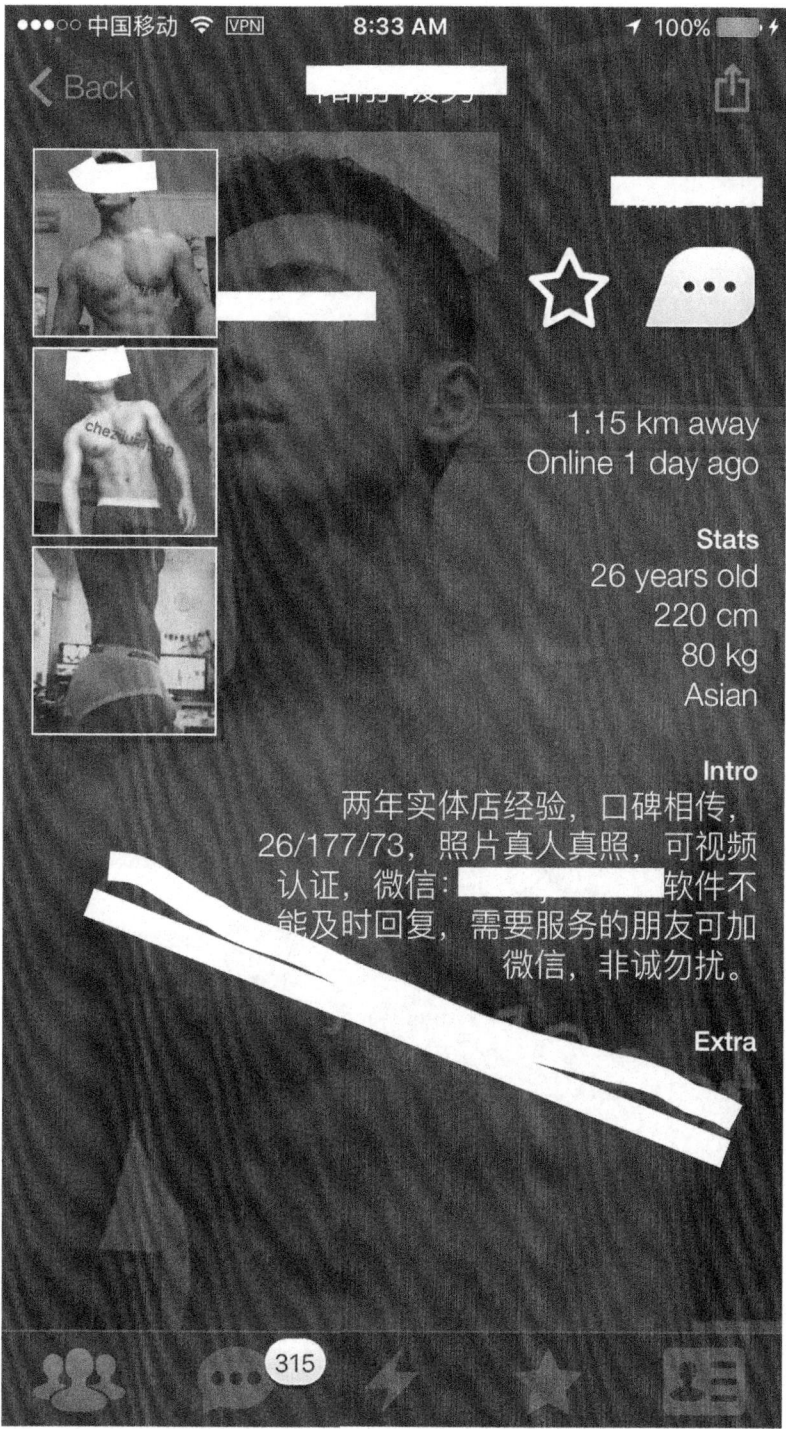

Figure 34.1 a–d Examples of male sex workers on the Jack'd app. The screen shots were taken from the author's phone and blurred to ensure confidentiality.

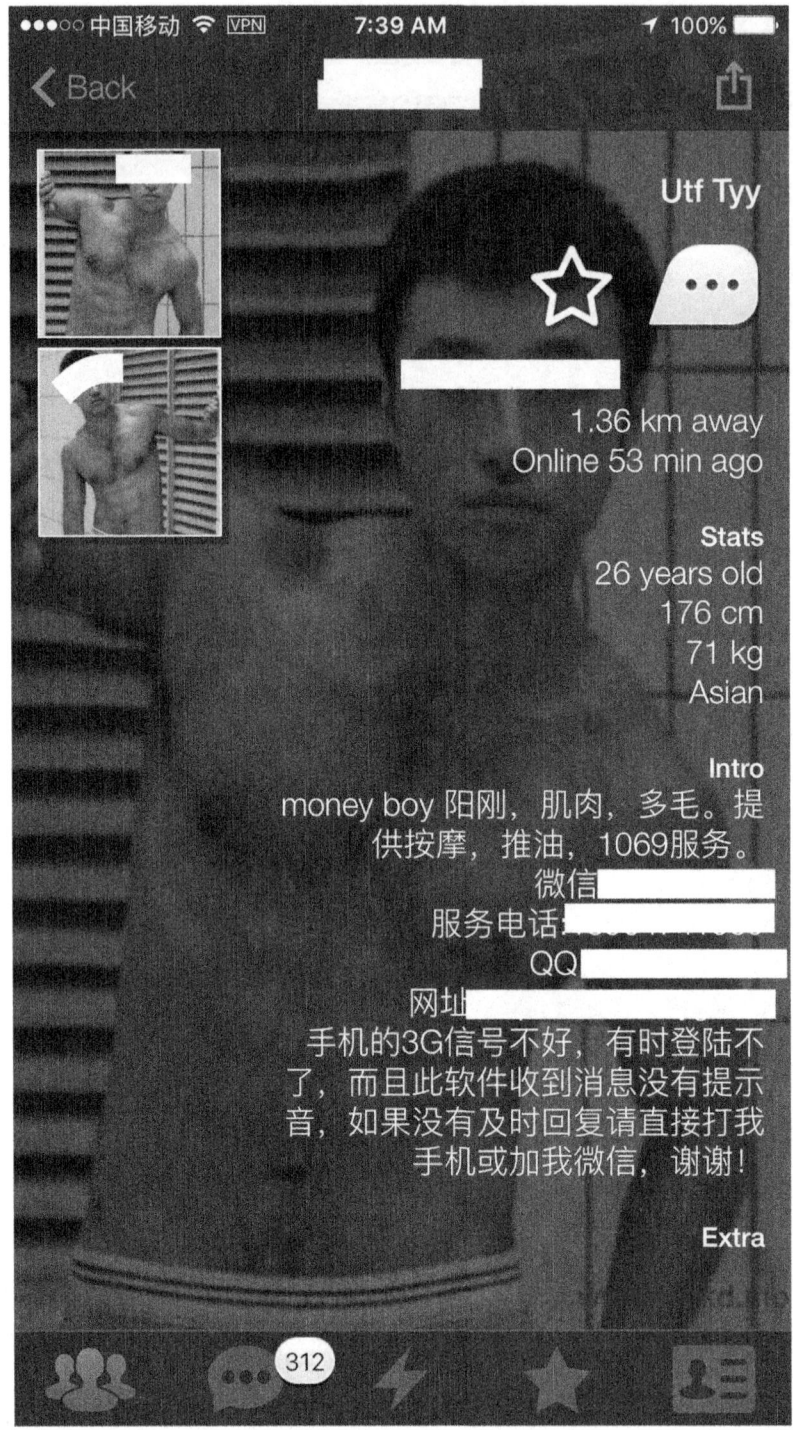

Figure 34.1 (Continued)

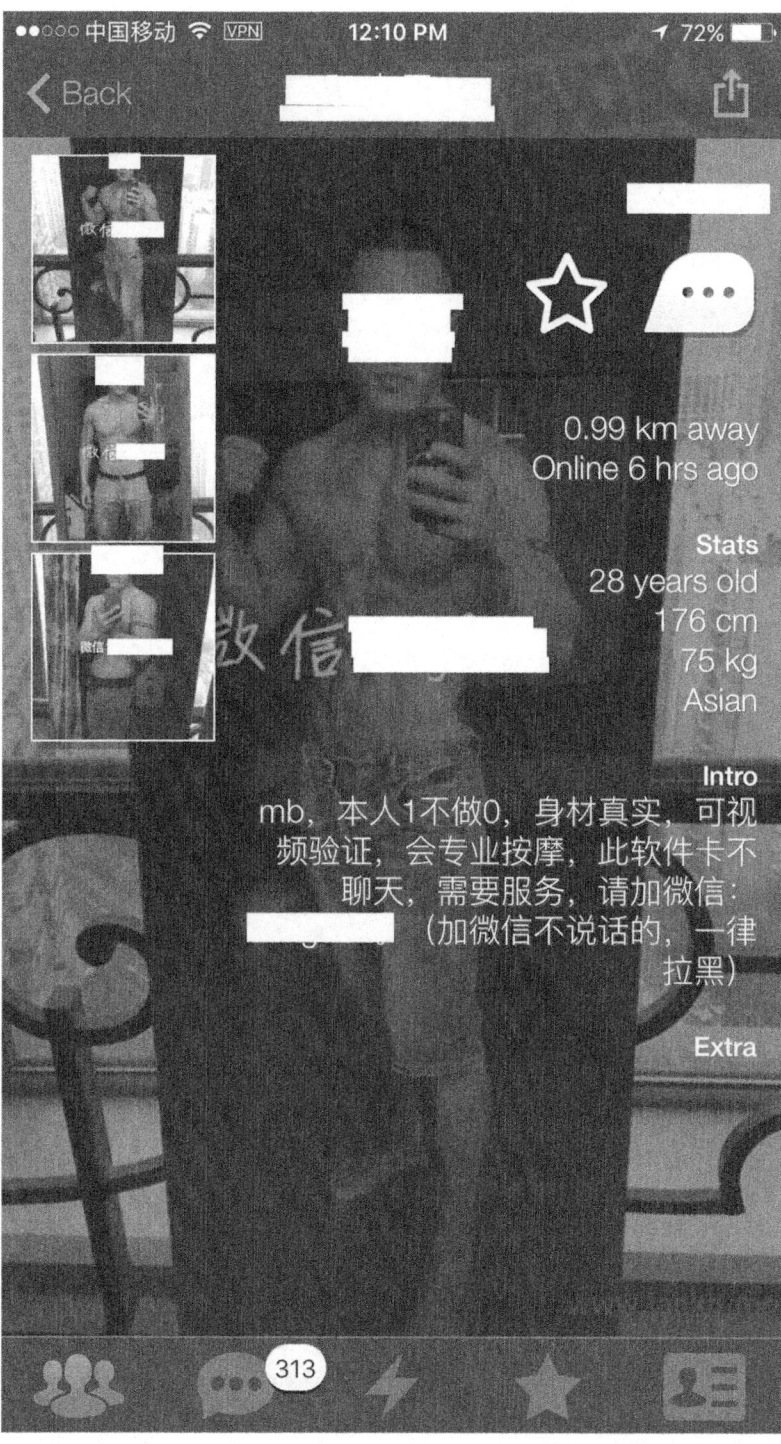

Figure 34.1 (Continued)

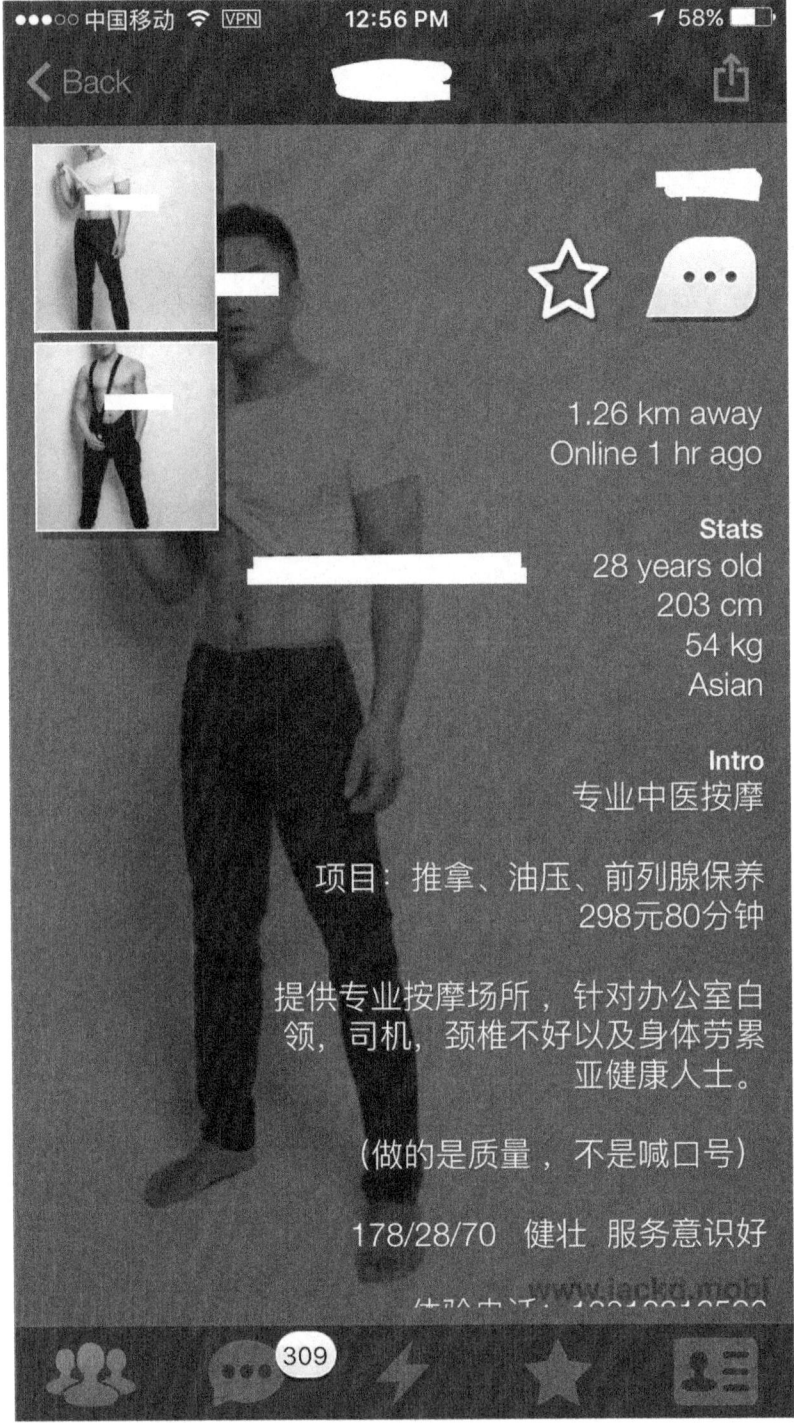

Figure 34.1 (Continued)

Blurry boundaries in the sex trade: selling sex or hooking up?

In the past, to become a (male) sex worker in China, one usually would need to work under an employer in a commercial sex venue such as a massage parlor or karaoke bar (Fang, 2011; Kong, 2010; Zheng, 2009). With the digitalization of male sex work through apps, one can become a sex worker simply by clicking on one's smartphone screen. MSWs can stay home, log onto a gay dating app, and negotiate a deal with potential clients. Theoretically, this convenient and individualized mode of male sex work makes it possible for just a gay man to sell sex, whether or not he identifies as a sex worker or has experience selling sex. As a result, the boundaries between selling sex and hooking up become blurry and sometimes indistinguishable, producing new lived experiences for app-based MSWs.

The first example is Zhang, a 20-something-year-old MSW with whom I became acquainted through a hook-up app. During the interview, Zhang took over the role of the interviewer and asked me to try my luck in the transactional sex scene:

Zhang: Of course you can! Just give it a try.

Me: (embarrassed laugh) It's not my thing. I can't fake it with guys I don't like.

Zhang: (impatiently) You don't know. Just start with the ones you are attracted to. Those young and pretty ones. That's how I started.

Me: Really? You only do it with the guys you like? Then how is that. . . . What is. . . . What is that?

Zhang: You think I do that all the time? I have a job. I'm a real-estate agent. When I'm horny I log on the hook-up apps, and see who message me.

Me: Then this is called hooking up!

Me: If you like them why would you still charge them?

Zhang: It's like hooking up and getting paid at the same time. How cool is that!

(interview 2017; translated from mandarin Chinese by the author)

Here, we see a rather special case. "Hooking up and getting paid to do it" is an illuminating phrase. Zhang was not earning "survival money." Nor was he uneducated or desperate. It was even harder to decide if he considered sex work or fun. Nor is it easy to tell if he was doing it for money or pleasure. With day jobs that pay decently, gay men like Zhang combine fun, having sex, and making money. They do not need to switch into the identity of a sex worker to separate the commercial part of sex from their "normal" sex lives. Instead, engaging in transactional sex on apps is a part of their sex life.

The story of another MSW, named Feng, further challenges some of the common assumptions about the lived experiences of MSWs in China. Feng is a 20-something gay man I met during a Gay Pride event in Shanghai the summer of 2018. After hearing about my research project, Feng suggested that I should interview him. Unlike Zhang, who has an up-and-running profile on dating apps, Feng's profiles do not indicate that he is available for paid sexual services. However, he too engaged in male sex work in a way that blurs the boundaries between sex, money, pleasure, and fun:

A guy once messaged me on Jack'd with a blank profile, and offered 1,500 RMB (approximately 220 USD) for sex straight ahead. I chatted with him for a while and asked him to unlock the pics. He's quite decent looking. That night he came over, we had sex, and then we chatted for a long time after that. We just talked about everything, drug policy, the economy in China, the gay scene in Shanghai. I didn't mention a word of the 1,500 coz

I didn't actually care at all. I liked this guy and wanted to be friends too. But at one point he just took out his phone and transferred the money to my WeChat. I didn't say anything and just kept it. Why? Coz it's fun. Why not haha. He offered it, right? I didn't even ask! But that's like the only time I did it though. We stay in contact but never have this pay thing anymore

(interview, 2018)

Compared with Zhang's case, Feng's is even more distant from how male sex work usually takes place as documented in previously published studies. Even though Zhang downplayed the transactional part of the encounter, compensation was still explicit in Zhang's conceptualization of it. For Feng, however, a business relationship with a man who started out as a paying client evolved into an unpaid relationship based on friendship, because Feng did not "care at all" about money. Instead, money symbolically added a "fun" element into the initial interaction. In the cases of both Zhang and Feng, we see that sex, fun, money, pleasure, and intimacy were all present in some of their encounters with other gay men.

In the examples provided previously, MSWs did not necessarily rely on transactional sex for their livelihood. Rather, they used dating apps to do what they were originally designed for: to have fun with other gay men. This selling sex/hooking-up model of male sex work is highly visible in Shanghai, a metropolis with China's fastest-growing market economy in which ideas about exchange and transaction are deeply woven into very fabric of everyday life. Indeed, this kind of transformation among male-male sexual exchange reflects larger social changes regarding intimacy, money, and exchange in post-socialist countries. Social studies of intimate relations in post-socialist contexts have pointed out that societal-scale politico-economic reconfigurations, such as marketization, privatization, and the loss of permanent employment or universal healthcare, have brought out the transactional aspects of intimate relations (Allen, 2011; Stout, 2014; Weiner, 2007; Zheng, 2009).[3] A decade ago in Shanghai, for example, the anthropologist James Farrer (2002) observed that young (heterosexual) people's dating practices already displayed highly transactional features. For example, as Farrer reports, young people in Shanghai would date people they did not consider attractive if the date offered money or gifts or treated them to fancy services. What I describe in this chapter, then, suggests the deepening of this kind of transactional consideration among Chinese people at a larger scale. While it might be observable only in highly marketized places such as Shanghai in the early 2000s, during my fieldwork between 2017 and 2018, I observed the same selling sex/hooking-up model in other major cities in northern, southern, and southwestern Chinese cities, including Beijing, Chongqing, Guangzhou, and Shenzhen. With geosocial dating apps, it is easier to negotiate transactions with potential intimate partners—pluralized here deliberately—more conveniently. Future studies are needed to examine whether app-based male sex work and the blurriness of boundaries also exist in less economically and digitally developed areas in China.

As money, transaction, and exchange have become increasingly important and morally acceptable in everyday life, they have also become salient parameters through which a growing number of Chinese gay men navigate their lives in contemporary urban China.[4] Repeatedly, my informants in Shanghai told me that gay men's attractiveness and social value are closely tied to how much others are willing to spend on them. For instance, many younger gay men will post pictures on social media (e.g., WeChat, Aloha, and so on) of money or gifts they receive, without labeling themselves or being labeled as sex workers or money boys.

Conclusion: reflections and challenges

In this chapter, I focused on the impact of geosocial dating apps on the male sex industry in contemporary urban China. It is worth restating that app-based male sex work is not replacing other forms of male sex work documented by previous studies, at least not yet. Rather, it is a burgeoning form of male-male sexual transaction that is gaining momentum and producing new meanings and experiences of being a male sex worker in today's China. To conclude, I reflect on theoretical and methodological implications as well as some challenges for future research.

App-based MSW requires a critical reflection on research design. More often than not, researchers visit physical locations with highly observable sexual transactions to access MSW populations. These physical locations include bathhouses, cruising parks, karaoke bars, and massage parlors. Additionally, commercial sex venues tend to spatially congregate and form "red light districts" in China (Fang, 2011; Pan, 1999, 2000). As a result, the common method for studying sex work is to enter these venues and neighborhoods to identify and recruit informants. Demographically speaking, male sex workers providing services in these venues and locations tend to come from the lower end of the socioeconomic spectrum. Most of them are rural-to-urban migrants seeking economic upward mobility in urban China—the population commonly referred to by Chinese people and scholars as "money boys" (Ge, 2007; Kong, 2014; Rofel, 2010; Zheng, 2016). However, a number of existing studies on women's sex work have pointed out that people from across the socioeconomic spectrum work in the sex industry (Bernstein, 2007; Showden, 2011; Status, 2009). My study here implies that the same can be said about the male sex industry. If we do not include the lived realities of MSWs from across the socioeconomic spectrum in our research, our understanding about male sex work will remain incomplete in today's rapidly digitalizing world.

An app-based approach to studying male sex work may provide a way to include a broader range of socioeconomic status. Sex-based apps are used by MSWs from all walks of life, including former street-based rural-to-urban migrant sex workers, men with well-paid day jobs, and those who are highly selective about their clients' physical attractiveness and/or social class. Therefore, compared with a research design that studies only physical venues, an app-based method can theoretically cover MSWs with varying socioeconomic status.

Additionally, app-based male sex work necessitates a holistic understanding about what I call "the infrastructure for male sex work," by which I mean the sociocultural and politico-economic conditions from which a particular kind of transactional sex emerges, whether because of or in spite of those conditions. Specifically, this infrastructure may include technological developments, legal and administrative policies and regulations, racial and ethnic dynamics, and the norms and traditions of the local social word. One area I would like to emphasize is the relationship between the state and the sex industry. More often than not, studies focus on the hindrances that the state places on the sex industry. However, in reality, the state may play a pivotal role in the development of the sex industry. Pan Suiming (1999, 2000), for example, argues that government officials are often important patrons who sustain local sex industries, especially in less developed towns and counties in PRC (see also Osburg, 2013; Uretsky, 2015; Zheng, 2009). Likewise, the development of app-based male sex work heavily relies on the app-based infrastructure the Chinese state supports. Without the state's encouragement of the "app economy" (Goldsmith, 2014) or its effort to replace paper currency with app payments, app-based sex work may not have become as prosperous as it is in today's China. This is not to say the state directly supports or encourages the sex industry. However, intentionally or not, these state actions have contributed to the development and transformation of male-male transactional sex. Therefore, future studies should pay more attention to how male sex work is influenced, mediated, or supported by multiple and complex social conditions, some of which may seem hostile or irrelevant to the male sex industry but which may nevertheless shape the industry in profound ways.

Without comparative studies at a global scale, it is hard to tell whether app-based male sex work and the blurriness of boundaries are particular to PRC or an emerging global phenomenon. However, ethnographic studies in various parts of the world have documented the increasingly blurry boundaries between work and intimacy in the sex industry (Cabezas, 2009; Gregory, 2007; Walby, 2012). Therefore, it is reasonable to predict that the lived experiences of MSWs worldwide may increasingly manifest such ambiguity and blurriness.

Such ambiguity and blurriness pose challenges for future studies of male sex work. First, who should be considered a male sex worker? Recall the example of my informant who saw what he did as "having fun and getting paid to do it." How should researchers recruit men who sell sex via dating apps but who do not identify as sex workers or even see what they do as selling sex? What are the criteria, implications, and consequences of including/excluding such men? Furthermore, does the concept of "male sex work(er)" accurately reflect the diverse lived realities of the men who engage in transactional sex? Historically, research on sex-for-money exchange among men has used various paradigms (Bimbi, 2007). Does the digitalization of contemporary human life require a new paradigm to understand sex-for-money exchanges in today's world? What is revealed and/or concealed by understanding male-male transactional sex primarily as work but not as pleasure or fun? Much work remains to be done.

Acknowledgments

I am indebted to multiple individuals for their help at different stages throughout this ongoing research project. Specifically, I would like to thank my PhD advisor, Prof. Katherine A. Mason, and PhD committee members, Profs. Matthew Gutmann and Bhrigupati Singh, for their guidance since I started this project in 2016. I also would like to thank Dr. Drew Walker, Director of Gender and Sexuality Studies at Brown University, for providing detailed and insightful comments for an early version of the chapter. This project has thus far received generous funding from various sources, including the American Council for Learned Societies, the Luce Foundation, the Institute for Humane Studies, the Global Health Initiative at Brown University's School of Public Health, the Graduate School of Arts and Sciences at Brown University, and the Institute for Sexuality and Gender at Renmin University of China and Harbin Medical University. Last but not least, I am grateful to the gay men in Shanghai who participated in this study.

Notes

1 The common expression, 恋老癖, *lian lao pi*, gerontophilia, refers to the "condition" or "fetish" of young men preferring older men for sexual partners. Frequently, this preference is regarded negatively by Chinese society, including the gay population.
2 The sociologist Fang's (2011) book Male Publicists: A Study of Chinese Masculinities (《男公关: 男性气质研究》) provides a more in-depth, ethnographic study of male sex work in private clubs (会所, hui suo) in south China.
3 Along with other social research on the relationship between intimacy and money (Bear, Ho, Tsing, & Yanagisako, 2015; Cabezas, 2009; Meiu, 2017; Zelizer, 2005), I argue that transactional aspects are always part of intimate relations (see also Cai, 2017). Instead of seeing intimacy among gay men as being turned into something transactional, then, I argue that politico-economic transformations such as those in China bring out these transactional aspects and make them more observable to social scientists.
4 Surely this cannot be said to be true for all gay men. Although I personally encountered gay men who embraced transactional logic within intimate relationships, there are still gay men who believe that

money has eroded genuine intimacy. What I am trying to point out, then, is an observable trend signaling the increasing acceptability of money and transaction in intimate relationships among gay men.

References

Albury, K., & Byron, P. (2016). Safe on my phone? Same-sex attracted young people's negotiations of intimacy, visibility, and risk on digital hook-up apps. *Social Media + Society*, *2*(4), 1–10. doi:10.1177/2056305116672887

Allen, J. (2011). *¡Venceremos?: The erotics of black self-making in Cuba*. Durham, NC: Duke University Press.

Bear, L., Ho, K., Tsing, A. L., & Yanagisako, S. (2015). Gens: A feminist manifesto for the study of capitalism. *Cultural Anthropology*. Retrieved from https://culanth.org/fieldsights/652-gens-a-feminist-manifesto-for-thestudy-of-capitalism

Bernstein, E. (2007). Sex work for the middle classes. *Sexualities*, *10*(4), 473–488. doi:10.1177/1363 460707080984

Bimbi, D. S. (2007). Male prostitution: Pathology, paradigms and progress in research. *Journal of Homosexuality*, *53*(1–2), 219–240.

Blackmore, C. (2011). How to queer the past without sex: Queer theory, feminisms and the archaeology of identity. *Archaeologies*, *7*(1), 75–96. doi:10.1007/s11759-011-9157-9

Boellstorff, T., Nardi, B., Pearce, C., & Taylor, T. L. (2012). *Ethnography and virtual worlds: A handbook of method*. Princeton, NJ: Princeton University Press. doi:10.1080/08838159609364336

Cabezas, A. L. (2009). *Economies of desire: Sex and tourism in Cuba and the Dominican Republic*. Philadelphia, PA: Temple University Press.

Cai, Y. T. (2017). *How China's male sex workers mix business with pleasure*. Retrieved from www.sixthtone.com/news/1000797/how-chinas-male-sex-workers-mix-business-with-pleasure?from=timeline&isappinstalled=0

Cao, Y. (曹忆蕾). (2018). Blued 宣布完成1亿美元D轮融资 [Blued announced its successful 100 million financing]. 新京报 [*Beijing News*]. Retrieved from www.bjnews.com.cn/invest/2018/02/02/475082.html%0A新京报快讯(记者曹忆蕾)2

Chan, L. S. (2018). Ambivalence in networked intimacy: Observations from gay men using mobile dating apps. *New Media & Society*, *20*(7), 2566–2581. doi:10.1177/1461444817727156

Dean, T. (2009). *Unlimited intimacy: Reflections on the subculture of barebacking*. Chicago and London: University of Chicago Press.

Delany, S. R. (1999). *Times Square red, Times Square blue*. New York and London: New York University Press.

Engebresten, E. (2014). *Queer women in urban China: An ethnography*. New York: Routledge.

Fang, G. (方刚). (2011). 男公关:男性气质研究 [*Male publicists: A study of Chinese masculinities*]. Beijing: Qunzhong Publishing House.

Farrer, J. (2002). *Opening up: Youth sex culture and market reform in Shanghai*. Chicago, IL and London: University of Chicago Press.

Garcia, J. R., Reiber, C., Massey, S. G., & Merriwether, A. M. (2012). Sexual hookup culture : A review. *Review of General Psychology*, *16*(2), 161–176. doi:10.1037/a0027911

Ge, T. (童戈). (2007). 中国男男性交易状态调查 [*An inquiry to commercial sex in MSM community in China*]. Beijing: Beijing Gender Health Education Institute.

Goldsmith, B. (2014). The smartphone app economy and app ecosystems. In G. Goggin & L. Hjorth (Eds.), *The Routledge companion to mobile media* (pp. 171–180). New York: Routledge.

Gregory, S. (2007). *The devil behind the mirror: Globalization and politics in the Dominican Republic*. Berkeley, CA: University of California Press.

Guo, X. (郭晓飞). (2007). 中国法视野下的同性恋 [*Homosexuality under the gaze of Chinese law*]. Beijing: Intellectual Property Publishing House.

Hammersley, M., & Atkinson, P. (2007). *Ethnography: Principles in practice*. New York: Taylor & Francis.

Hinsch, B. (1990). *Passions of the cut sleeve: The male homosexual tradition in China*. Berkeley, Los Angeles and London: University of California Press.

Kang, W. (2010). Male same-sex relations in modern China: Language, media representation, and law, 1900–1949. *Positions: East Asia Cultures Critique, 18*(2), 489–510. doi:10.1215/10679847-2010-011

Kong, T. (2010). *Chinese male homosexualities: Memba, tongzhi, and golden boy*. London and New York: Routledge.

Kong, T. (2014). Male sex work in China. In V. Minichiello & J. Scott (Eds.), *Male sex work and society* (pp. 314–341). New York and York: Harrington Park Press.

Light, B., Burgess, J., & Duguay, S. (2018). The walkthrough method: An approach to the study of apps. *New Media & Society, 20*(3), 881–900.

Lin, D. C. D. (2018). "妖"性工作者研究: 视角与方法 [A study of "Yao" sex workers: Perspectives and methodologies]. In Y. (黄盈盈) Huang & S. (潘绥铭) Pan (Eds.), 积淀与反思 [*Accretion and reflection: Sexuality studies of China*] (pp. 175–185). Hong Kong: 1908 Inc.

McGuire, M. L. (2016). The problem of technological integration and geosocial cruising in Seoul. *New Media & Society*, 1–15. doi:10.1177/1461444816675436

Meiu, G. P. (2017). *Ethno-erotic economies: Sexuality, money, and belonging in Kenya*. Chicago, IL and London: University of Chicago Press.

Osburg, J. (2013). *Anxious wealth: Money and morality among China's new rich*. Stanford, CA: Stanford University Press.

Pan, S. (潘绥铭). (1999). 存在与荒谬: 中国地下"性产业"考察 [*Existence and absurdity: China's underground sex industry*]. Beijing: Qunyan Press.

Pan, S. (潘绥铭). (2000). 生存与体验: 对一个地下红灯区的追踪考察 [*Subsistence and experience: Investigation on an underground red-light district*]. Beijing: Social Sciences Academic Press.

Race, K. (2015). Speculative pragmatism and intimate arrangements: Online hook-up devices in gay life in gay life. *Culture, Health & Sexuality, 17*(4), 496–511. doi:10.1080/13691058.2014.930181

Rofel, L. (2010). The traffic in money boys. *Positions: East Asia Cultures Critique, 18*(2), 425–458.

Showden, C. R. (2011). *Choices women make: Agency in domestic violence, assisted reproduction, and sex work*. Minneapolis and London: University of Minnesota Press.

Status, S. (2009). *Women with money, women with minds: Social status, gender, and marriage choices among elite urban women in contemporary China*. Canberra: The Australian National University.

Stout, N. M. (2014). *After love: Queer intimacy and erotic economies in post-Soviet Cuba*. Durham and London: Duke University Press.

Uretsky, E. (2015). "Sex"—It's not only women's work: A case for refocusing on the functional role that sex plays in work for both women and men. *Critical Public Health, 25*(1), 78–88. doi:10.1016/j.pestbp.2011.02.012.Investigations

Walby, K. (2012). *Touching encounters: Sex, work, and male-for-male Internet escorting*. Chicago, IL and London: University of Chicago Press.

Wang, S. (2018). Calculating dating goals: Data gaming and algorithmic sociality on Blued, a Chinese gay dating app. *Information, Communication & Society*, 1–17. doi:10.1080/1369118X.2018.1490796

Weiner, E. (2007). *Market dreams: Gender, class, and capitalism in the Czech Republic*. Ann Arbor, MI: The University of Michigan Press.

Wu, S., & Ward, J. (2018, May). The mediation of gay men's lives: A review on gay dating app studies. *Sociology Compass*, 1–10. doi:10.1111/soc4.12560

Zelizer, V. A. (2005). *The purchase of intimacy*. Princeton, NJ and Oxford: Princeton University Press.

Zheng, T. (2009). *Red lights: The lives of sex workers in postsocialist China*. Minneapolis and London: University of Minnesota Press.

Zheng, T. (2015). *Tongzhi living: Men attracted to men in postsocialist China*. Minneapolis and London: University of Minnesota Press.

Zheng, T. (2016). Same-sex attracted men and money boys in postsocialist China. In T. Zheng (Ed.), *Cultural politics of gender and sexuality in contemporary Asia* (pp. 23–40). Honolulu: University of Hawai'i Press.

极光数据解读国内最大同性交友应用 [Xtecher Statistical Analysis of China's Biggest Gay Dating App Blued]. (2017). Retrieved from https://acamh.onlinelibrary.wiley.com/doi/abs/10.1111/j.1469-7610.2010.02280.x

35

Male sex workers in China

Repercussions of local germ theories on safe sex, hygiene, and fatalism

Paul Bouanchaud

Male and transgender people who sell sex in China, as elsewhere, are subject to multiple risks and occupy disadvantaged positions in society (Baral et al., 2015). HIV infection constitutes both a real and a perceived risk for these sex workers, who in China commonly have unpaid sex with men in addition to selling sex, thus elevating their risk of infection. A recent review indicated that in addition to elevated risk of HIV infection, this group also has low rates of testing and low access to adequate HIV treatment (Tang et al., 2016), likely because the group is largely invisible to Chinese public health services. Although HIV and STI prevention and treatment services and policy in China focus on risk groups, they do not acknowledge male and transgender sex workers (MTSWs) as a group.

While Chinese government policy toward people living with HIV (PLHIV) has developed substantially since the early days of official denial, significant gaps remain in how PLHIV and their families are treated and in the implementation of the existing policy on the ground (Mendelsohn et al., 2018). There have been efforts to increase condom use among female sex workers and men who have sex with men (MSM). These efforts have had some success in reducing rates of unprotected sex and STI transmission (Chow et al., 2015). However, male and transgender sex workers, who frequently occupy multiple risk groups, remain absent from policy-level discourse around HIV prevention in China. While some local community-based organizations (CBOs) focus on providing information and support, their coverage is inevitably patchy, and their funding is frequently uncertain due to government restrictions on their work and sources of income, particularly following the 2016 NGO laws that further limit their activities (Feng, 2017). The importance of CBOs should not be underestimated, however. While community-based testing services accounted for only 0.7% of China's total number of HIV tests, they identified 30% of new HIV cases in the country in 2015 (UNAIDS, 2016).

While HIV infection remains a threat and is considered as such by many male and transgender sex workers in China (Liu et al., 2015), these workers face multiple other sources of risk in their daily lives, including arrest, violence, financial and social marginalization, and the psychological burdens of their work. The risk of HIV infection therefore can be understood as one of a range of factors that the MTSWs in this study negotiate in their daily lives.

MTSWs in Shenzhen, as elsewhere in China, have complex sexual networks with high levels of partner concurrency, and the majority are MSM (Baral et al., 2007; Morris, Epstein, &

Figure 35.1   A wall-mounted condom vending machine near the field site in South China.
Photo credit: Paul Bouanchaud.

Wawer, 2010; UNAIDS, 2013). MTSWs are at increased risk of HIV infection and transmission; the evidence from locally collected data suggests that the HIV prevalence rate among MTSWs in Shenzhen was 10% and rising in 2011 (Key Informant Interview, 2011), higher than levels reported historically for this group in China (Baral et al., 2015) but lower than the national rate in China estimated in a recent review of the male sex worker literature (Minichiello et al.,

2015). Compared to the less than 0.1% prevalence rate in the Chinese general population, and 6.3% among MSM nationally (AVERT, 2012; UNAIDS, 2012), HIV is as a significant epidemiological concern for MTSWs, a fact reflected in MTSWs' own discourse as a significant threat in their daily lives.

The risk of HIV transmission in the context of male sex work in Shenzhen, which is grounded within the wider social, economic, and cultural context of their lives, depends on a number of factors. Sex in and of itself is not necessarily risky; the sexual transmission of HIV can occur only when one of the partners is infected with the virus (Whiteside & Barnett, 2006). This fact highlights the important role that HIV testing can play. Unless one knows the HIV status of one's partner (and oneself), it is difficult to assess the risks of HIV transmission in a given situation. Also, the use of condoms during sex is highly effective in preventing transmission, and many MTSWs recognize their use as a tactic to prevent infection from HIV and other STIs. Condoms are quite cheap and readily available. For example, Figure 35.1 shows an on-street condom vending machine, a common sight in Shenzhen. However, the ways that some of the MTSWs in the study discuss the utility of condoms raises questions about their understanding of HIV risk and the possibilities for prevention. Furthermore, my research suggests that these local understandings tie in with ideas of hygiene and, in the absence of HIV testing, with practices and beliefs around assessing the risk that sex with different partners might pose.

This chapter looks at the ways that MTSWs manage those risks. I present empirical evidence from a population of MTSWs in a city in southern China. I address the question of how MTSWs understand and negotiate their HIV risks within and outside of their work. I explore the multiple meanings of *anquan xingxingwei* (safe sex) for these workers, highlighting some tensions and some areas of agreement between individual and more objective perspectives on HIV risk behaviors and safe sex practices. Female sex workers' use of condoms, both as a physical barrier to the transmission of pathogens and as a psychological barrier as they perform sex work, has been documented elsewhere (Sanders, 2002). However, there is little evidence of similar processes among MTSWs. There have been calls for more nuanced and geographically diverse reporting on male commercial sex workers (Koken & Bimbi, 2014), a goal to which I hope this chapter can contribute.

Methods

This chapter reports findings from a mixed methods study that I conducted in Shenzhen, a large new city in southern China, in the second half of 2011. Figure 35.2 shows the skyline of the field site, a densely populated urban area. In total, 251 participants were recruited to take part in a quantitative survey, from which 21 participants were selected for in-depth interviews. The study also included key informant interviews and focus group discussions with groups from the MTSW community in the city. Those representatives approved all research instruments (questionnaires and interview guides), and results were fed back to them and validated. The sub-sample of interview participants was selected to represent the diversity found within the wider MTSW quantitative sample with respect to work venue, age group, trans/cisgender identity, and self-identified sexual orientation. (*Cisgender* denotes a person whose sense of personal gender identity corresponds to their birth sex.)

All interviews were conducted in Mandarin, the main language spoken in Shenzhen. Mandarin is a lingua franca among migrants in the city, who originate from all over China, a country in which almost every city has its own dialect. The in-depth interviews were recorded and then transcribed verbatim in written Chinese before being translated into English and coded.

Paul Bouanchaud

Figure 35.2   Skyline of downtown Shenzhen, 2011.
Photo credit: Paul Bouanchaud.

Participants were eligible for recruitment into the study if they were born male (including male-to-female transgender), had sold sex in Shenzhen in the three months prior to recruitment, had not already taken part in this research, and were age 18 or over. The potential recruits were screened to ensure that they fit these criteria.

All participants were verbally informed of the purpose of the study before being invited to participate. If they wished to take part, they then were asked to give their full informed consent. They were informed that no personally identifying data would be collected, that all information would be anonymous, that they could refuse to answer any questions, and that they could terminate the interview at any time with no negative consequences. The study was approved by a community advisory board of male sex workers and NGO staff in Shenzhen and the London School of Economics and Political Science.

The meaning of "safe sex"

Anquan xingxingwei (safe sex), a term commonly employed in discussions of sexual health in China, was as a frequent part of sex workers' discourse regarding their commercial and non-commercial sexual partnerships. Many described HIV as being the main danger of their work:

> AIDS. That worries me the most. I am afraid my family would find out . . . I'm afraid they would I know I am a prostitute. . . . If we are doing *1069* [anal or oral sex], even with condoms on, it's still haunting. You wouldn't know when or how you got infected.
>
> *Male sex worker, 22, from Jiangxi Province*

The excerpt from this interview highlights not only a fear of AIDS but also its intersection with the stigma of sex work, suggesting that HIV transmission is understood as a physically and socially dangerous condition. For this sex worker, two key concerns are potential HIV infection and the shame that his family's discovery of his work would bring.

Anquan xingxingwei has many layers of meaning among Shenzen's MTSWs. By examining this concept of "safe sex," we can illuminate some of the behavioral and attitudinal motivators for these sex workers' different risk-avoidance practices. Whether a behavior is considered dangerous depends on the decision-maker's individual perspective, the context of the decision (for example, selling sex, buying sex, or having sex with a non-commercial partner), and who their partner is. The survey respondents were asked to provide up to three meanings for the phrase *anquan xingxingwei*, and their responses were recorded verbatim. Of the 238 respondents who answered this question, 71% said that "safe sex" meant using condoms. One interviewee commented:

> AIDS is rampant now everywhere, and then there are promotions on TV and from [name of local NGO]. People are scared, and they would bring condoms. And the *xiaodi* [little brothers, local term for male sex workers] wouldn't just casually have sex without a condom. It's just natural to wear condoms, just like how you put on more clothes in winter.
>
> *Male sex worker, 38, from Hunan Province*

This example, typical of discussions of safe sex among the respondents, emphasizes both a consciousness of the presence and danger of HIV and the role of condoms in protecting against its transmission. It also shows how condom use has become the norm for this respondent. There is also evidence that some MTSWs feel safer because of their professional knowledge:

> In prostitution we know the risks. We constantly meet clients; we know how to protect ourselves. For people who go out to have fun and do *419* [one-night stands], they just think they are clean but god knows what happens. For us, with the constant promotion and the free condom/lube provision, it's easy to protect ourselves.
>
> *Male sex worker, 38, from Jilin Province*

This respondent compares sex workers' professional knowledge of how to stay safe with non-sex workers who have one-night stands and who perhaps are less aware of the risks that they are taking. However, being able to effectively negotiate condom use in commercial encounters is not always easy, and requires a level of tact if clients are to be retained:

> [I have clients who said] not wearing condoms would be cool, they have asked not to use condoms, then you have to find a lot of ways to convince them. . . . They say they're very clean, it's no problem, then they say they've already washed, very clean, then they ask whether or not I have an illness.
>
> *Transgender sex worker, 22, Jiangsu Province*

This study found high levels of knowledge that condoms protect against HIV. However, how condoms provide protection, and the implications arising from that understanding, highlight some important gaps in safe sex practices among MTSWs in Shenzhen. Asked how to stay safe, one interviewee commented:

> First of all, condoms. This is the first point, and then it is usually some degree of *ziji weisheng xiguan* [one's own personal hygiene practices]. Then we need to observe our

clients. You're two naked people facing each other, we need to see if there are any kinds of anomaly. Look at certain body parts. If there are any differences, if they have this, then I would definitely reject the client.

Male sex worker, 21, from Hunan Province

This interviewee indicates that he uses several safe sex practices. Condom use is the first part of ensuring safety, but then personal hygiene and examining the client's body for abnormalities are also important. Indeed, the prominence of hygiene in discussions of safe sex was evident in the verbatim survey responses, where "hygiene" (washing, showering, avoiding body odor, and so on), was mentioned by 17% of the MTSWs surveyed. Respondents also mentioned other practical measures, such as avoiding particular behaviors (for example, kissing) and visually checking partners for STIs.

Nonetheless, many MTSWs considered hygiene a major concern, and they saw condoms as one important way to ensure good hygiene. The concept of hygiene extends beyond condom use, however. As in Simić and Rhodes' study among Serbian FSW, MTSWs in Southern China used hygiene as a framework to conceptualize risk avoidance among the participants (Simić & Rhodes, 2009). Evidence emerged of a local germ theory, which ties HIV prevention to hygiene through condom use, and this conceptual frame links hygiene to "safe sex." One of the most common explanations for the importance of hygiene in the MTSWs' narratives involved the understanding that disease is caused by germs, and that washing removes these germs:

First, *weisheng* [hygiene] is the most important, if you happen to get infected with something, to get infected with some disease, it is very *mafan* [troublesome]. . . . I am worried about other bacteria, that they would get into my body.

Male sex worker, 21, from Guangdong Province

This local germ theory explains the importance of washing not only the body but also clothing:

R: You can't talk about STIs in a group of people. It's like before, at work in the bar, do you know how we washed out underwear? It was all washed together, all put in the washing machine and washed! It wasn't all of my underwear being washed together in the machine, your underwear, my underwear [separately from] their underwear, socks, clothes . . . it was all put together in the washing machine, mixed mixed mixed!

I: Oh, didn't this sterilize them?

R: At that time, I didn't think that much about STIs, for example if another person has an STI, it's very easy to infect [others], even if you wash underwear, it can't disappear, everything is mixed together inside the machine.

Male sex worker, 24, from Henan Province

The dialogue between a respondent (R) and an interviewer (I) touches on two key themes. First is the statement that it is not possible to discuss STIs in a group of people, which suggests that fears of the social contagion of HIV make sexual health a difficult topic to talk about with peers (Steinberg, 2011). The interviewee then goes on to express concern about the risks of contracting infections from his co-sex workers' clothing, highlighting the importance of cleanliness and specific hygiene practices for ensuring safety. As one respondent said:

If you are not hygienic you catch diseases. . . [for example, having] body odor. . . . Or you shower only once a few days.

Male sex worker, 27, from Hunan Province

Here, body odor is linked with a lack of cleanliness and hence disease. This link highlights the ways in which dirtiness, in its literal sense, also applies to ideas about safe sex. In short, the idea is that physical evidence of poor hygiene is associated with higher sexual risk, and thus makes HIV infection detectable via an assessment of a person's hygiene. Examining another person's hygiene therefore becomes one of the tactics that MTSWs employ to manage their risk of disease.

One interviewee explained the link between hygiene and safe sex:

> Safe sex and hygiene are definitely related. If you are not clean there would be lots of bacteria . . . and if the clients have it, then it would be infectious. We do shower before and after work. . . . And then we would brush our teeth and wash our face . . . It's cleaner.
>
> *Male sex worker, 38, from Jilin Province*

The discourse around bacteria and cleanliness reveals a local conceptualization of disease spread and germ theory. This understanding not only allows MTSWs to take protective hygiene measures but also fits with understandings of germs and dirt. The same MTSW goes on to say:

R: I feel dirty.
I: Why do you feel that way?
R: I don't like the clients.
I: We also ask if you tell others about your job. Do you?
R: I don't. It's shameful. That's it.

Male sex worker, 38, from Jilin Province

Here, hygiene also emerges as a metaphor to counter the dirtiness of sex work. This interviewee talked not only about the importance of hygiene in a literal sense for the removal of bacteria, and hence the avoidance of infection, but also in its metaphorical sense, saying that he feels dirty because he does not like his clients.

Some of the participants also relied on communication from other sex workers to assess how clean or safe their customers are:

> [We] talk about it every day. . . . If they see a customer who seems like he might be not clean, they would tell us immediately, it could be bad for the next [worker] after all. . . . It's just between masseurs, it's similar to you and I talking right now, for example I had an hour of work today. . . . And then I'll come to you and talk about how it felt in that job, also talk about what the customer was like. . . . And if it's good he'd say good, if it looks like [the customer] is sick, he will tell you, tell me what it's like.
>
> *Male sex worker, 22, from Hunan Province*

The role of hygiene intersects with MTSWs' understanding of sexual risk behaviors, and it underlines how common this discourse is among these men, who discuss the cleanliness of clients among themselves. This quote also underlines the importance of MTSWs' social networks in information sharing about potentially unhygienic (and therefore potentially HIV-infected) clients. Hygiene plays an important role in two ways, one literal and one metaphorical. First, these interviewees know enough about disease transmission to associate cleanliness with the removal of bacteria. Second, they physically wash themselves to counteract the "dirty feeling" that their work creates. This approach to hygiene raises questions not only about the efficacy of the measures that these men are taking to avoid contagion but also about the psychological weight of their work.

Another interviewee discusses what he considers safe sex:

> First of all, if they are an old customer of mine, I would know about them. And then I know about their physical condition. And then for example when I do it with them, I'll take care of the hygienic problems. . . . I would clean the hidden area properly when I give them a shower. . . . And then, if I can do stuff like that, I would feel comfortable to have [oral] sex with you not wearing a condom. Second, without a condom is like, if you strictly insist to not wear a condom. And if you look very clean, and I washed you, and this I can choose to not wear a condom, it feels safe that way. . . . If I think there's something wrong with you, that will feel unsafe. [If he] looks dirty . . . I'll choose to wear a condom.
>
> *Male sex worker, 22, from Jiangxi Province*

Here, hygiene is discussed as a way to prevent disease transmission, and good hygiene means that condoms are not always considered necessary. Notions of hygiene, along with the importance of familiarity with a client, both appear to play important roles in minimizing sexual health risks. Familiarity with clients can be linked with feelings of attraction and intimacy, which were determinants of condom use for some of the interviewees:

> Before, when I did it [sex] I didn't like to wear condoms when I'd encountered someone I liked . . . but I didn't do 0, when I was a 0 I always wore condoms, I didn't wear them for being the 1. [*Note*: Colloquially, the terms 0 and 1 are used among MSM in China to denote receptive and insertive roles during anal sex, respectively.]
>
> *Male sex worker, 25, from Heilongjiang Province*

Here the interviewee describes that feeling attracted to a sexual partner, or wanting to become more intimate with him, means that he would not use condoms as the insertive partner (although he would always use condoms as the receptive partner). The theme of intimacy recurs in another interview:

> I think that using [condoms] is more safe, but between friends, if a *nvpengyou* [girlfriend] and *BF* [boyfriend] are together doing it, if there are times when you use condoms, then it would feel like it seems like that there is this question of "Do you not trust me?" . . . If you use them it feels like the relationship isn't intimate, if you don't use them then it should feel like it's more intimate, there's more trust between you.
>
> *Male sex worker, 23, from Hunan Province*

Here, condom use is explicitly described as a barrier to intimacy in emotional or non-commercial relationships. Intimacy is frequently documented in the literature as a barrier to condom use in sexual relationships (Theodore, Durán, Antoni, & Fernandez, 2004; Li, Lau, Holroyd, & Yi, 2010; Kong, Laidler, & Pang, 2012), and the evidence here appears to support that finding. A desire to maintain emotional distance from commercial partners can play out through the avoidance of intimacy. The need for hygiene and the potential riskiness of kissing are both representative of such boundaries, as several interviewees mentioned.

Luck or fatalism

The degree to which the sex workers with whom I spoke feel they have control over their safety is brought into question by some of their narratives. A number of the study participants used luck to conceptualize their work-related and HIV risks. Thinking in terms of luck may be a device that MTSWs use to manage risks in a context in which they do not have full control over their exposure to HIV. In discussing his fears about HIV, one respondent commented:

> It is the case that once you get it [HIV], you have it for your lifetime, for your whole life. . . . Everyone knows about it. Everyone's scared. But if by any chance it comes, then there's nothing you can do to prevent it. Anyway, I've been having sex for 8 or 10 years and haven't got it.
>
> *Male sex worker, 24, from Henan Province*

This interviewee presents a view of HIV framed around chance, saying that it is unpreventable but that he has managed to avoid being infected so far.

R: Even if you wore a condom, when your partner has AIDS, there's still a chance he could infect you if you are unlucky.
I: So if that's the case, what would you do?
R: I guess I will just *shunqi ziran* [let nature take its course].

> *Male sex worker, 22, from Jiangxi Province*

Letting nature take its course implies a degree of fatalism regarding infection. Condoms are not completely protective, and that luck plays a part in the risk of infection from a partner:

> If you have it [HIV], you have to acknowledge your fate, you resent your own lot in life and there's nothing you can do, it's that God is punishing us.
>
> *Male sex worker, 25, from Heilongjiang Province*

MTSWs in Southern China use luck, God, and fate to explain why they either contracted STIs or might become infected in the future. Fatalism has been associated elsewhere with increased HIV risk behaviors (McKirnan, Vanable, Ostrow, & Hope, 2001; Yi, Sandfort, & Shidlo, 2010) and lower levels of life satisfaction (Kalichman, Kelly, Morgan, & Rompa, 1997; Nguyen, Dunne, Debattista, Nguyen, & Dao, 2012), with implications for the adoption of safer sex practices. Such narratives are perhaps symbolic of a lack of perceived control over one's risks or a lack of knowledge of ways to avoid infection.

Conclusion

There is substantial evidence that MTSWs are at an elevated risk of HIV infection in Southern China. These sex workers frequently have multiple commercial and non-commercial sexual partners; the nature of transactional sex means that even if they want to, they may not always be able to insist on condom use with clients. And in non-commercial encounters with male or female partners, they may choose not to use condoms in order to differentiate these encounters from those with paying customers.

By examining the local understandings of HIV risk, we can move beyond calculating transmission probabilities and toward a more socially constructed understanding of sexual health and risk avoidance. From this perspective, the stigma and thus fear of infection (or suspected infection) produces a "social contagion" (Rao, Angell, Lam, & Corrigan, 2008) and safe sex practices that extend beyond focusing only on consistent condom use.

Evidence of what I term a local germ theory emerges in this group in Southern China, where MTSWs link hygiene to condoms and disease avoidance. MTSWs use this germ theory both to conceptualize safe sex and to cognitively manage the perceived dirtiness of their work. Mary Douglas's classic anthropological work exploring ritual cleanliness, purity, and taboo provides an anthropological antecedent to findings around the importance of hygiene in the work of MTSWs in this study. Dirt can be understood as "matter out of place" (Douglas, 1966) or in a state of disorder, interpretable both literally and metaphysically. Dirt is a moral-social construct, as is its corollary in sexual practice—promiscuity (Douglas, 1966; Slavin, Richters, & Kippax, 2004).

A tension emerges between the public health discourse and local representations of safe sex. HIV has been called a "disease of post-modernity" (Bancroft, 2001, p. 95), and it is through this lens that we can view the apparent dissonance between sex workers' conceptualizations of "safe sex" and the wider public and public health definitions, although these viewpoints are not mutually exclusive. Local understanding of HIV is informed by messages from public health services and campaigns and contact with NGO staff and the media, but these messages are then reinterpreted at the local level (Lorway & Khan, 2014), in a process akin to Boellstorf's "dubbing" of globalized sexual subjectivities in Indonesia (Boellstorff, 2003). Furthermore, representations of HIV in the Chinese media are frequently far from scientific, both informed by and influencing the broader public discourse around the disease (Hood, 2013), further muddying the waters informing safer sex practices in this MTSW high-risk group.

We therefore find a complex and sometimes contradictory set of understandings of *anquan xingxingwei* (safe sex) among MTSWs in our study. Awareness and fear of HIV infection was commonplace, but condom use was not exclusively framed as a method to avoid disease. Condoms were also presented as a means to be hygienic. Likewise, cleanliness and hygiene were presented as important ways to avoid disease, including HIV. The invisibility of MTSWs and transgender people in Chinese health policy, and in contemporary Chinese society more broadly, means that opportunities to challenge myths around sexual health and HIV, and to provide services to these groups, are being missed.

References

AVERT. (2012). *HIV & AIDS in China*. Retrieved from www.avert.org/hiv-aids-china.htm

Bancroft, A. (2001). Globalisation and HIV/AIDS: Inequality and the boundaries of a symbolic epidemic. *Health, Risk, and Society*, 3(1), 89–98. Retrieved from www.tandfonline.com/doi/abs/10.1080/713670174

Baral, S. D., Friedman, M. R., Geibel, S., Rebe, K., Bozhinov, B., Diouf, D., . . . Cáceres, C. F. (2015). Male sex workers: Practices, contexts, and vulnerabilities for HIV acquisition and transmission. *The Lancet*, *385*(9964), 260–273. doi:10.1016/S0140-6736(14)60801-1

Baral, S. D., Sifakis, F., & Cleghorn, F. (2007). Elevated risk for HIV infection among men who have sex with men in low- and middle-income countries 2000–2006: A systematic review. *PLoS Med*, *4*(12), e339. doi:10.1371/journal.pmed.0040339

Boellstorff, T. (2003). Dubbing culture: Indonesian gay and lesbian subjectivities and ethnography in an already globalized world. *American Ethnologist*, *30*(2), 225–242. doi:10.1525/ae.2003.30.2.225

Chow, E. P., Tung, K., Tucker, J. D., Muessig, K. E., Su, S., Zhang, X., . . . Zhang, L. (2015). Behavioral interventions improve condom use and HIV testing uptake among female sex workers in China: A systematic review and meta-analysis. *AIDS Patient Care and STDs, 29*(8), 454–460. doi:10.1089/apc.2015.0043

Douglas, M. (1991, c. 1966). *Purity and danger: An analysis of the concepts of pollution and taboo.* London: Routledge.

Feng, C. (2017). The NGO law in China and its impact on overseas funded NGOs. *Cosmopolitan Civil Societies: An Interdisciplinary Journal, 9*(3), 95. Retrieved from https://search.informit.com.au/documentSummary;dn=309840437088070;res=IELHSS

Hood, J. (2013). Distancing disease in the un-Black Han Chinese politic: Othering difference in China's HIV/AIDS media. *Modern China, 39*(3), 280–318. doi:10.1177/0097700413483275

Kalichman, S. C., Kelly, J. A., Morgan, M., & Rompa, D. (1997). Fatalism, current life satisfaction, and risk for HIV infection among gay and bisexual men. *Journal of Consulting and Clinical Psychology, 65*(4), 542. doi:10.1037/0022-006X.65.4.542

Key Informant Interview. (2011, December). *Primary data collected during a key informant interview with anonymous source.* Shenzhen. Retrieved from https://healthpolicy.ucla.edu/programs/health-data/trainings/Documents/tw_cba23.pdf

Koken, J., & Bimbi, D. (2014). Mental health aspects of male sex work. In V. Minichiello & J. Scott (Eds.), *Male sex work and society* (pp. 222–239). New York: Harrington Park Press.

Kong, T. S., Laidler, K. J., & Pang, H. (2012). Relationship type, condom use, and HIV/AIDS risks among men who have sex with men in six Chinese cities. *AIDS Care, 24*(4), 517–528. doi:10.1080/09540121.2011.617411

Li, H., Lau, J. T., Holroyd, E., & Yi, H. (2010). Sociocultural facilitators and barriers to condom use during anal sex among men who have sex with men in Guangzhou, China: An ethnographic study. *AIDS Care, 22*(12), 1481–1486. doi:10.1080/09540121.2010.482121

Liu, Y., Sun, X., Qian, H. Z., Yin, L., Yan, Z., Wang, L., . . . Amico, K. R. (2015). Qualitative assessment of barriers and facilitators of access to HIV testing among men who have sex with men in China. *AIDS Patient Care and STDs, 29*(9), 481–489. doi:10.1089/apc.2015.0083

Lorway, R., & Khan, S. (2014). Reassembling epidemiology: Mapping, monitoring and making-up people in the context of HIV prevention in India. *Social Science & Medicine, 112*, 51–62. doi:10.1016/j.socscimed.2014.04.034

McKirnan, D. J., Vanable, P. A., Ostrow, D. G., & Hope, B. (2001). Expectancies of sexual "escape" and sexual risk among drug-and alcohol-involved gay and bisexual men. *Journal of Substance Abuse, 13*(1–2), 137–154. doi:10.1016/S0899-3289(01)00063-3

Mendelsohn, J. B., Cheng, H., Calzavara, L., Wang, S., Bullock, S., Mishra, S., . . . Steele, S. J. (2018). Key gaps in the HIV cascade of care among men who have sex with men and migrants diagnosed with HIV: Findings from a surveillance study in Shanghai. *The Lancet, 392*, S85. doi:10.1016/S0140-6736(18)32714-4

Minichiello, V., Scott, J., & Callander, D. (2015). A new public health context to understand male sex work. *BMC Public Health, 15*(1), 282. doi:10.1186/s12889-015-1498-7

Morris, M., Epstein, H., & Wawer, M. (2010). Timing is everything: International variations in historical sexual partnership concurrency and HIV prevalence. *PLoS ONE, 5*(11), e14092. Retrieved from https://journals.plos.org/plosone/article/file?id=10.1371/journal.pone.0014092&type=printable

Nguyen, V. H., Dunne, M. P., Debattista, J., Nguyen, T. H., & Dao, T. M. A. (2012). Social contexts of risk behaviors for HIV among male, unskilled, unregistered laborers in urban Vietnam. *Qualitative Health Research, 22*(7), 871–879. doi:10.1177/1049732311424510

Rao, D., Angell, B., Lam, C., & Corrigan, P. (2008). Stigma in the workplace: Employer attitudes about people with HIV in Beijing, Hong Kong, and Chicago. *Social Science & Medicine, 67*(10), 1541–1549. doi:10.1016/j.socscimed.2008.07.024

Sanders, T. (2002). The condom as psychological barrier: Female sex workers and emotional management. *Feminism & Psychology, 12*(4), 561–566. doi:10.1177/0959353502012004016

Simić, M., & Rhodes, T. (2009). Violence, dignity and HIV vulnerability: Street sex work in Serbia. *Sociology of Health & Illness, 31*(1), 1–16. doi:10.1111/j.1467-9566.2008.01112.x

Slavin, S., Richters, J., & Kippax, S. (2004). Understandings of risk among HIV seroconverters in Sydney. *Health, Risk & Society, 6*(1), 39–52. doi:10.1080/1369857042000193057

Steinberg, J. (2011). *Three letter plague: A young man's journey through a great epidemic.* New York: Random House.

Tang, S., Tang, W., Meyers, K., Chan, P., Chen, Z., & Tucker, J. D. (2016). HIV and syphilis among men who have sex with men and transgender individuals in China: A scoping review. *The Lancet, 388*, S74. doi:10.1016/S0140-6736(14)60801-1

Theodore, P. S., Durán, R. E., Antoni, M. H., & Fernandez, M. I. (2004). Intimacy and sexual behavior among HIV-positive men-who-have-sex-with-men in primary relationships. *AIDS and Behavior, 8*(3), 321–331. Retrieved from https://link.springer.com/article/10.1023/B:AIBE.0000044079.37158.a9

UNAIDS. (2012). *HIV in China: Facts and figures.* Retrieved from www.unaids.org.cn/en/index/page.asp?id=197&class=2&classname=China%E2%80%99s+Epidemic+%26+Response+

UNAIDS. (2013). *HIV/AIDS in Asia and the Pacific.* UNAIDS Report. Bangkok, Thailand. Retrieved from www.unaids.org/sites/default/files/media_asset/2013_HIV-Asia-Pacific_en_0.pdf

UNAIDS. (2016). *Ending, A.I.D.S., 2016. progress towards the 90-90-90 targets.* Geneva: UNAIDS. Retrieved from www.unaids.org.cn/pics/20170721164838.pdf

Whiteside, A., & Barnett, T. (2006). *AIDS in the twenty-first century: Disease and globalization* (Fully revised and updated ed.). New York: Palgrave Macmillan.

Yi, H., Sandfort, T. G., & Shidlo, A. (2010). Effects of disengagement coping with HIV risk on unprotected sex among HIV-negative gay men in New York City. *Health Psychology, 29*(2), 205. doi:10.1037/a0017786

36

Male sex work and masculinities in Hong Kong and Mainland China

"One country, two men"*

Albert C. H. Yau and Travis S. K. Kong

In China, the tradition of same-sex love and same-sex prostitution dates back to ancient times (Kong, 2014, pp. 317–321). Today, male-male sex work is thriving in both Hong Kong and mainland China. Estimates suggest that more than 1,500 men were selling sex in Hong Kong in the early 2000s, and the population of male sex workers (MSWs) continues to expand (Amnesty International, 2016, pp. 15). In Hong Kong, men who sell sex are generally called *go-go-zai* (GGZ), a term initially promoted by some non-governmental organizations and later circulated within the sex worker community. The GGZ predominantly serve a male clientele. In mainland China, approximately 380,000 men are estimated to be selling sex nationwide, and, again, most serve male clients (Chow, Iu, Fu, Wilson, & Zhang, 2012). In local parlance, they are called Money Boys (MBs), a term used in both mainstream media reports and academia (Kong, 2014, p. 316).

In both societies, male-male sex work is stigmatized as deviant and typically feminine behavior. Men who engage in such work are seen as neither "good men" nor "real men." Their masculinity is suspect, and they are subject to marginalization for deviating from Chinese masculine norms and ideals (Kong, 2009, 2012). How, then, do male-male sex workers experience and make sense of their male identity in relation to their work? How do they negotiate—(re-)define and (re-)construct—their masculinity in the sex industry? Is there any difference in the accomplishment of occupational masculinity—the configuration of masculine practices in the workplace—between male-male sex workers in Hong Kong and those in mainland China? If so, how do we make sense of those differences in relation to the wider social contexts of the two Chinese societies, in which Hong Kong has changed from a British colony to Special Administrative Region of China under the One Country, Two Systems design since 1997, while mainland China has transformed from a socialist to post-socialist era since the 1980s?

This chapter addresses these questions through GGZ narratives in Hong Kong and MB narratives in mainland China. We first review the extant literature on masculinity, work, and male sex work. We then argue that male sex work forces the men who engage in it to employ a variety of gendered strategies to reassert their male identity. Specifically, we argue that GGZ accomplish a "craftsmanship masculinity," and MBs a "guerrilla masculinity" in negotiating occupational masculinity. We conclude by examining the reasons for the differences between the two groups and how they reflect the differing sociocultural and political contexts of Hong Kong and mainland China.

Masculinity, work, and sex work

Masculinity is a key concept that helps us unravel men's daily experience of being a "man." It illuminates the "gendering process" that takes place in men's lives, a process that concerns "the transformation of biological males into socially interacting men" (Kimmel & Messner, 2013, p. xi). In this sense, "doing gender" (West & Zimmerman, 1987) or doing masculinity is central to men's daily experience as they measure and account for themselves as men, both personally and socially. Connell (1993, 1995, 2000) offers a comprehensive account of this gendering process. Masculinity is best understood, she posits, as a "configuration of practice within gender relations, a structure that includes large-scale institutions and economic relations as well as face-to-face relationships and sexuality" (Connell, 2000, p. 29). Accordingly, doing gender/masculinity includes not only personal expression and the performance of being a man, but also the way in which it is conditioned by the dynamics of social institutions such as the workplace and family (Connell, 1993, pp. 602–603). Moreover, Connell reminds us that masculinity is usually expressed in multiple forms, as masculinities are differentiated and subject to a hierarchical ordering process in which "one form of masculinity rather than others is culturally exalted" in most societies (1995, p. 77). Men embodying the cultural ideal of masculinity are seen to be asserting a position of superiority with material benefits, whereas those who fail to do so may be forced into a subordinate or marginal position and therefore suffer social exclusion and economic discrimination (Connell, 1995, pp. 67–86). Hence, doing gender/masculinity is not merely a matter of lifestyle; it also concerns one's social status and the allocation of resources in the given society (Connell & Messerschmidt, 2005).

As a core institution, work is a critical site for both the construction and contestation of masculinities. A man's work or occupation is not only central to his own life but is also regarded by society as the primary basis of male identity, "of what it means to be a man" (Morgan, 1992, p. 76). Work practices and the making of masculinities are two sides of the same coin, although we cannot assume that all work-related masculinities are equally rewarding or valued. Some working cultures and organizational settings are safer than others, and some are "embattled" environments in which to perform masculinities (Dellinger, 2004). For instance, if working as a manager in a transnational company helps a man achieve a dominant position in the hierarchy of masculinities (Connell & Wood, 2005), then engaging in a "deviant" occupation such as male sex work is likely to force a man into a subordinate position in that hierarchy (Kong, 2009).

Studies of male sex work around the globe suggest that sex work or prostitution is a contested site for men's construction of masculinities, because sex work is widely stigmatized as a deviant, typically feminine activity/occupation (Dennis, 2008). Male sex workers often face severe challenges in asserting their male identity, both personally and socially (Alcano, 2011; Kumar, Scott, & Minichiello, 2017). Some studies have shown that male sex workers employ a variety of strategies to reclaim their masculine status, such as celebrating a sense of control and power in front of customers (Tewksbury, 1993), highlighting the lucrative nature of their profession (Takeyama, 2010), and recasting their daily routine as including such masculine components as "endurance" and "technical skill" (Kumar et al., 2017).

In addition to these gendered strategies, MSWs also perform different patterns of sex work-related masculinity in relation to different occupational conditions. For example, the pattern performed by MSWs working on the street may feature violence, aggression, and bellicos-ity (Alcano, 2011), whereas indoor-based MSWs may emphasize their business orientation by highlighting their career aspirations, professionalism, and entrepreneurship (Browne & Min-ichiello, 1996; Koken, Bimbi, Parsons, & Halkitis, 2004). In her ethnography of street-based MSWs in Chicago, Oselin (2016) demonstrates the marked effect of socioeconomic factors on shaping men's adoption of different masculine tactics. While some of the MSWs in her study adhered to a traditional street masculinity displayed through the initiation of violent acts, oth-ers, particularly those for whom sex work was their exclusive source of income, deliberately performed a "pacifist masculinity" to maximize their economic capital, echoing the traditional masculine discourse (e.g., the importance of entrepreneurship) at work in the wider society (Oselin, 2016, p. 219). Although MSWs must negotiate their male identity in the workplace, it is essential to note that they, like other men, construct tailored forms of masculinity to suit their daily work practices.

Drawing on this understanding, we argue that GGZ in Hong Kong and MBs in mainland China confront a very similar situation. Kong's work (2009) on Hong Kong MSWs illustrates that these men's strategies for handling the stigma of sex work are simultaneously their gender strategies for accomplishing masculinity. However, little is known about MSWs in mainland China. For the study summarized in this chapter, we examined the lived experiences of male-male sex workers in both locales, and we conceptualize two different forms of occupational masculinity: the "craftsmanship masculinity" of GGZ and the "guerrilla masculinity" of MBs. Our comparison of the narratives of GGZ and MBs contributes to the literature by offering new insights into how MSWs devise gendered strategies to respond to the sociocultural and political contexts of their work.

Methodology

This chapter is based on doctoral research conducted by Albert C. H. Yau. Using in-depth interviews as his main method of data collection, he carried out ethnographic research on the male-male sex industry in Hong Kong and mainland China from 2014 to 2017 after obtaining ethical approval from his university's review board. Thirty male-male sex worker informants (15 from Hong Kong and 15 from mainland China) recruited through snowball and purposive sampling were interviewed. The nature of the study was carefully explained to all participants, and they were assured of confidentiality and anonymity. Written consent was sought before audio-recording the interviews, which were later transcribed from Putonghua/Cantonese into written Chinese, with select quotes translated into English. The interviews were free-flowing but focused on the men's perceptions of their male identity in relation to their experiences with sex work. Most of the interviews lasted between 1 and 2 hours, resulting in roughly 65 hours of recordings. All names appearing herein are pseudonyms, and minor alternations have been made to the interviewees' biographies to protect their identity.

The Hong Kong interviewees ranged in age from 27 to 53. Most self-identified as gay ($n = 11$), with the rest referring to themselves as either bisexual ($n = 3$) or heterosexual ($n = 1$). Their education level varied from junior secondary ($n = 9$) and senior secondary ($n = 4$) to post-secondary ($n = 2$), and they had been engaged in the sex industry for 4 to 20 years. At the time of the interviews, one man had just quit the industry, and the others were still working in it full-time ($n = 12$) or part-time ($n = 2$). None of these interviewees had ever engaged in street prostitution.

The ages of the 15 mainland Chinese interviewees ranged from 23 to 43. Just over half self-identified as gay ($n = 8$), with the rest identifying as either bisexual ($n = 3$) or heterosexual

($n = 4$). Most ($n = 10$) had a senior secondary level of education, with the remainder having completed only primary ($n = 3$) or junior secondary ($n = 2$) school. They had been involved in sex work for between one and nine years. At the time of the interviews, two men were working part-time, one was kept as a "houseboy" by a male client, and the rest ($n = 12$) worked full-time. Like their Hong Kong counterparts, all of the mainland interviewees had worked only in an indoor setting such as a massage parlor.

Go-go-zai in Hong Kong

Perceived gender challenges

The notion of work and its gendered meanings have changed over time in Hong Kong, which was a British colony from 1842 to 1997. In the early colonial era, traditional patriarchal values were regarded as the masculine norms, and a man's male identity was measured mostly by his fulfillment of his familial responsibilities, such as being a good son to his parents (Kong, 2009, pp. 726–727). Work had peripheral status in men's lives. From the 1950s onwards, however, colonial Hong Kong witnessed fast-paced urbanization and industrialization. As Hong Kong developed into a modern capitalist city, a man's occupation took on a more prominent role in the construction of his male identity. Within the realm of work, individual competence and material success through entrepreneurship and upward mobility have become the cornerstones of how a man is defined (Equal Opportunities Commission, 2012). Although twenty-first-century Hong Kong has entered a post-industrial stage, and notions of post-materialism (including individual autonomy, aesthetic satisfaction, and self-expression) are increasingly part of people's construction of self-identity, work status remains crucial to the measure of masculine status (Equal Opportunities Commission, 2012).

The interviewees in this study subscribed to traditional notions of masculinity; all of the interviewees agreed that a man's job or occupation is centrally important to his life. However, their engagement in sex work subjects them to an "embattled" environment in which to perform their masculinities. First, society perceives their occupation as immoral. Although selling sex is not illegal in Hong Kong, nearly all activities related to it (e.g., soliciting, pimping, operating a brothel) are criminal offenses. The strict regulations on sex work not only attach a sense of illegality to the work itself but also imbue sex workers with a strong sense of their own immorality (Chiu, 2006, p. 549). Second, GGZ experience an even higher level of moral condemnation, as they predominantly serve male customers. Although Hong Kong decriminalized homosexual acts in 1991, much societal prejudice against homosexual behaviors remains (Chan, 2005, p. 94). Indeed, such derogatory terms as "duck" and "goose" are widely used in the media when reporting on MSW,[1] thereby re-confirming the sexual deviance of male-male sex work. "Duck" and "goose" are two derogatory local slang terms referring to men who sell sex to women and to men, respectively. For instance, Dark, a 27-year-old gay part-time sex worker, talked about his experience as a guest speaker at a university lecture:

> When I told them [the students] I sold sex, they were like, "Oh, you are so dirty!" . . .
> When I told them I was gay and I served men, their reaction was even more extreme, like,
> "What the hell? Do you have AIDS?" . . . I felt bad about this.

In addition to being seen as immoral, another major difficulty that GGZ face is the perceived feminized nature of their work. Sex work is a female-dominated occupation in Hong Kong, with women representing the largest number of sex workers (Amnesty International, 2016,

p. 15). In addition, sex work's association with service work, also female-dominated, strengthens feminine associations. In short, the selling of sex is associated with the female body, which is expected to be passive, deferent, and submissive (Kong, 2009, p. 738). Some of the GGZ interviewees reported feeling stress because of their engagement in a feminine occupation, and others reported that the act of selling one's body sometimes evokes a female or submissive role, especially when being penetrated. For instance:

> You have to serve the clients, please them, give them a massage and even have sex. . . . It's a kind of service work, a job that suits women a bit more . . . it has never been a good job for a man.
>
> *Ricky, age 36, bisexual, independent worker*

> I only experienced once as a "bottom," really . . . just once [he emphasized]! . . . You might say this is not normal sexual intercourse. . . . It's natural for a woman to be fucked. But not me, not a man.
>
> *Bruce, age 53, straight, former independent worker*

Given the context of sex work, which combines the connotations of immorality that society attaches to homosexual acts and engagement in sex acts for commercial purposes with the stigma of working in a traditionally feminine occupation, GGZ find themselves in a subordinate, marginalized position. How, then, can they construct their own male identity and accomplish occupational masculinity?

Negotiating masculinity in sex work: craftsmanship masculinity

To negotiate their marginal position, the Hong Kong interviewees perform an adjusted form of masculinity, which we conceptualize as "craftsmanship masculinity," defined as an emphasis on (1) craftsmanship, or the use of technical skills in service provision, and (2) commitment to a set of professional work ethics. Our interviews with GGZ suggest that they perform craftsmanship masculinity in two major ways: by managing the meaning of and recasting the content of male-male sex work.

Managing the meaning: "it's a profession!"

Although the GGZ interviewees were well aware of the connotations of deviance and femininity underlying their work, they all stressed that sex work itself is by no means an ordinary occupation, with many adding that they see their work as a profession or even a craft. Two major themes were identified in the men's articulation of their support for these ideas: technical skill and professional work ethics. With regard to the former, they emphasized the various skills required to serve their customers, including massage skills and communication skills. While acknowledging that a young body and handsome face were advantageous, the interviewees also stressed that technical skills were more important and that such skills can be learned only through on-the-job training and/or the accumulation of experience. These GGZ distinguished themselves from amateurs and displayed a sense of pride in their professionalism and the skilled nature of their labor:

> I spent two weeks learning how to massage before meeting my first customer. . . . . Our boss [the parlor owner] always reminds us that "what we sell is our massage and our professional service. You're cheap if you only focus on sex."
>
> *Berry, age 28, gay, independent worker*

> If you use too much strength or do it [a hand-job] too fast, it may be painful. . . . I did
> spend a lot of time to practice and improve my skill. . . . Of course I can always make my
> client orgasm [immediately], I'm skillful!
>
> *Carl, age 51, gay, independent worker*

Like the sex workers in Ho's study (2000), who often imbue sex work with a positive mean-ing by appropriating professionalism (p. 288), the GGZ in the present study identified them-selves as skilled laborers. Such appropriation is a gendering process in which male sex workers "professionalize" their sex work experience in a masculine way. Carl continued:

> We [GGZ] focus more on our [physical] labor and our skills. Unlike those women [female
> sex workers] who rely more on their appearance. . . . I don't mean they are not profes-
> sional. . . . I mean, we do things differently.

Men who work in female-dominated occupations often distance themselves from their female counterparts by emphasizing their masculine attributes (Lupton, 2000, pp. 42–43). Although some studies on female sex workers suggest that they also believe that skills are required to complete their work (Ho, 2000), the GGZ's perception of (or even prejudice against) women, and the GGZ's emphasis on technical skills, have helped them redefine male-male sex work as a masculine profession.

The GGZ in this study also claimed that male-male sex work is a profession with professional work ethics. Such ethics function as codes of practice or conduct, determining to some extent what a GGZ ought or ought not to do in the male-male sex industry. Although the profession lacks any written code, and there was no consensus among the interviewees concerning its ethics, several themes arose frequently in discussions of the criteria by which one's profession-alism is measured, including the separation of work and leisure sex (e.g., "Never take him as 'honey.' . . . Take it as work, and serve him!"), differentiation between work and private rela-tionships ("Once a client, forever a client. . . . Being friendly is fine but go beyond that? No."), and the practice of safe sex ("I am happy to negotiate, but using a condom is always a 'must.'").

Some studies have suggested that adopting a professional work ethic allows sex workers to create a "work persona" through which they are able to minimize the emotional trauma and sexual health risk inherent in their jobs (Browne & Minichiello, 1995, pp. 611–612). This sug-gestion applies to the GGZ in this study, but the GGZ also used professionalism to reclaim their manhood and their role as a respectable man in society:

> If you come here for fun, for leisure, or for money to gamble . . . you might say this man
> is a moron. . . . I'm not like that though. I take my job seriously and treat my customers
> well. . . . So, what's wrong with me then? Who dare to say I'm bad?
>
> *Frankie, age 33, gay, owner of and worker in a massage parlor*

In sum: By viewing their occupation as a job that requires technical skill and professional work ethics, GGZ have appropriated the idea of professionalism to redefine male-male sex work as both a craft and a masculine occupation. By developing technical skills, they build a certain level of craftsmanship, and by adhering to professional work ethics, they recapture respectabil-ity. Ultimately, they reclaim their male identity by associating themselves with skilled labor or craftsmanship like many other working-class men in Hong Kong (Equal Opportunities Com-mission, 2012, pp. 8–9).

Recasting job content: "skill is the most important thing"

Due to their orientation toward craftsmanship, the GGZ also incorporated related ideas into their work routine, particularly in promoting their services, designing the service package, and planning long-term strategies. First and foremost, when asked how they described themselves in their advertisements or to potential customers, many said they chose such occupational titles as "masseur" or "professional" (see Figure 36.1), giving the massage aspect of their work priority over the sex aspect. By highlighting their professionalism and craftsmanship, they neutralized or even desexualized sex work. For instance, Anthony (age 50, gay, independent worker) said:

> I will only say I am a masseur providing a massage service. It's better to keep a low profile for yourself. . . . Also, I very much prefer to proclaim myself as a masseur. It sounds more professional, and it also implies you have a specific skill.

Retitling one's job is a gender strategy often used by men involved in "deviant" or traditionally feminine occupations to reduce social stigma and minimize the connotations of femininity (Lupton, 2000; Kong, 2009). The advertising strategies adopted by the GGZ in this study can be understood in a similar manner. By reframing themselves as masseurs and emphasizing the professional nature of their services, they reconfigure their sex work experience, shifting it from a no-/low-skill occupation (e.g., only appearance matters) to an advanced-skill occupation (e.g., massage expert) and from a passive practice (e.g., selling one's body) to one that requires mastery (e.g., selling one's skills). Through such gendered tactics, GGZ not only "professionalize" their sex work experience but also realign themselves with normative masculine traits. Anthony continued:

> There are "manly" men who're also masseurs. They do foot massage and body massage. . . . They only do massage but not sex. And they are very professional. . . . So, I feel like it is more professional to be called a masseur, and also more "man[ly]"!

Secondly, these GGZ advocate the idea of "massage first, sex second" in their provision of services. According to them, the standard service package is "massage plus sex." The set price for a massage service is HK\$300–500 (around US\$40–65), with an additional charge for various sexual services such as a handjob (HK\$100–200, around US\$15–25), blowjob (HK\$200–300, around US\$25–40), or anal intercourse (HK\$400–500, around US\$50–65). They said the duration of the standard service package is 60–90 minutes, with 60 minutes of massage followed by 10–20 minutes of sexual service:

Figure 36.1 Screenshot of GGZ advertisements on a Hong Kong gay website (captured in 2017).

> Massage is the core of my job. I am not saying that I don't do that [provide a sexual service]. . . . Of course I do. But it is not the main thing in my job.
>
> *Louis, age 39, gay, worker in a massage parlor*

> If I say I am going to spend 60 minutes with you, then I will give you a massage for at least 50 minutes. . . . It's a "must." I rely on my hands to earn myself an income, not just sex.
>
> *Berry, age 28, gay, independent worker*

Like their job descriptions, this "massage first, sex second" occupational script not only functions as a distancing strategy to downplay their involvement in stigmatized, feminine sex acts but also enables GGZ to improve their masculine status by celebrating their labor and skills. The more committed they are to that script, the easier it is for them to (re-)claim their occupation as skilled and masculine labor.

Last, the GGZ's orientation toward craftsmanship and professionalism is also manifested in their long-term strategies. The interviewees were well aware of the short life cycle of their job, as most customers prefer new faces. To maintain their competitiveness, they developed a number of long-term business strategies, including building up regular customers and continuing to improve their massage and sexual skills. For instance, Kenny (age 52, gay, independent worker) said:

> Don't rely on new customers. That is not a good way to build your career; you should focus on how to keep your customers instead. . . . I keep exploring new techniques to give my customers some surprises. . . . I also keep trying something new with my customers, like using a sex toy!

Although the effectiveness of such strategies is unclear, they are important to acknowledge as part of the GGZ's determination to treat male-male sex work as a profession or craft. Some expressed the belief that achievement should be measured by the number of regular customers one has rather than by the amount of money one makes. Many even articulated a sense of pride that they had been able to "survive" in such a competitive industry. Their articulation of their long-term strategies was gendered, which granted them a positive masculine status. Kenny insisted:

> Of course, I'm professional! Otherwise, how could I stay working here for this long [11 years]? . . . Not everyone can stay in this business . . . only the competent ones can remain!

Based on the GGZ narratives, we conceptualize these men's reconfiguration of work/masculine practices in the male-male sex industry as the performance of craftsmanship masculinity. The Hong Kong interviewees reframed male-male sex work as a profession or craft by emphasizing their technical skills and professional work ethics. They also imbued their work routines with masculine components by (re-)positioning themselves as masseurs, prioritizing massage over sex, and emphasizing their competence in maintaining a place in the market. In doing so, these GGZ developed a sense of professionalism and craftsmanship, identified themselves as skilled professionals or craftsmen, and took their rightful place among other working-class men.

Money boys in mainland China

Perceived gender challenges

As in Hong Kong, patriarchal family values were once the predominate shaper of masculinity in mainland Chinese society, with work a secondary factor in defining men's lives (Hinsch, 2013, pp. 7–8). However, a drastic transformation of manhood resulted from the establishment of the People's Republic of China (PRC) in 1949. Under Mao's leadership, a new socialist subject without gender—known as "Chairman Mao's good soldier"—was created through ideological campaigns (Yan, 2010, p. 492). In this political landscape, ideal manhood was manifested through altruism and loyalty to the country. That landscape was upended in the late 1970s when the PRC government launched a series of economic reforms in line with its central policy shift from socialist ideology to a more market-driven approach, leading to the country's rapid industrialization and urbanization (Yan, 2010, pp. 494–495). The socialist ideologies of Maoism were gradually undermined by emerging new values (e.g., materialism), thus altering the perception of manhood, which today is increasingly measured by material success and affluence obtained through individual intelligence and hard work. Work has thus become as crucial as family to men's lives (Song & Hird, 2014).

With respect to notions of work and masculinity, all of the MBs interviewed for this study agreed that having a job or running a business is central to a man's life. Yet, like their Hong Kong counterparts, they saw their engagement in male-male sex work as seemingly detrimental to their performance of masculinity. The MBs identified two major difficulties in their narratives. First, sex work requires them to engage in an illegal and immoral activity. The PRC government has implemented a prohibitionist model of prostitution since the Mao era. Third parties involved in prostitution (e.g., brothel operators) are committing a criminal offense subject to severe punishment (e.g., imprisonment). First-party prostitution is not criminalized, but it is regarded as socially immoral, and both sellers and buyers are subject to mandatory educational detention and/or fines (Kong, 2014, pp. 322–323). At the same time, homosexuality still attracts social prejudice and moral disapproval in mainland China, regardless of the regulations on related acts being lifted in recent decades, such as the removal of "homosexuality" from the list of mental illnesses endorsed by the Chinese Psychiatric Association in 2001 and the abolishment of "hooliganism" (the crime usually cited in penalizing same-sex sexual activities) from the Criminal Law in 1997. The public discourse on homosexuality still tends to carry connotations of deviance, effeminacy, criminality, and even fears of an HIV epidemic (Zheng, 2015, p. 72). In this social context, MBs feel under constant pressure to claim their masculinity:

> Even if you perform a small service like a handjob for your customers, that's already illegal. . . . People will only see the bad side of you. You are nowhere near a good man.
>
> *Xiao Yi, age 25, heterosexual, brothel worker*

> People still see this [homosexuality] as an illness in my village. . . . If they [the villagers] learnt that I'm doing this [selling sex to men] . . . seriously, I would kill myself!
>
> *Zi Han, age 28, gay, independent worker*

Second, as in Hong Kong, another major difficulty is the feminized perception of sex work, as most sex workers in mainland China are women (Jeffreys, 2012, pp. 2–6), and sex work is associated with femininity because a passive, submissive, and even powerless position is usually assumed to be inherent in the act of selling one's body. Men who engage in such acts are often not considered "real men" (Kong, 2012, p. 31). The MB interviewees were well aware of this perception. Many explicitly articulated a degree of strain associated with their entry into a feminine occupation, and some reported the selling of sex or engagement in certain sex acts as detrimental to their masculinity:

> People consider it more acceptable for a woman [to sell sex]. But you're a man! . . . You will be condemned as having no ambition! It's simply disgraceful.
>
> *Ah Chong, age 31, bisexual, independent worker*

> Because I'm a man, I don't think I should let anyone to fuck me . . . It might sound weird. Even though I am into men, I still think being penetrated is really disgraceful.
>
> *Zi Han, age 28, gay, independent worker*

These social constructs relegate MBs to an inferior position in the hierarchy of masculinities in mainstream Chinese society. The MBs are readily dismissed as engaging in an illegal, immoral, feminine activity.

Negotiating masculinity in sex work: "guerrilla masculinity"

Notwithstanding the foregoing issues, MBs, like GGZ in Hong Kong, have been able to negotiate their masculine status by creating a nuanced version of masculinity within the male-male sex industry, which we conceptualize as "guerrilla masculinity." We define guerrilla masculinity as the reconfiguration of masculine practices centered primarily on fulfillment of the entrepreneurial dream, with aspirations to become a small business owner or entrepreneur facilitated by amateur, transient, and irregular involvement in sex work. The term "guerrilla" articulates the illicit status of sex work in mainland China, where the term "guerrilla workers" often refers to the various (usually migrant) workers participating in the informal urban economy (Guang, 2005, p. 503). Two major aspects of MBs' routine work are discussed in the following to illustrate their accomplishment of guerrilla masculinity: managing job meanings and recasting job content.

Managing job meanings: "it's a stepping stone!"

When asked to comment on their sex work experiences, nearly all of the MB interviewees emphasized their involvement in the male-male sex industry as a temporary, opportunistic means of pursuing, or as a "stepping stone" to, their desired future career: namely becoming a *xiaolaoban* (small boss) or entrepreneur. Two main themes were identified within this rationale: "future-oriented success" and "rational calculation."

In terms of future-oriented success, the MBs in this study always emphasized future success rather than present hardship in talking about their sex work experiences. They all had a rural-migrant, working-/lower-class background, and none was a stranger to poverty. Despite having big dreams (e.g., running a small business), they found their aspirations difficult, if not impossible, to realize. Hence, many had entered the sex industry to improve their material conditions by earning a higher income than would be possible in other work, but they also considered sex work a stepping stone to fulfilling their dreams:

> Many of us know well that this is only a temporary measure, like a *tiaoban* ["springboard"] for you to change your life. . . . When I have an opportunity to start a small business one day, I will quit [sex work].
>
> *Mi Mi, age 34, gay, independent worker*

Becoming an entrepreneur is not only a personal strategy for improving one's living conditions; it is also a gendered strategy for enhancing one's masculinity. Conditioned by its neoliberal reconfiguration, entrepreneurial masculinity is culturally exalted in mainland China today, and "besuited entrepreneurs and businessmen" have become the ideal form of manhood in the realm of work (Song & Hird, 2014, pp. 121–122). Against this backdrop, the MBs' articulation of their entrepreneurial dream is gendered, with these men to some extent realigning themselves with the prevailing masculine norms in mainstream society. Even though they had not yet realized their entrepreneurial dreams, they could still reclaim their male identity by stressing their future aspirations. Mi Mi continued:

> I don't consider myself a bad man. I would rather say I'm a mature man. . . . I am willing to do a job like this for the sake of my future and my career, and I think this is what a mature man would do.

In fact, prioritizing career prospects over one's current job is a common gendered strategy for reclaiming manhood among men working in a feminine or stigmatized occupation (Lupton, 2000, p. 36; Takeyama, 2010, p. 236). Regardless of whether MBs are ever able to realize their entrepreneurial dream, their declared attachment to future-oriented success enables them to project a positive masculine status.

In addition to dreams of entrepreneurship in future, the MB interviewees also emphasized the rational calculation behind their decision to pursue their goals through sex work, often in terms of the lucrative opportunity it offered to accumulate capital:

> If I worked as a waiter, I could earn round RMB3000 [around US$450] [per month] at best. . . . In this job [sex work], I can earn at least RMB8000 [around US$1,200] [per month]. . . . It's obvious: Work here, and you can accumulate capital much faster!
>
> *Xiao Hei, age 25, gay, independent worker*

> You always have a chance to meet people [customers] from various backgrounds. . . . Some of them are very outstanding. I can always learn something talking to them . . . like how to develop [my career] better . . . and invest [my] money. . . . I wouldn't be able to meet all of these people if it were not for this job.
>
> *Xiao Bao, age 27, heterosexual, independent worker*

By articulating all of these "potentials" in sex work, the MBs presented themselves as having made a rational, and indeed the right, choice on the path toward achieving success in future. Their emphasis on having made a rational choice was also gendered; seeing themselves as rational choice-makers enabled them to reclaim an active, masculine role regarding their decision to enter and remain in the sex work industry (Kong, 2009, pp. 732–733). Believing themselves to be men of ambition and vision resulted in a more positive masculine status. Xiao Bao continued:

> Although I don't have a decent job now, I am working on this step by step. . . . I have made the right decision. . . . This decision is not just for my career and my future but also for my family.

In short, the MB interviewees reconstructed the meaning of their sex work by connecting their present involvement to their entrepreneurial dream and by believing themselves to have made not only a rational decision but also the right choice for realizing their goals in future. They also reclaimed their masculinity by realigning themselves with the normative masculine discourse in mainstream society (that is, entrepreneurial masculinity) (Song & Hird, 2014, pp. 121–122).

Recasting job content: "money is the most important thing!"

In reconstructing the meaning of their work, the MBs also recast their involvement, and its gendered meaning, in the sex industry in a way that related their work to their entrepreneurial aspirations. The (re-)making process was manifested in the ways they promote their services, design their service package, and formulate long-term strategies. For example, when asked how they promote themselves in the competitive sex market, they often reported using semi-naked or naked photos, sexualized descriptions (e.g., huge cock, nice butt), and particular job titles (e.g., fitness trainer, armed policeman) to convey a hypersexualized or erotic image in their advertisements (See Figure 36.2). Their rationale was simple and direct: Such descriptions are the only way to attract customers' attention, as Ah Tu (age 26, bisexual, independent worker) explained:

> If you do not add [naked] photos to the ads, no one is going to give you a call. You will have no business. . . . As long as customers are coming to you, everything is fine. . . . Earning money is the most important [thing]!

Although the act of selling one's body carries connotations of immorality and femininity, MBs are still inclined to project a hypersexualized image to attract more customers because of their greater interest in earning more money. Due to their entrepreneurial aspirations, an emphasis on being "money-oriented" or profit-maximizing is indeed a rational, yet gendered, strategy. If sex work is merely a stepping stone to starting a business, then selling one's body becomes less of a concern than the ability to accumulate sufficient capital. The ability to devise and employ an effective advertising strategy to maximize income also allowed the MBs to reclaim their masculine role in the sex work process, as Ah Tu explained:

> It's all about your brain! . . . Smart people learn faster . . . and I think I'm okay; otherwise I'd be out of the game already. . . . Can't you see there are so many advertisements [on the website he uses]? Not everyone is earning good money. I'm sure.

Figure 36.2 Screenshot of advertisements by MBs on a mainland Chinese gay website.

(Translations of the ad headlines (left to right): "Ah Nick with Big Cock," "Hulk in China," "Big Cock, Good Looking and Nice Body," and "Your Private Butler") (captured in 2017).

In addition to their advertisement strategies, the MBs also incorporated this money-oriented mentality into their service package. They reported two major service packages: "a quickie" (priced at RMB300–600, around US$45–90), which provides sexual service only, and "full service" (priced at RMB600–800, around US$90–120), which includes a massage plus sex. Service duration was usually 60 to 90 minutes, they said, while admitting that the transaction would likely end once the customer had ejaculated. Accordingly, most MBs adopt the tactic of "full service but fast trade" to maximize their profits—that is, to encourage their customers to opt for the full service but then to minimize the duration of the massage and jump straight into sex. For instance, one MB described his work routine as follows.

> When he [a customer] arrives, I give him a brief massage . . . then I turn him on and we have sex until he ejaculates. . . . After he has been satisfied, I get my money and ask him to leave. . . . Then I can look for the next customer.
>
> *Xiao Fan, age 37, gay, independent worker and pimp*

Maximizing their monetary return by adopting this tactic allows MBs to further reframe their engagement in sex work as a "business-like activity." Xian Fan continued:

> This is also a kind of business. . . . As you are doing business, you have to think about how you can make more money. . . . Making love is no big deal at all; the money is a big deal though!

In her study of host clubs in Japan, Takeyama (2010, pp. 240–243) suggests that male hosts reconstruct their masculinity by celebrating their "entrepreneurial spirit" and speculative style of earning, considering themselves "self-employed entrepreneurs." Similarly, the MBs in the present study maintained their masculinity by reframing their sex work experience as a business-like activity. If one is running a business, then providing a (perhaps truncated) sexual service is no big deal. What is important is profit maximization.

Last but not least, to maximize their monetary returns over the long run, MBs also adopt a "guerrilla-style" business strategy in the sex market, traveling from place to place in search of business opportunities:

> We cannot stay in a particular place for too long. . . . Customers are always looking for a new face . . . so you should travel around markets in different cities. . . . Spend a month in Chongqing, then go to Xi'an, and then Shanghai.
>
> *Ah Chong, age 31, bisexual, independent worker*

Because the longer one works in the sex industry, the less marketable one is (Kong, 2012, p. 31), MBs must become highly mobile to maintain their "freshness" in the sex market, always on the lookout for new places to find customers. Rural-to-urban migration is very common in China, even though migrants are usually deprived of social welfare and protection (Chan & Buckingham, 2008). Although moving from place to place can be seen as a reactive tactic, it should be noted that, in alignment with MB's entrepreneurial aspirations, such a guerrilla-style strategy is also gendered and gives those who deploy it a sense of physical freedom. Some of the MBs described themselves as autonomous "self-employed entrepreneurs." For example, Ah Chong said:

> I am free to go wherever I want. . . . If I think a particular city will provide more business opportunities, I will move there for business. . . . I decide my next stop by myself.

In summary: The MBs reconstructed their work/male identity within the male-male sex work arena by adopting gendered practices that we conceptualize as guerrilla masculinity. They reframed their sex work experience as a rational and good choice for realizing their entrepreneurial dreams and achieving future success. In terms of job content, they recast their work routine as requiring them to play an active, masculine role by highlighting their money and business orientation and physical freedom. These tactics allowed the MBs in this study to reclaim their masculinity by prioritizing their future prospects over their current situation while presenting themselves as men engaged in a businesslike activity rather than men who passively sell sex and their bodies.

Discussion and conclusion

The comparison of GGZ in Hong Kong and MBs in mainland China in this chapter has revealed both similarities and differences. Male-male sex work is stigmatized in both societies, regarded as a typically feminine activity that is both immoral and illegal/criminal. Hence, GGZ and MBs can hardly be said to be performing socially acceptable occupational masculinities. Situated within such difficult conditions, the two groups of MSWs have adopted different gender strategies to reclaim their masculinity. We conceptualize their respective masculinities as "craftsmanship masculinity" (GGZ) and "guerrilla masculinity" (MBs). In their advertisements, GGZ predominantly display desexualized descriptions, whereas MBs predominantly project a hypersexualized image. In service provision, GGZ for the most part follow a "massage first, sex second" occupational script, whereas MBs tend to employ a profit-maximizing "full service but fast trade" business strategy. In terms of their long-term business strategies, GGZ prefer building up a regular clientele by developing advanced skills and honing their craft, whereas MBs prefer to look for new customers by moving from place to place. These differences are reflected in the different masculinities that the two groups perform. For example, GGZ are oriented toward the professionalism and craftsmanship of male-male sex work, seeing it as akin to the occupations of other working-class men in Hong Kong. MBs, in contrast, are oriented toward entrepreneurship and thus rationalize their engagement in sex work as offering a promising way to realize future career success, thus aligning themselves with the entrepreneurial masculinity that prevails in mainland China.

The distinct versions of occupational masculinity endorsed by GGZ and MBs must be understood in light of the different social contexts in Hong Kong and mainland China rather than as a matter of personal preference alone. For example, the legal frameworks in the two societies create varying degrees of freedom and constraints for developing careers in the sex industry. Because all forms of prostitution are unlawful in mainland China, which has thus adopted a prohibitionist stance (Kong, 2014, pp. 322–323), the treatment of sex work as a permanent job would carry considerable risk for MBs. A less restrictive environment is found in Hong Kong, where selling sex is not illegal in itself (Chiu, 2006, p. 549). Hence, the more neutral status of prostitution and less risky sex work environment in Hong Kong encourage GGZ to devote more time and money to advancing their skills.

Moreover, the ideology of the "modernization dream" has also played a crucial role in shaping the varying orientations of the two groups of men. Following modernization and industrialization, notions of the "Hong Kong Dream" and "Chinese Dream" emerged in public discourse in the 1970s and 1980s, reflecting the general belief that anyone could realize social and economic success through ability and hard work, regardless of social class (Lee, 2005; Yan, 2010). However, the impoverishment of the economic and political environment in Hong Kong in recent years, such as the widening poverty gap and the failure of democratization, seems to make such dreams impossible to achieve (Lee, 2005, pp. 306–307). In mainland China, in contrast, the "Chinese Dream" seems alive and well if PRC government propaganda is to be believed (Taylor, 2015). Although we are not suggesting that GGZ in Hong Kong have no aspirations for the future, the varying extents to which such aspirations have been internalized appear to explain the stronger emphasis on (and faith in) future occupational success by the MBs than the GGZ in this study.

Finally, it is important to note that conventional gender norms remain durable in both Chinese societies, as amply manifested in the interviewees' narratives. Just as guerrilla masculinity is a compromise version of mainstream masculine norms in mainland China, craftsmanship masculinity is an appropriation of socially accepted masculinity in the workplace in Hong Kong. In line with our previous findings (Kong, 2009, 2012), the GGZ and MBs in the present study conform to and support, rather than undo and challenge, socially accepted answers to the questions of masculinity or male identity. Regardless of these men's efforts to reclaim their manhood, the hierarchy of masculinities in mainstream society remains firmly in place, and the subordination of their sex work experience persists.

Notes

* The title "One Country, Two Men" mirrors Hong Kong's current constitutional status of "One Country, Two Systems." This chapter examines two occupational masculinities accomplished by Hong Kong and mainland Chinese male sex workers under one country, China.
1 For examples of media reports on male-male sex work in Hong Kong, see http://hk.on.cc/hk/bkn/cnt/news/20140218/bkn-20140218221024203-0218_00822_001.html and https://hk.news.apple daily.com/local/daily/article/20161007/19793798.

References

Alcano, M. C. (2011). "Slaves of our own making": The fabrication of masculine identities between Java and Bali. *Indonesia and the Malay World*, *39*(115), 373–389.

Amnesty International. (2016). *Harmfully isolated: Criminalizing sex work in Hong Kong*. London: Amnesty International. Retrieved from www.amnestyusa.org/wp-content/uploads/2017/04/hong_kong_report_-_sex_workers_rights_-_embargoed_-_final.pdf

Browne, J., & Minichiello, V. (1995). The social meanings behind male sex work: Implications for sexual interactions. *The British Journal of Sociology*, *46*(4), 598–622.

Browne, J., & Minichiello, V. (1996). The social and work context of commercial sex between men: A research note. *Australian and New Zealand Journal of Sociology*, *32*(1), 86–92.

Chan, K. W., & Buckingham, W. (2008). Is China abolishing the *hukou* system? *The China Quarterly*, *195*, 582–606.

Chan, P. C. W. (2005). The lack of sexual orientation anti-discrimination legislation in Hong Kong: Breach of international and domestic legal obligations. *The International Journal of Human Rights*, *9*(1), 69–106.

Chiu, M. C. (2006). (Han-)Chinese cultural appropriation of sexual legal politics: Postcolonial discourse on law controlling sex work in Hong Kong. *Asian Journal of Social Science*, *34*(4), 547–572.

Chow, E. P. F., Iu, K. I., Fu, X., Wilson, D. P., & Zhang, L. (2012). HIV and sexually transmissible infections among money boys in China: A data synthesis and meta-analysis. *PLoS ONE*, *7*(11), e48025. doi:10.1371/journal.pone.0048025

Connell, R. W. (1993). The big picture: Masculinities in recent world history. *Theory and Society*, *22*(5), 597–623.

Connell, R. W. (1995). *Masculinities*. Cambridge: Polity Pres.

Connell, R. W. (2000). *The men and the boys*. Berkeley: University of California Press.

Connell, R. W., & Messerschmidt, J. W. (2005). Hegemonic masculinity: Rethinking the concept. *Gender & Society, 19*(6), 829–859.

Connell, R. W., & Wood, J. (2005). Globalization and business masculinities. *Men and Masculinities, 7*(4), 347–364.

Dellinger, K. (2004). Masculinities in "safe" and "embattled" organizations: Accounting for pornographic and feminist magazines. *Gender & Society, 18*(5), 545–566.

Dennis, J. P. (2008). Women are victims, men make choices: The invisibility of men and boys in the global sex trade. *Gender Issues, 25*(1), 11–25.

Equal Opportunities Commission. (2012). *Exploratory study on gender stereotyping and its impact on male gender*. Hong Kong: Equal Opportunities Commission. Retrieved from www.eoc.org.hk/EOC/Upload/UserFiles/File/ResearchReport/201205/MenInPain_eFullReport.pdf

Guang, L. (2005). Guerrilla workfare: Migrant renovators, state power, and informal work in urban China. *Politics & Society, 33*(3), 481–506.

Hinsch, B. (2013). *Masculinities in Chinese history*. Lanham, MD: Rowman & Littlefield.

Ho, J. C. J. (2000). Self-empowerment and "professionalism": Conversations with Taiwanese sex workers. *Inter-Asia Cultural Studies, 1*(2), 283–299.

Jeffreys, E. (2012). *Prostitution scandals in China: Policing, media and society*. London and New York: Routledge.

Kimmel, M. S., & Messner, M. A. (Eds.). (2013). *Men's lives* (9th ed.). Boston: Pearson.

Koken, J. A., Bimbi, D. S., Parsons, J. T., & Halkitis, P. N. (2004). The experience of stigma in the lives of male Internet escorts. *Journal of Psychology & Human Sexuality, 16*(1), 13–32.

Kong, T. S. K. (2009). More than a sex machine: Accomplishing masculinity among Chinese male sex workers in the Hong Kong sex industry. *Deviant Behavior, 30*(8), 715–745.

Kong, T. S. K. (2012). Sex entrepreneurs in the new China. *Contexts, 11*(3), 28–33.

Kong, T. S. K. (2014). Male sex work in China. In V. Minichiello & J. Scott (Eds.), *Male sex work and society* (pp. 314–341). New York: Harrington Park Press.

Kumar, N., Scott, J., & Minichiello, V. (2017). Masculinity and the occupational experience of male independent escorts who seek male clients. *Social Sciences, 6*(2), 58. doi:10.3390/socsci6020058

Lee, E. W. Y. (2005). The renegotiation of the social pact in Hong Kong: Economic globalization, socio-economic change, and local politics. *Journal of Social Policy, 34*(2), 293–310.

Lupton, B. (2000). Maintaining masculinity: Men who do "women's work". *British Journal of Management, 11*(S1), 33–48.

Morgan, D. H. J. (1992). *Discovering men*. London and New York: Routledge.

Oselin, S. S. (2016). You catch more flies with honey: Sex work, violence, and masculinity on the streets. *Sociological Forum, 31*(1), 203–222.

Song, G., & Hird, D. (2014). *Men and masculinities in contemporary China*. Leiden: Brill.

Takeyama, A. (2010). Intimacy for sale: Masculinity, entrepreneurship, and commodity self in Japan's neoliberal situation. *Japanese Studies, 30*(2), 231–246.

Taylor, J. R. (2015). The China dream is an urban dream: Assessing the CPC's national new-type urbanization plan. *Journal of Chinese Political Science, 20*(2), 107–120.

Tewksbury, R. (1993). Male strippers: Men objectifying men. In C. L. Williams (Ed.), *Doing "women's work": Men in nontraditional occupations* (pp. 168–181). Newbury Park, CA: Sage Publications.

West, C., & Zimmerman, D. (1987). Doing gender. *Gender and Society, 1*(2), 125–151.

Yan, Y. (2010). The Chinese path to individualization. *The British Journal of Sociology, 61*(3), 489–512.

Zheng, T. (2015). *Tongzhi living: Men attracted to men in postsocialist China*. Minneapolis: University of Minnesota Press.

37

Male sex work in Australia

Impact of legalization, criminalization, and peer support in community and public health

Denton Callander, Ryan DeVeau, Garrett Prestage, Juliet Richters, and Basil Donovan

For decades, the epicenter of male sex work in Australia could be found along a stretch of road in Sydney's "gayest" district, Darlinghurst. Along "The Wall" (Figure 37.1)—a beautiful sandstone structure built by Australian convicts in the 1820s and a stone's throw from the hospital where Australia's first case of AIDS was diagnosed—men would buy and sell sex only blocks from Sydney's locales of sex work for both cisgender and trans women. Today, hustling is left to the numerous parking meters along the Wall's tree-lined street. Yet the Wall remains a powerful symbol of a business that in Australia now mainly operates in a virtual world.

This chapter is the story of male sex work in Australia, which, like so much of sex in the twenty-first century, finds itself written increasingly online. Each year seems to spawn new types of sex-work connection and communication, demanding multifaceted methods of self-promotion across many platforms (Callander & DeVeau, 2019). The digital age has reshaped not just sex work itself but also the systems of support and outreach that have underpinned Australia's community-driven approach to sex work for over three decades. Peer support and social advocacy have been at the heart of how the Australian sex industry—male and female—has organized for some time, and the Internet has allowed these same tenets to be enacted through diverse digital spaces.

While there is no question that the Internet has significantly changed male sex work in Australia, the reality is that (at least for now) it still requires flesh-and-blood participants, real people who buy sex in either online or offline environments. In this chapter, we sketch a picture of who these people are, using research conducted with male sex workers and their clients. The Australian male sex industry is among the most studied anywhere in the world, with dozens of high-quality social studies conducted over several decades. We spend some time describing the services provided by the community groups that support sex workers in Australia, with a special focus on publicly funded sexual health clinics. By attending to these organizations and what they symbolize, we can get some sense not just of past and present male sex work in Australia, but possibly its future as well.

Figure 37.1 The Wall, Darlinghurst, Sydney, Australia.

The history of male sex work in Australia

It is useful to start by looking at the history of male sex work in Australia, which for a long period was largely undocumented. By not fitting into the heavily gendered analyses of "prostitution" that featured in Australian discourse during the nineteenth and much of the twentieth century, male sex work was rendered invisible in the public imagination. Indeed, it was often conflated with legal and psychiatric arguments around homosexuality in Australia, a common theme in the histories of male sex work told around the world (Friedman, 2014). While some early books on homosexuality included references to sex work (French, 1993; Wotherspoon, 2016[1]), these were largely brief and in passing.

In 1977, a report from Australia's Royal Commission on Human Relationships acknowledged that "prostitution is not exclusively confined to the activities of women engaged in commercial sexual transactions" but then went on to describe related issues relevant only to women as the sellers of sex. Similarly, 35 years later, the sections on prostitution in Frank Bongiorno's *The Sex Lives of Australians: A History* (2012) concern only female prostitution before the mid-twentieth century. Only when discussing sex in postwar Australia did male sex work garner a reference from Bongiorno: "There was also a substantial, if little known, trade in male prostitution. In the larger cities, men bought sex from street boys or transvestites" (p. 213). He also included male sex workers when discussing Australia's liberalization of sex work in the 1990s but otherwise referred to sex workers exclusively as women.

It took a combination of gay community activism in the 1970s and research funds made available in response to the AIDS crisis in the 1980s to shed light on commercial sex between men. Some of the first published empirical research on gay male sex work in Australia was presented in Perkins and Bennett's *Being a Prostitute*, which reported on three small survey and interview studies with respondents recruited in gay venues in Sydney. This work was groundbreaking because of its sociological (rather than psychological or criminological) approach and its sympathy with the workers' point of view. The interviewees included gay men who had chosen—at least for a while—to make money from their youth and beauty while having sex they largely enjoyed and also men who did not necessarily identify as gay or bisexual, especially in street work. This early study illuminated the often informal and opportunistic nature of male sex work of the time, opportunities for sex that occasionally blurred the lines between "free" and (explicitly) paid sex. Some of the interviewees described their first experience of being paid for sex as coming about through a man offering them money when they were newly exploring the gay scene. Interestingly, as we explore later in this chapter, casual and opportunistic organization of sex work among men remains one of its defining features in Australia.

A significant component of past (and, indeed, present) male sex work in Australia is its legal status. From the 1970s through the 1990s, strong and effective social organization by (mainly female) sex workers and their allies resulted, over time, in the decriminalization of sex work in one Australian state (New South Wales) (Frances, 1994), which remains one of only two places in the world to have granted this legislative freedom (the other is the country of New Zealand). Although as of 2019, no other Australian jurisdiction had decriminalized sex work, it was a legal practice in several jurisdictions—Victoria, Queensland, and the Australian Capital Territory—but subject to regulation. As is often the case with legalized sex work, the exact details of such regulation differed over time and between jurisdictions, but broadly speaking, within these three jurisdictions, private, independent sex work and (licensed) brothels were permitted. In the remaining parts of Australia (Western Australia, Tasmania, South Australia, and the Northern Territory), independent sex work was legal as of 2019 (with restrictions), but brothels and other forms of collective sex work were not. It is important to recognize that these laws are not static; they have faced and continue to face many challenges and revisions. In 2018, for example, sex worker activists and their allies came together to advocate for sex work decriminalization in the South Australia, an ongoing movement that enjoyed the support of the state's attorney-general but also faced considerable community opposition (Boisvert, 2018).

Generally speaking, Australia enjoys some of the most liberal sex work laws in the world. Nevertheless, there are significant differences between jurisdictions, and these differences can introduce uncertainty among male sex workers traveling between different states and territories: what is permissible in one place may be illegal in others. Furthermore, in jurisdictions with more restrictive laws, it is easy to find examples of their use to stigmatize and harass sex workers, especially when such laws have been applied inconsistently. (Such inconsistency is something of a hallmark for how sex work laws tend to be enforced around the world.) For example, in Adelaide, the capital city of South Australia, in 2017, police conducted sudden raids on several female brothels that had been operating in plain sight for several years (Jones, 2017). It is not clear what sparked this sudden attention to these sex-work establishments, and while male sex workers in Australia may largely avoid the attention of police because they mainly operate independently, highly publicized actions like raiding a brothel likely foster anxiety among sex worker communities. Further, they serve as a powerful reminder of the disparate legislative attitudes that have shaped and continue to shape male sex work in Australia.

Australia's male sex workers and male sex work clients

What is known about male sex workers in Australia today? When a representative sample of men in Australia was surveyed in 2012–2013, 1.3% reported that they had been paid for sex at least once in their lives (Richters, de Visser et al., 2014). Of course, selling sex once or twice does not a sex worker make, and it seems clear that there is a subset of men in Australia for whom sex work is a casual or contextual experience, something they engage in once or twice or maybe something they dip in and out of as need or opportunity arises (McLean, 2015). This phenomenon has been observed in other countries, suggesting that it is not unique to Australia. It is notable, however, just how sizeable this group of men is; in one survey of gay and bisexual male sex workers in Sydney and Melbourne, 77% reported that they had sold sex only once or twice in the previous six months (pers. comm, Professor Martin Holt, Centre for Social Research in Health, 2016).

At the other end of the spectrum there is a (smaller) contingent of men for whom sex work is ongoing and regular. In the same survey of men in Sydney and Melbourne, 15% reported selling sex at least weekly, while the remaining 8% of men were somewhere in the middle, selling sex every few weeks or monthly. These differences reveal that sex work is not uniformly practiced among men in Australia and that it is useful to think of it as a continuum, ranging from the least to most invested in terms of frequency and time commitments. Ultimately, sex work is a not a full-time job for most men who sell sex in Australia: Only one in ten report sex work as their main source of income (Prestage et al., 2015).

Beyond helping us describe the nature of sex work among men in Australia, these proportional estimates also allow us to get some sense of the total population size. Estimating population size has important applications in epidemiology (for calculating the incidence of infection), healthcare (outlining the nature of the population requiring care), and support service delivery (by helping to gauge the scope and scale of required services). Describing the size of sex work populations is often hampered by unreliable data confounded by social stigma against those who buy and sell sex. But using information from surveys allows us to make some informed estimates about the breadth and depth of Australia's male sex work population.

It is helpful to think about three different categories of current sex work among men in Australia. The first, as we have discussed, comprises those who do so casually. These men make up the majority of male sex workers in Australia. The second category is composed of those men for whom sex work is more serious, which is to say they sell sex on an ongoing and regular basis but more as a side job than as a main source of income. Third, there is the "core" group of male sex workers who regularly sell sex and who do so as their primary or only source of income. As Figure 37.2 shows, when applied against national population estimates of gay and bisexual men

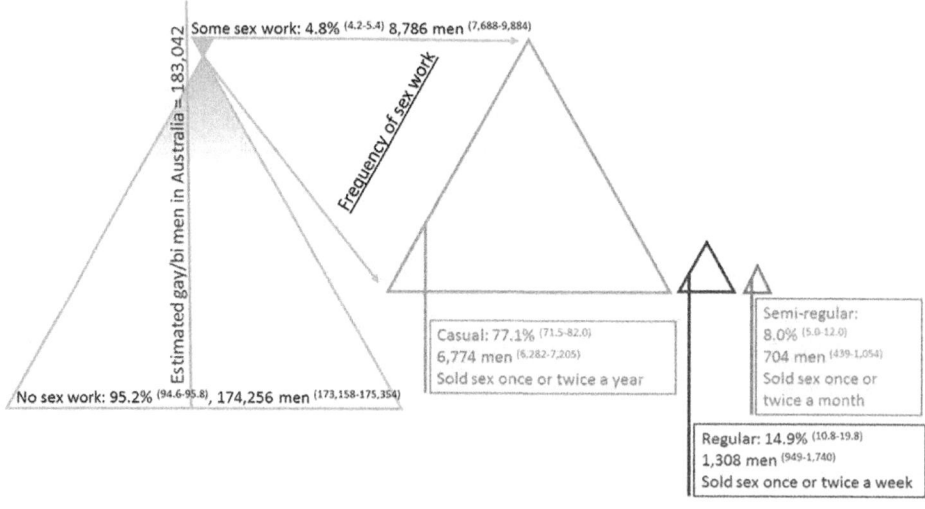

Figure 37.2 The estimated population sizes of casual, semi-regular, and regular male sex workers in Australia with 95% confidence intervals.

in Australia (Richters, Altman et al., 2014), we start to get a clearer picture of Australia's male sex work population. While there may be nearly 10,000 male sex workers currently working in Australia, only around 1,300 of those sell sex as a steady, ongoing job. Notably, these estimates do not include men who sell sex exclusively to women, a necessary omission given the lack of available information on this topic. While it seems likely that this group is a relatively small one (Caldwell, 2018), future efforts must endeavor to more completely account for the diverse kinds of male sex workers who operate in Australia.

Beyond the population size, characterizing men who sell sex in Australia is not straightforward, at least in part because sex workers rarely form a neatly homogenous group. What information we do have comes predominantly from two studies of male sex workers, one conducted in the late 1990s and the other in 2014 (Minichiello et al., 2002; Prestage et al., 2015). Consistent with much international evidence, men who sell sex in Australia tend to be mainly but not exclusively in their 20s and 30s and to identify as gay or bisexual. Around a quarter were born outside Australia. Nothing empirical is known about transgender male or transmasculine sex workers in Australia.

As is so often the case with sex work research, it is difficult to say much about the representativeness of these estimates. Recruiting a truly representative sample of sex workers to research is made difficult by the (often unclear) boundaries of what constitutes "sex work" and the enduring social stigma that permeates these practices. Previously, we have used information collected from online profiles to describe the demographics and practices of sex workers in Australia and elsewhere (Callander, Moreira et al., in press), which has proven to be a useful approach but one limited to only those men who engage in sex work on a regular basis. It is plausible that casual and contextual workers—those who make up the majority of male sex workers in Australia— are unlikely to maintain formal profiles of this kind and therefore are likely be excluded from that kind of analysis. In spite of the inconsistencies and uncertainties, one thing that does seem clear is that male sex workers in Australia tend to work on their own or through agencies: In 2018, across the entire country, there was only one male brothel in operation.

Another question we might ask is: Why do men sell sex in Australia? The most commonly reported consideration is financial, particularly among young people engaged in full- or part-time study (Prestage, Jin, Bavinton, & Hurley, 2014; Prestage et al., 2015; Minichiello et al., 2002) On its own, however, financial need is an unsatisfying explanation for sex work, particularly given the large proportion of men in similar circumstances who do not sell sex. One possible reason for this disparity comes from Prestage et al.'s (2014) survey study, which found that men who sold sex tended to be more sexually adventurous than their non-sex-working peers. Thus, for some men, an already outgoing sexual nature may be part of what facilitates their entry to sex work.

If it is difficult to describe male sex workers in Australia, then their clients are even more mysterious. This mystery is due, in part, to a paucity of data on sex workers' clients and the fact that clients rarely form anything resembling a community or even a network. Older research found that most male clients of male sex workers were middle class and middle aged, with a minority self-identifying as gay (Minichiello et al., 1999). Men who paid for sex with other men also tended to be older, educated, and employed. While not terribly illuminating, characteristics such as these remain the limit of what is known about male sex work clients in Australia.

Beyond men hiring male sex workers, the Australian public—including researchers—has recently started to ask questions about women who buy sex. In 2016, researchers drawing upon a digital archive of male sex work profiles (described in more detail by Kumar, Minichiello, Scott, & Harrington, 2017) found that a quarter advertised to female clients (Minichiello, Scott, Callander, & Harrington, 2018). When surveyed in 2012–2013, 0.3% of women aged 16–69 in Australia reported ever having paid for sex (Richters, de Visser et al., 2014), and while it is not safe to assume that all of this business has flown to men, what little research that does exist suggests that the majority of women who pay for sex do so with male sex workers (Caldwell, 2018). As research continues to expand in this area, new questions will be asked about how the experiences of male sex workers' male clients and female clients converge and diverge.

Peer-led support of male sex work in Australia

The size and nature of the male sex worker market is only one part of its story in Australia. One cannot properly account for male sex work in Australia without attending to the collection of community-run sex work organizations that seek to support and assist male sex workers and the sex industry more broadly. Generally speaking, each of Australia's eight states and territories is supported by at least one local organization, many of which are coordinated nationally by a peak body known as Scarlet Alliance. Formed in 1989, Scarlet Alliance state as its mission the achievement of:

> equality, social, legal, political, cultural and economic justice for past and present sex workers in order for sex workers to be self-determining agents, building their own alliances and choosing where and how they live and work.
>
> *(Scarlet Alliance, 2018)*

Funding for this organization comes from their member organizations and from Australia's peak HIV organization, the Australian Federation of AIDS Organisations. Importantly, since 2002, Scarlet Alliance has included a "male sex worker representative" dedicated to issues relevant to male sex workers. This voluntary two-year position is filled by election from the organization's membership, and its primary responsibilities include providing advice to Scarlet Alliance on issues affecting male sex workers in Australia, promoting involvement of male sex workers, and maintaining an email list to distribute content to male sex workers. As a peer-run organization, Scarlet Alliance stipulates that whoever fills this position must have some experience as a sex worker.

At a more local level, individual states and territories also host community-run sex work organizations. The role, influence, and offerings of these organizations are directly related to the size of their constituencies, with the most active organizations for male sex workers based in the largest Australian states of New South Wales, Victoria, and Queensland. The Sex Workers Outreach Project in New South Wales (SWOP NSW), for example, hosts a program dedicated specifically to male sex workers. SWOPmale provides a unique array of services, including postal safer sex packet distribution, outreach in sex venues, in-person support services, and traveling outreach to the state's rural and regional areas. Such efforts are coordinated by one paid position, SWOP NSW's male support officer.

While some states and territories have comprehensive and targeted peer support for male sex workers, others have much less or none at all. Smaller jurisdictions like Tasmania and the Northern Territory have much smaller sex worker organizations than other places, and it may not be efficient or possible for them to dedicate resources exclusively to men selling sex. But the size of the jurisdiction does not entirely explain the availability of services for male sex workers. South Australia, for example, is one of the smallest states but boasts a dedicated (volunteer) male sex work officer and a suite of digital offerings. Interestingly, that state also has some of the most restrictive sex work laws found anywhere in Australia. Generally, it is difficult to say what produces different levels of community support and organization between jurisdictions—quite likely it is a combination of funding, local will, and the number of male sex workers who live there—but it is important to recognize that peer and community support for male sex workers is not uniformly distributed across Australia. Accepting that these programs are mainly positive influences on the lives of male sex workers, it is necessary to consider the issues that may arise when men cannot access this kind of support.

Digital channels offer one way to overcome the geographic specificity of traditional support and outreach. In recent years, many Australian support programs for male sex workers have expanded to include different forms of digital outreach and support. Typically, this support ranges from the very simple, such as including a male sex work-specific section on an organizational website to something far more comprehensive. SWOPmale in New South Wales, for example, has for several years hosted several different social media accounts and groups, a dedicated resource section on their website, and an e-newsletter available to sex workers only. The male support officer also provides digital outreach through email and instant messaging.

Borrowing from models of online outreach developed in the United Kingdom (Mowlabocus, Dasgupta, Haslop, & Harbottle, 2018) and introduced in Australia for gay men generally (Casey & Cook, 2017), SWOPmale also maintains a number of outreach profiles on websites popular with male sex workers, which serve as connection points for male sex workers and clients "in the field." This approach to outreach and support reflects the changing nature of the industry, and, as noted, may help to overcome spatial barriers to support provision beyond Australia's cities. Given that half of male sex workers surveyed in Australia reported that they used the Internet as source of information on sex work (Prestage et al., 2015), digital approaches are vital.

Overall, Australia boasts a world-class network of peer support for sex workers, including programs tailored to the specific needs of men. While certainly not perfect, this network has been and continues to be a key part of maintaining the health and well-being of male sex workers while advocating for their rights across Australia's diverse legislative frameworks. In spite of its successes, this model of support faces ongoing challenges, namely funding. Public sympathy—and by extension funding—for sex work rarely abounds, and there exists a perception that because of the very low rates of HIV and other sexually transmissible infections (STIs) among sex workers in Australia, funding is not needed. This contention was highlighted by the chief executive officer of SWOP NSW, Cameron Cox, during a 2014 event in Sydney to mark World AIDS Day:

> Sex worker health is only a small part of overall HIV funding. Some people believe funding is low because of sex worker successes in HIV transmission reduction, but that success was built on a great and continuous 30-year effort, often unfunded and unpaid, and it would be dangerous [to decrease funding further] especially in the current volatile, changing, and often problematic HIV prevention landscape.

Indeed, funding for sex worker organizations is slight when compared to the funding received by Australian organizations representing other populations deemed to be a priority for the prevention HIV and STIs. As Cox suggests, successes in support and advocacy for male and other sex workers have likely happened in Australia in spite of funding, not because of it. Nonetheless, Australia is internationally rather unique in providing some public funding to organizations that directly support male sex workers.

Service delivery, health, infection, and regulation

The third part of our story turns to Australia's large and comprehensive network of publicly funded sexual health clinics, which operate in every state and territory. The first of these clinics opened in the 1920s, and there are now more than 60 such clinics across Australia, 40% of which are in urban centers, 50% in regional areas, and the remaining 10% in remote parts of the country. There is no charge for attending these clinics, which provide a full service of diagnostic testing, treatment, and management of HIV and other STIs. No identification is required. Some even provide additional services like psychologists and sex-worker-specific programs.

The significance of these clinics cannot be overstated. They provide a local, anonymous, and free way for male sex workers to access testing without judgment. It seems likely that these clinics have played a significant part in maintaining low levels of infection among male sex workers in Australia.

Globally, STI rates among male sex workers range from less than 1% in some countries to 60% in others, while HIV prevalence ranges from less than 1% to 50% (Minichiello, Scott, & Callander, 2015). These wide intervals highlight just how essential local context is for interpreting infection rates among any population. In 2016, some of us conducted a study of male sex workers attending Australian sexual health clinics in order to estimate the prevalence of chlamydia, gonorrhea, infectious syphilis, and HIV. We found that these infections among male sex workers in Australia were on the lower end of this global scale and sometimes significantly lower than countries we might consider socially, economically, and ideologically comparable (Callander et al. 2016). In 2011, for example, 25% of male sex workers attending a men's health clinic in the United Kingdom were diagnosed with chlamydia (compared with 13% in Australia) and 3% with syphilis (compared with 0.5% in Australia) (McGrath-Lone, Marsh, Hughes, & Ward, 2014). Similarly, one study from the United States estimated a 26% prevalence of HIV among male sex workers in the country (Timpson, Ross, Williams, & Atkinson, 2007), compared with 6% in Australia.

Comparing infection rates between countries is rarely straightforward and should be done with caution. A slightly more direct way to assess the impact of peer support and education is through condom use, which globally is as varied as infection rates. Of note, while in some countries only 15% of male sex workers reported consistently using condoms for anal intercourse with clients, this proportion ranged from 59% to 95% among different samples of sex workers in Australia (Minichiello et al., 2015; Prestage et al., 2015). With the introduction of biomedical forms of HIV prevention, however, it is unclear how condom use will change among male sex workers in Australia.

Regarding infection and risk, the most pertinent question is whether male sex workers have higher rates of infection than their peers who do not sell sex. When all things are equal, does sex work pose a risk to the sexual health of men in Australia? While globally, male sex workers appear to be at a greater risk for HIV than their non-sex-working peers (Baral et al., 2015), a similar association has not been observed in Australia, including for other STIs (Callander et al. 2016). While it is difficult to draw direct associations, this (non)relationship is another piece of evidence supporting the efficacy of peer support and publicly funded sexual health clinics.

Male sex workers in Australia have also demonstrated a high degree of sexual health service access and uptake. When surveyed in 2014, 84% of male sex workers in New South Wales and Victoria reported a sexual health screen within the six months prior to participation, and no men reported that they had never been tested (Prestage et al., 2015). Similarly, writing to the New South Wales Ministry of Health we reported that, on average, male sex workers had nearly two full sexual health screens per year (Callander, Cox et al. 2016). In some states, however, governments mandate quarterly testing as a prerequisite for sex work among both men and women. For women, this policy has been found to be highly cost ineffective, with one analysis suggesting that it costs nearly A$90,000 (US$68,000) to avert just one chlamydia infection (Wilson et al., 2010).

Analyzing the costs and benefits of highly frequent STI testing among male sex workers is likely to yield somewhat different results, owing to the generally higher incidence of STIs among gay, bisexual, and other men who have sex with men in Australia. A better question might be whether mandatory testing produces its desired outcome, which is frequent testing among male sex workers. This question can be answered by calculating the average number of sexual health tests that male sex workers have in a year and comparing that number between jurisdictions with mandatory testing and those with voluntary testing. This analysis is possible through the use of routine health data extracted from Australia's publicly funded sexual health clinics (Callander, Harrington et al., in press).

When comparing jurisdictions with mandated sexual health testing and those where it is voluntary, test frequency is indistinguishable (Figure 37.3). While testing rates have increased among male sex workers across Australia, it would seem that laws mandating testing fail to achieve more frequent sexual health screening among a group of people who already have highly frequent testing regimens. Male sex workers, it would seem, are quite able and willing to regulate their own sexual health testing without edicts from governments.

As noted earlier, male sex workers in Australia work within some of the most liberal legislative frameworks found internationally. This point is especially important when considered alongside a growing scientific consensus that legalizing and decriminalizing sex work supports greater health—including sexual health—among men and women who sell sex (Platt et al., 2018). A similar effect has been observed specifically within Australia (Harcourt et al., 2010), suggesting that Australia's legislative approach, its publicly funded sexual health clinics, and its world-leading peer support have produced exceptional uptake of sexual health services and some of the lowest infection rates found anywhere in the world.

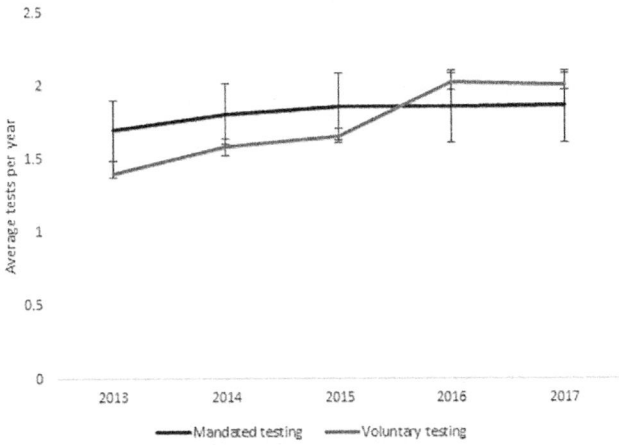

Figure 37.3 Average number of sexual health screens per patient per year (with 95% confidence intervals) among male sex workers attending Australian publicly funded sexual health clinics, stratified by jurisdictions with mandatory or voluntary testing, 2013–2017.

The future of male sex work in Australia

Digitally driven changes to the sex industry are well documented, and they have played out profoundly in Australia. The impact on individual well-being is not entirely clear, and some have pointed out that online sex work might increase feelings of isolation and loneliness (Jones, 2015). To offset these potential challenges, Australia's network of peer support for men doing sex work will need to continue to innovate and develop against an ever-evolving backdrop. Their innovation thus far is exciting and a hopeful sign of their impact and relevance into the future.

Proposed changes and the occasional challenge to sex work laws in Australia continue and seem unlikely to abate anytime soon. Support for and opposition to decriminalization plays out in many areas, and even states with more progressive laws face periodic challenges from mainly conservative political players. Promisingly, these challenges produce consistent outcomes: an evidence-based assessment that the laws (or their absence) work to protect individuals, maintain public order, and sustain public health (NSW Parliamentary Research Service, 2015).

What comes next for male sex work in Australia is difficult to predict, but it will likely involve closer integration of more innovative technologies. As noted, biomedical technologies of HIV prevention are increasingly central to sex in Australia, and it seems that male sex workers have started to adopt them as well. Studies of HIV pre-exposure prophylaxis have found that 5–6% of men accessing that drug in New South Wales and Victoria have engaged in sex work (pers. comm, Ms. Stefanie Vacher, The Kirby Institute; Mr. Michael Traeger, The Burnet Institute, 2018), while among those in a large national cohort of gay men, 44% of sex workers and 33% of non-sex workers report PrEP use (pers. comm, Mr. Mo Hammoud, The Kirby Institute, 2018). These data suggest that male sex workers are accessing PrEP at a similar or possibly higher rate than their peers, but it is unclear if or how their use of PrEP has changed the sex they have with clients. While anecdotal evidence abounds of condomless sex sold at a premium, it remains to be seen how antiretroviral-driven HIV prevention will reshape male sex work for workers and clients in Australia.

It seems that technology is and will remain a central theme in Australia's male sex industry. Digital and health technologies may offer new ways to engage with sex work clients, who remain largely outside of support and advocacy efforts, as well as those who sell sex infrequently and may not identify with the label "sex worker." If Australia's past is any indication, through the combined efforts of many different players—community advocates, peers, lawmakers, clinicians, researchers, and, of course, sex workers themselves—it is entirely feasible that male sex workers and their clients will continue to enjoy, for the most part, what appear to be healthy, quality sexual-professional experiences.

Note

1 Originally published as Wotherspoon G (1991) *City of the Plain: History of a Gay Sub-Culture*. Sydney: Hale & Iremonge.

References

Baral, S. D., Friedman, M. R., Geibel, S., Rebe, K., Bozhinov, B., Diouf, D., . . . Cáceres, C. F. (2015). Male sex workers: Practices, contexts, and vulnerabilities for HIV acquisition and transmission. *Lancet*, *385*(9964), 260–273.

Boisvert, E. (2018, June 1). *SA attorney-general declares supports for decriminalisation of sex work bill*. Australian Broadcasting Corporation. Retrieved from www.abc.net.au/news/2018-06-01/sa-attorney-general-supports-sex-work-bill/9824782

Bongiorno, F. (2012). *The sex lives of Australians: A history*. Melbourne: Black Inc.

Caldwell, H. (2018). *Women who buy sex in Australia: From social representations to lived experiences* (PhD thesis). Centre for Social Research in Health, University of New South Wales, Sydney.

Callander, D., Cox, C., Schmidt, H., & Donovan, B. (2016). *Sex worker health surveillance: A report to the New South Wales ministry of health*. Sydney: University of New South Wales.

Callander, D., & DeVeau, R. (2019). Male sex work and digital regulation. In *Male sex work and society* (Vol. 2). New York: Harrington Park Press.

Callander, D., Harrington, T., Scott, J., DeVeau, R., & Minichiello, V. (in press). Male sex work online. In *Navigating sex work—gender, justice and policy in the 21st century*.

Callander, D., Moreira, C., Asselin, J., El-Hayek, C., Watchirs Smith, L., van Gemert, C., . . . Guy, R. (in press). Australian Collaboration for Coordinated Enhanced Sentinel Surveillance (ACCESS): A protocol for monitoring the control of sexually transmissible infections and blood borne viruses. *JMIR Research Protocols*.

Callander, D., Read, P., Prestage, G., Minichiello, V., Chow, E. P. F., Lewis, D. A., . . . Guy, R. (2016). A cross-sectional study of HIV and STIs among male sex workers attending Australian sexual health clinics. *Sexually Transmitted Infections, 93*(4), 299–302.

Casey, J., & Cook, T. (2017, November 7). *". . . If you get tested and you are positive does that mean I'm going to basically die?": Improving HIV and sexual health literacy among gay and bisexual men using hook up app outreach in regional NSW*. Paper presented at 2017 HIV & AIDS Conference, Canberra. Retrieved from https://az659 834.vo.msecnd.net/eventsairaueprod/production-ashm-public/6737eb38f64a4c31b6ab719c22728c9b

Cox, C. (2014). *Speech at world AIDS day 2014*. Retrieved October 5, 2018, from http://talkabout.posi tivelife.org.au/current-articles/7-being-a-sex-worker-in-australia

Frances, R. (1994). The history of female prostitution in Australia. In *Sex work and sex workers in Australia*. Sydney: University of New South Wales Press.

French, R. (1993). *Camping by a Billabong: Gay and lesbian stories from Australian history*. Sydney: Blackwattle Press.

Friedman, M. (2014). Male sex work from ancient times to the near present. In *Male sex work and society* (Vol. 1). New York: Harrington Park Press.

Harcourt, C., O'Connor, J., Egger, S., Fairley, C. K., Wand, H., Chen, M. Y., . . . Donovan, B. (2010). The decriminalisation of prostitution is associated with better coverage of health promotion programs for sex workers. *Australian and New Zealand Journal of Public Health, 34*(5), 482–486.

Jones, A. (2015). Sex work in a digital era. *Sociology Compass, 9*(7), 558–570.

Jones, R. (2017, February 14). *Adelaide brothels raided in "heavy handed" attack on industry, sex workers say*. Australian Broadcasting Corporation. Retrieved from www.abc.net.au/news/2017-02-15/ adelaide-brothels-raided-in-sex-industry-crackdown/8271262

Kumar, N., Minichiello, V., Scott, J., & Harrington, T. (2017). A global overview of male escort websites. *Journal of Homosexuality, 64*(12), 1731–1744.

McGrath-Lone, L., Marsh, K., Hughes, G., & Ward, H. (2014). The sexual health of male sex workers in England: Analysis of cross-sectional data from genitourinary medicine clinics. *Sexually Transmitted Infections, 90*(1), 38–40.

McLean, A. (2015). "You can do it from your sofa": The increasing popularity of the Internet as a working site among male sex workers in Melbourne. *Journal of Sociology, 51*(4), 887–902.

Minichiello, V., Mariño, R., Browne, J., Jamieson, M., Peterson, K., Reuter, B., & Robinson, K. (1999). A profile of the clients of male sex workers in three Australian cities. *Australian and New Zealand Journal of Public Health, 23*(5), 511–518.

Minichiello, V., Marino, R., Browne, J., Jamieson, M., Peterson, K., Reuter, B., & Robinson, K. (2002). Male sex workers in three Australian cities: Socio-demographic and sex work characteristics. *Journal of Homosexuality, 42*(1), 29–51.

Minichiello, V., Scott, J., & Callander, D. (2015). A new public health context to understand male sex work. *BMC Public Health, 15*(1), 282.

Minichiello, V., Scott, J., Callander, D., & Harrington, T. (2018, November 1). Research shows distribution of online male escorts, by nation. *Me, Us and Male Escorting*. Retrieved from https://research.qut. edu.au/aboutmaleescorting/2017/11/01/number-of-online-male-escorts-by-nation-2/

Mowlabocus, S., Dasgupta, R., Haslop, C., & Harbottle, J. (2018). *Reaching out online: Digital literacy, and the uses of social media in health promotion.* Brighton: Centre for Material Digital Culture, University of Sussex. Retrieved October 7, from www.sussex.ac.uk/rcmdc/projects/reachingoutonline

NSW Parliamentary Research Service. (2015). Brothel regulation in NSW. *Issues Backgrounder, 1.* Retrieved from www.parliament.nsw.gov.au/researchpapers/Documents/brothel-regulation-in-nsw/Brothel%20Regulation%20in%20NSW%20Aug%202015.pdf

Platt, L., Grenfell, P., Meiksin, R., Elmes, J., Sherman, S. G., Sanders, T., Mwangi, P., & Crago, A. L. (2018). Associations between sex work laws and sex workers' health: A systematic review and meta-analysis of quantitative and qualitative studies. *PLoS Medicine, 15*(12), e1002680.

Prestage, G., Bradley, J., Hammoud, M., Cox, C., Tattersal, K., & Kolstee, J. (2015). *Hook-up: A study of male sex work in NSW and Queensland.* Sydney: Kirby Institute, University of New South Wales.

Prestage, G., Jin, F., Bavinton, B., & Hurley, M. (2014). Sex workers and their clients among Australian gay and bisexual men. *AIDS and Behavior, 18*(7), 1293–1301.

Richters, J., Altman, D., Badcock, P. B., Smith, A. M. A., de Visser, R. O., Grulich, A. E., . . . Simpson, J. M. (2014). Sexual identity, sexual attraction and sexual experience: The second Australian study of health and relationships. *Sexual Health, 11*(5), 451–460.

Richters, J., de Visser, R. O., Badcock, P. B., Smith, A. M. A., Rissel, C., Simpson, J. M., & Grulich, A. E. (2014). Masturbation, paying for sex, and other sexual activities: The second Australian study of health and relationships. *Sexual Health, 11*(5), 461–471.

Scarlet Alliance. (2018). *Who we are.* Retrieved October 5, 2018, from www.scarletalliance.org.au/who/

Timpson, S. C., Ross, M. W., Williams, M. L., & Atkinson, J. (2007). Characteristics, drug use, and sex partners of a sample of male sex workers. *American Journal of Drug and Alcohol Abuse, 33*(1), 63–69.

Wilson, D. P., Heymer, K. J., Anderson, J., O'Connor, J., Harcourt, C., & Donovan, B. (2010). Sex workers can be screened too often: A cost-effectiveness analysis in Victoria, Australia. *Sexually Transmitted Infections, 86*(2), 117–125.

Wotherspoon, G. (1991). *City of the plain: History of a gay sub-culture.* Sydney: Hale & Iremonge.

Wotherspoon, G. (2016). *Gay Sydney: A history.* Sydney: New South Publishing.

Decriminalization as a goal

Opportunities, varieties, and pathways

John Scott, Christian Grov, and Victor Minichiello

As Chapter 13 suggests, male sex work numbers are increasing worldwide as technologies allow for interaction with new demographic and geographic markets. A Swedish report estimated that male sex workers accounted for 10–20% of the overall sex worker population, and online escort forums are likely to be the dominant venue where male escorts are found (Minichiello & Scott, 2017). However, these estimates are likely to vary between countries. A Foundation Scelles report estimated the number of sex workers worldwide at about 42 million, with about 8 million thought to be men (Bancroft-Hinchey, 2014).

Suggestions of a decline in sex work as a result of the growth of new technology seem exaggerated. The popularity of dating and sexual rendezvous sites, with their absence of cost and mitigation of moral concerns, renders such sites a popular alternative to traditional sexual service providers. One argument is that online technologies and sites such as Manhunt, Gaydar, Gay Matchmaker, Grindr, and Scruff make male sex workers (MSWs) largely redundant, because these sites make access to (unpaid) sex easy. In addition, same-sex sexual activities are de-stigmatized and legal in many countries today. But it is also true that technology has raised awareness of MSWs and provided greater access to "closeted" and other consumers who have benefited from the safety, variety of services, and discretion offered by MSWs who work the online market. Moreover, clients are a heterogeneous group, and there are many reasons for choosing commercial sex encounters, many of which may not relate to cost (Scott, MacPhail, & Minichiello, 2014).

To return to a key point made in the introduction to this book: In the mid-1990s, sex workers made their first tentative steps onto the World Wide Web. The use of cell phones was not widespread, and although there were no smart phones—or applications to facilitate meeting sex partners—these devices gave sex workers greater geographic reach and mobility. These changes affected the structure and experience of sex work and provided new opportunities and risks for sex workers. Yet, while sex work was changing, legal reforms were often stagnating.

As some chapters in this book have highlighted, there are some problems with the sex industry worldwide, mostly related to the health and safety of sex workers and their clients. To understand the causes of these problems and prevent them, we need to divert our gaze from the bodies of sex workers and their clients. Instead we must focus on the ways in which social structures, especially regulatory structures, affect sex work. An overview of sex work in 100 nations in varied global regions found that sex work was legal in 53% of countries, home to

2.13 billion people. Meanwhile, sex work had limited legality in 12% of countries, home to 698 million people, and it was illegal in 35% of countries, home to 2.13 billion people. Male sex workers also have to contend with the criminalization of homosexuality. While this book was being written, 70 United Nations member states (and two non-member states) still criminalized consensual same-sex sexual activities (Avery, 2019).

But something else significant happened during the mid-1990s. In 1995, the year before the first escort website was established, the Australian state of New South Wales decriminalized sex work. That decriminalization "works" cannot be doubted. All the research, including that presented in this volume, points to this fact (Harcourt et al., 2010). So the rest of the world should be following suit, right? Unfortunately, it is not. The only other jurisdiction—and first country to decriminalize sex work—was New Zealand in 2003. The research speaks loudly for the benefits of decriminalization, but denial, drawing on a mix of morality and misconceived ideology, persists, and the science has not translated into much-needed reforms. In 2015, Amnesty International declared its support of decriminalization, citing state obligations to respect, protect, and fulfill the human rights of sex workers. Sex workers have advocated for decriminalization since the emergence of sex worker rights movements during the early 1970s (Scott, Cox, & Minichiello, 2017). Decriminalization is also supported by UNAIDS, the World Health Organization, Human Rights Watch, the United Nations Population Fund, and the medical journal *The Lancet*.

So, what is holding back sex industry reform? Historic concerns around sex work, grounded in the moral view that the commercialization of sex is degrading, have persisted. Although the dichotomy between erotic and commercial life has remained, recent concerns include the idea that sex work is inherent victimization, and thus reform equates to increased oppression of children and women. There are claims that decriminalization increases the overall volume of sex work activity and leads to more trafficking and more child prostitution, but there is no evidence of such effects in New South Wales or New Zealand (Scott et al., 2017).

Two difficulties lie in the conflation of trafficking with sex work and competing definitions of what trafficking means. The historic tendency of research to focus on street work, which is more likely to involve survival sex and violent exploitation, has also muddied the waters. Furthermore, some research has cherry-picked data for worst cases of exploitation and generalizes these to all sex work and sex worker experiences, perpetuating the idea that sex workers are inherent victims and that sex work is not freely chosen. It is better to frame concepts of trafficking and forced prostitution as exploitation. Exploitation can be experienced by other occupational groups and is not exclusive to sex work (Scott et al., 2017). It can also be difficult to frame male sex work as exploitation, and the research in this volume suggests that, while exploitation does exist, many MSWs experience their work in a positive manner.

Researchers have the opportunity to further collaborate with sex workers and governments to show the impact of decriminalizing the sex industry. We now have "laboratory" environments in which some countries have decriminalized sex work, while others have not. By studying how these countries are performing on a wide range of variables—economic, legal, health, workforce, social, recreational—we will be in a better position to create policies that remove the stigma and hardship frequently associated with the sex industry. Then perhaps we can answer the question: Are the stigma and hardship socially constructed and driven by human policies that are moralistic in their assumptions, and if so, what are the necessary steps required to ensure that sex work is organized in the most professional and optimal level of service delivery?

A government review of decriminalization in New South Wales resulted in continued support of the policy. It found that decriminalized adult sex work has improved human rights;

removed police corruption; netted savings for the criminal justice system; and enhanced the surveillance, health promotion, and safety of the NSW sex industry. Contrary to early concerns, the size and visibility of the NSW sex have not increased. NSW men are infrequent consumers of commercial sexual services, with only 2.3% purchasing sexual services in any given year, similar to the Australian average. The number of sex workers in Sydney brothels is similar to estimates from 20 years ago. Estimates range from 1,500 female sex workers working at any one time to 10,000 in the whole of NSW, a state of approximately eight million people. There were at least 101 brothels (possibly as many as 200) operating within 20 kilometers of the Sydney central business district. Sydney brothels are widely dispersed in inner urban and suburban areas, and they attract few complaints from neighbors. In addition to brothel-based sex workers (who are almost all female) SWOP (Sex Workers Outreach Project) estimates that up to 40% of all sex workers (including most male sex workers) in NSW work privately; approximately 5% are street-based. Condom use during sex work approaches 100% in Sydney brothels, and prevalence of four sexually transmitted infections is at least as low as the prevalence in the general population. In general, NSW brothel workers enjoyed levels of mental health that were comparable to the general population. There have been only a handful of successful prosecutions for trafficking (Parliament of NSW, 2016). Earlier research found no evidence of recent trafficking of female sex workers in the Sydney brothel survey or in a clinic study. This was in marked contrast to the 1990s before policy reform, when trafficked women from Thailand were common in Sydney (Donovan et al., 2012).

One of the difficulties with decriminalization is that it is not easy to define. Decriminalization is best conceptualized in terms of a "harm reduction" approach. In the simplest sense, it is about recognition of sex work as an occupation, as opposed to an identity. In this system, there are no special laws aimed solely at regulating sex workers or related activities. Instead, sex workers are subject to laws that regulate other businesses. In this system, sex workers are entitled to the full protection of the law and human rights. This system is premised on the definition of sex work as activity that involves consensual sexual exchanges between adults for some form of remuneration. Decriminalized systems can still apply criminal and penal codes, but these protect workers (and clients) against exploitation and violence (*The Economist*, 2015; Harcourt et al., 2010).

Unlike decriminalization, legalization involves state regulation of the sex industry. In places, such as the U.S. state of Nevada and parts of the Netherlands, legalization can mean increased police surveillance, forced health evaluations, higher taxes on sex workers, and financial penalties for sex workers. The law can also force sex workers to work in unsafe, often isolated, locations, making them more vulnerable to violence (Donovan et al., 2012).

In contrast to decriminalization and legalization, prohibitionist models of sex work criminalize all aspects of sex work, often on moral or religious grounds. Abolitionist approaches might legalize sex work, but they prohibit third-party involvement, for example, by making the buying of sex illegal. Where sex work is criminalized, sex workers and clients have been shown to be at increased risk of harm and violence. Additionally, stigma and corrupt law enforcement mean that abuses to sex workers and clients are often not prevented or acted on in places where sex work is criminalized (Scott et al., 2017).

Policy denial is built on myths around sex work. Notably, there needs to be recognition that sex workers are not a homogenous population, as this book has demonstrated. The experiences of sex workers and clients are diverse, and any generalization or simplistic policy calling for prohibition requires caution. Research, such as that presented in these pages, should endeavor to promote the removal of repressive laws around sex work, in the same way that laws that criminalized same-sex relations have been repealed.

The regulatory status of male sex work helps to remind us that there are global dimensions to the problems associated with sex work. This volume has demonstrated that the experience of sex work varies considerably from country to country and is often informed by cultural constructs of the masculine. Yet, overall, there has been little research conducted into global variations in sex work. Harcourt and Donovan (2005) set out to "compile a global typography of sex work," identifying at least 25 types of sex work according to worksite and principal mode of soliciting of sex, but little research on this topic has been done since, despite the increasing visibility of sex work in diverse global contexts. Official reports as well as academic typologies of prostitution have almost entirely ignored global variation in sex work. When sex work is acknowledged in the global south, even briefly, it is usually presented merely as an extension of a northern phenomenon, with few distinguishing organizational or regulatory characteristics.

Kempadoo (1998) noted that contemporary writers' constructions of the "prostitute/sex worker" mostly derive from the analysis of struggles of First World women in the global north. Such writings do not take historical and geopolitical context into account and therefore run the risk of universalizing sex workers. Contemporary research on male sex work derives much of its thinking from the masculinities and queer theorizing of the global north. Furthermore, as elsewhere in the global south, most research on sex work has focused on sexual health, especially HIV risk. Raewyn Connell's southern theory may be useful when considering what a global view of sex work might look like. As Connell (2007) argued, the global production of knowledge in the social sciences is—like the distribution of wealth, income, and power—structurally skewed toward the global north. Indeed, the influence of North Atlantic countries over knowledge production is even greater in research than that exerted in trading and financial economies (Marginson, 2014). Knowledge is a commodity, and knowledge production does not occur in a geo-political vacuum.

Connell (2007) used the term "southern" to bring to fore the center-periphery relations expressed in relations of authority, hegemony, partnership, sponsorship, appropriation, exclusion, and inclusion between the intellectuals and institutions of the metropole and those in the periphery, noting that the hegemony of metropolitan knowledge marginalizes alternative ways of thinking. Southern theory raises important questions for sex work researchers to consider regarding how and where knowledge is produced and disseminated and whose voices are heard in dominant academic discourses. Intellectual projects are intimately related to political and cultural struggles for recognition and social and economic justice. Boaventura de Sousa Santos observed, "There is no global social justice without global cognitive justice" (2014, p. viii). The next step in sex work research might involve a de-colonization and democratization of the field. Sex workers are, after all, often subject to harsh regulatory regimes in the global south and also face a lack of resources to manage often complex problems. The global diversity of sex work is yet to be fully documented, but the growth and visibility of global sex work over the last two decades have made this challenge possible.

References

Avery, D. (2019). *Countries where homosexuality is illegal: Acceptance of the LGBT community continues to spread around the world, but homosexuality is illegal in many parts of the world*. Retrieved from www.newsweek.com/73-countries-where-its-illegal-be-gay-1385974

Bancroft-Hinchey, T. (2014). Scelles foundation: 42 million people worldwide are prostitutes. *Pravda.ru*. Retrieved from www.pravdareport.com/society/126700-prostitutes/

Connell, R. (2007). *Southern theory: The global dynamics of knowledge in social science*. Sydney: Allen & Unwin.

Donovan, B., Harcourt, C., Egger, S., Watchirs Smith, L., Schneider, K., Kaldor, J. M., Chen, M. Y., . . . Tabrizi, S. (2012). *The sex industry in New South Wales: A report to the NSW ministry of health*. Sydney: Kirby Institute, University of New South Wales.

The Economist. (2015). "The Economist" explains: Why decriminalizing sex work is a good idea. *The Economist*. Retrieved from www.economist.com/blogs/economist-explains/2015/08/economist-explains-13

Harcourt, C., & Donovan, B. (2005). The many faces of sex work. *Sexually Transmitted Infections, 81*, 201–206.

Harcourt, C., O'Connor, J., Egger, S., Fairley, C., Wand, H., Chen, M., . . . Donovan, B. (2010). The decriminalisation of prostitution is associated with better coverage of health promotion programs for sex workers. *Australian and NZ Journal of Public Health, 34*(5), 482–486.

Kempadoo, K. (1998). Introduction. In K. Kempadoo & J. Doezema (Eds.), *Global sex workers: Rights, resistance, and redefinition*. New York: Routledge.

Marginson, S. (2014). The West's global HE hegemony—nothing lasts forever. *University World News: The Global Window on Higher Education*, 313.

Minichiello, V., & Scott, J. (2017). *Research shows distribution of online male escorts, by nation*. Retrieved from https://research.qut.edu.au/aboutmaleescorting/2017/11/01/number-of-online-male-escorts-by-nation-2/

Parliament of NSW. (2016, November). *Legislative assembly of New South Wales: Select committee on the regulation of brothels*. Report 1/56. Retrieved from www.parliament.nsw.gov.au/ladocs/inquiries/1703/Final%20Report%20-%20Inquiry%20into%20the%20Regulation%20of%20Brot.pdf

Santos, B. (2014). *Epistemologies of the South: Justice against epistemicide*. London: Paradigm Publishers.

Scott, J., Cox, C., & Minichiello, V. (2017). Criminology and the case for the decriminalisation of sex work. *PacifiCrim, 13*(2), 8–9.

Scott, J., MacPhail, C., & Minichiello, V. (2014). Telecommunications impacts on the structure and organisation of male sex work. In P. Maginn & C. Steinmetz (Eds.), *(Sub)urban sexscapes: Geographies and regulation of the sex industry*. London: Routledge.

Index

Printed in Great Britain
by Amazon

55668967R00355